Henry Fielding
A Life

Hogarth's frontispiece to Fielding's *Works* (1762).

Henry Fielding

A Life

—◦●◦—

Martin C. Battestin

with

Ruthe R. Battestin

ROUTLEDGE
London and New York

First published 1989 by Routledge
11 New Fetter Lane, London EC4P 4EE
29 West 35th Street, New York NY 10001

© 1989 Martin C. Battestin

Printed in Great Britain by
St Edmundsbury Press, Suffolk
Bound by Butler & Tanner Ltd, Frome and London

British Library Cataloguing in Publication Data
Battestin, Martin C.
Henry Fielding: a life.
I. Title   II. Battestin, Ruthe R.
823′.5
ISBN 0–415–01438–7

Library of Congress Cataloging in Publication Data
applied for

To Louis Landa

CONTENTS

ILLUSTRATIONS

Besides Hogarth's famous likeness (1762) which serves as frontispiece to this book, three other pictures of Fielding (or very probably of him) are collected here for the first time, all three drawn from the life. Of these the most delightful is again by Hogarth, who in *Characters and Caricaturas* (1743) facetiously returned the compliment his friend paid him in the Preface to *Joseph Andrews* (see Plates 35 and 36). The most authentic likeness, however, is of Fielding in his later years, when his aspect as a magistrate was described as "rueful" and "woeful." This portrait of him (Plate 47), drawn in red chalk and pencil, was attributed tentatively to Joshua Reynolds when the British Museum acquired it in 1892; it is, in any case, the work of a skillful artist, and one disinclined to flatter.

To these two pictures of Fielding, which I discussed in a recent article (*Eighteenth-Century Studies*, 17 [1983], 1–13), I believe we may add another: the figure of the magistrate in Captain Marcellus Laroon's drawing, *Night Walkers before a Justice* – also known as *A Frenchman at Bow Street* (Plate 52). This lively sketch depicts a typical scene at Bow Street: at the left the justice is seated before a table on which his clerk is writing, while in the center a gentleman pleads his case amidst a crowd of spectators, prisoners, and watchmen with their staves. Laroon (1679–1772) assigned this picture to the year 1740, when Sir Thomas DeVeil, not Fielding, presided at Bow Street. Laroon, however, according to his biographer, had a very faulty memory and made "major errors in dates" (R. Raines, *Marcellus Laroon* [1967], p. 3). The justice in the picture – a bulky, scowling figure with a long nose and large chin, as well as a dropsical belly and gouty leg – resembles Fielding rather than DeVeil. In a letter to my wife of 19 March 1987, Mr. Sidney F. Sabin, the eminent authority on prints and drawings of this period, remarked that when Laroon's *Night Walkers* (undated) was submitted to the British Museum for an opinion in 1912, whoever examined the picture noted the resemblance to Fielding. It is possible, Mr. Sabin suggests, that Laroon, who lived to be ninety-three, merely guessed at the date of the picture when, not long before his death, he bequeathed his entire collection to a friend (see Raines, p. 56). Laroon's memory often failed him even as a younger man, and the fact that the date is the rounded figure "1740" may also seem to support Mr. Sabin's hypothesis. Laroon, moreover, was only too well known to Fielding. In *Nollekens and his Times*, J. T. Smith records Saunders Welch's observation "that whenever Captain Laroon was named by Henry Fielding, he said, 'I consider him and his friend Captain Montague, and their constant companion, Little Cazey [i.e., Casey], the Link-boy, as the three most troublesome and difficult to manage of all my Bow-street visitors'" (ed. W. Whitten [1920], II.202). According to Smith, incidentally, these three revelers are depicted in Boitard's print, *The Covent Garden Morning Frolick* (1747), in which Laroon is shown brandishing an artichoke, while Montague rides atop the sedan chair of the bawd, Betty Careless, and "Little Casey" leads the way (Plate 20).

PREFACE

In 1975 my wife and I began the research for this book with some misgivings. In more than fifty years since the publication of W. L. Cross's biography (1918) scholars had made incidental discoveries concerning Fielding's life and works, but few of these added appreciably to the story Cross had told, spinning out the thin thread of his knowledge through three volumes. The thanklessness of the task ahead of us seemed plain enough from the example of F. Homes Dudden, who in 1952 produced a biography of Fielding which, after 1,100 pages, left his subject where he found him.

The "life-writer," as Fielding might have said, generally requires a plentiful supply of his subject's papers – letters, diaries, commonplace books, manuscripts. But in 1975 there were only twenty-four letters by Fielding to draw on, most of them short, perfunctory, and dull. Indeed, less was known about Fielding's personal circumstances than about those of any other figure of comparable importance in the century. I found myself therefore turning for comfort to the words of the pious biographer Agnellus, who a thousand years ago, when faced with similar difficulties in discovering hard facts about his subjects, hit upon a simple, not to say inspired, solution: "I invented lives for them," he explained, "and I do not believe them to be false." In a sense, of course, this is the condition of all biography. "What are facts," C. S. Lewis asked, "without interpretation?" – and the interpretation of facts being a subjective business, the lives we read in books will always be the invention of the author. Yet it will be true that these lives more closely resemble the originals the more fully and faithfully they reflect the subjects' actual circumstances, deeds, relationships.

Whatever may be the shortcomings of this book, it will relate the story of Fielding's life more fully than was possible heretofore. For one thing, owing chiefly to the discovery of two important caches of Fielding's correspondence, I have been able to refer to, and to quote from, nearly three times the number of his letters previously known. Of greatest importance to the revelation of Fielding's character are the twenty-six letters he wrote to James Harris, the "Salisbury *philosophe*" as Clive Probyn calls him, and the man who from 1741 became Fielding's closest friend; to this rich source was added Harris's unpublished "Essay on the Life and Genius" of Fielding. No less important to an understanding of Fielding's public career as lawyer and magistrate are the numerous letters and documents revealing the extent of his indebtedness to his great patron, the Duke of Bedford.

Valuable as they are, however, the discovery of the Harris and Bedford papers brought to little more than seventy the number of extant Fielding letters – a meagre supply when compared with the voluminous correspondence of, say, Pope or Swift or Richardson. Trying to compensate for this deficiency, we turned to possible sources of information in the public domain. My wife, who specializes in documentary research, carefully explored the contents not only of such formidable repositories as the Public Record Office and the British Museum, but of dozens of other archives in London and the provinces. Only those already acquainted with the biographies of Cross and Dudden will fully appreciate how successful her investigations proved to be. Her discoveries illuminate virtually every aspect of Fielding – his family and the circle of his acquaintance, his private and public affairs, his works.

I concentrated my own research on published sources. I methodically scanned "the diurnal historians" (as Fielding liked to call the authors of newspapers) from 1726 to 1755 looking for fresh facts about him and for clues that might point to his current interests and activities. I similarly examined as many as possible of the scores of fugitive pamphlets, tracts, poems, broadsheets, etc. that were published each year during this same period. Fly-casting in unpromising waters was the analogy for this systematic drudgery that came readily to mind, but in the end the "catch" was remarkable. I had expected this procedure – supplemented by scrutiny of the *Old Bailey Sessions Papers* and by my wife's investigations in the record offices – to result in a fuller account of Fielding's magistracy, and it did: we were able to identify many hundreds of cases in which Fielding was involved. Other results were wholly unexpected, however, and deepened our appreciation of other dimensions of his life. By far the most exciting of these potentially ("potentially" because the claim must pass the test of time) was the disclosure of one of the best-kept secrets of eighteenth-century literature: namely, that for a period of six years, from 1734 to 1739, Fielding was a regular contributor to *The Craftsman*, the principal organ of the Opposition as it tried to bring down the Prime Minister, Sir Robert Walpole. The argument for Fielding's authorship of these essays – forty-one witty political satires attributed to him on the basis of internal and circumstantial evidence and the results of a stylometric analysis independently conducted by Michael G. Farringdon – is set forth in *New Essays by Henry Fielding: His Contributions to the "Craftsman"*

(1734–39) and Other Early Journalism (University Press of Virginia: Charlottesville, 1989).

This biography, moreover, affords new perspectives on Fielding in a literal sense; for until recently we have had no very clear idea of how he looked. Hogarth's famous likeness of him, which served as the frontispiece to Arthur Murphy's edition of the Works (1762), was produced from memory nearly eight years after Fielding's death. It also serves as frontispiece to the present volume because, however imprecise it may be in detail, it captures the essence of Fielding's character as one of his closest friends wished to remember it – a countenance strong and wise, yet smiling still. Contrary to what was once supposed, however, other pictures of Fielding have come down to us, and they are gathered here for the first time in a biography of him (see the headnote to the List of Illustrations).

The debts we incurred in the course of this work are numberless – so many it is impossible to acknowledge them all as they deserve.

We began the research for the book during fifteen months in 1975–6, when I was a member of the Center for Advanced Studies at the University of Virginia and a Bicentennial Research Fellow of the National Endowment for the Humanities. Since then the time and the means necessary to complete the work we owe chiefly to the terms of my appointment as William R. Kenan, Jr., Professor of English at the University of Virginia. To the University I am also indebted for the services of an able research assistant, Dr. James Foster. For enabling me in a fundamental sense to "realize" this work I am grateful to Mrs. Barbara Smith of the English Department, whose wizardry metamorphosed my handwritten manuscript into a legible, computerized print-out, and whose loyalty and friendship sustained me.

Our obligations to librarians and archivists on both sides of the Atlantic will be apparent from the notes. We are especially grateful, however, to Ray W. Frantz, Jr., and the staff of the University of Virginia Library and to Ian Willison and the staff of the British Library. We also wish to acknowledge in particular the expert assistance and unfailing courtesy of Hugh Amory (Houghton Library, Harvard), Patricia Bell (Bedford County Record Office), the late John Brooke (National Register of Archives), R. J. E. Bush (Somerset Record Office), Marie P. G. Draper (Bedford Estates Office), J. M. Farrar (Cambridge County Record Office), John Fowles (Philpot Museum, Lyme Regis), Catherine Jestin (W. S. Lewis-Walpole Library), Evelyn Newby (Mellon Centre for Studies in British Art), Messrs. P. Pollak and D. S. Goodes (The King's School, Canterbury), Penelope Rundle (Wiltshire County Record Office), Richard Samways (Greater London Record Office),

Marjorie Wynne and Mrs. Louis Martz (Beineke Library, Yale), and
the archivists of the following banks: Barclays, Coutts, Hoare's, the
Royal Bank of Scotland, and Williams & Glyn's. For their kindness in
opening their private collections to us, as well as for the hospitality
shown us on these occasions, we are grateful to the late Earl of Harrowby and to Viscountess Eccles.

The timeliness and accuracy of this biography are owing in no small
measure to the generosity of fellow Fielding scholars who shared with
me their discoveries and insights, and allowed me to read their (at the
time) unpublished work. I am much indebted to Hugh Amory, W. B.
Coley, Bertrand A. Goldgar, Robert D. Hume, Thomas Lockwood,
Frederick and Anne Ribble, and Pat Rogers. I am grateful as well to
Kim Scott Walwyn of the Oxford University Press, who provided me
with proofs of the most recent volumes of the authoritative "Wesleyan"
edition of Fielding's works. To Professor Goldgar and Dr. Ribble I am
doubly indebted; their exceptionally close and judicious readings of the
manuscript could not have been more helpful.

My account of Fielding's experience of Eton is sounder because Eric
Anderson, the Head Master, and Paul Quarrie, the College Librarian,
did me the great kindness of criticizing those pages at an early stage.
Indeed, thanks to the hospitality shown us on several occasions by
Eric Anderson, his wife Poppy, and the masters and boys of Eton, we
have come to know, and greatly to admire, Fielding's school as it is
today.

For improving our knowledge of Fielding's experience of the Uni-
versity of Leyden, we are indebted to Arthur A. Mietes (Rijkarchief,
Zuid-Holland), Lotte Hellinga (British Library), Anne Goldgar, and
Frans DeBruyn.

Others, too, made important contributions to this work and deserve
our thanks: Anthony Amberg, Edward and Lillian Bloom, Benjamin
Boyce, Arthur Cash, Robert Adams Day, Hans Walter Gabler, Morris
Golden, Robert Halsband, the Right Reverend Colin James, Paul
Korshin, Gillian Percy, Linda Peterson, Hermann Real, Gordon Reed,
Betty Rizzo, Sidney F. Sabin, Major Ronald Watson, Howard
Weinbrot, and John Wilders. Nor will we forget the cordial assistance
given us by Fielding's descendants: Martin Fielding, Mrs. Rosa White-
man, and most particularly the late Mrs. Barbara Fielding Thoresby
and her son Henry Fielding Thoresby.

Finally, it is impossible for me adequately to express my gratitude
to the Earl and Countess of Malmesbury, who not only permitted me
to consult and to quote from the Fielding papers in their family archives,
but received me most hospitably into their home. Without their kindness this book would be a sadly diminished thing. And in this same
context, I wish to thank the biographer of James Harris, father of

the first Earl of Malmesbury: Professor Clive T. Probyn has greatly enhanced my understanding of Fielding's relationship with the man who was his closest friend.

M. C. B.
Charlottesville, Virginia

PART I

***

A West Country boyhood and Eton
(1707–26)

Like the history of Tom Jones, his foundling hero, Henry Fielding's own story begins in Glastonbury, Somerset, where – at Sharpham Park, the country seat of his maternal grandfather Sir Henry Gould – he was born on 22 April 1707. So Arthur Murphy, Fielding's first biographer, asserted; and so we can now affirm with certainty – together with the additional circumstance that he was baptized on 6 May at St. Benedict's church, where, in the Sharpham chapel, the Goulds customarily worshipped.[1]

As the setting for the birth of this very English author there could hardly have been a more suitable place than Glastonbury – the legendary Isle of Avalon, which monkish historians such as John of Glastonbury (whose *Chronicles* Fielding knew)[2] had claimed to be both the "fountain and origin" of the Christian faith in Britain and the burial place of King Arthur. There, it was said, in A.D. 63 Joseph of Arimathea founded a church that formed the nucleus of what in time became one of the most magnificent abbeys in England. Though the Abbey itself was reduced to ruins after the Dissolution in 1539, the superstitions associated with St. Joseph were more durable. As late as 1751 one of these – that a sacred spring issued from the place at the foot of Tor Hill where he buried the Grail – may have influenced Fielding's belief in the efficacy of the Glastonbury waters, whose curative properties had been revealed in a dream to a local valetudinarian.

Again as in the story of Tom Jones, Sharpham House, in which Fielding was born, was fashioned in the *"Gothick Stile"* – a sprawling, pleasantly irregular building with tall gables. Situated to the southwest of the town, less than two miles from St. Benedict's church, its grounds extended to that part of the Abbey lands known as "Paradise" – one of the names for Glastonbury in local tradition. In Fielding's imagination Sharpham House would have been, quite literally, no less "Paradise Hall" than Squire Allworthy's manor.

Sharpham would have held many other associations for Fielding. Its architect was the distinguished humanist and friend of Erasmus, Richard Bere, who as Abbot (1494–1525) dedicated himself to improving and beautifying the buildings belonging to the Abbey. Today, Sharpham House is a much diminished thing; but as Bere fashioned it, and as Fielding knew it, it might well have merited the description in *Tom Jones* (I.iv): "There was an Air of Grandeur in it, that struck you with Awe, and rival'd the Beauties of the best *Grecian* Architecture; and it was as commodious within, as venerable without." Bere, who used it as his summer residence, described the estate as follows in his account of the Abbey lands:

There is another park, called *Sherphame*, containing, with some mead inclosures in the circuit thereof, three hundred and eighty-two

acres. In this park, Abbot Richard lately built, at his own expense, a
very handsome manor-house, with a *chapel*, hall, parlours, chambers,
storehouses, kitchen, and other rooms and offices, having a stone
wall on one side, and oak pales on the other, with an orchard and
fish-ponds. In which park might be kept four hundred deer, and forty
large cattle.[3]

Bere's successor, the martyred Richard Whiting, was living at Sharpham when he was seized by Henry VIII's agents at the Dissolution –
at which time the manor was granted to Sir Thomas Dyer, whose son,
the poet and courtier Sir Edward Dyer, was born there. King Henry's
surveyors recorded that the manor was then "in circuite ii long myles
of good meade and pasture" and included eighty acres of oaks, ashes,
and maples.[4]

It was in 1657 that Sharpham passed from the Dyer family into the
possession of Fielding's great-grandfather on his mother's side, Richard
Davidge, a wealthy London merchant with roots, and a good deal of
property, in Dorset.[5] In 1692, after Davidge, Katherine his widow, and
five of their children had died, his estate came to his three daughters,
two of whom would figure prominently in Fielding's early life: namely,
Sarah Gould (*c.* 1654–1733), Fielding's grandmother; and Katherine
(d. 1739), the second wife of Charles Cottington (d. 1698) of Fonthill
Gifford, Wiltshire, a gentleman of a distinguished and powerful Roman
Catholic family.[6] It is clear, however, that Sarah and Henry Gould had
established themselves at Sharpham not long after their marriage in
February 1676/7,[7] for the register of St. Benedict's church reveals that
their daughter Katherine was buried there in November 1681 and that
Fielding's mother, Sarah, was baptized there on 28 December 1682.

They must have found Sharpham in a fair condition – so it would
appear from Warner's observation in 1826 that the "mansion was
formerly approached by a magnificent avenue, a mile in length, the
remains of which are seen in some vast elms, and stupendous oak
pollards." Even so Henry and Sarah – and later their son Davidge (*c.*
1684–1765), who inherited the estate in 1710 – made a number of
improvements: the stables, for example, were erected in 1701; the
staircase was installed by Davidge in 1726; and a pert-looking iron
weather vane inscribed with the legend, "D. G. 1733," still surmounts
the tallest gable of the house. Also remaining is the upper chamber –
called the "Harlequin Chamber" by Warner, but now simply the
"Fielding Room" – in which, according to a tradition preserved in the
Gould family,[8] Fielding was born: it is a pleasant room, with oak
paneling from the early sixteenth century and a window overlooking
gardens.

But in the setting of the early books of *Tom Jones* what is more vivid

than "Paradise Hall" itself is the splendid, almost visionary, prospect
it commands (I.iv). Ultimately, to be sure, the scene Fielding describes
is an imaginary one, incorporating several features more suggestive of
Hagley Park and Prior Park – the far-flung estates of his patrons
George Lyttelton and Ralph Allen – than of any place near Glastonbury.
Fielding's enemies pointed ironically to the unreal landscape he
described as proof of his "great Skill in *Chorography*";[9] and even Coleridge, who otherwise admired the novel and who knew the region well,
was puzzled as he tried to reconcile the scene of wild mountains whose
tops rose above the clouds with the tamer aspect of the Mendip and
Quantock Hills, which bound the Glastonbury levels to the northwest
and south, respectively.[10]

As Cross realized, however, the celebrated prospect from "Paradise
Hall" was not wholly the product of Fielding's fancy.[11] The improbable
vantage point from which he painted the scene, and which is therefore
the symbolic location of "Paradise Hall," is one of the noblest land-
marks in Britain – Tor Hill. The view he describes is one he would have
seen many times as a child, and on later visits to his uncle, as he looked
from the slopes of the Tor in a westerly direction across the vast levels:
the River Brue flowing into Meare Pond,[12] which "filled the Center" of
the "Plain," and then issuing from the lake to resume its meandering
course "till it emptied itself into the Sea" (or more precisely, into the
Bristol Channel at Burnham), "with a large Arm of which, and an
Island beyond it [namely, Stert Island], the Prospect was closed." The
legendary Tor, standing thus as the hub of Tom Jones's world, was the
focus of his author's earliest memories. Surmounted by the ruined
Tower of St. Michael, the great hill rises solitary and awful some five
hundred feet above the flat terrain that stretches for miles in every
direction. To this day it looms starkly visible from the threshold of
Sharpham House and from every window on the north.

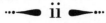

ii

Already implicit in the way Fielding transformed these Glastonbury
memories into the setting for his greatest novel is the autobiographical
dimension of his fiction that Richardson remarked – his great and
jealous rival, who insisted indeed that Fielding's dependence on his
own experience for his plots and characters was so complete it proved
the impotence of his imagination:[13] in a sense that we will come to
apprehend more fully, Tom Jones *is* Fielding – as, in their different
ways, are Mr. Wilson before him and Billy Booth after. For Fielding's
own character and progress – his personal development from a pas-

sionate and unruly young man into the sagacious and indefatigable reforming justice of his last years – are shadowed in the pattern of *Tom Jones*, whose bumptious hero, before he can be united with the beautiful young woman whose name signifies Wisdom, must learn to discipline his appetites and the energies of his heart through the acquisition of Prudence – the supreme rational virtue of antiquity, and, by tradition, supremely the virtue of magistrates. "Prudentissimi," aptly enough, is the distinguishing superlative on the slab that once marked the grave of Fielding's grandfather and namesake – Sir Henry Gould, Judge of the Queen's Bench.[14]

Fielding's character comprises a fascinating paradox: on the one hand, the essential quality of his nature, which he came with difficulty to control, was his improvident delight in living, fully and recklessly, for the moment; on the other hand is the equally impressive quality of his mind, a love of learning and a clarity and penetration of thought that in his own day earned him the respect of accomplished classicists and sober clergymen, of Lord Chancellors and Prime Ministers, and which more recently have prompted at least one professional phil-osopher to prefer the view of human nature embodied in *Tom Jones* to the abstract ethical systems of Shaftesbury or Bishop Butler – or even, in some respects, of Kant.[15] Perhaps it was because Fielding so well understood the anarchy of the passions that he came to value the prudential virtues of will-power and rational judgment, and to devote himself, with an energy that shortened his life, to enforcing and refor-ming the laws on which the social order depends.

It might seem from what we know of his family that these con-tradictory sides of Fielding's character were in his blood – the lawyer that he became being already present in his grandfather, Judge Gould, and the high-living, intemperate rake that he was in his early years being the legacy of his father's own pleasure-loving disposition. We must, in any case, pause to consider Fielding's family on both sides.

As we have remarked, Sarah (1682–1718), Fielding's mother, was the daughter of Sir Henry Gould and his wife Sarah – one of eight children of the merchant Richard Davidge of Dorchester. Sir Henry was himself of an old and respected West Country family. His forebears were substantial yeomen of Winsham, Somerset, where he was born in May 1643, the eldest son and heir of Andrew Goold (as the name was formerly spelled) and his wife Maude (née Linbearde, of the nearby town of Crewkerne).[16] He began the study of the law at an early age and became one of the most distinguished lawyers of his time. Admitted to the Middle Temple in his seventeenth year (1660),[17] he was called to the Bar in 1667 and, during the reign of William and Mary, rose rapidly in the profession, being appointed Bencher of the Temple (1689), Serjeant (1692), and King's Serjeant (1693). He was knighted in 1694 and in

1699 was made Judge of the King's Bench, his patent being renewed upon the accession of Queen Anne. In his sixty-seventh year Sir Henry died in his chambers at Serjeants' Inn, Chancery Lane, on 26 March 1710, his body being returned to Glastonbury for burial in the Sharpham Chapel, St. Benedict's.[18]

Sharpham then passed to Judge Gould's only son Davidge, himself a lawyer of the Middle Temple.[19] Indeed, in 1734 Davidge became a Master of the Bench at the Temple and, by being instrumental in enabling Fielding to qualify as a barrister, would assist his nephew at perhaps the most difficult time of his life. By his marriage to Honora Huckmore in 1709 he had numerous children,[20] three of his sons – Henry, Davidge, and Thomas – continuing in the family tradition by becoming lawyers of the Middle Temple.[21] With Henry (1711–94), especially, Fielding would become good friends: "This young Gentleman," Fielding wrote in 1748 upon a false report of his cousin's death, "(who was of the Middle-Temple) had great Parts, and had with great Diligence applied them to the Study of his Profession; in which he was arrived at a very extensive Knowledge, and had very early in Life acquired much Reputation."[22] But Henry Gould was very much alive when Fielding wrote these words, and would live to become King's Counsel (1754), Serjeant (1761), Baron of the Exchequer (1761), Judge of the Court of Common Pleas (1763) – and a very rich man.

Fielding always remained close to his mother's family. They were substantial, prudent people – merchants, landowners, lawyers – who must have represented for him that stability and orderliness of life which, however much his own early conduct might mock such virtues, he nevertheless admired from a distance. Only those with appetites and passions as powerful as his can perhaps feel so intensely the need to control them.

His father, Edmund Feilding, set no such steadying example; but through him Fielding was connected to one of the noblest families in the kingdom – the Earls of Denbigh and Desmond, who claimed descent from the Hapsburgs of Germany. This claim, now disproved,[23] was not doubted in Fielding's day; and though Gibbon in a famous compliment put it in proper perspective – predicting that "the romance of *Tom Jones* ... will outlive the palace of the Escurial, and the imperial eagle of the house of Austria"[24] – the author of *Tom Jones* proudly used a seal in which that eagle was displayed.

Fielding (who early adopted that spelling of the name) was in fact descended from the ancient Feilding family of Leicestershire and War-wickshire, which had grown rich through a series of prosperous marriages. (Thus, according to the anecdote told by Fielding's son, when the Earl of Denbigh asked how the novelist accounted for the different form of the name as Fielding wrote it, he replied: "I cannot

tell, my Lord, except it be that my branch of the family were the first
that knew how to spell.")[25] The title itself was a fairly recent one,
having been conferred on William Feilding (1582–1643), the first Earl
of Denbigh, in 1622, owing chiefly to his marriage with the sister of
George Villiers, the future Duke of Buckingham. When William died
in the Civil War of wounds he received fighting on the Royalist side
under Prince Rupert, the title passed to his son Basil (c. 1608–75), who,
however, even while his father was alive, preferred Parliament's cause
to that of Charles I. Holding a command under the Earl of Essex, Basil
fought against his father at Edgehill, and later served the government
during the Commonwealth. Steadiness in politics was no more a part
of Basil's character than filial piety; for after Cromwell's death he was
forward in welcoming Charles II from exile. Nor, for that matter, was
he notable for simple honesty: it was Basil who used forged papers to
establish the Feilding descent from the Hapsburgs.

Fielding descended from George (1616–65), Basil's younger brother,
who – again through the friendship of Buckingham – was raised to the
Irish peerage as a boy of six, eventually coming to hold the titles of
Earl of Desmond, Lord Feilding of Lecaghe, and Viscount Callan of
Ireland. By marriage with Bridget Stanhope of Suffolk, George had
three daughters and six sons, the youngest of whom was John, Fielding's
grandfather. Of John's brothers, William the eldest (1640–85) would
inherit the titles, becoming third Earl of Denbigh and second of
Desmond; he was also the grandfather of Lady Mary Wortley Montagu,
who would one day serve Fielding well as friend and counsellor. Charles
(1643–1722) became one of the most powerful men in Ireland: knighted
in 1673, he married the following year Ursula Stockton, daughter of a
Judge of the King's Bench; he served as Governor of Limerick, as Privy
Councillor of Ireland, and as Colonel of the King's Regiment, playing
an important role in the defeat of the Jacobites in 1690–1. Charles's
influence may help to explain why the first important promotions
Fielding's father enjoyed in the Army were in regiments on the Irish
establishment. Nothing very remarkable is recorded of George (d. 1688),
who married a lady of Bury St. Edmunds, Suffolk, and died there. Two
other brothers, however, distinguished themselves very sensationally
indeed, in a manner suggestive of that disposition to passion and
violence that was part of Fielding's own nature. Thus on 9 May 1667
Pepys recorded in his diary a murderous tavern brawl in which Basil
Feilding, page to Lady Sandwich, was stabbed to the heart by his
brother Christopher in a drunken fury – "a sad spectacle," wrote Pepys,
"and a broad wound, which makes my hand now shake to write of
it."[26]

Another sort of man altogether, John (c. 1650–98) matriculated at
Queens' College, Cambridge, in 1668 and became a Fellow in 1671, the

year he was awarded the M.A.[27] His principles, it appears, were Whiggish in politics and latitudinarian in church affairs; for, having resisted the pro-Catholic measures of James II, he was appointed one of King William's chaplains upon the Revolution of 1689 – the year in which, while on a visit to Cambridge with the King, he received the degree of Doctor of Divinity. These same political and religious principles Fielding later found congenial.

He would also esteem his grandfather for a more palpable reason. Originally from Suffolk, John Fielding was the first of his family to settle in the West of England, in the country his grandson loved so well. Sometime after his marriage to Dorothy Cockayne, who appears to have descended from an ancient family residing near the Cambridgeshire/Bedfordshire border,[28] John moved to Dorset as Vicar of St. Mary's, Puddletown (1675–91). Here at least five of his seven children were born – including, on 20 January 1679/80, Edmund, Fielding's father.[29] Of Edmund's brothers and sisters we need mention only three. John, who twice married well-born Irish women, became Secretary to the Duke of Portland, Governor of Jamaica, where he died in June 1725.[30] George (d. 1738) was Lieutenant Colonel in the Royal Horse Guards and Groom of the Bedchamber to Queen Anne and George I. A warm-hearted man, he was fond of Fielding and of Edmund's other children by his first marriage and behaved generously toward them by the terms of his will.[31] Edmund's sister Bridget, who in 1699 married Major Frederic Lapenotier, a Huguenot,[32] will have a small part to play, together with her mother, in the bitter litigation that troubled Fielding's childhood.

While his family increased, John Fielding grew in distinction in the Church and developed strong ties with two places that provided a setting for his grandson's early years: namely, the beautiful cathedral city of Salisbury, Wiltshire, and the parish of Gillingham Major, Dorset, the vicarage of which incorporated the chapelry of East Stour. From 1677 John was a Prebendary of Salisbury who held the successively more lucrative livings of Yatesbury, Wilts. (13 October 1677), Beaminster Prima, Dorset (15 February 1677/8), and Gillingham Major (24 January 1681/2); the latter he continued to hold until his death. On 27 March 1683 he was appointed Archdeacon of Dorset on the recommendation of a brace of bishops, William Gulston of Bristol and Seth Ward of Salisbury, who assured Archbishop Sancroft that John had the "Character of a vertuous good man" and was "an honor to the Church."[33]

John was ambitious enough, and well enough connected in Ireland, to aspire to a bishopric in that country – a circumstance that also suggests what has been insufficiently stressed by Fielding's biographers: the strength of the Irish connection in his family background. To support John in his ambition the Earl of Nottingham, Secretary of State, wrote to Sir Robert Southwell from Whitehall on 24 July 1690: "You know," he emphasized, "his family is of Ireland, and himself a man of worth as well as quality."[34] The King was too busy suppressing the Jacobites in Ireland to heed this request, and nothing ever came of it. But it enables us better to appreciate Fielding's frequent censures of his countrymen for prejudice against their Hibernian neighbors. In this spirit, for example, he opens a passage in "An Essay on Conversation":

> It is very common among us to cast Sarcasms on a neighbouring Nation, to which we have no other Reason to bear an Antipathy, than what is more usual than justifiable, because we have injured it: But sure such general Satire is not founded on Truth: for I have known Gentlemen of that Nation possessed with every good Quality which are to be wished in a Man, or required in a Friend.

This passage was remarkable enough for its pro-Irish sentiment to be quoted at length by someone styling himself "An unprejudiced *Englishman*" in an article published in *The Craftsman* on St. Patrick's Day, 1750. A similar defense of the Irish occurs in *The Champion* (29 March 1740). What is more, by keeping in mind the Irish element in Fielding's background, we will relish all the more the story of the Fitzpatricks in *Tom Jones*.

Disappointed in his hopes for an Irish bishopric, John Fielding continued on at Salisbury. As one of the six Canon Residentiaries, he shared responsibility for managing the affairs and revenues of the cathedral, and would certainly have been personally known to Gilbert Burnet, the latitudinarian Bishop of Salisbury (1689–1715), whom Fielding regarded as the greatest of English historians. He also enjoyed the privilege of a residence in the cathedral Close, where, presumably (at Myles' Place, No. 6), he died on 31 January 1697/8.[35]

iii

The most important figures in Fielding's childhood, of course, were his mother, about whom we know next to nothing, and his father – a fascinating man only now emerging from the shadows, with whom Fielding struggled for much of his life to come to terms. Edmund Fielding (like John his father he used this spelling of the name as often as not) would eventually become one of the dozen or so ranking officers in the Army. He began his military career during the War of the League of Augsburg, being commissioned ensign in the First Regiment of Foot

Guards on 15 December 1696.[36] Not yet seventeen years old at the time, he might have seemed one of those callow "Boys," as his son contemptuously called them, who because their families were rich enough to purchase their commissions, commanded seasoned veterans old enough to be their fathers.[37] In 1702, by the time Marlborough's second Flanders campaign was under way, Edmund had become a captain in General Webb's Regiment of Foot (the Eighth or Queen's Regiment), and probably took part in the storming of Venlo and Liège.[38] He was certainly with Webb at Blenheim in August 1704, when Marlborough won his greatest victory; for, in acknowledgment of his conduct during the battle, he was awarded a bounty of £30. There is reason to credit the statement of a contemporary that Edmund "serv'd in the late Wars against France with much Bravery and Reputation."[39] No doubt presuming on that reputation – and believing that, since he had "no other dependance than in the Army," he should lose no opportunity to advance himself – he approached Marlborough personally in January 1704/5, asking to be promoted to major "in the new levies."[40]

No portrait of Edmund has come down to us, but he must have been an attractive figure – gallant and charming, with a courteous manner and a no doubt aristocratic air. He was also more than a little self-indulgent, with a taste for fine things and expensive pleasures – and for handsome women, who appear to have found him irresistible. In 1706 (presumably) Sarah Gould, twenty-three years old and a woman of independent ways, was so much in love with him that she risked her parents' displeasure by marrying him not only without their consent but, as her mother later publicly declared, "contrary to their good liking."[41]

How, one wonders, did the lovers bring off this union? Where did it take place? In that same year on 12 April, Edmund's hopes for promotion were realized when he was commissioned major in Lord Tunbridge's newly raised regiment of foot. After waiting for orders in town, he was commanded with his company probably to Bristol in order to be transported to Ireland. There, his rapid advancement in the Army continuing, he was promoted to Lieutenant Colonel on 31 August. No record of the time and place of his marriage has come to light – and it may be that Edmund remained in England until July, when the officers formally received their commissions after a long delay that plunged many of them into debt.[42] But it is also possible that he eloped with Sarah to Ireland, and that it was in Ireland, in July 1706, that Henry Fielding was conceived.

Another circumstance squares well enough with such an hypothesis. It was not until 8 March 1706/7, little more than a month before Sarah's son was born, that Sir Henry Gould was moved to provide for his only daughter and her children by drawing up a new will expressly for that purpose.[43] By the terms of the will he would leave to his son Davidge and a certain William Day of London £3,000 in trust to be applied toward the purchase of an estate for Sarah's "sole and separate use". The restriction is important. For though Judge Gould was thus willing to forgive his daughter's disobedience in marrying against his wishes, he meant to protect her from the consequences of her folly: "And I do declare," the document continues, "That the interest and the profits of the Estate shall be during her life paid to her self, and her script only shall be a discharge ... It being my will that her husband shall have nothing to do with it." After Sarah's death, moreover, the estate was to go to her children, not to Edmund.

Edmund later insisted that Judge Gould in time relented toward him – that he was at length "well approved of and received" by Sir Henry and his family, and that the old man told him he meant to pass his declining years partly with his son at Sharpham Park and partly with Sarah and Edmund. Indeed, Edmund would claim a still more impressive conquest – the winning over of Sarah's formidable mother. However that might be, the Goulds for the present distrusted his motives in marrying their daughter and regarded him sourly. And Sarah, though she continued annually to bear Edmund's children, came home to Sharpham, and to her father, to have them. There, as we have said, Fielding was born on 22 April 1707; there, too, she gave birth to his sisters Catharine, on 16 July 1708, and Ursula, on 3 October 1709.[44]

Shortly before he died in the spring of 1710, Judge Gould, as he had promised, acquired for his daughter a handsome farm at East Stour, Dorset,[45] for which he paid £4,750, a sum well in excess of the £3,000 stipulated in his will. Edmund believed, nevertheless, that Sir Henry intended to pay the whole amount himself. He had become so well reconciled with his son-in-law that he sent him oxen to plow the land and promised to stock the dairy with cows. But though Edmund was put in possession of this fine seat, Sir Henry died before he could declare these intentions in form; and in the conveyance finally executed on 26 September 1713, the trustees of the estate, Davidge Gould and William Day, held strictly to the terms of Sir Henry's will. Edmund had himself to pay the amount of the purchase price in excess of £3,000 (for which he was allotted a proportionate share of the lands), and he was at the further expense of stocking the farm and providing the utensils needed to work it.

These demands must have seriously strained his resources; for, ever ambitious to rise in the Army, he had on 1 August 1709 laid out £2,800 in Dublin to purchase the commission of Kilner Brazier, colonel of a regiment of foot on the Irish establishment.[46] It was, as so many of Edmund's financial ventures proved to be, an imprudent investment.

In December 1710 he received orders to fill up his regiment with fresh recruits preparatory to embarking for Portugal in April. Not long after he arrived at Lisbon, however, his regiment, being judged one of the two weakest under Lord Portmore's command, was reduced and ordered home, where, after languishing for several months without pay, it was disbanded in August 1712.[47]

For the next three and a half years Edmund, like Billy Booth in *Amelia*, was a "broke" officer on half-pay, and he and his family must have experienced something of the financial distress Fielding describes in that novel. The regiment for which he had recently paid so dearly was no longer a source of income, and the farm never repaid the substantial investment he had made in it. Its rents came to just £150 a year – a pittance to a man of Edmund's prodigal habits – and most of the money was legally his wife's. What is more, his family steadily increased: Sarah, the future novelist and Henry's favorite sister, was born at East Stour on 8 November 1710; Anne in June 1713; Beatrice on 20 June 1714.[48]

That Edmund wanted money during these years is clear. In November 1714 he sank to borrowing £600 from his housekeeper.[49] But even that was insufficient: at about the same time he touched his neighbour Thomas Freke of Wyke, Gillingham, for £50, and then for £50 more in July 1715.[50] He was perhaps at this time also already in debt for £700 to Katherine Cottington, his wife's aunt.[51]

····➤ iv ➤····

However pinched the family's financial circumstances may have been during these early years of Fielding's childhood, they were never severe enough to cause Edmund to reduce the number of his servants or the amenities expected in the household of an officer and a gentleman. Besides his housekeeper, Marie Bentham, and several inferior servants, he maintained a French governess, Anne Delaborde, to look after his daughters (a woman whose presence in the family may help to account for Fielding's later command of French). The children, certainly, had plenty to eat, and it was a matter of pride in the household that they had plenty of beer and ale to drink.

Their spirits, too, were nourished. They were taught their catechism, and perhaps, like the young Joseph Andrews (I.iii), were encouraged to read the Bible, *The Whole Duty of Man*, and the *Imitation of Christ*. Fielding in later years had an impressive knowledge of the Scriptures. And like Joseph Andrews, who found the book lying open in the hall window, he also marveled as a boy at "the Casualties" related by Sir

Richard Baker in his *Chronicle* – most memorable of which were the stories of "how the Devil carried away half a Church in Sermon-time, without hurting one of the Congregation; and ... how a Field of Corn ran away down a Hill with all the Trees upon it, and covered another Man's Meadow."[52] In due course John Oliver, curate of St. Mary's, Motcombe,[53] would visit the farm two or three times a week to teach the boy Latin. It is Parson Oliver, surely, who served Fielding as the model for the sensible clergyman of the same name who in *Shamela* (1741) exposes the true character of Richardson's celebrated heroine.

And all round Fielding as a boy stretched some of the most beautiful country in England. The house was situated on the road between Shaftesbury and Sherborne (the present A30), and was only a few feet from the parish church, Christ's, its yard shaded by a towering yew tree. Facing south, the house was of stone with oak timbering – a great homely barn of a place, "very picturesque" as it seemed to one who saw it a century later,[54] and as it seems now in Plate 3. Nearby grew another remarkable tree, an enormous locust, from the middle of which sprang an elder tree. And there were numerous outbuildings, including a malt-house, a brew-house, a coach-house, and a large, circular stone dovecote. Now, except for the splendid countryside itself, little of this remains: the yew was cut down in 1760, yielding, it is said, ten wagonloads of wood; the church was rebuilt in 1841 in a Norman style; and five years earlier, in 1836, the house was demolished and the present unremarkable dwelling erected on the site. But his novels still testify to the impression made on Fielding by this place, with its green pastures rolling away to the Downs to the southeast and, beyond "the pleasant Banks of sweetly winding *Stower*"[55] that marked the western boundary of the property, opening to the magnificent Blackmore Vale. "Hardy country," the locals will tell you now (some of whom live in a housing estate called "The Fieldings"); but it was Fielding country long before, as Hardy knew, who declared that the authentic regional character of Fielding's scenes and dialogues was "apparent to any Dorset man."[56] This is the site of Dr. Harrison's parsonage in *Amelia* (III.xii), "placed among Meadows, washed by a Trout-stream, and flanked on both sides with Downs." Over those Downs still graze the flocks of sheep, famous for the sweetness of their meat and the fineness of their wool, that tempted the sheepstealers in *Joseph Andrews* (III.ii). The Downs, declares Parson Adams, "I take to exceed ... all other Prospects in the Universe" (III.xiii).

But what were Fielding's childhood impressions of life within doors at East Stour – his impressions, most particularly, of his parents? He must have been his mother's darling, whose first born he was and for many years her only son, to whom she gave her father's name. All we hear of her, however – though from an unfriendly witness who had it

Plate 1 Fielding's birthplace: Sharpham House, near Glastonbury.

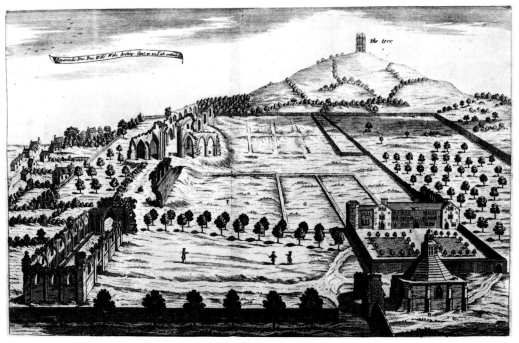

Plate 2 Glastonbury Abbey and The Tor (1723).

Plate 3 Fielding's house, East Stour, Dorset.

Plate 4 Salisbury Cathedral and The Close.

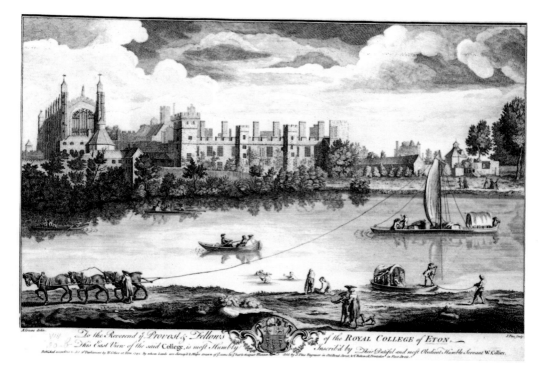

Plate 5 Eton College (1742).

Plate 6 The Court of Chancery
(*c.* 1725).

Plate 7 Sarah Andrew.

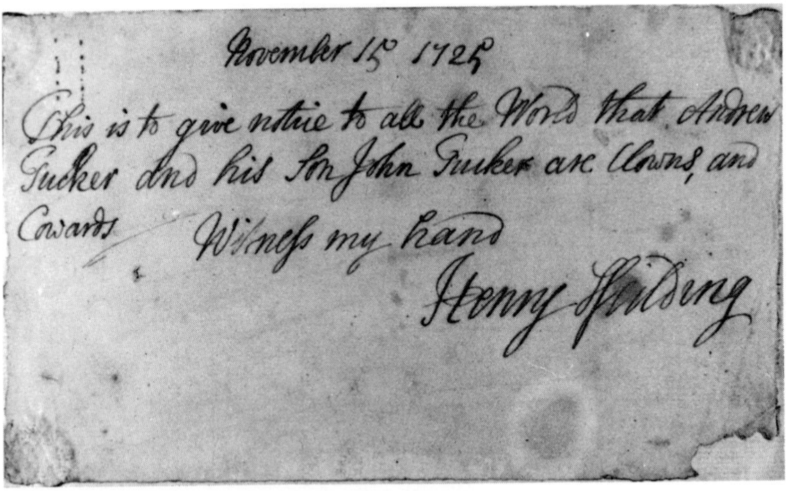

November 1st 1725
This is to give notice to all the World that Andrew Tucker and his Son John Tucker are Clowns, and Cowards — Witness my hand
Henry Fielding

Plate 8 Fielding's earliest extant manuscript, denouncing the Tuckers (1725).

at second hand from the governess, Anne Delaborde[57] – is that she did not shrink from beating the children when they "were rude or disobliged her." No image of her appears in Fielding's works – none, at least, that we can recognize. There is perhaps oblique evidence of his attachment to her, however, in the curious œdipal theme of *Tom Jones*, and in the marked animus against stepmothers expressed in the fiction of both Fielding and his sister Sarah.

We have a much better notion of Edmund's character and of his troubled relationship with Henry, as the tacit rivalry that normally obtains between fathers and sons worsened toward the end of Edmund's life into open resentment on Fielding's part. What must have made such bitterness particularly hard to acknowledge to a person of Fielding's usual good nature, and his sense of the duty children owe their parents, is that Edmund was to all appearances a charming, inoffensive, in some respects even an admirable man. He impressed one witness who knew him well as being "of a very easy temper and courteous behaviour," conducting himself toward Sarah as "a tender and loving husband" and toward the children as "a kind and indulgent father" – so his servant testified, and though a biased witness, she was probably truthful enough in describing Edmund's characteristic manner, which seems to have been gentlemanly and ingratiating. In later years, indeed – to judge from the extraordinary tone of his letter to Edmund – the usually self-possessed Aaron Hill was nothing less than infatuated with his "grace" and "gayety."[58]

Even when he meant to represent Authority, Edmund was seldom a fearsome figure – whether acting in his role of paterfamilias, or magistrate, or colonel of the regiment and acting-Governor of the Isle of Jersey. To be sure, at a time when the Hanoverian succession was new and memories of the 1715 rebellion were still fresh, he wanted it known that as a country justice he never failed to punish those who "were in the least suspected to be disaffected to his present Majesty King George."[59] But he preferred demonstrating his loyalty in jollier ways: on such occasions as the anniversaries of George I's accession and coronation, and the birthdays of the King and the Prince and Princess of Wales, he had all the household drink the healths of the Royal Family; he ordered bonfires to be lit, and mugs of beer and cider to be given to the bell-ringers at the church. As Governor of Jersey, he would later carry such celebrations to operatic heights, when, for example, on hearing that the King had arrived safely in England from Hanover, he declared a day of public rejoicing:

which was performed . . . with firing of Cannon in his Majesty's Castle, the Flags flying from Sun rising to Sun setting, the two Towns, St. Hillico and St. Obin's, raised each a Battery of 21 Cannons, which

kept continually firing all the Day, and till the Night was far spent;
and the Evening concluded with Bonfires, Illuminations, ringing of
Bells, and all other Demonstrations of Joy; and ... Fuziliers attended
at the Bonfires, firing of Vollies after the Healths of his Majesty,
our gracious Queen Caroline, and all the Royal Family, which was
answered by a Discharge of the Cannon of the two Towns.[60]

When it was necessary, moreover, to consider the serious affairs of his
command at Jersey, Edmund distinguished himself from his predecessors by acting both conscientiously and with clemency toward
prisoners.[61]

Edmund, clearly, had many virtues, and no one who enjoyed a
holiday as heartily as he did can have seemed a very awful figure to a
boy. The problem was that he was too fond of his pleasures and
indifferent to what they cost. It was his family who paid the price. So
it would seem to Fielding, who, as eldest son and heir of a man of rank,
substance, and noble connections, had great expectations – expectations
which, through his father's improvidence and self-indulgence, came to
nothing. Perhaps exacerbating Fielding's sense of rivalry and alienation
was the fact that he had very little of his father's company. As Thomas
Freke, the Fieldings' neighbor and disappointed creditor was aware,
Edmund "was frequently from home, sometimes in Ireland and other
places beyond the seas" and "at other very remote and distant places
for a considerable time together."[62] Sarah was left to discipline the
children herself. Perhaps she was aware that it was not always the call
of duty that deprived her of her husband's society, but also, as Aaron
Hill put it some years later, Edmund's "taste" for the gaiety a "mistress" can provide.[63] If so, it is tempting to sense something of her own
bitterness in Dr. Harrison's otherwise oddly gratuitous observation in
Amelia (II.iv) that "most young Gentlemen of the Rag" deserve their
reputation as fortune-hunters: "for, as little famed as the Army is for
Religion, nothing is, I believe, more common than for the Officers to
make good Christians of their Wives, and to teach them Repentance" –
a passage which, upon reflection, Fielding struck out of the second
edition.

We may imagine what Sarah's mood must have been in 1716 – the
year in which she gave birth to her last child, Edmund, in April, and
in August buried her three-year-old daughter Anne.[64] Edmund was
with her for part of the year; for on 10 May, in his capacity as justice
of the peace, he signed the Account-Book of the overseers of the poor
at Gillingham.[65] But much of the year he was in London, perhaps on
business relating to his being commissioned colonel of a newly raised
regiment on 16 February 1715/16[66] (the Jacobite rebellion continued
until April to pose a threat to the government).

Whatever it was that brought him to town, while he was there he gave Sarah yet another instance of his improvidence. Heavily encumbered with debts as he already was, Edmund allowed himself to be fleeced by a certain Captain Robert Midford, in circumstances curiously resembling Booth's gulling by Captain Trent in *Amelia* (X.v). While waiting to transact some business at Prince's Coffeehouse, a favorite resort of his in St. James's, Edmund was approached by Midford and several fellow officers who drew him into a game of faro – at first for small stakes, which, however, they raised by degrees until he had lost the considerable sum of £500. And Midford was no one to trifle with: to judge from another incident in which he was involved that year – on 11 May he desperately wounded a man in Chancery Lane, drawing his sword and beating him[67] – Edmund's gamester was not only a wily, but a dangerous character. Edmund paid part of this debt, but when Midford began an action of outlawry against him, he sued in turn, on the grounds that gaming debts were unlawful by Act of Parliament.[68] The judgment in the case has not come to light, but Edmund considered he had been victimized by sharpers who had brought him – and with him, his wife and family – to the brink of "utter ruin."

It would not be long before the family finances were in a ruinous state, thanks to Edmund's penchant for gaming of a more respectable, but no less foolish, sort – his plunge, that is, into the South Sea scheme. Except, however, as such worries affect the adults around them and make for tension in the home, children are not much troubled by the loss of money; and even in the worst of times the Fielding children never wanted for material comforts.

····◄ V ►····

Why is it, then, that the first clear image we have of Henry Fielding is of a lad on the verge of adolescence and utterly out of control, his behavior in every way not only willful and high-spirited, but rebellious, outrageous even – deliberately disrespectful of all authority? Even in later life, as his friend James Harris recalled,[69] Fielding's "Passions ... were vehement in every kind," and "easily passing into excess." He felt powerfully the emotion of the moment, whether anger or love or gratitude, or that sudden apprehension of what he liked to call "the Ridiculous" which provoked a hearty laugh. He was also physically robust and, with perhaps a trace of the blood that flowed in the veins of his great-uncles Christopher and Basil, he could react violently when he believed he had been insulted. Passionate by nature, he would have learned to discipline his temper with difficulty under the best of circumstances. But consider his situation as a boy – son and heir of a gallant soldier and the most powerful man in the parish, who, however, was seldom at home long enough to be a proper father to him; his mother's favorite, no doubt, and doted on as well by her no less adoring mother and aunt, Lady Gould and Mrs. Cottington; not only an older brother, but for nine years the only boy in a family of five sisters. It is hardly surprising that at age eleven, when we first catch a glimpse of him, Fielding expected to have things his own way – or that he was deeply attached to his mother and sisters.

Nor is it surprising that such a boy should be profoundly disturbed by the series of domestic events that began with his mother's death on 14 April 1718. She was buried four days before his eleventh birthday in the churchyard adjoining the house. The sense of loss Fielding and his sisters felt would be heavy, and with their mother's grave ever in sight, it would be prolonged. To this distress was soon added the sense of betrayal, their father's betrayal both of them and of their mother's memory – a feeling made all the keener and more disturbing by the open bitterness of their mother's aunt and surrogate, Mrs. Cottington, who had moved into the house earlier that year to supervise the household when Sarah fell ill. For sometime in the autumn of the year in which Sarah died, Edmund went to London to court a new wife. He was also seeking a new commission, his regiment having been reduced in November.[70] In December or thereabouts he established himself in the fashionable parish of St. James's, in a house on the west side of Blenheim Street, near Great Marlborough Street, where his neighbor across the way was his former commanding officer General Webb.[71] He seems thereby deliberately to have sought to recover memories of past glory: of the young captain's gallantry in Marlborough's wars – an exciting, glittering time before he ever wooed Sarah Gould or submitted, however intermittently, to the tedium of a squire's life in the country.

Not later than January of the new year, presumably (since their first child was born on 18 October 1719),[72] he married again – a certain Anne Rapha, a widow and a Roman Catholic. On 11 March 1718/19 he took another step toward starting a fresh life; on that date he was commissioned colonel of a new regiment raised from the out-pensioners of the Chelsea Royal Hospital. For the rest of his life Edmund retained command of this Regiment of Invalids, as it was called, which included many veterans of Marlborough's campaigns.[73]

After the death of Fielding's mother it was a matter merely of a few months, then, until Edmund (it must have seemed) had thoroughly expunged Sarah's memory, abandoned his children to the care of their old aunt and a houseful of servants, and, with his new wife, settled down to enjoy the pleasures of the town and the dignity of a new command. That, certainly, was how it struck Mrs. Cottington. And it was not long before he added to these injuries to the children's spirit damages of a quite material kind. For not only did Edmund continue to receive the rents and profits of the farm, contrary to the stipulations of Judge Gould's will, by which, in the event of Sarah's death, they were to be strictly applied in trust to the benefit of her children. Early in August 1720 – at the height of the national mania over the South Sea stocks, in which he invested heavily and would soon suffer in "the general calamity," as he called it, that followed the crash[74] – Edmund and his new wife sold for £2,100 a large part of the property at East Stour, together with lands in the adjacent parish of West Stour.[75] The children's favorite uncles, Davidge Gould and George Fielding, were parties to the transaction, and one would like to assume that the property Edmund thus disposed of was that part of the estate which he had paid for himself – though the purchase price was well in excess of the £1,750 he had put down seven years earlier.

The purchaser was Awnsham Churchill, a wealthy Dorset landowner and eminent bookseller, who with his brother John had published in 1704 the first volumes of their celebrated *Collection of Voyages and Travels*. It was surely these men whom Fielding had in mind in the last year of his life, when he criticized certain "judicious booksellers" who publish others' travels under their own names, "thus unjustly attributing to themselves the merit of others."[76] It may be that the bitterness of this sarcasm owes something to Fielding's sense that Awnsham Churchill, however legally and properly, had also appropriated a substantial portion of the lands he considered his birthright.

Lady Gould, who had distrusted Edmund from the start, objected to his receiving the income of the farm in defiance of Sir Henry's will and the terms of the deed of conveyance. And besides the rancor she felt over Edmund's marrying again so soon after her daughter's death, she feared that his new wife, a Roman Catholic, would complete the children's ruin by bringing them up as papists. For a while that dire possibility seemed remote, because in the latter part of 1719 Edmund – glad enough to begin a new marriage in gay St. James's without having half a dozen children by his first wife under foot – sent Henry off to Eton and committed his sisters and little brother to their grandmother's care in Salisbury, where she had recently settled: the four girls were placed at Mary Rookes's boarding school in The Close, while the boy Edmund stayed with Lady Gould in the house she rented in St. Martin's parish, quite near The Close through St. Anne's Gate.[77] But before long their father, as she heard, was talking seriously about removing the children from school and bringing them to town.

For these reasons Lady Gould took action against Edmund in the courts, suing him in Chancery to establish both her own right to custody of the children and the children's right to what was left of the farm at

East Stour. The proceedings set in motion by her complaint, filed on 10 February 1720/1, supply an invaluable, intimate picture of Fielding's troubled circumstances – and his unbecoming behavior – during the period 1718 to 1722, the years in which he entered adolescence.

The complaint[78] opens by rehearsing the facts concerning Judge Gould's acquisition of the East Stour estate: that, though Sarah had married Edmund without her parents' approval, Judge Gould wanted nevertheless to provide for his daughter and her children by purchasing the farm; that through his executors, Davidge Gould and William Day, whom he also appointed trustees of the estate, he had done so in such a way that Edmund could not, legally, "intermeddle" with it; that in the event of Sarah's dying without declaring how the property was to be apportioned, it was to belong to all her children as "Tenants in Common"; and that in signing the deed of conveyance, Edmund had agreed to these terms. Contrary to these stipulations, however, the trustees, ever since Sarah's death, had permitted Edmund "to continue in the possession" of the estate and "to receive the rents and profits thereof"; the children, therefore, were "in great danger of being defeated of the said Trust Estate or to have or receive any profit or advantage thereby and to be deprived of their maintenance and education."

But Lady Gould's case against Edmund as an unfit father does not end with the accusation that he was thus depriving the children of their birthright. Since their mother's death, she continued, he had married again – "one [Anne] Rapha, a widow, an Italian, a person of the Roman Catholic profession who has several children of her own, and one who kept an eating house in London ... and has now two daughters in a monastery beyond sea." To such a woman, Edmund now meant to commit the care and education of Sarah's children; and, Lady Gould feared, their father would himself prove no antidote to the poison: he "doth give out in speeches that he will do with [the children] what he thinks fit and has openly commended the manner of education of young persons in monasterys." Appealing to the Lord Chancellor as "the Supreme Guardian ... of the Infants of Great Britain," she asked that the Court affirm the children's title to the farm and prevent Edmund from removing them from school.

To these charges, which aspersed not merely his competence as a parent but his character as a man – for who but a scoundrel would attempt to defraud his own children of their inheritance and bring them up in the ways of Antichrist – Edmund replied on 23 February no less spitefully. His mother-in-law's true motive in bringing the action against him was her jealousy at his taking a new wife. The old woman, he insisted, deserved no credit, as she had claimed, for moving to Salisbury, because she had done so not out of any wish to be able to look after her grandchildren more easily, but merely "to convenience herself by living in a town." As for his rights to the farm, he pointed out that the money to finance it over and above the £3,000 stipulated in Judge Gould's will had come from his own pocket, and that he spent more each year on the children's maintenance and education than the £150 the farm annually brought in. Since October 1719 he had kept Henry at Eton for "the yearly expence" of "upwards of sixty pounds." He further assured the Court that the children were in no danger of being corrupted by their stepmother, who was neither an Italian nor the keeper of any eating house. (He did not, however, deny the more damaging charge that she was Roman Catholic.) He intended to "breed and educate" his children in his own religion, as good Protestants "of the Communion of the Church of England." Indeed, he reminded the Court, "by reason of his relation to and interest in several noble familys" he was better able to provide for his children than their grandmother was.

By the spring of 1721 this dispute had become more heated still, so that on 30 June, Edmund felt impelled to lodge a complaint of his own against Lady Gould.[79] At the Lent Assizes in Dorset, with the cooperation of the trustees of the estate, she had instituted ejectment proceedings to remove him, once for all, from the farm.[80] In order, furthermore, to keep his children completely in her grasp, she had withdrawn Henry from Eton sometime in early April and had since "suffered him to go about in the way of idleness to the irreparable loss of his time." On 17 May, when his servants had approached both Lady Gould and Mary Rookes in Salisbury, demanding in his name that his children be sent to him in London, they were refused "utterly." To be sure, Edmund's urging the Lord Chancellor to grant him his children's estate because they were proving an expense to educate and he had been out of pocket making repairs to the property must have made a less than edifying spectacle in court. But it is hard not to sympathize with him as he realized that the enmity of Sarah's family – to which his own fecklessness and self-indulgence had made him vulnerable – was depriving him of his sons and daughters.

More to the point, we need to appreciate the effect of these unsettling events and recriminations on Henry Fielding. For this purpose, the testimony of a parade of witnesses on both sides, as the proceedings dragged on for more than a year, is revealing. In evaluating this evidence we must remember that none of it is wholly disinterested, and that much of it, consequently, is contradictory. Thus, testifying on behalf of Lady Gould were Katherine Cottington, her sister; Margaret Sanger, her servant; and Marie Bentham and Anne Delaborde, who had lost their positions as housekeeper and governess, respectively, when Edmund remarried. For Edmund, on the other hand – who also testified in his own behalf – the roll of witnesses included his mother

Dorothy and his sister Bridget Lapenotier; Peter Wiggett, curate of his parish church; Thomas Grafton, his steward at the farm; and several of his servants – Richard Gough, Joseph Burt, Henry Halstead, and, most particularly, the nursery maid Frances Barber.[81] Different as these witnesses are with respect to their station, education, and prejudices, the testimony they gave, under oath, affords a clear picture both of the distressing circumstances at East Stour after the death of Fielding's mother and of the passionate, rebellious way in which he responded to them.

When Sarah fell ill early in 1718, Mrs. Cottington, her aunt and the godmother of two of her daughters, moved to East Stour to supervise the children and the general affairs of the household. With the assistance of Marie Bentham the housekeeper and Anne Delaborde the governess – and of the nursery maid Frances Barber, who joined the family in May – she stayed on in that capacity for more than a year after Sarah's death, while Edmund remained in London courting a new wife. These months after their mother's death would have been, under the best circumstances, a difficult period of adjustment for the children. During that time Henry would be especially susceptible to the influence of Mrs. Cottington, his mother's surrogate; for she saw to it that he was moved to her own apartment in the house, where, indeed, he slept in her own bedchamber – into which, after a little while, she also introduced his youngest sister Beatrice. This being a household inhabited almost entirely by females, his other sisters were lodged separately with the several servants: Catharine with Mrs. Delaborde in an upstairs room next to the nursery, where the infant Edmund lay with Mrs. Barber; Ursula with Mrs. Bentham in a room up one pair of stairs; and Sarah, his favorite, with Mrs. Cottington's maid in the chamber adjoining his own.

On deserting the farm for the pleasures of St. James's, Edmund could have done few things more surely calculated to alienate his children from him than leaving them in Mrs. Cottington's care. For one thing, she appears to have indulged Henry's every whim, and spoiled him badly. For another, she did her best to poison the children's minds against Edmund. When, for instance, news reached the farm that their father was about to marry again, the old woman made no secret of her anger, cursing Edmund openly for his faithlessness: "she wished," Mrs. Barber recalled, "that he might never sleep in his house, and if he had ten thousand devils to haunt him every night, she would not be sorry." As the time drew near when Edmund was to bring his new wife home, she played on the children's anxieties concerning this exotic woman their stepmother (an Italian, they had been told, and a papist – with children of her own whom she must prefer to them). When they wept, Mrs. Cottington advised them, "keep your tears till you have more cause; when your mother-in-law comes you must not dare to speak." They would then learn to trust their old aunt, their only protector; for if their father's new wife should "ever offer to strike" them (as of course she would often wish to do), Mrs. Cottington swore "she would certainly stab her with a knife."

No wonder that in such a pernicious atmosphere the children became "so very much indulged and so unruly" that even Mrs. Delaborde, who had known them for years, complained "she could not govern them." Henry, especially, whom his aunt actually encouraged "to be rude and do mischief" – so it seemed to Mrs. Barber – behaved outrageously. Mrs. Barber saw him "spit in the servants' faces," and she recalled that when Edmund was away in London to marry his new wife, Henry had written a letter to his grandmother, Lady Gould, which he began by referring to his infant brother as a "shitten brat."

····◄ vi ►····

But it is one part in particular of this tragi-comical episode from Fielding's boyhood that could be a clue to the deepest sources of both his personality and his creative imagination. For prominent in Mrs. Barber's garrulous rehearsal of his willful behavior is the accusation, if not perhaps of incest in the strict sense – he was barely twelve at the time and the sister in question only four and a half years old – then of some sort of shocking erotic experimentation with his youngest sister, with whom he shared Mrs. Cottington's bedchamber. At a time when his father was away, completing the rejection of his mother by marrying again, Henry, Mrs. Barber deposed to the Court, "was guilty of committing some indecent actions with his sister Beatrice." Even so, instead of correcting the boy, Mrs. Cottington – whose indulgence of her nephew appears to have been limitless – "rather seemed to encourage" him in such behavior. Mrs. Barber, in short, found him "very much subject to passion," and she feared – in words reminiscent of the prediction that Tom Jones "was born to be hanged" – that if "the said Henry Fielding had continued much longer ... under the care and management" of his aunt, "he would ... come to some ill or unfortunate end."

Happily, these dire predictions came true no more for Fielding than for Tom Jones. But the hint of incest that colors Fielding's relationship with his sisters – the plural is necessary, for Sarah is also involved – is plain enough, and, potentially at least, too important to an understanding of his life and works to be ignored. Before continuing the story of these tempestuous early years, we must pause to explore this possibility.[82]

From what we have already seen of his childhood, it is clear that, as he approached adolescence, Fielding was subject to influences which would have deepened his emotional attachment to his sisters. That this attachment, which is normally not simply emotional but specifically sexual in nature, might express itself in overt erotic experimentation or incestuous fantasies will surprise no one acquainted with the findings of modern psychoanalysis. That Fielding, a boy of independent spirit and violent passions, should indulge these feelings, having been deprived of his mother and left by his father to the care of a doting and permissive aunt, might seem inevitable. In weighing such possibilities, moreover, we should keep in mind not only the psychological realities of the situation in which Fielding found himself, but also the distinctive mores and attitudes of the time. The situation in the Fielding household at East Stour closely resembles what Lawrence Stone represents as characteristic of many country households in the seventeenth and early eighteenth centuries, when childhood sexuality was generally free and precocious (even, in some families, a source of amusement to adults), and when relationships between brothers and sisters were "particularly intimate." Stone surmises that owing to overcrowding and the need to share rooms, "incest . . . must have been common."[83] When we consider, furthermore, that Fielding's aunt, the figure of authority in the house and his dead mother's representative, appears to have smiled complacently on his fondling of Beatrice, it seems likely that at an age when his own moral sense could not have been very highly developed, Fielding's fraternal affections were associated for him with erotic pleasures.

Such an hypothesis helps to account for Fielding's later fascination with the theme of incest in his plays and novels – a fascination unusual in the literature of the period 1700 to 1765 and curious in the author of comedies. Critics have puzzled over the occurrence of this theme in *Joseph Andrews* (1742) and *Tom Jones* (1749), those two brilliant works which together established the genre of the English comic novel. On the eve of their marriage, the peddler discloses (so it appears) that Joseph and Fanny are brother and sister – a revelation no less frustrating to these lovers than disconcerting to the reader, and which causes Parson Adams to fall to his knees in an ecstasy of gratitude "that this Discovery had been made before the dreadful Sin of Incest was committed" (IV.xii). Why is it, we may wonder as we await with Joseph and Fanny confirmation of the peddler's story, that Fielding chose to inject, however mockingly, an element of Sophoclean fear into this light-hearted tale? "They felt perhaps little less Anxiety in this Interval than *Œdipus* himself whilst his Fate was revealing" (IV.xv). In *Tom Jones* (XVIII.ii) this same discordant element irrupts more violently still into the narrative, and Fielding, by temporarily subduing that reassuring irony of his and allowing the scene to unfold dramatically, forces us to face the awful probability that his hero has indeed suffered the "Fate" of Oedipus: "O good Heavens!" cries Jones, horrified at what has been revealed, "Incest – with a Mother! To what am I reserved?"

The narrow – or, as Parson Adams would have it, "miraculous" – escapes of Fielding's fictional characters from falling inadvertently into incestuous relationships are well known. But even before he turned novelist, this titillating device for complicating a plot was a feature of his comedies; it first appears in two of his earliest plays. In *The Wedding-Day*, written as early as 1730 but not produced until 1743, old Stedfast discovers before his marriage to Clarinda is consummated that his bride is in fact his daughter – a timely discovery indeed, preventing his "Fall, even at the Brink of Ruin" (V.xii). And as *The Coffee-House Politician* (1730) winds to a close, we may think it an awkward economy of the plot that Hilaret, whom the amiable rake Ramble had earlier mistaken for a streetwalker and nearly ravished, proves to be his sister. Or consider, in Fielding's early burlesque of Juvenal's *Sixth Satire*, the frivolous allusion to Berenice, daughter of the king of Judah, who lived with her brother Agrippa – a sin, Fielding flippantly remarks in a parenthesis, about as serious as a Jew's eating pork:

> However liberal your Grants,
> Still what her Neighbour hath she wants! . . .
> Or what Agrippa gave his Sister,
> Incestuous Bribe! for which he kiss'd her.
> (Sure with less Sin a Jew might dine,
> If hungry, on a Herd of Swine.)

When Fielding introduces this potentially disturbing theme into his works, he usually does so in this mocking way – as if by flaunting the comic artist's mastery even of life's tragic possibilities he could exorcize whatever personal demons the idea of incest may have had for him. Once, however, in *Amelia* (1751), his final novel, he resumed this theme obliquely – even perhaps unconsciously – and in a wholly serious manner. Here, especially, in the strange narrative of the death of Booth's sister (II.iv–v), the psychoanalytic implications for Fielding's own experience seem unmistakable – particularly as the character of Booth is in so many other ways a projection of Fielding himself. The episode, one of the most curious in his fiction, is brief. While relating the story of his courtship of Amelia, Booth breaks the thread of his narrative to tell of a melancholy event which almost caused him to lose her. On the eve of their marriage he receives an urgent message informing him that his favorite sister Nancy lies seriously ill at the house of a friend some distance away. Leaving Amelia in the middle of the night,

Booth rushes to his sister's side, who, however, though she has been calling for him piteously, fails to recognize him – in her delirium mistaking him for "a Highwayman who had a little before robbed her." She knows him at the last, however, and dies in convulsions in his arms. This instance of Booth's devotion to his sister almost costs him Amelia, whose mother has taken advantage of his absence to arrange a more lucrative match for her daughter. To prevent this, Booth hastens back to Amelia, leaving others to bury Nancy's corpse.

What is this episode, introduced quite unexpectedly into the narrative on the eve of Booth's marriage, doing in the novel? It obviously accomplishes two things: first, it reveals in Booth an unusual, and previously unsuspected, emotional conflict, the claim of his "Passion" for his sister being set in opposition to his "Love" for Amelia; second, his sister's claim on his affections being temporarily stronger and more urgent – indeed, drawing him precipitately away from his intended bride in the middle of the night and literally separating him from her by fifty miles – it complicates the plot by putting the marriage in jeopardy. But, surely, this element of suspense in the plot could have been achieved more plausibly in some other way. Except for this sudden appearance of his "beloved *Nancy*" – the reader has not heard of her before and will not hear of her again – Booth's family plays no part in the novel. It is the more extraordinary, then, that Fielding should arrange matters so that Nancy must die and her "dear lifeless Corpse" be buried – so that, indeed, her very "Idea" is expunged from Booth's mind – before he may enjoy in earnest "the tumultuous Delight" of "possessing" Amelia.

Seen in this way the episode seems a remarkable symbolic anticipation of a phenomenon well known to psychologists, who define the individual's attainment of sexual maturity by reference to the process by which he transcends the familiar pathology of the Œdipus complex – the process of displacing sexual desire from mother, to sister, to a "proper" object outside the family. In this sense the object of incestuous feelings in all men must be "buried" before a healthier relationship may occur. The strange way in which Fielding manages the scene of Nancy's dying, moreover, encourages such an interpretation, as it vividly points up the ambivalence of her feelings toward her brother. Booth relates that, though the fever has "ravish'd away" Nancy's "Reason," it "left my Image on her Fancy." In fact, however, he appears to his sister not in one image, but in two. In her thoughts he is her "dear *Billy*," the beloved protector who would prevent her suffering; but what her eyes actually *see* as she looks at him is the terrifying and guilty figure of "a Highwayman who had a little before robbed her." The occurrence of so incongruous an image in this context seems inexplicable otherwise than as an oblique (and unconscious) projection of sexual anxiety and guilt. At the time Fielding composed this passage the idea of highwaymen personifying guilt would have been quite natural to him, who as a magistrate passed judgment on them almost daily; and references to the robbery of a woman as a metaphor for sexual violation recur in his works.[84] Yet here, oddly, these associations attach to Booth, the hero of the novel — and his author's surrogate — whose sight inspires in his sister "the greatest Horrors." Indeed, Nancy's hallucination corresponds precisely to one of the commonest erotic fantasies identified by modern psychologists.[85] And, finally, the last image in this disturbing phantasmagory, as Nancy recognizes Booth at the moment of death, reinforces the episode's sexual suggestiveness, rendering the act of dying as a kind of orgasm: "At last she seemed for a Moment to know me, and cry'd, 'O Heavens! my dearest Brother!' upon which she fell into immediate Convulsions, and died away in my Arms."

The intensity of Fielding's fascination with the idea of incest — particularly with incest between brother and sister, or, as in the passage above, the incestuous longings between brother and sister — is matched in only one other author of the period. That author, interestingly enough, is his sister Sarah. In two of Sarah's works the theme takes the specific form of the destruction (actual in the first instance and only narrowly averted in the second) of a sister and her brother who have been falsely accused of an incestuous relationship. As is generally assumed (no doubt correctly), Sarah is the author of the final section of Fielding's *Journey from This World to the Next* (1743) — a chapter which, lacking all connection with what has gone before, purports to be the history of Anna Boleyn narrated posthumously by herself. At the conclusion of her story Anna reveals that her public humiliation and beheading were the consequence of the vilest slander: "I was brought to my trial, and to blacken me the more, accused of conversing criminally with my own Brother, whom indeed I loved extremely well, but never looked on him in any other Light than as my Friend."

The second instance of this theme in Sarah's works is far more striking. In the midst of her first novel, *The Adventures of David Simple* (1744), which otherwise reads like the sort of edifying, wholesome tale one might expect of a talented bluestocking, Sarah introduces the story of Camilla and her brother Valentine, and soon plunges the unsuspecting reader into a grotesque, nightmare world of psychological persecution, of humiliation and disfigurement. In Aurélien Digeon's phrase, who at this point abruptly broke off his interesting biographical analysis comparing Camilla and Valentine to their author and her own brother, the narrative here "sombre vite dans le plus affreux romanesque."[86] What has occurred, we may ask, in Camilla's story of her life with

Valentine to cause M. Digeon to drop the curtain and cease his commentary in horrified dismay?

A summary of this lengthy episode must suffice. Having employed all her wiles to alienate Camilla and Valentine from their father's affections, their stepmother — a lovely looking woman but odious as any harpy in old fable — makes life so intolerable for them they flee their home and take refuge with their aunt. When that good woman visits their father's house to try to effect a reconciliation, the stepmother completes their ruin by falsely accusing them of having run away in order to indulge without restraint the "criminal Conversation" in which she says she discovered them.[87] Appalled, the aunt returns to denounce the innocent pair and to turn them friendless into the world — asking them:

> "What it was we meant, by ... endeavouring to impose on her, and make her accessary to our wicked Conversation with each other: Brother and Sister! — it was unnatural, she did not think the World had been arrived at such a pitch of Wickedness." ...
> Then she launch'd out into a long Harangue on the crying and abominable Sin of Incest, wrung her Hands, and seemed in the greatest Affliction, that ever she should live to hear a Nephew and Niece of hers could be such odious Creatures.
>
> (pp. 160–1)

The consequences of their stepmother's slander are as terrible as she could wish. Penniless and shunned by their acquaintance, they drift to London, to a filthy garret room where Valentine lies seriously ill of fever. To make herself more pitiable in appearance in order to beg money for her brother in the streets, Camilla completes her degradation by disfiguring herself: "I made myself a Hump-back, dyed my Skin in several places with great Spots of Yellow; so that, when I look'd in the Glass, I was almost frighten'd at my own Figure" (p. 166).

Drawn out at length and in the darkest colors, the episode is quite extraordinary, impressing the reader with its almost pathological intensity. While it lasts the author seems to have lost control of the narrative. In this instance, surely, Sarah Fielding's disturbing representation of the powerful and destructive passions which the idea of incest arouses demonstrates that peculiar "Merit" for which her brother praised her in the Preface he contributed to the second edition: "a vast Penetration into human Nature, a deep and profound Discernment of all the Mazes, Windings and Labyrinths, which perplex the Heart of Man to such a degree, that he is himself often incapable of seeing through them."

What, then, does this mutual — and in the literature of the period highly unusual — fascination with the idea of incest between brother and sister imply about Fielding's relationship with Sarah? Did the sexual play he indulged in as a boy with Beatrice extend, perhaps more seriously, to Sarah as well, who bore his dead mother's name and who, for a year or more after her death, lodged in the chamber adjoining Henry's? Under the circumstances an intimacy between them even this absolute would not be improbable. There can be no doubt, of course, that their affection for each other was close and abiding – amply attested in later years both by their frequent literary collaborations, what Digeon called "cette amitié fraternelle,"[88] and more expressly in certain passages in their works. In the Preface to *David Simple*, for instance, Fielding refers to Sarah as "one so nearly and dearly allied to me, in the highest Friendship as well as Relation," and praises her for, among other amiable qualities, the goodness of her heart – as does Sophia in *Tom Jones* (VI.v). Sarah returned the compliment in the headnote to Letters XL–XLIV of her *Familiar Letters*; and the modern editor of Sarah's *The Governess* (1749) is surely right in supposing that Jenny Peace's fondness for her older brother "Harry" reflects Sarah's own sentiments.[89] The strength of the bond between them is perhaps also suggested by the fact that Sarah never married. Though this is true as well of Fielding's other sisters, Catharine, Ursula, and Beatrice seem to have been content in each other's companionship, living out their lives together in the same house. It was Sarah alone who, when Fielding's beloved first wife died in November 1744, moved into his house at Boswell Court to console her brother, remaining with him there until he married again three years later. And it is Sarah, very likely, to whom Fielding refers in a letter written from there to his friend James Harris on 11 January 1745/6 when he finds he must close abruptly: "Farewell, I am prevented from saying more by the Company of the Woman in the world whom I like best."[90]

All one can say with any certainty, however, is that the distinctive form which the incest motif takes in Sarah's works suggests her horrified awareness of how easily, and with what destructive consequences, an innocent friendship between sister and brother may be construed as a "criminal" relationship. It is worth noting, moreover, that the elaborate development of this fantasy in *David Simple* corresponds in certain respects to what we know of the critical juncture in Fielding's and his sisters' childhood. As Digeon observed before decorously discontinuing his analysis at the point in the novel where the incest motif begins, the relationship and family history of Camilla and her brother Valentine invite a biographical interpretation. To pursue Digeon's line of speculation a little further, we may observe that the cause of all that Camilla and her brother suffer is their stepmother, who alienates them from their father and slanders their pure affection for each other, accusing them of "the crying and abominable Sin of Incest." Could Sarah have been recalling a similar embarrassment her brother suffered as a

consequence of the public proceedings in Chancery precipitated by her
father's second marriage?

•••••➤ **vii** ➤•••••

The year 1719 was in any case a critical time in the childhood of
Fielding and his sisters. In May, having sent word of his marriage to
Mrs. Cottington and the children at East Stour – with what effect on
the behavior of his eldest son we have already seen – Edmund prepared
to bring his new wife home. As herald and pledge of the new regime,
he sent on ahead his wife's maid, a widow woman named Mary Howard,
with his authority to take over the government of the household. For
ten days, however, until Edmund arrived to insult her thus in person,
Mrs. Cottington refused to give up the keys. Suspecting, furthermore,
that Mary Howard was not a Presbyterian, as she claimed, but a papist
like her mistress, Mrs. Cottington also refused her the horse she required
to ride to mass in a neighboring parish, no doubt at Marnhull, a well-
known center of recusancy two miles away. Mrs. Cottington's violent
prejudice against Roman Catholicism probably owed much to her own
early marriage into a powerful Wiltshire family of that faith, her
husband indeed having been convicted in 1696 of harboring a priest
against the laws of recusancy;[91] she was certain now that the new Mrs.
Fielding and her instrument, Mrs. Howard, meant to "pervert" the
children to Antichrist. She watched carefully for them to reveal themselves, and, when she detected Mrs. Howard with a rosary, forced her
to admit she was a papist – after which the woman defied her by riding
to mass openly.

The children's stepmother made no secret of her faith, provoking
Mrs. Cottington on one occasion to stop Edmund as he was about to
reserve additional seats in the family pew: "he had no occasion" for
any, she told him, for "though his family was increased at home yet
they did not go to church, for this person" (pointing contemptuously
at his new wife) "is a member of the Church of Rome." What was
worse, Mrs. Cottington swore that their stepmother had already begun
her crafty work of seducing the children away from the Anglican faith.
She forbade the children to go to their aunt to be instructed in their
catechism, and she locked away from them the King James's Bible and
commentaries. Instead, Mrs. Fielding left "her own Romish prayer-
book, etc.," in the windows of the rooms that the children frequented.

It is uncertain how much of this testimony should be discredited as
owing to the malice Mrs. Cottington obviously bore Edmund. Mrs.
Bentham supported her in this evidence; but Mrs. Barber, Edmund's

witness, claimed to have seen no signs at all of any such insidious intent to convert the children to Rome. On the contrary, she had "often heard" Edmund declare that "he would as soon suffer his children's legs and arms to be cut off as he would suffer them, or any of them, to be brought up in the popish religion." Certainly, Edmund's numerous offspring by his second wife were baptized in the Church of England, as Peter Wiggett, curate of St. James's, Piccadilly, testified and as the register of the church confirms. What is no less plain, however, is that an element of religious bigotry was part of the poisonous atmosphere of hatred and jealousy and fear that infected the household in which Fielding was growing up.

Lady Gould's witnesses all insisted that the second Mrs. Fielding and her housekeeper abused the children physically as well. On this point their governess, Mrs. Delaborde, was outspoken. In league with Mary Howard, the new mistress of the farm had "insulted the whole family, but more especially the children," whom "they used after a most barbarous, cruel and inhumane manner," denying them even necessities. Not long after they established their new regime, they tried to force the children to eat unpalatable food, while making a point of eating well themselves. The bread, Mrs. Delaborde recalled, was inedible, and with it the children were given "stinking whey butter"; for drink they were offered small beer "so intolerably bad" that no one could swallow it, and consequently "for several days together" were reduced to what she considered the miserable alternative of drinking plain water. Mrs. Delaborde was convinced that Edmund's "papist" wife and housekeeper inflicted this diet on the children not merely because they enjoyed the cruelty of it, but because they wished to widen the rift between the children and their father: the two women, she declared, "caused [the children's] father to beat and abuse them for not eating."

As with most other charges brought against Edmund during this acrimonious litigation, his servants entirely denied these. They assured the Court that there was never any distinction made between the victuals offered the children and those served to Edmund and his wife. They maintained that for dinner the children had not only plenty of wholesome food and drink at every meal, but a delicious variety of it as well: beef, mutton, pork, veal, fowl, rabbits, pigeons, fish, larks; good bread, of course, and good things to drink, such as small and strong beer, ale, and sometimes wine – or at breakfast, chocolate or tea or boiled milk. In direct contradiction to Lady Gould's witnesses, Mrs. Barber, in short, testified that far from the children's having been "ill treated, beaten, or insulted," she had never seen Edmund or his new wife, or any member of the household, behave toward them in any but "a very kind and respectful manner."

With differences as wide as this in the sworn testimony of eye-

witnesses of the new regime at East Stour, we will never know the truth
of the situation. The new Mrs. Fielding may well have been "a very
good woman" who behaved kindly toward the children, as Edmund's
mother and sister said they had been assured formerly by Mrs. Delaborde herself. It seems likely from other sources, however, that what are
the normal feelings of suspicion and resentment harbored by children
against stepmothers were in this instance deepened into permanent
hostility − owing, in some considerable part, to what appears to have
been the vocal, unremitting campaign of character assassination
directed by Lady Gould and Mrs. Cottington against Edmund and his
wife. Thus even at the end of his life, in *Amelia* (VII.ii–iii), Fielding's
attitude toward his own stepmother is perhaps expressed by Mrs.
Bennet, who relates the "artful" way in which her father's new wife
contrived to turn him against his daughter:

> I will not entertain you, Madam [she tells Amelia], with any Thing
> so common as the cruel Usage of a Step-mother; nor of what affected
> me much worse, the unkind Behaviour of a Father under such an
> Influence.... he no longer acted from his own excellent Disposition;
> but was in every thing governed and directed by my Mother-in-
> Law.[92]

This same pattern of relationships − a kindly but weak father deliberately alienated from his children by the new wife on whom he dotes −
also appears in Sarah Fielding's macabre tale of Camilla and her brother
Valentine. Here, surely, Sarah's own sense of grievance may be heard
in the confession of Camilla's father, who fears his passion "will be to
your disadvantage; for altho' with Œconomy I am able to support you
and your Brother in a tolerable manner, yet my Fortune is not large;
and if I should marry, and have an Increase of Family, it might injure
you" (p. 139). From bitter experience Camilla comes to wonder "how
many *Mothers-in-Law* [there are], working underhand with their Husbands, to make them *turn their Children out of Doors* to *Beggary* and
Misery" (p. 190). Indeed, she comes to generalize her case to the point
where it seems the very pattern of all daughterly misery: she thus
inquires about the melancholy Isabella, "if this *young Lady had not a
Father alive*, and *whether it was not probable his marrying a second Wife
might be the cause of her Misfortunes*" (p. 194). In a country where the
laws of primogeniture obtained, Fielding, as Edmund's eldest son and
heir, had even more reason to resent his father's second marriage and
the woman who, whether innocently or not, caused him to forget his
duty to his children. But again, as with their mutual fascination with
the idea of incest, it is Sarah whose jealousy and sense of injury are
most vividly revealed in Camilla's description of her stepmother − a
fantastic image of evil incarnate:

I often thought, could she have beheld herself in the Goddess of Justice's Mirror of Truth, as it is described in that beautiful Vision in the *Tatler*, she would have loathed and detested, as much as now she admired herself. Her fine Chestnut-brown Hair, which flowed in natural Ringlets round her Neck, was it to have represented the Strings that held her Heart, must have become as harsh and unpliable as the stiffest Cord: Her large blue Eyes, which now seemed to speak the Softness of a Soul replete with Goodness, had they on a sudden, by the irresistible Power of a Goddess's Command, been forced to confess the Truth, would have lost all their Amiableness, and have looked askew an hundred ways at once, to denote the many little Plots she was forming to do mischief: Her Skin would have become black and hard, as an Emblem of her Mind; her Limbs distorted, and her Nails would have been changed into crooked Talons, which, however, should have had power to shrink in such a manner, as that the Unwary might come near enough (without Suspicion) to be got into her Clutches. Not a Metamorphosis in all *Ovid* could be more surprizing than her's would have been, was this Mirror of Truth to have been held to her. I have really shuddered with Horror at the Image my own Fancy has presented me; and notwithstanding all her Cruelty to me, nay, what is much more, to my dear *Valentine*, my Indignation never could rise so high, as to wish her the Punishment to see herself in this Glass, unless it could have been a Means of her Amendment.

(pp. 143–4)

Troubled thus by a variety of powerful, conflicting emotions – the sadness and sense of loss at their mother's death; the hurt felt at their father's evident faithlessness; the jealousy, resentment, and fear their stepmother inspired – Fielding and his sisters grew closer to each other and hostile to everyone else in the household. Edmund saw that while under the influence of their grandmother and aunt at East Stour they had grown "very headstrong and undutiful." These old women – "out of pure malice" he was sure – had imposed upon the children "evil impressions of disregard and undutifulness" toward himself and his wife. Mrs. Barber, too, had observed Lady Gould and Mrs. Cottington "alienating" the children's affections in this way; and as a consequence Henry, especially, whose behavior was bad enough before Edmund brought his stepmother home, now became insolent "towards the whole family in general." He was given to fits of passion, and seemed to revel, like some petulant Lord of Misrule, in creating disorder in the family. Often, Mrs. Barber declared, he deliberately "hindered his father's servants from doing their duties, and upon his being opposed by any of them, did all the mischief that lay in his power to do." Not even his

adoring and indulgent aunt was spared. At such times, Mrs. Barber
had no doubt, he well deserved the disciplinary measures his patient
father was driven to: she reported that when Edmund overheard his
son "give aloud some reproachful words" against Mrs. Cottington, he
reproved him for "abusing" the old woman and gave him "one stroke
or two with a whip."

···◆ viii ◆···

As this unhappy summer drew to a close, Edmund, after consulting
with Lady Gould, took steps to bring his children under control and to
begin their formal education. In August the household at East Stour
dispersed. Mrs. Cottington, together with the four girls and the infant
Edmund, moved to Salisbury. She and the boy moved in with Lady
Gould, in the house she had taken in St. Martin's Church Street. The
girls, too, were placed where they would remain under their grandmother's influence – in Mary Rookes's boarding school in The Close.
There, besides learning to read and write, they were taught to do
needlework and to dance and to speak French – and so, as Mrs. Barber
put it, be "brought up as gentlewomen." Edmund later protested that
he consented to these arrangements – which proved so damaging to his
relations with the children – only "out of regard" to their grandmother;
but the arrangements could not have been displeasing to his new
wife, then seven months pregnant with her own child by him. Henry,
however, accompanied his father and stepmother to London, to the
house in Blenheim Street, where, Mrs. Barber recalled with evident
satisfaction, he was given a room to himself. In October, the month in
which his stepmother gave birth to the first of the six sons she bore his
father, he was sent off to Eton, "to be educated amongst gentlemen's
sons and brought up as a gentleman."
    This was perhaps the last time, during his boyhood, that Fielding
saw his father – though we cannot be certain where he spent his school
vacations for another year or so,[93] whether in town with Edmund and
his stepmother or with his grandmother in Salisbury, as he seems to
have preferred. Considering the fine writer and classical scholar he
became, we can say that his years at Eton were well spent intellectually;
and considering his wild temper as a boy, we may think he needed the
disciplining he suffered there – however vividly he would recall
in later years Learning's "birchen Altar," at which, "with true
Spartan Devotion, I have sacrificed my Blood" (Tom Jones, XIII.i).
We will return to the subject of Fielding's experience at Eton. But

there is more to be said about the tragi-comical drama of Fielding's childhood and his relations with his family, most particularly with his father.

In this respect one of the most revealing episodes occurred in April 1721, shortly after Lady Gould had taken her grievances against Edmund to Chancery, and together with the trustees of the East Stour estate had moved to eject him from the farm before he could appropriate more of the rents or attempt to sell off more of the property. On 7 April, in the midst of his second year at school and a fortnight before his fourteenth birthday, Henry ran away from Eton and its birchen altars to seek comfort from his grandmother and Mrs. Cottington at Salisbury. As if to ensure that they would never again allow him to come under his stepmother's roof, he began at once mischievously to bait the old women on the one subject he knew would infuriate them. To her "great surprize," as Mrs. Cottington informed the Court, Henry had "entered into argument" with her "in defence of the Church of Rome, alleging it was the ancient church and that the Church of England was only since the Reformation." These "principles," she believed, had been "instilled" in the boy by his stepmother and her "emissaries in order to pervert him."

Soon after word of his son's elopement reached Edmund, who no longer doubted that Lady Gould meant him to have nothing more to do with her daughter's children, he responded by dispatching to Salisbury two of his most trusted servants, Frances Barber and Henry Halstead. Their mission was to deliver to his son, Lady Gould, and Mary Rookes letters demanding (but, he assured the Court, "in a very obliging manner") that Henry, together with his sisters and infant brother, all be brought to him in London. The children must be rescued from the malignant influence of his first wife's relations. He meant to see to it that his son returned to Eton (or perhaps enrolled in Westminster School, closer to home), and that his daughters were introduced "to the acquaintance of some noble family, as might be much to their advantage."

So he meant to do, but as usual he underestimated his formidable adversary. When his servants reached Salisbury on 18 May, they found Mrs. Rookes adamant in refusing to give up the four girls. And when his man Halstead approached Lady Gould at 9 o'clock in the evening, he had to hand his letters in at the window, for the door was shut fast against him. We are obliged to Lady Gould's servant, Margaret Sanger, for the last glimpse we have of Fielding as a boy: it is of Henry and the affectionate dragon his grandmother shut up together in her house, besieged at night by his father's servants, who threaten to fetch him forcibly to town. Barred from the house, Edmund's agent raged outside in the darkened street, shouting curses in at the windows: "Damn the

old bitch," he cried. "I hope to see her gray hairs brought with sorrow
to the grave. – Damn the old bitch, body and soul!"

Like some episode in romance, this scene serves as emblem of an
inner conflict, dramatizing as it does the affection and emotional refuge
Fielding found in Lady Gould, his mother's representative ("most"
daughters, Dr. Harrison assures Booth, "take after" their mothers),[94]
who stood firm and indignant between him and his father – that distant,
all too charming man, who had rejected his mother and was now his
rival for his mother's estate; who sought to subjugate him, either with
a whip or with other rude instruments: the stern and alien housekeeper
at East Stour, the birch-wielding pedagogues at Eton, the officers of
the Court of Chancery. However one may wish to account for it, whether
by the sinister influence of a possessive grandmother and great-aunt,
or by the familiar pathology of the Oedipus complex, this division in
Fielding's emotional life was not soon healed. It is reflected in his
continuing devotion to Lady Gould, whose body, when she died in
1733, he arranged to have carried thirty miles from Salisbury to be
buried beside his mother in the churchyard at East Stour. And it is
reflected in what appears to have been his deepening bitterness toward
his father.

This family antagonism seems to have prompted Fielding's first trials
as an author – and typically as a comic author; for he early recognized
that he could best master his enemies or exorcize his private demons
by mocking them. The period of his elopement from Eton may thus
have been the occasion for the following anecdote recounted by Horace
Walpole in the margins of his copy of Colley Cibber's *Apology*:

> Fielding had not only natural humour and a vein of satire, but gave
> very early indications of them. Dr. Bland, Master of Eton School,
> and afterwards Provost there and Dean of Durham, told his Friend
> and Patron Sir R[obert] Walpole, that when Fielding was Scholar,
> returning from some holydays, he had not learnt a word of his task.
> The Dr. on examining how he had passed his time, found he did not
> care to own. This raising the Dr.'s curiosity, he promised to remit
> the punishment, if Fielding would confess how he had employed his
> time. Fielding owned that he had been writing a Comedy, in which
> he had drawn the characters of his Father and Family – and on
> producing it, Dr. Bland said that even that juvenile Essay discovered
> many symptoms of Genius and Wit.[95]

What one would give to find that lost play! What form, one wonders,
did Edmund assume in his son's satiric imagination in early adolescence? Perhaps there are hints in Fielding's later works. Though not
of course an unfamiliar topic in literature, the rivalry between fathers
and sons, for instance, is a central, recurrent theme in Fielding's plays –

as in *The Miser* (1733), where Lovegold lusts after the woman his son Frederick loves and keeps him penniless: "Well may we wish [our fathers] dead," Frederick exclaims, "when their death is the only introduction to our living" (II.i). In *The Intriguing Chambermaid* (1734) the situation is reversed, as Valentine, who is in many ways an ironic self-portrait of Fielding, squanders his father's estate while the latter is away. The old man, Goodall by name, threatens to disinherit his son, but "paternal tenderness" prevails, and Valentine is forgiven. More interesting still is the similar situation, bordering on a wish-fulfillment fantasy, in *The Fathers*, one of Fielding's early works though not performed until long after his death. Here we find contrasted two sorts of fathers, Boncour and Old Valence: the former is a "good-natured," indulgent parent whose generosity seems to have spoiled his son George – again like Fielding himself a poet and a "profligate rascal" who keeps a mistress; the latter, in contrast, treats his offspring with "severity" and gloats that by threatening to disinherit them, he has kept them dutiful. Boncour, clearly, is the very antithesis of Edmund Fielding: "whoever denies his son a reasonable allowance," he admonishes his brother, "is answerable for all the ill methods he is forced into to get money" (I.i). A sentiment, we may be sure, Fielding much regretted never having heard from his own father's lips, as well as Boncour's later assurance to George: "no, my son, though perhaps I may not much increase, I shall be at least a faithful steward of my wife's fortune to her children" (V.i). As we will see, it was precisely Edmund's faithlessness in this respect that eventually caused Fielding to denounce his father bitterly, in the shabby forum of a sixpenny pamphlet which only penury could have impelled him to write.

But to conclude the sorry story of the Chancery litigation, the spite of Edmund's adversaries must have been well satisfied by his public denunciation on a far grander scale. For on 28 May 1722 the Lord Chancellor gave his judgment against Edmund on all counts:[96] he lost all rights to the East Stour estate, which he was required to relinquish by September of that year; he was ordered to give an accounting of the rents and profits he had received from the farm since Sarah's death; his children were to continue at their present schools, Henry at Eton and the girls at Mrs. Rookes's; and, that they might not again be exposed to the influence of their papist stepmother, they were to spend their school recesses with their grandmother in Salisbury. What is more, the Lord Chancellor further ordered that a debt of £700 which Edmund owed Mrs. Cottington be applied at once, as she requested, to the purchase of lands for the children's benefit. Edmund, in short, had been thoroughly defeated by Lady Gould; his humiliation was complete.

···➡ **ix** ➡···

Let us return now to October 1719, when Henry Fielding, having grown in Edmund's opinion "headstrong and undutiful," was sent off to Eton College to learn better manners – and to begin in earnest that intimate acquaintance with the classics which was a formative influence on his mature thought and prose style. For Eton at this time, besides being well known for the severity of its discipline, deserved its reputation as, in Defoe's words, "the finest school for what we call grammar learning, for it extends only to the humanity class, that is in Britain, or, perhaps, in Europe."[97]

And it could hardly be equalled as a setting for an English boy's schooling. Founded by a king (Henry VI) almost three centuries before Fielding arrived, its ancient buildings nestling near the magnificent Chapel, the College lies amidst green fields across the Thames from the looming, romantic pile of Windsor Castle. It was a scene then worthy of some of Thomas Gray's sweetest verses:

> Ye distant spires, ye antique towers,
> That crown the watry glade,
> Where grateful Science still adores
> Her Henry's holy Shade;
> And ye, that from the stately brow
> Of Windsor's heights th'expanse below
> Of grove, of lawn, of mead survey,
> Whose turf, whose shade, whose flowers among
> Wanders the hoary Thames along
> His silver-winding way.[98]

Regrettably, we know very little about Fielding's personal experience of Eton, though, unlike the poet's, it did not leave him "A stranger yet to pain!" We cannot even be certain how long he remained there, since the School Lists are missing for the period 1719–24.[99] From the records of Chancery we know only that he began at Eton in October 1719, that he ran away early in April 1721 but had returned by autumn, and that by decree of the Lord Chancellor in May 1722 he was to continue at school "till further orders" and to spend his vacations with Lady Gould. Presumably, he remained at Eton at least until the end of the school year at "Electiontide" in August 1723; and quite possibly, as he was only sixteen years old at the time, he returned in the autumn of 1723 to pursue his studies for another year.

As an "Oppidan" – that is, a boy who paid his way and not one of the seventy "Collegers" on the Foundation – Fielding would have lodged in the town, at one of the authorized boarding-houses kept by

"Dames" (or "Dominies" if, as was sometimes the case, the keeper of the house was a man).[100] So it is less easy to imagine the particular circumstances of his stay there, the "Collegers" being involved in the daily life of the school in somewhat more predictable ways: they all wore the same long gowns, they ate together in Hall, and, to the number of fifty or more, they slept together in one miserable, unheated room called Long Chamber. The "Oppidans" were rather more comfortable, though no boy's lot at Eton was easy: they wore their own clothes, they ate better, and, though they generally shared rooms and even beds (there were more than 300 of them and only thirteen boarding-houses), they were spared the wretchedness of the College dormitory.

To judge from Edmund's various statements that the yearly cost of keeping Henry at Eton was "upwards of sixty pounds" or "about seventy pounds," the boy was living better than most of his fellow "Oppidans." In 1719, for example, even William Pitt, the future Earl of Chatham, did not manage to spend quite £60, though at £25 annually his board was dearer by four pounds than what most boys spent; indeed, in 1726 £45 was sufficient to cover the expenses of one Walter Gough.[101] Money would always find a way of slipping through Fielding's fingers, but one wonders how he could spend so much of it as a lad just entering his teens in the regulated society of an English public school, when the "Dames" locked their houses at 6.00 p.m. and the lessons to be learned were long and heavy. No doubt, as he was always a voracious and eclectic reader, he spent more on books than the £3 or so Pitt spent in a year; and in Pitt's bill nothing is put down to the account of either the French tutor or the local dancing master – two skills which boys could elect to acquire after school hours and in which, in later years, Fielding was proficient. But however well spent the money may have been, Fielding's spendthrift ways probably further strained his relations with his father. Such, at least, is the inference to be drawn from a passage in *David Simple* in which Sarah Fielding, very likely recalling the circumstances of her own childhood, sends Valentine off to a public school, thus leaving his sister Camilla "inconsolable" and his father with too many bills to pay: Valentine, Camilla remembers, "would sometimes send for Money a little faster than my Father thought convenient; upon which he would say to me, 'This Brother of yours is so extravagant, I don't know how I shall do to support him' " (pp. 137–8).

Fielding's experience of Eton, then, could not have been the worse for want of money. And he began his studies there at a propitious time in the school's history. By the early part of the century Eton, together with Westminster, had become the most fashionable school in England. It had benefitted in recent years from a number of capital improvements sponsored by Henry Godolphin, Provost since 1695 and brother to the

Whig minister: the Chapel had been restored in 1699 and the School
Yard drained and paved in 1706–7; in Fielding's first year the Hall was
repaired and faced with brick, and, to add an appropriate touch of
elegance and dignity, Francis Bird's copper statue of the Founder was
erected at the center of the School Yard, where it still handsomely
stands.

At just this time, moreover, Eton experienced a radical and – from
Fielding's point of view, considering his later political and religious
sympathies – a congenial change in leadership. Since 1711 the Head
Master had been Andrew Snape, a celebrated preacher who had been
chaplain to Queen Anne. But Snape was a Tory and High Churchman
who refused to temper his views to the political climate that prevailed
after the accession of George I. In the Bangorian controversy of 1717
he was an outspoken opponent of that champion of the Whig Establishment, Bishop Benjamin Hoadly; and he went so far as to force the
resignation of one of his Assistant Masters who had expressed agreement
with Hoadly's latitudinarianism. But it was Snape himself whose views
could no longer be tolerated at Eton by those in power; in 1720 he was
removed from the headmastership and made Provost of King's, her
sister college at Cambridge. His farewell address to the boys in May
1720 is said to have moved them to tears.

Snape's successor as Head Master, Henry Bland, would instill in
them principles more likely to help them flourish in the England of the
Georges and Sir Robert Walpole: Bland was a Whig in politics and, by
reputation, an Arian in religion. He owed his appointment to two
circumstances: his politics were considered exemplary – indeed, in the
1730s he became one of the chief contributors to the ministerial organ,
the *Daily Gazetteer* – and he had been a schoolfellow of Walpole's at
Eton, the minister being well known for giving preferment to Etonians.
Nevertheless, Bland was an able man and right for the job. William
Cole, an antiquarian friend of Horace Walpole, remembered Bland's
tenure as Head Master (1720–8) as a moment unsurpassed in Eton's
history:

> The Schole was never known to be in a more flourishing and thriving
> condition than under his management; having all the requisites that
> a master of such a schole ought to be endowed with; being a man of
> an exceeding fine and stately presence, of a becoming gravity, allayed
> with a sweetness and amiableness of temper peculiar to himself,
> having a continual smile upon his countenance, which yet was tem-
> pered with a proper severity and dignity upon suitable occasions.[102]

In later years Fielding would remember sardonically certain of those
no doubt "suitable occasions," when he suffered floggings under Bland's
regime. What he thought of "the party of the Thwackums," whose

"Meditations were full of Birch," is plain enough from *Tom Jones* (III.v). Less familiar but no less exemplary of his author's sentiments on this subject is Thwackum's namesake in *The Jacobite's Journal* (7 May 1748), "Roger Strap," for whom the "first Principle ... of good Education is Scourging" and who therefore regrets how far the cause of pedagogy has declined since the good old days when Spartan boys were "scourged to Death upon the Altar of *Minerva*": now, he complains, even in "the very best" schools, "Correction is confined to nine or ten, or at most a dozen Lashes." One form such scourging could take Fielding remembered bitterly: that was the "barbarous Custom of whipping Boys on the Hands, till they look as if they had the Itch."[103] Like Locke, Fielding condemned flogging as a means of disciplining boys at school and, to judge from what we have seen of his unruliness as a youth, he doubtless had numerous sharply felt personal reasons for doing so. For all that, he was lucky to have been at Eton when he was. By the standards of the day Bland seems to have been a mild man with a sense of fair play.

If scourging in Fielding's opinion was the first principle of an Eton education, its goal was something better – to initiate young men into the mysteries and enriching pleasures of the great Christian humanist tradition which had comprised the substance of the intellectual life of Europe for centuries. To this end the boys were made to learn the classical languages – "I say," exclaims Dr. Harrison over a crux in the *Aeneid*, "a Boy in the fourth Form at *Eton* would be whipt, or would deserve to be whipt at least, who made the *Neuter Gender* agree with the *Feminine*"[104] – and they were made not only to read the classics, but to get them by heart. Since the foundation of all wisdom was considered to be the Christian religion, they were also made to memorize the New Testament and the liturgy of the Church of England; they recited prayers and attended Chapel daily; on Sundays they went to church at 10.00 a.m., and in the afternoon, before another service at 3.00, they sat for an hour in Upper School while a member of the Fifth Form read aloud from *The Whole Duty of Man*. No wonder, then, that Fielding would always regard this work – written reputedly by Richard Allestree, a former Provost of the College – to be essential to a sound religious education.

Though knowledge of the classics and of scripture was the goal, little specifically is known of the curriculum at Eton in Fielding's time.[105] Early in the century the boys read selected texts of Xenophon and Ovid, some fables of Aesop, the *Electa Majora*, and *Electa Minora*[106] of Ovid, Tibullus, and Propertius, Castalione's New Testament in Latin, William Willymott's *Particles*, Plato's *Phaedrus*, and an anthology of stories and fables in Latin edited by James Upton, formerly a master at Eton, who became a close friend of Fielding's family. The boys probably also knew Sophocles' *Ajax* and *Electra* and Terence's *Andria*, as well as selections from Horace's *Odes* and from Virgil. Other Latin classics were read in the famous Delphin editions.

Considering the conservatism of most English institutions, and particularly of English academic institutions, we might expect to gain a pretty accurate notion of the authors and subjects Fielding studied from the detailed summary by Thomas James, based on his observations some forty years later.[107] According to the best authority on the subject, however, "a very considerable shift in reading" occurred at Eton at mid-century, though the nature of these changes remains obscure.[108] For our present purpose, therefore, we do well to regard James's lists warily. James's outline of the curriculum is nevertheless the best available guide to the sort of education Fielding received at Eton.

As general background, and as assurance that the strong-armed pedagogues of Eton had lofty expectations of their pupils, we may observe that the boys of the two highest Forms (the Fifth and Sixth) were required to attend school seventeen times in a normal week, ten times for construing and seven times for repetition. Since construing officially took place, ineffectually, in "division," in the one large over-crowded room of Upper School, the boys also paid for private tutoring in small groups, wherein the real business of an Eton education went on. The following were the authors and subjects studied in 1761–6:

> *Fourth Form.* In a regular week the boys construed Ovid's *Metamorphoses*, *Electa ex Ovidio*, Aesop, Caesar, Terence, Farnaby's *Delectus*,[109] and the Greek Testament.
>
> *Remove.* In this, the transitional division to the upper forms, the boys studied the *Poetae Graeci*, Virgil, Horace's *Odes*, Pomponius Mela, and Cornelius Nepos. Geography was emphasized at this level, the boys being required to draw maps every week.
>
> *Fifth and Sixth Forms.* In these Forms, which constituted the Head Master's division, the boys each week construed Lucian, the *Scriptores Romani*, Homer, Virgil, Horace (hexameters), and the *Poetae Graeci* – the last four also being the subjects for repetition. In the Fifth Form two of the remaining "saying-lessons" were taken from the *Electa Minora ex Ovidio, Tibullo, et Propertio*. Sixth Formers instead memorized selections from the *Epigrammatum Delectus*. Every Monday, furthermore, the boys were required to recite twenty verses from the Greek Testament. During the summer term, as a change from this routine, Horace's *Odes* were substituted for Lucian, Virgil, and the *Scriptores Romani*, and were memorized instead of the *Electa Minora* and the *Epigrammatum Delectus*. The last week before the summer and winter recesses was entirely given

to the study of Greek plays, particularly Aristophanes and Soph-
ocles – the latter being read in John Burton's *Pentalogia*,[110] containing
Sophocles' Oedipus plays and *Antigone*, Euripides' *Phoenician
Women*, and Aeschylus' *Seven against Thebes*.

And this, we must bear in mind, was merely the core of the curriculum. During their leisure hours (few as they must have been) the boys
of the upper Forms were expected to read, as Thomas James put it,
"all other books necessary towards making a compleat scholar," which
in his time (the 1760s) included "Dr. Middleton's *Cicero*, Tully's *Offices*,
Ovid's long and short verses, *Spectator*, etc. Milton, Pope, Roman
History, Grecian History, Potter's Antiquities, and Kennet's."[111] And
those who stayed the course were also introduced to algebra and to
Euclid before they left school.

Clearly, the extent and weight of the matter Fielding was required
to master at Eton are impressive. That he did master it – even if in
spite of and not because of the penalties exacted for failing to do so! –
is apparent in his works in the sheer range and aptness of his allusions
to the classical authors. One would expect that the reading of great
books would be forever associated in his mind with the painful sacrifice
of his blood upon "birchen Altars," but the evidence is that Eton
stimulated Fielding's strong love of learning. In later life, even by the
expectations of his own century, he was a widely read man who left
behind him a personal library that compares favorably with Dr. Johnson's. To judge, furthermore, from his facility of quotation and the
ready way he could summon a literary allusion to his purpose, the
training his memory received at school was also useful to him.

At Eton, too, he became, in the eighteenth-century sense of the word
that few even of today's doctors of philosophy can pretend to, a fully
"literate" man: he was, that is, an accomplished Latinist and could
read Greek. As the distinguished historian of the school observes, "the
art of Latin versification" was "the crucial test of Eton scholarship."[112]
The Fifth Formers wrote Latin themes and verses, and there was more
of the same in the Sixth Form, at which stage the boys were also
expected to produce compositions in Greek iambics. There were exercises as well in extemporaneous composition and in "Declamation." By
this latter practice, which Dr. Bland introduced, the Sixth Form boys,
before the entire school, gave speeches taken from Cicero or Sallust or
Livy, the object of the exercise being to teach them to "read with
propriety." In the years ahead such training would be useful to Fielding
the barrister and magistrate, and to his friends and schoolfellows – for
example, Charles Hanbury Williams the diplomat, and the eminent
Parliament men, George Lyttelton and William Pitt. It was surely this
special feature of an Eton education that Fielding recalled when he

paid his friend, the future Earl of Chatham, a handsome compliment in *Tom Jones* (XIV.i):

> Nor do I believe that all the Imagination, Fire, and Judgment of *Pitt* could have produced those Orations that have made the Senate of *England* in these our Times a Rival in Eloquence to *Greece* and *Rome*, if he had not been so well read in the Writings of *Demosthenes* and *Cicero*, as to have transferred their whole Spirit into his Speeches, and with their Spirit, their Knowledge too.

Fielding's schooldays were not all spent in such "earnest business," as Gray called it. Besides the three long vacations – a month at Christmas, at Whitsuntide (in May), and at Electiontide (in August) – there were certain times during the week regularly set aside for recreation: Tuesday was a whole holiday, Thursday a half holiday, and Saturday a "play-at-four." Historians of the College record an admirable variety of diversions with which Eton boys of Fielding's time filled their vacant hours – refreshing themselves with chums at the Christopher Inn on the High Street, or at the local coffee-houses; swimming or boating in the summer and skating in the winter; harassing the bargemen on the river; watching cock-fights and bull-baiting; playing tennis or billiards, or cricket or football; playing at cudgels and hoops (the latter a rougher game than one would think and one at which the "Oppidans" and the "Collegers" were annually matched), or at innumerable other sports having cryptic appellations known chiefly to Etonians, such as "Fives" or "Shirking Walls" or "Scrambling Walls." But we cannot know which, if any, of these pastimes Fielding enjoyed. Eton was also well known for the College theatricals, usually comedies, staged at Christmas time; indeed, what is usually taken to be the first English comedy, *Ralph Roister Doister*, was written for his scholars by Nicholas Udall, Head Master from 1534 to 1537. But despite his love of the theatre and his talent at writing comedy, Fielding, as an "Oppidan," probably had nothing to do with these productions, which were presented in Hall by the "Collegers."

He could scarcely have escaped, however, participating in two of Eton's strongest, and most bizarre, traditions: these were the annual events, held in January and August, respectively, called "Montem" and "Hunting the Ram." Since 1561 the boys on the day of Montem (the word being taken from the Latin *mons*) had marched in antic procession to a hillock called Salt Hill near Slough. Along the way they exacted a tribute of money from anyone they encountered and, in what must have been thought an ungrateful exchange, required them to eat a pinch of salt. Once they reached the hill, they proceeded to initiate the freshmen, who had not yet proved their courage by standing up to the birch for a whole year. The new boys were seasoned first literally

with salt, then figuratively by being made the butt of satiric verses
seasoned with wit (*salem*). Finally, their cheeks wet with salt tears,
they were received in triumph into the ranks of the old boys, and the
procession returned to school. One can imagine what Fielding, who
under better circumstances than these was never fond of practical
humor, must have thought of these mortifying rites as he, presumably,
experienced them in the winter of 1719–20.

It is hard, however, to imagine him taking any part, except that of
spectator, in the brutal festival known as "Hunting the Ram," which
occurred each August at Electiontide (the time when boys were elected
to scholarships for the following year); for though he admired the skill
and bravery of boxers and cudgel-players, he hated cruelty in any form.
What, then, were his feelings at this event, when a ram, provided by
the College butcher, was turned loose and hunted across the playing
fields by the boys, who at last, with their knotted "ram-clubs," ritually
bludgeoned the beast to death, dipped their hands in its blood, and had
it roasted for dinner? This custom, abolished in 1747, will remind us
that eighteenth-century sensibilities could be less squeamish than our
own.

What did Fielding at last make of his Eton experience? Once, in
Joseph Andrews (III.v), he addresses the subject in an oblique and
general way as Parson Adams, having attended with mounting dismay
to Mr. Wilson's narrative of his dissolute youth, engages Joseph in a
"Disputation on Schools":

> "*Joseph*," cries *Adams*, screwing up his Mouth, "I have found it; I
> have discovered the Cause of all the Misfortunes which befel him. A
> public School, *Joseph*, was the Cause of all the Calamities which he
> afterwards suffered. Public Schools are the Nurseries of all Vice
> and Immorality. All the wicked Fellows whom I remember at the
> University were bred at them. – Ah Lord! I can remember as well as
> if it was but yesterday, a Knot of them; they called them King's
> Scholars, I forget why – very wicked Fellows! *Joseph*, you may thank
> the Lord you were not bred at a public School, you would never have
> preserved your Virtue as you have."

This opinion, however, Joseph respectfully counters by invoking the
authority of Sir Thomas Booby, himself bred at a public school and
(who could doubt it?) "the finest Gentleman in all the Neighbourhood":

> It was his Opinion, and I have often heard him deliver it, that a Boy
> taken from a public School, and carried into the World, will learn
> more in one Year there, than one of a private Education will in five.
> He used to say, the School itself initiated him a great way, (I
> remember that was his very Expression) for great Schools are Little

Societies, where a Boy of any Observation may see in Epitome what
he will afterwards find in the World at large.

No doubt Fielding was of the same opinion; and the parson's enthusiasm
in preferring the moral instruction to be had in a private school is a
little silly. On the other hand, Booby, the product of a public-school
education, hardly inspires confidence in the superior efficacy of that
institution. And we are left concurring with Joseph's view that, like
the horses he has observed in the stable, boys are good or bad by nature,
and the scourging of pedagogues will not make them otherwise.

But these generalities are of small help to us in trying to understand,
in a specific way, Fielding's experience of Eton during those four or
five formative years of early adolescence. It was a crucial time for him,
important in so many ways – in the development of his intellect and
the quickening of a moral sense, in the making of lasting friendships,
in the whetting of his talent for humor and satire, and in the tempering
at least (if, as we shall see, by no means the taming) of his passionate
nature. For the most part, what these years meant to him we can only
infer from the qualities of the man as we know him in his works.

Though Fielding remained throughout this period a ward of Chancery
in the care of his mother's family,[113] he did not return to Salisbury on
leaving Eton. There is some evidence, very slight, that he was drawing
closer to his father. As he turned eighteen he appears to have been in
London, where curiosity drew him on Monday, 24 May 1725, to a scene
that left him with an indelible impression of the cruelty and malevolence
of which human nature is capable. On that date the notorious criminal
Jonathan Wild was hanged at Tyburn before a vast, unpitying multitude – the "Mob," as Fielding called such licentious assemblies – who
pelted Wild with missiles and roared in triumph as he was "turned off."
"I had the Curiosity," Fielding recalled, "to see the late *Jonathan Wild*
go to the Gallows; but instead of taking any Pleasure in beholding so
notorious a Criminal brought to Justice, I was shock'd at the Barbarity
of the Populace, who pursued him in his last Moments with horrid
Imprecations, and even with brutal Violence."[114] If Eton, with its
floggings and its ram hunts, comprised for him an "Epitome" of the
greater world, it had not quite prepared him for the savagery of a
London mob.

But where was he staying in town? In St. James's with his father
and his by now numerous half-brothers? Perhaps, though to have done

so would be a violation of the Lord Chancellor's order that he never again be exposed to the influence of his stepmother.

In any event, his visit to London was brief, for by the summer of 1725 he was, nominally at least, residing in a most unaccountable place, the village of Upton Grey, Hampshire, in which Edmund had rented a house for him.[115] But why Upton Grey? As an adventurous and independent young man at last rid of the constraints of Eton, Fielding was no doubt glad enough to escape as well from the supervision of the doting old ladies in Salisbury; and besides the fact that he could not lawfully reside with his father, his prolonged presence in town may not have been agreeable to Edmund and his wife. Of one thing we can be sure: however delightful this neat little village appears today to admirers of the English countryside, Fielding did not go up to Upton Grey by choice. Three years later he expressed his opinion of the place in a poem entitled "A Description of U[pto]n G[rey], (alias *New Hog's Norton*) in *Com. Hants.*" There he complained that "his hard Fates" had removed him from the livelier scenes of London "To barren Climates, less frequented Plains,/ Unpolish'd Nymphs, and more unpolish'd Swains." Just how complete he considered his rustication in such a place to be is plain enough from the picture he paints:

> As the dawb'd Scene, that on the Stage is shewn,
> Where this Side Canvas is, and that a Town;
> Or as that Lace which *Paxton* Half Lace calls,
> That decks some Beau Apprentice out for Balls;
> Such our Half House erects its mimick Head,
> This Side an House presents, and that a Shed.
> Nor doth the inward Furniture excel,
> Nor yields it to the Beauty of the Shell:
> Here *Roman* Triumphs plac'd with aukward Art,
> A Cart its Horses draws, an Elephant the Cart.
> On the House-Side a Garden may be seen,
> Which Docks and Nettles keep for ever green.
> Weeds on the Ground, instead of Flow'rs, we see,
> And Snails alone adorn the barren Tree.
> Happy for us, had *Eve's* this Garden been;
> She'd found no Fruit, and therefore known no Sin.
> Nor meaner Ornament the Shed-Side decks,
> With Hay-Stacks, Faggot Piles, and Bottle-Ricks;
> The Horses Stalls, the Coach a Barn contains;
> For purling Streams, we've Puddles fill'd with Rains.
> What can our Orchard without Trees surpass?
> What, but our dusty Meadow without Grass?
> I've thought (so strong with me Burlesque prevails,)

This Place design'd to ridicule *Versailles*;
Or meant, like that, Art's utmost Pow'r to shew,
That tells how high it reaches, this how low.
Our Conversation does our Palace fit,
We've ev'ry Thing but Humour, except Wit.

The house Fielding here (probably) describes with such comical woe is still visible today in Upton Grey. Known as "The Village Farm House," it features a shed and working yard on one side and a garden on "the House-Side"; in front it looks across the road at a muddy pond which, to an unkind wit, might seem more nearly to resemble a puddle.

···—◄ **xi** ►—···

At age eighteen Fielding was no more willing to suffer any such lonely rural exile as this. Eventually, it may be that he came to enjoy the rural sports and pleasures that North Hampshire had to offer: there was a tradition in the nineteenth century that he once rode in the Vyne Hunt.[116] But when the hunting season began in September 1725, Fielding was far from Upton Grey and pursuing another sort of game. Accompanied by a servant named Joseph Lewis, he traveled to the prosperous and picturesque town of Lyme Regis, on the Dorset coast, and settled down for an extended visit of several months – a visit, however, that was to end abruptly, and in circumstances worthy once again of some episode in romance.

Fully to appreciate the colorful and sometimes stormy scenes to follow, we need to imagine the kind of young man Fielding was and how he seemed to others. Then in the first flush of manhood, he was relishing his independence from schoolmasters and guardians and parents. He was inclined to swagger a little – conscious, as he would always be, of the fact that he was a gentleman born; conscious, too, of the finish an expensive public-school education had given him; and conscious above all of his powers of both mind and body. He was in stature tall ("rising above six feet," as Murphy remembered him) and powerfully built. He was not handsome in the conventional sense: he would himself joke about the length of his chin and nose – a nose long enough, it appears, to gladden the heart of Walter Shandy. But there was about him a certain personal magnetism more attractive than mere good looks – a vivacity and passionate intensity that shone in his countenance. This is what most impressed his friend James Harris about his appearance, who recalled in later years that though Fielding's face was "not handsome" he had "an Eye peculiarly penetrating [and quick], and which during the Sallies of Wit or anger never failed to distinguish it self."[117] These were the qualities his friends found most remarkable about him – his "lively Witt," which, as Harris recalled, was "native, spontaneous, and ever new, derived instantly from those events that are arising every moment," and "his Passions . . . vehement in every kind."

In these early years Fielding's quick temper often involved him in brawls and violent altercations with a variety of antagonists from servants to the prosperous burghers of town corporations. Among his enemies in later days such episodes earned him a reputation as a *"foul mouth'd Farmer"* who spent his youth in wrestling and quarreling and hard drinking.[118] One such incident provides us with our earliest reference to him outside the records of Chancery – as well as our earliest examples of his signature (at a time when he spelled his name in the Denbigh fashion, "Feilding"). For he had not been long at Lyme when, on the afternoon of 21 September 1725, "without any provocation" as he claimed, he was "violently assaulted" by one Joseph Channon, the servant of a local miller named James Daniel, who struck him "two several blows in the face and other part of his body." So he deposed on oath the next day before the magistrate, Robert Burridge.[119] What might have prompted this unseemly encounter between a young gentleman and a miller's man we can only surmise. It was not the first time Fielding had quarreled with servants – as a child he spat in their faces – nor would it be the last.

His sojourn at Lyme soon became more exciting still. The chief attraction the town held for him was the presence there of his cousin (by marriage) Sarah Andrew – a lovely girl, fifteen years old, and heiress to a considerable fortune. She was the only surviving child of the marriage in 1709 between Solomon Andrew, a wealthy Lyme merchant and landholder, and Mary Huckmore of Buckland Baron, Devon, sister of Honora, the wife of Fielding's uncle Davidge Gould.[120] Soon after her father died in 1712, Sarah's mother remarried, and Sarah became, like her cousin, a ward in Chancery, living at Lyme in the house of her uncle (by marriage) and guardian Andrew Tucker. According to a tradition apparently originating with Sarah herself and first recorded in 1843,[121] Fielding had fallen in love with the girl and, when his romantic overtures were peremptorily discouraged by her uncle, attempted to ravish her away by force one Sunday while she was on her way to church.

Sensational though it sounds, the episode may well have occurred in just this way. As Sarah's near relation, Fielding had the opportunity of knowing her and, before he made himself an unwelcome guest, of visiting her at her uncle's house. Judging from her beauty, moreover – captured charmingly by a contemporary artist (see Plate 7) – and from

Fielding's own impulsive amorous propensities, it is not surprising that he found her irresistible. (Psychologists would say she had the additional charm for him of having the same Christian name as the other women in his early life to whom he was closest – his mother and grandmother and sister Sarah.) But Miss Andrew's uncle had no intention of encouraging a romance between his ward and this brash, rowdy youth of no fortune. Allegedly the old gentleman had a more solid objection to Fielding as a suitor: he meant Sarah to marry his son John – a match permissible according to the canons of the Church, though John was Sarah's first cousin.[122]

The story receives its surest support, however, from certain documents preserved among the records of the Lyme corporation. On 14 November 1725 – a Sunday, which being the sabbath attests to the urgency of the case – Andrew Tucker appeared before John Bowdidge, the Mayor and Tucker's colleague in the town corporation, "and solemnly declared on his oath that he is in fear of his life or of some bodily hurt to be done or to be procured to be done to him by Henry ffeilding Gent and his servant or companion both now and for some time past residing in" Lyme Regis. Fielding succeeded in eluding the town constables, but his man, Joseph Lewis, was not so lucky. That same day he was brought before Bowdidge and identified by Tucker as "a servant of the above-named Henry ffeilding" and "one of the persons against whom he craveth surety of the peace for that the said Joseph Lewis will beat, wound, maim or kill him."[123] One would like to know more about this zealous retainer, who seems to have played a less pusillanimous Partridge to Fielding's ruder Tom Jones; but the only fact we have is that, when he was bound over the next day to keep the peace, he gave his residence as St. James's, Middlesex, where Fielding also resided when he was in town. Could he later, as one scholar wonders, have made his own small niche in literature as the little-known author of the same name?[124]

However that may be, what we do know of these events squares well enough with the story handed down in Sarah's family. Angered by her guardian's forbidding him any longer to woo the girl he loved, Fielding decided upon a desperate course of action. Knowing the way she usually took to St. Michael's church on Sundays, he waited for her with his man Lewis and made a violent, but unsuccessful, attempt to carry her away by force. The following day, Monday, 15 November, while the unlucky Lewis was being bound over to keep the peace (together with one Robert Cossens, a local customs officer who may also have been implicated in the plot),[125] Fielding could not resist flinging one last, defiant insult at Sarah's guardian before he fled the town. In some prominent place – probably under the colonnade of the Customs House, where the townspeople of Lyme convened daily to conduct business or to gossip – Fielding posted the following notice, written out plainly in his own bold hand and signed by him no less boldly (see Plate 8):

November 15 1725
This is to give notice to all the World that Andrew Tucker and his son John Tucker are Clowns, and Cowards
Witness my hand
HENRY ffEILDING

So ends this lively episode of what may have been Fielding's first serious romance. In the following year Sarah Andrew was out of harm's way, having been married to Ambrose Rhodes in Modbury, Devon; she died in 1783, aged seventy-three, at Bellair, Heavitree (near Exeter).[126] That she long remembered how much Fielding had loved her is evident from the legend inscribed on her portrait in an eighteenth-century hand: "From whom Fielding, her admirer, avowedly drew his character of SOPHIA WESTERN."[127] On the contrary, of course, Fielding tells us it was Charlotte Cradock, his beloved first wife, who stood for the portraits of Sophie Western and Amelia Booth. But Sarah was his first love, and she may be pardoned a little wishful thinking.

···➤ xii ◆···

We cannot be sure where Fielding went after leaving Lyme Regis. To Upton Grey, to divert his grief hunting hares and foxes? To Salisbury, to forget Sarah in the pursuit of other belles, whom he soon began celebrating in verse? It may be that he tried at first to deal with his disappointment in another sort of verse, by writing his rude burlesque of Juvenal's *Sixth Satire*, the notorious diatribe against women: this piece, as Fielding stated in the Preface to the *Miscellanies*, "was originally sketched out before I was Twenty, and was all the Revenge taken by an injured Lover." Or did he head for London, to plunge into the pleasures of the town, chief of which would always be for him the theatre?

He was in London a year later, certainly, making his presence felt in palpable and characteristic ways – by assaulting, for instance, one of his father's servants, Joseph Burt. Burt, who with his fellow servants Frances Barber and Henry Halstead testified in Chancery that Fielding was fast going to ruin under the influence of his grandmother, had been part of the family at East Stour even while his mother was alive; and like Mrs. Barber and Halstead, he followed Edmund to London. He may have had something to do, moreover, with Fielding's residence during this period in such an unlikely place as Upton Grey: the baptism register for the parish church there includes an entry on 5 December 1725 for Martha, daughter of Joseph Burt.[128] If this man and Edmund's servant are one and the same, he may explain Fielding's connection with the village – in which case, Fielding may have considered he had a grudge to settle. Whatever the reason, on 4 November 1726 in St. James's he again lost control of his temper. He was cited by Burt in the King's Bench for having "shook, wounded and manhandled him so that he was desperately frightened for his life, and committed other enormities against the said Joseph and against the King and his dignity."[129] Nothing came of this quarrel; Burt, perhaps recalling that his assailant was his master's son, appears to have dropped the charges. And in the winter the court records indicate that Fielding, now said to be "late" of St. James's parish, had removed himself safely out of reach of the King's officers.

Images such as this – so many of them preserved in the records of the King's Bench, or Chancery, or the Corporation of Lyme – tell us much about the effects of Fielding's troubled childhood on his character and personality. To the sad and acrimonious events that followed his mother's death shortly before his eleventh birthday, he responded, on the one hand, by drawing closer to his grandmother and his sisters; on the other hand, by rebelling against any and all figures of authority – his father, the schoolmasters at Eton, Sarah Andrew's guardian – or by openly brawling with those in subservient roles who in some way opposed him. We are left with the picture of a young man – no doubt fun-loving and affectionate, a delightful companion – but driven by his passions: running away from Eton, from Lyme, from London, to escape the consequences of his own rash and willful nature. It would be some time yet before, like his heroes Tom Jones and Billy Booth, he learned to bring himself under control. In 1727 he was about to enter a time of his life remarkable for gayer pleasures, for the broadening of his experience of the world – and, of course, for the beginning of his career as a comic author.

PART II

Playwright and libertine
(1727–39)

By the spring of 1727, as the new year officially began on 25 March, Fielding had returned to town and was pressing his father for money. The ledgers of Drummonds Bank reveal that on 23 and 25 March Edmund made cash payments to his son amounting to £14.0.0.[1] Murphy asserted that Fielding was allowed £200 a year by his father, which, as Fielding quipped, "any body might pay that would." Prodigal sons have a way of complaining about the inadequacy of their allowances, but it seems to have been the case that Fielding never had as much money to spend as the eldest son of a well-off and powerful man of the time might expect. In the eight years since he married again, Edmund's family had increased by no fewer than six sons. (Indeed, worn out with childbearing, Anne Fielding would not live out the year: she died on 13 July 1727,[2] scarcely ten months after giving birth to the last of Henry's half-brothers.) Edmund, meanwhile, continued to rise in the Army, having been promoted to Brigadier General on 16 March.[3] One consequence of this prosperity was, as Murphy delicately expressed it, that "with the necessary demands of his station for a genteel and suitable expence, he could not spare out of his income any considerable disbursements for the maintenance of his eldest son." Edmund's bank account from this period – or rather what little remains of it, which covers only the dates 22–29 March 1726–7 and 28 December–11 January 1728/9 – suggests that Fielding might with some justice have considered those disbursements inadequate: during those three weeks Edmund paid out to various people a total of £1,139.17.2½, of which Fielding's share was the sum of £14.0.0 already mentioned. To be sure, these accounts are too fragmentary to make much of, but they square with what we have seen of Edmund's fecklessness as a father. No doubt he would have preferred his eldest son to remain in the sleepy little Hampshire village where he placed him, well away from the expensive pleasures of London.

But that spring, as Londoners talked of the Siege of Gibraltar and the heinous murder of Widdrington Darby by Henry Fisher, a young attorney whom he had befriended, Fielding was in town. The siege later became the scene of Capt. Booth's heroism in *Amelia*; and in *Tom Jones* (VIII.i) the blackguard Fisher serves as a more improbable example of unmitigated villainy than even Nero himself. It may be that Fielding's circumstantial knowledge of this sensational crime was owing to his friendship with Richard Willoughby (*c.* 1703–62), whose family estate, as Partridge reveals in *Tom Jones* (VIII.xi), was at West Knoyle, Wilts., not far from East Stour: Willoughby was Fisher's landlord in London (at Southampton Buildings) and it was he who discovered the villain's guilt when he caused Fisher's apartment to be searched.[4]

In these same months Fielding's thoughts were occupied by matters calculated to divert the town in a more agreeable way – a way, he hoped, that would bring him both fame and the money he needed to be independent of his father. He was, that is, well advanced in the writing of a comedy, *Love in Several Masques*, which he had the good sense to understand was never likely to see the light of day unless it had the benefit of the advice and, more to the point, the sponsorship of some astute and influential patron. He had just such a friend in his second cousin, the splendid bluestocking Lady Mary Wortley Montagu (1689–1762). To Lady Mary, then, "whose accurate Judgment," as he declared in the Dedication to the play, "has long been the Glory of her own Sex, and the Wonder of ours," Fielding in the spring anxiously sent the first three acts of his comedy. Just twenty years old, he was relieved and grateful when she passed on this inchoate performance so "light a Censure." How much his literary ambitions meant to him at this juncture is evident when, upon sending her the finished play, he observed that her "Goodness" in encouraging him in his work was "the greatest and indeed only Happiness of my Life."[5] It was, indeed, entirely owing to Lady Mary's encouragement that he had the heart to finish the piece: "it arose," he assured her, "from a Vanity, to which your Indulgence, on the first Perusal of it, gave Birth."

From this time on, Fielding and his cousin remained fast friends. In his verse, he would praise her as "sparkling *W[or]tley*," unrivaled for her wit;[6] and in his Dedication to the play, she seems to have redeemed for him a character he usually thought unnatural – the learned female: "You are capable," he declared, "of instructing the Pedant, and are at once a living Confutation of those morose Schoolmen who wou'd confine Knowledge to the Male Part of the Species, and a shining Instance of all those Perfections and softer Graces which Nature has confin'd to the Female."

···◀ ii ◀···

Fielding's first publication, however, was not owing to his desire to emulate Farquhar and Cibber in a comedy of manners, but rather to an unexpected political event. On 11 June George I died. During the summer, while the Court mourned and Sir Robert Walpole was confounding his enemies by weathering the change in sovereigns and securing his place as Prime Minister, preparations went forward for the staging of one of the great solemn festivals in English life: the coronation of a new monarch. The commencement of the reign of George II, coinciding as it did with the moment when his own literary ambitions were taking shape, must have seemed to Fielding a particularly auspicious event. His "Hapsburg" (so he believed) relations – William the fifth Earl of Denbigh and his brother Charles Fielding, who had recently been appointed Gentleman Usher of Queen Caroline's Privy Chamber – were favored at Court. Walpole, Lady Mary's powerful friend and a fellow Etonian, was still head of the government.

The Coronation took place on Wednesday, 11 October, and was magnificent even by British standards. We remember it today chiefly through Handel's stirring anthem, composed for the occasion. But the celebrations were remarkable in other ways as well. " 'Tis impossible," declared the *British Journal* (14 October 1727), "to express the triumph and universality of Joy of the Publick upon this Occasion." Guns fired, bells rang, flags flew; there were bonfires and fireworks and illuminations of every kind. At Drury Lane, so as to prolong the festival and give those who were unable to attend at Westminster Abbey some idea of what they missed, the managers revived Shakespeare's *Henry VIII* and made a show of the scene representing the coronation of Anne Boleyn. And there was more pomp and pageantry to follow within a few days: Monday, 30 October, was Lord Mayor's Day, which the King attended though it was his own birthday – that occasion being duly "solemnized" at Court two days later on 1 November. On that day the courtiers and their ladies came out of mourning and dazzled each other with their finery and gaiety. At St. James's Palace they danced through the night, while in the Park cannons fired forty-four salvos, one for every year of the King's life.

These two royal events, signaling the commencement of the long reign of George II, became the occasions for Fielding's début as an author. On 10 November he published together under his own name a pair of poems advertised as follows:

> The Coronation. A Poem. And an Ode on the Birthday. By Mr. *Fielding*. Printed for *B. Creake* in *Jermayn-street*; and sold by *J. Roberts* near *Warwicklane*. Price 6d.

These poems – of which no copies have survived – were doubtless made up of the most fulsome praise of the Royal Family and the Court. Such an inference seems safe not only from the fact that the publisher, James Roberts, was associated with the Court interest, but from the appearance, as the advertisement attests, of Fielding's name on the title-page: he was, of course, fond of ridicule, and as a young man he was often impertinent; but he was not so imprudent as to satirize the King openly. Fielding's first poems were probably among those Swift sarcastically commemorates in *On Poetry: A Rapsody* (1733):

> A Prince the Moment he is crown'd,
> Inherits ev'ry Virtue round,
> As Emblems of the sov'reign Pow'r,

> Like other Bawbles of the Tow'r.
> Is gen'rous, valiant, just and wise,
> And so continues 'till he dies. ...
>   Then *Poet*, if you mean to thrive,
> Employ your Muse on Kings alive;
> With Prudence gath'ring up a Cluster
> Of all the Virtues you can muster:
> Which form'd into a Garland sweet,
> Lay humbly at your Monarch's Feet;
> Who, as the Odours reach his Throne,
> Will smile, and think 'em all his own.
>   (ll. 191–6, 219–26)

Though Swift later insisted the slur was inserted "maliciously," without his knowledge, the London edition of this poem specifically included Fielding among such flatterers.[7]

Fielding meant to "thrive" in just this way when he published his verses on the Coronation and the Birthday. They did not, however, have the desired effect of making his fortune at Court. Perhaps the story of his disappointment is obliquely reflected in *A Journey from This World to the Next* (I.xxiv), where Julian the Apostate, in his incarnation as a poet, recalls his first experience as an aspiring young author. The correspondences between the two cases are tantalizingly close if for the subject of Julian's panegyric, Pope Alexander, we substitute George II, and Fielding's cousin Lady Mary for Julian's relation, the Jesuit who "had the Pope's Ear":

My first Composition after I left School [Julian relates], was a Panegyric on Pope *Alexander* IV. ... On this Subject, I composed a Poem ... which with much difficulty I got to be presented to his Holiness, of whom I expected great Preferment as my Reward, but I was cruelly disappointed: for when I had waited a Year without hearing any of the Commendations I had flattered myself with receiving, and being now able to contain no longer, I applied to a Jesuit who was my Relation, and had the Pope's Ear, to know what his Holiness's Opinion was of my Work; he coldly answered me, that he was at that time busied in Concerns of too much Importance, to attend the reading of Poems.

••• iii •••

Whatever disappointment Fielding felt at the reception of his poems, which dropped dead-born from the press, he must have been elated in September, when his comedy was accepted[8] by Colley Cibber, Robert Wilks, and Barton Booth, the famous "Triumvirate" who governed jealously the Theatre Royal at Drury Lane.[9] To an untried playwright of twenty, Cibber, especially, would be an awesome figure. Though his enemies – most memorably Pope in the final version of *The Dunciad* – liked to represent him as an impudent coxcomb without taste or principles, Cibber was in fact, as dramatist, comedian, and manager, the most talented and powerful personality of the London stage – a "star," as we would say today, of the first magnitude. That this canny old professional (for it was Cibber who made such decisions at Drury Lane) should condescend even to hear a comedy by an unknown playwright scarcely out of school can have but one explanation – clear enough from the following piece of advice offered to hopeful dramatists by a knowledgeable contemporary. The managers at Drury Lane, he writes, are notorious for their "Prejudice against every new Beginner ... Hence, without using as much Interest with the *Great*, as would procure a Provision for Life, you are not so sure even of a Reading, as a Condemnation." The writer concludes: "In the present Circumstances, therefore, he that has the most Friends will always have the most Success, independent of Genius and Merit; and I would advise every Author to sue for a COMMAND from *above*, before he ventures to present his Play, for fear of a Denial without it."[10]

Fielding, luckily, was well connected at Court, and it was no doubt owing to the influence of Lady Mary, in particular, that *Love in Several Masques* ever had a hearing before Cibber and his colleagues. The grudging, not to say humiliating, process by which a new comedy came to be accepted for production at Drury Lane during Cibber's tenure there is so well captured by an anonymous contemporary that we may easily imagine what Fielding went through:

The Author of a new Piece was instructed to pay his Complements severally to the Menagers, who, with much Unwillingness, were prevail'd upon to appoint some leisure Day for the Reading of it, when they were all three to be present: Yet this was a Favour not easily to be obtain'd; for we are to know, when an Author had got thus far, he had made a considerable Progress, not one in Twenty being ever able to gain this Point; and never, I believe, during their Prosperity, without the Recommendation of Interest or Power. Well, the Day being come for reading, the *Corrector* [Cibber], in his *Judicial Capacity*, and the other two being present; that is, *The Court sitting*,

Chancellor Cibber (for the other two, like M———rs in *Chancery* sat
only for Form sake, and did not presume to judge) nodded to the
Author to open his Manuscript. The Author begins to read, in which
if he failed to please the *Corrector*, he wou'd condescend sometimes
to read it for him: When, if the Play strook him very warmly, as it
wou'd, if he found any Thing new in it, in which he conceived he
cou'd particularly shine as an Actor, he would lay down his Pipe,
(for the *Chancellor* always smoaked when he made a Decree) and cry,
*By G–d there is something in this: I do not know but it may do; but I
will play such a Part.* Well, when the Reading was finished, he made
his proper Corrections, and sometimes without any Propriety; nay,
frequently he very much and very hastily maimed what he pretended
to mend: But to all this the Author must submit.[11]

The part in *Love in Several Masques* that pleased Cibber in this way –
who had long been famous for playing a fop to perfection – was that
of Rattle; Wilks, his fellow manager, played Merital. In his Preface to
the published version, Fielding declared he could not "sufficiently
acknowledge their civil and kind Behaviour, previous to its Representation." In this, however, he was grateful for courtesies that few
other playwrights of the time experienced, and which were not impressive enough to be remembered by Fielding himself two years later, when
he next publicly alluded to Wilks and Cibber in the characters of
Sparkish and Marplay in *The Author's Farce.*

   Love in Several Masques went into rehearsal immediately after the
first, nearly calamitous, performance of the play that proved to be the
great hit of the season at Drury Lane: *The Provoked Husband*, Cibber's
"genteel" adaptation of the late Sir John Vanbrugh's "low" comedy,
A Journey to London. On the opening night of Cibber's play (10 January
1727/8) the audience reacted so violently to some scenes of "low" humor
in the fourth Act, that one eyewitness feared for his life. No wonder
that Cibber thought it necessary to prepare some new piece at once;
Fielding's comedy was thus announced in the *London Evening Post* (11–
13 January) as "now in Rehearsal." It would be another month,
however, before it came on the boards; for *The Provoked Husband* not
only survived that first-night riot, but, after Cibber excised the offending scenes, it continued to run to great applause for twenty-eight
consecutive nights, its success owing in large part to the performance
of Anne Oldfield: as Cibber put it in his immortal compliment, in the
role of Lady Townly Mrs. Oldfield "outdid her usual outdoing."[12]
Fielding, in his Preface to *Love in Several Masques*, also expressed his
gratitude to this celebrated actress, who, "tho' she had contracted a
slight Indisposition by her violent Fatigue in the Part of Lady *Townly,*

was prevailed on to grace that of Lady *Matchless*; which placed her in
a Light so far inferior to that which she had in the other."

But not even the abilities of the principal comedians at Drury Lane
or his own brisk dialogue could keep Fielding's piece afloat for very
long. It is not at all a bad play; as the inaugural performance of an
author just out of his teens, it is in fact quite impressive – if recognizably
a part of the school of "humane" comedy made popular since the turn
of the century by playwrights such as Steele and Cibber. But the
moment was hardly propitious for Fielding's début. His play would not
seem to shine after the dazzling success of *The Provoked Husband*. What
is more, it was competing for audiences with another piece that became
one of the great popular successes in the history of the English theatre;
for at Lincoln's Inn Fields on 29 January, Gay's *Beggar's Opera* began
its astonishing run of sixty-three consecutive nights, engrossing, as
Fielding observed in his Preface, "the whole Talk and Admiration of
the Town." *Love in Several Masques* opened at last on Friday, 16
February, and played four nights, with Lady Mary gamely attending
half the performances; it was enough, at least, for Fielding to enjoy his
"Benefits." The play was published on 23 February by John Watts,
the well-known theatrical publisher, who thus began a long association
with Fielding.

The success of Gay's odd yet irresistible "Entertainment," which
Swift called a "Newgate pastoral," prompted Fielding to dash off a
song which one of his Salisbury acquaintances preserved and published
years later. With a light ironic touch it celebrates Lavinia Fenton's
triumph in the role of Polly Peachum and the way, in general, that
Gay's clever ballad opera had so totally eclipsed in popularity the
regular productions of greater dramatists – a lesson that would not be
lost on Fielding. The final four stanzas give the flavor of the piece:

> Polly she grew extensive fair,
> She put in to be a player;
> Polly she grew extensive fair,
> She put in to be a player,
> In that same famous play, which ran both night and day,
> Call'd the Beggars Opera – O brave Gay!

> Shakespeare divine was cut to the soul;
> Addison and Dryden ran their heads into a hole;
> Shakespeare divine was cut to the soul;
> Addison and Dryden ran their heads into a hole;
> Steel swore bitterly; swoons! cry'd Whicherly,
> I'll kill 'en; which is he? which is he?

Then for the character of Captain Macheath,
It made Walker a player in spite of his teeth;
Then for the character of Captain Macheath,
It made Walker a player in spite of his teeth;
All the actors liv'd in jail,
Soaking jugs of nappy ale, mild and stale.

Now all the mob from the town and court,
Came for to see this hotch potch sport;
Now all the mob from the town and the court,
Came for to see this hotch potch sport;
To see this famous play, which ran both night and day,
Call'd the Beggar's Opera – Oh! brave Gay![13]

The winter of 1727–8 also saw Fielding's début as a satiric poet. On 30 January – five days after the event at the Opera House in the Haymarket that occasioned it – James Roberts, who had recently published Fielding's verses on the Coronation, issued a poem in hudibrastics, entitled *The Masquerade*, purporting to have come from the pen of "Lemuel Gulliver, Poet Laureat to the King of Lilliput." It was inscribed, appropriately, "to C[oun]t H[ei]d[e]g[ge]r" – that is, to the notorious John James Heidegger (by courtesy called "Count"), universally acknowledged to be the ugliest man in England and the principal promoter of the fashionable Venetian balls that Fielding always satirized as a licentious entertainment. In *Tom Jones* (XIII.vii), for instance, Fielding calls Heidegger "the great *Arbiter Deliciarum*, the great High-Priest of Pleasure." But though a Middlesex grand jury presented Heidegger in 1729 as "the principal promoter of vice and immorality" in the metropolis, his masquerades continued to be popular, and he himself was honored by being appointed Master of the Revels to the King. A rollicking, often indelicate satire of nearly 400 lines, *The Masquerade* might never have been recognized as Fielding's had it not been reissued in 1755 as an appendix to the authorized edition of *The Grub-Street Opera*.

···◀ iv ◀···

No sooner was Fielding's career as a "Poet" (as he liked to call himself) well and truly launched in this way – his first comedy staged, his first poem published – than he removed himself as far as possible from the scene of these promising literary achievements to resume formal study of the classics at the University of Leyden in Holland. This abrupt change in course seems odd – especially considering how reluctant a young writer with Fielding's rakish inclinations would presumably be to absent himself from London, the glittering center of wit and gaiety. Did Edmund want him out of town? Perhaps Fielding's own experience informs Young Kennel's remark in *The Fathers* (V.ii): "I lived with ... my grandmother, till I was seventeen, and then my father stole me away from her, and sent me abroad."

But then again perhaps not: Young Kennel in no other way resembles his author; and if Edmund wanted to complete his son's education by sending him abroad to study and to travel, he had no wish to pay his bills. To understand Fielding's paradoxical character, we must remember that he had a mind as well as passions and appetites. "Curiosity" is the mental faculty he celebrates, albeit facetiously, at the opening of *The Masquerade*: "To this ... whate'er we know/In arts or sciences, we owe. ... From this we borrow hopes of greater/ Discoveries of madam Nature." The epigraph he chose for *Tom Jones* is Horace's description of Ulysses: *Mores hominum multorum vidit* ("he saw the wide world, its ways and cities all"); accordingly, in that great work (XIII.i) "Experience" is the last of the four Muses he invokes as essential to the author who would treat that most exacting of subjects, Human Nature. Her sister Muse, moreover, is "Learning (for without thy Assistance nothing pure, nothing correct, can Genius produce). ... Open thy *Maeonian* and thy *Mantuan* Coffers, with whatever else includes thy Philosophic, thy Poetic, and thy Historical Treasures, whether with *Greek* or *Roman* Characters thou hast chosen to inscribe the ponderous Chests." Learning and Experience distinguish Fielding's best work, whether as novelist or as magistrate; and he understood that – unlike the other pair of Muses, Genius and Humanity, which also inspired him – these did not offer their favors unearned. Perhaps, then, Fielding's decision to embark for Leyden is less puzzling than it seems at first glance. He had the wit to see that his apprenticeship to his craft was still far from complete – that merely clever imitations of Cibber and Farquhar, not to mention lame ones of Butler and Swift, were not good enough.

Whatever his motive for going, he was soon at Leyden, possibly having made the journey from London in the same manner as Jonathan Wild and Mrs. Heartfree (II.ix–x), by taking a coach to Harwich and from there sailing to Rotterdam. By 16 March 1728 (N.S.), just ten days after the publication of *Love in Several Masques*, he had taken lodgings in a hotel called the Castle of Antwerp and was ready to enroll at the University as a student of literature. The entry in the Admissions Register reads as follows:

16 Martii *1728* Henricus Fielding, Anglus, annor. 20 Litt. Stud., bot nog toe in het Cast. van Antw.[14]

By thus formally enrolling in the University, Fielding became eligible to attend lectures and otherwise to receive instruction. What may have seemed no less desirable, since he had reached the necessary age of twenty, he would also be allowed, duty free, a tun of wine a year, as well as half a barrel of beer per month.[15] One further privilege, which he came to appreciate, was that in the event of his misbehaving he would be exempt from prosecution in the civil courts, being charged instead before the University Court.

Fielding's choice of Leyden as the place to improve his knowledge of the classics was not unusual. Writing at a time a few years earlier when the threat of Jacobitism was real, Dudley Ryder observed that the University of Leyden, already well attended by his countrymen, would in future be "very much frequented by the English, ours having so little advantage for learning and besides extremely corrupt in principle, that the Whigs will be afraid to send their sons there."[16] A Protestant university founded in 1575 to commemorate a hard-won victory over the Spanish, Leyden rapidly became one of the most distinguished centers of learning in Europe. Because Holland was not only a wealthy nation, but one which prized liberty and freedom of thought, the University of Leyden attracted many of Europe's most illustrious intellectuals and scholars. Numbered among its professors had been the great humanists, Justus Lipsius and Joseph Scaliger, as well as Grotius and Heinsius and Gronovius. Fielding's library contained works by all these savants. In Fielding's time Herman Boerhave was Professor of Medicine and Joannes Jacobus Vitriarius of Law.

But it was Pieter Burmann, Professor of History, Eloquence, and Greek – or rather of "polite Literature," as Samuel Johnson put it more simply[17] – whom Fielding would have been closest to. Burmann was reputed to be an excellent teacher (his lectures, of course, were given in Latin); and his many learned editions of Latin authors – at least three of which Fielding owned[18] – spread his fame throughout Europe. These editions, *cum notis variorum*, Fielding facetiously recalled both in the Preface to *The Tragedy of Tragedies* (1731), where he assures his reader that "the great Professor *Burman*, hath stiled *Tom Thumb*, *Heroum omnium Tragicorum facilè Principem*," and in the notes, where he parodies his commentary.[19] But, though Burmann is today esteemed more for his erudition and accuracy than for his critical powers, so fine a classicist as Dr. Johnson nevertheless respected him as a "useful" scholar; and he was especially proficient at teaching Latin composition, a subject in which Fielding already had an excellent grounding from his schooldays at Eton.

We have no certain knowledge of the subjects Fielding studied at Leyden. For that matter, it would be rash to assume that he was especially diligent in attending lectures and preparing the required exercises. He devoted some of his time there to such extracurricular matters as the drafting of a new comedy, *Don Quixote in England*,[20] inspired perhaps by the sight of so many windmills to tilt at. Moreover, he would not have time enough to progress very far in his studies; he spent no more than a few months in residence at Leyden. We can merely point to the kinds of subjects he could have studied there had he chosen to take advantage of the opportunities offered.

At Leyden in the eighteenth century professors of literature generally devoted little attention to Greek, but stressed instead three aspects of Latin studies: history, Roman antiquities, and the interpretation of texts.[21] This latter discipline consisted, first of all, in an intensive training in Latin style. Students attended to the matter of the texts (particularly the historians), as well as to the style; but they were seldom required to interpret the texts as literature, or to consider the history of literature. As for the theory of style that prevailed, the principles of Anti-Ciceronianism had been advocated at Leyden from the beginning: there, in other words, "the fight for a free and personal Latin style" had been won.[22] It is a point worth making; for, as with most of the great stylists in our own language from Addison to Waugh, "the lusty ease" of Fielding's "fine English," to use George Eliot's phrase,[23] owes its qualities of clarity and precision, of rational order and symmetrical form, to his mastery of Latin.

But there was more than Latin to be learned at Leyden in Fielding's day. Attracted not only by the reputation of its faculty and library, but by the neatness and elegance of the city itself, students came there in great numbers from every corner of Europe. Besides the English and the Scots, there were Poles and Hungarians, Germans and French, Swedes and Danes – even some Turks pretending to be Greeks; among them were princes and nobility of every degree.[24] Here, too, was the famous printing house of the Elzevirs, and the no less celebrated Physic Garden, in which grew medicinal herbs and simples of every variety. From this garden a gallery, itself filled with rareties, led to a hall called the Indian Cabinet in which were preserved innumerable curiosities, fetuses and mummies being, apparently, the least *outré*: there one would find, for example, "a vegetable Priapus," a winged cat, the hand of a mermaid, a monster that had issued from a hen's egg. And just across the canal the famous Hall of Anatomy contained still more grotesque specimens to astonish the curious – skeletons of all sorts, a cow anatomized "with a man upon her, who had committed uncleanness with her."[25] Having witnessed such spectacles as these, Fielding would ever afterwards scorn the "virtuosi," whose study was not, as they claimed, "natural Philosophy," but "rather *unnatural*, which deals in the Wonderful, and knows nothing of Nature, except her Monsters and Imperfections."[26] Such men, he scoffed, were "*Triflers*" who busied themselves "in hunting after Monsters of every Kind, as if they were at Enmity with Nature, and desirous of exposing all her Errors."[27]

In this way only – that is, in incidental remarks or witticisms interjected into his writings on other subjects – does Fielding ever comment upon his experience of Holland and the Dutch. Most of these observations are so commonplace they might have been made by one who had never visited the country: the rough manners of Dutch boors;[28] the preoccupation of Dutchmen with trade and "*Gelt*";[29] their clumsiness, which makes them unlikely "dancing-masters";[30] their lack not only of wit, but of even a rudimentary sense of humor, especially among the burgomasters of Amsterdam.[31] At times, however, his allusions are fresher than this, suggesting that they originate in personal experience: the fondness of the Dutch for "waterzuche" (boiled perch served in its own liquor);[32] the unsavory odors of their coffee-houses;[33] the wiles of "a Dutch lady of pleasure" and the abundance of "bawdy houses" in Amsterdam;[34] the impertinence of Dutch landlords[35] – an observation which, as we shall see, may only mean that the landlords expected to be paid for the lodgings they let.

Fielding, if he was not quite xenophobic, hardly ever preferred the customs of other countries to those of his native England. But he was not invariably critical of Dutch ways. He was, for example, very favorably impressed with their civil institutions. Unlike England, Holland was a country where law and order prevailed, and where the individual citizen, of whatever degree, understood his obligation to the polity as a whole. Like Justice Worthy in *Rape upon Rape* (V.v), Fielding would increasingly "long to see the time when here, as in *Holland*, the Traveller may walk unmolested, and carry his Riches openly with him." Adding to the wonder, this sense of safety in the streets had been achieved despite the fact that Dutch laborers worked "much cheaper" than the English.[36] In contrast to the licentiousness of the English press, he admired the "Severity" with which the Dutch prohibited "Libels" against their governors.[37] And at the end of his life, he was convinced that capital punishment in England would be more effectual as a deterrent against crime if, instead of allowing the grotesque public spectacle of a hanging-day at Tyburn, Parliament substituted a grimmer ceremony after the Dutch example. Fielding seems to have witnessed one such execution in Holland, which, conducted in an "incredibly solemn" manner, was "performed in the Area before the Stadthouse, and attended by all the Magistrates. The Effect of this Solemnity," he remarked, "is inconceivable to those who have not observed it in others, or felt it in themselves."[38]

Fielding's experience of Holland was not, of course, limited to the city of Leyden. Like Wild and Mrs. Heartfree, he would have visited Rotterdam, which was so much the hub of commerce between Britain and the Netherlands that it was called "*Little London*."[39] And he several times alludes to the customs and characters of the citizens of Amsterdam. In *Tom Jones* (XIII.i) he refers in an amusing passage to the *trekschuit* – a large, covered canal boat, drawn by horses, which was the principal means of travel in Holland. In another passage, he vividly recalls one of the disadvantages for the traveler who visits The Hague in summer. As the travelers in *A Journey from This World to the Next* (I.ii) approach the City of Diseases:

> a most offensive Smell began to invade our Nostrils. This very much resembled the Savour, which Travellers, in Summer, perceive at their Approach to that beautiful Village of the *Hague*, arising from those delicious Canals, which, as they consist of standing Water, do at that time emit odours greatly agreeable to a *Dutch* Taste, but not so pleasant to any other. Those Perfumes, with the Assistance of a fair Wind, begin to affect Persons of quick olfactory Nerves at a League's distance, and increase gradually as you approach.

This passage, associating the stench of the Dutch canals in hot weather with the City of Diseases, suggests a compelling reason why Fielding would not have wished to remain in Holland during the summer months. Leyden was even more notorious than The Hague for these noxious summertime conditions – noxious, because it was commonly believed that the effluvia from the stagnant waters bred contagious diseases.[40] Probably, then, the summer journey to The Hague that Fielding recalled in later years took place early in July 1728 (N.S.), as, after little more than three months abroad, he left Leyden for home.

···◄◖ V ◗►···

Before resuming his studies late the following winter, Fielding's "hard Fates" returned him to the house his father leased for him at Upton Grey. His verses describing that less than idyllic place were "Written to a young Lady" (whom he calls "Rosalinda") "in the Year 1728" – written, to be more specific, in the late summer or early autumn of that year: hence his allusions in the poem to haystacks and bottle-ricks, and to fruit trees that bear no fruit.

Until recently, we have known nothing more of Fielding's movements and activities during the interval of more than half a year between his visits to the Continent. It now seems likely, however, that in the summer of 1728 Fielding first tried his hand at political journalism with a pair of highly entertaining pieces. Both were published in Opposition papers and both are mildly satirical of the Prime Minister, Sir Robert Walpole.[41] The first of these, a rousing ballad entitled "The Norfolk Lanthorn" (to be sung to the tune of "Which nobody can deny"), appeared anonymously in *The Craftsman* on 20 July 1728; the second, an essay on "the Benefit of Laughing," was published a fortnight later in *Mist's Weekly Journal* for 3 August.

Introducing the ballad, Fielding informs the reader that he has just arrived in town from Norfolk, where, having visited Walpole's country seat at Houghton, he was impressed by "the Magnificence" of the house and its costly furnishings. What delighted him most, however, was "the Sight of an huge and most sumptuous LANTHORN, which immediately struck my Eyes, upon entering the *great Hall*." This lantern – which did indeed hang in the Hall at Houghton (it was made of copper-gilt and held eighteen candles) – he "could not forbear celebrating" in six stanzas which wittily transform it into an emblem of the minister's peculiar way of letting his light shine before men: declaring in its hugeness and opulence both the poverty of Walpole's taste and the riches he was amassing at his country's expense.

Compared to most other satires of the period, Fielding's ballad is playful and brisk; it is meant rather to entertain its readers than seriously to wound Walpole. Nevertheless, slight a thing as it is, it instantly caught on. Nothing he had so far written caused anything like this commotion. While choruses of Tories and disaffected Whigs sang the ballad heartily in the coffee-houses and taverns where they congregated, Walpole's journalists tried to cry it down. The *Daily Journal* (24 July) protested that the balladeer had said the thing that was not, that Houghton was in fact a monument to the minister's modesty and good taste; the *London Journal* (27 July) retaliated with a ballad of its own, if not as clever as Fielding's. And in a leader of the same date "Roger Manley" in the *British Journal* used the occasion to denounce the Opposition for abusing the liberty of the press in personal libels against his patron: "Men must be treated as *being what they are*; and we cannot but despise the *little paultry Jingles* of a certain *Writer* on a certain *Lanthorn*."

Fielding's probable authorship of "The Norfolk Lanthorn" could be the clue we have needed to fit together the pieces of a puzzling contemporary account of his early relations with Walpole. Some years later, while Fielding was editing the anti-ministerial journal *The Champion*, one of Walpole's apologists declared that, at a time before he "set up for a Play-Writer," Fielding had behaved ungratefully to the minister. Fielding, the writer insists,

is a strong Instance of Ingratitude to the Ministry, as he lies under the strongest Obligations to Sir R[obe]rt W[alpo]le, whom he now

treats with a Strain of Insolence and Scurrility superior to any other
Paper ever went before. ... I have some Reasons to know particular
Obligations he lies under to the Minister, who once generously reliev'd
him by sending him a considerable Supply of ready Money when he
was arrested in a Country-Town some Distance from *London*, and
must have rotted in Prison had it not been for this Generosity in the
Minister. Soon after he libelled him personally in a Satyr, and next
Week had the Impudence to appear at his *Levee*. Upon Sir *R[ober]t*'s
taxing him with his Ingratitude, and asking him why he had wrote
so and so; he answered very readily, *that he wrote that he might eat*.
However Sir *R[ober]t* still continued his Generosity to him, till he
grew quite abandon'd to all Sense of Shame. He then set up for a
Play-Writer.[42]

Though coming from an unfriendly source, this circumstantial
account has the ring of authenticity. Certainly, we cannot automatically
dismiss as malicious gossip the assertion that Fielding as a youth cooled
his heels in a jail: he spent too much time before magistrates explaining
the various brawls and violent altercations his hot temper involved him
in. But even those who are prepared to think there may be more truth
than slander in the above anecdote have found it puzzling. Which
"Country-Town" is meant? Why, if the escapade took place in Fielding's usual rural haunts of Dorset, Hampshire, Wiltshire, should he
send for aid to Walpole instead of applying to his friends and relations
in the West Country? Which of Fielding's satires can the writer be
alluding to, when the only one he is known to have published before
setting up in earnest as a playwright in 1730 is *The Masquerade*, a poem
ridiculing not Walpole but a fashionable diversion of the Town?

Fielding's authorship of "The Norfolk Lanthorn" would enable us
to offer plausible solutions to each of these puzzles. The author of the
ballad (published on 20 July 1728) states that he has "just returned"
from Norfolk, where he has seen the curiosities of Walpole's "*Palace*,"
Houghton Hall – so, too, may Fielding have done if he returned from
Holland for the summer by way of Harwich. Walpole was residing at
Houghton for a fortnight or so in early July 1728;[43] and if Lady Mary's
mischievous cousin had become embroiled in yet another brush with
the law while in the vicinity, he may well have appealed to Lady Mary's
most powerful friend to bail him out.[44] "The Norfolk Lanthorn," which
embarrassed Walpole and his party, would fit the description of the
"Satyr" in which Fielding is said to have "libelled" the minister
"personally"; that the author of the ballad had defamed Walpole
personally in this way was the very point of "Roger Manley's" attack
on the poem. Furthermore, since the minister, like the author of the
satire, returned to town shortly before "The Norfolk Lanthorn" was

published – he arrived in London on 16 July and set out at once to establish himself at Hampton Court for the summer – he might well have had occasion at his levee the following week to upbraid Fielding for his ingratitude. Finally, if Fielding's authorship of the essay in *Mist's Weekly Journal* (3 August) were suspected, the remaining details of the account also fall into place, since Walpole, even after the "Satyr," is said to have continued befriending Fielding "till he grew quite abandon'd to all Sense of Shame." All this is conjecture; but it has the virtue of squaring more nearly than any other explanation with the circumstances cited by the author of the anecdote.

Though it caused less of a stir in political circles than the ballad on Walpole's lantern, the essay on "the Benefit of Laughing" that appeared anonymously in *Mist's Weekly Journal* a fortnight later is a far better and far more significant piece. Except for the few introductory sentences prefixed to *Love in Several Masques* and his poems, this represents Fielding's first published work in prose – a work, indeed, in that inimitable vein of humor for which there had been no exact precedent in English (Swift's manner is too arch and biting, Steele's too elegant), and which would one day ensure his reputation as one of England's greatest comic authors. Fielding here assumes the guise of a peculiar sort of physician – one who proposes "to cure all Diseases incident to the Mind and Body of Man by a *Laugh*." Though he had only recently turned twenty-one, Fielding was already working toward that theory of comic laughter which he later set forth in the famous Preface to *Joseph Andrews*, where, adapting to comedy Aristotle's medical metaphor of a tragic *catharsis* purging the audience of the passions of fear and pity, he declares that burlesque

> contributes more to exquisite Mirth and Laughter than any other; and these are probably more wholesome Physic for the Mind, and conduce better to purge away Spleen, Melancholy and ill Affections, than is generally imagined. Nay, I will appeal to common Observation, whether the same Companies are not found more full of Good-Humour and Benevolence, after they have been sweeten'd for two or three Hours with Entertainments of this kind, than when soured by a Tragedy or grave Lecture.

In this his début as a prose humorist Fielding literally posed as a doctor of mirth who understands the therapeutic properties of laughter and applies them, hilariously, to good effect. Though the essay ends with a joke or two cracked at Walpole's expense (such would be the price exacted by Mist for publishing the piece), Fielding's essay is important not so much for anything it may reveal about his politics of the time, but for its place as a kind of overture to the comic masterpieces to come.

The essay on "the Benefit of Laughing" concludes with the good doctor in a particularly hopeful mood; for, though he is soon "to cross the Channel," he has had a promise from a "certain Person of Interest" (i.e., Walpole) "to make me Physician to some Body [Walpole again] the first Vacancy." Was this mere banter on Fielding's part; or, as the author of the anecdote in the *Historical View* would have it, had he been impudent enough to attend the minister's levee and solicit his patronage at the very time he was, however playfully, roasting him in the Opposition press? If so, it would hardly be surprising if Walpole discontinued his favors, or if, as Fielding elsewhere complained, the promises Great Men made him often proved empty.

Nothing but the lack of money can have caused him to submit that summer to a disagreeable rustication among the "Docks and Nettles" of Upton Grey. On 22 April of this year he reached his majority and was at last, officially, his own man, entitled to his share of the profits from the East Stour farm. Since that share, however, was a paltry one-sixth part of £120 a year, it would not see him very far. That he felt it necessary, as late as October, to obtain official certification of his dates of birth and baptism[45] may also indicate that some legal technicality prevented him from receiving even this small legacy at once.

But by October he was probably back in town, suffering from his most recent disappointment in love. So it seems from the poem, "To Euthalia, Written in the Year 1728." Like most of the other young women with whom Fielding flirts in the verse of this early period, "Euthalia" can be known today only by her attributes. Since he praises her not only for her loveliness but for "The various Beauties of her perfect Mind" – for her "Learning" and her "Numbers," for instance – she was presumably something of a poet and bluestocking. She has, however, spurned him, forcing him to fly in vain "to Books, to Wine or Women" to lose his despair. What suggests that these lines were composed in town rather than in Hampshire is that among the women he visits for consolation are "Rosalinda," the no longer absent beauty to whom he had addressed his description of Upton Grey, and the witty "Sappho" – that is, of course, Lady Mary, who was then residing at Twickenham.

It appears, then, that the elation he felt in early summer on returning to England as a young man who had reached his majority and seen something of the world – a mood suggested by the frolicsome tone of his ballad on the "Norfolk lanthorn" and by the hilarity of the essay on laughing – soon gave way to less agreeable feelings. Only thoughts of "Rosalinda" and "happier Days" – and the small satisfaction of venting his irritation in sarcastic verses about the place – could make Upton Grey supportable. And his lack of success with "Euthalia"

left him even more dissatisfied, "Burning with Love, tormented with
Despair."

His spirits probably were not much lifted by an event that took place
a few weeks before he again left for Leyden. Sometime during the
second week of January 1728/9, Fielding's father took his third wife.
She was Eleanor Hill, a well-to-do widow from Salisbury; like Edmund,
who was about to turn forty-nine, she is described in the marriage
license as "aged above forty years."[46] She is said to have had a jointure
of £500 per year. Fielding's attitude toward his father's polygamous
inclinations may be sensed, perhaps, in *The Covent-Garden Journal* (4
February 1752), where he prints a facetious Latin epigram "made by
a Gentleman of Distinction on his third Marriage," and supplies his
own version in English:

> *Three Times I took for better and for worse,*
> *A Bed-Fellow, a Fortune, and a Nurse:*
> *How blest the State, which such good Things produce!*
> *How dear that Sex which serves such various Use!*

···➤ vi ➤···

Not long after his father's marriage, Fielding was again on his way to
Leyden. This time he may have meant to extend his travels to other
parts of Europe. On 22 February 1729 (N.S.) his name was entered in
the annual "Recensiones" of the University, where it is recorded that
he was living at the house of one Jan Oson.[47]

Immediately he began to run up debts he left unpaid. On 28 July
1730 (N.S.), in a newly discovered document that sheds the first real
light we have had on Fielding's Leyden experience,[48] two of his creditors
entered a complaint against him before the University Court – an
august body presided over by the Rector of the University and including
four professors (representing the several faculties), four burgomasters
of the town, and two councilmen. Indeed, two of the professors who
sat in judgment on Fielding were among the most distinguished men
in Europe: Herman Boerhave (representing the Faculty of Medicine)
and Joannes Jacobus Vitriarius (representing the Faculty of Law). The
original action against Fielding was brought by Pieter Fernandez, a
fellow student whom he had employed to tutor him in Italian; Fernandez was seconded in his suit by Fielding's landlord, Jan Oson, a
shoemaker by trade. The sums demanded were not especially large:
Fernandez claimed 18:18 guilders (about £1.14.4 in sterling) for three
months of instruction; Oson wanted 130 guilders (about £11.16.4) for

rent for the room Fielding let and for certain unspecified loans. But word of Fielding's dereliction spread quickly, and other creditors took action, among them his booksellers, the brothers Jan and Hermann Verbeek, who specialized in publishing learned works.[49] It is clear from this document that Fielding, perhaps apprehensive that he was about to be prosecuted for these debts, abandoned his "goods" in his lodgings and by 30 April 1729 (N.S.) had left Leyden never to return. It was on that date that Fernandez, with permission of the Rector, seized Fielding's property then in Jan Oson's custody.

Having waited "about two years" (the phrase appears to be a legal formula and need not refer to an exact period) for Fielding to appear and settle his accounts, the plaintiffs on 28 July 1730 (N.S.) asked the Court to permit them to make an inventory of his goods and to sell them, applying the money toward payment of the debts. Satisfied of the validity of the claims against Fielding, the Court granted the suit. On 16 January 1731 (N.S.), after the bells of the University had been rung, the Beadle mounted the steps of the Town Hall to denounce Fielding and to advise any others who had claims against him to inform the Secretary of the University.

Murphy, devoting a single muddled sentence to Fielding's Leyden experience, stated that, his "remittances failing, he was obliged to return to London." But is it true that when he left Leyden, Fielding went directly home? Or did he use this opportunity in the fashionable way, completing his education by making the tour of Europe? That he meant to extend his travels is indicated by the three months he spent in Leyden trying to add Italian to the French he already had. Of course his skipping town before paying his creditors suggests that he may have had to change his plans for lack of money. There is, moreover, an uncomfortably close parallel between what we now know of Fielding's relationship with Jan Oson and that of Harry Luckless with Mrs. Moneywood, his landlady in *The Author's Farce* (I.i–ii), who has not been paid her rent for three months and who will not let Luckless walk out of her doors without leaving behind his "Moveables," including his books.

On the other hand, his leaving his belongings behind when he left Leyden is consistent with the friendlier view that he intended to return to settle his accounts and reclaim his goods when his travels were finished. Like most gentlemen of his day, Fielding was dilatory about paying bills. Also consistent with such an interpretation is the fact that, though the Rector permitted Fernandez to seize Fielding's property on 30 April 1729 (N.S.), the Court would not actually entertain a suit against him for more than a year afterward. Fernandez obviously suspected the worst when Fielding left town. But Fielding may have been less culpable in the matter than appears at first glance: intending to return to Leyden, he may have hired his venal *valet à louage* and postilion (to whom the Man of the Hill refers in *Tom Jones* [VIII.xv]) and set off on his travels; and only then, in the course of the tour, been compelled to change his plans.

I am inclined to think that this was the case, but the evidence is inconclusive. One can say, negatively, that during this entire year there is not a sign of Fielding's presence in England. Some passages in his works are also suggestive. In *The Temple Beau* (I.v), which he wrote this year, Veromil, who has just returned from his travels, remarks to Valentine: "I . . . made the Tour of *France* and *Italy*. I intended to visit *Germany*; but on my Return to *Paris*, I there received the News of my Father's Death," who has disinherited him. Is Veromil recalling here his author's own experience abroad – except, of course, that the reference to his father would be an exaggerated rendering of Fielding's own attitude toward Edmund, his bitterness not only over the "failing remittances" of which Murphy speaks, but over the impecunious state he found himself in owing to his father's neglecting to support him in a style suitable for the eldest son and heir of a gentleman? In *The Fathers* (III.ii, V.ii) Young Kennel's travels have been similarly limited to France and Italy: in France he has visited Paris, Versailles, Boulogne, and Orléans – in which city he saw "one of the largest men I ever saw in my life; I believe he was about eight foot high"; in Italy he has been to Venice and Rome.

The novels, as well as his essays, allude to the experiences of English travelers abroad, particularly those who have seen France and Italy. In *Joseph Andrews* (II.v) Fielding ridicules the affectations of a gentleman who has visited Viterbo and can speak a few words of broken Italian; in *Amelia* (III.viii–x) he takes his heroine to Montpellier, by way of Marseilles, to recover her health, and to Paris, briefly, on her way home. Here, in one of the rare instances in which Fielding's generalizations about a foreign country seem based on personal experience, he uses the occasion to have Booth reflect on the manners of the French:

> we began to pass our Time very pleasantly at *Montpelier*: for the greatest Enemy to the *French* will acknowledge, that they are the best People in the World to live amongst for a little while. . . . Being a Stranger among them entitles you to the better Place, and to the greater Degree of Civility; and if you wear but the Appearance of a Gentleman, they never suspect you are not one. Their Friendship indeed seldom extends so far as their Purse.

In *Tom Jones* (VIII.xv) the Man of the Hill, misanthrope that he is, comments sourly on human nature as it reveals itself in the landlords of Italy and France (and of Germany and Holland as well); he has attended a carnival at Venice, and has observed Spaniards and Turks in their native lands. Again, however, it is only his opinion of the French that seems to have originated in his author's first-hand observation (though we need not attribute the Old Man's petulance to Fielding):

> But of all the People I ever saw, Heaven defend me from the *French*. With their damned Prate and Civilities, and doing the Honour of their Nation to Strangers, (as they are pleased to call it) but indeed setting forth their own Vanity; they are so troublesome, that I had infinitely rather pass my Life with the *Hottentots*, than set my Foot in *Paris* again.

Some years earlier, in an essay he (probably) contributed to *The Craftsman* (15 July 1738),[50] Fielding referred to himself, showing some friends the sights of Westminster Hall, as "a very good *Ciceroni*," and in a footnote glossed that word in a way that suggests he had experienced the good offices of the Italian original.

But it is a passage in the *Journal of a Voyage to Lisbon* that affords the strongest presumptive evidence that Fielding's travels in Europe ranged well beyond the waterways of Holland. His comments on the niggardly innkeeper Mrs. Francis suggest that he had had personal experience of her continental counterparts. Judging from the exorbitancy of her charges, he supposes Mrs. Francis had heard

> that it is a maxim with the principal innholders on the continent, to levy considerable sums on their guests, who travel with many horses and servants, though such guests should eat little or nothing in their houses. The method being, I believe, in such cases, to lay a capitation on the horses, and not on their masters. But she did not consider, that in most of these inns a very great degree of hunger, without any degree of delicacy, may be satisfied; and that in all such inns there is some appearance, at least, of provision, as well as of a man cook to dress it, one of the hostlers being always furnished with a cook's cap, waistecoat and apron, ready to attend gentlemen and ladies on their summons.

> ([14] July)

If, then, as seems likely, Fielding saw more of Europe while he was abroad than merely Holland alone, how much more did he see, and what impressions did he return home with? The observations on French manners by Booth and the Man of the Hill, together perhaps with Young Kennel's astonishment at the giant of Orléans, suggest that Fielding saw something of France. He may also, like Veromil and Young Kennel, have visited Italy. But these are as far as responsible inferences from the evidence can take us. In any event, his experiences abroad impressed him chiefly in a negative way — by enhancing his pride in the character, genius, and institutions of England, right down to her roast beef and her bulldogs. He scorned those travelers who, like Young Kennel in *The Fathers* or Bellarmine and the Italianate gentleman in *Joseph Andrews*, return from the Grand Tour not only unimproved intellectually or culturally, but having contracted a hearty contempt for their native land. The following from *The Craftsman* (28 June 1735) may serve as a summary of his views on the subject:

> all the *polite World*, at least, seem to be running mad with an Itch of *Strolling*; or, as They call it *Travelling*; but, instead of improving their Minds, by enquiring into the Constitutions and Governments of *other Nations*, They commonly reap no other Advantage from their Peregrinations than squandering away their Estates, and coming home with an idle Contempt of the Manners and Customs of their *own Country*. I am very far from intending by This to condemn the Practice of *Travelling* in general, which is certainly one of the noblest Methods of Instruction, and from whence the greatest Men of Antiquity derived their Knowledge. Neither would I be thought to include all our *modern Gentlemen*, who have *travelled* in this Censure; having many illustrious Examples now before my Eyes, which demonstrate the *Advantages of seeing the World*; and I heartily wish, for the Honour and Interest of my Country, that there were much fewer Instances of the *contrary*.[51]

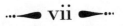

vii

Even if we suppose that Fielding continued his travels after leaving Leyden in April 1729, he probably had neither the desire nor the money to remain very long abroad. Exactly when he returned to England is not known, but he would be eager to be in London by September, before the start of the new theatrical season. He had substantial drafts of two plays, as well as an entire new comedy, ready to submit to the "Triumvirate" at Drury Lane. During his sojourn at Leyden in the spring of 1728 he had "sketched out" *Don Quixote in England* "into a few loose Scenes." At first, understandably intimidated by the task of recreating "Characters wherein the inimitable *Cervantes* so far excelled," he intended the work for his "private Amusement" only: "The Impossibility of going beyond, and the extreme Difficulty of keeping pace with him, were sufficient to infuse Despair into a very adventurous Author." In this opinion, Barton Booth and Cibber concurred when at last he found the courage to show them the piece.[52]

At about this time – for he tells us that it was "the third Dramatic Performance [he] ever attempted"[53] – Fielding had also begun drafting a five-act comedy, *The Wedding Day*, intending the parts of Millamour and Charlotte for Wilks and Mrs. Oldfield, both of whom had acted in *Love in Several Masques*. The new roles, he observed, dissatisfied with the piece, required the abilities of "that great Actor and Actress" to bring them off: "Characters of this Kind do, of all others, require most Support from the Actor, and lend the least Assistance to him." But though he intended *The Wedding Day* for Drury Lane, by the time he finished it, Mrs. Oldfield had died (in October 1730), and he had fallen out with Wilks – and with Cibber, too. The play was not ready to be heard until the season of 1730–1, when he read it not to the managers at Drury Lane, but to John Rich at the "New House" in Lincoln's Inn Fields.

Fielding's quarrel with Cibber and Wilks no doubt began in the autumn of 1729, in circumstances he recalled in *The Author's Farce*, where Marplay (Cibber) and his parrot Sparkish (Wilks) spurn a new play by the Author, whom Fielding names, transparently, "Harry Luckless." The abrupt reversal in Fielding's attitude toward the pair, whom he had complimented so warmly in the Preface to *Love in Several Masques*, is best explained by the fate of his most recent work, *The Temple Beau*, a comedy of intrigue in five acts. Because putting any new play into production meant giving the author a share of the proceeds, Cibber always needed compelling reasons to do so. These Fielding could no longer give: *Love in Several Masques* had hardly repaid the cost of staging it; and, with Lady Mary having fallen seriously ill in September and Walpole perhaps still smarting from those impudent satires of a year ago, he could no longer move the managers by applying pressure from above. Thus Act II, scene ii, of *The Author's Farce* opens with Marplay and Sparkish enjoying Luckless's disappointment:

MARPLAY. Ha, ha, ha!

SPARKISH. What dost think of the Play?

MARPLAY. It may be a very good one, for ought I know; but I know the Author has no Interest.

SPARKISH. Give me Interest, and rat the play. –

MARPLAY. Rather rat the Play which has no Interest. Interest sways as much in the theatre as at Court. – And you know it is not always the Companion of Merit in either.

The Temple Beau hadn't a chance at Drury Lane, and Fielding's bitterness toward the managers who spurned him is not hard to understand, particularly if he was made to feel that sneering contempt for his play with which Cibber on such occasions mortified young authors

as he handed them back their mutilated manuscript – a practice,
according to Thomas Davies, "he wantonly called *the choaking of singing
birds.*"[54]

To find a producer for *The Temple Beau* Fielding was obliged to
resort to the theatre recently constructed by Thomas Odell in Goodman's Fields, situated in London's East End. The theatre, which opened
on 31 October 1729 with a performance of Farquhar's *The Recruiting
Officer*, was hardly a setting Fielding considered worthy of his talents.
The company Odell assembled consisted "of raw unfledged players,"[55]
and the audience who attended were for the most part made up of an
obstreperous rabble of clerks and apprentices. By April 1730 the theatre
had become so obnoxious to the Citizens of Whitechapel that the Lord
Mayor moved to close it down. Even so, rowdy and unpolished as the
place might be, it was here at Goodman's Fields that Fielding's brief,
but remarkable, career as a dramatist began in earnest. Indeed, in the
view of the leading theatre historian of the period, Fielding "quickly
made himself the most dominant professional playwright in London
since Dryden."[56]

···◼ viii ◼►···

Before launching Fielding on that career we must consider the interesting implications of one of his non-dramatic works, begun soon after
he returned from the Continent, but never finished. Found recently
among Lady Mary's papers is Fielding's holograph draft of what might
have been (had he not given up on it and put it aside) one of the better
satires of the period.[57] It consists of more than 600 lines (parts of three
"Cantos") of mock-heroic verse done in imitation of Pope's *Dunciad*,
the first two versions of which caused a sensation when they were
published in 1728 and 1729. In this case, however, imitation was by no
means meant as flattery, for Fielding turned Pope's own weapons
against him, and against those other instruments of the Opposition,
Pope's friends Swift, Gay, and Bolingbroke, as well as the authors of
the two most virulent anti-ministerial journals of the period, *The
Craftsman* and *Fog's Weekly Journal*.[58] Pope appears in the poem as
Codrus, favorite son of the Goddess of Dulness and therefore friend to
"Popery" and "the God of Rhime," and foe to Walpole and King
George – foe, indeed, to the entire Royal Family, whom Fielding, in an
awkward strategy of praise, has Dulness laud one by one through a
passage of twenty-five lines. As the satire develops, Fielding, in parody
of the councils of the Greeks in the *Iliad*, introduces Pope's fellow

Scriblerians – Swift (Ochistes) and Gay (Ilar) – vying for superiority
with their colleagues in political mischief, Nicholas Amhurst (Caleb)
and Charles Molloy (Fog). Nor is John Rich (Plutus) forgotten, who,
having produced *The Beggar's Opera* early in 1728, had compounded
his offence by attempting to stage its sequel, *Polly*, a play considered
so obnoxious by the government that it was banned by the Lord
Chamberlain in December of that year. Against this lot, who represent
the Enemy in politics and literature, Fielding invokes the examples of
Walpole and King George, Shakespeare and Jonson, Congreve and
Wycherley, Milton and Prior – and, most especially, Addison: "Sense
and Religion taught his Skilful Pen/ The best of Criticks, and the best
of Men" (III.58–9).

As Dr. Grundy remarks, in all these ways Fielding's mock-*Dunciad*
mirrors Lady Mary's "prejudices most faithfully."[59] Indeed, Fielding
almost certainly undertook this work, the most ambitious poem he ever
attempted, as a further bid for her patronage, hoping as well, perhaps,
that through her offices he might be reinstated in Walpole's good graces.
Why, then, did he abandon the work? To answer that question would
require a clearer notion than is at present possible of the date and
circumstances of Fielding's composing it. Internal evidence points to a
period of composition no earlier than June 1729, but possibly as late
as January 1729/30.[60] It is also possible, judging from the satirical
allusion to Cibber's brazen-faced impudence (II.98–9), that Fielding
did not begin writing the poem until the rejection of his plays at Drury
Lane dampened his hopes for prospering in the theatre. But one would
then expect him to apply himself in earnest to finishing the work.
Perhaps Lady Mary's illness in the autumn discouraged him from
proceeding, or he may simply have lost interest when, after all, *The
Temple Beau* found a stage at Goodman's Fields. Or perhaps, in an
access of prudence, he came to understand that all he was likely to
achieve from such an unequal contest with Pope was a niche of his own
in the next edition of *The Dunciad*.

One thing is clear: he did not put the poem aside because he had
abandoned hopes of finding favor with Walpole. It was probably earlier
rather than later "in the Year 1730" that Fielding wrote the first of his
humorous, begging verse epistles "To the Right Honourable Sir Robert
Walpole." In that poem he refers to himself as "Your Bard" and angles,
however facetiously, for some government "*Sinecure*" – glancing wryly
at a poem by that name written by another of the minister's bards,
Joseph Mitchell, who hoped to be appointed governor of Duck Island
in St. James's Park. That Fielding's witty overtures of this kind had
so far proved ineffectual is suggested by his situation in the poem,
where he claims to be a greater man than Walpole because he is literally
more exalted, trapped as he is by dunning creditors in a fourth-floor

"Garret" from which he "can look down/ On the whole Street of
Arlington," where, on the west side, the minister had a house.

This setting, though it has been regarded as merely part of the
conventional *topos* of the Distressed Poet,[61] may in fact reflect Fielding's
actual circumstances, as so many of his fictions do. Not only does the
plight of Fielding in the poem square with the impecuniousness of his
surrogate "Harry Luckless" in *The Author's Farce*, which he was writing
in February and March 1729/30. At this same time Fielding's father
and newest stepmother held the lease on a house on the east side of
Dover Street, Mayfair[62] – perhaps the only location in town from which
one could look down, literally, from an upper room and scan the whole
of Arlington Street, but most particularly Walpole's house. If Fielding
found himself thus confined in an upper room of one of his father's
houses in Mayfair, what a galling reminder it would be of how meanly
Edmund provided for him. And how keenly aware he would be of the
power of Walpole to relieve his distress – for from his garret window
he could observe, just a few yards away, a tantalizing procession of
placemen and pensioners coming and going through the minister's door.

····➡ ix ◀····

The winter of 1729–30 may well have been the time when Fielding
quipped to Lady Mary that, his promised allowance never materializing,
he had to choose between becoming "a Hackney Writer or a Hackney
Coachman."[63] If so, before the season was over the choice he made must
have seemed a shrewd one. *The Temple Beau* opened at Goodman's
Fields on Monday, 26 January 1729/30 – the first new play Odell staged
there – and it ran through 5 February, nine consecutive performances
bringing Fielding three benefits. By the standards of his day, this was
by no means a contemptible showing; indeed, the comedy pleased the
public enough to warrant its being revived from time to time thereafter – again in February and for occasional performances in March,
June, and July. It was published on 2 February, without either a
Dedication or a Preface that might throw light on Fielding's circumstances, but with a Prologue by James Ralph (*c.* 1705–62) deploring
the decline of taste in a town where true comedy is neglected for farce
and deserving authors starve for want of patrons. Though the *beau
monde* of the West End ignored true merit, Ralph appealed to the
Citizens of Whitechapel to let "this Infant Stage" set a better example.

The Prologue to *The Temple Beau* is the first sign of Fielding's
friendship with Ralph,[64] with whom he would one day collaborate in
such ventures as the management of the Haymarket Theatre and the

editorship of *The Champion*. There is reason to think that, this early in their relationship, Ralph was so important to Fielding that he helped to shape his attitudes as a literary critic, even providing the seminal influence in the radical transformation soon to occur in Fielding's conception and practice of comedy. That Fielding should fall under the influence of a man who was in no obvious way his equal, either in genius, learning, wit, or understanding, is a tribute to Ralph's charm. He was by all accounts a lively and entertaining conversationalist, who – hard though it is to imagine from the evidence of his published works – possessed qualities of humor and eloquence that Fielding, himself a brilliant talker, would admire. He was also one of a circle of clever libertines and free-thinkers whose company in these early years Fielding found congenial.

Though born in England about 1705, Ralph spent most of his youth in America, where, as a merchant's clerk in Philadelphia, he became the close friend of Benjamin Franklin, whose *Autobiography* is the earliest and still one of the best sources of information about him. Ambitious to become a poet, he deserted his wife and daughter and accompanied Franklin to London in 1724. By the time Fielding made his acquaintance Ralph had sweated his reluctant Muse in some six or seven unremarkable poems, all but one of which are written in pseudo-Miltonic blank verse on such subjects as death and liberty and the numberless virtues of the Royal Family. In 1728, soon after Pope published *The Dunciad*, Ralph had the bad judgment to defend the dunces in a feeble satire called *Sawney*, in which he ridiculed not only Pope but his fellow Scriblerians, Swift and Gay – for which favor Ralph and *Night*, the poem he hoped would bring him fame, were accorded a kind of immortality the following year, when Pope made a place for them in *The Dunciad Variorum* (II.159–60):

> Silence, ye Wolves! while Ralph to Cynthia howls,
> And makes Night hideous – Answer him, ye Owls!

Perhaps it was this insult to his friend – as much as his desire to curry favor with Lady Mary – that prompted Fielding to follow Ralph's example by satirizing Pope and Swift and Gay in his mock-*Dunciad*. The literary and political attitudes Fielding expresses in that work reflect Ralph's own prejudices just as faithfully as they do Lady Mary's, in some ways, indeed, even more obviously – as, for example, the sustained ridicule of Pope for his slavish devotion to feeble "Rhime," despite the superior example of "Milton's Strength." Ralph may also have influenced Fielding in another, far more important, respect.[65] For in Ralph's *The Touch-Stone: or, Historical, Critical, Political, Philosophical, and Theological Essays on the reigning Diversions of the Town* (1728) Fielding would find the germ of the idea that led him to explore new possibilities of theme and form in the theatre. In that work – a comprehensive, sometimes witty, review of the present state of the diversions of the Town: opera, theatre, dancing, masquerades, bear-gardens, fairs, auctions, puppet shows, etc. – Ralph intended to correct the public taste, making *"Pleasures advantageous, by rational Courses"* (pp. xxii–xxiii). His way of doing so is by ironic praise, a form of travesty and burlesque, to expose the absurdity of the empty diversions which the Town preferred to more substantial entertainments. In *The Author's Farce* and *Tom Thumb* Fielding would take this hint – as well as what he learned from such other sources as Buckingham's *Rehearsal* and Gay's *Beggar's Opera* – and make of it a new kind of comedy, irregular in form, "emblematical" in method (to use the critic Sneerwell's term from *Pasquin*), and satiric in intent.

Just why, after the fairly successful run of *The Temple Beau* at Goodman's Fields, Fielding next threw in his lot with an even less reputable band of rogue comedians at the New Theatre in the Hay-market is unclear. It was not until 28 April 1730 that the Lord Mayor successfully petitioned to close down Goodman's Fields; and on the 2nd of that month, after Fielding had already moved, Odell staged a play by Ralph, *The Fashionable Lady: or, Harlequin's Opera*, which was similar in conception and intent to the irregular satirical drama that Fielding had also recently completed, *The Author's Farce*: both these plays ridicule the foibles of the Town and the decline in taste, and through the device of the rehearsal play – of "Harlequin's Opera" in Ralph's work, and of "an Operatical Puppet Shew, call'd, The Pleasures of the Town" in Fielding's – they might also be said to dramatize Ralph's satiric program in *The Touch-Stone*. In thus applying similar dramatic strategies for similar satiric purposes, the two friends may have worked closely together this spring. But Fielding far outstripped his mentor.

····••➤ X ◆━···

With *The Author's Farce*, first performed at the New Theatre in the Haymarket on Monday, 30 March 1730, Fielding found his true element as a dramatist. He also began his intermittent association with the theatre that provided the setting for most of his greatest hits, including (besides the present production of *The Author's Farce*) *Tom Thumb*, *Pasquin*, and *The Historical Register*. It was an improbable house to be distinguished in this way. Built in 1720 by John Potter, formerly a carpenter and scene painter for the Opera House across the way, the Little Haymarket was the smallest of the permanent London theatres and usually charged a shilling less per ticket than its rival houses. It was cheaply constructed and cheaply equipped, its entire stock of scenery, machines, and costumes being valued by Potter himself in 1735 at just £500 – a mere "pittance" according to the principal historian of the theatre.[66]

In several respects, it was not a conventional theatre at all. It had no manager in the usual sense and no regular company of actors. Potter leased the theatre to various performers on an *ad hoc* basis, though he ultimately had control over the sort of fare offered on his stage, which for the first eight years of its existence was given over to performances by traveling French comedians, juggling acts, concerts, and the like. After the extraordinary success of *The Beggar's Opera* at Lincoln's Inn Fields, however, those who leased Potter's theatre – for the most part they were companies of freelance actors or individual authors whose plays had been rejected elsewhere – began catering to more legitimate tastes. Even so, the Little Haymarket continued to be the venue for an unconventional variety of new irregular and experimental pieces, often with risky political implications which, however popular such impudence was with audiences who relished topical satire, would not be countenanced by the prudent managers of the patent threatres. Fielding's attempts at regular comedy having failed to please Cibber and the Town, he turned now, in a cynical humor, to these surprising experimental modes. Though the details of his agreement with Potter and the comedians at the Little Haymarket are not known, Fielding probably accepted a percentage of the profits in lieu of author's benefits.[67] No doubt he did so because he hadn't money enough to guarantee expenses.

The Author's Farce: and the Pleasures of the Town was his first experiment in the irregular comic modes of farce and burlesque, the ballad opera and the rehearsal play, where his true genius as a playwright at last found scope. He had a talent for a kind of pointed, inventive foolery that audiences had not seen on stage before – a talent for ridicule and brisk dialogue, for deft and emblematic characterization, and for devising absurd yet expressionistic plots that have scarcely been matched in the experimental theatre of our own century: actors strutting and squeaking about the stage as life-size puppets; Arthurian characters translated into the wonderland of pigmies and giants that Gulliver recently explored and there made to speak the fustian of half a hundred overblown tragedies; Don Quixote and Sancho set down in an English country town at election time. It must be said that he did not move eagerly in these new directions. He would have preferred that his regular comedies had succeeded; and before the year was out he returned to the five-act form twice more, packing it indeed with weighty matter beyond what the Town could bear. Stretching the forms he inherited to the limits – and sometimes, by stretching them beyond their limits, creating new forms altogether – would ever be Fielding's way as an author. It is an ambition that only a master craftsman with something to say would entertain.

But the public preferred gaping at tumblers and puppet shows, or swooning over castrati at the opera. Harry Luckless in *The Author's Farce* is Fielding's projection of himself and his own circumstances in the winter of 1729–30 – hounded by his landlady; sick of his poverty, "the most abominable Distemper"; his play spurned by the managers at Drury Lane, who had been long enough in the "Trade" to "know what Goods will best please the Town"; his only hope lying now in the success of a puppet show. For Fielding, like Luckless, took the advice he put into the mouth of Witmore in the play:

> 'Sdeath! In an Age of Learning and true Politeness, where a Man might succeed by his Merit, it wou'd be an Encouragement. – But now, when Party and Prejudice carry all before them, when Learning is decried, Wit not understood, when the Theatres are Puppet-Shows, and the Comedians Ballad-Singers: When Fools lead the Town, wou'd a Man think to thrive by his Wit? – If you must write, write Nonsense, write Opera's, write Entertainments ... and you may meet with Encouragement enough.
>
> (I.v)

It would be more accurate to say that Fielding *seemed* to take this advice; for though *The Author's Farce* is a puppet show comprising every inane entertainment the Town could hope for – the altercations of Punch and Joan, the antics of Somebody and Nobody, singing and dancing and much more – it is a puppet show with a difference. Fielding's puppets are not the usual ones displayed by such puppetmasters as Isaac Fawkes at his booth in fairtime: wooden figures full five feet tall, moved by wires and made to speak the master's words in high-pitched tones. As if in some surrealist drama of Ionesco, Fielding's puppets are played by actors who, as they pass before the throne of Nonsense, express in their rigid motions and squeaking voices the very essence of those empty "Pleasures of the Town" which have driven legitimate drama from the stage. They are all here in their emblematical guises: Edmund Curll, the scandalous bookseller (Curry), Francesco Bernardi Senesino, the popular castrato (Signior Opera), Lewis Theobald, the hero of *The Dunciad* (Don Tragedio), Cibber again (Sir Farcical Comic), John Henley, the zany priest who preached nonsense from his tub for a shilling (Dr. Orator), John Rich, manager of Lincoln's Inn Fields and the principal Harlequin of the age (Monsieur Pantomime), Eliza Haywood, the romance-writer loose of life and pen (Mrs. Novel), the card-playing demi-rep Mrs. Kingcall, and the censorious Presbyterian parson, Murdertext. By the end of the play, to complete the confusion of boundaries and identities, the puppets merge imperceptibly with the characters in the frame play – with Luckless and Harriet his love, the landlady and the constable and the parson, who instead of closing down the show falls in love with the puppet Mrs. Novel; indeed, Punch and Joan themselves prove to be brother and sister to Luckless and Harriet. To top all off the audience is treated to a spectacle not to be attempted again on stage until 1981 – an epilogue spoken by a cat.

It is all good fun, of course. But Fielding, "Bred in *Democritus* his laughing Schools," as the Prologue assures us, uses ridicule in the effort to expose and arrest the decline of rational entertainment. Like Swift, who often used a similar strategy, Fielding took a contemporary situation already true in metaphor and rendered that metaphor literally on stage.

> Beneath the Tragick or the Comick Name,
> Farces and Puppet-shows ne'er miss of Fame.
> Since then, in borrow'd Dress, they've pleased the Town;
> Condemn them not, appearing in their own.

The Author's Farce was the first of Fielding's great "hits" as a playwright. Opening on 30 March 1730, it held the stage at the Little Haymarket throughout April, May, and June, ending on Friday, 3 July, with the forty-second performance – the season had been stretched to the limit to let it play as long as there was anyone left in town to pay to see it. Assisted, to be sure, by the no less remarkable success of *Tom Thumb*, with which it was often paired after 24 April, *The Author's Farce* enjoyed the most dazzling run of any new play since *The Beggar's Opera*. Even then it was revived – or rather the "Puppet Shew" was, "No Wires, all alive" – at the time of Bartholomew Fair in August;[68] and when the new season began in the autumn, the Little Haymarket opened its doors on 21 October with a proven "winner": "that celebrated Performance, call'd, The Author's Farce, and the Pleasures of the Town: With a new Prologue address'd to the Merchants 'Prentices of Great Britain."[69] All told, the play was staged seventeen times this season (1730–1) with performances every month from October to June.

Another sign of the play's popularity was the immediate demand for reading copies. The first edition, printed for James Roberts and not for John Watts (who had brought out both Fielding's regular comedies), appeared under the name "Scriblerus Secundus" on 31 March 1730, the day after the first performance. The pseudonym Fielding chose, like his earlier ascription of *The Masquerade* to "Lemuel Gulliver," declares his sympathy with the satiric program of the Scriblerians, Swift and Pope and Gay, whose genius, if not their Toryism, he admired. A second printing, hard to distinguish from the first and only recently identified,[70] was at once called for; and in July a "Second Edition" appeared, this time under the imprint of Watts. An unauthorized Dublin edition was also published before the year was out.

Indeed, as would not soon again be true of Fielding's productions, *The Author's Farce* was so immensely successful that few criticisms of it of any kind found their way into print. But the play had not reached its third performance before Henley, whom Fielding satirized as Dr. Orator in the Puppet Show, added a special feature to his silly monologues at the "Oratory" near Clare-Market, Lincoln's Inn Fields. Making fun of the fact that Fielding shared a surname with a certain well-known supernumerary actor and publican, Henley entitled the skit, "Jerry Fielding the Tapster turn'd Poet, a prating Kingdom managed."[71] Henley probably refers to Timothy (not Jerry) Fielding, an actor-dancer with the Drury Lane company who regularly kept a theatrical booth at the George Inn, Smithfield, during the time of Bartholomew Fair; he also kept the Buffalo Head Tavern near Bloomsbury Square.[72] It is well to be aware of this man, who often appears in contexts where we might expect to find his more famous namesake.

Fielding this season had another small masterpiece ready for production. *Tom Thumb* proved to be more popular by far than even *The Author's Farce*, with which it was often paired as an afterpiece from the first performance on Friday, 24 April 1730, at the Haymarket. The hint for the play he may again have found in *The Touch-Stone*, where, having noted the British prejudice against Italian opera, Ralph archly proposed that some patriotic author find his subjects in "our most noted domestick *Fables*, which must please an *English* Audience." Why not, he wonders, an opera on Tom Thumb?

> *Tom Thumb* would be a beautiful Foundation to build a pretty little Pastoral on; his Length too being adequate to that of a Summer's Evening, the *Belles* and *Beaus* might arrive Time enough from either Park, and enjoy the whole of his Affair: Nay, it would admit of some very new Scenes, as surprizing as true: Witness the Accident of the Pudding, which would be something as uncommon as ever appear'd on any Stage, not excepting even a *Dutch* Tragedy – N.B. Cu[zzo]ni *in Breeches would make a delightful* Tom Thumb.[73]

From this hint Fielding devised the cleverest, most hilarious dramatic burlesque in English, applying his talent for travesty not, as Ralph proposed, to the opera, but to the absurdities of the heroic drama. Present at the first night was the Earl of Egmont, who remarked in his Diary on 24 April 1730:

> Afterwards I went to the Haymarket playhouse, and saw a play called "The Author's Farce and the Pleasures of the Town," with an additional piece called "The Tragedy of Tom Thumb." Both these plays are a ridicule on poets, and several of their works, as also of operas, etc., and the last of our modern tragedians, and are exceedingly full of humour, with some wit. The author is one of the sixteen children of Mr. Fielding, and in a very low condition of purse.[74]

Though Lord Egmont a little exaggerated the number of children Edmund had produced by his first two wives (thirteen seems the correct figure), he accurately represented the state of Fielding's finances in the winter of 1729–30. But soon, with *Tom Thumb* making a double bill with the already successful *Author's Farce*, there would be plenty of money – enough to satisfy his creditors and to support the expensive recreations he enjoyed. Before the lengthened season ended on 24 July, *Tom Thumb* had seen forty-one performances, nearly equaling the extraordinary run of *The Author's Farce*; and, beginning with a version published by Roberts for distribution on the day of the first performance, 24 April, the play was issued in several editions.[75] By the seventh night – the thirteenth for *The Author's Farce* (6 May 1730) – the demand for seats had become so great that, "at the particular Desire of several Persons of Quality," pit and boxes were put together, making every seat in the house 5s., except for those in the gallery, which remained at 1s.6d.; for this performance, moreover, two new scenes were added to "the Tragedy," and a new prologue and epilogue had already been written for the night of 1 May.[76] (With these additions and revisions a new edition of the play was published, with a Preface by "Scriblerus Secundus" in mock Cibberian style.) On 13 May, Fielding had a special benefit, at "the particular Desire of several Ladies of Quality," at which pit and boxes were again put together; this time even the price of a seat in the gallery was raised to 2s. The "Quality," indeed, of whatever political inclination, competed with each other for the reputation of supporting these plays most avidly. The day following Fielding's benefit on the 13th, there was a Command Performance for the Prince of Wales, who had already seen the double bill on 25 April.[77] And as Walpole's enemies were amused to observe, the Prime Minister not once, not twice, but "three Times graced with his Presence that sublime *Drama* call'd the History of *Tom Thumb*, acted at the little House in the *Haymarket*."[78]

Opposition journalists pointed derisively at the minister's patronage of Fielding's play: in the reign of Augustus, so the message went, his minister Maecenas befriended the greatest authors of the age, Virgil, Horace, and Livy; in the reign of George Augustus, Walpole favored not Pope or Prior, but the authors of *Hurlothrumbo* and *Tom Thumb*.[79] That his bitterest adversaries should thus associate Walpole with Fielding's play, not as a target for its jokes but as its sponsor, suggests that modern critics have strained too hard to attribute the play's success to timely political satire.[80] It is amusing, to be sure, to consider Tom Thumb the Great, played by a diminutive actress swaggering about the stage in hero's attire, as an ironic figure for the Great Man himself, Sir Robert Walpole. Henley appears to have enjoyed the joke at his Oratory in May,[81] and a decade later, in *The Hyp-Doctor* (10 June 1740), he mentioned the play in the same breath with *Pasquin* and *The Golden Rump* in a brief list of anti-ministerial dramas. Indeed, a notice in the *Daily Post* (29 March 1742) prompted by a revival of *The Tragedy of Tragedies* described it as "a Piece at first calculated to ridicule some particular Persons and Affairs in Europe (at the Time it was writ) but more especially in this Island."[82]

The game of finding such satire in *Tom Thumb* is easier to play, however, the more remote one is from the original production. The Earl of Egmont, who was attuned to every political innuendo, heard none in *Tom Thumb*; nor, for that matter, did those of such opposing points of view as Walpole himself and the authors of *The Craftsman* and *Fog's Weekly Journal*. Even more telling against the notion that the play could have been thought embarrassing to Walpole or the Court is the fact that, in its new guise as *The Tragedy of Tragedies*, it had its grandest contemporary staging in May 1732 at the Establishment's own Theatre Royal at Drury Lane. Whatever political jokes there may be in *Tom Thumb* they are either so good-humored that they gave no offence, or so recondite that they were lost on Fielding's original audience.

There were of course captious souls who found plenty in the play to complain about. "But what can we say," asks the anonymous author of *Observations on the Present Taste for Poetry* (1739), "for being pleas'd with an Abuse of all our finest Performances together! an Attack, at once, on all the Great Geniuses *England* has produced, for a Couple of Ages! whose best Endeavours, and some of their greatest Beauties were selected, to provoke our contemptuous Mirth, by being set in a ridiculous Light: And this was done, with wonderful Applause, by H[enr]y F[iel]d[in]g, Esq.; alias, *Scriblerus secundus*." This critic, incensed at how well the travesty had done its work of exposing the worst excesses not only of Fenton, Lee, and Rowe, but of their betters Dryden, Congreve, and Addison, could not forgive Fielding for, so to speak, breaking windows to let out the stale air. He was anticipated in

these sentiments by "a Friend" on the occasion of the original run of
the play:

> At length, dull F[iel]d[in]g, give thy Labours o'er,
> And shew thy Spleen, and plague the Town no more!
> No more to Wit by Libels make Pretence,
> But grub thy Pen, and shew a Grain of Sense.[83]

Though few critics were quite so morose as this in fearing that
Fielding's burlesque would permanently stem the vogue of heroic
tragedy – which, as happened, it indeed helped to do – many believed
that the popularity of Tom Thumb signified a deplorable decline in
taste. Giles Jacob, who claimed that Tom Thumb was "more famous"
even than The Dunciad, declared that the "extraordinary Success" of
the play, together with that of The Dunciad and Hurlothrumbo, was
incontestable proof of the "corrupted" judgment of "That stupid Ass,
the Town."[84] On the anniversary of the Restoration the same topic
engaged "Orator" Henley, speaking "On the WIT of our Court, and eke
of Tom Thumb, compar'd with that of King Charles II";[85] but it seemed
to one epigrammatist who attended the Oratory that Henley himself
should not be neglected in this context, British palates having become
so jaded they could be satisfied with no less than "Three Non-Pareils"
at a time: "Here [sic] but their Names, and be with Wonder
dumb;/JACK, Foe to Gyants; HE[NLE]Y; and TOM THUMB."[86] By the
time James Miller's satire, Harlequin-Horace; or, The Art of Modern
Poetry appeared in February 1730/1, Fielding's play – most particularly
the scene of the Cow's swallowing Thumb, which set audiences in an
uproar – had already become the ultimate illustration of how not to
observe "heavy Probability" in the drama:

> When 'ere for sake of sweet Variety
> You'd draw some Wonder, or diverting Lie,
> Fly far from heavy Probability;
> And shew Tom Thumb, the more Surprize to give,
> From the Cows Belly taken out alive.
>
> (p. 45)[87]

Among the sophisticated admirers of Pope and the Scriblerians, the
revised version of the play which Fielding produced the following season
served to confirm his place, along with Cibber and Theobold, Dennis
and Hurlothrumbo Johnson, in the motley ranks of "The Modern Poets"
ironically celebrated in a satire published in the Grub-Street Journal (18
November 1731) by "a young Gentleman of Cambridge."[88]

Fielding cannot have been hurt by such gibes as these. For one thing,
it was because his opinion of the public taste was so low that, to make
money, he had set aside for the moment the writing of regular comedies

in order to give the Town what it wanted, farce and puppet shows and burlesque. He liked the play, of course – as everyone has done who is capable of relishing the humor of it; *Tom Thumb* (or *The Tragedy of Tragedies*) held the stage, season after season, throughout the century, and it remains one of the few of Fielding's plays which are revived from time to time. Just how fond he was of Thumb is clear in *A Journey from This World to the Next* (I. ix), where the narrator encounters that "great little Man" in Elysium, who assures him that the story of his being swallowed by the cow was only too true. Nevertheless, Fielding understood the distinction between a *jeu d'esprit*, however perfect of its kind, and a work of art. In April 1731 in the Epilogue he wrote for Lewis Theobald's *Orestes*, he urged the ladies in the audience to show for once that they were capable of tasting finer things:

> Once in an Age, at least, your Smiles dispense
> To *English* Sounds, and Tragedy that's Sense.
> These are Variety to you, who come
> From the *Italian Opera*, and *Tom Thumb*.

Indeed, in the Prologue he wrote for his own most ambitious work for the stage, *The Modern Husband* (1732), he explicitly put the burlesque in its place, explaining that, as a younger man, his lack of skill as a maker of regular comedies had obliged him to give the public the silly things it wanted:

> Hence, your nice Tastes he strove to entertain,
> With unshap'd Monsters of a wanton Brain!
>   He taught *Tom Thumb* strange Victories to boast,
> Slew Heaps of Giants, and then – kill'd a Ghost!
>   To Rules, or Reason, scorn'd the dull Pretence,
> And fought your *Champion*, 'gainst the Cause of Sense!

Seen in perspective, however, *Tom Thumb* deserves the distinction it soon achieved among students of the British theatre – the distinction, which it shares with Buckingham's *Rehearsal*, of being the standard work of its kind: that is, of dramatic travesty or burlesque.[89] It is the work to which Fielding alludes in the Preface to *Joseph Andrews* as exemplifying the theory of a comic *catharsis* he sketched out earlier in his essay on "the Benefit of Laughing." It is especially pleasant to record, therefore, that the therapeutic dose he administered in *Tom Thumb* proved effectual in one of the hardest cases imaginable – the case of Jonathan Swift. As Fielding observed in that essay, though Swift had a knack of making others laugh, he "never laughs himself": to Mrs. Pilkington the Dean confessed he could remember laughing only twice in his life – once at the trick of a mountebank's Merry Andrew; the other "at the Circumstance of Tom Thumb's killing the

Ghost. The Dean," Mrs. Pilkington concludes, "had a high Opinion of Mr. Fielding's Wit."[90]

···━● xii ●━···

A great many others formed a high opinion of Fielding's wit in this, his first full season in the theatre. Competent performances though they were, nothing about *Love in Several Masques* or *The Temple Beau* had prepared audiences for the inventiveness, the sheer comic energy and pertness, of the pair of little farces that Fielding sent flashing across the firmament of London's West End in the spring of 1730, at once changing his financial prospects from night to day and presaging other clever things to come. These were the days Pillage, Fielding's surrogate, recalls in *Eurydice Hiss'd* (1737), as he tries to woo back the Muse he has forsaken:

> Not more I felt thy Power, nor fiercer burnt,
> My vig'rous Fancy, when thy blushing Charms
> First yielded trembling, and inspir'd my Pen
> To write nine Scenes with Spirit in one Day.

Nine scenes, with spirit, in a day. Only a pace close to this could account for the extraordinary fertility of Fielding's Muse during these months. Not counting *Don Quixote in England* and *The Wedding Day*, which were then only in draft, he had staged *The Temple Beau* in January, *The Author's Farce* in March, *Tom Thumb* a month later; and these he regarded as merely preparatory to two more "regular" comedies, his most ambitious works to date. The first of these, *Rape upon Rape: or, The Justice Caught in His Own Trap*, was ready for staging by mid-June, the earliest announcement appearing in the *Daily Post* (12 June 1730). The second, *The Modern Husband*, would be ready for rehearsal by September.

Though *Rape upon Rape* was scheduled to open on 15 June 1730, the "sudden Indisposition" of one of the principal actors forced a postponement of more than a week before the play was staged on Tuesday, 23 June – the date also of its publication by Watts. Six performances during the rest of this week and the week following gave Fielding two welcome benefits (26 June and 2 July), but illness recurred and interrupted what might have been a better run, though it was now summer and the town rapidly emptying. There were two further performances of the play during July – a total of eight in all.

Rape upon Rape is at once a lively and a disturbing play that marks a watershed (however temporarily) in Fielding's development as a dramatist. It was his first exploratory venture into a new province of comedy – a kind of comedy not characterized by the verbal pyrotechnics of Wycherley or Congreve, or by the pleasant sentimentalism of Steele or the mannered gentility of Cibber. Still less would it resemble the expressionistic absurdities of *The Author's Farce* and *Tom Thumb*, which, though he was glad enough to have the money they brought, Fielding now spoke of apologetically, as if he considered them aberrations from a grand design he had been too young, too unskilled to realize. Though conceived within the conventional five-act matrix of "regular" comedy, Fielding's new species of comedy differed from what had gone before in two essential respects: its manner was more earnest, its subject more daring. Thus, in the Prologue to *The Modern Husband*, to which this play directly leads, Fielding warns his audience that he expects "no loud Laugh [to] applaud the serious Page"; and in the Prologue to *Rape upon Rape* he declares that his target is not the innocuous foibles of the upper classes that injure no one however ludicrous they may be, but rather something more dangerous – "*Vice*" that "hath grown too great to be abus'd;/ By Pow'r, defended from the Piercing Dart." This was comedy with a reforming purpose so ardent and bold as to require the ministrations not of cheerful Thalia, but of her sister:

> the Heroick *Muse* who sings To-night,
> Through these neglected Tracks attempts her Flight:
> *Vice*, cloath'd with Pow'r, she combats with her Pen,
> And fearless, dares the *Lyon* in his Den.

This was Fielding's conception of the play which is remembered today (if at all) as it appeared transmogrified in the rollicking musical *Lock up your Daughters* (1967). But *Rape upon Rape* was in fact the manifesto of Fielding's deeper intent as a satirist – not only now that benign doctor of mirth who prescribes laughter as a cure for vapors or the spleen; but, as in *The Champion* (27 March 1740), a "Physician" who will not flinch from applying caustic remedies to purge the mind of vice and the body politic of corruption.

Rape upon Rape may have been inspired by a particular contemporary scandal that exposed all too clearly the decadence and venality of English society.[91] In February 1729/30 Colonel Francis Charteris, so infamous as a sensualist and an unprincipled tool of the ministry that he appears in the works of Pope and the Scriblerians as the personification of Vice, had been convicted of raping his maidservant; he was committed to Newgate and required to pay a heavy fine. But Charteris was rich and close to Walpole, who, as Fielding reminds his audience in the Prologue, was notorious for "screening" his creatures from punishment; by April, Charteris, "Rape-Master General of Great

Britain," had received the King's pardon and was ready to debauch more young women with impunity, as Hogarth graphically implies in Plate I of the *Harlot's Progress* (1732). Neither Charteris nor Walpole is mentioned in *Rape upon Rape*, though no one in Fielding's audience in June 1730 could fail to sense their relevance to the theme of the play. Still hoping no doubt for that *"Sinecure"* to which he refers in his *Epistle* to Walpole of this same year, Fielding was not reckless enough to hurl darts openly at Leviathan. As the Prologue makes clear, however, he aims at more dangerous game than the amiable rake, Jack Ramble; his target is Justice Squeezum, type of those lewd and corrupt instruments of power who seemed beyond the laws:

> Then only Reverence to *Pow'r* is due,
> When *Publick Welfare* is its only View:
> But when the *Champions*, whom the *Publick* arm
> For their own Good with *Pow'r*, attempt their *Harm*,
> He sure must meet the *general Applause*,
> Who 'gainst those *Traytors* fights the *Publick Cause*.

...◦ xiii ◦...

A vigorous young man of twenty-three, Fielding occupied himself in more frivolous ways than in thinking with a reforming zeal about the craft of play writing. As a rule, like most of the gentry and nobility, he divided his time between London in winter and the country in summer, arriving in town for the start of the "season" in October and departing for one of his favorite West Country haunts in June or thereabouts – not, presumably, for Upton Grey any longer (since nothing any longer could constrain him to go there), but for the farm at East Stour, perhaps; or for Glastonbury or Bath; but most especially during the early 1730s for Salisbury.

Salisbury, or New Sarum – one of England's handsomest cities, set like a jewel in Wiltshire meadows washed by three rivers; its golden, high-spired cathedral of St. Mary pointing heavenward from within the walls of The Close, green and safe and gracious, if in those days often too damp for comfort. Here in The Close until his death in 1698 Fielding's paternal grandfather lived, a canon residentiary of the cathedral; here, too, though outside The Close, in a house near St. Martin's church, his maternal grandmother Lady Gould had been living for ten years, perhaps with her sister Mrs. Cottington. Here his sisters had grown up and been educated; and here he had fled to escape the birchings at Eton. Now, the latest of his stepmothers was from

Salisbury. What is more, The Close was home to the woman and the man whom he came to cherish above all others: his beloved first wife, Charlotte Cradock, and her neighbor James Harris. In *Amelia*, which is in part the story of Fielding's marriage to Charlotte, Harris is the heroine's name, and Salisbury is her home.

We know a good deal about what drew Fielding to Salisbury, but we know less certainly just when he was there and what he found there to occupy him – besides, that is, dancing at the Assembly and flirting with an impressive variety of young women. Charlotte would become the love of his life, but for several years before they married in 1734, she had numerous rivals for Fielding's affection; among them, apparently, her sister Catherine. There was "Clarissa," celebrated in a verse he engraved on a window pane of the summer house belonging to Milford Manor, less than a mile's walk from Lady Gould's residence. Possibly dating from the summer of 1729 – as suggested by the coquette of the same name in *The Temple Beau* and by Mrs. Moneywood's complaint in *The Author's Farce* (I. ii) that Luckless had spoiled her floor "with Ink – [her] Windows with Verses" – the inscription reads:

> Dear Clarissa Puellarum omnium formassima
> She's fairest where thousands are fair.[92]

At about the same period he was paying other pretty compliments to a girl named "Jenny," whose eyes were so lustrous they made a supply of fresh candles at the assembly ball unnecessary[93] – and to "Gloriana," whose charms were such that he would exchange a half-crown for the halfpenny she had given a beggar, because the baser coin had lain "within her Bosom blest."[94] In other poems he paid tribute to "*Vince's* Eyes" and "fair *Bennet's* Breast,"[95] and to the whole person of a certain Miss "*S–per*," Hampshire's candidate for the office of Venus's Vice-Regent on earth.[96] Indeed, from this last untitled poem he felt obliged to delete the entire "middle Part ... (which was writ when the Author was very young)," because it "was filled with the Names of several young Ladies, who might perhaps be uneasy at seeing themselves in Print."

These were the years when he kept up a brisk correspondence with "the lovely part of the Creation," whose "dear *Scrawls, Skrawls,* or *Skrales,* (for the Word is variously spelt,)" he remembered receiving "in my Youth."[97] No stronger evidence of Fielding's fondness for the sex can be imagined than this willingness of his to exchange letters with them – none of which, however, has survived: "For my own Part," he wrote James Harris as he began one of the rare correspondences of his life, "I solemnly declare, I can never give Man or Woman with whom I have no Business (which the Satisfaction of Lust may well be called) a more certain Token of a violent Affection than by writing to them."[98]

About 1730 one of these Salisbury belles in particular began receiving more of Fielding's good-natured flattery than any other, as is clear from this piece of "Advice to the Nymphs of *New S[aru]m*" which he versified in that year:

> Cease, vainest Nymphs, with *Celia* to contend,
> And let your Envy and your Folly end.
> With her Almighty Charms, when yours compare,
> When your blind Lovers think you half so fair,
> East *Sarum* Ditch, like *Helicon* shall flow,
> And *Harnam* Hill, like high *Parnassus*, glow.[99]

Later that same year, affecting a misanthropic mood induced by too long an exposure in town to the critics of the *Grub-Street Journal* and to "Players, from *Boheme* to *Booth*," he exempts only "Celia," his "Charmer," from his universal "Hatred of Mankind."[100] From 1730 on, Celia seems to have monopolized the attentions of Fielding's amatory Muse. To Celia is addressed a poem "Occasioned by her apprehending her House would be broke open, and having an old Fellow to guard it, who sat up all Night, with a Gun without any Ammunition" – the anxiety she feels having sympathetically spoiled Fielding's sleep and even, temporarily, Celia's beauty.

> Not so you look when at the Ball,
> Envy'd you shine, outshining all.
> Not so at Church, when Priest perplext,
> Beholds you, and forgets the Text.[101]

To Celia are also addressed verses "On her wishing to have a LIL-LIPUTIAN to play with," in which Fielding imagines mankind striving to be metamorphosed into her monkey, or her "faithful Dog *Quadrille*," or any pet of hers – an ambition that unites even the bitterest political rivals:

> *P[u]lt[ene]y*, who does for Freedom rage,
> Would sing confin'd within thy Cage;
> And *W[a]lp[o]le*, for a tender Pat,
> Would leave his Place to be thy Cat.

As for her large poet himself, he would gladly be the very thing she wished for:

> May, I, to please my lovely Dame,
> Be five foot shorter than I am;
> And, to be greater in her Eyes,
> Be sunk to *Lilliputian* Size.

For then he could hitch a ride in her pocket; "Or sit astride, to frighten People,/ Upon her Hat's new-fashion'd Steeple"; or at night, "Upon her Pillow sitting still," he could watch over her and survey her charms, "(for afraid she could not be/ Of such a little Thing as me)."[102]

There are other poems to Celia – some written in this same playful vein; some echoing Luckless's romantic protestations to Harriot in *The Author's Farce*;[103] one praising her "gentle Heart" and "accomplish'd Mind" as plainly disproving Gay's rude "Severity on her Sex."[104] And one quite touching, called "The Price" – suggesting, perhaps, that for a time, as their love deepened to thoughts of marriage, Celia had been forced to choose between her feelings for her amiable but improvident poet and her duty to her parents:

> Can there on Earth, my *Celia*, be,
> A Price I would not pay for thee?
> Yes, one dear precious Tear of thine
> Should not be shed to make you mine.

As for Celia's true identity, that is plain enough from the rebus Fielding wrote on "Her Christian Name":

> A very good Fish, very good Way of Selling
> A very bad Thing, with a little bad Spelling,
> Make the Name by the Parson and Godfather giv'n,
> When a Christian was made of an Angel from Heav'n.

The solution, of course, is "Char" (the very good fish), "Lot" (the way of selling), and "Te" (for "Tea" misspelled – a bad thing, presumably, because Fielding preferred stronger brews). Celia, as we have suspected all along, must then be none other than Charlotte Cradock.

But caution even in such an apparently plain case as this is appropriate. Unless we suppose that Fielding was capable of addressing to Charlotte the unabashedly erotic poems entitled "An Epigram" and "The Question"[105] and that he was then capable of *publishing* them, it seems wiser to assume that "Celia" was his name for any number of young women he was enamored of – and, for that matter, even some he was not, as in the case of the Jacobite of that name in *Amelia* (I. vi). This interpretation is borne out in the untitled poem beginning "The Queen of Beauty, t'other Day," written sometime about 1729–30. For here, though Celia receives her accustomed compliment (a glance from her eyes is swifter than lightning), she is clearly distinct from Charlotte, who, with her sister Catherine, is by Jove himself appointed to the office of Venus's Vice-Regent upon earth:

> And can you, Daughter, doubt to whom
> (He cry'd) belongs the happy Doom,

While C[rado]cks yet make bless'd the Earth,
C[rado]cks, whom long before their Birth,
I, by your own Petition mov'd,
Decreed to be by all belov'd.
C[rado]cks, to whose celestial Dower
I gave all Beauties in my Power;
To form whose lovely Minds and Faces,
I stript half Heaven of its Graces.
Oh let them bear an equal Sway,
So shall Mankind well-pleas'd obey.

This early it would seem – in 1730 or thereabouts – Fielding's affections were divided between both the Cradock sisters, Charlotte and "Kitty." Both girls had a reputation for being "pretty,"[106] and Fielding had a rival for their attentions in a certain "Land-Waiter" turned poet, Henry Price of Poole, Dorset. In both Latin and English, Price produced the following stanzas on "Charlotte and Kitty Cradock":

> SHOULD fortune this way
> The dear charmers convey,
> Let this speak how their absence I grieve;
> None but that lovely pair
> Could create half such care,
> None but they too that care can relieve.
>
> My ambition nor blame
> If at both I should aim,
> Since with various charms they delight;
> Sprightly *Kitty* should sway
> The conversable day;
> Lovely *Charlotte* should govern the night.[107]

These verses – though not published until 1744, when Charlotte and Henry had been married for ten years, and "Kitty" had long since died a spinster – attest that the sisters were a charming pair during the early 1730s when Fielding seems to have found them equally attractive. Soon, however, Charlotte's beauty would be marred by a painful accident which Fielding later recalled in *Amelia* and which his cousin, Lady Bute, who knew her, well remembered – "a frightful overturn, which destroyed the gristle of her nose."[108] This injury – as Fielding neglected to mention in the first edition of his novel, to the amusement of the reviewers who affected to admire the unique attractions of his noseless heroine – was, he assures us, "absolutely cured" by "a famous Surgeon," who repaired the damage so skillfully that Charlotte's nose was again well proportioned, though it bore "a visible Scar on one Side."[109] The surgeon in question was probably Fielding's friend and Charlotte's neighbor in The Close, Edward Goldwyre (1707–74).[110] Soon, however, for about a year or two from 1732 to 1733, Fielding seems to have forgotten Charlotte temporarily, falling hopelessly in love with another young lady known to us only as "Dorinda" or "Miss D.W."[111]

But Charlotte, the inspiration for Sophie Western and Amelia Booth, would at last eclipse all her rivals. And she was a prize worth winning, not only for her beauty and her "accomplish'd Mind"; but for the comfortable dowry she was likely to bring her husband. Very little is known of her family. Her mother, Elizabeth, was apparently a widow; her husband, like Amelia's father (IX. viii), may have "died suddenly when his Children were Infants."[112] She may have had, besides Charlotte and Catherine, another daughter, Mary Penelope, who died on 28 October 1729, aged twenty-four, and was buried in the cathedral on 1 November.[113] The house Mrs. Cradock occupied with her girls from 1714 to 1733 was one of the finest in The Close. Leased from the Vicars Choral of the cathedral, it adjoined St. Anne's Gate on the south; the Goldwyres were next-door neighbors to the west, and directly opposite was the fine Palladian house of James Harris, now called "Malmesbury House," adjoining the Gate on the north. Later in the century the house in which Fielding courted Charlotte was described as follows in an advertisement in the *Salisbury Journal*:

> a large and commodious dwelling house, adjoining St. Ann's Gate, consisting of an entrance hall, two good parlours, and two bed-rooms over, the same size, all in front; with many other good rooms and offices: excellent cellerage, stall stable, coachhouse, etc., fit for the reception of a large family.[114]

We will return often to Charlotte, and to New Sarum, in the course of this narrative. For, after the metropolis itself, no town in England meant more to Fielding than Salisbury. Besides the numerous personal and familial connections we have already mentioned, two of its bishops, for example, profoundly influenced his view of English political history and of the Christian faith. Gilbert Burnet, Bishop from 1689 to 1715, he considered "almost the only *English* Historian that is likely to be known to Posterity, by whom he will be most certainly ranked amongst the greatest Writers of Antiquity."[115] Benjamin Hoadly, Bishop from 1723 to September 1734 and the most powerful latitudinarian divine of his time, Fielding praised as an example of "true greatness" in the Church; Hoadly's controversial interpretation of the Eucharist was "written," Parson Adams declares, "with the Pen of an Angel."[116] In his masterpiece, Fielding found places as well for the zanies of the town: for Thomas Chubb, the prolific, if illiterate, tallow-chandler who probably served as a model for Square the Deist; and for Daniel Pearce, one of the corporation mace-bearers, who, disguised as "the great

Dowdy," enjoyed terrifying the clientele at taverns by pretending to be an escaped lunatic loose amongst the tipplers. Associations such as these, and many more that we can never now recover, are a measure of Salisbury's importance in Fielding's life.

◆ xiv ◆

It is hard to say just when in 1730 Fielding absented himself from Celia and the nymphs of New Sarum to return to London. Probably he was at Salisbury only for a few weeks that summer, from mid-July to September. He would have wished to remain in town to see *Rape upon Rape* through its first performances – and to collect the receipts from his two benefits; and it is likely he was back in London by 1 September. He had by then finished writing *The Modern Husband*, the work he regarded as his masterpiece in the new genre we may call "heroic" comedy, and he hoped to have it staged that season.

From London on Friday, 4 September, he dispatched a copy of the play to his cousin Lady Mary at Twickenham, hoping anxiously that she would approve such a radical experiment in a new kind of comedy and promising that he would call on her "next Monday to receive my Sentence." The letter begins:

> I hope your Ladyship will honour the Scenes which I presume to lay before you with your Perusal. As they are written on a Model I never yet attempted, I am exceedingly anxious least they should find less Mercy from you than my lighter Productions. It will be a slight compensation to the Modern Husband, that your Ladyship's Censure will defend him from the Possibility of any other Reproof, Since your least approbation will always give me a Pleasure infiniter superiour to the loudest Applauses of a theatre. For whatever has past your Judgment may, I think, without any Imputation of Immodesty, refer Want of Success to Want of Judgment in an Audience.[117]

We know, because Fielding twice proudly alludes to the fact in his writings,[118] that Lady Mary cordially approved the manuscript, declaring in particular (though the first-night audience was not of her opinion) that the character of Lady Charlotte Gaywit was exactly right, "the Picture," indeed, "of half the young People of her Acquaintance."

Though Fielding in his letter to Lady Mary does not trouble to specify the year in which he is writing, we know from a surprising source that it was 1730. On 19 September 1730, *The Craftsman* – principal organ of the Opposition and a paper that usually ignored theatrical events unless they were politically significant – went out of

its way to inform its readers that Fielding's play was ready to be staged:
"We hear that the Town will shortly be diverted by a Comedy of Mr.
Fielding's call'd, the MODERN HUSBAND, which is said to bear a great
Reputation." This "puff" annoyed the editor of the *Grub-Street Journal*
(24 September), a paper hostile to Fielding: "*I don't understand,*" he
complained, "*how a* Comedy *so* little known *can be* said to bear a great
reputation." The answer to the puzzle troubling the editor is that
Fielding was circulating the play in manuscript and that those who
read it shared Lady Mary's opinion of it.

What is genuinely puzzling about these months in Fielding's life is
a matter more fundamental than the early reputation of *The Modern
Husband.* The elusive questions concern the attitude of Fielding's mind,
his motives and circumstances, during the period in which he wrote the
play and tried to promote it in the autumn of 1730. Why, if his
influential friends so well liked the play, did *The Modern Husband* wait
almost a year and a half before it was staged at Drury Lane in February
1731/2? Were Cibber and Wilks, in September 1730, still smarting from
the roasting they received in *The Author's Farce?* If so, and if Fielding
was unwilling to trust his most ambitious work to date to the clumsy
ministrations of the comedians at the Little Haymarket, why did he
not offer the play to Rich's able company at Lincoln's Inn Fields, as
he would do with two other of his regular comedies this season? For all
we know, of course, he may have done just that and been rebuffed;
Rich's meat was a spicy harlequinade or Newgate opera, not a play in
which one could expect "no loud Laugh [to] applaud the serious Page."

Complicating the puzzle further is the fact of that curious notice in
The Craftsman. Why would Nicholas Amhurst choose to "puff" a new
play by an author whom we have recently seen satirizing him and his
friends and making overtures to Walpole – a play, indeed, which when
eventually staged and published would carry a fulsome Dedication to
the Great Man himself? For one thing, of course, Amhurst would have
been unaware of writings which existed in manuscript only in Lady
Mary's or the minister's closets, or which, in the case of the Dedication,
had not yet been thought of. More to the point, however, Amhurst may
have believed that Fielding was drifting into the Opposition camp.

In Fielding's writings since he returned from Leyden the first traces
of satiric innuendo against Walpole and his corrupt agents occur, albeit
in a manner prudently oblique, in *Rape upon Rape* in June 1730. A
month later, while he was no doubt already drafting *The Modern
Husband,* he struck at the minister again, this time as if motivated by
some personal resentment at the Great Man's self-conceit and abuse of
power. For it was very probably Fielding, impersonating a public-
spirited physiognomist named "Thomas Squint," who informed the
readers of *Fog's Weekly Journal* (25 July 1730) that he had discovered

Walpole's character in his countenance: there he "found Pride, a great Assurance, much Arrogance, and immense Quantity of Self-Love, no small Share of Avarice, with its Attendant Ambition, writ in his Face, and to tell you the Truth, I saw some Signs of a violent Death there, and, if my Art does not deceive me, it will be a dry Death too; I think he is in Danger of going up Stairs out of the World." [119] What embittered Fielding's satire here is not hard to surmise. "Squint's" depiction of the minister as an arrogant "*Man-brute*" lording it over a throng of abject flatterers has its parallel in *The Modern Husband* (I. viii) in Captain Merit's personal experience – the Captain, no doubt like his author, having suffered in vain the humiliation of attendance at the Great Man's levee: "What an abundance of poor Wretches go to the feeding the Vanity of that Leviathan – one great Rogue."

Besides helping to explain Amhurst's "puff" of *The Modern Husband*, a second pseudonymous piece of this same period also echoes the satiric themes of the play Fielding had by then only recently finished. It is likely that in *The Craftsman* (10 October 1730), under the guise of the sportsman squire "Harry Hunter," "Harry" Fielding published an "Essay upon HUNTING" in which he wittily expounds the similarities between politicians and the minister's other favorite breed of men, fox-hunters;[120] in *The Modern Husband* (I. ix), the country M.P. Mr. Woodall personifies the analogy Fielding draws at length in the essay.

However much he may have tempered this strain of anti-ministerial satire as he revised the play – for, as we might suppose about a work that he eventually felt able to dedicate to Walpole, the vestiges of such satire in the text as we know it are faint – Fielding conceived *The Modern Husband* in a mood of political disaffection rather like the one he recently ridiculed in his unfinished cantos on the Scriblerians. Indeed, at about this same time he had openly paid tribute to the circle of Pope, Swift, and Gay by adopting as his own the pseudonym "Scriblerus Secundus," under which name he published both *The Author's Farce* and *Tom Thumb*. As "Tom Squint" and "Harry Hunter," occasional contributors to the Opposition's leading journals, Fielding could safely level his charge at the minister; for the moment at least (he would soon be of quite another opinion), it was Walpole who personally epitomized the theme of moral debility and corruption in government. These same themes, the burden of his "heroic Muse" in *The Modern Husband*, would have a more generalized and impersonal expression in "the Scenes" he submitted for Lady Mary's perusal that September.

···➤ **XV** ◆───···

Notwithstanding Amhurst's assurances that the Town would "shortly be diverted" by Fielding's new comedy, something prevented its production at either of the two principal theatres to which he would be inclined to submit it. For John Rich, as well as Cibber, probably had the offer of it. We know, at any rate, that during this season Fielding found a temporary place at Lincoln's Inn Fields.

His temporary break with the Little Theatre in the Haymarket is evident at the end of November 1730, when the company there staged, without Fielding's consent, adulterated versions of two of his popular successes of the preceding season. On Saturday, 28 November, they announced for the following Monday the first performance of the season of *Rape upon Rape*, now renamed *The Coffee-House Politician* (or, as originally given out, *The City Politician*);[121] the afterpiece to the comedy would be "The Comical Tragedy of TOM THUMB." But in order to capitalize on public amusement over a timely, if entirely pointless, question – which, that is, of five inept candidates would be the Court's choice to succeed Laurence Eusden, "the drunken parson," as Poet Laureate? – the company inserted into Fielding's burlesque a new Act, entitled *The Battle of the Poets: or, The Contention for the Laurel*. The scene represents the wedding day of Tom Thumb and Princess Huncamunca, when, on discovering that no epithalamium can be sung because the laureate is dead, King Arthur opens a competition for that honor between Comment Profound (*alias* Lewis Theobald, recently elevated by Pope to the princedom of *The Dunciad*), Sulky Bathos (*alias* John Dennis, dour admirer of the religious sublime in poetry), Flail (*alias* Stephen Duck, the "Thresher-Poet" from Wiltshire), Fopling Fribble (*alias* Colley Cibber, famous for his interpretation of Lord Foppington in Vanbrugh's *Relapse*) – and Noctifer (*alias* James Ralph, whom Pope immortalized in *The Dunciad* as the author of *Night*). Cibber, as everyone knew before the farce was staged,[122] won the competition handily and for many years to come would, in exchange for his butt of sack, annually discharge his feeble odes on the occasions of the New Year and the King's birthday. But what would particularly annoy Fielding was the mockery of his friend Ralph. Accordingly, on 30 November 1730, the day of the first performance of the piece, he published in the *Daily Journal* the following denial that he had had any part in the production:

> Whereas it hath been advertized That an entire New Act, called, THE BATTLE OF THE POETS, is introduced into the Tragedy of TOM THUMB; This is to assure the Town, that I have never seen this additional Act, nor am any ways concerned therein.
>
> *Henry Fielding.*

Who, then, was the author of this farce? The answer is uncertain –
partly because the evidence is scant and doubtful, but chiefly because
what evidence there is all points in an unlikely direction: namely, at
Thomas "Hesiod" Cooke (1703–56).[123] Cooke was a friend of Theobald,
Dennis, and Ralph, and he would soon be close to Fielding as well.
Moreover, on the very day the farce was announced (28 November),
Cooke began contributing regularly to the *British Journal*[124] and would
continue for some time to be associated with such pro-ministerial
publications; he seems not the sort of author to ridicule the Court's
choice of a Poet Laureate. But such surprising contradictions are by no
means rarities in the murky underworld of eighteenth-century hackney authorship, and the finger points, if shakily, at Cooke as the culprit.

No less uncertain is the generally accepted view that Cooke, as
"Scriblerus Tertius," wrote *The Candidates for the Bays*, a verse satire
on the contest for the laureateship published in December. Whoever
this poet was, he was as knowledgeable about literary and theatrical
affairs as he was unskilled in numbers. He also left us a vivid, if
uncomplimentary, sketch of Fielding as he appeared at the beginning
of his literary career – an arrogant, dissolute young man of twenty-
three. Since this is, however rough, the earliest extant impression of
Fielding by a contemporary, it is worth quoting, complete with the
author's pungent commentary:

> Bedaub'd o'er with Snuff, and drunk as a Drum,
> And mad as a *March* Hare Beau F[*ielding*] does come;
> He staggers, and swears he will never submit
> To Correction of (*a*) Friends, or the Censure of *Pit*;
> He says what is flat shall for ever be so,
> Who tells him a Fault he esteems as a Foe;
> He begs that *Apollo*'ll his Labours compleat,
> And give him the Bays, or the Wearer's Estate:
> He instances each little Thing he has wrote,
> And makes a new *Item* of every Thought;
> Commending himself as he passes along,
> From R[*ape*] upon R[*ape*] to (*b*) *Belinda* a song:
> He vamps upon wretched heroick Bombast,
> And sings the Success that attended the last:
> He'll shew both himself and (*c*) Assistants are no Wits,
> By valiant T[*om*] T[*humb*] and his (*d*) *Battle of Poets*:
> He steals all his Beauties when they're in their Fulness,
> As by (*e*) *Luckless* appears, and the Goddess of *Dulness*.

(*a*) This Gentleman is so self-conceited that he quarrels with
everyone that shews him a Fault.

(*b*) *Vain Belinda are your Wiles*, a favourite Air in the *Temple Beau*, but none of the best, for a Simile between a delicate Belle and a Ruffian Bully can never be coherent.

(*c*) Said to be assisted by several Hands in his Dramatick Performances, as a Scene from *this*, and a Scene from *that* Person of Quality, which he introduces as he thinks fit: How true it is we leave our Readers to judge, but will say this, his Plays seem Pieces of Sense and Nonsense, like Harlequin's Patch-work Jacket sow'd together.

(*d*) A new Scene introduced in *T[om] T[humb]* upon the *Scotchman's* Holy-day.

(*e*) Vide *Author's Farce*, the Scene between *Luckless* and his Landlady, pirated from *L[ove] in a B[ottle]*, and the Goddess of *Nonsense* from the Goddess Dulness in the *D[unciad]*.

If Cooke did write this satire (a presumption hard to reconcile with his also having written *The Battle of the Poets*, which the author here attributes to Fielding), the friendship that soon developed between the two men is all the more remarkable.

There was always a touch of arrogance about Fielding, and he loved a cheerful bottle. But as a playwright he had already proved that he had a fertile imagination – a knack, as the satirist put it, of making "a new *Item* of every Thought" – and that he could fill a theatre with paying customers. Sometime before the players at the Little Haymarket offended him by staging *The Battle of the Poets*, he decided to carry his wares to a better market. This was the season to which he refers in the Preface to the *Miscellanies*, where he reveals that having fallen out with Wilks, and Mrs. Oldfield having died (in October 1730) – they being the players for whom he created the roles of Millamour and Charlotte in *The Wedding Day* – he carried that play to Lincoln's Inn Fields and read it to Rich, "in the Presence of a very eminent Physician of this Age, who will bear me Testimony, that I did not recommend my Performance with the usual Warmth of an Author." He sensed that the play depended for its life on a kind of dynamic acting no one at Lincoln's Inn Fields was capable of. (The physician to whom Fielding refers, by the way, was probably his friend Dr. Benjamin Hoadly [1706–57], son of the Bishop of Salisbury and a dramatist in his own right, whose best-known comedy is *The Suspicious Husband* [1747].)

In any case, though Rich rejected *The Wedding Day* he was enough impressed with Fielding's success of the preceding season that he was ready to make an extraordinary concession in the attempt to procure his talents for Lincoln's Inn Fields: he agreed to stage a revival of *Rape upon Rape* under its new title *The Coffee-House Politician*, and to grant Fielding the gift of a benefit. A gift it was, for nothing prevented Rich from pirating the play and keeping the proceeds to himself. For his part Fielding must have jumped at the chance to leave behind the motley amateurs at Potter's little theatre and to establish himself at one of the two principal houses in town.[125] On Friday (4 December) of the same week in which the Haymarket players stole a march on Rich by staging *The Coffee-House Politician* for a single night, the company at Lincoln's Inn Fields were ready with their own production, with the fine comic actor John Hippisley in the role of Squeezum and Anthony Boheme as Politick – whose performance (or is it simply the man himself?) Fielding reviles in his poem, "To Celia." On the same day, Watts brought out the published version.[126]

The play ought to have fared better than before with one of London's better companies producing it. But such was not the case. *The Coffee-House Politician* saw only four performances at Lincoln's Inn Fields, and was then withdrawn, never to be staged again. The record of receipts tells the tale plainly enough, though, agreeably, its most lucrative night was the third, Fielding's benefit: 4 December (£39.5), 5 December (£59.13), 7 December (£54.13 [money], £23.5 [tickets]), 17 December (£28.9).[127] Just how "dead" the play had become is clear from Arthur Murphy's droll account in the *Gray's-Inn Journal* (20 April 1754) of the desperate subterfuge to which the hack "Jack Spatter" resorted in order to finance a holiday at Tunbridge Wells: "instantly [Spatter] sets down and writes a Farce; and because *Fielding's Coffee-house Politician* is not very likely to be acted again on either of our Stages, what does the merry Wag do, but he takes the Character, gives it a new Name, makes a little Alteration in the Scene, where the *Politician* reads the News-Papers, and instantly *Genial Jacob, and a warm third Day*, as the Poet has it, equips the GENIUS for Tunbridge."[128] However superciliously he may have regarded this weakness in "Spatter," it was not long before Murphy succumbed to the same temptation: his own farce, *The Upholsterer, or What News?* (1757), borrows from Fielding's play – as does William Hodson's *The Adventures of a Night* (1783).

···◆ XVI ◆···

The failure of *The Coffee-House Politician* dashed Fielding's hopes of finding with Rich at Lincoln's Inn Fields the welcome he no longer enjoyed at Drury Lane. But if the reputation he coveted as a serious author of regular comedies had so far eluded him at the two principal theatres, no one – least of all the daring young company at the Little Haymarket, whose house he had packed to capacity night after night during the previous season – would dispute his genius in the new, irregular modes of farce and burlesque. As the New Year turned, therefore, Fielding was back at the Haymarket, preparing a fresh and surprising version of *Tom Thumb* and drafting an entire new play in three acts, *The Letter-Writers: or, A New Way to Keep a Wife at Home.*

Slight as it is and unsuccessful, *The Letter-Writers* is worth noting for the clarity with which it exemplifies certain characteristics of Fielding's work as a comic author. It illustrates plainly, for example, two distinguishing features of his creative imagination: the fact that he draws much of his inspiration from fugitive (often personal) contemporary events, and the more remarkable circumstance that much of his art is a kind of benign literary alchemy, transforming base and potentially distressing materials into the stuff of laughter – sometimes, as in the present instance, laughter that is frivolous and light-hearted in effect; but sometimes, as often in his greatest work, laughter that is, in R. S. Crane's fine phrase, "the comic analogue of fear."[129] For the principal device on which the comedy turns in *The Letter-Writers* – that is, the use of threatening letters to keep the wives at home – was suggested to Fielding by the outbreak in 1730–1 of many instances of this same terrifying practice, used by real criminals and cutthroats to extort money from wealthy victims. One such letter, which may have served as model for those the husbands send in the play, was sent on 29 October 1730 to Fielding's second cousin, Lady Diana Fielding, daughter of the fourth Earl of Denbigh, at her house in Duke Street, Westminster.[130]

The Letter-Writers is also worth noting as perhaps Fielding's only experiment in the genre of pure "Farce," as he calls it on the title-page; for his other plays so denominated are more accurately classified as ballad operas. One of these, *The Lottery*, nevertheless contains in the Prologue Fielding's clearest statement of his conception of the genre:

> As *Tragedy* prescribes to Passion Rules,
> So *Comedy* delights to punish Fools;
> And while at nobler Game she boldly flies,
> *Farce* challenges the Vulgar as her Prize.
> Some Follies scarce perceptible appear
> In that just Glass, which shews you as you are.
> But *Farce* still claims a magnifying Right,
> To raise the Object larger to the Sight,
> And shew her Insect Fools in stronger Light.

The earliest reference to both Fielding's new plays of 1731 is a news item in the *Daily Post* (12 February 1730/1), reporting that they would be staged sometime "in the Beginning of March next." It was Friday, 19 March, however, before the same paper had heard that *The Tragedy of Tragedies: or, The Life and Death of Tom Thumb the Great* was "now in Rehearsal, and will be perform'd on Wednesday next" at the New Theatre in the Haymarket. The "puff" continued:

This Tragedy is so far superior to that which already bears the Name of Tom Thumb, that, omitting the Queen of the Giants, with several other grave Personages, together with Rivalships, Rebellions, Battles, Similies, &c. not to be found in the first Tom Thumb, it is enrich'd with a Ghost, which alone is worth that whole Performance. In short, it hath given great Satisfaction to the best Judges in the Closet, and doubtless will do the same in the Theatre.

This sanguine prediction proved truer than Fielding and his comedians could possibly have supposed. *The Tragedy of Tragedies* – which opened with *The Letter-Writers* as promised on Wednesday, 24 March 1730/1 – remained popular throughout the century, its performances at Drury Lane during Garrick's time there outnumbering even some of the favorite comedies of Wycherley, Congreve, and Shakespeare. It was, moreover, twice rendered in musical form, in 1733 as *The Opera of Operas* by Eliza Haywood and William Hatchett, and in 1780 as *Tom Thumb, a Burletta* by Kane O'Hara.[131] *The Letter-Writers*, on the other hand, though not a poor thing of its kind, seemed an insipid morsel indeed, being served up to the audience as afterpiece to all the hilarity of *The Tragedy*; it played just four times that season before vanishing permanently from the stage.

Both these plays – announced in the title-pages as the further productions of "Scriblerus Secundus" (or, to be quite precise in the case of *The Tragedy*, of "H. Scriblerus Secundus") – were published in separate editions by Roberts in time to be offered for sale on opening night for a shilling apiece. This timing, though not an unusual practice in the period, was especially desirable in the case of *The Tragedy*, not only because, as the advertisements promised,[132] "the Annotations of H. Scriblerus Secundus" would serve the audience "by Way of Key" to Fielding's innumerable parodies of the heroic dramatists, but also because Fielding had this time created two quite distinct, though complementary, kinds of satiric drama – kinds we might refer to in terms of the categories the publisher Bookweight understands in *The Author's Farce* (rev., I. vii): "your Acting Plays, and your Reading Plays." The "acting" version of *The Tragedy of Tragedies* continued to delight audiences with more of the same ocular and declamatory absurdities that had tickled them in its predecessor: the bombast and the swaggering, the ghosts and the thunder and lightning, the dances and the songs, the choreographed bloodbath of a catastrophe – seven stabbings seriatim! The "reading" version would enhance the pleasure of the parody by identifying the particular passages being mocked.

But, as Fielding's claim to be a scion of the Scriblerus family suggests, the book of *The Tragedy* was meant to parody the entire enterprise of Modern Criticism – as represented by those native-born pedants whom Pope and Swift roasted in *A Tale of a Tub* and *The Dunciad Variorum* (Bentley, Wotton, Dennis, and Theobald), as well as by those Dutch scholiasts whom Fielding listened to or pored over at Leyden (Burmann, Scaliger, and Lipsius). All these and more jostle for attention in Scriblerus's Preface and notes. Years earlier, in imitation of Addison's erudite praise of the ballad of *Chevy Chase* in *The Spectator* (21 May 1711), "William Wagstaff" had subjected the chapbook tale of *Tom Thumb* to a mock-critique rather like Fielding's.[133] Whether or not Fielding knew this pamphlet, the intent of his own uproarious performance – with its mock-learned prolegomena and annotations, and annotations *upon* annotations – is clear: he meant, like Nabokov in *Pale Fire*, to declare his literary kinship with Swift, Pope, and the Scriblerians.

The importance Fielding attached to the "reading" version of *The Tragedy of Tragedies* is also indicated by the fact that it is the only one of his plays – for that matter, it is the only one of his works of any kind – to be published originally with a frontispiece (see Plate 16). This plate, designed by Hogarth and engraved by Gerard Vandergucht, amusingly depicts Fielding's burlesque (in Act II, scene vii) of one of the celebrated moments from Dryden's *All for Love: or, The World Well Lost:* the confrontation between Cleopatra and Octavia, rivals for Mark Antony's love – in this case the principals having been transmogrified into the Giantess Glumdalca, Princess Huncamunca, and the diminutive Thumb. The real importance of this frontispiece, however, is that it marks the beginning, so far as we know, of Fielding's association with Hogarth, England's most distinguished artist of the middle decades of the century and a man who remained one of his closest friends.

The Tragedy of Tragedies – though circumstances prevented a run as prolonged as that of *Tom Thumb* a year earlier – was just as successful as its shorter, less elegant predecessor. Anticipating a keen demand for tickets, the Haymarket company added an extra sixpence to the normal charge for a seat in the gallery, but the audience was by no means limited to those who might be content with a place "in the gods." By the date of Fielding's second benefit (7 April) the following notice was placed in the *Daily Post*: "The Boxes not being equal to the great Demand of Places, (at the Desire of Several Ladies of Quality) Pit and Boxes will be laid together, and none admitted into either but by printed Tickets," thus adding two shillings to the usual price of a seat in the Pit. Among the "Ladies of Quality" who attended the play before the season ended were the Royal Princesses, Amelia and Caroline.[134]

That Fielding's burlesque enjoyed the patronage of the Royal Family makes it all the more doubtful that in *The Tragedy of Tragedies* he meant to satirize Walpole and the Court: to the point even of cracking tasteless jokes on the obesity of Princess Anne (who is said to be represented by Huncamunca), or her "pouting Breasts," or on the deformity of her future husband, the Prince of Orange.[135] There are, to be sure, lapses of delicacy in Fielding's works, but he was incapable of such gratuitous, gross public abuse of a princess of the Royal Family, particularly one whose mien he had not long before complimented privately in his unfinished mock-*Dunciad*: there "Anne's majestick lively Looks inspire" the "tuneful Muse."[136] And if in *The Tragedy* there is now and then a joke at Walpole's expense – as in applying the ministerial epithet, "the Great," to a hero of Lilliputian stature – a heavier irony is reserved for the minister's conniving adversaries, the leaders of the Opposition, represented by the choleric and conspiratorial Lord Grizzle, who in the account of the "Dramatis Personae" is said to be, like his party, "Extremely zealous for the Liberty of the Subject." Who, for instance, would have seemed to the audience the sillier of the two antagonists in the penultimate scene when Grizzle, the envious rebel, is summarily dispatched by Thumb, amiable and intrepid champion of the King's just cause?

GRIZZLE. Draw all your Swords, for Liberty we fight,
    And Liberty the Mustard is of Life.
TOM THUMB. Are you the Man whom Men fam'd *Grizzle* name?
GRIZZLE. Are you the much more fam'd *Tom Thumb*?
TOM THUMB. The same.
GRIZZLE. Come on, our Worth upon our selves we'll prove,
    For Liberty I fight.
TOM THUMB. And I for Love.

Thumb, after a hard-fought duel, runs the villain through; and Grizzle, after a moving speech of fourteen lines, gives up the ghost. Upon which, Thumb:

> With those last Words he vomited his Soul,
> Which, like whipt Cream, the Devil will swallow down.
> Bear off the Body, and cut off the Head,
> Which I will to the King in Triumph lug;
> Rebellion's dead, and now I'll go to Breakfast.

It is a nice matter in all this to distinguish the proportion of absurdity between Fielding's hero and his villain, but there can be no doubt where the sympathies of the audience lie. Though the satire of *The Tragedy of Tragedies* sometimes extends to targets other than the fatuities of heroic drama and modern pedantry, it was not meant as a serious indictment of contemporary politics.

Indeed, for some time in 1731 one suspects that Fielding was again actively courting Walpole. The plainest indication of such an intent is the Epilogue he contributed, under his own name, to *Orestes*, a new dramatic opera by, of all unlikely persons, Lewis Theobald: Pope's Prince of Dunces, whom Fielding also ridiculed in *The Tragedy of Tragedies*, mocking both his commentary on Shakespeare (I.i.8, n. c.) and his abortive attempts to soar in verse in his tragedy *The Persian Princess*.[137] *Orestes*, with Fielding's Epilogue, opened on 3 April 1731 at Lincoln's Inn Fields, the scene of Fielding's recent failure with *The Coffee-House Politician*. When published a week later, it boasted not merely the modest "puff" Fielding gave it in his Epilogue, but also the official blessing of the Great Man himself, to whom, with Walpole's express permission, the play was dedicated. Theobald's connection with Walpole was no secret; the minister had personally sponsored him in the recent competition for the laureateship.

This friendly gesture by Fielding seems surprising if we recall not only the uncomplimentary allusions to Theobald in *The Tragedy* and in the poem of the previous year to "the Nymphs of New S[aru]m," but also the rough treatment he would receive at Fielding's hands in the early 1740s, in such works as *The Champion, Shamela, A Journey from This World to the Next, The True Patriot* (11–18 February 1745/6), and *Plutus*. Nevertheless, this epilogue signals the beginning of a period of friendship between the two men. Consider, for example, in Fielding's unpublished "Epistle to Mr. Lyttleton" written in 1733, this impassioned defense of his new friend against the strictures of Pope:

> Why, when thou lashest Tibbald's lifeless Lays,
> Dost thou not give the Solid Critick Praise?
> His Name with Shakespeare's shall to Ages Soar
> When thou shalt jingle in our Ears no more
> Shakespeare by him restor'd again we see
> Recover'd of the Wounds he bore from thee.
> And sure much brighter must his Merit shine
> Who gives us Sha[kes]peare's Works, than his who thine.[138]

But this praise of Theobald's scholarly virtues is far less eloquent testimony of Fielding's esteem than the two guineas he was willing to part with in order to subscribe to his friend's edition of Shakespeare published in 1734. Four times only does Fielding's name appear on subscription lists of the period, and this is one of them.[139]

Another incident from the spring of 1731 – comical enough to serve Fielding years later in an essay illustrating the subjective element in taste and humor – again places him in the company of a figure so well known as a creature of the minister that he was called "Walpole's Poet." This was the fawning Scotsman, Joseph Mitchell, whose poem, "The Sine-Cure," petitioning Walpole for the governorship of Duck Island, Fielding facetiously alluded to in his own epistle to the minister of the preceding year. In *The Covent-Garden Journal* (7 March 1752) Fielding recalls that he was present at Drury Lane on 20 April 1731 for the fourth (and, as it mercifully proved, terminal) performance of Mitchell's comic opera, *The Highland-Fair* – this being Mitchell's benefit night. In this "Piece" his Scots friend

> intended to display the comical Humours of the Highlanders; the Audience, who had for three Nights together sat staring at each other, scarce knowing what to make of their Entertainment, on the fourth joined in a unanimous exploding Laugh. This they had continued through an Act, when the Author, who unhappily mistook the Peels of Laughter which he heard for Applause, went up to Mr. Wilks, and, with an Air of Triumph, said – *Deel o' my Sal, Sare, they begin to tauk the Humour at last.*

There is of course nothing political about the "pleasant Fact," as Fielding calls it, of Mitchell's foolishness that night at Drury Lane; Fielding's subject is the elusive quality of humor, and he seems to have been convinced that Scotsmen as a race lacked a sense of it.[140] Nevertheless, the story places him there at the Establishment theatre supporting the benefit of a man who, like his friends Theobald and Ralph, was an author for the Court side. What is more, it is clear that Mitchell thought of Fielding as, like himself, another of the singing birds who flocked round the minister for protection. Thus in *A Familiar Epistle to the Right Honourable Sir Robert Walpole, concerning Poets, Poverty, Promises, Places, &c.* (1735) he asked the Minister:

> Your Praises who has better sung?
> —— Pardon is begg'd of *Messieurs* YOUNG,
> TIBBALD and WELSTED, FIELDING, FROWDE,
> And fifty more who round you crowd.
>
> (p. 6)

Fielding's being in Mitchell's company on that droll occasion of the latter's "benefit" for *The Highland Fair* may, or may not, be a sign of his political inclinations at the time. He must have known, however, that by affixing his name to the epilogue for Theobald's *Orestes*, a work by Walpole's protégé and dedicated to Walpole, he would be seen by friend and foe alike to have taken sides in the political wars. Could these early months of 1731 – after his failure at Lincoln's Inn Fields and before the lucrative "benefits" of the spring season at the Haymarket – be the moment when he composed the second of his two begging verse epistles to the minister, dated only "*Anno* 1731"?

> Great Sir, as on each Levée Day
> I still attend you – still you say
> I'm busy now, To-morrow come;
> To-morrow, Sir, you're not at Home.
> So says your Porter, and dare I
> Give such a Man as him the Lie?
>   In Imitation, Sir, of you,
> I keep a mighty Levée too;
> Where my Attendants, to their Sorrow,
> Are bid to come again To-morrow.
> To-morrow they return, no doubt,
> And then like you, Sir, I'm gone out.
> So says my Maid – but they, less civil,
> Give Maid and Master to the Devil;
> And then with Menaces depart,
> Which could you hear would pierce your Heart.
>   Good Sir, or make my Levée fly me,
> Or lend your Porter to deny me.

If this was the time of such overtures to the minister, they were not answered to Fielding's satisfaction until later in the year, when another of his clever plays at the Haymarket brought home to Walpole just how troublesome an author Fielding could be if allowed unchecked to apply his talent for ridicule to the game of politics.

····➤ xvii ◀···

Fielding had been at work on *The Welsh Opera* at about the time he composed his epilogue for Theobald; for as early as 6 April 1731 the *Daily Post* informed the public that the play, planned for an earlier staging, had been "deferr'd till Easter Week." In fact, surely as much from a sense of the appropriateness of the occasion as from mere happy coincidence, it was "not ... entirely ready" until 22 April, Fielding's twenty-fourth birthday and also his third "benefit" from *The Tragedy of Tragedies*, to which the new ballad opera served as afterpiece. Considering that in two abbreviated seasons with the Haymarket comedians this represented the sixth new play Fielding had written for them (counting *The Tragedy of Tragedies*), the Player's opening speech to Scriblerus had point:

Upon my word, Mr. *Scriblerus*, you write Plays, (or something like Plays) faster than we can act them, or the Town damn them; I hope your Opera will take up more time in Running than it hath in Writing.

There can be no doubt about Fielding's remarkable facility as a dramatist; and in this instance the play had an encouraging, if reckless, run. Coupled with *The Tragedy of Tragedies* it was performed three more times in April, and was staged again on 19 May for the benefit of William Mullart, the company's principal actor, and his wife – for which occasion Fielding made "several Alterations and Additions."

Well before this performance Fielding must have realized he had underestimated the potential of the piece. He was already at work on a much enlarged and revised version, which he entitled *The Grub-Street Opera* – possibly taking the name from a gibe at John Gay in *The Fool's Opera*, written by the "droll," Anthony Aston, and published aptly on April Fool's Day.[141] A notice in the *Daily Post* (21 May) indicates that Fielding believed he had a possible "hit" on his hands and was impatient to get it before the public before the novelty of the idea was lost and the town emptied for the summer:

> We hear that the Grubstreet Opera, written by Scriblerus Secundus, which was to have been postponed till next Season, will, at the particular Request of several Persons of Quality, be perform'd within a Fortnight, being now in Rehearsal at the New Theatre in the Haymarket. This is the Welch Opera alter'd and enlarg'd to three Acts.

What was the formula, then, that Fielding hit upon and that seemed instantly worth the trouble of refining in this new and elaborate production? For one thing, Fielding was a gifted song writer, with a knack of composing a lively, witty lyric.[142] To judge from the nature of his revisions, audiences at *The Welsh Opera* called for more: in *The Grub-Street Opera* Fielding more than doubled the number of songs (from thirty-one to sixty-five), adding a half-dozen airs by Handel, and others by such popular composers as Henry Carey, Tom D'Urfey, Attilio Ariosti, and Pepusch, Gay's collaborator on *The Beggar's Opera*. It is worth noting, furthermore, as a sign of the continuing association between the two men, that in his haste to complete the revisions, Fielding borrowed nine songs that James Ralph had used a year earlier in his own ballad opera, *The Fashionable Lady*.[143] Hurried as these alterations were, the end product was admirable: "it is fair to say," observes an authority on the musical drama of the period, "that *The Grub-Street Opera* is musically the most satisfactory of all the ballad operas written in the decade following *The Beggar's Opera*."[144] Indeed, one of Fielding's songs from the play was so popular that, with some

belated help from Richard Leveridge, it became traditional for theatre
audiences throughout the century to sing it heartily before and after
any new play, and even between acts.[145] That song is, of course, "The
Roast Beef of Old England":

> When mighty roast beef was the Englishman's food,
> It ennobled our hearts, and enriched our blood,
> Our soldiers were brave, and our courtiers wee good.
>> Oh the roast beef of England,
>> And old England's roast beef!
>
> But since we have learnt from all-conquering France,
> To eat their ragouts as well as to dance,
> Oh what a fine figure we make in romance!
>> Oh the roast beef of England,
>> And old England's roast beef![146]

As it happened, however, audiences were denied the pleasure of
hearing this ballad for another three years, when Fielding made a place
for it in *Don Quixote in England*. For *The Grub-Street Opera* was never
staged. No doubt the reason for this disappointment was the second
element in the successful theatrical formula Fielding first hit upon in
The Welsh Opera: the play was not only musical; it was also political –
and in a way far more flagrant than Gay's *Beggar's Opera*, or even its
much lamented sequel *Polly*. For this reason, surely, the Haymarket
company chose for the second run of *The Welsh Opera*, beginning on
26 May, to couple it with *The Fall of Mortimer*, a thinly disguised and
abusive attack on Walpole. From this moment, whatever chance there
may have been of the government's continuing to suffer Fielding's
satire for the sake of his songs vanished; his play – and now it is the
fate of the new, improved version, *The Grub-Street Opera*, that concerns
us – was doomed.

In itself the political satire in Fielding's opera, though undeniably
impertinent, is neither very abrasive nor at all partisan. It turns on a
traditional analogy comparing the polity to a family. So, for instance,
the author of *Fog's Weekly Journal* (15 August 1730) had recently
begun another of his criticisms of the government, which, in his view,
was administered and staffed at every level by misfits interested solely
in their own private aggrandizement: "The Master of a Family, he who
has many Servants under him, is to consider their several Capacities;
it is his Business to judge of their different Qualifications, and apply
them accordingly. – He will not set a good Cook to clean the Stables,
or appoint him to dress the Dinner whose Business it is to dress
the Horses." The metaphor is pursued through all the offices of the
household, much as Fielding would himself later do in *Amelia* (I.ii). In

The Grub-Street Opera he similarly spins out his mischievous allegory of contemporary England: the Master of the Family, the Welshman Sir Owen Apshinken, stands transparently for King George II; his wife Lady Apshinken, who rules the family household and is "a zealous advocate for the church," shares those attributes with Queen Caroline; their philandering son Owen is no less obviously Frederick, Prince of Wales. And the male servants of the household ludicrously characterize the principal figures in the government and Opposition: there are Thomas the gardener (Thomas Pelham-Holles, Duke of Newcastle, Secretary of State) and John the groom (John, Lord Hervey, a favorite creature of the minister); and, most especially, there are Robin the butler (Sir Robert Walpole) and his bitter adversary William the coachman (William Pulteney, leader of the Opposition). "For the first time," as Professor Goldgar observes, "Fielding unambiguously jeered at politicians and court figures, reducing them to the level of a Welsh family with its domestic squabbles."[147]

Those stately figures may have winced at the laughter of audiences alert to every topical nuance, but Fielding's satire is fairly innocuous when compared to the egregious standard of scandal-mongering and vituperation current at the time. And – an important circumstance often overlooked – his satire is even-handed in roasting both parties alike. Parson Puzzletext thus advises Lady Apshinken on the relative merits of Robin and William: "I think it is a difficult matter to determine which deserves to be hang'd most; and if Robin the butler hath cheated more than other people, I see no other reason for it, but because he hath had more opportunity to cheat.' A sentiment with which Robin, the wiser bird, heartily concurs, making it the burden of the song he sings to the tune of "Ye Madcaps of England":

> The world is so cramm'd brim-full of deceit,
> That if Robin be a name for a cheat,
>   Sing tantarara, Bobs all, Bobs all,
>   Sing tantarara, Bobs all.

It is not true, as is sometimes said of the play, that in it Fielding at last plainly showed his true political colors, preferring William to Robin – declaring himself for the Opposition's cause of liberty and honesty in government against the cheating rogue, Walpole. Fielding was not quite cynical about the possibility of there being political causes worth holding to; he was unshakable in his principles as a good Whig of the sound Lockean stamp. But he took a pragmatic view of his talents as a writer when politics was his subject. It never mattered much to him which Whig was in place, so long as he was a friend. Now, as we reflect on the political ambiguities in *The Welsh Opera* and its sequel that have led critics to very different conclusions about Fielding's politics, and as we consider the bewildering inconsistency of the attitudes he expresses toward Walpole and the King, the Opposition and the Scriblerians, all of whom, depending on Fielding's mood or motives of the moment, are the object of either his mockery or praise – now is the time to recall the declaration he made some years later in *The Jacobite's Journal* (26 March 1748), that "a Writer, whose only Livelihood is his Pen," must, like "every other Advocate," be allowed the right to sell his services to those who will pay for them:

> To confess the Truth, the World is in general too severe on Writers. In a Country where there is no public Provision for Men of Genius, and in an Age when no Literary Productions are encouraged, or indeed read, but such as are season'd with Scandal against the Great; and when a Custom hath prevailed of publishing this, not only with Impunity but with great Emolument, the Temptation to Men in desperate Circumstances is too violent to be resisted; and if the Public will feed a hungry Man for a little Calumny, he must be a very honest Person indeed, who will rather starve than write it.
>
> In a Time therefore of profound Tranquillity, and when the Consequence, at the worst, can probably be no greater than the Change of a Ministry, I do not think a Writer, whose only Livelihood is his Pen, to deserve a very flagitious Character, if, when one Set of Men deny him Encouragement, he seeks it from another, at their Expence; nor will I rashly condemn such a Writer as the vilest of Men, (provided he keeps within the Rules of Decency) if he endeavours to make the best of his own Cause, and uses a little Art in blackening his Adversary. Why should a Liberty which is allowed to every other Advocate, be deny'd to this?

Twenty years earlier, as a wild young man whose only saleable commodity was a talent to amuse, Fielding was no more inclined to play the idealist in such a mercenary game as politics. His own sentiments on the subject conformed pretty closely to those of his surrogate, "Scriblerus Secundus," author of *The Grub-Street Opera*, who thus explains to the Master of the Playhouse how it happens that the Grub Street brethren should "pull one another to pieces as you do, especially in your political pamphlets":

Scriblerus. ... alas! you mistake Altercation or Scolding a little in Jest, for quarrelling in Earnest – Sir, was you ever at *Westminster Hall*?
Master. Often, Sir.
Scriblerus. Did you never hear our People scold there?
Master. I have heard the Lawyers.

SCRIBLERUS. The Lawyers! Why those are our People; there hath long been the strictest Union between *Grubstreet* and the Law; thus our Politicians are as good Friends as our Lawyers, behind the Curtain; they scold and abuse one another in the Persons of their Masters and Clients, and then very friendly get drunk together over their Booty – Our People no more quarrel in Earnest, than they quarrel with Civility – Why, Sir, you might as well suppose *Robin* and *Will*, in my *Opera*, to be in Earnest.[148]

In *The Welsh Opera* (or *The Grub-Street Opera* to be), Fielding's "clients" were not the patrons of either political party. They were the audience that crowded the Little Theatre in the Haymarket to see those politicians, on both sides, given a good roasting as the grasping opportunists they so obviously were: "Sing tantarara, Bobs all, Bobs all." Robin, if anyone, emerges the more attractive figure because he is bolder and better at the game than William, who sulks about, too much the cur in the manger. Even so, the play cannot have been acceptable to the authorities; it is too impudent in making a public spectacle of the foibles of the Royal Family. Critics who doubt that the ministry can have found Fielding's play objectionable on political grounds seem not to appreciate the importance of this offensive aspect of the satire. And as it began its second run on 26 May, it would be thoroughly contaminated by being yoked together on the same bill with *The Fall of Mortimer*, a play obnoxious to Walpole, whom the actor Mullart satirized in the title role as he did as Robin in the afterpiece.

So even as Fielding, perhaps sensing he had gone too far, was revising the play to make it more tuneful and less politically discordant, the patience of the authorities had been taxed to the limit; they would not suffer what was being advertised as a bigger and better version of Fielding's impudent opera. The *Daily Post* of 21 May promised that *The Grub-Street Opera* would "be perform'd within a Fortnight"; but it was not quite ready by 5 June, when the Haymarket company discontinued playing *The Welsh Opera* with *The Fall of Mortimer*, because, as they "advertise[d] the town," they were now rehearsing Fielding's new version in earnest. Next week they fixed the opening for Friday, 11 June – "the said Opera" being "thought by the best Judges to contain more Humour, delicate Satire, and a better Collection of Tunes, as well Italian as English, than any Performance with which the Town hath been lately diverted."[149] The day before the promised opening, apparently now apprehensive that the abnormally hot weather would discourage attendance, they assured the public they would be entertained "At Common Prices" and in comfort, the "House" being "extraordinary cool." To this "Bavius" of the *Grub-Street Journal*

(10 June) replied on the same day, "strictly charging" all his fellow Grubbeans to assemble on the morrow "at the Sign of the Cock and Bottle, an Alehouse at Charing-Cross, between the hours of three and four, thence to proceed in a body" to the theatre, warning "Scriblerus Secundus" at the same time that he was expected to receive and seat the brethren "with that respect which is due them." It was *their* opera, after all, and being also Fielding's they were no doubt prepared to accord it the kind of reception they always gave his work.

But Martyn, Russel, and their critical colleagues of the *Grub-Street Journal* had no opportunity to play their catcalls at the Little Haymarket the following evening. Despite three weeks of preliminary "puffs" and fanfares in the papers, and more time than that spent by Fielding and the company in writing and rehearsing the work, *The Grub-Street Opera* was not acted on 11 June, though the *Daily Post* advertised the performance as scheduled. The next day a shuffling notice in the same paper explained that the performance had been cancelled because of the sudden illness of the "Principal Performer" (Mullart); the play would be staged instead on "Monday next," 14 June. Not so. On that day, though Mullart had recovered his health, the company presented a double-bill of *The Fall of Mortimer* and *The Jealous Taylor*; and they were no longer troubling to invent excuses for disappointing the Town. The *Daily Post* of 14 June carried their simple notice: "We are oblig'd to defer the GRUBSTREET OPERA till further Notice."

What had happened to oblige the company to withdraw Fielding's play at the eleventh hour? They would not lightly cancel a production which had so much of their effort and capital invested in it. Only one explanation seems possible: the play was considered too offensive to the authorities and was suppressed – suppressed, however, as the complete lack of any hard evidence to that effect suggests, in some unconventional way.

The first hint of the government's attitude toward the play, and perhaps of its part in quashing it, came from the weirdest of Walpole's journalists, "Orator" Henley. In *The Hyp-Doctor* (8–15 June 1731) Henley was inspired by the event to compose some gloating verses to the "*Hay-Market* Actors *of the design'd* Grub-street *Opera*."

> THE censuring World, perhaps, may not esteem
> A Satire on so scandalous a Theme,
> As these Stage-Apes, who must a Play-house chuse,
> The Villain's Refuge, the Whore's Rendezvous:
> So dull in ev'ry Shape, that you may see
> Sorrow turn'd Mirth, and Mirth turn'd Tragedy;
> M[ullar]t's chief Business is to swear and eat,

He'll turn Procurer for a Dish of Meat,
Else the poor hungry Ruffian must, I fear,
Live on grey Pease and Salt for half the Year.

Henley's doggerel hints plainly enough that if the comedians at the
Haymarket were chiefly the objects of the government's abhorrence,
Fielding's play was considered to be their vehicle for scandal. Immedi-
ately following the poem, a mock-advertisement declares that the
company, having distinguished themselves in "assaulting THEIR
BETTERS" in *The Fall of Mortimer*, would next be seen at Paddington-
Road in "a Ballad Opera of one Act, call'd TYBURN IN GLORY, *or*,
THESPIS IN A CART": "The Style is Poet *Fielding*'s sublime, very
lofty."

A week later, in *The Hyp-Doctor* (15–22 June 1731), Henley resumed
this theme. Addressing "Caleb D'Anvers" (i.e., Nicholas Amhurst,
editor of *The Craftsman*), he drew up a short list of the chief literary
offenders against the ministry – Caleb's "Help-Mates and Yoke-Fellows
in the good Work of joyning the People in a Scheme of Division" –
including in a biblical vein the likes of "*Jonadab Swift, Jeroboam
Arbuthnot, Nebuchadnezar B[olingbrok]e, Achitophel P[ulteney], Rab-
sakeh Blocksem, Esau Budgel.*" Distinguished in Henley's catalogue of
political infidels by the sheer quantity of invective heaped on him is
"*Doeg* FIELDING," Caleb's

> Under-Spur-Leather, your Dagger of Lath, your Crier of Mustard to
> bite the Noses of the *Hay-Market* Actors, your Threader of Acts and
> Scenes, your Tragedy-Trimmer, your Farce-bundler, from the *Fall
> of Mortimer* to the *Grub-street Opera*; in short, your Flayer of dead
> Wits for live Conceits, your Rat-Catcher of Poetic Images, that either
> run from Him, or fly in his Face.

Critics have been reluctant to admit the ministry's irritation at the
brazen satire of *The Grub-Street Opera*, but these vituperative attacks
by Henley in successive numbers of *The Hyp-Doctor* should remove
such doubts once and for all.

Fielding received and understood the government's message: it was
he, apparently, who not only quashed the production of *The Grub-Street
Opera*, but who also actively discouraged its publication. His behavior
in the latter respect is especially puzzling, since he might have expected,
from the recent example of the money Gay made from the publication
of his suppressed play *Polly*, that publishing the play would be profitable. Had he been paid to keep it *out* of print? The curious history of
the play's publication – and of his own initially reluctant part in it –
is at least not inconsistent with such an hypothesis. The *Daily Post* for
21 May declared that *The Grub-Street Opera* "is now in the Press, and

will be sold at the Theatre with the Musick prefix'd to the Songs (being about sixty in Number) on the first Night of Performance." But just as the play itself never had a "first Night of Performance," so the book of the play to which this advertisement refers never saw the light of day. On 26 June, a fortnight after the promised opening night, there did issue from the press of the disreputable Opposition bookseller, E. Rayner, a slovenly and unauthorized version of *The Welsh Opera: or, The Grey Mare the better Horse* (the proverbial subtitle referring to Queen Caroline's dominance over her husband) – a version apparently based on the prompter's copy.[150]

In the Preface to this pirated edition, Rayner (or the hack representing him) asserted one very probable truth about *The Grub-Street Opera*: that its "Performance ... has been prevented, by a certain Influence which has been very *prevailing* of late Years" – and one very palpable falsehood: that the text of the play Fielding had so thoroughly revised was "in effect the same" as the one now being offered the public. Rayner was answered at the first opportunity in the *Daily Post* of the following Monday (28 June). The author of this riposte chose to remain anonymous; but he was irate enough, and knowledgeable enough about the circumstances pertaining to the authorship and production of the two works, to have been Fielding himself:

> Whereas one Rayner hath publish'd a strange Medley of Nonsense, under the Title of the WELCH OPERA, said to be written by the Author of the Tragedy of Tragedies; and also hath impudently affirm'd that this was great Part of the Grub-street Opera, which he attempts to insinuate was stopt by Authority: This is to assure the Town, that what he hath publish'd is a very incorrect and spurious Edition of the Welch Opera, a very small Part of which was originally written by the said Author; and that it contains scarce any thing of the Grub-street Opera, excepting the Names of some of the Characters and a few of the Songs: This latter Piece hath in it above fifty entire new Songs; and is so far from having been stopt by Authority (for which there could be no manner of Reason) that it is only postponed to a proper Time, when it is not doubted but the Town will be convinced how little that Performance agrees with the intolerable and scandalous Nonsense of this notorious Paper Pyrate.

If this declaration is in fact by Fielding (as it appears to be), it is particularly interesting in the claim that he had only "a very small Part" in composing *The Welsh Opera*, which the company's advertisements always attributed wholly to him, and in the firm denial that the performance was "stopt by Authority (for which [he adds parenthetically, affecting pained innocence] there could be no manner of Reason)". The defensive tone of these disclaimers suggests what is probably closer to the truth: that Fielding, having made a bargain with the ministry to withdraw his play and stop its publication, was anxious to state publicly that he had not gone back on his word, and that the impertinence of *The Welsh Opera*, which they could now read for themselves, was none (or little) of his own work.

A number of signs point to Fielding's having struck such a bargain – to his having come to some arrangement which exempted him from the measures the government took against the Haymarket comedians, not merely to muzzle them, but to prosecute them in the King's Bench for "false, infamous, scandalous, seditious and treasonable Libels."[151] The only reason officially given for the steps taken to arrest the actors and to close their theatre was the offensive character of *The Fall of Mortimer*; neither Fielding nor his scarcely less political play, whether we call it *The Welsh Opera* or *The Grub-Street Opera*, was ever mentioned in this context. On 17 June, for instance, it was reported that the Haymarket company "have been forbid acting any more *The Fall of Mortimer*,"[152] a prohibition which they defiantly disregarded. On 7 July Walpole's agent, Nicholas Paxton, reported that warrants had been granted the High Constable of Westminster to apprehend the players who acted in *The Fall of Mortimer* – all of whom, however, had fled and remained at large;[153] that same day the Grand Jury for the County of Middlesex delivered a presentment against the play. On 21 July Mullart and his colleagues again narrowly escaped capture by the High Constable, who raided the theatre as they were about to perform *The Fall of Mortimer*.[154] These persecutions continued even when the Haymarket company, trying now merely to ply their trade, attempted to stage an enter-tainment Walpole himself was known to have enjoyed and sponsored: on 20 August the constables raided the theatre in the midst of a performance of *Hurlothrumbo* and "dispers'd the Actors."[155]

Why, in this relentless official campaign to hound the Haymarket comedians out of existence, is no mention ever made of Fielding, their most popular author and, still more to the point, the author of *The Welsh Opera* – a play which ridicules the Royal Family and certain well-known politicians, including Walpole, and which was also tainted by being performed five times in association with *The Fall of Mortimer*? Light was thrown on this mystery in August, when, hoping to reap some return for their trouble in preparing Fielding's revised version of the play for the stage, members of the Haymarket company arranged surreptitiously with Rayner[156] to publish it under the title *The Genuine Grub-Street Opera*. In reference to the players' intention to publish this work, the *Daily Journal* (12 August), besides stating that the play was printed for "the Benefit of the Comedians ... and handed about privately," asserted that it had not been acted as originally planned because "suppressed." Soon, however, that paper (16 August) felt obliged to retract both statements:

> It having been inserted in this Paper of last Thursday, that the genuine Grub-street Opera, which was intended to have been performed at the New Theatre in the Hay-Market, but suppress'd, was printed for the Benefit of the Comedians of the said Theatre, and handed about privately: This is to inform the Publick, that we were imposed on in the said Account; and we are since well assured that the said Company are no ways concerned in the printing or publishing thereof: And as to its being suppress'd, the said Company know no more than that the Author desired it might not be performed.

This attempt of the Haymarket comedians to dissociate themselves from the publication of the work was motivated, according to one report, "thro' Fear" only – a plausible enough explanation, considering that they had now been harassed by the authorities for two months; from the same anonymous source the Town was assured that *The Genuine Grub-Street Opera* "was printed from a genuine original Copy ... altho' so great Pains have been taken to stifle and contradict it."[157]

According to the players, then, it was Fielding himself who insisted at the last minute that *The Grub-Street Opera* not be staged. Nor did he have anything to do with either of the two pirated published versions, which were the result of collusion between members of the Haymarket company and Rayner. What is more, it now appears that Fielding had nothing to do with the publication *this year* – or indeed any other year during his lifetime – of the one authoritative text of *The Grub-Street Opera*: this is the edition which also includes the verse satire *The Masquerade* and which claims on the title-page to have been printed by James Roberts in 1731. Through an ingenious piece of bibliographical detective work, a recent editor of the play concludes that the Roberts–1731 imprint is a later fabrication – that, indeed, Roberts never printed *The Grub-Street Opera* and that this, the only authorized text, did not appear in print until, in 1755, Andrew Millar published it in Fielding's *Dramatic Works* from copy Fielding himself had supplied.[158] If this analysis is correct (it is certainly cogent), and if it is also true, as the Haymarket players claimed, that it was Fielding who quashed the production of the play, there is only one plausible explanation for his reluctance to reap the fruits of his labors in writing the work: Walpole, or someone acting in his behalf, had made it worth his while to suppress the play.

In later years, among many malevolent charges leveled against Fielding by his enemies – some reflecting fact, some not – one in particular comes to mind in the present context. This is an anecdote related by "Aretine" of *Old England* (5 August 1749):

If there be such a Wretch, who, having wrote a Farce of personal Ridicule against a Minister and all his Family, finds Means to insinuate to them, by the Canal of a credulous Agent, that the dirty Work being extorted from him by griping Want and Penury, he was desirous to, and afterwards actually did, suppress it for a small Consideration of *Relief*; and if, after he had run thro' his Subsidy with an Extravagance of Voracity, he should threaten to revive the abusive Scenes of Scurrility, unless he was purchased a second Time into Silence....

Was *The Grub-Street Opera* the "Farce" to which "Aretine" refers? Perhaps. We shall see that Fielding was not above taking money to suppress his own works. And this play – with its ridicule of Walpole, his brother Horatio, his mistress Molly Skerrett – fits the description well enough if one allows for the malignant hyperbole usual with the author of the anecdote. Certainly no other known "Farce" of Fielding's squares as well with the circumstances as they are represented.

In any event Fielding's highly successful association with the Haymarket Theatre ended abruptly in June 1731, when *The Grub-Street Opera*, after many rehearsals, mysteriously vanished from the stage at the eleventh hour, never having been performed before an audience. Though hounded by the authorities for their brazen persistence in staging, or attempting to stage, such political entertainments – particularly *The Fall of Mortimer* – the Haymarket company clung to the delusion that the ministry's actions against them were merely monitory, that they were not meant to be crushed altogether. They were mistaken. The *Daily Post* (6 October) announced that the players would open their new season on the 16th with a performance of *The Author's Farce*; but the play was not performed. In the ensuing months their stage was given over to exhibitions of prize-fighting, tumbling, and rope-dancing.

••••◆ xviii ◆•••

Not everyone in the company suffered. A few of the best of them – Mullart, for instance, and their German music director, the obscure "Mr. Seedo"[159] – found less precarious places at Drury Lane. By far the luckiest of these refugees was Fielding himself, who, now in only his twenty-fourth year, was about to begin an extraordinary period of creative activity which, together with his position as dramatist of the company at the Theatre Royal, would establish his reputation as London's principal living playwright – a reputation attested all the more impressively by the venom and inveteracy of the attacks upon him in the *Grub-Street Journal.*

The first indication of his move to Drury Lane is a report in *Read's Weekly Journal* (27 November 1731) that "three new Plays [were] now on the Stocks there, which are to be acted one after the other with all Speed; a Tragedy by Mr. Aaron Hill; a Comedy of Captain Bodens; and another by Mr. Fielding, the Author of Tom Thumb." The play to which the paper refers was probably Fielding's major production of the new season, *The Modern Husband*, which would be staged in February not long after *The Modish Couple* (supposedly by Bodens but in fact by the Reverend James Miller) had suffered a riotous demise. *The Modern Husband* had been ready for the stage more than a year earlier (in September 1730); it was in rehearsal at Drury Lane shortly before Christmas.[160]

In the event, however, Fielding's first piece of the new season was something much lighter, if no less timely in the topic of its satire: this was the one-act ballad opera, *The Lottery*, on which he collaborated with Seedo. It was probably not Fielding's first collaboration with that little-known musician, whose modest talents are suggested by his leaving London in 1736 to become director of the "royal band" in Potsdam. As Seedo was musical director at the Haymarket when Fielding wrote *The Grub-Street Opera*, it is likely they worked together on that ill-fated production, an inference strengthened by the fact that they incorporated into *The Lottery* no fewer than seven tunes from *The Grub-Street Opera*. In rehearsal as early as 18 December 1731,[161] *The Lottery* was first performed as the afterpiece to Addison's *Cato* on 1 January and was published on the 7th of that month.

Lotteries of the kind Fielding ridicules were held at intervals from 1694 to 1826, often for such worthwhile purposes as the building of Westminster Bridge or the British Museum. But again the inspiration for Fielding's play was a particular newsworthy event of the recent past, the State Lottery of 1731, by which the government proposed to raise two-thirds of the cost of a loan of £1,200,000.[162] Drawings began at the Guildhall on 11 October and continued until 25 November. Whether or not Fielding had been personally burned in the fever of speculation that touched all classes, from dukes and duchesses to their coachmen and chambermaids, it is certain that from this time forward the institution of the state lottery became, like Heidegger's masquerades, one of his favorite satiric targets.[163] As Fielding saw it, the system promoted false hopes of riches in the "Adventurers," many of whom were poor; and the manipulation of tickets by unscrupulous brokers, such as Stocks in the play, was so adroit that the simple were easily victimized. In *The Lottery* it is the coachman who is bit (scene iii); in *The Intriguing Chambermaid* Lettice risks her little all (I.iii). On the whole, however, the fate of *The Grub-Street Opera*, together with his awareness of the proprieties to be observed by a playwright of the Theatre Royal, taught Fielding a lesson in how to direct his shafts prudently and with a lighter touch. Except for a passing hit at Walpole's lecherous friend, Colonel Charteris – an allusion that anticipates Plate I of *The Harlot's Progress*, reinforcing our sense of the early friendship between Fielding and Hogarth[164] – and except also for a fleeting glance at the recent scandal involving the directors of the Charitable Corporation (scene ii), Fielding avoids targets that might be considered politically sensitive.

As for the play's reception, the only contemporary opinion to have survived tells us as much of the tastes of the critic as of the success of Fielding's little opera. Lord Hervey, still perhaps annoyed at the part he had been made to play as John the groom in *The Welsh Opera*, attended the third night, when *The Lottery* was paired with *Henry VIII*; he was more amused by the havoc caused in the latter, as the Champion's horse went out of control during the coronation scene, than he was by any humor he detected in the afterpiece. He had to admit, however, that Fielding's play was a "hit." On 4 January 1731/2 he wrote Stephen Fox that he and his friends "adjourned after dinner to the play to see the new farce called *The Lottery*, ill-written, ill-acted and ill-sung, but well attended and well applauded."[165] So delighted were the audiences who saw even this original, abbreviated version of Fielding's ballad opera that *The Lottery* was performed fifteen times before the month was out: one of these performances was by Royal Command on the author's benefit night for *The Modish Couple*; another was for Fielding's own benefit on the 21st. By 1 February, Fielding had completed a revision of the play, enhancing its appeal in a number of ways but especially by adding a new scene representing the drawing of the lottery at the Guildhall. *The Lottery*, slight as it is, was performed regularly for half a century; it remains one of Fielding's happiest achievements in the ballad opera form.

While his musical afterpiece was entertaining audiences in January, Fielding was peripherally involved at Drury Lane in another production that proved to be – for reasons having little to do with its theatrical qualities – the most resounding failure of the season. This was the new comedy *The Modish Couple*, a work purporting to be the improbable creation of Charles Bodens, Captain in the Coldstream Regiment of Footguards and Gentleman Usher Quarter Waiter in ordinary to the King, but best known at Court for his magnificent corpulency and his resourcefulness as pimp to the Prince of Wales. Horace Walpole summed Bodens up as "a man of some humour, and universal Parasite."[166] But whatever other useful qualities he possessed, Bodens was no author. According to one report which Viscount Perceval had heard while visiting Hampton Court the preceding October, Bodens was merely the screen behind which the real authors, Lord Hervey and the Prince of Wales, were concealing themselves. Those closer to Drury Lane, however, heard a different story – a story recorded on good authority by the contemporary theatrical historian Benjamin Victor.[167] The author of *The Modish Couple* was in fact the theatrical parson and translator of Molière, the Reverend James Miller, who struck a bargain with Bodens, knowing that only someone of the Captain's interest at Drury Lane and at Court could get the play performed and ensure it a successful run.

Long before the play opened on 10 January 1731/2 it was obvious that *The Modish Couple* was the darling of the Court. In September 1731 the newspapers reported that it would be presented privately at St. James's for the entertainment of the Royal Family. By December, Cibber and Wilks were rehearsing it at Drury Lane, and a claque of eminent courtiers had formed to support it: on the 6th of that month the *Daily Post* reported that the Duke of Richmond and his inseparable chum the Duke of Montagu, who hugely loved a hoax such as this, were seen together at rehearsal along with many other "Persons of Quality ... and were very much diverted, desiring some of the Scenes to be rehearsed over again." To guarantee (they supposed) a successful first night for Captain Bodens's play, these noble friends invited two hundred of their acquaintance to dinner at the Bedford Head Tavern and The Rose, after which their parties converged on the theatre and were privately admitted before the doors were opened – a flagrant gesture of favoritism that incensed the general public. Though not itself a political play, *The Modish Couple* by these events became thoroughly politicized. And Fielding, it must have seemed, who had been given the job of writing the Epilogue, was now a Court poet.

In these verses Fielding shrewdly foretold that greater courage would be demanded of Captain Bodens facing the critics in his new capacity as poet than in his usual one as soldier. It did not require oracular powers to predict, by this time, something like the uproar that occurred at the playhouse on 10 January, when *The Modish Couple* opened to a crowded and polarized audience, one half of which was determined to damn it with jeers and catcalls, the other half to save it with cheers and the flourishing of oaken clubs. The din emanating from the political quarters of the house was augmented by the clamorous protests of the critical beaux of the Temple who found themselves ridiculed in the character of Grinly. So remarkable indeed was this occasion that "the first Night of Captain B——'s Play" would be the first of the "Histories" engraved on Joseph Andrews's cudgel "where you would have seen Critics in Embroidery transplanted from the Boxes to the Pit, whose ancient Inhabitants were exalted to the Gallery, where they played on Catcalls" (III.vi). The Opposition press was naturally incensed that the efforts of its own faction to damn the performance were, if just barely, thwarted.[168] The play's enemies soon prevailed, however. Though the Prince's royal presence, as well as the judicious positioning of a dozen Grenadier guardsmen with fixed bayonets on the stage and in other parts of the theatre, ensured that Captain Bodens (and through him Parson Miller) had his benefit, *The Modish Couple* was driven from the stage when the curtain rose on the fourth night.

Though Fielding played a part in this calamitous production, his true opinion of the play's quality is apparent in *Pasquin* (V.i). There the Queen of Ignorance orders Harlequin to arrange for the staging at both patent theatres of one particular drama – her favorite because "There is not in it either Head or Tail."

> The *Modish Couple* is its Name; my self
> Stood Gossip to it, and I will support
> This Play against the Town.

···➤ xix ◄─···

In February the moment came for which Fielding had waited eighteen months – the staging of *The Modern Husband*; and it came under circumstances more auspicious than he could have dreamed possible when he began writing the play back in 1730. For Fielding then, disappointed in his overtures to Walpole and Cibber, had found himself reduced to making a living by scribbling farces and burlesques for the worst of the London theatres. To be sure, *The Author's Farce* and *Tom Thumb* are among his most successful theatrical experiments; but he was too ambitious to settle for the reputation of a writer of drolleries. As *Rape upon Rape* made clear, he was even then evolving in his thoughts the conception of a new kind of "regular" comedy, whose aim was to expose and reform not merely the follies of society – the targets of the more conventional comic dramatists who preceded him – but rather vice and corruption at the highest levels. For this reason he had invoked "the Heroick *Muse*": "*Vice* cloath'd with Pow'r, she combats with her Pen,/ And fearless, dares the *Lyon* in his Den." In the summer of 1730 "the Lion" he meant to combat was the Great Man himself, "the *Man-brute*" at the center of the labyrinths of power.

When the play at last opened, however, on Monday, 14 February 1731/2, Fielding had not only escaped the hard fate suffered by other members of the Haymarket company in the summer of 1731, but had been welcomed back to the government's own theatre, Drury Lane, the scene of his début as a dramatist. *The Modern Husband*, the work that may fairly be considered the masterpiece of his career as a dramatist, now had every chance to succeed that the Establishment could provide. The best actors in the company would play it – Cibber as Lord Richly, Wilks as Mr. Bellamont, Theophilus Cibber as Captain Bellamont, his wife Susannah as Lady Charlotte Gaywit. Cibber, the Poet Laureate, was so far willing to forgive and forget the ridicule of *The Author's Farce* that he consented to supply the Epilogue.

Most delicious irony of all, the play's patron would be, if Fielding had his way, none other than the Great Man himself, who, by epitomizing moral debility in high places – "*Vice* cloath'd with Pow'r" – had inspired the satire. "To the Right Honourable *Sir* ROBERT WALPOLE, *Knight of the most Noble* ORDER *of the* GARTER," Fielding thus dedicated *The Modern Husband*, in phrases consciously echoing Horace's famous *Epistle to Augustus*:

> *SIR*,
> While the Peace of *Europe*, and the Lives and Fortunes of so great a Part of Mankind, depend on Your Counsels, it may be thought an Offence against the publick Good to divert, by Trifles of this Nature, any of those Moments, which are so sacred to the Welfare of our Country.

How close this seems to Pope's later imitation of these same Horatian compliments! But Fielding's prose has no such ironic intent. The Dedication concludes in a fulsome strain that its author would one day have reason to blush at:

> Protect therefore, Sir, an Art from which You may promise Your self such notable Advantages; when the little Artifices of Your Enemies, which You have surmounted, shall be forgotten, when Envy shall cease to misrepresent Your Actions, and Ignorance to misapprehend them. The Muses shall remember their Protector, and the wise Statesman, the generous Patron, the stedfast Friend, and the true Patriot; but above all that Humanity and Sweetness of Temper, which shine thro' all your Actions, shall render the Name of Sir ROBERT WALPOLE dear to his no longer ungrateful Country.
> That Success may attend all Your Counsels; that You may continue to preserve us from our Enemies Abroad, and to triumph over Your Enemies at Home, is the sincere Wish of, *SIR*,
>   *Your most obliged,*
>   *Most obedient humble Servant,*
>   HENRY FIELDING.

With *The Modern Husband* Fielding meant to make his peace with Walpole. He also meant to shake off the reputation he had earned at the Little Haymarket as an author capable only of farce, burlesque, and ballad opera. Spoken by Wilks – the other of the actor-managers at Drury Lane who introduced Fielding to London audiences in 1728 and then disowned him – the opening lines of the Prologue serve as Fielding's *apologia* for, and in part his repudiation of, his theatrical career to date:

> In early Youth, our *Author* first begun,
> To Combat with the *Follies* of the *Town*;
> Her want of Art, his unskill'd *Muse* bewail'd,
> And where his *Fancy* pleas'd, his *Judgment* fail'd.
> Hence, your nice Tastes he strove to entertain
> With unshap'd Monsters of a wanton Brain!
> He taught *Tom Thumb* strange Victories to boast,
> Slew Heaps of Giants, and then – kill'd a Ghost!
> To Rules, or Reason, scorn'd the dull Pretence,
> And fought your *Champion*, 'gainst the Cause of Sense!
> At length, repenting Frolick Flights of Youth,
> Once more he flies to Nature, and to Truth:
> In Virtue's just Defence, aspires to Fame,
> And courts Applause without the Applauder's Shame!

In *The Modern Husband* Fielding risked a new kind of drama that, using his own term, I have called "heroic" comedy – comedy that not only eschews "low Farce" and the "loud Laugh," but dares even to be "serious," taking as its subject something intrinsically detestable, "*Modern Vice*," and representing the Town "vicious, as it is." In this instance the subject was one that interested him throughout his career, occurring even in the comparatively light-hearted gypsy episode of *Tom Jones* (XII.xii) and in the story of the blackguard Captain Trent in *Amelia* (XI.iii): as the Prologue has it, "A Pair of Monsters most entirely new! ... *A willing Cuckold* –sells his *willing Wife*!"

Fielding was something of a rake in his youth; but he always regarded the institution of marriage as inviolable. Though he freely indulged his own powerful sexual appetites, he so well understood the distinction between lust and love that in *Tom Jones* (VI.i) he wrote one of his finest essays on the subject; and adultery was so far from being with him the comical game of intrigue Restoration wits and modern gallants had made it, that in the period of his magistracy he openly deplored the lack of laws for punishing adulterers, in *Amelia* (IX.v, X.ii) and the *Covent-Garden Journal* (21 and 28 October 1752) mounting an earnest literary campaign against the practice. But he understood the weakness of the flesh. Two things chiefly he found "detestable" in these matters: on the one hand the element of intrigue – the deliberate, artful corrupting of any woman, most particularly another man's wife, and the cuckolding of a husband; on the other hand, and even viler because avarice was the basest of passions, a lust for money so abject that it stoops to the prostitution of marriage itself, husband and wife conniving at her infidelity as long as they are well paid for it.

In Fielding's view this was a perversion so abhorrent, yet so common in his day, that it was the symptom of a fundamental malignancy – one which Pope, too, would consider in his *Epistle to Bathurst* on "The Use of Riches." In *The Modern Husband*, though the mutual complicity of Mr. and Mrs. Modern in her lucrative affairs is the shocking focus of Fielding's "serious" satire, it is her partner in adultery, Lord Richly, who epitomizes this darker theme of the play, a theme Fielding would not fully develop until the last major work of his life, *Amelia*. The universal cupidity of the age is the message of the play's strongest scene, the scene of Lord Richly's levee, where Captain Merit is unheard amidst a crowd of placemen and sycophants. Such scenes, as his verse epistles of 1730–1 suggest, Fielding had himself experienced at Walpole's house in Arlington Street. It may also be, as one of the most perceptive critics of Fielding's drama believed,[169] that his main plot was taken from an incident in "real life" – the notorious case of Lord Abergavenny which came to trial on 16 February 1730: the noble lord, having laid a trap to catch his wife and her paramour, brought an action for criminal conversation against the man and was awarded swingeing damages of £10,000. It is said that, unlike Mrs. Modern, who is incapable of shame, Lady Abergavenny died of grief before the trial.

One purpose of *The Modern Husband* – a purpose that distinguishes it from the comic tradition Fielding knew – is the exposure and correction not just of private folly or immorality, but of a specific public evil: "a state of affairs," Charles Woods remarked, "which enabled a man to make money from his wife's adultery without loss of social prestige, a noxious growth which festered in the English legal system until 1857, when Parliament at last put an end to actions for criminal conversation."[170] Fielding's "heroic" comedy was of a new kind, comedy written with an intent to reform the vicious institutions of society by means of a sobering ridicule. As Professor Woods observed, there is nothing in the English theatre quite like this until "the dramatic program of the author of *Mrs. Warren's Profession*."[171] Perhaps it was the recognition of this congenial didactic impulse, as well as the appreciation of Fielding's comic powers and his daring experiments with form, that drew from Shaw the most famous compliment Fielding was ever paid as a playwright: that he was "the greatest dramatist, with the single exception of Shakespeare, produced by England between the Middle Ages and the nineteenth century."[172]

The Modern Husband is the best of Fielding's regular comedies, and, far from being the failure it is usually said to have been, its initial run at Drury Lane must have been gratifying. Opening on Monday, 14 February (considering the subject of the play, the choice of Valentine's Day was apt), it ran almost continuously for the rest of the month, and there were two further performances in March – fourteen in all, four of which were Fielding's benefits. No main piece since *The Provok'd Husband* (1728) enjoyed a longer run. The penultimate performance, on 2 March, was a glittering occasion indeed: staged at the command of the King and Queen for the benefit of the unfortunate actress, Mrs. Porter, it was "acted to a splendid crowded Audience," including the entire Royal Family. This, the thirteenth night, proved unlucky, however; for the run had to be "discontinued, on account of the Indisposition of a principal Actress."[173] One last performance took place a fortnight later (18 March), for Fielding's benefit; *The Modern Husband* then disappeared forever from the stage. There was sufficient interest in the play, however – which Watts published on 21 February – to justify a second edition in August.

In short, the first months of Fielding's return to Drury Lane had been triumphant. According to one observer (perhaps Aaron Hill), Fielding this season quickly made a small fortune – only to squander it all, just as quickly, at the gaming tables. In the midst of a survey of the theatrical season of 1732 the author declares:

> *Fielding* has had very good and very bad Success, a *Farce* of his call'd the *Lottery* and a Comedy intituled the *Modern Husband*, have both met with extraordinary Success; and, between both, he has made little less than a thousand Pounds, but the poor Author has fall'n into the Jaws of *Rattle-snakes*, His Elbows have destroy'd the Off-spring of his Brain; and in Spight of all his good Sense he has been stript at Play by Sharpers.[174]

A thousand pounds made and lost in the course of a few weeks. Few contemporary witnesses so succinctly capture for us both the brilliance and the self-destructive recklessness that characterize Fielding's the-atrical years.

When the second edition of *The Modern Husband* was published, "Bavius" of the *Grub-Street Journal* (10 August 1732) sardonically demanded the bookseller's gratitude: after all, he reasoned, *The Modern Husband* would have sunk into oblivion had it not been that his journal kept it constantly in the public eye. Whatever extra sales Watts may have owed to "Bavius" and the authors of the *Grub-Street Journal*, Fielding owed them nothing for the relentless denigration of his works and character that commenced in that paper on 30 March. Provoked in part by envy at the "favourable reception *The Modern Husband* has met with from the Town" (for "Dramaticus," whoever he may have been,[175] resented that a play of his own had been rejected at Drury

Lane), and in part by anger at Fielding's political allegiances declared
in his Dedication to Walpole, "Dramaticus" began the fun at Fielding's
expense. Assisted by kindred Grublings – "Prosaicus," "Publicus," the
ubiquitous "Bavius" – he kept up the mud-slinging throughout the
spring and summer, finding fresh provocation in Fielding's other new
plays of the long season – *The Old Debauchees, The Covent-Garden
Tragedy, The Mock Doctor.*

In a sense, the campaign of vilification did more justice to Fielding's
reputation as a dramatist than friendlier critics of our own time have
done; for while the latter seem scarcely aware of Fielding's extraordinary popularity as a playwright, "Dramaticus" and his colleagues
acknowledge the fact. Fielding, it must be said, is himself partly to
blame for the notion that *The Modern Husband* did not take with
its audience: he more than once complained that, despite a superb
performance by Susannah Cibber and the approbation of the best
judges, the character of the affected belle Lady Charlotte Gaywit "was
condemned on the Stage for being unnatural, by a very large Assembly
of Clerks and Apprentices."[176] However keenly a sensitive author felt
those catcalls from the gallery directed at a favorite character, Fielding's enemies had a very different impression of the play's reception.
All that first week of the production "Dramaticus" was galled to hear
the play "so cried up, both within and without the House"; the levee
scene was especially "popular." Supporting this impression is the play's
strong run before audiences of the highest distinction – a run cut short
only by the illness of a principal actress. In a later letter to the journal
(13 April) "Dramaticus" regrets the "many benefits" Fielding enjoyed;
and the same note is heard from "Prosaicus" in the summer (29 June),
who grudgingly recalls the "vast encouragement [Fielding] met with
last winter" at Drury Lane.

As the virulence and persistence of the attacks suggest, the cause of
the *Grub-Street Journal*'s quarrel with Fielding was hardly a dis-
passionate concern to evaluate his qualities as a writer of comedies. It
seems rather to have been motivated by an animus toward Fielding
personally and, more to the point, toward what he now represented
politically as the Establishment's darling, the prolific, successful playwright of the Theatre Royal. It was no coincidence that Fielding was
introduced into the gallery of the journal's favorite targets – Captain
Bodens, "Orator" Henley, Colley Cibber – after he openly declared
himself to be Walpole's man. Though encouraging the notion that it
had been founded with Pope's blessing in order to carry on the crusade
against duncery, the *Grub-Street Journal* was in fact the organ of a
certain disgruntled divine of literary pretensions, Richard Russel – a
graduate of University College, Oxford, who, having lost his living in
1716 because he refused to take the oath to George I, now ran a

boarding-house near Westminster School for the sons of nonjurors.[177] The staunchest of Tories – in his sympathies, indeed, a self-confessed Jacobite – Russel remained editor and chief author of the *Journal* throughout the eight years of its publication. These prejudices were of course reflected in his paper.

Though Fielding's politics are never referred to by Russel and his colleagues in their criticisms of *The Modern Husband*, the political implications of the play's reception are suggested by the fact that its only defenders were Court journalists: these were his friends Thomas Cooke in *The Comedian* (June 1732) and James Ralph in the *Weekly Register* (8 July 1732), and the pseudonymous "Dramaticus *senior*" in the *Daily Courant* (29 July 1732). Ralph's protestations on behalf of his injured friend are especially poignant, and reflect a truer image of Fielding's standing as a dramatist during this period: "the Author of the *Modern Husband*," he declares, referring to the punishment Fielding received from the Grublings, is "a Gentleman as much above their Level in Reputation, as Genius, and ... by the Consent of the best Judges, is allow'd to deserve abundantly more Applause than will ever fall to the Lot of their whole Society." Unfortunately, by the time Ralph wrote these words, the *Journal* had sunk the reputation of *The Modern Husband*, Fielding's daring experiment in a new mode of comedy. "Dramaticus" (27 July) smugly reminded the managers at Drury Lane "how unanimous every body has since been in all private companies, in condemning" the play. It has never been revived.

·····➤ **XX** ◄····

Far different is the history of the ever popular *Tragedy of Tragedies*, which, in May 1732 at Drury Lane, enjoyed its most magnificent production. Performed on Wednesday, 3 May, "For the Benefit of Mr. Chetwood," it featured Mullart and his wife as King Arthur and Queen Dollallolla, roles they created originally at the Little Haymarket; Miss Robinson played Thumb and Theophilus Cibber, Lord Grizzle. The advertisements reveal that both Fielding in particular and the Drury Lane company as a whole spared no trouble or expense in order to ensure that William Rufus Chetwood, who served as prompter of the theatre from about 1722 to 1742, enjoyed a successful benefit. Fielding was fond of this man, who was also an author in his own right, best remembered for his useful *General History of the Stage* (1749): Fielding later introduced Chetwood into the opening scene of the ill-fated farce, *Eurydice*; but even surer as a sign of their friendship is the fact that Chetwood's *Voyages* of Falconer and Vaughan comprise half the total number of works for which Fielding in his lifetime ever advanced money as a subscriber.[178] For Chetwood, Fielding and his colleagues gave their all. There were decorations "in a new Manner"; a "new Overture with Kettle-Drums and Trumpets" by Seedo; a "New Grand Heroic Comic Dance" introduced into the third Act; and at the conclusion of every Act the orchestra played compositions by Vivaldi, Corelli, and Handel (his *Water Music*). Other entertainments followed – singing, harlequinades, a "grand Dance of Moors." For his part, Fielding supplied "a new Introduction," which, unfortunately, we know today only in the advertisement:

> With a new Introduction, written by the Author of Tom Thumb; The Speakers, Lord Monkeytail, Mr. A. Hallam; Mr. Critick, Mr. Watson; Mr. Heroick Diction, Mr. Wetherilt, jun.; Miss Sprightly, Miss Raftor; Mrs. Witwould, Mrs. Shireburn.[179]

This lively production was staged twice more in May (on the 12th and 25th) at "the particular Desire of several Persons of Quality."

During this month, however, Fielding was chiefly occupied with preparing two new works for the stage, *The Old Debauchees* and *The Covent-Garden Tragedy*.[180] As seems clear from his assignment of the copyrights to John Watts (for the modest sum of twenty guineas), these plays existed, in draft at least, as early as 4 April – the former being then entitled "the despairing Debauchee."[181] From the beginning Fielding seems to have conceived of these works, "a Farce" and "a Tragedy" he calls them, as complementary pieces designed for an evening's (rather bawdy and irreverent) entertainment. They opened together on Thursday, 1 June – with decidedly mixed results.

The Old Debauchees is Fielding's tasteless attempt to capitalize on the sensational case of Father Girard, a Jesuit recently tried at Aix for having seduced and debauched Marie Catharine Cadiere, a young woman under his spiritual care.[182] In this Fielding was merely doing for his own theatre what others had already done at Goodman's Fields and the Little Haymarket, which in February and March produced entertainments on the same subject, entitled *Father Girard the Sorcerer* and *The Wanton Jesuit*. But nowhere is Fielding's anti-Catholic bias more obvious than in *The Old Debauchees*. His great-aunt, Mrs. Cottington, once complained to the Lord Chancellor that, as a lad at Eton, Fielding had so far fallen under the influence of his stepmother that he was arguing for the superior claims of the Church of Rome; but there is no trace here – or, for that matter, elsewhere in his writings – of any such attitude. His prejudice in this respect squared, profitably, with the anti-papist feelings of his audience. Even "Miso-Cleros," who attacked the play in the *Grub-Street Journal* (13 July 1732), admitted that it was well received – one reason being Theophilus Cibber's clever performance in the role of Father Martin, a comic character (Thomas Cooke believed) as "masterly drawn" as Shakespeare's Pistol or Jonson's Abel Drugger.[183] Yet "Miso-Cleros" describes the effect of *The Old Debauchees* accurately when he complains that Fielding seems to direct his satire not at "the Popish Clergy" alone, but at priests and priestcraft in general. This may well have been his motive. It is one that would have been applauded by two of his closest companions of this early period, Ralph and Cooke.

But if the audience at Drury Lane enjoyed the roasting of a lecherous priest in *The Old Debauchees*, they were appalled when, in the afterpiece, Fielding introduced them to scenes meant to conjure up two of the most notorious brothels of the day, Mother Needham's bagnio in St. James's and the Rose Tavern in Russell Street, adjoining the Drury Lane Theatre. Inspired perhaps by Hogarth's series, *The Harlot's Progress*, which he appears to have seen and admired sometime before the six prints were published in April,[184] *The Covent-Garden Tragedy* is a hilarious burlesque of one of the most popular pseudo-classical tragedies in the repertory, Ambrose Philips's *The Distrest Mother* (1712).[185] In Philips's play, the heroine of the title is Andromache, who, a prisoner of the Greeks after the fall of Troy, mourns her dead husband Hector and fears for the safety of her son Astyanax. In Fielding's travesty, the focus is instead on the bawd Mother Punchbowl, who, unhappy at the decline in trade, expresses her exasperation in one of the most arresting opening lines in theatre: "Who'd be a Bawd in this degen'rate Age!"

There was also an esoteric dimension to the play's humor, meant to be savored by Fielding's fellow rakes in the audience. As "Prosaicus" reported in the *Grub-Street Journal* (8 June) he was surprised on opening night "to see the most notorious Bawds, Pimps, and Whores, brought on the stage to please as polite an audience as I ever saw for the time of the year." Much of this naughtiness would have been lost on him had not his companion, a man of pleasure, been able to explain "the secret history, the reality of the characters, and some personal scandal." Thus, as played by the actor Bridgwater, Mother Punchbowl, like Hogarth's bawd, recalled the infamous Elizabeth Needham, who died the previous year after being exposed in the pillory to the rage of the populace; Leathersides was just as obviously modeled on the notorious Leathercoat, porter and pimp at the Rose. As for the "personal scandal" in the play, Horace Walpole identified the bully, Captain Bilkum, with Captain Edward Braddock (later the famous General of the French-and-Indian War), who was known for his mercenary and tempestuous relations with the women who kept him.[186] In Bilkum's lament for Stormandra, whom he believes has hanged herself, there may then also be a tastelessly frivolous allusion to the suicide of Braddock's sister

Fanny, who at Bath in September 1731 hanged herself in despair at gambling away all her money.

Funny as it was (and can still be, as attested by the National Theatre production of 1968), *The Covent-Garden Tragedy* was too ribald for the tastes of an audience accustomed to the genteel comedies of Cibber or, nearer the mark, the more refined merriment of Gay's "Newgate Pastoral." There is nothing in *The Beggar's Opera* to equal, for example, the raw bawdry of Lovegirlo's speech to Kissinda at the close of Act I:

> Oh! I am all on Fire, thou lovely Wench,
> Torrents of Joy my burning Soul must quench,
> Reiterated Joys!
> Thus burning from the Fire, the Washer lifts
> The red-hot Iron to make smooth her Shifts,
> With Arm impetuous rubs her Shift amain,
> And rubs, and rubs, and rubs it oe'r again;
> Nor sooner does her rubbing Arm withhold,
> 'Till she grows warm, and the hot Iron cold.

As a boy Fielding needed his father's whip and birchings at Eton to teach him better manners. In his mid-twenties he was still, as a playwright, violating the proprieties, whether at the Little Haymarket theatre a year earlier in his satire of the Royal Family and the political Establishment, or now at Drury Lane in this uproarious celebration of the underworld of bawds and pimps, of whores and their bully-boys, all impudently dignified by the mock sublimity of his verse. Again Fielding had gone too far. Though, unlike *The Grub-Street Opera*, *The Covent-Garden Tragedy* was allowed to reach the stage, the audience found it in such bad taste he voluntarily withdrew it from production, intending, apparently, that it should "be acted no more."[187] As it happened the play was revived, as the afterpiece to *Don Quixote in England*, when Fielding left Drury Lane and returned to the Little Haymarket in 1734. It also found a place in the repertory of the English puppet theatre.[188]

Since *The Old Debauchees* was too insubstantial to make up an evening's entertainment by itself, the withdrawal of its companion piece left a gap that had to be filled. The following notice in the *Daily Post* (16 June 1732) explains why Fielding consented to the premature staging of yet another new comedy, his fifth of the season:

We hear there is now in Rehearsal, at the Theatre Royal in Drury-Lane, a new Farce, call'd The MOCK DOCTOR: Or, The DUMB-LADY CUR'D. The Piece of Moliere from which this is alter'd, and adapted to the English Stage, is justly esteem'd to contain the purest and most

natural Humour that has appear'd in any Language. As The OLD
DEBAUCHEES (which is not long enough in itself for a whole Night's
Entertainment) has met with great Applause from the Town, the
Author, lest it might suffer by the Addition of any old worn-out
Entertainments, has permitted this Performance to come on at a
more disadvantageous Season than he at first intended.

The Mock Doctor, which in time became the standard of its kind,
the light farce,[189] was not finished to Fielding's satisfaction until the
following season, when the final, revised version was produced for his
benefit on 16 November 1732. But, rushed though it was untimely into
the world, it succeeded instantly with those audiences who remained
in town into the summer: it opened, as afterpiece to *The Old Debauchees*,
on 23 June and, all told, played a dozen times during the summer. The
Daily Post (26 June) reported that the play was first acted "to a full
House, with great applause," and added: "*Le Medecin Malgré Lui*, of
Moliere, from whence the *Mock-Doctor* is taken, bears the greatest
reputation of any petit Piece in the French language; and many good
Judges allow the English Farce is no way inferior to the Original."
   The "many good Judges" in question included, of course, none of
the authors of the *Grub-Street Journal*: "Dramaticus" (29 June) found
the play "miserable stuff"; "Publicus" (20 July) pitied poor Molière's
original, which Fielding "has mangled and misunderstood from the
very *Title-Page* to *Finis*." As to the favorable reception *The Mock
Doctor* continued to enjoy, since no one with ears to hear the applause
could deny it, the Grublings preferred to attribute the phenomenon not
to any virtue in Fielding's play, but to the acting of young Cibber as
Gregory in the title role and of "Kitty" Raftor as Dorcas, whose
brilliance in those parts Fielding handsomely acknowledged in his
Preface to the published version. At last, however, even one of Russel's
regulars, "Prosaicus" (24 August), was obliged to "confess" that the
play was "an entertaining Farcical Piece" whose success was not
entirely owing to the acting of it. Such an admission from such an
inveterate enemy is a tribute to how well *The Mock Doctor* succeeded,
even before Fielding further strengthened its appeal in revision.
   This early version of *The Mock Doctor* was published by Watts on 11
July, carrying an ironic Dedication to the well-known Gallic quack,
Dr. John Misaubin – whom Hogarth had also recently ridiculed in Plate
III of *The Harlot's Progress*. Fielding concluded his Preface with a
statement which inadvertently fostered the mistaken notion that he
was at this time participating in another of Watts's publications, the
Select Comedies of Mr. de Molière, an eight-volume work "by several
Gentlemen" who provided literal English translations side by side with
the French texts. What Fielding wrote was this:

One Pleasure I enjoy from the Success of this Piece, is a Prospect of transplanting successfully some others of *Moliere* of great Value. How I have done this, any *English* Reader may be satisfy'd by examining an exact literal Translation of the *Medecin malgré Lui*, which is the Second in the Second Volume of *Select Comedies of Moliere*, just published by *John Watts*.

Fielding was soon to produce one of the finest versions in English of Molière's *L'Avare*. But he had no part whatsoever in the *Select Comedies of Molière*,[190] the first two volumes of which had been published, respectively, on 8 May and 3 July 1732,[191] the latter just eight days before Watts published *The Mock Doctor*; publication of the series was complete by December. The authors chiefly concerned in the *Select Comedies* were Henry Baker, F.R.S., editor since 1728 of *The Universal Spectator* and possibly an acquaintance of Fielding's,[192] and the Reverend James Miller, who, as the real author behind "Captain Bodens's" *The Modish Couple*, for which Fielding furnished an epilogue, may also have been personally known to him. In his Preface, Fielding meant only to "puff" a commercial enterprise of his publisher. The only connection between *The Mock Doctor* and the play which Watts's translator entitles *A Doctor and No Doctor* is that Fielding's Dedication to Misaubin parodies the latter's Dedication to the celebrated physician, Dr. Richard Mead.

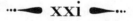

xxi

In tracing Fielding's circumstances during this first astonishingly active year at Drury Lane, it is pleasant to recall such wholesome triumphs as he enjoyed with *The Mock Doctor*. But this was not to be the focus of the attention he continued to receive from those venomous guardians of public taste, the authors of the *Grub-Street Journal*. From this period, it appears, in the Grublings' outraged response to *The Old Debauchees* and *The Covent-Garden Tragedy*, stems that image of the young Fielding as a disreputable rake that endured for more than a century and a half until Professor Cross replaced it with a more decorous portrait of his own invention. To determine which of these contrasting pictures of Fielding, the wholly black or the wholly white, comes closer to a true likeness of the man, we need to examine more closely the nature of the charges leveled against him in the *Grub-Street Journal*, attacks so virulent and unremitting they at last forced from him a proud, if embarrassing, defense of his powers as an author and his character as a man.

In their criticisms of *The Old Debauchees* and *The Covent-Garden*

Tragedy, "Miso-Cleros" and "Prosaicus" typified the Grublings' condemnation of Fielding as a lewd and impious author. Indeed, "Dramaticus" insisted (15 June), still furious with loathing after seeing those plays performed, that Fielding and the managers at Drury Lane who encouraged him were chiefly responsible for "the horrible profanation of the Stage at present." Such attacks, couched in the most abusive language, stung the young author of twenty-five. At first, Fielding – in concert with an ally who may have been Theophilus Cibber – responded not in kind, but in a bantering vein. Under the borrowed name of "Wm. Hint, Candle-Snuffer" at Drury Lane, the friend (or was it, as his enemies believed, Fielding himself?)[193] wrote to the *Daily Post* (21 June) and the *London Evening Post* (20–22 June) disclosing the true reason for Russel's campaign against Fielding: Mother Punchbowl in the opening scene of *The Covent-Garden Tragedy* had revealed her pimp Leathersides to be one of the authors of the *Grub-Street Journal*. So innocent was that play of any offensive language, "Hint" insisted, that he rashly challenged "Dramaticus," "with the Help of all your *Dictionaries*, to wrest one Word of it into an indecent Meaning."

The attacks of Russel and the Grublings were soon answered more wittily by Fielding, who, though content after the opening night to let his damned play sink, now felt obliged to let the Town see for itself what a harmless thing it was. Though Watts purchased the rights to both *The Old Debauchees* and *The Covent-Garden Tragedy* together early in April, he had so far published only the former play, on 13 June, holding back the latter presumably at Fielding's request. But on 24 June, three days after "Wm. Hint" defied "Dramaticus" to find a single indecent word in *The Covent-Garden Tragedy*, Watts made the task easier by publishing the text. As "Prolegomena" to the play itself, Fielding included "A CRITICISM on the *Covent-Garden Tragedy*, originally intended for the *Grub-street Journal*," an amusing parody of what he considered to be, with some justice, the malicious, incompetent criticisms which that paper had been directing against him and his works for nearly three months. One reason for this sustained enmity was, he believed, political: his "Critic" admits to being charmed by "the beautiful Manner wherein this Play sets out.... But alas! what follows? No fine Moral Sentences, not a Word of Liberty and Property, no Insinuations, that Courtiers are Fools, and Statesmen Rogues."

Refreshing as it is to read Fielding's travesty of the Grublings rather than the Grublings themselves, they were not to be quieted by ridicule. The issue of the journal (29 June) that followed publication of *The Covent-Garden Tragedy* teemed with abuse from several of their company, including "Dramaticus," who had accepted the candle-snuffer's challenge and raked through the text of the play searching for all the naughtiness it contained. The attacks continued through July, the critics' zeal mounting as the Dog-Star raged. On 20 July "Publicus," newly enlisted in Russel's legion of Fielding-baiters, declared that *The Old Debauchees* and *The Covent-Garden Tragedy* "were so far improper for an *English Stage,* or to be exhibited to a *polite,* an *honest,* and a *christian* people, that, (unless Sodom and Gomorrah had been now undestroyed) they were only fit for the hangman's flames." As for the language of the tragedy which "Wm. Hint" claimed was inoffensive, why it was "more gross than even goats and monkeys, if they could speak, would express their brutality in." But it was "Dramaticus" who added the last straw. In the *Journal* for 27 July, he descended to personal insults, accusing Fielding of being too ashamed to justify himself under his own name, and declaring that he was "a venal Poet" who prospered only because he had struck some unholy bargain with the managers at Drury Lane, "whose favour he may have absolutely secured to himself by arts, either unknown to, or unbecoming a gentleman."

For four months Fielding had suffered the incessant vilification of the *Grub-Street Journal* with as much good humor as he could muster and with a degree of patience seldom equaled outside the annals of hagiography. But these last aspersions on his character were too much. Under the name of "Philalethes" (Lover of Truth) in a letter to the author of the *Daily Post* (31 July), he defended himself – his talent, his learning, his birth, his manners, his morals, his character as a gentleman. He had been reduced to the unseemly shift of praising himself in public. The letter makes fascinating reading; in it we catch a glimpse of Fielding's own conception of himself as an author and as a man. For this reason, and because it reveals precisely where he stood in the public eye at the close of this first troubled, yet on the whole triumphant, season at Drury Lane, it merits quoting in full:

SIR,

I Have read, with the Detestation it deserves, *an infamous Paper* call'd the *Grubstreet Journal*: A Paper written by a Set of obscure Scriblers in the true Style and Spirit of Billingsgate, without either Learning, Wit, Decency, or often common Sense, and design'd to vilify and defame the Writings of every Author, except a few, whose Reputation is already too well establish'd for their Attacks, the Characters of whom they have, in the Opinion of all wise Men, blacken'd more with their Applause, than they have the others with their Censures.

The Love of *Scandal* is so *general an Appetite,* that no one can wonder at the Success of any Nonsense or Ribaldry which hath that to recommend it: To this all the infamous Scriblers of the Age owe a very comfortable Maintenance; and to this, and this only, the *Grubstreet Journal* owes its Being.

I believe every Man of good Sense and good Nature hath view'd with Abhorrence the scandalous undeserv'd Attacks, which they have lately so often repeated on a Gentleman, to whom the Town hath owed so much Diversion, and to whose Productions it has been so very favourable: An Attack which the Favour of the Town, and the good Reception he hath met with from the Players, hath drawn on him.

This Torrent of Ribaldry hath come abroad under several Names, such as *Dramaticus, Prosaicus, Publicus, &c.* Whether these be the same Person is insignificant to determine; however, as they have all said the same Things, or rather call'd the same Names, an Answer to one will serve them all.

Mr. *Publicus* (whom by the ingenious and cleanly Metaphors he takes from the Streets, such as *Nastiness, Dirt, Kennel, Billingsgate, Stews, &c.* one would have imagin'd to have sometimes thrown Dirt with other Instruments than a Pen) sets out with a most *notorious Falshood*, where he says *the two Performances* (*the Tragedy and Debauchees*) met with the *universal Detestation of the Town*; whereas the *Debauchees* was received with as *great Applause* as was ever given on the Theatre: The Audience, which, on most Nights of its Representation, was as numerous as hath been known at that Season of the Year, seem'd in continual Good-Humour, and often in the highest Raptures of Approbation; and, except on the first Night, and ev'n then in one particular Scene there never was one Hiss in the House.

He goes on, *Many that were there* (at the Tragedy) *had neither so much Taste, nor so little Modesty, as to sit it out;* as a Proof of which, three Ladies of the Town made their Exit in the first Act, while several of the first Rank and Reputation saw the Curtain fall: And this, had he not wanted common Sense, or common Honesty, he never had wonder'd, or pretended to have wonder'd at; for why should any Person of Modesty be offended at seeing a Set of *Rakes* and *Whores* exposed and set in the most *ridiculous Light?* Sure the Scene of a Bawdy-house may be shewn on a Stage without shocking the most modest Woman; such I have seen sit out that Scene in the *Humorous Lieutenant* [by Beaumont and Fletcher], which is quoted and commended by one of the finest Writers of the last Age.

The Author is said to recommend *Whoring and Drunkenness*; how! Why a Rake speaks against Matrimony, and a Sot against Sobriety: so Moliere in Don Juan recommends all Manner of Vices, and every Poet (I am sure every good one) that hath exposed a vicious Character, hath by this Rule contributed to debauch Mankind.

After the following excellent Remark, *Methinks the Writer tho'*

*might as well have left Seas of Sulphur and Eternal Fire out of the mad
Joke, for Fear he should meet with them in sober Sadness*, he proceeds
to *the Epilogue*, where he says the Author tells the Ladies, without
any Ceremony, *that there's no Difference between the best of them, and
the Bawdy-house Trulls they had been seeing on the Stage; and that
pretend what they would, they were all a Parcel of Errant Whores:* This
is *a most infamous Lye*, as any one who reads the Epilogue to the
Covent Garden Tragedy must see, where nothing more is asserted,
than that it is natural for one Sex to be fond of the other,

> *In short you* (Men) *are the Business of our Lives,*
> *To be a Mistress kept the Strumpet strives,*
> *And all the modest Virgins to be Wives.*

This is the Compliment for which he hopes the Ladies will reward
him the next Benefit Night. I am sorry any Man so well born as this
Author, should be obliged to receive a Benefit Night; but should be
much more sorry that he should depend on such Ladies as this
Critick's Wife and Daughter to support it: However, the Wish is
human enough, and shews how void of Malice the Writer is.

But he is not contented with representing the Poet as having
abus'd the Ladies, (which I believe the Poet is so much a Gentleman
as to think the worst Thing could be said of him) the Critick, after
having terribly mangled the Play by tearing out several Passages,
without inserting the whole Speeches, or making the Reader
acquainted with the Character of the Speaker, accuses the Author
with being free with the Bible; how free with the Bible? Why he
has given a ridiculous Description of Purgatory: Well, and hath
Purgatory any Thing more to do with the Bible than a Description
of the Infernal Shades or Elisian Fields of the Heathens, or of the
Paradise of the Mahometans. If the Critick had shewn as much Sense
as Malice, I should have imagin'd the *Popish Priest* had peep'd forth
in this Place; for sure *any Protestant, but a Nonjuring Parson, would
be asham'd* to represent a Ridicule on Purgatory as a Ridicule on the
Bible, or the Abuse of *Bigotted Fools* and *Roguish Jesuits* as an Abuse
on Religion and the English Clergy.

Not having vented enough of his Malice on these two Pieces, he
adds, *Had I either Leisure or Inclination I could go a little farther with
this Writer, and make it appear from all his Performances, that his Pen
is not only void of Wit, Manners and Modesty, and likewise of the most
common Rules of Poetry, but even Grammar:* This is a most barbarous
Assertion; how true it is I shall leave to the Opinion of the World:
As for the strict Rules which some Criticks have laid down, I cannot
think an Author obliged to confine himself to them; for the Rules of
Grammar, the Education which the Author of the Debauchees is

Plate 9 Lady Mary Wortley Montagu. Pope commissioned Kneller to paint this portrait (1720).

Plate 10 Sir Robert Walpole, his hand on the Chancellor's purse (1740).

Plate 11 George Lyttelton.

Plate 12 Colley Cibber.

Plate 13 University of Leyden, The Academy.

Plate 14 The City Hall, Leyden.

Plate 15 The Little Haymarket Theatre.

W. Hogarth inv.t.   Ger. Vanderbucht sculp.

Plate 16 Hogarth's frontispiece to
The Tragedy of Tragedies (1731).

Plate 17 Philip Dormer Stanhope, fourth Earl of Chesterfield (*c.* 1742).

Plate 18 Catherine "Kitty" Clive as Mrs. Riot in Garrick's *Lethe*.

Plate 19 The Stage Mutiny (1733). Theophilus Cibber as Ancient Pistol leads the actors' rebellion against Drury Lane—at far right Colley Cibber presents the scene.

Plate 20 The Covent Garden Morning Frolick.

Plate 21 The church at Charlcombe, near Bath, where Fielding married
Charlotte Cradock.

Plate 22 *The Judgment of the Queen o' Common Sense* (1736), addressed to
Fielding on the occasion of *Pasquin*.

THE FESTIVAL OF THE GOLDEN RUMP.
Rumpatur, quisquis Rumpitur invidiâ.

UNA EURUSQ.
NOTUSQ. RUUNT
CREBERQ. PROCELLIS
AFRICUS.

Plate 23 *The Festival of the Golden Rump* (1737).

Plate 24 The Middle Temple (1738).

Plate 25 Westminster Hall on the first day of Term (*c.* 1745).

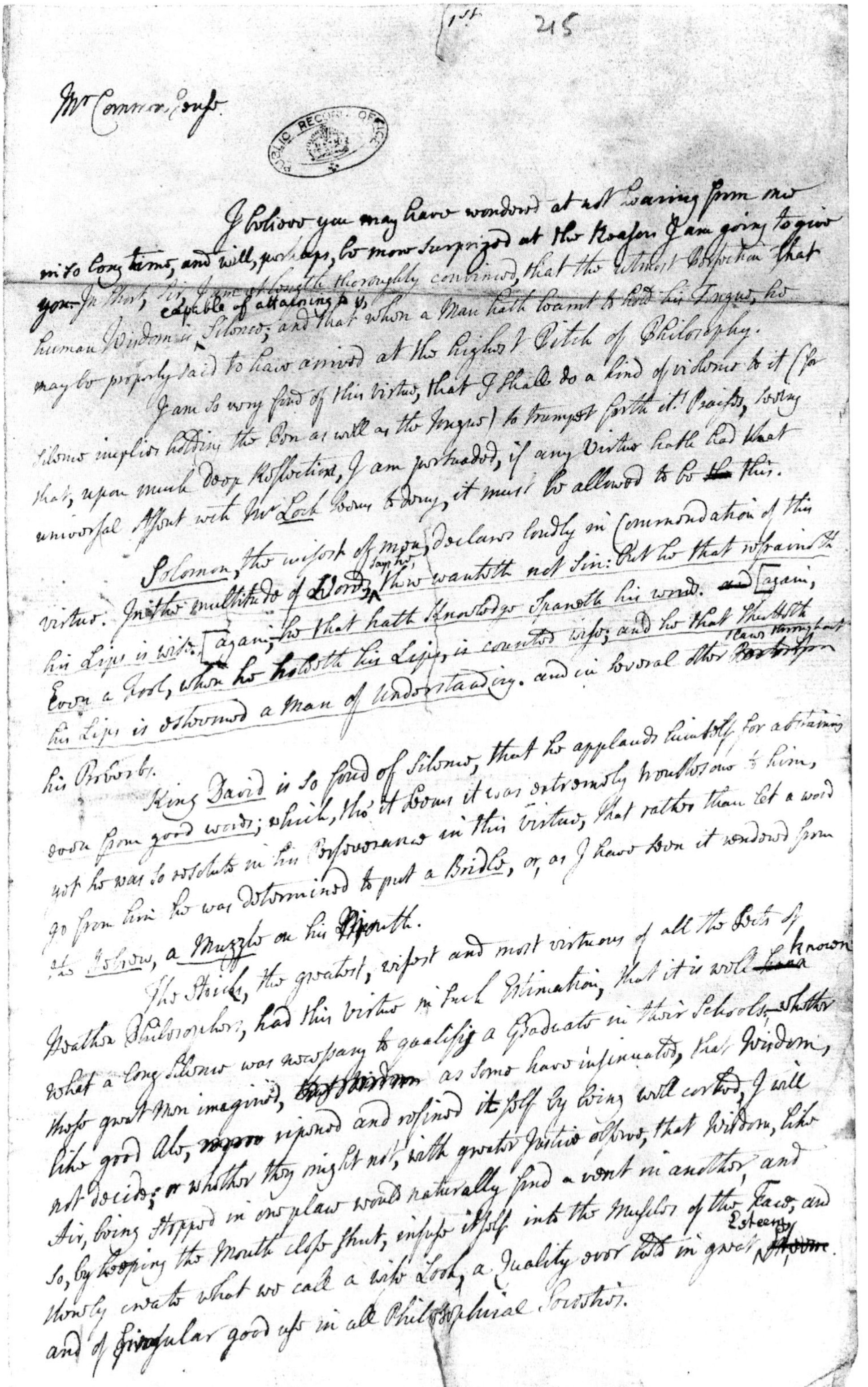

Mr Common-Sense.

I believe you may have wonderd at not hearing from me into so long time, and will, perhaps, be more surprized at the Reason I am going to give you for not ... I am ... me of being thoroughly convinced, that the utmost Perfection that human Wisdom is capable of attaining is Silence; and that when a Man hath learnt to hold his Tongue, he may be properly said to have arrived at the highest Pitch of Philosophy.

I am so very fond of this virtue, that I shall do a kind of violence to it (for silence implies holding the Pen as well as the Tongue) to trumpet forth it's Praises, and my that, upon much deep Reflection, I am persuaded, if any virtue hath had that universal Assent with Mr Lock ... to deny, it must be allowed to be this.

Solomon, the wisest of men, declares loudly in Commendation of this virtue. In the multitude of Words, saith he, there wanteth not Sin: But he that refraineth his Lips is wise. Again, he that hath knowledge spareth his word. Even a Fool, when he holdeth his Lips, is counted wise; and he that shutteth his Lips is esteemed a Man of Understanding. and in several other Places having that his Proverbs.

King David is so fond of Silence, that he applauds himself for abstaining even from good words; which, tho' it seems it was extremely troublesome to him, yet he was so resolute in his Perseverance in this virtue, that rather than let a word go from him he was determined to put a Bridle, or, as I have seen it rendered from the Hebrew, a Muzzle on his Mouth.

The Stoics, the greatest, wisest and most virtuous of all the Sects of Heathen Philosophers, had this virtue in such Estimation, that it is well known what a long Silence was necessary to qualify a Graduate in their Schools. Whether those great Men imagined, as some have insinuated, that Wisdom, like good Ale, requires ripened and refined it self by being well corked, I will not decide; or whether they might not, with greater Justice observe, that Wisdom, like Air, being stopped in one place would naturally find a vent in another, and so, by keeping the Mouth close shut, infuse it self into the Muscles of the Face, and nicely create what we call a wise Look, a Quality over told in great Esteem, and of Singular good use in all Philosophical Societies.

Plate 26 Manuscript page of Fielding's essay on the wisdom of silence, published in *Common Sense* (1738).

known to have had, makes it unlikely he should err in those, or be able to write such wretched Stuff as, *I used to offer in its Behalf*, &c. a Sense wherein that Verb is never found in any good Writer of the English Language; nor indeed will its Derivation from the Latin *Utor* at all admit of it. Again, *Trulls they had been seeing*, Expressions a Boy in the second Form at Eaton would have been whipt for: As for the other Part of the Charge, I must tell our Critick, there is a Vein of Good Humour and Pleasantry which runs through all the Works of this Author, and will make him and them amiable to a good-natur'd and sensible Reader, when the low, spiteful, false Criticisms of a *Grub-street Journal* will be forgotten.

Yours,

PHILALETHES.

P.S. Whether his Scurrility on the *Mock Doctor* be just or no, I leave to the Determination of the Town, which hath already declared loudly on its Side. Some Particulars of the Original are omitted, which the Elegance of an English Audience would not have endur'd; and which, if the Critick had ever read the Original, would have shewn him that the chaste *Moliere* had introduced greater Indecencies on the Stage than the Author he abuses: I may aver he will find more in *Dryden, Congreve, Wycherly, Vanbrugh, Cibber*, and all our best Writers of *Comedy*, nay in the Writings of almost every Genius from the Days of *Horace*, to those of a most *Witty, Learned, and Reverend Writer of our own Age* [i.e., Swift].

Fielding was not of course allowed the last word in this embarrassing public anatomy of his character. Russel – whom he seems to have known to be the moving force behind the *Journal* (witness the scornful allusion to the *"Nonjuring Parson"*) – was delighted that he had goaded his victim into exposing himself in this way. On the slurring went in that paper, through August and into September, until the Grublings had sucked the subject dry.

···◆ xxii ◆···

Which is the truer likeness of Fielding as a young man: the raffish portrait of him as an impious libertine painted by his enemies, or the one of nobler aspect preferred by Professor Cross and, as would appear from the apology of "Philalethes," by Fielding himself in his more defensive moments? Unfriendly witnesses who observed his conduct at the beginning and at the end of the decade of the 1730s took a morose view of what they saw. The former of these, annoyed by the success of

Tom Thumb, considered himself among "the Wise" who regard Fielding "with honest Scorn":

> Whose baneful Morals are a Peoples Jest,
> His Life a Scandal, and his Works a Pest.[194]

At the end of the decade a correspondent in the *Daily Gazetteer* (9 October 1740) dwelled at some length on Fielding's character, which he found unrelievedly *"Low"* and *"Bad"*; he was, in this writer's opinion, "one whose Private Conduct on many Occasions, is charitably pass'd over, lest it should make his Readers (those at least who are sincere in the Cause of Virtue) blush." It was this reputation for abject profligacy that lived on after him, prompting the Victorian wife of a descendant of one of his best friends to burn whatever she could find of their correspondence in an attempt to purge the relationship from the family annals.[195]

Arthur Murphy confirmed the view that Fielding, as a young man, was something of a rake, given to "excesses of pleasure." He writes of Fielding after his return from Leyden as having "launched wildly into a career of dissipation." Finding himself though "under age ... his own master, and in London," he became a favorite both "with the men of taste and literature, and with the voluptuous of all ranks." But what credit can we allow Murphy in this regard, whose acquaintance with Fielding began late and who made no serious attempt to gather reliable information about his subject, even though, in 1762, he had enviable opportunities to do so?

In fact, Murphy's vague references to Fielding's youthful "dissipation" square pretty well with the recollections of one who not only had an opportunity to observe Fielding's conduct for many years, but became his closest friend for the last fifteen years of his life: this was James Harris of Salisbury — no hackney life-writer bent upon sensationalizing his subject, but a scholar and a gentleman, whose probity and love of truth were matched only by his affection for his friend. As he drafted his own memorial of Fielding's "Life and Genius" four years before Murphy's appeared, Harris gave the following summary of the same period of his friend's life:

> Leaving School, he went to Leyden, whence returning soon to England, he fell into that Life, to which great Health, lively Witt, and yt flow of juvenile Spirits, so copious at this period, naturally lead every young man, unchecked by graver authority. His Company was highly pleasing, and his acquaintance of course became very extensive. He conversed not only with persons the first in fashion and quality, but with infinite others of indiscriminate rank, with whom either by chance or choice he was associated. Thus was he

soon furnished with a wide and diversified view of Life and Manners, where his apt Genius did not fail to mark those characteristic Strokes, which vulgar Minds behold with! feeling or attention.

Even in the much briefer memorial that Harris later published he respects truth too much to blink Fielding's youthful excesses; instead, like a friend, he justifies them for what they eventually meant to the future novelist: "Had his *Life* been *less irregular* (for irregular it was, and spent in a promiscuous intercourse with persons of *all* ranks) his *Pictures of Human kind* had neither been so *various*, nor so *natural*."[196] For Harris, it was Fielding's "Knowledge of Mankind, or (if I may be allowed the Phrase) his knowledge Experimental,"[197] of every rank and degree of society, from top to very bottom, that uniquely equipped him to write the masterly works of his maturity – and, we might add, that helped to make him a wiser magistrate. So Fielding himself believed as in *Tom Jones* (XII.i) he makes "Experience" one of the four Muses indispensable to the novelist. Like his namesake, Shakespeare's "Harry" the 5th, he would govern his "new Province of Writing" the better for having once "sounded the very base string of humility."

Fielding, it must be said, made no attempt to conceal the libertinism of his youth. Even as a sober magistrate writing his last sobering novel, he paused in *Amelia* (I.vi) to recall how deceptively innocent the notorious courtesan "Betty" Careless seemed when she was young and a neophyte in her trade:

> it was impossible to conceive a greater Appearance of Modesty, Innocence and Simplicity, than what Nature had displayed in the Countenance of that Girl; and yet, all Appearances notwithstanding, I myself (remember, Critic, it was in my Youth) had a few Mornings before seen that very identical Picture of all those ingaging Qualities in Bed with a Rake at a Bagnio, smoaking Tobacco, drinking Punch, talking Obscenity, and swearing and cursing with all the Impudence and Impiety of the lowest and most abandoned Trull of a Soldier.

This memory presumably dates from the early 1730s, since by 1734 "Betty" Careless was established as proprietress of her own bagnio, situated in Covent Garden.[198] Fielding did not have to tax his powers of invention to summon up the characters and setting of Mother Punchbowl's brothel; he had no doubt sown his wild oats at Mother Needham's and had been entertained at the Rose through the obliging offices of the pimp Leathercoat. According to one scandalized critic, he also knew Mother Haywood's bagnio in Charles Street, Covent Garden, so intimately he was able to reproduce the "Plan" of it "exactly" in the setting of *Miss Lucy in Town*,[199] a ballad opera not produced until

1742 but originally intended as an afterpiece to *An Old Man Taught Wisdom: or, The Virgin Unmask'd* in 1735.

Fielding's morality of this early period probably resembled pretty closely that mixture of jolly hedonism and easy benevolence that he put into the mouth of Old Laroon in *The Old Debauchees* (III.xiv), who declares: "I have no Sins to reflect on but those of an honest Fellow. If I have lov'd a Whore at five and twenty, and a Bottle at forty; Why, I have done as much good as I could, in my Generation; and that, I hope, will make amends." In *A Journey from This World to the Next*, published some ten years later, a life lived according to these same principles is good enough to earn the narrator instant admission to Elysium, though his death was owing to "the *Maladie Alamode*," at whose house he recognizes among the portraits hanging on the walls "the Faces of one or two of my Acquaintance, who had formerly kept Bagnio's" (I.iii). But Minos the Judge finds nothing damnable in a little loose sexuality:

> I confess'd [the narrator informs us] I had indulged myself very freely with Wine and Women in my Youth, but had never done an Injury to any Man living, nor avoided an Opportunity of doing Good; that I pretended to very little Virtue more than general Philanthropy, and private Friendship. – I was proceeding, when *Minos* bid me enter the Gate, and not indulge myself with trumpeting forth my Virtues.
> (I.vii)

In reviewing the fortunes of *The Modern Husband*, we noted another manifestation of the reckless exuberance with which Fielding plunged into the dissolute life of the town: "in Spight of all his good Sense," a friendly observer remarked, he allowed himself to be "strip at Play by Sharpers" – stripped indeed of the better part of a thousand pounds. Not to be outdone in the fashionable vices by his father, who had been bilked at cards before him, Fielding in these years found the thrill of gaming irresistible. In 1734 this would again be the activity (along with philandering of course) that chiefly characterized him for another observer who, when asked "Where is Fielding?" replies: 'he's now at *All-fours,/* With a parcel of *Dam-me Boys*, and *bob-tail'd Whores*."[200] These are the years Fielding remembered in *Amelia*, drawing on his own experience to fashion his fallible hero, Billy Booth, for whom "some Love of Gaming had been formerly amongst his Faults" (I.iv).

The best one can say of Fielding in this early period is that he was "a good-natured Libertine," the phrase Sophie Western uses to sum up the character of Tom Jones (XVIII.x) – a character which for her, as for her author in his maturity, was not good enough. "True Wisdom," Fielding remarked in his masterpiece, consisted in observing "Moderation" in the indulgence of one's appetites – a doctrine, he continues, to which it may be objected that "the wisest Men have been in their Youth, immoderately fond of Pleasure. I answer, they were not wise then" (VI.iii). Temperance, of all the cardinal virtues, would have been the most difficult for him to acquire if he had thought it worth the trouble; for "his Passions," as Harris remembered, were "vehement in every kind," "easily passing into excess." As a young man, indeed, Fielding seems to have felt himself to be completely at the mercy of his passions – his reason, for all the stoic philosophy he had read, powerless to guide or check his desires, his will too feeble to exercise control. This is a theme often heard in his first plays. "Of what Use is Reason then?" asks Heartfort in *The Wedding Day* (V.iv), who answers the question with a striking image that conjures up the literal predicament of all "the good-natured Libertines" of Fielding's fiction from Mr. Wilson to Tom Jones to Billy Booth: "Why, of the Use that a Window is to a Man in Prison, to let him see the Horrours he is confined in; but lends him no Assistance to his Escape." It is also Jack Ramble's predicament in *The Coffee-House Politician* (IV.iii):

> 'Tis as I have acted in all Affairs of Life; my Thoughts have ever succeeded my Actions; the Consequence hath caused me to reflect when it was too late. I never reasoned on what I should do, but what I had done; as if my Reason had her Eyes behind, and could only see backwards.

Ramble's simile inverts the traditional emblem of Prudence, that foresighted virtue that Tom Jones would with difficulty acquire some twenty years later. Given a philosophical turn in *Amelia*, the predicament of Ramble and Heartfort is also the core of Booth's belief in the doctrine of necessity, the doctrine "that every Man acted merely from the Force of that Passion which was uppermost in his Mind, and could do no otherwise" (I.iii). That this same belief tormented Fielding as a young man – no doubt helping him justify to himself "his wildest dissipations," as Murphy calls them – was one of the things about him that impressed his sister Sarah. So Aurélien Digeon surmised, I believe plausibly, when he remarked that in sketching the character of "Le Vive" in *David Simple*, Sarah gave us, "indubitablement," a portrait of her brother:[201] "He gives way to every Inclination that happens to be uppermost; and as it is natural for People to love to justify themselves, his Conversation turns greatly on the Irresistibleness of human Passions, and an Endeavour to prove, that all Men act by them" (IV.iv).

The passion Fielding felt most powerfully himself was sexual desire, "this all-subduing Tyrant," he calls it in *Amelia* (VI.i), "to whose Poison and Infatuation the best of Minds are so liable" – because lust is so nearly allied to the best feelings human nature is capable of: love, the root of benevolence, generosity, friendship, the social affections. The entire passage affords an insight into Fielding's character, as he warns his "young Readers" that the force of sexual passion is so irresistible we can hope to escape it only by "running away" from the object that has aroused it. It is a fire that will "scorch as well as warm":

> of all Passions there is none against which we should so strongly fortify ourselves as this, which is generally called Love: for no other lays before us, especially in the tumultuous Days of Youth, such sweet, such strong, and almost irresistible Temptations; none hath produced in private Life such fatal and lamentable Tragedies; and what is worst of all, there is none to whose Poison and Infatuation the best of Minds are so liable. Ambition scarce ever produces any Evil, but when it reigns in cruel and savage Bosoms; and Avarice seldom flourishes at all but in the basest and poorest Soil. Love, on the contrary, sprouts usually up in the richest and noblest Minds; but there unless nicely watched, pruned, and cultivated, and carefully kept clear of those vicious Weeds which are too apt to surround it, it branches forth into Wildness and Disorder, produces nothing desirable, but choaks up and kills whatever is good and noble in the Mind where it so abounds. In short, to drop the Allegory, not only Tenderness and Good-nature, but Bravery, Generosity, and every Virtue are often made the Instruments of effecting the most atrocious Purposes of this all-subduing Tyrant.

Fielding — "his person," as Harris recalled, "strong, large, and capable of great fatigues" — was a man as remarkable physically as he was for the strength and vigor of his mind. He enjoyed his body, and pursued the pleasures of all his senses with a zest that seemed excessive even to those who wished him well — pursued these pleasures exuberantly until the pace of his living undermined his robust constitution. When in later years he was racked with excruciating attacks of the gout, his friend Edward Moore understood that "intemperance" was "the cause"; Fielding, as he put it to the Reverend John Ward, was being "visited for his sins."[202] Fielding was never a sot, but he greatly loved a sociable bottle and cracked too many of them. He would, as one unfriendly observer insisted, *drink with any body.*[203] And when he drank he preferred "the best Old Port," strong and full bodied, to any other liquor — a good bottle of which, he declared, "will make you drunk but never sick."[204] He was also addicted to tobacco, which he sometimes chewed,[205] but more often took in the form of snuff — the stimulating "Dust," as one grateful bard put it, that "in a Breath invigorates the Pow'rs,/ And Motion to the languid Nerves restores."[206] But there was something reminiscent of Rabelais' Gargantua about

Fielding's love of eating. He was not, as is sometimes said of him, a gourmet — though he admired the skills of French chefs, whose fare he occasionally sampled at the tables of his aristocratic acquaintance: the "best" of these, the Duke of Newcastle's celebrated cook, "Cloë," he compliments in the opening chapter of *Tom Jones*. But Fielding's appetite did not require whetting by such saucy devices as "the extraordinary *Kickshaws*"[207] of French cookery. In his opinion, there was something unmanly, as well as unpatriotic, in the polite rage for foreign delicacies. He preferred plain, hearty English cooking: beef and plum pudding, venison and beans, chines of bacon and joints of mutton, chicken and roast pig (a "Dish I am particularly fond of").[208] From the sea he relished oysters and sole and lobsters — and, when he was near Plymouth and could get it fresh, the "john dorée," which "resembles a turbot in shape, but exceeds it in firmness and flavour."[209] To top off a good dinner few things suited him better than an apple pie. As to the sophistication of his palate, *Amelia* gives us a pretty accurate idea when she goes to some trouble to prepare Booth's favorite dish: a fowl with egg sauce and mutton broth — a meal which, Fielding predicts, "may bring the Simplicity of his Taste into great Contempt with some of my Readers" (XI.viii).

However elementary his tastes may have been, no author has celebrated the pleasures of eating quite so magnificently as Fielding, whether he tells us in song that the distinguishing virtues of his countrymen are attributable to "The Roast Beef of Old England," or in *Tom Jones* serves up no less a "Feast" than "Human Nature" (I.i) while presenting his hero as a worthy rival to Homer's in "that eating Poem of the Odyssey" (IX.v). From Fielding's dwelling on such gastronomic themes in that novel, "Aretine" of *Old England* (27 May 1749) ironically feared that readers "unacquainted with the laudable *Parsimony* and *Abstinence* he observes in eating" might conclude he was of "a *gluttonous Disposition*." Fielding would be unembarrassed by the criticism. To him, the pleasures of eating were not only too great to be despised; they were natural to man and, like laughter, sweetened the soul. Just as, in 1728, he wrote his first published essay on "the Benefit of Laughing," so under the apt name of "Will. Lovemeal," he would in 1736 set forth these axioms of his epicureanism in one of the most entertaining pieces he ever wrote, an "Essay on Eating":

But tho' I cannot think that the *ultimate End* of Man is to *eat*, and that his whole *Ambition* shou'd be in extending the *Circumference* of his *Body*... yet I freely allow that there is a good deal of *Pleasure* in *Eating*, which reasonably may be indulg'd; for, as in the Performance of any Office of Nature, there must a sensible and necessary Pleasure attend it, how is it possible to satisfy Hunger without enjoying that Pleasure? ...

Tho' *Gluttonizing* [he continues], if I may use that Expression, is what I am an utter Enemy to, yet a moderate Meal is not only necessary for the *Body*, but the *Mind*; for *Eating* I have often observ'd was conducive to *Good-Humour* and had a surprising Effect on the *Tempers* of Mankind.[210]

It was not of course the Rabelaisian vigor of his bodily appetites that recommended Fielding to a wide circle of refined and sophisticated men and women. Not all his pleasures were coarse. He loved dancing, for example, not only country dancing to the rasp and thump of a fiddler, but also the more elegant measures of "a Minuet," with which he "did to the utter Confusion of all his Brother Beaus open the first Ball at Bath."[211] How remarkable it must have been to witness a man of Fielding's robust figure conducting himself gracefully on the dance-floor! Like Locke in his treatise on education,[212] Fielding believed that lessons in that art were necessary if men were to shake off any innate clumsiness; otherwise, like the clownish Atkinson in *Amelia* (V.ii), they will be "apt to discover this Want in their Education in every Motion, nay, even when they stand or sit still." His tastes in music, moreover, ranged from the traditional tunes for which he supplied so many new lyrics in his ballad operas, to "the enchanting Harmony" of Handel, whom, like his heroines Sophie Western and Amelia Booth, he preferred to all other composers.[213] Indeed, like Shakespeare's Lorenzo in the famous speech to which he alludes approvingly in an early essay,[214] Fielding distrusted "The Man that hath no music in himself,/ Nor is not moved with concord of sweet sounds." So it appears from *Amelia* (I.vii), where a sign of Miss Mathews's dangerous temperament is that she takes no delight in music.

A man who could gracefully tread a minuet and rejoice in the harmonies of an oratorio, Fielding was no crass voluptuary. In his personal relations he was also something more than a sociable fellow of indiscriminate tastes, though it is true he took no pleasure in solitude, except of course the pleasure afforded by the many books he read. He was a serious student of the art of social intercourse, as is clear from his anatomy of the subject in his "Essay on Conversation" – a term by which he meant not merely chat, but the many ways by which men and women relate to each other in civilized society.

Few of his contemporaries – perhaps not even the great Johnson himself had Fielding only had *his* Boswell – were more agreeable companions or spoke so well and so wittily. Lyttelton, who knew them all, later declared to James Beattie that Fielding "had more wit and humour" than Swift, Pope, and the other wits of his time put together.[215] This was the quality, together with his lively look and personal magnetism, that his friend Harris particularly admired about Fielding. "His Company," Harris recalled in his unpublished memorial, "was highly pleasing" and his wit "native, spontaneous, and ever new, derived instantly from those events that are arising every moment." It "never deserted him" even "in his most unprosperous hours, nor even when Death itself openly lookt him in ye face." Nor did he require the stimulus of drink to shine in conversation: "tho' Wine could not suppress his Ingenuity, it never improved it, nor did he ever succeed so well whether in a Serious way or even a humorous one, as when he was sober, cool, and free from ye loads of Intemperance." And like Johnson in conversation, who when his pistol misfired would knock his adversary down with the butt end of it, Fielding relished a lively argument. Harris marveled at how his friend could hold out triumphantly against a throng of foes: "He would parry with admirable humour a whole host of assailants, would maintain his ground with invincible magnanimity and like Falstaff of old against his men in Buckram, wd. take all their Points upon his Target at once." Fielding was, in short, as Harris affectionately summed him up,

> a Man, the Source of infinite entertainment to his Friends, whatever was ye Conversation, whether grave or gay, for even in graver Conversation they knew him to have excelled, a fact not to be admired at, if we reflect on his natural good Understanding, that specific Principle, that Particle divine, which distinguishes real Wit from its Shadow, Buffoonery.

···◆ xxiii ◆—···

Who, then, was lucky enough to have the pleasure of Fielding's company during the 1730s, whether in revelry or in those "graver" conversations he also enjoyed? Because of the scarcity of his correspondence during this decade, or indeed of any letters even referring to him, we cannot answer that question confidently. Some clues, however, have come to light that help to lift the mists obscuring his personal relationships of the time. We have already noted his friendships with a number of literary figures in Walpole's orbit – Lewis Theobald, for instance, Pope's Prince of Dulness whom Fielding for a time admired for his abilities as a scholar and editor of Shakespeare, if not for his talents as a playwright.

Far more important to him was James Ralph, the first of his closest friends of this period and a consummate literary opportunist who may

have initiated Fielding into the ways of Grub Street after he returned
from Leyden to "set up for a Play-Writer." Fielding seems to have
thought this "Pretender to Genius," as Ralph's biographer calls him,[216]
a clever man: so much so that he may have taken from him the idea
for *Tom Thumb*, as, when transforming *The Welsh Opera* into *The Grub-
Street Opera*, he borrowed several songs from Ralph's own ballad opera,
The Fashionable Lady. It was Ralph who in his pro-Walpole periodical
the *Weekly Register* (8 July 1732) angrily defended Fielding and *The
Modern Husband* against Russel's Grublings.

That Fielding should take such a fancy to a man of Ralph's distinctly
modest abilities is best explained by his friend's engaging personality
and his brilliance in conversation. Benjamin Franklin, the companion
of his youth with whom Ralph sailed from Philadelphia in 1724,
declared categorically that he "never knew a prettier talker," and even
the bookseller Thomas Davies, who disliked him in most other respects,
gave Ralph credit for being "in his conversation, agreeable and instructive" and "entertaining."[217] These were social virtues which Fielding
valued, and they won for Ralph many other notable friends, such as
Hogarth, Garrick, and Thomas Birch, all of whom Fielding also loved.
Like Fielding and Hogarth, who in their works could draw from memory
scenes from the disreputable Rose Tavern, Ralph was also a libertine.[218]
And in his graver moments, when he was not playing the critic or
historian, he was outspoken in his religious skepticism and his contempt
of the priesthood.

It was at Ralph's urging that Franklin, his mentor in free-thinking,
committed to paper his deistical principles in a pamphlet entitled *A
Dissertation on Liberty and Necessity, Pleasure and Pain* (1725), a
work dedicated to Ralph and, as his biographer believes, probably
representing the substance of Ralph's own heterodox beliefs.[219] It is
Franklin's notion in this little tract (which, to his credit, he later
repented of and tried to destroy) that, God being infinitely wise and
good and powerful, "nothing could possibly be wrong in the World, &
that Vice and Virtue were empty Distinctions, no such Things existing."
Twisting to his own purpose an example he found in Wollaston's
Religion of Nature Delineated, Franklin insisted that there was nothing
morally reprehensible in a thief's stealing a horse, because, after all,
the thief, feeling "an Uneasiness [or pain] in the want of [the] Horse,"
is only obeying the impulse of nature. This way of thinking soon proved
convenient for Franklin himself – as it would also do for one of Mr.
Wilson's deistical friends in *Joseph Andrews* (III.iii) – who was moved
by a no less natural impulse to relieve himself from the uneasiness he
felt in being excluded from the embraces of Ralph's mistress. In Ralph's
absence, Franklin attempted to seduce the lady – upon which Ralph
felt justified in parting company with Franklin without troubling to

repay a debt he owed him of £27.[220] Such is the cement binding the friendships of deists.

Another of Fielding's closest friends of the period, Thomas Cooke (*c.* 1702–56), provides a further link with Walpole and with free-thinking, as well as with a number of like-minded associates. An accomplished classicist best known for his translations of Hesiod and Plautus, Cooke was a Whig in politics and a poet of some small fame. With other Whig critics and poetasters who had the bad judgment to club together against Pope – such as his friends Theobald, Dennis, Welsted, and Concanen – Cooke found a place in *The Dunciad*. If it was Cooke who appended *The Battle of the Poets* to *Tom Thumb* back in November 1730, thereby offending both Fielding and Ralph, it is clear that by the time he began publishing *The Comedian* in April 1732, Cooke and Fielding had become friends. This was a monthly magazine favoring Walpole in politics and Cooke's personal brand of deism in religion; as a critical organ it defined itself by opposing Pope and the *Grub-Street Journal*. It was accordingly Fielding's ally in his quarrel with Russel and his minions: Cooke was first to come to Fielding's defense, praising *The Modern Husband* in his third number (June 1732); and he fired the final shot three months later in the same periodical (September 1732), printing "*An* EPIGRAM" the gist and quality of which can be savored in the opening couplet: "When *Grubs*, and *Grublings*, censure *Fielding*'s Scenes,/ He cannot answer that which Nothing means."

Nothing establishes the depth of their friendship so clearly, however, as the discovery that Fielding was a contributor to Cooke's magazine.[221] For Fielding is very probably the "Friend" who in *The Comedian* No. 5 (August 1732) published not one but two pieces, an essay and a poem. In the first of these, entitled "Observations on Government, the Liberty of the Press, News-papers, Partys, and Party-writer[s]," Fielding in an uncharacteristically earnest vein admonishes the Opposition journalists, "these weekly Venders of Sedition," for abusing the Liberty of the Press in libels against Walpole and his ministry:

> Tho I have been always an Advocate for every Branch of Liberty, and among others for that of the Press, yet I conceive that this, as well as all other good Institutions, may, for Want of some Regulation, be in the End attended with evil Effects.
>
> ... I do not see [he goes so far as to say], if a Stop was put to our present weekly Incendiarys in a legal Way, why the Liberty of *England* may not be sayed to stand on a very sound Bottom.
>
> (pp. 34–5)

If Fielding was the author of this essay (as he appears to be), there could be no clearer evidence both of the sincerity of his recent fulsome dedication of *The Modern Husband*, and of the awkward ironies involved in being a political writer for hire in Walpole's England; for the arguments he uses against the minister's adversaries would be, in time, precisely those directed at himself in the columns of the *Daily Gazetteer*. The other piece probably by Fielding in this number of *The Comedian* is a poem of sixty-two lines, entitled "An Epistle to Mr. ELLYS the Painter." About Fielding's friendship with this colorful figure we will have more to say.

Cooke was the sort of person to whom Fielding at this period would have been drawn. He was a clubbable man and, early in life at least, something of a rake – or, as his biographer puts it, a man of strong passions "which, it is supposed, he gratified very freely."[222] With Fielding's own sociable nature in mind, compare Mawbey's account of Cooke:

> No one enjoyed the pleasures of the table more than he, nor was more entertaining at it. Though he spoke with much freedom of men and things . . . he had such a fund of general knowledge and anecdote, without being in reality ill-natured, that it was impossible for such as knew him thoroughly to avoid being pleased.

There was, however, for all his "infinite humour," a less amiable side to Cooke that Fielding, five years his junior, must have found tiresome. He could be "dictatorial," bent on dominating the company with displays of his superior learning and requiring that deference be paid to his opinions. Chesterfield, who knew him well, found him "the most irritable of the *genus irritabile vatum*, offended with trifles, and never forgetting or forgiving them." Even so, Fielding and Cooke remained friends throughout the decade and perhaps longer: he subscribed to Fielding's *Miscellanies* (1743), as Fielding had done to Cooke's long-delayed edition of Plautus; and, as we shall see, they were members of a club of wits who were meeting together as late as 1744.

By that time, however, their friendship must have been sorely strained, by a passage in *Joseph Andrews* (III.iii) if for no other reason. For as the reformed rake Mr. Wilson recounts the story of his youthful days in London, he reserves his most scathing ridicule for a certain society of free-thinkers who, having rejected the Christian religion, admit no other guide to conduct than the *"Rule of Right"* – a doctrine which was the foundation of Cooke's own deist philosophy as set forth in the monthly numbers of *The Comedian* (1732) and reprinted the following year in a collected edition entitled *A Demonstration of the Will of God by the Light of Nature*. Samuel Richardson was convinced that, in many respects, Wilson's narrative in *Joseph Andrews* was the story of Fielding's own early life.[223] Wilson's brief encounter with the "Rule of Right" club is surely among the most revealing of these autobiographical episodes, pointing toward what may well have been

Fielding's own early flirtation with the alluring doctrines of deism. Wilson first recalls that he had grown weary of the company of a club of sots who did nothing but sleep all day and drink all night:

> This Way of Life the first serious Reflection put a period to, and I became Member of a Club frequented by young Men of great Abilities. The Bottle was now only called in to the Assistance of our Conversation, which rolled on the deepest Points of Philosophy. These Gentlemen were engaged in a Search after Truth, in the Pursuit of which they threw aside all the Prejudices of Education, and governed themselves only by the infallible Guide of Human Reason. This great Guide, after having shewn them the Falshood of that very antient but simple Tenet, that there is such a Being as a Deity in the Universe, helped them to establish in his stead a certain *Rule of Right*, by adhering to which they all arrived at the utmost Purity of Morals. Reflection made me as much delighted with this Society, as it had taught me to despise and detest the former. I began now to esteem myself a Being of a higher Order than I had ever before conceived, and was the more charmed with this Rule of Right, as I really found in my own Nature nothing repugnant to it. I held in utter Contempt all Persons who wanted any other Inducement to Virtue besides her intrinsick Beauty and Excellence; and had so high an Opinion of my present Companions, with regard to their Morality, that I would have trusted them with whatever was nearest and dearest to me. Whilst I was engaged in this delightful Dream, two or three Accidents happen'd successively, which at first much surprized me. – For, one of our greatest Philosophers, or *Rule of Right-men*, withdrew himself from us, taking with him the Wife of one of his most intimate Friends. Secondly, Another of the same Society left the Club without remembring to take leave of his Bail. A third having borrowed a Sum of Money of me, for which I received no Security, when I asked him to repay it, absolutely denied the Loan. These several Practices, so inconsistent with our golden Rule, made me begin to suspect its Infallibility; but when I communicated my Thoughts to one of the Club, he said "there was nothing absolutely good or evil in itself; that Actions were denominated good or bad by the Circumstances of the Agent. That possibly the Man who ran away with his Neighbour's Wife might be one of very good Inclinations, but over-prevailed on by the Violence of an unruly Passion, and in other Particulars might be a very worthy Member of Society: That if the Beauty of any Woman created in him an Uneasiness, he had a Right from Nature to relieve himself;" with many other things, which I then detested so much, that I took Leave of the Society that very Evening, and never returned to it again.

In thus characterizing Wilson's club of fallible philosophers, Fielding combines the at times contradictory ethical systems of his two closest friends of the 1730s, Cooke and Ralph – Ralph's own brand of deism corresponding, as we remarked, to that set forth by his mentor Franklin in his *Dissertation on Liberty and Necessity*. Cooke, however, was the dominant influence, and his views in *A Demonstration of the Will of God by the Light of Nature* are echoed by Wilson. Thus, in his "Introduction" to that work Cooke declares that his system is based on "an Enquiry after Truth"; and to this end advises that "we should divest ourselves of all Prejudices ... we should disjoin the monstrous Association of Ideas which a wrong Education has grafted in us; we should separate the Idea of the tru [*sic*] God from the Idea of such a God as the Schools teach us to worship." In this noble enterprise, Cooke continues, our only guide must be "that original Revelation which the Almighty implanted in [our] Constitution, which is Reason, the Power of distinguishing Right from Wrong." Once, by following this unerring guide, we have rejected the false doctrines about the Deity which we have been taught as children – among them the doctrines concerning Christ, miracles, and Providence – once, in other words, we attend to "no other Guide but Nature," then "the Beauty of Virtue will appear unpolluted" to us. Having thus swept away divine revelation and the teaching of the Church, Cooke substitutes in their stead a vague imperative he calls "the Rule of Right."[224] For him, virtuous men are "such Men as make the Rule of Right their Rule of Conduct," by adhering to which "the cursed Root of all moral Evil would be destroyed, and an universal Harmony be among Men."[225] An utter enemy to Christian doctrine, Cooke was attempting to popularize a kind of neo-stoic rationalism (the Stoics were, in his view, "the wisest Sect that ever was on Earth").[226] How doggedly he pursued this will-o'-the-wisp is clear when, as late as 1 October 1745, he assured a correspondent: "I have, and shall all along make the Rule of Right my Rule of Conduct."[227]

However attractive Fielding as a young man may have found this flattering philosophy of man's natural goodness and self-sufficiency, he discovered in it no very practical moral imperative. Certainly he found it difficult to discipline his own passionate nature. Neither the stoic's misplaced confidence in the efficacy of reason, nor the neo-platonist's contemplation on the natural beauty of virtue, could turn the trick for him – as he remembered in drawing the characters both of Square in *Tom Jones*, who at the eleventh hour rejects Cicero and Shaftesbury in favor of the Christian religion, and of Booth in *Amelia*, who experiences a similar conversion. Other members of Cooke's little circle of philosophical rakes were even less amenable than Fielding to reforming their characters by "the Rule of Right." It was to one of these, the notorious libertine Anthony Henley, that Cooke dedicated his *Demonstration* in

April 1733, exhorting him, in tones quite splendidly avuncular, to be more moderate in his "Pursuit of Pleasure" and to govern his passions "by the Rule of Right." For this purpose Cooke pointedly prescribes a salutary perusal of his sixth discourse, "On Liberty and Necessity, and some Observations on the Use and Abuse of the Passions," where Henley would have found himself being admonished against indulging in the kind of adulterous relationship Mr. Wilson had deplored. It was not Cooke's "Rule of Right" but the hedonist doctrine of moral relativism espoused by Ralph's friend Benjamin Franklin that could be made to justify such conduct.

Fielding's flirtation with the deistical principles of his clever friends, Cooke and Ralph, probably did not last long. By the end of the decade, when he began writing *The Champion*, his authorities in moral and religious matters were those latitudinarian divines of the Church of England – John Tillotson, Samuel Clarke, Benjamin Hoadly – whose rational, Low Church attitudes in some respects resembled deism. For that reason, these divines were the ones even Cooke could sometimes find appealing.[228]

Fielding's other friends of this early period preferred the jollier, more tangible fruits of their hedonism to such paddling about in strange seas of thought. We have already mentioned two of these friends in passing who deserve a closer look: the burly painter John Ellys and the rake-hell politician Anthony Henley. "Jack" Ellys (1701–57), well known for his portraits in the old-fashioned manner of his master, Kneller, had many interests and acquaintances in common with Fielding, and the two men remained friends for life – as attested by Fielding's complimentary verses in *The Comedian* (August 1732) and a playful allusion to him twenty years later in the *Covent-Garden Journal* (29 August 1752). Both were close to Cooke, Hogarth, and Ralph – the latter two being Ellys's fellow champions of a native English school of painting.[229] Ellys, moreover, provides a further link between Fielding and Walpole during the early 1730s: it was Ellys who acquired for the minister his famous collection of pictures at Houghton, a service for which he was rewarded by being appointed Keeper of the Lions in the Tower. Like Fielding, he was a large, strong man – a frequenter of gymnasiums, in fact, who consorted with prize-fighters such as the champion James Figg. He was also a lover of the histrionic arts; in the early 1730s he owned shares in the patent of Drury Lane, and, after Wilks died in September 1732, acted as his widow's deputy in managing the theatre.

Ellys needed no coaxing to join in the fun with the other rakes in Fielding's circle. So Anthony Henley implied when he wrote to Cooke from "The Grange," his seat in Hampshire, on 19 August 1733, supposing that "*Jack Ellis*, to whom I beg my Service, entertains you with

much Gallantry."[230] Henley (d. 1748),[231] eldest son and heir of Sir
Anthony Henley, to whom Garth dedicated *The Dispensary*, was the
brother of Fielding's more famous friend, the distinguished lawyer
Robert Henley (1708?–72). M.P. for Southampton until he lost his seat
opposing Walpole during the Excise crisis, he married the daughter of
the Earl of Berkeley in 1728 and in less than twenty years of dissolute
living accumulated debts amounting to nearly £30,000.[232] Hogarth may
have drawn him as the leering little man who stands with Colonel
Charteris at the door of Mother Needham's brothel in Plate I of *The
Harlot's Progress*.[233]

Nevertheless, if Cooke is to be believed, Henley, besides unbridled
lasciviousness, possessed qualities Fielding would have found congenial:
"blessed with an Understanding and Vivacity of Genius superior to
most Men," Cooke observed, he was one "whose Wit and Gayety give
Life to the Company with whom he is."[234] Henley's feelings toward
Fielding, on the other hand, were ambivalent. On 17 November 1733
he wrote Cooke that Fielding, on his way up to town, had tried to visit
him at "The Grange": "*Fielding* who I suppose you have seen before
now, did me the favour to call on me here, but to my misfortune I was
then from home; he has a vast deal of humour, but I believe you'l [sic]
join with me in this point, he is *too free* with his *friends*."[235] Both
Anthony and Robert Henley subscribed to Fielding's *Miscellanies*
(1743), but it was Robert only whom Fielding complimented in those
volumes.[236] Though he rose to become the first Earl of Northington and
to serve as Lord Chancellor, Robert, too, was bibulous and profane as
a young man.

From Anthony Henley's letter to Cooke in November 1733, it appears
that a favorite resort of these jovial companions was the Mitre Tavern
in Fleet Street, later frequented by Johnson and Boswell. It was not
long, however, before Fielding's social orbit, as well as Cooke's,
occasionally took them across the river to Southwark – a region well
known to debtors confined within the Rules of the Marshalsea, across
London Bridge, and to those who by water visited the splendid new
pleasure gardens at Vauxhall. The "Master" of the Spring Gardens, as
they were called, was Jonathan Tyers (d. 1767), a man who remained
Fielding's cherished friend. In *Amelia* (1751), a novel set in the spring
and summer of 1733, just a year after Tyers opened the gardens to the
public, Fielding takes his heroine on a visit to Vauxhall and interrupts
the narrative to pay his friend a compliment:

> To delineate the particular Beauties of these Gardens, would, indeed,
> require as much Pains and as much Paper too, as to rehearse all the
> good Actions of their Master; whose Life proves the Truth of an
> Observation which I have read in some Ethic Writer, that a truly

elegant Taste is generally accompanied with an Excellency of Heart;
or in other Words, that true Virtue is, indeed, nothing else but true
Taste (IX.ix).

We do not know when or how Fielding's friendship with this good
man began, but perhaps it was owing to their common friend Hogarth,
who, tradition has it,[237] first convinced Tyers that the gardens at
Vauxhall would be an excellent place to exhibit a variety of contemporary arts; for besides the gardens themselves and the concerts of
music which Amelia found so ravishing, the grounds were adorned with
elegant buildings furnished with paintings and statues. Sometime later,
probably in the late 1730s, Cooke settled down permanently as Tyers's
neighbor in South Lambeth.[238] Chances are that Fielding's acquaintance
with Tyers dates from the early 1730s; but the first evidence of their
friendship occurs in the "Memoirs" of Dr. Charles Burney, the distinguished musicologist and father of the author of *Evelina*. Soon after
he arrived in London in 1744 to serve apprentice to Thomas Arne,
Burney began attending the concerts at Vauxhall and recorded his
impressions of the Master of the Spring Gardens. Part of his account
reads as follows:

> He [Tyers] had established a weekly meeting, a kind of club of Wits,
> at the Royal Oak, before I was acquainted with him, consisting of
> M[r]. Dawson of Lambeth; Harry Hatsel, equally witty, corpulent,
> sensual, and profligate, with Falstaff; Moore, author of Fables for
> the female sex; Cook, the translator of Hesiod; & Harry Fielding.[239]

Tyers was not witty himself, and far from being a dissolute or irreligious
man, he was a sincere Christian of unblemished morals. But, as Cooke's
biographer observes, he enjoyed the company of "literary characters"
and, "keeping a plentiful table,"[240] he easily drew about him the club
of wits to which Burney refers. By the time Burney became aware of
it, the club had already twice moved; it originally met in the Spring
Gardens themselves, and then moved to the Vine, a tavern in South
Lambeth – quite near the Royal Oak.[241]
Confirmation of Fielding's membership in this lively society is found
in the list of subscribers to his *Miscellanies*, published in 1743 but
probably projected two years earlier. There we find, with one exception,
all the names Burney mentions: Tyers and Richard Dawson are both
down for the more expensive sets in royal paper; Cooke and Henry
Hatsell settled for the cheaper sets. Only Edward Moore (1712–57), the
literary linen draper, is missing; he may have joined the group late,[242]
or perhaps he could not afford the price. In any case, he was a close
friend of both Cooke and Fielding, and his membership in the club, as
well as Hatsell's, is attested by Mawbey.[243] Richard Dawson (d. 1752)

was a member of a prosperous Vauxhall family of glass manufacturers; other Dawsons – John and Edward – were also friends of Cooke, but Richard, who was close to Hatsell as well as Fielding, is probably the man Burney had in mind.

Thanks are due another member of the club – the penniless, madcap priest Leonard Howard[244] – for providing us with a glimpse of the prodigiously fat and "facetious" Harry Hatsell, one of the most colorful and indeed (as Dr. Burney would have it) Falstaffian of Fielding's friends of this period. The second son of a judge, Sir Henry Hatsell, Harry (d. 1772) was himself, if his titles meant anything, a distinguished lawyer of the Middle Temple, appointed Bencher (1755), Reader (1763), and Treasurer (1768).[245] But as Howard more accurately described him in a mock "Epitaph," Hatsell's true "*study* was to *entertain*"; he lived chiefly to avoid the company of his wife, "To *crack* his *jokes* and drink his beer."[246] The flavor of his company is preserved in an anecdote told by an anonymous admirer for whom there was "not perhaps a person of more humour and sprightliness in conversation breathing."[247] Upon contracting a venereal disease, Hatsell, whose pleasures were not confined to cracking jokes and swilling beer, complained to the physician attending him that Nature had erred in providing man with ten toes but only a single vulnerable organ of generation. The doctor retorted that if Hatsell had had his wish, he would have succeeded only in being ten times more miserable than he was. True enough, Hatsell replied, but he "could not help wishing for ten of 'em to try, because ... it would be ten to one if all of them were lame together."

The circle of Fielding's friends in this early period was far wider than this. He was a gregarious, clubbable man, with friends, as Harris remarked, in virtually every rank and profession, from the Court to the theatre, from the Church to the garrets of Grub Street, from the polite assemblies at Salisbury and Bath to the bagnios of Covent Garden. The group we have just now been considering are worth singling out, however, for they are new to Fielding's biographers – either because their connection with him has not been suspected, or because the importance of their relationships with him has not been fully appreciated. These men – Ralph, Cooke, and Theobald; Hogarth and Ellys; Anthony and Robert Henley; Jonathan Tyers, Harry Hatsell, and Edward Moore – will suggest in the variety of their characters as libertines and free-thinkers, artists and poets, scholars and wits, the kinds of thoughts and activities that occupied Fielding in his leisure hours, when he was not plying his craft as a writer of comedies and political satires.

One subject which occupied Fielding's thoughts during the summer of
1732, and for some months to come, was a young woman who had
temporarily supplanted Charlotte Cradock in his affections – a young
woman with whom he had fallen hopelessly in love. In Fielding's verse
of the period she is called only "Dorinda," but a tantalizing footnote
to his "Epistle to Mr. Ellys the Painter" discloses at least the initials
of her true name: she was a "Miss D.W.," whose portrait Ellys began
but never finished. Perhaps he was prevented from doing so by the
circumstances to which Fielding alludes in the poem, in an uncharacteristically maudlin vein that suggests how much in love he was. The
passage in question begins as a compliment to Ellys, whose "Art" can
renew decaying Nature, preserve the images at least of our dead friends,
"And bid departed Beauty live again":

> *Leander* here, when *Melesinda*'s coy,
> Doats on the smiling Object of his Joy:
> And far, alas! by cruel Fate remov'd,
> (Too lovely Nymph! and O! too much belov'd!)
> Here, in the slightest Sketch, I fondly trace
> All the dear Sweetness of *Dorinda*'s[248] Face:
> Tho Parents, Fortune, and tho she, conspire
> To keep far from me all my Soul's Desire,
> Still shall my ravish'd Eyes their Darling see,
> If not so beauteous, look more kind thro thee.

Neither her parents nor, it would seem, "Miss D.W." herself considered
Fielding a suitable match; but to be on the safe side – for as his
attempt to abduct Sarah Andrew attests, Fielding was a lover not easily
discouraged – they prudently removed her "far" from him.

Even so, he continued to admire her. In February or March of the
following year, he paid her a pretty compliment in his "Epistle to Mr.
Lyttleton," where, while praising his friend's poem, "Advice to a
Lady," Fielding substitutes his own mistress's name for that of Lyttelton's heroine, Belinda:

> To thee [Lyttelton], the Lover blest shall Pleasures owe
> Which uninstructed Beauty can't bestowe.
> What they Should prove, Coquettes and Prudes shall see;
> And what She is, Dorinda read, in thee.[249]

But the reluctant "Miss D.W." was not to be the love of Fielding's

life. That distinction (which the lady must have found a mixed blessing)
belongs to Charlotte Cradock.

However unlucky Fielding was in this affair of the heart, as the
theatrical season of 1732–3 began he was at the peak of his fortunes as
London's favorite living dramatist. The Queen herself commanded that
the new season open at Drury Lane on 8 September with *The Mock
Doctor*, played as afterpiece to an old favorite, *The Rehearsal*; Colley
Cibber appeared again as Bayes, and in the new farce his son Theophilus
resumed the part of Gregory he had originally acted so well.[250]

But changes were occurring in the management of that theatre which
would in little more than a year's time dispel all this euphoria and
radically alter Fielding's career as a dramatist. Although royal approval
of the patent of Drury Lane was granted in July 1732 to the "triumvirate" of Cibber, Booth, and Wilks, that celebrated partnership at
once began to dissolve. Booth sold his share for £2,500 to John
Highmore, a young man with no other qualifications for the job than
his considerable wealth and passion for the theatre. Soon after Wilks
died in September, "Jack" Ellys began acting in his stead as Mrs.
Wilks's deputy. Cibber, who was preparing to retire, at first assigned
his share, temporarily, to Theophilus; then, in March 1733, by selling
out to Highmore, he dashed his son's hopes of continuing to prosper in
that office. By the end of the season, Theophilus and his fellow actors
would be in open revolt, and the fortunes of the managers, together
with those of Fielding, their leading author, would be at low ebb.

For the time being, however, in the autumn of 1732 Fielding was
riding high. He cannot have enjoyed his friend Cooke's bluntness in
The Comedian (October 1732), attributing the success of *The Mock
Doctor* more "to the extraordinary good Action" of Theophilus Cibber
and "Kitty" Raftor "than to the Merit of the Writer"; but he had by
his own admission rushed that play into production before it was ready,
and he was well along with revisions that would establish its reputation
as a minor classic for many years to come. This finished version of *The
Mock Doctor* was staged for Fielding's benefit on 16 November 1732;
and on the 30th of that month it was performed again at the King's
command. About the same time Watts published a "Second Edition
... "With Additional Songs and Alterations."

Signs that Drury Lane was not prospering under its new management
became all too plain the following month, when the first new play of
the season failed dismally. This was Charles Johnson's tragedy, *Cœlia:
or, The Perjured Lover*, which, with an Epilogue contributed by Fielding, opened and closed on 4 December. While the ministerial organ the
Daily Courant (25 December 1732), for which Ralph was now writing,[251]
reprimanded the Town for failing to support the Theatre Royal, the
Grub-Street Journal (8 March 1732/3) gloated over the failure of John-

son's tragedy, which so clearly proved "how insufficient the present managers of Drury-lane playhouse are to discharge their trust, as directors of our public entertainments."

In January the gloom at the Theatre Royal deepened as an epidemic spread through the town, affecting the companies of all the theatres so seriously that many performances had to be cancelled.[252] As early as 3 January, Fielding's *The Miser* was in rehearsal, scheduled to open "in a Fortnight's Time"; but owing to illness among the cast, including the indisposition of Theophilus Cibber,[253] who played the part of Ramilie, the production was not ready for another six weeks. When at last it reached the stage on Saturday, 17 February, it proved to be precisely the cordial the ailing company needed. *The Miser*, freely based on Molière's *L'Avare*, was by far the most successful of Fielding's regular comedies; all told, it was performed at least twenty-three times[254] during an abbreviated season, including performances on 26 April before the Royal Family and on 16 May before the Prince of Wales.

The opinion of the Earl of Egmont, who on 20 February attended the first of several benefits Fielding enjoyed, reflected the judgment of the Town in general: "the new play called 'The Miser,'" he wrote in his Diary, "is well translated from Moliere by Mr. Fielding, and well acted."[255] Particularly notable were the performances of "Kitty" Raftor as Lappet and of Benjamin Griffin as Lovegold in the title role.[256] Griffin, indeed, as Aaron Hill remembered in *The Prompter* (1 April 1735),"*topp'd* the Part of the *Miser*," acquiring "great Applause from his *close* and *fine* Representation" of the character – the quality of which is captured for us by a poet who saw one of the original performances:

> What then, Sir, do you call the *Miser*'s Rage?
> He frets, he raves, he storms, he shakes the Stage;
> Now his lost Hoard he mourns in plaintive Tone,
> Now pours his Curses on a spend-thrift Son.[257]

Years later on the occasion of a revival of the play, Fielding, for whom avarice was the most despicable of vices, remarked that he did not know "any Character, which is received both on the *French* and *English* Stage, with so general a Satisfaction. The Spectators always shewing a very visible Pleasure in all the Disappointments which he meets with through the whole Comedy."[258]

Watts published *The Miser*, with a Prologue by "a Friend" and an Epilogue once again by Cibber, on 13 March 1732/3. As a further sign of his commitment during this period to the Court party, Fielding dedicated the play to Charles Lennox, second Duke of Richmond (1701–50), taking this "first Opportunity of boasting the Countenance I have met with from One who is an Honour to the High Rank in which he is born."[259] Thus began Fielding's long and friendly association with a man he genuinely admired, particularly for that virtue he later celebrated in another work addressed to Richmond, the poem "Of Good-Nature." In the course of praising the Duke, however, Fielding could not resist paying one or two compliments to himself on having achieved "an extraordinary Success in so difficult an Undertaking"; the "Theatre," he continued proudly, "hath declared loudly in Favour of the MISER." In addition to the handsome profits he reaped from his benefit nights, Watts probably paid him liberally for the publishing rights — £100, according to Thomas Davies, was "the usual price paid to authors for plays which met with uncommon success."[260] Indeed, the sum may have been higher; the bookseller in *Joseph Andrews* (I.xvii) declares he has "formerly known a hundred Guineas given for a Play."

During this season Fielding wrote one other play which was, on the evidence, anything but a success. The play in question, a ballad opera entitled *Deborah: or, A Wife for You All*, was performed just once — as afterpiece to *The Miser* on 6 April, the occasion of "Kitty" Raftor's benefit.[261] The abrupt demise of *Deborah*, however, may have been owing more to contemporary politics and the intrigues of courtiers than to its deficiencies as a play. For it seems likely that, by making some ill-advised alterations to a work already in rehearsal, Fielding rashly involved himself on the wrong sides of two separate but related contemporary controversies: one between Walpole and the Opposition over the Excise Bill, the other between the King, protector of Handel, and a certain party of opera-loving noblemen that included Fielding's new-found patron, the Duke of Richmond.

Apparently written expressly for "Kitty" Raftor's benefit — as a vehicle allowing her to show off her fine singing voice after she first displayed her skills as an actress in *The Miser* — Fielding's play was originally entitled simply *A Wife for You All*.[262] Its setting seems to have been a magistrate's court, since Griffin, the star of *The Miser*, played Justice Mittimus and another role was that of Lawyer Trouble. In mid-March, however, two events occurred that electrified the climate in the worlds of politics and music: on 14 March, Walpole introduced his controversial Excise Bill on tobacco and wine; on 17 March, by the King's command, Handel's oratorio *Deborah* was performed at the Opera House in the Haymarket, at double the usual prices, with the Royal Family in attendance. It was the first time an oratorio had been scheduled for a Saturday night, a time usually reserved for Italian opera.[263] Walpole's attempt to impose a tax on the gentry's favorite pleasures was bitterly resented in the political sphere; and lovers of the Italian opera no less bitterly resented what they considered Handel's dictatorial attempt to force his expensive oratorios on them. In the Opposition press the two great men were linked as arrogant colleagues in oppression. In Eustace Budgell's *The Bee* (24 March 1733) there appeared "*A Dialogue* between two *Projectors*" which much amused the Town:

> *Quoth* W[alpole] to H[ande]l shall we two agree,
> And join in a Scheme of *Excise*. H. *Caro si.*
> *Of what Use is your Sheep if your Shepherd can't sheer him?*
> *At the* Hay-Market *I, you at* We[stminst]er? W. hear him.

But more formidable than such political opponents were those opera-loving courtiers and their ladies who not only organized subscriptions to support their favorite form of musical theatre, but mounted a campaign to boycott Handel's performances.

As far as Fielding was concerned, the Duke of Richmond had joined the anti-Handel faction.[264] Still more to the point, as reported in *The Craftsman* (7 April 1733), "The King's sworn Servants, of the two Theatres of *Drury-Lane* and *Covent-Garden*, reap'd the Benefit of this general Discontent, and were resorted to in Crowds, by way of Opposition to the *Oratorio*." However much Fielding came to love Handel's music, for the moment he had excellent practical reasons for wishing this "general Discontent" to continue: many of those applauding *The Miser* at Drury Lane would otherwise be attending the oratorio at the Opera House. By the day of its one and only performance, then, Fielding had given his ballad opera a new title: *Deborah: or, A Wife for You All.* The Town would understand that if they came to "Kitty" Raftor's benefit, they would be treated to a burlesque of Handel's oratorio. If, as seems likely, that is what Fielding gave them, we may imagine the reactions of the King to this mockery of his favorite composer, and of Walpole to any further possibility that his pet "project" and Handel's might be satirically associated. Only pressure from this high up can plausibly account for the fact that Fielding's *Deborah* not only never had a second performance, but was never published.

In these early months of 1733 Fielding wrote another work that might also have been lost to us – a work more important than *Deborah* in what it reveals about his loyalties and friendships of the period. Recently discovered among the papers of Lady Mary Wortley Montagu is Fielding's own fair copy of his "Epistle to Mr. Lyttleton,"[265] a poem occasioned by the now famous couplet in Pope's imitation of the *First Satire of the Second Book of Horace*, published on 15 February 1732/3: "From furious *Sappho* scarce a milder Fate,/ P[o]x'd by her Love, or libell'd by her Hate." This public insult to his cousin (for everyone knew who Sappho was) elicited from Fielding one of his handsomest compliments to her sex – "To greater Wisdom Men make false Pretence/

Nature with Beauty gave Superiour Sense" (ll. 24–5) – and his most vituperative verse:

> Say, Wretch, why should her Charms thy Anger move?
> Too ugly thou! too impotent for Love!
> 'Twere capital to suffer thy Embrace,
> For thou art Surely not of human Race.
> An evil Sprite, like Satan; sent to tell
> Those Lies on Earth, thy Brother spreads in Hell
> Sworn Foe to Beauty: Yet, thy Form believe,
> Thou hast no Fruit to tempt a Second Eve.
>
> (ll. 38–45)

The poet he can admire – especially the poet of *Windsor Forest, Eloisa to Abelard,* and *The Rape of the Lock* – but he abhors the "malicious Soul" of the man who would "assassinate" the good name of a lady or pillory Theobald in *The Dunciad* for being a better critic of Shakespeare than himself. Fielding always considered Pope "a great Poet,"[266] and in time he would come to know the man better and to value his acquaintance. But for the moment, in the simile which concludes the poem, he saw Pope as a little snapping "Curr" and himself, the protector of Lady Mary, as "the gen'rous Mastiff" that gives the upstart a shake and flings him into the kennel. No one, however, ever bested Pope in poetic combat, and such wishful sweet revenge as Fielding here exacts for the injury done his cousin he wisely confined to verses meant for the eyes of a few friends only. With the spectacle in mind of his chums Ralph, Cooke, and Theobald suffering perpetual mortification in *The Dunciad* for similar offences, Fielding, we may be certain, never meant to publish the work.

Besides illuminating Fielding's relations with Lady Mary and Pope, the "Epistle" is notable as the first sign of his enduring friendship with George Lyttelton (1709–73), whom he knew since their schooldays together at Eton. Already in 1733 Fielding was addressing him as "dear Lyttleton"; by 1749 he would confer a kind of immortality upon him, not only by dedicating *Tom Jones* to him, but by declaring that he served as model for Squire Allworthy, "a stronger Picture of a truly benevolent Mind than is to be found in any other" work. By that time Lyttelton and Fielding had been drawn still closer together by common political interests, interests first apparent a little later in the 1730s in the campaign of the "Patriots" to bring Walpole down. For the moment, however, Lyttelton had not committed himself to opposing Walpole, and Fielding leaves no doubt that his own loyalties remain with the minister and the Court. Thus in a contemptuous distich he contrasts the constructive achievements of General George Wade, the government's mild pacifier of Scotland, with the empty rhetoric of the

Opposition's disaffected leaders, William Pulteney and Henry St. John, Viscount Bolingbroke: "The more one Action of a Wade delights/ Then all that Poultney speaks, or St. John writes" (ll. 70–1). Such party sentiments in Fielding's writings are generally as fleeting as they are warm. Before another winter passed, he would himself (it appears) become a regular contributor to the journal Pulteney and Bolingbroke founded, *The Craftsman*, and would devote his talents for ridicule to making their politics more palatable to the public.

••• XXV •••

The series of events that precipitated this radical change in Fielding's political outlook began in the spring of 1733 when, for a great deal of money, Colley Cibber sold to John Highmore his share of the patent of Drury Lane. Theophilus Cibber, whose great expectations of prospering in his father's stead as manager of the theatre were thus thwarted, considered that he had been deprived of his "Birthright." [267] By the end of May – now, as his enemies saw it, enacting in real life the role of the swaggering Ancient Pistol he played so well on stage – he was in open revolt against the patentees and successfully persuaded most of the other principal actors of the company to secede with him. On 29 May the *Daily Post* reported that, as a consequence, "there will be no more Plays acted this Season" at Drury Lane. So ended, catastrophically, Fielding's most triumphant season at the Theatre Royal – a season in which no fewer than six of his comedies were at one time or another in production: at Drury Lane, besides the revised *Mock Doctor*, *The Miser*, and the ill-fated *Deborah*, there were revivals of *The Lottery* and *The Tragedy of Tragedies*; at the Little Haymarket rival comedians staged *The Old Debauchees*, as well as paying Fielding the tribute of producing a musical version of *Tom Thumb* called *The Opera of Operas*, with a score by Thomas Arne. Few playwrights in the history of the English theatre have enjoyed such popularity as this.

The worries he felt at the collapse of his theatre were temporarily forgotten in a deeper, personal sadness. On 7 June, in her seventy-ninth year, his grandmother Lady Gould died in Salisbury, where she had been living in the house in St. Martin's Church Street to which she moved soon after her daughter's death. She it was who had appealed to the Lord Chancellor to preserve her grandchildren's inheritance and keep them from the evil influence of their papist stepmother. To her Fielding had fled from the birchings at Eton; with her he had spent his holidays during a formative period of his life. What she meant to him we may infer from the trouble he took to have her body carried thirty miles from Salisbury to East Stour, to rest beside his mother in the churchyard adjacent to his farm. She was buried there on 12 June by the curate, William Young[268] – the learned and quixotic parson who in time served as the original of the most delightful character in Fielding's fiction, Abraham Adams. Since Lady Gould died intestate, the business of administering her effects was put into the hands of the reputable Salisbury solicitor, Robert Stillingfleet[269] – Fielding and his sisters Catharine, Ursula, and Sarah having signed the necessary legal forms on 13 August and their uncle Davidge Gould on 13 September.[270]

While Fielding was out of town that summer attending to such family affairs, audiences at Rich's new theatre in Covent Garden were being entertained at his expense – and were enjoying other laughs on just about everyone else associated with the recent troubles that had shut down Drury Lane. The author of this fun was Edward Phillips, "late of Trinity-College, Cambridge," who turned the misfortunes of Rich's rival theatre into a ballad opera entitled *The Stage-Mutineers: or, A Play-House to be Lett* (27 July). Phillips and Rich no doubt enjoyed roasting Fielding all the more for his having been the apparent source of an allegation, published earlier that season in the *Grub-Street Journal*, that they had conspired in pirating a play written by his friend Ralph.[271] In *The Stage-Mutineers*, at any rate, Fielding is brought on stage in the character of Crambo,[272] the "confident" and "self-opinionated" author of the House. The speech Phillips puts into his mouth on the consequences of "Pistol's" revolt must have struck close to the nerve: "It has ended very unhappily for the Town and me, for now Igad the Town will lose their Entertainment, and I my Benefit" (p. 37).

How long Fielding remained in the country that summer we cannot tell. From Anthony Henley's letter to Cooke we know that he called at "The Grange" on 17 November on his way to town; but he may have made more journeys than one to the West that year, not only to bury his grandmother and settle her affairs, but to court Charlotte Cradock, who had now, surely, supplanted the mysterious "Miss D. W." in his affections. It is pleasant to suppose that in *The Intriguing Chambermaid*, the new play he wrote for "Kitty" Clive, Valentine's true love is named Charlotte for apt personal reasons. Yet, if such matters took him to Salisbury and East Stour for a while, he would nevertheless wish to attend at Drury Lane on Saturday evening, 27 October, when, to bolster the Theatre Royal's sagging fortunes, *The Miser* was performed before an illustrious audience, including the King and Queen, the Duke of Cumberland, "all the Princesses," and "a great Concourse of Nobility."[273]

Fielding's movements remain doubtful until November, but we know he continued to write. Encouraged by the success of *The Miser*, he tried his hand at another five-act comedy, *The Universal Gallant: or, The*

Different Husbands. Though not in fact staged until February of 1734/5, it is clear from a notice in the *Daily Advertiser* (8 December 1733) that this ambitious work was ready for production by the end of 1733.[274]

To retrieve both his own falling fortunes and those of the struggling company at Drury Lane, Fielding agreed to set aside *The Universal Gallant* and to spruce up an old favorite. It was a desperate effort to lure audiences back to the Old House they had deserted, having been drawn away by too many competing attractions – Rich's harlequinades at Covent Garden, the entertainments at Goodman's Fields, the productions of young Cibber and the rebel actors at the Little Haymarket, and now also the Italian opera at Lincoln's Inn Fields. For the quarrel between Handel and the nobility which prompted Fielding's abortive burlesque of *Deborah* in the spring had led to the formation of yet another and more crushing rival attraction, the so-called "Nobility Opera." Just how grave Fielding understood the situation to be and who it was he blamed for it are clear from the Dedication to *The Intriguing Chambermaid*, the bright little ballad opera he wrote for "Kitty" Clive (née Raftor) at a time when the company's prospects were bleakest:

> It is your Misfortune to bring the greatest Genius for acting on the Stage, at a time when the Factions and Divisions among the Players have conspired with the Folly, Injustice, and Barbarity of the Town, to finish the Ruin of the Stage, and sacrifice our own native Entertainments to a wanton affected Fondness for foreign Musick; and when our Nobility seem eagerly to rival each other, in distinguishing themselves in favour of *Italian* Theatres, and in neglect of our own.

This was no time to bring on the boards such heavy fare as *The Universal Gallant*. Instead, Fielding fell back on the play that in 1730 had given him his first great success, *The Author's Farce*. According to the *Daily Advertiser* (8 December 1733) that "celebrated Performance" would be revived at Drury Lane "immediately after Christmas with very great Additions." This new version of *The Author's Farce* – revised especially to reflect Fielding's "War," as "Orator" Henley put it, with the Cibbers, *père et fils*[275] – was first produced at Drury Lane on Tuesday, 15 January 1733/4, with *The Intriguing Chambermaid* as an afterpiece adapted from Regnard's *Le Retour imprévu*. In addition to the satire against the Cibbers as Marplay senior and Marplay junior, Fielding improved the part of Harriot to allow more scope for Mrs. Clive; and Seedo composed a new overture. Even so, the play had a disappointing run of only six days, affording Fielding a single benefit. Its companion piece, on the other hand, continued to be performed from time to time

during the rest of the season and for many years thereafter – though
in 1751 Lettice's impertinent remark to Oldcastle that at sixty-six he
was too old for her mistress elicited from King George (then sixty-eight)
the harsh verdict, "This is damned stuff!"[276]

Watts attempted to capitalize on the Town's curiosity about the new
version of Fielding's first great popular success by reissuing "The
Second Edition" of 1730 more or less simultaneously with the first
performance and misrepresenting it in his advertisements as "just
publish'd."[277] In fact, however, the text of the play would not appear
in print until 1750, with "The Third Edition ... Revised, and greatly
Alter'd."

Publication of The Intriguing Chambermaid, "with the Musick prefix'd to each Song," followed a "few Days" after the play opened.[278]
Fielding's dedicatory "Epistle to Mrs. Clive" (1711–85) was so effusive
it inspired one of the Grublings to compose what even Russel considered
"a very vulgar Epigram," too naughty to publish. But we need not
suppose that Fielding's fondness for this delightful actress, whose
singing voice pleased even Handel, was at all improper. He admired
her both as a person and as a performer; indeed, he claimed to have
"made the first Discovery of your great Capacity, and brought you
earlier forward on the Theatre, than the Ignorance of some and the
Envy of others would have otherwise permitted." As "Kitty" Raftor
she had played Chloe in The Lottery, Kissinda in The Covent-Garden
Tragedy, Dorcas in The Mock Doctor, Lappet in The Miser, Deborah in
the ballad opera of that name; and now under her married name (she
married the barrister George Clive in 1732), she was Harriot in The
Author's Farce and Lettice in The Intriguing Chambermaid. But Fielding
was also grateful to her for her loyalty to the patentees – Highmore,
Mrs. Wilks, and his friend "Jack" Ellys – at a time when most of the
other talented actors of the company had deserted them. To the end of
his life Fielding would praise "Kitty" Clive: in Amelia (I. vi) she is said
to be to acting what Shakespeare is to poetry and Hogarth to painting.

Published with The Intriguing Chambermaid was a poem from an
anonymous admirer of Fielding that deserves closer scrutiny than it
has received; for it points to these early months of 1734 as a pivotal
moment in Fielding's assessment of himself both as a dramatist and as
a political writer. The poem, "To Mr. Fielding, occasioned by the
Revival of the Author's Farce," is said to have been "Sent to the Author
by an unknown Hand." Whoever the poet may have been, he was as
ardent in his appreciation of Fielding's talents, and as sympathetic in
reflecting Fielding's own recent disappointments and aspirations, as
only a close friend could be.[279] The theme of these verses is regret that
the author of The Modern Husband – an author whose "strong Genius"
was meant "To form our Manners, and amend our Laws,/ And aid,

with artful Hand, the publick Cause" – should have found no patron
to help him realize this potential. In part, the poet reproaches "The
publick Taste" for preferring farces, puppet-shows, and operas to more
rational entertainment. But most particularly he alludes to Fielding's
hope that Walpole would at last respond generously to the appeal for
his patronage made in the Dedication to *The Modern Husband*. So –
somewhat disingenuously, considering the lucrative benefits Fielding
enjoyed at Drury Lane until the present troubles began – he declares:
"Long have I seen, with Sorrow and Surprize,/ Unhelp'd, unheeded,
thy strong Genius rise." Fielding has survived, the poet continues, only
by stooping from time to time to gratify the Town's appetite for
spectacle and song, even though he has introduced a redeeming element
of "Sense" into all this drollery. The poet urges the playwright to
persevere until that happy moment when the Minister, recognizing at
last the waste of talent his negligence has caused, frees him from any
future necessity of scribbling farces for bread:

> Proceed, even thus proceed, bless'd Youth! to charm ...
> [Till] *Walpole*, studious still of *Britain's* Fame,
> Protect thy Labours, and prescribe the Theme,
> On which, in Ease and Affluence, thou may'st raise
> More noble Trophies to thy Country's Praise.

The poet's appeal to the minister on Fielding's behalf apparently fell
upon deaf ears, for in the winter of 1733–4 Fielding was ready to heed
Lappet's advice in *The Miser* (II.vi):

> Fools only to one Party will confide,
> Good Politicians will both Parties guide,
> And, if one fails, they're fee'd on t'other Side.

This, indeed, is the cynical theme of his essay on "Turn-coats" in
The Champion (12 January 1739/40) in which the irony (if any were
intended) is blunted by our knowledge of Fielding's tergiversation in
politics:

> Surely he who hath been on both Sides the Question, may, when he
> finds his former Principles the justest, revert to these Principles....
> Surely a Man is no more obliged to stick to his Principles, when they
> disappoint him, than to his Friends. Any ill Usage from his Party,
> any Refusal of what he thinks himself entitled to, no doubt
> sufficiently justify this Exchange. How much indeed a good large
> Offer from the other Party, when he hath nothing to complain of
> from his own, may speak in his own Behalf, I cannot say; but surely,
> such is the Weakness of human Nature, that it ought to be considered
> in his Favour, and will, no doubt, if not sufficiently justify him, very
> considerably lessen his Fault.

In the early months of 1734 every circumstance conspired to draw Fielding away from Walpole and the Theatre Royal and into the camp of the Opposition. At the time *The Author's Farce* was having its disappointing revival, the patentees at Drury Lane, aware that they had lost the battle with the rebel actors, were making plans to give up the fight. In the last week of January they sold out to Charles Fleetwood, who soon put an end to the hostilities: by 9 March young Cibber and his renegades, whom Fielding had ridiculed on stage and denounced in the Dedication to *The Intriguing Chambermaid*, had returned in triumph to the Theatre Royal.[280]

By the time this revolution in the fortunes of Drury Lane was accomplished, Fielding had lost his chance to bring on that stage his most important play of the season, *Don Quixote in England*, now transformed into a ballad opera in three acts. As he explained in the Preface to the published version, only "the Solicitations of the distrest Actors in *Drury-Lane*" could have moved him to rescue from "Oblivion" this piece which he had originally drafted at Leyden in 1728 and then abandoned on the advice of Cibber and Booth. He had now, however, transformed this unpromising sketch into an engaging piece of theatre, partly by including some of his best songs – among them "The Roast Beef of Old England" (salvaged from the ill-fated *Grub-Street Opera*) and "The Dusky Night rides down the Sky" – and partly by giving the play a political turn. It occurred to him that the timeliest way of presenting Cervantes' hero in an English setting was to set him down in a country borough town at election time, where the Don's unworldliness would contrast with the venality of the electors and politicians. The scenes he wrote for this purpose (I. viii–ix, II. iii, III. iv) – "representing Don Quixote, as a Candidate for Member of Parliament, which contain the Humours of Mayors and Corporations" – are impartial in the sense that they ridicule corrupt electoral practices generally. But coming on the eve of the parliamentary elections of 1734, they raised awkward issues to which Walpole was particularly sensitive: "Gods!" exclaims the Don in a strain that harmonizes with the ostensible idealism of Bolingbroke's political program, "to what will Mankind degenerate! where not only the vile Necessaries of Life; but even Honours, which should be the Reward of Virtue only, are to be bought with Money" (II. iii).

Though the play, as Fielding assures us, was "often rehearsed" at Drury Lane "and a particular Day appointed for its Action" (probably in the latter part of February),[281] it never came on the boards at the Theatre Royal. The reason given was that it must not be allowed to compete with the Dutch giant "Cajanus," who, in the role of Gargantua in *Cupid and Psyche*, was attracting crowds to Drury Lane from 5 to 12 February. Afterward commitments to the actors for their benefits, as well as the return of young Cibber and his victorious renegades, spoiled Fielding's chances of seeing the play performed that season at the Old House.

······➤ XXVi ◆······

But were these merely practical difficulties the only reasons why Fielding took *Don Quixote in England* instead to the Little Theatre in the Haymarket, where it opened at last on Friday, 5 April 1734 (the first of nine performances that season)? Probably not. Uncertain of his future with the troubled company at Drury Lane, and apparently dissatisfied with the way Walpole had responded to such appeals for patronage as the one recently published with *The Intriguing Chambermaid*, Fielding sensed that his talent as a satirist might prove saleable in this election year. It may be that, for this purpose, he made overtures to the Opposition, or they to him, as early as the first week of February: a faint, but none the less distinct, signal to this effect is the fact that the earliest notice of Fielding's "new Comedy," *Don Quixote in England*, appeared in *The Craftsman* (9 February), a journal which normally ignored theatrical affairs unless they in some way served the cause of anti-ministerial politics. In any case, this "puff" marked the beginning of what was very probably Fielding's long and clandestine affiliation with that periodical.

An unmistakable signal that Fielding had changed parties was the Dedication to *Don Quixote in England*, addressed to the Earl of Chesterfield (1694–1773): for, having infuriated Walpole by opposing the Excise Bill, Chesterfield had been rudely dismissed from the government in April 1733; he was now a leader of the Opposition. The intended thrust of Fielding's satire in the play is clear as he praises his new patron for having "so gloriously distinguished Himself in the Cause of Liberty, to which the Corruption I have here endeavoured to expose, may one Day be a very fatal Enemy." In passing, Fielding hints that, like Chesterfield, he had found the minister an uncongenial master: "There are among us who seem so sensible of the Danger of Wit and Humour, that they are resolved to have nothing to do with them: And indeed," Fielding continues, "they are in the right on't; for Wit, like Hunger, will be with great Difficulty restrained from falling on, where there is great Plenty and Variety of Food."

By the time Fielding thus declared his new-found political "Patriotism" – "a Word" especially associated with the Opposition and therefore, as he observes, "scandalously ridicul'd by some" – he had been applying the dangerous weapons of wit and humor in more sur-

reptitious ways for some weeks. Timed no doubt deliberately to appear
on the day the writs for the election were issued, *Don Quixote in
England*, with its Dedication to Chesterfield, was not published until
17 April 1734. It now appears, however, that Fielding's career as an
Opposition satirist had begun in *The Craftsman* a month earlier.[282] As
"Septennius" in a letter to that journal of 16 March 1733/4, he ironically
defended the practice of holding general elections every seven years,
rather than triennially as the Opposition advocated. Thus, anticipating
the new scenes he had recently added to *Don Quixote in England*, he
observed that

> whatever Reasons there may be for restoring *triennial*, or even *annual
> Parliaments*, the Attempt is certainly very unseasonable at this Time,
> when an *Election* is drawing so near, and several Gentlemen have
> been at so much Cost, as well as Trouble, for two or three Years past,
> in gaining over Corporations to their Interest. It would therefore be
> very hard to abridge their Expectations in this Manner, and restrain
> Them from being chosen for more than *three Years*, when They have
> actually proportioned their Expences to *seven*.

What, for that matter, could the mercenary electors themselves hope
to gain by the restoration of the triennial system? – a system advocated
by the honest Patriots in Parliament, who, with a view to curtailing
Walpole's influence, had "lately ty'd up their Hands by an *Act against
Bribery and Corruption*; from whence it is plain that *frequent Elections*
are not intended for their Benefit. They ought therefore – to shew a
just Indignation against the Promoters of an *Act*, which prohibits a
poor Man from selling his *Vote* to buy a little *Liquor*." A week later, in
The Craftsman of 23 March, Fielding resumed his ridicule of the ministry
in a witty essay on "Screens" which satirized Walpole's notorious
practice of shielding his friends (such as Colonel Charteris), as well as
himself, from the punishment their corrupt conduct deserved. The
evidence suggests that before the year was out Fielding published at
least three other satiric pieces in *The Craftsman*: one (3 August 1734)
an hilarious demonstration that the ministerial author James Pitt,
who wrote the *London Journal* under the pseudonym "Francis [or,
irreverently, Mother] Osborne," was in fact an old woman; another (5
October 1734) a letter from the Underworld from that arch politician,
"N. Machiavel," who, having observed the skill of Walpole and his
brother Horatio in conducting foreign affairs, could no longer contain
his admiration.

    As the Dedication of *Don Quixote in England* attests, as well as other
signs of his discontent during the winter of 1733–4, Fielding appears
to have begun contributing to *The Craftsman* at a time when he was
ready to seek patrons from among the party opposing Walpole. He

continued these contributions more or less steadily for six years, until, in 1739, he launched *The Champion*, a journal also favorable to the Patriot cause. *The Craftsman*, indeed, was the most important of the Opposition journals – the journal founded in 1726 by the leaders of the Opposition, Pulteney and Bolingbroke, and edited by Nicholas Amhurst under the pseudonym of "Caleb D'Anvers." It would be Fielding whose talent for irony and ridicule raised the reputation of the paper for wit and once, when that wit was too recklessly applied on occasion of the Licensing Act of 1737, came near to causing its abrupt demise. So well kept was the secret of his connection with *The Craftsman* that only once did a contemporary witness hint at it – when a correspondent to the *Daily Gazetteer* (12 October 1737) relates that he overheard Amhurst and Fielding conferring.

···■ **xxvii** ■···

But in 1734, as Fielding began to play this clandestine role in *The Craftsman*, he was vividly in the public eye in other respects, both as a playwright and as a cocky, dissolute young man too much bent upon his pleasures. Perhaps the most colorful of the few impressions of him to survive from this early period occurs in *The Dramatick Sessions: or, The Stage Contest*, an anonymous satire published in July but sketched out as early as February, when it was submitted to Russel at the *Grub-Street Journal*, who did "not think it proper for our Paper."[283] The author of this brash little piece imagines the scene at the Covent Garden Theatre as Nonsense, "the *Goddess* that *reigns* o'er the *Stage*," tries to choose "Her *most hopeful Blockhead* with *Poppy* to *crown*." The likely candidates are of course legion, numbering virtually every living dramatic author, and Fielding is prominent among them:

> Where is *F[ie]ld[i]ng*, She cries, with *heavy Quixote?*
> A biting his Audience, one said, he was got:
> Hold there, cries another, he's now at *All-fours*,
> With a parcel of *Dam-me Boys*, and *bob-tail'd Whores*.
>   In short some said one thing, and some said another,
> But at last he appear'd and ended the pother:
> With a Stride of three Yards then he broke thro' the Rout,
> Crying, "G— D-mn ye, Sirs, *What are ye about?*
>   "Reach, reach me the *Chaplet*—I'm going to write,
> "I'll shew ye the Odds in a crowded Ninth-night:
> "I alone please the Town in the Goddess's Vein,
> "And if Critics damn me – why, I damn them again.

His Assurance, 'twas thought, wou'd have gain'd him the Prize,
Had the *Goddess* been us'd to see with our Eyes;
But she bid him be gone for a *mad blust'ring Fool*,
Who by *Idleness* more than by *Nature* was *dull*.
　　On the *Goddess enraged*, he turn'd then his Br—ch,
Took a large pinch of Snuff, and then call'd her a B-tch;
Then, grinding his Teeth, swore he some one wou'd maul,
And *damn'd Goddess* and *Crown, Brother Scribblers* and all.

　　　　　　　　　　　　　　　　　　　　　　(pp. 11–12)

The author of these verses later protested that, before publication, "some alterations" were made without his consent in some of the characters, including that of Fielding;[284] even so the image was recognizable enough as caricatures go. Fielding's colossal stature, his exuberance and self-confidence, the violence of his passions, his love of snuff, his association with whores and riffraff, the imputation that, as he later wrote of Booth in *Amelia* (X. v), he "had naturally some Inclination to Gaming, and had formerly a little indulged it": all these traits square with what we know of Fielding from other sources.

　But we may notice, in particular, the goddess's judgment on his abilities as a dramatist, "Who by *Idleness* more than by *Nature* was *dull*." It was the opinion of some of Fielding's contemporaries that writing plays came too easily for him, that the sheer facility with which he could, by his own count, dash off nine clever scenes in a day, prevented him from more substantial achievements as a playwright. This is the view of one "Scriblerus Scribleri," the Grub Street author who remembers Fielding in his last will and testament, dated 28 June 1734 and published in the *Universal Spectator* (6 July):

Item, I give and bequeath to my very *negligent* friend *Henry Drama*, Esq; all and every Part of a certain Thing I am possess'd of, called INDUSTRY, which will be of very great Service to him as a *Dramatick Writer:* And whereas the World may think this an unnecessary Legacy, forasmuch as the said *Henry Drama*, Esq; brings on the Stage *four Pieces* every Season, yet as such Pieces are always wrote with uncommon *Rapidity*, and during such fatal Intervals only as the *Stocks* have been on the *Fall*, this Legacy will be of use to him to revise and correct his said Works. Furthermore, knowing how little thoughtful your great Wits are, for fear the said *Henry Drama* should make an ill Use of the said *Industry*, and expend it all on a *Ballad Farce*, it's my Will the said Legacy should be paid him by equal Portions, and at such Times as his Necessities may most require.

Fielding, however, now in his twenty-seventh year, could not be written off so easily as a hasty, undisciplined wit who preferred the pleasures of the town to the exacting business of his craft. Other judges, such as the author of *The Connoisseur: A Satire on the Modern Men of Taste* (1735), saw that he was the only dramatist of genius writing for the stage:

> F[ieldi]ng with Comedy now best can please,
> *England's Moliere!* he writes and charms with ease;
> Tho' Careless, every Thought is bold and new,
> His Beauties many, and his Faults are few.
>
> (p. 20)

By the mid-1730s, Fielding had established himself as the most prolific, the most inventive, the most entertaining of living playwrights.

⸺➤ xxviii ➤⸺

In the autumn of 1734 Fielding married Charlotte Cradock, the woman whose "Idea" is preserved for us in Sophia Western and Amelia Booth. They were to have only ten years together, too many of which were troubled by illness and by anxieties over money. But she provided for him what he had so badly needed all along – a sound foundation for his life. She was, he declared not many months before he lost her, "one from whom I draw all the solid Comfort of my Life."[285] Lady Bute, Lady Mary's daughter, knew Charlotte well and attested years later, commenting on the "picture" of her Fielding drew in *Amelia*, that "even the glowing language he knew how to employ did not do more than justice to the amiable qualities of the original, or to her beauty, although this had suffered a little from the accident related in the novel"[286] – that is, the injury to her nose, which, however, had been skillfully repaired. Fielding indeed, as he observes of Amelia (IV. vii), knew not "whether the little Scar on her Nose did not rather add to, than diminish her Beauty."

In Charlotte he found a worthy object for the strong and generous passions which were at once the best and weakest part of his nature, a woman who taught him the difference he insists on in *Tom Jones* (VI. i) between love and those feelings "commonly called" by that name, "namely, the Desire of satisfying a voracious Appetite with a certain Quantity of delicate white human Flesh." As Lady Bute recalled, "he loved her passionately, and she returned his affection." In an age of Richardsonian delicacy – of a prudishness which, long before the Victorians, regarded sexuality as a matter for sniggering and shame – Fielding felt obliged, in revising *Amelia* (IV. vi), to delete the following sentence which in the first edition concludes his description of a typical evening Booth and Amelia spend together at home, enjoying a simple supper with a pint of wine and the company of their children: "At length they retired, and with mutual Desires, and equal Warmth, flew into each other's Arms." Like Amelia and Sophie Western – or, for that matter, like her namesake in *The Intriguing Chambermaid* – Charlotte was no doubt a woman of spirit who would, if need be, dare risk the disapproval of parent or guardian to cherish the man she loved: "Love," as Charlotte sees it in the play (I.x), "reigns alone in every Breast it inhabits, and in my Opinion makes us amends for the Absence of Madam *Prudence*, and all her Train."

But it is best not to go so far in confusing fiction with fact as some of Fielding's biographers have done, who find in the story of Booth's elopement with Amelia a true account of the circumstances of Fielding's marriage with Charlotte. The evidence points in another direction entirely.

On Thursday, 28 November 1734, in the little church of St. Mary the Virgin, Charlcombe, about two miles north of Bath, Henry and Charlotte were married by a license obtained from the Bishop of Wells.[287] Conducting the ceremony was the Rector, Walter Robbins (c. 1692–1762), a native of Salisbury and a learned, eminently respectable divine who served as Master of the King Edward VI Grammar School in Bath.[288] Robbins stated in the register that Henry and Charlotte were "of St. James's, Bath"; but we need not suppose, with Cross and Dudden,[289] that the couple obtained the license "under the fiction" of their residence in Bath. Robbins lived in St. James's parish himself, in a house on Abbey Green; it was with Robbins in this house that Henry and Charlotte stayed some years later.[290] Clearly, the Reverend Walter Robbins was no Fleet Parson who would condone, let alone perform, a clandestine marriage for a runaway couple; and the fact of his continuing friendship with Henry and Charlotte suggests that their relationship was founded on mutual respect.

There are good reasons why the marriage took place at Bath, quietly, rather than at Salisbury. Charlotte's mother was dying of asthma; it would be natural for her to come to Bath to try to recover her health – as Charlotte herself would do ten years later during her own illness. Henry and Charlotte would otherwise enjoy being in Bath this autumn when that city was said to be the gayest, most fashionable place in all England.[291] That they were married by license, rather than by the more orthodox procedure of publishing the banns, need have no sinister connotations. It is probably Fielding himself who in *The Craftsman* (18 December 1736) reveals the real reason why the couple chose to be married in this way, in a small country church by a priest they knew well: "the profitable Trade of *Licences*," he remarks, "is chiefly supported by the natural Bashfulness of People, upon such Occasions, who don't care to have their *Amours* exposed in a full Congregation."

There is, furthermore, no reason to suppose that Mrs. Cradock opposed her daughter's marriage. She remembered Charlotte affectionately in her will, drawn up less than three months later in London, where she had gone to be treated by the distinguished physician William Wasey.[292] What evidence there is of a rupture in the family suggests that it was Charlotte's sister Catherine who had incurred her mother's displeasure. On 8 February 1734/5, Mrs. Cradock, then living at York Buildings (Buckingham Street), made a new will, bequeathing to her daughter Catherine "One Shilling"; "all the rest and residue" of her money, plate, jewels, and estate that remained after her debts and funeral expenses were paid she left "unto my dearly beloved Daughter Charlotte ffeilding, wife of Henry ffeilding of East Stower in the Co. of Dorset Esqr." She appointed Charlotte her executrix.

As we know from the dateline ("Buckingham-Street, Feb. 12") of the Dedication to *The Universal Gallant*, Fielding and Charlotte were living with Mrs. Cradock during the last days of her illness. Urgent business compelled Fielding to return to East Stour shortly before she died (see below, pp. 185–6), and so he was not himself present on 20 February when Mrs. Cradock was buried in the vault of James Gibbs's splendid new church of St. Martin-in-the-Fields. But the esteem in which Fielding held his mother-in-law is attested by the magnificence of the funeral he and Charlotte gave her.[293]

As for "Kitty" Cradock, we do not know why her dying mother spurned her. Two months later "Kitty" also died – a spinster who had been living under mysterious circumstances at Codicote, Hertfordshire. She was buried there at St. Giles's church on 24 April 1735. In the register her name was entered as "Mrs. Mary Cradock" and a note, subsequently scratched out, was written in the margin after the entry.[294] Why, one wonders, had she retired to this place, so far from her sister and from the scene of her triumphs at the Salisbury Assembly balls? Why was she known there as "Mary" and why "Mrs." (a title of course politely accorded spinsters in the eighteenth century after they reached a certain age, but not found elsewhere in the burial register)?[295] In his novels Fielding often observes what he calls in *Jonathan Wild* (rev., II. iii) "the common Failure of Sisters in envying, and often endeavouring to disappoint each other's Happiness." Molly Seagrim has such a sister in *Tom Jones* (V.v), and Betty Harris in *Amelia* is an egregious instance of sisterly malice. Can it have been "Kitty's" relationship with Charlotte that gave him this morose opinion of the enmity sisters can bear toward one another? His own "sisterhood," as Ursula called them[296] – including Catharine, Sarah, and Beatrice, besides Ursula herself – appear to have been very close and to have lived amicably together, though this appearance of amity, based on a single letter, could be misleading. In any event, to return from speculation to fact, "Kitty" Cradock having died intestate, her worldly goods and chattels were granted to Charlotte as "next of kin" in July 1735.[297]

"Kitty's" estrangement from her mother meant that Charlotte alone had to assume the responsibility of looking after Mrs. Cradock in her final illness. In trying to understand why Fielding's marriage took place when and where it did, we probably come closer to the truth in recognizing this fact than by assuming that the lovers were driven to elope in defiance of Mrs. Cradock. Sympathy for Charlotte's vulnerable situation in the world, the knowledge that after her mother's death she would be on her own, may well have precipitated Fielding's decision to propose marriage to her. For all his faults, he was a loving and a generous man.

···◗ XXIX ◖···

There was no time for a proper honeymoon. Sometime in December 1734 Fielding brought his bride to London, where, with Mrs. Cradock, they established themselves temporarily in York Buildings. After the series of awkward circumstances that had compelled him to take *Don Quixote in England* to the Little Theatre in the Haymarket in the spring, he was anxious to repair his broken connections with Drury Lane, now in its first full season under Fleetwood's management; for that purpose he was also willing to declare a truce in his "War" with the Cibbers.

He had two plays ready for production: *The Universal Gallant*, which the troubles at Drury Lane prevented from being staged as planned the preceding season; and a new ballad opera, entitled *An Old Man Taught Wisdom: or, The Virgin Unmask'd*. The latter, better known by its subtitle, was first performed as the afterpiece to Otway's *Venice Preserved* on Monday, 6 January 1734/5. It is another of Fielding's musical farces designed as a vehicle for his favorite "Kitty" Clive: as Lucy – the pert country heiress who spurns the fatuous cousins her father intends for her and marries instead the footman she loves – she charmed audiences with her singing and her flair as a comedienne. But it was first necessary for the play to survive a precarious first night, when the audience groaned at the length of some of the scenes and hissed the character of Lucy's scholarly suitor Bookish, a supercilious Oxonian whose speeches disparaging Lucy for her lack of learning were offensive to her sex. Fielding and the actors saved the play by, among other revisions, eliminating Bookish altogether, and by drastically cutting the number of songs (from twenty to twelve).[298] In this more palatable form, *An Old Man Taught Wisdom* ran all that week and was often performed during the season; indeed, throughout the century it remained one of the most popular short pieces in repertory.

Less happy was the fate of Fielding's long-awaited comedy *The Universal Gallant: or, The Different Husbands*. In late January it was being rehearsed at Drury Lane simultaneously with James Miller's comedy, *The Man of Taste*,[299] and, after the usual preliminary "puffs" in the papers, it opened on Monday, 10 February 1734/5. Despite the efforts of an excellent cast – including Quin as Mondish, Griffin as Sir Simon Raffler, and young Cibber as Captain Spark – the play was roundly damned by an obstreperous first-night audience; it lingered painfully for two further performances, to allow Fielding his benefit on the third night, and then was put to rest.

Fielding was angered at this failure of one of his more ambitious works. Convinced that the play had been victimized by a conspiracy of malicious bucks and failed authors who were envious of his former successes, he took the damning of the work as a personal affront. With the published version, which Watts issued on 19 February, he included an "Advertisement" reminiscent of the embittered response of "Philalethes" to the persecutions of the *Grub-Street Journal* some years earlier:

The cruel Usage this poor Play hath met with, may justly surprize the Author, who in his whole Life never did an Injury to any one Person living. What could incense a Number of People to attack it with such an inveterate Prejudice, it is not easy to determine; for Prejudice must be allowed, be the Play good or bad, when it is condemn'd unheard.

I have heard that there are some young Gentlemen about this Town, who make a Jest of damning Plays – but did they seriously consider the Cruelty they are guilty of by such a Practice, I believe it would prevent them. Every Man who produces a Play on the Stage, must propose to himself some Acquisition either of Pleasure, Reputation, or Profit in its Success: For, tho' perhaps he may receive some Pleasure from the first Indulgence of the Itch of Scribling, yet the Labour and Trouble he must undergo before his Play comes on the Stage, must set the Prospect of some future Reward before him, or I believe he would decline the Undertaking. If Pleasure or Reputation be the Reward he proposes, it is sure an inexcusable Barbarity in any uninjured or unprovoked Person to defeat the Happiness of another: But if his Views be of the last kind, if he be so unfortunate to depend on the success of his Labours for his Bread, he must be an inhuman Creature indeed, who would out of sport and wantonness prevent a Man from getting a Livelihood in an honest and inoffensive Way, and make a jest of starving him and his Family.

Authors, whose Works have been rejected at the Theatres, are of all Persons, they say, the most inveterate; but of all Persons I am the last they should attack, as I have often endeavoured to procure the Success of others, but never assisted at the Condemnation of any one.

This poignant (not to say whimpering) representation of his affairs may be less than faithful to the facts. In *The Prompter* (18 February 1734/5) William Popple gives a different version of the behavior of the audience that first night. Having congratulated the Town on the excellence of their taste in rejecting such sorry stuff as "the prolifick Mr. *Fielding*" has recently offered them, Popple makes a point of applauding the "*Impartiality*" they showed on the occasion: "for till almost the third Act was over, they sat very quiet, in hopes it would mend, till finding it grew still *worse* and *worse*, they at length lost all Patience, and not an *Expression* or *Sentiment* afterwards passed without its *deserved Censure*." Once again Fielding had tried to get right the formula for that new species of comedy with which he had been experimenting ever since *Rape upon Rape* – comedy in which a nervous kind of laughter is meant to serve an edifying social and moral purpose. This time the mixture not only proved less effectual than ever; it caused the audience to explode in a manner "so very obstreperous, and accompanied with such *Hissings*, and *Clappings*," that it became, for Popple at least, the very quintessence of the theatrical bomb.[300]

We may imagine how Fielding felt that opening night as he stood in the wings and saw *The Universal Gallant* succumb to this clamorous abuse. That his "Family" were in any imminent danger of "starving" because of the play's failure is, however, difficult to credit. Even though it had been some time since a play of his had done as well as *The Miser*, he had just married Charlotte, who, if Murphy is correct, brought him a dowry of £1,500 and who was sole heiress of a woman who appears to have been well-to-do – a reasonable inference from the fine house Mrs. Cradock occupied in The Close at Salisbury and from the references in her will to money, plate, and jewelry. Indeed, only days after Fielding publicly regretted his impecuniousness in the "Advertisement" to *The Universal Gallant*, he and Charlotte were sparing no expense on Mrs. Cradock's obsequies. But it is impossible to exaggerate Fielding's habitual carelessness with money. As Lady Mary remarked shortly after his death, Fielding, of all her wide circle of acquaintance, could be compared in this respect only with that paragon of prodigality, Sir Richard Steele: "They both agreed in wanting money in spite of all their Freinds, and would have wanted it if their Hereditary Lands had been as extensive as their Imagination."[301] This same sense of Fielding's improvidence, his way of spending money when he had it and regretting it when it was gone, is captured more graphically by James Miller in *Seasonable Reproof*, published in November 1735:

> F[ieldin]g, who *yesterday* appear'd so rough,
> Clad in *coarse Frize*, and plaister'd down with *Snuff*.
> See how his *Instant* gaudy Trappings shine;
> What *Play-house* Bard was ever seen so fine!
> But this, not from his *Humour* flows, you'll say,
> But mere *Necessity*;—for last Night lay
> In *Pawn*, the *Velvet* which he wears to Day.
>
> (ll. 46–52)[302]

Fielding's protestations that he wanted money at this time are also the theme of the Dedication to *The Universal Gallant*, addressed once again to a prominent member of the Opposition: in this instance, Charles Spencer (1706–58), third Duke of Marlborough. This young man, grandson of the great military hero of the Whigs whose memory Fielding ever extolled, inherited the title in 1733. Soon thereafter – together with his brother-in-law the Duke of Bedford, Fielding's fellow Etonians Pitt and Lyttelton, and Lyttelton's cousins the Grenvilles – he became one of the circle of "Boy Patriots" who were forming under the leadership of Chesterfield to oppose Walpole. Marlborough never enjoyed a reputation as a statesman, but he was a generous man, and it is this quality, "the Fame of your Humanity," that Fielding in his present "Distress" found most attractive about him: "Poverty has imposed Chains on Mankind equal with Tyranny; and Your Grace has shewn as great an Eagerness to deliver Men from the former, as your illustrious Grandfather did to rescue them from the latter."

···━● XXX ●━···

This year, as last, Fielding's affiliation with the Opposition is evident not only in the dedication of his chief dramatic work of the season to an eminent "Patriot," but also in what appears to have been his continued occasional contributions to *The Craftsman*: specifically, the numbers for 28 June, 12 July, 2 August, and 20 December 1735, and probably also the numbers for 5 and 26 April – all ridiculing Walpole, his brother Horatio, and their measures and agents at home and abroad. Of particular interest in the context of Fielding's stormy career as a playwright is *Craftsman* No. 469 (28 June 1735), an essay prompted by Sir John Barnard's abortive Bill for restraining the number of playhouses and "regulating" the actors. The Bill would have abolished all theatres except Drury Lane, Covent Garden, and the King's Theatre (or Royal Opera House) in the Haymarket; so it would not have affected Fielding personally, who at this time probably still thought of himself as writing for Drury Lane. It was aimed at Henry Giffard's theatre in Goodman's Fields, but would also have put an end to performances of plays at the Little Haymarket, at the booths in fairtime, and at theatres in the provinces. Introduced by Barnard on 5 March and read on 3 April, the Bill caused panic among those actors and managers who would be ruined if it passed Parliament;[303] but the moment was not yet ripe for such a drastic measure and the Bill was dropped. In *The Craftsman* Fielding archly offered his own belated condemnation of the measure, which "bore a little too hard upon an Order of Men, who have always made a very considerable Figure in the World; I mean the People call'd STROLLERS" – a term which, by a little deft juggling, he made synonymous with "Ambassadors" and so turned the piece into an ironic encomium on Horatio Walpole. For the benefit of his most recent patron, Fielding concluded in a manner suggesting he had recently visited Blenheim, proposing that the ministry's bungling pleni-potentiary be accorded the same honors a grateful nation bestowed on the Duke of Marlborough.

The other political event of the year that most interested him was the ministry's decision to merge three of its most virulent journals into one. Thus on 30 June 1735 appeared the *Daily Gazetteer*, clubbing together the laborious talents of William Arnall (alias "Francis Wal-singham" of the *Free Briton*), James Pitt (alias "Francis Osborne" of the *London Journal*), and Ralph Courteville (alias "R. Freeman" of the *Daily Courant*), not to mention a host of auxiliaries, including Theophilus Cibber and Fielding's former Head Master at Eton, Henry Bland.[304] Less than a fortnight after Walpole's drudges published their first number, Fielding in *The Craftsman* (12 July) expressed his aston-ishment "even at their *Dullness*"; "[I] cannot forbear exclaiming, with our *incomparable Laureat*, that They have *outdone all their former Out-doings!*" This, too, was the theme of his letter to the same paper of 2 August, where, as the westward traveler "Jack Ramble," he recalls baiting at a post-house along the road and noticing that, since the government was propagating the *Gazetteers* gratis throughout the country, his landlady had ingeniously found a use for her copy in the kitchen, by twisting it and setting it alight to singe a chicken with.

From his own writings, then – both the addresses he made openly to Chesterfield and Marlborough and his covert satiric contributions to *The Craftsman* – the direction Fielding's politics had taken since the early months of 1734 is plain. His association with Walpole and Drury Lane during the preceding two years, however, was not soon forgotten.

Perhaps the earliest public recognition that he was no longer safely in Walpole's pocket is a set of verses by one "W.H.," published in the *Grub-Street Journal* (26 September 1734) – the poet's use of the present tense to describe the minister's continuing beneficence to Concanen, Cibber, Mitchell, and Ralph contrasts with the past tense in reference to favors received by Fielding, now indeed found in company including Pope:

> What tho' CONCANNEN, CIBBER, MITCHELL, RALPH,
> Are smil'd on, by the Primier with the staff?
> So POPE, YOUNG, WELSTED, THOMPSON, FIELDING, FROWDE,
> Have, each by turns, to his indulgence owed.

These lines are too ambiguous to reveal what the poet actually believed about the currency of Fielding's obligations to Walpole in the autumn of 1734. Other verses published a year later (October 1735), however, suggest that Walpole's fawning Scots bard Joseph Mitchell still thought of Fielding as actively competing for the minister's patronage. In *A Familiar Epistle to the Right Honourable Sir Robert Walpole*, Mitchell asks:

> YOUR PRAISES WHO HAS BETTER SUNG?
> – PARDON IS BEGG'D OF *Messieurs* YOUNG,
> TIBBALD and WELSTED, FIELDING, FROWDE,
> And fifty more who round you crowd.
>
> > (p. 6)

But it is unlikely that at the time Mitchell wrote these lines Fielding was anywhere near Walpole, either politically or in a physical sense, attending his levees.

••••◀ xxxi ▶•••

According to Murphy, Fielding in this first year of his marriage, like "Jack Ramble" of his *Craftsman* essay (2 August), spent most of his time westward of London – to be precise, in Dorset, at his farm at East Stour, to which he "retired" with Charlotte "with a resolution to bid adieu to all the follies and intemperances to which he had addicted himself in the career of a town-life." Though little in Murphy's account of this period of Fielding's life can be trusted, on this point at least we have corroboration from Aaron Hill, at the time a friend of both Fielding and his father. In his review of *Pasquin* in *The Prompter* (2 April 1736) Hill, referring to a letter of November 1734 from a correspondent who claimed to be keeping Common Sense in the country

till the theatres in town were again worthy to receive her, observed
that she must have been all along in Fielding's care: "I am the more
inclined to this Belief, as about the Time COMMON SENSE left the
Theatres, the abovesaid Gentleman [i.e., Fielding] retired into the
Country, where he has continued ever since, till this Winter."

Hill was not strictly accurate, for we know that soon after their
marriage Fielding and Charlotte came to town to attend Mrs. Cradock
in her illness and to settle her affairs. Immediately after the failure of
The Universal Gallant, however, Fielding hastened back to East Stour,
leaving Charlotte temporarily behind at Buckingham Street. On 20
February 1734/5, the day of Mrs. Cradock's funeral, he was making his
presence felt in Shaftesbury, the market town five miles from his farm,
by violently assaulting a certain Thomas Bennet, so severely indeed
that the man's "life was greatly despaired of" – or so Bennet alleged
in the action he brought against Fielding at the King's Bench.[305] There
was no love lost between Fielding and this man, who slandered him
and injured him in the most sensitive part – his reputation among his
creditors. It was perhaps some urgent business of this nature that
compelled him to leave Charlotte at such a sad time; and no doubt she
joined him at the farm as soon as her mother's affairs were settled.
There is nothing to place either of them in town after 25 February
1734/5, when Charlotte, as executrix, proved her mother's will, until
Fielding returned a year later as "the Great Mogul" at the head of his
rogue "Company of English Comedians" at the Little Theatre in the
Haymarket.

At East Stour during the months after Mrs. Cradock's death, Henry
and Charlotte came to know one another as man and wife, and (to
apply Booth's account of his first year in the country with Amelia)
Poet Fielding became Farmer Fielding – or more likely, Squire Fielding.
Recalling this period, Booth declared that he scarce knew "a Circumstance that distinguished one Day from another. The whole was
one continued Series of Love, Health, and Tranquillity" (III. xii). On
the other hand, the scene Murphy paints is rather jolly than idyllic:
Fielding's "chief pleasure consisting in society and convivial mirth,
hospitality threw open his doors," and with "entertainments, hounds,
and horses" he began that course of thoughtless extravagance which,
in three years' time, reduced him to penury and compelled him to sell
the farm. There is truth in both these contrasting versions of the
Fieldings' country life. The requirement of a decent period of mourning
for Charlotte's mother would put off, for a while, the revelry Murphy
imagines; but there is no denying that Fielding found little pleasure
out of the society of friends, that he was an avid sportsman, and that
he was so free with his money (when he had any of it to spend or lend)
he was seldom out of debt.

He came to love Charlotte very much – as completely, indeed, as it is possible to imagine a husband's loving a wife. That much is unforgettably attested in the compliments he paid to her memory in the characters of Sophie Western and Amelia. To judge from those memorials, she was for him the flesh-and-blood reality behind the ideal he recommends at the close of his poem, "To a Friend on the Choice of a Wife":

> May she then prove, who shall thy Lot befall,
> Beauteous to thee, agreeable to all.
> Nor Wit, nor Learning proudly may she boast;
> No low-bred Girl, nor gay fantastic Toast:
> Her tender Soul, Good-nature must adorn
> And Vice and Meanness be alone her Scorn.
> Fond of thy Person, may her Bosom glow
> With Passions thou hast taught her first to know.
> A warm Partaker of the genial Bed,
> Thither by Fondness, not by Lewdness led.
> Superior Judgment may she own thy Lot;
> Humbly advise, but contradict thee not.
> Thine to all other Company prefer;
> May all thy Troubles find Relief from her.
> If Fortune gives thee such a Wife to meet,
> Earth cannot make thy Blessing more complete.

Pretty yet modest, tender yet passionate, no wit or bluestocking, a woman of plain good sense yet true to the vow that once included the promise to obey, as well as to love and honor, her husband: stressing as it does the qualities of simplicity and submissiveness, Fielding's definition of an ideal wife may seem today "chauvinistic," at best rather quaint. Be that as it may, his marriage with Charlotte was anachronistic in another sense as well, in that it "worked," being founded on mutual love, understanding, and respect.

····⬤ xxxii ⬤─···

Though we know little about Fielding's life at East Stour, we do know that he made there a lasting friendship – a friendship that inspired one of the most delightful characters in fiction, Parson Abraham Adams. A native of Wiltshire, William Young (1702–57) attended St. John's College, Oxford. In 1731–2 he was appointed Master of the Gillingham Grammar School, one of the oldest schools in Dorset and one that boasted no less distinguished a graduate than Edward Hyde, Earl of

Clarendon.[306] At about this time, or somewhat earlier, he began serving as curate at East and West Stour (chapelries annexed to the vicarage of Gillingham), in which capacity he buried Fielding's grandmother in June 1733.[307] Young's zeal in both these offices is attested, on the one hand, by an advertisement of 1737 in which he warned the public against the attempt of the curate at Gillingham to set up a rival boarding school,[308] and, on the other hand, by two cases in the records of the Archdeacon's Court of Dorset in 1733: on 9 August he took action against the church-warden of East Stour for neglecting his duty to repair the church and purchase a new Bible; and on 20 September he charged his parishioners, James Gulliford and Mary Stacey, with "incontinency" and getting a bastard child, for which the young woman was required to do penance standing in a white sheet before her fellow parishioners in the church.[309] Young continued to act as Master of Gillingham Grammar School and curate of East and West Stour until the latter part of 1740, when he appears to have followed Fielding to London.

If Fielding in his youth was drawn to the company of rakes and free-thinkers, we find him now increasingly cultivating the friendship of learned clergymen: Walter Robbins we have already noticed; Young was such another. Fielding, with whom Young collaborated in the translation of Aristophanes' *Plutus* (1742) and in a projected, but abortive, version of Lucian (1752), went so far as to declare that he would have "the universal Concurrence of those learned Men of this Age to whom [Young] is known, that no Man now alive is better versed in that Language in which the Wit of Lucian lies as yet concealed."[310] At the time Fielding made this assertion Young had completed his revision of Ainsworth's *Latin Dictionary* (1752) and three years later produced a corrected edition of Hederich's *Greek Lexicon* (1755). What especially endeared him to those who knew him best was his "Modesty": he never, in the words of one anonymous admirer, "turns loquacious, where he nothing knows."[311] One can imagine how grateful Fielding must have been during the months of his rustication for the companionship of a man of Young's qualities.

But Young was also something of an "original," in the eighteenth-century sense of the word — a man no less remarkable for his unworld-liness and comical absentmindedness than for his erudition and con-scientiousness as priest and pedagogue. Several anecdotes illustrating these traits have been preserved by his contemporaries. He was, it is said, so improvident "as to run into every tradesman's debt, and had went to gaol if [his friends] had not raised money to redeem him. All he knew of the matter was, he wanted the goods and had 'em."[312] In this respect, among others, Fielding would have recognized in Young a kindred spirit. With the little money that came to him, he was, like

Fielding, liberal to a fault. When, for instance, Lord Talbot sent him five guineas in acknowledgment of the Dedication to *Plutus*, Young could hardly be prevailed on to accept a share in the present, insisting that it all belonged to Fielding, who wrote the compliments which extracted this "Aristophanic gold," as he called it. This dispute taking place in a tavern, Young at last consented to accept half the money on condition that part of it be applied to paying Fielding's bill. From the same contemporary witness we get an idea of how inept Young could be – and how hilariously forgetful! – at attempting even the slightest "piece of disingenuity." Wishing to take a holiday while serving as tutor to a young gentleman, he wrote a letter to himself containing an invitation to spend a fortnight in the country – and then handed the letter, still sealed and unopened, to his employer.

These were among the anecdotes about Young that began circulating soon after the publication of *Joseph Andrews* (1742), in which – as everyone acquainted with Young believed – Fielding immortalized his friend in the character of Parson Adams. Though Young himself did not appreciate the honor done him in this way (he threatened to knock a man down who addressed him as Parson Adams),[313] the fame that came to him as the original of Fielding's best-loved character proved profitable to him in more solid ways; for it led to his being appointed chaplain to an Army hospital in Flanders during the hostilities with France in 1743. But we may let James Harris, who knew Young well, sum up the character of this good man:

Among the various characters, with which [Fielding's] Works are adorned, there is none more admired than that of Mr. Abraham Adams, a Portrait drawn after actual life, after ye Revd. Wm. Young, a worthy Clergyman of Dorset. No character was ever so truly exhibited, and therefore to repeat it wd. be perfectly superfluous. We can only add that Mr. Young, after his public Exhibition in Print, becoming more known, was called from his obscurity and made chaplain to ye Army Hospital, then abroad in ye late War. Here he had an opportunity to enlarge his acquaintance, and was much respected by such officers, as could relish his Learning and unaffected Wit. Here, too, in ye places to which he moved at different times, many adventures befell him that were singular in their kind, tho none more remarkable than what happened to him near Frankfort. Thence on a day having crost the River Meine, to indulge in what he loved, a solitary walk, he found he had stroled insensibly into ye midst of ye French Camp, and that too at an unseasonable time, just after their defeat at Dettingen [June 1743]. The Incidents wch. he met with there, no one could relate but himself, as he did it with a vein of humour which was perfectly original. Tis enough to say, that as his character indangered him, so his character brought him off; that as his native Inattention led him into ye midst of Strangers and Enemies, so his native Intrepidity and honest Simplicity ushered him thro perills to his Countrymen and Friends. The War being over, by ye friendship of Mr Ranby he found a retreat in Chelsea-College where his Valet de Chambre (as he used to call him) was a one-legged Corporal and where he lived amidst books and ye fumes of his own Pipe, till he peaceably ended his days in ye yr. 1757 regretted by all those who were so fortunate as to know him.[314]

So Fielding's friend, having been appointed chaplain to Major General Lascelles's Regiment of Foot, ended his life amidst the gracious surroundings of the Chelsea Royal Hospital with its associations with Edmund Fielding's Regiment of Invalids. He was survived by his son William, also a clergyman, and by his widow, whose Christian name was Grace.[315]

....➤ xxxiii ◄....

Fielding seems to have remained in the country until January 1735/6, by which time, owing to both his own extravagance and the spite of an enemy, he badly needed money. Thomas Bennet, still smarting from the drubbing Fielding administered to him a year earlier, retaliated by deliberately bringing him into disrepute with his Dorset creditors. Again represented by the Salisbury attorney Robert Stillingfleet, Fielding commenced an action for slander against Bennet, asking £500 in damages. As an example of that tautological sublime only lawyers can rise to, Fielding's complaint is amusing, but it was no laughing matter to him. At Dorchester on 1 January 1735/6, the document reads, Bennet "openly, publickly, falsely & malitiously spoke, asserted, pronounced and with a loud voice published ... those false, feigned, scandalous and reproachfull English words following (that is to say) 'Mr.Fielding is not worth a farthing. He will go quickly off and cheat his Creditors.'" Indeed, Bennet advised what to judge from the wording of the complaint must have been the entire population of Dorchester, "'If Mr. Fielding owes you any money the sooner you get it the better, for there will be some for the first but none for the last ... [he] is a beggarly fellow and he owes more than he is worth. If you do not arrest him you will lose your debt.'" As a consequence of this slander – which the Court judged it to be – Fielding's creditors swooped at once, suing him for the debts he owed and seizing his goods. Since few tradesmen would trust him any longer, he was forced to go to a great deal of trouble and expense to reestablish his credit.[316] Fielding proved these charges to the satisfaction of the jury; but it was not until 3 November 1736 that judgment was entered in his favor.[317]

The seriousness of his financial circumstances as he instituted these proceedings in January is obvious from the language of his complaint against Bennet. And Charlotte was then nearly six months pregnant with their first child, a daughter born on 27 April 1736 and named after her mother. The records of St. Martin-in-the-Fields give the Fieldings' address as Charing Cross, suggesting perhaps that, like Booth fleeing his country creditors in *Amelia* (III. xii), they had taken lodgings in the Verge of the Court.[318] Anxious to repair his ruined fortunes, he had come to town with hopes pinned on a new play to which he refers obscurely in dedicating *Tumble-Down Dick* (1736) to John Rich, manager of the Covent Garden Theatre: Fielding recalls "the Indifference you shew'd at my Proposal to you of bringing a Play on your Stage this Winter, which immediately determin'd me against any further pursuing that Project." That he felt obliged to offer this new work to Rich suggests how far his stock had fallen at Drury Lane, where memories of the damning of *The Universal Gallant* were still fresh. If, as seems likely, the play in question was *The Good-natured Man*[319] – his final attempt to succeed in the mode of regular comedy – one can appreciate Rich's "Indifference." Indeed, one can credit him not only with sparing Fielding the mortification of a second consecutive major failure, but with forcing him to explore again the vein of innovative, irregular drama where his talents shone most brightly.

With the exception of *The Miser*, his delightful adaptation of Molière, this was where Fielding's reputation stood in the Winter of 1735–6, on the eve of what would be the most successful season of his theatrical career. So it appeared to one "Ned Downright," who in the *Universal Spectator* (21 February) magnanimously exempts Fielding ("Mr. Couplet" as he calls him) from the general vanity of mankind:

> That ingenious Author, Mr. *Couplet*, would never have spent so many Years together in composing ballad Farces, mock Tragedies, dramatic Medleys, in all which he has shewn a pretty *farcical Genius*, and prov'd himself to be a tolerable Hedger and Ditcher in Stage Poetry: This witty humorous Gentleman wou'd never for so many Seasons have skimm'd so near the Earth, had not his usual Modesty told him he cou'd never soar to the Sublime, and that heroic Poetry was too strong for his weak Constitution; and yet we see he stole up to *Comedy*, by the Assistance of *Moliere* and *Plautus*, with great Ambition and humble Success.

Though in gloating over Fielding's ineptitude in the heroic mode the critic might have excepted *Rape upon Rape* and *The Modern Husband* –

Fielding's interesting experiments in "heroic" comedy — the verdict about his achievements as a dramatist was on balance fair enough. In less than a fortnight, however, Fielding would produce another of his ludicrous irregular plays, one that would show the Town just how dazzling and hilarious, and how disturbing to the ministerial party, a "pretty *farcical Genius*" could be.

This time, having had enough of the reluctant managers at Drury Lane and Covent Garden, he ensured almost complete control over the production by turning manager himself. In this undertaking he was assisted by Ralph, whose career as propagandist for Walpole had been abruptly terminated the preceding year when he was excluded from the staff of hard-core ministerial journalists who combined to conduct the *Daily Gazetteer*.[320] We know from Thomas Davies, who was a member of Fielding's company at the Little Haymarket, that Ralph was "a managing partner" in the enterprise, but that he was completely overshadowed in this role by his more gifted friend.[321] Thus it was in February 1735/6 that Fielding set up as "the Great Mogul" at the head of a company of "English Comedians" — appellations calculated, on the one hand, to mock the reputations of his rival managers as "Stage Tyrants,"[322] and, on the other hand, to appeal to the patriotism of the public, who, to the neglect of legitimate drama, were lavishing their money adoringly on the castrato Farinelli and Italian opera. The unlikely vehicle with which Fielding hoped to entice audiences back to the playhouse was *Pasquin* — one of the oddest of his irregular pieces and a work he dashed off in a fortnight.[323]

The following notice broke the news on Tuesday, 24 February 1735/6:

HAY-MARKET
By the Great Mogul's *Company of* English *Comedians,*
Newly Imported.
At the New Theatre in the Hay-Market,
Friday, March 5, will be presented
PASQUIN,
A Dramatic SATYR on the Times.
Being a Rehearsal of two Plays, viz. a Comedy, called The ELEC-
TION; and a Tragedy, called The Life and Death of COMMON
SENSE....
N.B.   Mr. Pasquin intending to lay about him with great Impar-

tiality, hopes the Town will all attend, and very civilly give their
Neighbours what they find belongs to 'em.

N.B.   The Cloaths are old, but the Jokes intirely new.[324]

Despite its being introduced late in the season and acted upon Potter's
jerry-built stage by a barely competent troupe dressed in well-worn
costumes, *Pasquin* became the greatest "hit" of the decade, running
without a break for forty-three consecutive nights and a total of more
than sixty performances before the season ended. In 1730 *The Author's
Farce*, its momentum sustained with the help of its companion piece
Tom Thumb, had run at the same theatre for over forty nights; but not
since *The Beggar's Opera* had London witnessed anything like the
popularity of *Pasquin*. From Aaron Hill's review in *The Prompter* (2
April 1736) it appears that, of the two plays that comprise the satire,
Trapwit's comedy – on Fielding's favorite theme of the corruption at
elections – at first pleased audiences more than Fustian's blank-verse
tragedy representing the murder of Common Sense by the followers of
Queen Ignorance, namely Law, Physick, and the priest Firebrand.
Though Hill himself considered the tragedy "by much the finer Performance of the two," he had heard others call it "stupid, dull, non-
sensical," claiming "that the Comedy supported it." But, he continued,
referring to a passage Fielding inserted in notices of the third day's
performance, "A short, humorous Advertisement engaged a close Attention, and set it a going."

Whatever criticisms Hill had heard, *Pasquin* never struggled to catch
on. In the advertisement to which Hill refers Fielding announced: the
"Boxes not being equal to the great Demand for Places, the Pit and
Front-Boxes will (at the particular Desire of several Ladies of Quality)
be put together, at 5s. each. Gallery 2s." This already entertaining
production was enhanced on the eleventh night when Charlotte Charke,
Colley Cibber's daughter who made a specialty of playing male roles,
joined the cast as Lord Place and treated audiences to hilarious
mimickry of her father's mannerisms.[325] In short, Hill did not much
exaggerate the case when he declared that *Pasquin* "PLEASED EVERY
BODY." The Earl of Egmont, having attended the second performance
on 6 March, returned on the 25th – when he found the theatre
"extremely crowded, though the 17th day of its acting"; he went again
on 4 May.[326] The magnitude of the play's success can be gauged from
an item in the *Daily Advertiser* (30 March 1736), reporting that the
Prince of Wales had "honour'd" the Little Haymarket with his presence
the preceding evening, when *Pasquin* "was acted the twentieth Time
to a crowded Audience, amongst which were great Numbers of the
Nobility, with universal Applause, and many thousands of People
turn'd away for want of room." Mrs. Delany (then Mrs. Pendarves)

wrote to Swift on 22 April (Fielding's twenty-ninth birthday), summing up his triumph: "When I went out of town last autumn, the reigning madness was Farinelli; I find it now turned on Pasquin."[327]

Others were quick to make capital of the play's great vogue, among them the hackney authors and print-sellers of the town. Earliest of these was Edward Phillips, author of a farce entitled *Marforio*,[328] in which (so it appears from the advertisements; the work was never published) Fielding himself and his champion Hill were ludicrously impersonated on stage at Rich's Covent Garden Theatre.[329] This rude production expired after a single performance on 10 April. In the Dedication to *Tumble-Down Dick*, published before the month was out, Fielding would "not venture to decide" exactly what part Rich had in this satire – whether it "was written by your Command, or your Assistance, or only Acted by your Permission"; but he was gratified "to observe the Town, which had before been so favourable to *Pasquin* at his own House, confirming the Applause, by thoroughly condemning the Satire on him at Yours."

He would also be amused at a more graphic tribute to his success – a print entitled *The Judgment of the Queen o' Common Sense. Address'd to Henry Fielding Esq*[r] (see Plate 22). According to the advertisement in the *Daily Advertiser* (16 April 1736), the print, published "by Permission of the Great Mogul" himself, was "curiously engrav'd on a Copper-Plate, and printed in the Chinese Manner." Accompanying the picture are the following verses:

> With bounteous hands ye Queen of common sense
> Appears her honest favours to dispence,
> On Pasquin's Author show'rs of Gold bestows,
> And Hamlets Ghost th' impartial Poet shows
> Tho' Shakespears merit in his bosom glows.
> In this french mongrill and apeing age,
> Half meaning Pantomime ye town engage.
> Ev'n that by Criticks is so dearly bought,
> Parnassus hills scarce worth a Poets thought.
> But from ye Great Mogul a Bard is come,
> And brought ye banish'd Exiles to their home.
> Wit, Humour, Satyr in their own defence,
> Are all arived [*sic*] to wait on common Sense.

Though evidence of *Pasquin*'s vogue is plentiful, the only serious attempts by contemporaries to appraise its qualities as a play are colored by the biases of the critics. Aaron Hill saw in Fielding's satire a necessary first step toward the realization of what he had long been advocating in *The Prompter*: a thorough reformation of the theatre. The success of *Pasquin*, Hill observed in his review of 2 April 1736, confirmed the opinion he had "ventured, *singly*, to advance, *viz. That the Stage may*, (and as it may, ought to) *be supported without* PANTOMIME. While our Theatrick Sovereigns [that is, Rich at Covent Garden and Fleetwood at Drury Lane], with the best Actors the Age can afford, are forced to call in the Assistance of *wonderful Scenary* [*sic*], *surprising Transformations, beautiful Landscapes, Dancers*, (the very best, both in the graceful and humourous Manner) and in short, all the attendant Powers of *inexplicable Dumb Shew*, at a very great Expence; a Gentleman, under the Disadvantage of a very bad House, with scarce an Actor, and at very little Expence, by the single Power of *Satire, Wit*, and *Common Sense*" had routed all his rivals. Though a little precious in the analogy he spins between the techniques of Fielding's ridicule and the styles of the Italian and Flemish masters, Hill's appraisal of Fielding's radical experimentation with the forms of dramatic satire is worth preserving:

THE ingenious Author of *Pasquin*, conscious how dangerous it might be, to venture *Common Sense* in the Stile of *Corregio* at first, has, in Imitation of some of the best of Painters, form'd to himself a Manner, out of different Stiles, which (tho' the Particulars may be traced) is, in the whole, *Original*. Thus in the Tragedy we see the bold, daring Pencil of *Michael Angelo*. Satires start out of every Line; they are *seen* and *felt*. Even when they *smile*, they look *terrible*, and *strike* with *Force*. He has here and there given them a *Flemish* Touch, for the sake of the *Vulgar*. He has been rather too sparing of the *Corregio Manner*; for tho' in some Parts his Allegory is delicate in the highest Degree, he has heightned the Colouring so much, that it comes too *full* and *gross* upon us. We lose the Beauty of *Simplicity*, in the Strength with which *it* is lay'd on; but he is justifiable; for, as I observed before, the *Pathetick* and *Delicate* is not to be ventured yet. *Wit, Humour*, and *Satire*, on a *Sub-stratum* of COMMON SENSE, *warmly coloured*, must be preparatory, and have a due Course of Admiration. I cou'd have wish'd he had been a little less *Flemish* in his Comedy; for tho' the *Corruption* he strikes at would not have been *felt*, had it been less *coarsely hit*, than it is *practised* in the *World*, I question, whether so dangerous a Vice as *Corruption* will not lose of the *Disgust* it ought to inspire, by being laugh'd at with so much Wit: A Thing we laugh at only, is no longer terrible. If he had dipped his Pencil in the Colours of *Michael Angelo*, and shewn the terrible Effects of Corruption, in the Ruin of a Borough or Corporation, he had render'd the State a publick Service; but *Trapwit* will tell us, *It would not have been a true Picture of Life, for Boroughs thrive by Corruption*.

For all his posturing, Hill comes closer here than any other contemporary critic to distinguishing the qualities and intent of Fielding's experimental drama at its best, in which a bold, hilarious expressionism (Hill's "Allegory" with "heightned" coloring) serves a didactic purpose by exposing truths which in their potentially pernicious moral and social consequences are anything but laughable.

This favorable appreciation of *Pasquin* loses something of its cogency, however, if we consider that it was probably prompted less by Hill's impartial desire to see justice done to a daring theatrical innovator than by his wish to "puff" the work of a friend. It is clear from Hill's correspondence that at least as early as February of the following year he was on amiable terms with Fielding, who tried (unsuccessfully) to enlist Hill's aid in the Haymarket production of *A Rehearsal of Kings*. Indeed, from the extraordinary tone of Hill's letter to Edmund Fielding in May 1737 it is even clearer that his relationship with Fielding's father was one of cordial intimacy. Having been promoted to Major General in November 1735,[330] Edmund began serving as Lieutenant Governor of the Island of Jersey at about the time *Pasquin* began its spectacular run; he continued in that office until the autumn of 1737.[331] In the spring of that year, despite his "natural aversion to the sea," Hill visited Edmund on the island and afterward expressed the love he bore him in a letter whose effusive language attests to their long-standing friendship.[332]

If Hill's praise of *Pasquin* may have been prompted in part by his friendship with the Fieldings, there can be no doubting the motives of those who roasted the play in the *Grub-Street Journal*. The first notice of Fielding's satire to appear in that periodical (8 April 1736), however, was something of a surprise; for it declared that Pope himself not only had condescended to attend a performance, but had applauded it. To commemorate the event the correspondent offered the following verses, "On seeing Mr. POPE at the *Dramatic Satire* call'd *Pasquin*":

> To lure to virtue, and to lash our crimes,
> The Comic Muse was rear'd in former times:
> But now in this French, Mongril, Aping age,
> Buffoons, and Songsters only can engage:
> Banish'd the Stage, the Boxes and the Pit,
> Gladly the dull unthinking Herd I quit.
> But to inform them what a bliss they've lost,
> *Pasquin* shall still torment them with my Ghost;
> And lash secure the Witlings of our Isle,
> Whilst *Pope* vouchsafes to grace him with a smile.

This compliment to Fielding, unique in the pages of the *Grub-Street Journal*, was obviously published without Russel's knowledge. In the weeks to come (15 and 29 April) he could not conceal his annoyance at

the report, repeatedly assuring his readers that the great poet had never
seen the play.

Pasquin having been published by Watts early in April, another of
the Grublings signing himself "Marforio" began reviling it at length in
an article published in the Journal on Fielding's birthday. His
comments, for all their bias, shed light on Fielding's political and
religious attitudes of this period.

> The design of the Comedy [the critic explains], is to ridicule the late
> Election of members of Parliament, by representing the Candidates
> of both Parties as bribing their Electors.... In the two Parties, it
> seems of Court and Countrey, the Elected and the Electors are both
> equally corrupt, the one bribing and the other bribed; and therefore
> it is foolish and ridiculous for a person out of love to his country, to
> ingage himself in any dispute about the Election of Members of
> Parliament. An admirable moral!

As for the tragedy, which "Marforio" anatomized in the Journal for 6
May, Fielding in drawing the character of Firebrand meant to be
sweepingly iconoclastic, ridiculing not merely papists and heathens,
but the institution of the priesthood itself.

····━● XXXV ●━····

Coming from a source well known for its anti-ministerial bias, the
criticism in the Grub-Street Journal of a cynical even-handedness in
Fielding's political satire seems to support more recent critics who
dispute Pasquin's reputation as an attack on Walpole and his party.
Resuming the theme of the scenes he added to Don Quixote in England
two years earlier, Fielding here aims at electoral corruption in general.
But in both these plays he meant to serve the Opposition's cause –
albeit in a manner more circumspect than what he could safely hazard
in the anonymous leaders he was contributing to The Craftsman during
this same period. The plainest public signs of his political affiliation
had been, of course, the dedication of his dramatic works to Chesterfield
and Marlborough, both prominently associated with the Opposition.

By 1736, however, in addition to these powerful patrons, he had also
been taken up by two friends from his schooldays at Eton, Lyttelton
and Pitt, the so-called "Boy Patriots," who entered Parliament in the
spring of 1735. Both these ambitious men were related by blood or
marriage to the great Lord Cobham of Stowe; and Cobham, like Chesterfield, had been publicly disgraced by Walpole for opposing him in
the Excise crisis. It may have been at Stowe during the summer of

1735 – when Cobham gathered his family and friends around him, including not only Lyttelton and Pitt, but Richard and George Grenville, Gilbert West, Pope, and Martha Blount – that "Cobham's Cubs" formed themselves into a concerted Opposition against the minister.[333] Inspired by Bolingbroke's pose of disinterested patriotism in the *Dissertation on Parties*, which appeared in *The Craftsman* during 1733–4, the program of the group was promulgated by Lyttelton, among others, in *Letters from a Persian in England, to his Friend at Ispahan* (March 1735). Among more general criticisms of his countrymen's manners, Lyttelton defended Whig principles and deplored the corruption of a venal electorate by unscrupulous politicians, most notably of course by the Prime Minister. Anyone who came to *Pasquin* from a reading of the *Persian Letters* (especially those on political topics, such as Letters IX, XXIV, LV, and LXXIX) would be aware that the satire of bribery and corruption in the comedy merely renders Lyttelton's "patriot" doctrine in dramatic form.

Pasquin was clearly understood in this way by Walpole's journalists – as, indeed, by Fielding and his friends. In the *Daily Gazetteer* (9 September 1736) there appeared the following sarcastic profile of a "young Patriot," obviously drawn with Lyttelton and the rest of Cobham's cousinhood in mind:

> He will exclaim vehemently against Bribery and Corruption in Elections ... and will pretend to more than ordinary Zeal for any new Law that is proposed, for punishing, with the utmost Severity, those that are guilty of such Practices ... he will inveigh with great Wrath and Bitterness, against those who stand in Opposition to the neighbouring Gentlemen, who have, what he calls, a *natural Interest*.

(This is also the opinion of the honest Alderman at the election in *Pasquin* [Act I]: "I think we should stand by our Neighbours; Gentlemen whose Honesty we are Witnesses of, and whose Estates in our own Neighbourhood render 'em not liable to be bribed.") The writer in the *Gazetteer* understood that Fielding's play, for all its show of impartiality, was the vehicle of Opposition politics:

> the Success of [*Pasquin*] is more to be imputed to the Politicks that are in it, than to its Wit and Humour; for several great and noble Persons, equally distinguished for their *good Sense* and *delicacy of Taste*, have considered that *finished Piece* not as a Farce, or a Droll, but as a refined Satyr of State, which for excellency of Contrivance, and elegance of Writing, never had its Parallel.[334]

Among the "great and noble Persons" who cried up Fielding's play were Lyttelton and Chesterfield, who, when in February of the following year they launched a new Opposition journal, called the journal

Common Sense in compliment to the character in *Pasquin*.[335] Aptly
enough, then, a correspondent in this same periodical (25 October 1738)
advised "that the Play of *Pasquin* should be acted in every Borough
in *England*, a little before the next Elections – I think it might caution
the People against the Artifices of those who come to corrupt their
Honesty with adulterate Wine, and more adulterate Promises." Indeed,
when in a dream-vision in *The Champion* (13 May 1740) a contributor
somewhat prematurely anatomized the corpse of Walpole, he had no
doubt about the cause of the minister's demise: his heart had been
pierced by "a small Arrow or Dart, whose *Mucro* or Point was very
sharp, and had been dip'd in Gall, and on the Feathers or Beard thereof,
was wrote the Word, *Pasquin*."

···➤ xxxvi ◄···

At first glance, the other charge "Marforio" leveled against *Pasquin*
in the *Grub-Street Journal* – the charge that Fielding had written a
deliberately irreligious work – also seems plausible. Nothing in the play
balances Fielding's satire of the hypocritical priest Firebrand except
the reverence Common Sense pays her deity "the Sun" in gratitude for
his light and warmth. In piety as vague as this even Fielding's free-
thinking friend Cooke could share; and Ralph would applaud his sardonic contempt of the priesthood. It was a theme, too, which Lyttelton
anticipated in his story of the Troglodites.[336] Others besides "Marforio"
remarked on the clergy's vexation over Fielding's disparagement of
their office and of the mysteries of religion. Years later a writer recalled
"some infamous Inuendo's" in the scene in Act IV where Firebrand
insults Common Sense by declaring that the authority of the priesthood
is not derived from her, but from an instrument

> sent us in a Box
> From the great Sun himself, and Carriage paid:
> *Phaeton* brought it when he overturn'd
> The Chariot of the Sun into the Sea

– which accident, Firebrand explains, has rendered the document
illegible to any but priestly eyes. It was this passage in particular that
"called for Vengeance from an *All-burning Priesthood*."[337]

   But we probably come closer to Fielding's actual intent in characterizing Firebrand and Common Sense if we understand that to the
more orthodox, High Church party in this age of theological controversy, the latitudinarian Christianity even of Bishop Hoadly was scarcely less objectionable than the irreverent satire of *Pasquin*. The two

are explicitly linked in a satire "On Religious Disputes" published soon after *Pasquin* was staged. The poem takes the form of a dialogue between a free-thinking "Fop" and an orthodox "Parson." Remembering Hoadly's mystery-dispelling tract on the Eucharist, *A Plain Account of the Nature and End of the Sacrament* (1735) – a work that inspired controversy nearly as vehement as what occurred in 1717, when Hoadly, as Bishop of Bangor, published the doctrine that the true "Kingdom, or Church, of Christ" was comprehensive enough to include all believers – the "Fop" admires such comfortable, indeed profitable, doctrines:

> Cou'd I the Christian Scheme embrace,
> (And I wou'd do it for a Place)
> 'Tis H[oadl]y cou'd alone persuade,
> The Terms so cheap my Lord has made.
> Doctrines politely urg'd may please,
> Which civilly consult our Ease. ...
> 'Tis quite genteel to make Salvation
> A simple Act of Compotation,
> Where we, like happy Saints above,
> Quaff Immortality and Love.

To the "Parson," Hoadly for urging such doctrines is no better than a Socinian, an Arian. But the "Fop" has no time to continue the debate; for he finds Fielding's religious views as congenial as the Bishop's – and it is curtain time:

> It may be, but I cannot stay,
> I've an Appointment at the Play,
> 'Tis *Pasquin*, Parson, by the Way.
> I the last Act intend to steal –
> He bow'd and turn'd upon his Heel.[338]

However fortuitous, the satirist has sensed Fielding's sympathy for Hoadly's brand of easy, moralizing Christianity. In *Joseph Andrews* (I. xvii) what he thought of the Bishop's interpretation of the Eucharist is expressed by Parson Adams, who extols

that excellent Book called, *A Plain Account of the Nature and End of the Sacrament*; a Book written (if I may venture on the Expression) with the Pen of an Angel, and calculated to restore the true Use of Christianity, and of that Sacred Institution: for what could tend more to the noble Purposes of Religion, than frequent cheerful Meetings among the Members of a Society, in which they should in the Presence of one another, and in the Service of the supreme Being, make Promises of being good, friendly and benevolent to each other?

Fielding was probably personally acquainted with Hoadly, who was Bishop of Salisbury from 1723 to September 1734. He was certainly a friend of the Bishop's theatre-loving sons, Benjamin (1706–57) and John (1711–76) – the former a physician and later author of *The Suspicious Husband* (1747); the latter a lawyer who in 1735 turned clergyman in order to prosper under his father's patronage.[339] It was John Hoadly, in fact, to whom Fielding owed the idea of *Pasquin*. In 1731 (30 April, 4 and 8 May) Hoadly brought on Rich's stage at Lincoln's Inn Fields a play entitled *The Contrast: A Tragi-Comical Rehearsal of Two Modern Plays: Match upon Match; or No Match at All, and the Tragedy of Epaminodas*. A burlesque of living poets, including Thomson, this work was suppressed at Bishop Hoadly's instance and was never published. But it served Fielding well – so well that when Garrick offered to revive *The Contrast* in 1773, John Hoadly declined: "The principal life, spirit, and vigour of the piece [he explained], (I mean the contrast between the two opposite bards of tragedy and comedy,) retailed out in Fielding's 'Pasquin,' and that too well-known to render the original thought (which is the life of it) either a novelty, or a night's entertainment."[340] These circumstances clarify Fielding's candid, but obscure, acknowledgment of the debt he owed his friend. Thus he wrote, addressing Rich in the Dedication to *Tumble-Down Dick*:

It was to a Play judiciously brought on by you in the *May*-Month, to which I owe the Original Hint, as I have always own'd, of the contrasted Poets, and two or three other Particulars, which have received great Applause on the Stage. Nor am I less obliged to you for discovering in my imperfect Performance the Strokes of an Author, any of whose Wit, if I have preserved entire, I shall think it my chief Merit to the Town. Tho' I cannot enough cure myself of Selfishness, while I meddle in Dramatick Writings, to profess a Sorrow that One of so superior a Genius is led, by his better Sense and better Fortune, to more profitable Studies than the Stage. How far you have contributed to this, I will not presume to determine.

···◆ xxxvii ◆–···

Tumble-Down Dick: or, Phaeton in the Suds, Fielding's other new play of the season, is a burlesque of those pantomime entertainments which Rich had made popular, both as Harlequin (a role he performed under the name of "Lun"), and as manager at Covent Garden, where he specialized in productions featuring the spectacular stage effects commemorated by Pope in *The Dunciad*, Book III. The immediate inspiration for Fielding's piece, however, was the success of a "New Pantomime Entertainment," called *The Fall of Phaeton: or, Harlequin a Captive*, which opened at Drury Lane on 28 February 1735/6. That he intended to travesty this entertainment, and through it to "attack *Pantomime*" in general, was announced as early as 2 April by Hill in *The Prompter*. The play had taken form by 21 April, when an advertisement in the *London Daily Post* promised it would be staged as afterpiece to *Pasquin* on the 28th. When, however, it dawned on Fielding that on that date his company would likely play to an empty house – the Town being occupied in celebrating the wedding between the Prince of Wales and Princes Augusta of Saxe-Gotha – he deferred the performance until Thursday, 29 April.[341] Watts probably had the book of the play ready for distribution on the day of performance; he had certainly issued it by the end of the week.

An amusing parody of the "puffs" for *The Fall of Phaeton* – which featured machinery invented by Pritchard, music composed by Thomas Arne, and scenes painted by Francis Hayman – the title-page reveals Fielding's intentions:

TUMBLE-DOWN DICK:
OR,
PHAETON *in the* SUDS.
A
Dramatick Entertainment of Walking,
in Serious and Foolish Characters:
Interlarded with
Burlesque, Grotesque, Comick Interludes,
CALL'D,
HARLEQUIN A PICK-POCKET.
As it is Perform'd at the
New Theatre *in the* Hay-Market.
Being ('tis hop'd) the last Entertainment that will
ever be exhibited on any Stage.
Invented by the Ingenious
MONSIEUR *SANS ESPRIT.*
The Musick compos'd by the Harmonious
SIGNIOR *WARBLERINI.*
And the Scenes painted by the Prodigious
MYNHEER *VAN BOTTOM-FLAT.*

The fun here was also of course very much at Rich's expense. Fielding had a number of scores to settle with Rich, who, having that winter refused to put on a play of his at Covent Garden, had instead produced a satire against him and, adding insult to injury, now accused him of having plagiarized *Pasquin* from John Hoadly's *The Contrast*. With an irony tinged with contempt Fielding rehearses all these affronts in dedicating *Tumble-Down Dick* to "Mr. *JOHN LUN*, Vulgarly call'd Esquire." What is more, in the play itself Rich is introduced as "Machine," who arrogantly presides over the rehearsal of the inane Ovidian entertainment he has devised. *Tumble-Down Dick* mocks the absurd but highly successful formula Rich had invented for his "*English* Pantomime," which, Fielding observes in *Tom Jones* (V.i), "consisted of two Parts ... distinguished by the Names of *the Serious* and *the Comic*. The *Serious* exhibited a certain Number of Heathen Gods and Heroes, who were certainly the worst and dullest Company into which an Audience was ever introduced; and (which was a Secret known to few) were actually intended so to be, in order to contrast the *Comic* Part of the Entertainment, and to display the Tricks of Harlequin to the better Advantage." From this time forward Rich remained a figure of ridicule in Fielding's writings.[342]

••••➡ xxxviii ➡•••

Other plays than *Pasquin* and *Tumble-Down Dick* were performed at the Little Haymarket during Fielding's first season as manager. To the chagrin of his partner, one of these was not Ralph's *Astrologer*, which, though often rehearsed and scheduled to be acted for the author's benefit on 26 March, was kept off the boards by the prodigious success of *Pasquin*. In the *Daily Advertiser* (29 March) Ralph represented his disappointment as a consequence of his altruism, explaining, "I could not suffer myself to interrupt the Run of that celebrated Satire, though by Agreement with the Author I had it in my Power"; for his benefit he instead settled, wisely, for the twenty-second performance of *Pasquin* (31 March). Thomas Davies later recalled that his fellow comedians were in fact "disgusted with the obsolete style" of *The Astrologer*, "and the almost forgotten scheme of hunting for the philosopher's stone, with an intent to cheat bubbles of their money." "Poor Ralph," as Davies remembered him, "had no other share in the management than viewing and repining at the success of his partner."[343] Considering the dismal showing made by the only other play Ralph sponsored during this season – Elizabeth Cooper's comedy, *The Nobleman: or Family Quarrel* (17 May) – it was happy for the Haymarket company that he left its management to Fielding. Among other plays that interrupted *Pasquin*'s run, or as afterpieces shared in its success, were "J. Dormer's" (Joseph Dorman's?)[344] *The Female Rake* on 26 April and Henry Carey's

Chrononhotonthologos and *The Honest Yorkshireman*, paired with *The Tragedy of Tragedies* on 3 May.

Crowning Fielding's first season as theatrical manager was a production that reveals as much about his capacity for friendship as about his professional judgment and enterprise. This was the production of *Guilt Its Own Punishment: or, Fatal Curiosity* (best known by its subtitle), a new domestic tragedy by George Lillo, who five years earlier with *The London Merchant* had staged the most popular example of this genre in English theatre history. At first glance Lillo (1693–1739) may seem an unlikely man to have won Fielding's affection: of Dutch/English parentage, he was a City jeweler by trade and a dissenter in religion – a man known more for his modesty and the probity of his morals than for his wit and learning. Moreover, nothing about Fielding's theatrical career to date suggests that he relished the sublime, sad pleasures of the tragic mode. On the contrary, the hilarity of *The Tragedy of Tragedies*, which he had recently revived at the Haymarket, compounding the burlesque by coupling it with Carey's *Chrononhotonthologos* – not to mention *The Covent-Garden Tragedy* with its mockery of Philips's *Distrest Mother*, or Fustian's ludicrous attempts at trying on the buskin: such travesties as these scarcely prepared the public for the following letter, almost certainly by Fielding, which appeared in the *Daily Advertiser* (Tuesday, 25 May), just two days before *Fatal Curiosity* opened at the Haymarket:

SIR,
IN an Age when Tragedy is thought so much out of Fashion, that the great establish'd Theatres dare hardly venture to attempt it, an Author may probably seem bold who hazards his Reputation with a Set of young Actors on a Stage hitherto in its Infancy; where he is sure, besides the Judgment, to encounter the Prejudice of the Town; and has not only the Chance of not being liked, but of not being heard.

But as to the ill Success of Tragedy in general, I shall not attribute it entirely to the Audience; I cannot persuade myself that we are sunk into such a State of Levity and Childhood, as to be utterly incapable of any serious Attention; or are so entirely devoted to Farce and Puppet Shew, as to abandon what one of the greatest Criticks who ever liv'd has call'd the noblest Work of Human Understanding.

I am afraid the Truth is, our Poets have left off Writing, rather than our Spectators loving Tragedy. The Modern Writers seem to me to have quite mistaken the Path: They do not fail so much from want of Genius as of Judgment; they embellish their Diction with their utmost Art, and concern themselves little about their Fable: In

short, While they are industrious to please the Fancy, they forget
(what should be their first Care) to warm the Heart.

Give me leave, Sir, to recommend to you, and by you to the Town,
a Tragedy, written in a different Manner, where the Fable is contriv'd
with great Art, and the Incidents such as must affect the Heart of
every one who is not void of Humanity. A tender Sensation is, I
think, in one of a Humane Temper, the most pleasing that can be
rais'd; and I will venture to affirm, no such Person will fail of enjoying
it who will be present on Thursday next at the Hay-Market Theatre;
where, without the bombast Stile of Kings and Heroes, he will see a
Scene in common Life, which really happen'd in King James I's
Time; and is accompany'd with the most natural, dreadful and tender
Circumstances, and affording the finest Moral that can be invented
by the Mind of Man.

What in Fielding's view distinguished *Fatal Curiosity* from the "bombast" tragedies he loved to ridicule was chiefly its "Fable." Lillo based
his play on (supposedly) an actual incident that occurred at Penryn,
Cornwall, in 1618: a young man, having made a fortune traveling in
the East for many years, returns home without revealing his identity
and is murdered by his father at the instigation of his stepmother.
Lillo's drama was not fanciful, but true; its incidents are genuinely
affecting; it is constructed with economy and a sense of pace, with a
fidelity to the Aristotelian unities greater even than Addison could
manage in *Cato*; and in his dialogue Lillo kept up a powerful simplicity
and vigor of style, achieving one of the rare triumphs of dramatic blank
verse of his century.

Further proof of the incompetence of the managers at the established
theatres, Lillo, having peddled his play in vain elsewhere, brought it
as a last resort to Fielding at the Little Haymarket, "reduced to the
necessity," as Davies recalled, "of having his play acted at an inferior
Play-house, and by persons not so well skilled in their profession." It
was then that Davies, who played the role of Young Wilmot, met
Lillo and witnessed Fielding's treatment of him. Fielding had always
despised those genteel critics who sneered at *The London Merchant*
"because the subject was too low." He understood Lillo's merit, and
behaved toward him "with great politeness and friendship." Indeed,
he personally "took upon himself the management of the play," applying all his talents and resources to ensure its success. Fielding, Davies
remembered, "was not merely content to revise the FATAL CURIOSITY,
and to instruct the actors how to do justice to their parts. He warmly
recommended the play to his friends, and to the public. Besides all this
he presented the author with a well written prologue."[345]

The Prologue is simply a distillation in couplets of Fielding's "puff"
in the *Daily Advertiser*:

> – But from this modern fashionable Way,
> To Night, our Author begs your Leave to stray.
> No fustian Hero rages here to Night;
> No Armies fall, to fix a Tyrant's Right:
> From lower Life we draw our Scene's Distress:
> – Let not your Equals move your Pity less!
>
> (ll. 7–12)

Mrs. Charke later recalled that the actor John Roberts, who spoke these
lines, "discovered a Mastership in the Character of the Husband" Old
Wilmot, while she played the cruel stepmother Agnes: "We were kindly
received by the Audience."[346] The day following the opening performance the *Daily Advertiser* (28 May) reported that *Fatal Curiosity*
had been received

> with the greatest Applause that has been shewn to any Tragedy for
> many Years. The Scenes of Distress were so artfully work'd up, and
> so well perform'd, that there scarce remain'd a dry Eye among the
> Spectators at the Representation; and during the Scene preceding
> the Catastrophe, an attentive Silence possess'd the whole House,
> more expressive of an universal Approbation than the loudest
> Applauses, which were given to the many noble Sentiments that
> every where abound in this excellent Performance, which must meet
> with Encouragement in an Age that does not want both Sense and
> Humanity.

"Puffing" this strenuous suggests that Fielding himself furnished the
copy. Whatever impact the play had upon the audience that first
night, it enjoyed only a modest run of seven performances, a showing
attributable in part to its having been introduced so late in the season.
In a second effort to serve his friend, Fielding brought it on again in
March 1737, when it ran for eleven nights coupled with *The Historical
Register*.

Fatal Curiosity was never staged again before Lillo's death in September 1739. Its reputation among certain knowledgeable critics
remained, however, very high: Sarah Fielding took up her brother's
cause by defending the play in her novel, *The Adventures of David
Simple* (1744; II.ii); Davies, for whom Lillo was matched only by
Shakespeare as "a painter of the terrible graces," believed that for sheer
affective power only the murder scenes in *Macbeth* could equal the third
Act of *Fatal Curiosity*;[347] and James Harris declared that in Lillo's
tragedy "we find the model of A PERFECT FABLE," deserving comparison
with the *Oedipus Tyrannus*.[348] This praise, coming from Fielding's sister

and friends, may seem merely to echo his own enthusiasm for the play, but in our own times a more disinterested critic has confirmed their judgment: to Allardyce Nicoll *Fatal Curiosity* is the only tragic masterpiece produced in England between 1700 and 1750, its author "a genius of no common rank."[349]

Fielding's final tribute to Lillo's genius, as well as to his qualities as a man, was published in *The Champion* (26 February 1739/40), a few months after his friend's death:

His fatal Curiosity, which is a Master-Piece in its Kind, and inferior only to Shakespear's best Pieces gives him a Title to be called the best Tragick Poet of his Age; but this was the least of his Praise, he had the gentlest and honestest Manners, and at the same time the most friendly and obliging. He had a perfect Knowledge of human Nature, tho' his Contempt for all base Means of Application, which are the necessary Steps to great Acquaintance, restrain'd his Conversation within very narrow Bounds; he had the Spirit of an old Roman, join'd to the Innocence of a primitive Christian, he was content with his little State of Life, in which his excellent Temper of Mind gave him an Happiness beyond the Power of Riches, and it was necessary for his Friends to have a sharp Insight into his Want of their Services as well as good Inclinations or Abilities to serve him; in short, he was one of the best of Men, and those who knew him best, will most regret his Loss.

Or perhaps it would be more accurate to say that Fielding's "final" tribute to his friend is the character of Heartfree in *Jonathan Wild* – like Lillo an honest, good-natured man whose trade is that of a City jeweler.

Though *Pasquin* continued to be performed until July, the production of Lillo's *Fatal Curiosity* probably marked the end of Fielding's first season as manager at the Little Haymarket. It could scarcely have been a more impressive début, especially for a young man not yet out of his twenties. In just three months he had injected new life into the London theatre – with *Pasquin* rivaling the popularity of the Italian castrati and Rich's harlequinades; with *Fatal Curiosity* reviving the moribund form of tragedy by shrewdly discerning the potential of more realistic plots and characters. And he accomplished these things despite the disadvantages of an inferior house and company.

The season was also memorable not only for what he accomplished, but for the brash and irreverent way he went about it. In his management of the theatre the impudence one saw in him as a boy took the form of a reckless, if usually playful, defiance of authority and convention – both in his satires of the political establishment, and in his flouting of the prohibition against performing plays on Wednesdays

and Fridays during Lent. *Pasquin*, for all its show of impartiality, was
calculated to embarrass the ministry; and Fielding, as manager of the
company, must also have approved the passing hits at Walpole in
The Female Rake and *Fatal Curiosity*. At the same time Fielding's
"*Mogulites*" were accused of "a want of common Decency" for failing
to "pay a due Observance to the *Wednesdays* and *Fridays* in *Lent*":
"these Heathens," complained the critic, "had no respect to these Days,
but play'd on, and would continue so to do (even in the *Passion* Week)
had not they been expressly forbid by the Lord *Chamberlain*."[350] The
historian of the London Stage remarks that during the spring of 1736
"every company," not just Fielding's, "played on some of the forbidden
days." But Fielding's conduct in this respect was egregious: beginning
with the Friday following Ash Wednesday (12 March) he kept *Pasquin*
running every Wednesday and Friday right into Passion Week, when
he was "ordered to desist."[351] It may at least be said that if he felt the
ceremonial requirements of his religion less forcibly than the attractions
of grossing £80 a night[352] from the successful run of his satire, he was
generous in his treatment of the actors and authors at the Haymarket,
and on one occasion (25 May 1736) devoted the proceeds of a performance of *Pasquin* and *Tumble-Down Dick* to the relief of a distressed
gentlewoman whose father, General Nugent, had been killed defending
Gibraltar.[353]

····➤ xxxix ➤····

From time to time during this year Fielding turned from theatrical
affairs in order to continue his contributions to *The Craftsman* – and
begin a desultory association with another periodical, the *Universal
Spectator*. The first three of these essays coincide with "the Great
Mogul's" season at the Little Haymarket, and they ring changes on
political themes echoed in *Pasquin* and *Tumble-Down Dick*. In *Pasquin*
(Act II) the avid "patriot" Miss Stitch may well be thinking of her
author's own writing when she says she has spent three days "in reading
one of the *Craftsmen*; 'tis a very pretty one; I have almost got it by
Heart." On 21 February 1735/6, for example, Amhurst published a
facetious defense of the new Act to repeal the Jacobean statute against
witchcraft; the author, one "Rachel Foresight," attributes Walpole's
success as a politician to his skill in conjuring. On 13 March a certain
virtuoso signing himself "T.T." used *The Craftsman* to publicize an
ingenious pneumatic machine designed to pump fresh air into the
Houses of Parliament and to improve the quality of the speeches heard
there. On 5 June in the same paper the government's unpopular Gin Act

(9 George II, cap. 23), intended to restrict the consumption of spirituous liquors, is the subject of a witty complaint by "A Moderate Man."

These pseudonyms almost certainly belong to Fielding, who, whether
on stage or in the pages of *The Craftsman*, was fast becoming one of
the Opposition's most effective instruments. A fourth essay, published
in *The Craftsman* (18 September) – the month in which the Gazetteers
were linking the politics of *Pasquin* with the interests of Cobham's
"Boy Patriots" – took the form of a dream-vision in which the happy
"Island *Fortunata*" is ravaged by a "devouring Monster" representing
Walpole. This piece, in which Fielding's usual facetiousness gives way
to sardonic irony, elicited an angry reply from Ralph Courteville (alias
"R. Freeman") in the *London Journal* (2 October), who noted that the
buffoonery of the author had become characteristic of *The Craftsman*
in recent months: "there is something so unaccountably *wild*, and
so unmeaningly *extravagant*, in our late *Country Journals*, that I
have often thought they might be printed as the Sequel of a *French
Romance*" which bears the title "*Contes Mogols*." Was this "Freeman's"
way of hinting it was "the Great Mogul" of the Little Haymarket whose
flair for impertinent satire had thus altered the character of Amhurst's
journal? Perhaps not. Fielding's association with *The Craftsman* seems
to have remained a well-kept secret. Only once, in the *Daily Gazetteer*
(12 October 1737), does a ministerial author notice the intimacy of
Fielding's relationship with Amhurst. Two other papers, in a lighter
vein, conclude his contributions to *The Craftsman* during 1736: these
are the humorous defense of the honorable society of barbers by "Philo-
Tonsor" (30 October) and "Ned Friendly's" anatomy of the dullness
and mendacity of newswriters (18 December).

One of Fielding's most delightful essays (for the evidence of his
authorship of this pseudonymous piece is persuasive) appeared in late
summer in an unexpected place, the *Universal Spectator*, a periodical
with anti-ministerial overtones which had been published since its
inception in 1728 by "Henry Stonecastle, of Northumberland, Esq."[354]
The reasons for Fielding's connection with this journal are obscure, but
several possibilities suggest themselves. Of the founders of the *Universal
Spectator*, Daniel Defoe had died in 1732, but Henry Baker lived on,
assisted in the enterprise by, among other contributors, John Kelly.
Fielding may have been acquainted with Baker, whose translation of
Molière's *Select Comedies* he "puffed" in the Preface to *The Mock Doctor*.
That Kelly's anti-ministerial farce, *The Fall of Bob: or, The Oracle of
Gin*, was acted at the Little Haymarket on 14 January 1736/7, by a
company under Fielding's influence, suggests that the two men may
have been on friendly terms. Another possible link is Ralph, who is
known to have edited the *Universal Spectator* in 1739, though his
biographer found no earlier trace of his hand in that paper.[355] In any

event, Fielding's essay "On Eating" was published in the *Universal Spectator* in two installments (14 and 21 August 1736) under the apt name of "Will. Lovemeal," a gourmandizer of the widest knowledge and experience of his subject, who writes peckishly "From under the Clock at Dick's Coffee-House, Temple-Bar," at four o'clock in the afternoon, well past the dinner hour. Besides the humor of this piece, it is tempting to suppose that in it Fielding treated us to a rare glimpse of his domestic affairs – of what, to be precise, mornings were like at home with his new wife:

> A *Lady* of my Acquaintance, is, as soon as she is out of Bed, as *ill-natur'd* a Woman as any in *Great Britain*; she is peevish with every Body about her, she is *angry* at she don't know *what*, and *scolds* she don't know *why*; but from the Moment she has swallow'd her first *Dish* of *Tea*, and *eat* her first Piece of Bread and Butter, she begins to *smile*, her *Frowardness* imperceptibly vanishes as her *Hunger* decreases, and then *continues* the *kindest Mistress*, the *tenderest Mother*, and the *quietest Wife* in the three Kingdoms 'till she wants to *eat* again.

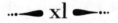

Fielding, of course, need not literally have been in London frequenting Dick's Coffee-House in midsummer. We know nothing of his movements from June, when he finished supervising the production of *Fatal Curiosity*, until December, when, as the records of the King's Bench reveal, he felt obliged to borrow £55 from one Charles Fielding, Esq.:[356] from this man at Southwark on 13 December 1736 Fielding borrowed £25, promising to repay the loan in nine months' time; from the same man at Westminster on the same date, he borrowed another £30, promising to repay the debt in thirteen months.[357] In time these debts, among too many others, came home to plague him. But why did he need to contract them now? How can he so soon have run through his share of the proceeds from the lucrative run of *Pasquin*, together with the £500 the Court awarded him on 3 November 1736 in his suit against Thomas Bennet?[358] Perhaps, since his complaint against Bennet was that the man's defamatory statements had stirred up a swarm of his creditors, most of this money had been paid out as soon as received. But Fielding was never able to live within his means. What is more, he was probably already devising an ambitious scheme he hoped would make his fortune as manager of a new theatre – a scheme requiring capital, as well as the nerve and talent he already had in abundance.

Not until late January 1736/7, however, did Fielding settle in London for what proved to be the most momentous, indeed catastrophic, season of his theatrical career. It is clear that he was not directly involved with the company which, trying to capitalize on the successful formula he had refined the previous spring, launched a brief season at the Little Haymarket on 14 January, staging a burlesque of Rich's pantomime entertainments entitled *The Defeat of Apollo* together with Kelly's satire on the late Gin Act, *The Fall of Bob*. The *Daily Journal* (11 January) represents Fielding's connection with this fugitive troupe as inspirational only:

> The judicious Author of *Pasquin* exposed, with a great deal of Wit and Humour, the Stupidity of Dumb Shew; and, as that Piece was received with publick Applause the last Season, it was hoped he would have followed the Blow, have driven Buffoonery off the Stage, and reinstated good Sense, Wit and Humour, which alone have Title to the Theatres: However, he has, by his Example, animated others; and we hear that the French Theatre in the Haymarket will soon be opened with a Piece or two in the same Taste with *Pasquin*.

In mid-January Fielding was far removed from the ludicrous entertainments of the metropolis. He was in Shaftesbury, Dorset, again embroiled in more violent sport with Thomas Bennet, who was no doubt less than satisfied with the judgment of £500 Fielding recently won against him. In Easter Term of 1736/7 Bennet brought before the King's Bench a plea of trespass and assault against his adversary, charging that in Shaftesbury on two occasions – the first on 20 February 1734/5, as we noted; the second on 10 January 1736/7 – Fielding, besides other unspecified "enormities," did "then and there beat, wound and evilly treat [him] so that his life was greatly despaired of." The damages Bennet claimed for these alleged offenses amounted, by a not very surprising coincidence, to precisely the sum Fielding had won from him in November – £500. Fielding was again represented by the Salisbury attorney Robert Stillingfleet. No record of a judgment survives, but it appears that even as he approached his thirtieth year, Fielding continued to find it difficult to control his temper.[359]

···◄ xli ►···

The first sign of Fielding's presence in town, and of his hopes of a more exciting and lucrative theatrical career than he had yet known, is a notice published in the *Daily Advertiser* (4 February 1736/7), but dated two days earlier:

Whereas it is agreed on between several Gentlemen, to erect a New
Theatre for the exhibiting of Plays, Farces, Pantomimes, &c. all such
Persons as are willing to undertake the said Building, are desir'd to
bring their Plans for the same by the 2d of May next ensuing, in
order to be laid before the said Gentlemen, the Time and Place of
which Meeting will be advertis'd in this Paper on the last of April.

Proportions of the Ground:
   The North side 120 Feet; the West, square with the North, 130
Feet; the South 110 Feet; and the East, on a Bevil, joining the
Parallels.
   Note, There must be a Passage left to go round the Building, and
the Stage to be 30 Feet wide at the first Scene; the Distance between
Wall and Wall 80 Feet; and the Scene-Rooms, Green and Dressing
Rooms, to be on the outside of the last mention'd Measure.
   The Stage to be either North or South.[360]

As Professor Hume has deduced, the theatre that might have been
constructed from these specifications would have "good proportions for
an attractive, fan-shaped auditorium," accommodating an audience of
850–900. Located presumably somewhere in the West End, it would be
a theatre capable of competing successfully with the patent houses.[361]
   That Fielding was the prime mover behind this project, in which he
was probably supported by his powerful friends in Opposition, is clear
from a letter to the editor of the same paper on 19 February:

SIR,
In a late Paragraph in one of your Papers it was insinuated, that
there was a Design on foot for erecting a New Theatre, which by
some Wise Heads was suppos'd to come from a certain Manager, in
order to revive the Playhouse Bill this Session of Parliament; I think
it proper therefore, in Justice to the Gentleman levell'd at, to inform
the Publick, that it is actually intended for a Company of Comedians
every Day expected here, late Servants to their Majesties KOULI
KAN and THEODORE, who in the mean time will entertain the
Town in the true Eastern manner, at the New Theatre in the Hay-
Market, with a celebrated Piece call'd *A Rehearsal of Kings.* I am,
Sir, yours, &c.

Agent for the Company

It was of course Fielding, "the Great Mogul" himself, who was now
forming around the nucleus of the best actors of the old *Pasquin* troupe
a new company of comedians, here facetiously represented as servants

of Kuli-Kan, fearsome Shah of Persia, and Theodore, the military adventurer who claimed to be King of Corsica. What was meant by "the true Eastern manner" of the company's productions would soon become disconcertingly plain to Walpole and his ministry.

While Fielding entertained hopes of a splendid new theatre of his own and made preparations for what was to be one last, impudent season at the Little Haymarket, he was also arranging with Charles Fleetwood of Drury Lane to stage another of his farces, entitled *Eurydice, or the Devil Henpeck'd*. An indication of how high his stock had risen at that theatre since the failure of *The Universal Gallant* two years earlier, the bargain Fielding struck was on the most unusual terms, highly advantageous to himself; for though *Eurydice* was, in his own words, "The trifling Offspring of an idle Hour,"[362] Fleetwood allowed Fielding a benefit on the first night. This arrangement proved provident indeed, as the play was never acted a second time.

The damning of *Eurydice* was owing, in part, to circumstances beyond Fielding's control. It was customary at Drury Lane that the footmen who attended their masters and mistresses were granted places free of charge in a gallery of their own. From this superior position, besides the drunken chatter they kept up, they hurled down noisy judgments on the play and made rude observations on their "betters" in the Pit. During the winter of 1736–7 this behavior had become intolerable. Responding to complaints of his clientele, Fleetwood offered to build a lobby where the footmen might be accommodated during the performance remote from the ears of the audience. This potentially explosive situation detonated on the opening night of Fielding's play, Saturday, 19 February, when the Pit rose up against their tormentors, drove them out of the house, and refused to allow the main piece, Addison's *Cato*, to be performed until Theophilus Cibber came to the front of the stage and promised that in future the gallery would be closed to the footmen. The footmen did not submit tamely to this discipline. Having regrouped outside, they stormed the theatre in force, and, using a hatchet to break down the door to their gallery, resumed their accustomed places while the players were performing the first Act of *Cato*. Though they kept some order while the play was in progress, at the end of each Act they expressed their triumph with, as one witness reported, "*huzzaing, tossing of Hats*, and the most *obstreperous* of *Vociferation*."[363] Before Act IV opened, the Pit rose again. The High Constable of Westminster was summoned, who, with the help of a posse, confined the footmen to their gallery until the play was over, when several arrests were made.

These clamorous proceedings having charged the atmosphere in the playhouse, Fielding's little burlesque, appropriately set in the Ovidian underworld, would have been damned had it been a better play. A mere

"*Oglio* of Tid-Bits," as the Author himself confesses, it succeeds well enough in its only design – to "come up to the Ridiculous" – and it continues Fielding's campaign against the Italian opera, which, expressing an opinion Fielding shared with Addison, Pope, Gay, and many others, Dr. Johnson characterized as "an exotick and irrational entertainment."[364] Fielding's account of what happened that night is given in *Eurydice Hiss'd*, the farce he wrote later this season to commemorate the occasion. Having taken the precaution of cramming the theatre with his friends, he found that the piece was received well enough at first; but it foundered when the character of Captain Weazle, the ghost of an army-beau, was taken as an affront to the military. " 'Tis true" – reports a witness in the play, who, like the messenger in Greek tragedy, enters to describe an event "too horrible" to be acted out on stage – "at first the Pit seem'd greatly pleas'd/ And loud Applauses thro' the Benches rung";

> But as the Plot began to open more,
> (A shallow Plot) the Claps less frequent grew,
> Till by degrees a gentle Hiss arose;
> This by a Cat-call from the Gallery
> Was quickly seconded: Then follow'd Claps,
> And long 'twixt Claps and Hisses did succeed,
> A stern Contention. . . .
> The Audience, as it were contagious Air,
> All caught it, hollow'd, cat-call'd, hiss'd, and groan'd.

One consequence of all this was that Fielding's bookseller, John Watts, "Who was this Morning eager for the Copy,/ Slunk hasty from the Pit, and shook his Head." *Eurydice* was not published until 1743, when Fielding used it to fill out the second volume of his *Miscellanies*. Nor was the play allowed a second trial. Though announced on the following Monday, 21 February, as the afterpiece to *Timon of Athens*,[365] it was replaced at the last minute by *The King and the Miller of Mansfield*. By this substitution, *Eurydice* was spared the even more violent riot of the footmen which occurred at Drury Lane that evening, when Colonel DeVeil, principal magistrate of Westminster, was obliged to read the Riot Act before order could be restored.[366]

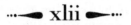

Before the week was out Fielding announced his intention to return to the theatrical wars. An advertisement in the *Grub-Street Journal* (24 February 1736/7) promised that on 9 March at the New Theatre in the Haymarket a new play would be performed "*By a Company of Comedians dropt from the Clouds, late Servants to their thrice renown'd Majesties* Kouli Kan *and* Theodore." The play was "a New Dramatic Comi-Tragical Satire of three Acts, entitled, A REHEARSAL of KINGS; OR, The Projecting Gingerbread BAKER; With the unheard of Catastrophe of *Macplunderkan*, King of Roguomania, and the ignoble Fall of Baron *Tromperland*, King of Clouts." To this would be added a new farce entitled *Sir Peevy Pet*. The advertisement also reveals that Fielding had gone to "the extraordinary Expence" of equipping his company with new costumes, an expense he passed on to his audience by raising the prices (boxes would now be 5*s*., pit 3*s*., and gallery 2*s*.). With memories of Saturday night's fiasco at Drury Lane fresh in mind, he also entered "his Caveat against all (by what Names soever distinguish'd) who may *hire* and *be hired* to do the Drudgery of *Hissing*, *Catcalling*, &c.," entreating that "the Town would discourage, as much as in them lies, a Practice at once so scandalous and prejudicial to Author, Player, and every fair Theatric Adventurer."

The "Great Mogul" had returned, having as the *Daily Advertiser* (8 March 1736/7) reported, "acceeded to the Treaty of the Hay-Market" – or in plainer English, having concluded with John Potter an agreement to rent his theatre for the season. The players Fielding assembled were a competent, if not a stellar, group: from the successful *Pasquin* company of the previous year they included Charlotte Charke, Roberts, Jones, Lacy, and Tom Davies, with the important addition of Eliza Haywood, who, for the time being at least, had forgiven Fielding for satirizing her as Mrs. Novel in *The Author's Farce*.[367] There can be little doubt about the sort of roles they would perform. The play he chose to inaugurate the season must have been a political allegory far exceeding *Pasquin* in the recklessness of its satire. This much is clear from a letter written to Fielding on 28 February 1736/7 by Aaron Hill, who declined his friend's invitation to furnish a Prologue and Epilogue for the piece, prudently choosing to avoid any connection with so "dangerous" a production.

> SIR,
> I SEE clearly, by some names among your performers, that you are not in so much danger as I apprehended, on that quarter. But, I am afraid, you are in more, than you imagine, on another; and that is, from the choice of your subject, and allegorical *remoteness* of your

satire. – What I mean is, that the necessity your prudence was under, to disguise your design with *caution*, has so perplexed it with *doubtfulness*, that I am fearful, in the hurry of action, some of the *most meaning* allusions, in your piece, may be mistaken for scenes, which want any meaning at all; while, on the other side, among the few, who can penetrate purpose, and unravel the *satire*, as fast as they hear it, you will find *some* persons malignantly disposed, upon a supposition, that royalty, in general, should never be the mark of contempt; and others, because they will conclude, you have levelled your aim against particular objects, at whose expense they must incline to be diverted.

FROM these apprehensions, I am compelled to depend on your good-nature for excuse, as to the Prologue and Epilogue: I have good reasons for declining every hazard, of being considered in a light this would very unseasonably shew me in; and I should do an injustice to your candour, if I made the least doubt of your pardon, upon a motive of this nature.

I am heartily sorry, I had not sooner an idea of your plan; and flatter myself, I might have had the good fortune of persuading you to change it, for some other, not only of less dangerous provocation, but more promising likelyhood, to fall in with the publick capacity. *Dramatic Levels* are to be taken by the apprehension of those we would divert; no matter how just, or how poignant our meanings, if they lie not open, and visible enough to be catched, in their *glancing*. – You know who, very much to your purpose, has told us,

> "That stars beyond a certain height,
> Give mortals neither heat, nor light."

UPON the whole, if it were possible, in so short a time as is left you, to substitute any other of your pieces, in place of this *Rehearsal of Kings*, I am convinced, you would avoid a disappointment, and, perhaps, a mortification. – And, persuaded as I am, of this, upon repeated and attentive reflection, I think it an honester error, to hazard my judgment, than, by disguising my sentiments, do injustice to my sincerity.[368]

Hill was mistaken in thinking that Fielding was the author of *A Rehearsal of Kings*: the *Daily Advertiser* (8 March 1736/7) declares it to be the work of "a Gentleman who never wrote for the Stage." It is clear from the same source, moreover, that Fielding by that date had been writing another play altogether, one destined to have for him precisely the dire consequences Hill foresaw: that play was *The Historical Register*, scheduled for performance immediately after *A Rehearsal of Kings*. Nevertheless, as manager of the Haymarket company, Fielding was responsible for a production which, it is reasonable to infer from Hill's account, satirized George II and his ministers. Even in the relatively innocuous *Eurydice* Fielding had touched this same forbidden ground – "how," inquires the Author in obvious reference to Queen Caroline's well-known influence over her husband, "could Hell be better represented than by supposing the People under Petticoat-Government?" Fielding was now promoting an entire play devoted to the same dangerous sport.

This impudence may help to explain the puzzling act of violence that delayed the opening of Fielding's season five days. On Wednesday, 9 March, *A Rehearsal of Kings* was about to be performed as advertised when a band of tradesmen and artisans, led by a certain "gentleman" named Joseph Hooke, forcibly took possession of the Little Haymarket, tearing up the theatre and kidnapping Potter, whom they held for ten hours against his will.[369] "On this Account," the *Daily Advertiser* (10 March) reported, "several hundred Persons were turn'd away." Or were these vigilantes motivated by a more pious cause, resenting the fact that Fielding had once again flouted convention by scheduling the performance for a Wednesday in the Lenten Season? In any case, the Lord Chamberlain issued an order the following day strictly forbidding the managers of all four theatres – Drury Lane, Covent Garden, and Lincoln's Inn Fields as well as the Little Haymarket – from staging plays on Wednesdays and Fridays during Lent.[370] This, surely, was the "unforeseen Accident" that caused Fielding to shift the new date for the play's initial performance from Friday the 11th to Monday, 14 March.[371] *A Rehearsal of Kings* had a second performance on 15 March, when the Earl of Egmont attended (regrettably without confiding to his Diary what he saw),[372] and then a third and final performance on 17 March, when the promised afterpiece, *Sir Peevy Pet*, was at last introduced. Neither play was ever staged again. On 19 March, they gave place to a revival of *Pasquin*.

····•➧ xliii ➧•····

On Monday, 21 March, as afterpiece to a revival of his friend Lillo's *Fatal Curiosity*, Fielding gave the Town the play it had been waiting for – *The Historical Register for the Year 1736*. The brashest of all his political dramas, it was precisely the opportunity Walpole wanted, a play that would put Parliament in a mood to place the theatres under restraint. Ever defiant of authority and heedless of the consequences, Fielding proceeded with this production despite early warnings that the ministry was moving in a determined, if cautious, manner to control the stage. A month before, Fielding's proposal to erect a new theatre started rumors of the government's reviving the abortive Playhouse Bill of 1735. Indeed, on 9 March – the day on which he planned to open his season at the Little Haymarket – a Bill was introduced into the House of Commons "for the more Effectual Punishing Rogues and Vagabonds." Though the Bill was dropped, its possible application to the actors of the London theatres was causing them "no small Pain" as late as 29 March.[373]

As if sensing he had gone too far, Fielding, at the moment when *The Historical Register* was beginning its fateful run, responded to such threats in an anonymous pamphlet entitled *Some Thoughts on the Present State of the Theatres, and the Consequences of an Act to destroy the Liberty of the Stage*. To ensure wider circulation of his views, the pamphlet was reprinted in the "Occasional Prompter" for 25 March, a series in the *Daily Journal* specializing in theatrical affairs.[374] Fielding vehemently argued against any attempt to censor the stage or to restrict the number of theatres to the two patent houses: the former course, he warned, would deprive society of one of "the best Means" of propagating virtue and shaming the vicious; the latter would establish "a Stage Tyranny" by which the managers of the privileged houses would stifle all inventiveness and pander to the Establishment. These lessons he implicitly applied both to his own spectacular success in reviving the biting style of Aristophanes, master of "the old Comedy," and also to his conduct as a manager courageous enough to provide the Town with the strong satiric fare it relished:

> But further, any other Restraint whatever, than from the Laws now in being, would have prevented several Pieces, to which the Town have shewn great Favour, from ever appearing: Managers are always extremely cautious (while they flourish without it) of giving the least Offence to the higher Powers. This Caution has (to my Knowledge) struck out many beautiful and justifiable Strokes of Satire, from some Performances which have been, after Castration, exhibited. This Caution would, I am sure, intirely destroy the old Comedy, which seems at present greatly to flourish, in which we have an Author who is an acknowledged Proficient, and which may be of very signal Service to our Country; for Imposture has no greater Enemy than Theatrical Ridicule.

As Fielding wrote these words, *The Historical Register* was proving his point. Having played on opening night to "the greatest Applause ever shewn" at the Little Haymarket,[375] it continued a spectacular run (thirty-six performances in all) until the ministry took measures not only to turn Fielding out of his theatre, but to muzzle him as a dramatist once and for all. The play is another of his variations on the rehearsal

formula; but this time, as the title jokingly promises,[376] the author
Medley, in flagrant contempt of the unities, means to represent nothing
less than all the momentous events that happened in Europe during
the past twelve months (the old year not having ended until 24 March).
The point is, of course, that in this the Age of Walpole, whose venality
and malfeasance have set the standard in high places and in low,
nothing at all of any moment has occurred. Politicians are occupied
with the usual business of bribes and taxes; the *beau monde* divert
themselves at mindless and extravagant entertainments – Farinelli's
warbling and the auctions of Christopher Cock; and, epitomizing the
general confusion of values, Theophilus Cibber aspires to be "Prime
Minister Theatrical" while his father attempts to cram adulterated
Shakespeare down the throats of the Town. First, however, as the
King's own Poet Laureate, he officially ushers in the New Year with a
stirring ode:

> This is a Day, in Days of Yore,
> Our Fathers never saw before:
> This is a Day, 'tis one to ten,
> Our Sons will never see again.
> > Then sing the Day,
> > And sing the Song,
> > And thus be merry
> > All Day long.

Having revived the mode of personal satire associated with Athenian
"old Comedy," Fielding, as it were, brought all these celebrities on
stage *in propria persona*, presumably instructing his actors to mimic
by their manner, attitudes, and dress the particular real-life figures
whom he had marked out for ridicule. Transparent in the character of
Ground-Ivy was Colley Cibber; his son Theophilus was no less obvious
as the blustering Pistol, a role he made famous; Christopher Cock, the
fashionable auctioneer, became by a simple change of gender Mr. Hen,
played by the transvestite, Charlotte Charke. Mrs. Charke, indeed, had
another part to play: though the published cast list gives no hint of
this particular indecency, the dramatic historian John Mottley later
declared that Cibber should not be blamed for vilifying Fielding in the
Apology, for in *The Historical Register* Cibber's "own Character was
brought upon [the stage] in a very ridiculous Light, opening the Play
with a *New Years Day* Ode, and, what was shocking to every one who
had the least Sense of Decency or good Manners, the Part was performed
by his own Daughter."[377]

In the *Apology*, with metaphors typically mixed, Cibber recalled this
season, when Fielding "like another *Erostratus* set Fire to his Stage, by
writing up to an Act of Parliament to demolish it."[378] What inflamed

Walpole most was the jesting Fielding indulged in at his own and his brother's expense. The political scenes that open and close Medley's farcical annals are set discreetly in Corsica, "being at present the chief Scene of Politicks of all *Europe*"; Fielding's players being "Servants" of King Theodore could not be supposed to have any interest in the politics of that other island, Britain. No one at the Little Haymarket was dim enough, however, not to see that the Second Politician, who opens the dialogue by exposing his ignorance of "foreign Affairs," was the very figure of Horatio Walpole, famed in the Opposition press for his bungling as Britain's ambassador abroad. Gibing at the ambassador in *The Craftsman* (28 May 1737), Fielding gloated that he had "made Him the Laughing-stock of crouded Audiences, for several Weeks together." But it was Horatio's powerful brother Robert who felt the full force of Fielding's ridicule. In the final scene of Medley's emblematical drama, he is brought on stage as Quidam, who bribes the disgruntled Patriots out of opposition and, taking up his fiddle, makes them dance to his tune. "Perhaps," Medley hints to Sourwit, "there may be something intended by this Dance which you don't take." To which the critic replies, "Ay; what prithee?"

> Sir, every one of these Patriots have a Hole in their Pockets, as Mr. *Quidam* the Fiddler there knows, so that he intends to make them dance till all the Money is fall'n through, which he will pick up again, and so not lose one Half-penny by his Generosity; so far from it, that he will get his Wine for nothing, and the poor People, alas! out of their own Pockets, pay the whole Reckoning.

Not content with mocking the minister in this "DUMB DANCING SHEW," as one of the Gazetteers called it,[379] Fielding, in a curious device of mutual mortification, soon made Walpole share with himself the role of Pillage, the shame-faced protagonist of the bold farce that replaced *Fatal Curiosity* as companion piece to *The Historical Register* on 13 April.[380] Under its original title ("a very short and merry Tragedy, call'd The DAMNATION of EURIDICE")[381] *Eurydice Hiss'd, or, A Word to the Wise* was ready for production a month earlier, on 15 March, Fielding having dashed it off while the humiliating event that occasioned it was fresh in mind. It opened, according to the *Daily Advertiser*, to "the highest Applause," and proved popular enough to be staged a further twenty times during the few weeks that remained in Fielding's career as dramatist and theatrical manager.

Eurydice Hiss'd is one of the oddest works Fielding wrote; for in it he applies to himself – rather than to Cibber or his son, as one would expect – a favorite satiric analogy between the political and theatrical worlds. At one level Pillage is Henry Fielding, who as playwright has justly suffered the consequences of forsaking the Muse that bore him

Pasquin in order to flirt with her rival, inspirer of the inane productions at Drury Lane; and who as manager has behaved like the "Stage Tyrants" he despises – putting off with empty promises the actors who solicit parts at his levee and abusing the public by charging higher prices for an insubstantial diet of farces. A puzzling exercise in self-ridicule, the public penance to which Fielding subjects himself in the play is all the more extraordinary when we see that Pillage also stands for Sir Robert Walpole and his damned farce for Walpole's defeat over the Excise Bill in 1733. This political dimension of the play was apparent to the Prince of Wales, now nominal head of the Opposition, and the Earl of Egmont, both of whom attended the performance on 18 April: in his Diary Egmont noted that the farce was obviously "an allegory on the loss of the Excise Bill. The whole was a Satire on Sir Robert Walpole, and I observed that when any strong passages fell, the Prince, who was there, clapped, especially when in favour of liberty."[382]

What can have disposed Fielding to dramatize this demeaning equation of Walpole and himself? He was of course capable of laughing at his own expense – even of poking fun at the outlandish figure he made, with his burly physique and length of chin and nose. But Walpole at this period of Fielding's life was The Enemy, the despised corrupter of his country. To present himself in this way, as essentially indistinguishable from the minister, seems a penitential act of self-mortification. Can it be that the ill-fated production of *Eurydice* at Drury Lane represents not merely a brief flirtation with Fleetwood, but with the man who, like Quidam in *The Historical Register*, stood behind Fleetwood, "laughing behind the Scenes"? Perhaps not; but it is worth noting that twice during this period Fielding was moved to assure his friends that he was above taking Walpole's bribes. Though he had "been often promised" employment in the ministry "whenever he would write on that Side,"[383] he could not bring himself to prostitute his pen by joining forces with the likes of laureate Cibber and Walpole's Gazetteers – those "Scribblers, who for Hire/ Would write away their Country's Liberties."[384] Lyttelton and the rest of Cobham's cousinhood would attend gratefully to the exhortation of Pillage's Muse and perhaps dig a little deeper into their purses:

> And thou, or else thy Muse disclaims thy Pen,
> Would'st sooner starve, ay, even in Prison starve,
> Than vindicate Oppression for thy Bread,
> Or write down Liberty to gain thy own.

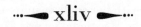

The day following the first night of the Haymarket program combining *The Historical Register* and *Eurydice Hiss'd*, the *Daily Gazetteer* (14 April 1737) published a satire against Lyttelton that suggests how close the association between Fielding and the "Boy Patriots" had become by this date. Imagined in conversation at the Bedford Head tavern, Lyttelton (or "Mr. Littledone," as the witty author has it) confesses that he "took the Hint" for the new journal *Common Sense* "from that ingenious Person, and my very good Friend, the Author of *Pasquin*." What is more, he is represented as the principal influence behind the satiric program at the Haymarket, which has become under his clandestine direction the vehicle for anti-ministerial propaganda. We hear him say:

> I have spoke to all the Writers for the Stage, of my Acquaintance, to put into their Plays all the strong Things they can think of against Courts and Ministers, and Places and Pensions, and all that; and they have hit my Humour to a Tittle; they have not spared them an Ace; the *Miller of Mansfield* and the *Historical Register*, have tickled them off ifaith.

Failing to convince his interlocutors of the goodness of his cause, he resorts at last to threatening them with the lash of Fielding's ridicule: "you may depend upon having some Stroaks of Satyr upon you, the next new Thing that is acted in the *Hay-Market*."

This feeble attack Fielding dismissed with a jest in the "Dedication to the Public" prefixed to the published versions of *The Historical Register* and *Eurydice Hiss'd* issued together on 12 May – not, it is worth noting, by Watts, the usual publisher of his plays who deserted him at the damning of *Eurydice*, but by Roberts. This Dedication, besides being a witty parody of the genre, has important implications for his biography. Written sometime in the latter part of April,[385] it reveals, for one thing, that Fielding had by then abandoned his plans to build a theatre and, encouraged by the success his productions had enjoyed over the past two seasons at the Little Haymarket, was instead circulating a public "Subscription for carrying on that Theatre, for beautifying and enlarging it, and procuring a better Company of Actors." No less significant, the Dedication stands as his most eloquent attack to date against the cancer of corruption in the body politic. In it Fielding dared to throw off the masks behind which he had been mocking the minister in the pages of *The Craftsman* and for the first time in his own voice named his Enemy:

But I am aware I shall be asked, who is this *Quidam*, that turns the Patriots into Ridicule, and bribes them out of their Honesty? Who but the Devil could act such a Part? Is not this the Light wherein he is every where described in Scripture, and the Writings of our best Divines? Gold hath been always his favourite Bait wherewith he fisheth for Sinners; and his laughing at the poor Wretches he seduceth, is as diabolical an Attribute as any. Indeed it is so plain who is meant by this *Quidam*, that he who maketh any wrong Application thereof might as well mistake the Name of *Thomas* for *John*, or old *Nick* for old *Bob*.

By the time this latest piece of impertinence was broadcast, the ministry's forbearance – never its most notable quality – had been strained to the breaking point. On 7 May the *Daily Gazetteer* published a letter from "An Adventurer in Politics" who states the ministerial view of the distinction between the political satire of *Pasquin* and that of *The Historical Register*: the former, though it "laid the Foundation for introducing POLITICKS on the Stage," could be tolerated because "the Author was general in his Satyr," exposing "the Practices of *Elections*, without coming so near, as to point *any Person* out"; in the latter, on the other hand, Fielding's aim is "to make a *Minister appear ridiculous to a People*." Indeed, the author continues, having "gone so far with Impunity" – in fact with the greatest applause – Fielding tried this "Vein further," and in *Eurydice Hiss'd* sank to insinuating

> to the *Vulgar*, who must ever be *led*, that *all Government is but a Farce (perhaps a damned one too)*. ... There are Things which, from the Good they dispense, ought to be Sacred; such are *Government* and *Religion*. No Society can subsist without 'em: To turn either into Ridicule, is to unloose the fundamental Pillars of Society, and shake it from its *Basis*.

Such was the higher, moral argument the government directed against "this *new* Method" of satire – which Fielding and his friends maintained was not new at all, but merely a timely revival in the Age of Walpole, which needed it so much, of the *vetus comoedia*, the "old Comedy" of Aristophanes. Behind this ministerial attitude of indignant altruism there lay a more pragmatic motive for the attack on Fielding. It had become obvious since the "great Success" of *Pasquin* that Fielding "was secretly *buoy'd up*, by some of the *greatest Wits* and *finest Gentlemen* of the Age, who ... have patronized a Method of Writing, themselves, were they in the Administration, would be the first to discountenance." In other words, as the laughing audiences at the Little Haymarket made evident, Fielding for some time had been regarded by the ministry as the all too effective instrument of the Opposition, and particularly of Chesterfield and Lyttelton. When he returned a month later to triumph over the broken poet, as the Bill to silence him was about to be enacted into law, the "Adventurer in Politics" drove home a lesson about the folly of playing too well on the wrong side in the game of party politics. It was a lesson Fielding learned too late:

> Alas! my Friend! Don't you see you are nothing but the *Cat's Paw*! No Office surely to be proud of! An Engine, supported by them, to bespatter with! Were you chosen by them for any other Reason but because your *licentious Satire* pleas'd their *Spleen*, I would allow the Choice, marking you out as an Object of Merit. But to be singled out for a *Squirt* to throw Filth about —[386]

Fielding twice replied to the attack in the *Daily Gazetteer* (7 May), which he appears to have attributed to some "Lord" in the ministry (John, Lord Hervey, Walpole's principal agent in the Upper House, is one likely candidate who comes to mind). A clear indication of the zeal with which Walpole set about the legal business of muzzling him is the fact that the first of Fielding's replies, signed "Pasquin" and appearing in *Common Sense* (Saturday, 21 May), was published the day after the Bill for licensing the stage had been admitted to the House of Commons; before he could again protest in print, this time anonymously in *The Craftsman* a week later (28 May), the Bill had already passed through the Lower House and was ready to be sent to the Lords. The first of the two essays in question is well known: "Pasquin's" defense of "Ridicule" as the "Fiery Trial, by which Truth is most certainly discovered from Imposture," and his expression of pride in being "patroniz'd by the Great, the Sensible, and the Witty in the Opposition."

The essay in *The Craftsman* (28 May) is less well known and, like all Fielding's contributions to that journal, it has only recently been attributed to him. It comprises a last, desperate attempt, by ridicule and moral suasion, to arouse the legislature to stop the passage of the Licensing Bill into law. Fielding reminds the public that once a censor has been placed over the stage and the number of theatres curtailed, "one of the great and original Ends of *dramatical Entertainments*" — that is, "to expose *Vice* and *Folly*, in all Ranks of People; especially *Those*, whose Riches or Power put Them out of the Reach and Cognizance of the *Law*" — will be forever lost; the consequence will be the encouragement of "*publick Vice*, by taking off this Check upon it, and discountenancing *publick Virtue*, at the same Time." It is, he observes,

> not to be supposed that *so great and near an Officer of the Crown*, who is to have absolute Power of LICENSING *Playhouses*, will ever suffer any Thing to be brought upon the *Stage*, which is not intirely

agreeable to the *Court*; much less such obnoxious Performances as the *Beggar's Opera, Pasquin*, the *historical Register*, and other Pieces of the like Kind.

···➡ **xlv** ◄···

As he wrote these words Fielding was aware that, unlike recent attempts to put the stage under restraint, this Bill had an excellent chance of succeeding because, conveniently for Walpole, a new piece of evidence had been introduced into the debate which served the government's purposes completely. What Walpole sought of course was the authority to suppress just such performances as *The Beggar's Opera, Pasquin*, and *The Historical Register*, performances all the more "obnoxious" because in them (to apply Dryden's analogy between the effects of a skillful satire and Jack Ketch's knack at hanging a man) the victim of ridicule is made to die sweetly. Such satires, having merit as art, are unlikely to rouse a legislature to abrogate what had come to be regarded as a basic liberty – the liberty of the stage. The instrument Walpole needed to achieve this end was precisely the sort of play he was now presented with by Henry Giffard, manager at Lincoln's Inn Fields – a farce of outrageous indecency not only larded with Jacobite sentiments, but exposing both the King's ministers and the Royal Family to gross abuse. This farce, now notorious in the annals of British theatre and British law, was *The Golden Rump*.

Though no copy of this work survives, it was inspired by a rude allegory in *Common Sense* (19 and 26 March 1737) rumored to be the work of the rabid Jacobite, Dr. William King of Oxford.[387] Its subject and manner may be inferred from the print published on 7 May,[388] entitled *The Festival of the Golden Rump* and embellished with the motto "*Rumpatur, quisquis, Rumpitur invidia*" (see Plate 23). Fielding's *Craftsman* essay of 28 May is the earliest published reference to this farce, and he was also first to surmise that, in a stratagem worthy of Machiavelli, Walpole himself had surreptitiously commissioned the piece in order to shock the legislature into licensing the stage. After reporting that the play "was actually in Rehearsal, at one of our Theatres" until suppressed by Walpole, who "is determined to take ample Vengeance upon all *such audacious Authors* and *Players*, by putting an effectual Restraint upon the Stage," Fielding accused the minister of basing his entire case for the Licensing Act on this "*obscure Piece*, which was never exhibited upon the Stage, and pretended to be suppress'd; so that it may have been written on Purpose, for aught we know, with such a particular Design."

The story of *The Golden Rump* and its role in precipitating the Licensing Act has often been told,[389] with responsibility for its authorship being assigned either to Fielding or to some hireling of Walpole's. Horace Walpole, who claimed to have found a copy of the farce among his father's papers, was convinced Fielding wrote it[390] — an opinion in which he was supported by two of Fielding's bitterest antagonists: "Marforio" in *An Historical View of the Principles, Characters, Persons, &c. of the Political Writers in Great Britain* (1740), and the author of the *London Evening Post* (1–3 August 1749). This, however, is not the opinion of several other writers who are likely to have known the circumstances. Lord Hervey, for instance, would have relished an opportunity to record Fielding's authorship of this "scurrilous" work, but he makes no reference to him in discussing it; nor does Sir Robert Walpole's biographer, William Coxe.[391] Perhaps less impressive is the further negative evidence of James Ralph, who ignores the question of its authorship:[392] in 1737 Ralph was probably no longer Fielding's partner at the Little Haymarket, but he would not wish to make any revelations that might embarrass a friend.

On the evidence, however, the notion that Fielding wrote *The Golden Rump* is so improbable it is hard to see how anyone could seriously credit it. In the first place, the farce was said to be fraught with Jacobitical propaganda, and Jacobitism was obnoxious to Fielding. In the second place, if he had written such a satire, he would not have carried it to Giffard at Lincoln's Inn Fields when he had his own company of comedians at the Haymarket, where he continued to stage rude satires on the most sensitive political subjects. Other contemporary sources are no doubt nearer the truth when they support the view Fielding himself hinted at in *The Craftsman* (28 May): namely, that the play was written at Walpole's instance in order that he might "discover" it and, by exposing it to an outraged King and legislature, provoke them to censor the stage.[393] What actually happened in the infamous affair of *The Golden Rump* is probably close to the following account by Thomas Davies, generally a dependable witness and one who in May 1737 was an actor in Fielding's company. Davies begins by recalling the financial difficulties Giffard was experiencing at Lincoln's Inn Fields:

> During this distress and anxiety of mind, a certain unknown writer brought to him a dramatic piece, called The Golden Rump. This was no less than a most outrageous satire against the king, the royal family, and many of the highest and most respected persons in the kingdom.
>
> Giffard imagined that this piece would excite the curiosity of the public ... but he had likewise the discernment to know, that the

author of The Golden Rump had wantonly exceeded every limit of
decency and loyalty, and put to defiance the laws of the land. The
piece was replete with Jacobite principles, at a time when they were
much more offensive to the people than the persons of Jacobites.
Upon reflection, Mr. Giffard thought it would be most honourable to
make a merit of laying this farce before the minister. He waited upon
Sir Robert Walpole; he acquainted him with his unhappy situation;
he was reduced, he said, to the necessity of acting a dramatic piece,
which would certainly fill his house, at a time when he was greatly
distressed; but, though he wished to mend his fortune, he could not
have any inclination to act against his conscience; for he abhorred
the principles and the slander with which it abounded. Sir Robert
desired he would leave the MS. with him, and promised to make no
use of it that should be to his disadvantage. The minister had no
sooner perused this curious drama, than he formed the plan of
limiting the number of theatres, and of suffering no plays, farces, or
any entertainment of the stage, to be acted without the permission
of a person appointed to license them.

Sir Robert was the best-natured gentleman that ever lived; but he
had received such provocations from Mr. Fielding, in his plays and
farces, just before that time, acted at the little theatre in the Haymarket, that he was not displeased to have it in his power to stop
the current of stage abuse against himself, which then ran very high.

Fielding, in his Eurydice Hissed, had brought the minister upon
the theatre in a levee-scene; and in his Historical Register, he had
introduced him as a fiddler, playing on his fiddle, and followed by
the members of parliament, who danced to the tune played by the
Premier.

Sir Robert watched the proper time, when he imagined the House
of Commons would be in a humour to receive the impression which
he intended to make. He informed the House, that he had something
to lay before them of great importance, which he should submit
entirely to their wisdom and determination. He then desired that
The Golden Rump might be read. The infamous scurrility contained
in this piece alarmed every body. . . .

We are told, that Sir Robert Walpole presented Mr. Giffard with
the sum of one thousand pounds. Thus, at a very cheap rate, the
ministry gained the power of hindering the stage from speaking any
language that was displeasing to them: and it has been said, that the
whole matter was a contrivance of Sir Robert Walpole.[394]

Davies's account of the sequence of events that put a stop to Fielding's theatrical career is plausible – and in this matter we must settle
for such hearsay evidence: despite Horace Walpole's claim that he had

his father's copy of the manuscript in his possession, no such manuscript has ever been found; the play was never acted (except perhaps in the rehearsal to which Fielding refers); nor was it ever printed. That Walpole himself caused the farce to be written in order to clinch his design to control the stage is not unlikely; but it is also possible that the minister was the eager victim, rather than the perpetrator, of such a stratagem. In the *Daily Advertiser* for 19 February 1736/7 Fielding took care to deny the rumor that his proposal to erect a new theatre was really only a device of rival managers "to revive the Playhouse Bill"; when, nearly a hundred years after the event, the subject was raised before a Select Committee of the House of Commons, the theatrical historian John Payne Collier reported:

> some have supposed [*The Golden Rump*] to have been a contrivance by certain parties to produce such an impression on the mind of the Minister of the day, as to the inconvenience of allowing an unrestrained state of the drama, that he would introduce the Act of 1737, which he did introduce accordingly."[395]

<h2 style="text-align:center">xlvi</h2>

Whoever devised it, the contrivance worked. Drafted in part by Henry Pelham and George Bubb Dodington, two of Walpole's creatures who would in turn, ironically enough, become Fielding's patrons, the Bill to explain and amend the Act of 12 Anne relating to common players of interludes was guided by Pelham through the Lower House in little more than a week's time and on 1 June was carried by him to the Lords, where it received a third and final reading on 6 June. Scarcely a voice was raised against it in either House – except for Pulteney's feeble opposition in the Commons and in the Lords the eloquent protest of Fielding's patron, Chesterfield, "who made," as Lord Hervey recalled admiringly, "one of the most lively and ingenious speeches against it I ever heard in Parliament, full of wit, of the genteelest satire, and in the most polished, classical style that the Petronius of any time ever wrote."[396] Chesterfield declared:

> This Bill is not only an encroachment on liberty, but it is likewise an encroachment on property. Wit, my lords, is a sort of property: the property of those who have it, and too often the only property they have to depend on. It is indeed but a precarious dependence.

Hoping to stir in his noble audience memories of the minister's odious proposals of 1733, Chesterfield continued: "by this Bill wit is to be delivered out to the public by retail, it is to be excised, my lords."[397] Chesterfield alone could not stem the tide, however, and on 21 June the Theatrical Licensing Act, having received the Royal Assent, passed into law. It would remain law for 230 years, from time to time invoked by other governments to stop productions of plays by Ibsen and Shaw, Samuel Beckett and Tennessee Williams.[398]

It must be said that Fielding had courted martyrdom recklessly throughout this his final season at the Little Haymarket. Disdaining every sign of mounting ministerial ire, he produced play after play in which Walpole and his courtiers – even the King himself – were turned into laughing stocks. Of these productions we have noticed such obvious instances as *A Rehearsal of Kings*, *The Historical Register*, and *Eurydice Hiss'd*, not forgetting the revivals of *Pasquin*. When *Pasquin* played on 4 May, the audience was also treated to an afterpiece entitled *Fame*, by James Lacy, one of Fielding's comedians whose benefit it was. No copy of this work survives, but from the advertisements it is easy to guess the kind of thing it was: "A new Satyrical, Allegorical, Political, Philosophical Farce," "the Sentiments grand, full of Patriotism."[399] As Fielding's letter to *The Craftsman* on April Fool's Day 1738 makes clear, even such an apparently innocuous piece as Henry Carey's *The Dragon of Wantley*, which ran for four nights at the Haymarket this season (16–19 May), was more than the simple burlesque of opera it seems: for in the Dragon – played by "Sig. Furioso (his other Name to be conceal'd)" – audiences discovered Leviathan himself, the marauding Prime Minister who lays waste the land. Politics were very much the theme on 25 April, when to the usual double bill of *The Historical Register* and *Eurydice Hiss'd* was added a third piece, entitled *The Female Free Mason* ("In which the whole Art and Mystery of Free-Masonry is delineated") – all for the benefit of William Hatchett, one of the victims of the Opposition's theatrical war against Walpole: it was Hatchett[400] whose politically pointed drama, *The Fall of Mortimer*, had in 1731 goaded the ministry into closing the Little Haymarket and prosecuting the players.

Nothing much is known about three other plays, *Sir Peevy Pet* (17 March), *The Lordly Husband* (16 May), and *The Sailor's Opera* (3, 5, 9, and 11 May). But there can be no doubt of the brazenness of the affront Fielding intended the Establishment in the production he advertised on Wednesday, 25 May, for performance the following Monday, 31 May – at the very moment when the minister's Bill to restrain the theatres was being hurried through Parliament. As announced in the *Daily Advertiser*, the two plays in question were:

MACHEATH turn'd PYRATE: or, POLLY in INDIA. An Opera. Very much taken, if not improv'd from the famous Sequel of the late

celebrated Mr. Gay, with a new Prologue proper to the Occasion.
And after the Run of that, the Town will be entertain'd with a new
Farce of two Acts, call'd The KING and TITI: or, The MEDLARS.
Taken from the History of King Titi. Originally written in French,
and lately translated into English.

Fielding was proposing to stage an "improv'd" version of the notorious
sequel to Gay's *Beggar's Opera*, *Polly*, which the government had
suppressed in 1729. Still more outrageous was the next scheduled
production; for *The King and Titi*, as readers of the "Royal Allegory"
emphasized in the English translation of 1736 would know,[401] was the
story of George II's unfatherly abuse of his popular son Prince Frederick, figurehead of the Opposition.

No one will wonder that these plays, though *Macheath twin'd Pyrate*
was scheduled for performance before the Theatre Bill reached the
House of Lords, were never acted. Exercising the sort of discretion
Walpole had recently rewarded in Giffard, John Potter, as we learn
from his correspondence with the Duke of Grafton on 7 January 1737/8,
hastened to the Lord Chamberlain "In Order to prevent what was
Intended to Be Represented In my theatre may last," being opposed
"to the utmost of my Power against all scandall & defamation" – and
being also assured that from the Duke and Sir Robert "I should
with the Rest of mankind find due Incurragement to bear an honnest
mind."[402] Potter prevented the performance of these plays simply by
rendering his theatre unusable: he dismantled the sets, took down the
decorations, and crammed the house full of lumber, bricks, and lime
by the cartload.[403]

Fielding's final production as manager at the Little Haymarket took
place, then, on Monday, 23 May, some weeks earlier than the new
law would make necessary. Attended by the Duchess Dowager of
Marlborough,[404] relict of Fielding's great hero and a virulent enemy of
Walpole, the night's entertainment consisted of the now familiar double
bill of *The Historical Register* and *Eurydice Hiss'd*, staged for the benefit
of Eliza Haywood, who played Mrs. Screen in the main piece and the
author's Muse in the farce. Considering the gratuitous interpolation
Mrs. Haywood made some years later in her novel, *The History of Betsy
Thoughtless* (1751), this latter bit of casting was ironic. She cherished
no very grateful memories of her employer, or of his final season at the
Haymarket, "then known by the name of F[ieldin]g's scandal-shop;
because," she explained,

> he frequently exhibited there certain drolls, or more properly, invec-
> tives against the ministry: in doing which it appears extremely
> probable, that he had two views; the one to get money, which he
> very much wanted, from such as delighted in low humour, and could

not distinguish true satire from scurrility; and the other, in the hope of having some post given him, but those whom he had abused, in order to silence his dramatic talent.

(I. 76–7)

Colley Cibber – whose provocation for the slur is more apparent – repaid Fielding in much the same coin in his famous *Apology*, calling him, among other names, a "broken Wit" whose indecent abuse of the stage was justly punished by a long-suffering ministry.

····◆ xlvii ◆····

What, finally, should be a more disinterested verdict on Fielding's theatrical career, which ended so abruptly in May 1737? As a dramatist he had the virtues of an irrepressible energy and fertility of invention: in a career that began with *Love in Several Masques* when he was a mere boy of twenty, but which did not get under way in earnest until two years later in 1730, he wrote more plays, and in a greater variety of the comic modes, than any other playwright of his era. In ten years he produced eight regular five-act comedies: *Love in Several Masques*, *The Temple Beau*, *Rape upon Rape* (or *The Coffee-House Politician*), *The Modern Husband*, *The Miser*, *The Universal Gallant*, *The Wedding Day*, and *The Fathers* – though the latter two were not staged until later. This, the classic form of his favorites Congreve and Farquhar, Jonson and Molière, was what he aspired unsuccessfully to master. Even in this form, however, he was not merely prolific, but daring as an innovator, in *Rape upon Rape* and especially *The Modern Husband* devising a new kind of "heroic" comedy – comedy with an earnest moral purpose – that deserves a place in the repertory. *The Miser*, of course, the public was better prepared for; it held the stage for years to come.

But Fielding is best remembered for the numerous "irregular" plays he wrote during the eight years from 1730 to 1737 – no fewer, indeed, than eighteen of them (or, if we count the revised versions of *The Author's Farce*, *Tom Thumb*, and *The Welsh Opera*, twenty-one) – ranging in scope from the five-act structure of *Pasquin*, down through three-act pieces such as *The Author's Farce*, *The Tragedy of Tragedies*, *The Letter Writers*, *The Grub-Street Opera*, *Don Quixote in England*, and *The Historical Register*, and the two-act ballad opera *The Intriguing Chambermaid*, to the one-acters, including *The Lottery*, *The Old Debauchees*, *The Covent-Garden Tragedy*, *The Mock Doctor*, *Deborah*, *The Virgin Unmasked*, *Tumble-Down Dick*, *Eurydice*, *Eurydice Hiss'd*, and

Miss Lucy in Town (the latter not being staged until 1743). No less impressive than the number of these productions is their variety. In them Fielding explored the potential of virtually every conceivable mode of comedy. The farce and the ballad opera were his staple fare; we often forget that he was among the most productive and entertaining song writers of his day. But he also experimented in other forms – a "live" puppet show (*The Author's Farce*), the comedy of the trans-actions of a year (*The Historical Register*), a sort of universal drama distilling the quintessential stuff of the contrasting genres of comedy and tragedy (*Pasquin*) – and of course burlesques and parodies aplenty, of bombast tragedies and Italian opera and Rich's harlequinades. To be sure, he learned much from *The Rehearsal* and *The Beggar's Opera*; but few dramatists in the history of English theatre can be said to equal Fielding in the range, variety, and daring of his formal experimentation. Prominent among these experiments was his revival of the "old Com-edy" – satire of a highly personal, highly topical, and often highly political cast, but disguised by expressionistic devices such as emblem-atical characters and allegorical situations.

Sometimes the gamble failed. But on the whole, as Professor Hume concludes, Fielding's achievement was extraordinary:

> Any assessment of Fielding's theatrical career must start with the realization that he was enormously and conspicuously successful. He had a few failures and rough times, but no other English playwright of the eighteenth century was so dominant in his own time, so frequently successful, or so well paid for his efforts.[405]

This surprising assertion, as it must seem to those who seldom read Fielding's plays and seldom if ever have an opportunity to see them performed, is confirmed by reference to the lists of performances at the London theatres during his last two spectacularly successful seasons at the Little Haymarket. In the single season of 1735–6, for instance, no fewer than ten of his plays were produced – more than Cibber, more even than Shakespeare. In the space of three days that season an avid theatre-goer might have attended *nine* separate performances of *seven* of Fielding's plays: on Tuesday, 27 April 1736, there was the fortieth day of *Pasquin* at the Haymarket, while at Goodman's Fields the program consisted of revivals of *The Temple Beau* and *The Mock Doctor* – the latter also being staged that day at York Buildings; on 28 April *The Lottery* played at Goodman's Fields; and on 29 April, besides *Pasquin* and *Tumble-Down Dick* at the Haymarket, there was *The Miser* to be seen at Goodman's Fields as well as *The Virgin Unmasked* at Drury Lane. What other dramatist of any period could equal such popularity? But perhaps a better measure of Fielding's success as a playwright is the steadiness with which his most popular plays (which is not necessarily to say his best) held the stage for years to come – among them such perennial favorites as *The Miser*, *The Mock Doctor*, *The Lottery*, *The Virgin Unmasked*, *The Intriguing Chambermaid*, and *The Tragedy of Tragedies*.

As a manager, too, Fielding deserves credit for bold policies that, for a time at least, breathed new life into the theatre, drawing audiences away from the mindless entertainments at the rival houses – from the castrati that ravished noble ears and the mimes and tumblers and rope-dancers that dazzled their eyes. Professor Scouten has succinctly summarized Fielding's accomplishments as "the Great Mogul"[406] – accomplishments, we should remember, achieved at the smallest and worst of the London theatres with a barely competent troupe of actors. Against such odds he succeeded in part of course by being a "trouble-maker"; for two seasons he staged a series of witty, inventive satires that made laughing stocks of the Establishment. Furthermore, while the managers at Drury Lane and Covent Garden shied away from taking risks, Fielding at the Little Haymarket produced a succession of new plays, not only his own successful satires, but a dozen or so other pieces, including Henry Carey's *Dragon of Wantley* and Lillo's *Fatal Curiosity*, the work that some critics regard as the finest tragedy of the century. Scouten observes, moreover, that as a producer of plays Fielding's experiments "were numerous and lively": he used the curtain between acts and sometimes between scenes; he improved lighting effects; he revived the induction scene of the rehearsal play; he not only staged an unusually large number of new plays, but limited his productions generally to very recent drama. Particularly striking was his innovation of offering two new plays in the same night. In short, Scouten advises, "Students of living drama, plays as they are actually produced on the stage, should make a careful examination of Fielding's programs, especially in his last season at the New Haymarket, the spring of 1737."

But for all this wit and energy that revitalized the stage, Fielding broke too many windows and pulled down too many idols. The minister, he ought to have known, was bound to silence him, as he most effectually did at a time when Fielding had only just completed his apprenticeship in the theatre and was dreaming of greater triumphs to come – other plays to be written and glittering new productions to be mounted in a refurbished theatre with a better company of actors. As Murphy reports, Fielding used to say "he left off writing for the stage when he ought to have begun." That the satiric and theatrical skills he had acquired by his thirtieth year were considerable may be judged from the intensity of Walpole's ire, who was goaded into applying the most extreme methods of silencing him – not only filling his theatre with bricks and lumber, but bringing down on him the full weight of Parliament. For no one either in or out of the government doubted that, whatever other convenient uses the minister might put it to, the Theatrical Licensing Act was instituted to put a stop to Fielding's play-writing. As James Harris understood, reflecting back on the uproarious seasons of *Pasquin* and *The Historical Register*, it was, however unwelcome, one of the most extraordinary tributes any dramatist has been paid:

> How those Performances were received, those who saw them, may well remember. Never were houses so crowded, never applause so universal, nor the same Peices so often repeated without interruption, or discontinuance. Tis enough to say that such was ye force of his comic humour and poignancy, that those in power in order to restrain him, thought proper by a Law to restrain the Stage in ye general, bearing even by this act of Restriction the highest testimony to his abilities. The Legislature made a Law, in order to curb one private man.[407]

····◄ xlviii ►····

The theatre now permanently closed against him, Fielding had to consider other means of maintaining his wife and infant daughter. It is possible, indeed, that his family was increasing – though this was not the year (as his biographers have asserted) of his daughter Harriet's birth. Among the unsubstantiated declarations of the devoted Fielding scholar J. Paul de Castro is the following: "As a fact [Fielding] had at least five children by his first wife – Charlotte, Harriott, Penelope, Katherine and Henry."[408] Charlotte we have accounted for. Henry, Fielding's only son of this marriage, was born in 1741–2.[409] "Harriet," as Fielding affectionately called his daughter whose given names were Henrietta Eleanor, was born in 1743.[410] Without firmer evidence than we have, however – and the search of registers has been extensive – the other two children De Castro claimed for the marriage remain questionable. Penelope and Katherine are names the Fieldings might well have chosen for their daughters: Charlotte, we recall, had a sister named Catherine and probably another named Mary Penelope; and Katherine (or Catharine) was the name of both Fielding's great-aunt, Mrs. Cottington, and his eldest sister. A child, "Penelope Feilding," was buried at St. Clement Danes on 6 February 1739/40 at a time when Henry and Charlotte were living in that parish. Another child, "Catharine Fielding ," said to be of "St. Margaret's, Westminster, was buried at St. Martin-in-the-Fields on 11 April 1743[411] – the Fielding's parish during their residence at Spring Garden, and the church in which

Charlotte's mother, her daughter, and her son, as well as Charlotte herself, were buried. Since De Castro stated that the dates on which Penelope, Katherine, and Henry died were "unknown" to him, he had presumably seen records (unknown to us) of the births of these three children which were unambiguous enough to justify the declaration that they were Fielding's offspring. Penelope and Katherine would therefore be Fielding's second and third children, the former born sometime during the period 1737–9, the latter during the period 1738–40.

But to return to the subject of Fielding's circumstances in the latter half of 1737. Doubtless supported by his friends in Opposition in whose behalf he had suffered the consequences of Walpole's ire, Fielding appears to have relieved his otherwise hopeless financial prospects by contributing more frequently, and more vigorously, to *The Craftsman*.[412] Indeed, one of his contributions so infuriated the ministry that it took steps to suppress the journal and to punish everyone connected with it from the editor Amhurst down to the printer's devil. During 1737 the following numbers of *The Craftsman* are probably Fielding's work: No. 569 (28 May), protesting the Bill to license the theatres; No. 571 (11 June), an allegorical dream-vision anatomizing corruption in the body politic; No. 574 (2 July), signed "C.C.*P.L.*" – i.e., "Colley Cibber, *Poet Laureate*" – who offers himself as the one best qualified to execute the Lord Chamberlain's new powers of censorship; No. 588 (15 October), signed "Philomath," a virtuoso who, writing on 16 August from the headquarters of the Royal Society, proposes a scheme for replacing the bench of bishops with puppets; No. 589 (22 October), anticipating the "Gypsy Episode" in *Tom Jones* by contrasting the enlightened government of ancient Egypt with England's present Establishment; and No. 591 (5 November), signed "Anglo-Germanicus," who in a dream-vision dated 30 October compares the oppressive policies of the recently executed Turkish minister to those Walpole implements with impunity. During this same year it is also likely that Fielding contributed to *The Craftsman* three other essays: No. 565 (30 April), No. 567 (14 May), and No. 586 (1 October). The first two are hilarious (and typically outrageous) companion pieces – No. 565 proposing a scheme for prohibiting the use of all liquors except water and for laying a tax on urine, No. 567 (signed "R. Dudley") proposing to amend the tax on urine and to substitute in its stead an impost on water; No. 586 is a further satire on corruption in Walpole's England.[413]

Of these nine essays, six were written after Fielding was shut out of the Little Haymarket. Further emphasized by the contributions he appears to have made to the *Universal Spectator* in the autumn, the accelerated pace of this journalism suggests that he was turning hackney author now in earnest. Though his satires were raising the reputation of *The Craftsman* for wit, one of them in particular goaded the ministry into taking swift punitive action against the paper.

In his essay of 28 May, Fielding warned that the Lord Chamberlain might not confine himself merely to preventing "such obnoxious Performances as the *Beggar's Opera, Pasquin,* the *historical Register,* and Pieces of the like Kind. He may likewise prohibit the Representation of *old Plays,* which breathe the same factious Spirit." Now in *The Craftsman* (2 July) – hilariously impersonating Cibber, who proposes himself for the job of "Supervisor of all Plays" under the Lord Chamberlain – Fielding demonstrates how, considering the government's knack at finding satires against itself in the most innocent places, many of the classic works in repertory were eligible for inclusion in "an *Index expurgatorius*" and should by no means be performed without first being subjected to "considerable Castrations and Amendments." This was, of course, precisely the sort of operation at which Cibber excelled. First among the classics he would alter in this way is Shakespeare's *King John*; but the list lengthens as he warms to his task: Shakespeare's *Richard II* and *2 Henry IV*, Jonson's *Sejanus*, Denham's *Sophy*, Dryden's *All for Love*, Lee's *Alexander*, Addison's *Cato*, and a good many others are tortured into seditious meanings. These are enough, declares Walpole's laureate,

> to shew that the *late Act, for restraining the Stage,* will not answer the Purpose intended by it, unless there be some Regulation of *old Plays,* as well as *new ones*; and that Nobody, without Vanity, is fitter for this Office than *Myself.* It will be a pretty Augmentation to *That,* which I now enjoy.

These strokes cut too near the bone. On 7 July one of Walpole's Gazetteers, purple with indignation, denounced the paper as "the greatest Insult and most notorious Abuse that was ever offer'd to the supreme Power or chief Magistrate of any Country, in any Age or Nation." On the night of 13 July the King's messengers raided the house of Amhurst's printer, Henry Haines. They seized Haines, as well as everyone else in his establishment, including the compositors, pressmen, and printer's devil, and they scoured the house from top to bottom, confiscating Haines's papers and ledgers. Amhurst was arrested and confined for ten days, at last having to resort to a writ of *habeas corpus* to regain his liberty. Haines was not so lucky: he was sentenced to twelve months in prison, fined £200, and required to raise £2,000 surety for his good behavior for seven years. Unable to raise the money, he languished in jail for more than two years.[414] The author of the offending paper was never identified, though at first suspicion naturally fell on Amhurst.[415] Amhurst, however, knew he was himself safe, and he was a steady, close-mouthed man who protected his friends. Appropriately, it is just at this period, in a letter to the *Daily Gazetteer* (12 October 1737), that we catch our only glimpse of his intimacy with Fielding; for it was almost certainly Fielding whose satire, having caused the restraint of the stage, had thus jeopardized the liberty of the press.

Throughout the summer, while Walpole's messengers kept Amhurst and his printers under surveillance, Fielding prudently refrained from submitting further contributions to *The Craftsman*. Probably, however, his witty, rather milder pieces appeared from time to time in the *Universal Spectator*[416] – as in the case of the ardent physiognomist "Proteus Dimplecheek" (8 October 1737), who, eager to put a stop to all unprofitable individuality of expression, offers an "entire new Project for the better *Government of the Face*." Among the students who would profit most from the curriculum of this Academy was Fielding himself, who, his career in the theatre ended, had determined to follow the example of his kinsmen the Goulds and become a lawyer:

> The young Gentlemen of the *Inns of Court* [proceeds Dimplecheek] may by my System be soon compleated in the Knowledge of all the *Quirks* of the Face, and with great Expedition attain the smooth, smiling pleasant Aspect of a *Chancery Pleader*, the warm, angry, positive Countenance of a *King's-Bench Council*; or the sage, demure, testy forgetful Visage of a *Common-Pleas Serjeant*.

⋯◆ xlix ◆⋯

In his thirtieth year Fielding became one of these "young Gentlemen of the *Inns of Court*" on 1 November 1737, when he was formally admitted to the Society of the Middle Temple as a "special" student. The entry in the Admissions book reads as follows:

1^e Nov^{ris} 1737

Henricus Fielding de East Stour in Com Dorset Ar [i.e., Armiger or "Esquire"] filius et haeres apparens Brig: Gen^{lis}: Edmundi Fielding admissus est in Societat Medij Templi Lond Specialiter et obligatur una cum &c.[417]

These words, denoting, as it were, Fielding's official "identity" in the autumn of 1737, are interesting on several counts. He continues, for instance, to claim the farm at East Stour as his home, and, as always, he takes pride in inscribing "Esquire" after his name. Curiously, he seems to have been unaware of his father's true rank in the Army, Edmund having been promoted from Brigadier to Major General two years earlier. Except for a brief visit home in March of this year,[418] Edmund had been out of the country, serving as military Governor of Jersey during most of 1736 and 1737, and may not have been much in his son's thoughts. But to readers of a psychoanalytic bent Fielding's slip may suggest an unconscious wish to diminish, by a degree, his father's dignity.

As a "special" student Fielding would be excused from the usual requirement that he continue in Commons for two years.[419] Furthermore, though the constitution of the Middle Temple stipulated that no more could be admitted to the Society than could be accommodated in chambers (allowing two members to a chamber), Fielding appears not to have complied with this regulation until much later – not indeed until the last possible moment enabling him to qualify for the Bar. The chamber he acquired, "situate in Pump Court No. 4 three pair of Stairs high," he obtained from a fellow Templar on 20 June 1740 for £2.0.0; on 28 November of the same year he relinquished it to one Thomas Potter for the same fee.[420] William Downing, Steward of the Middle Temple during this period, states that "Every Gentleman's chamber is his own free property and he disposeth thereof as he thinks fit, nor is it ever enquired whether the proprietor resides in them or no."[421] It seems to have been customary, however, to transfer the title to certain chambers, Fielding's at No. 4 Pump Court being one of them, whenever it became necessary for a member of the Society to qualify for the Bar. In short, Fielding may never actually have resided in the Middle Temple during the period of his legal studies; since he was not a bachelor, but a husband and father, it seems unlikely that he did.

The incongruity of England's leading comic playwright turning from the writing of licentious political farces to the business of preparing himself for the Bar was not lost on the hackney authors of the day. Particularly mordant was the sarcasm of *The Church Yard: A Satirical Poem* (May 1739), itself the surest testimony of the theme of *sic transit gloria poetarum* which the author finds confirmed in the fates of Cibber, Welsted, Theobald, "Namby Pamby" Philips – and Fielding:

> How hard on Poets, how severe their Fates,
> Since Death alike the Bard and Hero waits!
> F[ieldin]g must die, ah too untimely Doom!
> F[ieldin]g must die, like *Pasquin* or *Tom Thumb*.
> But as the Hydra of one Head depriv'd,
> With others not less terrible surviv'd,
> And from the recent Wound a new one sprung
> Hiss'd on, in spite of Fate, with venom'd Tongue;
> So he, tho' haply as a Poet dead,
> Shall teem more dreadful, with a Lawyer's Head,

Which all the former's Venom shall retain,
And hiss and spit to vex Mankind again.

(pp. 14–15)

However much others enjoyed the joke of Fielding's translation
from the Little Haymarket to Westminster Hall, at least one of his
contemporaries saw nothing preposterous in the change. In March 1738
there appeared *An Epistle to Mr. Fielding, on His Studying the Law*, in
which the poet, though he knows what Fielding's reaction will be
to the more ludicrous attributes of his new profession, prophetically
recognizes what the Town in general would scarcely have credited:
first, that Fielding's "vaster Mind" was capable of comprehending the
bewildering mysteries of the law, to a degree in fact matched by only
the ablest of his contemporaries in the profession; and second, that the
same "Rage" for justice, which heretofore had vented itself in satires
against Cibber and the Court, would find graver expression defending
the constitutional grounds of British liberty:

> Thus Thou abandon'st too the crampt up Stage,
> And more enriching Studies now Engage:
> Methinks, I see thy Satyre turn'd from Courts,
> And thy gay Muse deep bury'd in Reports.
> King *John* no more provokes thy dreaded Rage,
> Despis'd for *Magna Charta*'s Sacred Page:
> Th'unwieldy Law employs thy vaster Mind;
> The Subject Act where Treason is defin'd;
> The *Habeas Corpus*, and the *Bill of Rights*
> Are now preferr'd to past Poetick Flights.
>   Well judg'd Election! scarce the Sacred Nine
> Shall henceforth yield their Sons wherewith to dine;
> Wisely Thou leav'st the Great to blunder on,
> And live by Law, 'gainst which cou'd not be done.
> While Others feel the drowsy Pow'r of *Coke*,
> Thy Antidote shall be some well-tim'd Joke;
> And what to some shall seem *Herculean* Pain,
> Shall only be th' Amusement of thy Brain.
>   Canst thou behold the Statutes monstrous Size,
> And feel no ludicrous Emotion rise?
> Canst thou look forward to a Hundred Year,
> Compute their Growth, and yet the Smile forbear?
> Canst thou withold, to see our Sages weighty,
> Scarce know the Names of half of 'em at Eighty?
> Repeal'd are some, the Rest They dormant lie,
> As Daggers hanging o'er Posterity,
> Or Crocodiles, who sleep in Mud, but do not die.

> Say, if they're made, scarce hoping to be read,
> Will not *waste Paper* come into thy Head? ...
>   Accept the Hearty *Wish*, nor take it ill,
> Plainness is Elegance with pure Good Will.
> O! may the plural Fee so fertile rise,
> *Briareus'* Hands to take shall scarce suffice:
> May the vast Toil be paid with vast Reward;
> May Furry Honours crown the Muse-lost Bard:
> May to the *Orator* the *Member* follow,
> And yield at last a *Talbot* from *Apollo*.[422]

Never one to depreciate his abilities, Fielding, as he began his studies at the Middle Temple, probably did not aim so high as the Lord Chancellorship. But the poet's friendly wishes would be welcome.

From the latter part of the seventeenth century students at the Temple, though required to perform a number of exercises in order to qualify for the Bar, were left to their own devices to acquire the learning and skills necessary to their profession. As P. A. Smith observes, they were "left to the guidance of their own intelligence, with the help of private tuition, and of such published works as from time to time appeared, without the authority of any recognized board of instructors."[423] The experience of Dudley Ryder, who rose to great eminence in the profession, illuminates the realities of student life at the Middle Temple in the early eighteenth century. While preparing for the Bar in 1715–16, Ryder concentrated on the civil law and kept a diary of his activities. From this record, it is clear that he kept up a regular, often depressing, regime of heavy reading: he read such essential works as the commentaries and reports of Sir Edward Coke intensively, and to these added other such standard authorities as Dyer and Perkins.[424] He also belonged to a "club" that met afternoons at a favorite coffee-house to discuss questions of civil law. To judge from the regretful tone of his account, however, his own study-group could not compare with the elite little society, consisting of about nine members, to which his friend Bowes belonged. In Bowes's group, each member was assigned a topic which he was to research and discuss thoroughly. Ryder observed:

> They do it in the method of a commonplace by bringing in all the cases that are found in the law books on that head and proposing them to the company, who each of them in his turn gives his opinion of it till it comes back again to the person who first proposed it, who then gives a resolution and judgement upon it as it is in the books and arguments for it.

In addition, each week two members of Bowes's club were assigned to dispute a case "wherein there is some moot point not yet determined in the books."[425] As for the formal exercises which the students, dressed in their gowns, read before the Reader, who concluded by delivering his opinion on the point in question, this part of his education was in Ryder's opinion "all mere formality and signifies nothing."[426] Ryder unashamedly left the preparation of these exercises to an attorney whom he employed as tutor. Far more important were the regular trips to Westminster Hall, where the aspiring barristers observed the methods of the lawyers in presenting their cases and in arguing so as to impress a jury.[427]

Presumably Fielding followed roughly this same regime in preparing himself for the Bar as speedily as the urgency of his family's financial circumstances demanded. His friend Harris recorded that, having entered the Middle Temple, "he took to ye Study of ye Law with indefatigable industry," toiling at it, in fact, like a drudge.[428] Murphy's more colorful version of these years scarcely represents Fielding in an attitude of drudgery, but though he knew Fielding less well than Harris did – and knew him not at all during the period in question – Murphy's account is based on the recollections of Fielding's "intimates" and confirms Harris's essential point:

> His application [writes Murphy] when he was a student in the Temple, was remarkably intense; and though it happened that the early taste he had taken of pleasure would occasionally return upon him, and conspire with his spirits and vivacity to carry him into the wild enjoyments of the town, yet it was particular in him that, amidst all his dissipations, nothing could suppress the thirst he had for knowledge, and the delight he felt in reading; and this prevailed in him to such a degree, that he has been frequently known, by his intimates, to retire late at night from a tavern to his chambers, and there read, and make extracts from, the most abstruse authors, for several hours before he went to bed; so powerful were the vigour of his constitution and the activity of his mind.

Which were the "abstruse" authors whose works Fielding pored over and anatomized? From letters to his bookseller, John Nourse, we know he early acquired copies of three works that were considered indispensable in any comprehensive legal library of the period: the *Reports* of Sir Edward Coke (7 vols., 1738), described by the cataloguer of Fielding's library as the "best" edition; Anthony Fitzherbert's *Natura Brevium* with the commentary of Sir Matthew Hale (1730 edition), regarded as the most authoritative manual on the nature of briefs and legal procedures; and the first part of Sir George Croke's *Reports*, chiefly of cases in the King's Bench and Common Pleas (1669).[429] Though compiled long after the period with which we are now concerned, the *Sales Catalogue* of Fielding's library, as one might expect

of the library of a lawyer and a magistrate, lists scores of volumes on
legal subjects. Included among these are most of the volumes specified
by such authorities as Sir Matthew Hale and Sir Thomas Reeve as
recommended reading for students of the law. In Reeve's opinion, for
instance, the student who mastered Coke's commentary on Sir Thomas
Littleton's *Tenures* had possessed himself of the key to knowledge of
the law in general: without this, he admonished his nephew, "a common
sound lawyer can never be made"; to this, "all the faculties of the mind
must be applied."[430] The usual procedure for mastering such ponderous
works was one of abridging them, of making extracts (as Murphy's
sources report Fielding having done) suitable for preserving in a commonplace book. Fielding not only owned a copy of Coke upon Littleton
(*Catalogue*, item 268); as his frequent allusions to that work attest, he
mastered it. Two other works that Reeve especially recommended to
his nephew were Thomas Wood's *Institute of the Laws of England* and
the Abridgment of William Hawkins's *Pleas of the Crown*, both of which
Fielding studied intensively, not merely annotating them in the usual
way, but interleaving his copies with copious notes (*Catalogue*, items
276 and 102, respectively). On the other hand, Fielding's opinion of
two other works which Reeve considered useful – Giles Jacob's *Law
Dictionary* and *Attorney's Companion* – may be surmised from the ironic
references to their author in his works,[431] and from their notable absence
from his library. After such rudimentary preparations, Reeve's nephew
was advised to sample "the more useful statutes at large" in the order
Wood cites them and then to test the soundness of Wood's opinions by
comparing them with those expressed in the numerous volumes of
Reports, most particularly Salkeld's. Fielding may have followed a
similar method of study, and the presence in his library of nearly all
the Statutes at Large and all the Year-Books (*Catalogue*, items 103 and
105), together with the Reports not only of Salkeld (*Catalogue*, item
273), but, at a hasty count, some forty-five other voluminous commentators, suggests that his studies were assiduous, deep, and wide.

Reeve concluded his advice by citing other works found in Fielding's
library, but most especially Rolle's *Abridgment* (1668), the Preface to
which, by the celebrated Justice, Sir Matthew Hale, contained "the
best scheme for studying the law now extant." (See the *Catalogue*, item
117.) We may be sure that Fielding, too, attended closely to the advice
of Hale, whom he regarded, together with Coke and Hawkins, as the
chief authority on the law. In general, Hale's instructions, "Directed
to Young Students of the Common Law," are similar enough to Reeve's
that we need not rehearse them, except to note the emphasis again on
such authors as are represented in Fielding's library. Littleton, and
Coke's commentaries and reports, as well as Fitzherbert's *Natura
Brevium*, are, for example, among those that "will fit [the student] for

exercise, and enable him to improve himself by conversation and discourse with others, and enable him profitably to attend the courts of Westminster."[432]

Westminster Hall, which Fielding attended diligently during term time – that is, the four terms of Hilary, Easter, Trinity, and Michaelmas – was a bustling and variegated place at mid-century, an impression captured in the famous painting by Gravelot (Plate 25). In addition to the courts of King's Bench, Chancery, and Common Pleas, which were contained within low enclosures that left them exposed to the view of passersby and to the general din caused by so much miscellaneous business being conducted in the same room at the same time, Westminster Hall also contained the shops of tradesmen – booksellers, haberdashers, sempstresses, mathematical instrument makers.[433] Here, too, were displayed the standards taken at the battles won by Marlborough's forces. Despite such distractions, Fielding gained much practical knowledge of the law from observing the proceedings there. Thus in *Joseph Andrews* (I.ix) he archly recreates a typical mercenary scene of litigation:

> So have I seen, in the Hall of *Westminster*, where Serjeant *Bramble* hath been retained on the right Side, and Serjeant *Puzzle* on the left; the Balance of Opinion (so equal were their Fees) alternately incline to either Scale. Now *Bramble* throws in an Argument, and *Puzzle's* Scale strikes the Beam; again, *Bramble* shares the like Fate, over-powered by the Weight of *Puzzle*. Here *Bramble* hits, there *Puzzle* strikes; here one has you, there t'other has you; 'till at last all becomes one Scene of Confusion in the tortured Minds of the Hearers; equal Wagers are laid on the Success, and neither Judge nor Jury can possibly make any thing of the Matter; all Things are so enveloped by the careful Serjeants in Doubt and Obscurity.

Earlier, in a hopeful access of idealism concerning his new profession, it is probably Fielding who proposed in *The Craftsman* (17 June 1738) the erection of a sign for Westminster Hall in which its "Impartiality" would "be represented by a *Judge* holding a Ballance, with *Wealth* at one End, and *Honesty* at the other, and let the *latter* intirely weigh down the Scale."

However narrowly he observed the serious business of the law con-ducted at Westminster Hall he also regarded the place as one of the notable curiosities of the town. In *The Craftsman* (15 July 1738) it is probably Fielding again who writes that, having devoted much of the Whitsun holidays to showing some country cousins the sights of London, he at last took them to Westminster Hall, where term had begun and "the *Gentlemen of the long Robe*," the scarlet-gowned judges among them, were already in session. "I never omit shewing *this Place*," he declares; "not only as it is the most spacious Room in the World, but likewise the Repository for the glorious Trophies of our *late English Hero*. I am a very good *Ciceroni*, and have learnt to what Regiments many of the *Colours* and *Standards* belong'd, and by what *Corps* taken." As it happened, however, "one of the *reverend Sages of the Law*" passing by in his scarlet robe as Fielding was celebrating the victories of Marlborough's soldiers, his little cousin, who "had never before seen any Body in *Red*, except *military Persons*," inquired "with great Earnestness, if that was not one of the *Generals*, who beat the *French*, when *those Flags* were taken" – a remark so surprisingly apt it moved Fielding to a facetious consideration of "what Affinity there was between a *Judge* and a *General*," or, as we may put it in terms of his own family, between the professions of Judge Gould and General Fielding.

Besides his attendance at Westminster Hall and the intensive course of reading he pursued during his years as a student at the Temple, Fielding would also have been required to perform a total of nine "Exercises" in order to qualify for the Bar.[434] These, as both Dudley Ryder and Roger North observed, had dwindled into mere formalities by the time Fielding entered the Temple. Still, not everyone regarded these requirements quite as frivolously as Ryder did, who was surprised that "the other gentlemen" who participated with him in performing one of these exercises "seemed to have taken some pains upon it."[435] Clearly, it was possible to shine in the legal profession of Fielding's day without taking such pains; Ryder, who held the offices of Attorney General (1737) and Lord Chief Justice of the King's Bench (1754), rose to heights his more industrious colleagues never attained. Nevertheless, one suspects that Fielding acquired his deep erudition in legal matters the hard way. Professor Zirker's edition of the legal tracts makes it possible for the first time accurately to gauge the full extent of Fielding's command of the law; the impression is "that he was not merely competent but learned in his profession," that he had "an easy and confident command of the legal literature of his day and an assured comprehension of the legal principles and processes with which he dealt."[436] Zirker of course bases this appraisal on tracts such as Fielding's *Charge delivered to the Grand Jury* (1749), written more than ten years after the period with which we are at present concerned – tracts, in other words, which are the work of a seasoned veteran in the law, not of a tyro at the Temple.

Just how earnestly and well Fielding committed himself to the exercises of these student years is evident in what may be the earliest extant demonstration of his aptitude and abilities as a lawyer. Published in two parts anonymously in *The Craftsman* (8 and 22 April 1738), this is an essay on a subject which, above all others at this difficult juncture of his life, must have occupied Fielding's thoughts obsessively: the subject of the liberty of the press and the "modern Doctrine of Libels" according to which, by the arbitrary fiat of a ministry, such innocuous things as political farces, or a little free speaking in the forum of an Opposition periodical, may bring down on author and publisher the crushing weight of the Establishment:

> Some late uncommon Proceedings [observes the writer of these *Craftsman* papers], with Regard to *this Liberty*, which confirm'd the Jealousy of many Persons upon the *Restraint of the Stage*, that a *Restraint of the Press* would soon follow, make it necessary, before it is too late, to consider a little more minutely than hath hitherto been done, all the *former Acts of Parliament*, which did any Ways restrain it, and how they now stand; as well as the *arbitrary Proceedings*, upon that Head, in some Reigns, *without any Pretence of Law*.

The writer, who modestly disclaims "any great Knowledge in the *Common Law*," proceeds to examine all the statutes that relate to his subject, tracing "*this Affair* through the *several Acts*," and then making "Observations upon what hath been already mention'd." Methodically, he examines individual cases pertaining to the "*Doctrine of Libels*," his intention being to prove that through an unconstitutional application of legal precedents the oppressive arbitrary powers of the Star Chamber have been transferred, in effect, to the judges, of the King's Bench, who are mere creatures of the Establishment. This paper – its argument carefully documented and systematically conducted – is of a piece with the exercises on statute law required of students at the Temple. Its author, as becomes a neophyte in the profession, is suitably deferential, several times apologizing for his ignorance of the Common Law and protesting his willing "Submission to much greater Authority and Learning." Nevertheless, in a manner anticipating Fielding in his legal pamphlets, he applies his already impressive knowledge of the law to argue his case cogently. In this author – who shares so completely our own author's interests, erudition, and rhetorical skill – I believe we may detect Henry Fielding of the Middle Temple.

····■ 1 ■──···

These papers were but two of more than a dozen which, as the evidence suggests, Fielding published in *The Craftsman* this year.[437] Now that the government had excluded him from the stage, he was no longer merely contributing occasionally to that journal; he had become one of its principal authors. His contributions during 1738 begin with *The Craftsman* for 7 January: with the help of "an *honest, jovial Country*

Parson" – who, as we may imagine William Young often doing when
Fielding was at East Stour, has stopped by "to quaff a Bottle with
me" – a certain lover of the classics signing himself "A.B." attempts
to solve a crux in the *Aeneid* by reference to the hypocrisies of Walpole.
This essay, besides revealing how lightly Fielding could wear his knowledge of the classics, is notable for disclosing his previously unsuspected
acquaintance with two learned clergymen: his Dorset neighbor Christopher Pitt (1699–1748), rector of Pimperne, near Blandford; and "my
Friend," as Fielding calls him, the Reverend John Jones (1693–1752),
whose "beautiful and accurate Edition of *Horace*" he warmly commends – thereby also giving himself an opportunity to "puff" the
bookseller they had in common, John Nourse (1705–80). As we know
from Fielding's letter of 6 March 1737/8,[438] Nourse was now regularly
supplying him with books he needed for his legal studies; but he also
made a specialty of the classical authors. "Their best Works," Fielding
later assured his readers, "may be had of Mr. *John Nourse*, at his Shop
without *Temple Bar*, he being a Person very intimate with the said
Ancients."[439] Before long, Fielding would himself have a role to play
in helping to establish Nourse's reputation as the leading English
publisher of continental authors.[440] For the next several years the two
men had a close working relationship.

By the date of his letter to Nourse, Fielding had returned to town,
presumably to attend Westminster Hall during Hilary Term. It was
later that month at Covent Garden, however, while attending a performance of Henry Carey's *The Dragon of Wantley* – an immensely
popular play which Fielding first staged at the Little Haymarket – that
he hit on the idea for the best of his periodical papers for 1738. Inspired
by seeing Amhurst at the play break into a grin when the Dragon (alias
that other ravaging reptile, Sir Robert Walpole) receives "his *mortal
Kick*," this is a delightfully arch essay on one of Fielding's favorite
topics, the *"risible Disposition of Mankind."* To suit his theme, he poses
as "Democritus," the laughing philosopher, and ushers his facetious
observations into the world on April Fool's Day. Its playful tone
notwithstanding, this paper infuriated the ministerial writers, who
denounced it in the *Daily Gazetteer*.[441] In this clandestine fashion,
applying now in prose the talent for ridicule that in the productions at
the Haymarket had made the minister wince, Fielding in these years
established the reputation of *The Craftsman* as the wittiest of the
political journals.

How popular his humorous pieces had become with Patriot readers
was illustrated on Saturday, 13 May 1738, when – as the incident of
Captain Jenkins's ear incensed the public against Walpole's policy of
pacifying Spain – *both* the principal Opposition journals appear to have
carried leaders by Fielding. In *The Craftsman* for that date he is very

probably "Constans," who writes to insist that England avenge the Spanish depredations with the thunder of her men-of-war, not with the empty eloquence of Walpole's pensioners in Parliament. In *Common Sense* at the same time he is "Mum Budget," who was moved on April Fool's Day, for very good personal reasons, to compose an essay on silence – on the wisdom, that is, of holding one's tongue in Walpole's England:

> But this Virtue blossoms no where so much as among the Politicians. – A certain ludicrous Poet, in a Piece called *the Historical Register*, wherein he introduced several Politicians on the Stage, gives this Character of Silence to the chief of them; but I am afraid in so doing, he did not act very politickly for himself: for I have observed, that his Muse hath been silent ever since.[442]

Fielding concluded his regular association with *The Craftsman* with the issue of 23 December, in which "T.P.," a dramatist who has been ruined by the Licensing Act, drolly supposes he can rescue his lost career by writing political plays, a specimen of which, satirizing the ministerial hack Francis ("Mother") Osborne, he supplies. Reflecting Fielding's own regretful view of the circumstances that once led him to expect a happier fate, the autobiographical introduction reveals the mood of bitterness and doubt in which he found himself during this dark, transitional period – years as uncertain and arduous as any he would know:

> Know then, *Sir* [he addresses Caleb D'Anvers], that I was bred up to *Letters*, have been educated in a *good School*, and was then sent to a *foreign University*, where I kept close to my *Books*, and was well esteem'd by all the *Professors*, under whom I studied. But my Learning went no farther than *Humanity*, *History* and *Poetry*. My Imagination was too fertile, and my Parts too volatile, for any of the grave Professions. My Inclination tended most towards *Poetry*, and chiefly *dramatick Poetry*, in which I gave Way to my Fancy. I have now by Me several Pieces of various Kinds, the Productions of many Years Labour and Study, from which I was in Hopes of raising a large Fortune. To mention no more, I have compleatly finish'd *Thirteen dramatical Performances*, which I make no Question would, each of them, have as long a Run as *Hurlothrumbo*, or the *Dragon of Wantley*. But since I came over to *England*, I found there hath been a Law made to regulate the STAGE. ... I say, this *Reformation of the Stage*, however useful to refine our Taste, hath thrown away at least ten Years of my Life.

Fielding's participation in the political paper wars of the 1730s remained a secret. His association with the Patriot cause, however –

and in particular with Lyttelton, patron of *Common Sense*, and Amhurst, editor of *The Craftsman* – was well known. The ministerial author of *A Dialogue on One Thousand Seven Hundred and Thirty-eight* (August 1738) thus uttered the pathetic prophecy that, should the Opposition wits succeed in their campaign to turn Walpole out, the consequence would be England's ruin:

> Adieu then Virtue! Sense and Truth, good night! ...
> Religion soon to Scepticism shall yield,
> Which op'ning to wild Wits their wish'd-for-Field,
> Our ancient Constitution, sacred Laws,
> And all that Wisdom's Approbation draws,
> Shall be wip'd out, – and in their stead be writ
> The worthy Whims of Wou'd-be-Statesman's Wit.
> Then *L*[*y*]*tt*[*elto*]*n* our Government shall mend,
> On *F*[*ie*]*ld*[*in*]*g* our grave Lawyers shall attend;
> Our Poets all, from *Agamemnon* write,
> And Censor *Am*[*hur*]*st* then shall banish quite
> All College Learning, as pedantic Stuff,
> And treat each Prelate as a meer *Tartuff*.

···➤ li ◄···

From the marked increase in Fielding's journalism during 1738 – a time when he would have preferred to concentrate on preparing for the Bar – it appears he wanted money. As it happened, this was the year when he could find respite from such anxieties by being at last legally entitled to sell off his share of the farm at East Stour. Since his mother's death and the subsequent judgment of Chancery, the estate had been held in trust for Sarah's six children. In April 1737 Edmund, the youngest, turned twenty-one, thereby opening the way for the dissolution of the trust and the division of the property into six equal shares. (Edmund, who at seventeen had been commissioned ensign in his father's Regiment of Invalids, was already launched on a military career in which, under several other commands, he attained the rank of first lieutenant, serving in Scotland during the "Forty Five" and also, shortly after his marriage in 1753, in India.[443] Fielding's only mention of him makes clear that he was stationed at Minorca about the year 1740.)[444] On 3 February 1737/8, in order of seniority, Henry, Catharine, Ursula, Sarah, Beatrice, and Edmund signed two indentures preliminary to the sale of the farm: in one of these Davidge Gould and William Day were relieved of their responsibilities as trustees; in the other, the Fieldings, together with Gould, Day, and Peter Davies of Wells (in whose name the property had been held), conveyed the estate to Fielding's attorney, Robert Stillingfleet.[445]

A few months later, on 21 June 1738, the process began by which Fielding relinquished title to what remained of his birthright. This is the date of the first of four "Proclamations" by which Fielding and Charlotte conveyed to Thomas Hayter, Gentleman, that part of the farm consisting "of two messuages, two Dovehouses, three Gardens, three Orchards, fifty acres of Land, Eighty acres of meadow, one hundred and forty acres of Pasture, ten acres of wood, and Common of pasture for all manner of Cattle with the Appurtenanaces in East Stower." In return they received from Hayter a mere £260.[446] The farm, which originally cost Sir Henry Gould £3,000 and Fielding's father an additional £1,750, had thus been reduced over the years to something less than one third of its value (assuming that the shares owned by the other five children were worth as much as Fielding's). As appears from his letter to John Nourse dated from East Stour on 7 March 1738/9. Fielding continued to reside at the farm when he was in the country until the last possible moment – that being, presumably, 14 May 1739, the date of the fourth and final proclamation which formally completed the sale.

Before closing this melancholy episode of Fielding's life – one that meant for him both the end of his dignity as a landed gentleman and the severance, physically, of ties with his mother and grandmother, who rested in the churchyard at East Stour – we must consider the tradition that it was to the miser Peter Walter (1664?–1745), one of the most despised figures of his time, that Fielding through his improvidence had been forced to sell the farm. One source of this tradition ought to be reliable: Fielding's close friend from their school-days at Eton, Charles Hanbury Williams. In August 1743 Hanbury Williams put into verse "a Dialogue between Peter Walters & Henry Fielding," which he paraphrased for Henry Fox.[447] When this poem was eventually published, Hanbury Williams substituted the innocuous "Lord Quidam" for his friend; but since it is clear from the "plan" he sent Fox that he had Fielding in mind throughout, we may in the following excerpt restore his original intention. Fielding speaks:

> PETER, I've sign'd and seal'd; the work is done;
> My goods, my lands, and tenements are gone!
> I see my folly, and repent too late;
> But since you're now possess'd of my estate,
> And these few guineas all that now remain,
> Teach me to thrive, and to be rich again:
> To thee, the art of heaping endless stores

Is known, and Plutus opens all his doors.
                    PETER.
Already asking? – what! a fresh demand
With those five hundred guineas in your hand,
Of which, had I insisted on my due,
One shilling never could have come to you?[448]

It is true that, by his grasping practices as moneylender and land-steward, Walter, whose seat was at Stalbridge Park, Dorset, a few miles west of East Stour, acquired great riches and much property in Fielding's neighborhood. It is also true that, like Pope, Fielding regarded Walter as the very type of avarice. Indeed, he satirized him in his works so often and with such undisguised contempt that we might suppose he resented some personal injury the man had done him: Walter is the original of Peter Pounce in *Joseph Andrews*, Lady Booby's steward who lends money "at the moderate *Premiums* of fifty *per Cent.* or a little more" (I. x); and Fielding kept up the ridicule in other works of roughly this same period.[449] Furthermore, anecdotes associating the two, so antithetical in their characters, sprung up early. Horace Walpole recalled one of the most popular of these:

> Fielding was teazing Peter Walters, & said, prythee how canst thou pass thy whole Life in considering the Difference between a Shilling and Sixpence? Walters replied, that is a Difference you don't understand, but perhaps there may come a Time when you will – When is that? said Fielding. Why, if you happen to be worth Eighteen Pence. Well, said F[ielding], I have always said you had Wit – no, said He, I had not always, but I bought the Estates of several Men of Wit, & They gave me their Wit into the Bargain.[450]

The notion that it was the despicable Walter who acquired Fielding's estate persisted until much later in the century.[451]

It may be that Fielding borrowed money of this man at usurious rates, and that, by so doing, he was forced to relinquish the farm. Fielding throughout this period was running ever deeper into debt. The fact remains, however, that not a shred of hard evidence to support this tradition has come to light.

···◆ lii ◆–···

In August 1738, in the midst of these distressing financial circumstances, Fielding's prospects suddenly brightened. In that month his favorite uncle, Lieutenant Colonel George Fielding of the Royal Horse Guards, died at his home at Windsor, and by the terms of his will (proved 25 September 1738) left generous legacies to both Fielding and "dear" Charlotte – indeed, to all Edmund's children by his first wife. According to this will, Fielding could expect to inherit exchequer annuities worth £80 and Charlotte another £60 in annuities in her own right. The legacies, distributed among George Fielding's nephews and nieces and his sisters according to a complicated scheme of reversions, might be greater or less depending on which of Fielding's relations died and when. Unfortunately, for he and Charlotte needed the money at once, the will was contested by Colonel Fielding's estranged wife Ann, who, together with her daughter, had been entirely excluded from these benefactions. The case dragged on through the courts for ten years before, on 30 June 1749, judgment was pronounced against the widow, at which time Fielding – had he not grown impatient at the delay and sold his interest in the legacy for ready cash – would have come into a sizable inheritance.[452]

Perhaps buoyed up by these expectations, Fielding as the New Year turned discontinued his political writing in order to concentrate on the law. From East Stour on 7 March 1738/9 he wrote his bookseller:

Mr Nourse
Some Disappointments have prevented y^r. hearing from me before & likewise an immediate Complyance with what desired in yrs wch I recd last week, but at my Return to Town (a few days before Beginning of next Term) I hope to give y^o a very satisfactory Answer[.] I should be obliged to y^o in the mean time if y^o would send me down Croke Eliz by the Taunton Coach wch sets out ev^y. Tuesday from London and am

Y^r faithful humble serv^t
Hen: Ffielding[453]

When he wrote this letter Fielding was planning to go up to London in early May (Easter Term beginning late this year on 9 May), at which time he would resume attendance at Westminster Hall. We recall that 14 May was the date of the final proclamation completing the sale of his and Charlotte's interest in the farm. He remained in town, sinking deeper into debt, until late June. On 6 June, at Westminster, he borrowed £23.10s. from one Walter Barnes, signing a promissory note by which he agreed to repay the loan in five months' time. Following "the genteel Means" of collecting such debts that Fielding's creditors often employed against him, and which he bitterly recalls in *Amelia* (XI. iii), Barnes on the same day signed over the note to John Kempson, a druggist to whom Fielding, because of the precarious health of his family, already owed "divers other Sums of Money."[454] Before the month was out Fielding was sued for another debt – one he had contracted as long ago as 13 December 1736, when he borrowed £30 of Charles Fielding, promising to pay the debt by January 1737/8. Before that time Charles Fielding signed over this note to James Gascoigne, a tailor. On 1 January 1738/9 Fielding acknowledged the debt but, being unable to pay it, arranged for an extension. By Trinity Term (22 June to 11 July), however, Gascoigne felt he had been put off long enough and filed suit against Fielding, now said to be "late of Stower in the County of Dorset," to recover both the amount of the loan and substantial punitive damages: for, as the plea states, "the said Henry his Several promises and undertakings ... in no wise Regarding but contriving and fraudulently intending the same James in this Behalf Craftily & Cunningly to deceive and defraud," had not paid his debt. Fielding, the fledgling barrister, appeared at Westminster Hall "in his proper Person" to answer these charges. Having acknowledged the debt, he was ordered on 4 August 1739 to pay Gascoigne the sum of £38.10s.[455]

By this date Fielding had returned to the country, to some unspecified haven, to lick his wounds and continue his studies remote from the duns and distractions of the town. Perhaps he had been called to Bath and to Salisbury, to pay his respects to two of his near relations who were dying. At Bath on 7 August 1739 his stepmother Eleanor, of whom he and Charlotte appear to have been genuinely fond,[456] made out her last will and testament, bequeathing "to my dear Husband Lieutenant General Edmund Fielding his Heirs and Assigns all my Goods, Chattells and personal Estate whatsoever."[457] She died soon thereafter and her body was carried to Salisbury; her burial is recorded in the register of St. Martin's church for 10 August 1739. In Salisbury at this same time Mrs. Cottington, Edmund's arch-enemy but his son's doting great-aunt, was also in a perilous state of health; she died before the year was out. In January 1739/40 her goddaughter and namesake, Fielding's eldest sister Catharine, inherited her estate.[458]

Whatever may have drawn Fielding to the country in the summer of 1739, it is not surprising that he opened his second letter to Nourse of this year by again referring to "Disappointments" that continued to prevent him from settling his accounts – disappointments not merely associated with the indefinite delay in the receipt of his uncle's legacy, but now also beginning to assume the distinct, unwelcome shapes of bailiffs and creditors. In this letter, dated 9 July 1739, he assured his long-suffering bookseller that he had at last received Croke's *Reports* and would pay his bill "on my coming to Town ... next Month." He also had a favor to ask – one that marks the beginning of the unsettled, hand-to-mouth existence of shifting residences and piecemeal hackney authorship he and his family would lead in the metropolis for the next several years:

I desire the favour of y° [he writes Nourse] to look for a House for me near the Temple. I must have one large eating Parlour in it for the rest shall not be very nice. Rent not upwards of £40 p. an: and as much cheaper as may be. I will take a Lease for Seven years. Y^r Answer to this within a fortnight will much oblige.

The house Nourse acquired for him, and which the Fieldings were occupying that autumn, was in Essex Street (now No. 24) – a substantial dwelling, dearer than he hoped for at a yearly rent of £50, and situated adjacent to the Middle Temple in a neighborhood preferred by many successful lawyers. He remained there for about two years,[459] until his worsening financial circumstances drove him into the Verge of the Court (in anticipation of Booth's stratagem in *Amelia*) to take refuge from the bailiffs.

Perhaps another sign of Fielding's improvidence – as well as of his litigious temper and the aptitude he was acquiring in his profession – is the lawsuit in which he was involved not long after he came to town. A document filed in the King's Bench on the last day of Michaelmas Term (28 November 1739) reveals that Fielding brought suit against a man who ever after remained, like Peter Walter, a standing butt of his ridicule. This was William Deards (d. 1761), celebrated toyman and pawnbroker in the Strand – a tradesman, Fielding observed, of the sort who, though most obligingly eager to take "your Note" if you had no ready money, would later teach you to "repent having learnt to write your Name."[460] The motive for Fielding's action is unclear, but from the tenor of his subsequent allusions to Deards, we may suppose his grievance was financial.

By the time Fielding and London's most eminent toyman finished crossing swords in the King's Bench, Fielding's plans for entering a new phase of his public life would be accomplished. For the moment, on returning to London in August he marked time. After an hiatus of more than eight months, he appears to have resumed his occasional contributions to *The Craftsman* and *Common Sense*. In *The Craftsman* for 1 and 8 September, it is his wit, probably, that enlivens the letters from the projecting apothecary "Pharmacopola" and a scheming Methodist. In *Common Sense* (15 September), in a more humorous and personal vein, it may well be Fielding who reveals a basic truth about his character as a garrulous and clubbable scholar for whom the admonitions of sages are ineffectual in checking an immoderate love of pleasure:

I have read and heard a great many fine Things, in almost all Languages, against *Intemperance in eating and drinking*; I have seen the Force of the Arguments, and been fully convinced, that Gluttony and Drunkenness are the most nasty, and beastly, and murderous

Things in the World; and yet when I meet with a good Dinner, or a
Bottle of good Wine, and like my Company, and think they like me,
why I must own to you, that, though I have a thousand Precepts in
my Budget against going too far, not one of them comes into my
Head till next Morning, when I find, at waking, that it is much out
of Order. Then do I most philosophically condemn myself for a Fool,
and see very clearly, that *Temperance* is the Foundation of all Virtue.

   Oh, Dear *Common Sense!* what a wretched State it is, for a Man
to be so deeply immersed in the Dirt and Mud of *Sensuality*, and
Debauchery, and *low Pursuits*, as seldom or never to lift up his Head
and *bubble*, to see what a damn'd Condition he has brought himself
to?

Throughout his early life Fielding, like his heroes Tom Jones and Billy
Booth, felt powerless, for all his learning, to control his appetites
and passions, "vehement," as Harris remembered, "in every kind."
Nowhere in his writings is this dilemma more explicitly, or more
amusingly, expressed than here.

   As far as the public was aware, however, Fielding had not been heard
from since the last performance of *The Historical Register* at the Little
Haymarket in May 1737. The ministerial hack who wrote *The Satirists:
A Satire* (1739) thus spared a moment from abusing Pope and Swift in
order to sneer at Fielding's annihilation as a literary figure:

> Tell *F[ielding]* That – But *F[ielding]* is no more –
> Betaken now Reports and *Coke* to Pore –
> The scurril Jest, all the licentious Rage,
> Behold! absorpt in the dry cumbrous Page.

Amhurst and Molloy had kept Fielding's secret well. It would soon be
common knowledge, however, that the liveliest dramatist of the decade
was once again wittily serving the cause of morality, and of Opposition
politics – this time as author of a new periodical.

PART III

Politics, novels, and the law (1739–49)

Anthony Burgess likened Fielding's life to a play in four acts.[1] The curtain rose on Act III of that crowded little drama in November 1739. After (it would have seemed) an interval of silence lasting two and a half years, Pasquin of the Little Haymarket now reappeared in a new and improbable role – as "Captain Hercules Vinegar of Hockley in the Hole," the celebrated prize-fighter of bear-gardens and amphitheatres, who had exchanged cudgel and broadsword for a pen in order to set up as author of a witty periodical called *The Champion*. Fielding may have taken the hint for this bold (and as it proved, troublesome) persona from Aaron Hill, who in attacking the Italian opera in *The Prompter* (27 December 1734) invoked the example of this same formidable British hero.[2] In *The Champion*, however, Fielding would do more than imitate Hill's hero; he would *become* "Captain Hercules Vinegar." And he would assure his readers that his new censorial weapon would serve society much more effectually than the ones he was accustomed to wielding:

> IT is sufficiently known that some Years since, to the great Terror of the small Vulgar, I entered upon the Title of *Captain*; this I did without the Consent of any one Person living, or without any other Commission or Authority than what I immediately derived from myself. I have now determin'd to lay aside the Sword, which, without Vanity, I may boast to have us'd with some Success ... and take up the Pen in its Stead, with a Design to do as much Execution with the one, as I have already done with the other; or, in other Words, to tickle now, as I before bruised Men into good Manners.

In this undertaking, Fielding continues in a vein reminiscent of his great models Addison and Steele, the Captain would enlist the aid of "the whole Family of the *Vinegars*" in their several capacities: namely, his father Nehemiah Vinegar, well read in politics; his uncle Counsellor Vinegar of the Middle Temple; his cousin Dr. John Vinegar the phys-ician; his brother Nol Vinegar, classical scholar and critic; his son Tom Vinegar, who, having been five years a student at Lincoln's Inn, had become an authority on modern poetry and theatrical affairs; his younger son Jack Vinegar, idler and beau, who was therefore thoroughly acquainted with gossip from the polite parts of town; and finally his most intrepid ally, Joan Vinegar his wife, who would see to it that the interests of female readers were not neglected.

The range and variety of these topics – all of which and more Fielding would treat in his papers in *The Champion* – point up the fact that the journal was not originally planned as a political vehicle after the model of *The Craftsman* and *Common Sense*. What political coloring it did have was, as we would expect, very much of the Patriot hue. It was chiefly supplied not by the fictitious Nehemiah Vinegar, but by

Fielding's real-life partner in the journal, his friend and collaborator from the glory days of the Little Haymarket, James Ralph. Ralph was an experienced journalist who for many years had conducted periodicals on both sides of the political fence. Most recently he had been editing the *Universal Spectator*.

Unaware of the long apprenticeship Fielding served as a political humorist in *The Craftsman*, the public may have found his metamorphosis from "Pasquin" to "Hercules Vinegar" surprising. His abilities as an essayist must have been known, however, to certain members of the book trade who were prepared to sponsor this new periodical at a time when dozens of newspapers, journals, and magazines littered the coffee-houses of London. Another friend and fellow member of the club that regularly met under the auspices of Jonathan Tyers in Southwark, Thomas Cooke, seems to have been informed of the genesis and intended character of the paper soon after Fielding ceased his regular contributions to *The Craftsman*. In April 1739 Cooke, who like Ralph had shifted his political allegiance from the Court to the Country party, concluded an essay "on satire, and on the present state of our public entertainments," by offering his readers hope for the future:

> THIS is all that I shall say at present of our public entertainments; the particulars of all which will be more nicely examined into next winter; when a paper will be weekly published, perhaps oftener, by a society of gentlemen, not unequal to the design, who have already by them a stock sufficient for the publication of a year; nor will they confine themselves to public entertainments and the directors of them, but take a survey of men and manners in other circles of life, without invading the provinces of the authors of the *Craftsman* and *Common Sense*, tho they may sometimes venture to hunt their monsters of state with other beasts of prey.[3]

Cooke's remarks square very well with what we know of *The Champion* as it began publication in the winter of 1739–40. They are interesting in several respects. For one thing, coming so early in the year, they help to explain Fielding's abrupt break with *The Craftsman*, his regular contributions to that journal having ended in December 1738. For another, they also make clear that from its conception *The Champion* was not chiefly designed as a political vehicle: though, to be sure, like every self-respecting Patriot in the predatory age of Walpole, the authors would "sometimes venture to hunt their monsters of state with other beasts of prey," they did not intend to compete for readers with those established organs of the Opposition, *The Craftsman* and *Common Sense*. During the early months of his journal Fielding, representing himself as Champion and Censor of Great Britain, wielded his weapon of ridicule primarily to correct the bad manners, morals, and taste of his countrymen. His readers could never doubt that the paper supported the Patriot cause – and most specifically, the Patriot cause in the City of London, the commercial heart of the metropolis. But even when he wrote for Amhurst or Molloy, Fielding was more comfortable in the role of humorist and wit rather than political advocate. He was always at his best in the higher modes of ridicule, whose province is the inexhaustible comedy of human nature, beside which the farce of party politics was a piffling spectacle. *The Champion*, for the first time, provided Fielding with the vehicle he needed to write as he wished to write – free, for a while at least, from the obligation to serve a political cause that Amhurst and Molloy required of their contributors.

As to the "society of gentlemen" to whom Cooke refers, the records of Chancery enable us to identify them all with some confidence – thanks to a prolonged, abortive lawsuit attesting to the soundness of Dr. Johnson's opinion of the avaricious printer Thomas Gardiner.[4] Gardiner, who was appointed printer of *The Champion* in July 1741, later sued the other "proprietors" for money he believed they owed him.[5] The partners in the paper – besides the authors Fielding (who owned two sixteenth shares) and Ralph – were the booksellers Francis Cogan, Paul Vaillant, Henry Chappelle, John Wood, James Hodges, John Nourse, Lawton Gilliver, and Richard Chandler. According to another contemporary source, Fielding's "Gang" of booksellers also originally included "Common-Council-Man *Austin*" (i.e., Stephen Austen, a member of the Corporation of the City), who, afraid of losing his investment, quit the partnership, his share being acquired by "Count *Cogan*."[6] The printer to whom the paper was entrusted in the early, precarious days of its existence appears to have been "One *Smith*, a very obscure Typographer," whose shop was situated in Stanhope Street, Clare Market.[7]

It was Cogan, in particular, who along with Nourse and Chandler assumed primary responsibility for the enterprise. He was a man of such grotesque appearance and ill repute as to inspire the poet James Barber to reach the true sublime of obloquy:

> But see Count *Cog[a]n*, with his squinting Sight,
> Full fraught with Wine, pale, blear-ey'd Son of Light.
> Nature to thee her greater Charms assign'd,
> Than what has bless'd the rest of Human-kind;
> Two shining Lights to most she's giv'n to guide
> Their wandring Steps, with one some satisfy'd.
> Far larger Opticks bless thy happy Eye,
> Through which at once nine Ways with Ease you spy;
> But partial *Jove* enrag'd has curs'd thy Face,
> With a fell Visage, to the dire Disgrace;

> Of Man and all Mankind's succeeding Race:
> To this he adds, to make thee curs'd compleat,
> A Soul to ev'ry Virtue opposite;
> And at thy Birth the Fates confirm'd the same,
> Let Squinny says [*sic*] they, be thy loathsom Name:
> Not all the Learning that your Shop contains,
> Can teach th' indocile Breast, or clear your Brains.

The poet's hope is that "Squinny" Count Cogan, having first been poxed by his whore, will hang himself.[8] It is reassuring to find that Fielding's opinion of this man was less malignant: in *The Champion* (24 June 1740) he places "Mr. *Francis Cogan*, at *Temple-Bar*," at the head of the "three honest Booksellers" who direct the financial affairs of the paper.

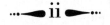

Having entrusted the distribution of the paper, curiously, to Thomas Cooper – the publisher of the *Daily Gazetteer*, whom Fielding indeed later called "*Publisher-General* to the *Ministerial-Society*"[9] – the partners were ready to launch *The Champion* by mid-November. The earliest notices appeared simultaneously in *The Craftsman, Common Sense*, and the *London Evening Post* for 10 November 1739:

> *On Thursday the 15th Instant will be publish'd,*
> (*To be continued every Morning on Tuesday, Thursday and Saturday*)
> The CHAMPION; or, British Mercury
> By the celebrated Capt. HERCULES VINEGAR
> of Hockley in the Hole.
> Containing Essays on various Subjects, and the freshest Advices both Foreign and Domestick.
> —Quod optanti Divum promittere nemo
> Auderet Volvenda dies en attulit. Virg.
> Printed for T. Cooper at the Globe in Pater-noster Row.

The epigraph from the *Aeneid* (IX.6–7) aptly declares Fielding's pleasure at the opportunity the journal would now afford him of making a fresh start as his own man in a genre relatively new to him – an opportunity he could not reasonably have expected: "what none of the gods would have dared to promise you as you wish, lo! rolling time has brought unasked."

The design and format of the paper were in several respects novel enough to elicit comment from its readers. Dividing the two parts of

the title was a *"hieroglyphical"*[10] picture of Hercules (a burly figure
suggesting Fielding's own large physique), who is shown under the
approving eye of a providential sun wielding his club against the
many-headed Hydra that threatens the nation's capital. In the middle
distance nearby is the new Westminster Bridge, symbol to the Opposition of ministerial folly and corruption; in the background beyond
the bridge loom the Monument, emblem of the City's destruction by
alleged papist intrigue (Pope's "tall bully [that] lifts the head, and
lyes"), and the dome of St. Paul's Cathedral, sign of the City's renewal
and piety.

In its original form – the earliest extant example of which is No. 20
(Saturday, 29 December 1739) – the paper consisted of just two pages,
opening typically with either a lead essay by Fielding or occasionally
some amusing piece of pseudonymous correspondence by him; he was
thus responsible for the front matter of fifty-two of the first sixty
numbers (to 1 April 1740) – after which his contributions become
noticeably less frequent, though they still amount to well over half the
articles published to 15 November, when the run of extant originals
abruptly ends. In addition to an occasional "Literary Article" which
might be the work of either author, the back page was chiefly Ralph's
responsibility and consisted of items of foreign and domestic news
culled mostly from other papers but digested in a peculiarly satiric
manner. Until April, when *The Champion* changed from a morning to
an evening paper and expanded to four pages, there was little room
for advertisements; but during the first months of its existence few
tradesmen or booksellers would be prepared to spend three shillings
(the price of an advertisement)[11] for the privilege of displaying their
wares where they would scarcely be seen. Throughout the period of
Fielding's association with it, *The Champion* sold at the rate of three
halfpence a copy – a price cheaper by a halfpenny than most comparable
papers, and one half what Fielding would later charge for *The True
Patriot* and the *Covent-Garden Journal.*

With little or no revenue from advertisers and a price below what its
competitors asked, *The Champion* had to attract a sizeable readership
quickly if it was to survive. In what proved to be an ineffectual move
to help the paper catch hold, the partners distributed the first number
gratis, and for a fortnight they advertised each number as it was
published in the early morning of the three weekly post days – Tuesday,
Thursday, and Saturday.[12] Despite these efforts *The Champion* nearly
sank without a trace. As early as his ninth number (4 December 1739)
Fielding was complaining of the "Contempt" his paper met with on all
sides, noting with particular bitterness "a certain Coffee-House near
Charing-Cross, where it was refused to be received *Gratis*, and scornfully
thrown out of the Doors." Some readers, even "such as allow a great

Deal of Merit" to the paper, objected to the vulgarity of Fielding's title
and to his choice of persona, and they protested that nothing worth
reading could possibly issue from Hockley in the Hole. Others complained that his essays were "not bold enough" – his distraught publisher imploring "that your Mightiness would infuse Gall in your Ink,
and, instead of Morality, Wit, and Humour, deal forth private Slander
and Abuse."

A week later, acceding to the demands of his genteel readers, "Hercules Vinegar" removed himself from Hockley in the Hole to take new
lodgings in Pall Mall, proclaiming this fashionable address on the
masthead of his paper (No. 12, 11 December 1739). In another week's
time he had altered the character of the paper in order to woo dissatisfied
readers among the coffee-house politicians. *Champion* No. 15 (18
December 1739) opens with a letter from a supposed well-wisher that
tells the sad story of the journal's first month:

> *SIR,*
>   THOUGH a Vein of Wit hath discover'd itself in your Papers,
> which the Town hath not, lately, seen any Thing equal to, I am
> afraid you have not yet met with the Success which your Writings
> deserve, and which I not only wish, but promise you on your Per-
> severance; nor would I have you discourag'd, that you are not receiv'd
> with that immediate Applause, which some of your Predecessors have
> met with on their first Appearance.

To which Fielding replied that, "though it was not, at first, [his]
Intention to deal much in serious Politics in this Paper," but rather to
treat subjects "of a more humerous [sic] Kind," he would bow to the
exigencies of the moment. The result, in this same issue of *The
Champion*, is the first of his serious anti-ministerial articles, signaled
by a special notice in the *London Daily Post, and General Advertiser* (18
December 1739) describing it as "An Address to the City of London
on their ensuing Election of Common-Council-Men." This paper was
effective enough to elicit from a contributor to Walpole's *Daily Gazetteer*
(22 December 1739) the first acknowledgment that journal had made
of *The Champion*'s existence. This abusive ministerial effusion Fielding
answered in his number for Christmas Day with a monitory epistle of
his own addressed "*To the ten-thousand Authors of the* Gazetteer," and
to "their PATRON," as another special advertisement (in the *London
Evening Post*, 22–5 December 1739) advised the public. Rallying Walpole's Gazetteers on their not being able to bear any hard words on the
subject of corruption, Fielding warned them to avoid in future "all
private Reflections on any Person supposed to be concerned in the
Champion" or else he would turn his attention from them to their

"Master." The enemy understood the message; six months would pass before Fielding or his paper was noticed again in the *Daily Gazetteer*.

Not until the end of March, however, was there any very hopeful indication that *The Champion* had survived its early trials and was about to achieve the popularity Fielding and his partners gambled on. A letter from "Tom Townly" in No. 57 (25 March 1740) declares that, for its "Wit and Morality," Fielding's "Paper begins to be the Talk of the learned World" and likewise of "several considerable Bodies of the fair Sex." It had not been an easy struggle. The paper seemed such a leaky vessel and the odds against its staying afloat so unpromising that by April it had been abandoned not only by Stephen Austen, one of the original partners, but also by two publishers, most recently by Charles Corbett, who had replaced Thomas Cooper with the twenty-first number.

Now, however, there was enough confidence in the venture that the partnership thought it worthwhile to introduce several shrewd changes in the design and character of *The Champion*. Since they found that the best of Ralph's news articles were being creamed off for publication later in the day by competitors such as *The Craftsman* and the *London Evening Post*, they would in future delay publication until the evening. To allow for more advertising space,[13] they also doubled the size of the paper from two to four pages. For the first time others besides Fielding and Ralph would contribute leaders. Of these, however, only the first to make an appearance, William Robinson of the Inner Temple (*fl.* 1740–58), has been identified:[14] a friend of Fielding and skillful imitator of his style, Robinson specialized in satirical dream-visions and under the name of "Morpheus" or "Somnus" contributed a number of essays in this form – the first of which, heralding the new policy of the journal, was published in No. 63 (8 April 1740). As for the content of the journal, that, too, would change: it would appeal more to the tastes of coffee-house politicians of a Patriot stripe, especially those in the City. Though Fielding contributed his share of these political papers, this shift in the policy of the journal – away from the essays of wit and humor, of morality and social commentary, that he preferred and toward a greater emphasis on Patriot polemics – may account for the abrupt decline in the proportion of his contributions from approximately 85 percent to little more than 50 percent.

So, with No. 64 (Thursday, 10 April 1740), the journal appeared for the first time as *The Champion: or, Evening Advertiser*, with a leader not by Fielding, but by Ralph, who under the name of "Lilbourne" gravely warned the public of the threat Walpole posed to the liberty of the press. The paper also had a new publisher, Josiah Graham, whose shop was situated "under the *Inner Temple Gate*, opposite *Chancery Lane*, in *Fleet street*, where Advertisements and Letters to the AUTHOR

are taken in." In this same issue Graham offered the following account
of the history of *The Champion* to date – its original goals, its struggles
and eventual triumph over a conspiracy of assorted competitors and
adversaries, and its plans for the future:

> IF NEWS-PAPERS, are only calculated to *kill Time*, the present Set
> will answer that End very effectually. But, if to *inform*, or even to
> *entertain* is the Tenure of their Charter, a *new One* is absolutely
> necessary to save it from being forfeited beyond Redemption.
>
> On this Presumption, this Paper was, a few Months ago, set up;
> which had, at least, something of Novelty, if no more, to recommend
> it. But, having a vigorous *Opposition* on all Hands to struggle with
> (*Booksellers*, who were Sharers in the Profit of other News-Papers;
> *Coffee-men*, who thought they were encumbred with too many
> already; *Place-men*, because it made War on their Patron; *Patriot-
> writers*, because it might possibly interfere with their own; and
> *Hawkers* in Fee with them all) it made its Way but slowly, nay was
> actually given out for *Dead*, long ago.
>
> And no sooner was it received with Approbation by some, and
> Indulgence by all unprejudiced Readers, but the *Craftsman*,[15]
> LONDON EVENING POST, &c. and many of the *Country Papers* began
> to enrich themselves with its Spoils; which (tho' their Sanction may
> be no Proof of its Merit) argued, at least, that it was not *unacceptable*
> to the Publick.
>
> Rather, therefore, than give Way to such *Piracies* any longer, it
> has been thought expedient to alter the *Time* of publishing this
> Paper, called the CHAMPION, from *Tuesday*, *Thursday* and *Saturday*
> Mornings, to the EVENINGS of the same Days, when it will be punc-
> tually sent to such publick or private Houses, as shall order it in. . . .
>   It will contain, as before,
> I.   An ESSAY on the *Manners* or *Politicks* of the Times.
> II.   Frequently, new Articles of Intelligence.
> III.   The News of Two Days, Foreign and Domestick, stated and
>   digested in a peculiar Manner.
> IV.   Extracts from, or Remarks upon such Books, Poems,
>   Pamphlets, &c. as are worthy the Notice of the Publick.

···◗ iii ◖···

Two months later, recalling the hostility through which *The Champion*
had struggled before arriving at last "at a Success and Reputation

which may justly make us vain," Fielding's memories were of total ruin avoided by the narrowest of margins:

> When I look back on the Precipice of Oblivion (if I may so call it) whence this Paper so narrowly escaped, (our little Stock being at one Time almost exhausted) I must own myself in a more than ordinary Manner elated with my present good Fortune.[16]

This metaphor of near annihilation held for Fielding a very personal meaning as he looked back on the bitter winter of 1739–40. It had been a time of hardship and humiliation such as he and Charlotte had not yet experienced – though, as the future proved, it was only the first of a sad series of adversity to afflict them.

Fielding had launched *The Champion* at a time when he was sinking deeper into debt. In August 1739 the Court ordered him to pay £38.10s. to James Gascoigne; the money he owed John Kempson was due on 6 November, but he could not pay it; and in that same month he was entering into litigation in the King's Bench with Deards. The house he had let in Essex Street was dearer than he could afford. What is more, always believing that a gentleman born and bred might expect to maintain a certain style of living, he was compounding the family's financial woes absurdly, by running into the books of London's most fashionable stabler, Elizabeth Blunt, from whom he had hired "divers Coaches, Chariots, Chaizes, Horses, Mares and Geldings."[17] No doubt Fielding later winced when, in *Amelia* (III.xii), Booth confesses to Miss Mathews what "I am almost ashamed to mention, as it may well be called my greatest Folly":

> You are to know then, Madam, that from a Boy I had been always fond of driving a Coach, in which I valued myself on having some Skill. This, perhaps, was an innocent, but I allow it to have been a childish Vanity.

To complete the dismal scene, in November 1739 began the worst frost England had experienced in living memory. By the time the first number of *The Champion* was published, the canal in St. James's Park had frozen over; soon after, ice choked the Thames as far as Greenwich. Snow driven by strong winds made the roads impassable. In *The Champion* Ralph began a special feature, a "Journal of the Frost," in which he reported the casualties and other phenomena caused by the freezing weather, which killed ducks along the river and postriders on their horses. "In short," he observed on 2 February 1739/40, "tho' many Frosts have lasted longer, few have been more severe, or inflicted greater Hardships on the Poor." Among those hardships was the extortionate gouging of coal merchants who doubled the price of fuel. With one of these – a certain Robert Henley of Milford Lane, near the family's residence in Essex Street – Fielding through the winter ran up a steep bill; by 1 March 1739/40 he owed Henley £20, which, despite frequent dunning that elicited only empty promises in return, Fielding could not pay.[18] Before the year was out Fielding was being sued by all these creditors, and more.[19]

Whatever income The Champion may have brought him, it did not stem this mounting tide of debt. We do not know what Fielding's two sixteenth shares of the profits of the journal may have been worth: many years later a knowledgeable enemy declared that Fielding furnished his three essays a week "at the humble Price of 5 s. each, and a Sunday's Dinner"[20] – an estimate that seems low when one considers that in 1739 Benjamin Norton Defoe, author of the rival paper to Amhurst's Craftsman, was paid a guinea a week and that Amhurst himself – who, however, was the most successful of the Opposition journalists – made as much as six guineas a week.[21] But, in the journal's early going at least, Fielding may not have made much more than the few shillings a week his enemy specifies. Even when The Champion was at the height of its popularity, its printer Thomas Gardiner, with three issues to produce each week, was running off fewer copies than Amhurst's weekly, and at a cheaper price per copy to the public.[22]

One of the surest signs of Fielding's financial anxieties during this period when he could rely only on the facility of his pen to provide for his family is the fact that, having undertaken the authorship of The Champion, he also felt obliged to accept an overture from his bookseller John Nourse to translate Gustave Adlerfeld's voluminous Histoire militaire de Charles XII, Roi de Suede – a work published in Amsterdam in November 1739, the very month Fielding launched his journal.[23] A striking instance of Fielding's extraordinary energies as a writer, he must have been well advanced in this project by Christmas day 1739, when the London Daily Post carried a notice by Nourse and his partners in the venture, John and Paul Knapton, promising that the translation would be "Speedily" published.[24] The announcement was premature, to say the least. Nearly ten months would pass before the work was ready for publication on 10 October 1740, in three handsome octavo volumes amounting to more than a thousand pages.

Long before then, Fielding's need for money compelled him to touch Nourse for £45, in payment for as much of the work as he had completed. The receipt, in Fielding's hand, reads:

Recd March the 10 1739 [i.e., 1740] of Mr. John Nourse the Sum of forty five Pound in Part of Payment for the Translation of the History of Charles the twelfth by me
Hen: Ffielding.[25]

Can it be that the experience of translating Adlerfeld's Military

History of Charles XII for Nourse became the inspiration for the similar episode in Wilson's story in *Joseph Andrews* (III.iii)? There Wilson relates that while languishing in a "miserable State" on the point of starvation, he became acquainted with a certain bookseller who, flattering him as a man of "Learning and Genius," offered to employ him as a translator:

> A Man in my Circumstances [Wilson continues], as he very well knew, had no Choice. I accordingly accepted his Proposal with his Conditions, which were none of the most favourable, and fell to translating with all my Might. I had no longer reason to lament the want of Business; for he furnished me with so much, that in half a Year I almost writ myself blind.

There can be little doubt of the autobiographical significance of several papers Fielding published in *The Champion* during these hard winter months. The earliest of these papers is Nehemiah Vinegar's dream-vision of the Palace of Wealth, published in installments on 27 and 29 December 1739. A remarkable feature of the Palace is "a vast Gallery, which surrounded a huge Pit so vastly deep, that it almost made me giddy to look to the Bottom":

> This [the narrator continues], as I afterwards found, was the Cave of *Poverty*. There were very high and strong Rails, which prevented any Possibility of the Spectator's falling from the Gallery to the Bottom of the Cave, and yet I observed a great Tremor and Paleness to seize every one who durst venture to cast their Eyes downwards; notwithstanding which, it was very remarkable, that not one of the Company could prevail on himself to abstain from surveying the Abyss.

Indeed, as he is informed and can easily believe, "from the Bottom of the Cave it was almost impossible for any one to ascend again."

Fielding soon dropped this allegory, which had all too quickly become a reality for him. In two later numbers of *The Champion* (16 and 19 February 1739/40) he addressed the subject more directly. In the first of these essays, ostensibly an objective analysis of the proper objects of charity, he declares the most deserving case to be not the *real* poor, who could be seen in their hundreds shivering in rags and begging in the snow-choked streets of the metropolis, but rather a figure very much resembling the imprudent gentleman, Henry Fielding:

> There are so few Things absolutely necessary to the Sustenance of Life [Fielding writes], that very few labour under a Want of them. Distrest Circumstances are, not being able to support the Character in which Men have been bred, and the Want of Conveniencies to

which they have been accustomed, and therefore the first and chief
Objects of our Charity are such Persons as, having been educated
in genteel Life with moderate Fortunes, partly through Want of
Resolution to quit the Character in which they were bred, and partly
for Want of duly considering the Consequences of their Expences,
have by following their Superiors into Luxury, in order to support,
as they call it, the Figure of Gentlemen, reduced themselves to
Distress and Poverty.

I own I am one of those who think there is some Merit in Misfortunes, especially when they are not ballanced with Guilt. I look
on Indiscretion with Pity, not Abhorrence, and on no Indiscretion
with so much Pity as that of Extravagance, which as it may bring
Men into the greatest Calamities of this Life; so may it arise from
the Goodness, the Openess [sic] and the Generosity of the Heart,
Qualities which naturally enlarge in every Man's Eye the Idea of his
Possessions, as Avarice lessens it.

As his most pitiable object of charity, Fielding concludes with a case
which, as he wrote the words, he had reason to fear might soon be his
own – the case of the pauper imprisoned for debt:

Lastly, and perhaps, chiefly such as sometimes by Inadvertency,
sometimes by Misfortunes, and sometimes by the noblest Acts of
Friendship, and through the Rapaciousness, Impatience and Unmer-
cifulness of Creditors, more savage than Wolves, and the impious
Severity of our Laws, are snatch'd away from their poor Families,
from the little Comforts of the Conversation of their Relations and
Acquaintance, from a Possibility of employing their Faculties for the
Service of themselves, their Wives or their Children, from the Benefit
of wholesome Air in common with the Brute Creation, stript of all
the poor little Supports of Wretchedness, and even that last and
greatest, Hope itself, and carried to Dungeons where no Conveniency
of Life is to be had, where even the Necessaries of it are dearer than
the Conveniencies elsewhere, where they are confined together with
the vilest of Criminals, who are indeed much happier, as a Judge is
shortly to deliver them either to Liberty, or, what is better than their
Dungeon, the Gallows.

To be sure, there is something embarrassing about the self-serving
tone of these remarks, whereby a degree of improvidence and self-
indulgence verging on the vicious (certainly Charlotte and the children
might be excused for thinking so, not to mention the tradesmen whose
bills went unpaid) is applauded as the natural effect of innate generosity,
or is justified by shifting the blame to bad examples set by the rich.
Still, it is hard not to pity Fielding as he wrote these words, feeling so

keenly the threat of debtor's prison, and feeling, too, the guilt of knowing that his own imprudence had inflicted suffering and ignominy upon Charlotte, whom he loved. Such a wife, he would observe in *Amelia* (IV.viii), was "the greatest Blessing" a man could possess: "A Blessing however, which tho' it compensates most of the Evils of Life, rather serves to aggravate the Misfortune of distress'd Circumstances, from the Consideration of the Share which she is to bear in them."

The succeeding number of *The Champion* (19 February) resumed this theme. In part it comprises the bitterest and most effective of Fielding's several attacks against the inhuman institution of imprisonment for debt, "that Prototype of Hell." The laws at present, he reminds his readers,

> do put it in the Power of every proud, ill-natur'd, cruel, rapacious Creditor to satisfy his Revenge, his Malice, or his Avarice this Way on any Person who owes him a few Shillings more than he can pay him; but let a Christian take Care how he uses it, and remember that as surely as he forgives not his Neighbour his Trespasses, so surely will his Father in Heaven deny to forgive him his; nor do I know any Crime in this World which can appear to a finite Understanding to deserve infinite Punishment, so much as that cursed and rancorous Disposition which could bring a Man to cause the Destruction of a Family, or the Confinement of a human Creature in Misery during his Life, for any Debt whatever, unless the contracting it be attended with great Circumstances of Villany.

Powerful as an appeal for the reform of an unholy institution, this essay is even more eloquent in the vivid image it affords of the physical discomfort and deprivation that Henry and Charlotte suffered during this desolate season – without the wherewithal to furnish or heat their lodgings, or even to dress decently. More telling still (for to a man of Fielding's pride the sting of contempt was more insufferable than physical hardship) is the impression the essay gives of how bitterly he resented the condescension of his friends. Addressed to those among his more affluent readers who take a malicious pleasure in humiliating their poorer, but better-born, acquaintance, Fielding's rebuke is too sharp, too circumstantial not to be founded in his own recent experience. He asks the rich:

> that whenever they condescend to visit Men of equal or superiour Birth, but infinitely their Inferiours in Fortune, they would not throw out certain Hints, *that* particular Parts of the Town (where Rents are cheap) *lie too distant,* that old Houses are *cold* and *incon-venient,* that they did not know there was *any such Place in Town.* I likewise insist that they never mention the Word *Pictures,* nor even

(during the Frost) insinuate that Carpets make a Room warm, that one cannot set his Wig without a Glass, or that small Grates waste Coals. I likewise earnestly recommend to all Grandees, never in the Company of their Inferiours, to wonder *how People can walk the Streets*; and do positively forbid any Person, of what Quality soever, unless he be a profest Wit, to condemn Port Wine. I desire, moreover, that no Man with a mourning Sword on, may be asked *who he is in Mourning for?* And so declare, that henceforth, a Hole in a Man's Stocking shall make no Flaw in his Reputation, unless the Stocking be a very fine one, or the Wearer rides in a Chair.

Fielding's penury was well enough known about town for one of Walpole's legion of propagandists – the reverend and well-connected poetaster Thomas Newcomb – to represent the author of *The Champion* actually conducting the journal from a cell in debtor's prison:

> Thro' his *Fleet* grate, let busy *F[ieldin]g* rave,
> And dictate what wou'd *Britain* sink, or save;
> Who by his happy wants more wisdom gets,
> His parts improving with his duns and debts.[26]

That Fielding's improvidence had reduced him, for a time, to the ignominy of incarceration in debtor's prison does not seem unlikely from the angry, personal tone of his denunciations of that institution. It would not be long, certainly, before he found himself cooling his heels in a bailiff's sponging house. The fact that no record exists of his having been committed to the Fleet or any other prison would be more reassuring, furthermore, if it were not that, for this period, records for the Fleet are imperfect and those for the Marshalsea do not exist at all.

But even in such straitened circumstances as these, Fielding's habitual cheerfulness and the "solid Comfort" he found in Charlotte's love and constancy could persuade him that their life together was happier than riches could have made it – happier and, given the hard lessons they had learned, wiser too. This, anyway, is how, in *The Champion* (10 May 1740), "the Man in the Moon" sees Hercules Vinegar and his wife through a window in Essex Street:

> I do assure you [he writes to Vinegar], that it is with no moderate Pleasure that I peep in at your Window, where I behold yourself and Madam *Joan*, enjoying the humble Comforts of a Mutton Chop and a Pint of Port, I often hear you recounting to each other, the mistaken idle Pursuits of Youth, before either of you had fully discovered the Folly and Vanity of the World. It is with Rapture I observe you consulting the Happiness of each other and of your Children, and shunning, with Contempt, even innocent Amusements that have not a Tendency that Way. I believe I could, if I would indulge myself,

draw a Picture of Happiness here from the Life, which the World hath rarely seen; and this even in Despight of Fortune.

The gloom of this season deepened that spring, however, when tragedy befell Fielding's favorite half-brother John, then nineteen years of age. For some time John had suffered from weakness of vision. Persuaded by the assurance of the eminent surgeon James Wilkie, who claimed he could cure the infirmity, Edmund Fielding committed his son to Wilkie's care on 10 March 1739/40. For three months John submitted to the ministrations of this man, one of the Governors of St. George's Hospital; as a consequence he was "rendered totally blind." Edmund, represented by Henry's own trusted advocate Giles Taylor,[27] brought an action against Wilkie in Hilary Term of the following year, when a jury, composed entirely of gentlemen, found him guilty of gross negligence and incompetence and awarded John damages in the amount of £500.[28] The award was considerable for the time, but small compensation for blindness permanently inflicted.

···◆ iv ◆···

There is more to be said about Fielding's association with *The Champion*, which in some ways is the liveliest and most interesting of the several periodicals he edited. By June 1740 the paper had not only survived its early difficulties, but was prospering. Before taking up that thread again – to consider some of *The Champion*'s topical themes, as well as what the paper reveals of Fielding's circumstances – we must glance at one of the most important events of his life which took place this same month, a time more propitious than any he had recently known.

On 20 June – after an unusually short probationary period of little more than two and a half years – Fielding was called to the Bar at the Middle Temple. The expedition with which he qualified as barrister was owing in part, no doubt, to the force of his intellect and the diligence with which he applied himself to master the law. But it was chiefly through the influence of his uncle, Davidge Gould, a Master of the Bench at the Temple, that an exception was made in Fielding's case – the claim being allowed, in particular, that he was a scholar of twelve years' standing in the University of Leyden, which he in fact attended for only a few months in 1728 and 1729. The order reads:

that M^r. Fielding H having produced a Certificate of his being twelve years Standing in the University of Leyden and being a near relation of M^r. Gould one of the Masters of the Bench who from his own knowledge assured their Masterships of the said M^r. Fieldings great application and progress in the Study of the Law be called to [the Degree of the utter Barr].[29]

On 20 June Fielding paid the necessary "Duties" of £48.4.10, as well as a "Fyne" of two pounds on his admission to chambers.[30]

Thus timely qualified in his new profession, Fielding attended the assizes on the Western Circuit, which included the largely familiar territory of Hampshire, Wiltshire, Dorset, Cornwall, Devon, and Somerset. In the summer of 1740, the itinerary was as follows: Winchester, Tuesday, 15 July; Salisbury, Saturday, 19 July; Dorchester, Thursday, 24 July; Bodmin, Thursday, 31 July; Exeter, Wednesday, 6 August; Bridgwater, Wednesday, 13 August; Bristol, Monday, 18 August.

Whether Fielding was present at all these times and places is uncertain, but it is clear that he attended the assizes at Dorchester. From Basingstoke on 15 July he sent an urgent message to his uncle at Sharpham Park, asking that he "would without fail send me the Conveyance I mentioned to y° to Dorsetshire Assizes, as I am advised my Success will greatly depend thereon." Replying on 23 July in a letter addressed to Fielding at Dorchester (the day before the assizes began), Davidge Gould assured his nephew that he had sent the deeds in question, which, however, had "received Damage by the Water" – a peril the soggy levels around Sharpham always posed. But, he continued, "I believe there's nothing in them that will be serviceable to ye point you told me was in question. I have cursorily cast my Eye on all the other old deeds, & I can see nothing of use to you."[31] Given the urgency of Fielding's tone and the nature of his business with his uncle, a former trustee of the East Stour estate, it is tempting to surmise from this exchange of letters that, in his début on the Western Circuit, Fielding was attempting, however ineffectually, to salvage something more of value from the recent liquidation of his inheritance.

We have it on the excellent authority of his friend Harris that Fielding was regular in his attendance at these peripatetic legal events (at least until illness disabled him), and that he enjoyed more "Success" in his profession than we have supposed: "He made some figure on ye western Circuit [Harris recalls], and had probably succeeded farther had not ye Gout rendered him incapable of pursuing those legal Journeys." Harris's recollections, indeed, afford an amusing glimpse of Counsellor Fielding – author in the summer of 1740 of *The Champion* and in years to come of some of the best comic novels in the language – as he tried cannily to ply both his trades at once, well aware of the problem that defeated Mr. Wilson in *Joseph Andrews* (III.iii), who, having once been a playwright, could find no employment in the legal profession; for, as one prospective client laughingly told him, "he was afraid I should turn

his Deeds into Plays, and he should expect to see them on the Stage."
According to Harris, Fielding learned this lesson early, and with the
help of a little sleight of hand and a suitably grave demeanor, contrived
to avoid Wilson's fate:

> At his Lodgings, upon ye Circuit he was often working on his Peices
> of Humour, which when Business was approaching, soon vanished
> out of Sight, while ye Law Books and the Briefs with their receptacle
> ye Green Bag lay on ye Table ready displayed, to inspire the Client
> with proper Sentiments.[32]

...◄● V ●►...

As Harris's vignette suggests, if Fielding had clients, he nevertheless
always found it necessary to supplement his income as a barrister by
writing for money – and what he preferred to write were those "Peices
of Humour" we best remember him for. As a playwright, and now as
an essayist in *The Champion*, when he felt free to follow his own
inclinations rather than those of his patrons, the subjects he chose to
treat were not usually political, but rather moral and social. For the
most part his manner was witty and playful, but when vice was the
target he could be earnest. The changes in format and organization
that altered *The Champion* in April 1740 also signaled a change in the
content of the paper, notably a new emphasis on Patriot polemics.
In a moment we will consider the perplexing implications of this
development.

First, however, it is important – important to our sense of Fielding's
technical versatility and amplitude of mind, as well as to our understanding of his distinctive conception of the novel, influenced as it was
by his mastery of the forms of the familiar essay – that we appreciate
the range and variety of topics he treated in *The Champion*. His early
papers were almost wholly given either to reflections on the manners
and morals of society, or to observations on serious philosophical
matters. Among the more than fifty essays he wrote before *The Champion* underwent its metamorphosis with No. 64 on 10 April 1740, we
find papers on such subjects as the importance of self-knowledge (No.
3) and self-control (No. 35), the deceptiveness of appearances (No. 4),
the insubstantial rewards of fame (No. 6), the role of chance in human
affairs (No. 10), and the fallacy of a misanthropic view of human nature
(Nos. 12 and 30). The essays from these months also include Fielding's
earliest attempts to articulate his creed as a Christian of the Low Church
latitudinarian tradition – the tradition of Archbishop Tillotson and

Samuel Clarke, whose confutation of atheism and deism he recommends
(No. 30); it was a benign and comfortable theology making salvation a
matter of sincerity and good works (Nos. 18, 24, 30, 48, 53, 58, 59, and
62). Since, moreover, one of his abiding concerns as an author was to
attempt to purify the moral vocabulary, so that men, having in common
a valid understanding of the nature of virtue and vice, might not only
know themselves better, but act toward one another in just and friendly
ways, he devoted several papers to defining such abstract terms as
Valour and Wit (No. 22), Authority (No. 27), Virtue (Nos. 32 and 53),
Charity (No. 41), and Good-Nature (No. 58). In other essays he ridicules
the follies or cruelties of men – as in his papers on pedantry and false
learning in the professions (No. 18), on avarice and greed (Nos. 19, 20,
41, and 42), on extravagance in living (No. 45), on slander (No. 49), and
on "roasting" and cruelty to animals (Nos. 52 and 56). Of unusual
interest are the two series of papers he began in March: "Extracts from
the Voyages of Mr. Job Vinegar," comprising a satiric survey of English
society written in imitation of his favorite Swift, were published at
irregular intervals over the course of a dozen numbers from 20 March
to 2 October 1740;[33] on 29 March appeared the first essay in an earnest
four-part series entitled an "Apology for the Clergy," in which he
examined the causes of a widespread contempt of the priesthood and
defined the characters of the true and false clergyman.

   Throughout the period of his authorship of *The Champion* Fielding
also acted as arbiter of contemporary taste in literary and theatrical
affairs. He thus hilariously recreates the opening night of James Miller's
farce *An Hospital for Fools*, whose damnation he witnessed at Drury
Lane on the day *The Champion* began publication (No. 43, 21 February
1739/40). He attended at that theatre as the season began on 6 September 1740 with an admirable production of *Hamlet*, and made the
occasion the subject of a paper praising James Quin, who he hoped
would replace the bungling Theophilus Cibber as manager (No. 129, 9
September 1740). Young Cibber, indeed, who so well became in life the
role of Ancient Pistol he played on stage, is a constant target in *The
Champion*, as is another familiar mark from Fielding's dramatic period,
John Rich and his pantomimes. But virtually all Fielding's former
targets are hit again in these pages – "Orator" Henley, madcap priest
and incoherent mouthpiece of the ministry; "Count" Heidegger and his
masquerades; Christopher Cock the auctioneer and the unscrupulous
ticketmongers in the lottery; Edmund Curll, the piratical bookseller;
the quacks John Misaubin and "Spot" Ward; the pedants Bentley and
Burmann, resurrected from the learned annotations of "H. Scriblerus
Secundus." The entire gallery of knaves and fools first exhibited in his
farces of the 1730s is hung up again – together with a number of
newcomers who, as Fielding put it in another context, had succeeded

in distinguishing themselves at the expense of being pointed at. Such are the preposterous metaphysician Dr. George Cheyne (Nos. 1 and 80), and the evangelist George Whitefield (No. 24), the fiery Methodist who would always represent for Fielding the most pernicious influence in contemporary religion.

But Colley Cibber remains the Prince of Folly. From time to time during the early months of *The Champion* Fielding took potshots at the Poet Laureate; no wit in Cibber's London could do otherwise. It was, however, a fresh Cibberian enormity engendered in the spring of the year that provoked Fielding to renew his attacks with a vengeance. This was Cibber's own self-congratulatory autobiography, published on 7 April 1740 and bearing the delectable title that Fielding enjoyed savoring: *An Apology for the Life of Mr. Colley Cibber, Comedian, and Late Patentee of the Theatre-Royal. Written by Himself.* He read the work eagerly on publication and found in Chapter VIII the following characterization of himself as a nameless "broken Wit" of the theatre whose scurrilous satires had precipitated the Licensing Act:

> This enterprising Person, I say (whom I do not chuse to name, unless it could be to his Advantage, or that it were of Importance) had Sense enough to know, that the best Plays, with bad Actors, would turn but to a very poor Account; and therefore found it necessary to give the Publick some Pieces of an extraordinary Kind, the Poetry of which he conceiv'd ought to be so strong, that the greatest Dunce of an Actor could not spoil it: He knew too, that as he was in haste to get Mony, it would take up less Time to be intrepidly abusive, than decently entertaining; that, to draw the Mob after him, he must rake the Channel, and pelt their Superiors .... Such then, was the mettlesome Modesty he set out with; upon this Principle he produc'd several frank, and free Farces, that seem'd to knock all Distinctions of Mankind on the Head: Religion, Laws, Government, Priests, Judges, and Ministers, were all laid flat, at the Feet of this *Herculean* Satyrist! This *Drawcansir* in Wit, that spared neither Friend nor Foe! who, to make his Poetical Fame immortal, like another *Erostratus*, set Fire to his Stage, by writing up to an Act of Parliament to demolish it. I shall not give the particular Strokes of his Ingenuity a Chance to be remembred, by reciting them; it may be enough to say, in general Terms, they were so openly flagrant, that the Wisdom of the Legislature thought it high time, to take a proper Notice of them.

Reprisals against contumely such as this were to be expected. They began in *The Champion* (15 April 1740), where the *Apology* is ironically lauded as the example of "*consummate Imperfection*" in writing, and they continue, weekly, until 24 May – after which Fielding kept his adversary's facetious memory alive with less regular flicks of the lash. The qualities he found most remarkable about the man whom Pope would soon elevate to the throne of Dulness in *The New Dunciad* were his prodigious vanity (if Fate had not made a comedian of him, he would have been a bishop or a general!), his fawning devotion to Walpole, and above all the amazing ineptitude of his English: "the *Ultra sublime*," Fielding declared, "will in future Ages be called the CIBBERIAN STILE" (3 May 1740). A deft parodist, Fielding demonstrated the propriety of this prediction by archly defending Cibber's ignorance of the language he wrote in (29 April 1740). He declared:

> That it is needless for a GREAT WRITER to understand his Grammar: for as we can generally guess his Meaning without it, so when his Genius (to speak in our Author's Stile) ascends into the elevated and nervously pompous Elements of the Sublime, the Ladder of Grammar offers it self in vain to the Feet of the Reader's Understanding: for tho' the Words which may be called the Brick and Mortar of Speech, are regularly conglutinated together, so as to erect the extraneous Frontispiece of a delicate excessively sweet Sugar-Loaf of a Pile; yet if there be no Sentiment, no aspiring, animating, softly, sweetly tempered Spirit, this Pile is only a naked Building, void of Furniture, where the wearied Understanding of the long travelled Reader will find no Featherbed to repose himself on.

The climax of Fielding's roasting of Cibber and his autobiography was promised for 17 May, when the Laureate would be brought before Hercules Vinegar's Court of Judicature for the crime of murdering the English language. Cibber, however, having kissed the rod by paying to advertise the *Apology* twice in *The Champion* (15 and 17 May), found the charge reduced to "*Chance-Medley*." One measure of the interest the Town took in this feud between Fielding and Cibber – the two liveliest figures in the theatrical world of the preceding decade – is the fact that five of the papers in *The Champion* which Fielding devoted to his antagonist were pirated by one "T. Johnson," a certain knowledgeable hack in the pay of Edmund Curll, who published them together in July in a shilling pamphlet entitled *The Tryal of Colley Cibber, Comedian* liberally seasoned with personal ridicule of Fielding and his "Gang."

If *The Champion* thus stands as a compendium of Fielding's satiric interests of the period, it is also a guide to many of his friendships and to the contemporaries whose talents in various fields he admired. Prominent among those he compliments are Pope and Swift; the actor Quin and his favorite "Kitty" Clive; the paintings of "the ingenious Mr. *Hogarth*," and "the enchanting Harmony of *Handel*'s Compositions ... that great Man" (10 June 1740). Also numbered among his friends here are some who have escaped the notice of his biographers. One is the wine merchant "honest *John Hunter*," who specialized in Fielding's favorite port and whose shop in Essex Street was perhaps a little too convenient to Fielding's lodgings (20 May). Another was the distinguished lawyer Giles Eyre (1673 to 25 February 1739/40) of the Middle Temple, King's Sergeant at Law and a member of an eminent Wiltshire family – three of whom would appear among the list of subscribers to Fielding's *Miscellanies*. Upon hearing that Sergeant Eyre was dying, Fielding inserted the following remarkable eulogy in the "Home News" column of *The Champion* (28 February 1739/40):

> Whose Loss will be heartily lamented by all who had the Happiness of his Acquaintance, or the Misfortune to want an Advocate, in which Character his Abilities were as eminent as his Integrity, in all the Actions of his Life. In short, he was truely worthy of Admiration, as a Lawyer and of Love as a Man, and one of those few, on whom we can indulge our Appetite of Commendation without the Danger of a Lie.

···➤ vi ◆─···

It is, however, the politics of *The Champion* – an aspect of the journal which became increasingly conspicuous after the spring of 1740 – which starkly reveals the perplexed personal circumstances in which Fielding found himself. *The Champion* was launched at a time when the hopes of the Patriots were high, for in October 1739 they had achieved two notable triumphs over Walpole. That month they defeated Sir George Champion, Walpole's candidate for the office of Lord Mayor of London – and a man whose name and connection with City politics gave ironic point to both the title Fielding chose for his journal and the audience to which it was chiefly addressed. The Patriots had also succeeded at last in forcing Walpole to abandon his unpopular pacific policy toward Spain: the War of Jenkins' Ear, as it came to be called, was declared on 23 October.

From its inception *The Champion* played a part, if a small one, in the Opposition's campaign to bring the minister down. Not until No. 15 (18 December 1739) did Fielding openly attack the ministry in his letter "To the Citizens of London," exhorting the electors to resist Walpole's bribes – a partisan gesture which provoked the only serious notice the *Daily Gazetteer* would deign to take of Fielding's journal during the first eight months of its publication.

But Fielding's political loyalties would have been obvious at once to

knowledgeable readers who perused his essays attentively. As early as
No. 6 (27 November 1739), for example, he praised the wit of his patron
Chesterfield, alluding to the noble lord's famous speech against the
theatrical Licensing Act. Far more revealing as a guide to his party
affiliations is the dream-vision in No. 13 (13 December 1739), in which he
imagines certain poets and their patrons attempting to scale Parnassus,
where, at the summit, Pope lolls in the lap of the Muses. The narrator
proceeds: "a Couple approached, who, tho' their Persons did not much
agree, (the one being of the taller Kind, and thin, the other shorter and
fatter) yet their Minds seemed to be more of a Piece, they seemed to
walk together with great Friendship and Affection." This congenial
pair, whom Pope eagerly welcomes, are George Lyttelton (who, Fielding
observes, had of late given up writing verse for "graver Studies, in
which he hath nobly distinguished himself") and Lyttelton's friend,
the City poet Richard Glover (1712–85) – author of *Leonidas* (1737), a
ponderous epic dedicated to Lord Cobham, and more recently of
London: or, The Progress of Commerce (1739). Thanks to Lyttelton's
puff in *Common Sense* (9 April 1737), Glover, despite the tedium of his
verse, was hailed as the poet of the Patriot cause, an honor he did his
best to deserve as a member of the Corporation of London by zealously
opposing every ministerial candidate for office. It was Glover who was
chiefly responsible for frustrating Sir George Champion's bid for the
mayoralty. In this same number of *The Champion* Fielding also singled
out for a remarkable compliment another member of Lyttelton's
immediate circle: this was Gilbert West (1703–56), Cobham's nephew,
who like Lyttelton and Pitt had been Fielding's schoolfellow at Eton.
Reviewing West's *A Canto of the Fairy Queen. Written by Spenser* (1739),
Fielding praised the poem as "almost ... a new Species of Satire,"
and he declared, "were it not for the superior Harmony of [West's]
Versification ... and the Correctness of his Language, I could, without
Difficulty, persuade myself, 'twas really a Fragment of that happy
Genius, whom I never yet read but with Love and Admiration."

There is no evidence that Fielding and Ralph were actually in
Lyttelton's pay, but when *The Champion* did address the political issues
of the day, it faithfully served the Cobhamite cause. Years later, when
"Aretine" of *Old England* (5 August 1749) sneered that part of Fielding's
payment for writing the journal was "a *Sunday*'s Dinner," we might
suppose it was Lyttelton's hospitality Fielding enjoyed.

We might just as reasonably suppose, however, that Fielding had
become by this time a regular guest at the table of another of his
powerful patrons, George Bubb Dodington (1691–1762). Having served
for fifteen years as a Commissioner of the Treasury, Dodington broke
with Walpole in 1739 and went immediately into opposition.[34] Through
his maternal grandmother, a Temple, he qualified as another of the

Cobham "cousinhood"; and, like Lyttelton's, his own political program was modeled on the "Patriot" manifesto of Bolingbroke. From the Preface to *Of True Greatness*, the poem Fielding dedicated to Dodington in January 1740/1, it is clear that the two men had by then been acquainted for "several Years" – a circumstance not very surprising when one considers that Dodington's palatial estate, Eastbury, at Tarrant Gunville in Dorset, was an easy journey from Fielding's farm at East Stour. Fielding no doubt had often enjoyed Dodington's hospitality. Accordingly, when he complimented his friend in *The Champion* (29 January 1739/40), he placed him in the company of two other leading figures of the Opposition, declaring that what the Duke of Argyll was to Valour and Lord Chesterfield to Wit, Dodington was to "Politeness."

Usually, however, the quality Fielding affected to find in this man, supremely, was one rather more astonishing – nothing less indeed than "true Greatness." In the *Daily Gazetteer* (13 May 1741), writing in response to Fielding's praise of Dodington in his poem on that subject, Ralph Courteville produced a mock Æsopian fable entitled "*The* Story *of the* BEAR *and his* MONKEY" which affords, in allegory, our fullest account of the close relationship between the two friends. In this narrative the Bear (Dodington), after long service at the court of "the young Lion" (George II) and his faithful minister the "honest Greyhound" (Walpole), began to imagine he had not been rewarded according to his merits and, in a surly mood, retired to his cave (Eastbury) – a den so "fine" "scarce any Bear had such another." Having fallen out with his old friends, he now took up with "Vermin," chief among whom is a particularly "mischievous" Monkey (Fielding), "more in favour with the Bear than all the rest."

What follows is Courteville's version of Dodington's patronage of Fielding during the period of *The Champion*. Of all his apery the Monkey most delighted in donning

a Gown and Band, in which he fancied he look'd the *Counsellor*. But as there is always somewhat out of Nature in the Buffoonery of that *Creature*, so in this grave Dress he would needs carry a Quarter-staff instead of a Roll of Briefs, which diverted the *Bear* extremely, and made indeed the Main of his Amusement. On the other hand, *Pug* [Fielding], who had tired a great many, was exceedingly attentive to his last *Patron* [Dodington]; he play'd over all his Tricks at a Nod, or Sign made with the Finger; no Creature of the highest Distinction was safe from his Feats of Ill-nature, especially if he imagined it would delight his *Bear*. Sometimes when that Beast was gloomy, the rest of the Vermine would get out of the Way; but *Pug* on such Occasions kept his Post, strok'd, comb'd, and coax'd the *Bear*, and

call'd his sullen Spirit, true Greatness of Mind forsooth, which made
his Master swell and look as significant as might be.

Since, the story continues, the "chief Object of the *Bear*'s Aversion"
was "Trusty" the Greyhound, Fielding (to drop the allegory) obliged
his new master by ridiculing Walpole and all his party. So, Courteville
concludes, after venting a long passage of personal abuse on his adversary, Fielding "is owned for [Dodington's] Secretary in *hope* as well as
his Jester for the *present*."

One inference is plain enough from this puerile satire: that Dodington
was behind the heightening of anti-ministerial polemics that began to
characterize Fielding's contributions to *The Champion* in March 1740 –
a trend which, with Ralph's greater collaboration, became so noticeable
after the paper's metamorphosis in April that for a brief period *The
Champion* supplanted *The Craftsman* and *Common Sense* as the principal target of the Gazetteers. That Dodington may have interested
himself in *The Champion* about this time is not unlikely. Not only did
he admire Fielding's satiric flair; he was so impressed with Ralph's
talents as a political writer that he would later make *him* his "secretary," collaborating with him on a number of publications.[35] Fielding's
compliments to Dodington – expressed briefly in *The Champion* in
January 1739/40 and expansively in *Of True Greatness* a year later –
suggest, furthermore, a deepening sense of gratitude to his patron.
Though Fielding had few unnecessary scruples about hiring out his
talent as a writer to whoever would pay him, it better suited that
deeper, and very real, part of his character which valued nobler actions
to espouse the cause of Patriotism, whose principles he found per-
suasively articulated by his friends Lyttelton and Dodington. To Fielding, however odd the opinion has seemed, Dodington always embodied
the idea of true greatness: as late as *Amelia* (XI.ii), more than ten years
after the period with which we are now concerned, Fielding would still
call his friend "one of the greatest Men this Country ever produced."

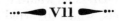

Might it be that Dodington was also the inspiration behind Fielding's
most ambitious work on this topic, *The Life of Mr. Jonathan Wild the
Great*, an ironic anatomy of false greatness figuratively embodied in the
Great Man himself, Sir Robert Walpole, once Dodington's friend but
now his enemy? We can at least state with confidence that few who
ever read that novel relished it more than Dodington. One of the
distressingly funny anecdotes to have come down to us is Richard

Cumberland's story that he had heard Dodington at Eastbury read *Jonathan Wild* aloud, in its entirety, to the elderly Ladies Hervey and Stafford[36] – a literary ordeal from life surpassed only by the appalling denouement of Waugh's *Handful of Dust*.

Jonathan Wild was not published until 1743, when it appeared as Volume III of Fielding's *Miscellanies*. But for many reasons – including the nature of the work itself, whose satire is aimed chiefly at Walpole – it seems likely that Fielding conceived the work and originally drafted it sometime during the period after the Licensing Act of 1737 and before Walpole fell from power in February 1741/2, the balance of opinion (among those who take this view) inclining to the period when Fielding was actively involved in *The Champion*.[37] To be sure, a number of topical allusions indicate that certain passages in the novel must have been written in 1742, after Walpole fell. But as part of the *Miscellanies*, which Fielding hoped to have in the hands of his subscribers no later than the winter of 1741–2, *The Life of Mr. Jonathan Wild the Great* would have been well under way by that time. Originally, moreover, the work must certainly have been conceived as a satire of Walpole, the Great Man with whom Wild – the notorious boss of a gang of thieves – had been identified by Opposition writers from the moment he was hanged at Tyburn in 1725. Like Wild (the analogy went), Walpole plundered the public; like Wild, his proper fate, if only the public could be roused, was the gallows. This sardonic jest was current and timely when Walpole was in power; it would be stale and irrelevant after February 1742. For far from suffering Wild's fate, Walpole, when his game was up, had been elevated to the peerage as Earl of Orford – an inequity not lost upon the Tory wit Paul Whitehead: "WILD falls a Felon, W[ALPOL]E mounts a Lord."[38]

Though we do not know precisely when Fielding began writing *Jonathan Wild* or precisely how that novel reached the form in which the public received it in 1743, it seems likely that by 1740, perhaps encouraged by that exemplar of "true Greatness" Dodington, Fielding had produced a stinging satire of Walpole under the familiar ironic guise of that notorious criminal. Twice during 1740 the Prime Minister is figured this way in *The Champion* – once in Fielding's leader on "Reputation" in No. 48 (4 March): "Actions have sometimes been attended with Fame, which were undertaken in Defiance of it. *Jonathan Wyld* himself had for many Years no small share of it in this Kingdom"; and later in some sarcastic verses in No. 132 (16 September):

> Nor *Wild*, great Man! who had his Day,
> And kept the lesser Rogues in Pay,
> Can live in *Newgate*'s Rolls so long
> As thou, thou greater R[ogue]! in Song.

At one moment this year we may even imagine Fielding celebrating his thirty-third birthday by reading a chapter of this new satire on contemporary politics to an appreciative audience in one of his favorite taverns. *The Champion* No. 70 (24 April 1740) contains the following sly observation on a news item reporting the cancelation of a parliamentary meeting scheduled for 22 April: "*About the same Instant, a very learned Comment was exhibited at a public House in the Neighbourhood, on* Aristotle's *Chapter of* Hats." Can this "*very learned Comment*" have been a draft of the chapter "Of Hats" in *Jonathan Wild* (II.vi) – in which Fielding ridicules, in a Swiftian spirit, the factitious distinctions between Whigs and Tories, and in an erudite footnote regrets the loss of "that Chapter written by Aristotle on this Subject, which ... might have given some light into" such a "mysterious" matter?

By the spring of 1740 Fielding probably already had in hand the most devastating of his prose satires – a work whose radical critique of contemporary politics and the social order struck Byron as stronger stuff than any the Jacobins of his own day could offer.[39] Why, then, did he not publish it? The answer may be that Walpole paid him to suppress it. Such is the inference to be drawn from a remarkable passage in *The Champion* (4 October 1740), the sense of which can be understood only in the context of Fielding's relations with Walpole during this difficult period.

viii

Though he was reluctant to make a partisan political vehicle of *The Champion*, Fielding's worsening financial circumstances and his anxiety over what appeared to be the imminent demise of the journal caused him to acquiesce in the politicizing of the paper in the spring of 1740. Throughout his authorship of *The Champion* he never wavered in supporting the cause of his friends in Opposition. It is clear, however, that he was under pressure from Walpole to desert the Patriots – preferably (from the minister's point of view) by turning his coat and appearing in print actively in Walpole's behalf, but, if defection seemed too flagrantly disloyal, then by withdrawing from the fray and keeping mum.

Hints of these overtures occur early in *The Champion* (as in the curious, only partly ironic tone of the essay on "Turn Coats" [12 January 1739/40]). But in the leader of 14 February 1739/40 – the month when the horrid spectre of debtor's prison seemed so real – Fielding quite plainly represented his predicament: an author who by inclination was "no Politican" yet who was being solicited by both parties to apply himself to politics; who remained sympathetically attached to the Patriot cause, yet who, out of concern for his family and a healthy respect for what the government could do to him if it chose, was tempted by Walpole's bribes:

As these two Parties assign different Reasons, so they offer different Rewards; one of them Reputation, Honour, Fame and the like, the other ask me, if I have no Love for my Family, and talk of Vacancies, good Things, snug Places, &c. One Mr. *Guts* particularly, says, *Do, do, do, Mr. Vinegar, write, write, write, and I'll warrant you – as soon as it happens – let me see but – ay that will do – depend – but then – through thick and thin – my Interest*; by which last Word I imagine him a Man of Consequence: There are likewise some Instructions to abuse certain Persons whose Names I dare not insert even the first Letters of, for Fear of having my Paper sentenced by the Common Voice, to be burnt by the Hands of the Common Hangman.

Tho' I have as great Contempt for the Promises of Mr. *Guts* as any Man living can have, and have therefore, instead of abusing any Person according to his Desire, absolutely concealed the least Hint of their Names, yet on the other Side I have some Regard likewise for the Advice of a very sensible Writer as he seems, who signs himself *Cavendum est*, for, I do not know many Parts of my Body, for which I have a greater Respect than my Ears.

Again, on 5 June 1740, less than a week after the publication of Fielding's rude, and highly successful, satire graphically representing Walpole as the "Trunk" through which the King's favors are transmitted to his courtiers,[40] Fielding ran a mock advertisement, the sense of which is that the minister's overtures were continuing:

A sober Man who hath a little Wit, and who understands at lest [sic] *English, can keep a Secret, and will go through thick and thin, may hear of an Employment by applying to* Robert Brass *at the Sign of the Gazetteer.*

Note, *Men of Parts are very much wanted, and all such who are pleased to serve the said* Robert Brass, *under the Direction of Mr.* Lead, *shall receive great Encouragement, and enter into present Pay.*

N.B. *All Persons qualified are desired to apply very shortly, or the said* Brass *will probably have no Occasion for them.*

During the summer months Fielding was busy on the Western Circuit, trying to establish himself in his new profession. For the most part his contributions to *The Champion* consisted of installments of the narrative of Job Vinegar's voyages which he had probably written earlier and left with Ralph to be printed as the need for copy arose. On 4 October, however, he published a most extraordinary paper – a

transparent allegory of his recent relations with Walpole, representing
the Prime Minister as a mountebank whose golden pills, when taken as
prescribed, are a nostrum to cure every malady – except, that is, a
deficiency of self-respect and love of one's country. This paper, one of
the most revealing autobiographical statements in Fielding's writings,
warrants quoting in full:

To one Capt. VINEGAR.

Capt. VINEGAR,
WHAT is the Reason, Sir, that you write against me? Prithee, what
dost mean by those cant Words of *Virtue* and *public Spirit?* Do'st
think they will go to Market? Kiss my A— I would not give a Fart
for all the Virtue in the Universe.

They tell me you have some Wit and Humour, and have you no
more Sense than to starve with them? To write on the Side of a Set
of Rascals and sturdy ———[41] D–mn them, I'll shew them who I am.

If you will not come over, and say some good Things of me, stay
at Home and be quiet and neuter, and I'll give you a hundred Pills.

But, if you will say a *single Word* in my Favour, I will give you
two hundred Pills.

If you can declaim handsomely upon my Nostrums, as they tell
me it is in you, nay, I know there is nothing easier, it is but
haranguing, I'll bring you upon the Stage myself, I'll give you three
hundred Pills, besides something very good to take twice a Year as
long as you live; and then I'll give your Booksellers fifty Pills a Piece
(which one of them looks as if he wanted), and I'll give your Publisher
forty Pills, and your Printer forty Pills, and his Devil twenty Pills,
and the Pressmen ten Pills each.—In short, I'll pill you and all that
belongs to you.

What is it to you then, whether I poison the Nation or no, provided
I give you wholesome Physick? Can't you hold your Tongue and be
d—n'd to you, without interfering in Matters that do not concern
you? You must be a Champion indeed for the Public, is there one of
all this Public, would give you a single Pill if you was sick? Not one,
then prithee know thy own Interest, and that it is better to be my
Merry-Andrew, than the Champion of the Public.

But I would not have you think, because I am willing to have you
in my Service, to abuse the regular Physicians, and to flatter myself
that I fear you; no, you may all kiss my A— for any Apprehension
I have of you, every one knows I never drank more Port, nor shook
my Sides more heartily than at present: And I shall shortly erect my
Stage, where I intend to dispense my Pills in the most public Manner,
and I will answer for it, as long as they are gilded, you, and all your
Confederates, will find it a difficult Task to prevent Mankind, in their

present sickly Condition, from joyfully taking them. Gild your Pill well, and Men will *swallow whatever you would cram down their Throats.* Experto credo Roberto.

Whoever the Quack is, from whom this Epistle is arriv'd, I believe the Public will sufficiently conclude that he is a very impudent Fellow. If I mistake not the Hand, it is one whose Pills I formerly refused on the like Conditions now offer'd, tho' I own, being in an ill State of Health, I accepted a few to stop the Publication of a Book, which I had written against his Practice, and which he threaten'd to take the Law of me, if I publish'd: These Pills, tho' a mere Matter of Bargain, he was pleas'd to consider as a great Obligation: But I can tell him, his Nostrums have now done so much Mischief, that whoever takes any Reward of him to secure his Practice any longer, deserves more to be hang'd, and is a more infamous VILLAIN than any on the Records of the *Old Bailey.*

Which "Book" was it that Fielding took Walpole's money to suppress, motivated both by the urgency of his financial circumstances and by the threat of being prosecuted for libel? In the dim light of our knowledge of Fielding's affairs, only one work seems to fit the case: namely, *The Life of Mr. Jonathan Wild the Great.* True, he had probably suppressed *The Grub-Street Opera* at the government's instance; but that episode occurred ten years before and at a time when Fielding, a carefree bachelor who had produced a string of plays the public flocked to see, was hardly in "an ill State of Health" financially. The term "Book," moreover, implies a more substantial work than the ballad opera, the publication of which, anyway, he did not succeed in stopping: two unauthorized editions were published despite his protests. *Jonathan Wild* seems the likelier candidate. That Fielding by 1740 had produced a version of this work satirizing Walpole and his "Practice" is probable. That he had been, financially, in a very "ill State of Health" indeed is beyond question. And Fielding himself, in his closing declaration, seems to supply the key to the riddle: hinting that the "Book" in question is his allegorical biography of that arch rogue, Jonathan Wild – than whom Walpole, or anyone who supports his corrupt ministry, "deserves more to be hang'd, and is a more infamous VILLAIN than any on the Records of the *Old Bailey.*"

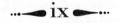

Fielding's ingratitude to Walpole was a recurrent theme of the increasingly numerous and virulent personal attacks leveled against him by the ministerial writers – attacks commencing in the *Daily Gazetteer* in June 1740 and rising to a crescendo of furious vilification in September, October, and November.[42] These were the months when the paper's reputation as an instrument of Patriot polemics surpassed that of *The Craftsman* and *Common Sense*. By 5 September, Courteville was complaining that the satire of the "*Pasquineers*" had "taken Root here; where by the Care and Cultivation of the Opposition, it flourishes beyond Expectation; insomuch that all the Parties and Factions amongst us divert themselves under its Branches, and delight themselves with its Fruit." By 17 October the same author grudgingly allowed, "It is an Honour justly due to the Paper call'd the CHAMPION, or EVENING ADVERTISER, that tho' it set out *last*, yet it has out-stripped all the *Vehicles* of *Sedition* in the Service of the *Opposition*." Another of the Gazetteers (9 October), in a minatory mood, pointed to the analogy between Fielding's farces of 1736–7, "*whose unbridled Licentiousness brought on* (what has been thought by some) *an unnecessary and hurtful Restraint on the Stage*," and the intolerable impertinence of his papers now in *The Champion*, wherein he "is endeavouring by frequent Provocations to draw the same on the Press."

Though Courteville and his Gazetteers thus credited him with *The Champion*'s rise to preeminence as the organ of the Patriots, Fielding was not chiefly responsible for the offensive political content of the paper during the summer and early autumn. That dubious distinction belongs to Ralph, and to certain unknown contributors – one of whom, signing himself "B.T.", published in *The Champion* (7 October 1740) a set of "Remarkable Queries" comprising, shortly before the City elections took place, a sort of legal bill of complaint in what the writer called the "Trial between the *whole Nation Plaintiff*, and *one single Man Defendant*." The awkward questions put to the Prime Minister in this paper were the kind of strong medicine *The Champion*'s readers relished; the queries were reprinted a week later in the issue for 14 October, and in November they formed the basis of a sixpenny pamphlet entitled *The Leviathan Hook'd*. Courteville was convinced, of course, that only "Counsellor F[iel]d[in]g" could be behind this further outrage against Walpole: "The very Stile of this Paper shows it to have fallen from the Pen of a *Smatterer* in the *Law*."[43]

The paper, however, was not by Fielding,[44] who indeed contributed infrequently to *The Champion* during the month of October. One of these contributions (16 October), in the form of a mock advertisement for an autobiography in the manner of Cibber, had the effect of sticking on Fielding's arch tormentor Ralph Courteville a mischievous label by which he would be forever known to the Opposition press:

> PROPOSALS for printing, by Subscription, An Apology for the Life, Actions, and Writings of RALPH FREEMAN, alias, COURT-EVIL, Esq; containing an authentic History of the several wonderful Stages, thro' which he hath passed in the World; together with the successful Progress of Corruption, Baseness, and Treachery, during his Time.
> Written by HIMSELF.

Fielding's absence (comparatively speaking) from the pages of *The Champion* this month did not mean that he was preparing to withdraw from the journal. For one thing, there was his translation of Adlerfeld's *Military History of Charles XII* to see through the press; it was published on 10 October. For another, he was occupied in writing a series of electioneering articles which would, when published in thirteen consecutive installments, comprise the whole of *The Champion*'s front matter for the month of November. Originally, this series, entitled *An Address to the Electors of Great Britain*, was not to have been his assignment at all. On 6 September he inserted the following notice in *The Champion*: "We shall shortly present our Readers with some Papers addressed to the Electors of *Great Britain*, written by a very eminent Hand, who hath thought fit to honour us by the introducing them into the World thro' our Hands." Who was this "eminent Hand"? Since, among the more literary leaders of the Opposition, Lyttelton and Chesterfield had their own vehicle in *Common Sense* and Pulteney his in *The Craftsman*, Dodington seems as likely a candidate as any. In any case, whoever he was, he did not fulfill his promise. The same announcement ran in *The Champion* on 9 and 11 September. And later that month – after a certain "Philopatriae" had published a pair of leaders addressed "To the Freeholders and Electors of Great Britain" in *The Champion* (20 and 23 September) – Fielding hastened to assure his readers that these were not "*the Papers, relating to Elections, lately promised*" in his journal; those, he said, "*will be published in the Beginning of Next Month*."[45] Still, however, they were not forthcoming.

Heralded at last by announcements in *The Champion* for 28 and 30 October – in which Fielding appealed to "*all* honest Men" to cooperate in forwarding the papers to his subscribers, since Walpole's agents in the Post Office were preventing deliveries – *An Address to the Electors of Great Britain* began appearing anonymously in No. 152 (1 November). The author was publishing it, he explained, months earlier than the parliamentary elections it was meant to influence, because the minister's agents were already at work in the newspapers and boroughs, giving "*Earnest* of their present good Affections, by entertaining, presenting, flattering, and promising." Calculated to inspire the electorate with Patriotic sentiments and with the resolve to resist Walpole's bribes, the *Address*, in the range of learning it displays and the skill with which its argument is conducted, is an impressive specimen of the author's powers as a polemicist. And there is no longer any reason to doubt that the author was Henry Fielding.[46] The *Address* was subsequently reprinted in Edinburgh (almost certainly without Fielding's consent) as a pamphlet of 108 pages.[47]

···━▶ X ◀━···

Had he been a more superstitious man Fielding would have seen something ominous in the violent hurricane that lashed the capital on the night of 1 November 1740, the date on which he began addressing the electors in what proved to be the last of his contributions to *The Champion* that can be identified with certainty. Chimneys were blown down, whole houses collapsed, one of the spires of Westminster Abbey fell, a long section of the wall enclosing Hyde Park from Kensington to Hyde Park Corner was flattened, many lives were lost: "a greater Desolation," reported *The Champion* (4 November), "has not been known of many Years." As winter deepened, the fragile fabric of Fielding's happiness would also be strained to the breaking point: before the year ended, the process had begun that would lead to his confinement for debt; in the same inauspicious month of November his father for the same cause would be committed to the Fleet Prison to measure out the last few months of his life in disgrace; the imaginative literary venture of a new fortnightly periodical, by which Fielding must have hoped to slow the decline of his finances, would not survive its fourth number; and in February, when the Opposition's motion that Walpole be removed from the King's counsels was easily defeated, the Patriot cause for which Fielding had been toiling appeared to be lost. He could not have guessed that another event of that otherwise catastrophic November would in time change his life for the better, bringing him, perversely, a kind of literary fame he never dreamed of: that event, advertised in *The Champion* for 6 November, was the publication of Samuel Richardson's novel, *Pamela: or, Virtue Rewarded*.

In December 1740, though *The Champion*, as Thomas Gardiner declared, was making a "considerable profitt" and paying dividends to the partners, Fielding was perilously short of money. By a favorite delaying tactic, the filing of a Writ of Error, he postponed for a few months execution of the judgment a jury found against him on 24 November, when they declared he owed Henley the coal merchant

£27.10s. On 1 December, however, another of his creditors, Hugh Allen, demanded payment of a larger, long-standing debt which he could not pay. On 2 January 1740/1, Allen brought an action in the Palace Court for £200 against Fielding and two other persons.[48] Like Billy Booth of *Amelia* (VIII.i), Fielding proved a "shy Cock," eluding the bailiff until early March – when he would also anticipate his feckless hero in being forced to change his lodgings for a sponging house.

Short of money as he was, Fielding in December began nevertheless to give less time to *The Champion* – reasoning, perhaps, that with his two sixteenth shares of the profits guaranteed, he could leave the work of conducting the paper to Ralph while he attempted other literary ventures that would augment his income. By mid-December, when Thomas Newcomb thought of satirizing the author of *The Champion*, it was Ralph, not Fielding, who came to mind;[49] and in *The Hyp-Doctor* (23 December 1740) "Orator" Henley gloated that Fielding, despairing that his efforts to win the forthcoming election for the Patriots could not succeed, was entertaining "some melancholy Thoughts of resigning his *Herculean* Club." Though the infrequency of his contributions might lead the well-informed ministerial hacks Newcomb and Henley to such a conclusion, Fielding probably did not cease writing for *The Champion* quite this early. Since only a handful of the original numbers survive from the period 15 November 1740 to June 1741 (by which time we have his own word that he had "desisted from writing one Syllable in the *Champion*, or any other public Paper"),[50] it seems best to rely on the testimony of the partners' minute-book: an entry dated 1 March [1741/2] states that Fielding had "withdrawn himself from that Service [of writing for *The Champion*] for above Twelve Months past and refused his Assistance in that Capacity since which time Mr. Ralph has solely Transacted the said Business."[51]

Sometime in January, or at the latest February, 1740/1 Fielding became a silent partner in the paper he originated. One sign that *The Champion* lost its sting at just this period is the fact that for two months in December and January the paper became conspicuous by its absence from the pages of the *Daily Gazetteer* – though Courteville and his colleagues resumed their attacks with a vengeance in February and continued them long after Fielding had certainly left the journal. Indeed, it is instructive to note – since it is sometimes assumed that in the hothouse world of contemporary political journalism secrets of authorship were impossible to keep – that as late as September Courteville continued to believe mistakenly that Fielding, not Ralph, was his principal adversary in *The Champion*.[52]

The first of Fielding's miscellaneous publications this year appeared in the bookstalls on 7 January 1740/1, less than a week after Hugh Allen initiated an action against him in the Palace Court. This was the poem *Of True Greatness. An Epistle to the Right Honourable George Dodington, Esq; By Henry Fielding, Esq*; – price, a shilling. The publisher was Charles Corbett (1710–52), a bookseller well respected in his profession, whose shop was located "at *Addison's Head* against St. *Dunstan's* Church, in *Fleetstreet*." Corbett, we recall, had been – from 29 January 1739/40 to 10 April 1740 – one of the several publishers of *The Champion*, and before this present month of January had run its course he would bring out two further works by Fielding. Just how close the two men had become is clear from the fact that Corbett would be one of the friends to whom Fielding turned when he needed rescuing from a sponging house.

As Fielding assures us in the Preface, *Of True Greatness* "was writ several Years ago" on a subject inspired by the "Conduct and Conversation" of Dodington, with whom, presumably, he had become well acquainted during his Dorset days. The poem itself – besides the definition it offers of a crucial term in Fielding's moral vocabulary – is chiefly interesting for what it tells us of the people he admires: namely, in theology, the controversial latitudinarian Bishop of Winchester, Benjamin Hoadly; in his own profession of the law, Sir William Lee (1688–1754), Chief Justice of the King's Bench, and later Lord Chief Justice; in poetry, Edward Young, also a favorite of Dodington's; and in politics, besides Dodington himself, a number of men notable for their opposition to Walpole – Argyll, Carteret, Chesterfield, and Lyttelton, as well as Sir John Barnard (1685–1764) and Sir Robert Godschall (*c.* 1692–1742), preeminent among the anti-ministerial aldermen of London whose interest Fielding and Glover had recently supported in the contest for the mayoralty.

In a passage tailored to suit his present circumstances, Fielding coyly includes himself among "the great" he honors, enjoying the pun on his large physique yet declaring his allegiance to the noble concept he celebrates:

> Thus the great tatter'd Bard, as thro' the Streets
> He cautious treads, least any Bailiff meets:
> Whose wretched Plight the Jest of all is made;
> Yet most, if hapless, it betray his Trade....
> And yet with Want and with Contempt opprest,
> Shunn'd, hated, mock'd, at once Men's Scorn and Jest,

Perhaps, from wholesome Air itself confin'd,
Who hopes to drive out Greatness from his Mind?

More interesting than the poem itself, in this autobiographical context, is the Preface that introduces it – "*a pretty remarkable one*," as Fielding himself archly observed soon after it was published:[53] remarkable, that is, for what it reveals both of his own recent relations with the Prime Minister and of the sordid devices by which a witty author might be brought to prostitute his talent in Walpole's England. Confirming the sorry parable of the mountebank "Robertus," dispenser of golden pills in *The Champion* (4 October 1740), Fielding in this Preface dropped all figurative disguises in order to rehearse that same tale in plainer English. He had been severely lashed by Courteville and his "Set of Ruffians" for no other offense than "refusing to be of their Number." He denied categorically that he had acted ungratefully to Walpole, who, the ministerial writers insisted, had behaved generously to him by rescuing him from distress: "Ingratitude," Fielding declared, was a vice "which my Nature abhors, as much at least as any one Man breathing." In other ways, too, Walpole had injured him by misrepresenting the nature of their relationship. The money Walpole gave him was not a gift, but the price he was prepared to pay not to see himself roasted in print. (And Fielding's deliberate use of the plural – "to silence my Productions" – suggests they had struck this curious bargain more than once.) The Preface is Fielding's troubled apology for his recent conduct as an author and a Patriot:

But to talk of himself is rarely excusable in a Writer, and never but in one, who is otherwise a Man of Consequence; and, tho' I have been obliged with Money to silence my Productions, professedly and by Way of Bargain given me for that Purpose, tho' I have been offered my own Terms to exert my Talent of Ridicule (as it was called) against some Persons (dead and living) whom I shall never mention but with Honour, tho' I have drawn my Pen in Defence of my Country, have sacrificed to it the Interest of myself and Family, and have been the standing Mark of honourable Abuse for so doing; I cannot yield to all these Persuasions to arrogate to myself a Character of more Consequence than (what in spite of the whole World I shall ever enjoy in my own Conscience) of a Man who hath readily done all the Good in his little Power to Mankind, and never did, or had even the least Propensity to do, an Injury to any one Person.

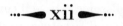

An impressive measure of Fielding's financial anxieties during this period is the recent surprising discovery that, as he wrote these words, he was about to launch a new fortnightly periodical – this time not a newspaper but a magazine, an ambitiously conceived miscellany of literature and current events in which he was assisted by "a Society of Gentlemen."[54] Taking its title from a celebrated work of his favorite English historian Gilbert Burnet, *The History of Our Own Times* appeared on Thursday, 15 January 1740/1, at the moderate price of fourpence a copy; Charles Corbett was publisher. As set forth in the title-page, the plan of this thirty-two page periodical was to instruct and entertain its readers in three ways – by offering:

> I. An Account of Foreign Transactions, from Time to Time, in an Historical Method, and on a regular Plan; by which our Readers may be enabled to form a Judgment of the Interests and Measures of the several Potentates of *Europe*.

> II. The present History of *Great Britain*, subdivided into the following Sections: 1. The History of the Great or Polite World; in which will be contained an Account of the Pleasures and Diversions of the Town. 2. Of the Learned World; in which we shall give an Account and Character of all new Books and Pamphlets in all Languages, wherever they are publish'd, (with Extracts from such as merit it) and a constant Review of the political and other learned Controversies which shall occur. We shall likewise present our Readers with several original Pieces both in Prose and Verse. 3. Of the three learned Professions, Divinity, Law, and Physic. 4. Military and Naval Affairs; in which will be introduced an exact Journal of the Operations of the present War. 5. Of Mercantile Matters; containing an Account of all Schemes advanced either for the Improvement or Hindrance of Trade; the freshest Advices from our Ports, from *Exchange-Alley*, from *Bear-Key*, and the other most considerable Markets; and the Prices of Goods at the said Places.

> III. Such new Parliamentary Speeches as may come to Hand.

The History of Our Own Times, regrettably, had a short life – owing, it may well be, to Fielding's being clapped into a sponging house at a critical juncture when the magazine had scarcely had time to establish itself. With its fourth number, appearing on 6 March 1740/1 after a week's delay and without a trace of Fielding's supporting hand, *The History of Our Own Times* ceased to exist. Fielding's part in the enterprise was obviously crucial. It was he, for example, who wrote the

"Introduction" to the work, an essay providing an informative, witty survey of the newspapers of the day. Not surprisingly, he preferred *The Champion* to all its rivals:

> At the Head of those Histories which appear three Times a Week in the Evening, I shall place the *Champion*, as the only one, which presents an Essay to his Readers. These Essays are sometimes on political, and sometimes on miscellaneous Subjects, and are often writ with great Spirit, but mixed with a little too much of the Vinegar: The historical Part is likewise well chosen, and methodized in a new Manner; but in a Stile grave Men think rather too humourous for History.

Fielding is also probably the author of the main essays in No. 2 (15–30 January) and No. 3 (30 January to 12 February), the former entitled "An Enquiry whether the Fear of Shame may not be turned to the Good of Society" and the latter relating "The Vision of the Golden Tree" – a political allegory figuring the conflict between Walpole, guardian of the Tree of Corruption, and his opponents: "The Leaders of this Party," we are assured, "were Persons of genuine Dignity; such as derived their Importance from their Merit and Capacity, not the false Glitter of Title and Ornament." Fielding probably contributed as well to other departments of the magazine, such as the notices of his own recent publications *Of True Greatness* and *The Vernoniad* (in Nos. 1 and 2, respectively), as well as some verse.

The identity of his collaborators in this venture is uncertain. But it is pleasant to accept Lockwood's conjecture that the author of the erudite reviews in the department entitled "The History of the Learned World" was Fielding's friend William Young, who may have come up to London from Dorset at about this time. Another collaborator whose hand is detectable chiefly in the section entitled "The Present History of Europe" may be the miscellaneous writer John Banks (1709–51), another of Corbett's authors, who made a specialty of foreign affairs. Banks was also a man friendly enough to Fielding to plump down a guinea subscription to the *Miscellanies*.

⸱⸱⸱ XIII ⸱⸱⸱

In the month he published *Of True Greatness* and launched *The History of Our Own Times*, Corbett issued another work by Fielding – one that served the Patriot cause more delightfully, with more wit and a double portion of impudence, than anything else he had written for many months. Appearing anonymously on 22 January 1740/1, priced at a shilling and a half a copy, was *The Vernoniad* – "Done into English," as the title-page declared, "from the original Greek of Homer. Lately found at Constantinople. With Notes *in usum*, &c. Book the First."

In the mock-epic mode with which as a youth he had experimented in his unfinished burlesque of *The Dunciad*, this far defter satire took its inspiration from a celebrated naval victory in the war against Spain – a victory the Opposition ingeniously managed to turn to Walpole's disadvantage. One month after war was declared Admiral Edward Vernon, scouring the Caribbean with only six ships, captured Porto Bello, a principal base of the marauding *guarda costas*. Vernon had become the people's hero, but with so small a force at his command he was unable to repeat his success. Though plans were approved to dispatch enough reinforcements to secure the West Indies for Britain – a large fleet of twenty-five men-of-war and 9,000 troops – an effectual combination of ministerial procrastination and contrary winds prevented them from sailing. Not until January 1740/1, the month of Fielding's poem, did they reach Vernon. Opposition journalists and balladeers seized the opportunity to make Walpole the villain of the piece, responsible for turning victory into fiasco. Jealous of Vernon's popularity and resenting his ties to the Patriots, he had connived at the delay in dispatching the reinforcements – so went, at least, the party line.

Despite the ruse of the title-page that *The Vernoniad* is a fragment of a lost work of Homer, no student of the *Aeneid* would have mistaken Fielding's true model. The poem opens:

> ARMS and the Man I sing, who greatly bore
> *Augusta*'s Flag to *Porto Bello*'s Shore,
> On Sea and Land much suffering, e're he won,
> *With Six Ships only*, the predestin'd Town;
> Whence a long Train of Victories shall flow,
> And future Laurels for *Augusta* grow.

Puffing the work in *The History of Our Own Times* No. 2 (15–30 January), Fielding made sure his readers saw what he was about. It is a poem, he writes, "which the Author humorously supposes to have been originally written by *Homer*; tho' it is indeed a Parody on the first Part of *Virgil*'s Æneid, where *Juno* bribes *Æolus* to disperse the *Trojan* Fleet." The author, he observes, "like *Montagne* ... hath entitled his Poem, *The Vernoniad*, without ever once mentioning the Hero, who may be supposed to be the Subject of his Poem." Fielding's purpose in writing the poem was not to celebrate the hero of the Patriots, but to satirize Walpole the Corrupter. Milton, therefore, as well as Virgil, is his model, as Satan, who espouses the cause of popish Spain, flies to Mammon (Walpole) to order him to "obstruct the Progress of the

War." Mammon's "Palace" sublimely recalls Houghton Hall in Norfolk, Walpole's sumptuous country house and the subject of Fielding's earliest satire of the minister, the ballad of "The Norfolk Lanthorn": "A huge dark Lantern hung up in his Hall,/ And Heaps of ill-got Pictures *hid* the Wall." Mammon accomplishes Satan's fell purpose by employing Walpole's proven device and bribing Æolus to send westerly winds to keep the British fleet in harbor.

Walpole and Vernon are not the only contemporaries whom Fielding ridicules or praises in the poem – or rather in the ludicrous annotations of his "editor," whom Bentley and Burmann inspire. No more delectable burlesque of pedantry had been seen since the scholia of "H. Scriblerus Secundus" in *The Tragedy of Tragedies*. There are hits at Cibber (of course) and at the minister's voluble instrument in Parliament, Sir William Yonge. But the barb aimed at William Deards, Fielding's antagonist in the law courts, is dipped in venom: Deards, together with certain nameless bishops who grow rich by religion, is among "Such kind of Traders as we read in Scripture were driven out of the Temple." Compliments, on the other hand, are paid to the Duke of Argyll, and to the Earl and Countess of Shaftesbury – the latter remembered perhaps because of Fielding's deepening affection for Shaftesbury's first cousin, James Harris. Here, too, is another tribute to "my Friend *Hogarth*, the exactest Copier of Nature," whose picture of *The Distressed Poet* Fielding pauses to contemplate, no doubt feelingly.

Though *The Vernoniad* was never publicly owned by Fielding, who not only published it anonymously but excluded it from the *Miscellanies* of 1743 – a time when his attitude toward Walpole and the Opposition had altered – only a dull reader could fail to detect his presence in the work. Conclusive evidence of his authorship, however, is the note Fielding sent to Nourse on 20 April 1741, asking him "Please to deliver Mr Chappell [the bookseller Henry Chappelle, another of the partners in *The Champion*] 50 of ~~my~~ True Greatness and 50 of the Vernoniad."[55]

····◄● xiv ●►····

This winter brought Fielding to the nadir of his fortunes. Hugh Allen pursued him through the Palace Court in Southwark until, on 27 February, a bailiff was ordered to track his quarry down and apprehend him. In a week Fielding found himself confined in a bailiff's sponging house – that halfway station on the way to debtor's prison. One helpful development had occurred, however, since Allen's original action: Fielding's case having now been separated from that of the others named with him, his debt had been reduced from £200 to only £28.16s.

Still he was obliged to seek securities sufficient to cover his debts so that he might regain his liberty and be restored to the comfort of Charlotte and his children. On 6 March he appeared in person before the Court in Southwark, together with his attorney Samuel Plummer and four friends who were willing to stand bail for him: these were Charles Bayntum, Esq., of Brewer Street; John Sangwine of Charing Cross, peruke-maker; Charles Corbett his publisher; and his eldest sister Catharine, who, we recall, was beneficiary of Mrs. Cottington's will and was now residing at Princes Court, St. Margaret's, Westminster.[56] The sheriff, however, who would be held responsible for the debt if Fielding or his friends could not pay it, required time to assure himself that the securities offered were adequate. Not until 20 March was he prepared to accept the bail of Sangwine and Catharine only. Fielding thus remained a fortnight in confinement. On 24 April a jury determined that he must pay Allen the debt, plus costs and charges amounting to £35.9.8. Fielding contrived to postpone this day of reckoning more than a year, until 26 May 1742.

By the time he regained his liberty on 20 March 1740/1, *The History of Our Own Times* was defunct. What is more, his friends in Opposition had been dealt what must have seemed a mortal blow when, on 13 February, Walpole easily survived the Motion to remove him from the King's counsels. In March the *Daily Gazetteer* twice hinted that Fielding was ready – or *ought* to be ready – to give up the hopeless cause *The Champion* had labored so long to promote. In a letter dated 19 February but published in the *Gazetteer* on 11 March, "Britannicus" depicted Fielding, author of *The Champion*, as a modern-day Sisyphus, perpetually disappointed in his efforts to shoulder the dead weight of the Opposition to the summit of the hill and now at last penitently relinquishing his burden. On 30 March, Courteville published a letter (written by himself) in which "Hercules Vinegar" declares he has deserted *The Champion* and hopefully offers his services to the *Gazetteer*:

> *Brother Scrib.*
> Having irredeemably mortgag'd my share of the Profit, arising from the Sale of the *Champion*; I have determin'd to bite the Mortgagee, (I'm a Lawyer you know, and understand Trap) by withdrawing my propping Hand from that falling Paper; and intend for the future to dedicate the Strength of my surprising Genius to you.

But this was merely Courteville's way of salting his enemy's wounds. Some months would pass before he would have cause to register real surprise at what was probably an offer very like this from Fielding – an offer, tendered and accepted, to turn his talent of ridicule against the Opposition, not, to be sure, in the odious vehicle of Courteville's *Gazetteer*, but rather in a sixpenny pamphlet.

For the moment, as the nation prepared in April 1741 for a general election, Fielding remained with his friends Lyttelton and Dodington. To further their interests he wrote one of the most curious of all his works, *The Crisis: A Sermon*.[57] *The Crisis* was Fielding's final exhortation to the electorate to resist Walpole and his bribes, to stem the "Torrent of Corruption" which is the curse of "that Enemy, which the Devil hath raised up against us." As Fielding construes his text (Revelation 14: 9–11) those who worship the minister and take his money to betray their country have received indelibly "the Mark of the Beast." Considering the ease with which Walpole survived the Motion to remove him from power, Fielding may well have regarded with dismay the prospect of the minister's continuing in office for yet another seven years. He had also learned from his experience as author of *The Champion* that, when addressing the electors of Great Britain in order to persuade them to vote for one's friends, one eschews "a Stile grave Men think rather too humorous." He may have been right. At any rate Charles Molloy, the friendly editor of *Common Sense*, devoted his entire leader for 9 May 1741 to recommending this "Preacher" and his "Sermon" against corruption. *The Crisis*, in more ways than one, is the product of a time in Fielding's life when his own and the nation's future seemed no laughing matter.

••••━▶ XV ◀━••••

One of the heaviest blows he suffered during this difficult time was the ruin of whatever hopes he entertained of a legacy from his father that might rescue him and his family from poverty. Edmund died in June 1741, in disgrace and penniless. What is more, by marrying a fourth time in the final months of his life, he added insult to the injury he had done his children by squandering not only the considerable emoluments of his position in the Army, but the sizeable estate he recently inherited from Eleanor, his third wife. Fully to appreciate the extraordinary decline in Edmund's worldly fortunes, we must return to a time two years earlier when he had reached the height of prosperity.

In July 1739 Edmund was promoted to Lieutenant General – an honor savored by his fond wife Eleanor when, during her final illness at Bath a month later, she bequeathed all her worldly goods and estate "to my dear Husband Lieutenant General Edmund Fielding" or in the event of Edmund's death to his "Heirs and Assigns." As Edmund's eldest son and heir, Fielding, despite being for the present dunned by creditors and hounded by bailiffs, must have had sanguine expectations of a happier future.

In little more than a year, however, these prospects would come to
nothing, as Edmund – like the unlucky ones in Nehemiah Vinegar's
vision of "the Cave of Poverty" – slipped into the abyss. More than
simply his own habitual carelessness with money, the cause of
Edmund's ruin was probably the bankruptcy of Kingsmill Eyre
(d. 1743), Secretary of the Chelsea Royal Hospital, who had served as
agent to Edmund's Regiment of Invalids since it was established in
1719; for as Colonel of the regiment Edmund was accountable for all
public money entrusted to his agent. Eyre handled the financial affairs
of the regiment, including such matters as receiving and dispensing pay
and contracting for uniforms and equipment. The office of regimental
agent was a lucrative one and, it was said,[58] Eyre by various extortionate practices added £2,000 annually to his salary. Eyre, however,
was a speculator with other interests than serving Edmund's regiment;
he sank a great deal of money, unprofitably, into a scheme for smelting
iron ore. In April 1738 he was declared bankrupt, the Court appointing
certain "assignees" to receive funds owing to Eyre in order to apply
them to discharging his debts; in fact, however, as is apparent from the
creditors' petition to the Lord Chancellor dated 4 November 1741, these
men abused their trust. They "possessed themselves" not only of Eyre's
liquid assets, amounting to several thousand pounds, but also of all the
income and produce of Eyre's valuable estate in Middlesex.[59] Edmund's
ruin would almost inevitably have been precipitated by the defalcation
of his agent and the malfeasance of the receivers appointed by the
bankruptcy Court. Often during this period these were the tragic consequences of the risky financial bond between colonels and their agents.[60]

By the early summer of 1740 the gravity of his situation dawned on
Edmund. He was then residing in a house probably provided for him
by his eldest daughter Catharine[61] in a street contiguous to the Verge
of the Court, a sanctuary for debtors. From Princes Court, Westminster,
he wrote on 26 May to Lord Harrington, Secretary of State for the
Northern Department, who was abroad with the King in Hanover. The
letter, with its quaint spelling, poignantly reveals Edmund's wish to
leave London for a haven offshore, as well as his anxiety over the future
welfare of his children:

My Lord
Whereas by the Death of Major General Cavallier; the Leiutenant
Governour's post of the Island of Jersey is Vacant.
and whereas I have Commanded that Island, by special Warrant
from his Majesty; I am intirely aquainted, in all things Necessary;
for his Majesty's Service there.
     If your Lordship would please to apply to his Majesty in my behalf;
that I might succeed to that imployment: that small Addition, to

my presant Command; would inable me the Better to Maintain, my
Numerous famely; as well as be, a very great Obligation to.
  My Lord
    your Lordshipps
      most humble and
    most Obedient Servant
      Edm^d: Fielding[62]

The brief exchange of correspondence thus begun gave Edmund hope
that his petition would succeed, which, as he explained in his fulsome
reply to Lord Harrington on 17 June, "will lay a foundation of a secure
provition for my 4 daughters." In a matter of days after he wrote these
words, however, the first of many creditors initiated an action against
him. Before the year was out Edmund would not be safely residing in
the Governor's mansion in Jersey, but in lodgings in the Old Bailey,
where for numerous debts he was confined within the Rules of the Fleet
Prison. His four daughters – Catharine, Ursula, Sarah, and Beatrice
(aged 31, 30, 29, and 25, respectively) – would have as their "provision"
only Catharine's inheritance from Mrs. Cottington and (later) Sarah's
meager income as a novelist. Edmund was disappointed even in asking
Lord Harrington that his son William (Fielding's half-brother) – who
in his sixteenth year had been commissioned second lieutenant in a
newly raised regiment of marines – be given a more secure post as
ensign in his own Regiment of Invalids, a post vacated by Fielding's
brother Edmund in March.[63]

Edmund's creditors, a flock of them, began to swoop early that
summer. On 26 June James Webb, apparently a contractor, accused
Edmund of owing him, on 1 January 1739/40, £2,000 for "certain
Work and Labour" and materials, a debt Edmund had since increased
by £300 – nor did Webb overlook the two guineas Edmund owed him
for renting four furnished rooms from him for a fortnight. Webb
claimed, however, that he was now injured to the extent of £300 only –
an estimate nearly confirmed by the Court, presided over by Fielding's
model of judicial "Greatness," Sir William Lee, who on 4 July awarded
Webb a judgment of £291. Others followed eagerly after: Thomas Oakes
(£20), Griffith Freeman and Robert Harrison, executors of Thomas
Haughton (£500), Stephen Hodges (£76.10s), Adam Richardson
(amount unknown).[64] Even this incomplete accounting indicates judgments against Edmund totaling £887.10s.

For such a sum he could find no bail even within the wide circle of
his rich and aristocratic friends and relations. By an order of 11
November 1740, confirmed on the 28th, Edmund was committed to the
Fleet Prison – not, it should be said, to some miserable cell within the
prison walls, but, because he had money enough to pay for the privilege,

to lodgings in the Old Bailey, within "the Rules" of the prison.[65] Though to be sure an ignominous experience, confinement in the Rules for a man of Edmund's rank is not likely to have been uncomfortable. If he could afford the price, he could rent from the warder a suite of rooms to which he would hold the key.[66] He would enjoy freedom of movement within the "Liberty of the Rules," and he could receive visitors as he wished. He could even keep servants.

Indeed, in his sixty-first year Edmund, who abhorred the celibate life as nature does a vacuum, would soon add to such comforts the solace of a new wife – a spinster named Elizabeth Sparrye, a woman somewhat more than thirty years old[67] and said to be his servant. Edmund being unable to perform the office himself, his bride-to-be crossed the river to Lambeth Palace, where she was granted the Archbishop's license on 7 March 1740/1.[68] Two days later they were married at St. Bride's church.[69]

What Fielding thought of this event, which put an end to his chances of inheriting the (as it eventually proved) not inconsiderable remnants of his father's estate, we may judge from a passage in *The Crisis: A Sermon*, published a month later. Though his ostensible purpose is to caution the electorate against exchanging their birthright, liberty, for Walpole's bribes, the bitter personal import of Fielding's analogy is plain:

> It is no less impossible for us to conceive, we have any Right to sell the Liberties of our Children. The Power of Fatherhood is the Power of Preservation, not Destruction. Let him look to it, who squanders the Patrimony left him by his Ancestors, and entails Beggary upon his [Posterity].[70]
>
> ... The smallest Degree of paternal Affection, will inspire us to abhor the Thought of bequeathing such a Legacy to our Children.
>
> (pp. 8, 12)

Sentiments such as these were what his enemies, the poisonous authors of *Old England*, later recalled when they denounced Fielding as a son who had been "*undutiful to his Father*" and "*impiously stigmatized him in his Old Age and Confinement with opprobrious Language*."[71] Indeed, when Fielding in later years felt obliged to imitate his father's example by marrying his own servant – Mary Daniel, his cook-maid – his filial impiety, as these authors saw it, inspired the following immortal verses in the same paper:

> When erst the *Sire* resided *near* the Fleet,
> In Want of something, like the Son, to eat,
> For Fifty Pounds in Hand, prime Fortune! paid,
> Before the Priest he led his Servant Maid.

Curse on the Scoundrel for the Deed he's done,
How I'm disgrac'd! cried out his *pious* Son.
... Another Way did operate the Curse,
In it's own Kind; *for better and for worse*,
The Kitchen Maid is coupl'd with the '*Squire*,
Who copy'd that for which he curs'd his Sire.
Just Retribution! for, by Heaven scons'd,
He makes the *Scoundrel* he himself pronounc'd!
This Diff'rence only 'twixt the Sire and Son,
The first had Money but the other none.[72]

For the moment Fielding regarded Edmund's most recent connubial adventure as a hateful act of self-indulgence, a repudiation of his paternal responsibilities which had entailed beggary on the children he so frequently brought into the world – and, most particularly, on his eldest son and heir. But Fielding was not an unforgiving man. No doubt the bitterness he felt soon changed to kindlier feelings; for on 18 June 1741 Edmund died – "in the Rules," according to a note in the court records, "at his Lodging in the Old Bayley."[73] A week later, on 25 June, he was laid to rest in the middle aisle of St. Bride's church.[74] His only memorial is the succinct but admiring notice in the *London Magazine* that he "serv'd in the late Wars against France with much Bravery and Reputation."

Later that summer Edmund's widow made a declaration in Doctors Commons that he died without leaving a will and that his worldly effects were not worth more than five pounds.[75] It is likely, however, that in time – perhaps when the irregularities associated with the bankruptcy of Kingsmill Eyre were resolved – the demands of Edmund's creditors were satisfied. Even in death Edmund continued to hold the colonelcy of the Invalids for some time – until 1 April 1743, to be precise.[76] It is certain, in any case, that Elizabeth Fielding was not left destitute. She lived on, comfortably, for nearly thirty years; her death – at Bridgnorth, Shropshire, on 29 April 1770 – was reported in the *London Magazine*. Her will reveals that she was quite well off by the standards of the time.[77]

...◆ **xvi** ◆...

For many reasons, then – personal, financial, political – these months were a distressing time for Fielding. In this same year of 1741 we also first hear of the chronic ill health that plagued him for the rest of his life, undermining a robust constitution. That he managed to rise above this sea of troubles to produce *Shamela* attests not only to an irrepressible sense of humor, but also to that "philosophical" temper, as he called it, which would see him through deeper afflictions. From our vantage point two and a half centuries later, moreover, this little book marked a turning point in the development of the modern novel: for as Fielding's initial response to Richardson's *Pamela: or, Virtue Rewarded*, it prepared the way for *Joseph Andrews* and that rival tradition of comic fiction evolving through Smollett to Thackeray and Dickens.

The story of a vulnerable but wonderfully resolute young servant maid who withstands her master's numerous inept attempts on her chastity till she brings him at last to his knees at the altar, *Pamela* was a phenomenal success from the moment it appeared on 6 November 1740. There had never been a literary event to compare with the enthusiastic reception of this romance, told by the beleaguered heroine herself in letters and in vivid particularity. Five authoritative editions (as well as an Irish piracy) were called for in less than a year. What is more, provoked by spurious sequels, the anonymous "editor" of Pamela's letters – who finally revealed himself to the public as the printer Samuel Richardson – reluctantly published his own continuation in December 1741.

In town, according to a notice in the *Gentleman's Magazine* of January 1740/1, it was "judged ... as great a Sign of Want of Curiosity not to have read *Pamela*, as not to have seen the *French* and *Italian* dancers," while in the country (so the charming story goes) the illiterate villagers of Slough gathered at the smithy to hear it read aloud and celebrated Pamela's marriage by ringing the church bells. That same winter Horace Walpole observed that, like the snow, Pamela covered everything with her whiteness; and no less sophisticated a critic than Alexander Pope was reported to have said that the novel would do more good than many volumes of sermons. Indeed, despite its "inflammatory" scenes of attempted seduction and rape, Richardson's romance was lauded as a moral work and recommended by the clergy from their pulpits – most notably by the Reverend Benjamin Slocock of St. Saviour's, Southwark. Scenes and characters from the novel were represented on fans and in waxwork, and were depicted in a series of a dozen paintings by Joseph Highmore. The story inspired several comedies and an opera. Eulogies, imitations, spurious continuations, piracies, translations – *Pamela* was paid every kind of tribute.[78] Most remarkable of all is the fact that, more than two centuries later, women who have never read the novel or heard of its heroine continue to name their daughters after her; for, though Richardson found the name in Sidney's *Arcadia*, it was so thoroughly unfamiliar to his readers that no one knew how to speak it. It was, as the peddler observes in *Joseph*

Andrews (IV.xii), "a very strange Name, *Paměla* or *Pamēla*; some pronounced it one way, and some the other."

Pamela caught the public fancy as no mere romance had ever done. To some readers, however – Fielding in every respect first among them – the book was an egregious performance. The writing was inept, the morality crass and mercenary, the piety it recommended not only a mask for hypocrisy but pernicious in emphasizing the doctrine of grace. In receiving *Pamela* so cordially, the nation seemed besotted; some strong antidote was required for what Fielding saw as "an epidemical Phrenzy now raging in Town" over the book. That antidote he provided in *Shamela*, an uproarious parody of Richardson's novel and one of the best of its kind in the language.

But the frenzy over *Pamela* was only the most recent and salient symptom of what Fielding regarded as a general social disorder manifest in virtually every area of public life, whether in letters or in politics or in religion. Consider, for example, the popularity of Cibber's *Apology* for his life and of Conyers Middleton's *Life of Cicero*, the latter published in February 1740/1 and delivered to more than 1,800 subscribers; consider the apparently unshakable supremacy of the Prime Minister, Walpole the Corrupter; consider the disturbing spread of Methodism, the new sect, sparked by the stern Calvinist Whitefield, who in March returned from South Carolina to resume preaching and proselytizing in the fields near London; consider as well that smug defender of the established Church, Joseph Trapp, who in a series of sermons accused the upstart Whitefield of being "righteous over-much."

All these targets are hit in the pamphlet published on 2 April 1741 at a shilling and sixpence by the bookseller Ann Dodd. The full title gave readers a foretaste of the rich variety of the tiny feast awaiting them within:

> An Apology for the Life of Mrs. Shamela Andrews. In which, the many notorious Falshoods and Misrepresentations of a Book called *Pamela*, are exposed and refuted; and all the matchless Arts of that young Politician, set in a true and just Light. Together with A full Account of all that passed between her and Parson Arthur Williams; whose Character is represented in a manner something different from that which he bears in *Pamela*. The whole being exact Copies of authentick Papers delivered to the Editor. Necessary to be had in all Families. By Mr. Conny Keyber.

The double joke of the "author's" name (for this early only Richardson's closest acquaintance knew he had written *Pamela*) would have been caught by any knowledgeable reader. On the one hand we are meant to think first of Colley Cibber, whose *Apology* for his life inspired Fielding's title and whose family name in Dutch was "Keiber," as he himself acknowledged and as his adversaries, including Fielding in *The Author's Farce* (I.iv), often reminded him. But when we find the author dedicating the work "To Miss *Fanny*," the name Pope had given the effeminate courtier John, Lord Hervey, a second prominent target comes into focus. For "Conny" points to the Cambridge divine, Conyers Middleton, who dedicated his *Life of Cicero* to Hervey in the most fulsome language – language Fielding here travestied to perfection.

Though he never acknowledged *Shamela* as his own, Fielding was certainly the author of this impudent little masterpiece.[79] It seems just as certain that when he wrote it, he had no notion at all who the author was who had perpetrated *Pamela*. The book itself and what it represented of the spirit of the times were his game. He dashed off his burlesque in a matter of days, sometime after *Pamela* appeared in a third edition on 12 March.[80] He had all the motive and leisure he needed to complete the work with dispatch, this being the period when he was confined in a sponging house trying to raise bail to satisfy his creditor – a situation lamented by Parson Williams in the narrative, who finds himself in the same predicament (pp. 37–8).

For the most part *Shamela* is a faithful burlesque of the epistolary form and ardent didacticism of Richardson's romance. In half a hundred pages Fielding distills the essence of *Pamela*, a tale at once so pious and so prurient – so seeming real. Even Richardson's trick of "writing to the moment" is scrupulously rendered:

> *Thursday Night, Twelve o'Clock*
> Mrs. *Jervis* and I are just in Bed, and the Door unlocked; if my Master should come – Odsbobs! I hear him just coming in at the Door. You see I write in the present Tense, as Parson *Williams* says. Well, he is in Bed between us, we both shamming a Sleep, he steals his Hand into my Bosom, which I, as if in my Sleep, press close to me with mine, and then pretend to wake.
>
> (p. 15)

Here too is that hallmark of formal realism, of which Richardson and Defoe were the earliest masters, the circumstantial enumeration of trivial particulars:

> Mrs. *Jewkes* went in with me, and helped me to pack up my little All, which was soon done; being no more than two Day-Caps, two Night-Caps, five Shifts, one Sham, a Hoop, a Quilted-Petticoat, two Flannel-Petticoats, two Pair of Stockings, one odd one, a pair of lac'd Shoes, a short flowered Apron, a lac'd Neck-Handkerchief, one Clog, and almost another, and some few Books: as, *A full Answer to a plain and true Account*, &c. *The Whole Duty of Man*, with only the Duty to one's Neighbour, torn out. The Third Volume of the

Atalantis. Venus in the Cloyster: Or, the Nun in her Smock. God's Dealings with Mr. Whitefield. Orfus and Eurydice. Some Sermon-Books; and two or three Plays, with their Titles, and Part of the first Act torn off.

(pp. 36–7)

As for Richardson's moral – namely, that his heroine's virginity is a commodity readily convertible into hard cash and social rank – how succinctly Shamela sums it up: "I thought once of making a little Fortune by my Person. I now intend to make a great one by my Vartue" (p. 33).

Fielding considered *Pamela* bad as art and pernicious in its affected religiosity and leveling social doctrine. His point was taken by the author of a poem addressed to him in the *London Magazine* for June 1741:

> Admir'd *Pamela*, till *Shamela* shown,
> Appear'd in every colour – but her own:
> Uncensur'd she remain'd in borrow'd light,
> No nun more chaste, few angels shone so bright.
> But now, the idol we no more adore,
> *Jervice* a bawd, and our chaste nymph a w——
> Each buxom lass may read poor *Booby*'s case,
> And charm a *Williams* to supply his place;
> Our thoughtless sons for round-ear'd caps may burn,
> And curse *Pamela*, when they've serv'd a turn.[81]

Though Fielding for the most part thus contented himself with impishly showing *Pamela* in her own colors, revealed in the funhouse mirror of parody, he departed radically from his original in one respect important to an understanding of his motives as a comic author: he used the occasion of this bawdy burlesque to continue the theme of his series "An Apology for the Clergy," published in *The Champion* a year earlier. Most notable of his improvisations in this vein is the framing of Shamela's story by an exchange of letters between the fatuous Parson Tickletext and his wiser friend the Reverend "J. Oliver," Fielding's spokesman. (It was the Reverend John Oliver, we recall, who taught Fielding Latin when he was a boy at East Stour and who continued to serve as curate of the neighboring parish of St. Mary's, Motcombe.) Shamela and her mother, moreover, are represented as avid readers of Whitefield's sermons and his confessional autobiography, "that charming Book about the Dealings" (p. 13). At best a contradiction still, Shamela is also charmed by the doctrines of Whitefield's adversary, Joseph Trapp, as they are conveyed to her by her lover Parson Williams – though, as she assures her Mamma, Williams's theology is "not the most charming thing belonging to him":

> Well, on *Sunday* Parson *Williams* came, according to his Promise, and an excellent Sermon he preached; his Text was, Be not *Righteous over-much*; and, indeed, he handled it in a very fine way; he shewed us that the Bible doth not require too much Goodness of us, and that People very often call things Goodness that are not so. That to go to Church, and to pray, and to sing Psalms, and to honour the Clergy, and to repent, is true Religion; and 'tis not doing good to one another, for that is one of the greatest Sins we can commit, when we don't do it for the sake of Religion. That those People who talk of Vartue and Morality, are the wickedest of all Persons. That 'tis not what we do, but what we believe, that must save us, and a great many other good Things; I wish I could remember them all.
>
> (p. 24)

Enemies though they were, the Methodist Whitefield and the High Churchman Trapp (or rather Fielding's caricature of him in the figure of Williams) thus concur in what Tickletext calls "the useful and truly religious Doctrine of *Grace*" which he rejoices to find "every where inculcated" in the pages of Richardson's romance (p. 2). As their willing scholar, therefore, Shamela naturally scorns the very different theology of Fielding's distinguished friend, Bishop Hoadly: heading the list of cherished inanities in the catalogue of her little library is one of the many virulent tracts written by High Churchmen against Hoadly's *Plain Account of the Nature and End of the Sacrament of the Lord's Supper* (1735). Even in the mood in which he wrote *Shamela* – a work as rude and bawdy as any to come from his pen – Fielding's comedy is thus colored by a serious moral intent.

Shamela also throws light on Fielding's political attitude during this period. Though Middleton's Dedication of the *Life of Cicero* was awful enough in its own right to have prompted Fielding's ridicule, the mockery of Middleton and his book was probably owing in part to his having alluded condescendingly to a work on the same subject by Fielding's patron: Lyttelton's *Observations on the Life of Cicero* would be issued in a second edition in this same month of April 1741. Politics is not Fielding's principal game in *Shamela*, but his loyalties remain with Lyttelton and his party. Following hard on the satire of Lord Hervey in the Dedication is this encomium addressed to the "Editor" of *Shamela* by "John Puff, *Esq*;" who is certain that the biographer who can do justice to the morals of Richardson's characters is qualified to write the life of Hervey's master, Walpole:

SIR,

I HAVE read your *Shamela* through and through, and a most inimitable Performance it is. Who is he, what is he that could write so excellent a Book? he must be doubtless most agreeable to the Age, and to *his Honour* [Walpole] himself; for he is able to draw every thing to Perfection but Virtue. Whoever the Author be, he hath one of the worst and most fashionable Hearts in the World, and I would recommend to him, in his next Performance, to undertake the Life of *his Honour*. For he who drew the Character of Parson *Williams*, is equal to the Task; nay he seems to have little more to do than to pull off the Parson's Gown, and *that* which makes him so agreeable to *Shamela*, and the Cap will fit.

As the burlesque thus opens by deriding the morals and virility of the Prime Minister and his lieutenant Hervey, so Shamela in her last letter describes the scene on the eve of the election that will determine control of Booby's borough, the corporation having gathered at his home to drink heartily and sell their votes. It comes as no surprise that Parson Williams is very much Walpole's man in the game of "*Pollitricks*."

Most readers agreed that *Shamela* hit all targets with devastating effect. Particularly interesting is the testimony of the son of Lord Chancellor Hardwicke, Charles Yorke. Writing on 12 April to his brother Philip in London, he reported the reception the book was enjoying in Cambridge, Middleton's own town:

> Shammela & the Dedications to it, the former as a ridicule on Pamela, & the latter on the Dedication to the Life of Cicero, meet with general Applause. – Your Embassador has not as yet seen the Book, and is credibly informed that it is in such universal Request at the Theatre coffee-house, that unless he were to purchase it for himself (which he has by no means any Intention of doing) it will be impossible for him to gain a sight of it these two months.

Just how thoroughly Fielding's travesty had done its work with Yorke and his fellow Cantabrigians of the Water-gruel Club, who met regularly to pronounce on the merits of current bestsellers, is clear as he reports that *Pamela* was "condemned without mercy": "No Advocate appeared on it's behalf – The whole Assembly concurred in Determination."[82] A huge success among the sophisticates of Cambridge, not to mention such literate judges as Thomas Dampier and Horace Walpole, *Shamela* obviously enjoyed a favorable reception from readers other than "the Weak and Vicious" sort to whom the hack John Kelly consigned it.[83] Later in the year (on 3 November) it was issued in a second edition. The work did have the regrettable consequence, however, of earning Fielding the enduring enmity of Richardson, and also, we may suppose, of costing him his friendship with Aaron Hill. For, though Fielding could not have known, it was Hill whose fawning letters of praise, prefixed to the second edition of *Pamela*, he mischievously burlesqued in Tickletext's opening remarks to Oliver.

xvii

Between the publication of *Shamela* and *The Crisis* in April and his leaving town in July to follow the Western Circuit, Fielding's activities are obscure. Together with his numerous sisters and brothers he no doubt was present at St. Bride's church to pay his respects at his father's funeral on Thursday, 25 June. The following Monday (29 June) at the Feathers Tavern he attended a meeting of the partners of *The Champion* – the others present being Nourse, Hodges, Cogan, Gilliver, Chandler, and Chappelle.[84] Their business was to auction off the "Impressions of the Champion in two Vollumes, 12⁰, No. 1000": in other words, to sell the reprint, published on 25 June 1741, of the articles from 15 November 1739 to 19 June 1740. Henry Chappelle, who recently had a share in publishing *The Crisis*, was highest bidder; the reprint was his for £110, to be distributed among the partners.

What is curious about this transaction is that it was opposed by one of the partners and one only: Henry Fielding, who for some months had taken no part in writing *The Champion*. Even so, why should he now oppose selling the reprinted articles comprising the bulk of his own contributions to the journal he had so enthusiastically founded? As a partner holding two sixteenth shares, he would profit from the bargain struck with Chappelle, and he needed the money.

Was there some ulterior reason why he wished to dissociate himself, in this formal way, from the publication of a book expressly calculated to support the Opposition's campaign to dislodge Walpole when the new Parliament convened in December? Ralph's prefatory address "To the New Members" leaves no doubt about the political purpose of the reprint, as he exhorts the newly elected legislators to prove themselves Patriots and honest men by siding with Chesterfield and the Cobhamites in rejecting Walpole and his corrupt policies: "YOU will find," Ralph concludes, "in both Houses, ready to join your noblest Endeavours, several young Gentlemen, who, disdaining to become Part of a Minister's State-Equipage, however gaudy the Livery, have already spoke and acted with a Spirit worthy of better Times." Having thus introduced the reprint with an anti-ministerial harangue, Ralph added the following "Advertisement," which helpfully distinguishes Fielding's contributions from his own:

SEVERAL Persons having been concern'd in writing the Champion, and it not being reasonable that any one should be answerable for the Rest, it has been thought proper to signify to the Reader, that all the Papers distinguish'd with a C. or an L. are the Work of one Hand [i.e., Fielding's];[85] *those mark'd thus* * * or sign'd* LILBOURNE, *of another* [i.e., Ralph's], *to whose Account, likewise, except a few Paragraphs, the* Index of the Times, *is to be plac'd.*

Ralph may well have published this notice at Fielding's instance, the only one who opposed the sale of the reprint and who possibly had good reasons for not wishing to be *"answerable"* (the word implies a threat, legal or otherwise) for the anti-ministerial politics that are the burden of Ralph's contributions to the journal.

Had Fielding by the latter part of June 1741 grown dissatisfied with the political cause he had been supporting actively for seven years – since the last general election in 1734? Had he again been tempted to take Walpole's money "to silence [his] Productions"? Giving some substance to this tenuous line of speculation are two hard facts. First, after June 1741 Fielding published nothing until in December, during the parliamentary session that decided Walpole's fate, he published *The Opposition: A Vision*, a work not only satirizing his former party but representing the Prime Minister in a decidedly amiable light. Second, in the list of subscribers to Fielding's *Miscellanies* – proposals for which appeared sometime before the winter of 1741–2 – one puzzling name is conspicuous: the name of Robert Walpole (identified according to the title conferred on him in February 1741/2, "The Right Hon. the Earl of Orford"), who ordered no fewer than ten sets on royal paper at two guineas a set.

····◄ xviii ►···

Early in July, Fielding's ambition to succeed in his profession would have drawn him from town to attend the assizes on the Western Circuit. The familiar itinerary in 1741 was as follows: Tuesday, 7 July, Winchester; Saturday, 11 July, Salisbury; Thursday, 16 July, Dorchester; Monday, 20 July, Exeter; Tuesday, 28 July, Bodmin; Wednesday, 5 August, Wells; Saturday, 8 August, Bristol. Of the two judges presiding over these courts, one was a man whom Fielding called "my ever-honoured and beloved friend":[86] Thomas Burnet (1694–1753), youngest son of the great Bishop of Salisbury, and a distinguished lawyer who in May 1740 succeeded another of Fielding's Wiltshire friends, Giles Eyre, as King's Serjeant at Law. Whenever it may have begun, Fielding's friendship with Sir Thomas Burnet (he was knighted in 1745) was cemented this summer.

So, too, was another friendship even dearer to him and of unparalleled importance to his biographers: for, though Fielding was a sociable fellow with a wide circle of acquaintance, we are indebted to just one of these friends for preserving his correspondence and, after Fielding's death, for recording his impressions of the character and genius of the man he knew and admired for more than twenty years. That friend was James Harris of Salisbury (1709–80). Harris was a wealthy, well-connected man whose mother was the daughter of the second Earl of Shaftesbury and whose son would be raised to the peerage as the first Earl of Malmesbury. But it was Harris's keen mind and kind heart that drew Fielding to him. He was a serious and innovative student of classical philosophy and a connoisseur of the arts. September 1741 was the moment when Fielding opened with Harris one of the rare correspondences of his life.

Soon after concluding his affairs on the Western Circuit, Fielding paused for some weeks in Bath, chiefly because he found the waters there beneficial. He and Charlotte stayed in the quiet little square called Abbey Green, at the house of the Reverend Walter Robbins, the scholarly clergyman who had married them seven years earlier. Here on 8 September 1741 Fielding first wrote James Harris at Salisbury, inviting him to join in a regular correspondence. The two men had been acquainted for many years, since Harris lived all his life in The Close at Salisbury, in the elegant house opposite the Cradocks at St. Anne's Gate.

As Fielding opens the letter he recalls a conversation he formerly had with Harris on a subject which, as a man of strong sexual appetites and tender feelings, would always interest him: namely, the distinction between love and lust. In *Tom Jones* (VI.i) he would devote an entire chapter to it. What is extraordinary, however – and he makes certain Harris appreciates the wonder of it – is that of all Fielding's acquaintance this gentle man should stir in him feelings of affection and respect powerful enough to overcome his deep antipathy to letter-writing.

You may have forgot [Fielding begins], that in one of our Evening Walks, whilst I was busy in explaining some Conceits of mine (for probably they are no other) concerning the clear Distinction between Love and Lust, our Conversation was interrupted by several fair Objects of both those Passions. Had I then proceeded, I should have told you, as perhaps one Instance of their distinct Existence in my Mind, that nothing was ever more irksome to me than those Letters which I had formerly from the latter Motive written to Women, nor any thing more agreeable and delightful than I have always found this Method of conversing with the absent beloved Object.... For my own Part, I solemnly declare, I can never give Man or Woman with whom I have no Business (which the Satisfaction of Lust may well be called) a more certain Token of a violent Affection than by writing to them, an Exercise which, notwithstanding I have in my time printed a few Pages, I so much detest, that I believe it is not in the Power of three Persons to expose my epistolary Correspondence. Receive this therefore as the Fruit of an Affection which hath been long growing, and hath taken the deepest Root whence it originally sprung.

He continues by assuring Harris he means not to flatter him, unless he allows himself the vanity of believing he flatters him by offering him his friendship:

I intend you therefore no Compliment in this nor any future Letter, unless my Friendship be one, which, as it bears no gawdy Outside, I shall endeavour to reconcile you to by its Qualities. First then, it is, like Bajazet's, not to be bought with the World; 2dly it hath not been much used and sullied hitherto, so that tho' it will not, like splendid Ornaments, recommend you much in the Beau Monde, yet, like a decent Dress, I hope you will not need be ashamed of it among the honester and plainer Part of Mankind. You see tho I promise not to entail Job's Curse on my Child[ren] by flattering my Friend, I reserve, like Mr Colley Cibber, the Liberty of flattering my self; but this I shall use with more Moderation.

Who else in 1741 had "the Power," as Fielding expressed it, "to expose" his familiar correspondence? (The very choice of verb suggests how jealous he was of his privacy – how reluctant to make himself vulnerable to the criticism or derision of strangers by committing his intimate thoughts and feelings to paper.) If we take literally his declaration that "not ... three Persons" received his "epistolary Correspondence," Harris would be one of only *two* persons who enjoyed that rare privilege, since Fielding with this letter had offered him "the Power" in question. If there was only one other friend to whom he wrote in this same intimate vein, "dear Lyttleton" (as Fielding addressed him in his verse "Epistle" of 1733) is the likely candidate; but those letters no longer exist, having been burnt as a sacrifice to the gods of Victorian propriety.[87] No other recipient of Fielding's familiar correspondence (as opposed to letters of "Business") has come to light.

This first letter to Harris is delightfully full, rich in gossip and in the sort of wit and humor we might expect from the author who was about to write *Joseph Andrews*. Fielding informs his friend that he dined that day for the third time with Serjeant Burnet. Though Burnet at forty-seven was thirteen years Fielding's senior, they were congenial companions: not only was Burnet from Salisbury and the son of Fielding's favorite English historian (Burnet had in fact edited his father's *History of My Own Time*); he had attended the University of Leyden, made the tour of Europe, and studied law at the Middle Temple. What is more, like Fielding he was a Whig and a witty man who as member of the madcap gang of Mohocks had liberally sown his wild oats in his youth.

At Bath – which Fielding declares a "pleasant City" but dull, "full of nothing but Noise, Impertinence and Confusion" – he was also relying for lively conversation on his chum from Eton days, Charles Hanbury Williams (1708–59). Fielding remained close to Hanbury Williams, who was also a wit and a Whig – and a very rich man. As one puzzles over the change in political attitude Fielding seems to have undergone during these months, it is well to remember that Hanbury Williams – "my old School fellow," as Fielding fondly calls him – held in Walpole's government the influential post of paymaster of the marine forces. To Burnet and to Hanbury Williams, Fielding declares, he is "chiefly obliged ... that the dulness of Bath doth not in some measure ballance the vivifying Quality of its Waters," which, he is pleased to report, "have really had so good and immediate an Effect" in restoring him to health.

As to the rest of the company in this fashionable resort, he has noticed "few Men of any Consequence, and fewer Women of any Beauty" – the principal ornaments of the place being Lord Hervey and Miss Cope, the daughter of General John Cope, a young woman apparently as homely as she was haughty. Fielding confides:

> I own I have the same Dislike to an ugly Woman which Women have for an handsome one, or as I have for a very silly Fellow: Female Ugliness and male Folly being seldom unattended with *Spite*, a word which I defie the Devil to equal or to punish as he ought.

What Fielding always admired in the sexes was beauty in women, good sense in men, and a benevolent disposition in both.

In concluding his letter, Fielding asked Harris to "look on this as a first Visit, which gives you a Power either to encourage or reject the Acquaintance. I shall not hereafter insist on Ceremonies, and may sometimes pay, and always gladly receive two for one: but the Repetition of a visit when the first hath not been returned is I think among the Ladies, the best Judges on such occasions, thought an Impertinence, an Imputation" which he will "always most cautiously" avoid.

On 17 September, Harris cordially replied to Fielding's overture: "I most Willingly accept the offer of your Correspondence." Besides asking Fielding to convey his compliments to Charlotte and Serjeant Burnet, he also sent a "kind Remembrance," as Fielding acknowledged, "of our little one." Chances are that Henry and Charlotte's only son, Henry, was born late this summer.[88]

On 29 September, Fielding, who had been seeing a good deal of Hanbury Williams, stepped with his friend into James Leake's bookshop, a favorite haunt in Bath, where one could browse and keep abreast of the gossip. When Hanbury Williams left him to drink the waters, Fielding sat down to write Harris, expressing the "great Pleasure" he felt at Harris's acceptance of his offer of a correspondence – though he warned that the "Entertainment" Harris could expect from it "will arise chiefly from my own Conceits, (a modest Phraze for my Philosophy)," not from any retailing of how the world wagged in Bath:

> for my own Part my Letters will contain so little of what the Ladies call *News*, that you will be often forced to consult the Top to know whence they come. In Truth I can not agree with the common Opinion, That it is a sufficient Reason to tell you a Story, *that you do not know it already*.

The "Conceits" that are the subject of this remarkable letter comprise a kind of anatomy of laughter as it serves to express both the worst and the best characteristics of human nature. The letter has a place, then, in Fielding's gradual formulation of what might be considered a theory of laughter – a subject that occupied him more than any other author of the period: his earliest published essay was on "the Benefit of Laughing" (1728); as "Democritus" in *The Craftsman* (1738) he had written "in Vindication of Laughter"; and soon he would define "the true Ridiculous" in the famous Preface to *Joseph Andrews* (1742). On this present occasion he anticipates the distinction between "Good-Humour and Good-Nature" which is an important theme in his "Essay on the Knowledge of the Characters of Men"; so close indeed are the correspondences that the letter may serve to date the period of composition of the essay, which Fielding intended for publication in the *Miscellanies*.

The "Conceits" with which he entertains Harris were the consequence, he explains, of his having indulged the day before in some ineffectual flirting:

> as I stood yesterday at the Pump, a beautiful young Girl caught me looking at her pretty earnestly, when turning about to her Companion, she smiled on her, and both presently burst into an affected Laugh. Instead of being angry, I began to philosophize on this Occasion, and to consider, as there was visible Ostentation in this Laugh what Idea she was desirous of conveying to me by it. I soon resolved with Mr. Hobbs, that it was the Effect of Pride, and she desired no more than to acquaint me with her Contempt. I carried

this still farther, and am in doubt whether that Laughter which entitles to the general Character of Good Humour, be not rather a Sign of an evil than a good Mind. Is it not indeed that *Solutus Risus* an endeavour to raise which Horace makes an Ingredient in his *black Man*, and Homer attributes to Thersites? Is it not this of which Solomon says *That it is mad*, and lastly which hath been observed to be never recorded of Jesus Christ. But do not imagine me excluding all Laughter. The blessed Man I have just mentioned is said to have had a Countenance *constantly smiling* and the same Horace ascribes the *Ridentem* to himself. I believe it likewise to be this latter which Democritus used to wear, which Juvenal tells us he never stirred abroad without, and is by him stiled

——— rigidi censura Cachinni

where *rigidus* seems to bear some Opposition to *solutus*, nor need I tell you that Laertius calls this Democritus the first and greatest of all the Philosophers, nor that Montagne prefers him to Heraclitus: for (says he) *there is more room for Laughter to exert itself as we are not so full of misery as inanity* (inanité): but I must observe that he describes this Philosopher with the visage *Moqueur*, a word I do not like, and which the best French Authors use to signifie a *Sneerer*. It is perhaps difficult to assign the just Bounds between these two Kinds of Laughter, which are in my Opinion the Indications of the best and the worst Disposition. It is sufficient for me that I know them when I see them, comfortable must it be to you likewise that this latter is a fattening Diet, since your Temperance will hardly keep you plump by any other. A Disposition which I hope no Accident will ever obstruct and to which I shall not be displeased to have afforded some Food by those Scraps of Learning which my Memory, where I wish I had laid up my Materials a little more regularly, furnishes me with. I will not however imitate my favorite Montagne who dishonestly accuses the best Memory in the World, as handsome Women some- times tell you how ugly they look. To be sincere, my Learning like my Life is less deficient in good Matter than good Method, for want of which I have the small Satisfaction of knowing both to be somewhat better than they are allowed by those who have no great Right to call either in Question. In some Places I might be told *those are all the World* which will not greatly disturb me after the Opinion you have delivered of the said *all the World* in which I so heartily concurr that I despise nothing so much as *all the World*.

This letter is one of the important personal documents of Fielding's life – important in what it reveals of his reading[89] and his mind, of his profound and subtle understanding of what are the twin essential bases of his art: the origins of laughter and the contradictions of human nature. Important, too, in revealing Fielding's awareness that, however spitefully exaggerated, there was justice in the world's opinion that the life he led was "less deficient in good Matter than good Method."

In the midst of these reflections Fielding was interrupted by General Cope's bursting into the bookshop with the distressing news that Hanbury Williams's mother had died suddenly of an apoplexy. Fielding hastened to close his letter, declaring, "I am in a true Sense not in the vulgar Phraze concerned for him, who is capable of being a *Son* and a *Friend.*"

···➤ xix ◀···

From Fielding's accounts to Harris of his recent experience of Bath one name is conspicuously missing – that of his future friend and benefactor Ralph Allen, "the benevolent man"[90] who one day would serve with Lyttelton as a model for Squire Allworthy of *Tom Jones*. Nor in these letters of September is there any hint that Fielding was even contemplating the greatest work of his literary life to date: *Joseph Andrews*. Yet, almost certainly, both his friendship with Allen and the commencement of the novel date from his long sojourn at Bath in the late summer and autumn of 1741.

One story current at Bath was that Allen, pleased with something Fielding had written, began their friendship by making him a present of £200.[91] The two men had many friends in common who might have introduced them or informed Allen of Fielding's straitened financial circumstances, but one of the likeliest candidates for this good office is Hanbury Williams, whose company Fielding was then enjoying. Allen had known Hanbury Williams and his family for many years, and advised the architect John Wood to model the stables of his new house, Prior Park, on those at Hanbury Williams's country seat in Monmouthshire.[92]

Situated on the hillside at Widcombe, where it commands a splendid prospect of Bath two miles to the north, Prior Park, Allen's magnificent Palladian house, had been under construction for years, but it was ready at last for his occupancy in the summer of 1741. It is obvious from the pair of compliments Fielding paid Allen in *Joseph Andrews* that he had been "courteously entertained" there before that novel went to press in early January. In Book III, chapter l, Fielding excepts not one but two Bathonians from his general condemnation of the pride of "high People," the first being Lord Chesterfield, the second Ralph Allen – a man who (as Pope emphasized in two versions of his famous couplet) was "low-born," of "humble" origins. Allen made a fortune devising an efficient system of cross-posts for England and Wales, and then purchased the valuable stone quarries of which not only his own house, but virtually all eighteenth-century Bath, was constructed. So Fielding warmly writes:

> I could name a Commoner raised higher above the Multitude by superiour Talents, than is in the power of his Prince to exalt him; whose Behaviour to those he hath obliged is more amiable than the Obligation itself, and who is so great a Master of Affability, that if he could divest himself of an inherent Greatness in his Manner, would often make the lowest of his Acquaintance forget who was the Master of that Palace, in which they are so courteously entertained.

Just when did Allen invite Fielding to dine with him in his new "Palace"? Allen did not occupy the house until June or early July, and Fielding did not arrive at Bath until he concluded his business on the Western Circuit in August. If he had been entertained by Allen and shown the splendors of Prior Park by 8 or 29 September we might expect him to have shared his impressions with Harris. During October, furthermore, Allen and his wife traveled to London, visiting Pope at Twickenham and returning with him to Prior Park, where they arrived on the 27th.[93] It was as Allen's guest during the winter that Pope wrote his masterpiece, *The New Dunciad*, which he called his "Widcombe Poem."[94]

Can it be simply coincidence that Fielding's second compliment to Allen in *Joseph Andrews* (III.vi) occurs in a passage that also contains the first compliment he ever paid to Pope as a *social* being? He always recognized Pope's greatness as a poet: even when, in the unpublished "Epistle to Lyttleton" (1733), he denounced Pope's ungentlemanly conduct toward Lady Mary, Fielding admitted his "Worth" as a poet, and *The Champion* abounds in complimentary allusions to Pope's poetry. Not until now, however, had Fielding seen any reason to praise Pope's humanity – and, we may note, to do so in the context of a dinner-table conversation that turns admiringly on Allen's charity and his "stately House." Joseph thus assures Fanny that not all "the great Folks" are wicked:

> Some Gentlemen of our Cloth report charitable Actions done by their Lords and Masters, and I have heard 'Squire *Pope*, the great Poet, at my Lady's Table, tell Stories of a Man that lived at a Place called *Ross*, and another at the *Bath*, one *Al— Al—* I forget his Name, but it is in the Book of Verses. This Gentleman hath built up a Stately House too, which the 'Squire likes very well; but his Charity is seen farther than his House, tho' it stands on a Hill, ay, and brings him more Honour too. It was his Charity that put him in the Book, where

the 'Squire says he puts all those who deserve it; and to be sure, as
he lives among all the great People, if there were any such, he would
know them.

Compliments such as these, worked obtrusively into Joseph
Andrews's narrative, seem so warm and gratuitous as to have been
prompted by Fielding's wish to cement a pair of important friendships
recently made. It is likely that sometime after 27 October, when he was
well advanced in his novel, Fielding was entertained at Prior Park in
the company of Pope. Such a meeting might account for the apparent
allusions in *Joseph Andrews* to two of Pope's works that then existed
only in manuscript – allusions to *The New Dunciad* (III.i) and to Pope's
satire of Hervey in *A Letter to a Noble Lord* (IV.ix).[95] The meeting would
also add a personal note to the only compliment Pope ever paid
Fielding: for in the opening lines of his "Widcombe Poem" he not only
praises Chesterfield for opposing the Theatrical Licensing Act, but also,
by declaring that satiric drama alone had kept the comic Muse alive,
he implicitly declares his approbation of *Pasquin* and *The Historical
Register*:

> There sunk Thalia, nerveless, cold, and dead,
> Had not her sister Satyr held her head:
> Nor cou'd'st thou, CHESTERFIELD! a tear refuse,
> Thou wep'st, and with thee wept each gentle Muse.

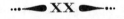

Fielding's final publication of 1741, *The Opposition: A Vision*, is one of
his most surprising works. At once satirizing his former party while
vindicating Walpole and his policies, it represents a complete reversal
of Fielding's political attitudes of the past seven years. As Cross
observed, "no one would have dared assign the pamphlet to him" had
Fielding not expressly declared his authorship of it in the Preface to
the *Miscellanies*.[96]

Students of Fielding's politics have tried to exonerate him from the
charge of tergiversation in this matter, first by reminding us that the
Opposition was not a single, unified party, but rather an uneasy
coalition of half a dozen bickering factions, and then by proposing that
in *The Opposition* Fielding was merely reflecting his friends' own
views of their rivals within the coalition as it began to disintegrate in
1741–2. Thus W. B. Coley distinguishes the several discrete elements
which comprised the Opposition: "the Pulteney–Carteret bloc of Whig
malcontents, the coterie still centering around the Prince of Wales,

Argyll and his Scots, Shippen and his Tories, 'the Boys' of the Cobham-ite alignment, and mercurial, almost centripetal figures like Chesterfield and Bolingbroke." Fielding can then be located within a circle including Chesterfield, Lyttelton, "and the more progressive advocates of a 'broad-bottom' policy of Opposition"[97] – men who wished, in other words, to form a government comprehending representatives of the various special-interest groups, a government ostensibly above party considerations and dedicated to the cause of true patriotism and the "Country Interest." To this "progressive" group Dodington had recently been added, with his own strong ties to Argyll, Chesterfield, and the Cobhamites. The threads of this tangled skein having been separated out in this manner, the claim then seems plausible that in *The Opposition* Fielding was not deserting his friends, but, on the contrary, was expressing their own disillusionment with the faction led by Pulteney and Carteret, whose lust for power became ever more obvious as Walpole's fall became certain.

Though based on a sophisticated appreciation of the complexities of Opposition politics in 1741–2, this reading of *The Opposition: A Vision* is not supported either by the known circumstances of Fielding's life during this period or by the evidence of the text itself.[98] Fielding in *The Opposition* not only deserted his political friends and patrons of the last seven years; he took their adversary's money to support his cause just when the time was ripe to pluck him down. The facts are that in the latter half of 1741 – the most crucial political juncture for many years – Fielding published nothing at all that could afford comfort or amusement to his friends among the Patriots; and that the single work he did publish, *The Opposition*, not only declared his bitterness at being neglected by these friends but (unprophetically as it proved) represented the triumph of their enemy, Sir Robert Walpole, as the victory of a truly great man, a man benevolent and magnanimous who in governing the nation would serve "the Country Interest" as his opponents only professed they would do.

Well before *The Opposition* appeared in mid-December there were signs that Fielding was dissatisfied with his relationship with the Patri-ots. We have noticed his curious solitary gesture of opposing the sale of the reprint rights to *The Champion* in June, and the no less curious gesture of Walpole's twenty-guinea subscription to the *Miscellanies*, proposals for which must have been distributed this year. During the weeks Fielding spent in Bath, moreover, his closest friends – Burnet, Hanbury Williams, Ralph Allen – were all strongly attached to the ministry.

By the end of October, Ralph Courteville, who knew about Fielding's sojourn in Bath, had heard that he resented being neglected by his former patrons and was prepared to accept comfortable accommodation in the minister's camp. The *Daily Gazetteer* (30 October 1741) consists of a remarkable dialogue to this effect between "Hercules Vinegar" (i.e., Fielding, who is said to have returned to town recently from Bath) and "Ralph Freeman" (i.e., Courteville). After reminding Fielding that, his "Patron" having abandoned him, his colleague Ralph had been promoted from mere "Deputy" to "Principal" author of *The Champion*, Courteville warns that none of the Patriots will "escape" once the populace recognizes them for the ambitious hypocrites they are. "Vinegar" replies with a prudent regard for his safety, and "Freeman" hints that, provided his old antagonist is duly contrite, he will be welcome to come over. As the past twenty years had proved, there were many mansions in Walpole's house.

H.V. Thou'rt a strange Fellow.—I escape.—Mind you but your own Affairs with the People, and never mind me.—But after all, if I thought it would come to that,—I wou'd not be—found o'th'wrong Side.

R.F. I dare say you wou'd not, Captain.—But what will the Publick think, when 'tis told them, that this *mighty Hector!* this *distinguish'd* Patriot of *Pall-mall!* the *renowned* Capt. HERCULES VINEGAR! has been whimpering to get over, without once desiring the least Favour to be shewn to his COADJUTOR R[alph] so that he is accepted of, — Nay! dear Captain, don't stare so. You know 'tis—. Perhaps at such a time we shou'd have Deserters of higher Rank.— Some Folks who have stout Stomachs, wou'd then talk in another Tone.—If an Administration's not to be bullied,—if the People are not to be rouz'd,—many a Malecontent would be glad of his Place again.—we have seen such things happen!

H.V. For all your severe Usage, Mr. *F.* I wish I was Conjurer enough to know—whether they will happen again.

R.F. Can't you ask some of your Correspondents of Quality.— Do,—try them, Captain.—Perhaps when you shew a thorough Repentance, something may be done for you—on our Side.

H.V. They,—rot them,—they'd abuse me,—or take the Hint.— Why, they never think me severe enough.—Should I write up to their Standard,—I might come to be—I won't say what,—even under your mild Administration.

R.F. Ay, then your's is a hard Task, indeed!—I ask your Pardon.—I pity you with all my Heart.—Poor Captain!—ah! as you was saying,—you might come to be—why, Faith, you are to be pity'd.—Adieu!

A fortnight later Courteville resumed the theme of Fielding's imminent defection. In the *Daily Gazetteer* (13 November 1741) he regrets that no writer of ordinary powers could possibly answer all the libels

heaped upon the minister by the Opposition: "It surpasses the Strength
of ordinary Men to atchieve such *Herculean* Labours, and consequently
this *Augean* Stable is like to go unclean'd, unless the *CHAMPION*
should once again change Sides, and endeavour to expiate past Offences
by undertaking the Job."

At a time very near 1 December, when the new Parliament met to
decide Walpole's fate, Fielding interrupted work on *Joseph Andrews* to
write the pamphlet which, from a ministerial point of view, was just
such an attempt "to expiate past Offences." Prominently advertised in
Walpole's *Daily Gazetteer, The Opposition: A Vision* (price sixpence)
appeared anonymously on 15 December, bearing the imprint of the
Gazetteer's own Thomas Cooper, the bookseller Fielding not long before
had mockingly dignified with the title *"Publisher-General* to the *Ministerial-Society."*

In one of Fielding's favorite forms, the dream-vision, the narrator
relates that he fell asleep soon after reading in Cibber's *Apology* the
"remarkable Expression ... *Here I met the* REVOLUTION" (p. 3). This
idea so stimulated his fancy that he dreams he is walking on a highway
near London "where *I met the* OPPOSITION," allegorically depicted as a
wagon heavily laden with passengers and baggage – "and (which surprized me greatly) ... drawn by *Asses* instead of Horses; the Asses
[being] of different Colours and Sizes, and so extremely ill matched,
that the whole made the most ridiculous Appearance imaginable, to
which the *shagged Coats* of many did not a little contribute" (p. 4).

In general, the terms of the allegory are clear enough. Representing
the disunity of the factions comprising the Opposition, the passengers
in the wagon sit *"Back to Back*, and (which was very remarkable) *scarce
two of them looked the same Way"* (p. 6). Their baggage consists of several
ponderous items. Primarily, there is a large trunk of *"Grievances,"*
which to the narrator's surprise

> contained little more than a few News-Papers, on one of which I read
> the Word *Champion*, and on another was the Word *onsense*, the
> Letter *N* being, I suppose, folded down; there were indeed one or
> two little Parcels at the *Bottom*, which seemed to have something in
> them; they appeared however *fastened* to the Trunk, and ... were
> not intended to be removed by any there, when they came to their
> Journey's End. I observed they were directed to the same Person at
> his House in *Downing-Street*; but ... they did not *honestly* belong to
> him.
>
> (pp. 14–15)

The bribery and corruption of which the Patriots had been accusing
the Prime Minister for two decades are thus dismissed as a necessary
fact of political life, a device that *any* ministry must employ to keep

the machinery of government well oiled. In a later electioneering pamphlet he wrote for Walpole's disciple in the art of politics, this would also be Fielding's way of defending the Pelham administration from the same charge: "Indeed," he declared in *A Dialogue between a Gentleman ... and an Honest Alderman* (1747), "to speak a bold political Truth, some Degree of Corruption always hath attended, and always will attend a rich and flourishing Nation .... Nothing, I apprehend therefore, can appear more unjust than this Charge of Corruption on the present Government; which neither introduced it nor can possibly cure it." The wagon of the Opposition in 1741 contains another formidable piece of baggage, a huge box of "*Public Spirit,*" which, however, the narrator discovers to be crammed with nothing but the passengers' "*own private Goods ... Ambition, Malice, Envy, Avarice, Disappointment, Pride, Revenge,*" and many other heavy Commodities."

But if the passengers are a motley and clamorous lot, and their baggage nothing but a load of rubbish, the quarrelsome knaves who drive the wagon are even less appealing as they urge the asses to haul their burden through filthy ways toward the summit of the hill symbolizing political supremacy. One "honest Gentleman," disgusted with the hypocrisy and greed of the company, leaps down from the front of the wagon, exclaiming against the Motion of February that had failed to disgrace the minister: "If such are your Intentions, I will go no *farther with you*; I think we have travelled thro' Dirt enough already; I was so bespattered with the *last Motion* the Waggon made, that I almost despaired of ever making myself appear clean again" (p. 7).

Fixing the identities of all the cryptic figures in the allegory cannot be done with certainty, but we can decipher enough of the code to be sure that, contrary to what is sometimes said, Fielding did not mean to exempt his former friends from the satire. The "honest Gentleman" who abandons the wagon in protest against "the *last Motion*" is no doubt the Jacobite William Shippen, leader of the Tory faction, who in a celebrated gesture walked out of the House in protest; but Fielding had no ties to Shippen, who thus escapes the general ridicule. Those members of the Opposition to whom Fielding was connected were less happy. The driver of the wagon, said to be "a Stranger *to the* English Roads" (p. 8), would be the Duke of Argyll, who was similarly depicted as the coachman in the satirical print called *The Political Libertines: or, Motion upon Motion* (see Plate 32), which may indeed have provided Fielding with the basic iconography for his allegory.[99] The resentment of the veteran passengers directed at "*that Gentleman who came in only at* Turn-em *Green,*" yet who has secured a front seat in the wagon despite his late arrival, is an allusion to Dodington, who resided at Gunnersbury, Middlesex, a village contiguous to Turnham Green but with a name less suggestive of Dodington's role (from Walpole's point of view) as "turn-coat." As for Fielding's fellow Etonians, Lyttelton and Pitt, both strongly supported the Motion against Walpole which the satire deplores: it was Lyttelton, indeed, who seconded it. Since they remained Fielding's friends, Lyttelton and Chesterfield obviously had a sense of humor and may have appreciated his mischievous transformation of the title of their journal *Common Sense* into "[*N*]on-sense"; but they could not have interpreted it as supporting their interests. No, if Fielding had wished his readers to construe *The Oppo-sition: A Vision* as an indictment of the Pulteney–Carteret faction only, his own friends and patrons escaping the ridicule, he would have given this narrative a very different shape and coloring.

Besides the fact that Fielding's satiric indictment of his former party is more general than some have supposed, two other aspects of *The Opposition: A Vision* are unmistakably clear: first, Fielding was annoyed that his former patrons had not paid him well enough for the distasteful political hack work they required of him; second, he wished now, as the minister's fate hung in the balance, to represent Walpole as an able and magnanimous leader of the nation.

The asses hitched to the Opposition wagon are, to be sure, "of different Colours and Sizes"; in the allegory they stand for all those dupes – whether newly elected members of Parliament or veteran journalists – who are being used by the leaders of the Opposition to further their ambitions. There is, however, no mistaking which of all these foolish drudges is uppermost in Fielding's mind:

> "Poor Asses! [exclaims one of the passengers] little do they think what cursed heavy Stuff they are endeavouring to draw." "What is it to the Asses (answered the sly Fellow) whether they draw Silver or Lead, provided they are fed as Asses ought to be?" "But," replied the other, "they appear to be the worst fed Asses I ever beheld; Why there's that long-sided Ass they call *Vinegar*, which the Drivers call upon so often to *gee up*, and *pull lustily*, I never saw an Ass with a worse Mane, or a more shagged Coat; and that grave Ass yoked to him, which they name *Ralph*, who pulls and brays like the Devil, Sir, he does not seem to have eat since the hard Frost. Surely, considering the wretched Work they are employed in, they deserve better Meat."
>
> (pp. 16–17)

The plain sense of this is Fielding's complaint that he has not been adequately rewarded for serving the Patriot cause. To whom other than his patrons – Lyttelton, Dodington, Chesterfield, Argyll – can such a complaint be directed?

When the wagon's progress is blocked by a coach and six spirited horses, there can be no doubt either about the identity of the intrepid rider. Sir Robert Walpole – familiar to readers of Fielding's earlier works as "Pillage," "Forage," "Brass," "The Grinner," "Mr. Guts," most recently indeed as "the Beast" of Revelation! – is now introduced as "a fat Gentleman who ... appeared to have one of the pleasantest best-natured Countenances I had ever beheld" (p. 20). Nor, when the drivers of the wagon threaten to drive on over the gentleman, can there be much doubt that of the many asses pulling the cart the one who balks at the dirty job expected of him is the one whose sentiments Fielding knows best – namely, "that long-sided Ass they call *Vinegar*," who had formerly championed the Opposition's cause but now, in this pamphlet, opposes it:

> The Gentleman smiled at these Threatnings, upon which the Drivers lifted up their Whips at the Asses, when one of them, methought, (such is the Extravagance of Dreams) raised himself on his hinder Legs, and spake as follows. "O thou perfidious Driver! dost not thou profess thyself a Driver of the COUNTRY WAGGON? Are not those Words written in large Characters upon it? Have not thy Passengers *taken their Places for the Country?* What will their Friends who *sent* them, and *bore the Expence* of their Journey, say, when they hear they are come up to their *own Account*, and neglect the Business of those who *sent* them? Will it be a sufficient Excuse that thou hast *misled* them? And hast thou no more Humanity, than to endeavour to trample on an honest Gentleman, only because his Coach stands in your Way? As to the Asses, it's of little Consequence where they are driven, provided they are not used to such Purposes, as the Honesty of even an Ass would start at."
>
> (pp. 20–1)

It is Fielding's complete vindication of Walpole and his policies that makes his own motives clear in this satire, and that makes untenable the view that, in writing *The Opposition: A Vision*, he somehow meant to serve the cause of the party he ridicules. Walpole is not merely tolerated and excused in this piece; he is lauded. The policies of the minister that Fielding had once denounced as bribery and corruption are now seen as manifestations of his natural beneficence and generosity; what Fielding had once condemned in Walpole as vile ambition and cynical self-aggrandizement is now represented as the determination of a true and able patriot to govern the nation skillfully and to serve its best interests. As the vision concludes, Walpole's coach thus "struck directly into that *very Road* whither the other had *pretended* it was going" – at which the people set up a cheer and set fire to the wagon together with its noisome baggage. Before the mob take their revenge, however, the "honest Gentleman" has kindly unhitched the hungry asses from the wagon, freeing them to feed in green pastures – "where they all instantly fell to *grazing*," the narrator observes, "with a Greadiness common to Beasts after *a long Abstinence*" (p. 23). However many of these grateful beasts there may be, we can be certain that prominent among them is "that long-sided Ass they call *Vinegar*," so notably ill-kempt and undernourished.

By his own admission in *The Champion* (14 February 1739/40), Fielding early found that he was "no Politician." Wit and humor, love and poetry, "Essays of Virtue and Vice" were his natural bent. But politics was what the Town and his patrons would pay for. There were limits to his wavering, of course: he never sank to betraying his country by aiding the Jacobites. But within those limits, when his friends disappointed him, his pen was for sale to others who vied for power within the Whig hegemony. As a political writer he took the same pragmatic view of his function that a barrister does of his, presenting his client's case in the most advantageous light. Late in 1741 – in dire financial distress, his wife seriously ill, his favorite daughter near death – he could no longer afford (as he put it in the Preface to *Of True Greatness*) to sacrifice to his friends' political ambitions "the Interest of myself and Family." He had already stooped, more than once apparently, to taking Walpole's money to "silence my Productions."

As the parable representing the Prime Minister as the mountebank with golden pills makes clear, however, Walpole's salutary prescriptions were proportionate to the degree of an author's incontinence in serving him: 100 pills was the dose for holding one's tongue; 200 for saying "a *single Word*" in his favor; 300, as well as "something very good to take twice a Year as long as you live," was the measure for declaiming "handsomely upon [his] Nostrums." These sums may be hyperbolic, to be sure. They are larger than what a writer in *Old England* (5 August 1749) implied some years later when, recalling Fielding's association with *The Champion*, he sneered that Fielding "at last took a small pecuniary Gratuity to betray his Paymasters and the Paper, out of which he had for some time extracted a precarious Subsistence." Whatever the exact sum, however, Fielding's reward for writing *The Opposition: A Vision* was probably greater than the twenty guineas Walpole gave as a subscriber to the *Miscellanies*.

xxi

Nothing but a desperate need for cash could have wrung from Fielding this embarrassing job of political hack work at a time when he was eager to finish *Joseph Andrews*. Sometime presumably during this bitter

December Fielding's luck changed for the better when he delivered the manuscript of his novel into the hands of the honest Scots bookseller Andrew Millar (1706–68), a man so generous in his dealings with authors that Dr. Johnson credited him with having "raised the price of literature."[100] Thus began a friendly and mutually profitable relationship that would not be broken during Fielding's lifetime.

According to a pleasant tradition, plausible enough in most respects, it was another Scot, the poet James Thomson, who brought the two men together. Millar had been Thomson's publisher for many years, and Thomson enjoyed another connection that would virtually have assured his knowing Fielding: George Lyttelton was their mutual friend. Echoes of Thomson's *Liberty* (1735–6) are heard in Fielding's own poetical essay of the same title – a poem addressed to Lyttelton and soon to be published in the *Miscellanies* Fielding was assembling.

As the story goes, Fielding, anxious to discharge a debt and not knowing what value to place on the new species of romance he had created, first gave the manuscript to another bookseller who, less than enthusiastic at what he read of it, offered a paltry £25 for the copy. Meanwhile Thomson, who had read the manuscript and recognized its merit, persuaded Fielding to retrieve the work and carry it to Millar. Millar in turn submitted the novelty to the judgment of his wife, who was usually his arbiter in such cases. Her verdict being favorable, Millar, with Thomson assisting, met Fielding at a coffee-house in the Strand, where, after a good dinner and a couple of bottles of Fielding's favorite port, he got down to business:

"I am a man," said Millar, "of few words, and fond of coming to the point; but really, after giving every consideration I am able to your novel, I do not think I can afford to give you more than 200 *l.* for it." "What!" exclaimed Fielding, "two hundred pounds!" "Indeed, Mr. Fielding," returned Millar, "indeed I am sensible of your talents; but my mind is made up." "Two hundred pounds!" continued Fielding in a tone of perfect astonishment; "*two hundred pounds* did you say?" "Upon my word, Sir, I mean no disparagement to the writer or his great merit; but my mind is made up, and I cannot give one farthing more." "Allow me to ask you," continued Fielding with undiminished surprise, "allow me, Mr. Millar, to ask you, whether you are *serious*?" "Never more so," replied Millar, "in all my life; and I hope you will candidly acquit me of every intention to injure your feelings, or depreciate your abilities, when I repeat that I positively cannot afford you more than two hundred pounds for your novel." "Then, my good Sir," said Fielding, recovering himself from this unexpected stroke of fortune, "give me your hand; the book is yours."[101]

The anecdote, rehearsed long after the event, is suspiciously detailed, but we might expect something like this actually to have occurred – especially if we suppose it was Thomson's friend Lyttelton, not Thomson himself, whose opinion of the manuscript Fielding sought (as he would later do with *Tom Jones*). In any case, there is nothing improbable about Thomson's acting as intermediary in bringing Fielding to Millar. Later, in *The Jacobite's Journal* (4 June 1748), Fielding's laudatory review of Thomson's *Castle of Indolence* suggests the puffing of a friend rather than the cool judgment of a critic. The amount of the bargain, furthermore, as a rounded figure, pretty accurately squares with what Millar in fact paid Fielding for the novel: that is, £183.11s. (with payments for two other works recorded in the same transaction bringing the total sum to £199.6s.).[102]

However it may have been that Millar acquired *Joseph Andrews*, by early January he had placed the copy with the printer Henry Woodfall the elder, with directions to run off an edition of 1,500 sets. Notices in the *Daily Advertiser* and *The Champion* for 12 January 1741/2 announced that the novel was "In the Press"; by 15 February, having made certain "alterations" Fielding required in the proofs, Woodfall's printers had completed the job.[103] Millar must have appreciated that the work was no ordinary romance, for he paid it the unusual tribute of heralding its publication with a ten days' fanfare in the newspapers. Appearing as promised on 22 February – in a pair of pocket-sized duodecimo volumes costing six shillings bound – was the first masterly comic novel in English:

> *The History of the Adventures of Joseph Andrews, and of his Friend Mr. Abraham Adams. Written in Imitation of the Manner of Cervantes, Author of Don Quixote.*

Fielding's name did not appear on the title-page, and would not until the third edition a year later. (Neither Defoe nor Swift nor Richardson before him put their names to mere prose romances; that Fielding should even then dignify the work by owning it publicly suggests that he understood what he had achieved.) His authorship, nevertheless, as well as the nature of his subject, was an open secret well before the novel reached the bookstalls. As far away as Bath, Dr. George Cheyne – who had felt in *The Champion* Fielding's ridicule of his Byzantine prose style – wrote eagerly to Richardson in town, requesting a pre-publication copy:

> I beg as soon as you get Fieldings Joseph Andrews, I fear in Ridicule of your Pamela and of Virtue in the Notion of Don Quixotes Manner, you would send it me by the very first Coach it is to be publish't the

22^{d} and perhaps if your People be artful they may procure it of the Trade on Saturday and send it by the Monday's Coach for Bath.[104]

Richardson could not have been amused by his friend's impatience to read the book he later called "a lewd and ungenerous engraftment" on *Pamela* (though he would be soothed by Cheyne's predictable verdict on Fielding's "wretched Performance," which he was confident "will entertain none but Porters or Watermen").[105] The public were just as keen to see what further sport Fielding could make of the work he had so hilariously ridiculed in *Shamela*. They were not prepared, however, for what he in fact gave them – a masterpiece of comic fiction far excelling the limited achievement of parody, which is, at best, a negative and parasitic mode, depending for its life on the host it mocks. For *Joseph Andrews* is much more than merely the best of the anti-*Pamela*'s. To be sure, Fielding continued amusing readers at Richardson's expense: his hero, a footman, is Pamela's equally chaste brother who suffers for virtue's sake at the hands of his mistress, a latter-day Mrs. Potiphar who happens to be Booby's lascivious aunt; indeed, toward the end of the comedy, her nephew and his new "Lady" make an appearance in person, adding to the fun and confusion at Booby Hall.

But, as the title-page declares with its bold invitation to compare his novel to one of the classics of literature, *Don Quixote*, Fielding in *Joseph Andrews* meant to write something altogether different from Richardson's book. Based on an alternative conception of the art of fiction, *Joseph Andrews* is a kind of work never before attempted in English. In the Preface, Fielding sets forth his theory of the "comic Epic-Poem in Prose" and its subject, "the true Ridiculous." Throughout the narrative itself it is Fielding's "voice" we hear – good-humored, benevolent, wise – as he unfolds for us the lively panorama of mid-Georgian England, the time and place of a universal human comedy. He could not have known it in 1737, when the Licensing Act put an end to his theatrical career, or in 1734, when he began the witty contributions to *The Craftsman* that led to his authorship of the *The Champion*, but the years he spent mastering the arts of characterization and dialogue, and perfecting his style as a familiar essayist on humorous and moral topics, were an apprenticeship in which he learned the skills of a new and (as far as his later fame is concerned) a greater species of writing.

As a novel, *Joseph Andrews* departs radically from its British predecessors – most notably from the tradition of Defoe and Richardson, whose work is distinguished by a circumstantial realism and fully individualized characters. Fielding here established two other distinctive traditions of the modern novel. On the one hand, *Joseph Andrews* begins the tradition of ironic social commentary extending most obviously through Smollett, Dickens, and Thackeray to Kingsley Amis, but also including in its subtler manifestations the novels of Jane Austen and George Eliot's *Middlemarch*. On the other hand, *Joseph Andrews* introduced into English what has been called the "self-reflexive" or "architectonic" novel – a kind of narrative deliberately flaunting its artificiality, in which the author is immanent in his creation, not aloof and paring his fingernails (like Joyce's novelist in *Portrait of the Artist as a Young Man*), but obtrusive in his contrivances (like Joyce himself in *Ulysses*), reminding us that the text we are reading cannot be a photograph of what really exists, but is instead a thing made and fabricated by the author, who, by means of the pleasure we take in the illusions of art, may more effectively express his own insights into reality: this, for all their differences, is the tradition of Sterne and Joyce, Nabokov and Barth.

For his models Fielding looked not homeward, but to the Continent – to Cervantes preeminently, whom he had loved as a lad and at Leyden tried to adapt to the stage; but also to Scarron's *Roman comique* (1651–7) and LeSage's *Gil Blas* (1715–35). As he declared in the introductory chapter to Book III, he found in *Don Quixote* a truer kind of history writing, a book that offered "the History of the World in general, at least that Part which is polished by Laws, Arts and Sciences; and of that from the time it was first polished to this day; nay and forwards, as long as it shall so remain." In his introductory essays, and especially in the Preface, Fielding played Aristotle to his own comic Homer; in these essays, that is, he offered a sort of *Poetics* of the kind of fiction he himself invented. Novels and romances being despised forms of entertainment, he coyly claims as his prototype no less a work than Homer's lost comic epic, the *Margites*, and, like Addison anatomizing *Paradise Lost*, he insists that this new species of narrative satisfies all the requirements "which the Critic enumerates in the constituent Parts of an Epic Poem ... such as Fable, Action, Characters, Sentiments, and Diction," except that it is not written in "Metre." As Aristotle had considered the function of tragedy to be a *catharsis*, a purging of the emotions of pity and fear, so Fielding (now restating less facetiously the doctrine of "the Benefit of Laughing" which had served as the theme of his first published essay fourteen years earlier) offers his own definition of comedy and of a comic *catharsis*:

Mirth and Laughter ... are probably more wholesome Physic for the Mind, and conduce better to purge away Spleen, Melancholy and ill Affections, than is generally imagined. Nay, I will appeal to common Observation, whether the same Companies are not found more full of Good-Humour and Benevolence, after they have been sweeten'd for two or three Hours with Entertainments of this kind, than when soured by a Tragedy or a grave Lecture.

The purging of spleen and melancholy is only one part of Fielding's theory of comedy, which also comprehends the moral function of satire – or what he calls "the true Ridiculous," whose source is affectation as manifested in those related forms of self-love, vanity, and hypocrisy. In all Fielding's works, hypocrisy is the characteristic of villainy. In his account of "the Ridiculous," Fielding's models are neither classical nor continental but English. In drama, his first love, it was Ben Jonson "who of all Men understood the *Ridiculous* the best." And in the sister art of painting it is his friend Hogarth – a "Comic History-Painter," Fielding calls him, who in his *Rake's* and *Harlot's Progress*, for example, understood the distinction between "the Comic" and "those Performances which the *Italians* call *Caricatura*; where we shall find the true Excellence of the former, to consist in the exactest copying of Nature; insomuch, that a judicious Eye instantly rejects any thing *outré*; any Liberty which the Painter hath taken with the Features of that *Alma Mater*."

Fielding insisted that his characters were not caricatures (as modern readers sometimes see them), but rather, beneath the mid-Georgian costumes they wear, representatives of timeless qualities in human nature. He wrote in the classical tradition that found reality not in the shifting particularity of things, but in the essences that underlie them and define their nature. These essences, since his subject is the characters of men and women, are moral:

> I declare here once for all, I describe not Men, but Manners; not an Individual, but a Species. Perhaps it will be answered, Are not the Characters then taken from Life? To which I answer in the Affirmative; nay, I believe I might aver, that I have writ little more than I have seen. The Lawyer is not only alive, but hath been so these 4000 Years, and I hope G— will indulge his Life as many yet to come. He hath not indeed confined himself to one Profession, one Religion, or one Country; but when the first mean selfish Creature appeared on the human Stage, who made Self the Centre of the whole Creation; would give himself no Pain, incur no Danger, advance no Money to assist, or preserve his Fellow-Creatures, then was our Lawyer born; and whilst such a Person as I have described, exists on Earth, so long shall he remain upon it.
>
> (III.i)

For all this generalizing impulse of Fielding's classicism, his works are rooted in his own experience: "I have writ little more than I have seen," he assures us. This autobiographical dimension of his fiction was so obvious to his rival Richardson that, reflecting on Fielding's novels after *Amelia* appeared, he sneered that their author had "little or no invention." Everyone knew, for example, that Fielding's friend the Reverend William Young was the original of Abraham Adams, the novel's most delightful character. As Richardson observed: "Parson Young sat for Fielding's Parson Adams, a man he knew, and only made a little more absurd than he is known to be."[106] Young's learning and strictness of piety, the pride he took in his skills as a pedagogue, his pugnaciousness and intrepidity in the face of danger, his carelessness with money, his comical absence of mind – all these qualities characterize Adams. As James Harris put it, who knew Young well, "No character was ever more truly exhibited."[107]

Another character Richardson recognized in *Joseph Andrews* was Fielding himself in the figure of Wilson. "His brawls, his jarrs, his gaols, his spunging-houses," said Richardson, summing up, "are all drawn from what he has seen and known." In the story of Wilson's follies Fielding not only remembered his friend Hogarth's *Rake's Progress*; he also recalled the libertinism of his own youth – the nights he had spent carousing with sots and whores, or, in more sober moods, attending naively to the deistical cant of Ralph and Cooke and the "Rule of Right" men. He was now living with the unpleasant consequences of his early profligacy – the ruin of a lucrative theatrical career, the drudgery and ignominy of life as a hackney author, the prospective clients who laughed to think that the author of *Tom Thumb* and *Pasquin* wished to be entrusted wih their legal business, the all too real threat of confinement in sponging houses and debtors' prison. As Wilson relates to Adams the story of a bailiff's arresting him for debt, Fielding surely had in mind his own recent incarceration for a debt of the same amount:

He arrested me at my Taylor's Suit, for thirty-five Pounds; a Sum for which I could not procure Bail, and was therefore conveyed to his House, where I was locked up in an upper Chamber. I had now neither Health ... Liberty, Money, or Friends; and had abandoned all Hopes, and even the Desire of Life. "But this could not last long," said *Adams*, "for doubtless the Taylor released you the moment he was truly acquainted with your Affairs; and knew that your Circumstances would not permit you to pay him." Oh, Sir, answered the Gentleman, he knew that before he arrested me; nay, he knew that nothing but Incapacity could prevent me paying my Debts; for I had been his Customer many Years, had spent vast Sums of Money with him, and had always paid most punctually in my prosperous Days: But when I reminded him of this, with Assurances that if he would not molest my Endeavours, I would pay him all the Money I could, by my utmost Labour and Industry, procure, reserving only what was sufficient to preserve me alive: He answered, His Patience was worn out; that I had put him off from time to time; that he wanted the Money; that he had put it into a Lawyer's hands; and if I did not pay him immediately, or find Security, I must lie in Goal and expect no Mercy.

Like his author, Wilson is redeemed from his confinement by the charity of a loving woman (in Fielding's case, his sister Catharine; in Wilson's, his future wife), and his story ends happily. Indeed, despite the melancholy circumstances in which Fielding wrote it, *Joseph Andrews* is the most cheerful of books. The laughter it provokes is often satiric, directed at certain specimens of "the true Ridiculous" whom Fielding knew in real life. The miser Peter Walter is thus immortalized as Peter Pounce, while Pope's "amphibious Thing," Lord Hervey, becomes the diminutive fop Beau Didapper. Though they have no comparable role to play in the narrative itself, a host of other favorites from the satiric gallery Fielding had been exhibiting in his works for a decade find their niches here as well: Cibber, as we might expect, has the central place, ironically celebrated for his odes as Laureate and the general spectacle of his "Life." But his son Theophilus is not forgot ("that face-making Puppy," as the player calls him [III.x]), nor is "Orator" Henley, or John Rich, or Conyers Middleton, or the auctioneer Christopher Cock, or William Deards the toyman – among other living targets.

But the triumph of *Joseph Andrews* is not owing to such strokes of personal ridicule, but rather to its great good humor – the delight Fielding takes in the comedy of humankind. In this novel, as later in *Tom Jones*, the Comic Spirit is a genial and sociable Muse, capable of redeeming for us the mess of life – life even as Fielding experienced it in the winter of 1741–2. Mrs. Tow-wouse's expressive parsimony ("'Common Charity, a F—t!' says she" [I.xii]), Trulliber's country-style hospitality (with a cry of "*I caal'd vurst*," snatching the cup from Adams's hand and swallowing down the ale [II.xiv]), Lady Booby's jealousy ("Beauty indeed, – a Country Wench a Beauty. – I shall be sick whenever I hear Beauty mentioned again" [IV.ii]): we judge them all, but even more we enjoy them. As we also do the predatory, bullying, lovable Slipslop, that "mighty Affecter of hard Words," incensed that her passion for Joseph "should be *resulted* and treated with *Ironing*" (I.iii, vi)! The finest tribute to the genius of Slipslop's character would be Sheridan's wholesale appropriation of her in *The Rivals* (1775), where she reappears as Mrs. Malaprop. Fielding's is the Comic Spirit we meet in Chaucer, but in few other English authors (Shakespeare is too brittle or too deep, Dickens too dark).

In this celebration of the human comedy Fielding also included many
friends. William Young of course is the life of the festival. Joseph
Andrews meets the publican Timothy Harris (d. 1748), keeper of the
Red Lion at Egham, a regular station on the road between London and
Salisbury (I.xi); and he has overheard "'Squire Pope, the great Poet"
at his lady's table praising the charity of Ralph Allen (III.vi). The
bitch "Fairmaid" that worries Joseph in his battle with the dogs was
a present to the roasting squire from John Temple (1680–1752), of Moor
Park, Surrey, nephew of the great Sir William Temple, whose works
Fielding admired (III.vi). The Muse who inspires the narrator in his
account of this epic contest is the same who infused "such wonderful
Humour into the Pen of immortal *Gulliver*" and who carefully "guided
the Judgment" while exalting "the nervous manly Style" of the Scotsman David Mallet (1705–65) in his *Life of Francis Bacon*. And Fielding
welcomes to the feast a whole company of his theatrical acquaintance –
the actors William Mills, James Quin, and Dennis Delane, as well as
"that ill-look'd Dog" Charles Macklin and "that saucy Slut" Kitty
Clive – and the shade of his dead friend Lillo (I.viii, III.x). It may be,
as Richardson believed, that Charlotte was the model for Mrs. Wilson.
It is more likely that Fielding invited the other favorite woman in his
life, his sister Sarah, to make her début in print by contributing a
section of the narrative – the letter from Leonora to Horatio, which
Fielding tells us in a footnote "was written by a young Lady" (II.iv).

As in *Shamela*, where his boyhood tutor John Oliver defined the
moral and religious basis of the satire, so in *Joseph Andrews* Fielding
enlisted for this purpose another Dorsetshire clergyman of his acquaintance. Transformed into Abraham Adams, Parson Young both defines
and embodies the doctrine of benevolism. From the moment Joseph
takes to the road and falls among thieves in Fielding's contemporary
parable of the Good Samaritan (I.xii) to the time when Adams fails to
persuade Pounce that charity is an active virtue (III.xiii), the central
movement of the narrative consists of a series of episodes ringing
changes on the theme of charity. Along the way, as he had done with
Tickletext and Williams in *Shamela*, Fielding ridicules such unworthy
brothers of the cloth as Barnabas, ignorant and pleasure-loving, and
the Falstaffian Trulliber, niggardly and porcine, who knows the Scriptures but whose thoughts are with the hogs he farms – characters who
act out the idea of the false priest as Fielding defined it in his "Apology
for the Clergy" in *The Champion*.

One scene in *Joseph Andrews* expresses more clearly than any other
passage in Fielding's works the nature of his religious thought, which
was in all respects consonant with the Low Church latitudinarianism
of the day. This was the religion of the Cambridge theologians Isaac
Barrow (1630–77), Samuel Clarke (1675–1729), and John Tillotson

(1630–94), Archbishop of Canterbury – divines to whom Fielding in his writings frequently refers as authorities on moral and spiritual matters; though on literary grounds he preferred the High Church Oxonian, Robert South (1634–1716), in whose sermons he found "more Wit, than in the Comedies of Congreve."[108] This was also the religion of his friend Bishop Hoadly. And it was the religion denounced by Whitefield (with some justice) as resembling deism more than it did the orthodox faith of the Church of England: for, Whitefield declared in castigating Tillotson and the author of *The Whole Duty of Man* before the multitudes assembled in the fields near London to hear him preach, theirs was a system prizing mere morality, the notions of sincerity and benevolence, over the doctrine of grace and the creed of Christ crucified.

From Fielding's point of view Whitefield, more than any other contemporary theologian, was the Enemy, whose charismatic Calvinism, by stressing man's depravity and emphasizing faith over good works, made religion a convenient mask for hypocrisy. The popular representation of the great Methodist's message was: "So you say you believe in the Lord Jesus Christ, you may live the life of devils."[109] This, to be sure, was a gross distortion: faith, Whitefield insisted, renewed the spirit and bore fruit in good works. But Fielding appears to have accepted it uncritically; repeatedly, Whitefield and the Methodists are targets of his sharpest satire. Yet in one respect he considered that Whitefield's message of reform was valid: the worldly clergy of the Church of England had by the example of their pride and luxury brought their order into contempt.

These themes come into focus in Book I, chapter xvii, as Parson Adams in the presence of the bookseller replies to Barnabas's objection that the Methodist is being righteous overmuch:

> "Sir," answered *Adams*, "if Mr. *Whitfield* had carried his Doctrine no farther than you mention, I should have remained, as I once was, his Well-Wisher. I am myself as great an Enemy to the Luxury and Splendour of the Clergy as he can be. I do not, more than he, by the flourishing Estate of the Church, understand the Palaces, Equipages, Dress, Furniture, rich Dainties, and vast Fortunes of her Ministers. Surely those things, which savour so strongly of this World, become not the Servants of one who professed his Kingdom was not of it: but when he began to call Nonsense and Enthusiasm to his Aid, and to set up the detestable Doctrine of Faith against good Works, I was his Friend no longer; for surely, that Doctrine was coined in Hell, and one would think none but the Devil himself could have the Confidence to preach it. For can any thing be more derogatory to the Honour of God, than for Men to imagine that the All-wise Being will hereafter say to the Good and Virtuous, *Notwithstanding the*

Purity of thy Life, notwithstanding that constant Rule of Virtue and Goodness in which you walked upon Earth, still as thou did'st not believe every thing in the true Orthodox manner, thy want of Faith shall condemn thee? Or on the other side, can any Doctrine have a more pernicious Influence on Society than a Persuasion, that it will be a good Plea for the Villain at the last day; *Lord, it is true I never obeyed one of thy Commandments, yet punish me not, for I believe them all?*" "I suppose, Sir," said the Bookseller, "your Sermons are of a different Kind." "Ay, Sir," said *Adams,* "the contrary, I thank Heaven, is inculcated‑ in almost every Page, or I should belye my own Opinion, which hath always been, that a virtuous and good *Turk,* or Heathen, are more acceptable in the sight of their Creator, than a vicious and wicked Christian, tho' his Faith was as perfectly Orthodox as St. *Paul's* himself."

For Adams, as for his author, the greatest theologian of the age was Hoadly. Hoadly was the sort of advocate of a complacent, comprehensive faith that Swift (in one of Fielding's favorite works) ironically represented as proposing the abolishing of Christianity. In 1717 Hoadly's sermon on "The Nature of the Kingdom, or the Church, of Christ" provoked the acrimonious Bangorian controversy by proposing that the true Church of Christ, whose kingdom was not of this world, was the whole community of believers. In 1735 he further outraged the High Church party by attempting to sweep away the theological foundations of the Sacramental Test Act. The Eucharist, he insisted, should be regarded as a simple memorial of Christ's sacrifice, an occasion for communicants to come together to reaffirm their fellowship in the faith and their moral obligation to love one another. Recognizing the heretical import of Hoadly's tract, as well as its Whiggish intent, a swarm of divines rose to the attack – among them Whitefield in his autobiography and the author (probably Thomas Bowyer) of another of Shamela's favorite works. Fielding's brand of Low Church Christianity informs Adams's spirited defense of the Bishop of Winchester:

"God forbid," says *Adams* [to the bookseller], "any Books should be propagated which the Clergy would cry down: but if you mean by the Clergy, some few designing factious Men, who have it at Heart to establish some favourite Schemes at the Price of the Liberty of Mankind, and the very Essence of Religion, it is not in the power of such Persons to decry any Book they please; witness that excellent Book called, *A Plain Account of the Nature and End of the Sacrament*; a Book written (if I may venture on the Expression) with the Pen of an Angel, and calculated to restore the true Use of Christianity, and of that Sacred Institution: for what could tend more to the noble Purposes of Religion, than frequent cheerful Meetings among the

Members of a Society, in which they should in the Presence of one another, and in the Service of the supreme Being, make Promises of being good, friendly and benevolent to each other? Now this excellent Book was attacked by a Party, but unsuccessfully."

Whiggish though he was, Fielding was "no Politician," and *Joseph Andrews*, one of the few works of this period in which he could afford to follow his own inclinations in this respect, is not in any important way a political novel. Indeed, the general tenor of Fielding's political intent in the work, when he can be said to have any, is to call down a plague on the houses of both parties. Depending on which of these few passages we choose to examine, he will seem disillusioned with either, whether Patriots or Courtiers. After the flattery of Walpole in *The Opposition: A Vision*, we might expect in Fielding's next published work a more positive attitude toward the Great Man, but we look in vain for it. The honest alehouse-keeper, formerly a seafaring man, criticizes the government's ineffectual defense of British shipping and its contempt for commerce; as for his opinion of the *Daily Gazetteer* (which Adams has never heard of) – "It is a dirty News-Paper ... which hath been given away all over the Nation for these many Years to abuse Trade and honest Men, which I would not suffer to lie on my Table, tho' it hath been offered me for nothing" (II.xvii). Fielding might have written such satire during the heyday of his fulminations in *The Champion*. And toward the end of the novel the parody of Middleton's Dedication which identifies Lord Hervey as the original of Beau Didapper confirms the suspicion that, however expedient Fielding found it to serve as Walpole's advocate in *The Opposition*, he had not altered his opinion that the minister's methods of keeping himself and his creatures in power were a nasty business. Here is Hervey transmogrified into Didapper out of Middleton:

Now, to give him only a Dash or two on the affirmative Side: "Tho' he was born to an immense Fortune, he chose, for the pitiful and dirty Consideration of a Place of little consequence, to depend entirely on the Will of a Fellow, whom they call a Great-Man; who treated him with the utmost Disrespect, and exacted of him a plenary Obedience to his Commands; which he implicitly submitted to, at the Expence of his Conscience, his Honour, and of his Country; in which he had himself so very large a Share."

(IV.ix)

Well might Fielding remark at the opening of Book II of *Joseph Andrews*, in a chapter probably written in the month that produced *The Opposition*, that there are "certain Mysteries or Secrets in all Trades from the highest to the lowest, from that of *Prime Ministring* to this of *Authoring,* which are seldom discovered, unless to Members of the same Calling." A pair of chapters in this same Book reflect those feelings of disenchantment and neglect his friends in Opposition had aroused in him by the latter half of 1741. In chapter vii, a kind of novelistic parable often found in his fiction, Fielding ridicules the false Patriot whose professions of courage and of selfless devotion to his country's welfare are shown to be hypocritical; in the next chapter, Parson Adams *"appears in a political Light"* and we discover that his efforts on behalf of candidates of the Country party were not only unwise, but unrewarded.[110]

In *Joseph Andrews* Fielding reserves his praise for two men in particular, Chesterfield and Ralph Allen – the former a leader of the Opposition, the latter with strong ties to the ministry. In the introductory chapter to Book III he attributes "Greatness" to them both, but it is not greatness of the political variety. He compliments Allen on his hospitality. His tribute to Chesterfield, whom seven years earlier in the Dedication of *Don Quixote in England* he lauded chiefly for his patriotism, is conspicuously innocent now of any political coloring:

> I could name a Peer [Fielding writes] no less elevated by Nature than by Fortune, who whilst he wears the noblest Ensigns of Honour on his Person, bears the truest Stamp of Dignity on his Mind, adorned with Greatness, enriched with Knowledge, and embellished with Genius. I have seen this Man relieve with Generosity, while he hath conversed with Freedom, and be to the same Person a Patron and a Companion.

···➤ xxii ◀─···

As *Joseph Andrews* made its way through Woodfall's press, events were occurring which confirmed Fielding in his evident disenchantment with the Opposition. A series of surprising anti-ministerial results in the elections sharply reduced Walpole's majority in the Commons – a process of erosion completed on 2 February 1741/2 when the vote on the contested Chippenham election went against him. On this defeat, the Great Man resigned his offices, bringing to an end his twenty years of control over the affairs of state – a tenure unequalled by any other Prime Minister in history. The King, it is said, wept on the occasion. On 9 February, however, to reward his trusted counselor (and to shield him from enemies howling to impeach him) he raised Walpole to the peerage as Earl of Orford. In the scramble for power that ensued, Pulteney and Carteret revealed the true motives behind the rhetoric of their patriotism by selling out to the Court. Pulteney, who for the same twenty years had distinguished himself as the Opposition's leader in the Commons, abandoned the cause: accepting the title Earl of Bath, he followed his great adversary impotently into the House of Lords. Carteret, a favorite with the King for supporting Hanoverian interests, was made Secretary of State, while Sandys, who the year before had sponsored the Motion against Walpole, became Chancellor of the Exchequer. As for the Prince of Wales, the figurehead around whom the Opposition had rallied, proposing him improbably to the public as the ideal of Bolingbroke's Patriot King: a supplement of £50,000 to his allowance reconciled him to his father and elicited a promise that he would cooperate with Walpole in supporting the new government.

The Cobhamites, on the other hand – with whose interests Fielding had long been identified – were thrown a sop but nothing more: Lord Cobham was restored to the colonelcy of his regiment. But there was nothing at all for Lyttelton or Pitt or Dodington or Chesterfield. These men, embittered at their own exclusion from office and disgusted at the hypocrisy of their former allies, formed the nucleus of a new and vigorous Opposition.

For the time being Fielding washed his hands of "pollitricks," though his sympathies remained with his friends. More than once in his writings of 1742 he intrudes to express the contempt he felt for the hypocrites Pulteney and Carteret. In revising *Joseph Andrews* for the second edition, for example (which was through Woodfall's press by 31 May 1742 and published on 10 June), he added passages that sharpen the point of the political parable of the false Patriot: the francophile fop Bellarmine has now become a turncoat member of the Opposition ("before I had a Place, I was in the Country Interest, he he he!" [II.iv]); and after the episode in which Adams rescues Fanny from a would-be ravisher, we find a new opening cobbled onto Book II, chapter x:

> THE Silence of *Adams*, added to the Darkness of the Night, and Loneliness of the Place, struck dreadful Apprehensions into the poor Woman's Mind: She began to fear as great an Enemy in her Deliverer, as he had delivered her from; and as she had not Light enough to discover the Age of *Adams*, and the Benevolence visible in his Countenance, she suspected he had used her as some very honest Men have used their Country; and had rescued her out of the hands of one Rifler, in order to rifle her himself.

The same motive accounts for the observation emphasized by glaring capitals in a footnote to Fielding and William Young's translation of Aristophanes' *Plutus*, published 31 May 1742: "TO MAKE USE OF POPULAR INTEREST, AND THE CHARACTER OF PATRIOTISM, IN ORDER TO

BETRAY ONE'S COUNTRY, is perhaps the most flagitious of all Crimes" (p. 57 n.).

Similar sentiments color the pieces Fielding was preparing for publication in the *Miscellanies*. Among his numberless reincarnations in *A Journey from This World to the Next*, for example, Julian the Apostate reveals that as leader of the Opposition during the reign of King John he behaved in a manner anticipating the conduct of Pulteney and Carteret in February 1742: "in truth, I sought nothing but my own Preferment, by making myself formidable to the King, and then selling to him the Interest of that Party, by whose means I had become so" (I.xxiii). Earlier, in the judgment scene before the gates of Elysium, Minos attends approvingly to a Patriot's "florid Harangue on public Virtue, and the Liberties of his Country," until he hears this "stately Figure" boast that "he had behaved as well in Place as he had done in Opposition; and that, tho' he was now obliged to embrace the Court-Measures, yet he had behaved very honestly to his Friends, and brought as many in as was possible" – whereupon Minos sends him packing (I.vii). Such incidental hits at self-serving "patriotism" suggest how profoundly disillusioned Fielding now was with the contemporary political scene. He levels all distinctions between Walpole and those who successfully brought him down only because they wanted to enjoy the spoils of office themselves.

In Book IV, chapter iii, of *Jonathan Wild* Fielding inserted a curious episode recounting Wild's deposition of his fellow criminal Roger Johnson as ruler of "the *Prigs*" in Newgate – an episode in which he changes the allegorical mask his hero wears, having Wild appear as Pulteney and Johnson as the fallen Walpole. Years later in revising the novel, Fielding advised readers that (whatever may have been his original intent in satirizing Walpole) the final political point of his novel was couched in this chapter in the speech of "the Grave Man" who addressed the debtors on the real significance of Newgate power struggles. The terms of this speech he borrowed from the rhetoric of Bolingbroke and, more to the point, of Bolingbroke's disciples in the ostensible cause of political idealism, Lyttelton, Dodington, and Chesterfield:

> NOTHING sure can be more justly ridiculous [declares Fielding's spokesman] than the Conduct of those, who should lay the Lamb in the Wolf's Way, and then should lament his being devoured. What a Wolf is in a Sheepfold, a great Man is in Society. Now, when one Wolf is in Possession of a Sheepfold, how little would it avail the simple Flock to expel him, and place another in his Stead? Of the same Benefit to us is the overthrowing one *Prig* in Favour of another. And for what other Advantage was your Struggle? Did you not all

know, that *Wild* and his Followers were *Prigs*, as well as *Johnson* and his? What then could the Contention be among such, but that which you have now discovered it to have been? Perhaps some would say, Is it then our Duty tamely to submit to the Rapine of the *Prig* who now plunders us, for Fear of an Exchange? Surely No: But I answer, It is better to shake the Plunder off than to exchange the Plunderer. And by what Means can we effect this, but by a total Change in our Manners? Every *Prig* is a Slave. His own *Priggish* Desires, which enslave him themselves betray him to the Tyranny of others. To preserve, therefore, the Liberty of *Newgate*, is to change the Manners of *Newgate*. Let us, therefore, who are confined here for Debt only, separate ourselves entirely from the *Prigs*; neither drink with them, nor converse with them. Let us, at the same Time, separate ourselves farther from *Priggism* itself. Instead of being ready, on every Opportunity, to pillage each other, let us be content with our honest Share of the common Bounty, and with the Acquisition of our own Industry. When we separate from the *Prigs*, let us enter into a closer Alliance with one another. Let us consider ourselves all as Members of one Community, to the public Good of which we are to sacrifice our private Views; not to give up the Interest of the Whole for every little Pleasure or Profit which shall accrue to ourselves. Liberty is consistent with no Degree of Honesty inferiour to this.

Throughout his career, however necessary he found it on occasion to employ his talents in behalf of his friends' interests (which he had a way of identifying conveniently with the true interests of the nation), these words express Fielding's deepest convictions about the duty of individual citizens to sacrifice their private ambitions in order to promote the general welfare of the polity. This will also be Dr. Harrison's message in *Amelia* (XI.ii), Fielding's last novel.

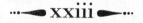

XXiii

In 1742, however, the disappointment of his friends' political purposes would seem trivial in comparison to his own distress. In June he felt obliged to apologize to his subscribers for the delay in publishing the *Miscellanies*: "The Publication of these Volumes," he explained in a notice in the *Daily Post* (5 June 1742), "hath been hitherto retarded by the Author's Indisposition last Winter, and a Train of melancholy Accidents scarce to be parallell'd." When the *Miscellanies* did at last appear in April of the following year – after he had failed twice to fulfill promises of delivering them first by Christmas 1742 and then by 28 February 1742/3[111] – Fielding in his Preface was more explicit in describing the afflictions of "last Winter" (i.e., 1741–2), when he was "laid up in the Gout, with a favourite Child dying in one Bed, and my Wife in a Condition very little better, on another, attended with other Circumstances, which served as very proper Decorations to such a Scene."

It was Charlotte, his first born, who died early in March 1741/2, a few weeks short of her sixth birthday – perhaps a victim of the epidemic fever that ravaged the metropolis that winter. By this time Fielding had moved the family from Essex Street to Spring Garden, Charing Cross, within the Verge of the Court, where he would be relatively safe from the creditors who hounded him. No financial worries would cause him to stint on his daughter's obsequies, however, for which he paid the high price of £5.18s: Charlotte was buried on 9 March 1741/2 in the chancel vault of St. Martin-in-the-Fields.[112] Trying to bring his grief under control, Fielding composed an essay in the tradition of the Christian-stoic *consolatio*, entitled "Of the Remedy of Affliction for the Loss of Our Friends," which he would include in the *Miscellanies*. In it he recalls the mood of sorrow and philosophic resignation that prevailed in his lodgings in the Verge:

> I remember [he writes] the most excellent of Women, and tenderest of Mothers, when, after a painful and dangerous Delivery, she was told she had a Daughter, answering; *Good God! I have produced a Creature who is to undergo what I have suffered!* Some Years afterwards, I heard the same Woman, on the Death of that very Child, then one of the loveliest Creatures ever seen, comforting herself with reflecting, that *her Child could never know what it was to feel such a Loss as she then lamented.*
>
> In Reality, she was right in both Instances: and however Instinct, Youth, a Flow of Spirits, violent Attachments, and above all, Folly may blind us, the Day of Death is (to most People at least) a Day of more Happiness than that of our Birth, as it puts an End to all those Evils which the other gave a Beginning to.

The remedies he proposed for curing grief, the mind's most painful disease, had "this uncommon Recommendation, that I have tried them upon myself with some Success." Chief among them was the expectation of a life hereafter happier by far than what he and Charlotte had recently known. In another of the works he was preparing for inclusion in the *Miscellanies*, the narrator of *A Journey from This World to the Next* (I.viii) describes his entrance into Elysium:

We pursued our way through a delicious Grove of Orange-Trees, where I saw infinite Numbers of Spirits, every one of whom I knew, and was known by them: (for Spirits here know one another by Intuition.) I presently met a little Daughter, whom I had lost several Years before. Good Gods! what Words can describe the Raptures, the melting passionate Tenderness, with which we kiss'd each other, continuing in our Embrace, with the most extatic Joy, a Space, which if Time had been measured here as on Earth, could not be less than half a Year.

A century later, Fielding's greatest admirer could think of no surer consolation for a grief such as this. Dickens – who esteemed Fielding enough to name his son after him – twice recalled this scene from the *Journey* when comforting friends mourning for the death of a child.[113]

In these early months of 1742 Fielding, author of that most cheerful of novels *Joseph Andrews*, thus fantasized about the "Happiness" of death. Suffering from the agonies of gout, he watched his favorite daughter die and buried her while at the same time her mother – "the most excellent of Women," he called her, from whom he drew "all the solid Comfort of my Life" – lay near to death herself. Meanwhile, despite the success of his novel and his continued hackney writing, he was unable to repair the family's ruinous financial circumstances. On 1 March the partners of *The Champion* voted to deprive him of the shares he owned in the profits of the paper; on 27 March (the date also of his dismal letter to Harris) he was obliged to borrow the considerable sum of £197 from one Joseph King.[114] As Fielding knew, the time was approaching when, having run through his lawyer's devices for postponing the Court's judgment, he would be obliged on 26 May 1742 to settle his debt with Hugh Allen.

No wonder that when Horace Walpole composed this spring an imitation of Horace's second Epode, he ironically put his "Praises of a Poet's Life" into Fielding's mouth, noting that he was "A Writer of great Humour, Extravagance, & Poverty":

> Thus *Fielding* spoke, & most devoutly bless'd
> The gracious Muse, not fruitlessly caress'd:
> A whole Half-Guinea, a Subscription-Fee
> That very Morn had set his Snuffbox free,
> Pledg'd to a Broker; which so late withdrawn,
> In Two Days' Time He seeks again to Pawn.[115]

This was also the period to which Horace Walpole assigned the following anecdote concerning Fielding and Thomas Winnington (1696–1746), a courtier under Sir Robert Walpole who continued in place after the Great Man fell:

Soon after Fielding had publish'd Joseph Andrews [wrote Horace Walpole in his commonplace book], he said to Mr. Winnington, I wish any Body woud lend me five hundred pound upon my Life. Mr. W. replied, I will tell you what I will do, I will lend you that Summ upon any Body's Life that you will write.[116]

From another point of view, Fielding's own, the spectacle of his improvidence and the circumstances attending it was less amusing. He was peddling subscriptions to the *Miscellanies* for less frivolous purposes than the redeeming of snuffboxes. He was in fact in a state of dejection that prevented him from sharing his friends' delighted expectation of Walpole's imminent punishment and disgrace. The Great Man's enemies – Lyttelton and Dodington among the most implacable of them – were eager to complete their revenge. Accordingly, they passed a resolution in the Commons that a Committee of Secrecy, chosen by ballot, should be formed to inquire into Walpole's conduct during the last ten years of his ministry.[117] To determine the composition of the Committee, a full House sat on Friday, 26 March; so charged was the atmosphere, however, that it could not complete the business until three o'clock the following afternoon. When the balloting was over, Lyttelton and Dodington were not among the twenty-one members chosen; but it appeared that the Committee was safely in the control of Walpole's enemies and that his fate therefore was sealed. (In the event, he escaped unscathed.)

As soon as he heard the news Fielding hastened to inform Harris of the results: "You will perhaps join the general Joy on the Majority you will perceive on the Side of the Opposition: for my own Part, I am not at present easy enough at home to regard what passes abroad." Adding to his grief over the death of his daughter earlier this month, his wife, he informed Harris, was "scarce yet recovered from a most dangerous Fit of Illness." Such indeed was his state of mind, "I know no other Man living who could at present induce me to write." Having completed the business of the letter, Fielding brought it to a close, imploring his friend to write him a few words of comfort:

> When I am cheerful enough to entertain you you shall hear from me again. In the mean time, you can scarce do a better natured thing than by sacrificing a few Minutes Leisure to a Correspondence which I faithfully aver gives [me] the most sensible Pleasure.

The "Train of melancholy Accidents" that had succeeded one another these past weeks brought Fielding to the lowest point of his life to date. Not least of this pain was the knowledge that much of Charlotte's unhappiness was owing to his own fecklessness. Finding himself in similar circumstances, the Man of the Hill declares in *Tom Jones*

(VIII.xi): "To see a Woman you love in Distress; to be unable to relieve her, and at the same Time to reflect that you have brought her into this Situation, is, perhaps, a Curse of which no Imagination can represent the Horrors to those who have not felt it." At which Jones cries out in reply, "I believe it from my Soul ... and I pity you from the Bottom of my Heart."

xxiv

As the winter of 1741–2 drew to a close, Fielding had another opportunity to earn a few guineas while doing a service for the widow of the Englishman he admired more than any other in his country's history – to judge from his reiterated and extravagant praise of the great Duke of Marlborough, it is not too much to say so. On 2 March was published *An Account of the Conduct of the Dowager Duchess of Marlborough, from her first coming to Court, to the Year 1710*. This self-serving narrative, purportedly written by the octogenarian Duchess herself in the form of a letter to an unnamed nobleman, was in fact the work of the historian Nathaniel Hooke (d. 1763), whom she rewarded for his pains with the astounding gratuity of £5,000. Justifying her conduct at the expense of the characters of Queen Mary, Queen Anne, Lord Oxford, and many others of high and low degree, the *Account* became the subject of controversy, eliciting numerous unfriendly replies. Within a week of its publication a reviewer in the *Gentleman's Magazine* observed that the work had "been so eagerly received, and so attentively considered, as to become even at this Time of Business, Contests, Wars and Revolutions, the most popular Topic of Conversation."[118]

Among the acrimonious pamphlets it spawned was one in particular that Fielding chose to answer: this was the anonymous *Remarks upon the Account of the Conduct of a Certain Dutchess. In a Letter from a Member of the last Parliament in the Reign of Queen Anne to a Young Nobleman*, published on 12 March.[119] The identity of the author, though unknown today, was no secret to Fielding (or so he believed), who dashed off a reply defending the Duchess at every point and reproaching her antagonist for his ill manners in slandering a lady – and, for that matter, not just any lady, but "the Consort of that Glorious Man, who carried the Honour of our Arms so high, and by such a Series of Courage, Conduct and Success, preserved the Liberties of *Europe*." Published under the imprint of J. Roberts on 2 April, this was indeed, as the title declares, *A Full Vindication of the Dutchess Dowager of Marlborough: Both with regard to the Account lately Published by Her Grace, and to her Character in general; against the base and malicious Invectives contained in a late scurrilous Pamphlet, entitled Remarks on the Account, &c. In a Letter to the Noble Author of those Remarks.* For good measure the advertisements added a pair of adjectives representing the "Noble" author of the *Remarks* as being also "Old and Spiteful."[120]

Slight as it is, Fielding's pamphlet is interesting on several counts. In writing it, he was not only defending the great Duke's aged widow, but taking sides with a half-dozen of his friends who were, in one way or another, concerned in compiling the *Account*, which in effect amounted to a Whig history of her own times. It is now clear from Frances Harris's analysis of the Blenheim Papers that in preparing the work over a period of four decades, the Duchess sought the advice and active assistance not only of Hooke, the friend of Pope and Chesterfield and a man whom Fielding admired,[121] but also of three of Fielding's intellectual heroes: Gilbert Burnet, Samuel Clarke, and Benjamin Hoadly. As Miss Harris plausibly conjectures, moreover, the noble lord to whom the *Account* is addressed was probably Chesterfield.[122]

By writing this work, Fielding thus also declared his allegiance to the "new Opposition" that was forming itself around Chesterfield – and which also included another of the Duchess's favorites, Fielding's former schoolfellow and his friend, William Pitt. Just how highly she regarded these two men is attested by the terms of her will: upon her death in 1744 she bequeathed £20,000 to Chesterfield and £10,000 to Pitt. Throughout the 1730s she had been the dreaded angel of Opposition, using her vast wealth at every turn to counter Walpole's bribery. One signal instance of her hatred of the minister is the bitter quarrel she engaged in with her grandson: in 1735, we recall, the spendthrift third Duke of Marlborough was Fielding's patron and a useful member of the "Boy Patriots"; however, in 1738 he defected to Walpole against the wishes of his grandmother, thus incurring her enduring enmity. The *Full Vindication* makes clear that *The Opposition: A Vision* – though almost certainly a piece of political job-work bought and paid for by Walpole – represented no very permanent change in Fielding's loyalty to the Cobhamites and Chesterfield, or in the opinion of the Great Man he had often expressed in his writings since 1734. The "honest Gentleman" of three months before, whose countenance shone with "Benignity," now reassumes his more familiar role of "Corruptor" as Fielding recalls the circumstances of the Duchess's illness at a time when Walpole's fate hung in the balance:

Had the Weight of the Dutchess of *Marlborough* been lately thrown into the Scale of Corruption, the Nation must have sunk under it: But, on the contrary, her whole Power hath been employed in Defence of our Liberties, and to this Power we in a very great measure owe their Protection; and this, the barbarous and inhuman Exultations of the Corruptor and his chief Friends last Winter exprest on her Grace's dangerous Illness, and their eager Expectation of her Death, which they declared would do their Business, sufficiently testify. So that this Nation may be truely said to have been twice saved within 40 Years by the glorious Conduct of this Illustrious Pair; and whoever considers this in a just Light, must acknowledge, that no Name ought to be so dear to the People of *England*, as that of the Dutchess of *Marlborough*.   (p. 38)

Did Fielding have more than merely these civic reasons for expressing so effusively his gratitude to this arrogant old woman? It is clear that, besides the friends they had in common, they were themselves personally acquainted, and it is also clear that Fielding understood the demeaning terms the Duchess exacted of him in their relationship. To those who called her proud, he could thus "truly affirm no such Pride hath been ever shewn to those who have acknowledged themselves to be her Inferiours, to whom none can equal her in Affability and Condescension" (p. 39). It is likely that he had visited Blenheim as early as 1735, when he was courting the favor of the third Duke; for in his article in *The Craftsman* published on 28 June of that year he refers admiringly to the magnificent memorials to the great Duke's military achievements he presumably had seen there – the tapestries depicting his victorious battles and the pillar erected to his memory. In *A Journey from This World to the Next* (I.iv), written much nearer the present time, he leaves no doubt that he had seen these curiosities. The walls of the Palace of Death are "adorned with various Battle-Pieces in Tapestry" which remind the narrator of "those beautiful ones I had ... seen at *Blenheim*" – though, he hastens to add, the battles Marlborough won have not been commemorated in this way by Death, who scorns a general who saved a thousand lives for every one his armies killed. There is, however, no evidence that the Duchess either commissioned the *Full Vindication* or rewarded Fielding for writing it. From a note by Andrew Millar on the back of the copyright assignment of *Joseph Andrews* – an instrument belatedly drawn up by Fielding and witnessed by his friend Parson Young on 13 April 1742 – we know only that Fielding received a total of £199.6s. for the novel and two other lesser productions of this year – one of them being the *Full Vindication*, for which he was paid five guineas.[123]

The other work included in the agreement was the farce *Miss Lucy in Town*, for rights to which Millar paid Fielding ten guineas. A bawdy sequel to his popular afterpiece, *The Virgin Unmask'd*, this play represents Fielding's first and last attempt to resume writing for the stage since the Licensing Act put an end to his theatrical career. Curiously, though he felt himself entitled to sell the copyright to the farce and also appears to have been the sole beneficiary of the author's benefit night when it was produced at Drury Lane in May, Fielding remarked in the Preface to the *Miscellanies* that he had only "a very small Share" in writing the piece. If this is so, who can have been his obscure (and with respect to financial arrangements, obligingly self-effacing) collaborator?

The most plausible candidate for this distinction is David Garrick.[124] In October 1741 Garrick had made his sensational London début in the role of Richard III at Goodman's Fields; and in May 1742 he would commence his long association with Drury Lane. By that time, certainly, he and Fielding had become acquainted; indeed, a friendship between them had begun which grew ever deeper and endured in Garrick's affections long after Fielding's death. This much is clear from Fielding's warm commendations of Garrick in the Preface to the *Miscellanies*, to which Garrick was a subscriber. Shortly before Garrick made his mark as an actor, however, he had come to the Town's attention as the author of a popular afterpiece entitled *Lethe: or, Esop in the Shades*, the earliest version of which contains episodes that anticipate Fielding's new farce by being themselves a sequel to *The Virgin Unmask'd*, as they introduce the principal characters of that play, the country heiress Miss Lucy and Thomas her footman husband, now shown in their married state predictably bored and disillusioned. In *Lethe* Fielding's favorite actress "Kitty" Clive performed the popular part of Lucy she had created originally, and in the best musical number of the play sang of Lucy's desire to lead the life of a town belle. But perhaps Garrick scholars are right in rejecting the notion that his connection with *Miss Lucy in Town* went so far as active collaboration in writing it. Just as Fielding readily admitted his debt to John Hoadly, whose play *The Contrast* gave him the idea for *Pasquin*, so in declaring that he had only "a very small Share" in creating *Miss Lucy in Town*, he may have meant merely to acknowledge that he had taken hints for it from Garrick's *Lethe*.

Though ready for performance two months earlier,[125] *Miss Lucy in Town* was first staged at Drury Lane, as an afterpiece to *Othello*, on 6 May 1742 – also the date on which Millar published it. Whatever

Fielding's reasons may have been for wishing publicly to share responsibility for the farce, it is a rollicking, risqué piece of theatre that bears every mark of his authorship. Like *The Virgin Unmask'd* it was conceived as a vehicle for his favorite, Mrs. Clive, in the role of Lucy. The setting, reminiscent of his *Covent-Garden Tragedy*, is a notorious brothel – this time Mother Haywood's (d. 1743), whom Fielding identifies in a note to his burlesque of Juvenal's *Sixth Satire* as "a useful Woman in the Parish of *Covent-Garden*"; in the play he calls her Mother Haycock, and at least one knowing spectator saw that, as depicted on stage, "the Plan" of her house "exactly" duplicated that of Haywood's.[126] Like Shamela, this loose woman is represented as a devotee of the Methodist Whitefield, who has convinced her that with regular repentance she may sin as much as she likes.

Fielding's amusing idea is that adultery has become so fashionable in polite society the bawds have been reduced to letting lodgings. (One recalls Mother Punchbowl's plangent cry, "Who'd be a Bawd in this degen'rate Age!") The silly country innocents Lucy and Thomas take rooms in Mother Haycock's house in town, where the madam tries to turn a profit by negotiating for the bride with the lecherous Jewish stock-jobber Zorobabel (played by Charles Macklin, who became the greatest Shylock of his day), and also with Lord Bawble, one of the Directors of the Opera. Indeed, the only feature of the farce Horace Walpole chose to report to Horace Mann was a duet between Lucy and Signior Cantileno (a castrato, played by the tenor John Beard) – "in which," wrote Walpole, "Mrs. Clive mimics the Muscovita admirably, and Beard Amorevoli intolerably."[127]

The play was brisk and amusing, and it took with the Town well enough to earn Fielding a modest benefit (the receipts came to just £40) on the sixth night, Wednesday the 19th, when it was paired with *The Miser*, and Mrs. Clive, who starred in both plays, spoke an Epilogue composed especially for the occasion. There was a seventh performance the next day, but by then the season was virtually over. More impressive was the success the farce enjoyed next season when, from 27 October to 1 December, it played a dozen times, once before the Royal Family.

December, however, was also the month in which appeared an anonymous attack on *Miss Lucy in Town*, entitled *A Letter to a Noble Lord, to Whom alone it Belongs*. The noble lord in question was the Duke of Grafton, Lord Chamberlain, whom the Act of 1737 had made Licenser of the stage. The author of this pamphlet – a sardonic latter-day disciple of Jeremy Collier – congratulated Fielding

on his happy Genius; which tho' the Legislature severely check'd on its daring to succeed in a Representation on the Principle of Liberty, *Pasquin*; yet it now, like a *Phoenix*, rises out of its own Ashes, and convinces the World, that it is not confined to the Lewdness of Liberty, but can equally shine and be approved in the Chasteness of Gallantry.

Thanks to this genius the author has no doubt that in the future "a *Play-house* and a *Bawdy-house* will be synonimous Words" – an understandable prediction given the reactions of the audience:

> Whilst the Farce was performing, I over-heard a Gentleman behind me cry out, by G——, it is quite natural! Damn it, I fancy myself at *Mother Heywood's!* S'Blood, the B——ch serv'd me once just as she does Lord *Bawble*, and gave me a damned P–x. A sober Person that sat by, taking a Pinch of Snuff, said, Faith *Fleetwood* had better have hired *Mother Heywood*, and her Company, personally to have appeared.

Besides the lasciviousness of the production, the author of the *Letter* complained about the slur against the Methodists and the Directors of the Opera – Lord Bawble being seen particularly as a caricature of the Earl of Middlesex, principal Director of the Italian Opera and paramour of the Muscovita, whom Mrs. Clive was mimicking on stage. There may not be a causal connection between the two occurrences, but after the publication of this *Letter* to the Lord Chamberlain, Fielding's popular little farce disappeared forever from the stage.

···◀ xxvi ▶···

During these early months of 1742 Fielding was engaged in another, far more ambitious literary enterprise. With the assistance of his learned friend William Young, who had given up schoolmastering in Dorset to find unexpected fame in the metropolis (chiefly as Parson Adams in the pages of *Joseph Andrews*), Fielding was preparing a translation of Aristophanes' *Plutus, the God of Riches* – "With large Notes, Explanatory, Historical and Critical." Published on 31 May not by Millar, but by the obscure bookseller T. Waller, whose shop was conveniently situated amidst the lawyers in the Temple Cloisters, *Plutus* was offered "as a Specimen" of a projected translation of all eleven comedies of Aristophanes, the translators declaring, however, that they intended "to proceed in the Work according to the Reception this Play meets with from the Public." There were to be no further volumes.

The project deserved a better fate. Young's knowledge of Greek ensured that *Plutus* would be a more accurate translation than its rivals, Madame Dacier's in French and Lewis Theobald's in English, whom Fielding and Young represent as limping blindly along after his Gallic guide even where she errs. With Fielding to enliven the dialogue, furthermore, the play might even have acted well – so he seems to have believed, as he pauses in the notes to comment on the subtleties of staging the work. Certainly the theme of the comedy was a favorite of his: the tendency of riches to corrupt the morals of the rich.

Abortive though the enterprise was, *Plutus* remains interesting for what it reveals of Fielding's political and literary concerns and his personal circumstances. He dedicated the work to William, Lord Talbot (1710–82), son of the Lord Chancellor who had died in 1737. Like Lyttelton, Talbot was a patron of the poet James Thomson, with whom Fielding was friendly, and he was also a supporter of the "new Opposition." In addressing this particular comedy of Aristophanes to the son of one of the most respected lawyers of his time ("that truly Great and Amiable Person," Fielding calls him), Fielding could at once give much-needed public assurance of his probity in his new profession and remind his readers of what he had suffered as an author in his country's cause. For, as he had often pointed out since 1734, when he declared his allegiance to Chesterfield and the Patriots in the Dedication to *Don Quixote in England*, Fielding saw himself as England's Aristophanes, in his ill-fated dramatic satires having revived the "Old Comedy" in order to expose false "Greatness" to ridicule and to purge the nation of corruption. This very personal point would not be lost on his readers in 1742 as he addressed Lord Talbot:

> The Greatness of this Author's Genius need not be mentioned to Your LORDSHIP; but there is a much stronger Recommendation to one of Your known Principles. He exerted that Genius in the Service in his Country. He attack'd and expos'd its Enemies and Betrayers with a Boldness and Integrity, which must endear his Memory to every True and Sincere Patriot.
>
> In presenting *Aristophanes*, therefore, to Your LORDSHIP, we present him to One, whom he, had he been an *Englishman*, would have chosen for his Patron.

Nor would Fielding, in commenting on the targets of Aristophanes' satire, lose the opportunity to contrast the wise tolerance the Athenian governors showed his author with the tyranny of the English politicians who, by muzzling him in 1737, had curtailed the nation's liberties:

> Such Instances, when they happen, fall very justly under the Lash of a Comic Poet. And it is by exposing such Persons and Things, that *unlicensed* Comedy will be found of great Use in a Society; and a Free Stage and a Free People will always agree very well together.
>
> (p. 86, n.)

Neglected though it is, *Plutus* is Fielding's finest tribute to the classical dramatist he regarded as the model and justification for his own most daring theatrical satires. As he declared in the Preface, one could find in Aristophanes the true Attic salt and manly simplicity of style which the influence of Cibber's "genteel Comedy" – written in feeble imitation of "that pretty, dapper, brisk, smart, pert Dialogue" Wycherley introduced – had banished from the stage. Just as in the Preface to *Joseph Andrews* Fielding observed that Ben Jonson "of all Men understood the *Ridiculous* the best," so here it is again Jonson who "of all our *English* Poets, seems chiefly to have studied and imitated *Aristophanes*."

The Preface to *Plutus* also signals the end of a friendship and reveals Fielding's continued efforts to ingratiate himself with the great poet whose moral character he once denounced. The criticisms of Theobald's incompetence as a translator go well beyond what was required to establish the superiority of the Fielding–Young version of the play. With Theobald's strictures against Pope's edition of Shakespeare in mind – strictures that had raised Theobald to the throne of Dulness in the original *Dunciad* – Fielding archly observes of his former friend that "being a Critic of great Nicety himself, and great Diligence in correcting Mistakes in others, [he] cannot be offended at the same Treatment." But if Pope enjoyed the sarcasms heaped upon his old antagonist in Fielding's commentary, he must have relished even more the extraordinary compliment Fielding paid him: "the inimitable Author of the *Essay on Man* [Fielding declares] taught me a System of Philosophy in *English* Numbers, whose Sweetness is scarce inferior to that of *Theocritus* himself." To be sure, Fielding went to school for his philosophy to other teachers besides Pope; but this tribute confirms one's sense of a strong affinity between the world view expressed discursively in the greatest philosophical poem of the century and that which is given life and form in Fielding's masterpiece *Tom Jones*.

Plutus did not quite drop stillborn from the press. Writing to *The Champion* from "Otter's Pool" three weeks later, Fielding's friend and former collaborator William Robinson – the satirical dreamer who contributed to that paper under the pseudonyms "Morpheus" and "Somnus" – was delighted with the new translation, which he appreciated all the more as he had been "a Truant in my *Greek*, since I left School." Indeed, he found it so irresistibly funny he was helpless to control his laughter:

The Drollery, the exquisite Strokes of Humour, Satire, and Ridicule, with the admirable Vein of Wit and Pleasantry, that run through that inimitable Piece, made me several Times burst out into a loud Laugh, tho' alone, insomuch that the People of the House, if they were not well accustomed to my way in such Cases, would certainly take me to be mad.

This experience, once he fell asleep, prompted him to dream that Plutus, having been restored to his sight, bestowed riches on everyone according to their just deserts. Walpole and his brother, the double-dealing Patriots, self-serving kings, generals, lawyers, princes of the Church – none escapes Plutus's judgment. The nightmare is not quite unrelieved, however, for "in the midst of these Disasters, I was not a little comforted to see my reverend and worthy Friend Mr. *Abraham Adams* translated from his Living of *twenty three Pounds per. Ann.* to the See of ———."[128] Young would not get a bishopric as a reward for *Plutus*, though he is said to have accepted a share of the five guineas of "Aristophanic gold" Fielding's Dedication elicited from Lord Talbot. Before long, however, his fame as Abraham Adams led to his appointment as "tutor to a young Gentleman at 70*l.* a year";[129] and also, sometime early in 1743, to the chaplaincy of an Army hospital abroad during the War of the Austrian Succession.

...◆ xxvii ◆...

The god of riches might well have been in Fielding's thoughts as he looked ahead to the summer and his travels on the Western Circuit. On 5 June he felt obliged to place a notice in the *Daily Post*, partly in order to solicit more subscriptions to the *Miscellanies*, which were to fill three volumes, but also to apologize for the delay in publishing them. The price was a guinea for the set, or two guineas for the printing on royal paper; and since subscribers paid half the price when they signed on (the other half coming due when the volumes were delivered in sheets), Fielding had taken a good deal of his friends' money without yet producing anything in return. In this notice he refers to an earlier set of proposals – his "last Receipts" – in which he had promised to deliver the work by Christmas 1742. He now reaffirmed that promise. Indeed, the notice concludes on a note of optimism that circumstances did not warrant: "As the Books will very shortly go to the Press, Mr. Fielding begs the Favour of those who intend to subscribe to do it immediately."

At just this time Fielding needed money to repay the £197 he owed Joseph King. Besides the subscribers to the *Miscellanies* and the friends he borrowed from, and whatever other income he derived from his new play and recent publications, he had another source of supply which, considering how he despised the breed of creditors who were unwilling to forgive debtors their debts, he must have regretted having to resort to. Despite his impecuniousness Fielding somehow had managed to lend the sum of £199 to one Randolph Seagrim, who contracted the debt in Dorchester on 1 June 1742.[130] Fielding may not himself have left London this early. He would have attended the performance of *The Miser* and *Miss Lucy in Town* staged for his benefit on 19 May, and we might expect him to remain in town for the publication of *Plutus* on 31 May. Since he had revised the novel extensively, he might also wish to see through the press the second edition of *Joseph Andrews* by the same date. Furthermore, though the proposals for the *Miscellanies* published in the *Daily Post* on 5 June direct potential subscribers to apply to Andrew Millar, the notice itself was obviously composed by Fielding. Seagrim probably borrowed the money from someone in Dorchester who acted on Fielding's behalf. He remains a shadowy figure, but perhaps he is the same Randolph Seagrim who had been Fielding's neighbor at East Stour;[131] that Seagrim is the surname Fielding would bestow on Black George, the dishonest gamekeeper in *Tom Jones*, may hint at his opinion of the man. However that may be, Fielding, through his attorney Giles Taylor, moved swiftly to recover the debt in Trinity Term. Judgment in the amount of £199 plus 63 shillings costs and damages was given in his favor on 8 July 1742. It came not a moment too soon, since in a judgment of 7 July the Court of Common Pleas determined that Fielding must settle his own debt with Joseph King in the amount of £197 plus 50 shilling costs and damages. Rarely in life would Fielding's accounts balance out, even just this barely, in his favor.

The Western Assizes happened late this summer. Commencing at Winchester on Tuesday, 27 July, they continued as follows: Saturday, 31 July, at Salisbury; Thursday, 5 August, at Dorchester; Monday, 9 August, at Exeter; Tuesday, 17 August, at Bodmin; Tuesday, 24 August, at Bridgwater; and Saturday, 28 August, at Bristol. While at Salisbury, Fielding visited Harris and was sorry to find him not well enough to think of stirring from home this season. For as usual Fielding's destination this summer was Bath, where he went not only to take the waters (his gout continued to trouble him), but also to enjoy the company and try to get on with the business of preparing his *Miscellanies*.

••• ➤ XXVIII ◀ •••

From Bath on 24 September he wrote Harris one of his most informative and delightful letters. Harris had written twice expressing his concern over Fielding's health. The second letter was necessary because Fielding neglected to answer the first – the reasons being, he explained, that he had been occupied with boring legal business in Bristol, attending courts of *nisi prius*[132] only to observe the proceedings as "*Auditor tantum*," and that he was "obliged to write more than is proper with the Bath Waters in order to finish my Works within the limited Time." In making these apologies, Fielding reveals how much he coveted Harris's friendship – "there is no Man living in whose Esteem I so eagerly desire a very high Place" – and how much in love he and Charlotte remained after nearly eight years of marriage. Charlotte, whom he had left behind in Bath while he attended to business at Bristol, used the arrival of Harris's first letter as an excuse to carry it to her husband herself. So happy was he to see her "after ten Days Separation" that, Fielding declared, "almost every other Matter" but the receipt of a letter from so good a friend "would have appeared indifferent" to him.

Besides the discomforts of the gout Fielding was experiencing pangs of conscience over the difficulties he was having with the *Miscellanies*, which he had twice promised to have in the subscribers' hands by Christmas, only three months away. He was anxious that he might not have sufficient material to fill the three volumes – though this worry was in large part owing to his decision not to publish or reprint several eligible works he might have included but which he deemed unsuitable for either political or personal reasons: he would not include, for instance, his earliest poems "The Coronation" or *The Masquerade*, or the unpublished verse "Epistle to Mr. Lyttleton" attacking Pope, or *The Vernoniad* or *The Opposition: A Vision*. Though he was grateful that Harris had been able to retrieve some "Verses" which had been preserved by no less august a personage than Philip Yorke (1690–1764), Baron Hardwicke – verses possibly comprising an Epistle to the Lord Chancellor comparable to the ones Fielding addressed to such other patrons as Lyttelton, Dodington, and the Duke of Richmond – yet he thought Harris too generous in commending "what was originally writ with the Haste and Inaccuracy of a common Letter, and which I shall be sorry if any Scarcity of Matter under the *Poetical* Article should oblige me to publish."

What always troubled Fielding about writing verse was the requirement Pope's formidable example had imposed on poets of the day to express themselves in couplets. As early as 1729 he represented the Palace of the "God of Rhime" as "A Gothick Structure! built in modern Time," and Pope as the god's votary, "Who one for thee one Verse for Sense compose[s]."[133] Now echoing Thomson's praise of John Philips, "Who nobly durst in rhyme-unfettered verse/With British freedom sing the British song,"[134] Fielding confesses to Harris that he finds the form of the heroic couplet too artificial and restrictive. If this is poetry, then, he admits, "I am no Poet." He will not, however, meekly depreciate the talent he does possess. A little like Wordsworth in his Preface to the *Lyrical Ballads*, he turns the tables on Pope and his tribe by declaring that a talent for writing good muscular prose is in fact superior to Pope's gift, fine as we know Fielding thought that gift to be:

> To confess a Truth, I wish that long Word [*Poetical*] had never been inserted in my Proposals: for my Talents (if I have any) lie not in Versification. My Muse is a free born Briton and disdains the slavish Fetters of Rhyme. And must not you or the greatest Admirer of Numbers allow that, even in the Hands of the best Versifier, a noble Sentiment, or a noble Expression at least, may be sometimes lost by the unfortunate length or shortness of a Word? for the Poet must imitate the Recruiting Officer who rejects Strength and Symmetry for a long ill-made Fellow of 6 Foot. What beautiful Expressions are to be found in the antient Prose-Writers which would not have yielded to Numbers.

To illustrate the point, Fielding quotes three elegant phrases from a chapter in Petronius Arbiter which he had been reading that morning, all containing "words which would not have *stood* (as we said at Eton) in an Hexameter."

> On the other Hand, how common is it with the Poets to admit a *shabby* word, as the Lovers of Music do sometimes a shabby Treble only for being musical: nay amongst those who write in Rhime one Line is often introduced only to chime to the other, according to the Poetical Observation,
>
> > for one for Sense and one for Rhime
> > I think is fairest at one Time
>
> which is likewise an Example of the Practice, half the last Line being superfluous.

That same couplet from Butler's *Hudibras* (II.i.29–30) had been in Fielding's mind earlier when he satirized Pope as being preeminent among the votaries of the "God of Rhime," a poet "Who one for thee one Verse for Sense compose[s]." And Pope is again Fielding's implicit target in marshaling these objections against the crippling constraints which "Rhyme" and "Numbers" impose on even "the best Versifier." Indeed, Fielding concludes this witty defense of prose, the medium *he* has mastered, by claiming Milton himself to be of his party:

> I apprehend it will be readily admitted that every Part of Stile except the Sublime may be reached by Prose: And what if even this may not only be atchieved by the Prose-Writer; but it should be found

that the Dignity and Majesty of Prose should be superiour to that
of Verse. Will you pardon me if I think Paradise lost is writ in Prose.

If Harris should think that claim excessive, Fielding was certain his
friend would grant the sublimity of a long passage quoted from Bacon's
Advancement of Learning, and Harris was not likely to protest too
strenuously at Fielding's final example, drawn from the manuscript of
Harris's own *Three Treatises* – "in which the Sublime is as greatly
exemplified as in any which I have ever seen."

Written early in the decade when the so-called "New Poets" –
Edward Young, the Wartons, Collins – followed Thomson's lead in
liberating English verse from what had become the tyranny of the
couplet, Fielding's critical excursus presages the revolution in taste
that was accomplished with the advent of Romanticism. What is more,
this antipathy to expressing himself in the "slavish Fetters of Rhyme"
is much of a piece with the passionate impulsiveness of his own deepest
nature, so uneasily submitting to all discipline and confinement. In
concluding these remarks – typically with a jest cracked at his own
expense – Fielding invokes the authority of Harris's uncle, the witty
Lord Shaftesbury, author of the *Characteristics* (1711):

> The Objection I have here made to Poetry hath, I think, at least
> Novelty to recommend it; having been never made either by those
> dull sad Fellows who have railed at Poets, or those dull merry Fellows
> who have laughed at them; if you are so much their Friend as to be
> offended at my Observations you may revenge your self on me by
> imitating Lord Shaftesbury who says of a Philosopher and a Poet
> who decryed Courage, that they were both Cowards, so may you
> conclude that I am no Poet.

Besides such passages of literary criticism, Fielding's letter is full of
gossip of the company at Bath. As he was making the acquaintance of
Ralph Allen and Pope a year ago, Fielding had not had the dubious
pleasure of meeting Pope's pompous friend and apologist, William
Warburton (1698–1779), polemical author of a number of ponderous
treatises, including most recently, *The Divine Legation of Moses demonstrated* (1738–41). Warburton, who later married Allen's niece, had
now become a regular visitor at Prior Park, and he presided like an
erudite colossus over the literary company that gathered at Leake's
bookshop.

> We have here [Fielding informs Harris] the *great* Warburton, Who
> resides at Mr Allen's, but sometimes visits Leake's where he
> harangued yesterday near two Hours: His Reading and Memory
> seem both very extraordinary, and his Knowledge of Things seems
> as extensive as Young's of Words. As to the rest, Pride, Arrogance,

Self Sufficiency and some other such Ecclesiastical Qualities compose his Character.

Such were Fielding's first impressions of the future Bishop of Gloucester. However frankly he was prepared to confide them to his friend Harris in the privacy of a letter, he was prudent enough in print to emphasize Warburton's more commendable qualities. As he prepared the *Miscellanies* for publication, he twice found opportunities to praise the mighty favorite of Allen and Pope: in the burlesque of Juvenal's *Sixth Satire* Fielding commends Warburton's account of the Eleusinian Mysteries, which are "explain'd" in the *Divine Legation* "in a most masterly Stile, and with the profoundest Knowledge of Antiquity" (p. 91, n. 3); in *A Journey from This World to the Next* (I. viii) he goes so far as to have Virgil himself confirm to the astounded Addison that these mysteries were indeed "couched" in the Sixth Book of the *Aeneid*, where Warburton had discovered them. In *Tom Jones* (XIII.i) Fielding would go farther still, imploring the Muse of Learning to "Give me awhile that Key to all thy Treasures, which to thy *Warburton* thou hast entrusted."

During this sojourn at Bath, Fielding also contracted "an Acquaintance here with a Parson of a very different Turn" from Warburton. This was the Reverend George Watts, who since 1735 had been Preacher of the Society of Lincoln's Inn – a position of some distinction once held by Tillotson. (Ironically enough, considering Fielding's antithetical view of the two priests, when illness forced Watts to resign in 1746, Warburton was elected to replace him.)[135] It was perhaps inevitable that Fielding and Watts should come to know each other, as they had many friends in common: Watts was not only "no Stranger" to Harris; he was also close to Thomas Birch, with whom he dined on occasion with Thomson and Lillo.[136] But Fielding probably was introduced to this latest of his clerical companions through the sociable offices of Charles Hanbury Williams, who had met Watts since arriving at Bath earlier this summer and immediately liked him. Writing to Henry Fox from Bath in November 1742, Hanbury Williams asked whether Fox knew Watts, who held the living at Orston, Nottinghamshire, near Fox's seat: "I have been acquainted with him ever since I've been here and admire him of all Men of his Cloth that I ever met with."[137] Fielding was similarly impressed, declaring to Harris that he found Watts "infinitely the most agreeable Companion I know in this Place."

In this same letter of 24 September 1742, so richly informative of his opinions and character, Fielding told Harris that he had seen at Bath their friend and Harris's neighbor in The Close, Edward Goldwyre, the surgeon who repaired the injury to Charlotte's nose. Playfully (for Harris would have known the facts) Fielding reports that "Mr Goldwyre a Surgeon of a City called Salisbury is lately married to one Miss Harris a young Lady of &c. –" The young lady in question was the daughter of one William Harris, Esq., also a resident of The Close,[138] but not, it appears, otherwise related to James Harris. Having met his friend Goldwyre, Fielding took the opportunity to enlist him as a subscriber to the *Miscellanies*.

Among the company at Bath this September were two other friends, barristers both, who like Fielding were enjoying the diversions of the place after riding the Western Circuit. These were Charles Pratt, who had recently given Fielding news of Harris, and the eloquent hedonist Robert Henley. Though at this early stage of their careers Pratt and Henley had to scour the county towns in search of briefs – indeed, in 1747 they would be indebted to Fielding for throwing a little business their way – both men eventually became, in Murphy's phrase, "the first ornaments" of the profession: Henley's eminence we have already noted; Pratt served as Lord Chancellor from 1766 to 1770 and was raised to the peerage as first Earl Camden.

Henley was courting the beautiful Jane Huband[139] (they would marry in November of the following year), who had come to Bath to take the waters. For the same reason Fielding was frequenting the Pump Room, and it was there he addressed to her a flirting poem, "Written *Extempore*." The physician who ministered to both their illnesses, and to whom Fielding cordially alludes in this poem as the "Glory of his Art," was Dr. Thomas Brewster (b. 1705) – himself something of a man of letters, having published a verse translation of the satires of Persius (1733–42) from which Fielding quotes in "An Essay on Conversation." Brewster, together with another well-known Bath physician, Dr. Edward Harrington (1696–1757), would later attend the philosopher Square in his final illness in *Tom Jones* (XVIII.iv). Fielding did not leave Bath without adding their names to his subscription list for the *Miscellanies*, and putting Jane Huband's affluent lover down for a set of the royal paper.

Thanks (as he believed) to the skill of Drs. Brewster and Harrington and the salutary effects of the waters of the Pump Room, Fielding had so completely recovered from the gout by the time he wrote Harris that he was cutting a figure on the dance floor. In the Dedication to *Shamela* he recalled Lord Hervey's being "carried into the Ball-Room at the *Bath*, by the discerning Mr. *Nash*," celebrated arbiter of that polite city's pleasures: "Here," Fielding teased the effeminate little courtier, "you was observed in Dancing to balance your Body exactly, and to weigh every Motion with the exact and equal Measure of Time and Tune." What we could not have guessed is that, in such a delicate art as this, Fielding could not only judge the fop Hervey's accomplishments; he could rival them. Applying to himself the epithet given the notorious rake Robert "Beau" Feilding (d. 1712), a disreputable member of the Denbigh family, Fielding informed Harris "that one Henry Fielding Esqʳ. commonly known by the Name of *Beau Fielding* did to the utter Confusion of all his Brother Beaus open the first Ball at Bath with a Minuet." The spectacle of a man of Fielding's large physique nicely treading a minuet – and doing it with so much self-assurance and good humor that he dared open the ball! – is comical to imagine. With the philosopher Locke, however, no less than the Earl of Chesterfield, Fielding understood that in order to qualify as a gentle-man, one had to correct the awkwardness of the body by submitting to the discipline of the dancing master. Commenting on the clumsiness of Atkinson in *Amelia* (V.ii), he thus observed:

> Tho' I do not entirely agree with the late learned Mr. *Essex*[140] the celebrated Dancing-Master's Opinion, that Dancing is the Rudiment of polite Education, as he would, I apprehend, exclude every other Art and Science; yet it is certain, that Persons whose Feet have never been under the Hands of the Professors of that Art, are apt to discover this Want in their Education in every Motion, nay, even when they stand or sit still. They seem indeed to be over-burthened with Limbs, which they know not how to use, as if when Nature hath finished her Work, the Dancing-Master still is necessary to put it in Motion.

Thanks to this one letter to Harris, we have a more complete view of Fielding during September 1742 than we have of him at any other period of his middle years. We also know that he planned to leave Bath for Winchester on Sunday, 26 September, and would pause along the way to spend Monday afternoon with his friend at Salisbury – unless, as he proposed, Harris, who was himself about to undertake a journey to the town of Marlborough, preferred to meet instead at Amesbury, Wilts., a place more conveniently situated for both their purposes.

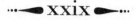

XXIX

When Fielding returned to London for the start of Michaelmas Term he found an unwanted tribute had been paid to the great popularity of *Joseph Andrews*. On 12 October his bookseller, Andrew Millar, brought an action in Chancery against the unscrupulous printer Jacob Ilive for pirating the novel and distributing it through the agency of three no less unscrupulous members of the trade, Daniel Lynch and his wife and William Owen, a hawker of books.[141] One Francis Smith, a hairdresser, testified he had purchased one of the pirated books, which proved to be "an exact Copy of the greatest Part" of Fielding's work; indeed, Millar complained that this rogue mutation of *Joseph Andrews* was selling so briskly that it had "for a considerable time stopped, lessened & hindered" the sale of the authorized version, to his "very great Injury." He wanted Ilive and his confederates suppressed and all unsold copies of the piracy confiscated.

In this action Millar had the support of the Attorney General, Sir Dudley Ryder, who on 23 October, amidst the din of Westminster Hall, wrote to his wife at Bath:

> I have this Moment satt down after endeavouring to rescue Jos: Andrews & ye Parson Adams out of ye Hands of Pirates, but in vain for this time occasion'd by a Mistake in ye Attack. However another Broadside next week will do ye Business.[142]

The mistake to which Ryder refers might well have been Millar's own carelessness in establishing his legal right to the property. Presumably the vogue Fielding's novel enjoyed caught his bookseller off guard. He did not formally purchase the copyright until 13 April 1742, almost two months after publication of the first edition. What is more surprising, he put off entering the book in the Stationers' Register; not until 10 June, when the second edition was published, did he take this necessary step to protect his property. Though records of the judgment in Millar's case against Ilive have not been found, it appears that the Attorney General's prediction proved correct. No copy of the piracy has ever come to light. Writing to Warburton on 6 November 1742 about Ilive's attempt to pirate *The New Dunciad*, Pope assumed, indeed, that justice had already been done: he states the opinion of William Murray, who was to be appointed Solicitor General before the month was out, that "if Millar has had redress, I may."[143] It is a measure of Ilive's impudence, not to mention his nose for business, that he thus attempted to steal both the best novel and the best poem of the year.

···◄ **XXX** ►···

Despite the success of *Joseph Andrews*, tempting him to court a new Muse – and despite the promises he had made to produce the *Miscellanies* by Christmas – the theatre, his first love, continued to hold an irresistible allure for Fielding. The laughter and applause that greeted his naughty farce, *Miss Lucy in Town* – the sight of the Royal Family witnessing the return of the author who had precipitated an Act of Parliament: Fielding might well have entertained hopes of reviving his career as dramatist. His friend Garrick – now in his first full season at

Drury Lane – must have sensed such feelings when, eager for that precious opportunity for an actor, a good new part to shine in, he asked Fielding if he could oblige him.[144]

As it happened, Fielding had at hand not one but two plays – both five-act comedies – which he had drafted some years before, but which had never been staged: these were *The Wedding Day*, which by his own reckoning was only the third "Dramatic Performance" he ever attempted, and *The Good-Natured Man* – a work, as he believed, "formed on a much better Plan, and at an Age when I was much more equal to the Task, than the former." *The Good-Natured Man* was the play that, by being turned down by Rich, made Fielding's fortune by sending him to the Little Haymarket in 1736 to experiment with *Pasquin*. Now he hoped it would establish his credentials as a comic dramatist in the more conventional mode. The play was, he declared, " a more favourite, and in the Opinion of others, a much more valuable Performance" than *The Wedding-Day*, the product of his "juvenile Years." The managers of the patent theatres seldom took risks staging new plays when the old repertory was a proven commodity. To Fielding's surprise, when he spoke to Fleetwood the next morning, he "embraced my Proposal so heartily, that an Appointment was immediately made to read it to the Actors who were principally to be concerned in it." On the day, however, – though the reading was so well received that Fleetwood ordered the play "writ into Parts" – Fielding saw that it needed more work and that there was no satisfactory part in it for Garrick.

The Wedding-Day, on the other hand, though it had "glaring Faults," had one virtue to recommend it: the character of Millamour – a brassy rake with a heart of gold and witty lines to speak. Originally, Fielding conceived the parts of Millamour and Charlotte with Wilks and Anne Oldfield in mind, both of whom had acted at Drury Lane in *Love in Several Masques*; but before he could finish the piece, Mrs. Oldfield died and Wilks had sent him packing. He tried peddling it to Rich at Lincoln's Inn Fields, but by that time he no longer believed in it himself: "Indeed," Fielding confessed in the spring of 1743, "I never thought, 'till this Season, that there existed on any one Stage, since the Death of that great Actor and Actress ... any two Persons capable of supplying their Loss in those Parts: for Characters of this Kind do, of all others, require most Support from the Actor, and lend the least Assistance to him." In Garrick and Peg Woffington, he believed he had the actors capable of carrying his comedy. Certain therefore that *The Good-Natured Man*, though a better play potentially, was not ready to be seen, and confident that, as Millamour, Garrick "would make so surprising a Figure ... and exhibit Talents so long unknown to the

Theatre, that ... the Audience might be blinded to the Faults of the Piece," he persuaded Fleetwood to substitute *The Wedding-Day*.

He intended "to work Night and Day" to improve the play in the week before Fleetwood required the copy. With all his facility, however, he had neither the leisure nor the peace of mind to accomplish the alterations that might have saved the piece: "unfortunately," he explained, "the extreme Danger of Life into which a Person, very dear to me, was reduced, rendered me incapable of executing my Task." Charlotte's illness was grave, and she could not throw it off. To the critics who rebuked him for allowing such an imperfect play to be acted, Fielding replied "honestly and freely, that Reputation was not my Inducement; and that I hoped, faulty as it was, it might answer a much more solid, and in my unhappy Situation, a much more urgent Motive."

Under these inauspicious circumstances Fleetwood on 19 January 1742/3 submitted *The Wedding-Day* to the Licenser of the Stage, William Chetwynd, who exerted himself in trying to purge it of all "Indecency." Indeed, on 25 January the Countess of Hertford wrote her son Lord Beauchamp that Fielding's comedy had been "refused by the Licenser, not as a reflecting one, but on account of its immorality."[145] The Larpent manuscript of the play reveals the heavy hand of the censor retrenching lewd and suggestive passages[146] – the effect, Fielding preferred to believe, of the Licenser's having been "very unjustly censured for being too remiss in his Restraints on that Head." But Fielding, who as a playwright was often unable to sense when he had stopped being funny and become merely outrageous, might have expected such treatment after the criticisms recently levelled against *Miss Lucy in Town* on these same grounds. Undaunted, he had produced another play featuring as its principal comic character the salacious bawd Mrs. Useful. As Lady Hertford had heard, it was only "by suffering his bawd to be carted, though she is his favorite character," that Fielding obtained the necessary license.[147]

Mrs. Useful not only offended the Licenser; she was too much even for the loyal "Kitty" Clive, whom Fielding wanted to play the role. Mrs. Clive had grown plump to be sure, and was at her best playing pert and saucy females; but she drew the line at being cast as an unprincipled procuress. Hanbury Williams, whose judgment as a critic Fielding respected, appears to have witnessed Mrs. Clive's dudgeon when Fielding tried to convince her she was right for the part. At any rate, he versified the scene for posterity:

> A Bawd! a Bawd! where is the scoundrel Poet?
> Fine Work indeed! By God the Town shall know it.
> F[ie]ld[in]g who heard, and saw her Passion rise,
> Thus answer'd calmly: "Prythee Cl[i]ve, be wise,

> The Part will suit your Humour, Taste, and Size."
> Ye lye! ye lye! ungrateful as thou art,
> My matchless Talents claim the Lady's Part
> And all who judge, by J—s G—d, agree,
> None ever play'd the gay Coquet like me.
>   Thus said and swore the celebrated *Nell*;
> Now judge her Genius: is she *Bawd* or *Belle*?[148]

In the event, it was Mrs. Macklin who played the part. Fielding's favorite comic actress was conspicuous by her absence from the stage.

This was the last time Fielding attempted to bring a new play of his upon the boards (*The Good-Natured Man* was produced long after his death), and from the start nothing went right. Charlotte's illness prevented him from making the revisions he knew it required. Mrs. Clive washed her hands of it. And, if we can credit Garrick's account, Fielding ensured the failure of the play by his own stubbornness. When Garrick urged him to delete a passage that the audience was certain to hiss, Fielding replied, "No, d—mn 'em ... if the scene is not a good one, let them find *that* out." Find it out they did on opening night, Garrick at the first opportunity fleeing from the chorus of catcalls and hisses to the Green Room, where, as Murphy relates,

> the author was indulging his genius, and solacing himself with a bottle of champain. He had by this time drank pretty plentifully; and cocking his eye at the actor, while streams of tobacco trickled down from the corner of his mouth, "*What's the matter, Garrick?* says he, *what are they hissing now?* Why the scene that I begged you to retrench; I knew it would not do, and they have so frightened me, that I shall not be able to collect myself again the whole night. *Oh! d—mn, 'em,* replies the author, *they* HAVE *found it out; have they?*"

This anecdote Murphy elaborated into a generalization that Fielding's "failure" as a dramatist was in part owing to "that sovereign contempt he always entertained for the understandings of the generality of mankind. It was in vain to tell him that a particular scene was dangerous on account of its coarseness, or because it retarded the general business with feeble efforts of wit; he doubted the discernment of his auditors, and so thought himself secured by their stupidity, if not by his own humour and vivacity."

There may be truth in this observation: Fielding had many admirable qualities, but the Christian virtue of humility was not among them. Yet Murphy's judgments are always suspect. An author who in less than a decade became the most popular and interesting playwright of his generation is not well described as a "failure" in his craft. Furthermore, since Murphy did not become acquainted with Fielding until long after he had quit the theatre, one must judge the candor of his sources – in this instance, Garrick.

Fielding and Garrick enjoyed each other's company and admired each other's talents. For his first attempt at acting after he came to London in 1737 Garrick chose the title role in *The Mock Doctor* for the private entertainment of Johnson and Edward Cave;[149] and he devoted his last days in the theatre to revising *The Good-Natured Man*, for which he also wrote the Prologue and Epilogue. In Fielding's opinion, Garrick was quite simply "the best Actor the World could have ever produced."[150] But Garrick had a way of preserving for posterity the least amiable features of his famous friends' characters. He enjoyed keeping center stage after hours, as it were, by entertaining whatever company he was in with animated and embarrassing tales of them. Everyone remembers that, having stooped to spying on Johnson through the keyhole of his bedchamber, Garrick regaled their acquaintance with the spectacle, mimicking Johnson as, like some great clumsy bear, he made passionate love to Tetty.

Garrick is also the source of several unflattering anecdotes about Fielding. There is the story of the dinner he gave for a number of his theatrical friends who, when the evening was over, all bestowed generous vails on his servant – all, that is, except Fielding, whose present was a penny folded up in a piece of paper. When Garrick reproved him the next day about the impropriety of jesting with a servant, Fielding affected surprise: "Jesting! ... so far from it, that I meant to do the fellow a real piece of service; for had I given him a shilling, or half a crown, I knew you would have taken it from him; but by giving him only a penny, he had a chance of calling it his own."[151] The point of the story – since Garrick makes clear that he was not in the habit of keeping his servant's gratuities for himself – is Fielding's cleverness at excusing his own meanness. But, though he often found himself without a shilling to spare, meanness was not characteristic of Fielding. Or consider another, still less savory trait of Fielding's for which we are again indebted to Garrick. Other contemporary witnesses noticed Fielding's untidiness in keeping his clothes free of snuff, but Garrick alone emphasized the grossness of his friend's personal habits. The scene in the Green Room on the occasion of *The Wedding-Day*, with the drunken author drooling tobacco juice from the corner of his mouth, is tame beside the one Garrick painted some years later in conversation with the German author Helfrich Peter Sturz. Having first deflated his interlocutor's opinion of Sterne by representing him as an insufferably vain reprobate whose obscenities drove women from the room, Garrick next enlightened Herr Sturz on the subject of Fielding:

Fielding [Sturz recalls Garrick saying] was a complete cynic, who would not be inferior to the old dog in the barrel in anything and chewed tobacco, wine, and epigrams together in a very unappetizing way. Once, at his home, when Garrick and a few friends were dining with him, a disagreeable smell tickled their noses; Fielding soon helped them out of their bewilderment when, as he stood up laughing, the company became aware that he was sitting at table on his chamber-pot.[152]

Even allowing that this anecdote may owe something of its repellent character to the Teutonic taste which in our own century could produce the paintings of Georg Grosz and Otto Dix, Garrick is its source. Fielding lived, of course, at a time when the water closet was scarcely a gleam in a plumber's eye – a time, for that matter, not far removed from that of Louis XIV, when the Sun King himself similarly tickled the noses of his courtiers in the public rooms of Versailles; moreover, for much of the time Garrick knew him Fielding was immobilized by the gout. Even so, that there is more mischievous hyperbole than truth in Garrick's tale is suggested by the fact that among the wide circle of those who loved Fielding and enjoyed his company were some of the most fastidious of men – James Harris and Thomas Birch, George Lyttelton and Ralph Allen come readily to mind.

However little Fielding's reputation for politeness may owe to his friend, he was at least much indebted to him for the two benefits he enjoyed from the brief run of *The Wedding-Day*, which opened at Drury Lane on 17 February 1742/3. An unknown but knowledgeable contemporary thus confided to his diary: "this bad new Play ... would have quite sunk the first Night, if it had not been supported by Mr. Garricks Acting. So it made a shift to hold out for Six nights."[153] Fleetwood and Fielding's bookseller Millar had sanguine expectations that the comedy would be well received: *The Wedding-Day* was the only new play staged by either of the patent houses this entire season; and Millar's optimism is reflected in the order he placed with the printer William Bowyer for 3,000 copies – an extraordinary number.[154] The play in fact opened to a crowded house, Fleetwood's receipts surpassing those for any other night of the season. But after the first night, attendance plummeted.[155] Millar must have fared even less well; for the book – which Fielding's fame and rumors of the play's lewdness might have caused to sell briskly had it been published on opening day – was not ready until a week later, by which time the Town had lost interest. By all accounts, opening night was calamitous – though Lady Hertford's acquaintance were not quite prophetic in believing "that it will be impossible to prevail on a second audience to hear it through."[156] Richardson's friend Thomas Edwards reported that the play had been "damned" that first night, "as the Clown says in Shakespeare, like an ill roasted egg, all on one side"; even so, he grudgingly admitted, "it has continued since, some approving, but among those that I know, the better judges disapproving it."[157] A delightful explanation of why *The Wedding-Day* was suffered to continue after this rude reception was offered by a certain Mrs. Russell, who witnessed the event: "Fielding's Play," she informed her absent husband, "had a fair hearing last night, first and second Acts tolerable but from thence every one grew worse to the End, but his friends will support it to a third night to which I hear of many going for the sake of Joseph Andrews."[158]

The Wedding-Day limped on until a sixth and final performance, on 26 February, gave Fielding his second, meager benefit. All told, he "received not 50 *l.* from the House for it."[159] To the end Fielding preferred to believe that his comedy had been ruined by malicious, exaggerated reports of its "Indecency," which "prevailed so fatally without Doors ... that on the sixth Night, there were not above five Ladies present in the Boxes." However that may be, it is clear in retrospect that he ought to have heeded Macklin's advice in the Prologue he wrote for the occasion:

> Ah! thou foolish Follower of the ragged Nine,
> You'd better stuck to honest *Abram Adams*, by half.
> He, in spight of Critics, can make your Readers laugh.

···━● xxxi ●━···

One measure of how delighted readers were with Parson Adams is the fact that, as Macklin spoke these words, a third edition of *Joseph Andrews* was on its way through the presses of William Strahan, to whom Millar also assigned the printing of a fourth and fifth edition during Fielding's lifetime. The third edition, consisting of 3,000 copies and completely reset in smaller type, was printed by 20 February 1742/3, though it was not published until a month later.[160] This edition – which Fielding revised, if much less extensively than he had the second – brought to 6,500 the number of copies of *Joseph Andrews* published in little more than a year, and it is the first edition to carry Fielding's name on the title-page. Indeed, Millar accorded this version of *Joseph Andrews* a distinction he did not grant to either *Tom Jones* or *Amelia* – though, thrifty Scotsman that he was, he would not spend an unnecessary shilling doing so: he employed the inept engraver James Hulett (d. 1771) to produce a dozen clumsy cuts illustrating scenes from the novel.[161] How much more indebted to Millar we would feel if he had given that assignment to Hogarth instead!

Hogarth, even so, would not be denied this opportunity of paying tribute to *Joseph Andrews* – or more precisely to its famous Preface. There, while distinguishing between true comic characterization and what "the *Italians* call *Caricatura*," Fielding had illustrated his point by complimenting his friend. "He who should call the ingenious *Hogarth* a Burlesque Painter, would, in my Opinion, do him very little Honour." For while it is the case that "the true Ridiculous," which copies Nature exactly, does not "so strongly affect and agitate the Muscles" as burlesque and caricature, the latter are inferior art forms: "it is much easier," Fielding explained, inviting a laugh at his own proboscis of a nose and vast expanse of chin, "much less the Subject of Admiration, to paint a Man with a Nose, or any other Feature of a preposterous Size, or to expose him in some absurd or monstrous Attitude, than to express the Affections of Men on Canvas." In the same jocular vein, Hogarth responded to this passage in his print *Characters and Caricaturas* (1743), repaying Fielding's compliment twice over. In his friend's own medium of prose, Hogarth wrote out in plain English beneath the picture: "*For a farthar Explanation of the Difference Betwixt* Character & Caricatura *see* y^e *Preface to* Jo^h. Andrews." In the picture itself, however, he not only illustrated Fielding's theory, but mischievously accepted Fielding's dare to show the world how easy it was to paint men with preposterous features and in absurd attitudes: for at the very center of the crowd of faces, Hogarth placed Fielding and himself, *vis-à-vis*, their features contorted with laughter, loud, it would seem, and irrepressible. (See Plates 35 to 36.) *Characters and Caricaturas* remains the most graphic and delightful testimony of the friendship between Hogarth and Fielding.

In this same year of 1743 *Joseph Andrews* was also paid the tribute of being translated into French by the Abbé Desfontaines, an astute critic and Fielding's ablest champion on the Continent. In his preface to the second edition (Amsterdam, 1744), which takes the form of an explanatory letter from an English lady to a friend at Montpellier, Desfontaines compares Fielding's achievement favorably to that of Cervantes and the paintings of the Dutch school; he admires *l'honnêteté* of Fielding's images and style, and the skill at rendering dialogue which Fielding had perfected during a decade of play writing; he applauds the novelist's ability to draw memorable characters from Nature – most particularly, of course, the character of Parson Adams. Anticipating a criticism that Fielding often heard from his fastidious contemporaries, he defends *Joseph Andrews* perceptively against the charge that it was a "low" and immoral work: two centuries would pass, for instance, before other critics would see behind the hilarity of the novel's opening

Plate 27 James Harris.

Plate 28 Benjamin Hoadly, Bishop of
Winchester (1741).

Plate 29 Sir Charles Hanbury Williams
(c. 1746).

Plate 30 Caricature of George Bubb
Dodington.

Plate 31 The Funeral of Faction (1741). Fielding carries the banner of *The Champion* as Opposition mourns defeat of the motion to impeach Walpole.

Plate 32 The Political Libertines: or, Motion upon Motion (1741). Fielding at left, in barrister's wig and gown, supports the Opposition.

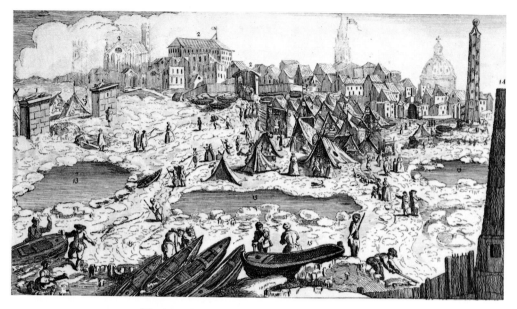

Plate 33 Ice Fair on the Thames (1739–40).

Plate 34 Pamela in the bedroom with Mr. B. and Mrs. Jewkes.

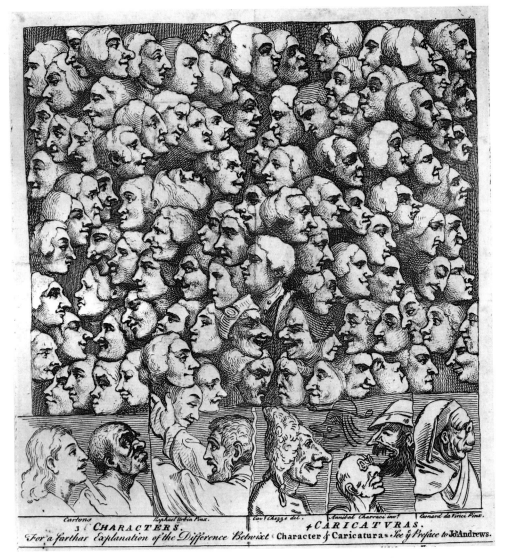

Plate 35 Hogarth's *Characters and Caricaturas* (1743).

Plate 36 Fielding and Hogarth (1743).

Plate 37 Ralph Allen (1740).

Plate 38 Richard 'Beau' Nash.

Plate 39 The King's Bath and the Pump Room, Bath (1747).

Plate 40 Fielding's house at Twerton, near Bath.

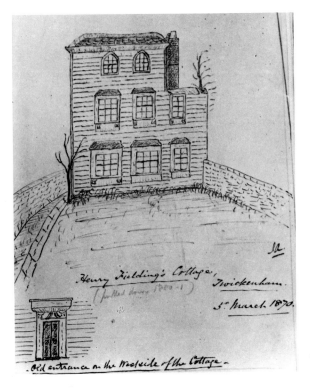

Henry Fielding's Cottage, Twickenham.

5th March 1870.

Old entrance on the Westside of the Cottage.

Plate 41 Fielding's house at Twickenham.

Plate 42 John Russell, fourth Duke of Bedford.

Plate 43 Philip Yorke, first Earl of Hardwicke (*c.* 1742).

Plate 44 Execution of the Jacobite Lords at Tower Hill (1746).

Plate 45 Garrick as Hamlet.

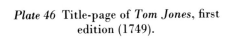

Plate 46 Title-page of *Tom Jones*, first edition (1749).

THE

HISTORY

OF

TOM JONES,

A

FOUNDLING.

In SIX VOLUMES.

By HENRY FIELDING, Efq;

—— *Mores hominum multorum vidit.* ——

LONDON:

Printed for A. MILLAR, over-againſt
Catharine-ſtreet in the *Strand.*
MDCCXLIX,

scenes a redaction of the biblical account of Joseph and Potiphar's wife – which, the Abbé reminds his readers, was a favorite subject of Christian art. In short, he declared *Joseph Andrews* to be "the most clever and pleasing Book" that England has produced: "It is certainly not a Book of simple amusement for the crowd: it is a Book of knowledge and unaffected morality, accessible to everyone, and what is more, a Book in which one comes to understand how we live in England."[162]

...◗ xxxii ◖–...

The new edition of *Joseph Andrews* and preparations for staging and publishing *The Wedding-Day* required Fielding's attention during February, but such literary labors were light in comparison with the pressure he felt to put the *Miscellanies* in the hands of his subscribers without further delay. In June a year before he had apologized publicly for his procrastination, and he subsequently failed to meet his Christmas deadline; in the *Daily Post* of 12 February he declared that the subscription would be closed on the 22nd and that the book would certainly be published by the end of the month. But these promises were again ill founded. He had badly overestimated his ability to supply copy enough to fill the three volumes. One expedient he resorted to was to pad out the work with odds and ends he had already published – such as his poem to Dodington *Of True Greatness* and his comedy *The Wedding-Day*, the latter serving, along with the damned farce *Eurydice*, to give a decent bulk to Volume II, originally advertised as containing only *A Journey from This World to the Next*.

But it is an amusing item inserted in Volume I that best illustrates the need Fielding felt to generate more matter for the work – and illustrates equally well his remarkable facility and resilience of spirit. Amused as always by what he considered the perverse preoccupations of the virtuosi of the Royal Society, he found in an article published in the *Philosophical Transactions* (No. 467, 13 and 21 January 1742/3) the inspiration he needed for a short piece that would serve double duty as a separate publication and as filler for the *Miscellanies*. The article in question was an account of experiments made upon the freshwater "Polypus" by the Swiss naturalist Abraham Trembley: the parts of the polyp, however many times and however many ways Trembley dissected it, always reformed themselves into individual organisms as complete in every respect as the original. In this phenomenon and the manner of reporting it Fielding found, to borrow Gay's phrase, "guineas intrinsical." Within a fortnight he wrote and published (on 16 February) a parody entitled:

Some Papers Proper to be Read before the R[oya]l Society, Concerning the Terrestrial Chrysipus, Golden-Foot or Guinea; an Insect, or Vegetable, resembling the Polypus, which hath this surprising Property, That being cut into several Pieces, each Piece becomes a perfect Animal or Vegetable, as complete as that of which it was originally only a Part. Collected by Petrus Gualterus, But not Published till after His Death.

Scarcely concealed behind the Latinizing of his name, the esteemed collector of these glittering creatures was the notorious miser Peter Walter, still very much alive and fresh from his role as Peter Pounce in *Joseph Andrews*. A third target of Fielding's satire is one that helpfully fixes his political inclinations of the moment. The allegory makes clear that a year after Walpole's fall Fielding was again serving his friends in the "new Opposition," among them Dodington, Lyttelton, Pitt, and Chesterfield, all of whom opposed the pro-Hanoverian policies of the King's favorite minister, John Carteret:[163] in England, and especially in the country, Fielding's persona writes, the *chrysipi* "are observed of late to be much rarer than formerly," whereas on the Continent, "particularly in a certain Part of *Germany*, they are much plentier; being to be found in great Numbers, where formerly there were scarce any to be met with." If the amused reaction of Thomas Edwards is any indication[164] – Edwards being for the most part no friend to Fielding or his works – this timely travesty found an appreciative audience, as well as putting a few welcome *chrysipi* into the author's pocket.

Despite his efforts the *Miscellanies*, even on the eve of the new deadline for publication, were not ready for the printers. On Sunday, 27 February, Fielding wrote Harris asking him to correct the manuscript of his translation of Demosthenes' *First Olynthiac* and to send the emended copy directly to Millar. It was a piece he probably sketched out in the late 1730s, when the Patriots were urging war against Philip of Spain as Demosthenes had urged the Athenians to act against Philip of Macedon.[165] Ordinarily, he would no doubt have applied to William Young for the favor he now asked of Harris, but Young this year was abroad, serving as chaplain to the Army in Flanders. From a second letter, dated 14 March and addressed to Harris in town (he had taken lodgings in Chancery Lane), it is clear that the future author of *Hermes* was responsible for whatever merit Fielding's version may claim: "I am infinitely obliged to you for the Trouble you have given yourself," Fielding wrote, "on my incorrect and lame Translation of the first Olynthiac."

These two letters are rather more interesting for the light they shed, if dimly, on Fielding's domestic circumstances. Fielding and Charlotte had left Spring Garden and were now temporarily residing on the western outskirts of town, in the Flask Inn. at Brompton (or "Brumpton," as Fielding spelled it), "being," as he assured Harris, whom he urged to join them there, "a very little Way from Knightsbridge." This curious move may best be accounted for by, as Fielding put it in the Preface to the *Miscellanies*, "the dangerous Illness of one from whom I draw all the solid Comfort of my Life, during the greatest Part of this Winter." The specific nature of Charlotte's lingering and, as it soon proved, fatal illness is not certainly known; but chances are she was consumptive. Because it was warm (relatively speaking) and its air fine owing to the freshening effect of the vast nursery located there, Brompton was considered one of the healthiest places in England, particularly beneficial to those suffering from consumption.[166]

From Fielding's letter of 14 March it is also clear that he was indebted to his friend for more than the favor of correcting his Greek; he acknowledges having received money from Harris. Perhaps he refers simply to payments for the *Miscellanies*, to which Harris and his brother Thomas generously subscribed; for the *Miscellanies* were at last about to be published. Entered in the Stationers' Register on 6 April, they were delivered to the subscribers the next day, 7 April. Fielding in the Preface speaks as usual of his "urgent" need for money, but it is hard to credit that he would at this time be so desperate for cash. Though the income from *The Wedding-Day* and from his parody on the "Chrysipus" may have been modest, his scheme of publishing the *Miscellanies* by subscription proved very profitable indeed. After analyzing the list of subscribers, Miller concluded that Fielding must have netted "a pleasant sum" from the venture – in fact, about £650, not counting payments from such friends and benefactors as Pope and Ralph Allen, who preferred to do good by stealth.[167] Of course, since subscribers were required to pay a moiety of the price when signing on, Fielding already would have collected – and, given his habitual improvidence, therefore spent – half this money in the many months since the receipts were originally distributed. That he continued to be financially embarrassed even after the *Miscellanies* had been delivered to the subscribers is evident from the fact that he continued to be hounded through the courts by impatient creditors: on 13 May a certain Charles Malson sued him for debt in the King's Bench, and in the autumn he would be obliged to answer the complaint of another creditor, William Goffe.[168]

Besides what it reveals about Fielding's financial circumstances, the list of subscribers to the *Miscellanies* is uniquely helpful as a guide – though in some respects an uncertain and puzzling one – to his circle of acquaintance. By no means all his friends are represented on the list, and in his Preface he thanked those who had so warmly forwarded the subscription on his behalf that he owed "not a tenth Part to my own Interest." Miller, therefore, who provides the most informative analysis of the list, is cautious in the inferences he is willing to draw from it. As we would expect, here are the names and titles of many of Fielding's patrons among the Opposition, old and new: the Dukes of Bedford and Argyll; Lords Chesterfield, Cobham, and Talbot; Dodington, Lyttelton, and Pitt. Indeed, the list is headed by the Prince of Wales. But here, too, we find the Great Man himself, Robert Walpole, newly created Earl of Orford, as well as such courtiers as the Dukes of Newcastle and Marlborough, and the Patriot turncoat Pulteney, now Earl of Bath and a target of Fielding's recent satire. The fact is that Fielding and his friends had been soliciting these subscriptions since 1741, and his political inclinations over that period had been unsteady. Even so, one conclusion seems inescapable: at the time these men saw fit to put down their money and have their names displayed as Fielding's patrons, they considered themselves his friends – Walpole very much among the rest, with his twenty-guinea purchase of ten sets on royal paper.

The list, however, is more than a sort of political hieroglyphics in which we try to puzzle out Fielding's party loyalties. In the Preface Fielding expressed his deepest gratitude to his colleagues in the law, "a Profession of which I am a late and unworthy Member, and from whose Assistance I derive more than half the Names which appear to this Subscription." Among these one finds, for instance, Richard Birt, who would later assist Fielding when he was appointed to his most distinguished office as a lawyer, the High Stewardship of the New Forest; and the clubbable, Falstaffian Harry Hatsell; and John Hayes, to whom he addressed one of the better poems in Volume I; and William Robinson, the satirical dreamer of *The Champion*; and Giles Taylor, who so often represented Fielding in his battles with creditors; and Richard Willoughby of West Knoyle, Wiltshire, whom Partridge remembers in *Tom Jones* (VIII.xi) as "a very worthy good Gentleman." Here, too, are a number of his fellow Etonians, including Lyttelton, Pitt, and Hanbury Williams. Bath, at first glance, makes a disappointing showing, with only Chesterfield, the Duke of Kingston, and Doctors Brewster and Harrington represented; but Ralph Allen made his twenty-pound contribution silently, and since the bookseller James Leake took a dozen sets, we may be sure the *Miscellanies* were more widely read in Fielding's favorite resort that those four names suggest. It was Fielding's Salisbury acquaintance who rallied to his cause most handsomely, owing not a little to James Harris's solicitations on his behalf. The names of Harris, his brother Thomas, and their mother Lady Elizabeth are here, and, as Miller deduced, this connection would account for such other Harris family names as Clarke, Knatchbull, Lord Wyndham, and the Countess and Earl of Shaftesbury. From Salisbury, too, were Dr. John Barker and the surgeon Edward Goldwyre, and Arthur Collier, LL.D. (brother of Jane and Margaret

Collier), as well as Mrs. Hooper, Mrs. Pitt, and Mrs. Rookes, at whose school within The Close Fielding's sisters had been educated.

As for literary and theatrical figures, the list is disappointingly thin, but not without luster: John Banks; "Kitty" Clive; Mr. and Mrs. Carey (Henry Carey and his wife?); Thomas Cooke; the manager of Drury Lane, Charles Fleetwood (who took twenty sets); Garrick; the Hoadly brothers, John and Benjamin; James Lacy; David Mallet; Peg Woffington – and perhaps Richard Savage, though Johnson's famous friend was in Bristol jail when the *Miscellanies* appeared and has no other known connection with Fielding. It is not exactly a constellation of luminaries. No doubt Miller is right in concluding that "the publication of the *Miscellanies* was not greeted as a literary event," and that for the most part Fielding's subscribers, "represent political or professional or merely personal connections."[169] However that may be, this list of 427 names is an invaluable index to those who touched Fielding's life and played a part in his work as author, lawyer, and magistrate.

With the important exception of *Jonathan Wild*, not much in the *Miscellanies* is of more than fugitive literary interest. Digeon summed up the quality of Fielding's collection when he called it "une liquidation de son passé littéraire"[170] – though the description is not literally accurate. As we remarked, Fielding chose to exclude certain unpublished poems, and there are signs in all three volumes that he had been exerting himself either in revising early work to make it more timely or in composing new pieces for this occasion. *A Journey from This World to the Next*, for instance, gives the impression of something fresh and promising that went wrong. Inspired by Plato's Myth of Er and attempted in the satiric manner of his favorite Lucian, the *Journey* is another of Fielding's imaginative renderings of the theme that goodness alone can bring true happiness.[171] But in 1742 he could summon neither the cunning nor the will to carry out the experiment successfully. The narrative begins briskly, but too soon dwindles into the tedium of Julian the Apostate's numberless transmigrations; that Fielding at last despaired of doing justice to this material himself is plain from his having (almost certainly) called upon his sister Sarah to stretch it out to the required length with the story of Anna Boleyn, the irrelevancy that concludes the work.[172] Because at another time he might have made it better, the *Journey* is the saddest confirmation in the *Miscellanies* of what Fielding called in the Preface "that Degree of Heart-ach which ... often discomposed me in the writing them."

However faulty they are, the poems and essays that comprise Volume I are nevertheless of interest to any serious reader of Fielding; for Fielding here expounds most of his essential themes. Of the thirty-eight poems in the collection all but the first five are merely playful. Those five, however, are anatomies in verse of important concepts in Fielding's ethical system: "Of True Greatness," addressed to Dodington; "Of Good-Nature," addressed to the Duke of Richmond; "Liberty," addressed to Lyttelton; "To a Friend [unknown] on the Choice of a Wife"; and "To John Hayes, Esq," on the force and confusion of the passions in human nature – these are all among the themes that inform Fielding's best work. Still more important in this respect are three essays in the collection. Those who doubt Fielding had any very nice sense of the proprieties of social intercourse should read "An Essay on Conversation," a guide to good manners in everyday relationships that defines good breeding less as a knowledge of the forms of courtesy (though these Fielding always insisted upon) than as a sympathetic willingness to put others at ease. "An Essay on the Knowledge of the Characters of Men" is the richest quarry for students of Fielding's fiction, for it is a searching analysis of hypocrisy, the vice Fielding most despised and the distinguishing characteristic of a Wild or a Blifil; it was a vice he considered especially pernicious because its "Prey" was that "honest, undesigning, open-hearted Man" who, in his several guises, is the hero of Fielding's fiction. Written on occasion of his daughter's death, "Of the Remedy of Affliction for the Loss of our Friends" is Fielding's attempt to articulate that "Philosophy", as he called it, which, in enabling us to endure the blows life deals, proved as useful to him as a sense of humor.

Despite the patchwork effect that was the consequence of Fielding's grafting new material onto old while enlarging his original design, *The Life of Mr. Jonathan Wild the Great* is the masterpiece of the collection – a witty and (for Fielding) rare experiment in Swift's darker kind of irony that has the force of a moral fable. What was conceived as a satire of Walpole became the profounder exploration of the antithetical ideas of "greatness" and "goodness," not merely in the narrow context of contemporary politics, but in the wide domain of human nature. In the most eloquent pages of the Preface, Fielding explained this deeper intent. The villain Wild – master of what he elsewhere calls "the *Art of thriving*"[173] – is not to be confused with any one individual: "Roguery, and not a Rogue, is my Subject." Nor, however, is his "Hero" meant "to represent Human Nature in general."

But without considering *Newgate* as no other than Human Nature with its Mask off, which some very shameless Writers have done, a Thought which no Price should purchase me to entertain, I think we may be excused for suspecting, that the splendid Palaces of the Great are often no other than *Newgate* with the Mask on. Nor do I know any thing which can raise an honest Man's Indignation higher than that the same Morals should be in one Place attended with all

imaginable Misery and Infamy, and in the other, with the highest
Luxury and Honour. Let any impartial Man in his Senses be asked,
for which of these two Places a Composition of Cruelty, Lust, Avarice,
Rapine, Insolence, Hypocrisy, Fraud and Treachery, was best fitted,
surely his Answer must be certain and immediate; and yet I am
afraid all these Ingredients glossed over with Wealth and a Title,
have been treated with the highest Respect and Veneration in the
one, while one or two of them have been condemned to the Gallows
in the other.

In the narrative itself, Fielding's corrosive irony and his enactment of
this vision in the story of Wild's persecution of Heartfree are what
prompted Byron, writing at a time when Jacobinism was rife, to
pronounce *Jonathan Wild* the strongest indictment he knew of "The
inequality of conditions and the littleness of the great."[174]

Though by no means an uninteresting or unentertaining farrago, the
Miscellanies are certainly uneven in quality. Fielding was dissatisfied
even with the best of them, *Jonathan Wild*, and ten years later subjected
it to a thorough revision. As he declared of *The Wedding-Day*, however,
enhancing his literary reputation was not his inducement in publishing
these pieces, but rather a more solid and urgent motive. Thanks solely
to his decision to publish by subscription, this purpose was handsomely
accomplished: the £650 or so that he cleared was more than he received
for any of his works with the exception of *Amelia*. Of the original
impression of 1,000 sets on "coarse" paper and 250 on "fine," subscribers bought up something more than 556 sets (including 214 of the
royal paper). Before the end of April, Millar disingenuously began
advertising a so-called "second edition" at the cheaper price of fifteen
shillings. This consisted, however, merely of the unsold remainder of
the original impression (without the list of subscribers) bound up with
new title-pages. As late as 1748 he was still offering it for sale.[175]

···◆ xxxiii ◆—···

If Fielding followed his usual practice this summer of 1743, he attended
the assizes on the Western Circuit, an itinerary that would take him to
Winchester on Tuesday, 12 July; Salisbury on Saturday, 16 July;
Dorchester on Thursday, 21 July; Exeter on Monday, 25 July; Bodmin
on Tuesday, 2 August; Wells on Tuesday, 9 August; and Bristol on
Saturday, 13 August.

The worsening of Charlotte's health may have restricted his movements, but it is clear from Harris's letter to William Young dated 1

October 1743 from Salisbury that he had seen Fielding "lately" and found him "well."[176] Rumors from the Continent had it that Young had been killed at the Battle of Dettingen in June. Happily, the report was ill founded, being based merely on that now famous instance of Young's absentmindedness, when, lost in thought while enjoying a solitary stroll through the countryside, he strayed into enemy territory.

> But how great, think you, was our joy [Harris writes] when we found that you were still alive? that you had not only escaped the dangers of the battle, but had even entered and returned again from the French camp with as much safety as old Priam visited the camp of his cruel adversaries the Grecians.

Harris proceeds to give Young news of their mutual friends – namely, besides Fielding and Dr. Arthur Collier, a trio of classical scholars: Canon John Upton (1707–60), Floyer Sydenham (1710–87), and Dr. John Taylor (1704–66). Harris, as his biographer points out, was "at the center of a busy provincial cell of classical scholarship," and it is likely that these friends, whom he and Young had in common, were also well known to Fielding.[177] To Sydenham, who translated Plato's dialogues (1767–80), Harris dedicated his treatise "Concerning Happiness," which Fielding had read in manuscript and greatly admired.[178] Taylor, editor of the orations of Lysias (1739) and works of Demosthenes and Aeschines (1741–57), was, along with Upton, the companion of Harris's "social, as well as ... literary hours"[179] – though his only known connection with Fielding is the posthumous one of his having attended the sale of Fielding's library and made several purchases.[180]

Of these three scholars Fielding was closest to John Upton. Upton's father James Upton (1670–1749) was himself a distinguished classicist who, having graduated from Eton and King's College, Cambridge, was from 1704 to his death at eighty Headmaster of the Free Grammar School of Taunton, Somerset – the school attended by Fielding's first cousin William Gould, as well as by Henry Price of Poole, Dorset, who so admired Charlotte and her sister.[181] The friendship between the Uptons and the Fieldings is attested both by Ursula Fielding's letter of 25 October 1748, expressing to a Salisbury acquaintance her concern over a near fatal illness suffered by "poor Upton,"[182] and also by John Upton himself, who on 28 December 1751 wrote Harris about the failure of "Our friend's Amelia." After attending his father's school, John Upton went up to Oxford, becoming Fellow of Exeter College in 1728; he was appointed chaplain to Lord Hardwicke (1734) and prebendary of Rochester (1737), a position he held until his death. But he was best known for his editions of Arrian (1739–41) and of Spenser (1758), and for his *Critical Observations on Shakespeare* (1746). In *Tom Jones* (X.i) Fielding seems obliquely to commend this work, which had been abused by Warburton;[183] and he surely meant to compliment the Uptons, father and son, when the Man of the Hill declares that having "gone through the School at *Taunton*," he "thence removed to *Exeter* College in *Oxford*" (VIII.xi).

Whether Fielding, in visiting Harris this summer, was pausing as usual on his way round the Western Circuit or this time making his way directly to Bath, it is certain that by early September he and Charlotte had taken a house there and would not return to London until the New Year. For, as Fielding explained in a letter to his friend of 6 September, Charlotte's health was rapidly deteriorating: she had, he wrote, only just recovered "from a very dangerous Illness in which she was given over." He continued, "You will easily believe the Happiness which I at present feel and I hope be persuaded that if it is capable of any Addition, it would receive it from the News of your speedy Arrival here." So great was the relief he felt at Charlotte's recovery, he was too agitated to write more: "I scarce know whether I write Sense or Nonsense to you." The Fieldings were staying in the village of Twerton (or Twiverton, as Fielding called it),[184] situated on the south bank of the River Avon just a mile and a half from the city, and close as well to Prior Park. Their house, which came to be known as "Fielding Lodge" (see Plate 40), no longer stands; but it is described by those who saw it as being a comfortable, even a luxurious, dwelling with a "spread eagle" over the door and a large garden in back.[185] It may be that, besides the sustaining presence of Ralph Allen nearby, Fielding and Charlotte also had the company of his sister Sarah, who, according to a strong but undocumented local tradition, had been living since 1739 in Church Lane, Widcombe, in a cottage provided for her by Allen.[186]

In November, Charlotte was somewhat better; her illness at least weighed less heavily on Fielding's mind. Having had news of Harris from the Clarkes, Harris's future father-in-law and his family who had just arrived in Bath, Fielding was inspired to write his friend on Monday, 14 November. It was a playful letter, warning Harris that from his Ball Room, Richard "Beau" Nash (1674–1761) – "Great Snash" and arbiter of all affairs pertaining to polite society at that resort – had issued a formal "Process" against him "in the Court of the Snash Bench at Bath," directing his deputies both in that city and at Salisbury to arrest Harris and to carry him before the Court "on the Morrow of our next Friday's Ball" to answer the charge that he had committed a heinous offense against gallantry by neglecting to pick up a certain lady's fan. The lady in question was Lady Brown, leader of the party of opera-lovers who opposed Harris's favorite, Handel; Nash's deputies, holding the no doubt highly coveted office of "Vice Snash," were: for Salisbury, Francis Swanton, Harris's neighbor in The Close, and for Bath the poet Edward Young (1683–1765), the Muses' "Darling" Fielding called him,[187] whose name he often linked with Pope's. The mock-summons Fielding sent Harris with this letter – by way of inviting his friend to visit him at Twerton and dance a minuet with the lady he loved, Elizabeth Clarke – perfectly exemplifies the more playful side of their relationship:

> SALISBURY to wit.
>   RICHARD without any Grace at all over all Assemblies Music Meetings Balls Hops Rendezvouses Routs Visits Parties &c Great Snash, to our right forward and well assured Edward Young and Francis Swanton Esqr our Vice Snash for the said City, Your Fav.
>
>   Whereas we lately commanded our Vice Snash of the City of Bath that he should take James Harris Esqr if he should be found &c and him safely keep so that he have his Body before us on the Morrow of our Great Tuesday's Ball wheresoever we should then be in Bath to answer to a Plea of Gallantry of Dame Margaret Brown Wife of Robert Brown Bar^t wherefore he the Fan of the said Margaret in his Presence dropt did not take up, and the said Vice Snash returned that the said James was not found &c and whereas it is sufficiently testified to us in our Ball Room here that the said James doth hide himself and run about in your Assemblywic. These are therefore to charge and command you that you take the said James and him safely keep so that you have his Body before us on the Morrow of our next Friday's Ball wheresoever we shall then be in Bath to answer &c and have you there this Precept: Witness Captain Patrick Oneal at Bath itself this 14th of Novr 1743.
> On the Back of the Writ [Fielding adds] there is indorsed.
>   Kepy Korpous
>   The Mark of X Edward Young.

This same jocular spirit – a sign that their friendship had become secure enough to allow him to play the fool a little – enlivens one other letter in Fielding's correspondence with Harris. Trying his hand at Fielding's own game, Harris had sent him a humorous piece of his own entitled *The History of the Life and Actions of Nobody*, which he dedicated to "H.F. Esqr." Aware that Harris was soon to publish his *Three Treatises* (on Art; Music, Painting, and Poetry; and Happiness), Fielding replied:

> Others may be surprized to see such Excellence in the Ridiculous flowing from the same Person from whose Genius and Knowledge the World will shortly derive Treasures of so very different a Kind, and of so much greater Value: but I am not of this Number: for to

me Wit and Philosophy have always seemed to bear a closer Alliance than they are allowed by those who have little Acquaintance with either.

Declaring that Plato and Bacon were of the same opinion, Fielding indulges in more "Foolery," playing changes on the things that Nobody does or says, much in the manner of his "Essay on Nothing" in the *Miscellanies*. Neither Harris's *History* nor Fielding's reply is dated; but the letter was almost certainly written at Bath, perhaps sometime earlier in the autumn of 1743.[188]

Whenever this amusing exchange in fact occurred, Harris in replying to Fielding's letter of 14 November took up a less frivolous matter, asking Fielding's assistance in gaining admission to the Bath Hospital for a poor man who suffered from a paralytic disorder, an affliction which the waters were thought to be especially efficacious in relieving. The Hospital, completed a year before, was yet another monument to Ralph Allen's charity, who from his own quarries supplied the stone for the building *gratis*. On 24 November, Fielding wrote back, setting forth the admissions requirements of the Hospital and renewing his invitation that Harris come visit him. Harris having declined because he was eager to complete work on his *Three Treatises* (1744), Fielding assured him that all the books he needed were available at Bath – unless of course Harris, like the proverbial Parson of Saddleworth to whom Fielding alludes in *Tom Jones* (III.ix), "could read in no Book but his own." Harris's resolve must have been weakened by the scene Fielding paints to tempt his friend to Twerton:

> As your Notes are the only impediment to your Journey hither, I hope that Objection will be removed by my assuring you that from the public Shops here and from some of my Acquaintance I can furnish you with any Books which shall be necessary to you for that Purpose; unless you should be in the Condition of a Parson who could read in no Book but his own. I need not tell you the Pleasure I should have in sitting at the same Fire with you while we were pursuing different Studies. I therefore repeat my Desire to you that you will fill a vacant Room in my House at Twiverton, and I sincerely assure you there is nothing in which the Interest of my Family is not immediately concerned which would give me half the Happiness.

He noticed, however, a missing element in this cheerful picture of scholarly companionship. To make the prospect irresistible he added in conclusion: "N.B. My Small Beer is excellent."

Harris, as far as we know, did not succumb to these temptations; but Fielding, on his friend's behalf, successfully performed the charitable office requested of him: the Governors admitted the poor invalid to the Hospital. This Fielding reported on 15 January 1743/4 in a letter written from Bagshot, as he journeyed by "Slow Marches" from Bath to London by way of Winchester. The military metaphor was inspired by his companion on the journey, the talkative Parson Young, mock hero of Dettingen, who had returned from the wars. " I should have writ you this from Bath," Fielding explained: "but ὁ ΙΟΥΝΙθ ὁ ΔΕΤΤΙΓΓΕΝΕΥΣ being with me made it impossible even to take my Pen in Hand." Even now, as he wrote in haste while preparing to set out for London, "the Greek" was at his side, insisting that he convey his respects to Harris.

One of the surest signs that their friendship had deepened into intimacy is the fact that, Fielding recently having had the opportunity to converse with Elizabeth Clarke and her family in Bath, Harris appears to have asked his opinion of the character of the woman he meant to marry. To which Fielding replied:

> I will when I see you (I hope now in a few Days) tell you every thing I think of the young Lady you mention; but as to the Question you ask of her Morals & Temper, I assure you in my Opinion neither Socrates nor St. Paul could have objected to them.

We may imagine what Miss Clarke would have thought of her husband-to-be asking a fellow of Fielding's reputation to pass judgment on her character. But Harris always saw more solid worth in his facetious friend than "all the World" could see.

····◄ xxxiv ►····

As far as we can trace them, Fielding's movements in this unhappy year of 1744 leave a bewildering impression of restlessness – of journeys between Bath and London interrupted *en route* by visits to Winchester, Salisbury, and even Gloucestershire. No doubt most of this toing and froing was occasioned by the conflicting claims upon his attention of his business as a lawyer and his deep concern over Charlotte's health, which was now in serious decline. In a way curiously inverting the situation in his final novel, in which Booth's sister must die before he is free to marry Amelia, Charlotte would die before this year had run its course and her place in Fielding's household would be taken by Sarah.

The period of this closer relationship between Henry and Sarah, 1744 to 1747, was also the period of Sarah's first serious experiments in fiction – experiments in which she explored for her own purposes the new directions marked out by her brother and by Samuel Richardson, her brother's rival and her friend. It would prove to be a fascinating, intensely personal triangular relationship in which all three authors, jealously interacting, spurred each other on to their best work, as well as to less appealing displays of pettiness and spite – and (to do justice to Fielding's overtures to Richardson on the occasion of *Clarissa*) to at least one gesture of magnanimity.

Published anonymously on 4 May 1744 by her brother's bookseller Millar, the first of Sarah's novels was *The Adventures of David Simple* – a "Moral Romance," as she called it in her "Advertisement," relating her hero's travels through the metropolis in search of a "Real Friend." In these preliminary remarks she apologized not only for the awkward style of the book, but for having had to write it at all – authorship, by the conventions of her day, not being considered a suitable activity for gentlewomen. Her excuse was the only one allowable, "Distress in her Circumstances"; indeed, in an access of self-pity she declared that should the book "meet with Success, it will be *the only Good Fortune* she ever has known." Edmund Fielding's selfishness had depressing consequences for more than one of his numerous progeny.

When drafting *David Simple*, Sarah naturally sought her brother's advice. As he assured her readers, however, in the Preface he contributed to the second edition (published on 13 July), the assistance she received from him was negligible – consisting merely in "two or three Hints" that occurred to him as he read the first half of the manuscript, "and some little Direction as to the Conduct of the second Volume, much the greater Part of which I never saw till in Print." Indeed, Fielding protested, his absence from town that spring had prevented him even from correcting "some Grammatical and other Errors in Style in the first Impression" – faults which, "tho' in great Haste," he did Sarah the favor of emending for the new edition.[189] Sarah might be forgiven if she resented the fact that the title-page of this edition took more notice of her famous brother's labors in redeeming the novel from its imperfections than it did of the author herself, whom the proprieties of the day required to remain anonymous: "THE SECOND EDITION, *Revised and Corrected*. With a PREFACE *By* HENRY FIELDING Esq."

Except for the coy acknowledgments he made of Sarah's contributions to *Joseph Andrews* (the letter from Leonora to Horatio, II.iv) and *A Journey from This World to the Next* (the history of Anna Boleyn) – assuming these are her work, as most scholars take them to be – the Preface to *David Simple* affords the first real glimpse we have of Fielding's close and complex relationship with Sarah, "a young Woman," he calls her, "so nearly and dearly allied to me, in the highest Friendship as well as Relation," and whose heart contains "all the Good which is to be found in Human Nature." That they loved each other deeply – a love, indeed, possibly colored by erotic feelings – is an inescapable inference from the evidence we considered earlier (see above, pp. 23–30), of which one of the most compelling pieces is the extraordinary story of Camilla and her brother Valentine in *David Simple*. This nightmarish tale, in which their innocent friendship is made to appear as an incestuous passion shamelessly indulged, is one reason, surely, why Fielding praised his sister most particularly for her understanding of the passions and characters of men: "the Merit of this Work," he wrote, "consists in a vast Penetration into human Nature, a deep and profound Discernment of all the Mazes, Windings and Labyrinths, which perplex the Heart of Man to such a degree, that he is himself often incapable of seeing through them." This, Fielding insists, "is the greatest, noblest, and rarest of all the Talents which constitute a Genius."

But even while giving Sarah this generous measure of praise, Fielding could not resist patronizing her by representing this strange romance of her own devising as a version of the new genre of the comic prose epic which he had defined in the Preface to *Joseph Andrews*; she was, he wished to think, merely following where he had led the way. Because of the very extravagance of his commendations, moreover – in her mastery of fable, character, and sentiment he calls her the equal of Homer and Shakespeare! – we cannot take them seriously. And though he makes light of the single fault he finds – namely, Sarah's weakness in "Diction ... the last, and lowest Perfection in a Writer" – he nevertheless dwells on it, blaming the incorrectness of her style on her want of "Learning," a deficiency so conspicuous in the work that it lies "open to the Eyes of every Fool, who has had a little *Latin* inoculated into his Tail."

Latin and Greek, the precious keys to the wisdom of the Ancients, were for Fielding a masculine preserve. One learned those mysteries at the birchen altars of Eton, not at Mrs. Rookes's finishing school in Salisbury. According to the Christian humanist tradition he inherited, learning and wit were qualities unseemly, not to say unnatural, in the female character. In *Amelia*, for example, the scholarly virago Mrs. Bennet amply demonstrates the proposition that a little learning can be a dangerous thing in a woman, whereas the heroine's education has been suitably confined to *belles lettres* in the vernacular, to divinity, and to the history of her own country, along with her knowledge of French and her love of good music (VI.vii).

Contemporary witnesses made much, indeed, of this source of friction between Fielding and his sister – though these witnesses, it should be said, are not wholly reliable. According to Dr. Arthur Collier, as reported by Mrs. Thrale (the former a feckless man whom Fielding came to despise, the latter a reckless gossip who rarely troubled to distinguish truth from falsehood), Sarah took up the study of the learned languages against her brother's wishes. She may well have been moved to do so by such criticisms of her illiteracy as Fielding expressed in his Preface to *David Simple*. Under Collier's tutelage, Sarah eventually became such a mistress of Latin and Greek that she could repeat "a thousand Lines at a Time" of classical poetry "without missing one";[190] and, with James Harris's help, she produced after her brother's death an excellent translation of Xenophon's *Memoirs of Socrates* (1762). According to Mrs. Thrale, Sarah accomplished all this to Henry's annoyance – as if to remove the deficiency he had exposed in her and which constituted one source of his masculine sense of superiority:

> Miss Fielding was wholly unassisted by her Brother whatever She Wrote [declared Mrs. Thrale (then Mrs. Piozzi), getting her facts wrong at the start]; for I know Dr. Collier has often told me that though they lived upon the tenderest Terms *before*, yet after She had by their common Friend's Assistance made herself a competent Scholar, so as to construe the sixth Book of Virgil with Ease – the Author of Tom Jones began to teize and *taunt* her with being a literary Lady &c. till at last She resolved to make her whole pleasure out of Study, and becoming justly eminent for her Taste and Knowledge of the Greek Language, her Brother never more could perswade himself to endure her Company with Civility – This Anecdote I do not recollect to have read in Mr. Murphy's Account of him, though curious enough; and most undoubtedly true.[191]

Given Fielding's views on the subject of scholarly females, there is probably a grain of truth in this chaff. That Sarah's mastery of the classics could have spoiled her relationship with her brother to this degree is, however, unlikely. All other evidence available to us suggests that there existed between them nothing but love and mutual respect. Sarah's writings contain frequent compliments to her brother and his works;[192] for his part, Fielding not only continued to assist Sarah in her novel-writing, but made her fiction the favorite reading of Sophie Western in *Tom Jones* (VI.v). Indeed, more than a year after Charlotte's death, it is surely Sarah whom Fielding declared to be "the Woman in the world whom I like best."[193]

Besides wishing to assure the public of his sister's talents as a romance-writer, Fielding had an urgent personal motive for writing the Preface to the second edition of *David Simple*. Despite the promise he had "solemnly made" a year before in the Preface to the *Miscellanies* that he would in future set his name to anything he published, readers persisted in attributing to him a number of anonymous works. One of these was *David Simple* itself.[194] But, to use his own metaphor, it was the fathering upon him of works far more damaging than this innocuous romance that prompted him to protest: "I have been", he declared, "reputed and reported the Author of half the Scurrility, Bawdy, Treason and Blasphemy, which these few last Years have produced." Though he had published nothing at all for more than a year, these rumors were making it impossible for him to shake off his reputation as a licentious and unprincipled satirist – so it appears from *An Essay on Calumny* (June 1744), whose author singled Fielding out, together with the notorious Paul Whitehead, as being the very type of the vice that was his subject:

> Whether the *nameless* or *fictitious* Page
> Convey the *printed* Venom thro' an Age,
> Where ceaseless *Strife* – and *Party-Rage* prevails,
> And best the Satire takes which wildest rails;
> Whether by Pr[e]l[a]te wrote, or garter'd P[ee]r
> By *F[ie]ld[in]g, Wh[i]th[ea]d,* – or the *G[a]z[e]tt[ee]r!*
> So Whores in Rags, or Velvet are the same,
> In *Fashion* only differ – not in *Name!*

In June had appeared another anonymous poem that Fielding feared would ruin him professionally if he did not put a stop to the rumors of his authorship. This was *The Causidicade*, an outrageous satire on the legal profession now ascribed to the Irish dramatist and attorney Macnamara Morgan (d. 1762), who later adopted the pseudonym "Porcupinus Pelagius." Occasioned by the resignation of the Solicitor General, Sir John Strange, and the appointment in his place of William Murray (afterward Lord Mansfield), this flagitious performance fell foul of every person of any eminence in the law: besides Strange and Murray, it hit the late Lord Chancellor Talbot; the present Lord Chancellor Hardwicke; the Attorney General, Dudley Ryder; Chief Justice Willes; the Master of the Rolls, William Fortescue; and many others, including the Earls of Bath (Pulteney) and Orford (Walpole). Small wonder Fielding hastened to disclaim any connection with the piece:

> Among all the Scurrilities with which I have been accused, (tho' equally and totally innocent of every one) none ever raised my Indignation so much as the *Causidicade*: this accused me not only of being a bad Writer, and a bad Man, but with downright Idiotism, in flying in the Face of the greatest Men of my Profession. I take therefore this Opportunity to protest, that I never saw that infamous, paultry Libel, till long after it had been in Print; nor can any Man hold it in greater Contempt and Abhorrence than myself.

Because he had been denied the benefit he hoped for from his promise to declare his authorship of any work he published, he revoked that promise: "I shall now look upon myself at full Liberty to publish any

anonymous Work, without any Breach of Faith." Before the year was
out, he would take advantage of this liberty in order to publish a
political satire calculated to assist his friends in Opposition. Thereafter
he produced several other anonymous or pseudonymous pamphlets.

In another revealing passage of this important Preface, Fielding
declared that, notwithstanding the success of *Joseph Andrews* and
Jonathan Wild, he had given up novel-writing in order to devote himself
to the law:

> a Profession [he declared], to which I have applied with so arduous
> and intent a Diligence, that I have had no Leisure, if I had Incli-
> nation, to compose any thing of this kind. Indeed I am very far from
> entertaining such an Inclination; I know the Value of the Reward,
> which Fame confers on Authors, too well, to endeavour any longer
> to obtain it; nor was the World ever more unwilling to bestow the
> glorious, envied Prize of the Laurel or Bays, than I should now be
> to receive any such Garland or Fool's Cap. There is not, I believe,
> (and it is bold to affirm) a single *Free Briton* in this Kingdom, who
> hates his Wife more heartily than I detest the Muses.

In the summer of 1744 thoughts of *Tom Jones* were far from Fielding's
mind. The Muse that brought him such recent fame he now spurned as
a fickle mistress whose favors were insubstantial. He meant instead to
concentrate all his formidable ability and energy on the less frivolous
business of the law – a business more becoming a gentleman than that
of romance-writing. Very likely he was already formulating plans to
publish a work he hoped would establish him as an authority in his
profession. Entitled "An Institute of the Pleas of the Crown" and in
conception copious enough to require two folio volumes, this work was
far enough advanced by February of the following year for Fielding to
announce that its publication was imminent.

···➤ XXXV ◄···

When the second edition of *David Simple* was published, Fielding's
colleagues in law were already progressing round the Western Circuit,
which commenced this summer at Winchester on 3 July and ended at
Bristol on 6 August. With Charlotte now in the final stages of her
decline, Fielding may not have attended the assizes as usual.

By autumn he was obliged for her sake to return to Bath, where they
resided not in the house at Twerton as before, but in lodgings. From
that city on 10 October he wrote Harris sadly: "My Wife's Illness ...
of whose Recovery I have scarce any Hopes, occasions me so much

Distress that you will expect no Entertainment in this Letter." Adding
to his worries was the dunning of his creditors: his principal reason for
writing his friend at this juncture was to accept "the Loan of a small
Sum of Money" which Harris had offered him when they last saw each
other in Salisbury. Promising to repay the loan by the first day of
Hilary Term, Fielding asked Harris to send Millar a note "payable to
him at sight and by the first Post." He did not specify the amount, but
presumably he felt some urgency in the matter.

In a few weeks Charlotte's long ordeal was over; it is said that, having
caught a fever, she died in Fielding's arms.[195] Fielding arranged for her
body to be carried from Bath to London for burial. But, strangely, he
appears not to have accompanied the corpse. Before following her to
London, he turned northward to pay a visit of four days to Harris's
acquaintance, Richard Owen Cambridge (1717–1802), at his seat at
Whitminster, Gloucestershire[196] – a journey from Bath that would take
him forty miles out of his way. A fellow Etonian and now a member of
the Society of Lincoln's Inn, Owen Cambridge was a gentleman of
leisure who occupied himself chiefly in beautifying his estate, boating
on the Severn, and composing humorous verse; this was the year in
which he wrote his best-known work, *The Scribleriad* (not published
until 1751). Though he drank nothing but plain water and kept up his
skill with bow and arrow by shooting ducks in the head, he nevertheless
had many friends in common with Fielding – besides Harris, there were
Charles Hanbury Williams, Lyttelton, Pitt, Chesterfield, and others.[197]
Fielding found him, he told Harris, "a Man of good Parts and Understanding."

But what is one to make of this apparent holiday in Gloucestershire
which Fielding found time for in the brief interval between Charlotte's
death in Bath and her burial in London? Of his behavior at this time
Murphy wrote that "the fortitude of mind with which he met all the
other calamities of life deserted him on this most trying occasion," his
friends indeed fearing he was "in danger of losing his reason." Lady
Stuart gives a similar account, declaring that Fielding's grief was so
intense it "approached to frenzy." This is the poignant picture preserved for us by Fielding's previous biographers, and given his love for
Charlotte and the "vehemence" of his passionate nature (to recall
Harris's characterization of him), it is not an improbable one.

Quite a different account originated among Fielding's acquaintance
at Bath, however, and persisted into the next century. According to
this story Fielding, immediately upon Charlotte's death, made every
effort to shake off his depression – to the extent that he seemed heartless.
R.E.M. Peach, the historian of Bath, wrestled uneasily with two versions of the anecdote, trying to turn it as much as possible to Fielding's
advantage. According to the first account (which Peach rejected as

unreliable) a friend encountered Fielding at a party in Bath on the evening of the day Charlotte died:

> "I am very glad to see you, Mr. Fielding, for there was a report ... that your wife died this morning." "It is very true," was the reply, "and that is the very reason that I have come ... to join the pleasure party."

In the other version (which Peach prefers, but which is inaccurate in every other detail concerning the circumstances of Charlotte's death) what Fielding actually said to the friend, who found him in the company of his sister, was that having lost his wife, he was determined to " 'dissipate,' using the word *dissipate* [Peach explains] in the obvious sense of a change of scene – a change from which he would derive solace and comfort, under the care and wise direction of his excellent sister."[198] This may well have been the motive that drove Fielding to visit Owen Cambridge in Gloucestershire, a man whose lively company would serve to unbend his mind after the sad months of watching Charlotte die. Indeed, Fielding himself confessed that, in London soon after he buried her, he spent with his Salisbury friends Dr. Barker and Arthur Collier "as pleasant a day ... as I have known some Months. Nay," he continued to Harris on 24 November, "I was so little a mourner that I believe many a Good Woman, had she been present, would have denied the Possibility of my having ever been a good Husband."

It was surely *because* he felt Charlotte's loss so bitterly that Fielding strove to dissipate his grief in these ways, unseemly as he knew they must appear to others. How much Charlotte meant to him is best seen in those great memorials of his love for her, *Tom Jones* and *Amelia*, in which he preserved her "Idea" in the characters of Sophie Western and Amelia Booth. And on the night of Wednesday, 14 November 1744 – when she was buried beside her mother and daughter in the chancel vault of St. Martin-in-the-Fields as the great tenor bell tolled – he honored her with the most solemn exequies: a stately funeral of such pomp that only the greatest families in the parish could afford.[199]

As for the cost, it was as usual money he did not himself have. Harris responded handsomely to his request for a loan, but he found that Fielding was too sanguine in expecting to be able to repay it in the near future.[200]

Harris having written to console his friend on the loss of this beloved woman whom he had known since childhood, Fielding replied on 24 November. No one who reads this letter will doubt the sincerity of his grief or fail to admire the strength of character which supported him in adversity. Nor will we doubt how much Harris meant to him: he was, Fielding declares, "the Man whom I esteem most of any person in this World."

You, my Friend, first taught me that Philosophy was not a bare Name, not a fruitless vain Pursuit of Something as chimerical as the Grand Secret of the Alchemist, or rather resembling those specious Fantoms the common Honour and Friendship of the World, which however gaudy and beautiful they appear vanish entirely if we endeavour to apply them to Use. In a Word, you first awakened an Idea in me that true Philosophy consisted in Habit only, without cultivating which in our own Minds, we should no more become Philosophers by reading the Pages of Plato and Xenophon, than great Poets by perusing the Works of Homer and Virgil.

When I had received this Hint from you Fortune presented me with sufficient occasion to exert it, by entring me in the School of Distress, through all the Classes of which, I have, I think proceeded with greater Diligence and Celerity than Boys generally use in going through the Schools of Eton or Westminster. Why should not I be as pleased with being arrived at the Head of this my School, and with equal Satisfaction look back on the several Whippings Head-achs and Heart-achs which I have suffered in my Progress, since I can now be lashed no more.

This is in good earnest the present Situation of my Mind, which you will find at our next meeting neither soured nor deprest; neither snarling like a Cynic nor blubbering like a Woman.

Among other things this eloquent document reveals about Fielding's intellectual bent is that, when he sought relief from the lashings he suffered in life's hard "School of Distress," he turned instinctively not to religion, but to philosophy – and particularly to the philosophy of Plato. Some months earlier, when he distinguished in the Preface to the *Miscellanies* between the Great and the Good in human nature, he also defined a third character, rarely to be found, in whose mind these different qualities united, "as they actually did, and all in the highest Degree, in those of *Socrates* and *Brutus*." This character, which he called "the Great and Good" was "the *true Sublime* in Human Nature." Then, as now in his letter to Harris, he defined it by reference to a favorite passage from Valerius Maximus describing the mind and spirit of Plato, "my Godlike Master" – a picture, he declares to Harris, of "the truest Sublime I ever met with."[201] In the Preface he rendered it freely:

That Elevation by which the Soul of Man, raising and extending itself above the Order of this Creation, and brighten'd with a certain Ray of Divinity, looks down on the Condition of Mortals. This is indeed [he observed] a glorious Object, on which we can never gaze with too much Praise and Admiration. A perfect Work! the *Iliad* of

Nature! ravishing and astonishing, and which at once fills us with Love, Wonder, and Delight.

It was, he explained to Harris, Plato's teacher Socrates whose example in adversity he tried to follow:

> You, my dear Friend, who are a Philosopher in earnest ... will not laugh when I tell you, I have often asked myself, How would Socrates have acted on this Occasion? An assertion I am almost afraid too confident. And yet why so? Would it be so in a Soldier to have his Marlborough; or in a Lawyer to have his Coke for a Pattern? Persons perhaps as difficult to rival in their several Sciences. This at least must be granted that if Socrates was a Man it is possible for a Man to be what he actually was. Is not here then a tacit Confession, My Friend, that Mankind notwithstanding their real and affected Depravity, do in their Hearts acknowledge that true Philosophy is of all things most valuable, and that it is more Honour to be, and more Impudence to pretend to be a Master of that Science than of any other.

We need not doubt that Fielding felt Charlotte's loss painfully; but it was neither in his nature, which was essentially cheerful and sociable, nor in his philosophy, which taught him to face misfortune with fortitude and equanimity, to wrap his grief around him and retire from the business of living.

···◆ XXXVI ◆···

However distraught he may have been in the first throes of his grief, he had brought himself so thoroughly under control by the time he wrote Harris on 24 November that he had been able to produce and publish a spirited satirical pamphlet calculated to serve his friends in Opposition. These men – Lyttelton, Pitt, Dodington, Chesterfield – having engineered Walpole's fall from power in February 1742, soon began pressing for the removal of the King's favorite minister, John Carteret, Lord Granville. To this end they held Granville responsible for the disastrous conduct of the war with France (formally declared in March 1744), and they denounced most particularly his unpopular policy of using English funds to subsidize the 16,000 Hanoverian troops in the Pragmatic Army. This issue, the depredations of the omnivorous "Hanover rat" which despoiled the countryside like a biblical plague, was Fielding's theme in a satiric anatomy written – like his *Papers* on the "Chrysipus" – in parody of the transactions of the Royal Society.

Entitled *An Attempt towards a Natural History of the Hanover Rat*,[202] the pamphlet was published on 23 November, not ten days after Charlotte's funeral. On the day following publication – though of course there was no causal connection between the two events – Granville resigned.

Before Parliament adjourned for the Christmas recess a new "Broad-Bottom" government had been formed, a coalition in which the "Old Whigs" under Walpole's protégé Henry Pelham, his brother the Duke of Newcastle, and Lord Hardwicke joined with the Chesterfield–Cobham faction[203] with whom Fielding had been allied for many years, if not recently in any very active way. Places were found in the new government for almost all Fielding's friends: Lyttelton was made a Lord of the Treasury; Dodington became Treasurer of the Navy; Chesterfield was appointed Lord Lieutenant of Ireland; Lord Cobham became Colonel of the First Dragoons; the Duke of Bedford was made First Lord of the Admiralty. Only Pitt, whom the King hated, had for the time being no share in the spoils, and he was content to await a riper season.

From this moment Fielding never wavered in his allegiance to the ministry. Though in the past he had been willing on occasion to draw his pen in defense of Walpole, for the most part he had been with Lyttelton, Dodington, and the Patriots, the gadfly of the Opposition. His friends at last in power, he would emerge in a few months' time as the government's most dutiful and effective apologist. The reversal of roles was not made without a certain awkwardness: in *Tom Jones*, for instance, it is no longer Fielding and his party, but the fatuous, ale-swilling Jacobite, Squire Western, who blusters against the "*Hannover Rats*" (VI.xiv).

At about the time these transformations were occurring in the political world, Fielding was settling into a comfortable house he had leased in Old Boswell Court,[204] near Lincoln's Inn Fields, on a site now occupied by the Royal Courts of Justice. In Fielding's day, Old Boswell Court, situated close to the Inns of Court, was a snug, highly desirable residential area inhabited by "People of Credit,"[205] chiefly successful lawyers. Fielding's neighbors included, for example, Justice William Wright and Serjeant William Wynne (both of whom subscribed to the *Miscellanies*), as well as Thomas Lane, Chairman of the Middlesex Quarter Sessions. Until his death earlier this same year Nicholas Paxton, Walpole's Solicitor to the Treasury, resided there. In this house and neighborhood, suitable for a gentleman who meant to prosper in the legal profession, Fielding lived for three years, until embarrassing domestic circumstances caused him to remove to discreet lodgings in Twickenham. With him were his infant son and daughter, Henry and Harriet (aged two and one, respectively), the cook-maid Mary Daniel, and now his sister Sarah, who had come to take Charlotte's place supervising the household.

····➤ XXXVII ◀····

Little more than a month after his friends had wrested the ministry from Granville, Fielding was made to cut a curious figure in print – in *The Seventh Satyre of Juvenal Imitated*, published anonymously on 31 January 1744/5. The author's literary tastes incline to such stalwarts of the old Opposition as Swift, Gay, and Glover. Yet Fielding and his friends, whom we might expect to find sympathetically treated in this company, are among the butts of the satire:

> Would you have F[ielding] match what *Congreve* writ?
> Oh, give him Cloaths, e're you deny him Wit.
> When press'd with Duns, and forc'd to write for Bread,
> The craving Belly checks the teeming Head.
> But he has Patrons, and of those not few –
> Patrons! d'ye call them? – an unthinking Crew,
> In Manners grov'ling, as they're high in Birth,
> Who give to Strumpets, what they keep from Worth;
> On Hounds and Horses fix their whole Regard,
> Nor spare one Guinea to relieve the Bard.

It is hard to see how this image squares either with Fielding's circumstances or with the character of his "Patrons" in 1745. Perhaps the satirist means to recall the period of *Miss Lucy in Town* and *The Wedding-Day*; the comparison with Congreve makes play-writing – not prose fiction, say – the frame of reference. Fielding had not recently been writing for bread in this way; and, though it is true he often complained "that there is no one Patron of true Genius, nor the least Encouragement left for it in this Kingdom,"[206] those men of rank and property whose favors he enjoyed are not well described as boorish and dissolute. Tantalizing as this satire is in its putative portrayal of Fielding's circumstances in 1745, it probably tells us nothing more than what we know from Horace Walpole's verses a few years earlier: that Fielding had become for his contemporaries the very type of the prodigal and impecunious hackney author who wrote to keep the bailiffs from his door.

It was this reputation that he was finding difficult to live down as he continued to apply himself to his profession, the law, "with so arduous and intent a Diligence."

That Fielding did not, to his own satisfaction, prosper as a barrister

is plain from his dry observation some years later that, when compared
with the annual income of actors, subaltern officers in the Army, and
the inferior clergy, "the Profits in the Law, to ninety-nine in a hundred,
amount not to a single Shilling." His friend Harris, however, as we
recall, had a more sanguine recollection of the "Success" Fielding
enjoyed as a lawyer. Regrettably, the business in which he was concerned is rarely documented in the records of the courts and assizes –
though these, it should be said, are spotty and incomplete. In connection
with cases involving the transfer of real property, Fielding's name'
appears during the period 1743-7 on only seven "declarations of
ejectment" pertaining to estates in the counties of Berkshire (1), Devon
(1), Somerset (2), Hampshire (2), and Northampton (1).[207] But it was
difficult for the brightest young barristers to make a name for themselves on the circuit, even when they did not toil under the handicap
of Fielding's reputation for improvidence and frivolity: neither Robert
Henley nor Charles Pratt, both of whom became Lord Chancellors,
could manage it.

To establish himself more securely in his profession Fielding had been
at work for some time composing an ambitious treatise on Crown Law,
which he entitled "An Institute of the Pleas of the Crown."[208] Though
he was himself learned in this field of the law, rumor would persist that,
in preparing the treatise, Fielding was indebted to the manuscript notes
and reports of his grandfather, Sir Henry Gould.[209] However that may
be, Fielding's "Institute of the Pleas of the Crown" was so far advanced
that in the *General Evening Post* for 26–8 February 1744/5 he announced
that it would be published "Shortly"; Millar had agreed to issue it in
two folio volumes. The advertisement, which Fielding no doubt drafted
himself, will indicate the nature of the work:

> Containing a compleat Series of the Law in all Criminal Matters, as
> it is laid down in the several Acts of Parliament, the Year Books,
> Books of Reports, &c. From the Times of Edward the First to the
> present. Together with the Methods of proceeding against Offenders,
> from the first Process to attack [sic] their Persons to the Judgment
> and its final Consequences; and in Cases where the Judgment is
> reversed, to the Restitution on such Reversal by Writ of Error.
>
> Digested in a Method most adapted to Practice; with correct
> Precedents of Indictments, and other Entries, on the Several Heads,
> taken from the Records.
>
> To which are added, Notes explaining the most difficult Passages,
> Terms of Art and Distinctions that occur through the Whole, and
> referring to particular Instances in which our Crown law hath bor-
> row'd from or agrees with the Institutions of other Countries relating
> to the Criminal Matters.

Though Fielding continued to advertise this impressive-sounding work in the newspapers until early April, it was never to appear. As Murphy was aware, the two manuscript volumes remained after Fielding's death "still unpublished," in the hands of his half-brother John. Eventually, the volumes suffered the fate of dismemberment, the leaves being dispersed on the autograph market by Fielding's grandson, William Henry Fielding.[210] Prompted by Murphy's reference to Fielding's abortive law book, a writer in the *Annual Register* for 1762 reported a tradition about it then still current among the lawyers who rode the Western Circuit:

> Having attended the judges two or three years without the least prospect of success, [Fielding] published proposals for a new law-book; which being circulated round the country, the young barrister was, at the ensuing assizes, loaded with briefs at every town on the circuit. – But his practice thus suddenly increased, almost as suddenly declined.[211]

What happened to discourage Fielding from completing this grand project remains a mystery. On balance, however, we can be thankful for the change in his plans; for it was probably about this time, the spring of 1745,[212] when, according to his own account in the Dedication to *Tom Jones*, he decided to oblige Lyttelton by resuming that very different species of composition at which he excelled, the comic prose epic – a decision which in time produced his masterpiece.

The fleeting celebrity which his projected law book brought him may have encouraged another of Fielding's schoolfellows to employ him in what was surely the grandest case of his career as counsellor. In June 1745 Hanbury Williams, together with other polite subscribers to the Italian Opera, was being sued by the five Directors of the subscription – namely, the Duke of Rutland, the Earl of Holderness, Viscount Middleton, the Right Honourable Charles Sackville (better known as Lord Middlesex), and John Frederick – for failing to pay both the £200 each subscriber originally promised and in addition his share (£56) of the amount by which the Directors had overrun the budget. Hanbury Williams chose Fielding to make his defense. This imbroglio of opera-lovers arose in 1742–3, when the Directors spent nearly £17,000 on a single season. In June 1744[213] the Directors tried to cut their losses by suing the subscribers, an eminent company including, besides Fielding's client, the Dukes of Bedford, Grafton, Marlborough, Montagu, and Newcastle; the Earls of Bath and Chesterfield; Henry Pelham and Horace Walpole – none of whom was eager to rescue the Directors from the consequences of their own extravagance. The court records show that Hanbury Williams had appointed his attorney by June 1745,[214] but Fielding did not submit his answer to the complaint until 13 August

1746.[215] It is an interesting document for what it reveals about the lucidity, force, and indeed audacity of Fielding's legal mind. He was the only defense attorney to attempt to turn the tables on the Directors by declaring that, since they had in effect canceled the subscription by violating the terms of the original agreement, his client not only denied any obligation to pay more, but demanded his money back, with the Directors to assume the costs and charges of the action. That Fielding succeeded in this tactic is unlikely, but it was an elegant riposte nonetheless.

••••➤ XXXViii ◆•••

In June 1745 Fielding also became embroiled in the law in a far more troublesome and personal way that eventually soured his long-standing friendship with Dr. Arthur Collier. Collier and his sisters Jane and Margaret figure so prominently in the story of Fielding's life, even to its melancholy end, that we must pause to consider them.

The Collier family were of Salisbury, in which city they had lived for many years before Fielding's grandmother Lady Gould settled there in 1720. Soon after, by decree of Chancery her home became the home of Fielding and his sisters, whose acquaintance with the Colliers presumably dates from this period. The most distinguished member of the family was the metaphysician, the Reverend Arthur Collier (1680–1732),[216] rector of Steeple Langford, Wilts., and author of *Clavis Universalis* (1713), a work which sets forth the Berkeleian hypothesis that ideas comprise the only reality. It was an especially quixotic system for a philosopher whose wife's extravagance sunk them so deeply into debt that he was obliged to sell the reversion of the advowson at Steeple Langford, which had been in his family for 125 years. His son Arthur (1707–77), LL.D., was Fielding's exact contemporary and a fellow lawyer who practiced as an advocate at Doctors' Commons, the ecclesiastical court; he was also tutor, as we have seen, both to Mrs. Piozzi (when she was Hester Lynch Salusbury) and to Sarah Fielding. According to the historian of Doctors' Commons, he was "an ingenious, but unsteady and eccentric man."[217] His sister Jane Collier (d. 1754–5) was an author of wit and spirit: she wrote *An Essay on the Art of Ingeniously Tormenting* (1753), in which she was assisted by James Harris;[218] and she collaborated with Sarah Fielding in *The Cry* (1754). Fielding was fond of Jane. On the eve of his fatal journey to Lisbon he presented her with a rarity indeed, a vellum-bound copy of his favorite Horace, inscribed by himself affectionately:

To Miss Jane Collyer,
This Edition of the best
of all the Roman Poets,
as a Memorial (however poor)
of the highest Esteem for
an Understanding more than
Female, mixed with virtues almost
more than human, gives, offers up
and dedicates her Sincere Friend
                    Henry Fielding[219]

Jane's sister Margaret (1717–94)[220] joined the Fielding household at
about this time (that is, 1745 or 1746), apparently as governess to his
daughter Harriet; in this capacity she accompanied him to Lisbon.
Though Fielding was fond of her sister, he came to regard Margaret as
meddlesome and ungrateful – or, to use the more expressive epithets
he uttered on his deathbed, as "the most artfull, wicked B—— in the
world." As for their brother Dr. Collier, Fielding sent him from Lisbon
a half-chest of onions, declaring as he did so his final opinion of the
man, "whose very Name I hate."[221]

The chain of circumstances that embittered this friendship began in
1745 when Collier found himself besieged by a small army of aggrieved
creditors to whom he owed a great deal of money. At least a half-dozen
actions were brought against him for sums totaling over £1,500.[222] The
fact that in the costliest of these Collier's mother Margaret was named
co-defendant suggests that not all this woe was of his own making; Mrs.
Collier's spendthrift ways had earlier reduced her husband to penury.

But it is another of these suits that particularly concerns us. For
when one Tristram Walton sued Collier for a debt of £400, Henry
Fielding "of Boswell Court, St. Clement Danes" and James Harris of
Salisbury came forward on 14 June 1745 to save their friend from
confinement by posting bail.[223] In the months to come, the need to
contrive ways of postponing the Court's judgment in this case would
often overshadow the greater sense of emergency Fielding felt as the
nation struggled in the throes of the Jacobite rebellion. In November,
acting as Collier's attorney, he filed two separate "Writs of Error,"
which, though they put off the day of reckoning, had the less happy
effect of adding more than £20 in damages and costs to Collier's debt.
The seriousness of Collier's predicament is evident from Fielding's letter
to Harris of 30 January 1745/6 – as is Fielding's uneasiness in having
to cope with the complexities of the law in an area with which, as a
barrister and no mere solicitor, he was unfamiliar:

As to surrendering the Doctor [Fielding warned Harris), it can not
be done without absolute Ruin to him: for being a Prisoner by
Surrender he will be in a worse Situation than if in absolute
Execution, and his Bail to the Writ of Error will not discharge him:
but I hope there is an Irregularity in their Proceedings which will
set them all aside and discharge us, of which you shall have Notice
in a Post or two. I know not whether you will blame my Ignorance
in these Quirks of the Law: but they are in Reality to us as Corn
Cutting is to a Physician.

Most helpful in clarifying the part Fielding played in Collier's case
is his final letter to Harris on the subject, written from London on 13
May 1746. In the absence of Collier's brother Charles, a soldier whom
the war in Flanders removed from the country,[224] Fielding had been
willing to act nominally as one of the two sureties the law required,
and he had also exerted himself in his capacity as attorney to delay
judgment on the suit. But from the start the friends had agreed it
would be Harris alone who must pay the money if Collier failed to raise
it himself; and with time running out, Collier lingered in Somersetshire,
far from the King's Bench. Still Fielding hoped that Collier would
behave responsibly; moreover, his brother, having learned of the emergency at home, had put his name to the bond. Fielding's letter reads
in part as follows:

The true Reason of my not answering your last sooner was the daily
Expectation I had of seeing Dr. Collyer. He promised to be in Town
a Fortnight ago, but is not yet, nor do his Family know when he will
return.
    The Writ of Error will be run out in the next Term at which time
Judgement will be affirmed, after which you have 4 days to surrender
the Principal and in Default of such Surrender will become together
with myself chargeable for the Debt, as will likewise his own Brother,
who is I think responsible enough and more entitled to pay the Debt
than either you or I.
    . . .
    The Dr. is at his Estate in Somersetshire, and I yet hope will be
enabled to pay this Debt before the Judgement is affirmed. If not
. . . As I told both yourself and the Doctor, at the time of your so
kindly becoming Bail for him, the Friendship was entirely yours: for
from you the Money would be expected in Failure of the Principal,
therefore I shall be very ready to act as you appoint. One of these
things, I repeat once more must next Term be the Consequence of
affirming the Judgement. The Doctor must pay the Debt, or he must
be surrendered or the Money must be paid either by Capt. Collyer or
yourself.

Judgment was affirmed against Collier on 4 June 1746, though, somehow, all his creditors were satisfied.[225] In the light of this letter, Fielding's representation of the affair seems disingenuous as, at the end of his life, he reflected bitterly on how Margaret Collier and her brother had abused his "Kindness." He wrote from Lisbon of the "obligations she and her Family have to me, who had Execution taken out ag^t [me] for 400*l.* for which I became Bail for her Brother, who took her starving in the Streets and nourished her in my own Bosom."[226] The peevish, self-serving tone of these words was not characteristic of Fielding. They came from a man who was dying of a hideous disease – and who, whether or not he paid the £400 to which he made himself liable by law, had in fact done the Colliers kindnesses he felt were insufficiently acknowledged. Nevertheless, it was a sad ending to what once had been a close and amicable relationship.

xxxix

But to return to June 1745. In that month Fielding in a more familiar vein facetiously applied his knowledge of the law to assist another friend, Dr. John Ranby (1703–73), Principal Sergeant-Surgeon to the King; in Fielding's opinion, indeed, Ranby was "the most eminent Surgeon in the Kingdom, or perhaps in the World."[227] The occasion was a rowdy medical controversy which Ranby had provoked by questioning in print the competence of several eminent physicians who attended Robert Walpole, Earl of Orford, in his final illness. The Great Man, who for better and for worse had loomed so large in Fielding's life, died in March of this year, suffering not simply from the natural agonies of his disease (kidney stones), but from those artificially induced by the medicine prescribed to cure him – a highly corrosive specific concocted by the physician James Jurin, who gave it the awesome denomination of *lixivium lithontripticum*. In *A Narrative of the Last Illness of the Right Honourable the Earl of Orford* (April) Ranby denounced the handling of the case by Jurin and his distinguished colleagues Sir Edward Hulse and William Chiseldon; they replied in kind, while others joined in a chorus of defamation and ridicule emanating from the pamphlet shops.

Fielding's contribution was of a piece with the irreverent treatment he generally accorded the medical establishment, from *Tom Thumb* and *The Mock Doctor* to *Amelia*. Its title tells the story:

> *The Charge to the Jury: or, The Sum of the Evidence, on The Trial of A.B.C.D. and E.F. All M.D. For the Death of one Robert at Orfud, at*

a Special Commission of Oyer and Terminer held at Justice-College, in W[arwi]ck Lane, Before Sir Æsculapius Dosem, Dr. Timberhead, and Others, their Fellows, Justices, &c.[228]

This lively satire, the last pamphlet of its kind he wrote, was in press at the end of June[229] and was published under Mary Cooper's imprint on 2 July. In it *"Sergeant John Narrative"* makes a sympathetic figure as prosecutor, as Fielding, summoning all the solemnity of the law, indicts *"A.B.* for that he, with a certain *deadly Instrument,* called a-Lickliverum Lithonskipticum, the Body of the said *Robert* at *Orfud* did pill and potion. And the said *C.D.* and *E.F.* for being comforting, aiding, abetting, prescribing, dosing, pilling, and potioning." To give his readers their shilling's worth, Fielding filled out the pamphlet by adding a pair of other satires on the College of Physicians: one takes the form of an "Advertisement" for the sale of a physician's library; the other, whose title recalls one of Fielding's favorite pieces of irony by Swift, is "A Project for the Advancement of Physic in this Island, by abolishing the Coll. &c."[230] According to this proposal, the College of Physicians would be disestablished in order to make room for a new and more catholic institution, namely, *"the Royal College of Empiricks."*

The happiness of his friend Harris, who on 8 July 1745 married Elizabeth Clarke, kept Fielding in this same facetious mood as the summer assizes drew near. From Boswell Court on Saturday, 13 July, he wrote to felicitate Harris on his nuptials – Harris and his bride having left Salisbury to begin their honeymoon at Southampton, where they were staying at the Star Inn. Playfully, Fielding salutes his friend as "My Dear Oroondates" – metamorphosing this prim scholar-gentleman of a bridegroom, now just short of his thirty-sixth year, into the hero of La Calprenède's romance, *Cassandre,* whose passion for his Statira made him the very type of romantic lover. So, in praising his Sophia, Tom Jones makes use of "Exclamations ... which would become the Mouth of *Oroondates* himself" (XVI.ix). Fielding offers to play a role himself in the tale. With a wink at his own large frame and hearty appetite, he declares:

> As you have no Giants in your Woods, I intend on thursday next you shall have a very large Counsellor at Law in them, a sort of Monsters whom I apprehend you fear more[;] however if you take Care to pacifie him with some Bacon and Beans and a Bottle of Southampton Port I hope he will do you no Harm.

It is, appropriately, the gayest letter Fielding wrote.

As he traveled on after visiting the Harrises in Southampton, making his summer's progress round the circuit – Winchester (23 July), Salisbury (27 July), Dorchester (1 August), Exeter (5 August), Bodmin (13

August), Wells (20 August), Bristol (24 August) – Fielding in his leisure moments no doubt also progressed in his writing of *Tom Jones*. Analysis of certain allusions and inconsistencies in the text of the novel as we now have it suggests that he had completed somewhat more than a third of his narrative before August of this year.[231] For that was the month when news reached the capital that Charles Edward Stuart, the "bonnie" Young Pretender, had landed in Scotland. The Jacobite uprising of the "Forty-Five" had begun. For months to come the crisis put a halt to such frivolous concerns as novel-writing. When he returned to his task, Fielding revised these early Books; the experience of the rebellion had altered his conception of the great work.

·····➤ xl ◄····

To understand Fielding's sudden reemergence as a political writer – a role he never relished and, except for anatomizing the Hanover rat, had eschewed since Walpole slipped from power almost four years ago – we need to sense the turbulent, uncertain climate of English affairs as autumn fell in 1745.[232] After their victory at Fontenoy in May, the French overran Flanders and entered the Netherlands without much resistance from the Dutch; Frederick of Prussia was again worrying Maria Theresa, Queen of Hungary and ruler of the Austrian empire, whose interest Britain was committed to protect; in Italy, the Genoese and Spanish armies were invading Lombardy. At home the effect of these continental troubles was compounded by the surprising early successes of the Young Pretender and his Highlanders, and by rumors of an imminent invasion of the French. As Fielding later reflected on these events it seemed that the nation was poised at "the very Brink of Ruin."[233]

But in September 1745 this was not how the situation appeared to his complacent countrymen, who at first disbelieved that Charles Edward Stuart had landed in the Western Isles and then, when they could no longer doubt the fact, belittled the danger he posed, supported only by seven retainers and the bands of ragged Highlanders who rallied to his standard. The King himself and his favorite Granville were so unconcerned they remained abroad in Hanover until the end of August, bent on pursuing continental wars. They suspected, indeed, that the anxious dispatches from home were deliberately exaggerated – that Granville's enemies in the ministry were inventing a spurious domestic crisis in order to discredit his pro-Hanoverian policies. Granville's enemies of course were Fielding's friends, who, having joined with the Pelhams and Lord Hardwicke to form a new government, had not yet established themselves in power. Henry Pelham and his brother the Duke of Newcastle saw that their hold was precarious and, should they lose the struggle with Granville, the whole fragile "Broad Bottom" accommodation would disintegrate. Hardwicke was especially alarmed that the monarch's disinclination to believe in the gravity of the Jacobite threat had infected the people with a perilous apathy. As late as 31 August he wrote Archbishop Herring: "There seems to be a certain indifference and deadness among many, and the spirit of the nation wants to be raised and animated to a right tone."[234]

After the rebels took Edinburgh (17 September) and routed General Cope's dragoons at Prestonpans (21 September), the danger they posed could no longer be doubted. It was time for a writer of Fielding's polemical talents to raise and animate the nation's spirit, as the Lord Chancellor put it. In so doing he would also serve his friends by stressing the potentially fatal consequences of Granville's policies.

Nothing so well attests to Fielding's zeal in behalf of this cause – and to his facility as an author – as the three anti-Jacobitical pamphlets that issued from his pen this October in less than a fortnight. The first of these, appearing anonymously on 3 October, was *A Serious Address to the People of Great Britain*, a hortatory tract calculated to impress on the public the pernicious consequences of a rebel victory and to rouse them to defend their Constitution and religion. Four days later, on 7 October, came *The History of the Present Rebellion in Scotland*, supposedly based on the experience of a certain Highlander, James Macpherson (entirely a figment of Fielding's imagination), who, having been among the first to rally to the Pretender's cause, had seen the error of his ways and defected after the battle of Prestonpans. A week later – certainly no later than 15 October and possibly as early as the 12th[235] – there also appeared *A Dialogue between the Devil, the Pope, and the Pretender*. Directed against the traditional unholy trinity of the Whig Establishment, this was the bluntest of satires, in which Old Nick, since he has the wit to distinguish between a mischievous plot that is feasible and one that is not, scoffs at his colleagues' "pretty trump'd-up Scheme" for subjugating so brave and freedom-loving a nation as England: "None of your wild Projects for me." Probably written in quick succession after news of the rebel successes at Edinburgh and Prestonpans reached the capital (*c.* 24–5 September), all three pamphlets were published under Mary Cooper's imprint, who, as the ledgers of the printer Strahan make clear, was working in cooperation with Fielding's principal bookseller, Andrew Millar.

In this flurry of propagandizing Fielding probably acted, at least in part, with the support and official encouragement of the government. The *Serious Address*, for instance, enjoyed an extraordinarily large first printing of 3,000 copies, and before the month was out Strahan had run off a second edition of 1,000. The demand for the piece is further attested by a pair of piracies as well. In contrast, the *History* and the *Dialogue* had printings of only 1,000 and 500 copies, respectively.

Fielding's correspondence with Harris supports the supposition that he was at this time in close touch with members of the government – especially with Hardwicke, who was anxious that the populace be stirred from its lethargy. On Saturday, 5 October, Fielding was in Essex House, near the Temple, enjoying the company of the distinguished Salisbury physician Dr. John Barker (1708–49).[236] The conversation having turned to their mutual friend Harris, to whom Barker owed a letter, Fielding undertook the obligation for him in his usual jocular way:

> Dr. Barker being obliged to write to you and having nothing to say desired me to take up the Pen in his Stead; and to confess the Truth I have as little, so that as you already know what will be the Contents of the following Lines, it is your own Fault if you read any farther.

But the lines that followed were not quite full of nothing. Fielding reports conversations he recently had both with General George Wade (1673–1748), long a friend of Ralph Allen and now Commander-in-Chief of the loyalist forces, and also with Hardwicke. Though he had concluded his *Serious Address* by urging his countrymen to "unite in Associations" of volunteers being hastily raised locally by subscription, he agreed with Wade, a man he greatly admired,[237] that these raw recruits would be ineffectual against the enemy: "I believe as Mr. Wade says we must trust to the Troops for the Extirpation of the Rebels, which I doubt not they will be able to perform: for he will have within ten Days no less than 16000 with him" – these having been summoned home from the continental wars. Moreover, he shared Hardwicke's optimism that, from the point of view of his friends in government, the dire events in Scotland would have the desirable effect of discrediting Granville's policies: "My Lord Chancellor and I are both of opinion," Fielding continues, that the success of the Young Pretender "will be of more Service than Disservice to the greater[?] Cause, by bringing My Cousin of Hungary to thoughts of Peace which she and Somebody else are very averse to with the K[ing] of Prussia tho I believe in the End he will prove our best Ally." What is revealing in these remarks is Fielding's presumption of an intimacy with the most exalted figures in the government. And when he refers to Maria Theresa as "My Cousin of Hungary," he is surely aware that his family's putative descent from the Hapsburgs gave a flattering point to his burlesque of the royal conventions of address. From the tone of all this – his way of sounding like someone well apprized of the private thoughts of generals and ministers – it appears he had been discussing with the ministry the part he might himself play, as author, in extirpating the rebels. Adding a few words of his own to this missive, Barker – though he omits mentioning Fielding's authorship of the pamphlet – informs Harris that early next week he may expect to have "a Compleat History of the Invasion ... taken from the Relation of one Mr. James Macpherson – Who escaped from the Pretender's Army." Significantly he adds: "We hear it will be publish'd by Authority ———."

If the rebellion was proving beneficial to Fielding by raising the value the government placed on his talents as a polemicist, it was having the opposite effect in the Royal Exchange, where stocks plummeted. Even so, Fielding was, for once, lucky: "wise and happy was it," he gloated, "that I sold out in time." How rare for Fielding, the role of the prudent and canny capitalist!

The day after writing this letter – in which he asked to be remembered to Harris's wife and his brother Thomas, a fellow lawyer of whom he was especially fond – Fielding planned to make another of his periodic trips to Winchester, no doubt on lawyer's business. The trip would take him within an easy journey of Harris; but for some reason (perhaps merely the notorious dampness of the place) the prospect of revisiting the city he knew so well was unappealing: "I ... would go the other 20 Miles any whither but to Salisbury to see you ... my dearest Friend."

He did not tarry in the country at this critical juncture. Parliament this year convened early, on Thursday, 17 October, and on the same day the company at Drury Lane staged another of Fielding's contributions to the war effort. Sensing that, however unpalatable the play's anti-papist humor had been in 1732, the public would now relish a second helping, the company revived *The Old Debauchees* – a much abridged version renamed *The Debauchees: or, The Jesuit Caught*. In this form it was performed as an afterpiece twenty-five times this season, often being paired with Cibber's *Nonjuror*. This same month Watts published a "second edition" of the play, indicating with inverted commas the considerable deletions in the acting version and proclaiming Fielding's authorship on the title-page in bold italic capitals.

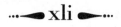

But Fielding's principal contribution to the nation's struggle against the rebels was the periodical he launched, with surprisingly little fanfare, on 5 November – Guy Fawkes Day, as it aptly happened, the anniversary of Britain's deliverance in 1605 from a Roman Catholic plot to blow up Parliament. Called *The True Patriot: and The History of Our Own Times*, the paper combined in its title allusions both to the ostensibly disinterested "patriotism" of his friends in government, and also to his favorite English historian, Gilbert Burnet, whose principles in politics and religion Fielding shared. Published every Tuesday at the comparatively dear price of threepence, *The True Patriot* was "undertaken on a new Plan," according to the single advertisement that heralded its appearance.[238] Besides the usual lead essay, the paper included a number of distinctive features: in a pair of complementary departments the "Present History" of Europe and Great Britain was summarized in lively narrative form, and readers were advised that these accounts would be more accurate than those in rival papers because of the author's privileged access to sources in the ministry; to emphasize the supposed authority of these histories, Fielding included a contrasting department of "APOCRYPHA. *Being a curious Collection of certain true and important* WE HEARS *from the News-papers*" – a section consisting of news items lifted from other journals, but seasoned here and there with his own sarcastic commentary. These witticisms, a distinctive feature of all Fielding's journalism, also served to enliven the dry lists of "Casualties," "Committed," "Preferred," "Married," "Dead."

Sending Harris a copy of the first issue on the day of publication, Fielding coyly declared that it was "written by a Friend of yours as well as mine in the Cause of your Country," for which good reasons he knew Harris would exert himself "to propagate" it. He added: "N.B. The News, which is not in the Apocrypha, will always be certainly true."

What might justify Fielding's claims that his paper enjoyed a privileged status compared with its rivals? *The True Patriot* was not an official organ of the ministry. That much is certain from his disgruntled complaint in No. 14 (28 January to 4 February 1745/6) that Henry Pelham the Prime Minister was contemptuous of such authors as himself: "Those who have the Honour to know him better than myself, assure me he hath the utmost Indifference for all Writers, and the greatest Contempt for any Good or Harm which they can do him." What is likely, however, is that the paper was sponsored by Fielding's friends in the "Broad Bottom" administration who, though allied with Pelham and the Old Corps in a common effort to exclude Granville from power, constituted a distinct faction within the ministry. In an arrangement probably similar to the sponsorship of *The Champion*, Fielding's friends appear to have established the paper through the agency of certain members of the trade who formed a partnership of shareholders. Most visible of these was Mary Cooper, under whose imprint the paper was published. But it is also clear from the pattern of advertisements and other notices in the paper that several other booksellers were concerned in the enterprise – among them Andrew

Millar, Robert Dodsley, George Woodfall, Ann Dodd, and Henry Chappelle.

As to the identity of his sponsors, Fielding provides clues in his introductory number, teasing readers who wonder who the author of *The True Patriot* may be:

> *First*, then, It is very probable I am Lord *B——ke*. This I collect from my Stile in Writing and Knowledge in Politics. Again it is as probable that I am the B——p of ****, from my Zeal for the Protestant Religion. When I consider these, together with the Wit and Humour which will diffuse themselves through the whole, it is more than possible I may be Lord *C——* himself, or at least he may have some Share in my Paper.
>
> From some, or all of these Reasons, I am very likely Mr. *W——n*, Mr. *D——n*, Mr. *L——n*, Mr. *F——g*, *T——n*, or indeed any other Person who hath ever distinguished himself in the Republic of Letters.
>
> This at least is very probable, that some of these Gentlemen may contribute a Share of their Abilities to the carrying on this Work.

The names Fielding here "emvowels" (to use the term he later coined for this practice of contemporary authors who thus prudently evaded the libel laws)[239] would have supplied the coffee-house politicians of the day with a transparent context for his paper. In order of occurrence, the names are as follows: Bolingbroke, the architect of the new "patriotism" which had defined the political ideology of Fielding and his patrons since the mid-1730s; Bishop Hoadly, of all contemporary divines the one Fielding most admired as defender both of the Hanoverian establishment and of a rational, Low Church theology; Chesterfield; Warburton, who, besides having become engaged to marry Ralph Allen's favorite niece, had recently fulminated against "the Present Unnatural Rebellion" in a sermon preached in Allen's chapel at Prior Park; Dodington; Lyttelton; Fielding himself; and James Thomson, who, since Pope's death, had no rival as the poet of the Patriot cause.

If Fielding had omitted the necessary qualification that any alleged candidate for the authorship of the paper must have "distinguished himself in the Republic of Letters," other names would surely have been added to this roll. Among these would be William Pitt, whose great "Abilities" Fielding extols in the leader for 24 December 1745, urging his inclusion in the Pelham administration from which he had been shut out; the Duke of Bedford, First Lord of the Admiralty, "whose Character," Fielding declares in the number for 7 January 1745/6 ("Present History"), "ought to be dear, nay even sacred, to every Englishman, as he certainly deserves every Honour his Country can bestow on it"; and of course Lord Chancellor Hardwicke, whom

Fielding, contemplating in his final number the judgment awaiting the defeated rebels, calls "that great and glorious Man, who is at the Head of our Law, and whose Goodness of Heart is no less conspicuous than those great Parts, which, both in the Character of a Statesman and a Lawyer, are at once the Honour and the Protection of his Country."

Of all these influential figures, however, Dodington is most likely to have taken the initiative in enlisting Fielding in a literary campaign to save the nation from the twin perils of the Pretender and Lord Granville. Not that he would be alone in backing such an enterprise: the usual procedure in establishing a political paper was to raise a subscription among members of a party in order to pay the author and insure the partnership of booksellers against possible loss. Others on Fielding's roll of "true patriots" had sponsored such journals in the past: Bolingbroke helped launch *The Craftsman* in 1726; Chesterfield and Lyttelton founded *Common Sense* in 1737. But it was a maxim in Dodington's system of practical politics that, to succeed, a party must have a paper of its own to promote its objectives. For this reason he later sponsored Ralph's *Remembrancer* (1747–51); and after the Prince of Wales's untimely death in 1751, Dodington proposed to establish a new political paper that would be funded by a subscription and, again, would be written by Ralph. There is, we have seen, reason to suppose that Dodington had been behind *The Champion*, in which Ralph, his favorite hackney ideologue, collaborated with Fielding. The case for Dodington's sponsorship of *The True Patriot* is strengthened, moreover, by the plausible hypothesis that when in late February and early March 1745/6 a sudden change became noticeable in the style and political content of the "History" departments of the paper, that change was owing to Fielding's having taken on Ralph as a collaborator.[240]

By his own admission Fielding was no more a politician than he was a poet – politics being, as he declared in *The Champion* (14 February 1739/40), "a Study beyond my Reach." He was seldom at his best writing on political matters in an earnest or hortatory vein. In the winter of 1745–6 – with the Jacobite "Banditti" penetrating into the heart of England and threatening the metropolis, while stocks plunged and rumors of a French invasion flew – the situation was grave enough to demand this most reluctant Muse of his. It was, moreover, a critical juncture for Dodington and his other friends in power, so precariously balanced in the places to which they had been raised a year before. In *The True Patriot* Fielding applied himself to promoting these two causes – the safety of the nation and the survival of the "Broad Bottom" ministry. As he insists in his second number, which defines the phrase he took for his title, a "true Patriot" in England at this hour was one who espoused *both* those causes. Having thus launched the paper by defining its goals and the character of its author, Fielding devoted his next few leaders to impressing on his readers the disastrous consequences of a Jacobite victory and to exposing those selfish and misguided attitudes in the public which left the nation vulnerable.

One of the most effective pieces in this vein was contributed by his friend Harris, whose "imaginary Journal" of Jacobite outrages comprises the lead essay of No. 10 (7 January 1745/6). Harris sent Fielding this essay, accompanied by the present of a chine of bacon, at a most opportune time – as "My Brother Tom" (so Fielding affectionately called Thomas Harris, who had recently returned to Salisbury) would have informed him. Writing from Boswell Court on 2 January to thank Harris for his wit and his bacon, Fielding complains that he has been "imprisoned a Month" with the gout "and am not yet able to stand." He assures his friend he would have acknowledged his kindness by an earlier post, "but was prevented by the Company of some Ladies of your Acquaintance" – company including, no doubt, his sister Sarah and perhaps Margaret and Jane Collier.

Having made some slight revisions to Harris's piece, Fielding published it a week earlier than planned, as he explained in a letter from Boswell Court on Saturday, 11 January – the day on which the editor of the *General Advertiser* did them the favor of reprinting it:

> The Town, I assure you, hath received your Wit with the Applause it deserves; however you may despise their Approbation, I know you will be pleased with it when you hear, that it hath had the consequence of serving me much by raising the Sale of the Paper. A News Writer, you see, hath transcribed it, which is the first Honour of that Kind conferred on me, and this merely on his own Motion without the least Application from myself.

He concludes:

> I set out to-Morrow for Winchester, tho I can not yet stand alone. Farewell, I am prevented from saying more by the Company of the Woman in the world whom I like best.

Apparently Fielding was trying not to allow either the torments of the gout or his editorial duties on *The True Patriot* to curtail his professional activities. As we will see, the journeys he regularly made into Hampshire on business proved a useful credential in qualifying him for a place his friends in government would soon bestow on him. And what of that final tantalizing sentence? He could trust Harris to know the woman he meant without naming her: Sarah had taken Charlotte's place in his affections.

Such glimpses into Fielding's personal life as the Harris correspondence affords make clear that politics and the rebellion were not the only topics on Fielding's mind as he continued conducting *The True*

Patriot. His anxious involvement with Harris in Dr. Collier's ruinous financial affairs no doubt inspired the angry leader in No. 5 (3 December 1745), one of the strongest of Fielding's many attacks on the practice of imprisonment for debt. Similarly, his satire against the Directors of the Italian Opera in No. 9 (31 December 1745) – scorning them not only for their wanton extravagance but, considering the gravity of the national crisis, for "the most depraved Levity of Mind" – is best understood in the context of Fielding's professional activities in behalf of Hanbury Williams, one of the harassed subscribers to the Opera. This was a frequent topic in the journal and one he broached in the second of two letters contributed by a certain Dorsetshire parson whom the biblical wickedness of the times had summoned from the pages of *Joseph Andrews* – namely, "Abraham Adams."[241] It is Adams in this same letter who calls attention to another of Fielding's friends: this is John Dalton (1709–63), poet and philandering divine, whose monitory sermons "on the Subject of educating Youth, lately preached ... at the University of *Oxford*" Adams warmly recommends.[242]

Among the personal matters which find expression in this paper chiefly devoted to momentous public concerns, perhaps none touched Fielding more deeply than the death of Swift, a man he never met as far as we know, but whose works he admired and delighted in more than those of any other contemporary author. Swift, indeed, influenced Fielding in forming his own ironic style and his sense of the uses of ridicule. In the introductory number of *The True Patriot* (5 November 1745) he paid his great mentor this tribute:

A few Days since [on 19 October] died in Ireland, Dr. Jonathan Swift, Dean of St. Patrick's in Dublin. A Genius who deserves to be ranked among the first whom the World ever saw. He possessed the Talents of a Lucian, a Rabelais, and a Cervantes, and in his Works exceeded them all. He employed his Wit to the noblest Purposes, in ridiculing as well Superstition in Religion as Infidelity, and the several Errors and Immoralities which sprung up from time to time in his Age; and lastly, in the Defence of his Country, against several pernicious Schemes of wicked Politicians. Nor was he only a Genius and a Patriot; he was in private Life a good and charitable Man, and frequently lent Sums of Money without Interest to the Poor and Industrious; by which means many Families were preserved from Destruction. The Loss of so excellent a Person would have been more to be lamented, had not a Disease that affected his Understanding, long since deprived him of the Enjoyment of Life, and his Country of the Benefit of his great Talents; But we hope this short and hasty Character will not be the last Piece of Gratitude paid by his Cotemporaries to such eminent Merit.

In February welcome changes occurring both in the course of the rebellion and in the political scene were reflected in a perceptible change in attitude and editorial policy in *The True Patriot*. The national crisis having passed, Pelham and the other members of the "Broad Bottom" ministry who felt the King's disfavor decided to take a bold gamble; they would bow to the King's wishes and withdraw, allowing him to form – if he could – a new government under the direction of his favorites, Granville and Bath. On Monday, 10 February, they began to resign *en masse*. The King at once appointed Granville Secretary of State and Bath First Lord of the Treasury. He could not, however, persuade anyone of comparable ability to join them, and control of Parliament remained in the hands of their adversaries. By 14 February, "the forty-eight-hour ministry" had guttered and gone out; Pelham and the "Broad Bottoms" were back in place, this time bringing with them the King's hated gadfly, William Pitt. The gamble had succeeded beyond expectation. Fielding's friends were triumphant and, for the first time, secure.

The Lords Granville and Bath – formerly Carteret and Pulteney, leaders of the Opposition to Walpole – had risen to the Great Man's eminence and come bumping ignominiously down in less than the interval between numbers of *The True Patriot*. At the first opportunity (No. 16, 11–18 February 1745/6) Fielding ridiculed the two mock-heroes in one of his most hilarious satires – its subject "the Instability of Human Greatness." How apt the discomfited Grizzle's lament, which he quotes from his own *Tragedy of Tragedies* (I.iv):

> *Greatness* (says a Burlesque Writer) *is a lac'd Coat*
> *from Monmouth Street,*
> *Which Fortune lends us for a Day to wear;*
> *To-morrow puts it on another's Back.*

Disputing Theobald's edition of *Macbeth*, he restores the "true Reading" of a famous passage in which Shakespeare anticipated the fates of Granville and Bath:

> *And all our Yesterdays have lifted Tools*
> *The Way to dusty Death. Out, out, brief Cabal.*

Better still, since their little drama was more farce than tragedy, he equates them with the usurping Physician and Gentleman Usher in Buckingham's *Rehearsal*, and with "that fine Raillery upon Greatness of Punchinello in a Puppet-shew."

The following week (No. 17, 18–25 February 1745/6), in what proved to be his last contribution to the department called "The Present History of Great Britain," he celebrated his party's triumph in a less facetious manner:

But the most satisfactory Contemplation is, that the Administration of Affairs is now in the Hands of Men who have given such Proofs of their Integrity, that have at once convinced us we are free Men, and may depend on being so under their Protection. It is indeed the rare Blessing of the Public, in the present Age, to be convinced that their Friends are in Power; that the greatest Men in the Kingdom are at the same time the honestest; that the very Person to whose Councils it is to be attributed, that the Pretender hath not been long since in Possession of this City, is at the Head of the Ministry; and that the greatest Enemies of the People are disabled from any longer hurting or oppressing them. Indeed it is now known in our Streets, to whom we owe the Preservation of this Kingdom, by the timely bringing our Troops from Flanders, and who they were who opposed and delayed that Measure.

It is now therefore, that Opposition is really and truly Faction; that the Names of a Patriot and Courtier are not only compatible, but necessarily conjoined; and that none can be any longer Enemies to the Ministry, without being so to the Public.

The last sentiment, now that Pelham and his friends were in power, would color Fielding's political writing in the future: those who opposed this best of all possible ministries he would represent as Jacobites or republicans or plain fools. His enemies reminded him that in *Pasquin* and *The Champion* he played a different tune. But the fact is that since 1734 (with the single aberration of *The Opposition: A Vision*) he had remained steady in his loyalty to his friends – Chesterfield, Lyttelton, Dodington – and to the principles of "true patriotism" they espoused.

That he felt the crisis in the country and at Court had passed is clear from his decision no longer to exercise complete control over the editorial content of *The True Patriot*, but to share those chores with a collaborator. With No. 18 (25 February to 4 March 1745/6) a new voice is heard in those secondary departments of the paper treating foreign and domestic "History" – a voice speaking earnestly and with authority on every topic of contemporary politics and recommending in a more methodical way the Bolingbrokean program of "patriotism." It is a voice sounding very like James Ralph's. Fielding no doubt welcomed the chance to give more of his attention to his profession, but he continued to contribute most of the lead essays. In No. 26 (22–9 April 1746) news of the rebels' defeat at Culloden on 16 April moved him – with gratitude to "GOD, the Deliverer of Nations" and to "those glorious Men whom it hath pleased him to make the Instruments of our Preservation!" – to rehearse eloquently the remarkable story of the nation's escape "from the very Brink of Ruin, to a State of present Safety, and to the fairest Prospect of future Felicity." A week later

(No. 27, 29 April to 6 May 1746) he continued in this grateful vein, offering up a "little Salver of Incense" to King George and the Royal family, but reserving special praise for the Duke of Cumberland, victor of Culloden, whose courage at that bloody battle he contrasts with the cowardice of the Young Pretender. "In short," Fielding declares, "as we should certainly have been one of the first in the String of Loyalists, who would have had the Honour of being hanged had the Rebellion succeeded, we shall at least be allowed some Place among those who triumph in its Defeat."

Its purposes achieved, *The True Patriot* ceased publication with No. 33 (17 June 1746) – no copy of which has survived. For the "*Substance*" of Fielding's "Farewel *to his* Readers" we must rely on the *London Magazine*.[243] His intention in undertaking the paper had been "to alarm my Fellow Subjects with the Dangers which that Rebellion threatned to their Religion and Liberties, indeed to every Thing valuable which they possessed." He takes satisfaction from the knowledge that he has thus "discharged my Duty" as an Englishman and a loyal subject of the King, and that he has done so with humanity – by urging tolerance toward those Roman Catholics and Scotsmen who remained loyal, and by recommending even the rebels themselves to the Lord Chancellor's mercy: "whoever knows me at all, must know that Cruelty is most foreign to my Disposition." These reflections, however, were cold comfort. He regretted that by keeping so moderate a temper in his paper, he had not recommended himself to the party whose interests he served; instead he had earned only the obloquy of their enemies: "I shall now retire with the secret Satisfaction which attends right Actions, tho' they fail of any great Reward from the one, and are prosecuted with Curses and Vengeance from the other."

It is hard to blame Fielding for thinking that talents such as his ought to be handsomely paid for; few of us, from refuse collectors to corporate directors, are inclined to undervalue the services we render. It is not true, however – as most who read Fielding's farewell have supposed – that his friends utterly neglected him. His reward was not "great," but it was real enough. Ambitious, as he later put it,[244] "of serving in an Office immediately under the Duke of Bedford" (who this year was appointed Warden of the New Forest), Fielding had successfully solicited him for the place of High Steward of the New Forest and of the Manor of Lyndhurst, Hants. The patent by which Bedford conferred this office on Fielding is dated 14 April 1746, two days before Culloden.[245] Fielding considered that "the Profits incident to it" were "small" (his stipend was £5 a year)[246] and it was by no means a sinecure: he was responsible for the prosecution of those who illegally despoiled the King's preserves of game and timber. (Hence when referring in *Tom Jones* [V.xi] to "the well-wooded Forest of

Hampshire," Fielding archly comments: "This is an ambiguous Phrase, and may mean either a Forest well clothed with Wood, or well stript of it.") But in practice the work would not have been very onerous, for the patent allowed him to appoint an "under Steward" to attend to the ordinary business of the office. As his deputy, Fielding chose the attorney Richard Birt of Lymington, Hants. (d. 1766),[247] a friend who had subscribed to the *Miscellanies*, and who is probably the Lymington lawyer complimented in *Tom Jones* (XVIII.vi) when Partridge, having spent three years in his service, characterizes him as "a very good Sort of a Man, and to be sure one of the merriest Gentlemen in *England*." However inconsiderable the High Stewardship of the New Forest now seemed to Fielding, when the time came for him to resign the office for a place far more exacting if more lucrative, he did so "with some Concern and Reluctance."

···➤ xlii ◂─···

From the time he bade farewell to readers of *The True Patriot* (17 June 1746) until mid-autumn there are few clues as to Fielding's activities or whereabouts. Owing to the trials of the Jacobite lords, held in Westminster Hall in July, Parliament was not prorogued until the late date of 12 August – the day before Fielding, on behalf of Hanbury Williams, answered the complaint of the Directors of the Italian Opera. On Monday the 18th he seems to have attended at Tower Hill, where, on "the Tragic Scaffold ... strewed with Saw-Dust," the Earl of Kilmarnock and Lord Balmerino were beheaded as the polite spectators flirted and laid wagers whether the condemned would die well.[248] By that time the assizes on the Western Circuit had been in progress for a fortnight, though they were not concluded until 6 September at Bristol.[249] After attending to Hanbury Williams's legal affairs, Fielding may have gone to Hampshire to discharge his duties as High Steward of the New Forest. There is also reason to suppose that in September he returned as usual to Bath.

The rebellion having interrupted his progress on *Tom Jones*, he now resumed the narrative on a new plan. Originally he had turned his errant hero out of "Paradise Hall" in mid-July of an unspecified year – with Jones, for want of anything better to do, resolving to go to sea. Now Fielding gave a topical turn to his story, setting it in what he regarded as the most critical moment of England's recent history: the "Forty-Five." When Jones encounters a company of soldiers near Bristol, we find that instead of summer weather he shivers in the cold of late November; for these soldiers are marching north to join the

Duke of Cumberland's forces against the Jacobites. To disguise this awkwardness in his time scheme, Fielding offers a coy apology:

> the Reader may perceive (a Circumstance which we have not thought necessary to communicate before) that this was the very Time when the late Rebellion was at the highest; and indeed the Banditti were now marched into *England*, intending, as it was thought, to fight the King's Forces, and to attempt pushing forward to the Metropolis.
>
> (VII.xi)

It now occurs to Jones, who has not considered the possibility before even though the rebellion has been in progress for months, that he might do something more useful with his life than to go seafaring. He enlists in the company as a volunteer; for, Fielding explains, he "had some Heroic Ingredients in his Composition, and was a hearty Well-wisher to the glorious Cause of Liberty, and of the Protestant Religion."

According to Richard Graves (1715–1804), who as rector of Claverton resided near Bath from 1750 to the end of his life and was acquainted with both Ralph Allen and Sarah Fielding, Fielding lived at Twerton and "dined almost daily" at Prior Park while he was writing *Tom Jones*. The notion is false, of course, that Fielding ever made Bath his home; and except for his letters to Harris in the autumn of 1743, we have no evidence that during his visits there he lived at Twerton. Another tradition, recorded by the historian of Bath, has it that when he visited the city, he sometimes stayed with his sister in a cottage called "Widcombe Lodge" in Church Lane, and sometimes stayed nearby with Philip Bennet (d. 1761), the Lord of the Manor, in the splendid Palladian mansion called "Widcombe House." Allen's brother-in-law and neighbor, Bennet, it is said, kept up "a considerable correspondence" with Fielding and (like most of those with whom Fielding engaged in the "irksome" business of writing letters) lent him money from time to time.[250] Wherever Fielding may have lodged during his sojourns there, it is certain that throughout the 1740s he regularly spent much of the late summer in Bath – partly because he believed the waters salutary, and partly because he enjoyed the glitter and society of the place. During these visits he saw as much as possible of his benefactor and friend Ralph Allen – the man who, together with George Lyttelton, served as his model for Squire Allworthy. Without doubt many chapters of *Tom Jones* were written at Bath, and in that novel Fielding is profuse in his praise of Allen, his hospitality, and his house.[251]

It is likely that Fielding was in Bath this September when news broke of a scandal that came to light at Glastonbury, his birthplace. There on 13 September, Mary Hamilton – lesbian and transvestite – was arrested for having duped a young woman of Wells and married

her. Posing as a physician and calling herself Dr. Charles Hamilton,
Mary successfully carried off this deception for two months before the
horrified bride discovered the truth. Though his uncle Davidge Gould
must have been apprized of every detail of this sensational affair, and
though his cousin Henry Gould was employed by the Corporation of
Glastonbury to advise the prosecution, Fielding appears to have known
the case only through reading accounts of it in Thomas Boddley's *Bath
Journal* beginning Monday, 22 September. [252] Leaving Bath for London
later that week, he missed Boddley's second report, but read the third
and final article as reprinted in the *Daily Advertiser* (7 November),
where he found that Mary Hamilton called herself George as well as
Charles, and that his cousin acted as "Council for the King."

In this case of unnatural sexuality Fielding found the hint for the
shoddiest work of fiction he ever wrote. Fiction it is, for despite the
claim of authenticity on the title-page, the story is almost wholly the
product of the darker fancies of his imagination. Published by Mary
Cooper on 12 November, this anonymous sixpenny pamphlet is entitled:

> *The Female Husband: or, The Surprising History of Mrs. Mary, alias
> Mr. George Hamilton, Who was convicted of having married a Young
> Woman of Wells and lived with her as her Husband. Taken from her
> own Mouth since her Confinement.*

For an epigraph, Fielding chose a passage from Ovid's *Metamorphoses*
(XII.168–70), the story of Caenis, who, having been ravished by
Neptune, implores the god to change her into a man so that she can
never again suffer the same violation. His tone in the narrative itself
alternates unpleasantly between the homiletic and the lewd.

Besides the few guineas he might expect from it,[253] what can have
prompted Fielding to turn the simple fact of Mary Hamilton's perversion into so elaborate a fantasy? As an instance (literally close to
home) of the power of lust to degrade human nature, it clearly held for
him an irresistible, yet disturbing, fascination. His own sexual appetites
were sufficiently ungovernable to have led him in his youth to incestuous
experimentation, and after his wife's death he would commit (as the
gentleman he believed himself to be) the humiliating impropriety of
seducing his servant. The opening paragraphs of *The Female Husband* –
with their curious anticipation of a theme he was then developing in a
light-hearted manner in his masterpiece – invite such speculation. The
passions, Fielding writes, are innocent enough "when govern'd and
directed by virtue and religion":

> But if once our carnal appetites are let loose, without those prudent
> and secure guides, there is no excess and disorder which they are not
> liable to commit, even while they pursue their natural satisfaction;

and, which may seem still more strange, there is nothing monstrous and unnatural, which they are not capable of inventing, nothing so brutal and shocking which they have not actually committed.

What were Sarah's thoughts as, sharing the house at Boswell Court with her brother and Mary Daniel, she read these lines in manuscript – Sarah, who, as Fielding observed in his Preface to *David Simple*, saw so deeply into "all the Mazes, Windings and Labyrinths, which perplex the Heart of Man"? What, for that matter, were her thoughts later this winter as she presumably also read in manuscript her brother's next publication – his prose paraphrase of Ovid's *Ars Amatoria*, Book I, where in a long catalogue of lewd women she would find such examples as that of Byblis, "who being in love with her Brother, punished her Crime with her own Hands, and hanged herself in her Garters," and Pasiphae, who "conceived a Passion worse, if possible, that that of Mrs. *Mary Hamilton*, for [a] Bull." "All these," Fielding's version reads, "have been the Effects of Womens raging Desires, which are so much more violent and mad than ours." During this winter of 1746–7 only two literary projects of his own interrupted Fielding's progress with his masterpiece: *The Female Husband* and his paraphrase, *Ovid's Art of Love*. By modern example and classical authority they attest to an intense, if temporary, fascination with subjects illustrating the rawest sexuality, most especially the sexuality of women, of a kind perverse and degrading. Three months separate the publication of these two works, which represent thematically a remarkable aberration even in the eccentric course of Fielding's literary career.

The only certain glimpse we have of Henry and Sarah together at Boswell Court we owe to the young Joseph Warton (1722–1800), and it is of a scene refreshingly wholesome and cheerful. Fielding had probably known Joseph's father, Thomas Warton (c. 1688–1745), for many years, since the elder Warton had left Oxford, where he was professor of poetry, to become Vicar of Basingstoke, Hants. He remained there, not far from Upton Grey, from 1723 until his death in September 1745. Joseph Warton, after attending Oriel College, Oxford, took holy orders in 1744 and that same year published the poem for which he is best remembered, *The Enthusiast: or, The Lover of Nature* – one of the better examples of the so-called "New Poetry" of the 1740s, most of which are experiments in the freer forms Fielding preferred to rhyme. Now in his twenty-fourth year, Joseph Warton had returned to Basingstoke after a brief tenure as curate in Chelsea. Before leaving town, he and a friend passed two entertaining evenings with the Fieldings – evenings he was eager to share with his younger brother Thomas (1728–90) in a letter written from Basingstoke on 29 October 1746, a Wednesday:

I wish you had been with me last week, when I spent two evenings with Fielding and his sister, who wrote David Simple, and you may guess I was very well entertained. The lady indeed retir'd pretty soon, but Russell and I sat up with the Poet till one or two in the morning, and were inexpressibly diverted. I find he values, as he justly may, his Joseph Andrews above all his writings: he was extremely civil to me, I fancy, on my Father's account.[254]

Long after Fielding's death the *Gentleman's Magazine*[255] printed a story about him which – if there is truth in it at all – allows us one other rare and entertaining glimpse of the time when Sarah was mistress of the household at Boswell Court. Short of money to pay the taxes on the house, Fielding, the story goes, went to his bookseller for an advance of a few guineas on a work he was writing. Before he got home with the money, he met an old schoolfellow he had not seen for some time, and in an access of conviviality, invited him to supper in a nearby tavern. As they talked into the night and drained their bottles of wine, he found his friend had no money – whereupon he cheerfully gave him what was left of the advance and rolled home shortly before daybreak. When Sarah reproached him for forgetting the mission she had sent him on, saying that the collector had called twice for the taxes that day, Fielding answered: "Friendship has called for the money, and had it; – let the collector call again." A second trip to the bookseller raised enough cash to pay the taxes. This is how some of Fielding's contemporaries remembered him – a man sociable, liberal, and improvident to a fault. In embellishing his story, the author of the anecdote does not inspire confidence, as he gets every name wrong: he calls Fielding's sister "Amelia," places the house in Beaufort Buildings (where Sarah lived later on her own),[256] and makes Jacob Tonson serve as the bookseller in question. But some legends ought to be true, and this one squares so well with what we know of Fielding's character it deserves keeping.

⋯⧫ xliii ◀⋯

Early in the New Year, Fielding attended to a variety of literary projects. *Tom Jones* no doubt continued gradually taking shape. On 25 February 1746/7 *Ovid's Art of Love Paraphrased, and Adapted to the Present Time* appeared anonymously, published by Mary Cooper, Ann Dodd, and George Woodfall. In the Preface Fielding states that what prompted him to resume this work, which he began "many Years ago," was "that Passage so justly applicable to the Glorious Duke of

CUMBERLAND," where in a fulsome panegyric he predicts that "the *British* Hero," recently appointed commander-in-chief of the allied forces, would vanquish the French in the coming campaign. He also disingenuously protests that "the Objection of Impurity" cannot fairly be made against the work, in which "there is nothing capable of offending the nicest Ear." He hints, moreover, that this "new Undertaking ... might perhaps, if properly encouraged, be carried on with other *Latin* Poets"; but if he hoped his Ovid would launch a profitable series of the classics Englished in prose, he was disappointed.

About this time he was assisting Sarah in a more decorous work entirely, her *Familiar Letters between the Principal Characters in David Simple*. Following her brother's example in the lucrative publication of the *Miscellanies*, Sarah arranged to have Millar act as her agent in issuing the work by subscription. Projected apparently before the Jacobite rebellion, it was well advanced by February 1745/6, when she explained to the subscribers that, owing to the national crisis, she was obliged to defer publication: "her Friends were totally prevented by the late Public Confusion, to favour her with their Interest, as they kindly intended; nor could she herself think it decent to sollicit a private Subscription, in a Time of such Public Danger."[257] They could, however, expect delivery of the book "in *January* next." In January, as it happened, the *Familiar Letters* had only begun to make its way through the press;[258] it was not published until 10 April 1747, when it appeared in a pair of handsome volumes. Sarah had found it difficult to draw out her story to a length sufficient to fill the two volumes her subscribers had paid for – and they had rallied splendidly to her appeal, signing on in their hundreds. She called on James Harris to contribute a couple of light satirical dialogues called "Much Ado" and "Fashion";[259] and she clapped on to the end of the work "A Vision," a moral allegory depicting the deceitful ways that lead to Wealth, Power, Pleasure, and Virtue.

She also enlisted her brother to contribute a Preface and five ill-assorted letters (Nos. XL–XLIV). In a note introducing the latter, she left no doubt as to Fielding's authorship of these pieces:

> I should have thought this Hint unnecessary, had not much Nonsense and Scurrility been unjustly imputed to him by the *Good-Judgement* or *Good-nature* of the Age. They can know but little of his Writings, who want to have them pointed out; but they know much less of him, who impute any such base and scandalous Productions to his Pen.

If this was anything more than an echo of Fielding's earlier complaint in the Preface to *David Simple*, the "base and scandalous Productions" being maliciously fathered upon him have not been identified.

As a demonstration of Fielding's powers as a critic and theorist of
the novel, the Preface to the *Familiar Letters* ranks just below the more
famous one to *Joseph Andrews*. The interest the Preface holds for
his biographer, moreover, is no less great; for Fielding's methodical
anatomy of "The Taste of the Public, with regard to Epistolary Writing
... much vitiated by some modern Authors," is colored by his awareness
of the rivalry now rapidly developing between himself and Richardson –
a rivalry not only for preeminence in the opinion of the critics, but for
his sister's loyalty. Though Fielding earlier claimed *David Simple* for
the genre of the comic prose epic which he founded in *Joseph Andrews*,
in her sequel Sarah took Richardson as her model, emulating him in
the fact itself of writing a sequel to the novel (as Richardson had done
in his continuation of *Pamela*), but more importantly, adopting the
epistolary form which he had made an effective vehicle for fiction.
Sarah probably became acquainted with Richardson sometime in 1744
or 1745, when he had already written a substantial part of his masterpiece, *Clarissa*;[260] the compliment she paid him by imitation he returned
by subscribing to her new novel. That Fielding winced at what
amounted to his sister's public repudiation of the kind of narrative art
he stood for is plain from the defensive attitude he takes in analyzing
the nature of the epistolary form and in rejecting it as suitable for
fiction. Ovid is his standard for this style, which, he insists, should be
"the Style of Conversation" – one by no means "adapted to the Novel
or Story-Writer; for what difference is there, whether a Tale is related
this or any other way? And sure no one will contend, that the epistolary
Style is in general the most proper to a Novelist, or that it hath been
used by the best Writers of this Kind." As a model for this kind of
writing he recommends the *Persian Letters* of Lyttelton – "one, who is
a Master of Style, as of every other Excellence." Richardson is not once
mentioned in all this, but there is no doubt he was in Fielding's eye as
he wrote it.

However injured his pride might be by Sarah's temporary defection
to the enemy, Fielding praised her novel warmly, especially commending his sister's genius at perceiving "the nicest and most delicate
Touches of Nature" – a genius comparable to those of Cervantes and
Hogarth. Some of these letters he declares to be "as fine, as I have ever
met with in any of the Authors, who have made Human Nature their
Subject." Those who measure Fielding's attitude toward women by the
ethos of twentieth-century feminism and find him wanting (as they
must do most writers of the Christian humanist tradition he inherited)
should attend to this Preface, which he concludes by invoking the
authority of (quite probably) his brilliant cousin Lady Mary Wortley
Montagu:

The Objection to the Sex of the Author hardly requires an Answer:
It will be chiefly advanced by those, who derive their Opinion of
Women very unfairly from the fine Ladies of the Age; whereas, if
the Behaviour of their Counterparts the Beaus, was to denote the
Understanding of Men, I apprehend the Conclusion would be in
favour of the Women, without making a Compliment to that Sex. I
can of my own Knowledge, and from my own Acquaintance bear
Testimony to the Possibility of those Examples, which History gives
of Women eminent for the highest Endowments and Faculties of the
Mind. I shall only add an Answer to the same Objection, relating to
David Simple, given by a Lady of a very high Rank, whose Quality
is however less an Honour to her than her Understanding. *So far,*
said she, *from doubting David Simple to be the Performance of a
Woman, I am well convinced, it could not have been written by a Man.*

Which is not to say, however, that Fielding was inclined to confuse the
proper characters of men and women as these had been historically
defined. In Sarah's *Familiar Letters*, he concluded, those who read
attentively would learn "that the Consummation of a Woman's Character, is to maintain the Qualities of Goodness, Tenderness, Affection and
Sincerity, in the several social Offices and Duties of Life."

As for the five letters, which Fielding must have dashed off even as the
first volume was committed to the press,[261] these consist of Valentine's
remarks on contemporary politics and taste (No. XL); a Frenchman's
travelogue on places of interest along the Thames (No. XLI); an
exchange between Miss Prudentia Flutter and Miss Lucy Rural, the
one spoiled by vanities of the town, the other sensibly preferring the
simple pleasures of the country (Nos. XLII and XLIII); and, what
must have been a refreshing change of theme to Sarah after her
brother's recent preoccupation with less edifying aspects of sexual
relations, Valentine's letter to his wife commending romantic love, true
and chaste, as the greatest happiness this world affords (No. XLIV). Of
these five letters only the first allows much insight into Fielding's
attitudes and friendships early in 1747 (though in a passage in Letter
XLI he manages to flatter a trio of noble patrons, including the Duke
of Richmond). Valentine tempers his general complaint about the
mismanagement of the theatres by praising Garrick at Covent Garden,
"one who never had, nor, I believe, ever will have an Equal," and at
Drury Lane "the vast Genius of Mrs. *Clive* (inimitable in all Humour)."
More extravagant still, however – and more significant for what it
reveals of the political sympathies that will inform all Fielding's published writing for the next two years – is Valentine's rhapsody on the
present ministry: "The Administration of our public Affairs is, in my
opinion, at present in the Hands of the very Men, whom you, and every

honest Person would wish to be intrusted with it." As he makes clear, in politics Fielding's hero of the moment was Chesterfield, who became Secretary of State for the Northern Department in October 1746. But it is also clear that, whatever reward he might enjoy in the future, his friends in power were not now supporting him according to his expectations: "I think I may affirm with Truth," Valentine declares, "that there is no one Patron of true Genius, nor the least Encouragement for it in this Kingdom." What Fielding felt most sharply this winter was "The cold Air of Neglect."

That he continued short of money is evident from the turn his correspondence with Harris had recently taken. It is a tribute to the closeness of their relationship – and most especially to Harris's ability to see past Fielding's annoying habitual impecuniousness to his better qualities – that the friendship remained firm despite the demands Fielding now began regularly to make on Harris's generosity. Since 1738, when his uncle George died leaving him a bequest that now – with Charlotte's portion and those of other beneficiaries added to his own – would bring him exchequer annuities worth more than £120, Fielding had hoped he would soon be better off. But, after nearly nine years, the will was still being contested in the courts.[262] Needing cash to pay his debts, he was trying to sell his interest in the bequest: "I think the Devil," he assured Harris in a letter from Boswell Court of 19 February 1746/7, "can not prolong that Affair much more."

These assurances were necessary because Harris, who had recently lent Fielding £100, would wish to know why he should "dare venture fifty Pounds more on the same bad Bottom." That begging money of his acquaintance did not come easily to this proud man, however frequently he sank to it, is plain from the extraordinary tone of the request, at once wheedling and arrogant:

> If this be either inconvenient or disagreeable to you, if you have not the Sum at present in your Command, or if you have any other use for it, or it will give you Pleasure to retain it tho you have no Use for it; in any of these Cases, I must insist on your granting me the Favour to burn this Letter without answering it, or ever mentioning it to me at our Meeting.
> Be assured there is no Sum of Money in my Estimation equal to your Friendship. Make therefore no ill Interpretation of my Asking.

With all his command of rhetoric Fielding struggled to make Harris understand that he was his "dear Friend" first and only incidentally a plentiful and patient source of money.

...➤ xliv ➤...

Fielding would never have enough money, no matter how much he had. But in June of this year there were heartening signs that patrons more powerful than Harris had not forgotten him. He was already ambitious, it appears, of supplying the place in the metropolitan magistracy left vacant by the death of Sir Thomas DeVeil (c.1684–1746), who had served for fifteen years as "Court Justice." Generations of "trading justices" had brought the office into contempt, but from the government's point of view it was essential to the preservation of both the public order and the present Establishment. Having demonstrated his loyalty and usefulness during the "Forty-Five," Fielding would be an attractive candidate to fill this vacancy. On 20 June 1747, therefore, his name was entered in the Commission of the Peace for the County of Middlesex.[263] This, unluckily, was a blunder. In order that he function as "Court Justice" efficiently (and with profit to himself), he needed two commissions: one for the City and Liberty of Westminster, the other for the County of Middlesex. But Fielding could not qualify for the latter commission because he did not possess property worth £100 clear value.[264] As we know because Fielding had to account for this muddle more than a year later, the person responsible for it was one of his oldest and greatest patrons, whose praises he had recently sung in the *Familiar Letters*: he was, he explained, "by a Mistake put into [the Middlesex commission] by my Lord Chesterfield's Instance."[265] Might it be that Chesterfield's unwillingness to correct this mistake, by enabling Fielding to satisfy the property qualification for the Middlesex commission, accounts for the puzzling fact that after the compliment in the *Familiar Letters* Fielding conspicuously ignored Chesterfield in all his subsequent works?

It is unlikely that mere coincidence accounts for Fielding's again taking up his pen for the government at the very time when the Secretary of State was recommending him to the Lord Chancellor for appointment to the magistracy. In January a new Opposition had begun to form under the aegis of the Prince of Wales, and, as always, there were public grievances enough for it to feed on. Taxes remained high as the continental wars dragged cheerlessly on. In April under the leadership of Hardwicke the ministry introduced in Parliament a controversial measure calculated to curtail the power of the great feudal families of Scotland: this was a Bill to abolish "the hereditable Jurisdictions" in Scotland – an anomaly in the legal system by which the right to administer justice (and therefore the opportunity to bend the populace to their will) rested with the lords of the clans rather than with the Crown. Those who supported the Bill – Lyttelton among the most ardent of them – found it convenient to label those who opposed it as Jacobites, but they were not without good reasons for believing that the ghost of the "Forty-Five" had not yet been laid. In March and April the public was enthralled by the trial and execution of the most inveterate of the Jacobite lords, Simon Fraser, Baron Lovat, while on a plane less sublime the "Independent Electors of Westminster," a Tory faction, made news when at their annual feast they recreated themselves by drinking treasonable toasts and severely beating a man they took to be an informer. Lyttelton figured prominently in both these events: as one of the managers of the proceedings against Lovat, he was appointed to the committee formed to investigate the alleged Jacobitism of the "Independent Electors."

In this highly charged atmosphere the ministry thought it prudent to steal a march on the Opposition by calling a general election a year earlier than required by law under the Septennial Act. The Prince of Wales's party, they reasoned, was as yet disorganized and ill supported. For this purpose Parliament was dissolved on 18 June. Five days later there appeared under Mary Cooper's imprint an anonymous electioneering pamphlet entitled:

A Dialogue between a Gentleman of London, Agent for two Court Candidates, and an Honest Alderman of the Country Party. Wherein the Grievances under which the Nation at present groans are fairly and impartially laid open and considered. Earnestly address'd to the Electors of Great-Britain.

From his seat in Bedfordshire on the day the pamphlet was published (23 June) Philip Yorke, son of the Lord Chancellor, wrote Thomas Birch that he had "heard Fielding was writing for the Government"; he was eager that he should publish before the "nonsense" of the Opposition journalists had "time to make an Impression." In reply Birch reassured his friend that Fielding had not only been quick off the mark; he had duped the enemy into supposing he was one of their own. Referring to the *Dialogue*, Birch wrote on 27 June, "Fielding has given us his Pamphlet under a Title he design'd to catch the Malignants under the Appearance of being levell'd against the Government."[266] If we can believe one ostensibly disabused correspondent to the *General Advertiser* (29 June), the ruse worked: "I am one, among many others, who have been deceived by the Title of a Pamphlet which is lately published, called, *A Dialogue between a Gentleman* ... But if this Pamphlet deceived me in its Title, it has undeceived me in many Points ... For my Part, I am not ashamed to own I have been led astray like the Alderman; like him I am convinced." No wonder, then, that despite his usual indifference to political writers, the Prime Minister himself paused in

a letter to the Duke of Richmond to recommend Fielding's clever
pamphlet.[267]

As Birch was aware, Fielding's strategy in the pamphlet is, under
color of a rational argument between two friends of differing political
parties, to reduce to absurdity the views of the factions comprising
the Opposition, whose candidates for election he calls Sir Thomas
Leadenhead and Mr. Toastum. Whether Tories or disappointed Whigs,
knaves or merely fools, their supporters serve the hated cause of
Jacobitism.

> The *Alderman* [Birch explained] acknowledges himself a *Jacobite*,
> but upon Republican Principles; which the *Gentleman* shows to be
> just as consistent as being *an Atheist upon Christian Principles*. The
> chief topics of Grievances are the Want of a place & Pension Bill, &
> of an Annual or at least Triennial Parliament, the War, Taxes, the
> Scots Bill, & the Dissolution of the Parliament.

How far Fielding had come since he treated most of these same issues
in the pages of *The Craftsman* and *The Champion* – or indeed as recently
as *An Attempt towards a Natural History of the Hanover Rat*! At every
point his arguments now are those he once had ridiculed.

But his friends in Opposition then were now his friends in power,
and there is little doubt that they commissioned him to write the
Dialogue. Though the possibility of a "surprize" election was a topic of
conversation in the coffee-houses early in June, Fielding must have
known it was a certainty sometime before the official announcement.
The *Dialogue* was rushed into print with all its typographical sins upon
it (not one, but two lists of errata were required). But it is a substantial
pamphlet of ninety-one pages, the most skillful of all Fielding's serious
political writings; that it could have been produced – written, printed,
published – in less than a week is unlikely. The ledgers of Strahan the
printer, furthermore, put the case for the ministry's subvention of the
work beyond reasonable doubt: it enjoyed a first printing of 3,500
copies – a very large number indeed, larger than that of any other
pamphlet by Fielding – and a month later Strahan ran off an additional
1,000 copies.[268] There is further presumptive evidence that Fielding
wrote the pamphlet at the behest of his friends, for a specific target of
the *Dialogue* is the "Independent Electors of Westminster," who
opposed the ministerial candidates (one of whom was Lord Trentham,
the Duke of Bedford's brother-in-law) in a district Bedford regarded as
his own fief. Hardwicke, who helped plan the surprise election; Lyttelton, who was concerned in many of the issues; Bedford, whose family's
interests were threatened – all three had reasons to set Fielding "writing
for the Government," as Philip Yorke put it, at the very moment when

Chesterfield was attempting, albeit ineffectually, to launch Fielding's career in the magistracy.

...▬► xlv ◄▬...

In December, six months later, Fielding would resume his role of hackney political author for the last time. During that interval he disappears from view. Perhaps he rode the Western Circuit as he used to do; but the gout, or his stewardship of the New Forest, or expectations of a new career in the law may have kept him closer to home. He had come to relish the change of scene Bath afforded in September and October, where he could get on with *Tom Jones* while enjoying Ralph Allen's company and the "vivifying" effects of the waters.

But Bath was a city teeming with gossips, and this season Fielding and his family had a very good reason to stay away. For some time his relationship with his servant Mary Daniel had taken an amorous turn; she was now noticeably with child. We may imagine what Sarah thought of this unseemly affair conducted in the household she had been mistress of since Charlotte's death; but though she would find other lodgings, the compliments she later paid her brother in her letters and published works suggest that the bond of affection between them was never broken. As for Lady Mary, who knew her cousin well, she was more amused than scandalized: Fielding's "natural spirits," she wrote, "gave him rapture with his cook-maid."[269] Many years later, Lady Mary's granddaughter, Lady Louisa Stuart, aware of Murphy's reticence on the subject, related Fielding's own version of the story as she had it from his friends:

> His biographers seem to have been shy of disclosing that after the death of this charming woman [Charlotte] he married her maid. And yet the act was not so discreditable to his character as it may sound. The maid had few personal charms, but was an excellent creature, devotedly attached to her mistress, and almost broken-hearted for her loss. In the first agonies of his own grief, which approached to frenzy, he found no relief but from weeping along with her; nor solace, when a degree calmer, but in talking to her of the angel they mutually regretted. This made her his habitual confidential associate, and in process of time he began to think he could not give his children a tenderer mother, or secure for himself a more faithful housekeeper and nurse. At least this was what he told his friends; and it is certain that her conduct as his wife confirmed it, and fully justified his good opinion.[270]

A plain and simple woman then in her twenty-sixth year, Mary Daniel does seem to have possessed all the amiable qualities Lady Stuart attributed to her. She came to be Fielding's wife, however, in quite another way than this – a way that vividly points up what was weak and what was best about his character. Certainly Fielding never coveted a reputation for continence in his relations with women, but this, as far as one knows, is the first time he was guilty of the folly he ridiculed in the randy hero of *Pamela*, who with his own servant "indulge[d] the Passion of Lust, at the Expence of Reason and Common Sense."[271] On the other hand, though a gentleman proud of his rank, he had the decency not to ruin this woman of humble birth who had accepted his embraces. Contemplating Fielding's life at the height of the Victorian era, Austin Dobson was so dismayed at discovering his indiscretion with Mary Daniel that he considered following Murphy's example and suppressing the fact. In a letter confirming the evidence, his informant made what surely remains the essential point:

> After his first wife's death Fielding found consolation in the arms of Mary Daniel. . . . Of course such connections were common enough in those days, but it was not as common when the natural consequences manifested themselves, to ratify the alliance at the altar. That Fielding did so, under the circumstances & manners of the period, seems greatly to his credit.[272]

In a passage in *Tom Jones* (XIV.vii) written about this time, this is also how Fielding's hero answers his friend Nightingale's objection that he would be laughed to shame if he stooped to marrying his landlady's daughter whom he has got with child:

> Fie upon it, Mr. *Nightingale*. . . . I am well assured there is not a Man of real Sense and Goodness in the World, who would not honour and applaud the Action. But admit no other would, would not your own Heart, my Friend, applaud it?

On 27 November 1747, with his friend Lyttelton attending (according to contemporary report) to give the bride away, Fielding married Mary Daniel in the sixth month of her pregnancy. The ceremony was performed in Wren's elegant brick church of St. Benet, Paul's Wharf, situated on the Thames near Doctors' Commons, the ecclesiastical court where, in *Tom Jones* (XV.viii), Nightingale followed his author's example and "in vulgar Language, soon made an honest Woman" of Nancy Miller.

That his wife might have the baby with as little embarrassment as possible, Fielding arranged for her to remove ten miles up-river to Twickenham, the pleasant village that seems to have been amenable to make-believe, where Pope had fashioned for himself a miniature

Roman villa and Horace Walpole was even then planning to transform Strawberry Hill into an exquisite Gothic castle. Here, in Back Lane (now Holly Road), Fielding leased a bright little wooden house with a garden.[273] (See Plate 41.) Here, on 25 February 1747/8 in the church of St. Mary the Virgin, their son William was baptized.

Fielding's enemies would gloat over his huddled match with Mary Daniel. Among the first to snigger was his new neighbor Horace Walpole, who, not content with mocking Fielding himself in print, would put his wife to shame as well. From behind the screen of anonymity, Walpole in *Old England* (23 April 1748) wrote that Fielding had been denied admission to a box at the theatre on the grounds that the woman with him was not his wife, but his maid and doxy, a person unfit to mingle with ladies. He later embellished the joke for his private amusement, adding in a note to his copy of the article an anecdote in which Fielding, after hearing Lyttelton praised for his integrity in political affairs, "started up & striking his Breast, cried, If you talk of Virtue, here's a Virtue! I married my Whore yesterday. – He had; Lyttelton made Him."[274] Smollett, too, enjoyed the scandal in the first edition of *Peregrine Pickle* (1751), where, alluding to Fielding and Lyttelton, he advises the poet Spondy to flatter Gosling Scrag heartily, so that "when he is inclined to marry his own cook-wench, his gracious patron may condescend to give the bride away."[275] Nor would Bonnell Thornton, in the *Spring-Garden Journal* (16 November 1752), fail to recall how Fielding had married his penniless bride in the nick of time.

...➡ xlvi ◆–...

Aptly enough, since Fielding liked to think of his masterpiece as "the Author's Offspring, and indeed as the Child of his Brain" (XI.i), November 1747 also affords the earliest documentary evidence that it was on the way – not under the name he eventually gave it, but entitled *The Foundling*. In that month Strahan recorded in his ledger the printing of 250 "Receipts for Mr Fielding's Foundling."[276] Apparently, as in the profitable instances of his own *Miscellanies* and his sister's *Familiar Letters*, he originally meant to publish the novel by subscription. That it was quite far advanced by the turn of the year is suggested by a curious passage in Thomas Birch's letter to Lord Orrery of 19 January 1747/8: "Mr. Fielding is printing three volumes of Adventures under the title of *The Foundling*."[277] The statement is tantalizing, because the novel would eventually appear in six volumes. If Birch can be believed in this assertion – and besides being in general a reliable literary gossip, he was a friend of Fielding – then it is clear that Fielding was now well enough satisfied with half his manuscript to think of submitting it to the printer. At this late date and with all the other exacting activities that required his attention this year, it would have been virtually impossible for him to alter his conception and conduct of the work so radically as to double its length.[278] Indeed, as Birch went on to say, Fielding had already progressed far enough with the novel to merit his patron's praise of his ingenious handling of the plot: "Mr. Littleton, who has read the manuscript, commends the performance to me as an excellent one, and abounding with strong and lively painting of characters, and a very copious and happy invention in the conduct of the story." That Fielding did in fact print the first half of *Tom Jones* well before he completed the narrative is confirmed by Birch's later advice to Philip Yorke in a letter of 17 September 1748: "Fielding's Novel is so far advanc'd in the Impression, that three Volumes are already finish'd, as the whole will be in about six Weeks."[279]

But to return to the autumn of 1747. Fielding was then well enough satisfied with the progress he was making on the novel that he was prepared to become involved again in the political paper wars. The strategy of "stealing a Parliament by Surprize," as the Alderman put it in the *Dialogue*, had succeeded so well that when the members convened on 10 November, Pelham and the "Broad Bottom" coalition found themselves with a majority of 125. Unlike his mentor Walpole, Pelham (as Fielding recently complained) had little use for political writers. Now, however, the need to prepare the country for the negotiation of an unpopular peace with France, as well as a spreading rash of treasonable demonstrations at home, warranted the founding of a new periodical to protect the government's interests against a pack of Opposition journalists. That Jacobitism could still be regarded by the ministry in 1747–8 as a serious threat to public order and the Hanoverian Establishment has seemed unlikely to some historians who interpret the cries of danger as merely a political device to discredit a loyal Opposition. However exaggerated such fears may have been, it is clear that the ministers themselves were sincerely concerned at several flagrant manifestations of Jacobitism: rioting had broken out at the Staffordshire elections in July, and at the Lichfield races in August a mob insulted, and then horsewhipped, the Duke of Bedford; at Oxford, where a virulent Toryism was officially condoned, undergraduates openly damned King George. Small wonder that in September 1747 Pelham wrote the Duke of Cumberland complaining that "a lurking Jacobite spirit begins to shew itself. Many insolences and petty riots have broken out; and those who, in open rebellion, thought it best not to appear, begin now to pull off the mask."[280]

Such anxiety at the highest level of government helps to account for Fielding's reemergence on Saturday, 5 December 1747, as editor of a ministerial paper – this time appearing not as the "true Patriot," but in the ironic guise of "John Trott-Plaid, *Esq*," bigotted and bibulous author of *The Jacobite's Journal*. Eleven months later in bidding farewell to his readers, Fielding recalled the inflammatory mixture of circumstances which prompted him to take up his pen:

> A strange Spirit of Jacobitism, indeed of Infatuation, discovered itself at the latter End of the Year 1747, in many Parts of this Kingdom, which was at the same Time engaged in a dangerous and successless War. A Spirit which gave the highest Encouragement to our Enemies, not only as such intestine Divisions must greatly weaken our political Strength; but as it afforded them a reasonable Hope, that if an Invasion of this Island was but coloured over with the specious Pretence of supporting the Pretender's Cause, a considerable Party among ourselves, would be found ready to join and assist the then avowed and declared Enemies of their Country.
>
> As it seemed necessary to apply some Remedy, in order to stop the Progress of this dangerous, epidemical Madness at so critical a Season; so none seemed more proper, or likely to be more effectual than Ridicule.

Echoing Pelham's own sense of the state of the nation in the autumn of 1747, this seems a sincere account of Fielding's motives in launching *The Jacobite's Journal*.

Published every Saturday for twopence, the *Journal* was the only paper lending full support to the ministry. As originally conceived, it was also wittier by far than any of its competitors. Prominently displayed at the head of the paper, a woodcut based on a drawing possibly by Hogarth,[281] served as an "Emblematical Frontispiece" depicting the ironies implicit in the title: against the background of the London skyline a popish friar leads an ass on which ride the Jacobite Trott-Plaid and his wife clad in their tartans, he holding his toasting glass and cheering the Pretender while she brandishes a sword; instead of a carrot, the ass is coaxed forward by a copy of the *London Evening Post*, an anti-ministerial paper he finds very much to his taste, while attached to his tail a volume of Harrington's *Oceana*, the classic manifesto of republicanism in covers embossed with the French fleurs-de-lis, has been ingeniously adapted to spur him on. The leader itself was a lively piece of ridicule exposing the inanities of Jacobitism. And following this were departments of "Foreign Affairs" and "Domestic News," copy for which was taken from other papers. To these departments others were often appended under such headings as "Credenda" or "Gallimatia," usually consisting of absurd items from the Opposition press to which Fielding added the spice of his own satiric commentary. Another notable feature, belatedly introduced in No. 7 (16 January

1747/8), was the "Court of Criticism," in which he singled out certain contemporaries for censure or commendation.

The remainder of the four-page format was reserved for advertisements, chiefly of publications in which Fielding's booksellers had an interest. Millar seems to have been a silent partner: this, at least, is a plausible inference not only from the number of his advertisements in the paper, but also from the colophon, in which appear the names of William Strahan his printer (in the first number only) and Mary Cooper, who appears to have had an agreement with Millar to issue Fielding's less prestigious works under her own imprint. Other booksellers are also represented – namely, George Woodfall, Charles Corbett, and Sarah Nutt – all of whom, with the possible exception of the last, had a hand in publishing one or another of Fielding's works.[282]

The success of the paper, however, was no doubt guaranteed by Fielding's patrons in the government. As a very old friend who now held a place in the Treasury, one likely sponsor of the enterprise would of course be Lyttelton, "whose Character," Fielding declares (No. 18, 2 April 1748), "is very dear to all who have the Honour of his Acquaintance." But Lyttelton by no means monopolizes Fielding's flattery in the *Journal*: Hardwicke is here, "that great and admirable Person who is at the Head of [the Law]" (No. 15, 12 March 1747/8); and Bedford, "a Nobleman of the highest Rank and Dignity, and eminent for the most exalted public as well as private Virtues" (No. 28, 11 June 1748); and newest name in Fielding's personal honor roll, Henry Pelham himself, who is not only "one of the greatest Men now alive" (No. 31, 2 July 1748), but also "one of the best and worthiest Men in this Nation" (No. 43, 24 September 1748). Missing from the list, on the other hand, are two powerful men on whom Fielding had not long ago lavished praise – Dodington and Chesterfield. Perhaps he was aware that both these former patrons were discontented with the Pelham ministry: Chesterfield would resign as Secretary of State in February 1747/8, and, though Dodington kept his place in the Admiralty until March 1749, he was already flirting with the Prince of Wales's party. Nor are there any compliments in Fielding's paper for the Duke of Newcastle, who had fallen out with his brother over Pelham's wish to conclude a peace with France. *The Jacobite's Journal*, then, the only ministerial organ of this period, was a paper dedicated to the interests of one part of the "Broad Bottom" coalition – Pelham's "pacific wing," as it has been called.[283] For these services – if one credits the persistent declarations of his rivals – Fielding was paid a weekly fee of two and a half guineas, and the government guaranteed the widest possible circulation of the paper by buying up 2,000 copies of each number and distributing them *gratis* throughout the kingdom.[284]

The Jacobite's Journal is in many ways a revealing source for Fielding's biographer. But before the paper had seen its fourth number a certain *cause célèbre* elicited from Fielding another publication – the last, and one of the least impressive, of his political pamphlets. On 30 November 1747 – as advertisements for the new periodical were appearing – an outrageous anti-ministerial pamphlet was published, entitled *An Apology for the Conduct of a late celebrated second-rate Minister*. The work purports to be the apology for his political life of Thomas Winnington, a prominent Whig and member of the government under Walpole and his successors – the manuscript allegedly having been discovered among Winnington's effects after his death on 23 April 1746. Whoever the real author was (Fielding took him for a Jesuit, and there is contemporary testimony that he guessed right),[285] he turned back on the ministry, at unconscionable length, their own trick of labeling their opponents Jacobites: "Winnington" confesses that not only he but every minister of the century including Walpole and the "Broad Bottoms" was secretly a Jacobite, dedicated to policies so ruinous for England that the nation would wish to expel their German kings and restore the Stuarts to the throne. The Opposition author of this piece of impudence meant to embarrass the ministry for mismanaging the war and for undermining the Church to the point where the people were fast sinking into immorality and atheism.

Fielding's response – as petulant as it is dull and perfunctory – was published by Mary Cooper on 24 December under the title *A Proper Answer to a late Scurrilous Libel, entitled, "An Apology for the Conduct of a late celebrated Second-rate Minister"*:

> When Popery without a Mask stalks publickly abroad, and Jesuits preach their Doctrines in Print, with the same Confidence as when the last Popish Prince was seated on the Throne, it becomes high Time for every Man, who wishes well to his Country, to offer some Antidote to the intended Poison.

What follows this alarming overture heavily underscores Fielding's abhorrence, so often expressed in his writings, of the entire family of Stuarts and their "Doctrines of absolute Power," as well as his particular animus toward Queen Anne's minister, Robert Harley, architect of the Tory Peace of Utrecht (1713), which, in Fielding's view, nullified all the advantages Britain had gained by the victories of "the Great, the Protestant, the Whig Duke of *Marlborough*." His aim here, as earlier in the *Dialogue*, is to answer the familiar litany of Opposition grievances against the government. On the whole, Fielding's *Proper Answer* is interesting chiefly for what it suggests about an important change in his relationships with two of the most powerful figures in the ministry. Though the author of the *Apology* slandered Chesterfield at length, Fielding completely ignores this smear of his former patron. Instead it is Pelham, "this truly great Man," whom he champions, exercising his talent for profitable adulation: "He hath indeed a Mind which no Difficulties can conquer, nor any Power corrupt."

If Fielding was commissioned to produce this pamphlet by someone in the ministry – and it is hard to imagine why he would add this uninspiring chore to his editorship of *The Jacobite's Journal* without some irresistible inducement – there is no evidence for it in the accounts of Strahan, who in December recorded a first printing of a mere 500 copies, followed in January by a so-called "Second Edition" of the same number.[286] Since this latter printing (a reimpression of standing type and not a true edition) was on sale by 2 January, the initial small run was presumably bought up eagerly. The "Shallowness" of Fielding's performance was all too obvious, however, and provoked in the anti-ministerial author of *The Patriot Analized* (1748) an amusing train of speculation: Was it not a sign that Fielding "approved of the *Apology* in his Head?" or that, indeed, he had cannily written that "unanswerable" piece himself in order to double his profits by answering it?[287]

By the time Fielding had finished drudging to clear Winnington and his fellow Whigs of the preposterous charge of Jacobitism, his periodical was not quite a month old. In all, he continued to publish *The Jacobite's Journal* every Saturday for eleven months, until, satisfied that it had served its purpose and eager to begin a demanding new career in the law, he abandoned the paper on 5 November 1748 with the forty-ninth number. Over that period, as part of his polemic in Pelham's behalf, Fielding defended a number of ministerial measures as, one after another, they came under attack in the Opposition press: such, for example, was the government's policy of allowing the exportation of English corn to feed the French enemy, or the Bills for naturalizing foreign Protestants, or implementing the window-tax, or transferring the summer assizes in Buckinghamshire from one town to another.[288] More urgent than any of these issues was the need to counter criticism of the ministry's foreign policy – Pelham being determined to put an end, however ingloriously, to the ruinous war with France: Fielding began defending Pelham's peace initiatives early in the *Journal*, and he made them his constant theme from the time the signing of the preliminary articles was announced in May until the Treaty was completed at Aix-la-Chapelle in October.

For these services to the ministry Fielding became the target of a vicious campaign of personal abuse and vilification. Most venomous of his Grub Street adversaries were the printer of the *London Evening Post* (John Meres); a writer in the *Daily Gazetteer* aptly calling himself "The Fool" (William Horsley);[289] the unknown editor of the *Westminster Journal*; and the several authors of *Old England*, who together may be said to have perfected the vile art of denigration. These last, writing under such names as "Argus Centoculi" and "Porcupinus Pelagius," have not all been certainly identified: Horace Walpole, an occasional contributor to *Old England*, joined in the sport (in the number for 23 April 1748), but Fielding believed the chief offender to be one he called "*Morgan* Scrub, Grubstreet-Solicitor," whom Thomas Birch identified as the attorney Hugh Morgan, perhaps, however, confusing this man with another of the same name who later printed the paper, or with Macnamara Morgan, author of the *Causidicade*, to whom Fielding also attributed the authorship of *Old England*.[290] Such are the difficulties of redeeming the clandestine political writers of the period from oblivion.

Fielding was no tyro in the wars of Grub Street: he had been harassed by the *Grub-Street Journal* in 1732 and by the *Daily Gazetteer* in 1740; and though he never sank to the depths where his antagonists wallowed, he generally gave better than he got. But he was unprepared for calumny as raw and unremitting as he now experienced. In the *Journal* No. 20 (16 April 1748) he complained that "a heavier Load of Scandal hath been cast upon me, than I believe ever fell to the Share of a single Man." The Opposition writers, he continued, have

> attempted to blacken [my Name] with every kind of Reproach; pursued me into private Life, *even to my boyish Years*; where they have given me almost every Vice in Human Nature. Again, they have followed me, with uncommon Inveteracy, into a Profession, in which they have very roundly asserted, that I have neither Business nor Knowledge: And lastly, as an Author, they have affected to treat me with more Contempt, than Mr. *Pope*, who had great Merit and no less Pride in the Character of a Writer, hath thought proper to bestow on the lowest Scribbler of his Time. All this, moreover, they have poured forth in a Vein of Scurrility, which hath disgraced the Press with every abusive Term in our Language.

Adding salt to these wounds, inflicted by writers he might with justice dismiss as contemptible, were the abler, trenchant articles appearing under the name of "George Cadwallader, Gent.," in *The Remembrancer*, a periodical founded just one week after his own in order to support the Prince of Wales's faction. This author – whom Fielding distinguished from the others toiling in the same cause, for he was "far from being like the rest of his Fellow-Labourers, void of all Abilities" – was his old friend and erstwhile collaborator, James Ralph. To counter Ralph's arguments, that "Drummer of Sedition," Fielding in No. 17 (26 March 1748) felt obliged to drop the entertaining ironic pose that distinguished his *Journal* from its competitors – as a few weeks earlier, with No. 13 (27 February 1747/8), he had discarded his drolly "Emblematical Frontispiece." In doing so, he observed that tho' Irony is capable of furnishing the most exquisite Ridicule; yet as there is no kind of Humour so liable to be mistaken, it is, of all others, the most dangerous to the Writer. An infinite Number of Readers have not the least Taste or Relish for it, I believe I may say do not understand it; and all are apt to be tired, when it is carried to any Degree of Length.

It was time "to pull off the Masque" of the silly Jacobite. The joke was worn, and besides, as he was finding on every side, the business he was engaged in was no laughing matter. Unfortunately, his comical headpiece gone and his ridicule blunted, Fielding's essays as Pelham's champion lose much of their appeal. Those wishing to comprehend the few unremarkable principles of Fielding's politics will of course persevere. And at least two minor themes of the *Journal* are notable for what they reveal of particular aspects of Fielding's social thought, which he usually expressed in pragmatic proposals for specific reforms: these are his series of articles recommending a charitable provision for the widows and children of poor clergymen (Nos. 21 and 29–32), and his insistence on the importance to the polity of a sound educational system – a system, in other words, inculcating Whig and Protestant principles.

The *Journal* also served Fielding as a vehicle for pronouncing judgment on the publications of his friends and enemies. In No. 7 (16 January 1747/8) he revived for this purpose "the Court of Criticism," over which he presided as "*Censor* of Great Britain." Originating in *The Tatler* with "our most dear Predecessor *Isaac Bickerstaff*, Esq; of facetious Memory" – that is, with Addison and Steele, the great models for all Fielding's journalism – this feature had been used by Fielding to good effect in *The Champion*. In a political context he would now use it to recommend a Whig pamphlet by Samuel Squire (No. 7) or a loyal sermon preached on the anniversary of the martyrdom of Charles I by Ferdinando Warner (1703–68), another of his ever-widening circle of clerical acquaintance (No. 17). On the other hand, having inquired into the merits of the Jacobite romance published by Thomas Carte under the title of a *General History of England*, Fielding ordered it to be "grubbed" (Nos. 12 and 13); and, though he probably did not know the identity of the offending author, he pronounced "Sentence of Infamy" on Horace Walpole, who, in his *Letters to the Whigs*, had defamed Lyttelton's fair name and political conduct (No. 18).

In a more amiable vein Fielding used the "Court" to promote the interests of his literary and theatrical friends. When his bookseller, Millar, reissued the English translation of a favorite work, the Abbé Banier's *Mythology and Fables of the Ancients Explain'd*, Fielding lavishly commended it in several numbers (e.g., No. 9). When his friend

Edward Moore produced his unsuccessful comedy *The Foundling*, Fielding, after weighing its faults and merits, adjudged it to be "a good
Play" and ordered the Town to receive it as such (No. 16); when the
same friend, in a bid for Lyttelton's patronage, produced a poem
entitled *The Trial of Selim the Persian*, Fielding delighted in its satire
of Lyttelton's detractors and recommended its author to the public –
"since I am convinced, that the Goodness of his Heart is, at least, equal
to that of his Head" (No. 33). Fielding also took this opportunity to
characterize Lyttelton, to whom he would dedicate the great novel now
nearing completion, as "almost the only Patron which the Muses at
present can boast among the Great." Among the most renowned of
Lyttelton's protégés was another friend, James Thomson, whose *Castle
of Indolence* was published by Millar in May. Predictably, Fielding
published an appreciation of this "excellent Composition" (No. 27).

Nor would he neglect those who gave him so much pleasure in the
theatre, his first and lasting love among all the arts, where he had by
now become something of a legend – the wiser, wounded veteran, as it
were, who had dared too much. Garrick, Quin, Susannah Cibber,
"Kitty" Clive, "Peg" Woffington – all luminaries of the company at
Drury Lane – he commended for mastering "the Business of an Actor,"
which is "to copy Nature, and not to imitate the Excellencies of their
Predecessors" (No. 10). Garrick, who with James Lacy acquired the
patent of Drury Lane in April 1747, he singles out for special praise,
thanking him "for his great Improvement of our Theatrical Entertainments, not only by his own inimitable Performance; but by his
proper Regulations of the Theatre under his Direction" – in which
respect he was a welcome contrast to Rich at Covent Garden, who
pandered to the corrupt tastes of the Town. As the benefit nights of
the Drury Lane company occurred this season – Mrs. Cibber's on 7
March, Mrs. Woffington's on 14 March, Mrs. Clive's on 21 March,
"Honest Billy" Mills's on 25 April – Fielding "puffed" each one in turn
and ordered "a good warm Box" to be made ready for himself and his
wife.

Whether in praise or blame Fielding in the *Journal* was seldom as
disinterested as his pose of censor and patriot would seem to require.
All the more remarkable, therefore, is the notice of *Clarissa* and its
author that appeared in No. 5 (2 January 1747/8), a month after
Richardson had published the first two volumes of his masterpiece. To
be sure, Richardson had advertised the work in the *Journal* (Nos. 2 and
3), and Millar was among the booksellers who distributed it. But it is
clear that Fielding, no doubt to his surprise, was genuinely impressed
by what the author of *Pamela* was in the process of achieving in his
second novel – impressed by the extraordinary development of his
narrative skills and by a new-found maturity in his understanding of

character. Not many months before, in the Preface to his sister's *Familiar Letters*, he had treated Richardson's kind of epistolary fiction with disdain. How wrong he had been to generalize:

> Such Simplicity [Fielding now exclaims of *Clarissa*], such Manners, such deep Penetration into Nature; such Power to raise and alarm the Passions, few Writers, either ancient or modern, have been possessed of. My Affections are so strongly engaged, and my Fears are so raised, by what I have already read, that I cannot express my Eagerness to see the rest. Sure this Mr. *Richardson* is Master of all that Art which *Horace* compares to Witchcraft.

This was not mere "puffing," he insisted, returning to the subject in No. 14 (5 March 1747/8), but "the most deserved Praises that can be bestowed." Indeed, he went further, complimenting the author on the goodness of his "Heart." Before the year was out, these first impressions of the new novel having been confirmed by the publication of Volumes 3–5, Fielding was moved to repeat his praises privately in a letter to Richardson that is among the finest tributes ever paid by one great writer to another, his rival, whose sense of his craft was antithetical to his own. Fielding this year extended the hand of friendship to Richardson, but he would not take it.

xlvii

While Fielding continued writing this year, producing his weekly articles for *The Jacobite's Journal* and composing the final books of *Tom Jones*, his duties as High Steward of the New Forest involved him in the most fully documented case of his career as a lawyer. James Perkins, a powerful landlord in the parish of Christ Church, Hants., had become convinced that part of the royal forest belonged to his own large estate. When in the spring of 1747 two of the King's woodsmen entered the disputed area and cut thirty cartloads of furze and holly to use as browse for the deer, Perkins filed suit against them.[291] The men were defended by Fielding's deputy, Richard Birt, who in turn charged Perkins with unlawfully appropriating the King's land, abusing the King's servants, and killing the King's deer. It devolved on Charles Coleman, Deputy Surveyor of the forest and Receiver of the Rents, to apprize the Duke of Bedford of the merits of the case; but Coleman was reluctant to oppose Perkins, who was, as he put it, "an electrified person, very full of fire and spirit."[292] When Fielding complained to Bedford, furthermore, that Coleman had never yet remitted his stipend, Coleman replied by accusing Fielding of neglecting his own responsibilities: the stipend, he explained, had formerly been paid at the meeting of the Swainmote Court, which the High Steward was supposed to attend in order to charge the inhabitants of the forest to observe the forest laws. "Mr. Fielding," he informed the Duke, "has not yet done so."[293]

The trial to decide between the claims of Perkins and the King being scheduled for Hilary Term 1747/8, Coleman went with an associate to survey the disputed land, where, however (as Birt advised Fielding),[294] he found Perkins waiting for him at the head of "a Banditti" consisting of his servants and tenant farmers who, with an "abundance of cursing and swearing," insisted on his right to the place. Birt was convinced that Coleman, who chose to support Perkins's claim against the testimony of the foresters, was a villain who had conspired with the man to defraud the King: "there never was so great a Vermin." Acting on Fielding's instructions, Birt prepared what he believed to be a strong brief for the Crown and arrived in Winchester on 1 March 1747/8 expecting to meet Fielding there to discuss procedures. Instead he was disappointed to find that John Sharpe, the Treasurer Solicitor, had "countermanded" the cause and that Fielding remained in London, hindered from attending the assizes by some business he hoped would prove to his "advantage and profit."[295] Fielding indeed at this time had more important matters on his mind than his not very lucrative duties as High Steward: he was about to stage a puppet show.

Coleman meanwhile came to London to explain himself to Bedford. Fielding, who had not yet vacated the house in Old Boswell Court, expected Sharpe and Robert Butcher, Bedford's agent, to call on him there on Wednesday, 9 March, to confer about the case. On 8 March he wrote Butcher that he had no objection to Coleman's being present at the meeting, though, he remarked, "I think his Arrival upon this Occasion very nearly amounts to a Proof of the Part which he hath taken in this Affair." No doubt uneasy at what Coleman might say to Bedford when they met next morning, Fielding offered to be present himself, so as "to prevent my Lord Duke ... from having more than one Trouble on this impertinent Matter."[296] But this proposal came to nothing, and the meeting with Sharpe and Butcher took place at Boswell Court as planned; it may explain the entries in Sharpe's accounts recording fees amounting to three guineas paid to Fielding for legal work done in connection with the case,[297] which appears to have been settled out of court – not, however, before Fielding took the opportunity to help his briefless friends Charles Pratt and Robert Henley by employing them in the case.[298] One consequence of Coleman's having made the journey to London is that he was obliged to borrow money of Butcher to pay Fielding his stipend. When he returned to

Hampshire, he was incensed to find that Fielding had in fact already been paid his money by Birt.[299]

Though Perkins withdrew his charges against the King's woodsmen, he was by no means chastened by this affair. A "Gentleman of great Resentment," as Birt characterized him,[300] and one who as justice of the peace could make his resentment felt, Perkins ruled his corner of southwest Hampshire like some cattle baron of the wild West, terrorizing not only those who might testify to his depredations, but even the officers of the law. Early in the spring Birt reported to Fielding that Perkins's men had been killing deer in the forest. When one of the culprits was apprehended, his accomplices rescued him. Perkins continued for many weeks to defy the authorities in this way. At one stage, when required to produce the guilty deer-stealer, he brazenly duped the magistrate by sending the fellow's brother in his place. It is probably this lively little melodrama, in its early stages, to which Fielding referred when from Twickenham on 3 April 1748, a Sunday, he sent Butcher a report he had just received from Birt "concerning an Affair of a very extraordinary Kind which I think it my Duty to lay before the Duke of Bedford." He requested an audience with Bedford on Thursday morning, "if the Gout with which among many other Evils I am plagued will permit me."[301]

···━➤ xlviii ◆━···

If "Evils" seems too strong a word, Fielding in these early months of 1748 was beset with a multitude of woes and responsibilities that were oppressive. He was plagued by the gout, which began to torment him more severely than ever before; he found the Perkins affair annoying, and it demanded his professional services; he was adjusting to changes in his household precipitated by his marriage and the birth of his son, events which, if they had their happy aspects, were also embarrassing and kept him shuttling between London and Twickenham; he was obliged to produce his weekly articles for the ministry, time better spent getting on with the novel he had nearly finished.

It is a tribute to Fielding's astonishing energy and resiliency of spirit – not to mention the catholicity and essential Englishness of his taste – that he chose this troubled moment to launch a new and wonderfully ludicrous enterprise. This was, as announced in the *General Advertiser* (7 March 1747/8), "*a Puppet Show after the Antient manner*; in which the true Humour of that most diverting Entertainment will be restored" – "*We are glad to hear this*," Fielding commented after quoting the "puff" in *The Jacobite's Journal* (12 March), "*as the true*

Humour of the Stage is almost lost."[302] In partnership with some eligible
puppet-master – a likely candidate would be Thomas Yeates the elder
(*fl.* 1725–55) – Fielding was planning to revive the comical humors of
Punch and Joan, "that fine Raillery ... of Punchinello in a Puppet-
shew, which," he regretfully observed in *The True Patriot* (11–18 Feb-
urary 1745/6), "hath been of late Years, for I know not what Reason laid
aside." For this purpose, while continuing to maintain his Twickenham
residence, he left the dignified surroundings of Old Boswell Court and
established himself in Panton Street, near the Haymarket.[303] The house
in Panton Street he "fitted up in the most elegant Manner," with
proper boxes and a coffee-room, where ladies could gossip and refresh
themselves before the performance. For this would be no ordinary
fairground drollery, but an entertainment aimed at fashionable audiences. And they came in numbers when word got round that London's
rogue dramatist of the 1730s – "the Great Mogul" himself, author of
Pasquin and *The Historical Register* – was returning to the theatre as
manager of a satiric puppet show. At the final rehearsal on Saturday,
26 March, the long room was crowded with "a great many Persons
of the politest Taste, who express'd the highest Satisfaction at the
Performance."

In order to evade the constraints of the Licensing Act, Fielding
adapted a device hit upon by Samuel Foote a year earlier, who, under
the pretext of "giving tea," performed as a mimic at the Little Theatre
in the Haymarket. Now, under the name of "Madame *de la NASH*" –
Mary Fielding doubtless lent her culinary talents to the venture –
Fielding opened a "large BREAKFASTING-ROOM for the Nobility
and Gentry" in which, for the price of a cup of tea, coffee, or chocolate,
not to mention "the very best of" jellies, customers would be entertained "Gratis with that Excellent old English Entertainment, call'd
A PUPPET-SHEW.... *With the Comical Humours of* PUNCH *and his
Wife* JOAN, With all the Original Jokes, F–rts, Songs, Battles,
Kickings, &c." From Monday, 28 March, until 2 June, "Breakfast"
was served in this way twice a day, morning and evening (no doubt for
the convenience of the late risers among his fashionable audience), at
prices of three shillings (boxes), two shillings (pit), and a shilling
(gallery). In addition to his share of the profits, Fielding, according to
Horace Walpole in *Old England* (23 April 1748), also "appropriated [a]
Fee of a Crown-Piece" for writing the advertisements.

As for the name of the proprietress, "Madame de la Nash" was surely
a facetious compliment to the monarch of Bath, "Beau" Nash. In *Tom
Jones* (XII.v), the puppet-master hints as much when he confesses to
Jones – who greatly prefers the antics of his "old Acquaintance Master
Punch" to the more genteel, indeed Cibberian, puppet shows now in
vogue – that this same unfashionable opinion was shared not long ago

by "some of the Quality at *Bath*," who "wanted mightily to bring *Punch* again upon the Stage."

Besides provoking hoots of derision from his Grub Street antagonists for years to come, Fielding's brief season as the author manager of "Madame de la Nash's" puppet theatre involved him in skirmishes with two of the most celebrated actors of the day. Timing his benefit night at Covent Garden to coincide with the opening of Fielding's puppet show on Monday, 28 April 1748, Theophilus Cibber had the irresistible idea of reviving *The Author's Farce* to use as an afterpiece – not the revised 1734 text, of course, which had not yet been published and in which Fielding ridiculed him as Marplay Junior, but an abridgment of the original version more amenable to Cibber's own satiric purpose, made all the more pointed by a few judicious "Alterations." In this revival Cibber played the part of Luckless the author, who presides over his "Operatical Puppet-Shew, call'd The Pleasures of the Town." At the very moment when Henry Fielding was introducing his puppet show in Panton Street, Cibber, as Fielding's surrogate Harry Luckless, was presenting his own little comedy of Punch and Joan at Covent Garden; as the curtain fell, he would be heard promising to "restore" Punch to his kingdom "at the Expence of my own." Cibber's revenge could not have been sweeter.

Fielding might himself have enjoyed Cibber's lucky stroke of ridicule – a palpable hit, but fair enough and momentary. Soon, however, he became embroiled in a ruder and prolonged satiric contest with Samuel Foote (1720–77), who for a year past, both as an actor at Covent Garden and as a solo performer on stage at the Little Haymarket, had been diverting the Town with his talent for mimickry – "taking off," often cruelly, various celebrities in the theatre and other walks of life. Fielding's friends Garrick, Quin, Delane, and "Peg" Woffington were among Foote's victims, as were "Orator" Henley, Christopher Cock the auctioneer, and the famous Bow Street justice Sir Thomas DeVeil, recently deceased. As early as 6 February 1747/8 in *The Jacobite's Journal* Fielding had expressed his contempt for Foote's antics and "admonished" John Rich, the manager at Covent Garden, "for suffering private Characters to be ridiculed by Mimickry and Buffoonery upon his Stage"; "all such Mimickry," he declared, "is indecent, immoral, and even illegal." As one of the more vicious follies of the age, it inevitably found a place in Fielding's satiric program at Panton Street.

In the *General Advertiser* for 14 April 1748, Fielding advertised for performance the following Monday (18 April) "a Comical Puppet-Show Tragedy, call'd FAIR ROSAMOND. With the Comical Humours of King *Henry* II. and his Queen. And likewise the Comical Humours of the Town, as Drums, Routs, Riots, Hurricanes, Hoops, Plaid Wastecoats, Criticizing, Whisk-Learning, Muffle-Boxing, Mimicking, &c." Clearly,

Fielding was using the "fine Raillery" of Punch and Joan, as he was using the pages of *The Jacobite's Journal* and *Tom Jones*, to ridicule the follies of fashionable society. All the specific topics of the satire are scored elsewhere in his writings – the popularity of card parties or assemblies known as drums and routs, riots and hurricanes; the wearing of hoop-petticoats or of plaid waistcoats, the defiant badge of unreconstructed Jacobites; the ignorance and impertinence of literary critics; the modern rage for whist; and the comfortable heroism of those whom he referred to in *Tom Jones* (XIII.5) as "the muffled Graduates of Mr. *Broughton's* School" of fisticuffs in the Haymarket, who protected themselves "from the Inconveniency of black Eyes, broken Jaws, and bloody Noses" by wearing boxing-gloves. To the polite audiences who crowded into "Madame de la Nash's Breakfasting-Room" in Panton Street to see this production, Fielding's puppet show must have seemed hilariously reminiscent of former days – the days before the Licensing Act, when Fielding had delighted them at the Little Haymarket with his brash and telling satires.

Last in the list of "Comical Humours" to be ridiculed in the puppet show was "Mimickry." Foote could expect that when *Fair Rosamond* opened on Monday he would receive a full measure of Punch's rough justice. He retaliated in his own way, conducting on that same day at the Little Haymarket an "Auction" of "a choice Collection of Pictures, all warranted Originals, and Entirely New." And so, on 18 April the Town could double their fun, as Fielding's puppets began mocking Foote and Foote began mimicking Fielding. A writer in *Old England* (25 June 1748) helps us visualize the scene in the "Auction Room" as he nominates Fielding for the directorship of a hospital for scoundrels: "His Picture is to be hung up in the Hall, drawn from Mr. *Foot's* Original, all in Black, except two or three Chasms in his *Galigaskins*, and the Flap of his Shirt hanging out, just as he was exhibited on the Stage." In these and other features Foote caricatured the figure, grotesque and disheveled, which Fielding presented to his contemporaries – his wig untidy, his worn black barrister's gown stained with snuff and tobacco juice, his gouty limbs wrapped in leggings.

On 21 April, just three days after Foote had hung up Fielding's portrait before the grinning assembly at the "Auction Room," Fielding, adding "a most extraordinary Diverting Scene" to the program at Panton Street, passed sentence of execution on Foote and proceeded to hang him up in earnest. To *Fair Rosamond*, the notice in the *General Advertiser* declared, "will be added, the Comical Execution of *Mr. PUPPET FUT, Esq; Grocer and Mimick. With a* New Scene *representing* TYBURN." The quarrel had begun to escalate. Not only was Fielding acting as judge and hangman; by his proclamations of Foote's execution, he was in a sense imitating the hawkers who distributed the dying speeches of condemned criminals. On 23 April Foote retaliated, protesting facetiously in the *Daily Advertiser* that the real Henry Fielding, author of *Joseph Andrews*, was long since dead, his place having been taken by a penniless impostor, the hackney writer of political journals and rogue biographies and the impresario of a puppet show:

> Whereas there is a dirty Fellow, in shabby black Cloaths, a flux'd Tye-Wig, and a Quid of Tobacco in his Jaws, that runs up and down calling himself Henry Folding, Esq; begging Money, and complaining of one Fut, a Grocer, from whom he says he has lately received a severe Drubbing: Now this is to inform the Public, that the said dirty Fellow is an arrant Imposter, it being well known that the true Henry Folding died about four Years since, soon after the Publication of Joseph Andrews; and that he now lies interr'd in St. Paul's, Covent-Garden, near the Remains of his old Friend and Patron, Edmund Curll, Bookseller, in whose service he lived and died.
>
> Note, The Said Imposter has gone by many Names; as, Hercules Vinegar, Jonathan Wild, Punch, &c. and was Yesterday Morning seen by two or three People in Panton-Street, officiating as Jack Ketch to a Puppet-Show; and in the Afternoon with his Wife and two Children hawking dying Speeches about the Streets.

The dispute between Fielding and Foote must have been good for business, and it is amusing in a puerile sort of way. But Fielding had had enough. The initial provocation may have been his, but Foote's was the dirtier game: he scored his points against the personal imperfections of his adversary, insulting and degrading his opponent. The innocent may look disheveled; they may possibly chew tobacco. Fielding vented his indignation by hauling Foote before the bench of the "Court of Criticism" in *The Jacobite's Journal* (30 April) and arraigning him on the charge of character assassination – the crime, doubtless, for which "Mr. Puppet Fut" had already been hanged in Panton Street. Foote's only defense is "to mimick the Court, pulling a Chew of Tobacco from his Mouth, in Imitation of his Honour, who is greatly fond of that Weed," and he stands convicted of "a very high Crime; a Crime not only contrary to Law, but certainly *contra bonos mores*." Fielding reminds the prisoner of the difference between ridiculing persons "under fictitious Fables and Characters" (as he had himself done in his dramatic satires, for example) and bringing "real Facts and Persons upon the Stage." The sentence of the "Court" is made to fit the baseness of the crime:

> I shall proceed therefore to pronounce the Judgment of the Court; which is, that you *Samuel Fut* be p—ssed upon, with Scorn and

Contempt, as a low Buffoon; and I do, with the utmost Scorn and Contempt, p–ss upon you accordingly.

The Prisoner was then removed from the bar, mimicking and pulling a Chew of Tobacco from his Mouth, while the P–ss ran plentifully down his Face.

But Fielding had reserved a still more appropriate fate for his adversary. On 9 May he dropped the traditional fare he had been offering at Panton Street and presented instead his own burlesque drama, *The Covent-Garden Tragedy*, assigning most of the principal roles to the puppet equivalents of some of London's most infamous characters. "At the particular Request of Mrs. Puppet Duggleass" (that is, of "Mother" Jenny Douglas, Covent Garden's most notorious bawd), Punch himself performed as Mother Punchbowl, while the parts of Stormandra and Kissindra fell to "Mrs. Puppet Fllips" and "Mrs. Puppet Morrey" (that is, to the scandalous "Con" Phillips, whose *Apology* for her conduct had begun to appear in installments in April, and to the courtesan Fanny Murray). But Fielding gave the part of the bully Captain Bilkum to "Mr. Puppet Fut"; in light of their recent quarrel, the role seems made for him. As Foote had been hanged twice daily on stage in Panton Street for his crimes *contra bonos mores*, so in his first exchange with Mother Punchbowl, Bilkum exclaims:

> Damnation on all Laws and Lawyers too:
> Behold thee carted – oh! forfend that Sight,
> May *Bilkum's* Neck be stretch'd before that Day.
>
> (I.iii)

And the finale, too, was exquisitely apt. Every difficulty resolved, Lovegirlo brings on a fiddler and the farce concludes in a dance with Mother Punchbowl declaring, "I too will shake a Foot on this blest Day"! We may imagine Punch, the champion of Fielding's theatre, kicking his puppet antagonist off the stage as the curtain closes.

With this amusing adaptation of his own play, the contest between Fielding and Foote had run its course, and so too had Fielding's own interest in his puppet theatre. After the final performance of *The Covent-Garden Tragedy* on 14 May, he left his partner to finish the season with more conventional fare.

····◆ xlix ◆–····

This summer Fielding was approaching the two virtually simultaneous events that marked a second radical change in his public life, both in letters and in the law: these events were the implementing of his appointments to the magistracy and the publication of *Tom Jones*. The gout continued to torture him. The pain was so excruciating he could not stir from his house at Twickenham for long periods. From Twickenham on 5 May – shortly before Punch began to perform in *The Covent-Garden Tragedy* – Fielding wrote the Duke of Bedford to request "a very small Favour."[304] This, probably, was the first step toward his appointment to the magistracy for the Liberty of Westminster. From Twickenham on 4 July, he wrote Bedford's agent to apologize for neglecting to acknowledge a "Favour," again unspecified.[305] He would have done so "long since," he explained, "had I not been in daily Expectation of coming to Town; but the Gout persecutes me most unmercifully." The favor in question must have been Bedford's having recommended him to the Lord Chancellor for the Westminster commission, for he asks Butcher "to present my humblest Duty to his Grace with my sincerest Thanks for the Trouble he was so kind to take on my Account." On 30 July, Hardwicke signed the fiat appointing Fielding to the Commission of the Peace for Westminster.[306]

By this time Fielding's fortunes had already brightened materially. The manuscript of *Tom Jones* – or rather "The History of a Foundling" as it was invariably called before publication – was sufficiently far along, and sufficiently promising, that on 11 June Millar was prepared to pay Fielding an advance of £600 for the six projected volumes.[307] The sum was generous for the time: at £100 per volume the rate was somewhat better than Fielding received for *Joseph Andrews*. According to Horace Walpole, moreover, Millar gave Fielding another £100 after he found the book "sell so greatly";[308] indeed, the record of Millar's payments to Fielding during 1749 makes Walpole's figure seem low (see Appendix II). A liberal gesture, to be sure, but as Joseph Spence observed at the height of the novel's popularity, Fielding "might probably have got 5 times as much [as £600] by it, had he kept the right in his own hands: but authors at first don't know, whether their works are good or bad; much less, whether they will sell or not."[309]

The pain of Fielding's malady may have eased enough to enable him to travel this summer as usual. There are signs, at least, that he was giving less time to *The Jacobite's Journal*. Substituting for the lead articles in No. 30 (25 June) and No. 32 (9 July), for instance, are letters from "Honoria Hunter" and "Abraham Adams," which may have been contributions from his sister Sarah and his friend William Young, respectively;[310] and No. 36 (6 August) reprints one of Addison's papers from *The Freeholder*. After the issue of 16 July, furthermore, Fielding discontinued the weekly "Proceedings at the Court of Criticism," one of the more attractive features of the *Journal*: "*As all the Grub-street Authors are now going into the Country to Harvest-Work,*" he explained, *"the Court of Criticism is adjourned till their Return to Town."* In fact, he never resumed these articles.

From our distant vantage point, Fielding disappears from view from early July until late September 1748. He may have journeyed to Worcestershire to visit Lyttelton, the patron of *Tom Jones*, at Hagley Park, where, in late August, Pitt also made one of the company.[311] From Hagley it would be an easy journey to Radway Grange, Warwickshire, the home of Lyttelton's friend Sanderson Miller (1717–80), amateur architect and pioneer of the new taste for the Gothic. According to a pleasant tradition in Miller's family, it was during a visit to Radway Grange that Fielding read aloud from *Tom Jones* to a group including Lyttelton, Pitt, and Miller – in order to sound their opinion of the manuscript before submitting it to the printers.[312] Lyttelton, of course, had been following the progress of Fielding's narrative for some time, and (to use Fielding's own word in the Dedication to the work) had "warmly" recommended it to his acquaintance. Perhaps, however, it was a visit to Hagley and Radway this summer that accounts for Pitt's now joining him in puffing the novel so enthusiastically that together they raised the expectations of the public and stimulated an extraordinary demand for *Tom Jones* before it was published.[313]

The earliest published reference to *Tom Jones* (as far as we know) came from a less friendly source. In a tantalizing remark linking the two works Fielding hoped would crown his careers as novelist and lawyer, a contributor to *Old England* (3 September 1748) complained of his boasting "so loud ... of his being to be brought to Bed soon of a Law-Book, begoten upon himself by the *Notes of an old Judge*, which is to be published at the same Time with Six Volumes of his Novels, spick and span new, fronted with special Dedications." Did the writer mean to parody, as his form of words suggests, some recent advertisement for the projected publication of *Tom Jones* and Fielding's abortive treatise on crown Law? Two and a half years after he prematurely announced its imminent publication, did Fielding still consider his "Law-Book" a viable project? Or by bringing it again to the attention of the public, did he merely wish to remind them of his qualifications for the magistracy? Regrettably, no such advertisement has come to light.

The private correspondence of the period reveals how eagerly the public awaited the publication of *Tom Jones* and *Clarissa*, sensing what would in fact prove to be the case: that Fielding and Richardson, for the better part of the decade acknowledged rivals in the art of fiction, were about to produce their masterpieces. On 17 September, we recall, Thomas Birch wrote Philip Yorke that three of the six volumes of *Tom Jones* had already been printed, "as the whole will be in about six Weeks." He added: "The Sequel of Clarissa is likewise in the Press, &

will be publish'd in the middle of November." On 30 September, having heard Lyttelton speak of Fielding's manuscript "in terms of high approbation," Birch wrote Lord Orrery, still believing that *Tom Jones* and the last volumes of *Clarissa* would be appearing together "about the middle of November."[314]

Unhappily for those who enjoy the coincidences of literary history, Birch erred (though not by very much) in predicting the simultaneous publication of these two works, the greatest comic novel and the only tragic novel of the age. As early as the first weeks of October certain privileged readers had received pre-publication copies of Richardson's fifth volume and of the first two volumes of *Tom Jones*. By 15 October, Fielding's friend John Dalton had "read over the two first Volumes of Fielding's Foundling," Birch told Philip Yorke, and he was "loud in his Commendations of it." Dalton particularly relished the comedy of Squire Western: "A West Country Squire, a Zealot in Politics, & whose chief Oracle is the London Evening, is a character of high Humour."[315]

By this same date the most improbable of all admirers of *Clarissa* had finished reading the fifth volume and wrote to congratulate Richardson on his achievement. In *The Jacobite's Journal* (2 January, 5 March 1747/8) Fielding had cordially recommended the initial installment of the novel. Now, however, having read more than half the narrative's million words, he was overwhelmed. As a fellow craftsman, he appreciated the skill with which Richardson drew his characters and constructed his plot; he even detected what few other readers have found – "a vein of Humour" running through the early volumes. But he struggled to comprehend and to articulate the extraordinary emotive force of the work – Richardson's ability, by the power of particularities, to create an illusion of actuality so compelling that his readers share empathically in the heroine's inner life and experience for themselves the disturbing, claustrophobic world she inhabits. Few people of the time were as widely read as Fielding, but no ancient or modern author had prepared him for this. His famous letter to Richardson of 15 October 1748 (though regrettably known to us only in copies of the original)[316] is of interest not only for its relevance to the history of the modern novel, but for what may seem the surprising facets it reveals of Fielding's character:

Shall I tell you? [Fielding writes] Can I tell you what I think of the latter part of your Volume? Let the Overflowings of a Heart which you have filled brimfull speak for me.

   When Clarissa returns to her Lodgings at St. Clairs the Alarm begins, and here my Heart begins its Narrative. I am Shocked; my Terrors ar[e ra]ised, and I have the utmost Apprehensions for the poor betrayed Creature. – But when I see her enter with the Letter in her Hand, and after some natural Effects of Despair, clasping her Arms about the Knees of the Villain, call him her Dear Lovelace, desirous and yet unable to implore his Protection or rather his mercy; I then melt into Compassion, and find what is called an Effeminate Relief for my Terror. So I continue to the End of the Scene.

When I read the next Letter I am Thunderstruck; nor can many Lines explain what I feel from Two.

... The Circumstance of the Fragments is Great and Terrible; but her Letter to Lovelace is beyond any thing I have ever read. God forbid that the Man who reads this with dry Eyes should be alone with my Daughter when she hath no Assistance within Call.

Here my Terror ends and my Grief begins which the Cause of all my Tumultuous Passions soon changes into Raptures of Admiration and Astonishment by a Behaviour the most Elevated I can possibly conceive, and what is at the same time most Gentle and most Natural. This Scene I have heard hath been often objected to. It is well for the Critick that my Heart is now writing and not my Head.

During the Continuance of this Vol. my Compassion is often moved; but I think my Admiration more. If I had rec'd no Hint or Information of what is to succeed I should perceive you paving the way to load our Admiration of your Heroine to the Highest Pitch, as you have before with wonderfull Art prepared us for both Terror and Compassion on her Account. This last seems to come from the Head. Here then I will end: for I assure you nothing but my Heart can force me to say Half of what I think of *the* Book.

Richardson could not have hoped for a more astute and sympathetic reader of his great work. More to our present purpose, however, what Fielding calls the "Narrative" of his "Heart," relating the tumult of successive passions that the story of Clarissa's rape raised in him – shock and terror, grief and compassion, moving him to find "an Effeminate Relief" in tears – reveals a depth of sensibility in him that until now he rarely drew upon in his own writings. Those who see him only as a man content to play about the surfaces of life, all shallow humor and easy benevolism, may here glimpse another side to his character – a side his friends Harris and Lillo knew. Fielding's passions, Harris recalled, were "vehement in every kind" and quickly roused; yet as Fielding himself revealed in recommending Lillo's *Fatal Curiosity* to the public, he believed a "tender Sensation ... in one of a Humane Temper, the most pleasing that can be rais'd."

Nearly as interesting is the question of how Fielding happened to be among those whom Richardson favored with an advance copy of his fifth volume. Was it because of the intercession of Sarah, or some mutual friend such as Edward Moore?[317] Or had Richardson, perhaps grateful for Fielding's puffing the novel in *The Jacobite's Journal* and hoping for more of the same, simply made him a present of it? Whatever the explanation, there are signs that, for a short while in 1748, relations between the two men took a better turn. In this respect the conclusion of Fielding's letter is particularly remarkable; for there – in an uneasy manner at once defensive, arrogant, and magnanimous – he ventured to explain to Richardson his personal character and his motives as an author, thereby exposing himself to his rival in an overture of reconciliation that must have been difficult to make:

I cannot be suspected of Flattery [he insists]. I know the Value of that too much to throw it away, where I have no Obligation, and where I expect no Reward. And sure the World will not suppose me inclined to flatter one whom they will suppose me to hate if the[y] will be pleased to recollect that we are Rivals for that Coy Mrs. Fame.   Believe me however if your Clarissa had not engaged my Affections more than this Mrs. all your Art and all your Nature had not been able to extract a single Tear: for as to this Mrs. I have ravished her long ago, and live in a settled cohabitation with her in defiance of that Publick Voice which is supposed to be her Guardian, and to have alone the Power of giving her away.   To explain this Riddle. It is not that I am less but more addicted to Vanity than others; so much that I can wrap my self up as warmly in my own vanity, as the Ancient could involve himself in his Virtue. If I have any Merit I certainly know it and if the World will not allow it me, I will allow it my self.
I would not have you think (I might say know) me *to be* so dishonest as to assert that I despise Fame; but this I solemnly aver that I love her as coldly, as most of us do Heaven, so that I will sacrifice nothing to the Pursuit of her, much less would I bind my self, as all her Passionate Admirers do, to harbour in my Bosom that Monster Envy which of all Beings either real or imaginary I most heartily and sincerely abhor.   You will begin to think I believe, that I want not much external Commendation. I will conclude then with assuring you. That I heartily wish you Success. That I sincerely think you in the highest manner deserve it. And that if you have it not, it it [sic] would be in me unpardonable Presumption to hope for Success, and at the same time almost contemptible Humility to desire it.

Fielding signed the letter "yrs. most Affectionately" and begged Richardson to send him "immediately" the two final volumes. It was a generous gesture and one which, presuming a degree of magnanimity in an author whose vanity he had twice sorely wounded, left him vulnerable to rebuff. How, or whether, Richardson replied to this letter is not known – though, since he later told Aaron Hill and Edward Young, among others, that Fielding urged him to let *Clarissa* end happily, he must have heard again from him on the subject. Richardson reveled in Fielding's praise of *Clarissa* and shared it with his acquaintance: some years later he would have it copied out for the edification of his Dutch translator, Johannes Stinstra. But far from accepting Fielding's offer of friendship, he remained his bitter enemy, hating the success of *Tom Jones*. He beamed on his admirers whenever they reviled Fielding's work and character. And he lost no opportunity himself to heap contempt on his rival – sinking even to lecture Sarah on the subject of his "continued lowness," which could only be excused "Had your brother ... been born in a stable, or been a runner at a sponging house."[318]

Sarah now was often caught between her admiration of Richardson and her affection for her brother. At the time Fielding wrote to Richardson she was struggling to complete *The Governess: or, Little Female Academy*, which enjoys the distinction of being the first English novel written for children – struggling, because before printing the book, Richardson required revisions which she was reluctant to make. In *The Governess* Sarah again submitted to Richardson's influence; as Edward Young put it prettily to the master, it was one of several pieces "which, like beautiful suckers, rise from [Clarissa's] immortal root."[319] But in the story itself, which is based on her experience of Mary Rookes's boarding-school in The Close, she has her heroine declare her love for her older brother "Harry," her friend and protector.[320] Richardson published *The Governess* on 2 January 1748/9. Five days later Sarah surprised him when she published a pamphlet entitled *Remarks on Clarissa*, answering the criticisms she had heard against the work, the final volumes of which had appeared on 6 December. Apprehensive that he might consider this friendly gesture an impertinence, she apologized for her "vanity in daring but to touch the hem of [Clarissa's] garment."[321]

After leaving her brother's household on his marriage to Mary Daniel, Sarah went to live for a time with her sisters – Catharine, Ursula, and Beatrice – in Duke Street, Westminster, close to Parliament and the Park. In a letter of 25 October to Mrs. Barker in Salisbury,[322] Ursula allows us a glimpse into the daily lives of these women, who appear to have lived together amicably: they called each other by their nicknames – "Kitty," "Patty," "Sally," and "Bea" – and Ursula refers to them collectively as "the sisterhood." They were all, of course, waiting impatiently for their brother and Richardson to finish their novels. Ursula apologized to Mrs. Barker that she "could not get the books you desired, but they will not be ready till after Christmas, for that rogue Tom Jones will follow his own will and pleasure." But "Oh!" she exclaimed, "the sweet Clarissa is almost ready to make her appearance. The Sweet Clarissa Harlowe. But no more of this subject for who can name Clarissa without a tear." Ursula goes on to tell Mrs. Barker the latest news of friends and relations: the Colliers often think of her; one of the Uptons nearly died last summer; and Henry Gould, playing "an old Trick of his," had planted a false report of his own death in the newspapers (eliciting from Fielding a brief obituary in *The Jacobite's Journal* [20 August 1748]). "We were all in mourning for a fortnight, after which the young gentleman was seen alive and merry, and is now come to the Term." "All the sisterhood," she assures her friend, "desire much love to you," while they carry on with their usual activities: "Kitty is at work. Sally is puzzling about it and about it" (struggling with the revisions Richardson required in *The Governess*, Sarah brought to mind Pope's dunces, who "explain a thing till all men doubt it,/And write about it, Goddess, and about it" [IV.251–2]). "Bea," the most accomplished musician in the family, is "playing on her fiddle, and Patty scribbling." Ursula, indeed, not only had a knack for writing an entertaining letter; she was emulating her more famous brother and sister by trying her hand at fiction – an "extremely pretty" story, her friend Jane Collier assured Richardson, which she promised to show him after her sister Margaret had read it.[323] Ursula closes with news of Henry:

> My brother and his family are come to Town for the winter, and have taken a house in Brownlow Street, near Drury Lane, where he intends to administer Justice. He keeps us all in awe for fear of being committed.

...◄ 1 ►...

Early in October 1748, Fielding came to London intending, at last, to begin a new career as magistrate. On the day of Ursula's letter to Mrs. Barker (25 October) he took the oath and paid the fees that enabled him to act as Justice of the Peace for Westminster.[324] For some weeks he had been in a less facetious mood than the japes about committing all his sisters and friends would suggest. The Duke of Bedford, though willing enough to install Fielding in the despised office of a Westminster justice, had become dissatisfied with the manner in which he was executing his duties as High Steward of the New Forest. On 28 September, Fielding wrote the Duke's agent from Twickenham to make certain that all was in order for his appointment to the Westminster commission, but he was obliged to explain that he had been prevented by the gout from attending the Swainmote Court. He was distressed to learn that Bedford planned to replace him in the stewardship: "his Grace's Pleasure will in this, as in every other Instance be a Law to me [Fielding assured Butcher]; but I hope nothing will be done 'till I have the Honour of waiting on his Grace which I hope to do within a Fortnight."[325]

Adding to his uneasiness was a letter from Harris, whose patience in waiting for his improvident friend to repay the money he had borrowed was finally exhausted. Harris may have reasoned that most men with as many sources of income as Fielding had in 1748 – the stewardship with its attendant fees for legal counsel, the editorship of *The Jacobite's Journal*, the puppet theatre, the thumping advance from Millar for *Tom Jones* – would have money to spare for their creditors. A reasonable inference, but in this instance, unsound. In London on 15 October, the day he extolled the virtues of *Clarissa* to Richardson, Fielding wrote in a very different style to Harris, whose vexing letter could not have reached him "at a more unlucky Hour":

> for besides that I never was more incapable of answering your Demand, it found me in a violent Fit of the Gout which had deprived me of Rest for many Nights; and it was far from Administring any Opiate to me. This Gout from which I am not yet recovered, hath been one principal Occasion of my not answering sooner; for indeed I have had a very severe Attack, and was many Days confined not only to my Bed but to my Back, so that I was forced in other matters to use an Amanuensis. I hope this will find you and your Family in a happier Situation, and that you will believe that nothing less than what must have made Socrates unjust can make me so to you.

That Fielding at this time could be so pinched financially as he here protests is hard to credit, though his ability to run through money at speed was extraordinary – almost a talent. There is no question, however, about the agonies he was suffering from the gout. Though not yet in residence at the house in Bow Street formerly occupied by Sir Thomas DeVeil – the house he would make famous in the annals of the metropolitan police – Fielding began holding court there on 2 November, three days before he concluded *The Jacobite's Journal*. At Bow Street on 2 November he signed the "summary conviction" of Mary, wife of Jasper Frame, and of James Twaits – both for swearing profane oaths – and a "recognizance" as well for the incorrigible Mrs. Frame, who was "a loose idle disorderly Person, not giving any good Account of herself or her Way of Life."[326] So commenced, meanly enough, the long parade of wretchedness and villainy that would pass before Fielding in Bow Street for the next five years. He carried on in this office for the rest of the winter despite being crippled by the gout. By 21 November, in his halting progress to Bow Street, he had moved temporarily from Brownlow Street to Meard's Court, Wardour Street, near St. Anne's church in Soho, where he remained until early December. From that address he wrote Butcher: "I am not yet, and God knows whether ever shall be, able to stand upon my Legs" – an affliction that prevented him from "paying my Duty at Bedford House."[327] By 9 December he was at last established in Bow Street.[328]

A month's experience of the Westminster magistracy had convinced him he could neither prosper himself in that capacity nor serve the public adequately unless he also became eligible to act in the commission of the peace for Middlesex County – the office for which Chesterfield mistakenly recommended him as long ago as June 1747. On 12 December 1748 he wrote to request an audience with Bedford's agent, "having," as he put it, "something of great Importance (to my self) to mention to you."[329] The matter Fielding wished to discuss with Butcher was the subject of his well-known petition to the Duke, dated from Bow Street the following day: only if Bedford assigned him property worth £100 a year clear value could he qualify as a justice of the peace for Middlesex, and "without this Addition," he reminded his patron, "I can not completely serve the Government." In asking this favor, Fielding promised to "give the full Worth" of the lease, though he would need to pay the sum over a two-year period; in addition, that the Duke might be certain of not losing by the transaction, he promised to put the property in good repair: "it will be in Reality an Improvement of that small Part of your Grace's Estate, and will be certain to make my Fortune."[330]

Before Bedford had time to ponder Fielding's proposal, letters arrived from the malignant Coleman shrewdly, and effectually, calculated to expose Fielding's incompetence as High Steward. Admitting to Butcher that he found it impossible to collect the forest rents, Coleman appears to have enclosed for Butcher's edification a copy of a letter sent to Fielding asking "what method I must take to get these Arrears" without "running a hazard of engaging my Self in Law Suits."[331] On 16 December, "not yet able to walk across the Room," Fielding wrote Butcher that Coleman's question "is impossible for any Lawyer in England to resolve without better Information than I have of the Fact. There are [he explained] three Kinds of Remedies for Rent viz. Distress, Seizure and an Action," but which of these is applicable in a particular case depends on the original agreement. As far as Fielding was concerned, such stuff was now a mere nuisance. His only concern was how the Duke would respond to his proposal about the Middlesex justiceship: "it is a Matter," he declared, "of such Consequence to me that I can not sleep while in Anxiety about it."[332]

Bedford was good enough not to cause him many more sleepless nights. The next day (Saturday, 17 December) Butcher sent word that the Duke had granted Fielding's request – on condition, however, that he resign the patent of High Steward. On Monday, 19 December, reluctantly enclosing his resignation, Fielding wrote to thank Butcher for informing him of "his Grace's great Goodness to me" and to remind him of "the Necessity of Dispatch in the present Affair, as the Sessions are now near at Hand."[333] Since the gout prevented him from coming to Bedford House in person to throw himself at the Duke's feet, as he put it in a rapture of gratitude, he also enclosed a letter to Bedford, thanking him for his "unparallelled Goodness" and promising that he would

> endeavour to the utmost of my Power to merit your Extensive Favours, not only by preserving an inviolable Duty to your Grace, but by acting in such a Manner that the Public of which your Grace is so noble a Protector in every Respect, shall in time own they have some additional Obligation to the Duke of Bedford for his having in so noble and generous a Manner constituted me a Magistrate.[334]

Bedford complied with Fielding's request that the business of leasing him the necessary property be completed with "Dispatch." On 9 January 1748/9, the day before the Quarter Sessions for Middlesex began, he conveyed to Fielding for a period of twenty-one years at an annual rent of £30 certain properties in the parishes of St. Paul's Covent Garden, St. Martin-in-the-Fields, St. Giles-in-the-Fields, and St. George's Bloomsbury.[335] Fielding was thus enabled, at last, to satisfy the requirements for the Middlesex magistracy. On 11 January he took the qualification oath; on 12 Janary he took the oath of office and paid the fees.[336] He then joined his fellow justices sitting at the Quarter Sessions at Hicks's Hall, St. John's Street. On 13 January he began acting in the Middlesex commission, signing recognizances and committing one Mary Williams to Bridewell for threatening to stab a person.[337] Now established in DeVeil's famous house in Bow Street and empowered to act in both the Westminster and Middlesex commissions, Fielding was ready to begin in earnest his brief, but distinguished, career as "Court Justice."

There is, however, a postscript to the story of Bedford's part in Fielding's appointment to the Middlesex commission. For some reason Bedford became dissatisfied with the original agreement concerning the property. In May, Fielding was obliged to surrender this lease and a new one was drawn up. For the same annual rent and twenty-one year period, he was given title to properties worth £135.17s. a year in the parishes of St. Paul's Covent Garden, St. Martin-in-the-Fields, and St. Giles-in-the-Fields, comprising three pieces of ground on which stood twelve houses – one in Hart Street, one in Great Wild Street, and ten on the west side of Drury Lane. These latter, appropriately enough, were all either adjacent or proximate to the Theatre Royal; one, it is pleasant to note, was rented by the managers of the theatre, Fielding's friends Garrick and James Lacy.[338]

What remains constant amid these complexities is the fact of Bedford's patronage, which in this instance was even more "princely" (to use Fielding's own word in the Dedication to *Tom Jones*) than at first appears. For besides enabling Fielding to enhance his income by collecting rents on these houses, Bedford during Fielding's lifetime never troubled him to pay the £30 required annually by the terms of the lease.

····➤ li ➤····

In the winter of 1748–9 Fielding thus entered on a new career in the law. At the same time he consummated, magnificently, the work he began seven years earlier when he founded "a new Province of Writing" – with *Joseph Andrews* introducing into English letters the "comic Epic-Poem in Prose."

In September 1748 Birch confidently predicted that *Tom Jones* would be published "about the middle of November." Three of the six volumes had already been printed, and copies of the first two had been delivered to such favored readers as John Dalton and Lady Hertford. But Fielding found it difficult to bend "that rogue Tom Jones," as Ursula expressed it on 25 October, to his own will and pleasure; the book, she regretted, would not be ready "till after Christmas." Moving his place of residence three times in two months – from Twickenham to Brownlow Street to Meard's Court to Bow Street; distracted by new duties and hopes for the magistracy; confined by the gout for days at a time, not only to his bed but to his back: it would be surprising had Fielding been able to keep up the pace and fire of his writing. Justly celebrated as *Tom Jones* is for the compass and intricacy of its design, the occasional incongruities and flatness of style that mar the final pages of narrative betray the hurry and the pain in which Fielding wrote. Can these last chapters of his masterpiece have been among the "other Matters" in which, he explained to Harris, his illness "forced" him "to use an Amanuensis"?

In any case, the novel was not ready by Christmas. Nor was it ready by 22 January, the date when Lady Hertford expected to have the final volumes – by which time the public could hardly contain its impatience. Of those who had already sampled the work and helped raise the Town's expectations, none "puffed" it so assiduously as Lyttelton. The author of *Old England* (27 May 1749) thus sarcastically complimented Fielding's patron on the obstetrical dexterity with which he ushered the *Foundling* into the world:

> Not only the Dedication, but common Fame is full of the warm Commendations you have given of the afore-mentioned *Romance*. You have run up and down the Town, and made Visits, and wrote Letters merely for that Purpose. You puffed it up so successfully about Court, and among Placemen and Pensioners, that, having catched it from you, they thought it incumbent upon them to echo it about the Coffeehouses; insomuch, that all the Women laboured under the Burthen of Expectation, 'till it was mid-wived into the World by your all-auspicious Hand, and proclaimed by them to be the goodest Book that was ever read.

Lyttelton's enthusiastic approbation of *Tom Jones*, echoed about town in coffee-houses and parlors, helped precipitate one of the most remarkable episodes in the publishing history of the period.[339] On 21 January, Millar announced that Fielding's novel would be published on Friday, 10 February (price bound eighteen shillings). The work was in fact ready this time well before the promised date. Strahan charged Millar in January for printing 2,000 sets,[340] and on 3 February (doubtless recalling that his neglect of this formality had cost him some pains and money to rescue *Joseph Andrews* from pirates) Millar duly entered *Tom Jones* in the Stationers' Register, depositing the requisite nine copies.[341] Not until the last day of February, however, did publication notices begin appearing in the newspapers, Millar cannily apologizing to his clients for his inability to have sets bound fast enough to satisfy the demand: "such Gentlemen and Ladies as please, may have them sew'd in Blue Paper and Boards" at sixteen shillings a set. This, however, was in fact the *second* edition, Strahan having rushed through a new printing of 1,500 sets. What had happened to obviate any earlier notice on the promised date of 10 February was, as Joseph Spence observed, "perhaps an unheard-of case." Writing to William Burrell Massingberd on 15 April 1749, Spence recalled the extraordinary circumstances of publication of the first edition:

> Tom Jones is my old acquaintance, now; for I read it, before it was publisht: & read it with such rapidity, that I began & ended within the compass of four days; tho' I took a Journey to St Albans, in ye same time. He is to me extreamly entertaining; & will be so, I believe, to you. A set of 2500 Copies was sold, before it was publisht; which is perhaps an unheard-of case. That I may not seem to write Riddles, you must know that the way here generally is, to send in their

number of Books to each of the Booksellers they deal with, four or
five days before the Publication; that they may oblige people, who
are eager for a new thing. In y^s case, the 10th of Febr^y was fixt for
ye Publication; & by the 10th, all the books were disposed of.[342]

So keen was the demand for the novel that by the following month
a third edition of 3,000 copies, completely reset in small pica and
reduced from six to four volumes duodecimo, was through Strahan's
presses. Before releasing this new edition for sale, however, Millar
asked Fielding to draw up the formal copyright agreement, which in
acknowledging Millar's £600 advance in June 1748, he had promised
to do on demand. By this agreement, dated 25 March 1749 and witnessed by Joshua Brogden, his clerk in Bow Street, Fielding signed
over to Millar all rights to *Tom Jones*, together "with all Improvements,
Additions or Alterations whatsoever which now are or hereafter shall
at any time be made."[343] Though copies of the second edition continued
to be available well into October, Millar wished to publish this new and
cheaper edition without delay. He released it to the public on 12 April
("*Price sew'd in Blue Paper Half a Guinea, or Bound 12 s.*").

By September, Strahan had printed a fourth edition of 3,500 sets,
bringing the total number of copies printed during the first nine months
of 1749 to 10,000 – a figure attesting to the novel's great popularity.
This supply, however, was sufficient to satisfy the public for many
years to come; and indeed, before publishing the fourth edition, Millar
waited to dispose of stock still on hand. Published on 11 December
1749, this edition, advertised as "Carefully revis'd and corrected/
By HENRY FIELDING, *Esq.*," represents his final conception of his
masterpiece.[344]

Clearly, though Richardson persisted in his refusal to read the book,
he set no very influential example. Even Fielding's enemies admitted
it was "in every Hand, from the beardless Youth, up to the hoary Hairs
of Age."[345] As to what readers have found to ponder and enjoy in *Tom
Jones*, there are as many answers as there have been critics of the novel.
Chief among its qualities, surely, is the festive entertainment Fielding
promises in his opening chapter, the "Bill of Fare to the Feast"; and
the hearty "Provision" he offers is nothing less than "HUMAN NATURE,"
in all its varities and degrees.

To apply another of Fielding's metaphors for the work, *Tom Jones*
may also be seen as his own "great Creation" (X.i). From this perspective, it seems indeed the summarizing expression of an entire world
view, of values characteristic of that period of English history (1660–
1750) called "the Augustan Age." This was the age of Newton and of
Pope – an age which saw the moral drama of the individual life enacted
within a frame of cosmic and social order conceived in the then still

compatible terms of Christian humanism and Newtonian science, and which saw the work of art as imitating this sense of things. According to a favorite metaphor of the philosophical tradition Fielding inherited, this drama was a comedy: for all its painful, eccentric episodes, it was an ordered progress, contrived and presided over by a Providence which, like Fielding's own "omniscient" narrator, conducts the actor-worldlings through complications of their own and others' making toward that final catastrophe when the cosmic equivalent of poetic justice will be meted out to all.

This is the confident, comfortable doctrine behind the poem that, Fielding remarked, "taught me a System of Philosophy in *English Numbers*":

> All Nature is but Art, unknown to thee;
> All Chance, Direction, which thou canst not see;
> All Discord, Harmony, not understood;
> All partial Evil, universal Good.

The world of *Tom Jones*, like that of Pope's *Essay on Man* (1733–4), is characterized not only by Energy – that animating power which everywhere enlivens its scenes and characters – but also by Order. "Art," ultimately, is the hidden, informing principle Fielding celebrates: with respect to the universe at large, the controlling hand of Providence, "the Art of God," is the source of harmony; with respect to the little world of man, Prudence – which Fielding, following Cicero, called "the Art of Life"[346] – is that practical, hard-earned virtue leading to the possession of Wisdom herself. Providence and Prudence, analogous attributes of macrocosm and microcosm, are also prominent themes of Fielding's novel, his own "great Creation" – novels being in his view, as he later put it in *Amelia* (I.i), "Models of HUMAN LIFE."[347] In *Tom Jones* these complementary motifs are rendered in the story of the hero's pursuit of Sophia and in the wonderful architecture of the book, in which, by means of the omniscient narrator and an almost geometrical symmetry of design, Fielding's form expresses the attributes of his world.

Though Fielding meant *Tom Jones* to stand as a timeless model of the human comedy as he understood it, a work transcending the private and idiosyncratic concerns of its author, yet it is also a very personal story and one rooted in the soil of mid-Georgian England. Consider, for instance, the setting of the first six books. Paradise Hall, where Fielding's foundling hero is born and raised, is, like Eden, an imaginary estate. Yet it is composed of elements associated in Fielding's mind with his own heritage and his own ideal identity. As he declares in the Dedication, the character of Allworthy, that paragon of benevolence and true paternity, is modeled on his benefactors, George Lyttelton and Ralph Allen, who had cared for him as his own father had never done. (The English word "patron" derives, aptly enough in this instance, from the Latin *pater*.) As Fielding describes it in Book I, chapter iv, Allworthy's seat is in many of its features a conflation of Hagley Hall and Prior Park, the estates of Lyttelton and Allen, respectively. On the other hand, the "*Gothick* Stile" of the building and its association with "Paradise" recall Sharpham Park, Fielding's own birthplace and the seat of his maternal grandfather, Judge Sir Henry Gould – that "most prudent" of men. The fine prospect Allworthy's house commands was in Fielding's day, before the levels had been drained, the prospect westward from atop the legendary Tor in Glastonbury, which, though Fielding does not mention it by name, is the specific locale in Somersetshire where the first third of his story takes place. From the threshold of Sharpham House the Tor rises in full view only a short distance away. Sophie Western, the girl Tom loves and marries, is, Fielding tells us (IV.ii), the very picture of his first wife Charlotte – "one whose Image never can depart from my Breast, and whom, if thou dost remember, thou hast then, my Friend, an adequate Idea of *Sophia*." Tom Jones himself – that headstrong, passionate young man whom all the family agree was "certainly born to be hanged" (III.ii) – very much resembles the willful lad Harry Fielding, whom Edmund's housekeeper had good reason to predict would "come to some ill or unfortunate End." Indeed, Fielding's own character and the course of his life – his progress from a wild, dissolute young man to the sagacious magistrate of his last years, preoccupied with the business of preserving public order and reforming the laws – are shadowed in the progress of his bumptious hero, who learns to discipline his passions in order to marry the girl he loves, whose name is Wisdom.

Like that of Joyce's Dublin, the world in which Tom Jones lives and through which he moves is a world in which fiction and actuality coalesce. The roads Tom Jones follows from Glastonbury to Wells, Gloucester, Upton-upon-Severn, and Meriden, and at last from Coventry to London, are roads Fielding traveled, and the time of Tom's journey is that perilous moment in the late autumn of 1745 when the Jacobite rebels had crossed the Tweed and were advancing deep into the heart of England. It is a world inhabited both by characters of Fielding's imagination and by living people of his acquaintance – by innkeepers and dancing-masters, actors and attorneys, toymen and prize-fighters, doctors and divines, coachmen and mantua-makers. Its events, whether trivial or momentous, are often those Fielding had experienced: in discordant strains Squire Western and his sister harp on the Court and on the war with France, and Jones marches north intending to fight the Jacobites. Sophia attends the riotous first night of Edward Moore's comedy (XIII.xi), and Partridge at a performance of *Hamlet* prefers the acting of "Billy" Mills to that of Garrick (XVI.v). Sophia is moved by a tender passage in *David Simple* (VI.v), and in her sentiments and demeanor Fielding invites us to compare his heroine with her rival, Richardson's Clarissa (XV.iii, XVI.v, XVIII.ix). What is more, the moral and religious issues that concern his characters are those that mattered to their author. Against the Methodistical cant of Captain Blifil, Allworthy, echoing Tillotson and Barrow, refutes the doctrine of absolute reprobation and defines true charity (II.ii, v). The deist Square mouths the ineffectual maxims of Shaftesbury, Tindal, and Chubb (III.iii), but in his conversion endorses arguments War-burton and Lyttelton had used to affirm the doctrine of immortality (XVIII.iv).

It is as if Fielding preserved for us, between the covers of a book, not only the time in which he lived – its events, its people of every degree, the feel of the countryside and the town – but the spirit of that time. For all its knaves and fools, it was a time when excellence in all things seemed attainable and was honored. Among the living contemporaries who help Fielding define it in *Tom Jones* are Hogarth in painting and Handel in music (I.xi, IV.ii); Hoadly and Warburton in divinity and Hardwicke in jurisprudence (II.vii, XIII.i, IV.vi); Pitt in oratory and Garrick on the stage (XIV.i, VII.i); Ranby in surgery (VIII.xiii) – all names that still command respect and (it is well to remember when imagining the kind of person Fielding was) all men whom he numbered among his friends and acquaintance. As for Fielding's taste in architecture, his standards were the works of James Gibbs, Roger Morris, and John Wood, of William Kent and Charles Bridgeman, who built the stately houses and laid out the gardens that adorned the countryside, visibly attesting to the magnificence of England – England as it was now governed by his powerful Whig friends: Pelham's seat at Esher, Surrey; Viscount Cobham's at Stowe, Buckinghamshire; the Earl of Pembroke's at Wilton, near Salisbury; Dodington's at Eastbury, Dorset – and most especially Ralph Allen's at Prior Park:

> Here Nature appears in her richest Attire, and Art dressed with the modestest Simplicity, attends her benignant Mistress. Here Nature indeed pours forth the choicest Treasures which she hath lavished on this World; and here Human Nature presents you with an Object which can be exceeded only in the other.
>
> (XI.ix)

In this way, his taste for an orderly magnificence in architecture outwardly expressing the natural goodness of his heart, Allen represents that spirit of liberality and benevolence which animates *Tom Jones* and which for Fielding was the final measure of every skill and virtue. From Allen and of course from Lyttelton – "two of the best and worthiest Men in the World" who, as he was pleased to boast in the Dedication, "are strongly and zealously my Friends" – he had drawn in this work what his readers declared to be "a stronger Picture of a truly benevolent Mind than is to be found in any other." Lyttelton would understand why, as he wrote these words in his parlor in Bow Street, Fielding now wished to "add a third to the Number":

and him one of the greatest and noblest, not only in his Rank, but in every public and private Virtue. But here whilst my Gratitude for the princely Benefactions of the Duke of *Bedford* bursts from my Heart, you must forgive my reminding you, that it was you who first recommended me to the Notice of my Benefactor.

PART IV

Magistrate and reformer
(1749–54)

The office to which Fielding had been appointed – and which elicited from him in the Dedication to *Tom Jones* such effusions of gratitude to Lyttelton and the Duke of Bedford – was among the most cheerless and despicable in the kingdom. After his death Lady Mary Wortley Montagu reflected sadly on the cousin whom she loved, regretting that "the highest of his preferment [was] raking in the lowest sinks of vice and misery." In her opinion, it would have been "a nobler and less nauseous employment to be one of the staff-officers that conduct the nocturnal weddings."[1] The life of a metropolitan justice was not for the squeamish. Throughout his brief but active career, Fielding would daily confront the worst and the most pitiable of humankind – a horrid parade of thieves and cheats, robbers and murderers, rapists and sodomites; many who reveled in cruelty, who battered women and ravished children. And with these came the misfits and outcasts, beggars and vagrants – such poor and naked wretches as haunted Lear.

For his pains in administering justice and keeping the peace in such circumstances he would also suffer the heavy load of opprobrium and contempt attached to the so-called "trading justices" of Westminster and Middlesex. Elsewhere in the kingdom – since magistrates were not salaried, but, if they were honest, earned a pittance from the fees legally associated with their office, such as licensing of public houses or issuing writs of commitment – the job generally fell to country gentlemen of independent means.[2] In London, where the demands upon justices were much greater and particularly repellent, only men of inferior rank could, for the most part, be enlisted, men who depended on "Justice Business" to make a living. Such men – whom Fielding characterized in Squeezum of *Rape upon Rape* (1731) – had a reputation for abusing their authority, for growing rich on the bribes of brothel-keepers and a variety of extortionary practices. By his own account (confirmed by disinterested witnesses) Fielding's conduct in the magistracy was very different from this. The income he might normally expect from the office was £500 a year. His predecessor DeVeil boasted that he made a thousand. By acting honestly and humanely, Fielding, who had far more business than DeVeil, could earn only a third as much:

> on the contrary, by composing, instead of inflaming, the quarrels of porters and beggars (which I blush when I say hath not been universally practised) and by refusing to take a shilling from a man who most undoubtedly would not have had another left, I had reduced an income of about 500 l. a year of the dirtiest money upon earth, to little more than 300 l.; a considerable proportion of which remained with my clerk.[3]

Indeed, Fielding on the bench often spent his prodigious energies in activities that were purely altruistic – activities calculated on the one hand to ensure that justice was done in hundreds of individual cases for which he received little or nothing in the way of fees, and on the other hand calculated to persuade the legislature of the need to reform both the laws themselves and the system for executing them. He brought to this office an exalted, even an idealistic, sense of its function in preserving the public order. Among the first to recognize the need for a stipendiary magistracy, he initiated by his example the slow process which led to the implementation of that reform, if inadequately, in the Middlesex Justices Bill of 1792. As "Court Justice" he "received from the government a yearly pension out of the public service-money." That his "great patron," as Fielding with a touch of irony calls the Duke of Newcastle when discussing these arrangements,[4] granted him this salary from the start seems unlikely. Fielding considered the amount of the pension small, but he tended to value his services highly. It may have been as little as £200; more likely it was £400, the stipend settled upon his half-brother John when, after Fielding's death, his responsibilities as "Court Justice" and director of police devolved upon him.[5] If Fielding's experience resembled his brother's, he was paid this money in equal half-yearly installments, but only after humbly applying for them in writing to jog the Duke's memory.[6]

····➤ ii ➤····

Some weeks before the publication of *Tom Jones* the public became aware of Fielding's latest professional metamorphosis as the cases that came before him began to be reported by "the diurnal Historians," as he liked to call the newswriters of the day. From the beginning of his magistracy he understood the value of advertising his office, not merely from the mercenary motive of increasing his business, but for public-spirited reasons. In this way he alerted the citizenry to the nature and prevalency of the evils that plagued society; moreover, by publishing descriptions of criminals and stolen goods, and by encouraging the victims of crimes as well as the pawnbrokers who were offered the booty to come forward to prosecute felons, he attempted to check the spreading epidemic.

The earliest such report – many of which seem to be based on copy supplied by Fielding or his clerk, Joshua Brogden – appeared in the *General Advertiser* for Friday, 2 December 1748.[7] It was a case in which Fielding, after the kind of rigorous and (in intent at least) impartial examination that characterized his conduct on the bench, committed to the Gatehouse Prison a certain genteel thief who had victimized a German householder and his maid.

Several other cases during this, his second month acting in the commission, reveal how seriously he took these new responsibilities, bringing to a despised office a sagacity, diligence, and compassion that distinguished him from most of his colleagues. On Saturday, 10 December, for instance, a certain Mrs. Molloy was carried before him charged with stealing six guineas; but, though her accusers insisted on her guilt, Fielding became convinced she was innocent:

> Two Persons swore positively to the Fact, but after a long Examination, which lasted several Hours, the principal Witness having contradicted himself in many Instances, and a great Number of creditable and substantial People appearing on the Behalf of Mrs. Molloy, who all concurred in giving her the best of Characters, the Justice at last was pleased to admit her to Bail.[8]

On Friday, 16 December, he dealt severely with one of the thousands of redundant sailors who had been turned loose on the town when the war with France ended in October. This man, John Jones by name, had the night before "barbarously and wantonly" wounded a young woman with a cutlass. Though the woman "had the Good-Nature to forgive the Assault," Fielding committed Jones to the Gatehouse for going about the streets armed with a dangerous weapon. Characteristically, he used the occasion not only to urge the culprit's less tender-hearted victims to come forward to prosecute him, but also to instruct the public on a point of law designed for their protection:

> it's hoped that all Persons who have lately been robb'd or attack'd in the Streets by Men in Sailors Jackets, in which Dress the said Jones appear'd, will give themselves the Trouble of resorting to the Prison in order to view him. It may perhaps be of some Advantage to the Publick to inform them (especially at this Time) that for such Persons to go about arm'd with any Weapon whatever is a very high Offence, and expressly forbidden by several old Statutes still in Force, on Pain of Imprisonment, and Forfeiture of their Arms.[9]

On Thursday, 29 December, in two separate cases, Fielding again exerted himself to protect the innocent, a girl of twelve and a young woman, from the accusations of malicious prosecutors. In a scene that might have served Dickens in *Oliver Twist*, the girl was falsely accused of robbing "one Fagan" of some silver: "which he refusing to verify upon Oath, and it being attested that the Child had been thrown into dangerous Fits by the Terror she had undergone on that Occasion, and as she and her Parents appeared to be of Substance and Character, and the said Fagan an idle and dissolute Fellow, the Justice discharged the

Girl, and committed her Accuser to Prison."[10] That same day one
William Darkis, having persuaded a lonely French woman to marry
him, repented of the deed when she began asking for money. Trusting
in the fact that the woman was alone and friendless, Darkis brought her
before Fielding, denying the marriage and charging her with extorting
money from him:

> The Woman being required to find Sureties, fell into an Agony of
> Tears, and declared she was a Stranger in this Kingdom, and had no
> sufficient Person to be bound for her, but alledged that she was really
> married to the said Darkis; to prove which she produced several
> Letters, and other Evidences under his Hand, all which he denied
> upon Oath; at last the Woman bethought herself of some Persons
> who lived in Southwark, that were Witnesses to her Marriage, for
> whom the Justice being touched with Compassion at so extraordinary
> a Case, sent a Messenger at his own Expence, and they upon their
> Oaths, confirmed the Truth of the Marriage, at which one of them
> had been actually present. The Woman was then discharged, and as
> to the Prosecutor he had taken Care to withdraw himself some Time
> before.[11]

Unremarkable as they are, these five cases from his earliest days as
a magistrate are representative of the qualities Fielding evinced on the
bench. We see in them his assiduity in examining witnesses and weighing evidence in order to distinguish truth from falsehood: this, the
crucial importance of forming true judgments – the function of *prudentia* in the humanist tradition – is a prominent theme of *Tom Jones*.
These cases also reveal Fielding's concern with protecting the weak and
innocent (even if it meant sending to Southwark for witnesses "at his
own Expence"). On the other hand, they reveal how severe he could
be with malefactors who showed any traits of cruelty, vindictiveness,
or malevolence. Here, too, is recorded the first of his many efforts to
raise the public's consciousness concerning the laws themselves, whether
they were sound and useful (empowering him, in this instance, to clear
the streets of the armed villain Jones, even though his victim refused
to prosecute), or whether, as often happened, they seemed inadequate
and in need of reform.

These cases hint at the character of Fielding's magistracy, but they
convey no adequate sense of the magnitude and enormity of the labors
he had now undertaken. They are merely five of his cases selected
from seventeen reported in the newspapers during the single month of
December 1748 – those seventeen cases themselves representing only a
fraction of the business Fielding conducted that month. And he had
not yet begun to act in the Middlesex commission, which greatly
increased the demands on him. Anyone wishing to assess how much of

his time and energy, not to mention his spiritual resources, Fielding gave to the magistracy must keep in mind that the great majority of cases which occupied him – the sad drudgery of issuing warrants to settle the vagrant poor in their country parishes,[12] or of binding over the contentious to keep the peace, or of examining and correcting prostitutes – were never newsworthy enough to be reported in the papers. The sobering effect of such constant exposure to human misery and depravity on a man of his generous sympathies must have been considerable, notwithstanding that innate cheerfulness his friends remarked in him. Out of curiosity Samuel Johnson attended a Westminster magistrate's court for an entire winter and found there such a "uniform tenor of misfortune, wretchedness and profligacy" he had no desire to repeat the experiment.[13] Fielding lived with these things daily for five years. The wonder is that the experience never hardened him, or made him cynical in the performance of his duties. He could be severe with villains, or when severity might serve to tame the lawless and preserve the social order; but he continued to judge the wretches he examined as individual men and women, assessing not only their veracity, but their character, and he was lenient when he could be. He never, for example, committed a prostitute to the house of correction if he believed a stern rebuke had any chance of shaming her into repentance; for Bridewell was "a School rather for the Improvement, than for the Correction of Debauchery."[14] In this, "tempering Justice with Mercy," he resembled Allworthy in *Tom Jones* (I.ix), who had too much humanity to sacrifice Jenny Jones "to Ruin and Infamy by a shameful Correction in a *Bridewel*." If, as a justice, he also resembled Allworthy in a less admirable respect, committing errors of judgment that were sometimes the consequence of an overweening confidence in his own perspicacity and the benevolence of his motives, the record of his magistracy will be, on the whole, the story of an exemplary, even a sacrificial dedication to the public welfare.

···◄● iii ●►···

January 1748/9 was an eventful month for Fielding. This was the month in which he began to function as a justice for Middlesex as well as Westminster, and it was the month when Strahan's presses at last delivered his masterpiece. Earlier, Fielding's wife gave birth to their second child, Mary Amelia, named after her mother and one of the royal princesses. She was baptized at St. Paul's, Inigo Jones's handsome church in Covent Garden, on 6 January; she would be buried there before the year was out, on 17 December.[15] She lived long enough, nevertheless, to inspire Fielding with the name for the heroine of his last work of fiction, *Amelia*, the novel he called his "favourite Child."[16]

January 1748/9 was also the month when Fielding's magistracy began to assume that graver aspect for which it is chiefly remembered. As "Court Justice" he was the one to whom the government and public turned in hopes that effective measures might be found to curb the depredations of large gangs of street robbers and smugglers. By a macabre coincidence one of the most sensational of these cases occurred when a gang of twenty armed pickpockets, all of them Irish and all discharged sailors, stormed the Gatehouse Prison and rescued one Thomas Jones – the favorite of the gang, who called themselves "The Royal Family." Later this year Fielding and his constables would be chiefly responsible for bringing the gang to justice.[17] More immediately, he put a stop this month to the violent career of Nicholas Mooney (otherwise known as "Terrible Nick" or "Nick the King of Glory"), the head of another gang which Fielding broke by means of one of his favorite devices: after Mooney was apprehended on the night of 20 January, Fielding publicized details of the robbery in the newspapers and invited the gang's victims to come forward to prosecute: if their evidence led to a conviction, they could claim a reward which, by royal proclamation adding £100 to the statutory £40, was no small inducement to public-spiritedness.[18] As experience soon painfully proved, it was also an irresistible temptation to unscrupulous thief-takers to swear away the lives of innocent men. On 11 January, Fielding had another success, eliciting from a smuggler testimony which led to the capture of a gang that raided the Customs House at Poole, Dorset.[19] The suppression of these smugglers was a cause in which Fielding's patron the Duke of Richmond was particularly interested.

At the moment, however, Richmond was not so earnestly occupied. Together with his chum, the Duke of Montagu, he was responsible for perpetrating one of the splendid hoaxes of the century. To demonstrate to his friends "the credulity of the English Nation," Montagu wagered 100 guineas that he could fill the Little Haymarket Theatre with paying customers if he advertised that at an appointed time a conjurer would appear on stage who would enter a quart bottle and entertain the audience with a song. Montagu won the bet – at an unforeseen cost, however, to John Potter, owner of the theatre, and to Samuel Foote, who, undeterred by Fielding's rebuke in *The Jacobite's Journal*, had continued to "auction" there his "pictures" of celebrities. On 16 January a large audience came early to the Little Haymarket and waited with mounting impatience to see the bottle-conjurer perform his trick. When a voice from behind the curtain apologetically explained that the conjuror was indisposed that evening, but if they stayed until tomorrow he would, for double the money, make amends for their disappointment by squeezing himself into a pint bottle, the audience went berserk. They gutted Potter's theatre and made a bonfire of his furnishings. Damages were estimated at more than £4,000 – an expense which the prankster dukes and their noble friends are said to have assumed. For Fielding, besides the hilarity of the joke, it had the further merit of curtailing Foote's apery by destroying his stage.[20]

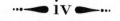

····■ iv ◖■····

Richmond soon involved Fielding in graver matters. For some time he had tried to suppress the brutal gangs of smugglers who infested the southern coast. On 10 March at a tavern in Kent, Richmond and Fielding jointly heard the testimony of Thomas Winter, a smuggler and murderer known to his colleagues as "Footsey" or "Frost."[21] Winter's evidence implicated a dozen members of a gang who, brandishing carbines and pistols, had on an August night in 1748 forcibly entered the isolated house of a Mr. Wakeford, terrorizing him and his servants and robbing him of silver and cash. Winter's testimony was used at the Winchester assizes to convict only one of these banditti, Joseph Rawlins.[22] But most of the others named were among the smugglers who had broken into the Customs House at Poole, a crime Fielding was actively engaged in solving. Of these, Thomas Kingsmill and William Fairall would hang for that crime, while another, Richard Mapesden, was acquitted on a technicality.[23] John Mills, another of the raiders at Poole, had taken part in the savage torture and murder of Daniel Chater, an informer, and William Galley, a Customs House officer, who while traveling to Sussex to give evidence in the case were intercepted by the gang. Instigator of the outrage against Wakeford was Jeremiah Curtis, who, together with Winter and the inhuman Mills, had in January 1747/8 whipped and kicked to death a fellow smuggler they suspected of cheating. Fielding's exposure to the most appalling depravity of human nature had begun in earnest.

Less than a month after they cooperated in the examination of Winter, Richmond asked Fielding to arrange to have another Crown witness, John Drury, taken from Newgate to the same tavern in Kent, where they might take his testimony – presumably against two other smugglers, George Chapman and James Double, who at the August assizes in Sussex were on Drury's evidence convicted of murdering a customs officer. On 8 April, Fielding replied from Bow Street. Having conferred with the Keeper of Newgate (Richard Akerman) and one of the High Sheriffs of London, he regretted that they could not comply with the Duke's request: since Drury was in Newgate not only on indictments for smuggling and murder, but in execution for debt, "the Goaler would be guilty of an Escape, if he suffered him to go out of the Liberties of the Prison."[24] Nor could Fielding himself examine Drury in Newgate, "Newgate being in the City of London and consequently out of my Jurisdiction."

Besides the light these documents shed on Fielding's professional activities and the role he played in the war Richmond waged against smugglers, the letter reveals that the friendly relations he enjoyed with the Duke were continuing, as cordially, of course, as the distinction in their social positions would permit. Included within the circle of their friendship were Richmond's companions, the Duke of Montagu and Captain Bodens, for whose (supposed) comedy *The Modish Couple* (1732) Fielding had supplied an epilogue:

> As I shall always esteem it one of the highest Honours to receive the Commands of your Grace, it gives much Uneasiness that it is in this Instance out of my Power to execute them. I hope, my Lord, nothing hath intervened to prevent me of the Honour which Mr Bodens gave me some Expectation that your Grace and the Duke of Mountagu intended me, and with the Hopes of which I so agreeably flattered myself. Your Grace hath done me many Favours; but I assure you, my Lord, you will do me no more than Justice in believing me to be with the utmost Gratitude and Respect ....

It is not clear what the "Honour" was which Richmond and Montagu jointly intended Fielding, and which he found so flattering. Probably it was nothing more than a promise to honor him with a visit to Bow Street; for this inseparable pair of fun-loving lords would be in town to witness one of the most remarkable spectacles ever staged in the capital – a spectacle for which Montagu, as Master of the Ordnance, was chiefly responsible.

Preparations had long been making to commemorate the Treaty of Aix-la-Chapelle, which in October 1748 ended the War of the Austrian Succession. The war having gone badly for England, the government was determined to celebrate the peace in the grandest style. For this purpose the renowned Cavaliere Jean-Nicholas Servandoni (1695–1766) – a native of Florence, but now director of stage design at the Paris Opera and architect of the church of St. Sulpice – was commissioned to construct a machine for a magnificent display of fireworks. This he accomplished at great expense. The machine Servandoni erected was in the form of a splendid Doric temple, 114 feet high, with wings extending to either side, each terminating in an elegant pavilion; in all, the structure sprawled over 410 feet of Green Park, near the Palace. (See Plate 54.) Despite the jeers of the Opposition press, which deplored the waste of public money to celebrate an event that should have been lamented as a national calamity, thousands of spectators crowded Green Park at the appointed time, the evening of Thursday, 27 April. At seven o'clock the King, accompanied by Fielding's patrons, the Dukes of Bedford, Richmond, and Montagu, toured Servandoni's great "Cracker Castle" and expressed his pleasure by distributing purses of gold. At 8:30 the jubilee commenced with the playing of Handel's Fireworks Music, which was immediately followed by the deafening salute of 101 brass cannon. Then the fireworks began – disastrously: a workman fell from the scaffolding and dashed his brains out; a drunken cobbler stumbled into a pond and drowned; a young woman watching from a boat on the Thames went overboard; a rocket shot off-course into the grandstand and set another young woman's dress alight. Still more inauspiciously, as the assembled multitude gaped, the pavilion at the right wing of the edifice caught fire.

Pushing through the crowd to try to stop the blaze from spreading, the Cavaliere Servandoni was halted in full career – indeed, "assaulted and collar'd" – by Charles Frederick, Esq., Comptroller of the Woolwich Depot, who under Montagu was in charge of the occasion. *"What,"* Servandoni exclaimed, *"will you let my Building burn!"* When he offered to draw his sword, he was seized and taken by soldiers to the guardroom at the Palace. After two nights in durance, on Saturday he was

> carried before Mr. Justice Fielding, whither his Prosecutor [Charles Frederick] soon after came in his Chariot, and swore the Peace against Signior Servandoni, declaring he went in Danger of his Life, and receiving bodily Harm. The two Matrosses, who were called in, declared they saw Signior Servandoni's Sword half drawn, and that they heard him say, he would run the Prosecutor through the Guts. Upon the whole, Signior Servandoni was discharged, after having found Sureties for his good Behaviour, one in 1000 l. and two in 500 l. each.

This account, published the following Tuesday in the *General Advertiser* (2 May 1749) as "the true State of the Case" (a phrase Fielding used later this year to entitle his pamphlet on Bosavern Penlez), may possibly have come from his pen. If so, he might have added that in order to cool the fiery Italian cavalier and ensure the safety of Montagu's agent, Fielding, over and above the sureties stated, required Servandoni to post a bond of £1,000 in his own name.[25]

This was the part Fielding played in the fiasco of the Royal Fireworks. The results were happier a few nights later on 6 May, when the Duke of Richmond, using what remained of the twenty-five tons of fireworks the Italians had provided, mounted his own magnificent display opposite his house on the Thames.

...◄● V ●►...

Meanwhile, Fielding continued – day in, day out – with the less glam-
orous business of his magistracy, doing so with a zeal which both the
public and his fellow justices found impressive. In March he was among
the advocates of a Bill calculated to feed the poor by breaking the
monopoly of the fishmongers: this, he later recalled, was that "excellent
scheme of the Westminster market, to the erecting which so many
justices of peace, as well as other wise and learned men, did so
vehemently apply themselves."[26] Though the plan passed into law on
24 June 1749 (22 Geo. II, c. 49) – with Dodington and Bedford's
brother-in-law, Viscount Trentham among the appointed trustees – the
fishmongers conspired to render it ineffectual; for which act of callous
self-interest, if only the legislature would declare "the starving thousands of poor ... to be felony," Fielding would hang them all.

As Fielding toiled in Covent Garden to dispense justice and help the
poor, Horace Walpole, snug in his mansion in St. James's, thought of
diverting George Montagu with droll scenes from the slums. On 18 May
he wrote: "I could not help laughing in myself t'other day, as I went
through Holborn in a very hot day, at the dignity of human nature;
all those foul old-clothes women panting without handkerchiefs, and
mopping themselves all the way down within their loose jumps." This
vignette of low-life called to mind another his friend Richard Rigby
(1722–88) had sketched for him:

> Rigby gave me as strong a picture of nature: he and Peter Bathurst
> t'other night carried a servant of the latter's, who had attempted to
> shoot him, before Fielding; who, to all his other vocations, has, by
> the grace of Mr. Lyttelton, added that of Middlesex justice. He sent
> them word he was at supper, that they must come next morning.
> They did not understand that freedom, and ran up, where they found
> him banqueting with a blind man, a whore, and three Irishmen, on
> some cold mutton and a bone of ham, both in one dish, and the
> dirtiest cloth. He never stirred nor asked them to sit. Rigby, who
> had seen him so often come to beg a guinea of Sir C. Williams, and
> Bathurst, at whose father's he had lived for victuals, understood that
> dignity as little, and pulled themselves chairs; on which he civilized.[27]

Rigby draws rather a different picture of Fielding at home from the
one Joseph Warton gave of the evening he was so "very well entertained" at Boswell Court. The company Rigby and young Bathurst
found when they interrupted Fielding at supper included of course his
half-brother John (the "blind man") and his wife (the "whore"). Who
knows what rabble the trio of Irishmen might be! Rigby, however, was

not in all respects accurate in representing the circumstances of this intrusion. The son of Fielding's friend Peter Bathurst (c. 1688–1768) of Clarendon Park, Wilts., brother of the great Earl, young Peter (c. 1724–1801) lived near Rigby in fashionable Hanover Square. On 10 May 1749, far from being victimized by his French servant, Louis Carpentier, Bathurst and Rigby together beat him within an inch of his life. It was Carpentier, supported by three witnesses, who brought a complaint against these gentlemen.[28] Bathurst was incensed by this impertinence: a fortnight later (24 May) he again assaulted Carpentier, who swore the peace against him before a magistrate.[29] What other circumstances did Rigby omit or embellish when he amused Walpole with this story of Fielding's rudeness and vulgarity? (The cloth was not too dirty or the company too vile for the intruders to pull up chairs.) Besides the possibility that Fielding found the abuse of a servant reprehensible, the fact that he was prevented from refreshing himself with family and friends after attending the Middlesex Sessions[30] could account for his irritation at the intrusion.

The attitude of his colleagues on the bench, at any rate, was more respectful. When the Westminster Quarter Sessions began on 29 March 1749, they elected him Chairman;[31] he had not yet been six months in the commission. Indeed, soon after the Middlesex Sessions began on 9 May several newspapers reported that the justices had "unanimously chosen" him to replace Thomas Lane as Chairman for Middlesex as well.[32] That, however, was a false report, owing perhaps to confusion over the fact that his election to the Westminster chairmanship was not officially recorded until 17 May, when the justices for Middlesex, not Westminster, were sitting. Though Fielding never chaired the Middlesex Sessions, he served in that capacity for Westminster for nearly three years.

It is important to grasp this distinction, since the dignity of Fielding's place in the magistracy – if not his importance to the government or his extraordinary accomplishments in that office – has often been exaggerated. The Middlesex chairmanship was the more eminent one. The Middlesex General Sessions met eight times a year – six at Hicks's Hall, St. John's Street, Clerkenwell, and twice (in April and October) at Westminster Hall – and was concerned with serious crimes. The Westminster Quarter Sessions met four times a year in the town Court House, near Westminster Hall, and was concerned with minor offenses, public nuisances, and misdemeanors. Notwithstanding the modesty of the honor thus conferred on him, Fielding understood the scope it afforded him to promote the reformation of society at the most fundamental level.

When the Westminster Sessions convened on Thursday, 29 June 1749, Fielding delivered the Chairman's customary charge to the Grand Jury. It was, the papers reported, "an excellent and learned Speech."[33] To judge from the version Millar published "By Order of the Court" on 21 July[34] under the title *A Charge delivered to the Grand Jury*, it was remarkable for another quality as well: its monitory vision of a morally corrupt society. The setting for this address to the custodians of order in the capital was emblematic of Fielding's theme: the Westminster Court House was an unwholesome building in decay – dark, overcrowded, oppressively hot and noisome at this season, its foundations were literally sunk in a common sewer.[35]

Published not six months after *Tom Jones*, the charge Fielding delivered to the Westminster Grand Jury signals the radical change which his experience of the magistracy had already effected in his understanding of his role as an author – a change, as we will see, even in his conception of the art of fiction. Though he speaks of Grand Juries, not of magistrates, Fielding's sense of his own function is plain as he reminds his audience of their role as "Censors of this Nation," emphasizing their responsibility to correct not so much the crimes as the *manners* of the people. As magistrate, he had become in fact what in his early days as journalist he facetiously claimed to be in metaphor – that is, the "Censor of the Age," Britain's "Champion" and "True Patriot." He exhorts the jurors to preserve peace and the established order by presenting offenders against God, the King, and the general public. His aim is to improve the moral character of society. The targets of the purge he recommends are not the rogues and felons who were ravaging the streets, but those who more insidiously undermined the stability and moral fibre of the nation – blasphemers and free-thinkers and all who bring the Church of England into contempt; those who swear and curse profanely; the politically disaffected, particularly all Jacobites; those who behave publicly in a lewd or indecent way, "to the Scandal of Good-manners"; the keepers of brothels, which have become "the Seminaries of Education," and of gaming houses; the perpetrators of masquerades, whose houses are "the Temples of Iniquity"; the exhibitors of licentious theatrical entertainments, such as Foote's abusive mimickry; libelers who rob "us of our good Name," whether by word of mouth or in print – for, as the hackney writers of the day had for some years been demonstrating at his expense, "there are Men who make a Livelihood of Scandal." All these were in law mere "Misdemeanours," not what Fielding calls "Crimes of the deeper Dye"; but together their total effect on society was more destructive because more pervasive and endemic. "This Fury after licentious and luxurious Pleasures," he declares, "is grown to so enormous a Height, that it may be called the Characteristic of the present Age." Applying a favorite analogy, he represents them as

> Evils of a more durable Kind, which rather resemble chronical than epidemic Diseases; and which have so inveterated themselves in the Blood of the Body Politic, that they are perhaps never to be totally eradicated. These it will be always the Duty of the Magistrate to palliate and keep down as much as possible.

The *Charge* is memorable for the sense it conveys of a great nation in decay and of Fielding's determination to apply his talents, whether as magistrate or author, to repair England's constitution. As he concludes in a passage whose language seems to echo the Gardener's speech in *Richard II* (III.iv) but whose tone of apocalyptic foreboding evokes Pope's final vision in *The Dunciad*, we may gauge the difference in mood that distinguishes his next novel, *Amelia*, from the buoyant comedy of *Tom Jones*. What was at stake in the duties he enjoins upon the jurors and justices of England was the survival of civilization:

> For as in a Garden, however well cultivated at first, if the Weeder's Care be omitted, the Whole must in Time be over-run with Weeds, and will resemble the Wildness and Rudeness of a Desert; so if those Immoralities of the People, which will sprout up in the best Constitution, be not from Time to Time corrected by the Hand of Justice, they will at length grow up to the most enormous Vices, will overspread the whole Nation, and in the End must produce a downright State of wild and savage Barbarism.

There was, to be sure, a certain awkwardness in the fact that the author of this jeremiad had himself formerly led the kind of life he now gravely deplored. Fielding's enemies mocked the hypocrisy of his performance and delighted in supplying from his own conduct and writings examples of the vices he censured.[36] The *Charge*, however, was otherwise well received, most particularly by the *Monthly Review*.[37] Thomas Birch, who earlier this year (if not before) had begun to dine occasionally at Fielding's table, wrote to Lady Grey, daughter-in-law of the Lord Chancellor, summarizing the piece: it was, he assured her, "an excellent performance, & worthy the Character of Mr. Alworthy himself."[38] Weightier still is the authoritative opinion of Fielding's modern editor, who, having surveyed the field and considered the range of Fielding's learning, pronounces the *Charge* "a masterly and assured model of its kind."[39]

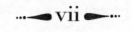

The weather when Fielding addressed the Westminster justices had
turned uncomfortably, indeed ominously, hot – "as hot," the papers
noted, "as it usually is at Jamaica."[40] To escape the heat and fetid air
of Covent Garden, Fielding left Bow Street to spend the weekend in
the country. While he was gone, rioting erupted in the Strand, as huge
mobs of sailors, joined by the wilder elements of the populace, began
pulling down the bawdy-houses.

The trouble started on Saturday afternoon, 1 July, when sailors
belonging to H.M.S. *Grafton* were bilked and bullied at a brothel. Bent
on revenge, they roused their mates and returned to wreak rough justice
on the house. A constable testified that by early evening the mob was
so great they "filled up the whole Space of the Street for near two
hundred Yards."[41] They swarmed into the house and demolished it,
throwing the furniture out the windows – pictures, mirrors, tables,
chairs, feather beds, and the hoops and gowns of the whores, who were
turned out of doors naked. These goods and furnishings, piled up in the
street, they set ablaze, causing (the constable reported) "so violent a
Flame, that the Beams of the Houses adjoining were so heated thereby,
that the Inhabitants were apprehensive of the utmost Danger from the
Fire"; the firemen fortunately managed to contain it. In an effort to
quell the disturbance, a dozen troops were dispatched from Somerset
House and, when these proved insufficient, forty reinforcements were
summoned from the Tilt-Yard. Far from being cowed by this show of
force, the mob moved on to the Bunch of Grapes, another bawdy-house
in the Strand. Only the combined force of guards and peace officers,
who were pelted with stones, preserved the building – not, however,
before all the windows were shattered. It was three o'clock before the
rioters dispersed. Two of them were seized and committed to the watch-
house, but at midnight the next day (Sunday, 2 July) their friends
broke open the prison and rescued them. By that time a second "vast
Mob" had completed the destruction of the Bunch of Grapes, making
a bonfire of the goods and furnishings even larger than the one the night
before. The neighbors, afraid the destruction would spread, appealed for
troops, but they could not find a magistrate to give authorization.

On this second night of rioting, Saunders Welch – High Constable
for the Holborn Division and one of Fielding's closest friends – enters
the story of his life. Welch (1711–84), born of poor parents in Buckinghamshire, had prospered in London as a grocer. As Sir John Hawkins's daughter remembered him, he was, despite his obscure origins,
"in person, mind, and manners, most perfectly a gentleman."[42] He

became one of Johnson's "best and dearest friends"[43] and the father-in-law of the sculptor Nollekens.

On the present occasion Welch, returning at midnight from the City, was horrified to see the huge fire in the Strand. Though he lacked the required authority, he hastened to the Tilt-Yard and prevailed on the commander of the garrison to dispatch an officer and forty men to accompany him to the scene of the riot, where they arrived to find the mob in process of demolishing yet a third bawdy-house – the Star, owned by Peter Wood – whose furnishings they were throwing into the street, intending, as Welch believed, to start another fire. Had they done so, it was clear – since the Strand narrowed at that point – houses on both sides of the street would be consumed, one of which was a bank. Luckily, when they heard the beat of the drum, the mob fled the house and had no time to light the fire. Several of them were apprehended and conveyed under guard to New Prison, Clerkenwell. Recalling this critical moment, Fielding declared:

That had not Mr. *Welch* (one of the best Officers who was ever concerned with the Execution of Justice, and to whose Care, Integrity and Bravery the Public hath, to my Knowledge, the highest Obligations) been greatly active in the Discharge of his Duty; and had he not arrived Time enough to prevent the Burning of that Pile of Goods which was heaped up before *Wood's* House, the most dreadful Consequences must have ensued from this Riot. For not to mention the Mischiefs which must necessarily have happened from the Fire in that narrow Part of the Town, what must have been the Consequence of exposing a Banker's Shop to the Greediness of the Rabble? Or what might we have reasonably apprehended from a Mob encouraged by such a Booty, and made desperate by such atrocious Guilt?[44]

Among those arrested in the early hours of the morning was Bosavern Penlez, a young man somewhat the worse for drink, who was taken by the watch as he tried to flee with a large quantity of linen and lace which Mother Wood, mistress of the Star, swore he had stolen from the house during the riot. The arrest of Penlez would involve Fielding in the most regrettable case of his magistracy.

On Monday morning, 3 July, Fielding returned to town to attend the opening of the Middlesex Sessions.[45] Though he immediately took measures to prevent further public disturbances, he had other business on his mind of a private nature. However keen he once had been to secure the place of "Court Justice," he was now, after a few months' experience of this vile office, eager to change it for something better. The place of Solicitor to the Excise having become vacant, he wrote to ask Bedford to bestow it on him:

I hope no Person is better qualified for it, and I assure you, my Lord, none shall execute it with more Fidelity. I am at this Moment busied in endeavouring to suppress a dangerous Riot, or I would have personally waited on your Grace to solicite a Favour which will make me and my Family completely happy.[46]

Bedford did not grant Fielding this favor, which would have freed him from the killing labors of "Justice Business" as he chose, heroically, to practice it. But if his promotion from the magistracy to a less arduous and more dignified post might have prolonged his life, it would have deprived the public of its ablest champion in the war against crime.

Soon after Fielding sent this request to Bedford, Welch came to acquaint him with the gravity of the disorders that had occurred in his absence from town. Fielding ordered a party of guards to conduct the prisoners from prison to Bow Street for examination, after which he committed them to Newgate.[47] Already the mob were reassembling and threatening a rescue. They filled Bow Street and spilled over into the streets adjacent, openly intent on continuing the sport of pulling down bawdy-houses that night. Fielding sent Welch to the Secretary at War, Henry Fox, urgently requesting more troops, but there was no response. From his window he read the Riot Act, warning the mob of their danger and urging them to disperse; but they were unmoved either by these threats or by Welch's entreaties, who bravely ventured into the street among them. As evening fell and Fielding received fresh information that a host of armed sailors was preparing to descend on the Strand, he wrote again to Bedford in a very different vein:

I think it my Duty to acquaint your Grace that I have recd repeated Informations of upwards of 3000 Sailors now in Arms ab.t Wapping and that they threaten to march to this End of the Town this Night, under Pretence of demolishing all Bawdy Houses. I have an Officer and 50 Men and submit to y.r Grace what more Assistance may be necessary. I sent a Messenger five Hours ago to the Secretary at War but have yet no Answer.[48]

Fearful that their houses would be pillaged and destroyed, citizens began removing their possessions and clearing out. Fielding, however, at last had the mob under control. Together with Welch and the officer of the guards, he sat up through the night while peace officers patroled the streets and a large party of soldiers, fully armed, was kept in readiness. Peace had been restored.

The dangers the city so narrowly escaped were real and terrifying. Nevertheless, the malevolent author of Old England (15 July 1749) was soon depicting Fielding and the government he represented as the corrupt oppressors of those honest tars who, having served their country gallantly on the high seas, wanted now, in an access of patriotic zeal, to rid the capital of vice. Fielding, declared "Argus Centoculi," protected the brothels because he took bribes to keep them in business:

> The late *worshipful Puppet-Shew* Writer may, in his present State of Transformation, imbitter his rueful Aspect at a Proposal to incorporate the incorrigible Spinsters of his Neighborhood into a legal Body, which may abridge the Perquisites of the good *old Shop*, and lessen the *Trade thereof*. To him I answer, that the scandalous Connivance at, if not the Protection of, Brothel Houses, has been but too long the prevailing Practice among a certain *worshipful Order* of Men, *for divers valuable Considerations thereunto moving*. Whether he knows this by *Experience*, and if from a Customer he is become a Patron, is submitted to himself.

Typical of the abuse to which Fielding was subjected in the Opposition press throughout his tenure as "Court Justice," this slander is worth preserving because it anticipates the similarly jaundiced view of a modern historian of these events.[49] Active though he was in exercising his powers as a justice and protecting the interests of the government, Fielding did not make a trade of the magistracy. On the contrary, by his example, reducing "an income of about 500 l. a year of the dirtiest money upon earth to little more than 300 l.," and by his efforts to purge the commission of such trading justices, he tried conscientiously to reform the office.

There is no reason to doubt his own explanation of why he took the measures he did to quell the riots. Having witnessed the actions of "a licentious, outrageous Mob, who in open Defiance of Law, Justice or Mercy, committed the most notorious Offences against the Persons and Properties of their Fellow-Subjects," he saw these sailors and the rabble who joined them in no very sentimental light:

> The Clamour against Bawdy-Houses was in them a bare Pretence only. Wantonness and Cruelty were the Motives of most, and some, as it plainly appeared, converted the inhuman Disposition of the Mob to the very worst of Purposes, and became Thieves under the Pretence of Reformation.[50]

In appealing to the common sense of his readers, he asks a question that vindicates his conduct on the occasion:

> When by our excellent Constitution the greatest Subject, no not even the King himself, can, without a lawful Trial and Conviction divest the meanest Man of his Property, deprive him of his Liberty, or attack him in his Person; shall we suffer a licentious Rabble to be Accuser, Judge, Jury, and Executioner; to inflict corporal Punish-

ment, break open Men's Doors, plunder their Houses, and burn their Goods?[51]

As for the bawdy-houses, which a few days earlier he had charged the Westminster Grand Jury to suppress: "The Law clearly considers them as a Nuisance, and hath appointed a Remedy against them; and this Remedy it is in the Power of every Man, who desires it, to apply."[52]

•••—● viii ●—•••

In July 1749 Fielding wrote two other letters that have been preserved. The earlier one, written on the 18th to Bedford's agent, is interesting only because it confirms that, in leasing Fielding the property that enabled him to qualify for the Middlesex magistracy, Bedford also enabled him to receive the rents – a welcome supplement to his income, though he did not yet have a complete list of his tenants or the key to one of the houses.[53]

Of greater interest is the letter Fielding wrote the Lord Chancellor on 21 July; for it points to one of the most ambitious projects of his magistracy. His *Charge delivered to the Grand Jury* having been published this day, Fielding sent Hardwicke a copy. He took the opportunity to renew his request "that the Name of Joshua Brogden may be inserted in the next Commissions of the Peace for Middlesex and Westmin\. for whose Integrity and Ability in the Execution of his office I will engage my Credit with your Lordship, an engagement which appears to me of the most sacred Nature."[54] No doubt Fielding hoped that as an associate justice Brogden could relieve him of much of the routine drudgery at Bow Street. Hardwicke meant to oblige; he put Brogden's name forward for the commission. In the end, however, he was deemed unsuitable: a note beside his name in the list of candidates states contemptuously that Brogden "Was no better formerly than an Hackney Clerk married to Sr Thos Deveils maid was his Clerk then Mr Burdus's now Mr. Fieldings ... It is much questioned how he can have a Qualification."[55] DeVeil, it appears, formerly managed to elevate Brogden to a captaincy in the militia;[56] but that humble dignity would be the highest of his honors. Brogden drudged on as Fielding's loyal clerk, receiving "a considerable proportion" of the £300 or so Fielding annually earned at Bow Street. Indeed, as Fielding declared, even if the whole £300 had gone to Brogden, "as it ought, he would be but ill paid for sitting almost sixteen hours in the twenty-four, in the most unwholesome, as well as nauseous air in the universe, and which hath in his case corrupted a good constitution without contaminating his morals."[57]

Fielding with this letter also sent the Lord Chancellor a document of supreme interest not only to his biographers and to critics of his final novel, *Amelia*, but also to historians of the metropolitan police:

> I have likewise [Fielding wrote Hardwicke] presumed to send my Draught of a Bill for the better preventing Street Robberies &c which y[r] Lordship was so very kind to say you would peruse; and I hope the general Plan at least may be happy in your Approbation.

This "Bill" – for Fielding did indeed intend that his proposal should be enacted into law – Hardwicke, as was his custom,[58] referred to the Duke of Newcastle, the Secretary of State. The draft of just such a Bill dating from this period has only now come to light, discovered among the welter of Newcastle's miscellaneous papers in the British Library (see Appendix I). To judge from numerous correspondences between the specific concerns of this plan and those Fielding expresses in his writings of 1749–51, this document is almost certainly the lost "Bill" which Fielding sent the Lord Chancellor.

The plan Fielding conceived in the six months or so he had been acting as magistrate reveals how quickly he identified the sources of disorder in the metropolis and how plainly he saw that little could be done to eradicate them unless Parliament could be persuaded to do two things. On the one hand, new laws were needed against specific evils overlooked in the constitution. Of more fundamental importance – because this deficiency endangered every member of society – the legislature needed not merely to reform the quaint existing system of law enforcement, which was ineffectual and corrupt; it needed to approve a radical reorganization of the system. What Fielding proposed, in short, was the establishment of London's first modern police force. In the second chapter of *Amelia*, which he probably began writing this summer,[59] Fielding dramatized the inadequacies of the present system of law enforcement. The watchmen, whose duty it was "to guard our Streets by Night from Thieves and Robbers," were unable to do so because they were "chosen out of those poor old decrepit People, who are from their Want of bodily Strength rendered incapable of getting a Livelihood by Work." Furthermore, since they were "armed only with a Pole, which some of them are scarce able to lift," they could not protect the King's subjects "from the Attacks of Gangs of young, bold, stout, desperate and well-armed Villains." In the same chapter Constable Gotobed sets free any malefactor with money enough to bribe him; and exercising "tremendous" authority over all is the tyrannical Justice Thrasher, who in his shameless venality and ignorance of the law characterizes Fielding's colleagues, the trading justices of Westminster.

The plan Fielding submitted to Hardwicke was calculated to remedy such defects of the system. Within the City and Liberty of Westminster and the adjacent parishes and liberties of Middlesex County he proposed "regulating the Watch and Ward" in the following ways. Supervising the new system of police would be "Commissioners" chosen from among those magistrates and barristers substantial enough to meet the requirements of the Justices Qualification Act (18 Geo. II, c. 20 [1745]). These Commissioners would meet annually in the vestry rooms of their parish churches, which would serve as administrative headquarters, and from a list of eligible persons would appoint for each parish a force of as many as forty "able bodied" watchmen. At the appointed hour each evening these officers would report to the parish watch-house where a constable would distribute arms to each man and assign him to his post. The Commissioners were to erect "Boxes or Watchhouses" to provide shelter for the officers. A notable feature of the scheme was the provision to facilitate communication between watchmen of the same and neighboring districts. Every officer would be equipped with "one large sonorous Bell" in order that the watch "may more easily assist each other." Furthermore, on hearing the alarm raised for any serious crime, they would be authorized to cross parish boundaries to come to the aid of a fellow officer. The disturbances earlier in July still fresh in mind, Fielding stressed the need for such instantaneous cooperation "in Case any Riot, Rout, unlawfull & tumultuous assembly or sudden affray shall arise." As he envisaged them, the newly organized watch would very much resemble a modern police force: they would be physically strong; they would have weapons with which to defend themselves against the pistols and cutlasses of marauding gangs of footpads; they could effectively raise the alarm and expect speedy assistance from fellow officers. And as an inducement to attract a better class of recruit, Fielding recommended that each watchman be paid eighteen pence per night – a rate more than doubling the current annual stipend of ten pounds. The scheme was to be funded in part by a tax levied in the same manner as the Poor Rate.

Fully aware of the well-earned reputation of the metropolitan watch and constabulary for negligence and corruption, Fielding meant to discourage such misconduct by punishing offenders. Watchmen who shirked their duties would be liable not only to dismissal, but to a month's imprisonment at hard labor. Those who connived at the escape of a prisoner would suffer three months' imprisonment at hard labor and would be publicly whipped at least twice. Constables who released prisoners before they could be examined by a Commissioner or a justice of peace would be deemed "guilty of an high offence": they could be fined ten pounds for a first offense or imprisoned for two months at hard labor, with whipping. Any watchman or constable who abused his authority by maliciously arresting the innocent could be fined five pounds or imprisoned until the next Quarter Sessions, when the justices would determine his guilt and punishment.

Having thus conceived a rational system of policing the metropolis – a system which would attract able men to the force by offering them good wages yet would enforce discipline by threatening severe punishment for misconduct – Fielding in this draft Bill also enumerated the kinds of offenders the watchmen, under laws already existing, were charged with apprehending. Virtually every one of these he cites and discusses in his tracts and newspaper notices of this same period: such offenders include anyone of low birth found in the streets armed, or in a public house with a concealed weapon; any gamester; anyone guilty of open acts of lewdness, or of profane cursing and swearing; brawlers and drunkards and street-walkers; ballad singers and street musicians; indeed, anyone found abroad or in a public house after ten o'clock who could give no good account of himself.

Other offenders mentioned in the final four paragraphs of the Bill specify what Fielding believed to be serious imperfections in the existing laws, and these he would dramatize in his new novel. Those who knowingly receive stolen goods are to be considered as committing an original offense and punished as felons (cf. *Amelia* [XI.vii], p. 484, as well as the *Enquiry into the Causes of the late Increase of Robbers*, Sect. v). Those who defraud another of his goods, or who like Amelia's servant Betty (XI,vii, p. 485) pawn goods entrusted to them, are to be "deem'd common Cheats" liable to corporal punishment, or, "if the Case be very atrocious," to transportation for seven years. Perjury is no longer to be a bailable offence (cf. *Amelia* [I.iv], pp. 34–5). Nor is it to be possible any longer for a defendant to remove an indictment by *certiorari* unless just cause be demonstrated (cf. *Amelia* [I.iv], p. 35, n.). In this last matter, Fielding's desire to eliminate the abuse of the lawyer's device of *certiorari* (by which a defendant could transfer an indictment from an inferior court to either Chancery or the King's Bench, thereby postponing his trial and increasing the costs of prosecution) was shared by the legislature, which the following March enacted a law (23 Geo. II, c. 11) designed in part to close this legal loophole in cases of perjury.

Abortive though the attempt was, in his draft Bill to reform the watch within Westminster and adjacent parishes and liberties in Middlesex County, Fielding in fact anticipated several of the conclusions reached in the earliest stages of their deliberations by the parliamentary Committee appointed in 1750–1 to consider reforms in the criminal law. Indeed, when Sir Richard Lloyd, the Committee's chairman, reported to the House on 1 April 1751, his first recommendation concerned the reforming of the watch in Westminster and its environs. Among the Committee's resolutions are the following: that the watch in this area was "defective, either as to Number, Strength, or Diligence"; that "there is not a sufficient Power to make and raise Rates for the Watch"; that "the Salaries paid to Watchmen are too small to induce able-bodied Men to undertake that Service"; that "Provision should be made for raising and enforcing the Payment of Money for maintaining an able Watch"; that constables and watchmen should be authorized to apprehend all "suspicious" persons whom "they shall find loitering and lurking about the Streets, Passages, and Alleys, and do not give a satisfactory Account" of themselves.[60] Though it would be excessive to claim that Fielding's "Bill" of 1749 was the model for the Committee's report – for one thing, the reforms he proposed are far more radical, more numerous, and more specific – yet the points of similarity between the two are striking enough to suggest that the Committee in their deliberations sought the advice of the person whose knowledge and experience made him the principal authority on the subject: namely, the "Court Justice," Henry Fielding.

····➤ ix ◄····

Fielding liked to get out of town during the summer, and he doubtless made short excursions into the country this year. He so much enjoyed his sojourns in Twickenham that he planned to purchase a house there. For the most part, however, he remained at his post in Bow Street; the newspapers place him there at least intermittently during July, August, and September.[61]

But this would not be a season soured completely by a preoccupation with the crimes and vices of the populace. Fielding was an affectionate man who rejoiced in the happiness of his friends, and this summer three of the dearest of them were getting married. On 22 June, Garrick gave the hearts of his female admirers a wrench when he married the celebrated French dancer Eva-Maria Violetti. Early in August, at a time when Fielding may have been in Twickenham, rumor had it that Edward Moore was married there to Jane Hamilton, the ceremony being performed by the same clergyman who married their mutual friend Garrick.[62] That report was premature. Moore and Jenny Hamilton were much in love; but he had no money, and her parents, upper servants to the princesses Amelia and Caroline, disapproved of so unsuitable a match.

There was nothing false, however, about the news of Lyttelton's marriage on 10 August to Elizabeth, daughter of Field Marshal Sir Robert Rich, a former Governor of Gibraltar. A sprightly and accomplished woman, she had been close to Lyttelton's beloved first wife Lucy, who died two years earlier. As it proved, the new Mrs. Lyttelton had little else in common with her husband; the marriage was disastrous. But this unhappiness was yet to come, and on 29 August Fielding wrote, belatedly, to offer his congratulations. The letter is the only extant specimen of what must have been a regular correspondence.[63]

Sir,

Bow St. Aug! 29, 1749

Permit me to bring up the Rear of your Friends in paying my Compliments of Congratulation on your late happy Nuptials. There may perhaps be Seasons when the Rear may be as honourable a Post in Friendship as in War, and if so, such certainly must be every time of Joy and Felicity. Your present Situation must be full of these; and so will be, I am confident, your future Life from the same Fountain. Nothing can equal the excellent Character your Lady bears among those of her own Sex, and I never yet knew them speak well of a Woman who did not deserve their good Words. How admirable is y^r Fortune in the Matrimonial Lottery! I will venture to say there is no Man alive who exults more in this, or in any other Happiness that can attend you than my self; and you ought to believe me from the same Reason that fully persuades me of the Satisfaction you receive from any Happiness of mine; this Reason is that you must be sensible how much of it I owe to your Goodness; and there is a great Pleasure in Gratitude tho it is second I believe to that of Benevolence: for of all the Delights upon Earth none can equal the Raptures which a good Mind feels in conferring Happiness on those whom we think worthy of it. This is the sweetest Ingredient in Power.

Whatever Fielding's faults, he was a loyal friend. He had another motive in writing Lyttelton, and that was to serve Edward Moore and to see him happily married to the woman he loved. A year earlier in *The Trial of Selim the Persian*, Moore had bid for Lyttelton's patronage by defending him against aspersions cast on him anonymously by Horace Walpole. In return Lyttelton is said to have promised to recommend Moore for the laureateship when Colley Cibber died – a promise that nicely epitomizes the extravagant insubstantiality of most favors conferred in the period by literary patrons on their flatterers. Now, with fitting irony, Fielding proposed Moore for a place he himself created in 1737 by his theatrical high jinks: the place of Deputy Licenser of the Stage. The act of "conferring Happiness" on our deserving friends being "the sweetest Ingredient in Power," Fielding continued:

I solemnly protest I never wished for Power more than a few Days ago for the sake of a Man whom I love, and that more perhaps from the Esteem I know he bears towards you than from any other Reason. This Man is in Love with a young Creature of the most apparent Worth, who returns his Affections. Nothing is wanting to make two very miserable People extremely blessed but a moderate Portion of the greatest of human Evils. So Philosophers call it, and so it is called by Divines, whose Word is the rather to be taken as they are, many of them, more conversant with this Evil than ever the Philosophers were. The Name of this Man is Moore to whom you kindly destined that Laurel, which, tho it hath long been withered, may not probably soon drop from the Brow of it's present Possessor; but there is another Place of much the same Value now vacant; it is that of Deputy Licenser to the Stage. Be not offended at this Hint: for tho I will own it impudent enough in one who hath so many Obligations of his own to you, to venture to recommend another Man to your Favour, yet Impudence itself may possibly be a Virtue when exerted on the Behalf of a Friend; at least I am the less ashamed of it, as I have known Men remarkable for the opposite Modesty possess it with' the Mixture of any other good Quality. In this Fault then you must indulge me: for should I ever see you as high in Power, as I wish, and as it is perhaps more my Interest than your own that you should be, I shall be guilty of the like as often as I find a Man in whom I can, after much Intimacy discover no Want, but that of the Evil abovementioned. I beg you will do me the Honour of making my Compliments to your unknown Lady, and believe me to be with the highest Esteem, Respect, Love and Gratitude....

In the event, Lyttelton did not, or could not, grant this request; but he did make it possible for Moore and Jenny Hamilton to wed. The young lady's parents apparently persisted in their disapproval, but in May of the following year the couple were married, with Lyttelton, as he had lately done for Fielding, standing in for Miss Hamilton's father to give the bride away. It is pleasant to record the suspicion of a knowledgeable modern student of Moore, that when he and Jenny christened their only son on 15 July 1751, they called him Harry after their friend Fielding.[64]

Soon after Fielding wrote his sunny letter to Lyttelton, less cheerful matters occupied him for several months. On 6 September the Sessions began at the Old Bailey. Of the six men he charged in the July riots, the Grand Jury found indictments against four – one of whom died in Newgate of jail fever before coming to trial.[65] On the testimony of the keepers of the Star brothel – Peter Wood, his wife, and a servant – two of the accused were convicted and sentenced to hang: these were John Wilson, a cobbler from Yorkshire, and Bosavern Penlez, a clergyman's son from Exeter who worked as a peruke-maker.

The testimony of so disreputable a trio of prosecutors hardly inspired confidence: a tax collector who lived opposite their house of ill fame declared he "would not hang a dog or a cat upon their evidence." Understandably the jury recommended that the Court – over which Lord Chief Justice Willes presided – show mercy. Public sentiment strongly supported the recommendation; indeed, several hundred worthy inhabitants of the parish of St. Clement Danes petitioned the Duke of Newcastle for a pardon, which the King was inclined to grant. Three times, it is said, he summoned Justice Willes, hoping he would advise accepting the recommendation of clemency; but Willes remained firm in his opinion that one of the condemned men must be made an example.[66] What the public did not know was that the Grand Jury, besides indicting Penlez for rioting, had also indicted him for burglary (for stealing the bundle of linen); Willes, thinking it supererogatory to convict Penlez of a second capital crime, decided not to try him for that offense. It was owing to Fielding's representation of this circumstance to members of the Privy Council that, as he put it, "the Distinction between an Object of Mercy, and an Object of Justice at last prevailed."[67] Wilson was reprieved at the eleventh hour and subsequently pardoned. But on 18 October, Bosavern Penlez – together with fourteen other malefactors, mostly sailors – was hanged at Tyburn before a sympathetic throng of spectators, including several thousand tars armed with bludgeons and cutlasses who threatened a rescue. Owing to the cool, manly behavior of the Sheriff, the executions took place without incident, but not without inflaming the populace against the government. Penlez was buried in the churchyard of St. Clement Danes, with honors due a martyr.

It was, as Saunders Welch succinctly put it, "a just, though unpopular execution."[68] Despite the cynical insinuations of Fielding's enemies, it is clear that he protected Wood and his house from the mob because it was his duty to enforce the laws and to prevent a dangerous riot from spreading. It is also clear that he bound over Penlez for trial because he was obliged to do so and because he believed him to be guilty: the testimony of Wood, his wife and servant was suspect, but it was sworn nevertheless; and there was no reason to doubt the evidence of the four peace officers who apprehended Penlez fleeing from the vicinity of the riot with goods concealed on his person. As to the larger question of why, except for ineffectually urging the Westminster Grand Jury to present the keepers of bawdy-houses, Fielding did not himself take action to suppress them, the answer is that he had no legal grounds for doing so. Citing the example of Peter Wood, Welch explained why even a magistrate as honest and as active as Fielding found it virtually impossible to shut down the brothels:

> The keeper of a notorious bawdy house, whose iniquitous practices, some few years since, produced a dangerous riot, and the most causeless and unjust abuse upon the administration, that malice ever invented; this very fellow did, by artfully shifting the names of the occupiers of his house; and, at other times, by entering an appearance in the crown office, (the whole charge of which, did not, perhaps, exceed eight pounds per annum) openly carry on his bawdy house, for years, unpunished, although presented at every meeting of the grand jury during that time.[69]

Such scoundrels as Wood knew how to run up the costs of an action against them, and they did not hesitate to bribe or intimidate witnesses; consequently, few citizens could be found who were altruistic and brave enough to carry on a prosecution. This being so, honest constables turned a blind eye to the vice, while those less honest took money to screen offenders. Given this combination of corruption and a sense of futility, Welch found that "The constables of Covent-Garden, do, upon their oaths, say, there are no brothels in their parish."[70]

Far from wishing to see Wood prosper, Fielding shared the public's sense of outrage and, when a lawful opportunity occurred, he acted swiftly to punish him. Early in November, Wood's brother James – one of the iniquitous family of bullies and whores at the Star – was accused of stealing a large quantity of human hair from William Burcket, a hair merchant. That no unprejudiced citizen suspected Fielding of being in Wood's pay plainly appears from the fact that Burcket chose to carry the thief to Fielding to charge him. Fielding bound over James Wood for trial at the Old Bailey, and, though Peter Wood attempted to bribe Burcket with £100 to drop the prosecution, his brother was duly convicted and sentenced to be transported for seven years. Wood's attorney pleaded that the prosecution, in which Fielding played an important role, was deliberately instigated to avenge Penlez's death by punishing Peter Wood through his brother. Before the sentence could be carried out, James Wood died in prison.[71]

The case of Bosavern Penlez proved doubly troublesome to Fielding in his capacity as "Court Justice," for it became an inflammatory issue in what has been called "one of the most violent and vituperative" political struggles in eighteenth-century England.[72] On 15 November 1749, owing to his promotion to the Admiralty Board, Bedford's brother-in-law Granville Leveson-Gower (1721–1803), Viscount Trentham, was required to resign his seat in Parliament as member for Westminster and to offer himself for reelection. Against him stood Sir George Vandeput (c. 1717–84), candidate of the anti-Court faction who styled themselves the Independent Electors of Westminster. The ensuing election, which lasted from 22 November to 8 December – "a Space of Time," remarked one observer, "without any Precedent of late Years"[73] – was so vigorously, as well as improperly, contested that when Vandeput lost by a narrow margin he demanded a scrutiny of the votes that delayed a final decision, confirming Trentham's victory, until May of the following year.

Fielding, it should be remembered, sincerely believed that since the formation of the Pelham ministry the "Administration of our public Affairs" was "in the Hands of the very Men, whom ... every honest Person would wish to be intrusted with it" – in the hands, that is, of his friends and patrons Lyttelton, Pitt, Hardwicke, and, now particularly relevant, the Duke of Bedford. When asking Bedford to qualify him for the magistracy, Fielding could promise, without a twinge of conscience, that he would "completely serve the Government in that Office"; in this instance, Westminster being Bedford's personal domain, serving the government meant serving his patron's interests. Both as justice and as author, Fielding therefore exerted himself in Trentham's behalf.

The Westminster justices (who voted for Trentham by a majority of seventy-six to seven) "played a partisan role in curtailing the activities of rival mobs at the hustings, arresting their opponent's ringleaders and countersigning affidavits against injured parties."[74] Of these justices Fielding was most active in promoting Trentham's cause. To the Opposition, Fielding in such activities seemed not so much to be attempting to control irregularities at the polls as to be countenancing them, so long as the disorders were committed by the Trentham faction. The figure he cut in the Opposition press was, as usual, less than amiable: among the "*Bruisers* of *Justice*" who toiled to protect the "*Bruisers* of Bodies" Trentham had hired to worry his rival's supporters was one, sneered *Old England* (9 December 1749) in reference to Fielding, "with such a Length of *Chin*, of *Nose*, and *Woefulness* of Countenance, as caused a loud Laugh at first sight among the Crowd."

One incident in particular infuriated Vandeput's sympathizers. On Friday, 24 November, the first busy day of polling, violence erupted at the hustings, which had been set up in the porch of St. Paul's, Covent Garden. The disturbance was instigated, the Opposition claimed, by Trentham's hired bullies, several of whom, together with their leader, Benjamin Boswell, were clapped into the roundhouse. They did not, however, suffer this confinement very long, for Fielding immediately bailed them out – a gesture causing one exasperated Vandeput supporter to assure the public: "If any Person happens to be taken into Custody for riotous Behaviour, Mr. Justice *Trotplaid* attends to prevent Commitment."[75] A fuller, if no less biased, account of the incident was later supplied by the Tory apologist, Paul Whitehead, who, as leader of the rival mob, had been directly involved in the events. In *The Case of the Hon. Alexander Murray* (1751), an angry vindication of the Jacobite martyr who had been punished by Parliament for improperly attempting to secure Vandeput's election, Whitehead breaks into a rash of italics symptomatic of his irritation at Fielding's conduct in protecting Trentham's bullies:

> *when carried before a neighbouring Justice, that excellent Magistrate from his tender Regard for the Liberty of the Subject, (of which he has ever been so zealous an Asserter) thought proper to discharge them; but, by a nice Refinement in the Administration of Justice, committed a Person, who had almost been murdered by them, to* Newgate, *only for a little too eager Impatience in preferring his complaint.*   (pp. 9–10)

Whitehead, of course, is anything but a disinterested witness: for one thing, he acted as the principal propagandist for the Vandeput faction and was himself forward in heading up and inciting the Opposition mobs; for another, he had personal reasons for hating Fielding. There is no proof that Fielding conducted himself improperly on the bench.

But however unfairly his actions were colored by scribblers such as Whitehead and the author of *Old England*, it is certain that Fielding played a very useful role indeed in Trentham's eventual election. He did procure Boswell's release from the roundhouse, but he did so in the belief that Boswell and his men were innocent of any offense – that the charges against them had been trumped up by Vandeput's agents, and by Whitehead in particular. Fielding's sense of the incident can be glimpsed from an affidavit sworn before him on 14 December by one William Bayley, yeoman, who had witnessed Boswell's arrest. By Bayley's account Boswell, far from inciting the *mêlée* near the hustings, might have been posing as the very allegory of innocent curiosity: standing peaceably apart, "with one of His Hands in His Bosom & the

Other Hand in His Pockett," he was set upon by a "Riotous Mobb" of Vandeput supporters who "Dragg'd & Pulled" him into the watch-house – not, however, before he had suffered the spiritual injury of Paul Whitehead's insults, who called him "a Scoundrell" and swore he "should be sent to Goal or He would be Damn'd else."[76] That the ringleader of a gang of toughs could have presented quite so pathetic a picture on this occasion strains credulity; but long after the event Bedford's attorney, George Ward, remained convinced that Boswell had been innocent of any mischief, "of heading a Mobb, or committing the least Act of Violence."[77] Fielding, at any rate, continued to interest himself in the case, advising Ward on matters of timing and procedure as the prosecution prepared for trial.[78]

Though his part in the Boswell affair seemed to the Opposition the most egregious instance of Fielding's readiness to apply his authority to support his friends in power, he served Bedford's party in other ways as well. On Monday, 27 November, accompanied by one of the Duke's agents responsible for getting out the vote, he went to the polls and cast his vote for Trentham.[79] On the same day, as Trentham's electors caroused at the Duke's expense in alehouses all over town, Fielding hosted the festivities at the Old George and Punchbowl, Drury Lane, and at the White Bear in Bow Street, where, if the money spent on bread and meat exceeded Falstaff's halfpennyworth, an intolerable deal more went for beer and wine and punch.[80] Months later, in expec-tation of renewed disturbances on 15 May 1750, when after a prolonged scrutiny of disputed votes Trentham's election would be officially declared, Fielding assured Bedford that he would obey his "Commands" to attend in person and "do the utmost in my Power to preserve the Peace on that Occasion."[81]

But it is a final incident relating to the election that best illustrates the fullness of his zeal in behalf of Bedford and the government. When Whitehead's *Case of the Hon. Alexander Murray* was issued anonymously on 27 June 1751, raking up again the accusations of ministerial malfeasance during the Westminster election and con-demning Parliament for its action against the hero of the Vandeput faction, the authorities moved to apprehend the author, publisher, and printer and to stop publication both of the pamphlet itself and of an abridgment being hawked about the streets for a halfpenny.[82] Doing his part to enforce the proscription, Fielding acted rather sensationally against this libel, in which not only Bedford's but his own conduct was aspersed. The *Whitehall Evening Post* (29 June to 2 July 1751) carried the following account of his actions:

Saturday Henry Fielding, Esq; committed one Anne Jenkins, a Hawker to Tothill-fields Bridewell, to hard Labour for one Month,

for crying abut the Streets, and vending a certain scandalous and
libellous Paper, purporting to be Part of the Case of the Hon. Mr.
Murray: And afterwards the same was publickly burnt, by Order of
Mr. Fielding, in the Street before his own Door, and in the Presence
of upwards of a hundred People.

Happily, since it is more agreeable to remember Fielding as writing
papers for his friends instead of burning those of his enemies, he played
another role in the election – not as magistrate, but as author. Soon
after the voting began on 22 November a "Paper War," as one observer
called it, was raging between supporters of the two candidates, filling
the papers with partisan squibs and advertisements and littering the
streets and coffee-houses with thousands of handbills – the work not
merely of the usual hacks and scribblers, but also of "some of the ablest
Writers, both for and against the Adm[inistratio]n."[83] Fielding played
his part in this electioneering, and his contributions, however trivial
they may be as literature, reveal what he believed to be the real issues
at stake in the election. They were not, he insisted, what the Opposition
would have the public believe.

Two incidents had recently occurred which the Opposition seized on
to embarrass Trentham and the Court: the first of these was the
execution on 18 October of Bosavern Penlez; the second was the violent
disturbance on 14 November at the Little Theatre in the Haymarket,
caused when a party in the audience attempted to prevent a troupe of
French comedians from performing. Trentham's opponents sought to
turn his part in both affairs to their advantage: they protested that,
together with Bedford, Trentham had been chiefly responsible for the
King's ignoring the public's wish that Penlez be pardoned; and they
insisted that Trentham had not only sponsored "the French Strollers"
at a time when, owing to the recent disastrous war, public sentiment
against all things Gallic ran high, but had drawn his sword against
unarmed patriots in the theatre who attempted to stop the play. These
two accusations nearly cost Trentham the election. The Independent
Electors appeared at the polls in great numbers, rallying round a broad
white standard on which was inscribed the legend: "UNITED FOR OUR
COUNTRY. NO FRENCH STROLLERS." Others of them, attended by lights,
carried a coffin in which lay a man in a shroud pretending to be the
ghost of Penlez, "who frequently sat up and harangued the Populace
for his unhappy Fate, &c."[84] So the people would not mistake their
enemy, Trentham's role in both affairs was kept constantly before
them. One doggerel ballad represented him as conscience-stricken over
the death of Penlez:

Poor *Penlez* I might have saved,
　　But I did refuse the same,
Tho' it were so justly craved,
　　By great Numbers of good Fame.
But, alas! it is too late, Sirs,
　　And I can't recall the Time,
Which has almost craz'd my Pate, Sirs,
　　For I own it a great Crime.[85]

As for the issue of the French comedians, the Opposition appealed to
the chauvinism of the mob and their natural suspicion of ministerial
power, by, as one writer put it, "magnifying a butterfly into a dragon,
that was to swallow up their liberties and properties."[86] To remove all
doubt that the ministry's candidate had forcibly suppressed the patriots
at the playhouse, they circulated the affidavit of William Davison, who
swore Trentham had hired one John Haines, a waiter at the King's
Arms Tavern in Pall Mall, together with fifteen other bullies, each
concealing bludgeons, to thwart any attempt to prevent the French
players from acting.[87]

Fielding did his part to answer both these charges. On 24 November,
the day when Davison made his damaging indictment of Trentham's
conspiring to bully the audience at the playhouse and when Boswell
and his bruisers were sent to prison for intimidating the electors at the
polls, the town was flooded with ten thousand copies of a handbill
Fielding wrote to discredit Vandeput and his party: it was entitled *Ten
Queries submitted to every Sober, Honest, and Disinterested Elector for the
City and Liberty of Westminster*.[88] Fielding's strategy in this little piece
was on the one hand to disparage Vandeput by emphasizing his obscurity and his foreign ancestry – the latter rather unfairly, since Vandeput's
family had lived in England for two hundred years; and on the other
hand, in a manner reminiscent of *The Jacobite's Journal*, to cast suspicion on the Independent Electors by associating them with Jacobites
and Papists bent on overthrowing the government. What plainer proof
of "jesuitical Craft and Policy," after all, than the campaign to impugn
Trentham's conduct at the playhouse? What better governor for the
nation than a *"truly English* Nobleman, of the highest Quality and
Fortune, and of the most unblemished Honour?" However far-fetched
Fielding's argument appears, it is a skillful piece of political rhetoric.
One may doubt that Trentham was the victim of a sinister alien
conspiracy, but there is no reason to suppose his opponents were any
more disinterested in the pursuit of the country's welfare than he –
and, witness Paul Whitehead and the author of *Old England*, they had
a flair for invective far more unconscionable than Fielding's.

In other ways, too, Fielding strove to refurbish Trentham's public image. On 26 November, for instance, Haines, the waiter named in Davison's affidavit as having been hired by Trentham to terrorize the audience at the playhouse, swore before Fielding that the allegation was utterly "false, scandalous and malicious"; Haines's affidavit, appearing over Fielding's name, was published the next day and ran for several days thereafter in the newspapers – indeed, twelve thousand copies of it were printed and distributed throughout the town.[89]

What is more, Fielding by this time had produced the only plausible defense of the ministry's unpopular action against Bosavern Penlez. Trentham knew in August that because of his promotion to the Admiralty Board he would have to stand for reelection in the autumn. By September, when Penlez came to trial, it was clear that the judgment against him for violating the unpopular statute called the Riot Act (1 Geo. I, c. 5) would be used by the Opposition to blacken the ministry and their candidate. In an attempt to defuse this explosive issue – which he had himself created by invoking the Act, however wisely given the circumstances – Fielding wrote a pamphlet explaining the laws pertaining to rioting. It appears to have been in September that Strahan recorded in his ledger the printing of 1,000 copies of "Fieldings Account of Penlez."[90] Prudence, however, leads us to conclude with the editors of the authoritative Wesleyan edition that the pamphlet in fact went to press in the latter part of October,[91] publication being timed to coincide with the announcement of Trentham's candidacy and the start of polling: the earliest notice of the work, promising publication "in a few Days," appeared in the *General Advertiser* for Tuesday, 14 November, the day before Trentham declared his candidacy. The full title of the pamphlet, published on 18 November, is as follows:

A True State of the Case of Bosavern Penlez, Who suffered on Account of the late Riot in the Strand. In which the Law regarding these Offences, and the Statute of George the First, commonly called the Riot Act, are fully considered.

It cannot be that the work as we know it was written in its entirety as early as September; for in the opening and closing pages Fielding alludes to the events of 17–18 October (the reprieve of Wilson and the execution of Penlez), and he is very much aware of the public anger Penlez's death aroused. He is also aware that he must respond to the attacks on the ministry and on his own character. "Sure I am," he insists in a quaint attempt at self-vindication that his enemies never tired of mocking, "that I greatly deceive myself, if I am not in some little Degree partaker of that Milk of human Kindness which *Shakespear* speaks of."

Complaints against the government – most particularly against the "trumped up" story of the stolen bundle – were cogently set forth in

The Case of the Unfortunate Penlez, a spirited pamphlet published on 7 November and recently attributed to John Cleland, an author chiefly remembered for another work of this year, *Memoirs of a Woman of Pleasure* (the notorious *Fanny Hill*).[92] Considering that Fielding's pamphlet was through Strahan's press by late October, it cannot exactly be that Cleland's work "provoked" him to write his *True State of the Case* in reply.[93] The time between the publication of Cleland's pamphlet and the announcement of Fielding's was just one week, and, except perhaps in his choice of title, Fielding makes no reference to Cleland's work. Cleland nevertheless supposed that Fielding published his pamphlet "by way of answer" to his own: so he asserted when reviewing both works in the *Monthly Review* (2 [November 1749], 61–5), where he not only declared his admiration for Fielding, whose "name would be alone sufficient to recommend this piece," but also generously allowed his adversary the last word in the debate, stating Fielding's conclusion that "nothing could be more unjust, or indeed more absurd, than the Complaint of Severity which hath been made" against the execution of Penlez.

For the most part, however, Fielding's interpretation of this unhappy affair did not find a sympathetic audience, and it incited Opposition journalists to effusions of scurrility. The author of *Old England*, for example, insisted that Penlez had been sacrificed because Fielding had "interested his foul Hands and bad Heart in the Protection" of the bawdy-houses, "these filthy Receptacles of Vice, and had shared in their Wages of Iniquity"; by this view, Fielding was the "Fiend" who prevented a pardon by interposing "his Cloven Foot" between Penlez and a merciful King.[94] As the election dragged on, slanders such as this, embarrassing both to Fielding and to the candidate he supported, kept the issues of Penlez and the "French strollers" continually before the public. Having tried to answer them in his pamphlet and in the *Ten Queries*, Fielding tried once more to do so, this time, since argument had proved ineffectual, by leveling against the enemy his favorite weapon of ridicule.

On Tuesday, 5 December 1749 – at a time when the contest between Trentham and Vandeput had become particularly obstreperous – hawkers began distributing throughout the town a curious broadsheet entitled: "The *Covent-Garden* JOURNAL. No° 1. *To be publish'd Once every Month, during the present* WESTMINSTER ELECTION. By PAUL WRONGHEAD, of the *Fleet*, Esq."[95] This bit of pseudonymous ephemera, though consisting of a single large page printed on one side only, otherwise has the format of a typical contemporary newspaper: two columns of text beginning with an "*Introductory Essay*" followed by separate sections of intelligence headed "FOREIGN AFFAIRS" and "HOME AFFAIRS" and concluding with an "ADVER-

TISEMENT." Along the bottom of the page the imprint reads: "Printed for *T. Smith, R. Webb,* and *S. Johnson,* and sold by all the People of *London* and *Westminster*; where Persons who bring Advertisements or Letters to the Authors are taken in." Indeed, those gullible enough to accept any of these representations at face value would have been "taken in" in quite another sense; for the *Covent-Garden Journal* of 1749 was a literary hoax, ordered and paid for by the Duke of Bedford to embarrass the Vandeput faction. The printer of this mock paper, which was never meant to have a monthly life, was Richard Francklin, who on 5 and 6 December ran off the astonishing number of 13,000 copies – of which exactly one survives in the British Library.

The Town at once attributed the *Covent-Garden Journal* to Fielding. This, for instance, is surely the witty paper to which the Duke of Richmond's agent referred as he hastened to send a copy to Goodwood on 7 December: "The enclosed [he informed Richmond] is a paper generally given to Mr. Fielding, as the author. The humor that is in it is at least akin to his. It may possibly divert you & your company."[96] Certainly, the author of *Old England* (9 and 16 December 1749) had no doubt that Fielding was responsible for this satire – though it seems more likely that he wrote only the "Introductory Essay," leaving the rest of the joke to be spun out by a collaborator. His target was the bard and firebrand of the Tories, Paul Whitehead (1710–74), who, as the by-line of the *Journal* attests, spent some years confined for debt in the Fleet Prison. Whether Fielding knew it or not, he also had a personal score to settle with Whitehead, who, as "Con" Phillips's ghost, had recently concluded her *Apology* with a savage attack on his character. (These services the lady is said to have "remunerated in kind.")[97] But by and large Whitehead was not himself lucky in the character given him by his contemporaries. Dr. Johnson remembered him only as "a small poet ... who hung loose upon society."[98] As for his conversation, a sample of which is preserved in William Bayley's testimony before Fielding, Sir John Hawkins represents it as "desultory, vociferous, and profane."[99] As a poet, Whitehead had wit; but, since he was a confirmed Tory whose party was always out of power, he invariably applied it in libels against the government. During the 1730s he satirized the Walpole ministry in *The State Dunces* (1733) and *Manners: A Satire* (1739); by the late 1740s he was sniping at Fielding's friends in the administration – in *Honour: A Satire* (1747), for example, castigating Lyttelton and Pitt for selling out to Pelham. Fielding's reasons for caricaturing Whitehead are plain enough, then. And it is delightfully apt that by metamorphosing "Whitehead" into "Wronghead," he turned the tables on his adversary, associating the Opposition's man with the family of Sir Francis Wronghead, the ale-swilling country politician of Cibber's *Provok'd Husband* whom Tory satirists had adopted as the type of the self-serving courtier.

The *Covent-Garden Journal* of 1749 fulfills the promise of its ironic by-line. The "Introductory Essay" parodies the patriotic cant of the Opposition propagandists, and of Whitehead in particular, by blustering inanely about the threat to "Liberty" and "Freedom" posed by ministerial "Power" – a threat manifested in the persecution of Penlez and the patronizing of the "French strollers." Under "Foreign Affairs" mock news items from Rome, Paris, and Amsterdam associate the anti-Court party with papists and Jacobites and (Vandeput being of Dutch ancestry) things un-English. Under "Home Affairs" a letter to Vandeput from a penniless debtor in the Fleet, presumably a familiar of the editor, contains the improbable offer of a supply of money to support his cause, and this is followed by reports that he enjoys the backing of other, equally reputable elements of the populace – black-shoe boys, pickpockets, a lamp-lighter and a chimney sweep. This heartening intelligence is interrupted by a muddled letter from "An Independent Elector," eyewitness to the recent uproar at the playhouse, who declares that, whether or not Trentham drew his sword on that occasion, his behavior ought to be resented.

In short, as fugitive political satires go the *Covent-Garden Journal* of 1749 is a clever performance. Certainly it pleased Bedford and his brother-in-law, who not only authorized an extraordinary printing, but also arranged to have the paper distributed throughout the country. Thus Trentham's friend Theobald Taaffe wrote Bedford's agent on 5 December:

> the Covent-Garden Journal this day published, is one of the best things y^t has been published. Lord Trentham desires there may be a great many distributed & sent into Different parts of England as it will have a very good effect & pray send down some [here?] if you have any to spare.[100]

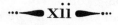

xii

If Fielding had reason to be grateful for Bedford's patronage, it is clear from his activities as magistrate and author during the Westminster election of 1749 that he gave full value in return. One consequence of these activities, however, was that, to judge from the response his pamphlet on Penlez provoked in *The Craftsman* (16 December 1749)[101] and *The Remembrancer* (16 June 1750), they appear to have completed his estrangement from two old friends, Thomas Cooke and James

Ralph. Ralph, perhaps, was merely earning his bread as an anti-ministerial writer and meant nothing personal by his criticisms. But Cooke's recriminations – for he is the likely author[102] – are full of venom. In *The Craftsman* (7 April 1750), for example, D'Anvers published some verses composed by Martinus Scriblerus to celebrate Folly on the first of April. Vying for preeminence with her votaries in divinity and physic (Orator Henley and Dr. Taylor the Oculist), Fielding represents the law and cuts much the same figure he had two decades earlier in *The Candidates for the Bays*:

> A Lawyer next stands Candidate for *Fame*;
> For now the Queen's amphibious Justice came:
> The Part he acts still changing with the Year;
> Now Whig, now Tory, *Trotplaid*, *Vinegar*!
> Brown as a J[a]kes, his Snuff-strown Chin he rais'd;
> While his big Plug he chew'd, the People gaz'd.
> The pungent Grains (a Present for his Vote)
> Heighten'd the yellow Horrors of his Coat.
> In Act to speak, he stopt; (while Laughter rag'd)
> Thinking on all the merry Wars he wag'd;
> On all the witty Malice he had shewn,
> And ev'ry Droll attempt to shake her Throne.
> Then thus at Length. "Forgive each *Pasquinade*;
> Forgive my antient, merry, honest Trade;
> Forgive the Sallies of ungovern'd Youth;
> Forgive, good Queen, my early love of Truth.
> Ah! let this leaden Journal of your own
> The Wit of *Joseph* or of *Jones* attone.
> O Lover of Assassins and the Love!
> Killing's no Murder, this true Case can prove.
> O Milk of human Kindness! well I wean,
> You, you, like Virtue, must be lov'd when seen!
> Too long a Foundling, Alien from your Throne!
> Now, Parent-Goddess, recognize your Son."

A learned and entertaining companion whom Fielding once loved, Cooke was also irascible and dictatorial – a man quick to take offense and unforgiving, who would suffer no rivals in wit. As Wilson's verdict on the "Rule of Right" men suggests in *Joseph Andrews*, the two were no longer compatible.

This was also a time when Fielding's inveterate carelessness about money put the best of his friendships to the test. Having waited with near biblical patience for Fielding to honor the debts he owed him, James Harris wrote to remind him of the matter. Fielding replied on 18 November 1749, enclosing something (probably a copy of his pamphlet on Penlez, published that same day) which he hoped would "plead my Excuse" for not having answered sooner. As to the purpose of Harris's letter, Fielding wrote:

> I hope it will be agreeable to you not to draw on me till February and then only for the £25 Note, I having laid out all my Money at present in purchasing a little Estate at Twickenham[.] This is a Fact, as it is that I will pay as above at the time above limited, and will within a year owe you nothing but my Gratitude for former Favours and hearty Good Wishes. The latter indeed I will not owe you for I will and do now heartily pay you.

Though jauntily expressed, a postscript hints at a cooling of the relationship: "As you can have nothing else to do, I wish you would write me longer Letters, and I will follow your Example." Besides the disagreeable impression it gives of a strain on the friendship, the letter is interesting for Fielding's statement that he had purchased a small estate at Twickenham. "This is a Fact," he insists; yet it is one which left no trace in any official records extant.

December was a sad and difficult month. On the 17th at St. Paul's, Covent Garden, Fielding buried his infant daughter, Mary Amelia. At about the same time, he fell "very dangerously ill with a Fever, and a Fit of the Gout." So grave was his case a rumor spread (fortunately ill founded) that he had contracted a "Mortification in his Foot."[103] Such attacks of gout were now chronic afflictions, crippling and exquisitely painful. The only token Edward Moore left of his intimacy with Fielding is an undated letter that reveals how dearly his friend was thus paying for the excesses of his youth (as Moore believed) and how entertaining Fielding's conversation continued to be despite the pain and fatigue. To the Reverend John Ward, a fellow dissenter who was eager to make the acquaintance of the author of *Tom Jones*, Moore wrote:

> Fielding continues to be visited for his sins, so as to be wheeled about from room to room: when he mends, I am sure to see him at my lodgings; and you may depend upon timely notice. What fine things are wit and beauty, if a man could be temperate with the one, or a woman chaste with the other! – But he that will confine his acquaintance to the sober and modest, will generally find himself among the dull and ugly. If this remark of mine should be thought to shoulder itself in without an introduction, you will be pleased to note, that Fielding is a wit, that his disorder is the gout, and intemperance the cause.[104]

The attack that struck Fielding in December 1749 seems to have been even more severe than the one Moore describes. From 9 December, when he committed the leader of a gang of pickpockets to Newgate, until 23 December, when he committed a counterfeiter to the same prison,[105] the papers printed no news of his activities at Bow Street. By the 27th, however – owing, he believed, to the ministrations of Dr. Thomas Thompson (c. 1700–63) – Fielding was "so well recovered, as to be able to execute his Office as usual."[106] For the time being, at least, Fielding's faith in the ability of this controversial physician to cure his ailments – particularly the gout, on which Thompson had published a treatise – was unshakeable. Indeed, he would make room in the original version of *Amelia* for an entire chapter (V.ii), "*Containing a Brace of Doctors, and much physical Matter*," whose chief function is to praise this man and to ridicule his many enemies among the apothecaries and physicians. In this version of the novel Mrs. Bennet (later Mrs. Atkinson) on three occasions delivers "many vast Eulogiums" on Thompson, "the true *Machaon*, of whom *Homer* speaks so greatly." Such was Fielding's admiration for this pugnacious empiric that he was willing thus to risk the derision of virtually the entire College of Physicians, who resented Thompson's outspoken disparagement of their methods and, insisting that it was Thompson's bungling which had killed Thomas Winnington in 1746, attempted to destroy his professional reputation.[107] In Thompson's behalf it may be said that, by trusting more to nature than to hypothetical systems and corrosive medicines, he probably killed fewer patients than his antagonists; and he enjoyed the confidence of a distinguished clientele – including the Prince of Wales, Sir Francis Dashwood, and Fielding's friend Dodington – most of whom, according to Hawkins, believed he "had reduced the art of healing to an epitome."[108]

Among those who remained skeptical of Thompson's skill, however, was Thomas Harris. On 16 January 1749/50 Fielding wrote James Harris the news that his brother "Tom" was again afflicted with the gout; but, Fielding complained,

> I can not persuade him to use my Doctor who hath lately cured me of that Distemper[.] I wish you would back my Solicitations, and Mrs. Harris must pardon me if I am so selfish to wish you would do this in Person: for believe me you have no Friend who wishes more ardently to see you.

To judge from this cordial profession of affection, the friendship between Fielding and Harris held firm. Indeed, Fielding wrote this letter in order to thank Harris "very kindly for your most acceptable Present of one of the finest Chines that ever graced the Back of a Hog with four Legs, or the Table of one with two." The nature of Harris's present, as well as Fielding's metaphor for his own appetite, suggests that an abler physician than Thompson would find it difficult to cure permanently the constitutional disorders which were shortening Fielding's life.

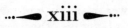

Though it is impossible to trace precisely Fielding's progress with *Amelia*, the novel appears to have been well under way by the time in late November or early December 1749 when Richardson, in a famous letter to Lady Bradshaigh, paused to review Fielding's literary career in that tone of disdain which thoughts of his rival ever elicited from him:

> Before his Joseph Andrews ... the poor man wrote without being read, except when his Pasquins, &c. roused party attention and the legislature at the same time, according to that of Juvenal, which may be thus translated:
>
>> Would'st thou be read, or would'st thou bread ensure,
>> Dare something worthy *Newgate* or the *Tower*.
>
> In the former of which (removed from inns and alehouses) will some of his next scenes be laid; and perhaps not unusefully; I hope not. But to have done, for the present, with this fashionable author....[109]

With *Tom Jones* Fielding had indeed become a "fashionable author": not one but two editions of a spurious sequel, *The History of Tom Jones the Foundling, in His Married State*, had appeared in November and December – by which time the novel also had become the target of one of the genuine monuments of ultracrepidarian criticism, *An Examen of the History of Tom Jones, a Foundling* by "Orbilius." But, as Richardson heard, Fielding's more recent concerns as a magistrate had given him a new sense of the purpose of fiction. In *Amelia* he would tell a "useful" story about the need to reform England's "Constitution," not only her laws but the moral temper of the nation; and his scenes, far "removed from inns and alehouses" – the festive setting of his comic epics of the road – would suit graver social themes: courtrooms, prisons, sponging houses, and that imperfect sanctuary for unforgiven debtors the Verge of the Court.

Certain specific problems he had addressed six months before in his abortive "Bill" to regulate the watch served now to shape and color the early chapters of the novel. An evil even more pernicious than the impotence and venality of the police, however, was the incompetence and corruption of too many members of the magistracy. At the Sessions in January, Fielding took a leading role in the efforts of the Middlesex justices to purge the bench of one such magistrate who may have been the real-life original of Justice Thrasher in *Amelia*. On 18 January 1749/50 the Court began to consider "Some Irregularities" alleged to have been committed in the execution of his office by Henry Broadhead

(d. 1754), a wealthy brewer in the disreputable district of St. Giles-in-the-Fields who had been plying his other trade as a justice and tool of the Duke of Bedford for twenty-five years.[110] Like Thrasher, Broadhead flouted the lawful procedures of his office in order to extort money from prosecutors and accused alike. Concluding their investigation some months later, the Middlesex justices protested to the Lord Chancellor that such behavior "is illegal, oppressive, and tends to render the Commission despicable." Hardwicke removed Broadhead from the commission.[111]

From this distant vantage point, the story of Fielding's life in the year 1750 is almost unrelievedly the story of his activities as a magistrate. For twelve months and more he published nothing, though presumably when he could find the time he continued writing *Amelia* until, in the autumn, he set aside his novel in order to draft the most ambitious of his social tracts, *An Enquiry into the Causes of the late Increase of Robbers.* Two events of this winter, however, interrupted the daily round of "what is commonly called Justice Business," to use his own phrase from the letter to Harris of 16 January 1749/50.

He refers to the first of these events in a postscript to that letter: his wife Mary was "in the Straw." She gave birth to a daughter who on 21 January at St. Paul's, Covent Garden, was christened Sophia[112] – her name, like that of her dead sister Mary Amelia, recalling both a favorite heroine of Fielding's fiction and the royal ladies of Hanover.

Of more general interest to the public was the opening on 19 February 1749/50,[113] of the Universal Register Office – an ingenious, if not unprecedented, business venture which Fielding apparently devised but which was managed by his half-brother John in partnership with certain other "Gentlemen." Originally called "The Office of Intelligence: or, Universal Register of Persons and Things," it was located "opposite Cecil-Street in the Strand." Agencies of a similar kind had been attempted before: Fielding might have read in the *Daily Gazetteer* (11 November 1736) an ironic proposal that Montaigne's scheme of an "Office of Intelligence" be put into practice; and he may have been aware of the short-lived "Universal Register" announced by Vander Esch and Company in the *Daily Advertiser* (29 April 1737).[114] But these hints came to nothing until the Fieldings took them up. Under John Fielding's energetic management the business prospered so enviably that it spawned a host of rival and unscrupulous imitators, "the ignorant and impudent Corrupters of so noble a Plan."[115]

"Noble" is perhaps not too grand a word for this business. Though his motives doubtless were chiefly commercial rather than altruistic, Fielding believed, however quixotically, that the Universal Register Office would be a panacea to cure the ills of the body politic. In its very conception this pragmatic affair of the marketplace reveals the close connection in Fielding's thought between "real" life and the world of ideas available through literature. For, as he makes clear in the *Plan* published a year later on 21 February 1750/1, Fielding's intent in establishing the Office was to realize an idea he ascribed to Montaigne (*Essays*, I.34): the idea of an agency that would promote the happiness of society by serving as a sort of clearing-house for all those who had services to offer and all those who required such services. For a small fee, by registering their names with the Office, servants and apprentices would find masters, priests curacies, soldiers commissions, schoolmasters schools, travelers conveyances, borrowers lenders; and those with houses to sell or lodgings to let, or with goods or curiosities to dispose of, could all be satisfied. Such an agency might well make its owners rich; but it would also be of great benefit to the nation:

> If any Society [Fielding writes in the *Plan*] ever hath been, or ever can be so regulated, that no Talent in any of its Members, which is capable of contributing to the general Good, should lie idle and unemployed, nor any of the Wants of its Members which are capable of Relief, should ever remain unrelieved, that Society might be said to have attained its utmost Perfection.

With so much to be gained if his scheme prospered, Fielding lost few opportunities to publicize the Universal Register Office. Indeed, disregarding the anachronisms they constituted in the time-scheme of his new novel, he insinuated into *Amelia* no fewer than six "puffs" of the agency.

····➡ xiv ◀─···

Throughout this year Fielding's business at Bow Street increased steadily as his reputation grew for diligence and efficiency. To give a complete account of these activities is impossible, so many of the original records having been lost. To chronicle the hundreds of his cases that a dogged search of contemporary newspapers, sessions reports, and archives has unearthed would be tedious. What we may hope to provide as from time to time we observe his appearance on the bench is a kind of profile sketch of Fielding as a justice, an outline of the more remarkable activities that characterized his most productive years in the magistracy.

After Fielding's death, John Fielding recalled how his brother began forming that doughty band of thief-takers who came to be called "the Bow-Street Runners":

The winter after the late Henry Fielding Esq; came to Bow-Street, the town was infested by a daring gang of robbers who attacked several persons of fashion, and gave a general alarm through the City and the Liberty of Westminster; and as that magistrate then enjoyed a good share of health, he spirited up the civil power, and sent several bodies of constables, with the advantage of having Mr. Welch at their head, into different parts of the town, by whose bravery and activity those disturbers of the peace were quickly apprehended and brought to justice: and though, the year after, most of these constables were out of office, yet some of them, being actuated by a truly public spirit against thieves, and being encouraged by the said magistrate, continued their diligence, and were always ready, on being summoned, to go in pursuit of villains.[116]

It is possible to reconstruct these events in some detail. On the night of Monday, 29 January 1749/50, Saunders Welch, High Constable of the Holborn Division, and Daniel Carne, who served in that capacity for the Liberty of Westminster, were authorized by Fielding to commence a series of raids on the known haunts of a large gang of street robbers and house-breakers who were terrorizing the populace. By notices in the papers Fielding urged the victims of recent robberies to attend at Bow Street the following day to identify the culprits. The first night's swoop netted one of the gang, Thomas Pendergast, as well as more than twenty other "Rogues, Vagabonds, Night-Walkers, &c." The raids continued and the number apprehended grew to "near 40 Highwaymen, Street Robbers, Burglars, Rogues, Vagabonds, and Cheats" whom Fielding committed to prison during that first week of concerted action by the constabulary. Two suspects he discharged "after an Examination which lasted several Hours."[117] Among the qualities that distinguished Fielding's conduct on the bench were his persistence in conducting such examinations and his skill at breaking false alibis and exposing inconsistencies in testimony.

The gang was broken thanks to William Pentlow, the most intrepid of Fielding's constables. Soon after the gang robbed the Countess of Albemarle on 14 February, Pentlow arrested one of its most vicious members, Thomas Lewis (known as "Captain Flash"), who before he was subdued snapped his pistol twice at the officer at pointblank range, the weapon luckily misfiring both times. To save himself, Lewis turned witness for the Crown, implicating among others the gang's fence, Samuel Cadosa.[118] Fielding understood that theft and robbery could not be curtailed unless the receivers of stolen goods were suppressed. But it was in examining Cadosa before a crowded and illustrious audience at Bow Street – an audience including the Duke of Richmond among other noblemen and magistrates – that the enormity of this problem became clear to him. He later observed in *An Enquiry into the Causes of the late Increase of Robbers* (Sect. V) that, besides the legion of small-time pawnbrokers who carried on their illicit trade by various dodges,

> there are others who scorn such pitiful Subterfuges, who engage openly with the Thieves, and who have Warehouses filled with stolen Goods only. Among the *Jews* who live in a certain Place in the City, there have been, and perhaps still are, some notable Dealers this Way, who in an almost public Manner have carried on a Trade for many Years with *Rotterdam*, where they have their Warehouses and Factors, and whither they export their Goods with prodigious Profit, and as prodigious Impunity.

By the terms of the "Bill" he submitted to the Lord Chancellor in July 1749, Fielding would have had receivers of stolen goods treated as guilty of the original offense and punished as felons without benefit of clergy. In the *Enquiry* he repeated this recommendation, but in light of his experiences with the likes of Cadosa, he devoted an entire section of the treatise to exposing more fully this fundamental cause of crime.

As for the villain Lewis, who as witness for the Crown had escaped prosecution, he was soon back plying his trade on the highway. On 22 March near St. Pancras church he and three other members of the gang still at large brutally robbed one John Matthews; Lewis thrust a pistol into the victim's mouth, breaking his teeth, while a colleague held a pistol to his ear. When his ordeal was over Matthews alerted Pentlow, who surprised Lewis in his bed and took his colleague in a brothel. At their trial their only defense was to impugn Pentlow's veracity as a witness, protesting that he *"would swear away any person's life for a trifle."* Fielding, however, *"upon oath declared, he sincerely believed there was not an honester, or a braver man than [Pentlow] in the king's dominions."* Lewis was found guilty and condemned.[119]

But Fielding's methods as a justice and his success in dealing with such dangerous criminals are perhaps best (and most aptly) illuminated by the role he played in the capture of Thomas Jones and his gang – "The Royal Family" as they called themselves – who rescued Jones from the Gatehouse in January 1748/9. That outrage prompted the King to proclaim an extraordinary reward of £100, over and above the statutory £40, for those instrumental in the arrest and conviction of Jones and his rescuers. Thoughts of such a bounty moved John Sargent, a butcher, to disclose that Jones and three of the gang had fled to Dublin. In concert with two other justices, Fielding dispatched a constable, Luke Dillon, in pursuit. In October 1749 Dillon and George Roe, keeper of Newgate jail in Dublin, seized Jones and his confederates and escorted them back to London to stand trial in March 1749/50. By that time six other members of the gang had been taken – one of them, Joseph Uptabake, by Pentlow singlehandedly. Jones and his "Royal Family" having preyed together were condemned to sway together at Tyburn; but only Jones suffered on 26 March, the sentences of his rescuers having been commuted to transportation. Pinioned to another prisoner and guarded by three sheriffs and several hundred peace officers, he would not be rescued twice.[120]

On 3 May, while supporting Pentlow's application for the reward, Fielding also backed another claim by this man, the ablest of his constables:

> I do hereby certifie that the above named Wm Pentlow was the Person by whom Thomas Lewis the first Person who discovered the great Gang of Street Robbers last Winter was taken in the bravest manner, and that the Public are in the highest Degree obliged to the said Mr. Pentlow for his Vigilance, Activity and Bravery in this Discharge of his Duty as a Peace Officer.[121]

Fielding thus certified the affidavits of nearly everyone claiming rewards in the affair of Thomas Jones and his rescuers: between 27 April and 29 May 1750 he endorsed no fewer than fourteen of these.[122] He would come to appreciate the risks of offering such tempting prizes to unscrupulous bounty-hunters, but for the moment the incentive was proving efficacious. During his tenure as magistrate the reward money paid out annually by the Crown increased at an astonishing rate – from £200 in 1748, to £600 in 1749, to £4,600 in 1750, to £6,500 in the period from 1751 to June 1752, when the last of the royal proclamations ended.[123]

In March 1749/50, affecting to advise the justices of England how to thrive, one wag observed that Fielding was so "extremely busy and pragmatical" in execution of his office that he had become "much the greatest Man in the three Kingdoms; at least, nobody else is talked of but he and G[arric]k."[124] The author was not far from wrong; no one else, certainly, was more often mentioned in the public papers than Fielding. Severe earthquakes having shaken the capital in February and March, terrifying the populace and prompting a spate of jeremiads from pulpit and press denouncing divine judgment against a dissolute nation, he thought the time propitious to act against two of the evils he deplored in his *Charge* to the Grand Jury and which also figure prominently in the social satire of *Amelia*: gaming and masquerades. On the night of 19 April he personally led a party of constables and foot guards in a raid on a notorious gaming house near the Strand. He seized a great many gamesters, others escaping out the windows and over the roofs, and ordered his men to break up the tables. "The Neighbourhood," reported the *General Advertiser* (21 April 1750), "test-

ified their Joy at the Demolition of this great Nuisance, by universal
Acclamations." The following week, when on 25 April a "Jubilee Mas-
querade Ball" was to be held at Ranelagh, the Middlesex justices –
Fielding among them – moved to suppress it, as tending "to the
Encouragement of Gaming, Lewdness, and all manner of Debauchery,
and the Corruption of the Morals of both Sexes."[125]

Among scores of individuals who appeared before Fielding at Bow
Street this year a few are interesting enough to mention. On 14 February
his constables thwarted a plot to assassinate the celebrated James
Annesley (1715–60), the so-called "lost heir" of Lord Altham, whose
brother, the Earl of Anglesey, had allegedly seized the inheritance.
Annesley claimed that in order to put him out of the way Anglesey sold
him into slavery in America and, when he returned to Ireland, entered
into conspiracies to take his life. Lord Anglesey by legal devices successfully contested these claims, which a jury had originally determined
to be valid. Fielding nevertheless believed Annesley's story; he committed the would-be assassin, "a most notorious Ruffian," to
Newgate.[126] In this belief Smollett shared; he included the story in
Peregrine Pickle (1751).

In March, Fielding was involved in two cases that were politically
sensitive. The first concerned John Thrift (d. 1752), the executioner
who not long before had hanged, drawn, and quartered the condemned
Jacobites. When a party of passing Irishmen jestingly called him "Jack
Ketch" – the name not only of his famous predecessor, but also, as it
happened, of a thief who recently escaped from Newgate – Thrift
became enraged and pursued the men with a cutlass, hacking one of
them so severely that he died of his wounds. This incident, witnessed
by a huge mob near Drury Lane, was instantly politicized by those
who resented Thrift as the cruel instrument of the Hanoverian establishment. Fielding, whose loyalty to the government did not extend to
violating the plain sense of the law, committed Thrift to prison to be
tried for murder; he was found guilty and condemned to death. Thrift,
however, having first had his sentence commuted to transportation,
was then awarded a full, and highly unpopular, pardon.[127] In March,
Fielding also committed to Newgate the incorrigible Jacobite Charles
Fitzgerald, who called himself Earl of Desmond. Having spent three
years in prison for attempting to assist the Pretender during the Forty-
Five, Fitzgerald resumed his treasonable activities as soon as he was
released. He was accused before Fielding of enlisting men into the
French king's service, of cursing George II and the House of Hanover,
and of drinking toasts to the Pretender, calling him Charles, the Prince
of Wales. The offense was a capital one, but he was acquitted.[128]

In June, Fielding was at the center of another sensational case – this
time involving Edward Walpole (d. 1784), Horace's elder brother,

whose bisexual proclivities were proving highly dangerous to himself. In April John Cather, a servant who followed Walpole to London from Ireland, accused him of an assault with intent to commit (according to the form of the indictment) "that sodomitical and detestable Sin called *Buggery*, (not to be named among Christians)." A jury acquitted Walpole of the charge, but he had also made himself vulnerable to another "infamous Prosecution" brought against him by Walter Patterson, an unscrupulous Irish attorney and confederate of Cather. Besides supporting Cather's accusation Patterson, with others, first attempted to blackmail Walpole, and then conspired to frame him on the improbable charge of forging a promissory bond of £150. On 14 June Fielding committed Patterson to Clerkenwell Bridewell, taking the precaution of ordering a party of soldiers to escort him there in order to thwart a rescue. Convicted of fraud, Patterson was sentenced to six months' hard labor, during which time he was to be whipped until bloody at the cart's tail three times – once around Hanover Square, once up and down Pall Mall, and once around Covent Garden Market – after which he was to be deported to Ireland. He escaped from custody before the sentence could be carried out, but was subsequently recaptured and tried, with Cather and others, for these offenses.[129]

But Fielding's most notable case of the year was wholly unremarkable, except in one respect: it represents the single documented instance of his having ever met face to face the author who would one day give us a name by which to call the age in which he wrote – and talked. On Monday, 12 March 1749/50, Fielding signed a recognizance certifying that "Samuel Johnson of Gough Square Gent" had appeared before him at Bow Street to post a bond of £20 for Mary Peyton, the apparently not so harmless wife of one of the drudges who toiled in Johnson's attic to produce his great *Dictionary*. Mrs. Peyton was bound to appear at the next General Quarter Sessions of the Peace for Middlesex to answer "what shall be objected against her and in the mean time to keep the Peace ... especially towards *Mary Humphreys*." Fielding later discharged Mrs. Peyton.[130] Could it be, however, that this brief encounter between these two proud men contributed to the forming of Johnson's famous opinion of Fielding, whom (remembering Malvolio's distempered slur on Feste) he called a "barren rascal"? One wonders too, whether it is only a coincidence that this encounter at Bow Street occurred earlier in the month in which Johnson wrote his famous essay, *Rambler* No. 4 (31 March): the essay in which he tacitly condemned the author of *Tom Jones* as chief among those who, for the sake of following Nature in their fiction, "so mingle good and bad Qualities in their principal Personages, that they are both equally conspicuous." Such authors, Johnson declared, "confound the Colours of Right and

Wrong" – a trait especially objectionable in an author whose business it also was to distinguish right from wrong in a court of justice.

····➤ XV ◆····

Such activities occupied Fielding for long hours daily. Understandably, he hoped to gain some less arduous and more dignified place in his profession – hoped, perhaps, to rise to such an eminence in the law as Judge Gould attained in his time and as his cousin Henry Gould would attain in his. To prove his qualifications for advancement he had attempted to cobble his grandfather's notes into a treatise on Crown law, and within a year of his appointment to the magistracy he published learned pamphlets on the institution of Grand Juries and on the Riot Act – not to mention his plan to reorganize the watch, presented to the Lord Chancellor in the form of a "Bill" to amend the constitution itself. He had neglected no opportunity to serve the government and to demonstrate his merit as a lawyer.

On 15 May another such opportunity occurred when, after a prolonged scrutiny of contested votes, Viscount Trentham was officially declared member for Westminster: Fielding on that occasion obeyed Bedford's "Commands" and attended in person "to preserve the Peace."[131] He soon saw a chance to escape such rude pragmatical employment once and for all. The promotion of Sidney Stafford Smythe from Steward of the Marshalsea Court to Baron of the Exchequer left a vacancy Fielding believed he was qualified to fill and which he saw as an important step toward further advancement. On Thursday, 24 May, he wrote Bedford:

> My Lord,
> If M[r]. Smith is made a Judge on the present Vacancies I hope your Grace will pardon my begging your Interest that I may succeed him as Judge of the Marshalsea. The Place is I believe of no great Profit since the Erection of the Courts of Small Debts, however it will be some Addition to my little Income, and will give me an Opportunity of shewing whether I deserve not some higher Promotion in the Law. It is in the Gift immediately of the Duke of Marlborough. If therefore I ask any thing improper of your Grace, I hope your Grace will punish me only by a Refusal.[132]

Bedford meant to grant this favor; he wrote promptly to recommend Fielding to Marlborough. But Marlborough informed him on 27 May that he had already promised to fill the place with the Prime Minister's own candidate. To judge from the grateful effusions in Fielding's letters to Bedford and his agent Butcher, both written on 29 May, he was not yet aware of this obstacle to his appointment – or perhaps he hoped Pelham would accept the Duke's recommendation:

> My Lord,
> I sit down in a Rapture of Gratitude to thank your Grace for the immediate Notice you was pleased to take of my Application, in the midst of Engagements with which if I had been acquainted I should not have presumed to have written on any Affair of mine. Success in this Matter, I most solemnly declare will be trifling compared to the Joy I taste in reflecting on so much Goodness, and on the Honour done me by the Duke of Bedford's Patronage and Protection. The great Business of my Life shall be, my Lord, to deserve these, at least to the utmost of my Power; and I heartily pray for some Opportunity to convince your Grace with what Zeal and Devotion, I am,
>
>   My Lord,
>   Y.r Grace's most obliged
>   most obedient, and dutiful
>   humble Servant
>   Henry Fielding[133]

Having read Fielding's letter to his noble patron, the critic will add to the list of styles he mastered – the Ridiculous, the Burlesque, the Marvelous, the Homerican and Mock Sublime – yet another category: the Fulsome. In the event, Pelham chose another man to fill the vacancy. Fielding's great expectations came to nothing. In an uncharacteristic mood of dejection, he resumed the dreary, debilitating round of "Justice Business" at Bow Street. Thomas Birch, who was now a close friend,[134] wrote on 7 July 1750 to Philip Yorke:

> Justice Fielding is so fatigued with that office, that he is determin'd to discontinue the Exercise of it, tho' the public can ill spare him, at a time when a most profligate Town wants the check of his Industry, Resolution, & Sagacity, Qualities not to be expected from any of his Competitors.[135]

Fatigued and disappointed, he would be further saddened by the deaths this summer of his eldest sister Catharine and of Henry, his only son by Charlotte. Both may have been among the victims of an epidemic of jail fever (a virulent strain of typhus) which at the Easter Sessions at the Old Bailey spread from the prisoners brought up for trial from Newgate, killing the Lord Mayor and a score of other eminent citizens who attended.[136] The contagion raged throughout the metropolis, which

suffered at the same time from a heat wave so oppressive that to find
relief great numbers of fish were said to have buried themselves in the
mud along the banks of the Thames.[137]

Catharine was living with Ursula and Beatrice in a house at Turnham
Green, near Hammersmith, when she died on 5 July, a few days short
of her forty-second birthday. She was buried on 9 July in the chancel
of St. Paul's, Hammersmith.[138] During a fit of illness three years earlier,
she had made her will (written in her own hand on 16 January 1746/7)
in which she named Ursula, next oldest of the sisterhood, as sole
executrix and beneficiary, bequeathing to her "all my real and personal
Estate all Linnen wearing Apparel Jewels Goods & all and every thing
that does now or ever may belong to me." On 25 July 1750 at Doctors'
Commons, Sarah Fielding and Susannah Jones, both of whom were
residing in the parish of St. Martin-in-the-Fields, appeared before
Arthur Collier to swear that the will was in Catharine's hand; on 27
July the will was proved before Collier on Ursula's oath.[139] Something
obviously remained of Mrs. Cottington's legacy to her goddaughter,
but the estate cannot have been large.

Late this same month the fever carried off Fielding's son Henry in
his eighth year. On 3 August he was buried near his sister, mother, and
grandmother in the chancel vault of St. Martin-in-the-Fields. Fielding
honored the boy with all the pomp of the most expensive funeral. A
procession of mourners followed the hearse to the church, which was
hung in black and illuminated with tapers while the great bell tolled.[140]

In August, Fielding took a holiday from Bow Street; at least there
is no trace of his activities there, either in the newspapers or in the
sessions reports, from 1 August, when he committed some pickpockets
to the Gatehouse, until 1 September, when he committed a gang of
robbers to Newgate.[141] Perhaps he took his family to Twickenham, to
nurse his grief and breathe fresher air. Perhaps he visited Ralph Allen
at Prior Park, to whom he would dedicate the novel he was writing.
Or, if there is truth in the tradition that in the early 1750s he lived for
a while at Barnes, Surrey, across the river from Hammersmith, this
could be the year he began leasing Milbourne House on Barnes Green –
a handsome dwelling that still stands, overlooking the village pond and
close to a tavern called The Sun.[142] At Barnes in 1750 Fielding would
be close to his sisters at Turnham Green and to his friend Dodington,
at whose house, "La Trappe," in Hammersmith, he and his wife dined
earlier this year on 28 April.[143] Fielding indeed was seeing more of his
former patron, who in March 1749 had resigned his place as Treasurer
of the Navy and allied himself with the Prince of Wales in order to
form a new Opposition.

In September 1750 Fielding was back at Bow Street, again master-
minding successful swoops of the constabulary against gangs of street

robbers.[144] His continuing neglect of his financial obligations to James Harris was now, however, seriously jeopardizing their friendship. Harris having written again to remind Fielding of the debt, Fielding on 22 September was brusque and ungracious in reply:

> Dear S^r,
> I wish it was owing to Forgetfulness that I had not yet desired you to draw on me: for I believe to forget one^s Friends is a great Happiness; but in Reality it arises from a more disagreeable Reason, and which still obliges me to desire you will defer drawing on me a little longer, as I think a Month or two can make no Difference to your Finances, and will I hope make a considerable one to mine. I am with all proper Compliments to your Family, Dear S^r.
>   Y^r most obed^t.
>   humble Servant.
>   Hen: Fielding

Fielding's letters to Harris, once so warm, full, and entertaining, had recently become cool, curt, and businesslike. Gone is the genial salutation – "My dearest Friend"; gone is the genial close – "and believe me/ My dearest Friend,/ Y^r most affectionate and/ obliged humble ser^{vt}." Money was the matter, as Harris's patience ran out and Fielding resented the obligations he had incurred. Happily, the friendship would survive this strain.

As it happens, this is the period when we can best apprehend the state of Fielding's finances, his habits of getting and spending; and his complaints about being short of cash are hard to credit. To begin with, in addition to Fielding's other sources of income, his bookseller had made 1749 a bonanza year for him: between May and January, Millar paid Fielding £838. 9s. (see Appendix II). What is more, the ledgers of Fielding's bankers, Hoare & Company, give a detailed record of his transactions from 20 April 1750 to 30 August 1751.[145] During this period, for once, Fielding appears easily to have balanced his account: when closing it out on 30 August 1751, he actually had to withdraw £21.15.3 in order to have debits cancel credits amounting to £813.18.6. Of course not all his financial transactions would be reflected in this ledger, which in fact raises more questions about his personal, professional, and commercial relationships than it answers. Of the forty persons to whom he paid money most are unidentifiable. Nor can one say *why* Fielding paid them: was he settling a bill for personal services rendered? Was the expense incurred in connection with his duties as magistrate or the business of the Universal Register Office? Was he lending money to a friend or repaying a loan?

However uncertain the inferences to be drawn from them, a few of the transactions are worth noting. Certain names seem to relate, for instance, to his work as a justice: Joshua Brogden, Saunders Welch, and perhaps John Jourdan – the last being a coachman whom Fielding may have employed to convey prisoners from Bow Street to jail. On 29 June 1750, not long after the troubles that were expected on the day Trentham was officially declared the elected Member for Westminster, Fielding paid £14.10s. to the prize-fighter John Slack, the "Butcher of Norwich," who in a famous bout on 11 April beat the champion, John Broughton: Fielding would honor both these pugilists in *Amelia* (XII.vi), but why did he owe Slack money as well as praise? Slack would have made a capital ally in a spot of bother, certainly, and he cast his vote for Trentham. The ledger also reveals that Fielding's friend, the "ingenious" Peter Taylor (1714–77), acted as his accountant; Taylor, a silversmith living at the corner of Cecil Street and the Strand, may have been one of the "Society of Gentlemen" who conducted the Universal Register Office.[146] Fielding made other payments to the printers Richard Francklin (£11 on 29 January 1750/1) and William Caslon (£13 on 23 November 1750), though the reasons for these payments are unclear: had they printed the various official forms and reward notices Fielding used at Bow Street, or advertisements for the Universal Register Office? Over this same period Fielding paid the bookseller, Samuel Baker, £53.16.9, whereas – since stocking the mind was a more important matter than furnishing the head – he allowed a mere thirty guineas to the fashionable peruke-maker, John Delaporte.

Two other names in the ledger are of interest. Five times Fielding gave money to a "Capt. William Fielding," amounting to the considerable sum of £63.19s. Presumably, this was not his half-brother, but rather the commander of H.M.S. *Fly*, who in advertisements invited "Gentlemen Seamen" to apply at the Universal Register Office.[147] Twice, moreover, Fielding helped Sarah with payments of £10 on 29 August 1750 and £9 on 19 March 1750/1 – the latter date corresponding to the time when she was being sued by Thomas Hayter, executor of the estate of his brother William Hayter, for recovery of an unspecified debt.[148] Thomas Hayter, who purchased the Fielding farm at East Stour, and his brother were of a wealthy Salisbury family and were friends of James Harris – to whom William bequeathed a small legacy and a favorite picture of Venice, with the request that Harris be kind to his wife and children.[149] One name conspicuously missing from Fielding's accounts is that of James Harris.

However much he may have teased her about her unladylike interest in acquiring Latin and Greek, the bond between Henry and Sarah remained close – closer, it appears, than their bonds to the others of the "Sisterhood" who lived apart, sharing the house at Turnham Green. Though her brother was a barrister, Catharine chose to draw up her own will in January 1746/7, in which she made no mention of Henry

and Sarah, who were then living together at Boswell Court. But she
made no mention either of Beatrice and Edmund, and probably merely
meant to endow Ursula, the next oldest sister, with the means to keep
their little household together. The playful, friendly tone of Ursula's
references to Henry and all her sisters in her letter of 25 October 1748
suggests that theirs was, as Fielding liked to say, "the Family of
Love."[150] That he deeply felt Catharine's death is clear from the passage,
pointedly inserted into the novel he was writing (*Amelia*, II.iv–v), in
which Booth grieves for a beloved sister who died suddenly of "a violent
Fever": "Upon my Soul, I cannot yet mention her Name without Tears.
Never Brother and Sister had, I believe, a higher Friendship for each
other." Sadly, within eight months of Catharine's death, he would feel
such sorrow twice more. Ursula and Beatrice died within weeks of each
other during the winter of 1750–1. Ursula was buried at St. Paul's,
Hammersmith, on 12 December and Beatrice on 24 February – both
receiving, by the standards of that suburban parish, the most expensive
obsequies. The three sisters rest together in the chancel of the church.[151]

···➤ xvi ◄➤···

In September 1750, after a brief holiday, Fielding resumed his duties
at Bow Street, and interrupted work on his novel in order to write the
most important of his social tracts. On 9 October 1750 the following
notice appeared in the *General Advertiser*:

> We hear that an eminent Magistrate is now employed in preparing
> a Pamphlet for the Press, in which the several Causes that have
> conspired to render Robberies so frequent of late, will be laid open;
> the Defects of our Laws enquired into; and Methods proposed which
> may discourage, and in a great measure prevent, this growing Evil
> for the future.

The pamphlet in question was *An Enquiry into the Causes of the late
Increase of Robbers*; and during the three months or so in which he
composed it, Fielding had fresh experiences of the evils it was designed
to combat. Of these by far the most important case was a consequence
of the highly effective raids he had mounted in the spring against the
gaming houses. On 23 November 1750 the Lord Chancellor received an
anonymous letter warning him of a plot against his life by a trio of
villains – individually the owners of brothels in the Strand, who also
jointly kept the profitable gaming house which Hardwicke had authorized Fielding to shut down, demolishing the tables in the process. The
three had set up new tables at Cuper's Gardens, opposite Somerset

House in the Strand, and they were paying two guineas a week to a certain magistrate for protection. Further to discourage prosecutions, their bullies were prepared to perjure themselves by swearing large debts and even robberies against anyone who dared lodge a complaint against them. But they would not be satisfied until they revenged themselves on Hardwicke.[152] Fielding investigated this alarming situation, and from Bow Street on 25 November he addressed an urgent note to the Lord Chancellor's Secretary, Hutton Perkins (d. 1757), at his chambers, No. 7 Lincoln's Inn Square:

> I have made full Enquiry after the three Persons and have a perfect Account of them all. Their Characters are such that perhaps three more likely Men could not be found in the Kingdom for the Hellish Purpose mentioned in the Letter. As the Particulars are many and the Affair of such Importance I beg to see you punctually at Six this Evening when I will be alone to receive you.[153]

We do not know what Fielding's detectives were able to discover about the plot to murder Hardwicke or how in his private interview with Perkins he proposed to prevent it.

There is no obvious connection between this case and the hard-earned success Fielding and his officers had against a gang of well-armed footpads whose leader was the powerful prize-fighter James Field, another of the thousands of sailors made redundant after the peace. On the evening of 6 December, Fielding was informed that several of the gang were carousing at the Fox, a public house in Drury Lane. He dispatched Welch and Pentlow to the place supported by a party of foot guards. It was Pentlow who spotted Field and raised the alarm – upon which Field drew a pistol and was about to fire when one of the soldiers struck him in the chest with the butt-end of his musket. The sergeant and several guardsmen rushed Field, who took them all on like some great bear baited by dogs: he knocked one man down, broke another's finger, and pistol-whipped a third before he was subdued by force of numbers. Only the timely arrival of Welch, who had been pursuing other members of the gang, saved Field from the fury of the soldiers he had mauled. Under examination by Fielding, he tried to save himself by impeaching more than a score of the gang; but he was tried and convicted of a brutal robbery for which he was condemned.[154]

As Fielding considered a range of measures to improve the system of law enforcement, Pentlow's conduct in such cases made him seem the perfect sort of man to implement one of the most urgently needed of these reforms. The early chapters of *Amelia* expose the oppressive practices of prison-keepers. By law prisoners could be fettered and made to subsist on a penny-loaf of bread a day. The keepers, therefore, extorted money for every amenity – from basic comforts such as the

right to move about unchained or to have a bed to sleep on and a bit
of meat to eat, to the comparatively luxurious private accommodation
which Miss Mathews enjoys in the novel. Typically, Fielding was not
content with exposing this evil in print; as with his prosecution of the
corrupt justice Henry Broadhead and the steps he was taking to
reorganize the police, he took practical measures to rectify the situation.
When the keepership of New Prison, Clerkenwell, became vacant he
wrote the Duke of Newcastle on 15 January 1750/1 recommending
Pentlow for the post: "He is a Man of whose Courage and Integrity I
have seen the highest Proofs, and is indeed every Way qualified for the
charge."[155] Ignoring Fielding's advice, Newcastle put forward his own
candidate, one John Bland, an illiterate man whom the Middlesex
justices rejected as "unfit" for the office; Pentlow, on the other hand,
they found "upon examination ... to be a person who writes a good
hand and is in other respects a fit and proper person."[156] Fielding felt
the urgency of this reform so strongly that he was prepared not only
to defy the Secretary of State in the matter, but to bind himself in the
amount of £100 to enable Pentlow to qualify for the keepership.[157] The
system itself was so defective, however, that an honest man could not
meet the expenses of the office and hope to make a living on the annual
allowance of £30.[158]

••••▶ xvii ◀••••

In the two years of Fielding's tenure at Bow Street a crisis had developed
of the greatest moment to the public. The incidence of crime and
violence in the metropolis had increased markedly, owing to circumstances that swelled the ranks of the vagrant poor: their number
was augmented annually by hundreds of migratory Irish who came to
England to harvest crops and were left to shift for themselves when
this seasonal labor was done; and now, the war with France at an end,
the situation was exacerbated by thousands of disbanded soldiers and
sailors. These desperate men, often in huge gangs, infested the streets
and highways, plundering the public and, since hanging was the punishment equally for murder or for the theft of goods worth a shilling,
using their victims cruelly. Horace Walpole complained: "One is forced
to travel even at noon as if one was going to battle."[159] The more
timorous of these outcasts joined the crowds begging for the penny that
would enable them to drown their troubles in a quartern of gin.
    Except as they were annoyed by beggars and pickpockets who
swarmed near the theatres and coffee-houses, the nobility and gentry
who made the laws were insulated from the poverty and the squalor,

snug within their townhouses or behind the windows of their carriages and sedan chairs. In his court at Bow Street, however, Fielding saw how deep and how far the rot had spread. He saw how it demoralized and brutalized "the Commonalty," as he called the lower classes, who, according to the myth of the ideal polity he inherited, ought to be the "useful" part of the nation. From his own observation – and from the reports of Saunders Welch, whose duties as High Constable took him into the dirtiest corners of town – he was only too well aware of the realities of life in the London underworld. Here crammed into stinking, ruinous tenements, "all properly accommodated with miserable Beds from the Cellar to the Garret," hundreds of men and women lay together promiscuously and drank themselves into oblivion, the price of a double bed and a quart of gin being fourpence.[160] In the outskirts of town the spectacle – which at Fielding's invitation several members of Parliament witnessed for themselves sometime later – was no less appalling. Looking into "the Habitations of the Poor," they beheld "such Pictures of human Misery as must move the Compassion of every Heart that deserves the Name of human":

> What indeed must be his Composition [Fielding asks] who could see whole Families in Want of every Necessary of Life, oppressed with Hunger, Cold, Nakedness, and Filth, and with Diseases, the certain Consequence of all these; what, I say, must be his Composition, who could look into such a Scene as this, and be affected only in his Nostrils?[161]

Soon after arriving in England in the winter of 1751, Giuseppe Baretti met Fielding and asked whether some of the beggars he saw of both sexes did not perish of hunger and want: "Over a thousand, or even two thousand, in the course of a year," Fielding answered, "but London is so large it is hardly noticed." He added that it was "the plentiful supply of money and the consequent dearness of living that are at the root of all this misery."[162]

London at mid-century presented scenes of wretchedness, savagery, and profligacy beyond any visible today in the worst urban ghettos. By one contemporary estimate there were 17,000 gin shops within the Bills of Mortality,[163] and as Welch reported, prostitutes, their bodies "a Composition of disorders," lurked "at every Corner," making "Sin Cheap."[164] In grotesque emulation of their "betters," apprentices and tradesmen with a few shillings in their pockets preferred the diversions of sleazy gaming-houses and pleasure resorts to the drudgery of fifteen-hour workdays.

Reflecting on these evils, Fielding produced the most remarkable of his social tracts – a work as important for what it reveals about his temperament and character as for the remedies it prescribes for the disorders of the commonwealth. Heralded by a notice in the *General Advertiser* for Friday, 4 January 1750/1 – the end of a week in which Fielding committed "upwards of fifty Criminals" to prison[165] – the work was published by Millar on 19 January under the following title:

> *An Enquiry into the Causes of the late Increase of Robbers, &c. With some Proposals for Remedying this Growing Evil. In which the Present Reigning Vices are impartially exposed; and the Laws that relate to the Provision for the Poor, and to the Punishment of Felons are largely and freely examined.*

This work, dedicated to the Lord Chancellor, defines Fielding's idea of society. The century in which he lived was moving toward revolutions in both the Old and New Worlds that ushered in republican and democratic forms of government; but Fielding, like the vast majority of his contemporaries, distrusted such systems. He scorned "the Mob" – "the fourth Estate," as he called them sarcastically.[166] He would have regarded those epoch-making events with horror, as cataclysms very like the triumph of Anarchy that Pope envisaged in *The Dunciad*. Though he was a staunch Whig in politics, preferring with Locke a constitutional to an absolute monarchy, his idea of the social order was drawn, as the Preface to the *Enquiry* makes clear, from much older sources – from Plato and the "*Greek* Philosophy," and, closer to home, from "the Constitutions of *Alfred*," whom Bolingbroke (and hence Lyttelton and Dodington) romanticized as Britain's most enlightened king. Far from being the forward-looking prophet of libertarianism he is sometimes said to be, Fielding was profoundly conservative as a social thinker. Indeed, as M. R. Zirker concludes in the most authoritative study of the subject, he "accepted unquestioningly a hierarchical, static society nearly feudal in some of its outlines."[167]

In this, we should bear in mind, he was entirely representative of his age: the doctrine of "subordination" – the doctrine which assumes that the ranks and degrees of society are ordered according to a divinely ordained hierarchy extending from the king and the nobility through the gentry down to "the Commonalty" – is the fundamental axiom of Fielding's social philosophy, as it is of Swift's and Pope's, of Smollett's and Johnson's, of Goldsmith's and Burke's. It was a doctrine impressed on the poor in numberless sermons calculated to remind them of their "useful" role – even of their happiness! – as "hewers of wood and drawers of water." (Even Fielding, who knew better, was capable of insisting in the *Enquiry* [Sect. IV] that "Health is the happy Portion of Poverty.") So well had the doctrine of subordination been inculcated that the distinguished economic historian Jacob Viner could find no work published in England during the hundred years after the Restoration which could be described as "egalitarian" in political sentiment. It should not be surprising, then, that Fielding was so far from thinking "perfect Equality" a desirable condition of society that he denounced it as one "inconsistent with all Government, and which befits only that which is sometimes called the State of Nature, but may more properly be called a State of Barbarism and Wildness."[168]

Fielding's ideal order, rather, is identical with that of Edward VI, "that most wonderful young Prince," whose statement of the commonplace analogy between the functional organicism of the microcosm, man, and that of the body politic he quotes approvingly:

> As there is no Part ... admitted in the Body that doth not work and take Pains, so ought there no Part of the Commonwealth to be, but laboursome in his Vocation. The Gentleman ought to labour in the Service of his Country; the Serving-man ought to wait diligently on his Master; the Artificer ought to labour in his Work; the Husbandman in tilling the Ground; the Merchant in passing the Tempests; but the Vagabonds ought clearly to be banished, as is the superfluous Humour of the Body; that is to say, the Spittle and Filth; which, because it is for no Use, is put out by the Strength of Human Nature.[169]

There is no better key to Fielding's social thought than this traditional notion of the body politic. Just as man is constituted, ideally, of the body's individual members, each working cooperatively in accordance with natural laws and the dictates of reason to effect the good of the whole, and just as this harmony reflects the health and temper of the soul, so Fielding thought of society as an organism whose well-being depended not only on the proper subordination and cooperation of its several members – each, under the government of law, performing duties appropriate to his or her rank – but also on the collective morality of the people, whose character in this respect comprised what might be called the "soul" of the nation.

To understand Fielding's work as a publicist in this final period of his life, we need to grasp the significance of this analogy. Whether as magistrate or as author, he saw himself as a kind of moral physician ministering to potentially fatal disorders in the "Constitution" of England. This is the theme he sounds at the beginning of *Amelia*, where he offers ironic "*Observations on the Excellency of the* English *Constitution*" (I.ii); and it is the theme he sounds in the Preface to the *Enquiry*, where he defines the concept as follows:

> Now in this Word, *The Constitution*, are included the original and fundamental Law of the Kingdom, from whence all Powers are derived, and by which they are circumscribed; all legislative and executive Authority; all those municipal Provisions which are com-

monly called *The Laws*; and, *lastly*, the Customs, Manners, and Habits of the People. These, joined together, do, I apprehend, form the Political, as the several Members of the Body, the animal Oeconomy, with the Humours and Habit, compose that which is called the Natural Constitution.

To emphasize that the term properly implies not only the laws of the nation, but its essential spirit and character, he recalls his favorite, Plato:

> By the *Constitution* is, indeed, rather meant something which results from the Order and Disposition of the whole; something resembling that Harmony for which the *Theban* in *Plato's Phaedo* contends; which he calls ... *something invisible and incorporeal*. For many of the *Greeks* imagined the Soul to result from the ... Composition of the Parts of the Body; when these were properly tempered together, as Harmony doth from the proper Composition of the several Parts in a well tuned musical Instrument: In the same manner, from the Disposition of the several Parts in a State, arises that which we call the *Constitution*.

Whoever would in this sense repair and sustain the constitution of his country must therefore combine both the lawyer's knowledge of her laws and the historian's knowledge of "the Genius, Manners, and Habits of the People"; otherwise, Fielding declares, he will make "but a wretched Politician" – and, we may infer, a wretched magistrate and wretched novelist as well, since these same principles governed Fielding's conduct on the bench and shaped his plan for *Amelia*.

In his study in Bow Street, at the heart of the depraved capital of Georgian England, Fielding liked to suppose that such an ideal polity once existed under "the Constitutions of *Alfred*," the fabled Saxon king who devised a decentralized, paternalistic scheme of government, dividing the counties "into Hundreds, and these again into Tithings, Decennaries, or ten Families." The basic unit of the social order was thus the "Family," whose "Master" was responsible for the welfare and good behavior of his servants, tenants, laborers (Sect. VI). So effective was this system, Fielding nostalgically observes, that a traveler might openly leave money in a public place and find it untouched a month later; indeed, as proof of the honesty of his people Alfred hung up bracelets of gold at the crossroads, knowing no one would meddle with them.

But this dream of an orderly and honorable past faded before the reality of the metropolis in 1750 – a wilderness of vice and roguery. Fielding attributed England's decline to the introduction of trade; for trade brought riches and riches, luxury, which spreading downwards from the Great had infected the lower orders with "Voluptuousness or the Love of Pleasure." Money, the corrupter, bred in the commonalty "Self-opinion, Arrogance, Insolence and Impatience of Rule"; "the Power of the Purse" supplanted the authority of the law. The Great, who were the source of the contagion, were beyond his reach; and besides, he subscribed to the Mandevillean maxim that, by indulging in their vices, the rich benefited the public by distributing the wealth. They injured no one but themselves, and he would expose their immoralities in the novel he was writing.

In the *Enquiry* Fielding therefore confined himself to the lower classes, the "useful Members of the Society," who had instead become its scourges and parasites. He advised the legislature to curtail the number of "expensive Diversions" that tempt the people from their work – pleasure resorts, masquerades, gaming houses. He is eloquent in denouncing "that Poison called *Gin*," the ruinous effects of which Hogarth depicted in his print *Gin Lane* (see Plate 58), published a month later than the *Enquiry*, together with his hideously monitory series *The Stages of Cruelty*; it may be the two friends had agreed to employ their different talents in making a concerted attack on these evils. In the longest section (IV) of the work Fielding anatomized the Poor Laws which had proved so ineffectual: indeed, he had thought of a plan that would provide universal employment for the poor and was ready to produce it, "when I shall have any Reason to see the least Glimpse of Hope, that my Labour in drawing it out at length would not be absolutely and certainly thrown away." He turned next to the people and conditions that fostered crime by encouraging and abetting criminals: receivers of stolen goods like the notorious Cadosa; deficiencies in the laws relating to vagabonds which enabled thieves to wander from their legal places of settlement and made escape easy; the difficulty of apprehending thieves without an adequate and respected force of police; the obstacles hindering the prosecution and conviction of felons. The concluding pages of the *Enquiry* reveal most clearly Fielding's final, disturbing vision of human nature and the tenuous grounds of order in society. From boyhood he had been too often the sport of "vehement" passions (to use Harris's word) which seemed irresistible. Like Mandeville – and more recently and cogently, like David Hume in the *Philosophical Essays concerning Human Understanding* (1748)[170] – he became convinced that reason and the will, the agents of morality in classical moral philosophy, were powerless to regulate man's emotional nature. This indeed was a dominant theme in the novel he was writing. He sensed that the moral conduct of individuals, and therefore the order of society as a whole, depended not so much on governing the passions – since for the most part they were too powerful to subjugate –

but rather on appealing to the strongest of them, hope and fear, to influence behavior.

In the penultimate section of the *Enquiry* ("Of the Encouragement given to Robbers by frequent Pardons") Fielding stressed the danger to the public of the King's exercising those humane affections he always found most admirable in men: tenderness, benevolence, compassion. For the good of society, "the Passions of the Man are to give Way to the Principles of the Magistrate." Far from believing in the benignity of human nature in the general, he was persuaded that the social edifice could be supported only by inspiring fear in the populace:

> To speak out fairly and honestly, tho' Mercy may appear more amiable in a Magistrate, Severity is a more wholesome Virtue. . . .
> . . . No Man indeed of common Humanity or Common Sense can think the Life of a Man and a few Shillings to be of an equal Consideration, or that the Law in punishing Theft with Death proceeds . . . with any View to Vengeance. The Terror of the Example is the only Thing proposed, and one Man is sacrificed to the Preservation of Thousands.

Fielding felt most keenly the urgency of implementing the reform with which he concludes the *Enquiry*. If the social order could be maintained only by terror deterring men from breaking the laws, then hanging, the ultimate sanction, must be made most terrible. As they were at present conducted, hanging days at Tyburn were mere theatrical spectacles, another diversion for the mob and an occasion for the condemned to triumph in their boldness and contempt for authority. Fielding's proposal, interestingly enough, is based on an understanding of the aesthetics of horror which anticipates Burke's famous analysis. Referring to the means by which the greatest poets raise in us the emotions of fear and awe, he cites Homer and Milton as his examples, but most particularly Shakespeare's management of Duncan's murder in *Macbeth*. As if reverting to his former role of theatrical manager, Fielding would stage this real-life tragedy in such a way that the public would be terrified into good order. Since the "great Business is to raise Terror" while stripping the object of it "of all Pity and all Admiration," he would have the execution carried out "behind the Scenes" at the Old Bailey immediately after sentence was pronounced, the event attended by the judges only and conducted with all the trappings of solemnity. "Nothing can, I think [Fielding writes], be imagined (not even Torture, which I am an Enemy to the very Thought of admitting) more terrible than such an Execution." And since the "Mind of Man is so much more capable of magnifying than his Eye," the impression on the public would be, in the highest degree, horrifying. In this proposal

Fielding was motivated not only by "Care for the Public Safety," but by "Common Humanity":

> for that many Cart-loads of our Fellow-creatures are once in six Weeks carried to Slaughter, is a dreadful Consideration; and this is greatly heightened by reflecting, that, with proper Care and proper Regulations, much the greater Part of these Wretches might have been made not only happy in themselves, but very useful Members of the Society, which they now so greatly dishonour in the Sight of all Christendom.

A hundred years later, in a letter to the editor of *The Times* (17 November 1849), Dickens approved the wisdom of Fielding's proposal – "to whose profound knowledge of human nature you, I know, will render full justice." [171] Indeed, except for the circumstance of "Celerity," Fielding's scheme in its essential features of "Privacy, and Solemnity" was eventually adopted. In passing the Murder Act of 1752, however, Parliament chose to ignore these, the most crucial of his recommendations.

Once seriously entertained by his biographers, the notion that Fielding was, in any definitive way, "the man behind the scenes" of the criminal legislation of 1751–2 is belied by his own bitter disappointment in this particular instance of the Murder Act, and it has been refuted by a methodical comparison of his recommendations in the *Enquiry* with the actual provisions of the Acts themselves. [172] There is, however, every reason to believe that the *Enquiry* gave impetus to these reforms and that it served to identify areas in which specific legislation was needed. [173] The Committee of 1751, chaired by Sir Richard Lloyd, was created in response to the King's address of 17 January 1750/1, which charged Parliament to consider measures for improving law enforcement and suppressing violent crimes. The *Enquiry* is in every respect so thoroughly germane to these concerns that it is likely Fielding, in preparing it, was not only aware of the government's intentions, but had been invited to offer his advice. He began writing the pamphlet in October and timed it to appear two days after the King's address. He was the ablest, most active magistrate in the metropolis; he was learned in the laws in question and had first-hand experience of their defects. What is more, the Committee that was constituted on 1 February 1750/1 included among its members several of his closest friends in government, among them Lyttelton and Pitt. [174]

The Committee reported three times this session, and Fielding's influence is evident in each report – though of course his recommendations were modified and supplemented as this large body of eminent legislators and judges deliberated. On 1 April, Sir Richard

Lloyd reported to the House nine resolutions calculated to strengthen
and reform the watch – resolutions which, as we earlier remarked,
reflect at several points the recommendations contained in Fielding's
"Bill" submitted to the Lord Chancellor in July 1749; these resolutions
were in fact embodied in a Bill managed by Lloyd and Sir John Strange,
Master of the Rolls, but it was not enacted into law. On 23 April the
Committee reported sixteen additional resolutions,[175] the first eight of
which are identical to recommendations Fielding had made in the
Enquiry. This report formed the basis of a "Bill for preventing Thefts
and Robberies" (25 Geo. II, c. 36), which embodies solutions to four of
the problems Fielding singled out for attention.[176] On 13 June the
Committee reported seven further resolutions concerning defects in the
Poor Laws,[177] a topic Fielding explored at length in the *Enquiry*, where
he offered, if invited to do so, to lay before Parliament a plan he had
devised to employ the industrious poor. In November of this year, as
Parliament reconvened, the Prime Minister extended this invitation to
Fielding, whose plan, as eventually published in January 1753, accords
with the Committee's proposal that responsibility for maintaining and
employing the poor should be shifted from the individual parishes to
the counties. Fielding's representation of the evils of gin-drinking,
furthermore – a section of the *Enquiry* widely acclaimed along with
Hogarth's *Gin Lane* and the Bishop of Worcester's sermon on the
subject, *The Expediency of preventive Wisdom* – provided a powerful
impetus in helping to ensure passage of the controversial Gin Act of
1751 (24 Geo. II, c. 40). In a few years' time that Act reduced the
annual consumption of gin in England from 11 million to less than
2 million gallons.[178]

When Parliament met in November to act on the recommendations
of the Committee, the public understood it would be "in a great
Measure, indebted to Mr. Justice Fielding" for these necessary
reforms.[179] Indeed, the reputation the *Enquiry* enjoyed among certain
legislators who were directly concerned in the reforms is clear from
Charles Gray's *Considerations on Several Proposals lately made for the
Better Maintenance of the Poor*. When he wrote this pamphlet (published
23 November 1751), Gray, a member of the Committee, had not yet
heard that Fielding was about to supply the one deficiency he found in
the *Enquiry*:

Mr. Fielding, in the excellent piece here alluded to [the *Enquiry*], has
shewn himself a most worthy labourer in the vineyard of the public:
and 'tis great pity that in a performance so masterly, the one thing
needful (as to the present point) should be omitted. It is to be hoped,
that he will soon oblige us with his plan, because at this time the

thoughts of a Gentleman of so much ability and experience, could not but be extreamly useful.

(p. 6)

It would of course be quixotic to suppose that Fielding alone, among so many proud and able men of more exalted rank, dictated the precise forms this legislation would take. For one thing, though he had influential friends in Parliament, they were matched by others whom he had personally offended, or who resented his role as agent and publicist for the ministry. Sir William Yonge, whom he had often ridiculed in the past, became the guiding force behind the new laws. One prominent member of the Committee of 1751, furthermore, was General James Oglethorpe (1696–1785), who with others in Opposition deplored Fielding's advocacy in the *Enquiry* of an increase in "the Civil Power" and his frequent use of troops to enforce the laws. Oglethorpe was the clandestine sponsor of *The True Briton*, a blatant organ of Jacobite principles conducted by the obscure hack George Osborne: for more than two years at Oglethorpe's bidding Osborne shrilly denounced Fielding and his plans for suppressing crime and providing for the poor.[180] There was no doubt in Osborne's mind that Fielding – author of that "very pernicious Book" the *Enquiry* – was securely "seated in the Chair of Authority, and countenanced with all the Favours of Ministerial Power."[181]

The *Enquiry* had other critics besides Osborne. Under the disguise of the publican "Ben. Sedgly," Richard Rolt, another Jacobite, produced an elaborate attack on Fielding's treatise.[182] And a much abler adversary, Johnson in *Rambler* No. 114 (20 April 1751), clearly had the *Enquiry* in mind when he complained that crime was increasing not because of the weakness or inefficiency of those who execute the laws, but because of the inhumanity of the laws themselves, which in the punishment prescribed made no distinction beween a thief and a murderer. For the most part, however, the *Enquiry* was acknowledged for what it really was: by the lights of the time a masterly, authoritative attempt to diagnose and cure appalling social disorders. Among those who recognized the value of Fielding's contribution were Ralph Griffiths, editor of the *Monthly Review*; Isaac Maddox, Bishop of Worcester; the barrister Joshua Fitzsimmonds; the poet William Henry Draper; and a certain "Philo-Patria," who, however, chides Fielding for having overlooked the root cause of the nation's evils – lewd women![183] Indeed, the work sold so briskly, even at a half-crown a copy, that the first printing of 1,500 copies was quickly exhausted. A second edition of 2,000 copies was through Strahan's presses and in the bookstalls by 6 February.[184]

···➡ xviii ➡···

For the next several months there is news only of Fielding's activities
as a magistrate – activities often calculated to attack the evils he
specifically addressed in the *Enquiry*. Even his *Plan* of the Universal
Register Office (published 21 February) might be said to have a place
in this context. As the advertisements pointed out, Fielding concluded
the *Enquiry* by recommending the office because it would prevent
prospective employers from being victimized by dishonest servants. In
the *Plan*, resuming the analogy which in the *Enquiry* informs his
account of England's "Constitution," he explained that the office in an
important way would promote the health of the body politic: "the
Members of the Body Corporate, like those of the Natural Body, having
their several different Uses and Qualifications, all jointly contributing
to the Good of the Whole," the office would ensure "that no Talent in
any of its Members, which is capable of contributing to the general
Good, [need] lie idle and unemployed."

Fielding's other activities in serving the public were rather less grand.
On the night of 1 February he sent Welch with a large party of
constables and soldiers to raid a gaming house in the Strand, where
they seized forty-five people, "many of whom were inferior Tradesmen."
Fielding, reported the *General Advertiser* (4 February 1750/1), "tho' at
that time disorder'd with a violent Cold, as well as the Gout, sat up till
two in the Morning to examine them"; he committed thirty-nine to the
Gatehouse under heavy guard – the Prince of Wales's groom among
them, who was mortally wounded in the leg while trying to escape.
Throughout these months the papers report such raids carried out by
Fielding and his officers. Other justices – as far away as the fashionable
resort of Tunbridge Wells in Kent – began to follow "the laudable
Example of that great and worthy Magistrate Mr. Justice Fielding ...
which may be the happy means of preventing the Ruin of many young
Persons of both Sexes."[185] In the campaign he was mounting against
gaming houses Fielding, indeed, enjoyed the full and often clamorous
support of the public. After Welch broke up one of these dens near
Soho Square and arrested eight players, the neighborhood turned out
to cheer the officers and, snatching up pieces of the demolished table,
carried them "with great Glee, as Trophies, before the Prisoners to the
House of the Justice."[186]

Fielding was nearly as active against the masquerades – those
"Temples of Drunkenness, Lewdness, and all Kind of Debauchery," as
he called them in the *Enquiry*. At midnight on Monday, 3 June, Welch
raided one of these places and carried a number of the masqueraders

before Fielding, "who sat up all Night to examine them." The report in the *General Advertiser* (5 June 1751) concludes:

> Several of them when stript of their Antic Dresses, were found to be young Gentlemen of Fashion, under twenty Years of Age, whose Names and Persons the Justice did not think proper to expose, and therefore, as he was unwilling to shew any Partiality, after a severe Reprimand, dismiss'd all the Prisoners; tho' some of them (particularly the Females) could not give a very good Account of themselves. Hence it appears how necessary it is to abolish these Scenes of Midnight Rendezvous.

But the cases that demanded Fielding's attention daily were numberless and of every kind: there was the sorry parade of prostitutes to rebuke or send to Bridewell;[187] there were uncooperative victims of robberies to be made to prosecute (or else, as the *General Advertiser* [6 June 1751] warned, "*the Labours of the best Magistrate, to suppress Robberies must be totally ineffectual*"); there were carters and draymen to fine for endangering the public by riding on the shafts of their vehicles (one of these men dragged Fielding's own coachman off his box and beat him).[188] There were counterfeiters to prosecute, and the campaign continued against gangs of smugglers.[189] On 28 February, Fielding was among the Middlesex justices who by formal complaint to the Lord Chancellor tried to purge the bench of the corrupt magistrate Sir Samuel Gower, who flagrantly connived at the protection of brothels and other disorderly houses.[190]

Among the routine cases which came before Fielding this year were two in which he would have been particularly interested as they concerned his friends Peter Taylor and Robert James (1705–76), the well-known physician and author of the *Medicinal Dictionary*. Having entrusted to a porter a parcel containing a £50 banknote, Taylor accused the fellow of conspiring with two other men to steal the note; the porter claimed he had simply lost it and the others that they had found it. On 21 May, Fielding committed all three to Newgate, but they were acquitted at the Old Bailey.[191] As for Dr. James, he had made himself answerable for a debt, the amount of which was in dispute. On 15 July, Fielding took the sworn statements of the parties concerned.[192] How the matter was settled is unknown, but in the novel he was then writing Fielding delivered his opinion of James and the specific for which he was famous – "that Powder [he declared in *Amelia* (VIII. ix)], for the Invention of which, my worthy and ingenious Friend Dr. *James* would, in almost any Country but this, have received public Honours and Rewards."

July was also the month when Fielding became involved in a potentially explosive cause of far more importance to the public in general –

a cause which reveals more clearly perhaps than any other the ambivalence of his attitude towards the working class. For some time there had been friction between the Master Tailors and their journeymen (some 7,000 of them) over wages and working conditions. At the July Quarter Sessions the Master Tailors applied for arbitration to the Middlesex justices, Fielding listed prominently among them. The justices voted to improve the lot of the journeymen, though to say so will suggest how miserable they must have been before this happiness befell them. In future they were to work during the summer months only fourteen hours a day, from 6 a.m. to 8 p.m. (with a half-hour off to breakfast on an allowance of three halfpence, and an hour for dinner). Their daily wage was raised by ten pence to 2s. 6d. – which, however, would be reduced to two shillings during the autumn and winter when working days were shorter. These terms were at first acceptable to both parties, but not for long. In autumn, when their wages fell, the journeymen tailors began entering into illegal "Combinations" against their employers, using intimidation to shut down the shops and threatening violence against the masters. On 16 October the King issued a proclamation commanding the magistrates to enforce the several statutes regulating the journeymen tailors and prohibiting combinations, riots, and the sending of threatening letters.[193] Complying with this order, Fielding committed a number of journeymen tailors to Bridewell, sentencing them, as the law directed, to suffer correction and a month's hard labor.[194] Though this was an action he was obliged to take, it was doubtless one he would have taken on principle. Fielding firmly believed in the prevailing mercantilist theory of the time, which maintained that the prosperity of a nation depended on keeping wages low and prices down: "In all Manufactures whatever," he declares in the *Enquiry* (Sect. IV), "the lower the Price of Labour is, the cheaper will be the Price to the Consumer; and the cheaper this Price is, the greater will be the Consumption, and consequently the more Hands employed." Having so recently been instrumental in improving the wages and conditions of the journeymen tailors, Fielding probably had little sympathy with their cause in the autumn.

But if the *Enquiry* and Fielding's related activities reveal the sterner aspect of his social attitude, its more amiable features appear in the part he played in establishing one of the city's newest charities: the Lying-in Hospital for Married Women, founded in 1749 under the presidency of the Duke of Portland. The *Account* of the hospital published in the summer of 1751 lists Fielding as a "Perpetual Governor," a title requiring a subscription of thirty guineas and entitling him "to recommend and have in the House one Woman at a Time."[195]

...➡ xix ◀—...

From Bow Street on 7 May, Fielding wrote Bedford requesting a favor on which (he assured Butcher, the Duke's agent) would depend "the future Happiness of my Life."[196] The nature of this remarkable favor is not known; but Fielding may simply have asked Bedford to sponsor his half-brother John's appointment to the Westminster magistracy. For many months Fielding had kept up the strenuous labors of his office despite the ill health that plagued him. Even as he wrote this letter he was suffering from the gout: "my Feet are so tender I am not yet able to walk." He was eager to have John in a position to help. In a letter to Butcher of 12 June this is doubtless the matter to which he refers when he hopes "his Grace hath sent his List to Lord Chancellor that the Commission may pass immediately."[197] (In closing, he also hints at dietary habits that were not helping to relieve the agonies of the gout: "and if you will take an Opportunity to remind his Grace of his Goodness to me last year in the Venison Season, I will gratefully drink y.ʳ Health on that Occasion.") So it happened that on 27 July, John Fielding took the oath of office and paid his fees; on 30 July he was appointed by Hardwicke to the Commission of the Peace for Westminster.[198]

Fielding at once left Bow Street business in his brother's care and set out with his family for Bath "for the Recovery of his Health."[199] On their way out of town he and Mary dined with Dodington at Hammersmith on 6 August.[200] The renewal of this friendship, together with Bedford's recent resignation from the government, would have an interesting effect on a curious political chapter in *Amelia* (XI.ii).

From Bath the Fieldings made the short journey to Glastonbury, where they no doubt stayed with Davidge Gould at Sharpham, and where, with "his Lady and Daughter," Fielding was seen amidst a throng of valetudinarians taking the waters.[201] In what by now had become an almost superstitious search for a cure for his ailments, Fielding, like some stricken pilgrim in romance, was enticed back to Glastonbury by rumors of the curative properties of a legendary spring of water at the foot of Tor Hill, the imaginary location of "Paradise Hall" in *Tom Jones*.[202] Public interest in the Glastonbury waters was aroused in 1751 by the case of Matthew Chancellor, an old man who for thirty years had suffered from asthma. Chancellor claimed he had been cured of this malady as the result of a dream: in the dream he saw himself in Glastonbury at a certain spring near the Tor, where an angel appeared and told him that if he drank a glass of that water, fasting, on seven successive Sundays, he would be well. To the superstitious the story gained credibility from the fact that the spring in question was the "Bloody Well" (so called from the reddish color of the stones where it issued from the ground), which, according to tradition, had begun to flow miraculously when Joseph of Arimathea buried the Holy Grail at the foot of the Tor. Thousands of invalids were soon crowding into Glastonbury to drink the waters, and testimonials of cures were published. By July those unable to make the journey from London could drink the waters in town through the exclusive agency of the Universal Register Office, which charged fourteen pence a bottle (two-pence back when the bottle was returned).

Wags and skeptics, of course, attempted to discredit the waters and scoffed at the gullibility of those who paid good money to drink them. A correspondent in the *London Daily Advertiser* (20 May) wondered if he should take his dose on Saturdays instead of Sundays, since he was a Jew; and the *General Advertiser* (5 June) reported that the famous "Haymarket Quart Bottle," of infinite capacity, had been dispatched to Glastonbury in order to be filled and returned to town, where it would provide a source of the waters as inexhaustible as the spring itself. Considering the profit the proprietors of the Universal Register Office stood to make if the vogue continued, it was inevitable they should reply to such criticism by reassuring the public of the waters' efficacy. Thus John Fielding, who managed the office and occasionally puffed it in the *London Daily Advertiser* – the Fieldings being at this time on friendly terms with the principal author of that paper, the pompous literary hack and virtuoso Dr. John Hill (1714?–75) – defended "the salubrious Springs of Glaston" against the undeserved "Contempt in which ... [they] are in general held," and he insisted that, to his knowledge, they had performed "many extraordinary Cures."[203]

But it is Henry Fielding's part in this quaint affair that chiefly concerns us. Whatever he stood to gain from the sale of the waters, he was in fact convinced of their curative properties. Announcing his return to town on 12 September, the *London Daily Advertiser* (13 September) reported that he had "received great Benefit" from drinking the waters at Glastonbury. So persuaded was he of their efficacy that when an anonymous writer aspersed them in print, insisting they were merely common spring water and had cured no one of anything, Fielding came to their defense in a sarcastic letter to the author of the *General Advertiser* (8 October).[204] The letter tells us a little about his recent movements, but a good deal more about his character: he had acquired a properly judicial respect for hard evidence, but his essential tem-perament was sanguine, even romantic; he trusted in wonders because he wanted to get well. While in Glastonbury he sought out and con-versed with Matthew Chancellor and found him "to be as well as any Man in England." He observed "Experiments" made on the waters

Plate 47 Henry Fielding (*c.* 1753).

Plate 48 Henry Pelham (1751).

Plate 49 Thomas Pelham-Holles, first Duke of Newcastle (*c.* 1752).

Plate 50 The Reverend Thomas Birch (*c.* 1735).

Plate 51 Saunders Welch (*c.* 1756–7).

Plate 52 Night Walkers before a Justice (or A Frenchman at Bow Street)—showing Fielding seated at left?

Chap.t 1. Of Outlawry in Criminal
Causes.

1. Upon an Indictment ~~for~~ for Treason Felony, ~~~~
or Trespass ~~~~ Trover of Outlawry lies. But if he be
once in Custody of Record, as where the Sheriff returns
(a) copy to the Capias, if he afterwards escape, the Sheriff
shall be punished, but no Exigent awarded (a) +

a. H.H.P.C. II. 202.

This refers to ye fifth
page back

2. In order to prosecute a Criminal to an Outlawry there must (b)
be either first an Appeal of the Party injured wch was
formerly usual in all ~~~~ holmes but hath of late
been totally discontinued unless in ~~~~ only. or 2dly
an Indictment ~~~~
~~~~ of Record in the Court wherein
the Writ issues (b) ~~~~   This refers to ye fifth page back
~~~~ in the Indictment should be set ~~~~

(b) H.H.P.C. 1. 5

Brast C 3
c 12 & Co.

3. If an Indictment be found in B.R. or removed into (c)
that Court by Certiorari, a Capias issues to the Sheriff
of the county where the Dft is indicted, and on the Sheriff's
Return that he is not found in his Bailywick ~~~~
~~~~ an Exigent shall go unless it be ~~~~
that he is in some other County, then a Capias shall
issue into that County, ~~~~ (c)

(c) H.H.P.C. II ~~~~

4) Justices of Oyer and Terminer may ~~~~ Caps & Exigent
& so proceed to outlaw any ~~~~ indicted before them this

(1) The Reason of this is that no averment is suffered ~~~~ the Truth of a Record. (2) When a Sheriff arrests
a man on a Writ he endorses on the Back of it copi corpus J have ta'en this Body, and at ye
Day ~~~~ of Writ is returnable he reads ~~~~ whereof ~~~~ or Return
of the Sheriff become ~~~~ part of the Record. (3) The Writ commanding him to arrest
the Body. 4) this is explained a little ~~~~ (5) In Latine Appell. i.e. a Call. a form then
in the Civil Law and hence a ~~~~ another to answer some allegation in a Court of Justice wherein
the Plaintiff or caller is named Appellant, the ~~~~ person called on is the Appellee. 6) ~~~~

Plate 53 Fielding's manuscript "Of Outlawry" from his unpublished
"Institute of the Pleas of the Crown."

Plate 54 Servandoni's structure for the Royal Fireworks in Green Park (1749).

Plate 55 The Sailors' Revenge: or, The Strand in an Uproar: the Penlez riots (1749).

Plate 56 A masquerade at Ranelagh (1751).

Plate 57 The pleasure gardens at Vauxhall (1751).

Plate 58 Hogarth's *Gin Lane*
(1751).

Plate 59 Hogarth's *The Idle Apprentice Executed at Tyburn* (1747).

Plate 60 Sir John Fielding.

Ford Hook *EALING*, the Residence of *FIELDING* Author of *Tom Jones* &c.

Plate 61 Fordhook, Fielding's house at Ealing.

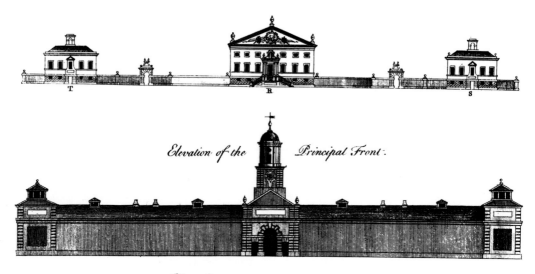

T   R   S

Elevation of the Principal Front.

Part of the Section within the Courts.

Plate 62 The Middlesex County workhouse and Governor's mansion as
Fielding envisaged them (1753).

Plate 63 *The Conjurers* (1753), showing Elizabeth Canning, Fielding, Sir Crisp Gascoyne, Dr. John Hill, and Mary Squires.

Plate 64 Lisbon harbor as Fielding might have seen it.

Plate 65 The Reverend Allen Fielding and his son Henry (1790).

which indicated "a strong Chalybeate"; and in smell and taste the waters, having "a sulphurous and steely Quality," differed from common water. He had seen and conversed with "a great Number of Persons" who assured him that the waters had cured them "of Asthmas, of the King's Evil, and of other scrophulous Complaints." Indeed, he could himself testify that two "Maid-Servants belonging to the Gentleman at whose House I was [presumably Davidge Gould], were by these Waters perfectly restored from the most deplorable Condition" – from ulcers and swellings and dropsical complaints. Both these women "had perfectly regained their Healths, and all the ruddy Bloom of Country Wenches." Since his return to town, furthermore, he knew of cures the waters had performed on a girl and an old woman at Hammersmith, where he had twice been to dinner with Dodington (and, incidentally, had renewed acquaintances with the politically minded Ralph).[205] In short, the waters seemed to Fielding almost a kind of panacea which would benefit the "whole Society," and he accordingly was moved to publish this testimonial concerning an "Affair, in which I think Mankind are so greatly interested; an Interest, which I have always been and always shall be forward to promote with equal Indifference, whether bad Men shall ridicule me for acting from this Motive, or shall insinuate that I am influenced by any other."

The Glastonbury waters were of course no panacea. They could not check the steady decline in Fielding's health. But for the time being he believed in them. In the penultimate paragraph of *Amelia* he went out of his way to assure readers that the Booth family itself had reason to be grateful for Matthew Chancellor's dream: in a passage deleted from the revised edition, he relates that after suffering two years from "a violent Humour," Booth's daughter "was last Summer perfectly cured by the *Glastonbury* Waters."

···◖ XX ◗–···

On returning to town in September, Fielding resumed his duties at Bow Street. John was now able to assist with the heavy burden of work, and he continued to manage affairs at the Universal Register Office. John would soon acquire a helpmate of his own in the person of Elizabeth Whittingham of Staffordshire, whom he married on 21 November 1751.[206]

The cases in which Fielding was involved this winter were, with few exceptions, unremarkable. It is interesting to find that two years after the regrettable affair of Bosavern Penlez he had not forgot Peter Wood and his nefarious family at The Star brothel. At midnight on Sunday,

13 October, Welch, acting on a warrant issued by Fielding, searched the house and arrested Wood, his wife, and five of the prostitutes. In the morning Fielding committed them all to Bridewell to hard labor.[207]

By far the most important of these matters, however – and one of the ugliest in what it reveals of the rampant anti-Semitism of the day – is the complicated case of Henry Simonds, a Polish Jew, and his adversaries Joseph Goddard and James Ashley, a country innkeeper and London brandy merchant, respectively.[208] Simonds accused these men of robbing him; they accused him of perjury. It is impossible, at this distance, to distinguish confidently the guilt or innocence of these parties. The case remained a *cause célèbre* for several years, with witnesses on one side claiming that Simonds was part of a Jewish conspiracy to ruin the Christian Ashley, while others took the more plausible view that Goddard and Ashley had in fact robbed Simonds and plotted to ruin him, taking advantage of the fact that he was a Jew and a foreigner, an "unhappy and much injured Stranger."[209] The Simonds affair would soon become a focus of the controversy which raged over the government's unpopular Bill to permit the naturalization of Jews.

It is evident from his earlier satires of Jewish stockjobbers and usurers that Fielding was not immune from the anti-Semitism that tainted the generality of his contemporaries. But the part he played in this case does him credit, attesting to his determination to see justice done – and done humanely – despite such prejudice. On 9 October, when Simonds was brought before him charged with perjury, Fielding ordered that he be freed from the iron handcuffs that cut into his wrists.[210] At the trial on 10 December, in an effort to test the prosecution's case, he advised them where to find a Polish interpreter – advice which they declined to take, thus forfeiting their cause against Simonds, who spoke no English.[211] The prosecution's reluctance to allow Simonds a fair hearing appears to have aroused Fielding's suspicions: with the Lord Mayor he issued a warrant to apprehend Goddard's principal witness on an indictment for willful and corrupt perjury – of which charge the man was convicted at the Old Bailey in April, when he was sentenced to be pilloried, imprisoned for a year, and then transported.[212] Furthermore, when in 1753 an article was published in the *Public Advertiser* supporting the Jew Bill, Thomas Birch, who knew Fielding well, was at first mistakenly convinced he had written it; he was unlikely to have made such a mistake had he been aware of any violent antipathy to Jews on Fielding's part.[213]

Long after Fielding's death, however, an anecdote was published suggesting that he had acquired some reputation for dealing sharply with the race traditionally supposed to be skilled in such practices. It is said that a "celebrated" Jew, Booz de Paiba, threatened to disinherit

his son if he married a certain Christian woman, the father objecting
to the match not because of the lady's religion, but on account of her
small fortune. The son in turn threatened not only to marry the lady
against his father's wishes, but to turn Christian himself, thereby, under
English law, gaining half his father's wealth. Paiba, confounded, sought
Fielding's advice, who assured him the law in question did exist:

> but, added he, if you will give me ten guineas, I'll put you in a way
> to frustrate the hopes of your son, and the ungrateful rascal will not
> be able to shew cause to get a single farthing from you. These words
> set Booz in raptures; he told down the money. Fielding laying hold
> of it, and putting it in his pocket, – "Now, friend, says he, all the
> advice I can give you to save your property is, to become Christian
> yourself, and the law will give nothing to your son."[214]

Fielding was clever enough to have thought of this device, reminiscent
as it is of Portia's turning the tables on Shylock; but bilking a client
was not characteristic of him.

Such stories of Fielding's conduct in his profession, most of them
satiric, became commonplace. One of the most comical of them was
current this winter of 1751–2. It includes all the essential elements of
contemporary caricatures of him: his stern and arrogant demeanor on
the bench, his habit of declaiming with his jaws crammed with tobacco,
his way of favoring the rich and great while bullying the lower classes.
The cause in question came before him on 16 December and pitted Sir
Samuel Prime, eminent Serjeant at Law, against his indolent cook-
maid. The scene at Bow Street that day is hilariously preserved in *The
genuine Trial of Mary, late Cook-Maid to Sir Simon Pride, Knight, before
the worshipful Mr. Justice Feeler, for lying a-bed in a Morning, &c. &c.*[215]

···➤ xxi ◆─···

Despite every impediment – the time required to ponder and produce
his most ambitious social tract, the continual hurry of justice business,
the crippling effects of the gout – Fielding made steady progress in
composing his new novel. A month after he returned from Glastonbury
it was nearly finished. Even at Bath, remote from the source of literary
gossip, Walter Harte learned that publication was imminent. On 29
October, a fortnight before the advance notices began appearing in the
papers, he passed the news on to Hanbury Williams, then at Dresden:
"Fielding is coming out with another work, in the tone and style of his
late performances. ... [it] is called Amelia."[216] What most of Fielding's
readers were expecting was another comic romance "in the tone and

style" of *Joseph Andrews* and *Tom Jones*. Excitement at such a prospect, needless to say, was keen; for with these novels Fielding had become the supreme standard of a new species of writing, admired not only for his wit and humor, but also for his wise understanding of human nature in all its great variety.

His enemies of course continued slurring him. The author of *An Apology for the Life of Mr. Bampfylde-Moore Carew* sarcastically dedicated a "second edition" (April 1750) of that work "To the Worshipful Justice Fielding." It was a piece of invective worthy of the dire "Orbilius" or the malignant writers of *Old England*, one of whom, when earthquakes shook the capital in April 1750, attributed these prodigies to God's wrath at the favorable reception the public had accorded *Tom Jones*.[217] Prigs such as Charles Bellers, who echoed Johnson's famous opinion that such books debauch the nation's morals, congratulated the French clergy for suppressing La Place's translation of Fielding's lewd romance[218] – a rumor circulated by Fielding's critics smugly but mistakenly, since the *arrêt du conseil* of 24 February 1750 was directed not against *Tom Jones*, but against the translator's bookseller, who had published the work without due license.[219]

Such criticisms as these, however, could scarcely be heard amidst the general acclaim. Even the Jacobite author of *A Journey through the Head of a Modern Poet* (April 1750), who scorned Fielding's politics, had to acknowledge his genius as a novelist:

> I do not mean the humorous Mr. *F*[*ieldin*]*g*, he who is so intimate with the Door-keepers of the great Stage of Nature, that, whenever he pleases, he can step, with the Authority of a *Beau*, behind the Scenes, sit down in the *Green Room* to observe the Actors, and afterwards publish his Discoveries to the World, in the Histories of *Jonathan Wild, Joseph Andrews*, and *Tom Jones*. (p. 19)

Among critics less concerned with politics, Fielding seemed to have attained the heights of Parnassus. William Kenrick gave him the place of honor in a pantheon of humorists including Cervantes, Scarron, Swift, and Steele.[220] Christopher Smart, who about this time joined the circle of Fielding's friends, similarly made room for him when naming the brightest constellation of wits – Lucian, Swift, Butler, Erasmus.[221] From distant Lincolnshire came a swelling tribute in fifty-eight lines of verse "On the Incomparable History of *Tom Jones*."[222] And the prolific John Hill, whose series "The Inspector" in the *London Daily Advertiser* helped form public taste, repeatedly commended Fielding's fiction in the most extravagant terms, comparing, for instance, a chapter from "the almost creative Pen" of the author of *Tom Jones* to scripture![223] To Hill, who feebly imitated Fielding's manner in his own novels, *The Adventures of Mr. Loveill* (March 1750) and of *Mr. George*

Edwards, A Creole (August 1751), Fielding, for the time being at least, was "one of the greatest Genius's in his Way, that this, or perhaps any Age or Nation have produced."[224]

Fielding inspired other imitators as well, most of whom acknowledged the debt: such, for example, was the unknown author of *The History of Charlotte Summers* (1750) and William Chaigneau in *The History of Jack Connor* (1751). By far the most delightful of these was Francis Coventry (d. 1759), a Cambridge-educated parson, in *The History of Pompey the Little: or, The Life and Adventures of a Lap-Dog* (February 1751). Coventry is also usually credited (if that is the word in regard to so jejune a performance) with the laudatory *Essay on the New Species of Writing founded by Mr. Fielding* (March 1751). But it is hard to believe that the author of this pamphlet – contemptuously dismissed by a reviewer as "a meer catch-penny job, probably the work of some forward school-boy"[225] – could have written so lively and sophisticated a book as *Pompey the Little*. In any case Coventry paid Fielding his handsomest tribute when dedicating to him the third edition of his novel (1752). Warburton in the notes to Pope's *Works* (1751) cited Marivaux and Fielding, in that order, as the two masters of the novel form – to which Coventry objected that, with respect to his superior skill at characterization and plot construction, Fielding deserved to stand foremost. "Few books of this kind," he observed, "have ever been written with a spirit equal to *Joseph Andrews*, and no story that I know of, was ever invented with more happiness, or conducted with more art and management than that of *Tom Jones*."[226]

····━● xxii ●━····

Founded on his comic masterpieces, this was Fielding's reputation as a novelist in the autumn of 1751, as the Town impatiently awaited publication of *Amelia*. But *Amelia* would be an altogether different sort of novel – at once the most personal work of fiction he ever wrote and the product of his heightened awareness of disorders in England's "Constitution."

By 29 October, when Walter Harte predicted that publication was imminent, *Amelia* was near enough to completion that Fielding projected a fresh literary enterprise – a smart new periodical calculated in part to promote the Universal Register Office and to keep the public apprised of his activities at Bow Street. Remembering his satire of Paul Whitehead in 1749, he called it the *Covent-Garden Journal*. Announcements of the paper were included in advertisements for the Universal Register Office as early as 31 October, promising publication on 23

November.[227] In the event, the *Covent-Garden Journal* would not appear until 4 January 1752, six weeks later than promised. The delay is chiefly owing to the fact that Fielding did not finish *Amelia* until 12 December, the date subscribed to the Dedication to Ralph Allen; and he tampered with the narrative even as it went through the press.[228] Millar began "puffing" the novel in mid-November, but it was not published (in four volumes duodecimo) until Thursday, 19 December. As that moment approached, he tried to ensure that demand for the work would be at fever pitch. He added to his advertisements the following somewhat disingenuous notice, to which a pointing finger directed the attention of prospective customers dull enough to doubt Fielding's new novel would be as popular as his last:

> *To satisfy the earnest Demand of the Publick, this Work is now printing at four Presses; but the Proprietor notwithstanding finds it impossible to get them bound in Time without spoiling the Beauty of the Impression, and therefore will sell them sew'd at Half a Guinea a Sett.*

No such devices had been necessary to drum up interest in *Tom Jones*, every copy of which was bought up before the day of publication. But this time Millar was worried. Citing as his source the publisher Thomas Cadell, who later this decade became Millar's associate in the business, Nathaniel Wraxall recounted the circumstances of Millar's agreement with Fielding and his subsequent apprehension that he had on his hands a work rather less saleable than Fielding's masterpiece. Having paid Fielding the munificent sum of £800 for the copyright – at £200 per volume a rate doubling what he gave for *Tom Jones* – Millar asked his friend Andrew Mitchell for his opinion of the manuscript. Mitchell recognized the quality of the novel, but he also saw that it was an odd performance, much inferior to *Tom Jones*. He advised Millar to get rid of it quickly. Millar, who had ordered a massive printing of 5,000 copies, kept his friend's advice to himself and by strategies whetted the appetite of the public for this work which he feared would prove a drug. In Wraxall's account, Millar announced to the trade at his first sale:

> "Gentlemen, I have several works to put up, for which I shall be glad if you will bid; but as to 'Amelia,' every copy is already bespoke." This manoeuvre had its effect. The booksellers were anxious to get their names put down for copies of it, and the edition, though very large, was immediately sold.[229]

It is not true that Millar, canny Scot though he was, managed to sell off this huge edition "immediately." On 23 December, just four days after publication, Fielding was aware of the Town's verdict. Sending a copy of *Amelia* to Harris (who had anticipated the favor by making

Fielding a present of *Hermes* and a chine of bacon)[230] he wrote the last extant letter of their correspondence. From the cordial manner of this exchange, it is good to find the friendship holding fast despite the recent awkwardness about money; but Fielding's disappointment at the reception of his novel reveals how quickly its fate was sealed:

> My Dear Friend,
> I do sincerely assure you, you would have recd my damned book (for so it is) by this very Coach, even without your having mentioned it. If you read it, you will do it more Honour than hath been done it by many here. Indeed I think I have been more abused in a Week than any other Author hath been; but tho' *our* favourite Authors have not taught me to write so as to avoid Censure, they have at least taught me to bear it with Patience.

On 28 December, John Upton wrote Harris from town, giving a more specific account of the disaster – and verifying that, in the company of his friends at least, Fielding was bearing up very philosophically indeed:

> Our friend's Amelia does not answer people's expectations in reading, or the bookseller in selling. They say 'tis deficient in characters; and see not a Parson Adams, a Square & Thwackum & Western, in it. In short, the word condemnation, tho not Damnation, is given out. Millar expected to get thousands, & there chiefly the disappointment lies; for as to Fielding himself he laughs, & jokes, & eats well, as usual; & will continue so whilst rogues live in Covent Garden, & he signs warrants.

The first call for the novel must nevertheless have been encouraging; Dr. Johnson assured Mrs. Piozzi that the work sold so briskly "a new edition was called for before night."[231] Millar did project a substantial new edition of 3,000 copies; but this optimism, he quickly saw, was ill founded. Strahan's ledgers for January 1752 show that work on a second edition had scarcely begun before it was terminated.[232] A mere two months after *Amelia* had been so breathlessly ushered into the world, Richardson gloated to Mrs. Donnellan that "The piece ... is as dead as if it had been published forty years ago, as to sale."[233] That huge first printing was sufficient to satisfy public demand for years to come. Not until 1762, when Millar published Fielding's *Works*, did *Amelia* appear in a true second edition.

How was it, then, that Fielding's hopes for *Amelia*, his "favourite Child,"[234] were so cruelly dashed? The answer is plain enough from the reactions of readers who either regretted the new direction he had taken in the novel – the unexpected earnestness of its satire and the novelty of its narrative method – or simply read it with a lust to misapply. The former sort found it dull and indelicate; the others, seizing on its faults in a spirit of spitefulness and puerile glee, turned it to scorn. Though the Town had already condemned it, the first reviews were in fact quite favorable. Remarking that "The author takes up his heroine at the very point at which all his predecessors have dropped their capital personages" – that is, after her marriage – John Cleland in the *Monthly Review* applauded *Amelia* as "the boldest stroke that has yet been attempted in this species of writing," and he commended both Fielding's virtuous purpose and his artful conduct of the narrative.[235] The reviewer in the *London Magazine* also saw merit in the book: "upon the whole," he concluded, "the story is amusing, the characters kept up, and many reflections ... are useful, if the reader will take notice of them."[236]

Yet despite these commendations, there are signs in both reviews of the troubles that had already begun to plague the novel. Cleland worried that Fielding's candor in treating scenes of low-life would "disgust" the fastidious. And his counterpart in the *London Magazine* drew attention to an unlucky slip which was all the wags needed to turn *Amelia* into a standing jest. Having censured Fielding for a "notorious" anachronism in the narrative (wherein the masquerades at Ranelagh take place several years before they in fact began), he moved on to the silliest fault of all: Fielding, who modeled his heroine after his beloved first wife, subjected Amelia to the same injury Charlotte had suffered – "by the overturning of a Chaise ... her lovely Nose was beat all to pieces" (II.i) – but he neglected to state that the injury had been skillfully repaired by the surgeon. Once exposed to view by the critic, the noselessness of Fielding's heroine diverted the Town for months to come – prompting Samuel Foote, for example, to prefix to the published version of his comedy, *Taste* (January 1752), a frontispiece depicting the bust of Praxiteles' Venus of Paphos without a nose.

The painful yet amusing tale of *Amelia*'s damning is familiar enough that we need not rehearse it in detail.[237] As the New Year turned, the mockery of the critics grew more clamorous, stimulated in part by the rowdy "Paper War" in which Fielding became embroiled as author of the *Covent-Garden Journal*. Bonnell Thornton, for instance – in the guise of "Madam Roxana Termagant," authoress of the *Drury-Lane Journal* – kept up a continual ridicule of the novel, delivering in his fifth number (13 February 1751/2) a gross burlesque of Fielding's style and characters, entitled "A New Chapter in *Amelia*." Smollett was even more impudent. Having recently roasted Fielding and Lyttelton in *Peregrine Pickle*, he resumed the sport in his pamphlet, *A Faithful Narrative of the base and inhuman Arts that were lately practised upon the Brain of Habbakuk Hilding* (15 January 1751/2), in which Fielding, lunatic and astride an ass, appears at the head of his Bow Street myrmidons:

riding up to a draggle-tail Bunter, who had lost her Nose in the Exercise of her Occupation, he addressed himself to her by the Appelation of the adorable *Amelia*, swore by all the Gods she was the Pattern of all earthly Beauty and Perfection; and that he had exhausted his whole Fancy in celebrating her Name – To this Compliment she answered in a snuffling Tone, "Justice, you're a comical Bitch; I wish you would treat me with a Dram this cold Morning"

(p. 18)

– upon which, to oblige his liquorish darling, Fielding gives his tobacco box to Booth to pawn at the next gin shop.

No one who scribbled for bread in these weeks after *Amelia* appeared could refrain from heaping abuse on the novel and its "doting" author. What might pass for rational criticism, instead of mere vituperation, centered on two principal objections: first, by discarding his old formula of comic romance to write in a sentimental vein, Fielding had mistaken his true talent; second, by exposing the most odious moral and social evils with uncompromising candor, he had offended against good taste. On the first count, the judgment of the Richardsonians was of course predictable, for Fielding had dared to poach in the master's preserve. "Poor Fielding, I believe, designed to be good," wrote Mrs. Donnellan, "but did not know how, and in the attempt lost his genius, low humour."[238] And Thomas Edwards advised Fielding not to overreach himself by attempting to describe "either the great or the tender sentiments of the mind," which he was too coarse to feel: "indeed," he declared to a clerical acquaintance, "I think, if Hogarth and he knew their own talents, they should keep to the Dutch manner of painting, and be contented to make people laugh, since what is really great seems to be above their powers."[239] The verdict was not quite unanimous. James Harris's cousin, the fourth Earl of Shaftesbury, was so moved by the "tender Scenes" between Booth and Amelia that he had to put the novel aside while he recovered his composure: "I find," he wrote Harris on 31 December 1751, "it is not a greatly admir'd Performance but I think there are many fine sentiments in it and it is a further confirmation to me of the Humanity and tender Disposition of the author." Lord Shaftesbury, however, saw a side to Fielding's character that few others would allow him. On the whole, the Town agreed that Fielding's experiment in the pathetic mode was a failure.

The other principal criticism of *Amelia* is more interesting, revealing, as it does, that the audience for fiction at mid-century was ill prepared either for the kind of realism Fielding here attempted, or for the disturbing moral and social purpose it was meant to serve. In trying to give his Gallic readers some notion of this quality of the book, Pierre Clément was reduced to sarcasm. He cautioned the squeamish that the author of *Amelia*, being a justice of the peace, "has surprised Nature in *flagrante delicto*, has closely copied her, and there is no execrable object with which he is not familiar." He hopes, therefore, they would be prepared to admire "the pictures of prison, tavern, and gibbet, of scoundrels deserving execution, gaolers deserving to hang, and magistrates to be pilloried, of which the work ... is formed."[240] The sensibilities of Fielding's English readers were hardly less offended by the frankness of the novel. The author of *Poetical Impertinence* (4 March 1751/2) reproached Fielding for corrupting the public taste: "Would it not be thought the highest *Impertinence* to tell a certain worshipful Author, that the horrid imprecations, made use of in the *Gatehouse* or *Newgate*, are far from being an agreeable entertainment to virtuous ears?" (pp. 3–4).

By modern standards, of course, the "realism" of Fielding's descriptions of prison life, or of the insides of police courts and sponging houses, seems very tame indeed, and no one who has read Dickens could mistake its social purpose. But Fielding's first readers expected romance-writers to make them laugh or cry, not to prick their consciences or offend their ears with the speech of whores and turnkeys. Disallowing the very premise of his didacticism, they preferred to think he wrote the way he did in such passages because, being a coarse and dissolute fellow, he enjoyed paddling in the mire. Richardson, having perused the first volume of *Amelia*, felt compelled to lecture Sarah Fielding on the "lowness" of her brother, who wrote as if he had "been born in a stable, or been a runner at a spunging house."[241] But even those who wished Fielding well found it embarrassing that he could so flagrantly disregard the proprieties of polite literature. In Dresden, Hanbury Williams was eager to obtain a copy of his friend's new novel and to have news of its reception. On 17 January 1751/2 Henry Harris reported that "Fielding has not succeeded, in his last story book, up to the wish of our criticks" – an opinion in which Harris generally concurred, implying that Fielding's insistence on rehearsing in his fiction the unseemly experiences of his youth had spoiled him for genteel readers: "For my own part, I allow in it great knowledge of human nature, and many masterly strokes of humour: but the low and habitual profligacy of his early life will ever hang round him; and when he talks of brothels, and spunging houses, one is sure that everything is painted from his own experience, and inhabitancy."[242]

To be sure, not every reader of *Amelia* condemned it. But those who approved, who understood what Fielding had attempted and how well he had succeeded, were indeed a "judicious few."[243] Matthew Maty came closer than any other critic to grasping the true qualities of the novel. In the *Journal Britannique* he declared his admiration of "an author whose pen is no less chaste than spiritual, and who equally unveils Nature and ennobles humanity." (What, one wonders, would Richardson have made of this!) Maty praised the "truth" of Fielding's descriptions, the "finesse" of his dialogue, the "variety" of his characters; but he also sensed what few others had seen in the book – that Fielding's purpose was, by exposing "the faults of his compatriots and those of their laws," to reform them: "The citizen and the magistrate appear no less in this work than the philosopher and the Christian."[244] At home, the boldest commendation came from an anonymous adversary of John Hill (who was by now regularly disparaging the novel in the *London Daily Advertiser*): defying Hill and "the Town," the writer protested that *Amelia* was "a most finished Performance," written to promote the cause of "Religion and Virtue" and evincing "all the Regularity and Beauties of epick, and all the Life of dramatick Poetry."[245] The most extravagant praise, however, would come much later and from the most surprising source: Dr. Johnson, who could not bring himself to read *Joseph Andrews* and who pronounced the author of *Tom Jones* "a blockhead" and "a barren rascal," read the novel through at a sitting and, despite his admiration for Richardson, preferred Amelia to Clarissa. She was, he declared to Mrs. Piozzi, "the most pleasing heroine of all the romances."[246]

Most readers, however, disparaged Fielding's last, ambitious experiment as a novelist. Though he put on a face of carefree indifference for the benefit of his friends Upton and James Harris, he was hurt by the novel's failure. How deeply is evident from the response he made to his critics in the early numbers of the *Covent-Garden Journal*. On 25 January, by which time the verdict was already in, he carried *Amelia* before the "Court of Censorial Enquiry," indicted by "Counsellor Town" upon "the Statute of Dulness." The ensuing trial – in which it is not *Amelia*, but the obtuseness and rancor of her critics which are judged – reveals what Fielding took to be the principal complaints against the novel: it was too earnest in promoting the cause of religion and virtue; its heroine lacked spirit, as well as a nose; Dr. Harrison was unnatural and Colonel Bath a fool; the prison scenes were "low." And to these weighty allegations were added the cavils of genteel ladies who damned the book without troubling to read it. In short, in the words of "Counsellor Town's" summation: "the whole Book is a Heap of *sad Stuff, Dulness, and Nonsense*; ... it contains no Wit, Humour, Knowledge of human Nature, or of the World; indeed ... the Fable, moral Characters, Manners, Sentiments, and Diction, are all alike bad and contemptible."

In concluding the trial on 28 January, Fielding was reduced to the always ineffectual – and always a little embarrassing – expedient of pleading his own cause. But the scene, as he defends the book that had sunk his reputation and wearily disowns his Muse, is poignant enough:

If you, Mr. Censor, are yourself a Parent, you will view me with
Compassion when I declare I am the Father of this poor Girl the
Prisoner at the Bar; nay, when I go farther, and avow, that of all
my Offspring she is my favourite Child. I can truly say that I
bestowed a more than ordinary Pains in her Education; in which I
will venture to affirm, I followed the Rules of all those who are
acknowledged to have writ best on the Subject; and if her Conduct
be fairly examined, she will be found to deviate very little from the
strictest Observation of all those Rules; neither Homer nor Virgil
pursued them with greater Care than myself, and the candid and
learned Reader will see that the latter was the noble model, which I
made use of on this Occasion.

I do not think my Child is entirely free from Faults. I know nothing
human that is so; but surely she doth not deserve the Rancour with
which she hath been treated by the Public. However, it is not my
Intention, at present, to make any Defence; but shall submit to a
Compromise, which hath been always allowed in this Court in all
Prosecutions for Dulness. I do, therefore, solemnly declare to you,
Mr. Censor, that I will trouble the World no more with any Children
of mine by the same Muse.

···◆ xxiii ◆─···

Amelia was, as he promised, Fielding's last work of fiction. For what
it reveals about his changing literary and social concerns, and most
especially for the light it sheds on the most private corners of his
personality, it is also perhaps his most interesting work.

In dedicating *Amelia* to Ralph Allen, Fielding declared that his
design in the novel was "to promote the Cause of Virtue, and to expose
some of the most glaring Evils, as well public as private, which at
present infest the Country." The idea for the book took form soon after
Fielding began at Bow Street. Its purpose is didactic and much of a
piece with that of his other writings of this period: namely, to urge
reforms in England's "Constitution" both in the laws themselves, which
he found inadequate to preserve order, and also in the "Customs,
Manners, and Habits of the People" – the essential character and
temper of the body politic. In the summer of 1749 he had charged the
Westminster Grand Jury to present those who pandered to that "Fury
after licentious and luxurious Pleasures" which had become "the
Characteristic of the present Age" – among them infidels and Jacobites,
the keepers of brothels and gaming houses, and the perpetrators of
masquerades. At the same time he submitted to the Lord Chancellor

the draft of a "Bill" which proposed to strengthen and reorganize the watch. Later that year, after lawless mobs endangered the city, he had defended the hated Riot Act and the exemplary punishment of Penlez. More recently he had tried to diagnose the causes of a spreading plague of violence and crime whose source, however – the hedonism of the rich which had corrupted the "useful" orders of society – was beyond the reach of the laws. All these sobering public concerns find expression in *Amelia*, which may fairly be called the first novel of social protest and reform in English – a kind of book scarcely attempted again on such a scale until Dickens. What is more, since as a novelist he could more freely attack the source of the disease, his satire is directed against the Establishment at every level – the watchmen and bailiffs, the magistrates and prison-keepers, worldly priests, profligate lords, the rotten members even of the government which as "Court Justice" he served. Thus in his dialogue with the noble lord who represents venal and wholly pragmatic ministerial policies, Dr. Harrison, Fielding's spokesman, advocates a kind of political idealism which had long been the stock in trade of the Opposition – and which Fielding had recently been hearing at the table of his friend Dodington, "one of the greatest Men," Harrison declares, "this Country ever produced" (XI. ii).[247]

In keeping with this didactic purpose, Fielding experimented with new narrative strategies and techniques. His manner of exposition, depending more on dialogue than on the narrator's commentary, resembles that of the dramatist – a grander version, as it were, of his early "heroic comedies," *Rape upon Rape* and *The Modern Husband*. His materials, drawn more from his own experience and observation, resemble those of the historian and (in tantalizing ways) the auto-biographer. His tone now, wavering between indignation and a maudlin sentimentality, is darker and more monitory, as such a subject required – no longer the follies of men, but their errors and cupidities and the doubtful efficacy of those institutions, the law and the Church, which were meant to preserve the social order. Reinforcing our sense of the novel as a social document to be distinguished from Fielding's previous comic "biographies" of Joseph Andrews and Tom Jones is the remarkable device of withholding the identity of his hero until the third chapter: Booth is introduced as merely another of the faceless victims of a corrupt system who are paraded before Justice Thrasher. The story of Booth and Amelia is in fact framed by scenes whose function it is, through negative and positive examples, to stress the importance of just laws and their proper execution to the health of society. Thrasher, ignorant and venal, sounds this theme at the start of the novel, and in its closing pages he is replaced by another magistrate, resembling Fielding himself, who, as the mob surges through the streets threatening to burst the dikes of civilization, distributes justice and restores innocence to its rightful estate. Cooperating in this work of redemption, furthermore, is another agent of social order, the good priest Dr. Harrison. Booth, infidel and debtor, is at a stroke released from prison and from his subtler bondage to error.

Nearly as prominent as the didactic social intent of *Amelia* is its extraordinary, and often puzzling, autobiographical dimension.[248] Fielding opens the novel by declaring that his subject will be "The various Accidents which befel a very worthy Couple, after their uniting in the State of Matrimony." As those who knew him immediately saw, the story of that worthy couple, Billy and Amelia Booth, is also the story – however much disguised and sentimentalized – of Harry Fielding and his beloved first wife Charlotte. To Richardson, indeed, this was only the latest and most egregious instance of an autobiographical element in all Fielding's fiction which proved the impotency of his "invention."[249] And Lady Mary assured her daughter, Lady Bute, that Fielding in *Amelia* had "given a true picture of himselfe and his first Wife in the Characters of Mr. and Mrs. Booth (some Complement to his own figure excepted) and I am persuaded several of the Incidents he mentions are real matters of Fact"[250] – incidents no doubt related to Fielding's imprudence and his incurable improvidence with money: the mounting debts incurred, the flight from bailiffs to a shabby sanctuary in the Verge of the Court, the confinement in sponging houses, the threat of imprisonment. Lady Bute knew Charlotte personally and spoke of her "amiable qualities" and "her beauty," which, however, "had suffered a little from the accident related in the novel."[251] In later years her daughter, Lady Stuart, recorded her mother's impressions of the marriage:

> He loved her passionately, and she returned his affection; yet led no happy life, for they were almost always miserably poor, and seldom in a state of quiet and safety. All the world knows what was his imprudence; if ever he possessed a score of pounds, nothing could keep him from lavishing it idly, or make him think of to-morrow. Sometimes they were living in decent lodgings with tolerable comfort; sometimes in a wretched garret without necessaries; not to speak of the spunging-houses and hiding-places where he was occasionally to be found. His elastic gaiety of spirit carried him through it all; but, meanwhile, care and anxiety were preying upon her more delicate mind, and undermining her constitution.

In too many ways, however, the story Fielding relates conceals more than it discloses about his essential character and most intimate relationships. It tantalizes more than it rewards the biographical reader. Consider, for example, the setting of the novel. Unlike Fielding's other works of fiction, in which the action is more or less contemporaneous with the period of composition, the action of *Amelia* occurs sixteen years, and more, in the past: time present in the novel is the period from 1 April to June 1733, while the reminiscences of the characters recreate scenes that took place six or eight years earlier still.[252] Why should Fielding choose for his setting this particular moment – a time in his own life when he was riding high as a playwright at Drury Lane, his marriage to Charlotte more than a year in the future? What fascination did these months hold for him?

More interesting still is the puzzle of Booth's identity. In many respects he is obviously his author's double: his fondness for snuff, for instance (I.v); his way of indulging himself by driving coaches he cannot afford (III.xii); his length of nose (XI.i) – not to mention such general matters as the delight he takes in Lucian's works (VIII.v) and his admiration for the edifying writings of Isaac Barrow (XII.v), Fielding's "favourite" divine.[253] It is Barrow's sermons on the Apostles' Creed which convert Booth from the infidelity that paralyzes him as a moral agent, an error founded in a belief his author, himself a man of strong passions, may well have shared: "Indeed," Booth assures Dr. Harrison, "I never was a rash Disbeliever; my chief Doubt was founded on this, that as Men appeared to me to act entirely from their Passions, their Actions could have neither Merit nor Demerit."

In certain other respects, however, Booth more nearly resembles Fielding's father than he does Fielding himself. Like Booth, Edmund was a military officer who had behaved gallantly in battle. The circumstances of his courtship of Sarah Gould, Fielding's mother, and the articles of their marriage settlement, also find parallels in the story of Booth and Amelia: Sir Henry Gould and his wife resisted Edmund's marriage to their daughter and, when they were finally reconciled to the match, made legally certain, as Amelia's mother does (II.iv), that Sarah's dowry would be applied exclusively to maintain her and her children. Like Booth, when Edmund's regiment was disbanded and he was reduced to half-pay, he tried his hand at farming, all too unprofitably. Again like Booth (X.v), he once allowed himself to be cheated at cards by a disreputable fellow officer and his accomplices in a fashionable St. James's coffee-house, his losses seriously embarrassing him financially. And like Booth, Edmund had been no stranger to bailiffs and sponging-houses.

Booth is, then, curiously, a character in whom Fielding and his father coalesce. In Booth, despite their estrangement during Edmund's lifetime, Fielding and his father quite literally become one. Might there be in this fictional reconciliation a symbolic significance? Earlier we saw that the strange interpolated episode of the death of Booth's sister on the eve of his marriage invites a Freudian explanation, hinting not only at the possibility of incest in Fielding's own story, but also, and more agreeably, at the maturing of the erotic side of his nature (see above, pp. 25–7). It may be that *Amelia* also represents a final, happier stage in Fielding's relationship with his father. One would like to believe that he came to understand Edmund better and to forgive him – that he came to recognize, indeed, that whatever Edmund's faults and follies, they were very like his own. I suspect that in *Amelia* Fielding tried to expiate his former bitterness toward Edmund, that in the character of Captain Booth – a soldier too weak to follow his own good intentions, who nearly ruins his family through his gaming and dissipation – Fielding sought not only to come to terms with his own all too fallible nature, but to reconcile himself to his father's memory.

····►● xxiv ●◄····

Projected three months earlier, the *Covent-Garden Journal* appeared at last on Saturday, 4 January 1751/2. The most ambitious of Fielding's periodicals, it was published twice weekly, on Tuesday and Saturday, for the dear price of threepence. Remembering the nature of his previous journalism, his enemies at first suspected that Lyttelton and the Prime Minister had launched the paper, as sailors do a tub, in order to divert an angry populace from worrying the ship of state.[254] To be sure, Fielding during the eleven months in which he conducted the paper would pay his respects to the Royal Family and reflect happily "on the Freedom, the Wealth, and indeed every political Happiness of the People," whom he saw flourishing under Pelham's government.[255] But there was no need at present to harp on these themes. The sudden death of the Prince of Wales in March 1751 had left the Patriots in such disarray the ministry was completely secure. By October even Dodington had abandoned hope of forming a new Opposition and was trying to ingratiate himself with Pelham. For the first time as a journalist Fielding was free of the political constraints he found so uncongenial.

The *Covent-Garden Journal* was launched for very different purposes.[256] In strictly pragmatic terms it was intended as a vehicle for promoting the Universal Register Office and for keeping the public apprised of Fielding's activities and concerns at Bow Street. Almost certainly Fielding's friend and bookseller Andrew Millar was a partner in the enterprise and used the paper to promote the sale of his publications. Though the colophon states that the paper was printed and sold by Ann Dodd, she was merely Fielding's "mercury," the agent who distributed it. That Millar was the actual publisher seems clear from the fact that the paper carried no fewer than 159 advertisements for his books, a number of which – such as *The History of the Portuguese*

(No. 23) and Charlotte Lennox's *The Female Quixote* (No. 24) – Fielding also singled out for favorable review. What is more, during the period of the journal's publication Millar's accounts show payments to Fielding amounting to £254 (see Appendix II).

Although the first notices represent it as "A Paper of Entertainment by several eminent Hands," Fielding alone was responsible for the true substance of the journal: he wrote the great majority of the leaders, as well as such related special features as the short-lived "Journal" of the "Paper War" and the "Proceedings at the Court of Censorial Enquiry"; he dictated to his clerk, Joshua Brogden, the Bow Street affairs reported in the column headed "Covent-Garden"; and (for the first twenty numbers) he enlivened with witty commentary the items reprinted from the newspapers under the heading "Modern History. *Cum notis variorum.*" The stupefying task of culling these items he entrusted to "a Man of so wakeful a Capacity, that he defies the Juice of Poppy itself to set him asleep."[257] Who this colleague was is uncertain, but a likely candidate is William Young, whom one contemporary associated with Fielding in this context.[258] Of other "eminent Hands" who occasionally contributed to the journal, only three can be identified with much certainty. James Harris supplied the "Dialogue ... between a Philosopher and a Fine Lady" in No. 30, and only he, surely, could have written the laudatory review of *Hermes* in No. 21. In Nos. 38 and 41 the letters from "Benevolus" recommending the plan of the Society of Navy Surgeons to advance medical knowledge are probably by William Hunter (1718–83), whom Fielding later called "my friend ... the great surgeon and anatomist of Covent Garden."[259] And one of the two letters signed "E.R." (Nos. 63 and 64) clearly betrays John Fielding's interest in promoting the Universal Register Office.

Though very much "A Paper of Entertainment," the *Covent-Garden Journal* is nevertheless colored throughout by the graver moral purpose that characterizes all Fielding's writings of these last years. Even the playful pseudonym he chose – "Sir Alexander Drawcansir, Knt. Censor of Great Britain" – hints at his determination to carry on the work of reforming the nation's "Constitution": like Drawcansir, the swaggering hero of Buckingham's *Rehearsal*, he would "dare" put on an air of invincible authority as self-appointed "Censor" of the manners, morals, and taste of the age. This, he declared in his fifth number (18 January), would be the theme of his paper:

However vain or romantic the Attempt may seem, I am sanguine enough to aim at serving the noble Interests of Religion, Virtue, and good Sense, by these my Lucubrations.

To effect so glorious a Purpose, I know no readier a Way than by

an Endeavour to restore that true and manly Taste, which hath,
within these few Years, degenerated in these Kingdoms.

To accomplish this program of reform "Ridicule" – or, as he put it
in a lighter moment, "a Wry-Sickle"[260] – would be his weapon. In many
of these essays, however, Fielding's satire is sharper, his tone perhaps
inevitably more magisterial, than before. There is a bite to his irony
reminiscent of Swift, whose example he often invokes, sometimes
silently, by imitating the most sardonic of his pieces such as *An
Argument against abolishing Christianity* (No. 8) and *A Modest Proposal*
(No. 11).[261] Swift, indeed, with Lucian and Cervantes, is one of "that
great Triumvirate" of wits who used their talents "to expose and
extirpate" folly and vice.[262] How radically Fielding had by this date
revised his conceptions of humor and the sense of his own role as
humorist is evident in his stern repudiation of Rabelais and Aristophanes, the author he formerly proclaimed as the model for his
reckless comedies at the Haymarket: these authors – declares the satirist
who fifteen years before had pulled down the weight of the legislature
on his own head – made "so wretched a Use" of their talents of wit and
humor "that had the Consecration of their Labours been committed to
the Hands of the Hangman, no good Man would have regretted their
Loss." Their "Design," he continues, "appears to me very plainly to
have been to ridicule all Sobriety, Modesty, Decency, Virtue and
Religion, out of the World." In *Amelia*, we noticed, the process was
already under way which culminates in these essays in Fielding's
assertion that in the sermons of Robert South "there is perhaps more
Wit, than in the Comedies of Congreve" – "more true Wit," indeed, in
the writings of St. Paul than in the works of Petronius.[263]

Fielding used the *Covent-Garden Journal*, as he had used *Amelia*, to
expose those glaring public and private evils which were beyond his
authority as a magistrate to correct, and often, as in his essay on
gaming and lewdness (No. 66), only "the Language of a Sermon" –
albeit a sermon in the trenchant and lively manner of a South or a
Barrow – seemed to serve his purpose. His leaders address a sobering
variety of such topics: the neglect of sound educational practices
(No. 42) and the debasement of the language of moral discourse (No. 4);
the decline in common courtesy and good breeding (Nos. 3, 26, 27, 33,
55, and 56) with its more vicious manifestations in slander (No. 14),
pride (No. 43), and contempt (No. 61); the indulgence in dissolute pleasures, such as pornography (No. 51) and prostitution (No. 57), gaming
(No. 66) and licentious masquerades (No. 32); the indifference to adultery (Nos. 67 and 68); the mere inanities of the fashionable (Nos. 17, 37,
and 54); the pretentious incompetencies of intellectuals, whether free-
thinking philosophers (No. 46), captious critics (No. 46), irresponsible

editors (No. 31), or the hypothesizing scientists of the Royal Society (No. 70); the spreading vogue of infidelity, undermining the grounds of order in society (Nos. 8, 9, and 11); and the threat of imminent anarchy precipitated by mob rule (Nos. 47 and 49).

For the most part, there is wit and a sort of sad good humor in all this long litany of evils. And from time to time Fielding relieves the gloom with a letter from "Axylus," the good-natured man, on his favorite theme of the pleasures of benevolence (Nos. 16 and 29). But the sheer scope of the indictment is a measure of Fielding's pessimism as he contemplated society during these last years of his life. Sensing this mood and aware of the reforming motive prominent in Fielding's writings of this period, Marxist critics have claimed him for the Revolution. (The U.S.S.R. was, as far as I am aware, the only nation to honor Fielding's memory on the bicentennial of his death by issuing a commemorative postage stamp.) Thus, according to Sabine Nathan, Fielding proposed "a series of changes which are, in fact, a foretaste of the moral standards finally established by the victors of the Industrial Revolution .... it was Fielding who made the vital step that led to the Nineteenth Century."[264] Stranger comrades are hard to imagine than Marx and Fielding – who championed the Whig Establishment, founded the metropolitan police, defended the faith, and would soon be advocating bigger and better workhouses for the proletariat. Yet, curiously, while accepting implicitly the social and economic systems which Marx would sweep away, Fielding came to resemble him in certain ways. He is the first writer of importance in the century to undertake a methodical diagnosis of imperfections in England's "Constitution" and to expound "all the moral Evils introduced by Trade"[265] – matters Marx, too, would have much to say about. In the *Covent-Garden Journal* No. 11 (8 February 1751/2) Fielding in a remarkable essay anticipated a celebrated doctrine of *Das Kapital*. Here he rebukes the rich who callously ignore the plight of the poor – "Wretches in a State of Hunger and Nakedness; without Bread to eat, without Clothes to cover them, without a Hut or Hovel to receive them." Swift's solution, he sarcastically regrets, will not serve in England, where the children of the poor are inedible, being "little better than a Composition of Gin"; it would be preferable, since the rich in their materialism and uncharitableness have repudiated the teachings of Christianity, to restore heathenism openly and, by "the Immolation of human Sacrifices," mercifully to end the misery of these wretches. His point, of course, is to warn his readers that it is the Christian religion alone which can preserve, or indeed justify, the inequities of the present economic order, since only Christianity promises the poor compensation in another world for their sufferings in this:

Could any Thing therefore be so weak in our late Governors, as to have suffered a Sett of poor Fellows, who were just able to read and write, to inform their Brethren, that the Place which the Rich had allotted them was a mere Utopia, and an Estate, according to the usual Sense of the Phrase, in Nubibus only! Could the Poor become once unanimously persuaded of this, what should hinder them from an Attempt in which the Superiority of their Numbers might give them some Hopes of Success; and when they have nothing real to risque in either World in the Trial?

To Fielding, of course, the Christian religion had come to be something more than merely the opiate of the masses. The *Covent-Garden Journal* is notable for passages in which the shocking author of *Pasquin* affirms the essential doctrines of the Church: belief in a Creator (No. 8), in Providence (No. 9), in the divinity of Christ, man's Savior and Redeemer (Nos. 29, 39, and 44), in the efficacy of prayer (No. 29), in the immortality of the soul (Nos. 4, 29, 44, and 69), and in the supreme duty of charity (Nos. 29, 39, and 44). But he also understood, in a pragmatic and utilitarian sense, that religion was the cement that held the polity together; in a godless as well as an unjust society the poor had indeed nothing to lose but their chains.

He seems to have sensed the approaching apocalypse, now only a generation away in France. Coining a famous phrase, he thus commented darkly on riots that had erupted at Norwich: "*The Writers on our Constitution, when they mention only three Estates, are guilty of a great Omission in leaving out the fourth Estate,* THE MOB; *which seem at present in a fair Way to get the better of all the rest.*"[266] He resumed this theme in a pair of essays in which, after an historical account of violent rebellions undertaken from egalitarian principles, he warned of the present dangers posed by "the Mobility," who have risen "to that exorbitant Degree of Power" they "threaten to shake the Balance of our Constitution." With deists like Thomas Chubb (No. 13) and freethinkers like Tindal and Bolingbroke (No. 46) having made a spirit of irreligion so fashionable it had intoxicated even the illiterate clowns and mechanics who made up the Robin Hood Society (Nos. 8 and 9), Fielding concluded there were now only

two Sorts of Persons of whom this fourth Estate do yet stand in some Awe, and whom consequently they have in great Abhorrence. These are a Justice of Peace, and a Soldier. To these two it is entirely owing that they have not long since rooted all the other Orders out of the Commonwealth.[267]

 XXV

As one of the "two Sorts of People" who stood between the nation and anarchy, Fielding also made the journal serve his purpose as magistrate. In the "Covent-Garden" columns his clerk reported specific cases of interest, and Fielding himself commented on imperfections in the laws which frustrated him in executing his office. As we have seen, he was particularly troubled by the conduct of the executions at Tyburn, which, instead of serving as a deterrent to crime, were providing the mob with macabre holidays and the condemned felons with a last opportunity publicly to flout authority. Fielding in the *Enquiry* had recommended specific reforms, but since then the evils he hoped to remedy had grown worse. "*More shocking Murders have been committed within this last Year,*" he observed in commenting on one such case, "*than for many Years before. To what can this be so justly imputed, as to the manifest Decline of Religion among the lower People.*"[268] A few weeks later, commenting on the brutal rape and murder of a young woman by two men – one of whom made her lay her Bible under her head for a pillow – he exclaimed: "*If something be not done to prevent it, Cruelty will become the Characteristic of this Nation.*"[269] Such was Fielding's reputation for diligence and acumen in the conduct of his office that when footpads in Essex murdered a higler and savagely mutilated the man's son and companion, the Lord Mayor, at the instance of several gentlemen of that county, ordered that suspects be brought to Fielding for interrogation; he spent nearly eight hours examining them separately (a standard technique with him), by which means promising "Discoveries" were made.[270]

When this barbarous crime came to his attention in mid-January, he appears to have been optimistic that the legislature would adopt his recommendations for reforming the procedure of capital punishment. In the event, however, the "Murder Act" (25 Geo. II, c. 37), while incorporating to a degree his proposal that punishment speedily follow conviction, completely ignored the crucial element in his scheme: that the execution be carried out in private in order to heighten the terror of punishment and hence its efficacy as a deterrent. Instead, the criminal's body was to be given over to surgeons to be dissected and anatomized (a provision graphically depicted in the last of Hogarth's *Stages of Cruelty*). Two days after the Act became law, Fielding in the *Covent-Garden Journal* No. 25 (28 March 1752) expressed bitter disappointment at its inadequacy in this respect, not only in his leader – a parable of England as an orchard ravaged by blackbirds because the gardeners scorn taking advice from "a jesting Kind of a Gentleman" – but also in the "Covent-Garden" column, where he vividly describes the

"Affectation of Mock-Heroism" in criminals recently hanged at Tyburn
and the boisterous behavior of the spectators who reveled in "these
horrid Farces, which do really reflect so great a Scandal to the Nation,
and so much Disgrace to Humanity." Frustrated that he lacked the
"Authority" to have his plan enacted into law, he wished "some greater
Man *would alter a few Words in it, and make it his own.*" For as these
punishments were now conducted, "we sacrifice the Lives of Men, not
for *the Reformation, but for the Diversion of the Populace.*" In No. 55
(18 July 1752), after witnessing the "ridiculous Drama" of another
licentious hanging day at Tyburn, he renewed his appeal to the legislature to adopt his plan, "Namely private Executions before the Face
of the Court." The plan, he heard, had been rejected chiefly because
the judges were repelled at the thought of having to witness such
a "disagreeable Sight" – an objection he considered frivolous when
compared to the good of the public:

> I will only add that if no Method can be found of making our capital
> Punishments more terrible and more exemplary, I wish some other
> Punishments were invented; and that we may no longer proceed to
> string up hundreds of our Fellow-Creatures every Year, a Matter as
> shocking to all Men of Humanity, as it is entertaining to a dissolute
> Rabble, who ... instead of being terrified, are hardened and encour-
> aged by the Sight.

While he thus endeavored in the *Covent-Garden Journal* to raise the
consciousness of the legislature, Fielding's concern over the recent
increase in violent crimes, particularly murder, prompted him to
produce one of his most curious works: *Examples of the Interposition of
Providence in the Detection and Punishment of Murder.* He dedicated
this little book to Isaac Maddox, Bishop of Worcester, who had liked
the plan of it and encouraged him to publish – "*a true* Labourer in the
Vineyard," Fielding elsewhere called this good man, to whose "*great
Care and Diligence*" the public were indebted for the recent Act which
had already "*very considerably lessened the pernicious Practice of Gin-
drinking.*"[271] Announced as early as 4 April 1752, the book was published by Millar on Monday, 13 April – price: a shilling, or ten shillings
a dozen "to those who give them away." Altogether 3,000 copies were
printed.[272]

The body of the work consists of thirty-three examples of the "miraculous" discovery and punishment of murderers, ranging from a pair
of soldiers in the army of Pyrrhus to the recent sensational case of the
parricide Mary Blandy, whose story Fielding reflected on in several
numbers of the *Journal*.[273] These Fielding, or some assistant, collected
from such popular sources as Reynolds's *The Triumphs of God's Revenge
against the Crying and Execrable Sin of Murther*; only the Introduction

and Conclusion are his own work. The former in particular is interesting for what it reveals of the increasingly religious bent of his mind in this period:

> For my part, I sincerely declare I can discover no more than one cause of the horrid evil of which I am complaining: ONE indeed most perfectly adequate to the production of every political mischief; and which I am convinced hath more than all others, contributed to the production, and to the encrease of all those moral evils with which the public is at present so extremely afflicted.
>
> My sensible reader will presently guess, that I mean that general neglect (I wish I could not say contempt) of religion, which hath within these few years so fatally overspread this whole nation; hath grown to be a kind of fashion among us, and like other fashions, having begun among the higher ranks of people, hath descended gradually through all orders, till it hath reached the very lowest in the society.

As to his own faith, Fielding seems prepared now not only to believe in "such manifest preternatural interpositions of Divine providence," but even in ghost stories, "some of which [he declares] have been so well and faithfully attested, that to reject them with a hasty disbelief, seems to argue more of an obstinate and stubborn infidelity, than of a sound and sober reason."

Such protestations of an almost superstitious piety sound more like Defoe than the enlightened author of *Tom Jones*, and, in part certainly, they may be explained as a rhetorical strategy calculated to instill fear into the minds of the simple audience to whom the book is addressed – fear and hope being, in Fielding's view, the strongest of the passions governing the conduct of men and the passions (as Dr. Harrison remarks in *Amelia* [XII.v]) to which the Christian religion "immediately applies." On the day of publication Fielding began distributing the work *gratis* at his court in Bow Street, and he urged other well-wishers to their country to do the same. He meant it most particularly as a primer for school children:

> For there is nothing of which Children are more greedy, than Stories of the Tragical Kind; nor can their tender Minds receive more wholesome Food, than that which unites the Idea of Horror with the worst of Crimes, at an Age when all their Impressions become in great Measure, a Part of their Nature: *For those Ideas which they then join together*, as Mr. Locke judiciously observes, *they are never after capable of separating.*[274]

In the "Covent-Garden" column of the *Journal* he remarks from time to time on the good his little book has done – in admonishing a wife-beater (No. 31), in improving discipline among the private soldiers of a regiment (No. 36), in wringing tears of remorse from a lad of seventeen, the first to suffer under the new Murder Act, who was hanged for cutting his wife's throat in a fit of jealousy (No. 42). Fielding's book was of course derided in the press for its simple-minded piety (by his old friend Ralph for one),[275] but it was reprinted in far-off Dublin by James Hoey – who, indeed, had already pirated the *Covent-Garden Journal*.[276]

···━● xxvi ●━···

Another piece of legislation drew Fielding's earnest attention this year and helps to make clear the complexity of his character. This was the Disorderly Houses Act (25 Geo. II, c. 36), which became law on 1 June, its purpose being to suppress the brothels and clear the streets of prostitutes. Perhaps no one feature of his magistracy better illustrates how much Fielding had changed from his rakish days, when he frequented Betty Careless's brothel and knew the insides of Mother Needham's and Mother Haywood's well enough to recreate them on stage at Drury Lane. Perhaps, too, no one feature of his magistracy better illustrates the ambivalency of his attitude toward those responsible for the evils that were infecting society (in this instance, literally).[277]

On the one hand, when he contemplated in the abstract the "profligate Lewdness" of the times and those brothels which had become "the Seminaries of Education," he could, in tones worthy of a Jeremiah, exhort the Westminster Grand Jury to suppress them. No less stern is the leader he published this summer (No. 57 [1 August 1752]) in reply to those who mistakenly supposed he had written a letter (No. 50 [23 June]) complaining of the hardships the new law was inflicting on prostitutes: he had become, he said, "the reigning Toast of all the Ladies" at Mother Douglas's, and a correspondent signing herself "Mari Murrain" was so pleased with him she was "ready to rub down my old Back at any Time without a Present." He soon makes it clear, however, that the whores of London are no laughing matter. As such "Prostitutes are the lowest and meanest, so are they the basest, vilest, and wickedest of all Creatures," who in hiring out their bodies not only "descend below the Dignity of Human Nature" but indeed debase themselves "below the Animal Creation, where no such Baseness is known." More important, the "Contagion" they spread "extends not only to an innocent Wife, but like the divine Vengeance, to the Children of the third and fourth Generation." "From me," Fielding declares, "the modest Girl under a Basket of Oysters attracts more Respect, than the Punk in her Coach and Six."

The severity of this indictment is now characteristic of Fielding's attitude when he speaks in a public voice of social "evils" he believes pernicious to society, not only robbers and murderers, but beggars and whores. On the other hand, when actually confronted with the pitiable wretches accused of such crimes and misdemeanors – those individual men and women who appeared to him the victims of injustice – he acted toward them with the compassion and good-humored tolerance that characterize the treatment of the "lower orders" in his novels. He was in general extremely reluctant to subject prostitutes to the prescribed punishment of Bridewell, "a School," he observed in the same leader, "rather for the Improvement, than for the Correction of Debauchery":

> I know a Magistrate who never sends a Woman thither, while she retains even any external Mark of Decency; and I have heard him declare, that he never yet saw a Woman totally abandoned and lost to all Sense of Shame, who had not already finished her Education in that College.

The "Covent-Garden" columns of the *Journal* show Fielding striving time and again, often beyond what a strict interpretation of the laws would warrant, to temper justice with mercy, and to influence changes in the laws themselves. In January, for instance, his constables raided a notorious brothel near the Strand, arresting the keeper and four of the women. Fielding singled out one of these who seemed "less abandoned than the rest" – she was a frightened girl of sixteen who had already been three years "upon the Town" – and assured her of his protection if she would give evidence against the keeper of the house: "she revealed all the Secrets of her late Prison-House, Acts of Prostitution, not more proper to be made public, than they are capable, as the Law now stands, of being punished." Fielding arranged to send the girl home to Devonshire. Her hardened companions he committed to Bridewell, "whence they will return, if possible, worse than they went thither"; their "severe Task-Master" he sent to jail for want of sureties, "whence he will have a Right, in a few Days, to come out." In concluding his remarks on this case, he recommended that the legislature close certain loopholes in the laws which were enabling such villains to carry on their nefarious trade, "the daily Cause of the Misery and Ruin of great Numbers of young, thoughtless, helpless poor Girls, who are as often betrayed, and even forced into Guilt, as they are bribed and allured into it."[278] Such clearly was the case of Mary Parkington, "a very beautiful Girl of sixteen," who had been seduced and deserted by a sea officer. Three weeks before she appeared before Fielding she had been ensnared by the keeper of a brothel, who kept her prisoner and prostituted her to several men. Again Fielding urged

reforms in the law – reforms in fact incorporated in the Disorderly
Houses Act – which would hinder brothel-keepers from "committing
such dreadful Outrages, and of driving Youth, Beauty, and Modesty
(for this Girl was possessed of all three) headlong to the Ruin of Body
and Soul."[279] In March, rather than ruin another young woman – a first
offender with every appearance of gentility – by sending her to Bridewell on a charge of street-walking, Fielding showed her "all the Compassion in his Power" and bound her to her good behavior; he warmly
approved his clerk's exclaiming of the man who debauched her: "*What
doth that Wretch deserve, that was the Destroyer of an innocent lovely young
Creature, who seems once to have so well merited Happiness herself? and
to have been so capable of bestowing it on an honest Man?*"[280] In July he
foiled a scheme to sell a sixteen-year-old servant girl into prostitution:
"the poor Girl returned with great Satisfaction to her sorrowful
Mother."[281]

It is impossible to read these reports without sensing the intolerable
fatigue of body, mind, and spirit to which Fielding daily subjected
himself at Bow Street – or to read them without admiring both his
leniency to those he believed had not yet become incorrigible offenders
and his charity to the unfortunate. His use of the *Journal* to try to help
the starving lunatic Samuel Redman or to raise money to enable the
burnt-out baker William Pierce to start again in business is a notable
example.[282] There are many others. When an urchin of twelve was
arrested for theft and appeared in court with his distraught parents,
Fielding, instead of sending the boy to prison, "which would have
probably ended in the Death of the Mother, and in the Destruction of
the Son," sentenced him to be birched privately by his father.[283] When
a poor woman, the mother of three small children, was charged with
stealing a cap worth threepence, Fielding exerted himself to find the
evidence against her insufficient – otherwise, he explained in a long
comment on the injustice of the laws pertaining to petty larceny, he
would have had no choice but to commit the woman to prison, thereby
ruining both mother and children "for a trifling Theft, dictated perhaps
by absolute Necessity."[284] When a woman, ravaged by venereal disease
contracted from her husband, was charged with stealing a blanket,
Fielding similarly found the evidence insufficient and instead of committing her to prison, recommended her to a hospital.[285] In a lighter
vein, when a girl who had been victimized by a cutpurse wept because
she hadn't the money for a ticket to *Harlequin Sorcerer*, "the new
Entertainment which is so much and so justly admired, at Covent-
Garden Theatre," Fielding gave her a pass to the gallery.[286] And when
(in one of life's little ironies, as it must have seemed to him who caused
the law to be enacted) Fielding was required by the Lord Chamberlain
to enforce the Licensing Act by arresting troupes of apprentices who

were staging theatricals, he chose not to commit them to Bridewell, but discharged them with a reprimand, "and Exhortations to abstain for the future from Diversions so very improper for Persons of their Condition, and which could not fail of bringing on them Habits of Idleness that must necessarily end in their Ruin."[287]

As it evolved serially in these twice-weekly episodes reported in the *Covent-Garden Journal*, the continuing drama in Fielding's courtroom at Bow Street was by no means unrelievedly of the tragic or pathetic kind. The low-life that seethed around him in Covent Garden had its droll moments, and these, with his keen ear for homely dialogue, he often rendered as if they were miniature scenes in a comedy. Such, for instance, is the sentimental reunion between an old man and the stolen ass Fielding restored to him:

> Sir, this is my Ass. I should know him among all the Asses in the World, and he would know me, wouldst not thou, poor Duke? Sir, we have lived together these many Years, ay that we have, as a Man and Wife, as a Man may say; for Sir, I love my Ass as my Wife; the best twenty Horses in the World, no nor a King's Ransom to boot, should not buy my poor Ass. Poor Duke! Thou hast had many an *empty Meal* since I saw thee, and so has thy Master too for Want of thee. For Sir, I do not love him without Reason. Poor Thing he has got me many a good Meal's Meat, and many a good one he will get me I hope. Poor Duke! We shall never part more, I hope, whilst I live.
>
> Then followed [Fielding observes] a Scene of Tenderness between the Man and the Ass, in which it was difficult to say, whether the Beast or its Master gave Tokens of the higher Affection.[288]

Another such episode is the stormy reconciliation of the hearty Welsh sailor and his reluctant bride-to-be: "*Woot ha'me, Peg, or no, d—n me, if woot not, I'll swear thy Life.*"[289]

The levity in Fielding's Bow Street reports offended his graver readers, who thought it unseemly that the character of the magistrate should thus be lost in the wit and romance-writer. But it will serve to remind us that even in this strenuous, sobering period of his life Fielding's sense of humor was irrepressible. His friend Mrs. Hussey (the mantua-maker he found a niche for in a footnote to his masterpiece) remembered that he "never suffered his talent for sprightly conversation to mildew for a moment," often stooping to broaden his knowledge of human nature by consorting with common folk: yet, Mrs. Hussey continued, "his manner was so gentlemanly, that even with the lower classes, with which he frequently condescended particularly to chat, such as ... the Vauxhall water-men, they seldom overstepped the limits of propriety."[290] As the only portrait of him done from the life

clearly shows (see Plate 47), Fielding's countenance when he assumed
his aspect of authority was dauntingly severe – "rueful" and "woeful"
his enemies described it, accurately enough.[291] Yet his reputation as "a
jesting Kind of a Gentleman," even while on the bench, remained. One
of his sourest critics thus imagined him presiding at Bow Street like
Jaques's justice.

> exciting mirthful Follies of Laughter and loud peals of Applause,
> from Constables, Informers, Goalers, Thief-takers, and all the Mob
> of *Covent Garden*; and, if not soon taken down, may boast of
> > Fair round Belly with good Capon lin'd,
> at the Expence of Justice, good Sense, common Honesty.[292]

Fielding, to be sure, served the cause of justice, sense, and honesty
very well indeed, despite his love of sprightly conversation and a joke.
Perhaps this was the time (if the time ever was) when one of the jovial
company at Bow Street remembered him having fun at Andrew Millar's
expense. Fielding, it seems, had declared his opinion that the Scots as
a race entirely lacked a sense of humor, but the point was disputed. It
was agreed to test the hypothesis on Millar, who was just then coming
upstairs to join them:

> Fielding, upon Millar's entering the Room, pretended to be going on
> with the Conversation, and said, I will be judged by my Friend here,
> whether my Scheme be not a good one. – What is it? says Millar. –
> I was thinking (answered the Wit) how I might keep a Coach with
> little or no Expence. How is that? replied the Bookseller; I would
> keep one myself upon those Terms. You shall go halves with me, if
> you will, Millar. You know that I send a great many Prisoners to
> Goal in Hackney-Coaches, and if I was to let my own Coach do that
> Business, I might pay for the Job in Shillings and Eighteen-Pences
> to Newgate, Bridewell, and Clerkenwell. – What think you? Millar
> looked very grave, shook his Head, and said, with great Solemnity,
> that he thought it very unbecoming a Magistrate to make his Coach
> a Carriage for Whores, Highwaymen, and Pickpockets. By G-d, says
> Fielding, I thought so. The Company laughed, and the Gentleman
> gave up the Dispute.[293]

···◆ xxvii ◆···

Though the *Covent-Garden Journal* chiefly served Fielding's graver
purpose as magistrate and moralist, his jurisdiction as "Censor" also
extended to the province of public taste in literature and the theatre,

and it is here that his talent for good-humored ridicule shines as bright as ever. In his first number he began a kind of crusade against "Dullness" and intended that a "Journal of the present Paper War between the Forces under Sir Alexander Drawcansir, and the Army of Grub-street" should be a regular feature of the paper. Against the legions of hackney authors and illiterate critics of the town (who of late had been "cruelly" abusing *Amelia*) he would oppose the heroes of Greek and Roman letters and their modern allies, Molière and Bossu among the French and "a large Body of English VETERANS, under Bacon and Locke, sent me in by Major-General A. Millar," who, as it happened, was advertising his editions of these authors in this same issue.

Modeled on Swift's *Battle of the Books*, the gambit was promising and Fielding, in a playful spirit, hoped it would stimulate sales. In the event he proved no match for the Goths and Vandals of Grub Street, and after his fourth number (14 January) he prudently exchanged his military persona for one more congenial: in future he would preside as judge over a "Court of Criticism" – or, as he put it more grandly, a "Court of Censorial Enquiry." Before retiring from the fray, Fielding had been bloodied by Smollett and demoralized at the prospect of being mimicked weekly by Bonnell Thornton. Reacting to Fielding's bantering allusion to "Peeragrin Puckle" and "Rodorick Random" in No. 2 (7 January), Smollett produced one of the liveliest and most malevolent pieces of invective in the language: *A Faithful Narrative of the Base and inhuman Arts that were lately practised upon the Brain of Habbakuk Hilding, Justice, Dealer, and Chapman, Who now lies at his House in Covent-Garden, in a deplorable State of Lunacy; a dreadful Monument of false Friendship and Delusion.* In Smollett, obviously, Fielding would have found the exception to prove his rule that Scotsmen lacked a sense of humor. A day later, sponsored by the proprietors of the rival Public Register Office, appeared the first of twelve numbers of Bonnell Thornton's weekly periodical devoted to mockery of Fielding and his writings, *Have At You All: or, The Drury-Lane Journal.*[294]

What chiefly prompted Fielding to put an end to the "Paper War," however, was a more personal matter involving his relationship with one of the most extraordinary personages of his time, Dr. John Hill (1714–75).[295] A prolific and versatile author who wrote on virtually any subject (from the art of acting to the history of fossils and the science of botany) and in virtually every literary mode (essays, novels, plays, operas), Hill for nearly a year had been publishing a daily column called "The Inspector" in the *London Daily Advertiser*. A foppish figure universally derided for his vanity and charlatanism, he had risen from humble origins as an apothecary and unsuccessful thespian to become a rich man and a critic who, presiding pompously over the wits at the

Bedford Coffee-House, had considerable influence in matters of taste. John Fielding, we recall, solicited Hill's puffs of the Universal Register Office, and his brother must have been prepared to like the man who had lavished such fulsome praise on *Tom Jones*.

Fielding and Hill had never met, however, until Hill appeared at Bow Street on legal business at the moment Fielding was launching the *Covent-Garden Journal*.[296] On Boxing Day 1751, returning in his chariot from a visit to Hampstead, Hill was robbed by a pair of highwaymen. Two days later (28 December) Hill and his footman, together with two men who claimed they could identify the robbers, went to Bow Street where, on oath before Fielding, they described their assailants. Though these affidavits proved fruitless, Fielding received Hill cordially and took the opportunity of this chance encounter to propose, *"with the utmost good Humour,"* that they might make their journals more entertaining by engaging in a little harmless literary horseplay in the context of a "Paper War."[297] Accordingly, in his "Journal" of the war dated 6 January, Fielding had his forces march to Hill's "Garrison" at the Bedford, where they *"blockheaded* up the said Coffee House."[298] At first, Hill seemed willing enough to play the game. In the *London Daily Advertiser* (Wednesday, 8 January) he reported that his "Lion" – which in imitation of Steele he had installed at the Bedford as a receptacle for contributions – had bitten his adversary's head off. On that same day the two men might be seen cooperating in other ways as well. While Fielding at Bow Street was examining one John Smith on the charge of forcibly marrying an old woman for her money, he began to suspect that the fellow was one of the highwaymen who had robbed Hill a fortnight earlier. Hill and his footman having been sent for, the latter confirmed Fielding's suspicions, who, after an examination lasting four hours, committed Smith to Newgate to await trial (the evidence was doubtful, however, and he was acquitted).[299]

Something must have happened at Bow Street that day to put an abrupt end to Hill's short-lived friendship with Fielding. In the *London Daily Advertiser* for 9 January, instead of replying to Fielding's playful ridicule of his "Lion" in the same good-humored spirit, as he had done only a day earlier, Hill now affected anger at "so formidable an Attack upon me" and devoted his entire leader to smearing Fielding and representing his strategy in the "Paper War" as "an insolent Deceit" upon the public. This stinging rebuke took Fielding by surprise. By his own admission he responded in the *Journal* No. 3 (11 January) "with a little more Bitterness than [was] usual to him":

> *If the Betrayer of a private Treaty could ever deserve the least Credit, yet his Lowness here must proclaim himself either a Liar, or a Fool. None can doubt but that he is the former, if he hath feigned this Treaty,*

and I think few would scruple to call him the latter, if he had rejected it.

Hill was, in short, "absolutely the vilest Fellow that ever wore a Head."

The fun having gone out of the game, Fielding with No. 4 (14 January) discontinued this feature of his paper. Events of the next year of so would nevertheless deepen the antagonism between the two men. In May, for instance, Hill became a laughing stock when, having gratuitously insulted Montfort Browne – an Irishman who later became a general officer and a high-ranking, if disreputable, official in the colonial service[300] – he was publicly kicked, caned, and dewigged by Browne at Ranelagh. Hill tamely submitted to this humiliation, though he threatened to prosecute Browne, claiming that he had been so cruelly used he had developed a dangerous "Empyema" in his chest and his life was despaired of. Browne surrendered himself to Fielding, who, after taking him to Hill's house to confront his accuser,[301] and being assured by a physician that Hill was not in danger, admitted Browne to bail. Indeed, Fielding devoted much of his "Covent-Garden" column in No. 38 (12 May 1752) to vindicating Browne's character from Hill's aspersions and to citing testimony from "many" persons "of Fashion" who witnessed the happening at Ranelagh that Browne had behaved like a gentleman. Inevitably, the Hill–Browne affair, with Fielding's part in it duly memorialized, became in the ensuing months the subject of a spate of satires.[302]

····➤ xxviii ◆····

The *Covent-Garden Journal* and his magistracy kept Fielding continually in the public eye. To put him on display in print or on the stage seemed to many this year a certain way of attracting an audience. In February, William Kenrick's attempt to dramatize the "Paper War" in a satirical entertainment called *Fun* was suppressed by order of the Lord Mayor, who was acting, perhaps, as Kenrick believed, on Fielding's behalf.[303] A month later, hoping to ensure a crowded house for his benefit at Covent Garden on 8 April, Charles Macklin traded on his friend Fielding's fame by producing a two-act afterpiece entitled *The Covent Garden Theatre, or Pasquin Turn'd Drawcansir*. In the play Macklin, posing as Fielding, the satirist and censor, invokes "sweet facetious Lucian" and passes judgment on the follies of the Town.

Fielding ran several advertisements for Macklin's play in the *Covent-Garden Journal*, which indeed he often used to compliment his friends and promote their interests. Of such praise we have already noted several examples, and many others mentioned in the leaders will be familiar: Hogarth's paintings (Nos. 6 and 52), Richardson's *Clarissa* (No. 10), the poetry of Edward Young (Nos. 23 and 60), the benevolence of Ralph Allen (No. 29), Jack Ellys's knowledge of the lions under his care at the Tower (No. 61), and the "excellent" and "very entertaining" *Account of English Ants* written by Fielding's first cousin, the Reverend William Gould (No. 70). And from his second number until his paper had run its course Fielding championed the cause of Garrick and Lacy at Drury Lane in their rivalry with Rich at Covent Garden, and found occasion to commend virtually every actor in their company. He used the "Covent-Garden" column for the same good-natured purpose – defending the character of Baron Lempster, who had killed a man in a duel (No. 17), admiring Henry Bathurst's conduct as prosecutor of Mary Blandy (No. 25), enjoying Dr. Thompson's triumph over a slanderer (No. 31), and extolling the lavish hospitality of "long" Sir Thomas Robinson – as he calls him in *Joseph Andrews* (III.vi) – so rapturously indeed that one suspects Fielding attended this great "Drum" on 21 April (No. 33). Similarly, in his comments on the items of news under "Modern History," Fielding puffed a benefit for "Kitty" Clive, whom he regarded in comedy as "the greatest Actress the World ever saw" (No. 11); he commended the views of the antiquities of Greece and Egypt published recently by the "ingenious" Richard Dalton (No. 20); and when the position of Secretary to the Royal Society fell vacant, he promoted the candidacy of Thomas Birch, "a Gentleman of great Merit in the learned World" (No. 6). Indeed, Fielding's friendship with Birch grew ever stronger. The only letter of Fielding's to come down to us from this year is addressed to Birch at Norfolk Street and dated 18 May 1752: it consists of a single gracious sentence asking Birch for "the Favour of his Company to dinner on Monday next [25 May]."[304]

····◆ xxix ◆····

As the town emptied for the summer Fielding thought of giving up the *Journal*. For six months the authorship of a twice-weekly periodical had added to the heavy burden of justice business – and, besides, he and Young, who was probably assisting with the paper, had been thinking for some time of collaborating on an ambitious new project. In *Amelia* (VIII.v) Booth hints plainly enough at this venture while conversing with an illiterate author who confuses Lucian with Lucan:

"I have been speaking of *Lucian* [says Booth], a *Greek* Writer, and in my Opinion the greatest in the Humorous Way, that ever the

World produced." "Ay!" cries the Author, "he was indeed so, a very excellent Writer indeed. I fancy a Translation of him would sell very well." "I do not know," cries *Booth*. "A good Translation of him would be a valuable Book."

Accordingly, on 27 June 1752 in the *Covent-Garden Journal* Fielding and Young began running a series of advertisements proposing the subscription publication of a new translation of Lucian's works, "With Notes Historical, Critical, and Explanatory." The work, in two large quarto volumes, would cost subscribers as many guineas, one to be paid at the time of subscribing and the other on delivery of the book in sheets. Receipts were obtainable either from the authors or from Millar, Robert Dodsley, and Samuel Baker. In his advertisement for 4 July, Fielding assured his more polite readers that "Every Thing which hath the least Tendency to the Indecent will be omitted in this Translation." In a further effort to stimulate interest in the work, Fielding in No. 52 (30 June) expounded the virtues of his author, who, he declared, "may be almost called the Father of true Humour." Very much an original genius, remarkable for both the "Attic Elegance" of his diction and the moral utility of his satire, Lucian was in Fielding's judgment inimitable – or nearly so. Only "the immortal Swift" deserved comparison: "To say Truth, I can find no better Way of giving the English Reader an Idea of the Greek Author, than by telling him, that to translate Lucian well into English, is to give us another Swift in our own Language." How, then, could Fielding hope to do justice to such a nonpareil? His answer ought to have interested critics more than it has done: "no Man," Fielding declares, "seems so likely to translate an Author well, as he who hath formed his Stile upon that very Author."

Before concluding this tribute, however, Fielding could not resist observing that those who conferred places in Pelham's ministry had made it impossible for him to emulate Lucian in one very material respect. For under Marcus Aurelius, "that Glory of human Nature," Lucian enjoyed "a very considerable Post in the Government. That great Emperor did not, it seems, think, that a Man of Humour was below his Notice, or unfit for Business of the gravest Kind." Nor would Fielding succeed in his present appeal for patronage – though the initial response was encouraging enough to make the project seem viable even six months later. To this Fielding's new friend and imitator Arthur Murphy attests in the *Gray's-Inn Journal* (30 December 1752), where in a dream he finds himself at the summit of Parnassus:

I perceived in a select Company *Lucian*, *Doctor Swift*, and *Cervantes*. ... I told *Lucian*, that the excellent Mr. *Fielding* has promised us a Translation of his Performances into the *English* Tongue, which gave the old *Grecian* great Pleasure, as he did not doubt but the Author

of *Joseph Andrews* and *Tom Jones*, would give the whole the true
Spirit of Humour.

Regrettably, the work was never published and no trace of it survives.

Fielding's plans for translating Lucian doubtless had much to do
with his decision, announced in No. 53 (Saturday, 4 July), that in
future he would publish the *Covent-Garden Journal* only once a week,
on Saturdays. His commitment to the paper had been slackening for
some time. As early as No. 21 (14 March) he had discontinued his
comments on the news in the "Modern History" section, and he had
given up the "Court of Censorial Enquiry" with No. 28 (7 April), when
he urged readers to attend a benefit for the actor William Havard.
After No. 57 (1 August) the "Covent-Garden" column shrinks to a few
perfunctory lines an issue. During September (when, as if to favor his
indolence, the Calendar Act took effect, shortening the month by eleven
days and bringing England at last into chronological accord with
the rest of Europe) he generally gave over the lead articles to other
contributors, and the news from Bow Street indicates that John Fielding or some other justice often supplied his place on the bench. By mid-
October, however, he was back in stride: whether denouncing the
worldliness of the age or ridiculing the Royal Society and the inanities
of a new "Theatre War," these last leaders are among the best examples
of Fielding's journalism.

On 25 November with the seventy-second number Fielding brought
the *Covent-Garden Journal* to a close. He had, he explained, "neither
Inclination or Leisure" to carry on any longer a kind of writing which
had come to seem frivolous. His "graver Friends" thought it "below
my Character" and urged him to "employ my Pen much more to the
Honour of myself, and to the Good of the Public." The advice was
superfluous, for he was already preparing an ambitious treatise designed
to solve the problem of providing for the poor. In less than three years
since the publication of *Tom Jones* he had, it seems, ceased to value
the gifts which brought him lasting fame as an author: "I solemnly
declare that unless in revising my former Works, I have at present no
Intention to hold any further Correspondence with the gayer Muses."
He was as good as his word. Before his death Fielding thoroughly
revised *Jonathan Wild*, completing the process of transforming into a
more general anatomy of false "Greatness" the work which began as a
satire of Walpole;[305] and while still smarting from the criticisms of
Amelia, he altered many passages in that novel against the day when
a new edition was called for.[306] Curiously, as if already anticipating the
edition of his collected works which was not published until long after
his death, he also retouched several passages in the *Covent-Garden*

Journal.[307] But Fielding never again undertook a work of, as he might now say, mere literature.

Fielding concluded this final number of the *Covent-Garden Journal* by announcing one of the new ways in which he meant to serve the public while serving his own financial interests. On 1 December 1752 the daily paper which for eighteen years had been published under the name of the *General Advertiser* would reappear as the *Public Advertiser*, the plan of the paper having been modified in part to aid Fielding in his war against crime and to provide a continuing vehicle for the Universal Register Office. On commencing his magistracy, Fielding saw that one sure way of curtailing the incidence of robberies was by suppressing the receivers of stolen goods: he had provided for this reform in the draft Bill he submitted to the Lord Chancellor in 1749 and also in the *Enquiry* (Sect. V), and he had dramatized the problem in *Amelia*. Early in 1752 the legislature seemed ready to act on his recommendations when the Commons passed a Bill for regulating pawn-brokers, but the Bill was rejected by the Lords.[308] One provision of this Bill – a provision Fielding was thought to have lobbied for[309] – was that stolen goods should be immediately advertised "in a publick paper to be specified for that purpose," so that all pawnbrokers in the metropolis would have knowledge of the theft and either could assist in recovering the goods and apprehending the thief, or would be liable to be prosecuted for receiving such goods knowing them to be stolen. Though it never enjoyed the official sanction of Parliament, the *Public Advertiser* was meant to serve this purpose, Fielding having secured the cooperation of fifty-nine of the "principal Pawnbrokers within the Bills of Mortality." Fielding had a financial interest in the paper[310] – fairly enough, one would think, since he devised this useful scheme and was trying to implement it. Nevertheless, his connection with the paper was seen by some as further proof of his alleged venality as a "trading" justice: as "Justice Fail-Paper" he is thus ridiculed in the puerile satire, *A Scheme for a New Public Advertiser, with a List of the Present Subscribers* (February 1753).

···━● XXX ●━···

Fielding's plans for the *Public Advertiser* would have meant his ending the *Covent-Garden Journal* in any case. But that decision – detaching him from the petty broils of Grub Street – must have seemed timely at this moment; for by siding with Garrick in the recently intensified rivalry between Drury Lane and Covent Garden, he had again become the target of Dr. Hill's abuse, all the more furious and personal now because of the part Fielding had played in Hill's humiliation at the hands (and well-aimed foot) of Montfort Browne. The episode, moreover, is especially notable as it marks the beginning, as far as we know, of the most important new relationships of Fielding's last years: his friendships with Christopher Smart (1722–71) and with Smart's friend Arthur Murphy (1727–1805). For it was as a consequence of an uproarious evening at Drury Lane on Friday, 10 November, that Hill found himself alone and fulminating against a formidable corps of adversaries including Fielding, Smart, and Murphy, together with Garrick and his troupe at Drury Lane.

As early as August, Hill invited such trouble when he anonymously published *The Impertinent* – a scurrilous attack on Smart and Fielding ("a particular Friend of mine," Smart called him)[311] in which Hill tried to conceal his authorship by including himself among the victims. This stratagem – a favorite device of his for drumming up interest in his publications – fooled no one, however;[312] and it started Smart and Fielding thinking of retaliating by writing new *Dunciads* of their own, with Hill enthroned in Cibberian impudence.[313]

Hostilities did not break out in earnest until November. To ridicule the company at Covent Garden, who were packing the house with a spectacle of wire-dancing and the antics of strange animals, Garrick at Drury Lane burlesqued Rich's entertainment in scenes added to *Harlequin Ranger*, a pantomime in which his star comedian Henry Woodward played Harlequin. The Town, however, was unamused, and incited by Hill's rebuke of Garrick in the *London Daily Advertiser* (9 November), a party went to Drury Lane the next night determined to damn the play. Amidst the din of hisses and catcalls a "gentleman" named Richard Fitzpatrick threw an apple at Woodward, who replied (depending on whether one accepts Woodward's version or Fitzpatrick's) either with mock courtesy ("Sir, I thank you") or with an insolent challenge ("I have noticed you in particular and I shall meet with you again"). In the *London Daily Advertiser* on 14 and again on 17 November, Hill took sides with Rich against Garrick and reprimanded Woodward for his effrontery. On that same day Woodward appeared before Fielding to swear to the truth of his version of the incident, and he was supported by the affidavits (also sworn before Fielding) of two members of the Drury Lane company.[314]

Fielding of course sided with Garrick and Woodward in the dispute, which quickly engendered the usual litter of pamphlets – one of which was, rashly, attributed to Fielding, or to Fielding in collaboration with Garrick: this was *A Letter from Mr. Woodward, Comedian ... to Dr. John Hill* (2 December).[315] It was in the final two numbers of the *Covent-Garden Journal* (18 and 25 November) that Fielding entered the fray, ridiculing Hill at first good-naturedly as "the Trumpeter" of "the

Ninnies" who opposed Garrick in the "War" of the theatres. Hill replied with furious invective, hinting darkly at unspeakable immoralities in Fielding's past:

> I would reproach you, but it is impossible. What is there I can say of you so ill, that all Men have not spoken it before me? Is there an Act that can degrade the Gentleman, and have you not been guilty of it? Is there a Thing that can disgrace the Man? Have you not gloried in it? But I repeat them not; they are notorious. Look back into the Years of your own Life ... look back into it; and, for I am not going to repeat the Story, blush in Secret. To stain you with new Infamy is impossible. All I can say is, you continue that which you always was: And can there be in Language so severe a Censure?[316]

For Fielding the year was ending as it began, his character smeared by those who would not let him live down the follies of his youth – smeared not only with vile innuendoes, but with what appear to be downright lies: Smollett, for instance, having reminded the Town that the celebrated magistrate and self-appointed censor of the age had once been "accustomed to Riot, Outrage, and all Manner of Profligacy," asserted more specifically that Fielding once hired himself out as "a Bawdy-house Bully ... for the Space of two whole Years";[317] now to the catalogue of indignities Fielding's enemies endlessly invented, Hill added that before being "exalted to move the Wires of a Puppet Shew" he had been "Runner to a Bailiff."[318] Small wonder Fielding's friends advised him that by undertaking the *Covent-Garden Journal* and opening himself to such vilification, he had sunk below his character. He was quite ready to retire from the "Paper War."

Or was he, quite? Among his friends Fielding now numbered Christopher Smart and Arthur Murphy. Smart, who had become a well-known figure in the literary life of the town – among other things contributing articles to *The Student*, editing *The Midwife: or, The Old Woman's Magazine*, and staging a regular entertainment called "The Old Woman's Oratory" – may indeed have been moving in Fielding's orbit for some time. As early as June 1750 he warmly complimented "the incomparable Mr. Justice Fielding,"[319] and in *The Midwife* for February 1750/1 he cordially puffed the Universal Register Office. Murphy, Smart's friend, had on 21 October 1752 taken over authorship of *The Craftsman*, giving it the new name of the *Gray's-Inn Journal*, substituting (as Smart put it)[320] "Wit and good Sense in the Place of abstract Politicks," and, incidentally, changing completely the attitude of that paper to Fielding, who after the denigration of recent years now found himself extolled as "the immortal Author of *Jonathan Wild*, *Joseph Andrews*, and *Tom Jones*."[321] Murphy indeed acknowledged that he had taken the *Covent-Garden Journal* as his model and would endeavor to conduct his own paper in the same spirit.[322]

In the flurry of journalism and pamphleteering, the three friends combined with Garrick and Woodward against Hill. The most memorable of their satires was the realization of the new *Dunciad* Fielding and Smart had contemplated in response to Hill's sneaking aspersions in *The Impertinent*. Announced by Smart as early as 7 December 1752, his poem *The Hilliad* – with a prefatory letter by Murphy containing one of the handsomest tributes Fielding ever received – was not published until 1 February 1753.[323] In the main, Murphy was probably also responsible for the satiric "notes variorum" which accompany the verse; but he may well have had help from Fielding, whose delight in such mock-scholarly mischief is evident in the annotations to *Tom Thumb* and *The Vernoniad*.[324] Fielding and his friends also had a final hilarious fling at their adversary on stage at Drury Lane. For Woodward's benefit on 20 March 1753, Garrick chose *The Mock Doctor* as afterpiece. Woodward in the title role took off Hill, the "new" mock doctor, to perfection – his foppish dress, his smirk, his waddle of a walk. Smart composed a Prologue for Woodward that exquisitely pointed up the satire, but the Lord Chamberlain quashed it.[325]

···◄xxxi►···

In bringing the *Covent-Garden Journal* to a close on 25 November 1752, Fielding hinted that he was forsaking the "gayer Muses" in order to employ his pen "to the Good of the Public." For some time he had been pondering one of the most urgent social problems of his (or any other) age: the problem of how best to provide for the nation's poor. His analysis in the *Enquiry* had sparked lively debate on the matter and had alerted the legislature to the inadequacy of the Poor Laws, by which, since the time of Elizabeth, responsibility for providing for the poor devolved on the individual parishes, which raised the money by means of a tax on householders. But these laws, grudgingly executed by the churchwardens, chiefly benefited the lawyers who disputed the attempts of magistrates to remove the vagrant poor to parishes in which they had a lawful "settlement." In the vain hope of improving their lot, the poor in their thousands deserted the villages and, like a malignancy in the body politic, swelled the ranks of beggars and thieves in the capital.

In the *Enquiry* Fielding had offered – if he could be certain his efforts in drawing it up would not be wasted – to produce a plan for providing "universal Employment for the industrious Poor." He received the

encouragement he needed as Parliament met in the Session of 1751–2
to consider a number of wide-ranging reforms, several of which, as we
have seen, Fielding had advocated in that treatise. The *London Daily
Advertiser* (25 November 1751) reported that he had "laid before" the
Prime Minister "a Scheme" (presumably in outline) "for employing the
Poor much to the Advantage of the Nation and themselves; and also
for putting an effectual Stop to the daring Outrages and Robberies we
have lately been too much alarmed with; and it is hoped it will meet with
an Attention due to its Importance." Throughout 1752, as Parliament
continued its prolonged deliberations on the subject, the plight of the
poor and the need to provide for them are recurrent themes in the
Covent-Garden Journal: Fielding insists, for instance, on the right of the
poor – a right derived from the law of nature and the teachings of
Christ – to be relieved from the superfluities of the rich (No. 39); he
offers his own sardonic version of Swift's *Modest Proposal* (No. 11); he
scores the inadequacy of the existing Poor Laws, attributing to them
the frightening ascendancy of the mob (Nos. 49 and 54). No less eloquent
testimony to his preoccupation with this problem are the succinct
reports from Bow Street during the winter months:

> This Morning the Body of a poor Wretch who perished last Night in
> the Street, with Cold, Hunger and Disease; was brought to the
> Round-House at St. Giles.[326]

> Yesterday [three Irishmen arrested for begging were] brought up
> again in order to be pass'd to their several Settlements, when they
> appear'd to be in so dreadful a Condition with Sickness as well as
> Poverty, that the Justice having first relieved, dismissed them. Such
> is the present State of the Poor, in a Nation where near a Million is
> yearly raised for their Support.[327]

To such scenes as these, daily enacted before him, Fielding responded
with pity, and with a sense of outrage at the system that inflicted the
suffering. They are what motivated him as he sought a pragmatic
solution to the problem, one that would enforce discipline in the lower
orders – as he was now thoroughly convinced the weakness and intract-
ability of human nature required – while affording them a measure at
least of hope and self-respect as well as the necessities of life.

Dedicated to Henry Pelham and dated 19 January, Fielding's *Proposal for Making an Effectual Provision for the Poor, for Amending their
Morals, and for Rendering them useful Members of the Society* was
published by Millar on Monday, 29 January 1753, in an edition of 2,000
copies.[328] Now "in the Decline of my Health and Life" (as he put it in
the "Introduction") Fielding had nevertheless taken pains not only to
read over and reflect on all the laws relating to the poor, but to consider

carefully "every thing which I could find that hath been written on this Subject, from the Original Institution in the 43d of *Elizabeth* to this Day" (pp. 232–3). To this knowledge he added a practical understanding of the problem gained from his experience on the bench. The plan he produced is characterized by the humane conservatism of its assumptions – humane, certainly, by the rough standards of the times – and characterized also by the ingenuity of its elaborate design.

Fielding begins by accepting the mercantilist maxim that "the Strength and Riches of a Society consist in the Numbers of the People" – a maxim which, however, as he reminds his readers, assumes "that those Numbers may contribute to the Good of the Whole." Otherwise, far from benefiting society, the poor must "lie as a useless and heavy Burden on the rest of their Countrymen" (p. 225). Here was the fallacy in the doctrine which moved Swift to recommend that the Irish solve their problem by cannibalism, and Fielding to propose in the *Journal* that his countrymen revive the heathen practice of human sacrifice. But the poor could contribute nothing but their labor to "the Good of the Whole," and on this labor "the Public," Fielding declares, "hath a Right to insist" – exempting of course the impotent and infirm, who are the proper objects of charity. Besides ensuring such a charitable provision, the legislature in Fielding's view had "a twofold Duty": first, it must procure the able-bodied poor "the Means of Labour"; second, it must "compel them to undertake it" (p. 228).

These basic assumptions underlie Fielding's *Proposal*. As for the most effectual means of implementing them, Fielding, since broaching the subject in the *Enquiry*, had altered his thinking in one important respect. In accord with Resolutions approved by the House of Commons in June 1751, he no longer advocated reforms in the smaller administrative units of the parishes, many of which were too small or too poor to answer the purpose. His scheme now called for the erection of workhouses, large and various enough in function to accommodate the poor of an entire county – in this particular instance, Middlesex, the most populous and disorderly of all, with whose problems he was well acquainted. For, Fielding reasoned, "In a large Body alone the Materials can be sufficiently supplied, the Hands properly adapted, new Manufactures taught, and the Work well disposed of to the Emolument of the Public, and the proper Encouragement of the Labourer" (p. 258).

But if, in advocating county workhouses, Fielding was following the lead of Parliament and a number of earlier projectors,[329] no previous author had drawn out the implications of such a scheme so judiciously and in such detail. Included with the *Proposal* was a fold-out frontispiece by Thomas Gibson, consisting of an elaborate plan complete with elevations of the buildings and courts (for the latter, see Plate 62). Much like a fortified city-state or colony in miniature, the institution

Fielding envisaged consisted of distinct departments with different functions. The "County-house," spreading over a vast area, included lodging-rooms (two persons to a bed) and work-rooms for "upwards" of 3,000 men and 2,000 women; lodgings for the warders; an infirmary and a chapel. The "County-House of Correction" included accommodation and work-rooms for "upwards" of 600 prisoners, who were to lie on mattresses, not beds, and were to be employed at "the hardest and vilest Labour"; for the refractory there was "a Fasting-room" (where the diet consisted of bread and water) and "several Cells or Dungeons" for solitary confinement. And, since Fielding attributed most of the ills of society to a spreading irreligion, at the hours appointed for worship and moral instruction the prisoners were to assemble in "a large Room with Iron Grates" which looked into the end of the chapel. Handsome and commodious houses would be provided for the Governor and his deputies, and for the chaplains.

The regime Fielding proposed was strict but by no means severe by contemporary standards; and it was designed not only to train and employ the poor in a variety of manufactures (they were to be hired out to contractors), but also to rehabilitate those who were delinquent or criminally inclined. Justices would have discretion to commit persons to either the "County-house" or the "County-House of Correction" for idleness and vagrancy, or wandering from their habitations without an official pass – and of course for the more reprehensible offenses that were punishable by confinement in a Bridewell. Those who were thus committed to the workhouse – to distinguish them from the eager unemployed who Fielding supposed would join this community voluntarily in order to find work – would wear a badge with the word "County-house" in large letters sewed on the left shoulder of their clothing. The day would begin with the ringing of a bell at 4:00 a.m., followed by chapel at 5:00 with lectures on morality every Wednesday and Friday. The working day of ten hours was extremely lenient for the period, and time was provided for refreshment and recreation: the inmates were to work from 6:00 to 9:00, from 10:00 to 1:00 p.m., and from 2:00 to 6:00 daily, with two hours free every Thursday afternoon and Sundays off, as well as all the usual holidays. Prayers would be said every evening at 7:00, and the day ended punctually at 9:00, when the gates were locked and all lights and fires extinguished. To prevent the notorious debauchery prevalent in the Bridewells of the day, the sexes would be strictly separated, and spirituous liquors were to be prohibited.

As a recent authority has observed, Fielding's scheme was designed to "concentrate the power of the poor as an engine might concentrate natural forces."[330] Here, as in his attitude toward the whores of London, one senses the difference between his compassion for the individual wretches he confronted daily at Bow Street and his conviction, as he contemplated the general problem they posed for society, that the poor as a class must be made to conform to his cherished abstraction of the body politic and its ideal "Constitution." In his time on the bench he had seen too much of the dark side of human nature, too much of the ignoble savagery men were capable of, to allow the objection that his scheme was dictatorial and oppressive:

> I should scarce apprehend, tho' I am told I may, that some Persons should represent the Restraint here laid on the lower People as derogatory from their Liberty. Such Notions are indeed of the enthusiastical Kind, and are inconsistent with all Order and all Government. They are the natural Parents of that Licentiousness which it is one main Intent of this whole Plan to cure; which is necessarily productive of most of the Evils of which the Public complains; of that Licentiousness, in a Word, which among the many Mischiefs introduced by it into every Society where it prevails, is sure at last to end in the Destruction of Liberty itself.
>
> ... But if we must on no Account deprive even the lowest People of the Liberty of doing what they will, and going where they will, of Wandring and Drunkenness, why should we deny them that Liberty which is but the Consequence of this; I mean that of begging and stealing, of robbing or cutting Throats at their good Pleasure.
>
> (p. 267)

Once the mischievous exponent and champion of liberty unbridled – whether in his political satires or in the excesses of his private life – Fielding had come to value order, restraint, stability. The wisdom in this new-found sense of the anarchic tendencies of human nature he had tested in his own conduct and confirmed many times over in his observations from the bench. He would not have been surprised at the bloody consequences when license and egalitarianism triumphed in 1789.

For all its pessimism about the ability of the "Fourth Estate" to govern themselves, Fielding's plan is remarkable for its humanity. In this respect, for instance, as in many of its practical details, it compares very favorably indeed with the monstrous scheme of "Pauper Management" propounded half a century later by Jeremy Bentham, hero of the Enlightenment.[331] It is remarkable, too, in its design to attempt the rehabilitation of an entire class of people – at present idle, useless, demoralized. Fielding meant to make of these people individuals who were capable of earning a living and of being constructive members of society. The laborers in his workhouse would be taught the skills which not only would qualify them for "the Manufactures and Mysteries now exercised in this Kingdom," but would enable them to introduce into

England "foreign Manufactures and Mysteries" (p. 24). Furthermore, by a novel system of rewarding the industrious, not merely punishing the idle, they would be encouraged to work well and to master their trades.

Essential to Fielding's plan, however – and the key to his mature thinking about human nature – was the inculcation of religion: attendance at chapel, morning and evening, was to be compulsory. One of the most revealing sections of the *Proposal* (pp. 269–72) – in which Fielding takes as his authority "the excellent Archbishop *Tillotson*" – argues that religion alone is capable of healing and sweetening the natures of men, and of preserving order in society. The "very Deist and Atheist himself, if such a Monster there be," must at least acknowledge its political utility. Without religion, Fielding observes, "such a Body of Men" as would be assembled together in this workhouse could be kept from "the most violent and inordinate Outrages" only by "a strong and constant military Force; in short by the same Degree of Coercion, as would restrain the Fury of wild Beasts, which are possibly as easy to be governed as wild Men." But, he continues,

> Heaven and Hell when well-rung in the Ears of those who have not yet learn't that there are no such Places, and who will give some Attention to what they hear, are by no Means Words of little or no Signification. Hope and Fear, two very strong and active Passions, will hardly find a fuller or more adequate Object to amuse and employ them.

However uncongenial it may appear today, Fielding's plan for the management and rehabilitation of an entire derelict class of society is a fascinating work, revealing almost literally the final shape of his moral and social thought. He was not sanguine enough to suppose it would be adopted, or even widely approved, and in conclusion he affected not to care very much, quoting some appropriately stoical verses from his "great Master," Horace. His enemies, he knew, would sneer "that instead of intending a Provision for the Poor, I have been carving out one for myself, and have very cunningly projected to build myself a fine House at the Expence of the Public" – supposing he saw himself elevated from Bow Street to the Governor's mansion. But, he assured them, that would be ignoring what in his present condition seemed the shrewdest of all Horace's satires: his ridicule of those who would (as Fielding paraphrased the lines in *Tom Jones* [II.viii]) "build Houses of five hundred by a hundred Feet, forgetting that of six by two." For Fielding no longer doubted he was dying. Those who know him, he concludes, "will hardly be so deceived by that Chearfulness which was always natural to me ... to imagine that I am not sensible of my declining Constitution."

Ambition or Avarice can no longer raise a Hope, or dictate any
Scheme to me, who have no farther Design than to pass my short
Remainder of Life in some Degree of Ease, and barely to preserve
my Family from being the Objects of any such Laws as I have here
proposed.

It must indeed have seemed that the months he spent in devising
and drawing up his *Proposal* had been wasted. In a brief notice the
Monthly Review recommended it to "the consideration of every well-
wisher to the good order and prosperity of our country";[332] and some
years later, the poor and the problem they posed still being with us,
another writer on the subject observed that Fielding's "famous Plan"
had been "approved by many Gentlemen of great Abilities in the House
of Commons."[333] But from the beginning, as his friend John Upton
feared – who as chaplain to the Lord Chancellor was in a position to
know – Fielding's *Proposal* was never taken very seriously even in
friendly quarters. "I much like Fielding's scheme for providing for the
Middlesex poor," Upton wrote James Harris on 12 February, "but I
am afraid it will meet with the fate of other schemes: I have heard cold
water & cold reflexions cast on it by those I wish would patronize it."[334]
As for Fielding's enemies in Opposition, they read it with their usual
lust to misapply. At General Oglethorpe's bidding, the Tory author
George Osborne – who, confined for debt in the Fleet, was in a position
to speak feelingly on the subject – attacked Fielding and his *Proposal*,
seeing in his workhouse scheme a sort of parable of life under Pelham's
oppressive government.[335]

···◆ xxxii ◆-···

Fielding was soon diverted from such abstract considerations as the
problem of the poor by the most famous case ever to occupy him: the
mystery of Elizabeth Canning.[336]

A simple servant girl of eighteen, Elizabeth Canning disappeared on
the night of 1 January 1753 while returning home to the City from a
visit to her aunt near Houndsditch. She was dressed in her holiday
finery and was carrying a few shillings her mistress had given her as a
Christmas present. The outskirts of town being infested with footpads,
her mother and friends (for she was a good, hard-working girl, well
liked in the neighborhood) had reason to fear the worst. Mrs. Canning –
a widow and devout Methodist who eked out a living as a sawyer –
placed notices in the *Daily Advertiser* offering a reward for information
concerning her daughter, but there was no response. Then, on Monday

evening, 29 January – four weeks after she had vanished – Elizabeth Canning came home: the few clothes she had on were in rags; she was emaciated, filthy, blue with the cold, and too weak to stand upright.

As she told her story, what happened to her was this. On her way home that New Year's night she was assaulted by two men as she passed the gate of Bethlehem Hospital in Moorfields. They took her money; stripped her of her hat, apron, and gown; and tied her hands behind her. One of her assailants struck her a hard blow to the head and she lost consciousness. When she came to, they were dragging her along the Hertford road, their destination a house where she found an old crone and two young women. The old woman, tall and swarthy in appearance, took her hand and promised her fine clothes "if she would go their Way" and become a prostitute. When she refused, the woman took a knife and cut off her stays, while her companions stood by and jeered. She slapped Elizabeth across the face, cursed her, and locked her in an empty loft, the window boarded up and nothing but a jug of water and some crusts of bread to eat. She threatened to cut her throat if the girl cried out. For twenty-eight days Elizabeth Canning remained imprisoned in the loft until she managed to pull the boards from the window and make her escape, staggering ten miles or more to London in the cold and dark and rain. As to the identity of her captors, she knew only that during her confinement she had heard people below-stairs calling for Wills or Wells. One of the excited company who gathered in Mrs. Canning's house after the girl's return was certain he knew the place: Mother Wells's brothel at Enfield Wash.

While Elizabeth Canning slowly recovered from her ordeal (she seemed on the point of death), her master and friends took action against the villains who, they had no doubt, were responsible for the outrage. Having obtained a warrant from the sitting alderman at the Guildhall on 31 January, they formed a posse and set out the next day for Enfield, with Elizabeth, still very ill and weak, following in a chaise. There, at Mother Wells's – despite discrepancies between her description of the place and the house itself – Elizabeth identified Mary Squires, a hideous gypsy woman, as the person who had robbed and abused her; she also identified the gypsy's daughter Lucy Squires and Virtue Hall as the young women who had laughed at her. After hearing Elizabeth's evidence, a neighboring justice committed Mary Squires to New Prison for stealing the stays and sent Susannah Wells to Bridewell for keeping a disorderly house. The story quickly spread of the girl's barbarous usage at the hands of these women, and of her heroism in preferring death by starvation to the loss of her chastity. The Town soon talked of nothing but this real-life Pamela and her persecutor, the grotesque gypsy woman who outdid Mrs. Jewkes in villainy. Elizabeth Canning's friends were determined to see justice done.

On Tuesday, 6 February, Fielding was taking tea with his wife and "Counsellor" Martin Madan (1726–90), "a Gentleman of Fashion," Fielding called him, "and of as much Honor as any in the Nation."[337] Madan, who not long before had given up practicing the law and living a life of pleasure in order to become a Methodist preacher, might seem a surprising companion for Fielding, considering his antipathy to that "Sect"; but he was an educated and interesting man and already something of a celebrity. Fielding was, as he put it, "almost fatigued to Death, with several tedious Examinations," and he planned to leave Bow Street the next morning to rest for a day or two in the country. To escape the incessant pressures of justice business and the unwholesome air of Covent Garden, he had recently leased Fordhook – a handsome house (see Plate 61) and forty-four acres of land at Ealing,[338] six miles west of town – and he was eager to refresh himself. He had not enjoyed the ease of his new retreat, "unless on a *Sunday*, for a long Time."

As too often happened, he would have to postpone his holiday. Brogden interrupted Fielding's conversation with Madan by announcing the arrival of "Mr. Salt," a solicitor who frequently sought Fielding's counsel on procedural matters. This time Salt came as Elizabeth Canning's attorney, seeking advice as to the surest manner of bringing Mary Squires and Mother Wells to justice. He asked that Fielding take Elizabeth Canning's sworn testimony without delay and that he examine Virtue Hall concerning her knowledge of the affair. Fielding, for his usual fee, advised Salt how to proceed in the case, but he had no wish to involve himself further – partly because another justice, whom he knew and respected, had already taken down this information, but chiefly because he was exhausted and eager to leave town. He finally consented, however, prevailed on by "some Curiosity, occasioned by the extraordinary Nature of the Case, and a great Compassion for the dreadful Condition of the Girl," as Salt had represented it.

The next day, 7 February, Elizabeth Canning was carried in a sedan chair to Bow Street, and Fielding heard her sworn information, upon which he issued a warrant authorizing the arrest of everyone residing in Wells's house. Among these was Virtue Hall, who he heard was ready to confess. When she appeared before him, trembling and in tears, he treated her gently, allowing her to sit down and compose herself before he began the examination. But her testimony was so full of contradictions she exhausted his patience. He broke off the examination and advised Salt to prosecute her as a felon. Terrified at this prospect, she begged to be heard again, promising this time to tell the truth. Salt took her into a room apart and returned two hours later with her statement, which wholly confirmed Elizabeth Canning's accusations. In all, the interrogation of Virtue Hall lasted from six o'clock until past midnight. It seems not to have occurred to Fielding that he had behaved irregularly by acting both as counselor for the prosecution and as magistrate in the same cause, or that he had acted foolishly by permitting the prosecuting attorney, who knew Elizabeth Canning's story in detail, to take down Virtue Hall's testimony in private. That their accounts corroborated each other so closely could now easily be explained away.

In the morning Fielding saw Virtue Hall again, briefly, and, satisfied with the truth of her evidence, ordered that Mary Squires and Mother Wells be detained in prison for felony. He then left at last for the country. While he was away public interest in the Canning affair rose to fever pitch. Unable to contain their curiosity a number of noble lords and gentlemen asked that, on his return to town, Fielding examine the principals in the case in their presence. On 14 February the drab courtroom at Bow Street was crowded to capacity as Elizabeth Canning and Virtue Hall confronted Mother Wells and the evil-looking old gypsy; afterwards Fielding committed them both to Newgate to await trial. On 26 February at the Old Bailey, Mary Squires was sentenced to be hanged, and Susannah Wells to be branded on the thumb and imprisoned for six months.

It was a popular judgment, but not all the judges were satisfied. Witnesses for the defense had testified that during the first ten days of January, Mary Squires was peddling handkerchiefs in Abbotsbury, Dorset, more than a hundred miles from the scene of the crime. The prosecution countered with a witness of its own who swore he saw her in the neighborhood of Wells's house almost daily in the month of January. But the doubt remained. Sir Crisp Gascoyne (1700–61), the Lord Mayor who presided at the trial, began inquiries which seemed abundantly to confirm the testimony of the Dorset witnesses.

At this point the officious Dr. Hill enters Fielding's story for the last time. Having heard of Gascoyne's new evidence, Hill on 6 March met with Thomas Lediard – the magistrate who had succeeded Fielding as Chairman of the Westminster Sessions and who was ambitious of succeeding him as Court Justice.[339] Together they questioned Virtue Hall, and then repaired to the Lord Mayor to inform him she was ready to recant. Gascoyne summoned her to the Mansion House and, examining her in private, got her to say, reluctantly, that Fielding had bullied her into giving false evidence. Hill triumphantly announced his enemy's discomfiture in the *London Daily Advertiser* (9 March), and on 13 March, Gascoyne issued a warrant for the arrest of Elizabeth Canning on a charge of perjury. Fielding was shaken by this turn of events and angered by Hill's insults. Once again he narrowly examined Elizabeth Canning in the presence of many witnesses, using every art he had perfected in his years of interrogating suspects "to sift the Truth out of her, and to bring her to a Confession if she was guilty." The girl "persisted," however, "in the Truth of the Evidence that she had given, and with such an Appearance of Innocence, as persuaded all present of the Justice of her Cause" (p. 307).

On 13 March, the day Gascoyne ordered Elizabeth Canning's arrest, a notice in Fielding's paper, the *Public Advertiser*, called on the town "to suspend their Judgment in the Case of the Gypsy Woman till a full State of the whole, which is now preparing by Mr. Fielding, is published." One week later – on Tuesday, 20 March – Millar published *A Clear State of the Case of Elizabeth Canning*. So brisk was the demand for this shilling pamphlet that Millar issued a so-called "Second Edition" two days later. It was the first of many ephemeral pieces published this year and the next on the question of Elizabeth Canning's guilt or innocence,[340] and for the moment it checked the tide of public opinion which, after the evidence of the Dorset witnesses and the haranguing of Hill, had begun to turn against the girl. Hill of course replied at once, abusively, in *The Story of Elizabeth Canning Considered* (29 March). And in his own account, published in July 1754 when Fielding could not defend himself, Gascoyne accused him of deliberately concealing "certificates" from more than sixty witnesses in Dorset confirming Mary Squires's alibi.[341]

Gascoyne's smear is the more unconscionable because he must have known at the time he made this accusation that Fielding – who took almost no part in the Canning case after publishing his *Clear State* of it and who did not have the "certificates" in his possession – had done all he could to make the girl's supporters produce them. When Gascoyne first learned of this evidence (which Canning's newly appointed attorney had unintentionally uncovered and tried to suppress), he appears to have told the King's counselors that Fielding was a partner to this duplicity. A messenger from the Lord Chancellor ordered Fielding to convey to Newcastle "all the Affidavits I had taken since the Gipsy' Trial which related to that Affair." But, as he explained in a letter to the Duke written from Ealing on 14 April, Fielding had not taken any such affidavits, which were in the possession of Canning's attorney.

> However in Consequence of the Commands with which your Grace was pleased to honour me yesterday, I sent my Clerk immediately to the Attorney to acquaint him with those Commands, which I doubt not he will instantly obey. This I did from my great Duty to your Grace for I have long had no Concern in this Affair, nor have I seen any of the Parties lately unless once when I was desired to send for the Girl (Canning) to my House that a great Number of Noblemen and Gentlemen might see her and ask her what Questions they pleased.

But Canning's supporters were slow to cooperate. At Ealing, his health now rapidly deteriorating, Fielding was chagrined to receive a letter from Newcastle's secretary informing him of their obstinacy and implying that he had failed to exert himself in the matter. On 27 April he wrote Newcastle as follows:

My Lord Duke

I am extremely concerned to see by a Letter which I have just received from Mr Jones by Command of your Grace that the Persons concerned for the Prosecution have not yet attended your Grace with the Affidavits in Canning^s Affair. I do assure you upon my Honour that I sent to them the Moment I first received your Grace^s Commands, and having after three Messages prevailed with them to come to me I desired them to fetch the Affidavits that I might send them to your Grace being not able to wait upon you in Person. This they said they could not do, but would go to Mr. Hume Campbell their Council, and prevail with him to attend your Grace with all their Affidavits many of which, I found were sworn after the Day mentioned in the Order of Council. I told them I apprehended the latter could not be admitted, but insisted in the strongest Terms on their laying the others immediately before your Grace, and they at last promised me they would, nor have I ever seen them since. I have now again ordered my Clerk to go to them to inform them of the last Commands I have received, but as I have no Compulsory Power over them I can not answer for their Behaviour, which indeed I have long disliked, and have therefore long ago declined giving them any Advice, nor would I unless in Obedience to your Grace have any thing to say to a Set of the most obstinate Fools I ever saw; and who seem to me rather to act from a Spleen against my Lord Mayor, than from any Motive of protecting Innocence, tho' that was certainly their Motive at first. In Truth, if I am not deceived, I suspect they desire that the Gipsey should be pardoned, and then to convince the World that she was guilty in order to cast the greater Reflection on him who was principally instrumental in obtaining such Pardon. I conclude with assuring your Grace, that I have acted in this Affair, as I shall on all Occasions with the most dutiful Regard to your Commands, and that if my Life had been at stake, as many know, I could have done no more.[342]

Fielding was exasperated at the conduct of Elizabeth Canning's friends, and for the moment at least was disposed to wash his hands of the affair. He remained convinced, however, that the girl was innocent, for a number of witnesses had come forward whose testimony exploded the gypsy's alibi and confirmed crucial details of Canning's story. (It would eventually be the case, indeed, that forty-one witnesses for

Squires were contradicted by twenty-seven witnesses for Canning.) In May, the King pardoned Mary Squires, and on 9 June the Grand Jury presented Elizabeth Canning for perjury. On 30 June, the question of the girl's guilt or innocence continued to occupy the Town as Birch wrote Philip Yorke:

> The Report of Fielding's having chang'd his Sentiments concerning it is without Foundation, for he professes himself still more convinc'd of his first opinion by affidavits in his hands, which were never call'd for by the Attorney [General] & Sollicitor [General], & which he was unwilling to obtrude in the Way of his Majesty's Mercy, which he thinks properly exerted in this & all other Cases the least dubious.

As late as 20 October, Birch assured his friend, "Mr. Fielding continues persuaded of her Innocence."[343] Fielding's belief in the justice of Elizabeth Canning's cause probably had more than a little to do with the fact that, shortly before her trial in April 1754, she petitioned the King to allow Henry Gould to represent her when certain points of law were argued.[344]

In the end Elizabeth Canning was convicted of perjury and sentenced to be transported to America. She settled in Wethersfield, Connecticut, where she joined the household of the Methodist minister Elisha Williams, a former rector of Yale University. There she married in 1756, and there in 1773 she died – never having changed her story.

···••••❧ xxxiii ❧••···

The illness which prevented Fielding from waiting on Newcastle in April 1753 he later described as "a lingering imperfect gout," for which he had been taking "the Duke of Portland's medicine" for many months, with results that seemed encouraging.[345] He was far from well, however, and the court records and newspaper reports of his activities as a justice suggest that from April to September he made the journey into town only sporadically and for short periods. Early in May his infant daughter died. This was Louisa (named presumably after another of the royal princesses, who died in 1751): christened at St. Paul's, Covent Garden, on 3 December 1752, Louisa was buried on 10 May 1753 at St. Paul's, Hammersmith,[346] where she rests with Fielding's sisters.

During the times he felt better, Fielding carried on his war against crime without sparing himself. At Bow Street on 16 May, for instance, he examined five highwaymen.[347] On 18 June, when the penny-postman was robbed and murdered by two youths near Enfield Chace, four of

Fielding's small force of intrepid constables – "runners" or "thief-takers" as they were usually called – acted efficiently to capture them.[348] In September, at the urging of his friend John Ranby – "the King's premier serjeant-surgeon," Fielding called him, "and the ablest advice, I believe, in all branches of the physical profession" – he was preparing to go to Bath, where he had taken lodgings for a month. But he was detained at Bow Street by a terrible outbreak of violent crimes, "five different murders, all committed within the space of a week, by different gangs of street robbers." The most sensational of these crimes, the robbery and brutal murder of the Earl of Harrington's cook by two soldiers of the Coldstream Guards, required Fielding's attention for several weeks, from mid-September to mid-October.[349]

During these same weeks, despite the state of his health and these other exacting duties, Fielding was able to realize his long-standing ambition to establish in the metropolis an efficient, professional police force. While "almost fatigued to death" with several murder investigations, and suffering now not only from the gout but from symptoms of cirrhosis of the liver[350] – a "dropsy," as it was then diagnosed – he was summoned by Newcastle to attend next morning at the Duke's house in Lincoln's Inn Fields, "upon some business of importance." Fielding asked to be excused, pleading illness and exhaustion; but Newcastle was peremptory. Though "in the utmost distress," Fielding was kept waiting in an antechamber until the Duke sent one of his staff to propose that he devise a plan for putting a stop to the present wave of violent crimes. Newcastle would present the plan to the Privy Council for approval.

This visit, Fielding recalled, "cost me a severe cold." Nevertheless, he set to work "and in about four days sent the Duke as regular a plan as I could form, with all the reasons and arguments I could bring to support it, drawn out in several sheets of paper." Much simpler than his abortive "Bill" of 1749 to reorganize the watch (which the Duke had consigned to the refuse heap of his miscellaneous papers), Fielding's plan was quickly approved. Though the document itself has not come to light, it is possible from various sources to deduce the terms of the scheme. As Fielding asserted, the "principal and most material of those terms was the immediately depositing 600 l. in my hands; at which small charge I undertook to demolish the then reigning gangs," and to put "the civil policy" into good order. He might well call this a "small charge," for in the two years or so in which the Crown had resorted to the expedient of increasing by £100 the statutory reward of £40 for apprehending a felon and prosecuting him to conviction, the treasury had paid out £11,100[351] – not only without curtailing criminal activity, but with the effect of encouraging unscrupulous thief-takers, such as the infamous Stephen Macdaniel, to frame and hang innocent men.[352]

It was Fielding who, for these reasons, had persuaded the Privy Council to discontinue the system of extraordinary rewards by royal proclamation, which ended in June 1752. And in the event the annual expense of Fielding's police "never exceeded" £400.[353]

Fielding used this money to form the nucleus of a professional police force, consisting of seven constables – "all men of known and approved fidelity and intrepidity" – whom he reinforced, when occasion demanded, from a pool of trustworthy ex-constables held in reserve.[354] He had actually organized this band of regulars earlier: William Pentlow, Keeper of New Prison, continued to be the most active member of the group.[355] But, as Fielding explained in his "Memorial" on the subject, these "Associated Constables had for some time desisted from their undertaking" because they were not only inadequately rewarded considering the risks they took, but were treated with contempt by the public they served. For their trouble, Fielding complained, his officers had

> gained only the Appelation of Thieftakers, a name become so odious not only to the common People but in Courts of Justice, that they had often little or no Share of the Money allowed ... for the apprehending Thieves, which was given away to Prosecutors, and their Witnesses, against the Letter as well as meaning of the Act, from these Men who had earned it often with yᵉ Loss of Part of their Blood.

The inequity to which Fielding refers became the subject of a judgment by the Attorney General in January 1754. No doubt encouraged by Fielding himself, six of his "myrmidons" stated their grievances with respect to the division of reward money, and he forwarded their petition to Newcastle, insisting on behalf of his men that the statutes specified "none but the actual Apprehenders of the Felons are ... entitled to any Share" in the rewards. This narrow interpretation of the law was rejected by the Attorney General, however, who ruled that those who discovered felons and those who prosecuted them were also entitled to a share of the money.[356] In any case, the government had already allotted Fielding all the money he needed to reengage his officers and establish the police on a secure basis.

Essentially, Fielding's method (succinctly summarized by his brother) was "quick notice and sudden pursuit."[357] But the announcement Fielding placed in the *Public Advertiser* (20 November 1753) affords a fuller explanation. Victims or witnesses of crimes were urged "to give immediate Notice of the Fact, with the best Description they can produce" of the criminals to Fielding at Bow Street or to his brother at his house in the Strand, "or to leave Notice at any of the Turnpikes within Five Miles of London." Such witnesses, on application to Fielding or his brother, "shall immediately receive a full Satisfaction for any

Charges" they have incurred. The *Public Advertiser* served as the vehicle by which notices and descriptions of things lost or stolen would be broadcast, "since that Paper alone will be taken in by all those who are concern'd in the Execution of the ... Scheme." In addition, accomplices to crimes were encouraged by promises of clemency and anonymity to impeach their guilty colleagues. A crucial feature of the plan was later emphasized by John Fielding in the *Public Advertiser* (20 December 1754): on receiving notice of a crime, the Fieldings "would immediately dispatch a Set of brave Fellows in Pursuit, who ... are always ready to set out to any Part of this Town or Kingdom, on a Quarter of an Hour's Notice."

Fielding chose the "runners" with great care, chiefly from among those reputable householders who had already served their parishes as constables and proved their mettle. And having chosen such men, he was careful to instruct them not only in their duties, but in the proper exercise and extent of their authority under the law. In dedicating to Fielding his *Observations on the Office of Constable* (March 1754), Saunders Welch declared that in his eight years' tenure as High Constable he had never had a complaint or action brought against him; he owed "that safety," he acknowledged, "to the ready access to, and friendly advice and caution of Mr. Justice FIELDING." (Indeed, though he died before he could perfect it, Fielding left behind his own *Treatise on the Office of Constable*, which his brother edited and published in 1761.) Besides making certain that his officers were fit and disciplined and amply rewarded, Fielding was concerned to minimize as far as possible the terrible risks they took, recommending to the legislature that assaulting an officer in the line of duty should be considered a special offense. When one of his men captured a vicious robber who wounded him with a knife, Fielding exclaimed in the *Public Advertiser* (28 December 1752): "If it be not possible to reward these brave Officers, who so well and faithfully discharge their Duty, it is Pity that the Law doth not at least afford them some special Protection, by punishing any Assault on them in the Execution of their Office with the most exemplary Severity." Indeed, the bond of mutual respect, even of affection, between Fielding and his "myrmidons" attests to the kind of man he was. As Fielding's illness grew steadily worse, Welch hoped that "heaven [would] spare a life, invaluable to his friends and family, hazarded, I may say with truth, sacrificed to the public welfare, I mean a magistrate, whose good heart, and great abilities, justly entitle him to the affection of every worthy mind."[358]

By mid-October 1753, soon after the government had enabled him to reengage these men, "the whole gang of cut-throats was entirely dispersed, seven of them were in actual custody, and the rest driven, some out of town, and others out of the kingdom."[359] His health "now

reduced to the last extremity," Fielding nevertheless made every effort
to ensure that the cases against these villains were airtight. He "often
spent whole days, nay sometimes whole nights" accumulating evidence.
On 20 October, writing to Philip Yorke, Birch declared his admiration
for Fielding's selfless exertions on behalf of the public, but confessed
his concern that these labors were shortening his friend's life: Fielding

> is at present fully employ'd in detecting the numerous Gangs of
> Banditti, who infest all the Roads about town, & is indefatigable in
> the Execution of his Office, tho' he has been for some time in a very
> ill state of Health, which alarm'd his Friends, & induc'd him to call
> in Dr. Heberden, who has remov'd his Jaundice, but not yet restor'd
> his appetite.[360]

To the roll of doctors who tried to stop Fielding's decline was now
added William Heberden (1710–1801), his near neighbor in Cecil Street;
a learned and charitable man, Heberden was one of the most respected
physicians of his time.

But Fielding had the satisfaction of knowing his sacrifices were
not in vain. By December he could boast in the *Public Advertiser* (7
December) that since his plan had been approved, "no one Robbery,
or Cruelty hath been heard of in the Streets, except the Robbery of one
Woman, the Person accused of which was immediately taken." He was
sanguine enough to suppose that if his fellow magistrates in the suburbs
and provinces cooperated in this effort, "not only the Town, but the
whole Kingdom may be restored to Safety, and the Subjects pass and
repass upon their lawful Occasions free from the dreadful Apprehensions
of being robb'd, murder'd, or maim'd." A week later (14 December)
the same paper exulted: "With great Pleasure we can assure the Public,
that since the apprehending the great Gang of Cut-throats, not one
dangerous Blow, or Shot, or Wound has been given either in the Roads
or Streets in or near this Town." In this respect the winter of 1753, he
later declared, stood "unrival'd, during a course of many years."

Having accomplished this miracle (as it might well have seemed to
the inhabitants of this violent town), Fielding at last left Bow Street
for the country, "in a very weak and deplorable condition" – afflicted
indeed "with no fewer or less diseases than a jaundice, a dropsy, and
an asthma, altogether uniting their forces in the destruction of a body
so entirely emaciated, that it had lost all its muscular flesh." His was
"now no longer what is called a Bath case," and he therefore discharged
the lodgings he had kept there but never used.

He did not leave town, however, without attempting to reward
Saunders Welch, who had served him so well throughout his magistracy – a man, Fielding declared, "whom I never think or speak of but
with love and esteem."[361] On 6 December 1753 he wrote the Lord

Chancellor, recommending that Welch be appointed to the magistracy for both Westminster and Middlesex.[362] Welch would not in fact be commissioned a justice until after Fielding's death. In January 1754, however, John Fielding was empowered to take his brother's place as Court Justice: on 5 January he was commissioned magistrate for Middlesex County; on 14 January he received the sacrament and took the oaths qualifying him to act in that capacity.[363]

xxxiv

As he recalled some months later, Fielding by this time had begun, "in earnest, to look on my case as desperate, and I had vanity enough to rank my self with those heroes who, of old times, became voluntary sacrifices to the good of the public." But it was a motive stronger than altruism that drove him to implement his plan for a police at the risk of his life. At the beginning of winter his "private affairs" had taken on, as he put it, "a gloomy aspect." Indeed, they had become so dire – despite what ought to have been the ample income he enjoyed from various sources – that on 31 December 1753 he felt it necessary to borrow from Millar the extraordinary sum of £1,892.[364] Fielding, with some truth, attributed his straitened circumstances to his being too honest to make a job of the magistracy (as his predecessor DeVeil had done); and he complained that the annual pension the government paid him was inadequate, because his "great patron," the Duke of Newcastle, was mistakenly convinced that, however demanding and disagreeable the office of principal justice for Westminster might be, it must be "very lucrative." No doubt Fielding would have fared better if Bedford, his "princely" benefactor and Newcastle's hated rival, had not left the government in 1751 to go into opposition; but Bedford no longer influenced the Treasury. Leasing Fordhook also taxed Fielding's resources; Ranby would pay £800 for it with only eleven years remaining on the lease. Even so, debts of this magnitude are hard to account for. Aware that he would leave his family "very slenderly provided for," Fielding chose to apply himself unsparingly to implement his plan and establish the new police force on a secure footing. He did so, hastening his death, in the hope that he would recommend his widow and children to the care of a grateful nation. Besides, he well knew "what a poor sacrifice" he made, "being indeed no other than the giving up what I saw little likelihood of being able to hold much longer, and which, upon the terms I held it, nothing but the weakness of human nature could represent to me as worth holding at all."

Fielding remained at Fordhook during most of January. The weather was bitter cold and heavy rains caused flooding along the Thames westward, making travel dangerous.[365] In February he returned to Bow Street and, when not wholly incapacitated by illness, continued his war against crime for more than two months, signing recognizances[366] and gathering the evidence needed to convict, among many others, the gentleman highwayman John Parry, who had terrorized the polite inhabitants of Mayfair.[367] By April, however, he could carry on no longer. Announcing Parry's capture, the *Public Advertiser* (2 April 1754) observed that, since Fielding's plan had taken effect, "the Publick ... have suffer'd fewer Outrages than have happened in any Winter this twenty Years." Fielding, the report continued, had "communicated" the plan to his brother John and Saunders Welch, "who are determined to bring it to that Perfection of which it is capable."

That Fielding continued performing these duties so long required great strength of will and heroic courage. When he returned to town in February, he was in an appalling state of health and desperate enough to seek advice from the notorious empiric, Joshua "Spot" Ward (1685–1761), whose "Pill and Drop," which Ward represented as a universal nostrum, were in fact virulent compounds of antimony and arsenic. Until now, Ward had been for Fielding a figure of fun, a standing butt of his satires since 1737. Ward wished his patient had consulted him sooner and recommended that he be "tapped" at once to drain the fluid which grotesquely distended his belly. The operation relieved him of fourteen quarts of water; in his weak and emaciated condition, however, the sudden relaxation nearly killed him. He was at the worst, he recalled, on 6 March, "that memorable day when the public lost Mr. Pelham" – after which he gradually regained strength. Two months later his belly was again full and the operation was repeated: this time thirteen quarts were drawn, but he found he bore it better, his surgeon having fortified him with a dose of laudanum.

The terrible winter hung on. Heavy snows fell and strong winds blew.[368] But two events of this otherwise evil season would have cheered him. On 19 March, Millar brought out the new edition of *Jonathan Wild*, which Fielding had thoroughly revised. And on 6 April at St. Paul's, Covent Garden, his new-born son was christened Allen,[369] in honor of his father's beloved patron, to whom he hoped to entrust the future welfare of his family.

It was probably during these weeks of March and April, as he slowly gained strength, that Fielding read Bolingbroke's posthumous *Works* with mounting indignation and resolved to form a reply. Since no prudent member of the trade wished, or dared, to meddle with so rank a farrago of blasphemy and irreligion, David Mallet took it on himself to publish the collection, which appeared on 6 March in five handsome quarto volumes. In the *Covent-Garden Journal* (Nos. 46 and 69), alluding to Bolingbroke's attacks on scripture in *Letters on the Study and Use of History*, Fielding warned of the consequences to society if such pernicious doctrines became fashionable. Now Mallet had enabled his lordship to infect the air with still stronger emissions of infidelity in the form of eighty-one "Fragments or Minutes of Essays"; before the month was out the free-thinking bakers, cobblers, and comedians of the Robin Hood Society were debating the merits of the proposition, That Bolingbroke had done more than the Apostles to serve mankind.[370] Fielding, by his own account, began reading these fragments with "a very high prejudice to the doctrines said to have been established in them," yet with "the highest, and strongest prepossession, in favour of the abilities of the author."[371] When he had finished reading, he found "my prepossessions greatly abated, and my prejudices not in the least removed." However insubstantial and "chimerical" he knew Bolingbroke's principles to be, Fielding understood that the author's name alone gave them a certain authority and made it likely that many readers would swallow the poison. Preparing to defend religion against so formidable an adversary, Fielding, according to Murphy, made "long extracts and arguments from the fathers and the most eminent writers of controversy" – worksheets Murphy later saw in the possession of John Fielding. As usual, however, Fielding's "antidote" to this poison would be ridicule. He would expose Bolingbroke's philosophy as a tissue of contradictions so hastily and contemptuously thrown together that it could only have been meant in jest, as a kind of game indulging the author's perverse taste for sporting with the gravest subjects. His lordship's life, Fielding declares, "was one scene of the wonderful throughout":

That, as the temporal happiness, the civil liberties and properties of Europe, were the game of his earliest youth, there could be no sport so adequate to the entertainment of his advanced age, as the eternal and final happiness of all mankind.

In his "Comment" Fielding got no farther than the first of the eighty-one fragments. Why he abandoned the task is not known. But to refute effectively a philosophical work, even one as nugatory as this collection of "Minutes of Essays," would tax the patience and powers of an ill man; and if he meant to finish the task later in Lisbon (as the absence of Bolingbroke's *Works* from the catalogue of books he left behind might suggest), he would probably have found it impossible. The censors of the Inquisition inspected every book brought into Portugal – a process that not only took several months, but would certainly have ended in the confiscation of volumes such as these.[372]

···=➤ XXXV ◆=···

Early in May, in the vain hope that spring would soon bring kinder weather, Fielding left Bow Street for the last time and returned to Fordhook, his "little house ... in the country," as with excessive modesty he called the mansion in which, in the next century, Lady Byron, the poet's wife, saw fit to reside. There at Ealing, he believed, he enjoyed "the best air ... in the whole kingdom," for the place was higher and drier than the Kensington Gravel Pits, "and more open towards the south, whilst it is guarded from the north by a ridge of hills, and from the smells and smoke of London by its distance."

His dropsy stubbornly resisted the powers of Ward's remedies, so he made "a short trial" of a milk diet, which proved equally ineffectual. Next he tried "the virtues of tar-water," which Bishop Berkeley – "one of the greatest scholars and best of men," Fielding called him – had extravagantly recommended in Siris (1744). Fielding had read this curious metaphysical treatise some years earlier; he was reminded of it now by Charlotte Lennox (1720–1804), "the inimitable and shamefully distress'd author of the Female Quixote," with whom he formed a friendship not long after praising her work in the Covent-Garden Journal (No. 24). Every morning and evening Fielding dosed himself, according to Berkeley's prescription, with half a pint of tar-water. The new regime seemed to help: he felt better and his appetite returned. But, inevitably, by the end of May his belly "became again ripe for the trochar"; he was encouraged, nonetheless, that this third tapping drew only ten quarts of water from him, and afterward he scarcely felt faint at all.

Fielding was naturally of a sanguine disposition, but he could not fail to notice that the intervals between these operations were becoming shorter; and the days continuing cold and wet, he could not throw off a lingering asthma. His "physical friends" (and he had many) concurred that his only chance of life was having a proper summer in which to gain strength enough to support the rigors of another winter. But even in June the weather did not improve, and Fielding resolved to seek a warmer climate abroad. He thought first of Aix en Provence, but the long journey overland would be too arduous and too dear. He thought next of Marseilles and the ports of the Mediterranean, but there were no ships scheduled to sail soon enough. Lisbon was farther still to the south, and because of England's thriving commerce with Portugal, an early passage could be easily arranged. On about 12 June, John Fielding learned that "excellent accommodations for passengers" were available on the Queen of Portugal, due to sail for Lisbon in three days' time.

As it happened, it would be a fortnight before Fielding embarked, but he began at once to prepare his family for the voyage and to put his affairs in order. It was probably at this time that he drew up his will, written in his own hand and witnessed by Margaret Collier, Richard Boor (the steward who managed the farm at Fordhook), and the maidservant Isabella Ash.[373] He bequeathed his entire estate to Ralph Allen, the richest and most benevolent man he knew, and appointed him his executor. He asked that Allen sell all his property (except his twenty shares in the Universal Register Office) and that the money raised be used in part to purchase annuities "for the Lives of my dear Wife Mary, and my Daughters Harriet and Sophia," and in part to keep in trust for his sons William and Allen until they reached the age of twenty-three. As for his shares in the Register Office, he asked that ten be given to his widow immediately, whereas Harriet and Sophia were to receive the accumulated profits of seven and three shares, respectively, when they reached the age of twenty-one. The haste in which Fielding prepared this document is evident from the fact that he had no time to inquire whether Allen would accept such a responsibility. In the event, he declined to do so, preferring to do good to Fielding's family in his own way.

There are other signs that Fielding and his friends understood his end was drawing near. By June, John had left his house in the Strand and taken his brother's place at Bow Street.[374] And counting on rumors of his author's imminent demise to stimulate a demand for his works, Millar began advertising Fielding's books at regular intervals in the *Public Advertiser* – a list of eleven titles from *Joseph Andrews* to the new edition of *Jonathan Wild*.[375] As Thomas Birch informed Philip Yorke, Fielding's "last Request to Mr. Millar, his Bookseller, was to take all Care, when he should hear of his Death, to prevent his Life from being undertaken by any of the Grubstreet Writers, who are so ready & officious on such Occasions."[376]

So grave was Fielding's condition that on 20 June one of the evening papers reported he had died – though, as the *Public Advertiser* (22 June) assured its readers, he was actually in better health than he had been "for some Months past." If somewhat exaggerated, the report of Fielding's death was at least understandable. To those who saw him, Fielding declared,

> I presented a spectacle of the highest horror. The total loss of limbs was apparent to all who saw me, and my face contained marks of a most diseased state, if not of death itself. Indeed so ghastly was my countenance, that timorous women with child had abstained from my house, for fear of the ill consequences of looking at me.[377]

For that matter, he could not bear to look at himself and had the mirrors covered with cloths.[378]

Among the friends who came to say farewell was James Harris. This at least is a reasonable inference from the tribute Harris later paid his friend. Trying to define the essence of Fielding's genius and character, Harris, in his unpublished memorial, distinguished several kinds of wits:

> There is a fourth order of men, and those of no mean import, whose Wit and Humour keep pace with their Condition. When Health and Fortune abound, then are Wit and Humour abundant also. If the Scene change, the Spring soon fails, and every attempt to exert themselves proves fruitless and vain. Nothing like this ever happened to our Author, whose Wit, though it might have had perhaps its intensions and remissions, yet never deserted him in his most unprosperous hours, nor even when Death itself openly lookt him in ye face.
>
> Two Friends made him a visit in his last Illness [on his leaving England], when his Constitution was so broken, that twas thought he could not survive a week. To explain to them his Indifference as to a protraction of Life, he with his usual humour related them the following story. A Man (sd. He) under condemnation at Newgate was just setting out for Tyburn, when there arrived a Reprieve. His Friends who recd. ye news with uncommon Joy, prest him instantly to be blooded; they were feard (they said) his Spirits on a change so unexpected must be agitated in the highest degree. Not in the least (replied the Hero) no agitation at all. If I am not hanged this Sessions, I know I shall ye next.

···➤ XXXVI ◆─···

The captain of the *Queen of Portugal* having twice put off sailing (he was Richard Veal, a blustering, kind-hearted old salt with half a century's experience at sea), Fielding invited him to dinner at Fordhook to settle details of the passage. For £30 Veal agreed to carry Fielding and five members of his family to Lisbon: his wife Mary; "her friend" Margaret Collier, as he pointedly refers to her; his daughter Harriet, now aged eleven and the only surviving child of his union with Charlotte; and the servants Isabella Ash and William. They were to board ship on Wednesday, 26 June – the captain assuring Fielding he "would not stay a moment for the greatest man in the world."

Harris might admire his friend's jesting in adversity, but as dawn broke on the 26th Fielding could not subdue his grief:

> ON this day, the most melancholy sun I had ever beheld arose, and found me awake at my house at Fordhook. By the light of this sun, I was, in my own opinion, last to behold and take leave of some of

those creatures on whom I doated with a mother-like fondness, guided by nature and passion, and uncured and unhardened by all the doctrine of that philosophical school where I had learnt to bear pains and to despise death.

In this situation, as I could not conquer nature, I submitted entirely to her, and she made as great a fool of me as she had ever done of any woman whatsoever: under pretence of giving me leave to enjoy, she drew me in to suffer the company of my little ones, during eight hours; and I doubt not whether, in that time, I did not undergo more than in all my distemper.

At noon his coach stood ready to carry the party to Rotherhithe, where they would board ship. It was Mary now "who behaved more like a heroine and philosopher, tho' at the same time the tenderest mother in the world" as they kissed their children goodbye – William, Sophia, and Allen – whom they left behind at Fordhook in the care of Mary's mother, Elizabeth Daniel. Some friends had come to see them off, but Sarah Fielding was ill herself and remained at Bath to take the waters.[379] Accompanying the party on the two-hour journey to Rotherhithe (and seeing them on their way as far as Gravesend) were Saunders Welch and Jane Collier, good friends both. Jane – a lively, intelligent woman – had recently expressed her admiration for Fielding's works in several passages of her novel The Cry (March 1754), a work in which she and Sarah Fielding collaborated; and on the eve of this melancholy day Fielding presented her with a rare edition of his favorite Horace, inscribed "as a Memorial (however poor) of the highest Esteem for an Understanding more than Female, mixed with virtues almost more than human."[380]

When they reached Rotherhithe, Fielding, like so much dead freight, had to be hoisted on board, in a chair lifted with pulleys – a spectacle which moved the assembled sailors and watermen to mockery and jeers. It was, Fielding remarked (who once subscribed to a more optimistic view of human nature), "a lively picture of that cruelty and inhumanity, in the nature of men, which I have often contemplated with concern; and which leads the mind into a train of very uncomfortable and melancholy thoughts." He now believed that to remedy this taint in our blood, men must be "polish'd and refin'd, in such manner as human nature requires, to produce that perfection of which it is susceptible, and to purge away that malevolence of disposition, of which, at our birth we partake in common with the savage creation." He would not in fact think of "enroling myself among the voyage-writers" until a week later, when, cabin-bound in the Downs near Deal, he found himself without a companion to talk to and sought by writing to relieve the oppressive solitude; he was of a "social disposition" and hated to be alone ([28 July]). But the journal Fielding then began to keep is remarkable for such passages, in which the once genial creator of Parson Adams and Tom Jones reflects irritably on the characters of men: he exclaims against the petty tyranny of sea captains, of river pilots and customs officers; he seethes at the exactions of scullers and innkeepers and fishmongers. The world through which the helpless travelers move, like the original outcasts from Eden (the analogy is Fielding's own [27 June]), resembles Hobbes's state of nature, in which "every man spunges and raps whatever he can get," the laborer struggling "as hard to cheat his employer of two pence in a day's labour, as an honest tradesman will to cheat his customers of the same sum in a yard of cloth or silk" ([16] July).

Despite such fitful moods, mingling a cynical disenchantment and (given the wretched state of his health) an understandable world-weariness, Fielding meant not merely to vent his indignation but to serve the public. The *Journal* – "which, if I should live to finish it, a matter of no great certainty, if indeed of any great hope to me, will be probably the last [work] I shall ever undertake" ([21] July) – would have a useful purpose: by alerting the legislature to the evils he complained of, he hoped to amend the maritime laws and to curb the licentiousness and greed of the people which threatened to introduce "a pure state of anarchy" ([16] July).

But Fielding's tone in the *Journal* is not always so sharp. He was not by nature a morose or cynical man, and much that he saw and experienced on his voyage to Lisbon gave him pleasure. He heartily acknowledged the many kindnesses of Mrs. Roberts,[381] "that polite and good lady" who charitably supplied the family with fresh provisions as they remained wind-bound for days at Ryde on the Isle of Wight ([18] July). He warmed to Captain Veal, who, for all his imperiousness and roughness of manner, "was one of the best-natur'd fellows alive," caring tenderly for his crew and extending "his humanity, if I may so call it," even to his cats ([24 July]). Fielding could still delight in such instances of good nature though he found fewer of them now. He swelled, too, with patriotic pride at the grandeur of Wren's Royal Hospital at Greenwich and the spectacle of so many fine ships in the Thames and Solent:

> For my own part [he declared, stirred by the view from Ryde], I confess myself so entirely fond of a sea prospect, that I think nothing on the land can equal it; and if it be set off with shipping, I desire to borrow no ornament from *terra firma*. A fleet of ships is, in my opinion, the noblest object which the art of man hath ever produced; and far beyond the power of those architects who deal in brick, in stone, or in marble.   ([18] July)

Indeed, remembering now the magnificent display of British naval might Walpole annually staged off Spithead, he set down his final opinion of his old antagonist: "one of the best of men and of ministers." Fielding had come to terms at last with the Great Man.

In nothing does he seem so unchanged as in the pleasure he takes in eating. His appetite having returned, he relishes again in relating them the meals he has taken in good-humored company. Though diminished a little by the badness of his teeth, which made the act of chewing a sometimes tragic adventure, there are the familiar joys of bacon and beans, of roast mutton and venison (a welcome present of half a buck from the New Forest). But he waxes eloquent on the subject of Devon cider and the local seafood – "of soals, and whitings, and lobsters, far superior to those which adorn a city-feast" (13 July) – and he commends most particularly the john dory, on which he "gloriously regaled" himself, "washing it down with some good claret" ([23] July).

As for the character of the work he was composing, it is unique among his writings. The genius that enlivened the characters of his fiction and shines through some of the finest prose in the language had not yet deserted him. (There are, to be sure, occasional awkward turns of syntax and one or two obscure passages which are sometimes taken as signs of his declining powers, but they may as easily be blamed on those who saw the manuscript through the press.) The deftness of his portraiture is as sure as ever. Most memorable and fully rounded is the captain (unnamed in the *Journal*, but identified in Fielding's letters as Richard Veal), with his cockade, scarlet coat, and outsize sword, swaggering like a bashaw in his cabin – "a man of gallantry," moreover, who "at the age of seventy ... had the finicalness of Sir Courtly Nice, with the roughness of Surly; and while he was deaf himself, had a voice capable of deafening all others" (27 June). Hardly less striking are Mrs. Francis, the furious mistress of the inn at Ryde, and her nonentity of a husband,[382] whose dispositions perfectly complemented one another: "She was indeed as vinegar to oil, or a brisk wind to a standing-pool, and preserved all from stagnation and corruption" ([14] July).

But these are not characters in a work of fiction. They are figures vividly copied from life – and if Veal remains (transparently) anonymous, Mrs. Francis and her husband are named for all to point at. For one of the most remarkable facts about the *Journal* – a fact perhaps symptomatic of the sobering effects of his years at Bow Street – is that it represents Fielding's repudiation of the pleasantries and indirections of mere literature. Homer's *Odyssey* and Fénelon's *Telemachus* were among Fielding's models when in *Joseph Andrews* he defined his new species of writing, "the comic Epic-Poem in Prose," and, as a mirror of "Truth," preferred it to the deceitful narratives of biased historians.

Now, defining this new genre in the Preface to the *Journal*, his conversion is complete:

> But, in reality, the Odyssy, the Telemachus, and all of that kind, are
> to the voyage-writing I here intend, what romance is to true history,
> the former being the confounder and corrupter of the latter. I am far
> from supposing, that Homer, Hesiod, and the other antient poets
> and mythologists, had any settled design to pervert and confuse the
> records of antiquity; but it is certain they have effected it; and, for
> my part, I must confess I should have honoured and loved Homer
> more had he written a true history of his own times in humble prose,
> than those noble poems that have so justly collected the praise of all
> ages; for though I read these with more admiration and astonishment,
> I still read Herodotus, Thucydides and Xenophon, with more amuse-
> ment and more satisfaction.

We could not hope for a more striking measure of the reordering of
Fielding's literary and intellectual values than this wish to see Homer
transformed into the Bishop Burnet of ancient Greece, writing "a true
history of his own times in humble prose."

···➧ XXXVii ➧─···

Under favorable conditions the voyage to Lisbon would have taken a
fortnight, but the *Queen of Portugal* took forty-two days to complete
the passage. Not until Sunday, 30 June, did they proceed downriver to
Gravesend – by which time Mary was in agony from a raging tooth and
Fielding, apprehensive that his belly would fill again while he was at
sea with no surgeon at hand, had been tapped a fourth time by his
friend William Hunter and relieved of ten quarts of water. On Monday,
1 July, Saunders Welch and Jane Collier said their sad goodbyes and
returned to London.

Now, however, contrary winds sprang up and persisted, as if Nature
herself wished to prevent the departure of the most English of authors
from his native country. The ship lay off Deal for a week before a shift
in the wind enabled it to make the Mother Bank off Ryde, the Isle of
Wight, where it dropped anchor on 11 July and where it would remain
for another week. On 12 July, a Friday, Fielding wrote his brother
"Jack" to assure him and Mary's mother that they were all safe aboard
ship:

> where we had last Night in Safety the Pleasure of hearing the Winds
> roar over our Heads in as violent a Tempest as I have known, and

where my only Consideration were the Fears which must possess any Friend of ours, (if there is happily any such) who really makes our Well being the Object of his Concern especially if such Friend should be totally unexperienced in Sea-Affairs. I therefore beg that on the Day you receive this M^{rs}. Daniel may know that we are just risen from Breakfast in Health and Spirits this 12th Instant at 9 in the Morning. Our Voyage hath proved fruitful in Adventures all which being to be written in the Book, you must postpone y^r. Curiosity.

Fielding could not know just how depressed Mrs. Daniel felt at her daughter's departure and at the burden of domestic responsibilities she had had to assume at Fordhook; but he knew she was anxious and hoped to cheer her up. He wished also to assure John that he had placed him and the other members of the party in capable hands. Captain Veal, he writes, is

a most able and experienced Seaman to whom other Captains seem to pay such Deference that they attend and watch his Motions, and think themselves only safe when they act under his Direction and Example. Our Ship in Truth seems to give Laws on the Water with as much Authority and Superiority as you dispense Laws to the Public and Examples to y^r Brethren in Commission.[383]

On Saturday the 13th Mary urged her husband to go ashore, to lodge at Mrs. Francis's house of (as it proved) dubious hospitality until they could continue the voyage. Though "a great lover of the sea," Fielding was eager to escape the confinement of his cabin and to breathe fresh air; but being, as he put it, "dead luggage" and "incapable of any bodily motion without external impulse," he was carried ashore with difficulty. It was Mary – "a faithful friend, an amiable companion, and a tender nurse" – who saw to it that he was comfortably settled in a dry, warm barn belonging to Mrs. Francis, situated in a spot commanding a beautiful prospect.

Having suffered for five days the ill nature and exorbitancies of Mrs. Francis, whom Fielding likens to a Fury in Paradise – and having happily survived the last-minute emergency of a misplaced chest of china tea, that "sovereign cordial" – Fielding and his family departed Ryde on 18 July, and, blown by a fickle wind in crazy stages, found themselves three days later anchored in Tor Bay, off the Devon coast, where they remained confined, agreeably enough, for another week.

On the 21st Fielding took the opportunity to write Welch on some point of business. On the 22nd he wrote "Jack." He had "soon remembered the Country," so very agreeable and so abundant in "the finest of Fish, Turbut, vast Soals and Whitings for less than you can eat Plaice in Mdd^x." that the banishment of the Jacobite Lord Cromarty from

Scotland to Devon struck him as "somewhat less cruel than that of Ovid from Rome to Pontus." As they were now "in the midst of the South hams a Place famous for Cyder and I think the best in England," Fielding spent nearly four pounds for two hogsheads of the liquor which he sent home as presents to John, Welch, Dr. Hunter, and Millar – "and I wish you all merry over it." The gesture was typically generous and typically imprudent; for he was worried, with good reason, about money. John caused him "much Uneasiness" in a recent letter by doubting the honesty of Boor, the steward at Fordhook, who was incurring unusual expenses hiring laborers to bring in the harvest.

> If he is not trusty [Fielding wrote] he is a Fool; but that is very possible for him to be, at least to catch at a lesser, and dishonest Profit, which is present and certain in Preference to what is in all Respects it° Reverse. Pray give me as perfect Ease as you can in this particular. I begin to despair of letting my House this Summer. I hope the Sale of my Wine may be more depended on: for the almost miraculous Dilatoriness of our Voyage, tho it hath added something to the Pleasure, hath added much more to the Expence of it.

Indeed, he was tempted to borrow twenty pounds from Welch. But Welch was already helping to float the farm, apparently, and Fielding "would not for good Reasons be too much a Debtor to the best of Friends." In closing, he hoped for "a ten Hours Gale from North or East," which would carry them to Land's End, where he promised "most cheerfully" to drink John's health "with all our Friends left behind us in England."[384]

But the wind would not change, and for the next several days Fielding occupied himself aboard ship with his journal. The goodness and cheapness of the local fish inspired thoughts of how to feed the nation's poor – and the delicious john dory prompted facetious compliments to Quin and Macklin, the epicures among his actor friends. By 25 July his belly was full again and was causing shortness of breath. A surgeon tapped him, and this time (it was the fifth such operation he had borne) relieved him of nine quarts of water. Still the wind blew from the southwest. So perverse was the behavior of the elements that Captain Veal thought himself bewitched – the witch in question being Mrs. Francis, who he believed had cursed his ship out of anger at Fielding's not having spent more money at her house.

At last, on Saturday, 27 July, the wind turned, and in fair weather they set sail for Portugal, moving now so swiftly "that the shore appeared to move from us, as fast as we did from the shore." Fielding was glad the waiting was over; and the wind's blowing the passive vessel onward seemed to him a kind of parable of life: he thought, "with what different success we proceeded, under the influence of a superior

power, which while we lay almost idle ourselves, pushed us forward on
our intended voyage."

...➤ XXXVIII ◄...

Once under way the voyage was soon completed, and too uneventfully
to inspire much comment. Fielding admired the simple piety of Captain
Veal and his excellent crew. The seasickness of the women sank him
again into melancholy solitude: it could not have happened, Fielding
mused, "to one who disliked it more than myself, or to myself at a
season when I wanted more food for my social disposition, or could
converse less wholsomely and happily with my own thoughts." It was
owing to this same set of circumstances, depriving him of the sociable
talk he enjoyed at the best of times and needed now to distract him
from the sad thoughts that filled his mind, that he had begun writing
his journal some weeks before: "some of the most amusing pages [he
reflected] ... were possibly the production of the most disagreeable
hours which ever haunted the author" ([28 July]). The majesty of
sunset and moonrise over the waters thrilled him, however, bringing to
mind the story of creation in Genesis: "Compared to these the pageantry
of theatres, or splendor of courts, are sights almost below the regard of
children" ([31 July]).

Fielding's first impressions of Portugal were less edifying. It seemed
a country not only alien but ominously infernal. On Monday, 5 August,
they sighted land for the first time since leaving Devon – the Berlenga
Islands, a place fifty miles north of Lisbon which served as a penal
colony for "malefactors, who are banished hither for a term, for divers
small offences." Arriving next morning at the mouth of the Tagus, they
passed the Rock of Lisbon, on the summit of which, in a hermitage,
lived an old Englishman who, having many years previously converted
to Catholicism, had ever since prepared himself for death by doing
penance for the sins of his youth. As they paused at the mouth of the
great river until the tide turned, they surveyed the uninviting country
that awaited them – a burnt-over scrubland of stunted trees scorched
by the heat and drought; it was nothing like the green and pleasant
country they had left behind:

[we] had the pleasure of surveying the face of the country, the soil
of which, at this season, exactly resembles an old brick kill, or a field
where the greensward is pared up and set a-burning or rather a-
smoaking, in little heaps, to manure the land. This sight will, perhaps,

of all others, make an Englishman proud of and pleased with his own country, which in verdure excels, I believe, every other country.

From the "Paradise" of Arthur's Glastonbury, his birthplace, Fielding in his forty-seventh year had come to this. Even the pilot who came aboard, the first Portuguese they spoke to, resembles in Fielding's account a latter-day Charon and the Tagus he will help them navigate another Acheron.

In the afternoon they entered the Tagus and passed along a coast of old fortresses and ruined buildings. The firing of a gun gave warning that they were to proceed no farther than the Tower of Belém ("the castle of Bellisle," Fielding called it),[385] where they cast anchor with Lisbon, three miles away, spread out before them. Before they could complete the voyage, they had to pass inspection by "magistrates of health" and insolent customs officers, who deprived Fielding of one of the solaces he most relied on, his snuff and tobacco.

As dawn broke on Wednesday, 7 August, they were anchored at Lisbon and from the deck surveyed the city. It was medieval Lisbon Fielding saw – the city as it was one year before the earthquake reduced it to rubble. And it was unlike any other city he had seen, with its large white buildings – houses, churches, convents, all of them white – rising tier on tier up the steep hillsides. From a distance it was beautiful; but on a closer approach he thought the buildings lacked "every kind of ornament" and "all idea of beauty vanishe[d] at once." He imagined how dismayed a man might be if translated here through time from ancient Palmyra: "in how glorious a light would the antient architecture appear to him? and what desolation and destruction of arts and sciences would he conclude had happened between the several æra's of these cities?"

At seven in the evening, after a series of annoying delays, Fielding found himself at last in a chaise on shore, being "driven through the nastiest city in the world, tho' at the same time one of the most populous." They reached "a kind of coffee-house" a mile from the city – perhaps, as tradition has it, one of the inns on the Rua Sacramento à Lapa where Byron later stayed, in the district then known as Buenos Ayres. It was pleasantly situated on the brow of a hill, from which he could view the Tagus from Lisbon to the sea, and the way home. He had a good supper, and the bill was dear enough to summon up thoughts of hostelries along "the Bath road, between Newbury and London." He remembered, too, that other traveler Aeneas, who, after an arduous voyage, disembarked with his friends on the welcome shore of Carthage. But it was a verse of Horace (*Satires*, I.v.104) that he chose to bring his journal to an end:

– hic Finis chartaeque viaeque.
[– this is the end of the story, and the journey.]

···■ **xxxix** ■─···

We know too little – yet in a way too much – of Fielding's time in Lisbon, the last two months of his life. He wrote home – to his brother, to Welch, to Millar. Yet only three letters to John survive, all three undated but written very near the end: the earliest, though imperfectly preserved, is long and informative; the next exists only in a censored transcript; the last is a mere note. The merchants and their families who comprised the English Factory at Lisbon were a thriving and numerous community, and the arrival in their midst of a man of Fielding's eminence cannot have gone unnoticed; but they left no memorial of his presence there.

As soon as he landed, half his family came down with dysentery, "the Flux" as Fielding called it.[386] Mary, Margaret Collier, and William were all stricken. It reduced Mary "to almost the lowest Ebb of Life" before she recovered. William could not shake it off and, frightened of dying in a strange country, returned to England on Captain Veal's homeward journey. Though annoyed at his servant's deserting him at this difficult juncture, Fielding agreed to pay for William's passage and on his departure presented him with a bank draft for ten pounds. He learned after the ship had sailed, however, that William had schemed to saddle him with his nurse's bill for £3.12s. – at which piece of trickery annoyance turned to ire. Fielding instructed John to stop payment of the note and to strip William of his livery: "In all the World," Fielding fumed, "there is not such a scoundrel as William.... and there is [no] Punishment which his Ingratitude doth not deserve."

Compounding the inconvenience of William's defection, Isabella Ash also followed the septuagenarian Veal back to England; he had promised to marry her. But "Bell" was "only a Fool," not a scoundrel, and Fielding asked his brother to make use of the Register Office to find her a new place. With "Bell" and William gone, Fielding's "Family," he wrote John, "now consists in a black Slave and his Wife."

Adding heavily to these anxieties was the dismal state of Fielding's finances:

I found my self in the dearest City in the World and in the dearest House in that City. I could not for my Soul live for less than 2 Moidores [about 54 shillings] a day and saw my self likely to be left Pennyless 1000 Miles from home, where I had neither Acquaintance

nor Credit among a Set of People who are tearing one another's Souls
out for Money and ready to deposite Millions with Security but not
a Farthing without. In this Condition moreover, I saw no Likelihood
nor Possibility of changing my Situation.

Doubtless in hopes of eliciting an advance from his bookseller,
Fielding twice wrote Millar. The letters themselves are lost, but Millar
shared them with Thomas Birch, who on 7 September summarized the
contents when writing Philip Yorke:

> Fielding arriv'd at Lisbon about a month ago, after a very tedious
> passage, the contrary Winds having kept him long in the Channel. I
> have seen two Letters from him to his Bookseller written with his
> usual Spirit & Vivacity, one from Torbay of the 25th of July, & the
> other from Lisbon of the 12th of August. He exclaims greatly against
> the extravagant prices of every thing there, where the Expence of
> living is near thrice what it is in England. He has almost finish'd the
> History of his Voyage thither, which he offers to Millar as the best
> of his performances; & directs him to send him over all the Books
> which relate to Portugal for some other Work, which he has in
> view.[387]

On 12 August, apparently, Fielding despite his worries was in a
cheerful, optimistic mood. He had nearly finished the *Journal* – indeed,
the only parts of that work which from internal evidence were written
in Lisbon are the Preface and Introduction. Given his urgent need of
money, the opinion that it was "the best of his performances" may
seem a pardonable piece of puffery calculated to whet Millar's appetite
for the manuscript. It is possible, however, that in this period of his
life and in his present mood Fielding sincerely believed he had produced
a masterpiece: he had already puzzled readers by declaring *Amelia* to
be his "favourite Child," and in the Preface he was now writing he
preferred Herodotus to Homer. This preference of "true history" over
fiction surely underlies the most interesting revelation of Birch's letter:
namely, that Fielding was projecting "some other Work" on Portugal –
nothing less, perhaps, than a history of that nation.

That he could now entertain thoughts of such an ambitious work
suggests how much better he was feeling. He was convinced indeed that
he was on his way to a complete recovery. After being tapped at Tor
Bay for the fifth time, he was hopeful "the Dropsy" had left him for
good; eight weeks later he had "not a Drop of Water in me to my
Knowledge":

> In short as we advanced to the South, it is incredible how my Health
> advanced with it, and I have no Doubt but that I should have

perfectly recovered my Health at this Day, had it not been obstructed
by every possible Accident which Fortune could throw in my Way.

The sickness of his family, the defection of his servants, the unexpectedly high cost of living in Lisbon were just a few of the misfortunes
that plagued him. More worrisome was the domestic unhappiness that
developed sometime after these other difficulties had been overcome.

Fielding was rescued from certain financial ruin by the timely intercession of John Stubbs – "the greatest Merchant of this Place and the
greatest Cornfactor in the World," with whom he became acquainted
"by a strange Accident." Stubbs (who a year later would himself be
reduced to penury by the earthquake) found Fielding a small unfur-
nished house in Junqueira ("Jonkera" Fielding spelled it), two miles
west of Lisbon, near Belém, "which is the Kensington of England, and
where the Court now reside." Stubbs, who lived there with his family
in a *quinta* ("a little Kintor or Villa"), would be Fielding's neighbor.
Before Stubbs came to his aid Fielding had been living in town at a
rate of two moidores a day; now, though the house in Junqueira was
so ill equipped there were too few beds and no grate to cook on, his
rent would be only nine moidores a year, and he found "the Produce
of the country ... preposterously cheap."

Though Fielding attributes to "Fortune" the "strange Accident"
that introduced him to the man who thus served his family, it was
Samuel Richardson who claimed the credit[388] – a friendly gesture and
"strange" enough if true. But Fielding appears to have known nothing
of it. More than once in recent years Fielding, by lavishing public and
private praise on Richardson and *Clarissa*, had tried to heal the rift
between them; but these overtures had come to nothing. At Lisbon, far
from acknowledging any obligation to this rival, he concluded the
Preface to the *Journal* with sarcastic reflections on Richardson's vanity
and on the heavy, incompetent didacticism of his novels. He has
Richardson in mind when he ridicules "the conduct of authors, who
often fill a whole sheet with their own praises, to which they sometimes
set their own real names, and sometimes a fictitious one." And Richardson is "the great man" who, insisting that "entertainment" in a
"romance" should be only the vehicle of instruction, attempts to reform
"a whole people, by making use of a vehicular story, to wheel in among
them worse manners than their own."

By the time Fielding removed his family to Junqueira he had "scarce
suff: Money to buy me the Necessaries of Life." He had tapped his last
thirty-six shilling piece when he received from John a draft enabling
him to discharge his debts and leaving him with a few pounds to spare.
"The Tables were now turned," he assured his brother; "my Expences

were become moderate or rather indeed in the contrary Extreme to
what they were before.''

Where then you will say was the Misfortune of all this? or what was
there which could retard my Recovery, or shock a Philosophy so
established as mine which had triumphed over the Terror of Death
when I thought it both certain and near.

What had happened was discord in the family. The quarreling had
reached the point where Fielding was certain Mary and Margaret
Collier were conspiring to convince the English community he was
incompetent – ''a good-natured Fool'' no longer capable of governing
his family. Though Mary had recovered from her illness, she was
desperately homesick:

> so dispirited that she cries and sighs all Day to return to England.
> Is blind to the good I have received so manifestly, and on which I
> receive daily Compliments as well from my Physical as from my
> other Acquaintance, insists upon it that the same, if it hath happened,
> would have happened in England, and that by returning thither I
> shall perfect my Recovery, that I want the Exercise of my Coach
> [&c] which nothing can supply, and that my children as well as
> Affairs can be by no other means preserved.

Mary was understandably anxious at the thought of finding herself a
destitute widow far from home, and her fears for her children's welfare
were well founded. Mrs. Daniel, as she may have heard, had become
seriously unstable.

But nothing is clearer from the abruptly shifting moods, the solecisms
and broken syntax of this rambling letter than that Fielding, as Mary
and her friends could plainly see, was not himself. He supposed that
the hot Portuguese summer was restoring his health, working the
miracle that a dozen English doctors could not perform; but he was in
fact dying, his mind unsteady and unclear, moved from moment to
moment by fits of petulance or euphoria. Mary seemed weak and willful
in her nagging to return home. But the behavior of Margaret Collier
infuriated him. A spinster of thirty-six she had set her cap at the most
eligible bachelor among the English in Lisbon – a man charming as
well as learned who had become Fielding's favorite companion. This
was John Williamson (c. 1713–63) of Balliol College, Oxford, Doctor of
Divinity and Chaplain to the British Factory.[389] Fielding disapproved
of Margaret's designs, and he resented her taking sides with Mary in
their quarrels, not only by encouraging her to defy him, but by malign-
ing him in the community:

The Part which another acts on the Occasion is inconceivable, she is become a fine young Lady of Portugal, a Toast of Lisbon, and is at the English Minister here an intimate Acquaintance of Millar̤ one M̤ Williamson, who is every Way the cleverest Fellow I ever saw, and is my chief Companion. He is smitten, and she would succeed, if I did not prevent it. She is indeed the most artfull, wicked B—— in the world, blows the Coals of my Wife̤ Folly. . . . By these means my Spirits which were at the Top of the House are thrown down into the Cellar.

These broils were proving so intolerable, indeed, "I really think my Life at Stake." Only John could save him by rallying his friends back home to foil Margaret's schemes, to repair his damaged reputation in the community, and to send him skilled and agreeable comforters. Fielding's instructions to his brother pour from his pen, full of gall at first and unreasonable in kind, attesting plainly enough to his declining powers:

First, shew this Letter to M̤ Millar and desire him to write M̤ Williamson the Character of the B—— what obligations she and her Family have to me, who had an Execùtion taken out ag̤ me for 400£ for which I became Bail for her Brother, who took her starving in the Streets and nourished her in my own Bosom – This he knows but perhaps you may instruct him somewhat in the Returns she has made to my Kindness.

2ᵈˡʸ do procure as many Letters to be written to the Merch̤ and Ladies of Lisbon among the English of what character you and the Writers think I deserve as a Husband.

3ᵈˡʸ Get me a conversible Man to be my Companion in an Evening, with as much of the Qualifications of Learning, Sense and Good humour as yᵒ can find, who will drink a moderate Glass in an Evening or will at least sit with me 'till one when I do.

4ᵗʰˡʸ send over [H] Jones or M̤ˢ Hussy. I will pay their Passage hither, and will return them whenever they desire it and that not empty handed: for in Truth I never was so likely to grow rich as [now nor was any] one more likely to recover his Health than my self. I have actually regained s[om]e Elasticity in my Limbs, get with̤ Difficulty in and out of a [Ch]aise, and when in it can ride a whole Day; but all this will be lost, and I shall be destroyed unless I can be reliev[ed] from the greatest Folly and the greatest Bitchery that ever w[er]e united in 2 Women by a 3ᵈ who hath some Degree of Hon̤ and Understanding[,] at least shall have sense enough to see their own Interest, and not form a Contempt of me as a good-natured Fool, shall lay such wild Schemes as to get me to send my Wife to England by Force, and to become the M̤ˢ of my Family here under

Colour of a Companion of my Daughter. [I] shall only add that my Comfort is as my Life absolutely depend[ent on] y.' Success, so y.' Success in what you attempt seems to me [alm]ost infallible. – If my male Friend understands Portuguese or Spanish (which if he doth not he may easily, if he hath the Latin Grammatical Rudiments, learn) he may put Money in his own, mine and the Great Millar.' Pockets. Note he must be my Amanuensis.

It is an extraordinary story. With his weak wife's consent, Margaret Collier meant to persuade the English community that, because Fielding was no longer capable of governing his family, they should enable Mary to return home against his wishes and install Margaret, his daughter's governess, as mistress of the household. With her adversary thus isolated and discredited she would be free to ensnare the infatuated Williamson. (Such, at least, was Fielding's view of the situation.) To prevent these calamities, John must rally all his brother's friends at home to rain down letters on the English Factory at Lisbon, disabusing the merchants and ladies of their dangerously mistaken opinions of his own and Margaret's characters. He must send indeed not only letters, but flesh-and-blood allies – a companionable and learned amanuensis for one; and, as an antidote to Mary's "Folly" and Margaret's "Bitchery," some sensible woman who will take Fielding's side: his friend Mrs. Hussey (no doubt the "celebrated Mantua-maker in the *Strand*" for whom he found a place in *Tom Jones* [X.iii]) would be a perfect choice.

Feeling thus beleaguered and maligned, friendless and impotent in a city of troubles, yet Fielding could not remain dejected for long. His thoughts abruptly turn to more cheerful matters – to the half-chests of onions he has sent by Captain Veal to friends and family back home (to John, Millar, Welch, Peter Taylor, Mrs. Daniel; there is even one for Arthur Collier, "whose very Name I hate"); to the half hogsheads of calcavella he has sent to Millar and a certain Mr. Rose. In November, "which is the right season," he will send orange trees and lemons and "some Wine, Port or Lisbon, which y° like best." And, oh yes, he is sending half a dozen watermelons by Captain Allen, "who sails next Week."

In an access of optimism about the future he thinks of settling down indefinitely in this strange place which has done him so much good. He will need supplies from home to pass the winter comfortably and to cut a figure in the community. John must send potatoes and parsnips and nonpareils. And

from Fordhook likewise 4 Hams, a very fine Hog fatted as soon as may be and being cut into Flitches sent me[.] As likewise a young Hog made into Pork and salted and pickled in a Tub. A vast large cheshire Cheese, and one of Stilton if to be had good and mild.

With these provisions to supplement "the Produce of the Country" the family would dine heartily through the winter, especially since John must also be sure to dispatch "a very good, perfect Cook by the first Ship" (but not by Captain Veal, who he was now convinced was a scoundrel and "a Madman").

And he must have an eye to appearances; for, surely, he would soon have many important visitors to entertain. As yet he had had few callers, but he had been in Lisbon only six weeks. John must send him:

> My old rug Wastecoat and a dark blue Frock with a drest Sleeve. Desire Curtis to make my cloaths wider in the Shoulders. Let me have likewise my Tye and a new Major Perriwig from Southampton Street, and a new Hat large in the Brim from my Hatter the Corner of Arundel Street. I have had a visit from a Portuguese Nobleman, and shall be visited by all as soon as my Kintor is in order.

A little more cash, then, was all he needed to settle splendidly into this exotic place, whose history he would write – so profitably to himself, "the Great Millar," and even the imagined amanuensis:

> Scrape together all the Money of mine you can and do not pay a Farthing with! my orders. My Affairs will soon be in a fine Posture, for I can live here and even make a Figure for almost nothing.

The idea of the projected work on Portugal was already taking a definite shape and color in Fielding's mind, but with nothing more to guide us than the few observations recorded in the *Journal* and in the scraps of correspondence that survive we can have no true sense of it. His health having improved so much that he could venture out whole days in a chaise, he would certainly have made a tour of Belém and Lisbon itself, in the company perhaps of his new acquaintance, kindly Mr. Stubbs or clever Parson Williamson. He would have taken a closer view of those elegant examples of Manueline architecture the Tower of Belém and the Church and Monastery of Santa Maria (the Mosteiro dos Jerónimos), which he had admired from offshore, calling it "one of the most beautiful piles of building in all Portugal." And at Belém, where Vasco da Gama set sail for India, he would be reminded of the prowess and daring of the great navigators who founded Portugal's far-flung, opulent empire. On landing he had found the city itself repellent – its filthy narrow streets were infested by vermin, its grander buildings seemed merely ostentatious. Perhaps he saw these now with a less jaundiced eye: the Royal Palace and Hospital, the Cathedral, the Convent of St. Domingo (which contained "one of the largest and noblest libraries in Europe"), the magnificent churches of the Carmelites and of the Canons of St. Augustine ("reckoned by connoisseurs, the finest piece of Architecture in Europe"),[390] the Castle of St. George, and

King John V's recently erected Opera House and Aqueduct (all but the
last destroyed by the great earthquake of November 1755).

Having reached Lisbon a week before the death of the pious Dowager
Queen, Fielding may have witnessed "the great Magnificence" of her
funeral,[391] after which the Court retired in deepest mourning to the
Palace at Belém. Nowhere, Fielding observed in the Preface to the
Journal, was there "more pomp of bigotry" to be seen than in Lisbon,
where the Church exacted of the people a superstitious belief in doctrines
and facts "contrary to the honour of God, to the visible order of the
creation, to the known laws of nature, to the histories of former ages,
and to the experience of our own, and which no man can at once
understand and believe." He had arrived a few weeks too late to witness
a recent instance of the most infamous means by which the Inquisition
exacted such beliefs, the terrible ceremony of the *auto-da-fé*: in June a
Jew had been publicly burnt for relapsing from the faith.[392] In his
response to the numberless daily spectacles of superstitious devotion
which Lisbon presented, Fielding for once would be of a mind with the
Methodist Whitefield, who during Lent of this same year beheld in
horrified fascination the hooded penitential processions, the idolatry
and other "ecclesiastical Curiosities" which he vividly described in
letters home, giving thanks "for the great Wonder of the Reformation"
and for England's "glorious Deliverance" in 1745–6, when the Jacobite
rebellion threatened to restore a "papist" to the throne.[393]

These things, or others very like them, Fielding would have seen and
reflected on as the chaise carried him through town and suburbs.

> He was in the sumptuous pre-earthquake Lisbon [wrote Rose Macau-
> lay] ... a Lisbon of churches, convents, gold and jewelled ornaments,
> abject poverty, negro slaves, priests, friars, the sumptuous pro-
> cessions which had a few months before the Fieldings arrived scan-
> dalized and fascinated the Reverend Mr. Whitefield, superstition,
> squalor, corruption, women eating sweets and playing guitars at
> windows, and rich galleys sailing in from Brazil. How much of this
> rich and entertaining pageantry Fielding was able to see, we shall
> not know.... These are the sad lacunae of history.[394]

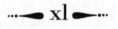

In mid-September, though harassed by domestic worries, Fielding could
still dream of profitable new work and of hearty dinners soon to
be shared with more agreeable companions whom John would send.

Characteristically, he remained sanguine to the last, however irksome his circumstances.

Soon after he delivered to Captain Allen his long, erratic letter, dispatched homeward together with a present of watermelons, an "accident" happened which, he wrote his brother, "will explain more to you than I can by any other means, what is my situation here." He described this amusing episode in a letter to "My dear Jack" known today only in a truncated transcript,[395] and known to very few; for it has never found a place in biographies of Fielding:

About a week ago [he wrote] I bought a parrot for Harriet and should have bought one for my sister [i.e., his sister-in-law, John's wife] could I have found an easy way of sending it, but the Captains are too great to take money for such things and too little to take any trouble without it, so that what can't be called freight can not be sent at all, unless by their particular friends, amongst whom I have not the honour to be numbered.

I did not, however, think that water melons required much trouble to bring, and, accordingly, I ordered my black to buy me the six finest he could get for you. He brought them in whilst Mr. Stubbs was sitting with me, who asked me jocosely whether I was to entertain the Court that day, being the day before yesterday. I told him they were for England by Capt. Allen who, as he had told me, was to sail in a day or two for England. "I thought," said he, "you did not know Captain Allen." I told him I did not. "Then I promise you," said he, "your water melons will stay behind." This vexed me heartily, but my vexation lasted not long; on the contrary, my sister owes both her bird and her beast to the accident; both of which were bought yesterday.

The one consigned by mamma is to the use of Billy, the other to Sophy.

This morning at breakfast Mr. Stubbs introduced Capt. Allen to me, whom you will find to be a — captain of a ship. Harriet's parrot was on a stand by her chair; my sister's in the balconey, but neither Harriet nor mamma in the room. "If you send a parrott to England," says Mr. Stubbs, "let me advise you to send one more likely to live for I will not ensure that. Indeed it hath drooped these two days" (and I think it had).[396] The mistake was soon rectified and they soon went away.

Now it happens that Harriet's parrott is the larger bird, for this is scarce full grown, and my wife, who doth not approve a preference of which she is jealous, fancied (though the price was to a farthing the same) that Sophy was unfairly dealt with, having the smaller bird, and exprest some uneasiness about it. But Harriet was obstinate, and you will believe I did not interfere.

They came back into the room soon after my company left it. I whispered my wife what Stubbs had said. Harriet overheard imperfectly, or suspected, and fell into tears and declared she would not part with her parrot, for no notice had been taken of the drooping before by any but myself, nor was it agreed to now.

And now, Jack, what do you think? Why truly, mamma, suspecting my partiality, discovered that I had laid a plot to deceive her. Mr.——— and Mrs. ——— and Miss ——— had all declared they liked Miss Harriet's parrot when first it was bought, and Mr. Stubbs would say anything I bid him. Here a crying bout between mother and daughter, both contending against themselves.... At last I condescended so low as to take the opinion of my black, for these blacks being the countrymen of the parrots are really good judges in them, but, so the devil ordained, my honest black knowing who was master, and desiring to please accordingly, declared against Mr. Stubbs and against me.

The matter was too ridiculous to be withstood. I called for my pipe and enjoyed it. Mamma went away in a rage vowing vengeance against poor Stubbs. B [i.e., Margaret Collier] is not at home.

This is the last glimpse we have of Fielding, and it is good to find that even at the last the qualities for which he is remembered shone undiminished. His generosity of spirit, occupied even now in choosing exotic presents for his children and family – watermelons and parrots and a monkey (that is likely to have been "the beast" referred to; one was among the items later offered for sale at Fordhook). The special affection he had for Harriet, the only surviving "Pledge" (as Booth puts it in *Amelia* [II.iii]) of his and Charlotte's love for one another. His ability to savor the humor in the "crying bout" between his daughter and her stepmother over the choice of parrots, Mary jealously protesting that her own flesh and blood should not be slighted in a matter of such distinction, while both contestants obstinately insist on having the inferior bird. His ability to laugh at his own misplaced sagacity in referring the case to the expert judgment of the black, who proves too wise to declare against the opinion of the real "master" of the house, Mary. His ability still to make the episode live for us on paper, so vividly it might stand as a chapter from the novels – a scene of the "ridiculous" in the human comedy he always "enjoyed."

There was just one further message from Fielding. For "Fortune," as he liked to say, had determined he would write no more:

Dear Jack — You must wait for an account of new wonders which every Day produces 'till the arrival of my amanuensis: for there is no such thing as a Pen to be bought in all Lisbon, nor can I use their Paper or Ink with! Difficulty.[397]

These are the last words of a man for whom, since boyhood, writing had been a way of life. There were wonders still to tell; but the rest is silence.

...➤ xli ➤...

Fielding died at Lisbon on 8 October 1754, leaving not a trace in the records of the Factory.[398] Regarded as heretics, the English had as yet no church of their own (services were held irregularly in the chapel of the house of the envoy, Abraham Castres), but they had with difficulty won the right to have a "Burial Ground" — about an acre of land pleasantly situated on the hill of Buenos Ayres — which they held in common with the Dutch. In order "to hide the graves of the heretics from the eyes of the faithful" the Inquisition required that the plot be enclosed within a wall and a screen of cypress trees.[399]

The English at Lisbon customarily buried their dead with great simplicity. The coffin, placed on the shafts of a coach, was conveyed to the burial ground unattended and without pomp; there it was met by the priest — in this case, presumably, John Williamson — and by the family and friends of the deceased. After prayers were said, it was lowered into the grave and the body exposed briefly to the view of those in attendance. The lid was then closed and locked, and the key was given to the nearest relation. The grave was filled with earth, and the mourners departed.[400] Fielding's family could afford only the humblest of markers, which was soon concealed with nettles and weeds.

Fielding's death came as a surprise to his friends at home. More than a week after the event the *Public Advertiser* (16 October 1754), prompted by the sanguine tenor of his recent correspondence from Lisbon, announced that he was "surprisingly recovered since his Arrival in that Climate. His Gout has entirely left him, and his Appetite returned." Not until Monday, 28 October, did the news break, the *Public Advertiser* reporting tersely: "From Lisbon we hear, that on the 8th instant died Henry Fielding, Esq." Similarly brief notices appeared soon after,[401] the *Whitehall Evening Post* (29–31 October) adding the information that Fielding had named Ralph Allen his executor.

It is one of the peculiar ironies of literary history that Fielding's only eulogy (as far as we know) was delivered by "Orator" Henley from his

tub near Clare Market on Sunday, 3 November 1754. As his text Henley
chose Luke 20:38 ("For he is not a God of the dead, but of the living:
for all live unto him"). The substance of Henley's tribute – for there
seems no hint of sarcasm about this memorial to his old antagonist –
may be gleaned from the following advertisement:

> Tomorrow, Catholic Perfection: Late Mr. Fielding's; No Death to the
> Immortal Denbigh; I[.] a Relation; his Talents: Merit, unadvanc'd,
> a Reproach to Courtiers: Pimping promoted: He, best of Husbands,
> Fathers, Masters: What, as a Writer, Dramatic: Dean Swift's Appro-
> b[atio]n: Why he did not write Tragedy: Why so Satirical: His Talk
> to me, and Satirising me: His Novels: Why Pope not write Prose
> well: Mr. Fielding's Papers, Pamphlets, &c. What, as a Lawyer; a
> Magistrate; and the King's Duty to provide for deserving Men, or,
> that – II. Prayer; that the H[ouse] of Hanover be kind to Men of
> Wit.[402]

Fielding's virtues were real enough. In time they would be celebrated
in verse (regrettably uninspired) composed both by an anonymous
admirer and by his friend Christopher Smart.[403]

PART V

---•◦•---

Consequences

Among Fielding's virtues, however, was not prudence in the management of money. His widow soon saw that her anxieties about his "Affairs" were well founded. Fielding died so heavily in debt there would be nothing left of his estate after his creditors were satisfied.

Before she could begin to fathom these financial troubles, Mary was plunged still deeper into grief. A week before her husband died, her mother killed herself. Left behind at Fordhook to supervise the household and care for Mary's children, and with no prospect (as far as she could tell) of seeing her daughter again, Mrs. Daniel grew despondent. About 1 October she walked to the bottom of the garden and shut herself in the "Necessary-House." She knelt down with her head over the hole, and cut her throat – "in which Posture she was found," the papers reported, "having bled to death."[1] Distressed as she was in mind, she would leave no mess behind for others to clean. Though a suicide, she was nevertheless buried on 3 October in consecrated ground, at St. Mary's, Ealing.[2]

It was well for the children that Mary was now free to come home. And it was well for them and their mother that, suffering the consequences of Fielding's improvidence, they also benefited from the goodwill and gratitude he had widely inspired, not only by his writings and his services to the public, but by the simple gift he had for friendship. Though Ralph Allen declined to act as Fielding's executor, he provided conscientiously for his family: according to Murphy, Allen annually made " a very generous donation" to the children's education, and on his death in 1764 he bequeathed £100 each to them and to Mary. Millar, too, who had behaved munificently toward Fielding, made handsome presents to Harriet and her mother when Harriet married in 1766,[3] and when he died in 1768, left legacies of £200 each to William and Allen. But it was John who assumed the burden of supporting his brother's family – properly enough, to be sure, considering that he owed all he now had to opportunities Fielding created for him.

On 14 November 1754 Fielding's will was proved. Ralph Allen and Mary having "renounced" the office, John was sworn to administer his brother's "Goods Chattels and Credits."[4] It was soon obvious that in order to satisfy Fielding's creditors he would have to dispose of all his worldly goods and property. On 20 December the *Public Advertiser* announced that Fordhook, together with all its furniture, would be put up for auction. The notice, which reads in part as follows, will suggest the scale on which Fielding had been living:

To be *SOLD* by *AUCTION*, by Mr. LANGFORD, (By Order of the Administrator) *on Thursday* the 26th *Inst. and the* following Day, The Lease of the Dwelling House, Out-houses, Gardens, with about

forty Acres of Land thereunto belonging, situated at the hither End
of Ealing Common, a little beyond Acton, of
              HENRY FIELDING, Esq;
Late of Bow-street, Covent Garden, deceased; Together with all the
Stock on the Farm, consisting of two large Ricks of Hay, two of
Wheat, one of Oats, and one of Pease; about eighty Sheep, seven
Cows (four of them Alderney) five Hogs, three Sows, three Asses, a
Monkey, seven Coach and Cart-Horses, two Saddle Horses, three
Carts, and other Farming Utensils. As likewise all the genuine Hous-
hold Furniture, his Landau and Harness, Plate, Wines, and other
Effects.

Fielding's friend John Ranby acquired the lease of Fordhook and the
farm for £800.[5] But there is no record of how much he or others paid
for the stock and furniture, or for Fielding's landau and plate and
wines – or for the monkey.

This same issue of the *Public Advertiser* (20 December) also promised
that Samuel Baker would publish "Next Month" the catalogue of
Fielding's "entire and valuable Library," which was to be sold at
auction "for the Benefit of his Family, in February next." The *Catalogue*
was not in fact published until 6 February, the sale commencing on
Monday the 10th at Baker's house in York Street, Covent Garden.
Among many curious works in the collection were "most of the Greek
Commentators on ARISTOTLE, and several Books with Mr. FIELDING's
MSS. Notes." Though the bookseller exaggerates the number of the
commentators, Fielding obviously shared with his friend "Hermes"
Harris an unfashionable interest in the Stagyrite; as for the tantalizing
reference to books annotated by Fielding, the most diligent search has
traced but a single one.[6] The *Catalogue* by no means represents Fielding's
"entire" library: it is clear from the authors Fielding mentions in his
works and correspondence that the range of his reading was far more
extensive than the 653 lots Baker listed for the four nights of the sale.
The *Catalogue* nonetheless is an invaluable guide to Fielding's interests –
in philosophy, religion, history, the classics, and of course the law –
and it attests to his impressive erudition in all these areas. The sale
totaled "in the neighbourhood of £364,"[7] nearly £100 more than Samuel
Johnson's library brought thirty years later. It has been said, indeed,
that the collection of books Fielding assembled in his relatively short
life represents "the largest working library possessed by any man of
letters in the eighteenth century."[8]

On the day the *Catalogue* was published, the papers announced the
imminent publication of Fielding's *Journal of a Voyage to Lisbon*,
together with "a Fragment of his Answer to Lord Bolingbroke."[9] A
week later the *Public Advertiser* was more definite, promising pub-

lication on Tuesday, 25 February (price: three shillings bound), and stipulating that the work was "*Printed for the Benefit of his Wife and Children,*" with Millar acting as their agent.[10] Besides appealing to the charitable inclinations of the public in advertisements such as these, John Fielding privately enlisted the support of his friends in promoting the work: on the eve of publication he sent Thomas Birch a complimentary copy, hoping that "you will assist this little volume by your recommendation through the Beau Monde."[11]

The most strenuous puffing would be required if Millar was to dispose of the massive stock he already had on hand. In January he ordered the printing of *two* separate editions of 2,500 copies each: the first in smaller type, the second in a handsomer format.[12] These constitute radically different versions of the *Journal*, both ready for distribution a month earlier than the date of publication. Bibliographically, it is an extraordinary case. What is more, it implies, within the circle of Fielding's family and friends concerned in publishing this posthumous work, an embarrassed state of utter confusion.

The mystery of the two *Journals* remains unsolved, but the following hypothetical sequence of events would plausibly account for it. On returning to England, Mary delivered her husband's manuscript to John. Unable to read it himself and eager to act quickly to satisfy Fielding's creditors, John in turn delivered the work to Millar for publication. Millar, to whom Fielding owed nearly £1,900, would be equally keen to hurry it into print. Someone – probably Arthur Murphy[13] – was then enlisted to write a brief introduction to the book in the form of a "Dedication to the Public": a muted sort of fanfare calculated to stir in the reader appropriate (and profitable) sentiments both of admiration for Fielding's "strong and lively genius," now seen as "a lamp almost burnt out ... struggling against its own dissolution," and of compassion for "those innocents he hath left behind," whose welfare depended on the book's brisk "circulation through the kingdom." In extenuation of the decision to print so imperfect a work without editorial revision (a decision which conveniently saved both time and money, or so it would have seemed at first), the writer states:

> It was thought proper, by the friends of the deceased, that this little piece should come into your hands as it came from the hands of the author; it being judged that you would be better pleased to have an opportunity of observing the faintest traces of a genius you have long admired, than have it patch'd by a different hand; by which means the marks of its true author might have been effac'd.

Accordingly, Strahan, using Fielding's unadulterated manuscript as copy-text, printed an edition of 2,500 copies. As this edition was making its way through the press early in January, John Fielding became aware of certain objectionable or merely clumsy passages which required retrenching: Strahan charged Millar for "Extraordinary Corrections" that only John, presumably, could have authorized. It follows, then, that the text as Fielding wrote it is not wholly preserved even in this first printing. In this respect, nevertheless, the first edition is preferable by far to the one Strahan rushed into print later this same month. Thoroughly alert to the offensiveness of many passages in the work – Fielding's unflattering characterization of Captain Veal, for instance; or his even harsher portrait of the landlady at Ryde, whom he explicitly identified: "Mrs. Francis (for that was the name of the good woman of the house)" – John now set about patching and effacing the text in earnest, among many other changes metamorphosing Mrs. Francis into "Mrs. Humphrys."

It is generally supposed that, having discovered too late the objectionable passages of his brother's text as preserved (for the most part) in the first printing, John suppressed that edition, releasing to the public on 25 February only the expurgated second printing, the so-called "Humphrys" version. This version was in fact circulating then; an excerpt from it was reprinted in the *London Magazine* (February 1755). It is also generally supposed that Millar, having later acquired the rights to the work, withheld publication of the more authentic "Francis" version until December of this year, when news of the earthquake stimulated the public's curiosity about all things relating to Lisbon.[14] But is it likely that Millar, who could not foresee this helpful calamity, would hold this edition in storage for so many months? As A. W. Pollard observed, all that is known with certainty of the publishing history of the two editions of Fielding's *Journal of a Voyage to Lisbon* is that the "Francis" version was printed before the "Humphrys" version, that both versions were printed in January 1755, and that it was from a copy of the "Humphrys" version that the reviewer in the *London Magazine* described the book: "Everything else is conjecture."[15]

····◄ ii ◄►····

Though the *Journal* was published in February, the income Fielding's widow derived from it was insufficient to make up the sum total of his debts. A month later John was exasperated to learn that the depths of Fielding's neglected obligations had not yet been plumbed. As his brother's administrator he received a demand from the Duke of Bedford's agent "for near Six Years Ground Rent" at £30 per annum for the estate in Drury Lane by which Bedford had enabled Fielding to qualify for the Middlesex magistracy. John's reply, written to

Bedford on 28 March 1755, attests to the distress Fielding's improvidence was continuing to cause his widow and children. After examining his brother's accounts, John found to his "great surprize"

> that not one Shilling Ground Rent has hitherto been paid; a circumstance I was a stranger to ... and an omission, I own, for his Sake, I am ashamed of. – And as my Brother's circumstances are left in a very bad State for his Family, there being scarce sufficient for the Creditors, I don't know how I can answer M: Butcher's demand in any other manner than by begging in the Children's behalf, that your Grace wou'd cover an Act of indiscretion in the Father by an Act of generosity to them, and kindly accept a Surrender of the Lease as an equivalent for the Arrears, and thereby discharge me, as Administrator, of one Debt, as it can never be in Your Grace's power to discharge that other, which your distinguished Friendship to my Brother has made ever due to you from all his Family.[16]

Bedford was good enough to accept this proposal, excusing the debt (£172.10s) when John surrendered the lease on 3 May 1755. Indeed, he generously offered the lease to John on the same terms. But John felt obliged to decline: "as there was at that Time some Disputes with his Brother's Widow and Family he could not accept," he later explained, "without exposing himself to fresh Family Broils."[17] These quarrels, he recalled, "soon ... were settled"; but one wonders what caused this unpleasantness between Fielding's brother and his widow and "Family." Mary and the children were now entirely dependent on John, who allowed them £100 a year out of the £400 salary the government gave him.[18] But if he was a generous man with a sense of responsibility, he was also imperious. He may have made Mary feel too keenly the debt of gratitude she owed, and she may well have resented his treatment of her two closest friends, Margaret Collier and Saunders Welch.

Not long after she returned to England with Mary and Harriet, giving up hopes of marrying Chaplain Williamson, Margaret Collier was literally isolated from the family she had been part of for some years. She found herself in lonely, chastening exile on the Isle of Wight, a boarder occupying a draughty room in the cottage of an elderly couple at Ryde. Her sister Jane was dead. Mrs. Roberts and her daughters lent her books to read, but otherwise ignored her. Adding insult to injury, when she arrived at Ryde in the late summer of 1755 she was "sadly vexed" to find that local gossip attributed to her the authorship of the *Voyage to Lisbon*: "the reason which was given for supposing it mine," she explained to Richardson, "was to the last degree mortifying, (viz. that it was so very bad a performance, and fell so far short of his other works, it must needs be the person *with him* who wrote it."[19]

Whatever the part John Fielding may have played in separating

Mary from her friend – after his brother's reports of Margaret's conduct in Lisbon, he would be disinclined to continue supporting her – it is clear that he treated Saunders Welch, whom Mary regarded as her protector, with unforgivable insolence. When Welch was appointed to the Middlesex magistracy in April 1755, the post for which Fielding had recommended him, he understood that he and John were to collaborate equally in executing Fielding's former office of Court Justice, dividing between them the annual salary of £400. John, however, could brook no brother near the throne. In lodging a formal complaint with Newcastle, Welch described the abuse to which he was being subjected at Bow Street:

> Mr. Fielding unhappily mistaking my Assiduity, for an Attempt to supplant & injure, has treated me publicly, when in Office, & under his own Roof, where I imagined every Gentleman must have found protection, in a Manner too opprobrious to repeat, & too offensive for any but the ill-deserving to bear. So far did Mr. Fielding forget himself, as to descend to ill language, such as he would have reproved in a Criminal before him; Judge, My Lord Duke, if any but the Person conscious of his deserving it could return to the House of Mr. Fielding; Yet by the advice of my Friends, I was prevailed upon to return to my Duty that the Business of the Public might not be neglected. But this Condescention was misconstrued into a Submission, And so far was I from meeting a reception my good Interest merited, that I was insulted in the grossest Manner, & forbid coming into his House any more, except upon Terms I could not in Honour comply with.
>
> Thus have I presumed to lay before your Grace, in the fewest Words I could, the Treatment I have met with, & have borne ever since I have been connected with him in Office, out of regard to the Family of his late Brother, wch I am still desirous, if continued to be enabled by your Grace, of contributing to support in any manner you shall be pleased to direct.[20]

Newcastle responded to this petition by allowing annual salaries of £200 to Welch and £400 to John,[21] with John allowing £100 a year to his brother's widow and children.

But wounds such as these do not soon heal. Mary resented her dependence on her brother-in-law, and by autumn 1756 she had become desperate and angry enough to defy him by petitioning her husband's former patron, Lord Barrington, Secretary at War, for a pension that would relieve her of these demeaning obligations. John was incensed when he learned what she had done. From Bow Street on 16 December 1756 he wrote Barrington on a matter of business:

before I conclude this Letter I must beg leave to mention a circumstance that has given me some concern – I find that my late Brothers widow has applied to your Lordship for a thing which I have told her my Self was irregular and could not be granted but I assure you she did it without either my knowledge or consent least therefore your Lordships humanity should suffer from a supposition of her being in distress at present I thought it my duty to say a word or two on that subject when my Brother died he left little more than would answer his Just Debts and left a Widow and Four children one of which [Sophia] is since dead this Family I have taken to my self and hope from my own Labours so long as I shall live to support them handsomly and I do assure your Lordship that the tenderest regard is paid to their healths the exactest care taken of their Educations and the most unwearied diligence used by me to make her forget the loss of a Husband them of a Father nor has she or them been deny'd one Earthly thing in my Power since my Brother's death but on the contrary I have told her, her Friends and all my acquaintance that so long as I have one Shilling in the world they shall have the same Share of it as if she was my own wife they my own Children doubtless as life is precarious and as their subsistence depends on mine it would make me very happy if she could obtain some certain establishment for her own Life but should be glad to be acquainted with the nature of her applications.[22]

We may well wonder how "soon," as John later insisted, "Family Broils" such as these were "settled." In the spring of 1757, when she petitioned the Duke of Bedford to appoint her elder son William to a place in the Charterhouse School, Mary was living apart from John in rented lodgings in Theobald's Row, Holborn, and it was Welch, not John, on whom she relied to act as her intermediary.[23]

In any event John conscientiously continued supporting his brother's family, including Sarah. A notebook in which he recorded one year's disbursements to them (apparently in 1761, the year in which he was knighted) specifies the amounts: "To the widow pr. ann., £60. To the educating Wm. at Eaton School, £40. To the educating Allen at Mr. Skelton's school at Warfield, £20. To Harriet's clothes and maintenance, £40. To Sarah, sister of the said Henry, £20."[24] When William came of age, moreover, John saw to it that he was appointed Assistant Magistrate at Bow Street, and he supported his nephew's application to the Duke of Bedford (unsuccessful in the event) that he be granted "the same kind of favour which he so nobly conferr'd on my Father – namely a qualification to act as Magistrate for the County of Middlesex."[25]

Some years later, when the "tatter'd" manuscript of The Fathers: or, The Good-Natur'd Man was discovered among Sir Charles Hanbury

Williams's papers and subsequently identified by Garrick as Fielding's lost comedy, John – who had fallen out with Garrick over the question of staging so pernicious an entertainment as *The Beggar's Opera!* – made up the quarrel in order that they might cooperate with Richard Brinsley Sheridan in producing his brother's play for the benefit of his widow. Garrick and Sheridan – "the most distinguished dramatic talents of the age," as they are rightly represented in the "Advertisement" to the published version – collaborated in making this "Fragment" stage-worthy, if just barely. Garrick wrote both Prologue and Epilogue, these tributes to his departed friend being, aptly enough, his last contributions to the theatre; he died a few weeks later (20 January 1779). In all this John exerted himself in behalf of his brother's widow. *The Fathers* was hardly a success, having a fitful run of just nine nights at Drury Lane (30 November to 12 December 1778); but it brought Mary the proceeds of three benefits, the house crowded on each occasion owing to John's private appeals to Fielding's friends and other likely patrons. A letter he wrote to Dr. William Hunter for this purpose is particularly interesting for the light it throws not only on Fielding's friendship with that eminent surgeon, but also on the question of his literary effects left unpublished (as far as John knew) at the time of his death:

> Sir John Fielding presents his Compliments to Dr. Hunter, and acquaints him that the Comedy of the Good-natured Man written by the late Mr. Henry Fielding will be performed at Drury Lane next Monday being the Author's Widow's Night.
>
> He was your old and sincere friend. There are no other of his Works left unpublished. This is the last Opportunity you will have of shewing any Respect to his Memory as a Genius, so that I hope you will send all your pupils, all your patients, all your Friends, & every body else to the Play that Night, by which Means you will indulge your benevolent feelings & your Sentiments of Friendship.[26]

The Fathers was published on 12 December 1778. It carried a Dedication from Sir John Fielding recommending "this little orphan posthumous work" to the "protection" of the Duke of Northumberland, Lord Lieutenant of Middlesex County.

Sir John Fielding, having married a second time in 1774, died without issue on 4 September 1780 at his country house, Brompton Place, and was buried in the Chelsea parish church.[27] He was careful by the terms of his will to provide for his brother's family, leaving £200 to each of his nephews, William and Allen, and asking that his wife continue to look after Mary.[28] In June of that year the house at Bow Street in which he and his brother had dispensed justice for more than thirty years was gutted during the Gordon Riots by an enraged mob who made a bonfire of the contents. It may be (though the hypothesis contradicts John's assurance to William Hunter to the contrary), that some valuable literary papers of Fielding's were destroyed in the fire. Forty years later W. H. Fielding, the novelist's grandson, declared to a collector who requested a specimen of Fielding's handwriting "that some Novels and other works, ready for the press, were in the House of *Sir John Fielding* when it was destroyed ... and they thus fell a sacrifice to the flames."[29]

··· ● iii ● ···

A final word needs saying about the fortunes of the family Fielding left behind, and of his works, the children of his brain, as he liked to call them, for which he is chiefly remembered.

Harriet, the only child of his union with Charlotte who lived to maturity, grew to be "of a good stature ... a sweet temper, and great understanding";[30] but she also inherited her mother's frailty. For a time she was a favorite companion of the notorious Elizabeth Chudleigh, mistress of the Duke of Kingston, through whom she met Colonel James Gabriel Montresor, an accomplished military engineer and a widower forty years her senior. While "in a deep decline" from the effects of consumption, Harriet accepted Colonel Montresor's gallant proposal of marriage. The wedding took place on 25 August 1766 at the parish church of St. Marylebone. She was twenty-three and had less than four months to live.[31]

Fielding's two sons by Mary lived on into the next century, making their marks in law and divinity. William, the elder, followed his father's example in many ways. He went to Eton, studied law at the Middle Temple, and was called to the Bar. Despite a paralytic stroke which left him crippled in his early thirties, he served for fifty years with reputation as a Westminster justice; for the last twelve years of his life he was principal magistrate at the Queen's Square police court. Like his father he was witty in conversation and had a knack at composing gay songs. Hazlitt, indeed, who often passed him in St. James's Park (and never without taking "off my hat to him in spirit" in honor of his father), fancied he "had a strong resemblance" to Fielding. William died on 1 October 1820, aged seventy-two.[32]

William resembled his father in another, less fortunate respect. He conceived, apparently out of wedlock, a son William Henry Fielding, whose mother he afterward married.[33] On his father's death W. H. Fielding appears to have come into possession of the two manuscript volumes on Crown law which Fielding had been compiling as early as

1745 and which Murphy reported in John Fielding's custody in 1762. At the earliest opportunity, Fielding's grandson began dismembering these volumes and dispersing the leaves on the autograph market.[34] One who knew him described W. H. Fielding as "a very eccentric character."

Allen, born shortly before Fielding's departure for Lisbon, became a pious and prolific clergyman who achieved considerable eminence in the Church in the vicinity of Canterbury. In 1762, on the nomination of Lord Bute, Lady Mary's son-in-law, he was admitted to the Charterhouse School as a "poor Scholar."[35] In 1770 he matriculated at Christ Church, Oxford, taking his B.A. in 1774 and M.A. in 1800. He served as Chaplain to Lord Nelson of the Nile, and among other notable livings and appointments was Vicar of St. Stephen's, Hackington (1787–1823); Master of Eastbridge Hospital (1803–23); and a Six Preacher (1815–23) attached to the Cathedral. A witty, yet dignified man, he spoke so deliberately he came to be called "the minute Gun."[36] He died 9 April 1823, aged sixty-nine.

In 1783 Allen married Mary Ann Whittingham, the adopted niece of John Fielding's first wife. Four of their children became clergymen: Henry (1786–1863), the eldest, attended the King's School, Canterbury, and in 1816, when his father resigned the living in his favor, became Rector of Blean, Kent (see Plate 65); Charles (1791–1866) became Vicar of Headcorn, Kent; George (1793–1869), a graduate of St. John's, Cambridge, became Vicar of North Ockendon, Essex, and married the grandniece of Fielding's friend, Sir Charles Hanbury Williams; and Allen (b. 1801) became Chaplain of Chatham Dockyard.[37] Mary Fielding made her home with Allen in Canterbury until she died in 1802, aged eighty-one, and was buried at St. Stephen's. From Allen and his progeny have sprung Henry Fielding's numerous descendants.

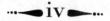

Fielding's image – the impression, that is, of his character and genius, even of his physical aspect – descended to later generations of readers in less satisfactory ways, preserved imperfectly in Millar's truncated edition of the *Works* (1762), with its famous frontispiece drawn from memory by Hogarth and its incompetent assessment of his life and art by Arthur Murphy. At the turn of the century the Reverend Thomas Rackett, who wished to include an account of Fielding in a history of Dorset, appealed for help to Allen Fielding.

You ask [came the reply] whether an authentic account of my father has been published, to which the answer is – "certainly not." All that is to be found relative to him, in print, is contained in the Life written by Arthur Murphy & prefixed to an Edition of all his Works, published by Millar – Murphy, himself knew nothing of my father; but patched that history up, from the accounts given to him by Millar, & a variety of *good jokes* that were handed about concerning him, & which would perhaps have lost much of their *merit* if they had been confined within the bounds of truth.

... I hardly need to say that I *wish* it were in my power to give you more information on *this subject* as the life of such a Man, may be supposed to have afforded much matter worthy of remembrance – but alas it has all perished –[38]

For more than a century the "shadow" of Arthur Murphy (to borrow Cross's figure for the baneful influence Murphy's "Essay on the Life and Genius of Henry Fielding, Esq." has had) darkened our understanding of the man and obscured the full range and variety of his writings. It has taken another century of research to discover the most rudimentary facts of Fielding's life and to establish a canon that more accurately represents his achievement.

How much lighter would these labors have been – how much better, and sooner, would we have come to know him – if the original plan for Fielding's biography had not been thwarted by his publisher? For that work, which now survives only in fragments and labored drafts, was undertaken by Fielding's closest friend in collaboration with his sister. The story can be pieced together from the unpublished correspondence of Sarah Fielding and James Harris.[39] It begins well before we have reason to suppose that Millar was contemplating an edition of Fielding's *Works*;[40] indeed, that edition was probably inspired by the plans Harris and Sarah formed for a memorial to Fielding.

Early in 1758 while visiting Bath, Harris first discussed with Sarah the desirability of publishing a short critical biography of Fielding. The original draft, which Harris composed at Bath, is entitled "An Essay on the Life and Genius of Henry Fielding Esqr." (the identical title Murphy would use) and is dated 5 February 1758. At this stage Sarah was supplying Harris with "Notes" concerning her brother, from among which Harris selected those which seemed to him "proper" for Sarah "to add" to the essay. Writing from Bathwick on 1 July 1758, Sarah was eager to finish the work as soon as possible that it might "be printed early in the Winter." In reply, Harris hoped she would attend particularly to the dating of events in Fielding's life – for which purpose Sarah regretted that "our Friend" William Young was no longer living; he "would have been a great help" (30 July 1758).

Sarah at first thought the memoir might serve as Preface to a volume of Fielding's unpublished writings; but she had to agree with Harris and his brother Thomas that there was "nothing worthy Printing to be collected." On 6 September she informed Harris that she had written Millar "concerning the Length of your Essay on my Brother, and also concerning the prefixing it to Tom Jones, or Joseph Andrews"; but Millar had gone to Scotland and they could expect no answer for several weeks. Millar, it appears (for Sarah makes no mention of the project in her two letters of this month), had not yet begun to think seriously of publishing an edition of Fielding's works. From the time he first saw Harris's "Essay," however, he had misgivings about its length.

As the idea for the *Works* took shape in Millar's mind over the next few months, the "Essay" would seem too short to stand at the head of so pompous an edition. Only a professional writer with editorial experience could serve his purpose. On 19 May 1759, therefore, Millar published proposals for:

An elegant edition of the WORKS of the late HENRY FIELDING, Esq. Revised throughout, with Annotations upon such Passages as require Illustration, and an Essay on the Life and Genius of the Author. By ARTHUR MURPHY, of Lincoln's Inn, Esq.[41]

This was to be an edition in five quarto volumes, published by subscription; but the public response was disappointing, and by July 1760 Millar had modified his plans for the *Works*, which he would now issue in two formats – one in four volumes quarto, the other in eight volumes octavo. At that time he hoped to publish next winter.

Curiously, though Sarah and Harris were aware of these plans, they remained ignorant of the part Millar, months earlier, had assigned Murphy to play in the project. They continued to suppose Harris's "Essay" might be "publish'd with my Brother's Works," as Sarah wrote on 16 October 1760 from "the little Cottage" she had recently purchased at Walcott, near Bath. As late as 9 April 1761 she informed Harris that "Millar took your Essay" some time ago, since he had intended to publish the *Works* "this Winter" (i.e., 1760–1); "but as they do not appear," she assumed he had "postponed the Publication to a time he thinks will be more profitable." By the date of this letter, indeed, Harris's manuscript was being corrected with an eye to publication, as Sarah apologetically explained:

I was obliged to send you back even the part in which I had the favour of your signing your Name, with your kind Assurance of Friendship because it is corrected with the other Side. I am greatly oblig'd to you for giving me leave to credit my-self with your Authority.

Harris and Sarah continued laboring under this delusion until a matter of weeks before Millar published the *Works* in April 1762 – though Millar had the grace to disabuse her in time for Murphy to eliminate or alter the most egregious passages in his "Essay," the very title of which, as well as several substantive parts of his narrative, he appears to have pillaged from Harris without consent. On 13 February 1762 Millar paid Murphy £100 "for writing the Essay, correcting an Edition of Fielding's Works, and adding such notes and illustrations as he found necessary."[42] On 4 March 1762 Sarah, in a state of shock and dismay, wrote Harris from Walcott:

> Notwithstanding the reiterated request to obtain your leave for prefixing the Essay you so obligingly wrote, to my Brother's Works, yet they are going to be published without it, and another long Essay *weighing* heavy in every Sense will be published instead of it. Millar was here lately, it was sent to him here, he shewed it to me, you never saw such a shocking Creature as it had made my Brother, and not only of him but of his Father too. Millar himself desliked it, but peculiar Reasons (besides his having agreed to pay for it) too long to be explained unless I could have the pleasure of seeing you, made it necessary to print it. The Writer, a Mr. Murphy, knew little or nothing of my Brother, yet as Mr. Millar informs me, rejoyces much to have hear'd the truth, and confesses he had his strange Information from Bow-Street; so that however dull it may be, it will be altered from giving such a wretched Picture of him. Millar says he has printed but a Small Number now, and if you will write another Life of my Brother, for he doats on Length, and with your leave, add your Essay to it, he shall rejoyce to prefix it to another Edition.

Understandably angered at what he considered a piece of duplicity not only insulting to himself but detrimental to Fielding's future reputation, Harris replied immediately, eliciting from Sarah on 15 March a promise: "what you wrote with so kind an Intention with regard to me, shall never be blended with Murphy's." But Murphy, almost certainly, had long before perused Harris's account and appropriated what he would. At least Sarah could assure her friend:

> The Opprobrium put into Murphy's Essay will be altered, so that it will only be tedious and dull. To make his own Works the Basis of conveying it, and making it become as you say "Coeval with *their* Merit" would have been indeed a Cruelty without a Name adequate to express it.

Much of what Sarah called the "Opprobrium" of Murphy's essay – the "strange Information" which John Fielding gave him concerning, presumably, the excesses and embarrassments of his brother's early life and his strained relations with his father – was probably accurate enough in the main. Such shameful passages of his life's story, which he had come to regret, Fielding hoped might be forever buried in oblivion; before embarking for Lisbon he asked Millar to prevent just such a hackney author as Murphy from writing his biography. Yet derived as they were from at least two sources who knew him well, John Fielding and Millar, what genuine insights into Fielding's character might Murphy's essay have afforded had not Sarah blotted them out? Naturally enough, Fielding's sister and his best friend wished to conceal his frailties. They aimed to perpetuate an image of the author of *Tom Jones* very like the image Cross invented in the work which has remained the standard biography for seventy years – the image of a man who never was or could have been, a man nearly flawless. Even so, Murphy knew, if not nothing, certainly very little of his subject. However softened and incomplete the portrait of Fielding might have been which Harris and Sarah meant to give us (the outlines of which are discernible in the extant fragments of Harris's "Essay"), it would have faithfully preserved lineaments and qualities of the man which are no less true for being admirable.

How sincerely Harris admired those qualities and loved the friend who possessed them is attested by his daughter Gertrude, who recalled how, on his deathbed, her father asked her sister to read aloud to him from *Joseph Andrews*: "he himself selected the different chapters from which Louise read several passages, to which he listened with attention, especially to that part of the 3^d chapter in the second book wherein Parson Adams discourses his Host on religion, and the Immortality of the Soul."[43]

The bond between Sarah and Henry was stronger still, if unspoken. On 9 April 1768 in her fifty-seventh year Sarah died at Bath, where, in the Abbey Church, a memorial composed by Dr. John Hoadly celebrates her virtues. She chose to be buried, however, in the little church of St. Mary, Charlcombe – where, many years before, her brother had married Charlotte Cradock.

Fielding's friends did not forget him, and his countrymen came to acknowledge, with gratitude and pride, the inestimable legacies he left them in literature and the law.

For seventy-five years, however, his grave in Lisbon was neglected, overgrown with weeds, disturbed only by tremors of the earthquake. Surrounded by the opulent monuments commemorating the dead of the English Factory, its very site may have been forgotten.[44] The present handsome sarcophagus, with its elaborate Latin inscription honoring Fielding's virtues and his genius (and, in sentiments worthy of Richardson's latter-day disciples, regretting that he sometimes did those things he ought not to have done), was erected in 1830. It stands now under the tall cypress trees of the English Cemetery of St. George's church, visited by countless pilgrims from George Borrow to Kingsley Amis[45] – and in the spring of 1988 by someone unknown to us who laid forty-seven roses on the cold grey stone.

But Fielding's true monument – like that of the architect of St. Paul's – has always been his masterpiece, *Tom Jones*, the great work which Gibbon prophesied "will outlive the palace of the Escurial, and the imperial eagle of the house of Austria." And in *Tom Jones* (II.vii) Fielding wrote his own truest epitaph:

> For Men of true Wisdom and Goodness are contented to take Persons and Things as they are, without complaining of their Imperfections, or attempting to amend them. They can see a Fault in a Friend, a Relation, or an Acquaintance, without ever mentioning it to the Parties themselves, or to any others; and this often without lessening their Affection. Indeed unless great Discernment be tempered with this overlooking Disposition, we ought never to contract Friendship but with a Degree of Folly which we can deceive: For I hope my Friends will pardon me, when I declare I know none of them without a Fault; and I should be sorry if I could imagine I had any Friend who could not see mine. Forgiveness, of this Kind, we give and demand in Turn. It is an Exercise of Friendship, and, perhaps, none of the least pleasant. And this Forgiveness we must bestow, without Desire of Amendment. There is, perhaps, no surer Mark of Folly, than an Attempt to correct the natural Infirmities of those we love. The finest Composition of human Nature, as well as the finest China, may have a Flaw in it; and this, I am afraid, in either Case, is equally incurable; though, nevertheless, the Pattern may remain of the highest Value.

NOTES

1 When Fielding reached his majority he arranged to have the following affidavit sworn at Wells, Somerset, on 26 Oct. 1728 before D. Sherston, Master of the Rolls (PRO: C.41.43. 1030):

> Alexander Robertson of Glastoⁿ in ye Co. of Somersett &c. maketh Oath y^t Henry ffeilding Son of Edm^d ffeilding Esq and Sarah his Wife was born ye 22^d of April in ye year of our Lord 1707 & Baptized ye 6th of May following as Appears by ye Reg^{tr} of St. Bennings parish in Glastoⁿ afsd.

2 A copy of John of Glastonbury's *Chronica*, ed. Thomas Hearne, 2 vols. (Oxford: 1726), was in Fielding's library. Fielding also owned a copy of Adam of Domerham's history of Glastonbury in Hearne's edn. (Oxford: 1727), which includes William of Malmesbury, *De antiquitate ecclesiae Glastoniensis*. (See *A Catalogue of the Entire and Valuable Library of Books of the Late Henry Fielding, Esq.*, in H. Amory, ed. *Sale Catalogues of Libraries of Eminent Persons*, vol. 7 [London, 1973], pp. 140–58, items 522 and 520, respectively.)

3 The account, in Latin, is in Vol. II of Hearne's edn. of John of Glastonbury (see above, n. 2), pp. 310–11. I quote the translation in Richard Warner, *An History of the Abbey of Glaston; and the Town of Glastonbury* (Bath: 1826), pp. lxx–lxxi.

4 John Collinson, *History and Antiquities of the County of Somerset* (1791), II.258.

5 See F. J. Pope, *Notes & Queries*, 12th ser., 6 (Feb. 1920), 34; and the Davidge family pedigree in *A Visitation of the County of Kent, begun in 1663, finished in 1668*, Publications of the Harleian Society, Vol. 54 (London: 1906), p. 46. See also Richard Davidge's will, made 17 Apr. 1666, naming as his beneficiaries his wife Katherine and his eight children (PRO: P.C.C.1666). The Davidge family lived principally at Dorchester and Bridport, and owned other property in Dorset – in the Isle of Purbeck, for example. He left Sharpham Park to his wife.

6 In Jan. 1692 Charles and Katherine Cottington were suing her sisters Sarah and Anne over the terms of her brother Thomas's will of 1683, by which, they claimed, all the Davidge lands should have come to Katherine (PRO: C.22.234.33). Obviously, the suit was unsuccessful, at least with respect to the disposition of Sharpham Park.

7 Their marriage settlement, dated 16 Feb. 1676/7, is in the Somerset Record Office, Taunton (DD/BR/vi 33).
CONCERNING THE TREATMENT OF DATES IN THIS BOOK. Until the calendar reform of September 1752, the new year in England (Old Style) officially began on 25 March and the dates were eleven days earlier than on the Continent (New Style). Throughout this book the form "1676/7", etc., is used with dates from 1 January to 24 March (O.S.) occurring before 1753.

8 Warner identifies the room as that "lighted by the small window which

appears over the chapel" (and just below Davidge Gould's weather vane) in Plate 1.

9 See "Aretine" in *Old England* (27 May 1749); and "Orbilius" in *An Examen of the History of Tom Jones, a Foundling* (1749).

10 See the marginal comment in Coleridge's copy of the novel (BL: C.28.c.5).

11 See W. L. Cross, *The History of Henry Fielding* (New Haven, Conn.: 1918), II.165–6.

12 Meare Pond, now drained, is shown on maps of the period, as in *Magna Britannia et Hibernia, Antiqua & Nova* (1720), opp. p. 720.

13 See Richardson to Mrs. Donnellan, 22 Feb. 1752, in J. Carroll (ed.), *Selected Letters of Samuel Richardson* (Oxford: 1964), p. 197.

14 This slab, at present under the tower of the church, records the fact that Judge Gould (spelled "Gold") died on 26 Mar. 1710 in his sixty-seventh year.

15 See B. Harrison, *Henry Fielding's "Tom Jones": The Novelist as Moral Philosopher* (London: 1975), pp. 75 ff., 113–15.

16 Information relating to the Gould family (the name being formerly spelled Goold or Goole) may be found in the Somerset Record Office. The Winsham parish registers record that Sir Henry's father Andrew – son of Henry Goold and Agnes (née Bagge), who married 23 Apr. 1599 – was baptized 3 Mar. 1615/16 and was buried 11 Dec. 1682. Andrew married Maude Linbearde (or Magdalen Linbear) in the church of St. Mary Major, Exeter, Devon, on 12 Jul. 1642 (see the register in the Exeter Public Library). Besides Sir Henry, they had two other sons, Andrew and James.

17 See the Middle Temple Admissions Book (24 May 1660), where he is described as "Mr. Henry Goold soone and heire of Andrew Goold of Winsham in ye County of Somerset, Gent."

18 The St. Benedict's register records Judge Gould's burial on 8 Apr. 1710.

19 Davidge was admitted to the Middle Temple 21 Nov. 1692; called to the Bar 15 May 1702; and made Bencher 24 May 1734. (See J. B. Williamson,

The Middle Temple Bench Book, 2nd edn. [London: 1937], p. 166.)

20 See the Lambeth Palace Library, the Vicar General's Calendar of Marriage Allegations, 3 Aug. 1709, where Honora is said to be sixteen years old (her surname is incorrectly given as Hockman). The register of St. Benedict's, Glastonbury, records the births and burials of eight of Fielding's cousins, the children of Davidge and Honora Gould – among them Henry, born 28 Dec. 1711; William, born 6 Jan. 1713/14; and Davidge, born 18 Oct. 1715. Honora died on 16 Jul. 1731; Davidge (the elder) was buried on 23 Oct. 1765.

21 Henry, Davidge's eldest son and heir, was admitted to the Middle Temple 16 May 1728, called 14 Jun. 1734, Bencher 3 May 1754, etc. Davidge, the third son, was admitted 27 May 1734, but seems not to have been called. Thomas was admitted 27 Nov. 1745, called 29 Jun. 1750, Bencher 28 Jan. 1785, Reader 1793, Treasurer 1799. (See Williamson, *Middle Temple Bench Book*, pp. 172, 190; and Sir Henry F. MacGeagh (ed.), *Register of Admissions to the Honourable Society of the Middle Temple* [London: 1949], I.304, 316, 336.)

22 *Jacobite's Journal* (20 Aug. 1748).

23 See J. H. Round, *Studies in Peerage and Family History* (London: 1901), pp. 216 ff.

24 G. B. Hill (ed.), *Memoirs of the Life of Edward Gibbon* (London: 1900), p. 5.

25 J. Nichols, *Literary Anecdotes of the Eighteenth Century* (1812), III.384.

26 See R. Latham and W. Matthews (eds.), *The Diary of Samuel Pepys*, Vol. VIII, 1667 (London: 1974), pp. 208, 321.

27 See J. A. Venn, *Alumni Cantabridgiensis* (Cambridge: 1922), Pt. I, Vol. ii; also Cross, *History*, I.10–13.

28 Cross mistakenly identified Fielding's grandmother as "Bridget, daughter of Scipio Cockayne (or Cokayne), a Somerset squire" (*History*, I.13). No record of John's marriage has been found. It is certain, however, that his wife's name was Dorothy Cockayne, and probable that she was the daughter of Scipio and Dorothy Cockayne

residing at Wendy-cum-Shingay, Cambridgeshire, only a few miles distant from Cockayne Hatley, Bedfordshire, which had been the principal seat of the family from as early as 1417.

That her name was Dorothy we know both from the parish registers of Puddletown, Dorset, which identify her as the mother of Dorothy (20 Dec. 1677) and Edmund Fielding (20 Jan. 1679/80); and from the records of the Court of Chancery (PRO: C.41.37.406). That she was a member of the Cockayne family is clear from the will of George Cockayne of the Cursitor's Office, Middlesex, Gent., who mentions as his sisters "Dorothy ffeilding," Elizabeth Godwyn, Anne Rives, and Katherine Bernard (PRO: P.C.C.1718). That she sprang from the branch of the Cockayne family residing at Wendy-cum-Shingay, Cambridgeshire, is not certain; but the parish registers, though imperfect for the period in question, record the baptisms of several children of Thomas Cockayne, among them Scipio (17 Dec. 1620), and they further reveal that on 21 Dec. 1643 a daughter Katherine was born to Scipio and Dorothy Cockayne. We know that Fielding's grandmother had a sister Katherine, and she may herself have been named after her mother.

29 The parish registers record the baptisms of the following: Bridget, 26 Jun. 1675; Dorothy, 20 Dec. 1677; William, 1 Sep. 1685. The entry for Edmund gives the date of his birth. According to Venn, Edmund's elder brother John was born at Puddletown c. 1674; he attended school in Salisbury before being admitted to Christ's College, Cambridge, on 21 Feb. 1688/9 in his fifteenth year (B.A. 1692/3). There is no record of the births of Edmund's brother George or his sister Elizabeth.

30 At the time of his death at St. Iago de la Vega, Jamaica, John Fielding owed £2,400 to one Maurice Conyers of Middlesex. Mentioned in John's will are his widow Dorothy, two sons William and Charles, and a daughter Elizabeth – none of whom lived in England, but rather in Ireland or Jamaica. (PRO: Prob. 31.83.659; also 31.85.772.)

31 PRO: P.C.C.1738.

32 See Huguenot Society of London, Vol. 26 (Manchester: 1922). Registers for the Church of the Savoy, etc., p. 138.

33 See W. H. Jones, *Fasti Ecclesiae Sarisberiensis* (Salisbury: 1879), esp. pp. 358, 384, 433; C. H. Mayo, *Notes & Queries for Somerset and Dorset*, 6 (1899), 183, and 14 (1915), 231; and Bodleian Library, Oxford, Ms. Tanner, 35, f. 230, letters dated 17 Mar. 1682/3. Additional information was supplied by P. Rundle, Archivist, Wiltshire County Record Office, Trowbridge (esp. Register of Bishop Seth Ward, 1674–88: DI/2/23).

34 HMC: Reports of the Mss. of the late Allan George Finch, Esq. Report 71, Vol. 2 (1922), p. 383; see also p. 389.

35 D. Slatter (ed.), *The Diary of Thomas Naish* (Devizes, Wilts.: 1965), pp. 34, 40; and the notebooks of C. R. Everett, Chapter Records, Cathedral Library, Salisbury, [A, p. 13], [A2, p. 14ᵛ], and [J, p. 4]. There is no record of his burial in Salisbury.

36 C. Dalton, *English Army Lists and Commission Registers, 1661–1714* (London: 1904), Vol. 5, Pt. 2, p. 43, n. 8.

37 See *Tom Jones* (VII.xii) and *Amelia* (IV.vii).

38 *Historical Record of the King's, Liverpool, Regiment of Foot*, 2nd edn. (1883), p. 214.

39 *London Magazine*, 10 (Jun. 1741), 310.

40 BL: Blenheim Papers, Add. Mss. 61287, f. 112.

41 Unless otherwise noted, my account of Edmund's relations with the Goulds and of the purchase of the East Stour estate is based on documents referred to below, nn. 78–81.

42 See PRO: W.O.25.3149, pp. 57–8; and BL: Mss. Bibl. Eg., 1631, p. 24ᵛ.

43 PRO: P.C.C.1710. The will, by which Judge Gould also left £100 to his wife and the rest of his estate to his son Davidge, was proved on 5 May 1710.

44 See the register of St. Benedict's, Glastonbury.

45 In *Magna Britannia et Hibernia, Antiqua & Nova* (1720) the manor at Stour is said to have been "anciently" part of the extensive lands of

the rich Abbey of Shaftesbury and to have been granted after the Dissolution to Thomas Wriothesley, Earl of Southampton (p. 568); it is referred to as the "Seat" of "Ed. Fielding, Esq." (p. 602).

In the late seventeenth century the lands of East Stour were in the possession of Sir Robert Napier (*c.* 1642–1700) of Punknoll, Dorset – barrister of the Middle Temple (1660), sheriff of Dorset (1680), baronet (25 Feb. 1681/2), and twice MP for Dorchester (1690, 1698–1700). He had begun to sell off these lands at the time of his death (PRO: P.C.C.1700). Judge Gould purchased the estate in the winter of 1709–10 from Sir Robert's daughters Ann and Theodosia and his son Sir Charles (PRO: Deeds enrolled in Court of King's Bench. Hil., 8 Anne 1709. Dorset; and Docket Book. Ind. 6112. Hil., 8 Anne 1709. The relevant plea roll is missing). A receipt signed by Ann Napier on 4 Jul. 1714 attests that Davidge Gould had paid in full the principal and interest on "the bond"; the bond itself is lost, but presumably this transaction concluded the purchase of the farm. (The receipt, together with other documents pertaining to Davidge Gould's affairs, is at the offices of Dodson, Harding & Reed, Solicitors, Bridgwater, Somerset, whose assistance I gratefully acknowledge.)

46 See *Succession of Colonels from their Rise to 1744* (1745), s.v. "Foot, Broke: 37 Foot" (BL: B.S.45/152 [4]).

47 See the following documents in the PRO, all relating to the affairs of Edmund's regiment during this period: W.O.25.3151, p. 6; S.P.44.110, pp. 308–9; W.O.26.12, pp. 252^v, 300; W.O.4.13, p. 98; W.O.4.14, pp. 7, 20, 24, 204; W.O.25.3183; W.O.30.89, pp. 178, 374.

48 See the register of Christ's church, East Stour.

49 The housekeeper, Marie Bentham, sued to recover the debt in Trinity Term, 1721 (PRO: K.B.122.99, Roll 572^v). The Court ruled in her favor on 3 Jul. 1721, and added 53 shillings damages.

50 Freke died in May 1721, never having succeeded in getting Edmund to

repay the money. His executors sued to recover the debt in May 1724 (PRO: C.11.2171/12).

51 See below, p. 37.

52 *Joseph Andrews* (I.iii). In the *Covent-Garden Journal* (11 Feb. 1752), Fielding calls this work "the great Favourite of my Youth."

53 See below, n. 81, testimony of Frances Barber, dated 28 Nov. 1721. Documents of the Wiltshire County Record Office show that Oliver was curate of Motcombe as early as 1707 (Visitation Mandates, 1699–1744) and that he remained there until his death in 1750 (Churchwarden's Presentment records, Gillingham, 1719–89). See also the Visitation Book, 1734–89 of Gillingham, and the Clergy and Churchwardens' Lists, 1718–61.

54 The Rev. Edward Peacock, quoted in the Notebooks of C. R. Everett [A, p. 69]: Chapter Records, Cathedral Library, Salisbury.

55 *Tom Jones* (IV.viii).

56 *Yearbook* of the Society of Dorset Men in London (1908–9), p. 7.

57 See below, n. 81, testimony of Frances Barber, 28 Nov. 1721.

58 See Hill's letter to Edmund at Jersey, 30 May 1737; in Hill's *Works* (1753), I.350–1.

59 See below, n. 81, Edmund Fielding's testimony, 29 Jun. 1721.

60 *Daily Gazetteer* (11 Feb. 1737).

61 In letters addressed to the Duke of Newcastle on 24 and 25 Mar. 1736 Edmund interceded first on behalf of a soldier and a woman accused, wrongly he believed, of murdering their bastard child (they had spent three miserable winters in jail, shackled hands and feet), and then on behalf of three other prisoners who had been languishing several years in a dungeon (PRO: S.P.47.4).

62 See above, n. 50.

63 See above, n. 58.

64 The registers of Christ's church, East Stour, record Edmund's baptism on 22 Apr. and Anne's burial on 6 Aug. 1716.

65 In the Museum of the Gillingham Local History Society.

66 C. Dalton, *George I's Army* (London: 1912), II.141.

67 Robert Lilburne of Gray's Inn Lane was the victim of this assault; on 8

Jul. 1718 he sued Midford for £500 damages (PRO: K.B.1.1, Mich., 4 Geo. I).

68 PRO: C.11.2726/91. *Feilding v. Midford.* The complaint is dated 22 Oct. 1722.

69 In Harris's unpublished Ms., "An Essay on the Life and Genius of Henry Fielding, Esqʳ." (1758). Quotations from this work and from the Harris/Fielding correspondence are by the kind permission of the Earl of Malmesbury.

70 See above, n. 66.

71 The Poor Rate Books for St. James's, Gt. Marlborough Div., show that from 1718 to 1723 Edmund occupied a house on the west side of Blenheim St., rateable value £1.0.0; in 1724 he had moved to more expensive quarters (value £1.3.0) in Poland St. nearby (Westminster History Collection, Buckingham Palace Road: D26-32.) The books for 1725–6 are missing, and thereafter his name does not appear.

72 The register of St. James's, Piccadilly, records the births and baptisms of Edmund's children by his new wife: (1) George, born 18 Oct. 1719; (2) Charles, born 13 Oct. 1720; (3) John, born 16 Sep. 1721; (4) William, born 11 Nov. 1723; (5) Basil Thomas, born 19 Sep. 1726. Another son, James, was baptized on 15 Nov. 1724 at St. Martin-in-the-Fields. In *The Life and Works of Sir John Fielding* (London: 1934), R. Leslie-Melville stated that all John's brothers died young (p. 3). Not all were so ill fated. On the nomination of the Earl of Pembroke, George attended the Charterhouse School as Exhibitioner from 1730 to 1737, when he matriculated as Scholar of St. Catherine's, Cambridge; the Charterhouse records indicate that he "died young and unmarried" (B. Marsh and F. A. Crisp [eds.], *Alumni Carthusiani: A Record of the Foundation Scholars of Charterhouse, 1614–1872* [London: 1913], p. 94). William had a military career that lasted until 1778 (see below, Part III, n. 63).

73 See Dalton, *English Army Lists*, Vol. 5, Pt. 2, p. 43, n. 8; and *The History of the Welch Regiment* (Cardiff: 1932), Ch. i.

74 In a letter of 4 Oct. 1720 Edmund cited heavy losses in the fall of South Sea stocks as the reason for his being unable to repay the debt he owed Thomas Freke (PRO: C.11.2171/12).

75 The sale is cited in *Index of Fines*, 1–7 Geo. I, Trin. 7 Geo. I. Dorset, p. 199ᵛ ((PRO: C.P.25 [2]). A much fuller account is the Declaration of Trust by Awnsham Churchill in the Dorset Record Office, Dorchester (s.v. Deeds, East Stour). The dates of the sale were 5–6 Aug. 1720. Together with Martin Folkes and Thomas Bennet, Churchill was acting as agent for William Wake, Archbishop of Canterbury, and his daughter Magdalen.

76 Preface, *Journal of a Voyage to Lisbon* (1755); see also *Covent-Garden Journal* (21 Oct. 1752).

77 Lady Gould's name appears in various Salisbury records as early as 1720 (but not earlier), and thereafter until her death in 1733. See the Highway Assessment Book, 16 Mar., 19 Jun. 1720; the Poor Book of St. Martin's parish, 25 May 1720; and the Vestry Accounts of that parish for 1720, where it is acknowledged that her servant paid 2s. 6d. for seats in a pew. (Wiltshire County Record Office.) Considering the rather high assessment in the Poor Book (£1.8.0. in 1730), the house was probably a good one – which, however, she rented rather than owned. The Salisbury antiquarian T. H. Baker was of the opinion that the house was situated "In St. Martin's Church St. between St. Mary's Home [and] the Church" (Ms. "Salisbury Notes", Annex 52, p. 223). J. P. de Castro further speculated that it was the fourth house from the still extant Elizabethan trades hall in St. Anne St. (*Notes & Queries*, 12th ser., 3 [Nov. 1917], 468).

78 PRO: C.11.259/37. Also collected under this call number are the replies of Edmund Fielding, summarized below, and of the trustees, Davidge Gould and William Day.

79 PRO: C.11.2283/45.

80 PRO: K.B.122.99, Roll 302.

81 See the following in the Register of Affidavits for Chancery at the PRO, all having the call number C.41.37: Katherine Cottington (Easter 1721, No. 546, 22 May; Trinity 1721,

No. 15, 29 May); Margaret Sanger (Trinity 1721, No. 17, 11 May); Anne Delaborde (No. 16, 29 May); Marie Bentham (No. 14, 9 Jun.); Richard Gough (No. 405, 26 Jun.); Thomas Grafton (No. 404, 24 Jun.); Dorothy Feilding and Bridget Lapenotier (No. 406, 26 Jun.); Frances Barber, Henry Halstead, and Joseph Burt (No. 403, 26 Jun.); Edmund Feilding (No. 402, 28 Jun.; Michaelmas 1721, No. 1014, 18 Dec. [C.41.38]). See also the following Depositions in Chancery, all having the call number C.24.1396, Pt. 1, No. 29: Frances Barber, 28 Nov. 1721; Bridget Penotier [sic], 6 Dec.; Peter Wiggett, 12 Dec.

82 The following discussion is based on my article, "Henry Fielding, Sarah Fielding, and 'the dreadful Sin of Incest,'" Novel: A Forum on Fiction, 13 (1979), 6–18.

83 See L. Stone, The Family, Sex and Marriage in England 1500–1800 (New York: 1977), pp. 115–16, 491, 507–18, and passim.

84 As, for example, in The Temple Beau (1730), IV.vi, and the opening paragraph of Joseph Andrews, II.x.

85 Cf. the distinguished psychologist Sandor Ferenczi: "Sexually unsatisfied women ... very commonly dream of thieves breaking in, of attacks by robbers or wild beasts, not one of the well-concealed incidents of the dream betraying the fact that the outrages to which the dreamer is subjected really symbolize sexual acts" (Sex in Psycho-Analysis, trans. E. Jones [Boston: 1916], pp. 107–8).

86 A. Digeon, Le Texte des romans de Fielding (Paris: 1923), p. 99.

87 Sarah Fielding, The Adventures of David Simple, ed. M. Kelsall (London: 1969), pp. 162–3.

88 A. Digeon, "Fielding a-t-il écrit le dernier chapitre de 'A Journey from This World to the Next'?", Revue Anglo-Américaine, 8 (1931), 430.

89 Sarah Fielding, The Governess: or, Little Female Academy, ed. J. E. Grey (London: 1968), pp. 5, 124–8. Complimentary allusions to Fielding's works abound in Sarah's writings: e.g., Familiar Letters (1747), I.285–7; The Cry (1754), I.16, 169, II.1, 99, 297, III.118, 122–4; The Lives of Cleopatra and Octavia (1757), pp. ii–

iii; and The History of the Countess of Dellwyn (1759), I.6, 53–4, 97, 249 n., 258, 282, II.162.

90 Sarah was a friend of Harris's. He assisted her in her translation of Xenophon's Memoirs of Socrates (Bath: 1762), where she refers to him as "one not more known for his Learning, than esteemed for his Candour and Benevolence" (p. 2, n.).

91 See J. A. Williams, Catholic Recusancy in Wiltshire, 1660–1791 (Newport, Mon.: 1968), pp. 175–6.

92 Consider in Amelia (VI.vii) Booth's commending a passage in Diodorus Siculus on the folly of placing a stepmother over one's children: "a very wise Law of Charondas ... by which Men, who married a second time, were removed from all public Councils: for it was scarce reasonable to suppose, that he who was so great a Fool in his own Family, should be wise in public Affairs."

93 Beginning with Christmas 1721, it would have been unlawful for Henry to spend his vacations with his father. On 30 Nov. 1721 the Court ordered that "Henry Fielding who is now at Eaton School be at liberty to go" to Lady Gould at the Christmas recess (PRO: C.33.337. Pt. 1, p. 70). On 18 Dec. of the same term (Michaelmas) Edmund's attorney declared that he intended to ask the Court the following term to rescind this order so that Henry "might be with his father during his recesses from school" (PRO: C.41.38.1014). He seems, however, to have failed in this motion. On 26 Apr. 1722 the Court ordered that Henry spend the Whitsun recess with Lady Gould in Salisbury (PRO: C.33.337, Pt. 1, p. 206ᵛ). And on 28 May 1722 the Lord Chancellor decreed that Henry and his sisters spend all their recesses from school with their grandmother (see below, n. 96).

94 Amelia (II.v.).

95 As noted by W. B. Coley, "Henry Fielding and the Two Walpoles," Philological Quarterly, 45 (1966), 166, n. 45, Walpole's copy of Cibber's Apology (in which the anecdote is recorded on pp. 164–5) is at the King's School, Canterbury.

96 See PRO: C.33.337, Pt. 2, p. 377.

97 Defoe, A Tour through the Whole

Island of Great Britain (1724; ed. P. Rogers, Harmondsworth: 1971), p. 284.

98 "Ode on a Distant Prospect of Eton College," written in 1742, but based on Gray's experience as a schoolboy at Eton from 1727 to 1732.

99 See R.A. Austen-Leigh, *The Eton College Register, 1698–1752* (Eton: 1927).

100 The authoritative *History of Eton College*, 4th edn. (London: 1911), is by Sir H.C. Maxwell Lyte. Also useful is P.S.H. Lawrence (ed.), *The Encouragement of Learning* (Wilton, Salis.: 1980), an anthology of items from *Etoniana*, the periodical published by R.A. Austen-Leigh from 1904 to 1955.

101 See Maxwell Lyte, *Eton College*, p. 285. The above estimates of expenses are based in both cases on bills for half a year: i.e., for Pitt £29.0.3, for Gough £22.5.4.

102 Quoted ibid., pp. 281–2.

103 *Ovid's Art of Love Paraphrased* (1747), p. 4, n. (b).

104 *Amelia* (X.i).

105 In the following account of texts read at Eton early in the eighteenth century I am indebted to P.J. Quarrie, the College Librarian.

106 Cf. *Covent-Garden Journal* (8 Aug. 1752), where Fielding published a translation of Tibullus' Elegy 1 of Book I: "an incomparable Elegy," the author remarks, "which you must formerly have got by Heart in a certain Book called *Electa Minora*, or more commonly at *Eton, Elector Minor*."

107 Maxwell Lyte, *Eton College*, Ch. 16 ("Eton Life in 1766").

108 This is the view of P.J. Quarrie in his helpful letter to me of 21 Dec. 1987. Quarrie observes that Fielding could not have read at Eton the following texts cited by James: *Poetae Graeci* (1755), *Scriptores Romani* (c. 1760), and Pomponius Mela, ed. John Reynolds (1711), but not in use at Eton until c. 1740.

109 An anthology of the classics by Thomas Farnaby (1575?–1647).

110 Fielding knew the tragedies of Sophocles, but not in this edition by John Burton (1696–1771), which was published in 1758.

111 Copies of John Potter's *Antiquities of Greece*, 2 vols. (Oxford: 1697–9), and Basil Kennett's *Antiquities of Rome* (1721), were in Fielding's library (items 48 and 179); he refers to the former work extensively in his and William Young's translation of Aristophanes' *Plutus*.

112 Maxwell Lyte, *Eton College*, p. 332.

113 On 22 Nov. 1723 the trusteeship of the East Stour estate was temporarily transferred, at his request, from Davidge Gould to Lady Gould and Mrs. Cottington, together with Marie Bentham "their surety," all of Salisbury (PRO: C.33.341, Pt. 1, p. 45). On 19 Dec. 1724 Davidge Gould resumed the trust, asking the Court to appoint a Receiver to receive the rents and profits of the farm and apply them to the children's benefit. (PRO: C.33.343, Pt. 1, p. 175. See also Register of Affidavits, C.41.40.1206.)

114 See the letter from "A Moderate Man" in *The Craftsman* (5 Jun. 1736); attributed to Fielding in Battestin and M.G. Farringdon, *New Essays by Henry Fielding: His Contributions to "The Craftsman" (1734–1739)* (Charlottesville, Va.: 1989).

115 As late as 28 Apr. 1729 the name of "Coll. Edward Feilding" appears in an account of the rental property in the Manor of Upton Grey by John Opie, Bread Street Hill, London, in connection with the sale of the Opie estate to one "Heathcote, Esq"" of Great Russell Street, Bloomsbury. The rental paid was £2.15.0 yearly, relatively little in comparison with most of the other properties listed. (See the J. Heathcote papers, Hampshire Record Office, Winchester: 58M71M.E/B44.)

116 In an article, "Fielding and Lyme Regis," *Times Literary Supplement* (4 Jun. 1931), De Castro cites a work entitled *Early Days of the Vyne Hunt* (1865), where it is said that Fielding hunted in North Hampshire. I have not found such a statement in the rare publication, *Recollections of the Early Days of the Vine Hunt* (1865), "By a Sexagenarian," in the library of The Vyne; but perhaps De Castro had in mind the unpublished version, entitled "Recollections of the Vine Hunt," by the Rev. J.E. Austen Leigh, to which C.W. Chute refers in

A History of the Vyne (Winchester: 1888), Ch. vi.

117 From Harris's Ms. "Essay on the Life and Genius" of Fielding (1758).

118 *Daily Gazetteer* (30 Jul. 1740).

119 See C. Wanklyn, *Lyme Leaflets* (Colchester: 1944), pp. 68–9; and his earlier note in *Somerset and Dorset Notes & Queries*, 20 (Mar. 1930), 166–7. The original documents, reproduced opposite p. 69 of Wanklyn's book, were once in the Borough Misdeameanour Book at Lyme; but the top half of the page is now in the Robert Taylor Collection, Firestone Library, Princeton University.

120 Sarah Andrew's parents married at Heavitree, Devon, on 5 Oct. 1709. Her father died in 1712; his sons William and Solomon died in 1713 and 1714, respectively, leaving Sarah as his heiress. Sarah's mother's father was William Huckmore of Buckland Baron, Devon. Soon after Solomon Andrew died, Sarah's mother remarried, this time Brent Reynell, Esq. (see De Castro, *Somerset and Dorset Notes & Queries*, 20 [Mar. 1930], 17–18). Sarah's mother was one of two sisters of Honora, Davidge Gould's wife, the other being Jane (who married three times, her surname becoming first Palmer, then Pitt, then Speke): see the indenture in the Somerset Record Office (DD/BR/vi/33) and the *Dictionary of National Biography* (s.v. Henry Gould the younger). The mother of these girls, "Madam Hockmore," went to live at Sharpham Park after Honora's marriage in 1709 and was buried at St. Benedict's, Glastonbury, on 1 Nov. 1710.

121 See A. Dobson, *Fielding* (London: 1907), Appendix I.

122 In 1699 Andrew Tucker married Florence (1680–1768), the sister of Sarah's father Solomon Andrew. I am grateful to Mr. G. Reed for his advice on the pedigree of the Tucker family.

123 See Wanklyn, *Lyme Leaflets*, pp. 69–71. Tucker's declaration is in the Lyme Regis Misdemeanour Book, now at the Dorset County Record Office (B7/A3/1).

124 See B. Rizzo, "Joseph Lewis in *Real Calamity*," *Bulletin of the New York Public Library*, 81 (1978), 84–9, esp. p. 84, n. 2; also K. Williamson, ibid., pp. 74–83.

125 Lewis was bound in the sum of £80, Cossens for £40. (See "Fugitive Pieces", Dorset County Record Office: B7/N23/4, f. 25).

126 I am grateful to Mrs. M. M. Rowe, Devon Record Office, Exeter, for supplying this information from the Heavitree parish register. On the south wall of St. Michael's church, Heavitree, a tablet commemorates members of the Rhodes family, including Ambrose and Sarah, who is there mistakenly said to have died on "the 22nd of August 1785 aged 83." (See B. F. Cresswell, *Exeter Churches* [Exeter: 1908], p. 39.)

127 I am grateful to Mr. V. Smith, formerly of Somerset West, South Africa, for furnishing me with photographs of the portrait in his possession (see Plate 7) and the caption accompanying it.

128 For this information I am grateful to Miss G. A. Rushton, Hampshire Record Office.

129 See the following documents in the PRO: K.B. Crown Side Index 6672, Mich., 13 George I, No. 127, Middlesex, ffielding, henricus; K.B.10.19, Pt. 1, Indictments; K.B.29.386, Mich., Middlesex, CXXVII.

PART II

1 Our thanks to Messrs. Phillips and Must of Drummonds Branch, the Royal Bank of Scotland, Charing Cross, London, for making these ledgers available.

2 *Historical Register*, 12 (1727), 27.

3 PRO: S.P.44.180, p. 99.

4 The murder took place on 10 Apr. 1727; Fisher was apprehended but escaped from Newgate on 17 May, the day before his trial. He fled to the Continent and was never brought to justice. For details see *Tom Jones*, eds. Battestin and F. Bowers (Middletown, Conn., and Oxford: 1975), p. 402, n. 3, and (on Willoughby) p. 458, n. 1.

5 For the text of Fielding's letter, mistakenly supposed to concern *The Modern Husband*, see R. Halsband

(ed.), *The Complete Letters of Lady Mary Wortley Montagu* (Oxford: 1966), II.96. See Battestin, "Dating Fielding's Letters to Lady Mary Wortley Montagu," *Studies in Bibliography*, 42 (1989), 246–8.

6 See "The Queen of Beauty," l. 17, and "To Euthalia," l. 14, in Fielding's *Miscellanies: Volume One*, ed. H. K. Miller (Middletown, Conn., and Oxford: 1972), pp. 78, 82.

7 See the London edition of 1733, l. 396, and the disclaimer in the collected edition of Swift's poetry (1735), where it is said that the London editor "maliciously inserted" Fielding's name, "for whose ingenious Writings" Swift "hath manifested a great Esteem."

8 See the *British Journal* (23 Sep. 1727).

9 *Covent-Garden Journal* (4 Feb. 1752).

10 *A Proposal for the better Regulation of the Stage* (1732), p. 10.

11 *The Laureat: or, The Right Side of Colley Cibber, Esq.* (1740), pp. 94–5.

12 Preface, *The Provoked Husband* (1728).

13 "AN ORIGINAL SONG, *Written on the first Appearance of the* BEGGARS OPERA, *by the late* HENRY FIELDING, Esq. *Author of* Tom Jones, &c. *then resident in* Salisbury," in the *Country Magazine*, 1 (Mar. 1787), 239. This magazine was published at Salisbury "By a Society of Gentlemen."

14 From the transcription by P. J. Blok, Professor of History at the University of Leyden, included among the correspondence of Austin Dobson at the Senate House, University of London (ADC Ms. 810/VI/10[ii]). Dobson summarizes this information in Appendix IV of his *Fielding* (London: 1907). The date is Continental New Style, see Part I n. 7 above.

15 See Thomas Nugent, *The Grand Tour; or, A Journey through the Netherlands, Germany, Italy, and France*, 3rd edn. (1778), I.102; and anon., *Les Délices de Leide* (Leyden: 1712), p. 71.

16 See W. Matthews (ed.), *The Diary of Dudley Ryder, 1715–1716* (London: 1939), p. 65.

17 See Johnson's brief life of Burmann in the *Gentleman's Magazine*, 12 (Apr. 1742), 206–10.

18 The Catalogue lists Burmann's editions of Petronius Arbiter (1709), of Quintilian's *Opera* (1720), and of Valerius Flaccus' *Argonauticon* (1724), [see Nos. 424–6].

19 See the note to I.i.10. For other references to Burmann, see *The Champion* (25 Dec. 1739), and the notes to *The Vernoniad*.

20 See the Preface to that play.

21 See Th. H. Lunsingh Scheurleer and G. H. M. Posthumus Meyjes (eds.), *Leiden University in the Seventeenth Century: An Exchange of Learning* (Leiden: 1975), esp. J. H. Waszink, "Classical Philology," pp. 161–75.

22 Ibid., p. 166.

23 Eliot. *Middlemarch* (1872), ch. XV.

24 See *A New Description of Holland, and the rest of the United Provinces in General* (1701), pp. 98 ff.; and *Travels through Flanders, Holland, Germany, Sweden, and Denmark*, 5th edn. (1725), pp. 14–15.

25 *A New Description of Holland*, pp. 99–100.

26 *Tom Jones* (XIII.v).

27 *Covent-Garden Journal* (24 Mar. 1752).

28 "An Essay on Conversation," in Miller (ed.), *Miscellanies: Volume One*, p. 127.

29 *Author's Farce* (1730), I.ii, II.vi; *Tom Jones*, XIII.i.

30 *Eurydice*, sc. 1.

31 *Author's Farce*, III; Preface, *Tragedy of Tragedies*.

32 *Grub-Street Opera*, III.xi.

33 Fielding's unfinished burlesque of the *Dunciad* (c. 1729), Canto I, line 88 (see I. M. Grundy, "New Verse by Henry Fielding," *Publications of the Modern Language Association of America*, 87 [1972], 222). See also "A Parody, from the First Æneid," l. 4, in Miller (ed.), *Miscellanies: Volume One*, p. 81.

34 *Universal Gallant*, III.

35 *Tom Jones*, VIII.xv.

36 *An Enquiry into the Causes of the late Increase of Robbers*, Sect. IV.

37 "Observations on Government", in *The Comedian*, No. 5 (Aug. 1732), p. 34.

38 *Enquiry*, Sect. XI.

39 See *Travels through Flanders*, p. 11; and *Directions for Travelling through Holland and Germany*, &c. (1734), Sig. A2ᵛ.

40 See *Travels through Flanders*, p. 103; and Nugent, *The Grand Tour*, I.99.

41 See Battestin, "Four New Fielding Attributions: His Earliest Satires of Walpole," *Studies in Bibliography*, 36 (1983), 69–109.

42 *An Historical View of the Principles, Characters, Persons, &c. of the Political Writers in Great Britain* (1740), pp. 49–50.

43 See the *Daily Journal* (1, 17 Jul. 1728).

44 Fielding's name does not appear in the court records of Harwich, Norwich, and King's Lynn for 1728–9; however, these records are incomplete and some other town may be meant.

45 See above, Part I, n. 1.

46 Edmund applied for the license in person on 1 Jan. 1728/9; he is said to be of St. James's, Westminster, and Eleanor Hill to be of St. Martin-in-the-Fields, Westminster. (Lambeth Palace Library: Faculty Office Calendar of Marriage Licences.) The marriage was to be solemnized in the church of St. Martin-in-the-Fields, but no record of it appears in the church register. That Eleanor Hill formerly resided in Salisbury is clear not only from the announcement of the marriage in the *Daily Post* (13 Jan. 1728/9), but also from the fact that she is buried in that city (see the register of St. Martin's church, Salisbury, 1702–58, entry dated 10 Aug. 1739). She appears to have been married formerly to one John Hill, whose will, probated in Jan. 1727/8, describes him as being "late of Salisbury and now of Richmond, Surrey" (PRO: P.C.C.1728).

47 The entry as transcribed by Blok (see above, n. 14) reads: "*1729*, 22 Febr. Henricus Fieldingh, by [i.e., living at the house of] Jan Oson."

48 In the archives of the Vierschaar der Universiteit te Leiden (inventory number 26, pp. 2ᵛ–3, 10ᵛ–11) in the Rijksarchief in Zuid-Holland, 's-Gravenhage. Though the complaint is against "Henricus Fielden," there can be no doubt that Fielding is meant: according to the official *Album Academicum* of the University, no one by the name "Henricus Fielden" was ever a student at Leyden. I am grateful to Arthur A.

Mietes of the Rijksarchief in Zuid-Holland for the search he made in my behalf, and to Mrs. Lotte Hellinga of the British Library for translating the Dutch.

49 On the Verbeeks, see A. C. Kruseman, *Aanteekeningen betreffende den Boekhandel van Noord-Nederland, in de 17de en 18de Eeuw* (Amsterdam: 1893), p. 568. I am grateful to Ms. Anne Goldgar for information about the Verbeeks.

50 See Battestin and M. G. Farringdon, *New Essays by Henry Fielding: His Contributions to "The Craftsman" (1734–1739)* (Charlottesville, Va.: 1989), pp. 336–48.

51 Ibid., pp. 71–91.

52 Preface to *Don Quixote in England*.

53 Preface to Miller (ed.), *Miscellanies: Volume One*, pp. 4–5.

54 *Memoirs of the Life of David Garrick, Esq.*, 4th edn. (1784), I.219–20.

55 Ibid., I.234.

56 R. D. Hume, *Henry Fielding and the London Theatre, 1728–1737* (Oxford: 1988), p. ix.

57 Grundy, *PMLA*, 87 (1972), 213–45.

58 *Fog's*, edited by Charles Molloy (d. 1767), succeeded *Mist's Weekly Journal* when the latter was suppressed in 1728.

59 Grundy, *PMLA*, 87 (1972), 214.

60 In Canto III, lines 76 and 81, respectively, Fielding alludes to the trial of Thomas Bambridge, keeper of the Fleet Prison, and to the publication of the astronomer John Machin's "Laws of the Moon's Motion according to Gravity," appended to Andrew Motte's translation of Newton's *Principia*: both these events occurred in May 1729. In the same canto, lines 52–3, however, Fielding possibly alludes to Pope's alleged sponsorship of the *Grub-Street Journal*, the first number of which was issued on 8 Jan. 1729/30 under the joint editorship of John Martyn and Richard Russel, who called themselves "Maevius" and "Bavius": Codrus in the poem declares that "While Maevius, Bavius (Stinking Names) survive/ So long in Grubstreet Annals shall I live." Cf., too, the first section of the poem (ll. 97–8) also in reference to Pope: "Sometimes the Lawrels on his

Notes to pages 80–90

Temples spring/ And Grubstreet Allies ecchoe to their King."

61 Miller (ed.), *Miscellanies: Volume One*, p. 57, n. 4.

62 On 3 Mar. 1729/30 for the sum of £31.10*s*. Edmund and Eleanor Fielding, now residing in the parish of St. George, Hanover Square, Middlesex, leased to Richard Lucas, a perukemaker of the same parish, a house on the east side of Dover Street. (Greater London Record Office (Middlesex): MDR/Bundle 474, No. 386.)

63 Halsband (ed.), *Complete Letters*, III.66.

64 The best study of Ralph is J. B. Shipley's "James Ralph: Pretender to Genius," unpublished dissertation (Columbia University, New York: 1963). I am indebted at many points to this work.

65 See H. S. Hughes, "Fielding's Indebtedness to James Ralph," *Modern Philology*, 20 (1922–3), 19–34. Also Shipley, "James Ralph," pp. 207, 214.

66 See R. D. Hume, "Henry Fielding and Politics at the Little Haymarket, 1728–1737," in J. M. Wallace (ed.), *The Golden and the Brazen World: Papers in Literature and History, 1650–1800* (Berkeley and Los Angeles: 1985), p. 81.

67 Hume makes this inference on the plausible grounds that Fielding did not receive a benefit until 13 May, the seventeenth night: see ibid, p. 90.

68 *Daily Post* (4 Aug. 1730).

69 *Daily Post* (17, 21 Oct. 1730).

70 See C. B. Woods (ed.), *The Author's Farce* (Lincoln, Nebr.: 1966), p. xi.

71 See Henley's advertisement in the *Daily Post* (3 Apr. 1730).

72 For references to Timothy Fielding see the following: E. L. Avery (ed.), *The London Stage, 1660–1800* (Carbondale, Ill.: 1960), Pt. 2, 1700–1729, pp. 985, 988; *Mist's Weekly Journal* (24, 31 Apr. 1728); *Craftsman* (2, 16, 23, 30 Aug. 1729); news items in *Daily Post* (13 Oct. 1732; 15, 20 Oct. 1733); and the Bloomsbury rent books, Bedford Estates Office, 1734–40 (s.v. "Buffalo Head").

73 Quoted from the 1731 edition, entitled *The Taste of the Town: or, A Guide to All Publick Diversions*, Essay I ("Of Musick; Particularly Dramatick"), pp. 22, 25–6.

74 Historical Mss. Commission, *MSS. of the Earl of Egmont. Diary of Viscount Percival* (London: 1920–3), I.97.

75 See L. J. Morrissey (ed.), Fielding's *"Tom Thumb" and "The Tragedy of Tragedies"* (Edinburgh: 1970), pp. 11–12.

76 *Daily Post* (1, 6–7 May 1730).

77 See news items in the *Daily Post* (27 Apr., 15 May 1730) and the advertisement in the same paper for 14 May.

78 *Fog's Weekly Journal* (1 Aug. 1730).

79 *Fog's Weekly Journal* (1 Aug. 1730); *Craftsman* (22 Aug. 1730).

80 For a sensibly skeptical review of such interpretations, see B. A. Goldgar, *Walpole and the Wits: The Relation of Politics to Literature, 1722–1742* (Lincoln, Nebr.: 1976), pp. 104–5.

81 Among the topics advertised for Henley's Oratory in the *Daily Post* (26–7 May 1730) is "Tom T. and Sir R. W."

82 See G. M. Godden, *Henry Fielding, A Memoir* (London: 1910), Appendix J.

83 See *Observations on the Present Taste for Poetry* (1739), pp. 16–21.

84 Jacob's *The Mirrour: or, Letters Satyrical, Panegyrical, Serious and Humorous, on the Present Times* (1733), esp. Preface (p. 3) and Letter III, *"To B[arnha]m G[oo]d, Esq; on the Judgment of the Town"* (p. 13). The date of the letter, 16 Feb. 1729/30, must be in error, as *Tom Thumb* had not then been performed.

85 *Daily Post* (29 May 1730).

86 *Read's Weekly Journal* (25 Jul. 1730).

87 In a note to this passage in the 3rd edn. of *Harlequin-Horace* (1735), ll. 537–8, Miller congratulated the directors of the theatres for improving *"this Marvellous* Incident, *wherein the* Cow *is said to have perform'd her Part beyond Expectation, and disgorg'd her little Inhabitant in full Health and Vigour, and in a Manner entirely Satisfactory to the transported Beholders."*

88 Other sarcasms against *Tom Thumb* occur in the *Grub-Street Journal* (7 May, 11 Jun., 17 Dec. 1730).

89 *Tom Thumb* is cited in this way by Samuel Foote in the Dedication to his comedy, *Taste* (1752), p. v; (by P. Hiffernan?) in the short-lived periodical *The Times* (21 Jan. 1754),

pp. 61–2; and by the reviewer of George Alexander Stevens's *Distress upon Distress* in the *Monthly Review*, 7 (Jul. 1752), 79.

90 Laetitia Pilkington, *Memoirs*, III (1751), 155.

91 See Goldgar, *Walpole and the Wits*, pp. 105–10, and p. 235, n. 52, where he modifies the conclusions set forth in his earlier article, "The Politics of Fielding's *Coffee-House Politician*," *Philological Quarterly*, 49 (1970), 424–9.

92 The verses in Fielding's script were in the upper left pane of the window to the left as one enters the elegant Georgian summer house; the pane is now in the Salisbury Museum. The verses would seem to confirm the essential part of the local tradition (R. C. Hoare, *History of Modern Wiltshire*, VI [1843], p. 602) that Fielding once lived at the Manor House at the foot of Milford Hill while composing *Tom Jones*: he did at one time use the summer house, which still stands and bears the coat of arms of the Swayne family, who were in possession of the property in the early eighteenth century. That he might have lodged at the Manor when in Salisbury is the more likely since his friends the Goldwyres, Charlotte's neighbors in The Close, held the copyhold estate (see the wills of William and Edward Goldwyre [PRO: P.C.C.1748, 1774]). But he probably used the summer house while composing, say, *The Temple Beau* rather than some much later work. The property is now owned by Messrs. Reed and Mallik, civil engineers. I am grateful to Mr. William Leak of Salisbury for calling the verses to my attention.

93 "To the Master of the Salisbury Assembly; Occasioned by a Dispute, whether the Company should have fresh Candles"; Miller (ed.), *Miscellanies: Volume One*, p. 76.

94 "Written *Extempore*, on a Half-penny, which a young Lady gave a Beggar, and the Author redeem'd for Half a Crown"; ibid., pp. 59–60.

95 "To Celia"; ibid., p. 71.

96 "The Queen of Beauty, t'other Day"; ibid., p. 79. Miller conjectures that the young lady referred to is Patience

Soper, who lived not far from Upton Grey (p. 79, n. 5).

97 *Journey from This World to the Next* (Introduction).

98 Fielding from Bath to Harris at Salisbury, 8 Sep. 1741.

99 Miller (ed.), *Miscellanies: Volume One*, pp. 68–9.

100 "To Celia"; ibid., pp. 63–5. The poem was presumably written sometime between the commencement of the *Grub-Street Journal* in Jan. 1729/30 and the death of the actor Anthony Boheme in Jan. 1730/31. Perhaps it can be dated more narrowly if we suppose that some friction developed between Fielding and Boheme upon the latter's playing the part of "Politic" in the Lincoln's Inn Fields production of *The Coffee-House Politician*, which ran only four nights in Dec. 1730.

101 Miller (ed.), *Miscellanies: Volume One*, p. 71.

102 Ibid., pp. 72–4.

103 Cf. his song in Act I, scene iii, with the poem, "Similes" (ibid., p. 74).

104 Ibid., p. 75.

105 Ibid., pp. 62–3.

106 They are so called in the advertisement at the end of *The Tryal of Colley Cibber* (1740).

107 *London Magazine*, 13 (Apr. 1744), 198. The verses do not appear in Price's *Poems on Several Occasions* (1741), to which, though neither Fielding nor Charlotte subscribed, many of their friends and acquaintances from the region did: e.g., Thomas Chubb, George Bubb Dodington, the Goldwyres, and Fielding's cousin, Henry Gould.

108 Lady Louisa Stuart, "Introductory Anecdotes," in Lord Wharncliffe (ed.), *The Letters and Works of Lady Mary Wortley Montagu*, rev. W. Moy Thomas (1861), I.105–6.

109 See the *Covent-Garden Journal* (11 Jan. 1752), where Fielding insists "that she had scarce a Scar left on it"; and Mrs. James's description of Amelia (XI.i).

110 See J. P. de Castro, *Times Literary Supplement* (13 Jan. 1927). Edward's father, William Goldwyre (1666–1748), was also an eminent surgeon and Charlotte's neighbor, but he seems to have retired from practice in 1732 or somewhat earlier (see the

Chapter Act Book, Salisbury Cathedral, XX [1696–1741], 27, 224); and in the *Covent-Garden Journal* Fielding clearly refers to a surgeon still living in 1752. That Fielding and Edward Goldwyre were friends is suggested not only by the latter's subscription to the *Miscellanies* (1743), but by Fielding's cordial reference to him in his letter to James Harris from Bath (24 Sep. 1742).

111 See below, p. 161.

112 Charlotte Cradock's father may have been Leonard Craddock, a major in General Erle's Regiment of Foot, who was killed at the Siege of Douai in Flanders in 1710/11; he also probably fought at the bloody Battle of Malplaquet in 1709, to which Fielding alludes in *Tom Jones* (VII.xii). His commissions: ensign, 25 Aug. 1693; captain, 18 Mar. 1699/1700; brevet major, 17 Mar. 1706/7; major, 23 Mar. 1709/10. (See C. Dalton, *English Army Lists and Commissions Registers, 1661–1714* [London: 1904], VI.337–8). In the P.C.C. administrations, dated 15 Mar. 1710/11 (PRO: Admons. Prob. 6.1711, s.v. March) he is said to be "late of Portsmouth" and his widow's name is Elizabeth. The earliest record of Elizabeth Cradock's residing in The Close, Salisbury, dates from 1714.

113 See the Register of Burials, 1719–1812 of the Cathedral Church of Sarum and the funereal tablet in the floor of the Cathedral itself, north side of the choir, east end. As she is said to be "of the Close," and as no other Cradocks are known to have resided there during this period, Mary Penelope was probably Charlotte's sister.

114 C. Everett, *Notebooks* [Q, p. 2], s.v. "Monday, 30 May 1791" (Wiltshire County Record Office). The Land Tax Assessments for the Liberty of The Close, New Sarum, were examined for the years 1712, 1714, 1716, 1719, 1721–6, 1728–33. Mrs. Cradock's name does not appear in 1712, but does in every case between 1714 and 1733; the exact position of the house is indicated, furthermore, by the fact that her name invariably occurs between those of James Harris and Mr. Goldwyre (WCRO: Salis-

bury District Council Records, X207; again I am grateful to Miss P. Rundle, Archivist, for assistance.)

115 *Amelia*, 1st edn., VI.vii.

116 *Of True Greatness* (1741); Miller (ed.), *Miscellanies: Volume One*, p. 28. *Joseph Andrews* (1742), I.xvii. See also *Tom Jones* (1749), II.vii.

117 Halsband (ed.), *Complete Letters of Lady Mary Wortley Montagu*, II.93.

118 See *The Champion* (1 Jul. 1740) and *Tom Jones* (VIII.i).

119 See Battestin, *Studies in Bibliography*, 36 (1983), 96–8.

120 Ibid., 103–6.

121 The *Daily Post* (28 Nov. 1730) announced the new title as "The City Politician: or, The Justice Caught in His Own Trap". When the play was performed on the 30th, it had been renamed *The Coffee-House Politician*.

122 See *Daily Post* (28 Nov. 1730).

123 Shipley is skeptical of the attribution to Cooke, which he believes to be entirely founded on a confusion of the farce with the poem by Cooke of the same title, published in 1725 and 1731 ("James Ralph", p. 224, n. 29). But the evidence, though inconclusive, is stronger than that: (1) The farce was published in Dec. 1730 under the pseudonym "Scriblerus Tertius", which Cooke used. (2) Cooke is also the probable author (accepted without question as such by Henry Pettit in the *New Cambridge Bibliography of English Literature*) of *The Bays Miscellany; or Colley Triumphant*, which contains not only the poem *The Battle of the Poets*, but also the play of that name, together with the "New Prologue" spoken at the New Theatre in the Haymarket at the opening of the season of 1730–1. (3) Finally, both the play and the "New Prologue" were published separately under the pseudonym "Scriblerus Tertius," identified in the British Library copy (11777.b.73) in what appears to be a contemporary hand as "Thomas Cooke." See also A. H. Scouten (ed.), *The London Stage, 1660–1800*, Pt. 3, 1729–1747 (Carbondale, Ill.: 1961).

124 From Southwark, where he was confined for debt within the Rules of the King's Bench, Cooke wrote Sir Hans Sloane on 2 and 13 Mar. 1730/1, revealing that he was the author of

the series called "The Traveller," which commences in the *British Journal* on 28 Nov. 1730 (BL: Sloane 4052, ff. 76–7).

125　See W. J. Burling, "Fielding, His Publishers and John Rich in 1730," *Theatre Survey*, 26 (1985), 41.

126　For bibliographical details, see J. A. Masengill, "Variant Forms of Fielding's *Coffee-House Politician*," *Studies in Bibliography*, 5 (1952), 178–83.

127　See Scouten (ed.), *London Stage*, Pt. 3.

128　*Gray's Inn Journal* (1756), II.170–1.

129　Crane, "The Concept of Plot and the Plot of *Tom Jones*," in R. S. Crane (ed.), *Critics and Criticism Ancient and Modern* (Chicago: 1952), p. 637.

130　See C. B. Woods, "Notes on Three of Fielding's Plays," *PMLA*, 52 (1937), esp. pp. 359–62.

131　See Morrissey (ed.), *"Tom Thumb" and "The Tragedy of Tragedies"*, p. 8.

132　*Daily Post* (22 Mar. 1730/1).

133　See *A Comment upon the History of Tom Thumb* (1711).

134　*Daily Post* (6 May 1731).

135　See Morrissey (ed.), *"Tom Thumb" and "The Tragedy of Tragedies"*, pp. 6, 114–15, notes to II.iv.10, 35, and II.v.2.

136　Grundy, *PMLA*, 87 (1972), 221, ll. 61–2.

137　See C. B. Woods, "Fielding's Epilogue for Theobald," *Philological Quarterly*, 28 (1949), 419–24; N. A. Mace, "Fielding, Theobald, and *The Tragedy of Tragedies*." *Philological Quarterly*, 66 (1987), 457–72.

138　Grundy, *PMLA*, 87 (1972), 244, ll. 124–31.

139　The other three works to which Fielding subscribed are: Thomas Cooke's translation of *The Comedys of Plautus* (1746) and two works by William R. Chetwood, *The Voyages, dangerous Adventures, and miraculous Escapes of Capt. Richard Falconer* (Dublin: 1752) and *The Voyages, Travels and Adventures of William Owen Gwin Vaughan, Esq.* (Dublin: 1754). Copies of the latter two very rare works are located, respectively, at Cambridge University Library (Bradshaw) and at the British Library and the National Library of Wales, Aberystwyth. For help in identifying these works, I am grateful to P. J. Wallis, co-author with F. J. G. Robinson, of *Book Subscription Lists: A Revised Guide* (Newcastle upon Tyne: 1975).

140　See below, p. 554.

141　Aston's ballad opera opens with an exchange between the Poet (who is meant to satirize Gay) and the Fool, who addresses the former as "Cudden Fool," accusing him of writing "Nonsense." The Poet replies: "Sirrah, you're not so great a Fool as you would make yourself" – to which the Fool returns: "Nor you so great a Wit, for all you wrote the Original *Grub-Street* Opera, Cudden."

142　In this same year of 1731, for instance, John Watts issued Vol. VI of *The Musical Miscellany; being a Collection of Choice Songs, and Lyrick Poems: with the Basses to each Tune, and Transpos'd for the Flute. By the most Eminent Masters.* Attesting to the reputation Fielding had already acquired as a writer of songs, this volume included songs from *Love in Several Masques* ("Ye Nymphs of Britain, to whose Eyes"), *The Temple Beau* ("Vain, Belinda, are your Wiles"), and *Rape upon Rape* ("Let a Set of sober Asses"). It also included the following humorous ditty never printed in any of Fielding's works: "*A* DIALOGUE *between a* BEAU'S HEAD *and his* HEELS, *taken from their Mouths as they were spoke at St. James's Coffee-House. By Mr.* FIELDING. To the Tune of, *Dear Catholick Brother*" (pp. 170–3). See H. P. Vincent, *Notes & Queries*, 184 (13 Mar. 1943).

143　See L. J. Morrissey (ed.), *The Grub-Street Opera* (Edinburgh: 1973), p. 8, n. 13.

144　E. V. Roberts (ed.), *The Grub-Street Opera* (Lincoln, Nebr.: 1968), p. 75.

145　Both Horace Walpole and Boswell attest to this tradition: see Walpole to Sir Horace Mann, 24 Feb. 1743, in W. S. Lewis, *et al.* (eds.), *Horace Walpole's Correspondence with Sir Horace Mann* (New Haven, Conn.: 1955), II.180 and n. 9; citing also Boswell's *London Journal, 1762–3*, ed. F. A. Pottle (New York: 1950), p. 154.

146　About 1735 Leveridge added five additional stanzas to these two by Fielding and also introduced a new tune. See E. V. Roberts, "Henry Fielding and Richard Leveridge: Authorship of 'The Roast Beef of Old England,'" *Huntington Library Quarterly*, 27 (1964), 175–81.

147 Goldgar, *Walpole and the Wits*, p. 110.

148 From *The Genuine Grub-Street Opera*; Morrissey (ed.), *Grub-Street Opera*, pp. 92–3.

149 *Daily Post* (9 Jun. 1731).

150 See the authoritative account of the publishing history of the play in Morrissey (ed.), *Grub-Street Opera*, pp. 13 ff.

151 *Grub-Street Journal* (15 Jul. 1731), quoting *London Evening Post* of 8 Jul. The charge was applied to *The Fall of Mortimer* among other Opposition writings.

152 *Grub-Street Journal* (24 Jun. 1731), quoting *St. James's Evening Post* for 17 Jun.

153 PRO: S.P.36.23, f. 252.

154 *Daily Journal* (22 Jul. 1731).

155 *Daily Post* (23 Aug. 1731).

156 According to the *Daily Journal* of 18 Aug. the play was published that day. Though the title-page contains no reference to the printer, stating only that it was "Printed and Sold for the Benefit of the Comedians of the NEW THEATRE in the *Haymarket*," Morrissey demonstrates that the work was printed by E. Rayner. (See Morrissey (ed.), *Grub-Street Opera*, pp. 16–17.)

157 This information from a newspaper clipping inserted in the British Library copy (C.45.d.12) of John Mottley's "List of all the Dramatic Authors" appended to Thomas Whincop's *Scanderbeg* (1747), opposite p. 233. The newspaper from which the clipping was taken is not known, and, though someone has written that the date is mid-April, it must in fact be mid-August 1731.

158 See Morrissey (ed.), *Grub-Street Opera*, pp. 18–21.

159 See E. V. Roberts, "Mr. Seedo's London Career and His Work with Henry Fielding", *Philological Quarterly*, 45 (1966), 179–90.

160 *Daily Post* (22 Dec. 1731).

161 See *Daily Post* for that date.

162 For this background, see E. V. Roberts, "Fielding's Ballad Opera *The Lottery* (1732) and the English

State Lottery of 1731," *Huntington Library Quarterly*, 27 (1963), 39–52.

163 See, for example, *Champion* (29 Dec. 1739, 3 Jan. 1739/40); *Joseph Andrews* (III.iii); *True Patriot* (12, 19, 26 Nov. 1745); *Tom Jones* (II.i).

164 In *The Lottery* (scene ii) Lovemore, having pursued his love Chloe from the country to town, exclaims "'Ha! by all that's infamous, she is in keeping already; some bawd has made prize of her as she alighted from the stage-coach. While she has been flying from my arms, she has fallen into the colonel's." So in Plate I of his famous series Hogarth depicts the bawd Mother Needham ensnaring Kate Hackabout the instant she arrives in town, while Colonel Charteris leeringly observes the proceedings. Since *The Harlot's Progress* was not published until April 1732, Fielding presumably saw in his friend's studio the painting which was the original of the print.

165 Earl of Ilchester (ed.), *Lord Hervey and His Friends, 1726–38* (London: 1950), p. 69. Lord Ilchester misdates this letter 4 Apr. 1731, as Scouten points out in *London Stage*.

166 See Walpole's note in the British Library copy of Lord Chesterfield's *Miscellaneous Works*, ed. M. Maty and J. O. Justamond (1777), II.361.

167 See C. Winton, "Benjamin Victor, James Miller, and the Authorship of *The Modish Couple*," *Philological Quarterly*, 65 (1985), 121–30.

168 See, for example, the criticisms in *Fog's Weekly Journal* (15 Jan. 1731/2); *Grub-Street Journal* (27 Jan., 10, 24 Feb., 16 Mar. 1731/2); and the anonymous verse satire, *Of Modern Wit. An Epistle to the Right Honourable Sir William Young* (Mar. 1732), pp. 6, 9.

169 C. B. Woods, *PMLA*, 52 (1937), 362–8.

170 Ibid., p. 366.

171 Ibid., p. 367.

172 Shaw, *Plays: Pleasant and Unpleasant* (New York: 1909), I.xiii.

173 *Daily Post* (3 Mar. 1732).

174 *See and Seem Blind: Or, A Critical Dissertation on the Publick Diversions, &c. ... In a Letter from the Right Honourable the Lord B—— to A—— H——, Esq*; (Jun. 1732), pp. 7–8. R. D. Hume has published a

facsimile of this obscure pamphlet in the Augustan Reprint Society Publications, No. 235 (Los Angeles: 1986); the author, he plausibly conjectures, may have been Aaron Hill. I am indebted to Professor Hume for calling my attention to this work.

175 He was not, as was once supposed, Sir William Yonge: see B. A. Goldgar, *Notes & Queries*, n.s. 19 (Jun. 1972), 226–7.

176 *Champion* (1 Jul. 1740); *Tom Jones* (VIII.i).

177 See B. A. Goldgar, "Pope and the *Grub-Street Journal*," *Modern Philology*, 74 (1977), 366–80.

178 See above, n. 139.

179 *Daily Post* (3 May 1732).

180 The *Daily Post* (16 May 1732) began promising that *The Old Debauchees* and *The Covent-Garden Tragedy* would open together on Monday, 29 May. The same paper (22 May) noted that the "two new Pieces" were in rehearsal and had been "very much approved by all who have read or heard them."

181 This hastily written document, dated 4 Apr. 1732 and signed by Fielding, is in the collection of Viscountess Eccles. In it Fielding refers to the two plays as "a Farce of three Acts called the despairing Debauchee and a Tragedy called the Covent-Garden-Tragedy"; but at this point he adds a note, "or by whatever other Names they shall be called."

182 The scandal is recounted in *The Case of Mrs. Mary Catharine Cadiere, against the Jesuit Father John Baptist Girard*, which went through ten editions by 1732.

183 *The Comedian*, No. 7 (Oct. 1732), pp. 38–9.

184 See above, n. 164.

185 See P. Lewis, "Fielding's *The Covent-Garden Tragedy* and Philips's *The Distrest Mother*," *Durham University Journal*, n.s. 37 (1975–6), 33–46.

186 See Walpole to Sir Horace Mann, 21 Aug. 1755; in Lewis *et al.* (eds.), *Horace Walpole's Correspondence with Sir Horace Mann*, IV.492–3.

187 *Daily Post* (5 Jun. 1732).

188 See G. Speaight, *The History of the English Puppet Theatre* (London: 1955), esp. pp. 104–8.

189 Thus twenty years later even Fielding's enemy, Dr. John Hill, acknow-

ledged that *The Mock Doctor* defined the qualities an English audience expected in a farce: see *London Daily Advertiser* (13 Jan. 1752).

190 See L. P. Goggin, "Fielding and the *Select Comedies of Mr. de Moliere*," *Philological Quarterly*, 31 (1952), 344–50; also J. E. Tucker, "The Eighteenth-Century English Translations of Molière," *Modern Language Quarterly*, 3 (1942), 83–103.

191 *London Evening Post* (4–6 May, 29 Jun.–1 Jul. 1732).

192 See below, p. 209.

193 Russel, who at first believed that Fielding and Theophilus Cibber collaborated on the letter from "Wm. Hint," came to attribute it to Fielding alone: see W. J. Burling, "Henry Fielding and the 'William Hint' Letter: A Reconsideration," *Notes & Queries*, 231 (Dec. 1986), 498–9.

194 From a poem written by a friend of the author "many Years ago" and quoted in *Observations on the Present Taste for Poetry* (1739), pp. 16–21.

195 So R. M. Davis, Lyttelton's biographer, was informed by De Castro: see *The Good Lord Lyttelton* (Bethlehem, Pa.: 1939), p. 216, n. 33. The late Lord Cobham assured me that no trace of the Fielding–Lyttelton correspondence remains at Hagley.

196 Harris's *Philological Inquiries in Three Parts* (1781), pp. 163–4 n.

197 From the Ms. "Essay" on Fielding's "Life and Genius."

198 See H. Phillips, *Mid-Georgian London* (London: 1964), p. 143.

199 See *A Letter to a Noble Lord, to whom alone it Belongs. Occasioned by a Representation at the Theatre Royal in Drury-Lane, of a Farce, called "Miss Lucy in Town"* (1742), p. 10. Mother Haywood died in Dec. 1743 (see *London Magazine* for that month, p. 621). For references to her in Fielding's works, see "Part of Juvenal's Sixth Satire, modernized in Burlesque Verse" (l. 191) and *Joseph Andrews* (III.iii).

200 *The Dramatick Sessions: or, The Stage Contest* (1734), p. 11.

201 See Digeon, *Le Texte des romans de Fielding* (Paris: 1923), p. 99.

202 The best text of this letter, undated but probably written during the period 1748–52, was published by Joshua Toulmin, "A Delineation of

the Character of the late Rev. John Ward, of Taunton," *Protestant Dissenter's Magazine* (Jul. 1797), p. 242, n.

203 *Daily Gazetteer* (9 Oct. 1740).

204 See *The Champion* (20 May 1740), an amusing letter from "H. Bottle," celebrating the pleasures of wine-bibbing. For other references to Fielding's fondness for port, see *Champion* (19 Feb. 1739/40, 10 May 1740) and his unpublished letter to James Harris dated 13 Jul. 1745.

205 *Old England* (11 Jan. 1752).

206 *Snuff: A Poem* (1732), pp. 4, 6. Fielding's fondness for snuff, a weakness he shared with Booth in *Amelia* (I.v), is often ridiculed by his contemporaries: e.g., James Miller, *A Seasonable Reproof* (1735), l. 47, who pictures him "Clad in *coarse Frize*, and plaister'd down with *Snuff*." This indeed was how he saw himself in *The Champion* (27 May 1740), with "a great Quantity of Snuff on his Coat."

207 See his "Essay on Eating," *Universal Spectator* (21 Aug. 1736): in Battestin, "Fielding's Contributions to the *Universal Spectator* (1736–7)," *Studies in Philology*, 83 (1986), 88–116.

208 *Champion* (26 Feb. 1739/40).

209 *Journal of a Voyage to Lisbon* (1755), s.v. Tuesday [28 Jul.].

210 See above, n. 207.

211 Fielding's unpublished letter to James Harris, Bath, 24 Sep. 1742.

212 *Some Thoughts concerning Education*, Sect. 67, in J. L. Axtell (ed.), *The Educational Writings of John Locke* (Cambridge: 1968).

213 See *Champion* (10 Jun. 1740); *Tom Jones* (IV.v); *Amelia* (IV.ix). Compliments to Handel occur frequently in Fielding's writings: e.g., in *True Patriot* (5 Nov. 1745, 28 Jan.–4 Feb. 1746); Letter XL of Sarah Fielding's *Familiar Letters* (1747); *Jacobite's Journal* (19 Mar. 1748); *Tom Jones* (IV.ii); *Covent-Garden Journal* (16 Sep. 1752).

214 See the essay in *Daily Journal* (25 Mar. 1737), attributed to Fielding by T. Lockwood, "A New Essay by Fielding," *Modern Philology*, 78 (1980), 48–58.

215 Beattie, *Dissertations, Moral and Critical* (1783), p. 571.

216 The subtitle of J. B. Shipley's dissertation, "James Ralph."

217 Quoted by Shipley, "James Ralph," p. 58, from Franklin's *Memoirs*, ed. M. Farrand (Berkeley and Los Angeles: 1949), p. 94, and Davies's *Memoirs of the Life of David Garrick* (1784), I.250.

218 Shipley, "James Ralph," pp. 181, 202.

219 Ibid., pp. 42 ff.

220 Ibid., pp. 47, 54–5.

221 First to suspect Fielding's authorship of the verse "Epistle to Mr. Ellys the Painter," in *The Comedian*, No. 5 (Aug. 1732), was J. B. Shipley, "Ralph, Ellys, Hogarth, and Fielding: The Cabal Against Jacopo Amigoni," *Eighteenth-Century Studies*, 1 (1968), 322. The crucial link converting suspicion to virtual certainty is the identification of Fielding as the author of the poem's companion piece, the essay "Observations on Government, etc." in the same number of that magazine. Of this I was myself intuitively convinced; but it is Lockwood, working independently, whose research, soon to be published, firmly establishes the attributions.

222 Sir Joseph Mawbey's account of Cooke was published over several numbers of the *Gentleman's Magazine*: viz. 61 (Dec. 1791), 1090–4; (Supplement 1791), 1178–85; 62 (Jan. 1792), 26–32; (Mar. 1792), 214–21; (Apr. 1792), 313–16.

223 See Richardson's letter to Mrs. Donnellan, 22 Feb. 1752, in J. Carroll (ed.), *Selected Letters of Samuel Richardson* (Oxford: 1964), p. 197.

224 Thus Cooke in his "Introduction" to the *Demonstration* summarizes his "two principal Propositions" (p. xi):

I. *An Obedience payed to the Rule of Right advances our Happyness here; and consequently every Deviation from it is a Deviation from the Road which leads to Happyness.*

II. *An Obedience payed to the Rule of Right is an Obedience payed to the Will of God; which appears from that Rule of everlasting Righteousness which the Deity makes the Measure of his Actions.*

225 See *Comedian*, No. 5 (Aug. 1732), p. 16; No. 7 (Oct. 1732), p. 10.

226 *Comedian*, No. 9 [Dec. 1732], p. 5.

227 BL: Add. Mss. 20723, f. 29.

228 These are the divines Cooke cites approvingly in his *Letter to the Archbishop of Canterbury, concerning Persecution for Religion, and Freedom of Debate* (Feb. 1732), in which he cautions the Archbishop against trying to curtail freedom of debate on religious topics.

229 See Shipley, *Eighteenth-Century Studies*, 1 (1968), 313–31.

230 Leonard Howard (ed.), *A Collection of Letters and State Papers*, Vol. II (1756), p. 599.

231 See *Gentleman's Magazine*, 19 (Jan. 1749), p. 44.

232 See the following documents in the Hampshire Record Office relating to Anthony Henley's marriage and debts: 11M52/110, 112, 114–15, 118–25.

233 R. Paulson, *Hogarth's Graphic Works*, rev. edn. (New Haven, Conn.: 1970), I.141.

234 "Dedication" to Cooke's *A Demonstration of the Will of God by the Light of Nature* (1733), p. vi.

235 Howard (ed.), *Collection*, II.695.

236 See "Part of Juvenal's Sixth Satire modernized in Burlesque Verse," l. 414, where Henley is praised for his eloquence as a barrister. Fielding's poem, "To Miss H—— and at Bath. Written *Extempore* in the Pump-Room, 1742," is addressed to Jane Huband, whom Henley married in Dec. 1743: see Miller (ed.), *Fielding's Miscellanies: Volume One*, p. 118; and below, p. 357. Robert Henley was also close to Cooke: as early as Jun. 1731 he wrote a prologue for Cooke's tragedy *The Mournful Nuptials* (1739); see Howard (ed.), *Collection*, II.693–4. He also subscribed to Cooke's *Plautus*.

237 See R. Paulson, *Hogarth* (New Haven, Conn.: 1971), I.347.

238 See Mawbey, *Gentleman's Magazine*, 61 (1791), p. 1090; 62 (1792), pp. 27–8. Cooke had established residence in South Lambeth by 1740, but, as Mawbey explains, he might have been living there as early as 1736–9, the rate books for those years having been lost.

239 I am grateful to S. Klima, who is editing Burney's *Memoirs*, for calling this important passage to my attention.

240 Mawbey, *Gentleman's Magazine*, 61 (1791), p. 1090.

241 Mawbey, ibid. On the Vine, see B. Lillywhite, *London Signs* (London: 1972), No. 15678, as well as the Foster Collection, Vol. 18, p. 198, in the Westminster History Collection, Buckingham Palace Road; on the Royal Oak, see Lillywhite, *London Coffeehouses* (London: 1963), No. 1107.

242 J. H. Caskey conjectures that Moore probably established himself in London as early as 1737 (*Life and Works of Edward Moore*, Yale Studies in English, No. 75 [New Haven, Conn.: 1927], p. 21); but the earliest evidence of his association with any of the members of Tyers's club is Cooke's note in his "Commonplace Book" that he was reading the manuscript of *Fables for the Female Sex* in Jun. 1743 (see Mawbey, *Gentleman's Magazine*, 61 [1791], 1180).

243 *Gentleman's Magazine*, 62 (1792), 30.

244 Howard was Rector of St. George, Southwark, and chaplain to the Princess Dowager of Wales. In 1765, confined for debt in the Rules of the Marshalsea Prison, he published his *Miscellaneous Pieces in Prose and Verse. To which are added, The Letters, &c. of that well known facetious Gentleman* HENRY HATSELL, *Esq.; deceased.* The declaration that Hatsell was "deceased" this early must be an error: see below, n. 245.

245 See B. J. Williamson, *The Middle Temple Bench Book*, 2nd edn. (London: 1937), p. 173. He was admitted to the Middle Temple on 10 Mar. 1717/18 and was called to the Bar on 12 Feb. 1724/5.

246 *Miscellaneous Pieces*, pp. 6–7.

247 *The Tell-Tale: or, Anecdotes Expressive of the Characters of Persons eminent for Rank, Learning, Wit, or Humour* (1756), I.112–13.

248 Here Fielding's footnote reads: "An unfinished Picture of Miss D. W. by Mr. Ellys." See *Comedian*, No. 5 (Aug. 1732), p. 37 and n.

249 Grundy, *PMLA*, 87 (1972), 240.

250 See *Daily Post* (6 Sep. 1732); *Daily Advertiser* (8–9 Sep. 1732).

251 Shipley, "James Ralph," pp. 303 ff.

252 *Daily Post* (25 Jan. 1732/3).

253 *Daily Post* (26 Jan. 1732/3).

254 The exact number of performances cannot be determined owing to gaps in the extant numbers of the *Daily Post*: according to that paper, the performance on 4 May was the twenty-second, and we know from the *Daily Advertiser* (17 May) that the Prince of Wales attended a later performance on 16 May.

255 Historical Mss. Commission, *Diary*, I.333.

256 So Theophilus Cibber testifies in his *Letter ... to John Highmore, Esq.* (1733), p. 2.

257 *The Satirist: In Imitation of the Fourth Satire of the First Book of Horace* (Jun. 1733), p. 11.

258 *Champion* (27 Dec. 1739).

259 That Richmond appreciated this gesture is suggested by the fact that members of his family and entourage staged a private production of *The Miser* in the orangerie at Goodwood on 4 Sep. 1741. (West Sussex Record Office, Chichester: Goodwood Ms. 141, f. 219).

260 *Memoirs of the Life of David Garrick* (1784), II.209.

261 See E. V. Roberts, "Henry Fielding's Lost Play *Deborah, or A Wife for You All* (1733), Consisting Partly of Facts and Partly of Observations upon Them," *Bulletin of the New York Public Library*, 66 (Nov. 1962), 576–88.

262 This is true of all the advertisements, beginning with the earliest in the *Daily Post* (14 Mar. 1732/3); see also *St. James's Evening Post* (13–15, 22–4 Mar.); *Craftsman* (17, 24, 31 Mar.); *Daily Post* (30 Mar.).

263 For the circumstances of the production, see O. E. Deutsch, *Handel: A Documentary Biography* (London: 1955), pp. 307–13.

264 See the letter from Lord de la Warr to Richmond on 16 Jun. 1733 (West Sussex Record Office: Goodwood Ms. 103, f. 173).

265 Grundy, *PMLA*, 87 (1972), 213–45. The Ms. is contained in Vol. 81, Harrowby Mss. Trust, Sandon Hall, Stafford.

266 See the Dedication to *Tom Jones*.

267 *A Letter from Theophilus Cibber, Comedian, to John Highmore, Esq.* (1733), p. 2.

268 Young recorded the following entry in the register of burials for Christ's church, East Stour: "1733. June 12. Dame Sarah Gould Relict of Sr Henry Gould K^t. She dyed June 7 at Salisbury aged 79."

269 Though residing at Salisbury, Robert Stillingfleet was of an eminent family of Cranborne, Dorset, whose most distinguished member was Edward Stillingfleet (1635–99), Bishop of Worcester and a prominent latitudinarian.

270 These documents, together with the Bond of Administration signed by Stillingfleet on 5 Oct. 1733, are at the Wiltshire County Record Office: Cons. Sarum Index to Wills/Ad. Bd. Ren. (2).

271 A correspondent in the *Grub-Street Journal* (26 Apr. 1733) accused Rich of stealing a ballad opera by Ralph called "The Gallant Schemers" and giving it to Phillips to be altered and staged under the title of *The Mock-Lawyer*. In the *Grub-Street Journal* (17 May) a correspondent defending Rich explained that "The Gallant Schemers" had been offered to him by Edward Combe, a clergyman – Rich recommending that Combe and Phillips collaborate on a revision for payment of £40. "In the mean while Mr. *Rich* happened to mention Mr. C[o]mbe's work to Mr. F[ieldi]ng, and to read part of it to him: upon which Mr. F[ieldi]ng told Mr. *Rich*, that it was Mr. R[al]ph's; and that he had shewed it to him as his own before." Thus enlightened, Rich canceled his bargain with Combe, and Phillips proceeded on his own to write *The Mock-Lawyer*. Ralph subsequently wrote to the same journal (24 May) in Combe's behalf, explaining that, after becoming discouraged at his own inability to get "The Gallant Schemers" produced, he had in fact given the play to Combe to treat as his own.

272 "Crambo" is the name Fielding gave to the hackney dramatist patronized by Lord Richly in *The Modern Husband* (II.v).

273 *Daily Advertiser* (29 Oct. 1733).

274 The notice reads: "We hear from the Theatre Royal in Drury-Lane, that the celebrated Performance call'd the Author's Farce, (which was some

Years ago receiv'd with universal Applause), will be reviv'd there immediately after Christmas with very great Additions, and that it will be succeeded by a New Comedy of the same Author's, call'd the Universal Gallant, or the Different Husbands."

275 See the advertisement for Henley's Oratory in the *Daily Journal* (16 Jan. 1733/4). Henley continued to be satirized in the "Puppet Show" as "Dr. Orator." In *An Apology for the Life of Mr. T[heophilus] C[ibber], Comedian* (1740) young Cibber is made to recall the measures taken by the patentees at Drury Lane to embarrass the rebel actors: "They next attack'd us by another old, worn-out rhapsodical Affair of one *Feildings*, call'd the *Author*'s Farce, in which I and my Father were daily ridicul'd" (pp. 88–9).

276 Lewis *et al.* (eds.), *Horace Walpole's Correspondence with Sir Horace Mann*, IV.289–90.

277 See Watts's advertisement for Ralph's *Cornish Squire* in the *London Evening Post* (10–12 Jan. 1733/4), in which he refers to the 2nd edn. of *The Author's Farce* as "just publish'd." See also *Daily Journal* (16 Jan.).

278 See *Daily Journal* (16 Jan. 1733/4). It was circulating before 31 Jan., when the *Grub-Street Journal* reported having received the "vulgar Epigram" on Fielding's Dedication to "Kitty" Clive.

279 It is tempting to think Ralph was the author: he was now also involved in the fortunes of the Drury Lane company, his play *The Cornish Squire* having opened there on 3 Jan. 1733/4.

280 See *Daily Journal* (1 Feb. 1733/4); *Daily Advertiser* (9 Mar. 1733/4).

281 Notices declaring that *Don Quixote in England* would be published "in a few Days" appeared in the *London Evening Post* as early as 14–16 Feb. 1733/4. See also *Grub-Street Journal* (21 Feb.). It seems reasonable to infer that Watts then believed the play would be in production.

282 See Battestin and Farringdon, *New Essays by Henry Fielding.*

283 *Grub-Street Journal* (28 Feb. 1733/4).

284 *Grub-Street Journal* (15 Aug. 1734).

285 Preface to *Miscellanies* (1743); Miller (ed.), *Miscellanies: Volume One*, p. 13.

286 Lady Louisa Stuart, "Introductory Anecdotes," I.105–6.

287 The register at the church of St. Mary the Virgin, Charlcombe, was examined through the courtesy of the incumbent, A. F. Bell; a transcript is in the Bath Public Library. The license "would probably have been obtained within 24 hours of the marriage either from the Registry in Wells or from the Bishop's Surrogate (or appointed deputy for this purpose) in the Bath area"; unfortunately, no trace of it survives. I am grateful for this information to Mr. D. M. M. Shorroks, Archivist, Somerset Record Office.

288 Robbins entered Queen's College, Oxford, in Jan. 1706/7 aged fourteen; he then proceeded to St. John's, Cambridge, to take his LL.B. In 1719 he came to Bath as curate to the Rev. John Taylour, Rector of Charlcombe, and in the same year married there a widow, Mrs. Elizabeth Colthurst of Widcombe. He was a wealthy man, and in 1721 was chosen Master of the School at Bath in return for his annexing to the school in perpetuity the advowson of Charlcombe. After becoming Master, he entered his name at Oriel, Oxford, and in 1725 took the degree of B.C.L. He succeeded Taylour as Rector of Charlcombe in 1728. During the forty-one years of his Mastership, the Bath Grammar School became the leading classical school in Somersetshire. See K. Symons, *The Grammar School of King Edward VI at Bath* (Bath: 1934), pp. 215 ff.

289 W. L. Cross, *The History of Henry Fielding* (New Haven, Conn.: 1918), I.169; F. H. Dudden, *Henry Fielding: His Life, Works and Times* (Oxford: 1952), I.149.

290 So Fielding wrote from Bath to James Harris on 8 Sep. 1741.

291 The *Daily Journal* (11 Oct. 1734) reported that Bath was "as full, if not fuller, than ever was known, there being at this Time upwards of 16000 Strangers (including Servants) there, and more Company daily arriving." On 15 Oct. the same paper reprinted a letter from Bath dated 12 Oct., the day after elaborate festivities had

taken place on the anniversary of the King's coronation: "This Place was never known to be so full as it is at present. Never so gay, never more loyal."

292 PRO: P.C.C.1735. The will was witnessed by Dr. Wasey and an attorney on 8 Feb. 1734/5 at York Buildings and probated at London on 25 Feb. by Charlotte's oath. Wasey (1691–1757), who became President of the Royal College of Physicians, is complimented by Fielding in his burlesque of Juvenal's *Sixth Satire*, l. 353.

293 Details, including the location of the grave, are to be found in the Burial Book for St. Martin-in-the-Fields, Westminster History Collection, Buckingham Palace Road, F 2463. The cause of her death is recorded as "Asthma." Fielding paid seven guineas in expenses; in the records examined this amount was exceeded only by the £11.17s. charged for the funeral of the Rt. Hon. Lady Anne Cavendish, also of York Buildings.

294 For this information I am indebted to Mr. N. Maddex of the Codicote Local History Society, and to his father the Reverend P. J. Maddex, Vicar of Codicote until 1982.

295 The entry must refer to Catherine, as we know from the legal documents pertaining to the administration of her estate that she died in Codicote early in 1735; no other Cradocks appear in the burial register.

296 See her letter reprinted by De Castro, *Notes & Queries*, 15th ser., 20 (9 Mar. 1940), 165.

297 PRO: P.C.C.1735 (Admons.). Catherine's estate was presumably not inconsiderable. On 25 Jul. 1735 in Charlotte's behalf, Henry and his sisters Sarah and Ursula (all said to be of East Stour, Dorset) bound themselves in the amount of £100 to produce an inventory of the estate. This document bears not only their signatures, but also the signatures of Fielding's cousin Henry Gould and his friend the Rev. William Young. (PRO: Prob. 46/104.)

298 The *Grub-Street Journal* (23 Jan. 1734/5) notices that the play was by then published, but the first edition of *An Old Man Taught Wisdom* must have appeared much closer to the opening night's production on 6 Jan., as it contains none of Fielding's revisions, merely referring to them in the following notice: "The Spectator of this Farce is desired to take Notice, that whereas the Audience at its first Performance seemed to think some Scenes too long, as well as to express a Dislike to one particular Character, to comply with their Opinion, that Character hath been since entirely omitted, and several Speeches and Songs left out, which are to be found in the Printed Book." A revised second edition, incorporating these changes, is also dated 1735.

299 *Daily Advertiser* (28 Jan. 1734/5).

300 *The Prompter* (22 Aug. 1735). On Popple's role in *The Prompter*, see C. R. Kropf, "William Popple: Dramatist, Critic, and Diplomat," *Restoration and 18th Century Theatre Research*, 2nd ser., 1 (1986), 1–17.

301 Lady Mary Wortley Montagu to her daughter, Lady Bute, 22 Sep. [1755]; in Halsband (ed.), *Complete Letters*, III.88.

302 Miller had much in common with Fielding and probably knew him personally: he was from Dorset; he was the real author of "Captain Bodens's" *The Modish Couple*, for which Fielding wrote the Epilogue; he was, with Henry Baker, the principal force behind the *Select Comedies of Moliere*, which Fielding "puffed" in his Preface to *The Mock Doctor*; and his plays, *The Mother-in-Law* and *The Man of Taste*, were produced at Drury Lane during the season of 1734–5. Indeed, in Dublin in 1734, Miller's *The Mother-in-Law* was published under Fielding's name.

303 For an authoritative discussion of the Bill, see V. J. Liesenfeld, *The Licensing Act of 1737* (Madison, Wis.: 1984), pp. 23–59. The Bill inspired a satiric print entitled *The Player's Last Refuge: Or the Strollers in Distress*, in which, among those depicted as mourning the destruction of the stage, are "H[i]pp[es]ly a Retailer of Coffee, F[iel]d[in]g, a Retailer of Wine, *chief Mourners*". There are also verses accompanying the print, including this couplet: "F[ieldin]g Whom once did Gods with *Nectar* cheer/ Pawns his full Bottom for a *Pot* of *Beer*." In both instances,

however, the person referred to is Timothy Fielding (see above, p. 86), who, like Hippisley, kept a booth at the fairs. (See F. G. Stephens and E. Hawkins [eds.], *A Catalogue of Prints and Drawings in the British Museum. Division I: Political and Personal Satires* [1877], No. 2146.).

304 See R. L. Haig, *The Gazetteer 1735–1797: A Study in Eighteenth-Century English Newspapers* (Carbondale, Ill.: 1960).

305 See below, p. 211 and n. 359. The name is so common it is impossible to identify this Thomas Bennet with any confidence. A Thomas Bennett was Mayor of Shaftesbury in 1734; and another Thomas Bennett, eldest son of Thomas Bennet, Esq., was Fielding's neighbor at East Stour, where he was buried in 1738 (on this latter, see Hutchins's *History* of Dorset, 3rd edn. [1868], III.634). But in none of the legal records relating to Fielding's adversary is he referred to as "gentleman" or "esquire," as one would expect of either of these men. Perhaps it is no coincidence that "Tom Bennet" is among the bumpkins laid low by Molly Seagrim in *Tom Jones* (IV.viii).

306 The Gillingham "Subscription Book" (WCRO: Diocesan Records) reveals that Young was appointed Master of the school on 18 Jan. 1731/2. He took the necessary oaths on 12 Jun. 1735 and received his license on 16 Jun. 1735. The "Visitation Book [1734–89]" of Gillingham reveals that, though his appointment as Master officially continued until Jul. 1749, Young actively served in that capacity only until 9 Jul. 1740: after that date the annual entries beginning with 3 Sep. 1741 are marked "not appeared, excused." Contrary to what Fielding's biographers assert, Young was never curate at Gillingham. For a history of the school, see A. F. H. V. Wagner, *Gillingham Grammar School, Dorset: An Historical Account* (Gillingham: 1958).

307 The parish registers for East and West Stour show Young serving as curate from 1731 to 1739; he was replaced in 1740 by one Richard Clark. (WCRO: Diocesan Records, "Dorset Transcripts 169, East Stour. i.1731–63, 1766–79"; "Dorset Transcripts 171, Stour West. i.1731–78".

308 Young's advertisement was answered by the curate, the Rev. John Prince, in the *Sherborne Mercury* (3, 10, 17 May 1737). See Wagner, *Gillingham Grammar School*, pp. 23–4.

309 Wiltshire County Record Office: Diocesan Records, "Acts of the Court, 1733—" [Archdeacon's Court of Dorset], f. 5ᵛ.

310 *Covent-Garden Journal* (30 Jun. 1752).

311 See "A Prophecy," in the *London Daily Advertiser* (5 Mar. 1752); in the *Covent-Garden Journal* (30 Jun. 1752) Fielding also observed that Young was "greatly endow'd with that Virtue" – i.e., "Modesty."

312 From a manuscript dated 18 Dec. 1742, quoted in *Salisbury and Wiltshire Herald* (25 Feb. 1837); see Battestin (ed.), *Joseph Andrews* (Middletown, Conn., and Oxford: 1967), pp. xxi–xxii, n. 2.

313 See Cross, *History of Henry Fielding*, I.346.

314 From Harris's Ms. "Essay on the Life and Genius" of Fielding, dated 5 Feb 1758, not long after Young's death. The "Mr. Ranby" to whom Harris refers is Fielding's friend, John Ranby, Principal Sergeant-Surgeon to George II. See also C. T. Probyn, "James Harris to Parson Adams in Germany: Some Light on Fielding's Salisbury Set," *Philological Quarterly*, 64 (1985), 130–9.

315 PRO: P.C.C.1757. (Admons.).

316 See PRO: K.B.122.160, Roll 457.

317 PRO: K.B.125.144. Rule Book. (Wed. one month after the day of St. Michael, 10 Geo. II).

318 Westminster History Collection, Buckingham Palace Road: Account Book, Marriages and Christenings, St. Martin-in-the-Fields (F 419/207). Charlotte was baptized by the vicar, Dr. Pierce, on 19 May – an occasion for which Fielding spared no expense: the half-guinea it cost him is more than any other such charge recorded for several months. Dr. Pierce, the King's chaplain, was the sort of priest Fielding admired. In his Diary, the Earl of Egmont characterized him as "a zealous minister against Popery and a good man" (2 Mar. 1735/6); "a grave clergyman of good learning and irreproachable behav-

iour, always a hearty Whig," but one who "never courted Sir Robert [Walpole]" (8 Dec. 1737).

A cautionary note: the registers of burials and baptisms for St. Giles-in-the-Fields – a disreputable district, including Drury Lane and many of the brothels and hedgetaverns near the theatres (see *Amelia*, I.iii) – reveal a considerable number of "Fieldings" or "Feildings" living in that parish during the period 1734–41, their Christian names being Elizabeth, Mary, Edward, Robert, Roger, Charles, Ann, Thomas, etc. An entry in the Burial Register for 19 Feb. 1735/6 might otherwise tempt one into an extravagant speculation; for on that date was buried "James of Henry Fielding." But nothing except the coincidence of the name should connect this man with our Henry Fielding: Fielding at this time was living at Charing Cross and his church was St. Martin-in-the-Fields; James, with its Stuart and Jacobite associations, is not a name we would expect him to give a son, especially his first-born; and, though the entries in these registers are in general cursory, Fielding usually insisted on recording his rank as "Esq." or "Gent."

319 In the Preface to the *Miscellanies* (1743) Fielding speaks of *The Good-Natured Man* as a "Play" which had "lain by me some years, tho' formed on a much better Plan" than the five-act comedy *The Wedding-Day*, "and at an Age when I was much more equal to the Task." Of Fielding's known works, only the "Play" he offered to Rich in the winter of 1735–6 and then set aside fits this description. (See below, pp. 615–16.)

320 See Shipley, "James Ralph," p. 306.

321 See Davies, *Memoirs of the Life of David Garrick* (1784), I.234–5.

322 See Henry Carey's poem of that title (1735).

323 Pasquin contains allusions (I.i, IV.i) to two events that may be precisely dated in Feb. 1735/6: the Act (9 Geo. II, cap. 5) passed on 11 Feb. repealing the old statute against witchcraft, and the floods of 16 Feb. that inundated Westminster Hall.

324 *London Daily Post* (Tues., 24 Feb. 1735/6); also *Craftsman* (28 Feb.).

325 See her autobiography, *A Narrative of the Life of Mrs. Charlotte Charke*, 2nd edn. (1755), p. 63. The author of *Sawney and Colley* (1742) observed that Mrs. Charke was "celebrated for her Performances in the *Hay-Market Theatre*, where, in the Farce of *Pasquin*, the *Historical Register, &c.* she play'd off her Father and Brother [Theophilus] with surprising Humour to the high Recreation of many Audiences: And has since chose to communicate herself to the Publick by Day-light in Men's Cloaths" (p. 4, n.).

326 Historical Mss. Commission, *Diary*, II.240, 250, 268.

327 *The Autobiography and Correspondence of Mary Granville, Mrs. Delany*, ed. Lady Llanover (1861), I.554.

328 See J. Milhous and R. D. Hume, "Edward Phillips and the Authorship of *Marforio* (1736)," *English Language Notes*, forthcoming.

329 See "The Statue of Œdipus to Marforio," in *Daily Advertiser* (8 Apr. 1736), *Prompter* (9 Apr.), and *Daily Post* (9–10 Apr.).

330 PRO: S.P.41.9, f.317.

331 For several documents relating to Edmund's service as military governor of Jersey, see PRO: S.P.47, and the Index to the correspondence (Ind.6899). He was governing the island as early as 24 Mar. 1735/6 but was no longer in command by 15 Nov. 1737.

332 See Hill's letter to Edmund, dated from Guernsey, 30 May 1737; in Hill's *Works* (1753), I.350–1.

333 See Davis, *The Good Lord Lyttelton*, esp. Pt. II, Ch. 1. On the importance of Lyttelton and Cobham's "Cousinhood" to Fielding's political career, see T. R. Cleary, *Henry Fielding: Political Writer* (Waterloo, Ontario: 1984).

334 The more esoteric aspects of the play's political satire were probably the subject of a fourpenny pamphlet published, according to the *London Daily Post*, on 17 May 1736, but now lost: "A KEY to PASQUIN, address'd to HENRY FIELDING, Esq; printed for and sold by E. Lynn, against Devereux Court, without Temple-Bar; and the Pamphlet-Shops at the Royal Exchange and

Charing-Cross." At least one feature of Fielding's satire appeared more strongly to contemporary audiences than to modern readers of the play: this was the skill with which Miss Burgess, the actress who played Miss Stitch (Act II), ridiculed James Pitt of the *Daily Gazetteer*. Thanks to his scolding manner of defending Walpole's interests, Pitt, who wrote under the name of "Francis Osborne", had been metamorphosed in the Opposition press to the old woman, "Mother Osborne." In *The Craftsman* (24 Apr. 1736) Amhurst remarked how in *Pasquin* Pitt "hath been made the Butt of the whole Town, for above forty Nights together, upon the publick Stage, by a *pert little Baggage*, in the Character of Miss *Stitch*". Somewhat later, the political satire in *Pasquin* was considered offensive enough to have precipitated the Theatrical Licensing Act: see *The Laureat: or, The Right Side of Colley Cibber, Esq.* (1740), pp. 51–2; and *Theatrical Correspondence in Death: An Epistle from Mrs. Oldfield, in the Shades, to Mrs. Br[a]ceg[ir]dle, upon Earth* (1743), pp. 16–17; also John Mottley, "List of all the Dramatic Authors" appended to Thomas Whincop, *Scanderbeg* (1747), p. 233.

335 See Chesterfield's tribute to Fielding in the first number of *Common Sense* (5 Feb. 1736/7).

336 *Persian Letters* (Letters XVI–XVII).

337 See *A Letter to a Noble Lord, to whom alone it Belongs* (1742), p. 2.

338 *Four Satires* (1737), Satire IV, pp. 46–7.

339 In the list of subscribers to Fielding's *Miscellanies* (1743), Benjamin Hoadly is down for three sets of the royal-paper issue, his brother John for two. Fielding pays a compliment to Benjamin Hoadly in his burlesque of Juvenal's *Sixth Satire*, l. 353; and in the *Covent-Garden Journal* (18 Jul. 1752) he alludes favorably to his comedy, *The Suspicious Husband* (1747). John Hoadly wrote the inscription for Sarah Fielding's memorial in Bath Abbey.

340 Hoadly to Garrick, 3 Jun. 1773, in *The Private Correspondence of David Garrick with the Most Celebrated Persons of His Time* (1831), I.542. My thanks to Thomas Lockwood for calling this letter to my attention.

341 See *London Daily Post* (28 Apr. 1736).

342 See, for example, *Champion* (22 Apr., 3, 24 May 1740); *Joseph Andrews* (I.vii); *Tom Jones* (V.i, XII.xii); *Covent-Garden Journal* (11 Jan., 18 Nov. 1752).

343 *Memoirs of the Life of David Garrick* (1784), I.234–5.

344 Scouten conjectures that the author was Joseph Dorman, but Dormer is the name in the advertisement, and the published version of the play is said to be printed for "J. Dormer." (See Scouten, *London Stage*, Pt. 3, 1729–47 [1961]).

345 Lillo's *Works*, ed. T. Davies (1775), I.xv–xvi, xvii.

346 Charlotte Charke's *Narrative*, 2nd edn. (1755), p. 65.

347 Lillo's *Works* (1775), I.xxvii.

348 Harris's *Philological Inquiries* (1781), pp. 154, 156.

349 *A History of English Drama, 1660–1900* (Cambridge: 1952), II.122, 124. See also C. F. Burgess, "Lillo sans Barnwell, or the Playwright Revisited," *Modern Philology*, 66 (1968), 5–29.

350 "Some Accounts of PLAY-HOUSES," in *The Usefulness of the Stage to Religion, and to Government*, 2nd edn. (1738), pp. 16–17.

351 Scouten, *London Stage*, Pt. 3, 1729–47, p. xlv.

352 In the *Grub-Street Journal* (8 Apr. 1736) this is the estimate of the nightly take at the Little Haymarket at the height of *Pasquin's* run.

353 Notices of this benefit, with poignant accounts of the lady's circumstances, appeared in *Fog's Weekly Journal* (15 May) and the *Daily Advertiser* (24 May).

354 For Fielding's connection with the journal, see Battestin, *Studies in Philology*, 83 (1986), 88–116.

355 Shipley, "James Ralph," pp. 311–13 and n. 27.

356 It is impossible to identify this man precisely. Fielding had a first cousin of that name (see below, n. 452), but the person here in question may have been Charles Fielding of the Inner Temple whose name appears in Nov. 1730 on the Rolls of Attorneys (PRO: K.B.IND.4583). A distant relation of Fielding's was the Hon. Charles Fielding of the Denbigh family; but "Esquire" would be a more appropriate title for an attorney.

357 See (1) *Hugh Allen v. HF*: PRO: K.B.122.189 (Part 2), Roll 689; (2) *James Gascoigne v. HF*: PRO: C.P.40.3502, Roll 1592.

358 PRO: K.B.125.144.

359 PRO: K.B.122.164, Roll 658. (The case was reported by De Castro in *Somerset and Dorset Notes & Queries*, 20 [Mar. 1930], 130–2.) The Index to the Books of Judgment, No. 9633, gives the date of this plea as 26 Jul. 1737. The progress of the case through the court may be followed intermittently in the Rule Book, K.B.125.145, until the trail is lost in Feb.1737/8.

360 See E. L. Avery, "Proposals for a New London Theatre in 1737," *Notes & Queries*, 182 (1942), 286–7.

361 Hume, *Henry Fielding and the London Theatre*, pp. 225–6.

362 *Eurydice Hiss'd* (1737).

363 See "Ingenuus" in *Daily Journal* (22 Feb. 1736/7).

364 Johnson's "Life of Hughes," in G. B. Hill (ed.), *Lives of the English Poets* (Oxford: 1905), II.160.

365 *Daily Post* (21 Feb. 1736/7).

366 *Weekly Journal or British Gazetteer* (26 Feb. 1736/7).

367 These are the players in the cast of *A Rehearsal of Kings* announced in the *Grub-Street Journal* (3 Mar. 1736/7), where notice is also given that "This Company will endeavour to entertain the Town the remaining part of the Season."

368 Hill's *Works*, I.239–41. See J. R. Brown, "From Aaron Hill to Henry Fielding?" *Philological Quarterly*, 18 (1939), 85–8.

369 PRO: K.B.28.144.20.

370 See PRO: L.C.5.160.318. Warrant Book (10 Mar. 1736/7).

371 *Daily Advertiser* (11 Mar. 1736/7).

372 See Historical MSS. Commission, Egmont's *Diary*, II.369.

373 *Daily Post* (29 Mar. 1737).

374 The pamphlet survives in a unique copy at the Houghton Library, Harvard. On the attribution to Fielding, see Lockwood, *Modern Philology*, 78 (1980), 45–58.

375 *Daily Advertiser* (22 Mar. 1736/7). On the same day Lord Egmont, having attended the second night's performance, recorded his approbation in his Diary: "It is a good satire on the times and has a good deal of wit" (II.375).

376 *The Historical Register* was an annual publication purporting to summarize the important domestic and foreign events of the preceding year.

377 See Mottley's "List of all the Dramatic Authors" appended to Thomas Whincop's *Scanderbeg* (1747), p. 235.

378 *An Apology for the Life of Mr. Colley Cibber, Comedian* (1740), p. 164.

379 *Daily Gazetteer* (12 Jan. 1738/9).

380 It is worth noting, as further testimony of Fielding's affection for Lillo, that he allowed *Fatal Curiosity* to run for ten consecutive performances during the height of the season, in that period granting his friend the unusually liberal favor of four benefits. There was a further performance of the tragedy on 2 May.

381 *Daily Advertiser* (15 Mar. 1736/7).

382 Historical Mss. Commission, Egmont's *Diary*, II.390.

383 "Dedication" to *The Historical Register*.

384 Pillage to his Muse in *Eurydice Hiss'd*.

385 *The Craftsman* (30 Apr. 1737) promised that the two plays would be published "*Next Week* ... With a Dedication to the Publick, and an Apology for the Author against some malicious Insinuations industriously spread about."

386 *Daily Gazetteer* (4 Jun. 1737).

387 See "Marforio," *An Historical View*, p. 22.

388 See *The Craftsman* for that date.

389 For a thorough account of this, and all other circumstances relating to the Licensing Act of 1737, see Liesenfeld's book on the subject.

390 Horace Walpole attributes *The Golden Rump* to Fielding in a marginal gloss in his copy of Cibber's *Apology* (1740), pp. 164–5, now at King's School, Canterbury; and in his *Memoirs of the Last Ten Years of the Reign of George the Second* (1822), I.11 n., he claims to have seen a copy of the play. (See Coley, *Philological Quarterly*, 45 [1966], 166–7.) I was assured by the late John Brooke, editor of Walpole's *Memoirs*, that no manuscript of *The Golden Rump* exists among the Walpole papers.

391 See John, Lord Hervey, *Memoirs of the Reign of George the Second*, ed.

J. W. Croker (1848), II.341; Coxe, *Memoirs of the Life and Administration of Sir Robert Walpole* (1798), I.515–16.

392 See *A Critical History of the Administration of Sir Robert Walpole* (1743), p. 312.

393 See, for example, *An Apology for the Life of Mr. T—— C——, Comedian* (1740), pp. 91–4; the "Anecdote of Sir Robert Walpole, the Minister; Gifford [*sic*], the Manager; and Garrick, the Player," in *The Rambler's Magazine*, 5 (1787), 484–5.

394 Davies, *Memoirs of the Life of David Garrick* (1784), II.214–17.

395 Report of the Select Committee on Dramatic Literature, *Sessions* (1831–2), VII.23.

396 *Memoirs*, ed. Croker, II.341–2.

397 Chesterfield's *Miscellaneous Works* (1777), I.228 ff.

398 See P. Hartnoll, "The Theatre and the Licensing Act of 1737," in A. Natan (ed.), *Silver Renaissance: Essays in Eighteenth-Century English History* (London: 1961), p. 182.

399 *Daily Advertiser* (30 Apr. 1737).

400 W. T. Lowndes, *The Bibliographer's Manual of English Literature* (1834), p. 1302.

401 In 1735 at Paris, H. Cordonnier de Saint-Hyacinthe had published the *Histoire du Prince Titi*. In the same year two English versions were published, one allegedly by Eliza Stanley and the other attributed to James Ralph (see E. Solly, *Notes & Queries*, 6th ser., 10 [26 Jul. 1884], 70–2). Shipley rejects the attribution. He does show, however, that Ralph was probably the author of certain manuscript memoirs entitled "the History of Prince Titus," being an account of Frederick's bitter relations with his royal parents: see "James Ralph, Prince Titi, and the Black Box of Frederick, Prince of Wales," *Bulletin of the New York Public Library*, 71 (Mar. 1967), 143–57.

402 From John Payne Collier's transcriptions of several documents by Potter relating to the Little Haymarket in 1737. I am indebted to R. D. Hume for supplying me with copies of his transcripts; the originals are at the Folger Library (Ms. T.b.3). De Castro published the letter in *Notes & Queries*, 182 (20 Jun. 1942), 346.

403 The expense of doing so (twelve guineas) was part of Potter's account dated 13 Jun. 1737 submitted to the Duke of Grafton on 24 Feb. 1737/8 (Folger Ms. T.b.3/3).

404 *Daily Advertiser* (23 May 1737).

405 Hume, *Henry Fielding and the London Theatre*, p. 256.

406 See Scouten, *The London Stage*, Pt. 3, 1729–47, I.lxxxvi–lxxxvii, cxlii–cxliv.

407 Harris's "Essay" on Fielding.

408 See De Castro's review of Cross's biography, in *Modern Language Review*, 15 (1920), 185.

409 See T. C. Duncan Eaves and B. D. Kimpel, "Henry Fielding's Son by His First Wife," *Notes & Queries*, n.s. 15 (Jun. 1968), 212; and below, p. 507.

410 She three times gave her Christian names as Henrietta Eleanor at the time of her marriage to Colonel James Montresor on 25 Aug. 1766. See for 23 Aug. 1766 both the Faculty Office Marriage Bond (Montresor/Fielding) and the Faculty Office Marriage Allegation (Montresor/Fielding), Lambeth Palace Library. In the latter document she is said to be of Odiam, Hants., and twenty-three years of age. See also the parish register of St. Marylebone, 25 Aug. 1766 (GLRO: Reel X/23/45).

411 See the relevant registers, Westminster History Collection, Buckingham Palace Road.

412 Apparently unaware of the evidence for Fielding's having contributed to *The Craftsman* during this period, Lockwood surmised that Walpole bribed him into silence: see "Fielding and the Licensing Act," *Huntington Library Quarterly*, 50 (1987), 379–93.

413 See Battestin and Farringdon, *New Essays by Henry Fielding*.

414 These events may be followed in detail in the following numbers of *The Craftsman*: 30 Jul., 6, 13 Aug., 3, 17 Sep., 1 Oct. 1737. See also Haines, *Treachery, Baseness, and Cruelty Display'd to the Full; in the Hardships and Sufferings of Mr. Henry Haines* (1740); and the reply to Amhurst in *The Craftsman* (18 Oct. 1740). For documents relating to the case see PRO: K.B.28.144.26; S.P.36.44,

f. 79; S.P.36.147, f. 91; S.P.44.82, ff. 155–8; IND.6658 (Hil., 11 Geo. II, s.v. Haines) and (East., 11 Geo. II, s.v. Amhurst); IND.6672 (Mich., 11 Geo. II, No. 107) and (Hil., 11 Geo. II, No. 65).

415 Among the Duke of Newcastle's papers is a letter of 22 Jul. 1737 from Lord Hardwicke referring to testimony by one Parry, who believed that the copy for *The Craftsman* of 2 Jul. was in Amhurst's handwriting (BL: Add. Mss. 32690, f. 303). Amhurst was taken into custody, but charges against him were dropped for lack of evidence, Parry apparently having died (ibid., 33054, f. 150). For reasons set forth elsewhere, Fielding, not Amhurst, was the likely author: see Battestin and Farringdon, *New Essays by Henry Fielding*, pp. 221–40.

416 See Battestin, *Studies in Philology*, 83 (1986), 88–116.

417 Middle Temple: "Admissions to House and Chambers, 1695–1737," f. 574. The fee is specified as £4.0.0; in the left-hand margin a further notation indicates that, by this transaction, Fielding was admitted "ad h." or "to the house" (as opposed to "ad. Cam." or "to Chambers"). The "Middle Temple Day Book, 1734–1739" confirms that Fielding paid the fee of £4 on 5 Nov. 1737. I am indebted to Mrs. B. Given, Archivist, Middle Temple Library, for assisting me in consulting these and other documents.

418 *Daily Gazetteer* (7 Mar. 1736/7).

419 See P. A. Smith, *A History of Education for the English Bar* (1860), p. 9.

420 Ibid., p. 9; and the Middle Temple "Day Book" for 20 Jun. and 28 Nov. 1740.

421 Downing, *Observations on the Constitution, Customs and Usage of the Honourable Society of the Middle Temple. Originally written in the year 1733 and revised 1739* (1896), p. 102.

422 From *The Young Senator. A Satyre, With an Epistle to Mr. Fielding, on his Studying the Law* (1738), pp. 16–18.

423 Smith, *History*, p. 42. See also J. Walton, "Notes on the Early History of Legal Studies in England," *Law Magazine and Review*, 5th ser., 25 (1899–1900), 404.

424 W. Matthews (ed.), *The Diary of Dudley Ryder, 1715–1716* (London: 1939), pp. 192, 49, 147, 184, 281; 87, 113, 116.

425 Ibid., pp. 8, 207, 223, 226, 256, 364.

426 Ibid., p. 258. At about the same period, Roger North similarly observed that the exercises were now "shrunk into mere form, and that preserved only for conformity to rules, that gentlemen by tale of appearances in exercises rather than by any sort of performances, might be entitled to be called to the Bar" (quoted by Walton, *Law Magazine and Review*, 5th ser., 25 [1899–1900], 404).

427 Matthews (ed.), *Diary of Dudley Ryder*, p. 8.

428 Harris's "Essay" on Fielding.

429 See Fielding's letters to Nourse dated 6 Mar. 1737/8, 7 Mar. 1738/9, 9 Jul. 1739; and the Sales Catalogue of Fielding's library (items 1, 84, 271). See below, n. 438, pp. 251, 252–3.

430 "Lord Chief Justice Reeve's Instructions to his Nephew concerning the Study of the Law," in *Collectanea Juridica. Consisting of Tracts relative to the Law and Constitution of England.* Vol. I (1791), p. 80. Reeve was called to the Bar in 1713 and died in 1737.

431 *Champion* (25 Dec. 1739, 12 Feb. 1739/40, 17 Jul., 12 Aug. 1740); *Joseph Andrews* (I.xv).

432 *Collectanea Juridica*, I.277.

433 E. Foss, "Westminster Hall," in *Old London*, Archaeological Institute of Great Britain and Ireland (1867), pp. 219–40, esp. pp. 234–5.

434 Downing, *Observations*, p. 86.

435 Matthews (ed.), *Diary of Dudley Ryder*, p. 258.

436 M. R. Zirker (ed.), Fielding's *An Enquiry into the Causes of the Late Increase of Robbers and Related Writings* (Oxford and Middletown, Conn.: 1988), p. xxx.

437 See Battestin and Farringdon, *New Essays by Henry Fielding*.

438 In the collection of Lady Eccles the letter reads:

MʳNourse
I desire you would send me by Bearer best Edit of Fitzherbert Natura Brevium[.] I wonder I have heard nothing of Cokes Reports

since they have been so long advertised as published. I am

y^r humble serv^t
Hen: Ffielding

439 *Champion* (21 Oct. 1740).
440 Nourse commissioned Fielding to
translate Adlerfeld's *Histoire militaire de Charles XII, Roi de Suède*
(see below, p. 266). On Nourse, see
J. Feather, "John Nourse and his
Authors," *Studies in Bibliography*, 34
(1981), 205–26; G. Barber, "Voltaire
and the 'maudites éditions de Jean
Nourse,'" in R. J. Howells *et al.*
(eds.), *Voltaire and his World: Studies
presented to W. H. Barber* (Oxford:
1985), pp. 133–45.
441 *Daily Gazetteer* for 5, 8, 20 Apr., 1
May 1738.
442 This essay, preserved among confiscated papers in the PRO
(S.P.9.35), is the only extant literary
prose manuscript of Fielding. See
M. C. with R. R. Battestin, "A Fielding Discovery, with Some Remarks
on the Canon," *Studies in Bibliography*, 33 (1980), 131–43.
443 Edmund served as ensign in his
father's regiment from 27 Nov. 1733
to 22 Mar. 1739/40, when he removed
to Col. Blakeney's Regiment of Foot
(PRO: S.P.41.8; W.O.25.19, p. 216).
He was made lieutenant in Blakeney's regiment on 18 Sep. 1741, but
left that command before 1 Oct. 1742
(W.O.25.20, p. 130; 64.9, p. 85). By
1743 he was with Col. Cochran's
Regiment of Marines, in which he
served until 1754 (C. Whitefoord,
Papers, ed. W. A. S. Hewins [Oxford:
1898], p. 25; W.O.25.21, p. 100; *Army
List* 1754 corrected). On 26 Jan. 1755
he joined Col. Aldercron's 39th Regiment of Foot, then stationed in
Madras (*Army List* 1754 corrected).
On 26 Feb. 1753 at St. George's
Chapel, Mayfair, he married Mary
Peylin (or Peglin) of St. James's
(Harleian Society Registers, Vol. 15
[1899]).
444 *Journal of a Voyage to Lisbon* ("Humphrys" version [24 Jul. 1754]).
445 These documents are in the Houghton Library, Harvard (FMS Eng
735).
446 PRO: C.P.25(2), Bundle 1118,
No. 134. To complete this transaction, four "Proclamations" were

necessary, the dates of which are
given on the verso of this document
as 21 Jun., 24 Nov. 1738, 7 Feb.
1738/9, 14 May 1739.
447 Hanbury Williams's letter to Fox,
20 Aug. 1743 (BL: Add. Mss. 51390,
ff. 118–19).
448 See "Peter and My Lord Quidam: A
Satire. (Written in August, 1743),"
in Hanbury Williams's *Works*, ed.
Horace Walpole (1822), I.37–8.
449 See the following, all published in
the *Miscellanies* (1743): "Epigram on
one who invited many Gentlemen to
a small Dinner," "Essay on Conversation," "Some Papers Proper to
be Read before the R——l Society,"
*A Journey from This World to the
Next* (I.i), and *Jonathan Wild*
(II.vii).
450 Walpole's "Common Place Book of
Verses, etc.," p. 68; quoted in Coley,
Philological Quarterly, 45 (1966),
169–70. See also Ferdinando Foot,
The Nut-Cracker (1751), p. 73, where
the same anecdotes are told of Walter
and a nameless "Gentleman, not so
remarkable for his Oeconomy, as his
Wit and Humour." In *Memoirs,
Anecdotes, Facts, and Opinions*
(1824), by Laetitia-Matilda Hawkins
(daughter of Sir John Hawkins), the
anecdote is again specifically told of
Fielding and Walter, and it is said to
have originated with Saunders Welch
(I.48–9).
451 See *Salisbury and Winchester Journal*
(11 Sep. 1780).
452 For the will, dated 16 Aug. 1733 but
radically altered by codicils of 19
Jan. 1735/6 and 1 Mar. 1737/8, by
which Fielding and Charlotte particularly benefited, see PRO:
P.C.C.1738. The clearest exposition
of George Fielding's complicated
scheme of benefactions may be found
in PRO: C.33.385, Pt. I, p. 305 (20
Mar. 1745/6). For the final judgment,
see PRO: C.33.391, Pt. II, p. 456.
  These documents throw much
light on Fielding's family relationships. His grandmother Dorothy had
a sister Mary Cockayne. His aunts
Dorothy Fielding and Bridget
Lapenotier had died by 1745, though
a third aunt, Elizabeth Crowther,
lived on. His first cousins were
Charles and William Fielding and
George Lapenotier.

453 Robert Taylor Collection, Princeton University Library.

454 PRO: *Kempson v. Fielding*, K.B. 122.178, Roll 253.

455 *Gascoigne v. Fielding*, PRO: Ind.6501 (Docket Books) and C.P.40.3502, Roll 1592.

456 They probably meant to honor her memory by naming their daughter (whose nickname was Harriet) Henrietta Eleanor. See above, n. 410.

457 PRO: P.C.C.1739. The will was proved by Edmund in London on 15 Aug. 1739. He had been promoted to Lt. General in Jul.: *Gentleman's Magazine* (IX.384); *London Magazine* (VIII.362).

458 Mrs. Cottington's will, dated 11 Aug. 1732, was witnessed by Ursula and Sarah Fielding. It was administered by Catharine on 7 Jan. 1739/40. (PRO: P.C.C.1740.)

459 N. Maslin, "Henry Fielding's Homes," *Notes & Queries*, 30 (Feb. 1983), 50.

460 *Ovid's Art of Love Paraphrased* (1747), p. 49. For the document in question, see *Fielding v. William Deards*, PRO: K.B.122.175, Roll 522. For other gibes at Deards, which begin in Fielding's writings as early as *The Temple Beau* (IV.vi) and *The Miser* (II.i), see the following: *The Vernoniad* (1741; p. 30 and n. 58); *Joseph Andrews* (III.vi); *Jonathan Wild* (II.iii, III.vi); *A Journey from This World to the Next* (I.i); *Tom Jones* (XII.iv); *Covent-Garden Journal* (4 Jan. 1752).

PART III

1 Review of P. Rogers's *Henry Fielding: A Biography* (New York: 1979) in *The Observer*, 8 Jul. 1979.

2 References to the real-life Capt. Hercules Vinegar often occur in the period before Fielding's *Champion*, the earliest I have noticed being in Erasmus Philips's periodical *The Country Gentleman* (14 Nov. 1726), and the most tantalizing for students of Fielding being the following pamphlet, published in Jul. 1731 but now lost: *An Answer to one Part of a late infamous Libel, reflecting on Captain Vinegar and the late Jonathan Wilde* (see J. E. Wells, "Fielding's 'Champion', and Captain Hercules Vinegar," *Modern Language Review*, 8 [1913], 165–72; and *The Nation* [New York, 16 Jan. 1913], pp. 53–4). After Fielding had made it famous, other authors appropriated the pseudonym: e.g., "Hercules Vinegar, Esq.," *The Cudgel: or, A Crab-tree Lecture to the Author of "The Dunciad"* (1742); and "Capt. H——s Vinegar," *Blast upon Blast, and Lick for Lick: or, A New Lesson for Pope* (1742). (See K. Chandler, "Two 'Fielding' Pamphlets," *Philological Quarterly*, 16 [1937], 410–12.)

3 Cooke's Preface to *The Mournful Nuptials: or, Love the Cure of all Woes* (1739), p. xiv. See T. Lockwood, "Fielding's Champion in the Planning Stage," *Philological Quarterly*, 59 (1980), 238–41.

4 See G. B. Hill and L. F. Powell (eds.), *Boswell's Life of Johnson* (Oxford: 1934), II.344–5.

5 PRO: C.11.2155/7, Chancery Proceedings, 1714–58: *Gardiner v. Farrin and others*. At a meeting in May 1741 the partners of *The Champion* agreed to reconvene on 14 Jul., at which time Gardiner was appointed printer and treasurer; he was to be paid 30s. for the first 1,000 copies, and 6s. per ream after that number. Before Gardiner became its printer, *The Champion* had made a "considerable profitt," and dividends were paid to the shareholders. After his appointment no dividends were paid, and, the paper steadily "declining in the sale" under Ralph's authorship, the partners discontinued *The Champion* on 31 Mar. 1743. Gardiner brought his complaint against the partners on 26 Nov. 1748 and amended it on 9 Dec. 1749, at which time Fielding's name was added to the bill. Suspended until Jan. 1754, the case dragged on through Feb. and Dec. (when Nourse promised to produce the minute-book of the partnership if the Court required, which it did not), through Feb. 1755, Jun. and Nov. 1758, Jan. and Feb. 1759 – after which it disappears from the records.

6 See T. Johnson (ed.), *The Tryal of Colley Cibber, Comedian* (1740), p. 39.

7 Ibid., p. 2 and n.

8 *Tom K[in]g's: or, The Paphian Grove,*

with the various *Humours of Covent Garden, the Theatre, the Gaming Table, &c.,* 2nd edn. (1738), pp. 35–6.

9 *Champion* (16 Oct. 1740).

10 *Champion* (27 May 1740).

11 Johnson, *The Tryal of Colley Cibber,* p. 36 n.

12 *London Daily Post* (12 Nov. 1739). This paper advertised the first four numbers; the *London Evening Post* the first six.

13 Most advertisements were placed by the partners themselves, since, as Gardiner revealed in his suit, every holder of one sixteenth share in the paper was obliged to place at least one advertisement in every issue. (See above, n. 5.)

14 See F. G. Ribble, "William Robinson, Contributor to Fielding's *Champion,*" *Studies in Bibliography,* forthcoming. Robinson subscribed to Fielding's *Miscellanies* (1743).

15 In a footnote Graham remarked that *The Craftsman* of 5 Apr. pirated no fewer than ten paragraphs published in *The Champion.* One of these (from *Champion* No. 60 [1 Apr. 1740], "Home News") the government considered so libelous Amhurst had to black it out. Indeed, John Meres, printer of the *London Evening Post,* was taken into custody for exhibiting, as Ralph gloated, the same "stollen Goods," while *The Champion,* the source of the trouble, escaped unnoticed (see *Champion* [8 Apr. 1740], "Home News," and Ralph's comment in the 1741 reprint).

16 *Champion* (12 Jun. 1740).

17 Mrs. Blunt carried on the business of her husband, who died in 1733 at his house "facing the Upper End of the Haymarket: He kept the most Coaches and Horses of any Person in England, which he lett out to Persons of Quality" (*Daily Post,* 30 Mar. 1733). Mrs. Blunt sued Fielding for debts dating from 1 Jan. 1739/40 and earlier; they amounted, she claimed, to £30 and she asked a further £20 in damages. Represented by the distinguished attorney Giles Taylor, Fielding admitted owing only 5 guineas, which he was ordered to pay together with £6 damages and costs. (PRO: K.B.122.178, Roll 255; and Ind.6173, May 1740.)

18 PRO: C.P.40, Roll 362. On 24 Nov. a jury determined that, with costs and damages, Fielding owed Henley £27.10s. By various legal delaying tactics Fielding postponed the day of reckoning until Easter Term of the following year: K. B. Docket Book. Hil., 14 Geo. II, 1740, Special Remembrances, No. 697; and K.B. 125.147, Rule Book, Easter, 14 Geo. II, 1741.

19 On 31 May 1740 a certain Brien Janson, in another action against Fielding, was awarded damages amounting to £9.8s. (PRO: C.P. Docket Book, Ind.6173.)

20 *Old England* (5 Aug. 1749).

21 For Defoe's salary, see PRO: S.P.36.50, ff. 29–33. For Amhurst's earnings, see Henry Haines, *Treachery, Baseness, and Cruelty Display'd to the Full* (1740), pp. 20–1.

22 Gardiner was paid for a basic 1,000 copies per issue, with provision made for larger runs (see above, n. 5); Haines, Amhurst's printer, stated that 4,500 copies of *The Craftsman* were run off each week, though some of these were wasted (see above, n. 21).

23 Though dated 1740 on the title-page, Adlerfeld's work was published in Nov. 1739 (see *Journal des Scavans* for that month, p. 690). Nourse specialized in importing French works: see J. Feather, "John Nourse and his Authors," *Studies in Bibliography,* 34 (1981), 205–26.

24 See also the *London Evening Post* (3–5, 5–8 Jan. 1739/40).

25 See Yale (Mss. Vault: Fielding). There is little reason to doubt that Fielding wrote the whole of the translation, presumably being paid the balance due him on completing the work: see J. E. Wells, "Henry Fielding and the History of Charles XII," *Journal of English and Germanic Philology,* 11 (1912), 603–13; M. and J. Farringdon, "A Computer Aided Study of the Prose Style of Henry Fielding and its Support for his Translation of the Military History of Charles XII," in D. E. Ager, F. E. Knowles, and J. Smith (eds.), *Advances in Computer-Aided Literary and Linguistic Research* (Birmingham: 1979), pp. 95–105.

26 The lines are a later addition to "Verses to the injur'd Patriot, written in 1733," in Newcomb's *A Miscellaneous Collection of Original Poems* (1740), p. 206. In this collection other hits at Fielding's anti-ministerial writings in *The Champion* occur on pp. 90, 104, 323, 347.

27 Fielding employed Giles Taylor to defend him against the suits of John Kempson and Elizabeth Blunt, and he would call on him again in the future. That they were on friendly terms is suggested by Taylor's subscribing to Fielding's *Miscellanies*. He died on 25 Nov. 1752 "at his Chambers in Lyons-Inn ... an eminent Attorney, of great Business, and fair Character" (*General Advertiser* [27 Nov. 1752]).

28 PRO: K.B.122.183, Hil., 14 Geo. II, 1740, Pt. II, Roll 778. See also PRO: Rule Book, K.B.125.147, Easter (1741–2).

29 Middle Temple, "Orders of Parliament" (20 Jun. 1740), p. 467.

30 "Middle Temple Day Book, 1740."

31 Both letters are in the Houghton Library, Harvard (FMS Eng 735).

32 Harris's "Essay."

33 These have been collected by S. J. Sackett (ed.), *The Voyages of Mr. Job Vinegar from "The Champion"* (*1740*), Augustan Reprint Society, No. 67 (Los Angeles: 1958). *Champion* No. 112 (31 Jul. 1740), Job Vinegar's characterization of himself, is probably not by Fielding.

34 J. Carswell, "George Dodington," in *The Old Cause: Three Biographical Studies in Whiggism* (London: 1954), pp. 129–265; also J. Carswell and L. A. Drable (eds.), *The Political Journal of George Bubb Dodington* (Oxford: 1965).

35 Ralph and Dodington collaborated, for example, on *The History of England*, 2 vols. (1744–6), and *Of the Use and Abuse of Parliaments*, 2 vols. (1744), as well as the periodical *The Remembrancer* (1747–51).

36 Cumberland's *Memoirs* (1806), p. 146.

37 The following have argued that *Jonathan Wild* was conceived and, as a satire of Walpole, drafted well before Fielding wrote *Joseph Andrews* and that it was subsequently modified both to generalize the political satire and to incorporate the Heartfree sections: T. Keightley, "On the Life and Writings of Henry Fielding," *Fraser's Magazine*, 57 (Jun. 1858), 763; A. Dobson, *Henry Fielding* (London: 1907), pp. 103–6; A. Digeon, *Les Romans de Fielding* (Paris: 1923), pp. 145–51; T. R. Cleary, *Henry Fielding: Political Writer* (Waterloo, Ontario: 1984), pp. 192–5. For a summary of this argument, see F. H. Dudden, *Henry Fielding: His Life, Works and Times* (Oxford: 1952), I.480–3.

38 *Honour* (1747), p. 7.

39 In "Detached Thoughts," No. 116 (1821) Byron wrote: "I have lately been reading Fielding over again. They talk of Radicalism, Jacobinism, etc., in England (I am told), but they should turn over the pages of 'Jonathan Wild the Great.' The inequality of conditions, and the littleness of the great, were never set forth in stronger terms; and his contempt for Conquerors and the like is such, that, had he lived *now*, he would have been denounced in 'the Courier' as the grand Mouth-piece and Factionary of the revolutionists. And yet I never recollect to have heard this turn of Fielding's mind noticed, though it is obvious in every page" (*Works*, ed. R. E. Prothero [London: 1901], V.465.)

40 *Champion* (31 May 1740). This number was so popular it was reprinted.

41 i.e., the Citizens of London, whom Walpole is said to have called "sturdy beggars."

42 The charge of Fielding's ingratitude to Walpole occurs in several numbers of the *Daily Gazetteer* (e.g., 24, 30 Jul. 1740, 13 May 1741); and in *An Historical View of ... the Political Writers in Great-Britain* (Oct. 1740), pp. 37–8. Beginning on 12 Jun., the *Daily Gazetteer* began its roasting of *The Champion*, which continued for many months. Among its more remarkable attacks on Fielding are those in the issues for 24, 30 Jul., 3, 5, 12 Sept., 9, 17 Oct., 12 (where Fielding is figured as "Campanus"), 14 Nov. 1740.

43 *Daily Gazetteer* (17 Oct. 1740).

44 See W. B. Coley, "The 'Remarkable Queries' in the *Champion*," *Philological Quarterly*, 41 (1962), 426–36.

45 *Champion* (23, 25 Sep. 1740).

46 T. R. Cleary, "The Case for Fielding's Authorship of *An Address to the Electors of Great Britain* (1740) Reopened," *Studies in Bibliography*, 28 (1975), 308–18.

47 The imprint of the very rare copy at Yale reads: "Edinburgh, Printed by Drummond and Company, in *Swan*'s Close, a little below the Cross-well, North Side of the Street, 1740."

48 PRO: Plea Rolls, K.B.122.189, Pt. 2, Roll 689; K.B.122.187, Roll 604; Palace Court, 2/34, Plaints, p. 379.

49 Newcomb, *A Supplement to a late Excellent Poem, entitled, Are these Things So?* (published 20 Dec. 1740), pp. 13–14.

50 Preface to *Miscellanies*; H. K. Miller (ed.), *Miscellanies: Volume One*, (Middletown, Conn., and Oxford: 1972), p. 14. Fielding's *Address to the Electors* took up all the leaders in Nov. 1740, after which only seven issues of *The Champion* survive for the period until Jun. 1741. These are as follows: No. 179 (3 Jan. 1740/1) in British Library; No. 187 (22 Jan. 1740/1) in Bodleian Library; No. 196 (12 Feb. 1740/1) in Bodleian Library; No. 204 (7 Mar. 1740/1) in Cambridge University Library; No. 213 (24 Mar. 1740/1) in British Library; No. 232 (7 May 1741) in New York Public Library; No. 237 (19 May 1741) in British Library. With the possible exception of No. 187, a letter from "Tim. Tell-truth" satirizing Walpole and his courtiers, none of these is by Fielding.

    J. B. Shipley, however, persuasively identifies an essay in the *Dublin Evening Post* (30 Dec. 1740–3 Jan 1740/1) as one written by Fielding and published originally in *The Champion* sometime during December 1740 (*Philological Quarterly*, 42 [1963], 417–22). Shipley elsewhere identifies nine other essays from *The Champion* reprinted in other newspapers of the period 2 Dec. 1740–28 Apr. 1741, but none of these is by Fielding (see *Notes & Queries*, 198 [Nov. 1953], 468–9; n.s. 2 [Jan. 1955], 25–8).

51 Quoted by Godden from a copy of the minutes in her possession, but now lost along with the original: see *Henry Fielding: a Memoir* [1910], pp. 138–9. This same entry states that Fielding's two sixteenth "Writing Shares" in the paper were at this time reassigned to Ralph.

52 Only twice in Dec. 1740 are Fielding and his journal attacked in the *Daily Gazetteer* (6, 10 Dec.), both times by out-of-date correspondents objecting to papers published in *The Champion* much earlier. Then a silence of seven weeks falls until *The Champion* is hit again in the *Daily Gazetteer* (28 Jan.). Thereafter the paper is often attacked and Fielding, not Ralph, is usually the intended target: e.g., *Daily Gazetteer*, 25 Feb., 11, 30 Mar., 25 Apr., 13, 20 May, 9, 12 Jun., 3, 15 Jul., 5 Aug., 11, 18, 23, 30 Sep.

53 See what is probably Fielding's review of the poem in *The History of Our Own Times*, No. 1 (1–15 Jan. 1740/1), p. 22. On Fielding's part in this periodical, see below, pp. 292–3.

54 Though the evidence for Fielding's connection with this short-lived magazine is circumstantial and stylistic, it is convincing. See T. Lockwood, "New Facts and Writings from an Unknown Magazine by Henry Fielding, *The History of Our Own Times*," *Review of English Studies*, 35 (1984), 462–93; and Lockwood's introduction and notes to the text, Scholars' Facsimiles & Reprints (Delmar, NY: 1985).

55 Huntington Library: Bixby Collection, HM 20358.

56 PRO: Palace Court 1/37, Bail Book, pp. 61, 63. Princes Court, contiguous to the Verge of the Court, no longer exists; its northern boundary was the southern wall of St. James's Park. (See Westminster Abbey, Muniment Room, Lease Book [14 Mar. 1754], ff. 131–3.) The rate books of St. Margaret's, Westminster, show that on 4 Apr. 1739 Catharine Fielding resided in a house in Princes Court. Coincidentally with her inheriting Mrs. Cottington's estate (Jan. 1739/40) and her father's financial distress, she had acquired a second house in Princes Court by 14 Apr. 1740, perhaps for Edmund who was also living there. She was in Princes Court

on 21 Apr. 1741, when, however, she was assessed for one house only, presumably because Edmund in Nov. 1740 had been confined in the liberties of the Fleet. Her name does not appear in the assessments for Princes Court dated 7 May 1742 and thereafter. (Westminster History Collection, Buckingham Palace Road: Highway Rate, St. Margaret's parish [1739], p. 36; also Poor Rate, St. Margaret's parish, Nos. 358, 360, 362–3, 365.)

57 Nichols possessed a copy of *The Crisis* bearing on the title-page the following inscription by one "R.B.": "This Sermon was written by the late Mr. Fielding, Author of Tom Jones, &c. &c. as the Printer of it assured me" (*Literary Anecdotes* [1814], VIII.446). Most scholars, some more hesitantly than others, have accepted the attribution: among these are Dobson, Cross, and Dudden; see also J. E. Wells, "Henry Fielding and *The Crisis*," *Modern Language Notes*, 27 (Jun. 1912), 180–1; G. E. Jensen, "The Crisis: A Sermon," *Modern Language Notes*, 31 (Nov. 1916), 435–7. Cleary, however, doubts Fielding's authorship (*Henry Fielding: Political Writer*, pp. 149–50), seconding my own former skepticism in the matter.

I now, however, accept *The Crisis* as Fielding's work, though it is unlikely the attribution can be proved. The pamphlet emphasizes Fielding's favorite political theme of this period: the ruin Walpole's bribery and corruption will bring upon the nation. Like the author of *The Crisis*, Fielding knew the Scriptures and was capable of adopting the pose of the preacher if the occasion warranted such a rhetorical strategy – as in his series "An Apology for the Clergy" in *The Champion*. Though the style of the "Sermon" is serious, it is not unlike Fielding's more earnest writings. Finally (a circumstance that has not been sufficiently weighed), of the three booksellers who published the work – namely, A. Dodd, E. Nutt, and H. Chappelle – two were associated with Fielding at exactly this period: Ann Dodd published *Shamela* on 2 Apr. 1741; and Henry Chappelle not only was a partner in *The Cham-*

pion, but from Fielding's note to Nourse of 20 Apr. 1741 it is clear that Chappelle acted as his bookseller in distributing *The Vernoniad* and *Of True Greatness*.

58 See John Woodman, *The Rat-Catcher at Chelsea College: A Tale. Alluding to the Manner in which the Out-pensioners of Chelsea have been a long Time oppress'd by Usurers and Extortioners* (1740), p. 43 and *passim*.

59 PRO: B.1.16, p. 295.

60 A. J. Guy, "Regimental Agency in the British Standing Army, 1715–1763: A Study of Georgian Military Administration," *Bulletin of the John Rylands University Library of Manchester*, 62 (Spring 1980), 423–53; 63 (Autumn 1980), 31–57. Guy makes the point that agents often speculated with regimental money or, when facing bankruptcy, used it as an additional asset. Colonels who neglected to demand adequate securities of their agents thus took dangerous risks with money belonging to their regiments – money for which the colonels were responsible. (See esp. p. 431.)

61 See above, n. 56.

62 PRO: S.P.36/50, p. 146. This, together with Edmund's subsequent letter to Harrington of 17 Jun., is transcribed by J. B. Shipley in *Notes and Queries*, 199 (Jun. 1954), 253–4.

63 See Harrington's reply of 2/13 Jul. 1740 to Edmund's letter of 21 Jun. (PRO: S.P.44.129, p. 192). William Fielding's commission in Col. Robinson's (later Col. Fraser's) Regiment of Marines is dated 25 Jan. 1739/40 (*Army List* 1740, p. 50); he was made first lieutenant in Mar. 1746/7. After this regiment was disbanded in Nov. 1748, he was commissioned lieutenant in Col. Dalzell's Regiment of Foot on 21 Jun. 1749 (PRO: W.O.25.22, pp. 76, 275). On 29 Oct. 1754 he was lieutenant in Lt. General Huske's 23rd Regiment of Foot (later the Royal Welsh Fusiliers), which he left in Sep. 1756 (W.O.25.25, p. 178; 25.24, n.p.). On 9 May 1758 he was commissioned "Lieutenant and Captain" in the 1st Regiment of Foot Guards (W.O.65.6, p. 40) with which he remained until 1778.

On 2 Aug. 1750 at Tewkesbury, Gloucestershire, William married

Hester (or Esther) Nichols of that place (register of St. Mary's, Tewkesbury, in Gloucester County Record Office, Gloucester; also *General Advertiser*, 10 Aug. 1750). Hester died a widow in 1799 and was buried at Tewkesbury. She was survived by their son Thomas. (PRO: P.C.C.1799.)

64 See the following sources in the PRO: (1) Rule Book, K.B.125.146; (2) Marshall's Surrender Book, K.B.139.49; (3) Marshall's Dockets of Commitments in Execution, Hil., 14 Geo. II, 1740, K.B.140.3; (4) K.B.122.181, Roll 505; (5) Commitment Books of the Fleet Prison for 1740, Case 82 (11 Nov.), f.193, and Case 194 (11 Feb. 1740/41), f. 253, Pris. 1.8; (6) C.P.40.3512; (7) Index to Docket Books, Hil., 14 Geo. II, 1740, Ind. 6503. To complete the history of actions for debts against Edmund, he was sued by one Henry Hyde in the autumn of 1728, the year his son Henry attained his majority; and in Easter Term 1736 an action was brought against him by Robert and Sarah Gosnell and Mary Boulton. (See, respectively, Exchequer of Pleas, Docket Book, Michaelmas, 2 Geo. II, 1728, Ind. 4534; K.B.122.159, Roll 440, and Docket Book, Ind.6165.)

65 The Fleet Prison occupied a site on the east side of what is now, roughly, Farringdon Street. In 1729 some 300 prisoners enjoyed the liberty of the Rules, an area bounded by Ludgate Hill on the south, Old Bailey on the east, Fleet Lane on the north, and the prison walls on the west. (H. B. Wheatley, *London Past and Present* [1891], s.v. "Fleet Prison.")

66 R. Evans, *The Fabrication of Virtue: English Prison Architecture* (Cambridge: 1982), pp. 30–1.

67 If she is the Elizabeth Spary, daughter of Benjamin and Anne Elizabeth Spary, christened at St. Andrew, Holborn, on 6 Jun. 1705, she would be thirty-five years old. On the marriage license (see below, n. 68) her age is given as "above 30 years."

68 Lambeth Palace Library: Faculty Office Calendar of Marriage Licences, 7 Mar. 1740/1.

69 Guildhall Library, Corporation of London: Ms. 6542/1. (St. Bride's, Marriages). The entry, dated 9 Mar. 1740/1, states that both Edmund and Elizabeth are of the parish of St. Martin, Ludgate. See also J. P. de Castro, *Notes & Queries*, 12th ser., 11 (26 Aug. 1922), 178, who transcribes a document certifying that the marriage took place; it is dated 10 Mar. 1740/1 and signed by W. E. Barnes, curate of St. Bride's.

70 The original reads "Prosperity," an apparent misprint.

71 *Old England* (25 Nov. 1749).

72 *Old England* (24 Sep. 1748).

73 PRO: Pris.1.8. Commitment Books, Fleet Prison, for 1740, Case 194, f. 253.

74 Guildhall Library, Corporation of London: Ms. 6543/1 (St. Bride's, Burials). Fr. Barnes, the curate who three months earlier had married Edmund, now buried him. The entry in the register, dated 25 Jun. 1741, mistakenly gives Edmund's age as sixty-three years; he was sixty-one.

75 PRO: Prob.29.139, Pt. II, ff. 522–3. The document is dated 4 Aug. 1741.

76 PRO: W.O.25.20, p. 245; W.O. 25.134, 1 Apr. 1743.

77 PRO: P.C.C. 1770. In the will (made 3 Mar. and proved 2 Jun. 1770) she is said to be "late of Charter House Square in the City of London but now of Bridgnorth," Shropshire. She was buried at St. Leonard's church, Bridgnorth. She had a sister, Martha Hodges, and a brother, John Sparrye, to whose daughter Ann she left the bulk of her estate.

78 See B. Kreissman, *Pamela–Shamela: A Study of the criticisms, burlesques, parodies, and adaptations of Richardson's "Pamela"* (n.p., Neb: 1960); T. C. Duncan Eaves and B. D. Kimpel, *Samuel Richardson: A Biography* (Oxford: 1971), esp. Ch. VII.

79 See C. B. Woods, "Fielding and the Authorship of *Shamela*," *Philological Quarterly*, 25 (1946), 248–72.

80 Parson Tickeltext advises Parson Oliver that copies of *Pamela* will be available in the country "as soon as the fourth Edition is published" (p. 4). For the date of the third edition, see the *Daily Post* (12 Mar. 1740/1).

81 "To the Author of Shamela," *London Magazine*, 10 (1741), 304.

82 BL: Add. Mss. 35633, ff. 31–2.

83 Introduction to *Pamela's Conduct in High Life* (1741), pp. xii–xiii, by "B.W." – attributed to Kelly.

84 See Godden, *Henry Fielding*, pp. 115–16.

85 In the originals the signature letters begin with No. 48 (4 Mar. 1739/40). Fielding also used the letter "M." – as in the numbers for 25 Mar. [no letter in reprint], 10 May [marked *L* in reprint], 27 May [leader omitted from reprint], and 28 Aug. (See J. B. Shipley, "The 'M' in Fielding's 'Champion,'" *Notes & Queries* n.s. 2 (Jun., Aug. 1955), 240–5, 345–51.) Many other unsigned articles should also be attributed to him: specifically, those for 15, 17, 20, 22 Nov., 27 Dec. 1739; 31 Jan. [mostly omitted in reprint], 28 Feb. 1739/40; 15, 20 May, 17, 24 Jun., 8, 12 ["Moll Mackerel" only] Jul., 11 ["Wm. Loverest"], 27 ["Jacob Carroll"?] Sep., 9 Oct., 1–15 Nov. 1740.

86 Introduction, *Journal of a Voyage to Lisbon* (1755).

87 See above, Part II, n. 195.

88 The boy died in Aug. 1750, before he was nine years old: see below, p. 507.

89 In order of their occurrence in the quoted passage Fielding alludes to the following: Hobbes, *Leviathan* (I.vi); Horace, *Satires* (I.iv.83–5); Homer, *Iliad* (II.211–15); Ecclesiastes (2:2); Horace, *Satires* (I.i.24); Juvenal, *Satires* (X.31); Diogenes Laertius, *Lives of Eminent Philosophers* (IX.xliii); Montaigne, *Essays* ("Of Democritus and Heraclitus" and "Of Liars").

90 B. Boyce, *The Benevolent Man: A Life of Ralph Allen of Bath* (Cambridge, Mass.: 1967).

91 Samuel Derrick's letter from Bath, 10 May 1763 (*Letters* [Dublin: 1767], II. 57–8).

92 Boyce, *The Benevolent Man*, p. 128.

93 Pope's *Correspondence*, ed. G. Sherburn (Oxford: 1956), IV.344, 350; 366, n. 1.

94 Pope to Allen, 8 Feb. 1741/2 (*Correspondence*, IV.387).

95 See Battestin (ed.), *Joseph Andrews* (Middletown, Conn., and Oxford: 1967), pp. 188, n. 2; 313, n. 2.

96 W. L. Cross, *The History of Henry Fielding* (New Haven, Conn.: 1918), I.298.

97 W. B. Coley, "Henry Fielding and the Two Walpoles," *Philological Quarterly*, 45 (1966), 162.

98 For conflicting interpretations of *The Opposition* see, on the one hand, Coley, ibid., esp. pp. 159–65; and Cleary, *Henry Fielding: Political Writer*, pp. 152–62; on the other, Battestin, "Fielding's Changing Politics and *Joseph Andrews*," *Philological Quarterly*, 39 (1960), 39–55; and B. A. Goldgar, *Walpole and the Wits* (Lincoln, Nebr.: 1976), pp. 197–208.

99 The print, which satirizes the Opposition on occasion of their defeat in February 1741, depicts Argyll as driver of the coach, as well as ridiculing Pulteney, Chesterfield, Carteret, Cobham, Lyttelton, and Fielding himself (who is shown in his barrister's wig and gown holding a scroll marked "*Pasquin*").

100 A. Dobson, "Fielding and Andrew Millar," *The Library*, 3rd ser., 7 (1916), 177–90.

101 C. F. Partington, *The British Cyclopaedia of Biography* (1837), I.706, where the story is mistakenly told of the sale of *Tom Jones*. As Frederick Lawrence pointed out, the circumstances, if true at all, can relate only to the sale of *Joseph Andrews* (*The Life of Henry Fielding* [1855], p. 164n.).

102 See below p. 345, and n. 123.

103 P. T. P., "Woodfall's Ledger, 1734–1747," *Notes & Queries.*, 1st ser., 11 [2 Jun 1855], 419.

104 C. F. Mullett (ed.), *Letters of Dr. George Cheyne to Samuel Richardson, 1733–43*, University of Missouri Studies, 18 (Columbia; Mis.: 1943), p. 85.

105 Richardson to Lady Bradshaigh, Nov. (?) 1749: Carroll (ed.), *Selected Letters of Samuel Richardson* (Oxford: 1964), p. 133; Cheyne to Richardson, 9 Mar. 1741/2: Mullett (ed.), *Letters of Dr. George Cheyne*, p. 88.

106 Richardson to Mrs. Donnellan, 22 Feb. 1752; in Carroll (ed.), *Selected Letters*, p. 197.

107 Harris's "Essay" on Fielding.

108 *Covent-Garden Journal* (3 Mar. 1752).

109 Whitefield's *Works* (1771–2), V.135.

110 Battestin, *Philological Quarterly*, 39 (1960), 39–55.

111 Miller (ed.), *Miscellanies: Volume One*, pp. xlvi–xlvii.

112 See the Burial Account Books (1735–Sept. 1744) of St. Martin-in-the-Fields, in which Charlotte is said to have resided at Spring Garden. (Westminster History Collection, Buckingham Palace Road: 419/264.)

113 See Dickens's letters of consolation to Basil Hall (26 May 1841) and the Rev. James White (4 May 1848) – the latter of which reads: "The traveller who journeyed in fancy from this world to the next was struck to the heart to find the child he had lost, many years before, building him a bower in heaven." (M. House and G. Storey [eds.], *Letters of Charles Dickens*, Vol. II [Oxford: 1969], p. 285; and G. Storey and K. J. Fielding [eds.], *Letters of Charles Dickens*, Vol. V [Oxford: 1981], p. 296. My thanks to Graham Storey for calling these allusions to my attention).

114 PRO: C.P.40.3524, Roll 522. King asked for damages of £98.12s. in addition to the amount of the debt; Fielding was represented by the attorney Thomas Buckle. On 7 Jul. 1742 the Court judged that Fielding owed King £197 plus only 50 shillings in damages. Fielding scholars misdate this debt, stating that he contracted it in 1741.

115 I am indebted to the late John Brooke for providing me with a photocopy of these verses in the collection of the late W. S. Lewis, who permitted me to see these and other unpublished papers in his collection. For a discussion of the poem, see Coley, *Philological Quarterly*, 45 (1966), 168–70.

116 Coley, ibid., p. 169.

117 J. B. Owen, *The Rise of the Pelhams* (London: 1957), pp. 105–9.

118 *Gentleman's Magazine*, 12 (Mar. 1742), 128.

119 *Daily Advertiser* (12 Mar. 1741/2). Cross (*History of Henry Fielding*, I.361) and Dudden (*Henry Fielding*, I.394) wrongly state that the author of the *Remarks* signed himself "Britannicus" – the pseudonym used by the author of another work, *A Review of a Late Treatise, entitled An Account of the Conduct of the Dowager D—— of M——* (published on 23 Mar.).

120 *Daily Advertiser* and *Daily Post* (2 Apr. 1742).

121 In *A Journey from This World to the Next* (I.ix) Livy praises Hooke's *Roman History* (Vol. 1, 1738); in *Tom Jones* (XV.iv) Lady Bellaston has read the work.

122 See Frances Harris, "Accounts of the Conduct of Sarah, Duchess of Marlborough, 1704–1742," *British Library Journal*, 8 (1982), 7–35.

123 The original document is in the Forster Collection, Victoria & Albert Museum, London; for a transcription, see Battestin (ed.), *Joseph Andrews*, pp. xxx–xxxi. Millar arranged with Roberts to publish the *Full Vindication*. Roberts this year reissued the original printing with a new title-page incorrectly representing it as a "Second Edition."

124 C. B. Woods, "The 'Miss Lucy' Plays of Fielding and Garrick," *Philological Quarterly*, 41 (1962), 294–310.

125 Fleetwood submitted the copy to the Lord Chamberlain on 5 Mar. 1741/2. (See the Larpent Ms., Huntington Library [LA33].)

126 *A Letter to a Noble Lord, to Whom alone it Belongs* (1742), p. 10.

127 Letter of 26 May 1742, in W. S. Lewis, *et al.* (eds.), *Walpole's Correspondence with Horace Mann* (New Haven, Conn: 1955), I.434–5.

128 *Champion* (29 Jun. 1742): Bodleian Library (Don. c. 72).

129 See above, Part II, n. 312.

130 PRO: K.B.122.192, Pt. II, Roll 963.

131 W. Phillimore, Dorset *Marriages*, VI (East Stour), records the marriage of Randolph Seagrim and Elizabeth Burden in 1732.

132 *Nisi prius*: "trials by jury ... originally ordered to be held at a central court 'unless previously' held before justices on circuit" (*Guide to the Contents of the Public Record Office*, Vol. I [London: 1963], p. 207).

133 Fielding's unpublished Cantos, I.133, 142; Grundy, *PMLA*, 87 (1972), 213–45.

134 Thomson's *Seasons*, "Autumn," ll. 646–7, praising Philips for writing *Cyder* (1708) in blank verse.

135 For references to Watts in the period 1733–46, see *Records of the Honourable Society of Lincoln's Inn. The Black Books*, Vol. III, 1660–1775 (1899), Index.

136 Birch's Diary: BL: Add. Mss. 4478, Part C. Diary entries for 14, 27 Apr., 15 May, 21 Nov. 1736.

137 BL: Holland House Papers 35190, f. 80.

138 Goldwyre's marriage to the eldest daughter of William Harris, Esq., a man said to be worth £20,000, took place on 8 Sep. 1742 (*Gentleman's Magazine*, 12 [Sep. 1742], 499).

139 J. P. de Castro *Notes & Queries*, 12th ser., 1 [17 Jun. 1916], 483–4) gave the lady's name as Husband, an error in which he was followed by Cross (*History of Henry Fielding*, I.378–9), Dudden (*Henry Fielding*, I.407, n. 2), and Miller ([ed.] *Miscellanies, Volume One*, p. 118, n. 1): he was corrected in *Notes & Queries*, 12th ser., 2 (1 Jul., 12 Aug. 1916), 16, 137–8.

140 John Essex, whom Hogarth depicts in Plate I of the *Analysis of Beauty* (1753). Fielding facetiously alludes to him in *Tom Jones* (XIV.i) and also, though not by name, in *A Journey from This World to the Next* (I.xxv).

141 For Millar's bill of complaint see PRO: C.12.307/62 (listed 52 in Index, but marked 62). See also the affidavits of Millar and Francis Smith (C.41.51, No. 66, sworn 15–16 Oct. 1742); and Chancery Decrees and Orders, Mich., 1742, 16 Geo. II, dated 23 Oct. (C.33.380, Pt. I, pp. 1, 113).

142 Harrowby Mss. LVI, 3rd ser., Letters, f. 19.

143 Pope's *Correspondence*, ed. Sherburn, IV.425. Both Ilive and Daniel Lynch are named in Pope's complaint (PRO: C.11.837/14).

144 The following account is based on Fielding's own in the Preface to the *Miscellanies*.

145 H. S. Hughes, *The Gentle Hertford* (New York: 1940), p. 238.

146 Huntington Library: LA39.

147 Letter of 19 Feb. 1742/3, in Hughes, *Gentle Hertford*, p. 242.

148 "Verses occasion'd by a Quarrel betwixt Mr. F[ie]ld[in]g and Mrs. Cl[i]ve, on his intending her the Part of a Bawd, in his new Play called *The Wedding Day*," in *The Foundling Hospital for Wit*, No. 1 (1743), p. 1. The verses are included in Hanbury Williams's *Works* (1822), II.190, where the allusion in the penultimate line is explained: "She acted the

character of Nell in the 'Wives Metamorphosed' most inimitably well."

149 Sir John Hawkins, *Life of Johnson*, in Johnson's *Works* (1787), I.45.

150 *Covent-Garden Journal* (11 Jan. 1752).

151 See W. Cooke, *Memoirs of Charles Macklin* (1804), pp. 146–7.

152 H. P. Sturz, *Schriften* (Leipzig: 1786), p. 131. Dr. Bernhard Fabian of the University of Münster called this passage to the attention of Arthur Cash, who kindly shared it with me. The translation is by Robert Waugh.

153 Comment on occasion of Fielding's first Benefit, 21 Feb. (BL: Egerton 2320, f. 81ᵛ).

154 Bowyer's ledger, 18 Feb. 1742/3: Bodleian Library, Johnson Collection: B.P.C.2108, Grolier IV(1), f. 11.

155 J. Milhous and R. D. Hume, "David Garrick and Box-Office Receipts at Drury Lane in 1742–43," *Philological Quarterly*, 67 (1988), 323–44.

156 Letter to Lord Beauchamp of 19 Feb. 1742/3; Hughes, *Gentle Hertford*, p. 242.

157 See Edwards's letter to John Clerke, 23 Feb. 1742/3: Bodleian Library (Ms. Bodl.1010, p. 23).

158 Letter of 18 Feb. 1742/3 from Mrs. Russell to her husband Col. Russell stationed at Ghent in Flanders, as transcribed from the papers of Lord Lee of Fareham by J. P. de Castro in his copy of Cross (*History of Henry Fielding*, I.374–5), in the Houghton Library, Harvard.

159 His own estimate in the Preface to the *Miscellanies*. After the second dismal Benefit, the witness quoted earlier was equally explicit about Fielding's discomfiture: "This author Mr. Fielding did not get above 30 lib each benefit night, though he expected mighty things from his play, as he formerly had met with great success" (BL: Egerton 2320, f. 82).

160 Battestin (ed.), *Joseph Andrews*, p. xxxiii.

161 On Hulett and his "naive and artless cuts to *Joseph Andrews*," see H. Hammelmann, *Book Illustrators in Eighteenth-Century England*, ed. T. S. R. Boase (New Haven, Conn.: 1975), pp. 40, 57.

162 For a translation of Desfontaines's

Preface, as well as of his earlier review of *Joseph Andrews*, see R. Paulson and T. Lockwood (eds.), *Henry Fielding: The Critical Heritage* (London: 1969), pp. 126–37.

163 Owen, *Rise of the Pelhams*, pp. 142 ff.

164 On 8 Mar. 1742/3 Edwards wrote John Clerke in the country, sending him "two little treatises, one on the Polypus, which I thought I should have been able by this time to have confirmed the truth of by having seen the experiments made, but they are not yet come ... the other dissertation is written by Fielding on the Crysopus [*sic*], an insect which ... [is] plenty enough with you to enable you to make the experiments mentioned in the treatise" (Bodleian Library: Ms. Bodl.1010, p. 25).

165 Miller, *Essays on Fielding's Miscellanies* (Princeton: 1961), pp. 344–6.

166 Wheatley, *London Past and Present* (1891), I.281; and B. Weinreb and C. Hibbert, *London Encyclopedia* (London: 1983), pp. 96–7. A century later Brompton was said to have the lowest mortality rate in England, and, being "remarkable for the salubrity of its air," was chosen as the site for the Hospital for Consumption and Diseases of the Chest.

167 See Miller, *Essays*, pp. 15–26. On 12 Apr., Pope wrote Allen: "Fielding has sent the Books you subscribed for to the Hand I employd in conveying the 20 ll. to him. In one Chapter of the Second vol. [i.e., *A Journey from This World to the Next*, I.v] he has payd you a pretty Compliment upon your House" (*Correspondence*, ed. Sherburn, IV.452).

168 PRO: Ind. 9761 (*Malson v. Fielding*, Easter, 16 Geo. II, 1743, Middx.); and PRO: C.P.40.3533 (*Goffe v. Fielding*, Mich., 17 Geo. II, 1743, Middx., in Rolls of Attornies, p. 4).

169 Miller, *Essays*, p. 25.

170 Digeon, *Les Romans de Fielding*, p. 118.

171 An illuminating account of this neglected work is B. A. Goldgar, "Myth and History in Fielding's *Journey from This World to the Next*," *Modern Language Quarterly*, 47 (1986), 235–52.

172 In a footnote to this part of the *Journey* Fielding coyly remarks that it "is in the Original writ in a Woman's Hand ... and as it is the Character of a Woman which is related, I am inclined to fancy it was really written by one of that Sex." Digeon first attributed this section to Sarah Fielding: see *Revue Anglo-Américaine*, 8 (1931), 428–30. See also J. F. Burrows and A. J. Hassall, "*Anna Boleyn* and the Authenticity of Fielding's Feminine Narratives," *Eighteenth-Century Studies*, 21 (1988), 427–53.

173 "Essay on the Knowledge of the Characters of Men," p. 154.

174 See above, n. 39.

175 See Miller, *Essays*, pp. 12–15.

176 C. T. Probyn, "James Harris to Parson Adams in Germany: Some Light on Fielding's Salisbury Set," *Philological Quarterly*, 64 (1985), 130–9.

177 Ibid., pp. 135–6.

178 In "An Essay on Conversation" Fielding complimented Harris on this work, which, though finished by Dec. 1741, was not published until 1744, as part of Harris's *Three Treatises* (see Fielding's *Miscellanies, Volume One*, ed. Miller, p. 122 and n. 1).

179 Harris, *Philological Inquiries* (1781), p. 33.

180 H. Amory (ed.), *Sale Catalogues of Libraries of Eminent Persons*, Vol. 7 (London: 1973), p. 129. As F. and A. Ribble explain in their annotated catalogue of Fielding's library (in progress), the "Upton" who also purchased books at the sale was not Canon Upton, but rather John Upton of Ingmire Hall, Yorkshire.

181 The Common Place Book and Accounts Book (1704–49) which James Upton kept as Headmaster of Taunton School reveal that he and his son John were well known to Fielding's uncle Davidge Gould. Fielding's cousin William entered the school on 22 Sep. 1725 (in his eleventh year) and remained there until 1732. John Upton, who was admitted to the school on 4 Oct. 1714, knew Fielding's uncle well enough to act as intermediary in conveying William's final tuition payment to James Upton on 9 Dec. 1732, John being then Fellow of Exeter College, Oxford. Henry Price entered the

school on 15 Aug. 1716 and in 1722 was appointed Assistant to the Headmaster at the "usual" salary of £5 a quarter. (Somerset Record Office: DD/X/SAY C/1701.)

182 De Castro, *Notes & Queries* 178 (9 Mar. 1940), 164–7.

183 *Tom Jones*, eds. Battestin and Bowers (Middletown, Conn., and Oxford: 1975), pp. 523–4 and notes.

184 The three letters Fielding wrote Harris in Sep. and Nov. 1743 were all sent from "Twiverton." They are the only proof of the tradition that Fielding once resided in Twerton: see Richard Graves, *The Triflers* (1806), p. 67.

185 See Graves, *Triflers*; and esp. R. E. M. Peach, *Historic Houses in Bath*, 2nd ser. (1884), pp. 34–5.

186 Peach, *Historic Houses*, p. 32.

187 "Of True Greatness" (l. 196); for other compliments to Young, see *Miscellanies: Volume One*, ed. Miller, pp. 78, 136.

188 Clues within the letter point to Fielding's having written it at Bath to Harris at Salisbury. As for the time of writing, Fielding in a postscript states: "I shall not go hence 'till 1ˢᵗ Novʳ. so hope to spend some Days with you here." Since he did not in fact leave Bath in 1743 until the turn of the new year, the letter cannot have been written that year unless Fielding changed his plans, as, for a number of reasons, I believe he may have done. (1) The only other eligible year would seem to be 1741, when the two friends were just beginning their correspondence and in doing so preserved a dignified formality which would not allow for the foolery displayed here on both sides. (2) In this letter as in his mock-writ of 14 Nov. 1743 Fielding jokes at the expense of a certain Patrick Oneal of Bath. (3) Fielding opens the letter by attributing his "long Silence" after receiving Harris's *History* to a "*Dulness*" he felt, owing in part "to some late violent Agitations of Grief and Joy." Such a mixture of conflicting emotions is evident in his letter from Twerton of 6 Sept. 1743, in which he refers to his "Happiness" at Charlotte's having "perfectly recovered from a dangerous Illness in which she was given over." (4) The long interval between this letter of 6 Sep. and his next of 14 Nov. 1743 would allow time for Harris to have sent his *History* and for Fielding not to have answered until some time before 1 Nov., after a "long Silence." But the date of this letter remains uncertain.

189 For a discussion of Fielding's revisions of *David Simple*, see M. Kelsall's edition (Oxford: 1969), pp. xix–xxiii.

190 See ibid., p. ix.

191 Mrs. Piozzi to the Rev. Leonard Chappelow, 15 Mar. 1795. I am indebted to Edward and Lillian Bloom for calling this letter to my attention.

192 See above, Part I, n. 89.

193 Fielding to Harris from Boswell Court, London, 11 Jan. 1745/6.

194 Even such knowledgeable literary gossips as Thomas Birch and Lady Grey were uncertain whether Sarah Fielding or her brother had written *David Simple*. Accompanied by Birch, Lady Grey arrived at her country seat, Wrest, on 21 May 1744 and wrote the following day to another well-known bluestocking, Catherine Talbot: "We follow'd your example, & amused ourselves upon the Road with David Simple, & it really did amuse me extreamly, but I think I could have spared or at least shorten'd some of the Stories for as the excellence of Mʳ. or Mʳˢ. Fielding (whichever I am to call the Person) seems to be their Odd Original Characters, David's own Adventures gave more Scope for exercising that Genius than anything of the Novel Kind, & yet they are not half the Book." (Bedford County Record Office: Lady Lucas collection [L30/9A/3, p. 107].)

195 Lady Louisa Stuart, "Introductory Anecdotes," in Lord Wharncliffe (ed.), *The Letters and Works of Lady Mary Wortley Montagu*, rev. M. Moy Thomas (1861), I.106.

196 So Fielding reported to Harris in a letter from London, 24 Nov. 1744.

197 George Owen Cambridge's "Memoirs" of his father, in the latter's *Works* (1803).

198 Peach, *Historic Houses*, pp. 37–8.

199 St. Martin-in-the-Fields, Burial Account Books, 1744–9: Westminster History Collection, Buckingham

Palace Road (419/265). The entry states that Charlotte's body was brought "from Bath" and gives the charges as £11.17.2. Until Sep. 1745, when there was an equally expensive funeral, the next highest amount recorded for such a service is £3.13.8.

200 Opening his letter to Harris of 24 Nov., Fielding acknowledged "some late Obligations to you as extraordinary in the Manner as the Measure." Closing the letter, he added a postscript: "If you think proper to stay a year for the Repayment with the Casualty of my Death in that time you must be assured the Favour you offer me will be as serviceable to me now as the offer is kind in you." The state of Fielding's finances during this period may be glimpsed in the ledgers of his bankers, C. Hoare & Co. (Ledger 43, p. 103). On 16 Nov. 1744 he paid in a note of £21, which he withdrew on 20 Nov. On 26 Jan. 1744/5 (the beginning of Hilary Term, when he had promised to repay Harris's loan) he paid in £100 in four notes (two of £30 each and two of £20 each); these he withdrew on 28 (£20), 30 (£20), 31 Jan. (£30), and 1 March (£30). Others less accommodating than Harris presumably had claims on him he could not so easily put off.

201 To Harris, Fielding quotes in Latin a passage from Valerius Maximus, *Factorum ac dictorum memorabilium*, IV.i. *externa* 2 ("De Moderatione") – translated by Samuel Speed as follows: "One would have thought his [Plato's] Soul had not kept her Station in a Mortal Body, but in a Celestial Tower, and as it were armed, that could so invincibly keep off the Incursions of Human Vices, keeping the whole number of Vertues in the close Fortress of the breast" (Speed trans. [1678], p. 161).

202 The pamphlet was attributed to Fielding by G. E. Jensen: "A Fielding Discovery," *Yale University Library Gazette*, 10 (1936), 23–32. The work is almost certainly by Fielding, as most scholars agree; but the definitive case for his authorship has yet to be made.

203 See J. B. Owen, *The Rise of the Pelhams* (London: 1957), Ch. vi.; and

Cleary, *Henry Fielding: Political Writer*, pp. 197–206.

204 J. P. de Castro, "Fielding at Boswell Court," *Notes & Queries*, 12th ser., 1 (1 Apr. 1916), 264–5. Examination of the Poor Rate accounts, parish of St. Clement Danes, Shier Lane Ward (Westminster History Collection, Buckingham Palace Road: B154–9, 1743–8), indicates that Fielding took up residence in Boswell Court sometime after 27 Sep. and before 20 Dec. 1744; he continued there until 20 Jan. 1747/8. The house was one of the more expensive ones in the court, with a rateable value of £45 (1744–5) and £55 (1746–7).

205 A handbill describes Boswell Court as one of those courts "Where there are but few in a Court, and the Inhabitants People of Credit" (*Proposals to Suppress Robberies all over England* [1750?]: BL: 516.m. 17. [43.]).

206 Letter XL (20 Dec. [1746?]), which Fielding contributed to Sarah Fielding's *Familiar Letters between the Principal Characters in David Simple* (1747).

207 See, respectively, the following documents in the PRO, under K.B.119/4: (1) Pt. 1, No. 83, Mich., 17 Geo. II [1743]; (2) Pt. II, No. 78, Mich., 18 Geo II [1744]; (3) Pt. II, No. 106, Mich., 18 Geo. II [1744]; (4) Pt. II, No. 124, Mich., 18 Geo. II [1744]; (5) Pt. I, No. 13, Easter, 18 Geo. II [1744/5]; [6] Pt. I, No. 48, Easter, 18 Geo. II [1744/5]; and (7) K.B. 119/5, Pt. I, No. 74, Mich., 21 Geo. II [1747].

208 W. B. Coley, "Henry Fielding's 'Lost' Law Book," *Modern Language Notes*, 76 (May 1961), 408–13.

209 References to the Gould Mss. recur in *Old England*: see issues for 3 Sep. 1748; 7 Jan. 1748/9; 5, 26 Aug, 25 Nov. 1749.

210 Amory has assembled and edited such fragments of the work as can now be identified: see *Henry Fielding, An Institute of the Pleas of the Crown* (Cambridge, Mass.: 1987). See also Amory's "Preliminary Census of Henry Fielding's Legal Manuscripts," *Publications of the Bibliographical Society of America*, 62 (1968), 587–601; and the additional information in the *Index to English*

Literary Manuscripts (Oxford: 1981–), Vol. 3, Pt. 1.

211 *Annual Register* for 1762 (1763), p. 18 n.

212 On the complex matter of the date of composition of *Tom Jones*, see Battestin and Bowers (eds.), I.xxxv–xlii. Also T. R. Cleary, "Jacobitism in *Tom Jones*: The Basis for an Hypothesis," *Philological Quarterly*, 52 (1973), 239–51; H. Amory, "The History of 'The Adventures of a Foundling': Revising *Tom Jones*," *Harvard Library Bulletin*, 27 (1979), 277–303.

213 See PRO: C.11.565/26 – the Bill of Complaint, dated 6 Jun. 1744.

214 Chancery Decrees and Orders in PRO: C.33.383, Pt. II, p. 446. Trin., 19 Geo. II [1745].

215 Fielding's answer, signed by Hanbury Williams and himself, was sworn before one Thomas Bennet at the latter's house in Cursitor Street on 13 Aug. 1746: PRO: C.11.565/26.

216 R. Benson, *Memoirs of the Life and Writings of the Rev. Arthur Collier, M.A., Rector of Langford Magna, in the County of Wilts, from A.D. 1704 to A.D. 1732. With Some Account of his Family* (1837).

217 C. Coote, *Sketches of the Lives and Characters of Eminent Civilians* (1804), pp. 116–17.

218 Harris's daughter Katherine (later the Hon. Mrs. Frederick Robinson) heard that her father "had written great part of the Art of Tormenting" ("Memoir of James Harris" [1801] – PRO: PRO.30/43/1/4).

219 The inscription, dated by Fielding "Fordhook/June 25. 1754," is on the flyleaf of Vol. I of Horace's *Opera Omnia*, in Latin and French, ed. Michael de Marolles (Paris: 1660), 2 vols. 8⁰. (Bancroft Library, University of California, Berkeley: PA6393/A2/1660.) I am indebted to my friends the late Irvin and Anne Ehrenpreis for supplying me with a photograph of the inscription, and for pointing out that in the original the article "a" inserted before "mixed" is in different ink, placed there by someone who apparently misread "mind" for "mixed." The inscription was noted by "Olybrius" (i.e., T. O. Mabbott) in *Notes & Queries*, 178 [27 Apr. 1940], 298), who observed Fielding's "elegant rendering of 'dat, donat, dedicat.'"

220 Margaret Collier was baptized in Salisbury Cathedral on 2 Sep. 1717: "Register Book, Cathedral Church of Sarum" in the Cathedral Library. She died at Ryde, Isle of Wight (Isle of Wight County Record Office, Newport: burial register, St. Thomas, Ryde, 8 Sep. 1794).

221 Fielding to John Fielding from Lisbon, *c.* 18–19 Sep. 1754: H. Amory, "Fielding's Lisbon Letters," *Huntington Library Quarterly*, 35 (1971), pp. 70, 72.

222 See the following Plea Rolls in the PRO: K.B.122.209, Pt. I, Rolls 123, 202; K.B.122.210, Pt. II, Rolls 739, 741–2. Also Ind. 9636 – showing two additional suits against Collier in Trinity, 18–19 Geo. II [1745]; Hilary, 19 Geo II [1745/6].

223 J. P. de Castro, "Fielding and the Collier Family," *Notes & Queries*, 12 ser., 2 (5 Aug. 1916), 104–06. See PRO: K.B.122.210, Pt. II, Rolls 741–2.

224 See Jane Collier's letter to her friend Mrs. Barker, dated Salisbury, 17 Mar. 1744/5: J. P. de Castro, *Notes & Queries*, 178 (11 May 1940), 337–9.

225 His name appears nowhere in the records of commitments to the several debtors' prisons.

226 Fielding to John Fielding, *c.* 18–19 Sep. 1754: Amory, *Huntington Library Quarterly*, 35 (1971), p. 71.

227 *Amelia* (V.v), first edition.

228 See R. C. Jarvis, "The Death of Walpole: Henry Fielding and a Forgotten *Cause Célèbre*," *Modern Language Review*, 41 (1946), 113–30.

229 *General Advertiser* (24–8 Jun. 1745).

230 Except that it does not show the archaic verb forms *hath* and *doth*, usual with Fielding in his post-theatrical period, this essay bears every other mark of his style and appears to be Fielding's work.

231 Battestin and Bowers (eds.), *Tom Jones*, I.xxxv–xlii.

232 For a survey of this background, see W. B. Coley (ed.), Fielding's *True Patriot and Related Writings* (Oxford and Middletown, Conn.: 1987), pp. xxx ff.; and Owen, *Rise of the Pelhams*, pp. 277 ff.

233 *True Patriot* (22–9 Apr. 1746).

234 Quoted in Coley (ed.), *True Patriot and Related Writings*, p. xxxi.

235 For an account of the composition, printing, and publication of these pamphlets, see ibid., pp. xxxvi–lx.

236 Barker and his wife were friends of the Fieldings and Harrises (Dr. Barker subscribed to Henry's *Miscellanies* [1743] and Mrs. Barker to Sarah's *Familiar Letters* [1747]). Educated at Wadham College, Oxford (A.B. 1731, A.M. and M.B. 1737), Barker settled in Salisbury. He took his M.D. at Oxford in 1743. At the time he was with Fielding in London, he was candidate for admission to the College of Physicians, becoming a Fellow of the College on 24 Mar. 1746. He wrote *An Inquiry into the Nature, Cause and Cure of the Epidemic Fever of 1740–42* and *An Essay on the Agreement between Ancient and Modern Physicians; or, A Comparison of the Practice of Hippocrates, Galen, Sydenham and Boerhave* (1748). Attached to the Westminster Hospital in 1746, in 1748 he became Chief Physician to the Army and contracted an illness in Flanders. He died at the Ipswich Military Hospital on 31 Jan. 1748/9. (W. Munk, *The Roll of the Royal College of Physicians of London* [1878], II.158; De Castro, *Notes & Queries* 178 [9 Mar. 1940], 164–7.

237 A distinguished soldier, Wade in 1715 quelled the Jacobites in Bath, a city he came to love and which he represented in Parliament. From 1724 to 1740 he commanded the Army in Scotland and improved the system of roads there. In his unpublished "Epistle to Mr. Lyttleton" (1733) Fielding praised Wade as a man of "Action," but the depth of his affection for him is best measured by his comment on the report of Wade's death in *The Jacobite's Journal* (19 Mar. 1747/8): "*He was ... in private Life, a Gentleman of the highest Honour, Humanity and Generosity, and hath done more good and benevolent Actions than this whole Paper can contain.*"

238 *London Evening Post* (2–5 Nov. 1745). For an account of the circumstances of publication, see Coley (ed.), *True Patriot and Related Writings*, pp. lx ff.

239 See *Jacobite's Journal* (5 Dec. 1747).

240 See Coley (ed.), *True Patriot and Related Writings*, pp. lxii–lxiv and n. l, lxix–lxx, xcii–xciii. Supporting Coley's hypothesis, perhaps, is a somewhat cryptic passage in *The Art of Stock-jobbing* (Apr. 1746). The writer seems to have heard that the authors of *The Champion* were collaborating again, this time on a ministerial paper: "Now R[al]p-h [sic] and F[iel]d[in]g are still kept in Pay,/To write for G[ran]v[ill]e's Honour Night and Day" (ll. 217–18). The notion that Fielding and Ralph were supporting Granville must be ironic. Or perhaps the author means Lyttelton's cousins the Grenvilles.

241 The two letters by Adams are in *True Patriot* No. 7 (17 Dec. 1745), No. 13 (28 Jan. 1745/6).

242 On John Dalton, see Coley (ed.), *True Patriot and Related Writings*, p. 206, n. 2. Fielding also knew his brother, Richard Dalton (1715–91), Librarian to the Prince of Wales and Keeper of the Royal Drawings and Medals, and in the *Covent-Garden Journal* (10 Mar. 1752 ["Modern History"]) praised his architectural engravings of Greek and Egyptian antiquities.

243 *London Magazine*, 15 (Jun. 1746), 298–9.

244 Fielding to Bedford, 19 Dec. 1748: in M.C. with R.R. Battestin, "Fielding, Bedford, and the Westminster Election of 1749," *Eighteenth-Century Studies*, 11 (1977–78), 143–85.

245 Bedford County Record Office: R4/6129.

246 See the Accounts of the New Forest, which record payments to Fielding in 1746–8; and the letter of Charles Coleman (receiver of the rents for the New Forest) to Bedford's agent Robert Butcher, 13 Sep. 1749 (Bedford Record Office: R5/6457A, R4/6140).

247 Birt's accounts relating to the New Forest (from Lady Day 1746 to Lady Day 1754) are at BCRO: Russell Papers, Box 282 (Out Counties: Hants.).

248 Fielding describes the scene in *Ovid's Art of Love Paraphrased* (1747), p. 21.

249 *London Gazette* (15–19 Jul. 1746).

250 R. E. M. Peach, *Bath: Old and New* (London and Bath: 1891), pp. 226–7.

Peach states that this correspondence was preserved and "is still in the possession of the family." We have not been able to corroborate this assertion.

251　See esp. *Tom Jones* (Dedication, VIII.i, XI.ix, XIII.i).

252　S. Baker, "Henry Fielding's *The Female Husband*: Fact and Fiction," *PMLA*, 74 (1959), 213–24.

253　William Strahan's ledgers show that in Nov. 1746 he printed for Millar 1,000 copies of *The Female Husband* and then ran off a further 250 copies: BL: Add. Mss. 48800, f. 71ᵛ.

254　J. Wooll, *Biographical Memoirs of the late Rev. Joseph Warton* (1806), p. 215.

255　*Gentleman's Magazine*, 56 (Aug. 1786), 659–60.

256　About 1754 Sarah wrote Richardson from "Beauford-Buildings": Amory, *Huntington Library Quarterly*, 35 (1971), 80 and n. 38.

257　"Advertisement" in *True Patriot* No. 16 (11–18 Feb. 1745/6), p. 4.

258　*General Advertiser* (24, 26–30 Jan, 20–23 Mar. 1746/7).

259　Samuel Johnson ascribed these pieces to Harris: C. Barrett (ed.), *Diary and Letters of Madame D'Arblay* (London: 1904), I.86.

260　T. C. Duncan Eaves and B. D. Kimpel, *Samuel Richardson: A Biography* (Oxford: 1971), p. 202.

261　In complaining that Rowe's *Fair Penitent* and *Jane Shore* had "furnished the Entertainment of a Month this Winter at *Covent Garden*," Valentine in Letter XL refers to runs of those plays that took place during 14–29 Nov. 1746 and 2–16 Jan. 1746/7, respectively.

262　Together with his brother Edmund, their four sisters, and their cousin Charles (son of their uncle John Fielding), Fielding answered the complaint of George Fielding's widow in Mar. 1744/5; they were represented by Henry Gould. Fielding signed this document at Breams Buildings on 3 Mar. 1744/5. (PRO: C.12.1768/43.)

263　Greater London Record Office (Middlesex): MJP/CP/124, ff. 1–2.

264　Since the Justices Qualification Act (18 Geo. II, c. 20 [1745]) did not apply to Westminster, no property qualification was required for that

commission: K. Goodacre and E. D. Mercer, *Guide to the Middlesex Sessions Records, 1549–1889* (London: 1965), p. 16.

265　Fielding to R. Butcher, the Duke of Bedford's agent. Twickenham, 28 Sep. 1748 (BCRO: R4/6141).

266　For this exchange, see BL: Add. Mss. 35397, ff. 49, 51ᵛ.

267　Pelham to Richmond, 2 Jul. 1747 (West Sussex Record Office: Goodwood Mss. 104, f. 304).

268　See W. B. Coley (ed.), *The Jacobite's Journal and Related Writings* (Middletown, Conn., and Oxford: 1975), pp. xxxiii–xxxv, 437–9.

269　Lady Mary to Countess of Bute, 22 Sep. [1755], in R. Halsband (ed.), *The Complete Letters of Lady Mary Wortley Montagu* (Oxford: 1966), III.87.

270　Wharncliffe (ed.), *Letters and Works of Lady Mary Wortley Montagu*, I.106.

271　*Shamela*, p. 53.

272　J. L. Chester to Dobson, 5 Apr. 1882: Senate House, University of London (ADC. Ms. 810/VI/14).

273　On the authority of Horace Walpole, whom he served as chaplain, Daniel Lysons (1762–1834) stated that Fielding rented the house (*Environs of London*, Vol. 3 [1795], p. 598 and n. 160). While it was still standing, R. S. Cobbett described it as "a quaint old-fashioned wooden house," in which Fielding resided until his appointment to the magistracy in 1748 (see *Memorials of Twickenham* [1872], pp. 358–9). A drawing of the house made in 1870 is in the Twickenham Public Library (LCF 4002, s.v. Holly Road). Fielding's name appears in the earliest extant record of the Poor Rate for Twickenham (1748):

Mrs. Adams for ye Garden 　£/s/d
& House
　or Counslʳ Fielding. 　　 ,, 10 ,,

The tax was later listed as "uncollected." (Twickenham Public Library.) Dr. D. H. Simpson, Hon. Archivist of the church of St. Mary the Virgin, Twickenham, informed me that in an entry of 4 Feb. 1749 "Mrs. Adams, or Counsellr Fielding" are also paired in the Church Rate Books, where it is also indicated that no payment was made; whether the date is Old Style (i.e. 1749/50) is not clear.

274 Coley, *Philological Quarterly*, 45 (1966), 173.

275 *Peregrine Pickle* (1751), IV.123. To his credit, Smollett in revising the novel deleted the passage.

276 BL: Add.Mss.48800, f.71ᵛ.

277 *The Orrery Papers*, ed. Countess of Cork and Orrery (London: 1903) II.14.

278 For this hypothesis, see Amory, *Harvard Library Bulletin*, 27 (1979), 277–303.

279 BL: Add. Mss. 35397, f. 164ᵛ.

280 Quoted by W. B. Coley (ed.), *Jacobite's Journal* (Middletown, Conn., and Oxford: 1975), pp. lv–lvi, n. 8; lxiv, n. l. Throughout this period and beyond the correspondence of Hardwicke and Bedford reveals their concern at anti-Hanoverian demonstrations not only in Staffordshire, traditionally a hotbed of Jacobitism, but also in Cornwall and Bedfordshire.

281 See R. Paulson (ed.), *Hogarth's Graphic Works* (New Haven: 1970), I.276; and Coley (ed.), *Jacobite's Journal*, p. lii, n. 5.

282 Coley (ed.), *Jacobite's Journal*, pp. liii-liv.

283 Ibid., p. lxiii.

284 Ibid., pp. lxxv–lxxvi, lxxix.

285 Ibid., p. 67, n. 1.

286 Ibid., pp. l–li.

287 *The Patriot Analized: or, A Compendious View of the Publick Criticism on a late Pamphlet, called, "An Apology for the Conduct of a late Second-rate Minister"* (1748), pp. 36–8.

288 See *Jacobite's Journal* Nos. 9 (30 Jan.), 11 (13 Feb.), 19 (9 Apr.).

289 For Fielding's opinion of Horsley, who "libelled [him] for many Years together," see *Covent-Garden Journal* (22 Feb. 1751/2, "Modern History").

290 Coley (ed.), *Jacobite's Journal*, pp. 181, n. 3; 197–200; 214, n. l; 481, 483.

291 PRO: K.B.122.225, Roll 880.

292 Coleman to Bedford, 22 Jul. 1747 (BRO: R4/6140).

293 Coleman to Bedford, 1 Dec. 1747 (BRO: R4/6140).

294 Birt to Fielding, Lymington, Hants., 3 Feb. 1747/8 (BRO: R4/6141).

295 Birt to Fielding, Winchester, 2 Mar. 1747/8 (BRO: R4/6141).

296 Fielding to Butcher, Boswell Court, 8 Mar. 1747/8 (BRO: R4/6141).

297 Sharpe recorded "Fees to Mr. Fielding to peruse Declaration and draw plea, etc. [2 guineas]" and "More to Mr. Fielding to move the Court of King's Bench for leave to plead double [1 guinea]." (*Treasurer Solicitor's Declared Accounts* [30 Jun. 1747–30 Jun. 1748] in PRO: A.O.1. 2324/62.)

298 Bedford's accounts relating to the Perkins case in 1748 (though the bills were not paid until 24 Oct. 1750) show fees paid to Birt, Henley, and Pratt – and probably to Fielding as well (£2.9.0), though he is identified only as Bedford's "Associate in Court." (BRO: R5/6475.).

299 Coleman to Butcher, Lyndhurst, Hants., 21 Mar. 1747/8 (BRO: R4/6140). Coleman was a scoundrel who in Dec. 1748 was detected abusing his trust by selling the King's timber for his own profit (BRO: R4/6124); but in this instance Fielding was at fault, as the accounts of the New Forest show that he was regularly paid his £5 annual fee as High Steward (BRO: R5/6457A).

300 Birt to Butcher, Lymington, 7 May 1748 (BRO: R4/6141).

301 Fielding to Butcher, Twickenham, 3 Apr. 1748 (BEO: Butcher Papers, I/2/45).

302 The following account of Fielding's puppet theatre is based on Battestin, "Fielding and 'Master Punch' in Panton Street," *Philological Quarterly*, 45 (1966), 191–208.

303 Fielding left Old Boswell Court some time after 8 Mar. 1747/8, the date of his letters to Butcher, but before 26 May 1748, when he was no longer listed in the Poor Rate for the Shier Lane Ward, St. Clement Danes (see Westminster History Collection, Buckingham Palace Road, B.159). The Poor Rate lists for St. Martin-in-the-Fields show that by 25 Mar. 1748 he had taken a house worth £24 annual rental in Panton Street; sometime after 4 Jun. 1748 but before the end of the month, he had "gone" (see ditto: Collectors' Books and Ledgers, F523).

304 Fielding to Butcher, Twickenham, 5

305 Fielding to Butcher, Twickenham, 4 July 1748 (BEO: Butcher Papers, I/2/102).

305 Fielding to Butcher, Twickenham, 4 July 1748 (BEO: Butcher Papers, II/3/11).

306 PRO: C.234/25.

307 The original document is in the J.P. Morgan Library, New York; transcribed in Battestin and Bowers (eds.), *Tom Jones*, p. xliv.

308 Walpole to George Montagu, 18 May 1749, in Walpole's *Correspondence*, eds. W.S. Lewis *et al.*, IX.84.

309 Spence to William Burrell Massingberd, 15 Apr. 1749; quoted in A. Wright, *Joseph Spence: A Critical Biography* (Chicago: 1950), p. 232, n. 29.

310 Coley (ed.), *Jacobite's Journal*, pp. 317, n. 1; 330, n. 5.

311 R.M. Davis, *The Good Lord Lyttelton* (Bethlehem, Penn.: 1939), p. 218.

312 G. Miller, *Rambles Round Edge Hills and in the Vale of the Red Horse* (Banbury: 1896), pp. 16–17.

313 *Old England* (27 May 1749).

314 *Orrery Papers*, ed. Countess of Cork and Orrery, II.43.

315 Birch to Yorke, London, 15 Oct. 1748 (BL: Add. Mss. 35397, f. 177ᵛ). Other readers besides Dalton received prepublication copies of Fielding's first two volumes. On 3 Nov., Elizabeth Carpenter wrote Lady Grey from London that she had heard "they are well worth reading" (BRO: Lady Lucas Collection. L30/9/24/35). On 20 Nov. Dalton's friend Lady Hertford wrote Lady Luxborough from the country: "I have been very well entertained lately with the two first Volumes of the *Foundling*, written by Mr. Fielding, but not to be published till the 22d of *January*; if the same Spirit runs through the whole Work, I think it will be much preferable to Joseph Andrews" (T. Hull [ed.], *Select Letters between the Late Duchess of Somerset, Lady Luxborough ... and others* [1778], I.85).

316 A copy of the letter was acquired by the late Professor E.L. McAdam, Jr., and Mr. George Milne: "A New Letter from Fielding," *Yale Review*, 2nd ser., 38 (1948–9), 300–10. Professor McAdam mistakenly believed the manuscript to be the original Fielding holograph, but it is unquestionably a copy. I am grateful to Mr.

Milne for generously providing me with a Xerox of the document and for granting me permission to quote it. When on 2 Jun. 1753 Richardson wrote his Dutch translator, Johannes Stinstra, he enclosed a substantial extract from Fielding's letter with the comment: "He had been a zealous Contender for the Piece ending, as it is called, happily." (W.C. Slattery (ed.), *The Richardson–Stinstra Correspondence and Stinstra's Prefaces to "Clarissa"* [Carbondale, Ill.: 1969], pp. 33–4.).

317 Richardson sent Moore a copy of Vol. 5 as early as 1 Oct: Eaves and Kimpel, *Samuel Richardson*, p. 219.

318 Richardson to Lady Bradshaigh, 23 Feb. 1751/2; quoted in Eaves and Kimpel, ibid., p. 302. For a survey of Richardson's relations with Fielding, see ibid., pp. 292–306.

319 Young to Richardson, 5 Nov. 1749; quoted ibid., p. 202.

320 *The Governess*, ed. J.E. Grey (London: 1968), pp. 124–8.

321 Sarah Fielding to Richardson, 8 Jan. 1748/9; quoted in Eaves and Kimpel, *Samuel Richardson*, p. 203.

322 See De Castro, *Notes & Queries*, 15th ser., 20 (9 Mar. 1940), 164–7.

323 Jane Collier to Richardson, 4 Oct. 1748; in A.L. Barbauld (ed.), *Correspondence of Samuel Richardson* (Oxford: 1804), II.61–5.

324 See the following documents in the PRO: (1) Return of Writs for Michaelmas Term, 22 Geo. II, recording the *dedimus potestatem* authorizing certain persons to receive Fielding's oaths for the Liberty of Westminster: C.202.267, Vol. 8. (2) Return of Writs for the same term, issued 25 Oct. 1748 to Sir Thomas Clarke, Charles Frewen, and Thomas Rugeley, authorizing them to receive Fielding's oaths: C.202.136.1. (3) On the verso of this writ, Charles Frewen's affidavit, filed 26 Oct. 1748, affirming that he had received Fielding's oaths. (4) Clerk of the Crown's Account of *dedimus* (called the "Dedimus Book"), dated 25 Oct. 1748, listing Fielding as having taken his oaths for the Westminster magistracy and paid his fees (amounting to £2.17.8): C.193.45.

For useful preliminary investigations of Fielding's appointments to the magistracy, see A. B. Shepperson, "Additions and Corrections to Facts about Fielding," *Modern Philology*, 51 (1954), 217–20; W. B. Coley, "Fielding's Two Appointments to the Magistracy," *Modern Philology*, 63 (1965), 144–9.

325   Fielding to Butcher, Twickenham, 28 Sep. 1748 (BRO: R4/6141).

326   GLRO(M): WJ/SR/2912. The earliest reference to Fielding in the Sessions Papers is to his examination on 7 Nov. 1748 of one Katherine Ballard for stealing a copper tea kettle: see GLRO(M): MSP/1748/DEC/108.

327   Fielding to Butcher, Meard's Court, 21 Nov. 1748 (BEO: Butcher Papers, II/4/129).

328   The earliest references to Fielding's occupying the house in "Bow-street, Covent-Garden, formerly Sir Thomas DeVeil's" occur in the *General Advertiser* (10 Dec. 1748) and the *General Evening Post* (8–10 Dec.). The lease of this house, together with a plan of it, is on file at the GLRO: E/BER/CG/L/23/7. By the terms of the lease, dated 4 Sep. 1745, DeVeil and his representatives were assigned the property for twenty-one years in exchange for £280 plus a low annual rent of £10, DeVeil promising to undertake extensive repairs to the building, which had been damaged in a riot. Nowhere in Bedford's Rental Books for the period 1748–54 is Fielding associated with this house, which, according to the terms of the lease, continued to be managed by DeVeil's representatives (GLRO: E/BER/CG/E/8/2/7). When the lease expired in 1766, Sir John Fielding took formal possession of the house, paying Bedford £300 down and the same annual rent of £10 (GLRO: E/BER/CG/L/23/21).

329   Fielding to Butcher, 12 Dec. 1748 (BEO: Butcher Papers, II/4/196). For a detailed account of Fielding's appointments to the magistracy and his relations with Bedford, see Battestin and Battestin, *Eighteenth-Century Studies*, 11 (1977–8), 143–85.

330   Fielding to Bedford, Bow Street, 13 Dec. 1748 (BEO: Ms. Letters, Vol. XXII, f. 95).

331   Coleman to Fielding, Lyndhurst, Hants., 9 Dec. 1748 (BRO: R4/6140).

332   Fielding to Butcher, Bow Street, 16 Dec. 1748 (BRO: R4/6140).

333   Fielding to Butcher, 19 Dec. 1748 (BEO: Butcher Papers, II/4/210).

334   Fielding to Bedford, 19 Dec. 1748 (BEO: Butcher Papers, XI/46/22).

335   GLRO: E/BER/CG/L9/9 (BEO).

336   See, respectively, GLRO(M): MJP/Q/I, f. 187; PRO: C202/136/2 – on the verso of this writ, Charles Frewen declared that he received Fielding's oath on 12 Jan. and filed on the 13th.

337   See, respectively, GLRO(M): MJ/SBB/1060; GLRO(M): MJ/SR/2915, MJ/CC/R/19.

338   GLRO: E/BER/CG/L56/68a (BEO). On 19 Nov. 1750 Fielding rented two of these houses, in Drury Lane, to one James Robinson for £21.4s. annually (E/BER/CG/L56/69). No doubt it was the fact of the new lease that accounts for Fielding's taking the Qualification Oath for the Middlesex commission over again on 13 Jul. (GLRO[M]: MJP/Q/I, f. 191).

339   This account of the novel's printing and publication is based on Battestin and Bowers (eds.), *Tom Jones*, I.xlvii–li.

340   BL: Add. Mss. 48800, f. 77ᵛ.

341   Stationers' Hall, Registry of Copyrights. Entries of Copies 1746–73, p. 55.

342   Quoted in A. Wright, *Joseph Spence: A Critical Biography* (Chicago, 1950), p. 232, n. 29.

343   The original document is in the J. P. Morgan Library, New York.

344   It should be noted that reviewers of the Wesleyan–Clarendon edition of *Tom Jones*, ed. Battestin and Bowers, 2 vols. (Middletown, Conn., and Oxford: 1975), made possible a number of corrections in that text. Particularly important was the discovery by H. Amory that sheet O in Volume III of the first edition (containing text from Book VIII, chapters xiii–xv) was a cancel substituted for an original which was preserved and accidentally printed in the third edition only: see *Harvard Library Bulletin*, 25 (1977), 101–13. For this reason the most authoritative modern text of *Tom Jones* is the one-volume paperback edition published by Wesleyan University Press (Middletown, Conn.: 1978).

345 *An Apology for the Life of Bampfylde-Moore Carew*, "2nd edn." (1751), p. 2.
346 *Amelia* (1751), I.i.
347 For a discussion of these themes in *Tom Jones*, see Battestin, *The Providence of Wit: Aspects of Form in* *Augustan Literature and the Arts* (Oxford: 1974), Chs. 5, 6. (Available now only from University Press of Virginia, Charlottesville.)

PART IV

1 Lady Mary to the Countess of Bute, 22 Sep. [1755], in R. Halsband (ed.), *The Complete Letters of Lady Mary Wortley Montagu* (Oxford: 1966), III.87.
2 My understanding of the eighteenth-century magistracy in general and of Fielding's practice in particular owes much to J. H. Langbein, "Shaping the Eighteenth-Century Criminal Trial: A View of the Ryder Sources," *University of Chicago Law Review*, 50 (1983), 1–136.
3 Introduction, *Journal of a Voyage to Lisbon* (1755).
4 Ibid.
5 No records of Fielding's pension survive. The salary Newcastle was allowing Fielding's office when he died was £400. Saunders Welch, who was commissioned magistrate in Apr. 1755, understood that Newcastle meant this money "to be equally divided between Mr. [John] Feilding and me"; however, this was not John Fielding's understanding and a bitter quarrel arose between the two justices (BL: Newcastle Papers, 33055, f. 273). According to the Treasurer's Minute Book, the dispute was settled in Oct. 1757, when the government approved an annual allowance of £400 for John Fielding and £200 for Saunders Welch (PRO: T.29.32, pp. 486 [21 Oct. 1757], 487 [27 Oct. 1757].
6 R. Leslie-Melville, *The Life and Work of Sir John Fielding* (London [1934]), p. 77.
7 See also *Whitehall Evening Post* (1–3 Dec.); *Penny London Post* (2–5 Dec.). From this date onward, hundreds of Fielding's cases are reported in the newspapers. For many of these, additional details as well as the outcome of the trials may be found in the *Old Bailey Sessions Papers* (BL: P.P.1349.a) – the earliest being the case of John Salter, a servant arrested for stealing 16s. and sen-

tenced to transportation for seven years: Salter's arrest and examination before Fielding were reported in the *General Advertiser* (10 Dec. 1748), *General Evening Post* (8–10 Dec.), and *Penny London Post* (9–12 Dec.); his trial in *OBSP* (Jan. 1749, No. 108).
8 *General Evening Post* (10–13 Dec. 1748).
9 *General Evening Post* (15–17 Dec. 1748).
10 *General Evening Post* (29–31 Dec. 1748).
11 *Whitehall Evening Post* (29–31 Dec. 1748).
12 Some idea of the extent of this part of Fielding's business may be gained from documents in the Greater London Record Office (MF/V/1752, 1753): during the period 6 Mar. 1751/2 to 6 Nov. 1753 his signature appears on eighty-one vouchers authorizing payments to constables for expenses incurred while removing vagrants from London to their legal places of settlement in the provinces.
13 Boswell's *Life of Johnson*, eds. G. B. Hill and L. F. Powell (Oxford, 1934), III.216.
14 *Covent-Garden Journal* (1 Aug. 1752).
15 Registers of St. Paul's, Covent Garden: Harleian Society, Vol. 33 (Births), Vol. 4 (Burials).
16 *Covent-Garden Journal* (28 Jan. 1751/2).
17 Jones (alias Harper) and two of his rescuers were captured in Dublin and in Oct. were returned to London to stand trial with six other members of the gang. Their trials are reported in *OBSP* (Feb–Mar. 1749/50, Nos. 194, 230–7).
18 On Mooney and his gang, see *General Advertiser* (21, 23 Jan., 15, 20 Feb. 1748/9); *Penny London Post* (24–27 Feb. 1748/9). His trial is reported in *OBSP* (Feb. 1749, No. 169).
19 *London Gazette* (31 Jan.–4 Feb., 4–7 Feb. 1748/9). Trials of members of

the gang are reported in *OBSP* (Apr. 1749, Nos. 280–4).

20 See G.W. Stone, Jr., *The London Stage, 1660–1800*, Pt. 4, 1747–76 (Carbondale, Ill: 1962), pp. cxcvii–cxcviii.

21 A copy of Winter's examination before Richmond and Fielding is in the West Sussex Record Office: Goodwood Ms. 155/H105. See M. M. Stewart, "Henry Fielding's Letter to the Duke of Richmond," *Philological Quarterly*, 50 (1971), 135–40. Also C. Winslow, "Sussex Smugglers," in D. Hay, *et al.* (eds.), *Albion's Fatal Tree: Crime and Society in Eighteenth-Century England* (London and New York: 1975), pp. 119–66.

22 John Wicker to Richmond, Horsham, 24 Jun. 1749 (WSRO: Goodwood Ms. 156/G38).

23 See *OBSP* (Apr. 1749, Nos. 280, 281, 303).

24 Fielding to Richmond, Bow Street, 8 Apr. 1749 (WSRO: Goodwood Ms. 110, f. 159).

25 Recognizance, pledging "Sir John Sarvandoni of Chelsea, Knt.," to be on his good behavior toward Charles Frederick, Esq., and signed by Fielding on 29 Apr. 1749 (GLRO: MJ/SR.2922, No. 360).

26 *Journal of a Voyage to Lisbon* (Tuesday [23 Jul.]).

27 Walpole to Montagu, Arlington Street, 18 May 1749. W.S. Lewis *et al.* [eds.] Horace Walpole's *Correspondence*, vol. 9 [New Haven, 1941], p. 84.

28 PRO: K.B. 10.29, Pt. II, No. 14. In Hilary Term the next year, the Court entered judgment against Rigby in this case (K.B.21.36, pp. 503 507, 512).

29 Recognizance signed by Justice Thomas Ellys (GLRO: MJ/SR/2922, No. 249).

30 Fielding was among the justices attending the Middlesex Sessions, which began on 9 May 1749 (GLRO[M]: MJ/SBB/1064).

31 A note added to the Westminster Sessions records for 29 Mar. 1749, but dated 17 May, states that Fielding was "elected chairman of this present Session & to continue until the 2d day of the next" (GLRO[M]: WJ/SBB/1062, p. 81). Though the records of subsequent sessions for Westminster are incomplete, they

indicate that he was regularly reappointed Chairman until 9 Oct. 1751. See the records for the following sessions: 11 Jan. 1749/50 (ibid., 1069), 5 Jul. 1750 (1074), 28 Jun. 1751 (1085), 9 Oct. 1751 (1088). An announcement Fielding placed in the *London Daily Advertiser* (14 Dec. 1751) indicates he was still Chairman of the Westminster justices at that time; however, on 10 Jan. 1751/2 Thomas Lediard was "unanimously chosen" in his place (*General Advertiser*, 13 Jan.). Thereafter Fielding's name does not appear in the list of justices who attended the Westminster Sessions on 1 Apr. 1752 (1093), 18 Oct. 1752 (1095), or 12 Jul. 1753 (1102).

32 M. M. Stewart, *Notes & Queries*, 214 (Sep. 1969), 348–50; 218 (Jan. 1973), 13–15.

33 See *General Advertiser* (30 Jun.) and *Old England* (1 Jul.), which give Thomas as Fielding's Christian name; and *Whitehall Evening Post* (29 Jun.–1 Jul.); *Penny London Post* (30 Jun.–3 Jul.).

34 Strahan's ledger for Jul. 1749 reveals that 750 copies were printed (BL: Add. Mss. 48800, f. 83ᵛ).

35 In 1752 the Westminster justices unsuccessfully petitioned Parliament to erect a new courthouse by levying a rate of twopence; Fielding supported this proposal in the *Covent-Garden Journal* (10 Mar. 1751/2), "Modern History [Saturday]." For a description of the old building, see *Journal of the House of Commons* (*JHC*), XXVI.355.

36 See *London Evening Post* (1–3 Aug. 1749); *Old England* (5 Aug., 4 Nov. 1749); *The Mitre and Crown*, I (Aug. 1749), 579–80; II (Oct. 1749), 22–3; *Craftsman* (14 Oct. 1749); *A Journey through the Head of a Modern Poet* (1750), p. 19.

37 *Monthly Review*, 1 (Jul. 1749), 239–40.

38 Birch to Lady Grey, 5 Aug. 1749 (BL: Add. Mss. 35397, f. 198). Birch recorded in his diary that he dined with Fielding on 23 Feb. 1748/9 (BL: Add. Mss. 4478, f. 155ᵛ).

39 M. R. Zirker (ed.), Fielding's *Enquiry into the Causes of the Late Increase of Robbers and Related Writings* (Oxford and Middletown, Conn.: 1988), p. xxviii.

40 *Whitehall Evening Post* (4–6 Jul. 1749).

41 *A True State of the Case of Bosavern Penlez* (Nov. 1749), in Zirker (ed.), *Enquiry*, p. 48; quotations from *Penlez* will be from this edition. My account of the riots is based on the sworn testimony of the peace officers in this pamphlet. Additional details are from *OBSP* (Sep. 1749, Nos. 480–2); *The Malefactor's Register: or, New Newgate and Tyburn Calendar* [1778], III.236–42; and H. Talon (ed.), *Selections from the Journals and Papers of John Byrom: Poet, Diarist, Shorthand Writer, 1691–1763* (London: 1950), pp. 260–1.

42 Laetitia-Matilda Hawkins, *Memoirs, Anecdotes, Facts, and Opinions* (1824), I.46–7.

43 Boswell's *Life of Johnson*, eds. Hill and Powell, III.217.

44 *Penlez*, p. 57.

45 Fielding was among the justices attending the session, which began 3 Jul. (GLRO[M]: MJ/SBB/1065).

46 Fielding to Bedford, Bow Street, 3 Jul. 1749 (BEO: Ms. Letters, Vol. XXIV, f. 42).

47 On the oaths of Joseph Stanhope, keeper of the Bunch of Grapes and Peter Wood, keeper of the Star, Fielding on 3 Jul. 1749 committed six persons into the custody of Richard Akerman, Keeper of Newgate, in two separate writs charging them with riotous assembly, pulling down bawdy-houses, and "High Treason in Levying War against his Majesty." The six were: Edward Wrench, John Willson, James Hetherington, Bosavern Penlez, Benjamin Launders, James Irons. (GLRO: MJ/SP1749 JY/90, 91).

48 Fielding to Bedford, Bow Street, 3 Jul. 1749 (BEO: Butcher Papers, IV/9/9).

49 Linebaugh, "The Tyburn Riot against the Surgeons," in Hay *et al.* (eds.), *Albion's Fatal Tree*, esp. pp. 89–98. "It appeared [writes Linebaugh] that the magistrate's duty lay less in bringing down bawdy-houses than in keeping them standing" (p. 96).

50 *Penlez*, p. 58.

51 Ibid., p. 59.

52 Ibid., pp. 58–9.

53 Fielding to Butcher, Bow Street, 18 Jul. 1749 (BEO: Butcher Papers, IV/9/43).

54 Fielding to Hardwicke, Bow Street, 21 Jul. 1749 (BL: Add. Mss. 35590, f. 334).

55 BL: Add. Mss. 35603, f. 229.

56 See *The Deviliad* (1744), p. 22 and n.

57 Introduction, *Journal of a Voyage to Lisbon* (1755).

58 Among Newcastle's papers is a minute of a conversation with the Lord Chancellor of 2 Apr. 1754, stating that Hardwicke "communicated Every Thing" to the Duke. Lady Gower, the note continues, "knew the concert with which the Chancellor acted with the Duke of Newcastle; and that [speaking to Hardwicke] was the same thing" as speaking to Newcastle. (BL: 32995, f. 78.)

59 For the date of composition, see Battestin (ed.), *Amelia* (Middletown, Conn. and Oxford: 1983), pp. xl–xliv.

60 *JHC*, 26 (1 Apr. 1751), p. 159.

61 Reports of cases in which he was involved as magistrate occur in the following papers: *General Advertiser* (5, 18, 24 Jul., 16, 22, 24, 25 Aug., 4, 5, 19 Sep. 1749); *Whitehall Evening Post* (1–4, 27–29 Jul.); *Penny London Post* (19–21 Jul., 18–20 Sep., 29 Sep.–2 Oct.).

62 *General Advertiser* (5 Aug. 1749).

63 The letter is at the Historical Society of Pennsylvania, Philadelphia. In her biography R. M. Davis notes a record at Hagley of the sale of a letter by Fielding of 1749 for £20 (*The Good Lord Lyttelton* [Bethlehem, Penn.: 1939], p. 218, n. 43.)

64 In a letter to me of 7 Apr. 1978, A. Amberg pointed out that no one in either Moore's or Jenny Hamilton's family had ever been named Harry or Henry or Harold.

65 *OBSP* (Sep. 1749, Nos. 480–2), reporting the trials of John Willson, Bosavern Pen Lez, and Benjamin Launder. The death of John Hetherington, the fourth man indicted, was reported in the *Penny London Post* (8–11 Sep. 1749).

66 *The Malefactor's Register*, III.239.

67 *Penlez*, p. 60.

68 *A Proposal to render effectual a Plan, to remove the Nuisance of Common Prostitutes from the Streets of the Metropolis* (1758), p. 9.

69 *Observations on the Office of Constable* (1754), pp. 30–1.

70 Ibid., p. 32.

71 For the trial of James Wood, see *OBSP* (Dec. 1749, No. 40). Also *General Advertiser* (10 Nov. 1749); *Penny London Post* (19–21 Feb. 1749/50).

72 N. Rogers, "Aristocratic Clientage, Trade and Independency: Popular Politics in Pre-Radical Westminster," *Past and Present*, 61 (1973), 70–106, esp. p. 77. My account of Fielding's role in the Westminster election of 1749 is based on my article, "Fielding, Bedford, and the Westminster Election of 1749," *Eighteenth-Century Studies*, 11 (1977–8), 143–85.

73 *The Two Candidates: or, Charge and Discharge* [1749], p. 20.

74 Rogers, *Past and Present*, 61 (1973), p. 81.

75 *The Two Candidates*, pp. 11–12.

76 BEO: Westminster Election (Nov.–Dec. 1749), Accounts and Papers.

77 Ward to Butcher, 19 May 1750 (BEO: Butcher Papers, VI/18/53).

78 Ward to Butcher, 7 Jan. 1749/50 (BEO: Butcher Papers, V/14/12).

79 BEO: Westminster Election (Nov.–Dec. 1749), St. Paul's, Covent Garden, item 14.

80 BEO: Westminster Election (Nov.–Dec. 1749), St. Paul's, Covent Garden, item 8; St. Martin-in-the-Fields, items 14, 18.

81 Fielding to Bedford, Bow Street, 14 May 1750 (BEO: Ms. Letters, Vol. XXV, f. 93).

82 John Sharpe to Butcher, 5 Jul. 1751 (BEO: Butcher Papers, VIII/31/15).

83 *The Two Candidates*, p. 6.

84 *T[ren]t[ha]m and V[an]d[epu]t* [1749], p. 42.

85 "Peg Trim Tram's Sorrowful Lamentation," ibid., p. 35.

86 *An Impartial State of the Case of the French Comedians, Actors, Players, or Strollers, Who lately opened a Theatre at the Haymarket* (1750), p. 4.

87 *A Genuine and Authentic Account of the Proceedings at the Late Election for the City and Liberty of Westminster* [1749], pp. 28–9.

88 For the text of *Ten Queries*, together with evidence of Fielding's authorship, see Battestin, *Eighteenth-*

89 BEO: Westminster Election (Nov.–Dec. 1749), Sundry Printers' Bills, item 2.

90 BL: Add. Mss. 48800, f. 83ᵛ.

91 Zirker (ed.), *Enquiry*, pp. li–lii; F. Bowers, ibid., pp. cxvii–cxviii.

92 R. Lonsdale, "New Attributions to John Cleland," *Review of English Studies*, 30 (1979), 268–90, esp. pp. 270–5.

93 Ibid., p. 274.

94 *Old England* (25 Nov. 1749). Similar charges recur in the issues for 2, 9, 16 Dec. 1749, 3 Mar. 1749/50. See also *London Evening Post* (23–25 Nov. 1749).

95 The following discussion of the *Covent-Garden Journal* of 1749 is based on my article, *Eighteenth-Century Studies*, 11 (1977–8), 166–74.

96 Thomas Hill to Richmond, 7 Dec. 1749 (WSRO: Goodwood Mss. 103, f. 250).

97 *Dictionary of National Biography*, "Phillips, Teresia Constantia." The attack on Fielding concludes the *Apology*, published 13 Sep. 1749 (III.318–23).

98 See "Pope" in Johnson's *Lives of the English Poets*, ed. A. Waugh (Oxford: 1906), II.297.

99 Hawkins, *The Life of Samuel Johnson* (1787), p. 335.

100 Taafe to Butcher, 5 Dec. 1749 (BEO: Westminster Election [Nov.–Dec. 1749], Accounts and Papers).

101 References to *The Craftsman* during the period 7 Oct. 1749 to 30 Dec. 1752 are to the unique run in the John Dawson Collection, London Borough of Hackney Public Library. See S. Varey, "The Publication of the late *Craftsman*," *The Library*, 33 (1978), 230–3.

102 Cooke was editing *The Craftsman* in the spring of 1748, when Bedford threatened to prosecute him for writing too freely against the government: *Gentleman's Magazine*, 62 (1792), 27; Varey, *Library*, 33 (1978), 230.

103 *General Advertiser* (28 Dec. 1749).

104 Joshua Toulmin, "A Delineation of the Character of the late Rev. John Ward, of Taunton," *Protestant Dissenter's Magazine* (Jul. 1797), p. 242, n. This is Amberg's preferred text,

Century Studies, 11 (1977–8), 161–3.

who places the time of composition "*post* 1748 and *ante* 1752".

105 *General Advertiser* (11 Dec. 1749); *Penny London Post* (22–25 Dec. 1749).

106 *General Advertiser* (28 Dec. 1749).

107 For an account of Thompson, see R. A. Day, "When Doctors Disagree: Smollett and Thomas Thompson," *Études Anglaises*, 32 (1979), 312–24.

108 Hawkins, *Life of Samuel Johnson*, p. 337.

109 J. Carroll (ed.), *Selected Letters of Samuel Richardson* (Oxford: 1964), pp. 133–4.

110 On his death the *Whitehall Evening Post* (26–28 Nov. 1754) reported that Broadhead left an estate of £3,000 a year. When Bedford sought to prosecute members of the Opposition for offences committed during the Westminster election, his attorney proposed Broadhead as a justice whom he could rely on to serve his interests on the jury (George Ward to Butcher, 23 May 1750 [BEO: Butcher Papers, VI/18/62]).

111 The action against Broadhead dragged on for several months: see GLRO(M): MJ/OC/5, ff. 189, 194, 197, 199–200; BL: Add. Mss. 35603, ff. 227, 300, 302.

112 See the register of births, St. Paul's, Covent Garden: Harleian Society, Vol. 33.

113 See the announcements in *General Advertiser* (13–14 Feb. 1749/50).

114 On the Universal Register Office and Fielding's *Plan* of the office, see B. A. Goldgar (ed.), *The Covent-Garden Journal and A Plan of the Universal Register Office* (Oxford and Middletown, Conn.: 1988).

115 "Philanthropos," *An Appeal to the Public; against the Growing Evil of Universal Register-Offices* (1757), p. 6.

116 John Fielding, *A Plan for preventing Robberies within Twenty Miles of London. With an Account of the Rise and Establishment of the real Thieftakers* (1755), pp. 1–2.

117 *General Advertiser* (30, 31 Jan., 5, 7, Feb. 1749/50).

118 *General Advertiser* (21 Feb. 1749/50); *OBSP* (Feb.–Mar. 1749/50, Nos. 200, 201).

119 *General Advertiser* (24 Mar. 1749/50); *OBSP* (Apr. 1750, Nos. 307–9).

120 Accounts of the rescue of Jones and his subsequent recapture and execution appeared in the *Whitehall Evening Post* (21–24 Jan. 1748/9; 24–27 Mar. 1750), *London Gazette* (31 Jan.–4 Feb. 1748/9), *General Advertiser* (12 Oct. 1749; 1, 5 Mar. 1749/50). Also *OBSP* (Feb.–Mar. 1749/50, Nos. 194, 230–7).

121 PRO: T.1.342, f. 27.

122 PRO: T.1.342, Nos. 64, 68, 70, 72, 74, 76, 77, 79, 81, 83, 85, 87, 90, 92.

123 PRO: S.P.36.153, f. 16.

124 *Directions to Mankind in General: And in particular to The Courtier, the Lawyer, the Divine, the Physician, the Justice of Peace* by "Dr. Fitzpatrick, Q.D.G.," p. 63.

125 *General Advertiser* (24 Apr. 1750).

126 *Penny London Post* (14–16, 16–19 Feb. 1749/50); *DNB*, s.v. "Annesley."

127 The trial, including Fielding's testimony, is reported in *OBSP* (Apr. 1750, No. 325). See also H. W. Bleakley, *The Hangmen of England* (London: 1929), pp. 84–6 – who erroneously states that Thrift was acquitted of the charge of murder. Thrift's pardon came on 14 Sep.; it incensed the populace and provoked a sarcastic leader in *Old England* (22 Sep. 1750).

128 *Whitehall Evening Post* (15–17, 17–20 Mar. 1749/50); *OBSP* (May–Jun. 1750, No. 372).

129 For Cather's accusation against Walpole, see GLRO(M): MJ/SR/2940, No. 63. For the judgment against Patterson, see GLRO(M): MJ/SBB/1075, f. 49. Also *General Advertiser* (16 Jun. 1750); *Whitehall Evening Post* (24–26 Jul. 1750). For a full summary see *The Tryal of John Cather [et al] ... on Friday the 5th of July 1751 for a Conspiracy against the Hon. Edward Walpole* (Dublin: 1751): BL: 1578/3772.

130 GLRO(M): MJ/2938, Recog. 68. On the identity of Mary Peyton, see J. L. Clifford, *Dictionary Johnson* (New York: 1980), pp. 53–4.

131 Fielding to Bedford, Bow Street, 14 May 1750 (BEO: Ms. Letters, Vol. XXV, f. 93).

132 Fielding to Bedford, 24 May 1750 (BEO: 4th Duke's Additional Correspondence [May 1750]). See M.P.G. Draper, "Letters of the 4th Duke

of Bedford," *Eighteenth-Century Studies*, 12 (1978–9), 206–8.

133 Fielding to Bedford, London, 29 May 1750 (BEO: 4th Duke's Additional Correspondence [May 1750]. For Fielding's letter to Butcher, written from Bow Street on the same date, see BEO: Butcher Papers, VI/18/94.

134 In his Latin Diary, Birch records dining with Fielding on 23 Feb. 1748/9, 26 Dec. 1750, and 19 Jan. 1750/1. On this last occasion, Fielding brought him a copy of *An Enquiry into the Causes of the late Increase of Robbers*, published that day. (BL: Add. Mss. 4478, Pt. C, ff. 155ᵛ, 186, 187.)

135 BL: Add. Mss. 35397, f. 258ᵛ.

136 On 25 May 1750 Hardwicke doubted that the contagion had spread from Newgate, "the gaol not having been more sickly that time than usual"; but the public was convinced otherwise (BL: Newcastle Papers 32720, f. 405ᵛ). The author of *Old England* (2 Jun. 1750) described the disease as "a very malignant Fever so rife about the Town, as to have carried a great many People off in such very short Periods of Time as may shock the Survivors."

137 *General Advertiser* (13 Jul. 1750).

138 Burial Register, St. Paul's, Hammersmith, Jul. 1750 (Shepherd's Bush Branch Library: Archives, DD/71/7, p. 120). That Catharine was a victim of the epidemic is suggested by the fact that she was one of twenty-one people buried at the church that month.

139 PRO: P.C.C.1750.

140 The funeral cost £5.16s.8d. See Burial Book, St. Martin-in-the-Fields, 3 Aug. 1750 (Westminster History Collection, Buckingham Palace Road: F2466); Burial Accounts Book, Aug. 1750 (419/266); and Eaves and Kimpel, *Notes & Queries*, n.s., 15 (Jun. 1968), 212.

141 See *General Advertiser* (3 Aug., 3 Sep. 1750).

142 The tradition was recorded by Lysons in *Environs of London*, Vol. I (1792), p. 544. As curate of the adjacent parish of Mortlake from 1784 to 1790, Lysons was well placed to hear and to authenticate such local gossip, though his tenure there began thirty years after Fielding's death. N.

Maslin mistakenly places Lysons at Mortlake in 1748, during Fielding's lifetime: see *Notes & Queries*, 30 (Feb. 1983), 50.

143 J. Carswell and L. A. Dralle (eds.), *The Political Journal of George Bubb Dodington* (Oxford: 1965) p. 67.

144 *Penny London Post* (3–5 Sep. 1750).

145 C. Hoare & Co., Bankers: Ledger 51, pp. 55, 390.

146 Goldgar (ed.), *Covent-Garden Journal*, p. xvii, n. 4. Fielding playfully compliments Taylor in *The Journal of a Voyage to Lisbon* (Tues. [Jul. 23]).

147 *General Advertiser* (19 May 1752). On 26 Sep. 1749 Henry and a William Fielding shared equally the sum of £865.9s. paid by Millar (see Appendix II).

148 PRO: K.B.122.242, Pt. I, Roll 488.

149 PRO: P.C.C. 1750.

150 In *Jonathan Wild* (IV.xvi) Fielding describes the Heartfrees as "the Family of Love," and Tom Jones applies the phrase to the Millers (XIV.vi).

151 St. Paul's, Hammersmith: Burials, 1750–1 (Shepherd's Bush Branch Library: Archives, DD/71/7). The funerals of Ursula and Beatrice each cost eighteen shillings, far more than the normal charges; since accounts begin in Sep. 1750, there is no record of the cost of Catharine's funeral (DD/71/9). Neither Ursula nor Beatrice left a will.

152 BL: Add. Mss. 35591, f. 145.

153 Fielding to Perkins, Bow Street, 25 Nov. 1750 (ibid., f. 147). Also P. C. Yorke, *The Life and Correspondence of Philip Yorke, Earl of Hardwicke* (Cambridge: 1913), II.108–10.

154 *General Advertiser* (8, 15 Dec. 1750); *Penny London Post* (7–10, 12–14 Dec. 1750); also *OBSP* (Jan. 1750/1 No. 100).

155 BL: Add. Mss. 32685, f. 59.

156 GLRO(M): MJ/OC/5, f. 221 (23 May 1751).

157 Idem, ff. 232–4.

158 See Pentlow's complaint to this effect: GLRO(M): MJ/OC/6 (1753), MF/1 (19 Jul. 1753).

159 Walpole to Horace Mann, 23 Mar. 1752: in Lewis *et al.* (eds.), *Correspondence*, 20 (1960), p. 312.

160 *Enquiry*, Sect. VI.

161 *Proposal for Making an Effectual Provision for the Poor* (1753), in Zirker

(ed.), *Enquiry*, p. 230. Quotations from Fielding's *Proposal* are from this edition.

162 L. Collison-Morley, *Giuseppe Baretti, with an Account of his Literary Friendships* (1909), pp. 66–7.

163 *Penny London Post* (25–27 Feb. 1750/1).

164 Welch to Newcastle, 18 Feb. 1754 (PRO: S.P.36/153, No. 11) – reprinted as an Appendix to Welch's *Proposal ... to remove the Nuisance of Common Prostitutes*.

165 *Penny London Post* (7–9 Jan. 1750/1).

166 *Covent-Garden Journal* (13 Jun. 1752).

167 M. R. Zirker, *Fielding's Social Pamphlets*, University of California English Studies, No. 31 (Berkeley and Los Angeles: 1966), p. 136.

168 *Proposal*, p. 227.

169 Ibid., p. 227.

170 A copy of Hume's *Philosophical Essays* was in Fielding's library (*Catalogue*, item 539). For the relevance of Hume's theory of the passions to Fielding's ethical thought during this period, see Battestin, "The Problem of *Amelia*: Hume, Barrow, and the Conversion of Captain Booth," *ELH* (*A Journal of English Literary History*), 41 (1974), 613–48.

171 G. Storey and K. J. Fielding (eds.), *Letters of Charles Dickens*, V (Oxford: 1981), 652–3.

172 See H. Amory, "Henry Fielding and the Criminal Legislation of 1751–2," *Philological Quarterly*, 50 (1971), 175–92.

173 Both Langbein "Shaping the Eighteenth-Century Criminal Trial" (pp. 65–66 and n. 250) and Zirker (ed. *Enquiry*, p. lix and n. 2) are inclined to this view of Fielding's influence.

174 For the membership of the Committee, see Ms. Minutes, House of Lords (1 Feb. 1750/1), ff. 133–5.

175 *JHC* (23 Apr. 1751), Vol. 26, p. 190.

176 Amory, *Philological Quarterly*, 50 (1971), 188.

177 *JHC* (13 Jun. 1751), Vol. 26, p. 289.

178 T. G. Coffey, "Beer Street: Gin Lane. Some Views of 18th-Century Drinking," *Quarterly Journal of Studies on Alcohol*, 27 (1966), 669–92.

179 *Whitehall Evening Post* (9–12 Nov. 1751).

180 See the following numbers of *True Briton*: 1 (27 Feb. 1751), 194–204; (6 Mar. 1751), 218–27; 2 (26 Jun. 1751), 3; (24 Jul. 1751), 118; (27 Jun. 1752), 602; 4 (15 Nov. 1752), 290–1; 5 (7 Mar. 1753), 216; (21 Mar. 1753), 242–51, 261–2. For Oglethorpe's sponsorship of Osborne's *True Briton* and their hostility to Fielding, see Osborne's letters to John Caryll in 1753 (BL: Add. Mss. 28236, esp. ff. 23, 28, 29ᵛ, 34, 44, 48–9).

181 *True Briton*, 2 (26 Jun. 1751), 3; 3 (27 Jun. 1752), 602.

182 See Ben. Sedgly, *Observations on Mr. Fielding's Enquiry into the Causes of the late Increase of Robbers, &c ... To which are added, Considerations on the Nature of Government in general; and more particularly of the British Constitution: With a Vindication of the Rights and Privileges of the Commonalty of England, in Opposition to what has been advanced by the Author of the Enquiry, or to what may be promulgated by any Ministerial Artifices, against the Public Cause of Truth and Liberty*. By Timothy Beck, the Happy Cobler of Portugal Street (publ. 7 Mar. 1750/1) – copy in Goldsmiths' Library, Senate House, University of London. William Kenrick identifies Richard Rolt (1725?–70) as the author both of the *Westminster Journal* and of this attack on Fielding's *Enquiry*: see *The Pasquinade* (1753), p. 19, n.

183 See the following: *Monthly Review*, 4 (Jan. 1751), 229–39; Maddox, *The Expediency of Preventive Wisdom*, 3rd edn. (1751), Appendix; Fitzsimmonds, *Free and Candid Disquisitions, on the Nature and Execution of the Laws of England, both in Civil and Criminal Affairs* (Mar. 1751), pp. 38–53; Draper, *The Morning Walk* (May 1751), p. v; [Philo-Patria], *A Letter to Henry Fielding, Esq; Occasioned by his Enquiry into the Causes of the late Increase of Robbers* (Mar. 1751).

184 BL: Add. Mss. 48800, f. 83ᵛ.

185 *General Advertiser* (21 Jun. 1751).

186 *London Daily Advertiser* (13 Jul. 1751).

187 *London Daily Advertiser* (16 May 1751); *General Advertiser* (15 Oct. 1751); *Whitehall Evening Post* (15–17 Oct. 1751).

188 *General Advertiser* (15 Jun. 1751).

189 *OBSP* (Oct. 1751, Nos. 599–600); *London Gazette* (9–13, 13–16 Jul. 1751).

190 GLRO(M): Sessions Books and Orders, Vol. 5 (Sep. 1750–28 Feb. 1750/1), ff. 207d, 210d, 216d, 221–2d.

191 *London Daily Advertiser* (22 May 1751); *OBSP* (May 1751, No. 388).

192 Corporation of London: Records, Sessions Papers (Sep. 1751).

193 My account of this dispute is based on the following: *London Daily Advertiser* (18 Jul., 21 Oct. 1751); *London Gazette* (19–22 Oct.); *General Advertiser* (21 Oct.); *Whitehall Evening Post* (22–24 Oct.). Also *An Abstract of the Master-Taylors Bill* of 1721 [7 Geo. I, c.13]; *The Case of the Master Taylors residing within the Cities of London and Westminster, in relation to the Great Abuses committed by their Journeymen*; and *The Case of the Journeymen-Taylors residing in the Cities of London and Westminster* – all three collected in *Proclamations, Declarations, Political Tracts*: BL: 816.m.14 (1–3).

194 *London Daily Advertiser* (26 Oct. 1751); *Whitehall Evening Post* (24–26 Oct.).

195 *An Account of the Rise and Progress of the Lying-in Hospital for Married Women, in Brownlow Street, Long-Acre, from its First Institution in November 1749, to July 25, 1751* (1751). (BL: C.T.102.[6].)

196 Fielding to Robert Butcher, Bow Street, 7 May 1751 (BEO: Butcher Papers, VIII/29/11).

197 Fielding to Butcher, Bow Street, 12 Jun. 1751 (BEO: Butcher Papers, VIII/30/46).

198 PRO: C.193.45, C.234.25.

199 *London Daily Advertiser* (8 Aug. 1751); *Whitehall Evening Post* (6–8 Aug.).

200 Carswell and Dralle (eds.), *Dodington's Political Journal*, p. 130.

201 *London Daily Advertiser* (24 Aug. 1751).

202 See Battestin, "Fielding and the Glastonbury Waters," *Yearbook of English Studies*, 10 (1980), 204–9.

203 *London Daily Advertiser* (28 Oct. 1751). In a fulsome letter to Hill of 10 Nov. [1751], John Fielding gratefully acknowledged his cooperation in pro-

moting the Universal Register Office: BL: Mss. Stowe 155, f. 124.

204 The letter is reprinted in Battestin, *Yearbook of English Studies*, 10 (1980), 207–9.

205 Fielding dined with Dodington and Ralph on 14 Sep. 1751 and again with Dodington a fortnight later (29 Sep.): Carswell and Dralle (eds.), *Political Journal*, pp. 132, 134.

206 *London Daily Advertiser* (22 Nov. 1751).

207 *General Advertiser* (15 Oct. 1751).

208 My account of the Simonds affair is based in part on the following sources: *London Daily Advertiser* (10–11, 17 Oct., 11, 16 Dec. 1751); *General Advertiser* (10 Oct. 1751; 14 Apr. 1752); *Covent-Garden Journal* (22 Feb., 17 Mar. 1752); *OBSP* (Apr. 1752, No. 268). Also *A Narrative of the remarkable Affair between Mr. Simonds, the Polish Jew Merchant, and Mr. James Ashley, Merchant of Bread-Street, London* (1752); and *The Case of Henry Simons, A Polish Jew Merchant; and his Appeal to the Public Thereon* (1753). (BL: 1132.c.50[1] and 1418.g.33, respectively.)

209 For the former charge see the affidavit of Jacob Ree, a Polish Jew (23 Jan. 1754) in BL (1132.c.50.[2]); for the latter, see *Read's Weekly Journal* (14 Dec. 1751), *General Advertiser* (22 Feb. 1752).

210 *The Case of Henry Simons*, p. 34.

211 *A Narrative*, p. 35.

212 *OBSP* (Apr. 1752, No. 268). Fielding refers to this "famous Cause" in *Covent-Garden Journal* (22 Feb. 1751/2), "Covent-Garden."

213 Birch to Philip Yorke, London, 11 Aug. 1753: BL: Add. Mss. 35398, f. 145. The author of the article was the Rev. Josiah Tucker: see T. W. Perry, *Public Opinion, Propaganda, and Politics in Eighteenth-Century England: A Study of the Jew Bill of 1753*, Harvard Historical Monographs, 51 (Cambridge, Mass.: 1962), esp. pp. 127–8.

214 *London Chronicle* (7–10 Nov. 1778), p. 455. My thanks to Hugh Amory for bringing this story to my attention.

215 The satire was published in the *London Daily Advertiser* (10 Jan. 1751/2) and was reprinted in the same paper on 11 Jan., because of

the "extraordinary" demand of the public. See also *True Briton*, 3 (15 Jan. 1751/2), 48; *Ladies Magazine*, 3 (11–25 Jan. 1751/2), 67–8; Stephens and Hawkins (eds.), *Catalogue of Prints and Drawings in the British Museum. Division I: Political and Personal Satires*, Vol. III, Pt. ii (1877), No. 3187.

216 From the Hanbury Williams Mss. (Vol. 54, p. 86) in the collection of the late W. S. Lewis.

217 *Old England* (7 Apr. 1750).

218 Bellers, "Free Censures on a Romance lately publish'd, entitled, The adventures of Mr. Loveill," *British Magazine*, 5 (May 1750), 208.

219 See B. P. Jones, "Was There a Temporary Suppression of *Tom Jones* in France?" *Modern Language Notes*, 76 (1961), 495–8.

220 *The Kapelion, or Poetical Ordinary*, 1 (Aug. 1750).

221 *The Midwife*, 2 (1751), 118.

222 *Ladies Magazine*, 2 (20 Apr.–4 May 1751), 202; *Westminster Magazine*, 13 (11 May 1751), 250–1.

223 *London Daily Advertiser* (2 Nov. 1751).

224 Hill, *The History of a Woman of Quality* (Feb. 1751), p. 3.

225 *Monthly Review*, 4 (Mar. 1751), 375.

226 *History of Pompey the Little*, ed. R. A. Day (Oxford: 1974), p. xliv.

227 Goldgar (ed.), *Covent-Garden Journal*, pp. xxvi–xxvii.

228 Strahan, who was assigned the printing of Vols. I and III, charged Millar for "Extraordinary Corrections" made while the work was in press. For a detailed account of the history of publication, see Battestin (ed.), *Amelia*, pp. xliv–lxi.

229 N. Wraxall, *Historical and Posthumous Memoirs, 1772–84*. ed. H. B. Wheatley (1884), I.38–9.

230 Harris's *Hermes: or, A Philosophical Inquiry concerning Language and Universal Grammar* was published 16 Dec. 1751 (*London Daily Advertiser*, 13 Dec.). From Salisbury on 21 Dec., Harris wrote Fielding:

I hope you have received Hermes, for which in return I have the assurance to Desire that you would Send me Amelia. Should you ask with indignation, what four Books, for one – I might answere,

if I would, that put them in the Scales, and See how much heavier grammatical Speculation is than Wit, and Humour.

Replying to this letter on 23 Dec., Fielding acknowledged Harris's "very valuable Present. (I mean that of yʳ. Book) I sincerely think it among the best Books in our Language."

231 Mrs. Piozzi, *Anecdotes of the late Samuel Johnson*, ed. S. C. Roberts (Cambridge: 1925), p. 143.

232 BL: Add. Mss. 48800, f. 83ᵛ.

233 Letter of 22 Feb. 1752, in Carroll (ed.), *Selected Letters*, p. 196.

234 *Covent-Garden Journal* (28 Jan. 1752).

235 *Monthly Review*, 5 (Dec. 1751), 510–15.

236 *London Magazine*, 20 (Dec. 1751), 531–5, 592–6.

237 See F. T. Blanchard, *Fielding the Novelist: A Study in Historical Criticism* (New Haven, Conn.: 1926), Ch. 3; Battestin (ed.), *Amelia*, pp. l–lix.

238 Letter to Richardson, 11 Feb. 1751/2; in A. L. Barbauld (ed.) *Correspondence of Samuel Richardson* (Oxford: 1804), IV.56.

239 Letter to Rev. Mr. Lawry, 12 Feb. 1751/2 (Bodley Ms. 1011, pp. 331–2).

240 From Lettre XCI, 1 Jan. 1752, in *Cinq années littéraires* (The Hague: 1754), III.267–80.

241 Letter to Lady Bradshaigh, 23 Feb. 1751/2; in Carroll (ed.), *Selected Letters*, p. 198.

242 Hanbury Williams Mss., Vol. 54, p. 249; in W. S. Lewis Collection.

243 *Some Remarks on the Life and Writings of Dr. J[ohn] H[ill]* (1752), p. 60.

244 *Journal Britannique*, 7 (Feb. 1752), 123–46; translated in R. Paulson and T. Lockwood (eds.), *Henry Fielding: The Critical Heritage* (London: 1969), No. 119.

245 *Some Remarks*, pp. 59–61.

246 Mrs. Piozzi, *Anecdotes*, p. 143.

247 On this surprising political dimension of *Amelia*, see Battestin (ed.), pp. xxxvii–xxxix.

248 Ibid, pp. xvi–xxi.

249 Richardson to Mrs. Donnellan, 22 Feb. 1751/2; in Carroll (ed.), *Selected Letters*, p. 197.

250 Letter of 23 Jul. [1754]; in Halsband (ed.), *Complete Letters*, III.66.

251 Lady Louisa Stuart, "Introductory Anecdotes," I.105–6.

252 On the time scheme of *Amelia*, see Battestin (ed.), Appendix I.

253 *Covent-Garden Journal* (11 Apr. 1752).

254 *Old England* (11 Jan. 1751/2); *Craftsman* (25 Jan.).

255 *Covent-Garden Journal* (25 Feb. 1751/2).

256 The authoritative account of the journal is Goldgar's introduction and commentary to the Wesleyan edition (Middletown, Conn., and Oxford: 1988).

257 *Covent-Garden Journal* (7 Jan. 1751/2), "Covent-Garden."

258 In *The March of the Lion* (1752) Young, "the sober Abraham [Adams]," is depicted slumbering on a couch in Fielding's company at Bow Street, "with an *Euripides* dangling from his Hands; for the good Priest could never sleep without-book" (p. 17).

259 *Journal of a Voyage to Lisbon* (28 Jun).

260 *Covent-Garden Journal* (11 Feb. 1751/2).

261 See B. A. Goldgar, "Swift and the Later Fielding," *Yearbook of English Studies*, 18 (1988), 93–107.

262 *Covent-Garden Journal* (4 Feb. 1751/2).

263 *Covent-Garden Journal* (3 Mar. 1751/2).

264 S. Nathan, "The Anticipation of Nineteenth Century Ideological Trends in Fielding's *Amelia*," *Zeitschrift für Anglistik und Amerikanistik* (East Berlin), 6 (1958), 386, 398.

265 See the "Preface" to the *Enquiry*.

266 *Covent-Garden Journal* (1 Feb. 1751/2), "Modern History."

267 *Covent-Garden Journal* (20 Jun. 1752); also No. 47 (13 Jun.).

268 *Covent-Garden Journal* (1 Feb. 1751/2), "Modern History."

269 *Covent-Garden Journal* (7 Mar. 1751/2), "Modern History."

270 *Covent-Garden Journal* (28 Jan. 1751/2), "Covent-Garden."

271 *Covent-Garden Journal* (10 Mar. 1751/2), "Modern History."

272 Strahan's ledger: BL: Add. Mss. 48800, f. 83ᵛ.

273 *Covent-Garden Journal* (8 Feb. 1751/2 ["Court of Censorial Enquiry"], 25 Feb., 10, 14 Mar., 28 Mar. ["Covent-Garden"] 1752). Mary Blandy was convicted of poisoning her father and was hanged on 6 Apr. 1752.

274 *Covent-Garden Journal* (14 Apr. 1752), "Covent-Garden."

275 See Ralph in *The Protester* (7 Jul. 1753); Bonnell Thornton, *Spring-Garden Journal* (7 Dec. 1752).

276 Drawing on Fielding's leaders and other material from the *Covent-Garden Journal*, Hoey began publishing a periodical by that title on 23 Jan. 1751/2, with Fielding's name on the title-page. In his No. 16 (27 Apr. 1752) he advertised Fielding's *Examples of the Interposition of Providence* for publication the next day.

277 See B. A. Goldgar, "Fielding and the Whores of London," *Philological Quarterly*, 64 (1985), 265–73.

278 *Covent-Garden Journal* (11 Jan. 1751/2), "Covent-Garden."

279 *Covent-Garden Journal* (25 Jan. 1751/2), "Covent-Garden."

280 *Covent-Garden Journal* (10 Mar. 1751/2), "Covent-Garden."

281 *General Advertiser* (21 Jul. 1752).

282 On Redman, see *Covent-Garden Journal*, "Covent-Garden" columns (18 Jan., 11, 18 Feb. 1751/2; 12, 23 May 1752); on Pierce, see (2, 5, 9, 12, 16, 19, 23 May, 9 Jun. 1752).

283 *Covent-Garden Journal* (4 Feb. 1751/2), "Covent-Garden."

284 *Covent-Garden Journal* (25 Feb. 1751/2), "Covent-Garden."

285 *Covent-Garden Journal* (11 Apr. 1752), "Covent-Garden."

286 *Covent-Garden Journal* (3 Mar. 1751/2), "Covent-Garden."

287 *Covent-Garden Journal*, "Covent-Garden" columns (4, 14 Apr., 15 Aug. 1752).

288 *Covent-Garden Journal*, No. 15 (22 Feb. 1751/2), "Covent-Garden."

289 *Covent-Garden Journal*, No. 26 (31 Mar. 1752), "Covent-Garden."

290 J. T. Smith, *Nollekens and His Times* (1828), ed. G. W. Stonier (London: 1949), p. 61. For Fielding's tribute to Mrs. Hussey, see *Tom Jones* (X.iii).

291 *Old England* (15 Jul., 9 Dec. 1749).

292 *Craftsman* (2 May 1752).

293 "Democritus," in *Baldwin's London*

Weekly Journal (2 Dec. 1769). My thanks to Morris Golden for bringing this anecdote to my attention.

294 See W. C. Brown, "A Belated Augustan: Bonnell Thornton, Esq.," *Philological Quarterly*, 34 (1955), 335–48.

295 On Hill, see G. S. Rousseau, "John Hill, Universal Genius Manqué: Remarks on His Life and Times, with a Checklist of His Works," in *The Renaissance Man in the Eighteenth Century* (Los Angeles: 1978), pp. 49–129; G. S. Rousseau (ed.), *Letters and Papers of Sir John Hill* (New York: 1982). For a helpful account of his relations with Fielding, see B. Rizzo, "Notes on the War between Henry Fielding and John Hill, 1752–53," *The Library*, 6th ser., 7 (1985), 338–53.

296 It is important to understand that the date of this meeting was, by Hill's own testimony, 28 Dec. 1751 – not, as is generally thought, 8 Jan. 1751/2: see *OBSP* (Jan. 1752, No. 89).

297 *Covent-Garden Journal* (11 Jan. 1751/2), "Journal."

298 *Covent-Garden Journal* (7 Jan. 1751/2), "Journal."

299 See above, n. 296.

300 Browne was Lt. Governor of West Florida (1767–9) and Governor of the Bahamas (1774–8): Rizzo, *Library*, 6th ser., 7 (1985), 340–1 and n. 9.

301 Hill twice refers to this official visit by Fielding: *London Daily Advertiser* (12, 30 May 1752).

302 Goldgar (ed.), *Covent-Garden Journal*, p. xxxix, n. 2.

303 A notice in *Old England* (1 Feb. 1751/2) promised that *Fun* would represent on stage "the Match" between Fielding and his Grub Street adversaries, with odds favoring the latter. At an "Especial Court held on Shrove Tuesday" (11 Feb.), the Corporation of London directed the Lord Mayor to suppress the play, which was scheduled for performance at the Castle Tavern, Paternoster Row, on 13 Feb. (Corporation of London Record Office: Repertories, 156.1751–2, Lord Mayor and Aldermen [11 Feb. 1752], p. 179). In his Preface to the published version of *Fun* (6 Mar.), Kenrick implied that Fielding had used his influence to prevent the performance – an impu-

tation repeated in the Guildhall Library Catalogue, which, however, cites no authority. Fielding's interest in this case may be the specific impetus behind his essay on slander in *Covent-Garden Journal* (18 Feb.): "What an Encouragement indeed must it give to scandalous Writers to find that an Abuse on a private Character shall be a sufficient Recommendation of their Works."

304 BL: Add. Mss. 4475, f. 207.

305 This revised edition of *Jonathan Wild* was published by Millar in Mar. 1754. For a discussion of the revisions see A. Digeon, *Le Texte des romans de Fielding* (Paris: 1923); and the forthcoming Wesleyan edition by Goldgar and Amory.

306 The opportunity to publish this revised edition did not occur until Millar issued Fielding's *Works* (1762); in his introductory "Essay" the editor, Arthur Murphy, states: "*It is proper the reader should be informed that* Amelia, *in this edition, is printed from a copy corrected by the author's own hand.*" For an analysis and a list of the revisions see Battestin (ed.), *Amelia*, pp. lix–lxi and Appendix VI. For an argument, elaborate but unpersuasive, that Murphy himself made these extensive alterations to the text, see H. Amory, "What Murphy Knew: His Interpolations in Fielding's *Works* (1762), and Fielding's Revision of *Amelia*," *Papers of the Bibliographical Society of America*, 77 (1983), 133–66.

307 See H. Amory, "Fielding's Copy of the *Covent-Garden Journal*," *Bodleian Library Record*, 11 (1983), 126–8; Goldgar (ed.), *Covent-Garden Journal*, Textual Introduction.

308 *London Magazine*, 21 (Jul. 1752), 317–18.

309 In *Drury-Lane Journal* (19 Mar. 1751/2), Bonnell Thornton imagines Fielding in decline, saying "I have no other refuge than to sollicit an ACT OF PARLIAMENT for monopolizing News-papers, not for my own *Interest* to be sure, but solely and wholly for the *Good* of *Community*."

310 See John Fielding, *A Plan for preventing Robberies*, p. 21.

311 *Public Advertiser* (14 Dec. 1752).

312 *The Impertinent* was immediately attributed to Hill by the reviewer

(Samuel Johnson?) in the *Gentleman's Magazine*, 22 (Aug. 1752), 387.

313 In *Covent-Garden Journal* (15 Aug.), Fielding announced his intention to attempt a *Dunciad* "in Prose"; it is clear from No. 60 (22 Aug.) that Hill's authorship of *The Impertinent* prompted this resolution. This same work inspired Smart's *Hilliad* (1753).

314 *General Advertiser* (18 Nov. 1752).

315 For the attribution to Fielding, or to Fielding and Garrick, see Rizzo, *Library*, 6th ser., 7 (1985), 344, n. 19. Garrick, however, denied that he had written the work (see D. M. Little and G. M. Kahrl [eds.], *Letters of David Garrick* [Oxford: 1963], I.190); and its style does not support the attribution to Fielding.

316 *London Daily Advertiser* (20 Nov. 1752). Hill continued in this vein in the numbers for 21, 24 Nov., 6–7 Dec.

317 *A Faithful Narrative*, pp. 5, 11.

318 *London Daily Advertiser* (6 Dec. 1752).

319 A. Sherbo, *Christopher Smart, Scholar of the University* (East Lansing, Mich.: 1967), p. 67.

320 *Midwife*, 3 (1753), 136–7.

321 *Craftsman: or, Gray's-Inn Journal* (9 Dec. 1752).

322 *Craftsman: or, Gray's-Inn Journal* (30 Dec. 1752), "Domestic Occurrences."

323 See *Public Advertiser* (7 Dec. 1752); *Daily Advertiser* (1 Feb. 1753). For *The Hilliad* and its contexts, see K. Williamson (ed.), Smart's *Poetical Works*, vol. 4 (Oxford: 1987).

324 See Rizzo, *Library*, 6th ser., 7 (1985), 347–52.

325 B. Rizzo, "A New Prologue by Christopher Smart and a Forgotten Skirmish of the Theatre War," *Papers of the Bibliographical Society of America*, 68 (1974), 305–10.

326 *Covent-Garden Journal* (8 Feb. 1751/2), "Covent-Garden."

327 *Public Advertiser* (6, 10 Jan. 1753).

328 Strahan's ledger: BL: Add. Mss. 48800, f. 96^v.

329 For an authoritative discussion of the contexts of Fielding's *Proposal*, see Zirker (ed.), *Enquiry*, pp. lxxvi–lxxxi; Zirker, *Fielding's Social Pamphlets*, pp. 117 ff.

330 R. Evans, *The Fabrication of Virtue: English Prison Architecture, 1750–1840* (Cambridge: 1982), p. 56.

331 See G. Himmelfarb, "Bentham's Utopia," in *Marriage and Morals among the Victorians* (London and Boston: 1986), pp. 111–43.

332 *Monthly Review*, 8 (Feb. 1753), 150.

333 From *A Plea for the Poor* (1759), quoted by R. Dircks, "Henry Fielding's *A Proposal for Making an Effectual Provision for the Poor*: an Edition," Ph.D. dissertation (New York: 1961), p. x. (Zirker [ed.], *Enquiry*, p. lxxxii and n. 3)

334 I am grateful to Professor Probyn, Harris's biographer, for bringing this letter to my attention.

335 *True Briton*, 5 (21 Mar. 1753), 242–51. In a letter to Carryl from the Fleet dated 21 Feb. 1753, Osborne states: "I was desired by [Oglethorpe] to defend the Cause of the Poor when it should be opened by Fielding" (BL: Add. Mss. 28236, f. 23).

336 The story of Elizabeth Canning is fully (if imaginatively) related by Lillian de la Torre, "*Elizabeth is Missing*" (New York: 1945). Fielding's part in that story is discussed in Zirker (ed.), *Enquiry*, pp. xciv–cxiv.

337 Fielding recalls the scene in *A Clear State of the Case of Elizabeth Canning*. (Zirker [ed.], *Enquiry*, pp. 297–8; quotations from Fielding's *Canning* are from this edition.)

338 As stated in the agreement by which John Ranby acquired the property for £800 on 25 Jan. 1755, the lease by which Fielding acquired Fordhook for a term of fourteen years was dated 7 Jul. 1753 (GLRO[M]: Memorials 1755/1/162, Order No. MDR/Bundle 1024, No. 162). But it is clear from the Poor Rate records that Fielding began occupying the estate sometime after 22 Jul. 1752 (when Thomas Gurnell is listed) and before 14 Feb. 1753, when Fielding is first listed (Ealing Central Library: Local History Collection). Fielding's name first appears in the Ealing Church Rate Book on 25 Mar. 1753 (GLRO[M]).

339 After Fielding's death, Lediard petitioned the Duke of Newcastle, unsuccessfully, to "appoint him to succeed the late Mr. Fielding, in transacting the Government Business as a Magistrate, with such an

Allowance as has been usual" (BL: Add. Mss. 33055, f. 103 [1754]).

340 For a bibliography, see L. B. McCue, "Elizabeth Canning in Print," *Elizabethan Studies, and Other Essays, in Honor of George F. Reynolds.* University of Colorado Studies, Ser. B (Boulder, Col.: 1945), 2 (No. 4), pp. 223–32. An excellent exhibition of materials relating to this *cause célèbre* was mounted by H. Amory at the Harvard Law School Library in 1987.

341 *Address to the Liverymen of the City of London*, pp. 23–4.

342 PRO: S.P.36.127, Pt. II, 24, ff. 140–3.

343 BL: Add. Mss. 35398, ff. 127, 177.

344 For Canning's petition and Gould's declaration that he would not represent her without the King's permission, see PRO: S.P.136.127, Pt. II, 24, ff. 160–1.

345 Unless otherwise noted, my account of Fielding's circumstances during these last months of his life is based on his "Introduction" to *The Journal of a Voyage to Lisbon.*

346 Harleian Society, Vol. 33; Burial Register, St. Paul's, Hammersmith (Shepherd's Bush Branch Library: Archives, DD/71/11).

347 *Public Advertiser* (15, 18 May 1753).

348 *Public Advertiser* (19–21 Jun. 1753); *OBSP* (Jul. 1753, Nos. 348, 349).

349 The crime took place on 17 Sep. 1753. Details of the case are reported in the *Public Advertiser* (19, 22, 26, 29 Sep., 5, 19 Oct.) and at the trial, *OBSP* (Dec. 1753, No. 56). For informations of several witnesses sworn before Fielding on 25–27 Sep. and 10, 18 Oct., see GLRO: MJ/SP.1753. Oct.

350 For this diagnosis I am grateful to the late Dr. William B. Wartman, an eminent pathologist.

351 See above, p. 502. Early in 1754 the Treasurer Solicitor concluded his account of reward money paid out since 1748: "1753 – to Mr. Justice Fielding £600/-/-" (PRO: S.P.36.153, f. 16).

352 In *A Plan for preventing Robberies* John Fielding relates Fielding's suspicions of Macdaniel "and his hellish Crew," and his part in persuading the Privy Council to discontinue the royal proclamations of £100 rewards (pp. 4–6). On the reward system and the Macdaniel scandal, see Langbein, "Shaping the Eighteenth-Century Criminal Trial," pp. 106–14.

353 John Fielding, *An Account of the Original and Effects of a Police Set on Foot by His Grace the Duke of Newcastle in the Year 1753, upon a Plan presented to his Grace by the late Henry Fielding, Esq*; (1758), p. 33.

354 See Fielding's Ms. "Memorial" (Huntington Library: HM 11617); John Fielding's *Plan*, pp. 2–3.

355 See F. Felsenstein, " 'None of Your Knockers-Down': John Fielding and Smollett's Watch," *Études Anglaises*, 26 (1973), 273.

356 PRO: S.P.36.125, ff.23, 91; 153, ff.10–11.

357 John Fielding, *Plan*, p. 1.

358 Welch, *Observations*, p. 46.

359 These successes, which Fielding thus recalled in his "Introduction" to *The Journal of a Voyage to Lisbon*, are reported in *Public Advertiser* (17, 19, 22 Oct.; also 7 Dec. 1753).

360 BL: Add. Mss. 35398, f. 177.

361 *Journal of a Voyage to Lisbon* (26 Jun. 1754).

362 BL: Add. Mss. 35604, f. 127.

363 PRO: C.193.45; GLRO: MJ/SBB/1107, p. 53.

364 See Amory, *Huntington Library Quarterly*, 35 (1971), 80, n. 39. During 1753 Millar's accounts show payments to Fielding amounting to £245.10s., the last payment being made on 31 Dec., the date of the bond (see Appendix II). Perhaps Millar had agreed to help Fielding consolidate all his debts in one friendly hand.

365 *Public Advertiser* (22 Jan., 8 Feb. 1754); *Whitehall Evening Post* (5–7 Feb.).

366 The Sessions Rolls for Middlesex and Westminster show that Fielding was intermittently active in this way until as late as 3 May 1754 (GLRO: MJ/SBB/1107-9); WJ/SR/3015, 3017). As far as his activities as magistrate can be traced in the newspapers, he is last reported signing mittimuses at Bow Street on 16 Apr. (*Public Advertiser*, 17 Apr. 1754).

367 *Public Advertiser* (29, 31 Mar., 1–2 Apr. 1754); *Whitehall Evening Post* (28–30 Mar., 30 Mar.–2 Apr.); *OBSP* (Apr. 1754, No. 290 [n.s.]).

368 *Public Advertiser* (13, 15 Mar. 1754).

369 Harleian Society, Registers, Vol. 34.

370 See *The Connoisseur* (28 Mar. 1754); and the notice signed John Hopkins in *Public Advertiser* (17 Apr. 1754).

371 "A Fragment of a Comment on L. Bolingbroke's Essays" (1755).

372 See Udal ap Rhys, *An Account of the Most Remarkable Places and Curiosities in Spain and Portugal* (1749), p. 234; also *A Picture of Lisbon* by "A Gentleman" (1809), pp. 172–5.

373 PRO: Prob.10/2161.

374 See the notice in the *Public Advertiser* (10 Jun. 1754).

375 These advertisements begin on 5 Jun. 1754 and continue intermittently until Nov.

376 Birch to Philip Yorke, 6 Jul. 1754 (BL: Add. Mss. 35398, f. 182).

377 *Journal of a Voyage to Lisbon* (26 Jun.).

378 See the letter (dated Ryde, the Isle of Wight, 31 Mar. 1755) recounting malicious anecdotes of Fielding's visit to Ryde: J. P. de Castro, "Henry Fielding's Last Voyage," *The Library*, 3rd ser., 8 (1917), 157–9. The letter is erroneously ascribed to Margaret Collier; whoever wrote it had not witnessed the scenes described as she had done.

379 See Sarah Fielding's letter to Richardson from Bath, 6 Jul. 1754: Barbauld (ed.), Richardson's *Correspondence*, II.68–70.

380 See above, pp. 392–3.

381 On the identity of the lady, whom Fielding does not name, see Cross, *History of Henry Fielding*, III.38–9.

382 The couple in question were Mrs. Ann Francis (d. 1758) and her husband Jephtha (d. 1775), keepers of the Nag's Head inn, Upper Ryde. (In Isle of Wight County Record Office, Newport: see esp. leases of 21 Nov. 1736 and 27 Dec. 1739 [RYD/9/19; LIND/283] and the burial registers of Binstead parish church.) Our thanks to Mr. C. D. Webster, Archivist, for his assistance.

383 Letter of 12 Jul. 1754: Fielding "On board the Queen of Portugal Rich! Veal at Anchor on the Mother Bank off Ryde, to the Care of the Post Master of Portsmouth" to John Fielding "at his House in Bow Street/ Cov! Garden/London" (Harvard).

384 Letter of 22 Jul. 1754: Fielding at "Torr Bay" to John Fielding at Bow Street: Huntington Library, HM 11615.

385 This locution was not uncommon among the English in Lisbon, as Rose Macaulay observed in her lively account of the English in Portugal originally published in 1946: *They Went to Portugal* (Harmondsworth: 1988), p. 88.

386 Fielding to John Fielding, Lisbon [c. 18–19 Sep. 1754]: Huntington Library, HM 11616. For a transcript, see Amory, *Huntington Library Quarterly*, 35 (1971), 65–83. Unless otherwise noted, the following account of Fielding's circumstances in Lisbon is based on this document.

387 Birch to Philip Yorke, London, 7 Sep. 1754: BL: Add. Mss. 35398, f. 208ᵛ.

388 Richardson's friend Thomas Edwards implies as much in his letter to Daniel Wray, 16 Jun. 1755: "Fielding's malevolence against our friend was the more unpardonable as the Good Man had once by his interposition saved his bones and at the very last by his correspondence at Lisbon had procured him accommodations which he could not otherwise have had" (Bodleian Mss. 1012, p. 212).

389 J. D. Hampton, *History of the Lisbon Chaplaincy* (1965), pp. 20, 60.

390 The quoted opinions are from *An Account by an Eye-Witness of the Lisbon Earthquake of November 1, 1755*. British Historical Society of Portugal. (Lisbon: 1985), p. 20.

391 *Public Advertiser* (25 Sep., 7 Oct. 1754).

392 *Whitehall Evening Post* (29 Jun.–2 Jul. 1754).

393 Whitefield's *Brief Account of some Lent and other Extraordinary Processions and Ecclesiastical Entertainments seen last Year at Lisbon* (1755), pp. 2, 14.

394 Macaulay, *They Went to Portugal*, p. 91.

395 J. P. de Castro, "Fielding's Last Letter," *Times Literary Supplement* (15 Jan. 1920), p. 35. De Castro reproduced "about two-thirds" of this letter, suppressing the remainder on the grounds that it was "of a confidential nature, written for the eye of John Fielding only."

396 De Castro's transcript reads: "I will not ensure that. (Indeed it hath drooped these two days and I think it had)."

397 For this fragment, offered at Sotheby's (23 Jul. 1962, Lot No. 283), see Amory, *Huntington Library Quarterly*, 35 (1971), 66, n. 4.

398 In the register of burials of the Church of England chaplaincy in Lisbon, there is a hiatus in the entries from June 1754 until 1762 (British Historical Society of Portugal, Lisbon: *Marriages, Baptisms, and Burials, 1721–1807*). I am grateful to Miss Joan Croft de Moura for allowing me to examine these records.

399 Hampton, *History of the Lisbon Chaplaincy*, pp. 18–20.

400 *A Picture of Lisbon*, pp. 167–8.

401 *London Evening Post* (26–29 Oct. 1754); *Gentleman's Magazine*, 24 (Oct. 1754), 483; *London Magazine*, 23 (Nov. 1754), 533.

402 *Daily Advertiser* (2 Nov. 1754).

403 See John Hackett, *Select and Remarkable Epitaphs* (1757), II.223:

On Henry Fielding, Esq.

I.

Turn hither, Man! within this Tomb
  In Peace doth *Fielding* rest,
This must in time be *Stanhope's*
  Doom;
  Know then, all Wit's a Jest.

II.

Learning and Sense refin'd shall here
  Brittania's Loss deplore,
Humour's gay-self shall drop a Tear;
  And Vice shall crouch no more.

III.

Now may she rear her shameless
  Head,
  And throw her Lures abroad,
From Earth her constant Foe is fled,
  To Virtue and to God.

For Smart's well-known tribute, composed sometime between 1758 and its publication in the *St. James's Magazine* (2 [Jul. 1762], 312), see Williamson (ed.), Smart's *Poetical Works*, Vol. 4, p. 354.

PART V

1 *London Evening Post* (3–5 Oct. 1754); *Sherborne Mercury* (7 Oct.).

2 GLRO(M): DRO 37/A1/8.

3 Millar's account at Coutts Bank shows payments in 1766 of £100 to Harriet (25 Mar.) and £90.6s. to Mary (25 Jun.).

4 PRO: P.C.C. Nov. 1754.

5 See Part IV, n. 338.

6 On the subject of Fielding's library and his reading, see H. Amory, "Henry Fielding," in A. N. L. Munby (gen. ed.), *Sale Catalogues of Libraries of Eminent Persons*, Vol. 7 (Poets and Men of Letters), ed. Amory (London: 1973). Also the comprehensive analysis, now nearly complete, by Dr. and Mrs. F. G. Ribble of Charlottesville, Virginia.

7 Amory, "Henry Fielding," p. 127.

8 Cross, *The History of Henry Fielding* (New Haven, Conn.: 1918), III.77.

9 *Public Advertiser* (6 Feb. 1755); *London Evening Post* (4–6 Feb.).

10 *Public Advertiser* (13–15 Feb. 1755).

11 John Fielding to Birch, Bow Street, 24 Feb, 1755: BL: Add. Mss. 4307, f. 49.

12 Strahan's ledger: BL: Add. Mss. 48800, f. 103^v.

13 J. P. de Castro first detected the similarity between the Dedication to the *Journal* and the style and substance of Murphy's remarks on that work in his "Essay" of 1762: see F. S. Dickson, "The Early Editions of Fielding's 'Voyage to Lisbon,'" *The Library*, 3rd ser., 8 (1917), 24–35, esp. p. 29.

14 See H. E. Pagliaro (ed.), *Journal of a Voyage to Lisbon* (New York: 1963), pp. 17–18. News of the earthquake reached London on 25 Nov. 1755; Millar began advertising the *Journal* on 4 Dec.: see *Public Advertiser* for those dates.

15 A. W. Pollard, "The Two 1755 Editions of Fielding's 'Journal of a Voyage to Lisbon,'" *The Library*, 3rd ser., 8 (1917), 160–2. See also in this same volume of *The Library*, J. P. de Castro, "Henry Fielding's Last Voyage," pp. 145–59.

16 John Fielding to Bedford, Bow Street, 28 Mar. 1755 (BEO: Ms. Letters, Vol. XXXI, f. 34).

17 Sir John Fielding to Bedford [2 May 1770] (BEO: Robert Palmer Papers [1769–71], item 34).

18 So John Fielding stated in a letter to Newcastle on 29 Sep. 1757 (BL: Add. Mss. 32874, f. 379).

19 Margaret Collier to Richardson, Ryde, 3 Oct. 1755: A. L. Barbauld (ed.), *Correspondence of Samuel Richardson* (Oxford: 1804) II. 77–8. Other letters between Margaret and Richardson are included in this volume, the last written by Margaret from Ryde, 4 Feb. 1757. Margaret lived to see better days: in 1775–6 she acquired a plot of land in Upper Ryde and built a house; she died in Sep. 1794, aged seventy-seven. (In Isle of Wight County Record Office: see leases [LIND/37–39] and the burial register of St. Thomas, Ryde [Nch 1794].)

20 Welch's petition is undated, but must have been written between Feb. 1756 and Oct. 1757: BL: Add. Mss. 33055, f. 273.

21 PRO: T.29.32, p. 486 (21 Oct. 1757).

22 PRO: W.O.1.976, pp. 508–9. William Wildman, 2nd Viscount Barrington (1717–93), was appointed Secretary at War in 1755. He was a subscriber to Fielding's *Miscellanies*.

23 Mary Fielding to Bedford, Tibbalds Row, 20 May 1757 (BEO: Ms. Letters, Vol. XXXIV, f. 9).

24 Leslie-Melville, *Sir John Fielding*, p. 61. John Fielding's account at Coutts Bank (The Strand) records payments made irregularly to Mary, Harriet, William, and Sarah during the period from Dec. 1757 to Jul. 1769. These payments are less than the sums stipulated in John's notebook (e.g., in 1761 the only payments were of £15 to Mary on 16 Apr. and on 31 Oct.). But the Coutts account provides only an incomplete record of John's actual expenditures.

25 William Fielding to Robert Palmer, Bedford's agent, Bow Street, 2 May 1770 – supported by Sir John Fielding's recommendation to Bedford (BEO: Robert Palmer Papers [1769–71], item 34).

26 Sir John Fielding to [William] Hunter, 4 Dec. 1778 (Royal College of Surgeons, Library: Hunter-Baillie Collection, Vol. I, f. 30).

27 Leslie-Melville, *Sir John Fielding*, p. 299.

28 Ibid., pp. 309–10.

29 From a note by the collector John Scott, dated 5 Dec. 1820, attesting to the authenticity of a "Book" of Fielding's law manuscripts: see H. Amory, "Henry Fielding," in G. Austin (ed.), *Four Oaks Library* (Somerville, NJ: 1967) p. 36. Also Leslie-Melville, *op. cit.*, pp. 298–9.

30 Thomas Whitehead, *Original Anecdotes of the late Duke of Kingston, and Miss Chudleigh* (1792), p. 95.

31 Parish register of St. Marylebone, in the GLRO. Harriet was buried on 11 Dec. 1766 at St. James's, Piccadilly (Westminster History Collection, Buckingham Palace Road). In the Allegation sworn on 23 Aug. 1766 Col. Montresor declared his intention to marry "Henrietta Eleanor Fielding of Odiam [Hants.] a Spinster aged 23 yrs. & upwards" (Lambeth: Faculty Office Marriage Allegations, 23 Aug. 1766 [Montresor/Fielding]).

32 Cross, *History of Henry Fielding*, III.121–2; F. H. Dudden, *Henry Fielding: His Life, Works, and Times* (Oxford: 1952), II. 1070–1.

33 Cross, *History of Henry Fielding*, III.366. In his will, curiously, William mentions only his wife, Martha (PRO: P.C.C. Nov. 1820).

34 See Amory, "Henry Fielding," in Austin (ed.), *Four Oaks Library*, pp. 35–39; "Preliminary Census of Henry Fielding's Legal Manuscripts," *Publications of the Bibliographical Society of America*, 62 (1968), 587–601; the revision in the *Index to English Literary Manuscripts* (Oxford: 1981–), Vol. 3, Pt. 1; and Amory's "Textual Note" to his edition of fragments of Fielding's *An Institute of the Pleas of the Crown* (Harvard: 1987).

35 PRO: S.P.44.162, f. 279.

36 D. I. Hill, *The Six Preachers of Canterbury Cathedral, 1541–1982* (Ramsgate: 1982), p. 92; J. Shirley (ed.), *The Reminiscences of the Reverend George Gilbert (1796–1874)* (Canterbury: 1938), pp. 5–6.

37 For information on Fielding's descendants, see Cross, *History of Henry Fielding*, III.122–3; J. É. M. F[ielding], *Some Hapsburghs, Feildings, Denbighs & Desmonds* (1895),

pp. 97–101; Burke's *Peerage*, s.v. Denbigh. For additional information I am indebted to the late W. Urry, St. Edmund Hall, Oxford; to P. Pollak, Archivist, the King's School, Canterbury; and to members of the family: Mrs. Rosa Whiteman and Mr. Henry Fielding Thoresby.

38 Allen Fielding to Rev.ᵈ Thomas Rackett, St. Stephens, 27 Jan. 1802 (Dorset County Record Office).

39 The letters (from Sarah to James Harris), as well as the drafts of Harris's "Essay on the Life and Genius" of Fielding, are among the private papers of the Earl of Malmesbury.

40 On the bibliographical history of the *Works*, see H. Amory, "Andrew Millar and the First Rescension of Fielding's *Works* (1762)," *Transactions of the Cambridge Bibliographical Society*, 8 (1981), 57–75; *Papers of the Bibliographical Society of America*, 77 (1983), 133–66.

41 *London Chronicle* (17–19 May 1759), p. 472. On 18 May 1759 Strahan charged Millar for printing 1,000 "Proposals for Fielding's Works" (BL: Add. Mss. 48800, f. 120ᵛ).

42 Summarized in Jesse Foot, *The Life of Arthur Murphy* (1811), p. 314; quoted by Amory in the articles cited above, n. 40. Millar's account at Coutts Bank (The Strand) records payment to Murphy of £27.4s. on 6 Feb. 1762.

43 Katherine Gertrude Harris (later the Hon. Mrs. Frederick Robinson), "Portrait or rather some account of my Mother, 1806" (PRO: 30.43.1.4, p. 18). Other passages Harris asked for from *Joseph Andrews* were I.xv–xvi, II.xii–xiii.

44 R. Macaulay, *They Went to Portugal*, (1946) (Harmondsworth: 1988), pp. 92–5.

45 Borrow, *The Bible in Spain* (1843), I.8; Amis, *I Like It Here* (New York: 1958), p. 185.

BIBLIOGRAPHY

For abbreviations and references in the Bibliography, see below, pp. 703–5.

WORKS BY FIELDING

[NOTE: Published jointly by the Wesleyan University Press, Middletown, Conn., and the Clarendon Press, Oxford, the authoritative Wesleyan Edition of the Works of Henry Fielding (W. B. Coley, Executive Editor; F. Bowers, Textual Editor) is in progress. It includes full bibliographical descriptions as well as histories of the printing and publication of the works. To date the following volumes have appeared: *Joseph Andrews*, ed. Battestin (1967); *Miscellanies: Volume One*, ed. H. K. Miller (1972); *Tom Jones*, eds. Battestin and Bowers, 2 vols. (1975); *The Jacobite's Journal and Related Writings*, ed. Coley (1975); *Amelia*, ed. Battestin (1983); *The True Patriot and Related Writings*, ed. Coley (1987); *An Enquiry into the Causes of the Late Increase of Robbers and Related Writings*, ed. M. R. Zirker (1988); *The Covent-Garden Journal and A Plan of the Universal Register Office*, ed. B. A. Goldgar (1988).]

1728

The Masquerade, a Poem. Inscribed to C[oun]t H[ei]d[eg]g[e]r. By Lemuel Gulliver, Poet Laureat to the King of Lilliput. Publ. by J. Roberts and A. Dodd, 30 Jan. 1728 (*MChr*).

Love in Several Masques. A Comedy. Written by Mr. Fielding. First perf. Drury Lane, 16 Feb. 1728. Publ. by J. Watts, 23 Feb. 1728 (*DP*).

1729–30

"O to look oer the old Records of Time" [unfinished burlesque of *The Dunciad*]. Publ. Grundy 1972.

1730

The Temple Beau. A Comedy. Written by Mr. Fielding. First perf. Goodman's Fields, 26 Jan. 1730. Publ. by J. Watts, 2 Feb. 1730 (*DP*).

The Author's Farce; and the Pleasures of the Town. Written by Scriblerus Secundus. First perf. Haymarket, 30 Mar. 1730. Publ. by J. Roberts, 31 Mar. 1730 (*DP*).

Tom Thumb. A Tragedy. First perf. Haymarket, 24 Apr. 1730. Publ. by J. Roberts, 25 Apr. 1730 (*DP*). First perf. with new Prologue and Epilogue, 1 May 1730; with Additions, 6 May 1730.

Tom Thumb. A Tragedy. Written by Sciblerus Secundus. 2nd edn., publ. 6 Jun. 1730 (*LEP*, 4–6 Jun.). 3rd edn., publ. 11 Jul. 1730 (*LEP*, 9–11 Jul.).

Rape upon Rape; or, The Justice Caught in his own Trap. A Comedy. First perf. Haymarket, 23 Jun. 1730. Publ. by J. Watts, 23 Jun. 1730 (*DP*).

The Coffee-House Politician; or, The Justice Caught in his own Trap. A Comedy. Written by Mr. Fielding. First perf. Lincoln's Inn Fields, 4 Dec. 1730. Publ. by J. Watts, 4 Dec. 1730 (*LEP*, 1–3 Dec.). [*Rape upon Rape* reissued with a new title.].

1731

The Tragedy of Tragedies; or, The Life and Death of Tom Thumb the Great. With the Annotations of H. Scriblerus Secundus. First perf. Haymarket, 24 Mar. 1731. Publ. by J. Roberts, 24 Mar. 1731 (*DP*).

The Letter-Writers: or, A New Way to Keep a Wife at Home. A Farce. Written by Scriblerus Secundus. First perf. Haymarket, 24 Mar. 1731. Publ. by J. Roberts, 24 Mar. 1731 (*DP*).

Epilogue to *Orestes. A Dramatic Opera.* (By Lewis Theobald.) First perf. Lincoln's Inn Fields, 3 Apr. 1731. Publ. 10 Apr. 1731 (*GSJ*, 22 Apr.).

The Welsh Opera: or, The Grey Mare the better Horse. Written by Scriblerus Secundus, Author of the *Tragedy of Tragedies.* First perf. Haymarket, 22 Apr. 1731. Publ. by E. Rayner, 26 Jun. 1731 (*DJ*), unauthorized.

The Genuine Grub-Street Opera. Written by Scriblerus Secundus. Revision of *Welsh Opera* announced for performance at Haymarket, 11 and 14 Jun. 1731, but never performed. Publ. by E. Rayner(?), 18 Aug. 1731 (*GSJ*), unauthorized.

The Grub-Street Opera. By Scriblerus Secundus. To which is added, *The Masquerade, a Poem.* The authorized text, which, though bearing the imprint J. Roberts 1731 on the title-page, was first published by A. Millar in 1755 as part of Fielding's *Dramatic Works.*

"A Dialogue between a Beau's Head and His Heels, taken from their Mouths as they were Spoke at St. James's Coffee-House. By Mr. Fielding." In *The Musical Miscellany*, Vol. VI (1731), pp. 170–3.

1732

The Lottery. A Farce. First perf. Drury Lane, 1 Jan. 1732; perf. with alterations and an additional scene, 1 Feb. 1732. Publ. by J. Watts, 7 Jan. 1732 (*DJ*).

Epilogue to *The Modish Couple. A Comedy.* (Attributed to Charles Bodens, but in fact by James Miller.) First perf. Drury Lane, 10 Jan. 1732. Publ. 14 Jan. 1732 (*LEP*, 11–13 Jan.).

The Modern Husband. A Comedy. Written by Henry Fielding, Esq. First perf. Drury Lane, 14 Feb. 1732. Publ. by J. Watts, 21 Feb. 1732 (*DP*).

The Old Debauchees. A Comedy. By the Author of the *Modern Husband.* First perf. Drury Lane, 1 Jun. 1732. Publ. by J. Watts, 13 Jun. 1732 (*DP*).

The Covent-Garden Tragedy. First perf. Drury Lane, 1 Jun. 1732. Publ. by J. Watts, 24 Jun. 1732 (*DP*, 23 Jun.).

The Mock Doctor: or, The Dumb Lady Cur'd. A Comedy. Done from Molière. First perf. Drury Lane, 23 Jun. 1732. Publ. by J. Watts, 11 Jul. 1732 (*LEP*, 6–8 Jul.). 2nd edn., with additional songs and alterations, publ. *c.* Nov. 1732 (*LEP*, 30 Nov.–2 Dec. 1732).

Epilogue to *Cœlia: or, The Perjur'd Lover. A Play.* (By Charles Johnson.) First perf. Drury Lane, 11 Dec. 1732. Publ. 15 Dec. 1732 (*DP*, 13 Dec.).

1733

The Miser. A Comedy. Taken from Plautus and Molière. By Henry Fielding, Esq. First perf. Drury Lane, 17 Feb. 1733. Publ. by J. Watts, 13 Mar. 1733 (*DP*, 12 Mar.).

Deborah: or, A Wife for You All. Written by the Author of the *Miser.* Only performance: Drury Lane, 6 Apr. 1733 (*DP*, 14 Mar.; *DA*, 6 Apr.). Never publ.

"An Epistle to Mr Lyttleton occasioned by two Lines in Mr. Pope's Paraphrase on the first Satire of the 2d Book of Horace" (written *c.* late Feb. to early Apr. 1733). Publ. Grundy 1972.

1734

The Author's Farce. In which will be introduc'd an Operatical Puppet Show, call'd *The Pleasures of the Town.* With great Additions, and a new Prologue and Epilogue. First perf. Drury Lane, 15 Jan. 1734 (*DJ*). Publ. by J. Watts as "Third Edition" 1750.

The Intriguing Chambermaid. A Comedy of Two Acts. Taken from the French of Regnard. By Henry Fielding, Esq. First perf. Drury Lane, 15 Jan. 1734. Publ. by J. Watts, Jan. 1734 (*GM*).

Don Quixote in England. A Comedy. By Henry Fielding, Esq. First perf. Haymarket, 5 Apr. 1734. Publ. by J. Watts, 17 Apr. 1734 (*LEP*, 11–13 Apr.).

1735

An Old Man Taught Wisdom: or, The Virgin Unmask'd. A Farce. First perf. Drury
Lane, 6 Jan. 1735. Publ. by J. Watts, *c.* 23 Jan. 1735 (*GSJ*, 23 Jan.).
The Universal Gallant: or, The Different Husbands. A Comedy. By Henry Fielding, Esq.
First perf. Drury Lane, 10 Feb. 1735. Publ. by J. Watts, 19 Feb. 1735 (*LDP*).

1736

*Pasquin. A Dramatic Satire on the Times: Being the Rehearsal of Two Plays, viz. A
Comedy call'd, The Election; and A Tragedy call'd, The Life and Death of Common-
Sense.* By Henry Fielding, Esq. First perf. Haymarket, 5 Mar. 1736. Publ. by J.
Watts, 8 Apr. 1736 (*LDP*, 6–7 Apr.).
Tumble-Down Dick: or, Phaeton in the Suds. A Dramatick Entertainment of Walking,
in Serious and Foolish Characters: Interlarded with Burlesque, Grotesque, Comick
Interludes, call'd, Harlequin a Pick-Pocket. Being ('tis hop'd) the last Entertainment
that will ever be exhibited on any Stage. Invented by the Ingenious Monsieur Sans
Esprit. The Musick compos'd by the Harmonious Signior Warblerini. And the Scenes
painted by the Prodigious Mynheer Van Bottom-Flat. First perf. Haymarket, 29
Apr. 1736. Publ. by J. Watts, 29 Apr. 1736 (*LEP*, 29 Apr.–1 May).
Prologue to *Fatal Curiosity: A True Tragedy of Three Acts.* By Mr. Lillo. First perf.
Haymarket, 27 May 1736. Publ. Apr. 1737 (*GM*).

1737

Eurydice, a Farce: As it was d–mned at the Theatre-Royal in Drury-Lane. Only performance: as *Euridice, or The Devil Henpeck'd* at Drury Lane, 19 Feb. 1737. Publ.
in Fielding's *Miscellanies* (1743), Vol. II.
The Historical Register for the Year 1736. To which is added a very merry Tragedy,
called, *Eurydice Hiss'd, or, A Word to the Wise.* Both written by the Author of
Pasquin. First perf. Haymarket, 21 Mar. 1737; *Eurydice Hiss'd,* 13 Apr. 1737. Publ.
together by J. Roberts, 12 May 1737 (*DP*).
Letter from "Pasquin" in *Common Sense* (21 May 1737).

1738

Letter from "Mum Budget" on the wisdom of silence, in *Common Sense* (13 May 1738).
(Battestin and Battestin 1980.)

1739–40

The Champion; or, British Mercury. By Capt. Hercules Vinegar, of Hockley in the
Hole. (To be continued every Tuesday, Thursday, and Saturday Morning.)
Under this title (though the address of Capt. Vinegar was altered with the issue
of 11 Dec. 1739 from "of Hockley in the Hole" to "of Pall-mall") this two-page
periodical was published by a partnership of booksellers from No. 1 (Thurs., 15 Nov.
1739) to No. 63 (Tues. 8 Apr. 1740). In this initial phase of its publication, Fielding
contributed more than fifty leaders, James Ralph about ten, and William Robinson
the last. The earliest issue extant is at the Bodleian Library, Oxford (Hope fol. 106),
whose collection, beginning with No. 20 (Sat., 29 Dec. 1739) is thereafter complete
except for Nos. 25 (Thurs., 10 Jan. 1739/40) and 39 (Tues., 12 Feb. 1739/40).
The Champion: or, Evening Advertiser. By Capt. Hercules Vinegar, of Pall-mall. (To
be continued every Tuesday, Thursday, and Saturday Evening.)
Under this title the paper, expanded to four pages, continued publication. Fielding
continued writing for it until (probably) sometime in Dec. 1740, though Ralph,
Robinson, and others now contributed a greater proportion of the leaders. The
Bodleian Library (Hope fol. 10) has a complete run from No. 64 (Thurs., 10 Apr.
1740) to No. 158 (Sat., 15 Nov. 1740).
Most of the essays and selected news items from 15 Nov. 1739 to 19 Jun. 1740
were reprinted in *The Champion: Containing a Series of Papers, Humourous, Moral,
Political, and Critical,* 2 vols., 25 Jun. 1741 (*DG*). Reissued in 1743 with Index.

1740

The Military History of Charles XII. King of Sweden. Written by the express Order of
his Majesty, by M. Gustavus Adlerfeld, Chamberlain to the King. To which is added,
An exact Account of the Battle of Pultowa, with a Journal of the King's Retreat to
Bender. Translated into English. 3 vols. Publ. by J. and P. Knapton, J. Hodges, A.
Millar, and J. Nourse, 10 Oct. 1740 (*DG*).

1741

Of True Greatness. An Epistle to The Right Honourable George Dodington, Esq; by
Henry Fielding, Esq. Publ. by C. Corbet, 7 Jan. 1741 (*DA*). Reprinted in *Miscellanies*
(1743), Vol. I.
ΤΗΣ ΟΜΗΡΟΥ VEPNON-ΙΑΔΟΣ, ΡΑΨΩΙΔΙΑ ἢ ΓΡΑΜΜΑ Α' The Vernon-iad.
Done into English, from the original Greek of Homer. Lately found at Constan-
tinople. With Notes in usum, &c. Book the First. Publ. by C. Corbet, 22 Jan. 1741
(*DA*).
An Apology for the Life of Mrs. Shamela Andrews. In which, the many notorious
Falshoods and Misrepresentations of a Book called *Pamela*, are exposed and refuted;
and all the matchless Arts of that young Politician, set in a true and just Light.
Together with a full Account of all that passed between her and Parson Arthur
Williams; whose Character is represented in a manner something different from what
he bears in *Pamela*. The whole being exact Copies of authentick Papers delivered to
the Editor. Necessary to be had in all Families. By Mr. Conny Keyber. Publ. by A.
Dodd, 2 Apr. 1741 (*DP*). 2nd edn. publ. 3 Nov. 1741 (*Ch*).
The Opposition. A Vision. 1742. Publ. by T. Cooper, 15 Dec. 1741 (*DG*).

1742

*The History of the Adventures of Joseph Andrews, and of his Friend Mr. Abraham
Adams.* Written in Imitation of the Manner of Cervantes, Author of *Don Quixote.* 2
vols. Publ. by A. Millar, 22 Feb. 1742. 2nd edn., Revised and Corrected with
Alterations and Additions by the Author, publ. 10 Jun. 1742. 3rd edn., illustrated
with Cuts [by J. Hulett], publ. 21–8 Mar. 1743, the first edition to carry Fielding's
name on the title-page. 4th edn., revised and corrected (misdated 1749), publ. 29
Oct. 1748. 5th edn., publ. 19 Dec. 1751.
A Full Vindication of the Dutchess Dowager of Marlborough: Both with regard to the
Account lately Published by Her Grace, and to Her Character in general; against the
base and malicious Invectives contained in a late scurrilous Pamphlet, entitled
Remarks on the Account, &c. In a Letter to the Noble Author of those Remarks.
Publ. by J. Roberts, 2 Apr. 1742 (*DP*).
Miss Lucy in Town. A Sequel to *The Virgin Unmasqued.* A Farce; with Songs. First
perf. Drury Lane, 6 May 1742. Publ. by A. Millar, 6 May 1742 (*DA*).
Plutus, the God of Riches. A Comedy. Translated from the Original Greek of Aristophanes, with Large Notes Explanatory and Critical. By Henry Fielding, Esq; and
the Revd. Mr. Young. Publ. by T. Waller, 31 May 1742 (*DP*, 29 May).

1743

*Some Papers Proper to be Read before the R[oya]l Society, Concerning the Terrestrial
Chrysipus, Golden-Foot or Guinea*; an Insect, or Vegetable, resembling the Polypus,
which hath this surprising Property, That being cut into several Pieces, each Piece
becomes a perfect Animal, or Vegetable, as complete as that of which it was originally
only a Part. Collected by Petrus Gualterus, but not Published till after his Death.
Publ. by J. Roberts, 16 Feb. 1743. Reprinted in *Miscellanies* (1743), Vol. I.
The Wedding-Day. A Comedy. By Henry Fielding, Esq. First perf. Drury Lane, 17
Feb. 1743. Publ. by A. Millar, 24 Feb. 1743 (*DP*). Reprinted in *Miscellanies* (1743),
Vol. II.
Miscellanies, by Henry Fielding, Esq. 3 vols. Publ. by Fielding (sold by A. Millar) 7
Apr. 1743. "2nd edn." publ. by Millar.
   Vol. I contains a List of Subscribers; a Preface; poems, including Of True Great-
ness, of Good-Nature, Liberty, To a Friend on the Choice of a Wife, To John Hayes,

Esq., Part of Juvenal's Sixth Satire Modernized in Burlesque Verse, etc.; prose, including essays On Conversation, On the Knowledge of the Characters of Men, On Nothing, Some Papers Proper to be Read before the R[oya]l Society, The First Olynthiac of Demosthenes, Of the Remedy of Affliction for the Loss of Our Friends, A Dialogue between Alexander the Great and Diogenes the Cynic; An Interlude between Jupiter, Juno, Apollo, and Mercury.

Vol. II contains A Journey from This World to the Next, Eurydice, and The Wedding-Day.

Vol. III contains The Life of Mr. Jonathan Wild the Great.

1744

The Adventures of David Simple: Containing an Account of his Travels through the Cities of London and Westminster, in Search of a Real Friend. By a Lady [i.e., Sarah Fielding]. 2 vols. The Second Edition, Revised and Corrected. With a Preface by Henry Fielding, Esq. Publ. by A. Millar, 13 Jul. 1744 (GA).

1745

The Charge to the Jury: or, The Sum of the Evidence, on the Trial of A.B.C.D. and E.F. All M.D. For the Death of one Robert at Orfud, at a Special Commission of Oyer and Terminer held at Justice-College, in W[arwi]ck Lane, before Sir Asculapius Dosem, Dr. Timberhead, and Others, their Fellows, Justices, &c. Publ. by M. Cooper, 2 Jul. 1745 (GA). (Jarvis 1946.)

A Serious Address to the People of Great Britain. In which the Certain Consequences of the Present Rebellion, are fully demonstrated. Necessary to be perused by every Lover of his Country, at this Juncture. Publ. by M. Cooper, 3 Oct. 1745. 2nd edn., Corrected, with Additions, publ. c. 5 Nov. 1745.

The History of the Present Rebellion in Scotland. Publ. by M. Cooper, c. 7 Oct. 1745.

A Dialogue between the Devil, the Pope, and the Pretender. Publ. by M. Cooper, 12–15 Oct. 1745.

The Debauchees: or, The Jesuit Caught. A Comedy. By Henry Fielding, Esq. First perf. Drury Lane, 17 Oct. 1745. Publ. by J. Watts, Oct. 1745 (GM). An "acting" version of The Old Debauchees (1732) with deletions indicated.

1745–6

The True Patriot: and The History of Our Own Times. (To be Continued Every Tuesday.) Publ. by M. Cooper in partnership with others from 5 Nov. 1745 to No. 33 (17 Jun. 1746). The original of No. 33 is lost, but was reprinted in the London Magazine, 15 (Jun. 1746), 298–9.

1746

The Female Husband: or, The Surprising History of Mrs. Mary, alias Mr. George Hamilton, Who was convicted of having married a Young Woman of Wells and lived with her as her Husband. Taken from Her own Mouth since her Confinement. Publ. by M. Cooper, 12 Nov. 1746 (DA).

1747

Ovid's Art of Love Paraphrased, and Adapted to the Present Time. With Notes. And a most Correct Edition of the Original. Book I. Publ. by M. Cooper, A. Dodd, and G. Woodfall, 25 Feb. 1747 (GA).

Familiar Letters between the Principal Characters in David Simple, and Some Others. To which is added, A Vision. By the Author of David Simple [i.e., Sarah Fielding]. 2 vols. Publ. by S. Fielding (and sold by A. Millar), 10 Apr. 1747 (GA). Fielding wrote the Preface and Letters XL–XLIV.

A Dialogue between a Gentleman of London, Agent for two Court Candidates, and an Honest Alderman of the Country Party. Wherein the Grievances under which the Nation at present groans are fairly and impartially laid open and considered. Earnestly address'd to the Electors of Great-Britain. Publ. by M. Cooper, 23 Jun. 1747. 2nd edn. publ. c. Jul. 1747.

A Proper Answer to a Late Scurrilous Libel, entitled, An Apology for the Conduct of a late celebrated Second-rate Minister. By the Author of the *Jacobite's Journal.* Publ. by M. Cooper, 24 Dec. 1747. "2nd edn." publ. 2 Jan. 1748.

1747–8

The Jacobite's Journal. By John Trott-Plaid, Esq. Publ. by M. Cooper in partnership with others every Sat. from 5 Dec. 1747 to No. 49 (5 Nov. 1748).

1749

The History of Tom Jones, a Foundling. By Henry Fielding, Esq. 6 vols. Publ. by A. Millar, *c.* 3 Feb. 1749. 2nd edn., publ. 28 Feb. 1749. 3rd edn., 4 vols., publ. *c.* 12 Apr. 1749. 4th edn. (revised), publ. 11 Dec. 1749.

A Charge delivered to the Grand Jury, at the Sessions of the Peace held for the City and Liberty of Westminster, &c. On Thursday the 29th of June, 1749 by Henry Fielding, Esq; Chairman of the said Sessions. Published by Order of the Court, at the unanimous Request of the Gentlemen of the Grand Jury. Publ. by A. Millar, 21 Jul. 1749.

A True State of the Case of Bosavern Penlez, Who suffered on Account of the late Riot in the Strand. In which the Law regarding these Offences, and the Statute of George the First, commonly called the Riot Act, are fully considered. By Henry Fielding, Esq; Barrister at Law, and one of his Majesty's Justices of the Peace for the County of Middlesex, and for the City and Liberty of Westminster. Publ. by A. Millar, 18 Nov. 1749. 2nd edn. publ. 16 Dec. 1749.

1751

An Enquiry into the Causes of the late Increase of Robbers, &c. with some Proposals for Remedying this Growing Evil. In which the Present Reigning Vices are impartially exposed; and the Laws that relate to the Provision for the Poor, and to the Punishment of Felons are largely and freely examined. By Henry Fielding, Esq; Barrister at Law, and One of His Majesty's Justices of the Peace for the County of Middlesex, and for the City and Liberty of Westminster. Publ. by A. Millar, 19 Jan. 1751. 2nd edn. publ. 6 Mar. 1751.

A Plan of the Universal Register-Office, Opposite Cecil-Street in the Strand. Publ. 21 Feb. 1751.

Amelia. By Henry Fielding, Esq. 4 vols. (misdated 1752). Publ. by A. Millar, 19 Dec. 1751. "2nd edn." publ. *c.* Jan. 1752. 2nd edn. revised, in Fielding's *Works* (1762).

1752

The Covent-Garden Journal. By Sir Alexander Drawcansir, Knt. Censor of Great Britain. To be continued every Tuesday and Saturday. Publ. by Mrs. Dodd (probably in partnership with A. Millar) from Sat., 4 Jan. to No. 72 (Sat., 25 Nov. 1752). After No. 52 (Tues., 30 Jun. 1752) published only on Saturdays.

Examples of the Interposition of Providence in the Detection and Punishment of Murder. Containing, above thirty Cases, in which this dreadful Crime has been brought to Light, in the most extraordinary and miraculous Manner; collected from various authors, antient and modern. With an Introduction and Conclusion, Both written by Henry Fielding, Esq. Publ. by A. Millar, 13 Apr. 1752.

1753

A Proposal for Making an Effectual Provision for the Poor, for Amending their Morals, and for Rendering them useful Members of the Society. To which is added, A Plan of the Buildings proposed, with proper Elevations. Drawn by an Eminent Hand. By Henry Fielding, Esq; Barrister at Law, and one of his Majesty's Justices of the Peace for the County of Middlesex. Publ. by A. Millar, 29 Jan. 1753.

A Clear State of the Case of Elizabeth Canning, Who hath sworn that she was robbed and almost starved to Death by a Gang of Gipsies and other Villains in January last, for which one Mary Squires now lies under Sentence of Death. By Henry Fielding, Esq. Publ. by A. Millar, 20 Mar. 1753. "2nd edn." publ. 22 Mar. 1753.

1754

The Life of Mr. Jonathan Wild the Great. A New Edition with considerable Corrections and Additions. By Henry Fielding, Esq. Publ. by A. Millar, 19 Mar. 1754 (*PA*).

1755

The Journal of a Voyage to Lisbon, by the late Henry Fielding, Esq. Publ. by A. Millar, 25 Feb. 1755 (*PA*). The so-called "Humphrys" version – a revised, second printing but probably published first. Concluding with *A Fragment of a Comment on L. Bolingbroke's Essays.*

The Journal of a Voyage to Lisbon, by the late Henry Fielding, Esq. Publ. by A. Millar, 4 Dec. 1755 (*PA*)? The so-called "Francis" version – the unrevised, first printed edition which was probably withheld and published second. Also concluding with *A Fragment of a Comment on L. Bolingbroke's Essays.*

1758

"Plain Truth. By Henry Fielding, Esq;" in *A Collection of Poems in Six Volumes by Several Hands,* Vol. V (1758), pp. 302–5.

1761

"A Treatise on the Office of Constable" in Sir John Fielding's *Extracts from such of the Penal Laws, as particularly relate to the Peace and Good Order of this Metropolis.* (1761).

1762

The Works of Henry Fielding, Esq; with The Life of the Author (1762). Issued by A. Millar in 4 vols. quarto and in 8 vols. octavo. The first (though incomplete and imperfect) edition of Fielding's collected works, including a frontispiece by Hogarth and "An Essay on the Life and Genius of Henry Fielding, Esq;" by Arthur Murphy.

1778

The Fathers: or, The Good-Natur'd Man. A Comedy. By the late Henry Fielding, Esq. First perf. Drury Lane, 30 Nov. 1778. Publ. by T. Cadell, 12 Dec. 1778 (*PA*).

WORKS PROBABLY BY FIELDING

[NOTE: The following writings, unacknowledged by Fielding, have been plausibly ascribed to him either by his contemporaries or by present-day scholars or by both. In the evolutionary process of defining the Fielding canon, these works do not yet enjoy the same unquestioned status as, say, *An Apology for the Life of Mrs. Shamela Andrews* (1741), listed above. As readers of this biography will be aware, however, the author is persuaded they are by Fielding.]

1727

[*The Coronation. A Poem. And an Ode on the Birth-day.* By Mr. Fielding. Publ. by B. Creake (and sold by J. Roberts), 10 Nov. 1727.] Probably Fielding's first published work, but no copy survives. Known only through advertisements in *DJ* (10, 13 Nov.), *DP* (10, 15 Nov.), and *MC*, No. 55 (Nov. 1727), p. 126. (Foxon 1975, F119.)

1728

"An Original Song, Written on the First Appearance of the *Beggars Opera,* by the late Henry Fielding, Esq.," in the *Country Magazine* (Salisbury), I (Mar. 1787), 239. (Vincent 1943.)

"The Norfolk Lanthorn," a political ballad, in *The Craftsman,* No. 107 (20 Jul. 1728). (Battestin 1983.)

Letter on the benefit of laughing, *Mist's Weekly Journal,* No. 172 (3 Aug. 1728). (Battestin 1983.)

1730

Letter from "Tho. Squint," a physiognomist, in *Fog's Weekly Journal*, No. 96 (25 Jul. 1730). (Battestin 1983.)

Letter from "Harry Hunter" comparing hunters and politicians, in *The Craftsman*, No. 223 (10 Oct. 1730). (Battestin 1983.)

1732

Letter from "Mr. Wm. Hint, Candle-Snuffer" defending Fielding's *Covent-Garden Tragedy* against the authors of the *Grub-Street Journal*, in the *Daily Post* (21 Jun. 1732) and the *London Evening Post* (20–22 Jun. 1732). (Burling 1986.)

Letter from "Philalethes" defending Fielding and his plays against the authors of the *Grub-Street Journal*, in the *Daily Post* (31 Jul. 1732). (See above, pp. 140–3.)

"Observations on Government, the Liberty of the Press, Newspapers, Partys, and Party-writer [*sic*]," in Thomas Cooke's *Comedian*, No. V (Aug. 1732), pp. 32–6. (Shipley 1968: 322; see above, pp. 153–4.)

"An Epistle to Mr. Ellys the Painter," ibid., pp. 36–8. (Shipley 1968: 322; see above, pp. 153–4, 161.)

1734

[NOTE: Reasons for Fielding's authorship of the *Craftsman* articles listed below for the years 1734–9 are presented in Battestin and Farringdon 1989.]

Letter from "Septennius" ironically defending septennial elections, in *The Craftsman*, No. 402 (16 Mar. 1734).

Letter on screens, in *The Craftsman*, No. 403 (23 Mar. 1734).

Letter proving that "Francis Osborne" is an old woman, in *The Craftsman*, No. 422 (3 Aug. 1734).

Letter chastizing "Mother Osborne" and "Squire Walsingham," in *The Craftsman*, No. 423 (10 Aug. 1734).

Letter from "N. Machiavel" on Walpole's foreign policy, in *The Craftsman*, No. 431 (5 Oct. 1734).

1735

Letter inspired by Addison's *Dialogues upon Medals*, in *The Craftsman*, No. 457 (5 Apr. 1735).

Letter presenting the fantasy of a Great Man's public confession, in *The Craftsman*, No. 460 (26 Apr. 1735).

Letter on strollers, in *The Craftsman*, No. 469 (28 Jun. 1735).

Letter on living dead men and the founding of the *Daily Gazetteer*, in *The Craftsman*, No. 471 (12 Jul. 1735).

Letter from "Jack Ramble" on the founding of the *Daily Gazetteer* by Walpole and Paxton, in *The Craftsman*, No. 474 (2 Aug. 1735).

Letter celebrating *The Craftsman*'s tenth year, in *The Craftsman*, No. 494 (20 Dec. 1735). (Cleary 1984: 78–81.)

1736

Letter from "Rachel Foresight" on the repeal of the Witchcraft Act, in *The Craftsman*, No. 503 (21 Feb. 1736).

Letter from "T.T." presenting a project for ventilating Parliament, in *The Craftsman*, No. 506 (13 Mar. 1736).

Letter on the state of tragedy and Lillo's *Fatal Curiosity*, in the *Daily Advertiser* (25 May 1736). (Hume 1988.)

Letter from "A Moderate Man" on the Gin Act, in *The Craftsman*, No. 518 (5 Jun. 1736).

Letter from "Will. Lovemeal" on eating, in the *Universal Spectator*, Nos. 410–11 (14, 21 Aug. 1736). (Battestin 1986.)

Letter presenting a dream-vision of England ruined by Walpole, in *The Craftsman*, No. 533 (18 Sep. 1736).

Letter from "Philo-Tonsor" in defense of barbers, in *The Craftsman*, No. 539 (30 Oct. 1736).
Letter from "Ned Friendly" on the untruthfulness of newswriters, in *The Craftsman*, No. 546 (18 Dec. 1736).

1737

Some Thoughts on the Present State of the Theatres, and the Consequences of an Act to destroy the Liberty of the Stage. Reprinted in the *Daily Journal*, No. 5955 (25 Mar. 1737). (Lockwood 1980; Amory 1987a: no. 16.)
Letter proposing a scheme for prohibiting the use of all liquors except water, and for laying a tax on urine, in *The Craftsman*, No. 565 (30 Apr. 1737). (Cleary 1984: 114.)
Letter from "R. Dudley" proposing to amend the tax on urine and substituting an impost on water, in *The Craftsman*, No. 567 (14 May 1737).
Letter on the Bill to license the stage, in *The Craftsman*, No. 569 (28 May 1737).
Letter presenting a dream-vision of the body politic, in *The Craftsman*, No. 571 (11 Jun. 1737).
Letter from "C.C.P.L." (i.e., Colley Cibber, Poet Laureate) proposing himself censor of old plays, in *The Craftsman*, No. 574 (2 Jul. 1737).
Letter on the methods of nations in acquiring wealth, in *The Craftsman*, No. 586 (1 Oct. 1737).
Letter from "Proteus Dimplecheek" proposing a physiognomists' academy, in the *Universal Spectator*, No. 470 (8 Oct. 1737). (Battestin 1986.)
Letter from "Philomath" proposing a scheme to replace the Bench of Bishops with puppets, in *The Craftsman*, No. 588 (15 Oct. 1737).
Letter on the ideal government of the ancient Egyptians, in *The Craftsman*, No. 589 (22 Oct. 1737).
Letter from "Anglo-Germanicus" relating a dream encounter with the ghost of the Turkish minister, in *The Craftsman*, No. 591 (5 Nov. 1737).

1738

Letter from "A.B." offering a political exegesis of the *Aeneid*, in *The Craftsman*, No. 600 (7 Jan. 1738).
Letter comprising an historical survey of political satire in children's plays, in *The Craftsman*, No. 604 (4 Feb. 1738).
Letter from "Democritus" in vindication of laughter, in *The Craftsman*, No. 612 (1 Apr. 1738).
Letter on the laws pertaining to libel and the liberty of the press, in *The Craftsman*, Nos. 613, 615 (8, 22 Apr. 1738).
Letter praising Cardinal Fleury of France as the paragon of prime ministers, in *The Craftsman*, No. 614 (15 Apr. 1738).
Letter from "Constans" advocating war with Spain, in *The Craftsman*, No. 618 (13 May 1738).
Letter on signposts, in *The Craftsman*, No. 623 (17 Jun. 1738).
Letter on the characters of ministers, in *The Craftsman*, No. 624 (24 Jun. 1738).
Letter on the affinity between the legal and military professions, in *The Craftsman*, No. 627 (15 Jul. 1738).
Letter on proverbs and politics, in *The Craftsman*, No. 636 (16 Sep. 1738).
Letter on the mottoes of signposts, in *The Craftsman*, No. 638 (30 Sep. 1738).
Letter on the customs and polity of the Mosquito Indians, in *The Craftsman*, No. 644 (11 Nov. 1738).
Letter from "T.P." presenting a specimen of a political play, in *The Craftsman*, No. 650 (23 Dec. 1738).

1739

Letter from "Pharmacopola" on the political implications of modern botany, in *The Craftsman*, No. 686 (1 Sep. 1739).
Letter from a Methodist proposing the establishment of a court of equity, in *The Craftsman*, No. 687 (8 Sep. 1739).

Letters on ministerial whisperers and on talkativeness and intemperance, in *Common Sense*, No. 137 (15 Sep. 1739). (Battestin and Battestin 1980: 137–8.)

1740

An Address to the Electors of Great Britain. Publ. by Drummond and Co., Edinburgh, Dec. 1740. (Cleary 1975.)

Essay in *The Champion* during Dec. 1740, reprinted in the *Dublin Evening Post* (30 Dec. 1740–3 Jan. 1741). (Shipley 1963.)

1741

The History of Our Own Times. By a Society of Gentlemen. Publ. by C. Corbett for four numbers: No. 1 (1–15 Jan. 1741), No. 2 (15–30 Jan.), No. 3 (30 Jan.–12 Feb.), No. 4 (5 Mar.). Besides assuming general editorial responsibility for this short-lived magazine, Fielding probably wrote the introductory essay, the essay on shame, and the vision of the golden tree in Nos. 1–3. (Lockwood 1984, 1985.)

The Crisis: A Sermon, on Revel. XIV. 9, 10, 11. Necessary to be preached in all the Churches in England, Wales, and Berwick upon Tweed, at or before the next General Election. Humbly inscribed to the Right Reverend the Bench of Bishops. By a Lover of his Country. Publ. by A. Dodd, E. Nutt, and H. Chappelle, 16 Apr. 1741. (Wells 1912.)

1744

An Attempt towards a Natural History of the Hanover Rat. Dedicated to T***m. M******r, M.D. And S[ecretar]y to the Royal Society. Publ. by M. Cooper, 23 Nov. 1744 (*GA*). (Jensen 1936.)

1749

Ten Queries submitted to every Sober, Honest, and Disinterested Elector for the City and Liberty of Westminster. A handbill publ. 24 Nov. 1749. (Battestin and Battestin 1977–8.)

The Covent-Garden Journal. No. 1. To be publish'd Once every Month, during the present Westminster Election. By Paul Wronghead, of the Fleet, Esq. A broadsheet publ. 5 Dec. 1749. (Battestin and Battestin 1977–8; see also above, pp. 491–3.)

1751

Letter defending the efficacy of the Glastonbury waters, in *General Advertiser* (8 Oct. 1751). (Battestin 1980.)

WORKS ERRONEOUSLY ATTRIBUTED TO FIELDING

[NOTE: For lists of works erroneously attributed to Fielding, see Cross 1918: III.340–50, and Dudden 1952: II.1140–5). To these should be added the following:]

1732

Select Comedies of Mr. de Moliere. French and English. 8 vols. Publ. by J. Watts, May–Dec. 1732. Attributed in part to Fielding by Cross (1918: III.335–6) and Dudden (1952: II.1127); but not by him. (Tucker 1942; Goggin 1952.)

1734

The Mother-in-Law: or, The Doctor the Disease. A Comedy. By H. Fielding, Gent. [i.e., James Miller]. Publ. by J. Hoey, Dublin, 1734.

Darius's Feast: or, The Force of Truth. A Poem, Addressed to the Right Honourable the Earls of Salisbury and Exeter. Publ. by L. Gilliver, 1734. T. J. Wise tentatively attributed this work to Fielding in the Wrenn Library catalogue and it is so attributed at Cambridge and Leeds; but not by Fielding.

1737

A Rehearsal of Kings: or, The Projecting Gingerbread Baker. First perf. Haymarket, 14 Mar. 1737. Never publ. Attributed to Fielding by Cross (1918: III.336) and Brown (1939); but *DA* (8 Mar. 1737) announced it as the work of "a Gentleman who never wrote for the Stage."

Essays on affectation as the source of ridicule, in *Common Sense*, Nos. 32–3 (3, 10 Sep. 1737). Attributed to Fielding by Cross (1918: III.301) and Williams (1970); but by Chesterfield. (Maty and Justamond 1777.)

1747

A Compleat and Authentick History of the Rise, Progress and Extinction of the Late Rebellion, and of the Proceedings against the Principal Persons concerned therein. Publ. by M. Cooper, 1747. Attributed to Fielding by Cross (1918: III. 314–15) and Dudden (1952: II. 1131); but not by Fielding. (Jarvis 1945, 1956–7; Coley, 1987: xlvi, n.l.)

1748

The Important Triflers. A Satire. By Henry Fielding, Esqr; Author of *Tom Jones*. Publ. by J. Hoey, Dublin, 1749. Attributed to Fielding by Cross (1918: III. 316); but title-page of London edn., publ. by M. Cooper, reads "By Captain Cockade" and copy in BL identifies author as Timothy Brecknock.

1749

Stultus versus Sapientem: In three Letters to *The Fool*, on Subjects the most Interesting. By Henry Fielding, Esq. Publ. by E. Bate, Dublin, 1749. Attributed to Fielding by Cross (1918: III. 319); but by William Chaigneau. (Coolidge 1936; Baker 1953; included in Chaigneau's *History of Jack Connor*, 2nd edn. 1753.)

LETTERS

[1727?]

HF to Lady Mary Wortley Montagu. "Wednesday Evening," n.d., n.p. [London, Sep. 1727?]. Sending "a Copy of the Play" (*Love in Several Masques?*) for her criticism. (Harvard.) Publ., Halsband 1965–7: II.96; Battestin 1989.

[1730?]

HF to Lady Mary Wortley Montagu. "7ber [Sep.] 4," n.d., n.p. [London, 4 Sep. 1730?]. Sending her a copy of *The Modern Husband*. (Text facsimile, Dalloway 1803: I.106; Ms. fragment, Forster Coll., V&A.) Publ., Halsband 1965–7: II.93; Battestin 1989.

1737

Aaron Hill to HF. N.p., 28 Feb. 1736 [1737]. Declining to write the Prologue and Epilogue for *A Rehearsal of Kings*. Publ., Hill 1753: I.239–41; Brown 1939.

1738

HF to John Nourse. "March 6 1737 [1738]," n.p. [London?]. Requesting JN send law books. (Hyde.) Publ., Amory 1967: 35.

1739

HF to John Nourse. "East Stour March 7 1738 [1739]." Requesting JN send law book. (Taylor Coll., Princeton.) Publ., Taylor 1960: no. 29.

HF to John Nourse. "July 9 1739," n.p. [East Stour?]. Requesting JN find him a house near the Temple. (Hyde.) Publ., Cross 1918: I.248.

1740

HF to Davidge Gould. "Basingstoke 15 July 1740." Requesting DG send him deeds. (Harvard.) Publ., Cross (1918: I.258).

Davidge Gould to HF. "Sharpham Park July 23^d 1740." DG has sent deeds to HF at Dorchester. (Harvard.) Publ., Cross 1918: I.258–9.

1741

HF to John Nourse."Ap. 20 1741," n.p. [London?]. Requesting JN deliver copies of *True Greatness* and *Vernoniad*. (Huntington Library.) Publ., Cross 1918: I.288.

HF to James Harris. "Bath 7.ᵇʳ [Sep.] 8 1741." Opening their correspondence. (This and all other letters between HF and Harris are in the private collection of the Earl of Malmesbury.)

James Harris to HF. Salisbury, 17 Sep. 1741. Accepting HF's offer of correspondence.

HF to James Harris. "Bath 7ᵇʳ [Sep.] 29 1741." On laughter.

1742

HF to James Harris. "London March 27 1742." Reports voting of Comm. of Secrecy investigating Walpole's conduct.

HF to James Harris. "Bath September 24 1742." On superiority of prose to poetry.

1743

HF to James Harris. "Brumpton Feb 27 1742 [1743]." Requesting JH correct Ms. of *First Olynthiac of Demosthenes*.

HF to James Harris. "Brumpton March 14. 1742 [1743]." Thanking JH for correcting Ms.

HF to James Harris. "Twiverton [Twerton, near Bath] Septemb. 6 1743." Informing JH of Charlotte's improved health.

HF to James Harris. N.d., n.p. [Twerton? Sep–Oct. 1743?]. Thanking JH for dedicating *History of Nobody* to him.

HF to James Harris. "Twiverton Nov. 14 1743." Summoning JH to Bath.

HF to James Harris. "Twiverton Nov. 24 1743." Informing JH of requirements for admission to Bath Hospital.

1744

HF to James Harris. "Baggshot Jan 15. 1743 [1744]." HF setting out for London with William Young.

HF to James Harris. "Bath 8.ᵇʳ [Oct.] 10 1744." Accepting JH's offer of loan as Charlotte's health worsens.

HF to James Harris. "London Nov. 24.ᵗʰ 1744." On the consolations of philosophy after Charlotte's death.

1745

HF to James Harris. "Boswell Court July 13 1745." Congratulating JH on his marriage.

HF to James Harris. "Essex House October 5 1745." Containing news of the war and rebellion, with note from John Barker on verso.

HF to James Harris. "London Nov. 5. 1745." Enclosing copy of *True Patriot* with news of Arthur Collier's lawsuit.

1746

HF to James Harris. "Boswell Court Jan 2. 1745 [1746]." Thanking JH for contribution to *True Patriot*.

HF to James Harris. "Boswell Court. Jan. 11. 1745 [1746]." Concerning JH's contribution to *True Patriot*.

HF to James Harris. "London Jan: 30 1745 [1746]." Concerning Collier's lawsuit.

HF to James Harris. "London May 13 1746." Congratulating JH on birth of son and heir, with details of Collier lawsuit.

1747

HF to James Harris. "Boswell Court Feb 19 1746 [1747]." Requesting a loan.

1748

Richard Birt to HF. "Lymington [Hants.] 3 Febry 1747 [1748]." Concerning illegal acts of James Perkins in New Forest. (Bedford Record Office.)

Richard Birt to HF. "Winchester 2 March 1747 [1748]." Concerning Perkins case. (BRO.)

HF to Richard Birt. "Boswell Court. March 8. 1747 [1748]." Concerning Perkins case. (BRO.)

HF to Robert Butcher. "Boswell Court March 8 1747 [1748]." Concerning Perkins case. (Bedford Estates Office.) *N.B.* Unless otherwise indicated, HF's letters to Robert Butcher (whom HF invariably addresses as Richard Butcher) and to the Duke of Bedford are published in Battestin and Battestin 1977–8: 176–82.

HF to Robert Butcher. "Twickenham Ap! 3 1748." Concerning New Forest affairs. (BEO.)

HF to Robert Butcher. "Twickenham May. 5. 1748." Requesting favor of Bedford. (BEO.)

HF to Robert Butcher. "Twickenham July 4 1748." Thanking Bedford for favor and complaining of gout. (BEO.)

HF to Robert Butcher. "Twickenham Sept! 28 1748." Concerning HF's office as High Steward of New Forest and his appointment to magistracy. (BRO.) Not publ.

HF to James Harris. "London October 15 1748." Excusing himself from repaying a debt and complaining of gout.

HF to Samuel Richardson. "Oct. 15. (1748)," n.p. [London]. Praising *Clarissa.* (McAdam/Milne. Ms. copy of original.) Publ., McAdam 1948–9; Sabor 1985.

HF to Robert Butcher. "Meard! Court Nov! 21. 1748." Requesting RB call on him. (BEO.)

Charles Coleman to HF. "Lyndhurst, 9th Dec! 1748." Asking HF's advice on collecting New Forest rents. (BRO.)

HF to Robert Butcher. "Decb! 12 1748," n.p. [London]. HF to call on RB on a matter of importance to himself. (BEO.)

HF to Duke of Bedford. "Bow Street Decb! 13 1748." Asking Bedford to enable him to qualify for Middlesex magistracy. (BEO.)

HF to Robert Butcher. "Bow Street Decb! 16 1748." Explaining impossibility of answering Coleman's questions, eager to hear whether Bedford granted his request. (BRO.) Not publ.

HF to Robert Butcher. "Dec! 19 1748," n.p. [Bow Street]. Resigning patent as High Steward of New Forest. (BEO.)

HF to Duke of Bedford. "Decb! 19 1748," n.p. [Bow Street]. Thanking Bedford for constituting him a magistrate. (BEO.)

1749

HF to Duke of Richmond. "Bow Street Ap! 8 1749." Advising Richmond how to proceed against smugglers. (West Sussex Record Office.) Publ., Stewart 1971.

HF to Duke of Bedford. "Bow Street, July 3. 1749." Asking to be appointed Solicitor to Excise. (BEO.)

HF to Duke of Bedford. "Bow Street July 3 1749." Informing Bedford that a riot may occur. (BEO.)

HF to Robert Butcher. "Bow Street July 18 1749." Relating to properties granted HF by Bedford (BEO.)

HF to Lord Hardwicke. "Bow Street July 21 1749." Sending copy of *Charge delivered to the Grand Jury*, enclosing "Draught of a Bill for the better preventing Street Robberies," and recommending Joshua Brogden for magistracy. (British Library.) Publ., Cross 1918: II.243–4.

HF to George Lyttelton. "Bow St. Aug! 29. 1749." Congratulating GL on his marriage and recommending Edward Moore to be Deputy Licenser to the Stage. (Historical Society of Pennsylvania.) Publ., Cross 1918: II.245–7.

HF to James Harris. "London Nov! 18 [?] 1749." Excusing himself from repaying loan.

1750

HF to James Harris. "London Jan 16. 1749 [1750]." Thanking him for gift of bacon and recommending doctor for treatment of gout.

HF to Duke of Bedford. "Bow Street May 14. 1750." Promising to preserve the peace. (BEO.)

HF to Duke of Bedford. "May 24 1750," n.p. [Bow Street?]. Asking to be appointed Judge of the Marshalsea. (BEO.) Publ., Draper 1978–9.

HF to Duke of Bedford. "London May 29 1750." Thanking Bedford for recommending him for Judgeship. (BEO.) Publ., Draper 1978–9.

HF to Robert Butcher. "Bow Street May 29.1750." Thanking RB for supporting his application for the Judgeship. (BEO.)

HF to James Harris. "London Sept. 22. 1750." Postponing repayment of debt.

HF to Hutton Perkins (Secretary to Lord Chancellor Hardwicke). "Bow Street Nov. 25.1750." Concerning plot to murder the Lord Chancellor.(BL.) Publ., Cross 1918: II.249.

1751

HF to Duke of Newcastle. "Bow Street Jan 15 1750 [1751]." Recommending William Pentlow to be Keeper of New Prison. (BL.) Publ., Cross 1918: II.253.

HF to Robert Butcher. "Bow Street. May 7. 1751." Asking him to convey important request to Bedford. (BEO.)

HF to Robert Butcher. "Bow Street. June 12.1751." Regretting that legal technicality prevents his fulfilling Bedford's request and reminding Bedford to send list of commissions to Lord Chancellor. (BEO.)

HF to Robert Butcher."Bow Street June 13.1751." Asking him to deliver letter concerning public business to Bedford. (BEO.)

James Harris to HF. Salisbury, 21 Dec. 1751. Requesting copy of *Amelia* in return for *Hermes*.

HF to James Harris. "Bow Street Dec. 23. 1751." Sending copy of his "damned Book" *Amelia* and thanking JH for *Hermes*.

1752

HF to Thomas Birch. "May 18. 1752" [Bow Street]. Inviting Birch to dinner. (BL.)

1753

HF to Duke of Newcastle. "Ealing April 14 1753." Concerning affidavits in the case of Elizabeth Canning. (Public Record Office.) Publ., Cross 1918: II.290–1.

HF to Duke of Newcastle. "Ealing April 27. 1753." Assuring Newcastle he has tried to comply with his request to see affidavits in Canning case. (PRO.) Publ., Cross 1918: II.291–2.

HF to Lord Chancellor Hardwicke. "Dec. 6 1753," n.p. Recommending Saunders Welch be appointed to magistracy. (BL.) Publ., Cross 1918: III.13.

1754

HF to John Fielding. "On board the Queen of Portugal ... off Ryde ... July 12 1754." Reporting on progress of voyage to Lisbon. (Harvard.) Publ., Cross 1918: III.32–3.

HF to John Fielding. "Torr Bay July 22 1754." Dispatching cider to his friends, inquiring about business relating to Ealing farm. (Huntington Library.) Publ., Cross 1918: III.41–3.

HF to John Fielding. n.d., n.p. (*c.* 18/19 Sep. 1754? Lisbon]. A long, petulant account of his arrival in Lisbon and of family matters. (Huntington Library.) Publ., Amory 1971.

HF to John Fielding. n.d., n.p. [mid-Sep. 1754, Lisbon]. Relating family quarrel over gifts of parrots. Publ. (in part), De Castro 1920.

HF to John Fielding. n.d., n.p. [late Sep. 1754, Lisbon]. Fragment explaining hindrances to his writing. Publ., Amory 1971: 66, n. 4.

SELECT MANUSCRIPTS

HF's public denunciation of Andrew and John Tucker. 15 Nov. 1725. (Lyme Regis.) See above, Plate 8.

"Cantos" of an unfinished burlesque epic satirizing the Scriblerians. *C.* 1729–30.
(Harrowby.) Grundy 1972.
Receipt to John Watts for 20 gns. for copyright to "the despairing Debauchees" [i.e.,
The Old Debauchees] and *The Covent-Garden Tragedy*. 4 Apr. 1732. (Hyde.)
Verse "Epistle to Mr Lyttleton occasioned by two Lines in Mr Pope's Paraphrase on
the first Satire of the 2d Book of Horace," defending Lady Mary Wortley Montagu
against Pope. *C.* Mar. 1733. (Harrowby.) Grundy 1972.
Essay on the wisdom of silence, published under the pseudonym "Mum Budget" in
Common Sense (13 May 1738). 1 Apr. 1738. (PRO.) Battestin and Battestin 1980.
See above, Plate 26.
Receipt to John Nourse for £45 in part payment for translating Adlerfeld's *Military
History of Charles XII*. 10 Mar. 1739/40. (Yale.)
Assignment to Andrew Millar of copyrights to *Joseph Andrews* (£183.11s.), *A Full
Vindication of the Dutchess Dowager of Marlborough* (5 gns.), and *Miss Lucy in Town*
(10 gns.). 13 Apr. 1742. (Forster Coll., V&A.)
Fragments of an unfinished work entitled "An Institute of the Pleas of the Crown".
C. 1745. (Hyde, Harvard, Yale.) Amory 1987b.
Receipt to Millar for £600, promising to assign copyright to *Tom Jones*. 11 Jun. 1748.
(Morgan.)
Assignment to Millar of copyright to *Tom Jones*. 25 Mar. 1749. (Morgan.)
HF's will. *C.* Jun. 1754; proved 14 Nov. 1754. (PRO.) Cross 1918: III.22–3.

REFERENCES IN THE BIBLIOGRAPHY

Amory, H. (1967) "Henry Fielding," in G. Austin (ed.) *Four Oaks Library*, Somerville,
NJ: pp. 29–49.
Amory, H (1971) "Fielding's Lisbon Letters," *Huntington Library Quarterly*, 35, 65–
83.
Amory, H. (1987a) *New Books by Fielding: Commentary toward an Exhibition*,
Cambridge, Mass.: Houghton Library.
Amory, H. (ed.) (1987b) Fragments of Fielding's unpublished *Institute of the Pleas of
the Crown*, Cambridge, Mass.: Houghton Library.
Baker, S. W. (1953) "Fielding and 'Stultus Versus Sapientem,'" *Notes & Queries*, 198,
343–4.
Battestin, M. C. (1980) "Fielding and the Glastonbury Waters," *Yearbook of English
Studies*, 10, 204–9.
Battestin, M. C. (1983) "Four New Fielding Attributions: His Earliest Satires of
Walpole," *Studies in Bibliography*, 36, 69–109.
Battestin, M. C. (1986) "Fielding's Contributions to the *Universal Spectator* (1736–7),"
Studies in Philology, 83, 88–116.
Battestin, M. C. (1989) "Dating Fielding's Letters to Lady Mary Wortley Montagu,"
Studies in Bibliography, 42, 246–8.
Battestin, M. C. and Battestin, R. R. (1977–8) "Fielding, Bedford, and the Westminster
Election of 1749," *Eighteenth-Century Studies*, 11, 143–85.
Battestin, M. C. and Battestin, R. R. (1980) "A Fielding Discovery, with Some Remarks
on the Canon," *Studies in Bibliography*, 33, 131–43.
Battestin, M. C. and Farringdon, M. G. (1989) *New Essays by Henry Fielding: His
Contributions to "The Craftsman" (1734–9) and Other Early Journalism*, Char-
lottesville, Va.: University Press of Virginia.
Brown, J. R. (1939). "From Aaron Hill to Henry Fielding?" *Philological Quarterly*, 18,
85–8.
Burling, W. J. (1986). "Henry Fielding and the 'William Hint' Letter: A Recon-
sideration," *Notes & Queries*, 231, 498–9.
Ch. The Champion.
Cleary, T. R. (1975) "The Case for Fielding's Authorship of *An Address to the Electors
of Great Britain* (1740) Re-opened," *Studies in Bibliography*, 28, 308–18.
Cleary, T. R. (1984) *Henry Fielding: Political Writer*, Waterloo, Ontario: Wilfrid
Laurier University Press.

Coley, W. B. (ed.) (1987) Fielding's *The True Patriot and Related Writings*, Oxford and Middletown, Conn.: Clarendon Press and Wesleyan University Press.

Coolidge, A. C. (1936) "A Fielding Pamphlet?" *Times Literary Supplement*, 9 May, p. 400.

Cross, W. L. (1918) *The History of Henry Fielding*, 3 vols., New Haven, Conn.: Yale University Press.

DA. Daily Advertiser.

Dalloway, J. (ed.) (1803) *Works* of Lady Mary Wortley Montagu, 5 vols. London: R. Phillips.

de Castro, J. P. (1920) "Fielding's Last Letter," *Times Literary Supplement*, 15 Jan., p. 35.

DG. Daily Gazetteer.

DJ. Daily Journal.

DP. Daily Post.

Draper, M. P. G. (1978–9) "Letters of the 4th Duke of Bedford," *Eighteenth-Century Studies*, 12, 206–8.

Dudden, F. H. (1952) *Henry Fielding: His Life, Works, and Times*, 2 vols., Oxford: Clarendon Press.

Foxon, D. F. (1975) *English Verse 1701–1750: A Catalogue of separately printed poems with notes on contemporary collected editions*, 2 vols., Cambridge: Cambridge University Press.

GA. General Advertiser.

GM. Gentleman's Magazine.

Goggin, L. P. (1952) "Fielding and the *Select Comedies of Mr. de Moliere*," *Philological Quarterly*, 31, 344–50.

Grundy, I. M. (1972) "New Verse by Henry Fielding," *PMLA (Publications of the Modern Language Association of America)*, 87, 219–39.

GSJ. Grub-Street Journal.

Halsband, R. (ed.) (1965–7) *The Complete Letters of Lady Mary Wortley Montagu*, 3 vols., Oxford: Clarendon Press.

Harrowby. Harrowby Mss. Trust, Sandon Hall, Stafford.

Hill, A. (1753) *The Works of the Late Aaron Hill, Esq.*, 4 vols.

Hume, R. D. (1988) *Henry Fielding and the London Theatre, 1728–1737*, Oxford: Clarendon Press. Appendix IV.

Hyde. Collection of Donald F. Hyde, in care of Viscountess Eccles.

Jarvis, R. C. (1945) "Fielding, Dodsley, Marchant, and Ray: Some Fugitive Histories of the '45," *Notes & Queries*, 189, 90–2, 117–20, 138–41.

Jarvis, R. C. (1946) "The Death of Walpole: Henry Fielding and a Forgotten *Cause Célèbre*," *Modern Language Review*, 41, 113–30.

Jarvis, R. C. (1956–7) "Fielding and the 'Forty-Five,'" *Notes & Queries*, n.s. 3, 391–4, 479–82; n.s. 4, 19–24.

Jensen, G. E. (1936) "A Fielding Discovery," *Yale University Library Gazette*, 10, 23–32.

LDP. London Daily Post.

LEP. London Evening Post.

Lockwood, T. (1980) "A New Essay by Fielding," *Modern Philology*, 78, 48–58.

Lockwood, T. (1984) "New Facts and Writings from an Unknown Magazine by Henry Fielding, *The History of Our Own Times*," *Review of English Studies*, n.s. 35, 463–93.

Lockwood, T. (ed.) (1985) *The History of Our Own Times (1741)*, attributed to Henry Fielding, Delmar, NY: Scholars' Facsimiles & Reprints.

Lyme Regis. Lyme Regis (Philpot) Museum, Dorset.

McAdam, E. L., Jr. (1948–9) "A New Letter from Fielding," *Yale Review*, 2nd ser. 38, 300–10.

Maty, M. and Justamond, J. O. (eds.) (1777) Chesterfield's *Miscellaneous Works*, 2 vols.

MC. Monthly Catalogue.

MChr. Monthly Chronicle.

Morgan. J. P. Morgan Library, New York.

PA. Public Advertiser.

Sabor, P. (intro.) (1985) Sarah Fielding's *Remarks on Clarissa (1749)*, Appendix. Augustan Reprint Society, Nos. 231–2. Los Angeles: William Andrews Clark Memorial Library, University of California.

Shipley, J. B. (1963) "A New Fielding Essay from the *Champion*," *Philological Quarterly*, 42, 417–22.

Shipley, J. B. (1968) "Ralph, Ellys, Hogarth, and Fielding: The Cabal against Jacopo Amigoni," *Eighteenth-Century Studies*, 1, 313–31.

Stewart, M. M. (1971) "Henry Fielding's Letter to the Duke of Richmond," *Philological Quarterly*, 50, 135–40.

Taylor, R. H. (1960) *Letters of English Authors*, Princeton, NJ: Princeton University Library.

Tucker, J. E. (1942) "The Eighteenth-Century English Translations of Molière," *Modern Language Quarterly*, 3, 83–103.

Vincent, H. P. (1943) "Early Poems by Henry Fielding," *Notes & Queries*, 184, 159–60.

Wells, J. E. (1912) "Henry Fielding and *The Crisis*," *Modern Language Notes*, 27, 180–1.

Williams, I. M. (ed.) (1970) *The Literary and Social Criticism of Henry Fielding*, London: Routledge & Kegan Paul.

APPENDIX I

Fielding's "Bill" to reform
the Police (1749)

On 21 July 1749 Fielding submitted to the Lord Chancellor "my Draught of a Bill for the better preventing Street Robberies &c." This interesting paper – representing the first thoughts on the subject of the man who later founded the metropolitan police – subsequently disappeared without a trace into the muddled archives of officialdom. Just such a document from this same period has now been found among the miscellaneous papers of the Duke of Newcastle, Secretary of State, to whom the Lord Chancellor customarily referred all matters of this kind. Though unsigned and undated, the document contains numerous and distinctive parallels with views Fielding expressed on this subject in his writings in 1749–51, and it is almost certainly the lost "Bill" which he hoped (vainly) would serve as the basis of an Act of Parliament to establish an effective, modern police force (see above, pp. 477–80). What follows is a transcription of the document (BL: Add. Mss. 33054, ff. 406–13).

The King to appoint Comm^{rs} not exceeding five in the City & Liberty's of Westm^r. & the Parishes of St Mary le bone, St Giles in the fields, St George the Martyr, St George Bloomsbury with that part of St Andrew Holborn which lies within the County of Middlesex, & the several Liberties of the Rolls & of the Savoy in the said County & that part of the Dutchy of Lancaster within the same County for regulating the Watch & Ward therein.

Such Comm^{rs} or the major part to meet yearly within one Month next after Easter in the Vestry Room of their Respective Parishes & Liberties to appoint able bodied men for each parish not exceeding forty for any one Parish to keep Watch & Ward within their respective Parishes.

Such Com^{rs} or the major part annually to order two or more Constables or Headboroughs to return the Names of 50 able bodied Men, out of which Com^{rs} or major Part to appoint a Certain Number according to the Restrictions herein after mention'd[.]

Constables to return any person other than an Esqr or one of higher

Degree, or a Surgeon or Apothecary or an Attorney or any Person holding a Tenement rated in the Poors Book at the yearly Value of   or any Person bearing his Majestys Commission in the Army or Navy or having any Civil Employment under his Majesty of the Value of   p^r annum or a Lawful Apprentice or Journeyman or hir'd servant to any Inhabitant occupying any Tenement of the Yearly Value of   or any Person who shall by Age, sickness or Infirmity be reduced incapable of the Office.

Comm^{rs} impower'd to order the Vestry Clerks to provide Arms to be kept in the Vestry rooms in a Chest Nightly to be distributed by the Constables, & Com^{rs} to ascertain from time to time the hour at which the watchmen are to assemble by appointment under their hands & seals directed to the high constables who are to summon the petty Constables & headboroughs, who are to take a Copy of the appointment & to summon the Watchmen & to attend precisely at the hour appointed, viz. one petty Constable or headborough in each parish Nightly by Rotation at the Watchhouse who are to deliver forth arms to the Watchmen & to order them to their posts: Com^{rs} to take orders for erecting Boxes or Watchhouses for the Watchmen, & may allot their several stations & in default of such allotment the high Constables to allot the same, & that the Watchmen may more easily assist each other, Every of them are to be furnish'd with one large sonorous Bell to be provided by the Vestry Clerks by order of the Commissioners.

Com^{rs} to allow a nightly stipend not exceeding 18^d p^r night p^r Man which the Vestry Clerks are to pay to the Watchmen pursuant to the order of the Com^{rs} out of the Moneys receiv'd by them by Virtue of this Act.

Towards defraying the expences incurr'd by Virtue of this Act a certain Yearly Sum is to be rais'd in the same manner as the Poors Rate is, for which purpose the Churchwardens, Overseers & Inhabitants are to assemble Yearly in Easter Week or within one fortnight after Easter to settle such assessment to answer all Charges impos'd by this Act, to be collected by the Churchwardens & Overseers & paid into the hands of the Vestry Clerk, who is to render Account Yearly within 14 Days after Easter to Churchwardens, Overseers & Houskeepers, & if the Disbursments exceed the Moneys receiv'd, the Churchwardens, Overseers & Housekeepers or any 5 of them immediately to levy a Sum sufficient to reimburse the Vestry Clerk, & if any surplus Money shall remain in his hands it shall be paid to the Overseers of the Poor towards the Poors Rate—

Vestry Clerk to be paid the Sum   in Reward for his trouble[.]

Churchwardens Overseers & Inhabitants neglecting to make such Assessment or to receive or collect the same, the Com^{rs} calling the

Vestry clerk & principal Inhabitants are impower'd to do the same, &
upon Refusal or neglect of Paying such Rates, the same to be levy'd
by distress & Sale of the offenders Goods. Any person thinking himself
aggriev'd by Means of the Rate or in the Levying thereof, may appeal
to the Comm^{rs} or any one of them. Com^{rs} to meet monthly at least or
oftner, at which meeting the high Constables having due Notice thereof
are to attend as likewise the Vestry Clerks Churchwardens Overseers
petty Constables or Headboroughs as shall be summon'd two Days
before, where the Com^{rs} are fully to execute the Powers given them by
this Act, & to determine all complaints against the Vestry Clerks,
Churchwardens, Overseers, Constables, Headboroughs or Watchmen
touching this Act, petty Constables to make a just return at every
monthly meeting of all such Watchmen as shall be remov'd, die, fall
sick, or be incapacitated, & shall at the same time return the names of
2 others to supply the place of the said disabled watchman, whose place
the Com^{rs} are to fill up with one of them, & if such Vacancys shall fall
out within 20 Days next after those meetings, the Constables are to
make a return thereof with 2 other persons to one of the Com^{rs} who
shall supply the vacancy till the next monthly meeting, when & where
the com^{rs} are to ratify the same or appoint another, the Com^{rs} authoriz'd
at their monthly meetings to make orders for the Regulation of the
Watch which orders are to be duely entred in a Book to be kept by an
able Clerk who shall be appointed by the Com^{rs}, & intitled to the Yearly
Salary of   for his Attendance[.]

High Constable or Vestry Clerk wilfully neglecting or refusing to
perform their Duty to forfeit a sum not less than 5$^{£}$ nor exceeding 10$^{£}$
to be impos'd at the discretion of the Com^{rs} at their monthly meetings
to be levy'd by distress & sale, petty Constable or Headborough offending in like manner, to forfeit a Sum not exceeding 5$^{£}$ nor less than 40$^{£}$
[sic] to be impos'd & levy'd in like manner; Watchman guilty of
Misbehaviour or Breach of Duty (other than by letting at large any
Prisoner) Com^{rs} to punish him by removing him from his office, & if
they see fit by committing him to the house of correction there to
remain & to be put to hard Labour for one Month; Watchman wilfully
assisting or suffering any Prisoners to escape to be committed to the
house of Correction for three Months to be kept to hard Labour, & to
be publickly whipt at least twice during his Confinement.

In Case any Murder, Robbery, Burglary or other Felony be committed or attempted in any of the Places in this Act mention'd, the
Watchmen within Call are upon outcry thereof to repair to that place
whether within the place for which they serve or any other, & endeavour
to seize any Person suspected to be a Party concern'd in any such
felony, & in Case any Riot, Rout, unlawfull & tumultuous assembly or
sudden affray shall arise within the View or hearing of any of the said

Watchmen, they are to repair forthwith to the place, giving an alarm with their handbells to summon their fellows, & shall endeavour to quell & disperse the same, & if any person shall be killd or wounded or otherways hurt or beaten, they are to endeavour to seize and apprehend the offenders & to convey them before some Justice of ye Peace or one of the Commissioners.

The Watchmen after the time appointed for their Watch & while they remain thereon may apprehend all manner of Persons in the Streets arm'd with any dangerous Weapon & all who shall be found in the streets, Inn, Alehouse or any Shop where Brandy or other strong Liquors are sold or any other publick house or place with Arms conceald in their possession & all who shall be found playing or betting at any Game whatsoever, & all who in the places aforesaid shall be guilty of any open or direct Act of Lewdness, or who shall be guilty of profane cursing & swearing & all Women who shall stand in the streets or in Corners & Byeplaces to pick up Men for lewd purposes & who shall walk the street for such purpose & by their indecent behaviour manifest their said Intention & all persons who by any Brawls shall raise a Mobb or who shall break windows or commit any outrage Insult or trespass whatsoever, or Balladsingers, & Persons going about with Musick, all Persons being Drunk in any of the Places aforesaid, & lastly all who shall be found after ten at Night in any Alehouse Victuallying house or Shop where any strong waters or Liquors are sold or all suspicious Persons after that hour walking or standing in the streets Lanes or bye allys who shall by their behaviour give any just Cause of any evil design all which persons so apprehended the said Watchman shall convey before some one justice or Com^r unless it shall happen at too late an hour in which case the watchmen shall convey the prisoners to the Watchhouse to be kept till the next morning & then to be carryed by the Constable before such Justice or Com^r, any Watchmen [*sic*] neglecting his Duty in the Premises or Constable letting at Large any Prisoner before he shall have been brought before such Justice or Com^r is hereby declar'd to be guilty of an high offence, for which he shall be fin'd by the Commissioners.

The Justice or Com^r shall have full power to determine all ye foregoing offences & to punish offenders upon his own View or by the Oath of one Witness or by Confession either by fine not exceeding 10^£ for one Offence, or if such Offender shall be unable or unwilling to pay the same by committing him to the house of correction there to remain two Months & to be put to hard Labour with whipping or otherwise at the Discretion of such Justice or Com^r[.]

Nothing in this Act shall extend to prevent any Nobleman or Gentleman from wearing any usual Weapon or any of his Majestys Guards or other officers or Soldiers from bearing their Arms or to prevent any officers of the peace, or any Persons in their assistance from arming themselves as they are now intitled by Law. That no Constable or Watchman shall have power of entring into any Tavern or any other House than publick Inns Alehouses or Shops where Brandy or other strong waters are sold by Retail unless by Warrant. Nor shall any thing in this act prevent any Persons from going about their Lawfull Buisness [sic] or from walking the Streets at any hour who shall behave themselves soberly & discreetly & who shall not be guilty of any of ye Offences before mentiond, nor to any Hackney Coachman or Chairman, who shall behave themselves soberly & orderly in the publick streets being attending upon his or their Coach or Chair; nor to any Travellers who shall have their Lodging in Inns, or shall be just arriv'd there or just setting out from thence nor to certain persons who shall go up & down with musick in the night call'd the Waiters; nor to certain foreigners who are us'd to travel about with Rare shows; And if any Constable or Watchman shall knowingly or maliciously arrest, or cause to be arrested any Person contrary to the meaning of this Act, he shall forfeit any Sum not exceeding 5^£ to be levyed by distress & sale, for want of such distress the Offender is to be committed to Prison there to remain to the next General Quarter Sessions unless he finds sufficient Suretys for his appearance at such sessions, where the Justices on a Complaint exhibited to them against him shall have full power to punish the Offender.

All fines payable by Virtue of this Act unless in Cases where the act itself otherwise directs shall be applyed towards the defraying the Wages of the Watchmen in that parish in which the offence shall arise, but if the offence shall be committed in any other place not mention'd in this Act, they [sic] to the Use of that place in which the offender shall be convicted, the said Com^rs [&?] Justices, to pay all such conviction Money to the Vestry clerk intitled to receive the same within one month after Receipt thereof; Com^rs, Justices, Vestry Clerks, Constables, or other Persons, who shall receive any Moneys by Virtue of this Act, not paying or accounting for the same as this Act directs, but fraudulently imbezzleing the same shall forfeit 100^£, one Moiety to the King & the other to such persons as will Sue for the same[.]

Com^r, Justice, Vestry Clerk, high Constable, Churchwarden, Overseer, petty Constable or Watchman sued for any thing done in Pursuance of this Act they may plead the general Issue & give the special Matter in Evidence at the Tryal & if a Verdict shall pass for the Defendant, or the Plaintiff or Prosecutor shall be nonsuited or discontinue his suit, Defendant shall be intitled to his full treble Costs.

After the   Day of   it shall be lawfull for any Justice of any County or for the Mayor or any two Justices in any City Town Corporate or Liberty on Complaint against any Person who shall be guilty of insulting the Person so complaining with any gross abusive & scandalous Language to cause the Party so offending to come before him or them & upon Lawful conviction to impose some reasonable fine not exceeding ten Shillings, & upon Refusal or neglect to commit such offender to the house of correction there to remain & pe [*sic*] put to hard Labour for any time not exceeding seven Days.

No Person qualified to be a Comm^r by Virtue of this Act or to exercise any of these Powers who shall not be a Justice of the Peace for some County & shall have registerd his Qualification or who shall be a Barrister at Law on Penalty of the Like Forfeiture as by a certain Act of Parliament made in the Year of his present Majesties Reign, is appointed to be forfeited by all who shall presume to act as a Justice without having first register'd his Qualification[.]

Receiving stolen Goods knowing them to be stolen to be consider'd as an original Offence, & the Receivers punish'd as Felons without Benefit of Clergy[.]

No Certiorari for the future to be granted to remove any Indictment whatsoever taken before Com^{rs} of Oyer & Terminer or of the Peace at the suit of the Defendant, unless just cause be first shewn & verifyed by oath of one credible Witness to the satisfaction of some Judge of the Kings bench & allow'd by him.

No Person indicted for Perjury, Forgery at Common Law, an assault with intent to Commit a Rape, an assault with intent to commit Sodomy or of a Cheat by false Tokens shall be liable to be admitted to Bail.

All Persons getting into their possession the goods of others by means of any fraudulent pretence, or where the goods are deliver'd for any special purpose by the owner, who shall embezzle pawn or sell the same shall be deem'd common Cheats & may be indicted as such before Comm^{rs} of Oyer & Terminer & of the Peace and shall be liable to such corporal punishment not to extend to Life or Limb as the Court before whom &c. shall think fit or if the Case be very atrocious to be transported for seven Years.

APPENDIX II

Andrew Millar's payments to Henry
and Sarah Fielding (1749–54)

From 11 May 1749 until his death in 1768 the publisher Andrew Millar had an account at Coutts Bank. Ledgers 24–28 at Coutts (The Strand) record the following payments made by Millar to Henry and Sarah Fielding.

To HENRY FIELDING		To SARAH FIELDING	
11 May 1749	£52.10.0	5 Oct. 1750	£20.0.0
24 Jun. 1749	40.12.6		
26 Sep. 1749	432.14.6	5 Jan. 1750/51	57.0.0
[26 Sep. 1749 to		7 May 1751	50.0.0
Wm Fielding also	432.14.6]	16 Nov. 1751	50.0.0
15 Dec. 1749	300.0.0	3 Jun. 1752	58.1.0
		6 Oct. 1752	21.0.0
17 Jan. 1749/50	12.12.0		
		Total	£256.1.0
23 Mar. 1750/51	50.0.0		
12 Nov. 1751	105.0.0		
21 Nov. 1751	23.0.0		
25 Mar. 1752	21.0.0		
2 Jul. 1752	10.10.0		
20 Aug. 1752	150.0.0		
4 Oct. 1752	52.10.0		
10 Nov. 1752	20.0.0		
25 Jan. 1753	63.0.0		
19 Apr. 1753	50.0.0		
13 Jul. 1753	52.10.0		
22 Nov. 1753	50.0.0		
31 Dec. 1753	30.0.0		
15 Jun. 1754	50.0.0		
Total	£1565.19.0		

INDEX

NOTE: References are to the main text and selected notes, as well as to the headnote to the Illustrations. References to the notes take the form "670:328," indicating the page and the note number. Within entries, the names of Henry Fielding and his father Edmund are abbreviated as "HF" and "EF" respectively.